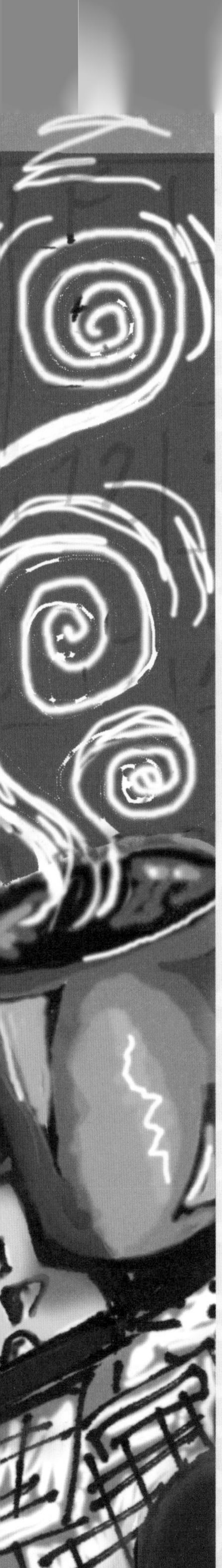

SOUTH-WESTERN'S FINANCE RESOURCE CENTER

A unique and rich online resource for finance students, **http://finance.swlearning.com** provides learning tips and tools, access to all of South-Western's text-supporting Web sites, and other cutting-edge educational resources, such as Finance Interactive, NewsEdge, Investment Analysis Calculator, Finance Links Online, Finance Online Case Library, and our highly regarded NewsWire: Finance in the News.

GITMAN SUPPORT WEB SITE

The Gitman Web site, **http://gitman.swlearning.com**, provides you with access to online quizzes with immediate scoring feedback, direct links to all the Internet addresses and activities mentioned in the text, downloadable learning support tools, and much more!

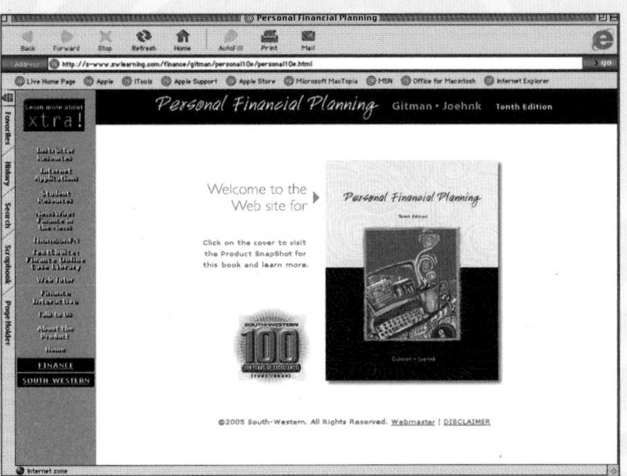

Tenth Edition

Personal Financial Planning

Lawrence J. Gitman, CFP® · *San Diego State University*

Michael D. Joehnk, CFA · *Arizona State Universtiy*

Australia · Canada · Mexico · Singapore · Spain · United Kingdom · United States

Personal Financial Planning, 10e

Lawrence J. Gitman and Michael D. Joehnk

VP/Editorial Director:
Jack W. Calhoun

VP/Editor-in-Chief:
Michael P. Roche

Executive Editor:
Michael R. Reynolds

Sr. Developmental Editor:
Elizabeth R. Thomson

Marketing Manager:
Heather MacMaster

Production Editor:
Starratt E. Alexander

Manufacturing Coordinator:
Sandee Milewski

Technology Project Editor:
John Barans

Design Project Manager:
Bethany Casey

Production House:
GEX Publishing Services

Cover and Internal Designer:
Bethany Casey

Printer:
R.R. Donnelley

Printed in China by R.R. Donnelley

2 3 4 5 07 06 05 04

ISBN: 0-324-28247-8
Book Only ISBN: 0-324-28248-6

Library of Congress Control Number:
2003116853

For more information contact South-Western, 5191 Natorp Boulevard, Mason, Ohio, 45040.
Or you can visit our Internet site at: http://www.swlearning.com

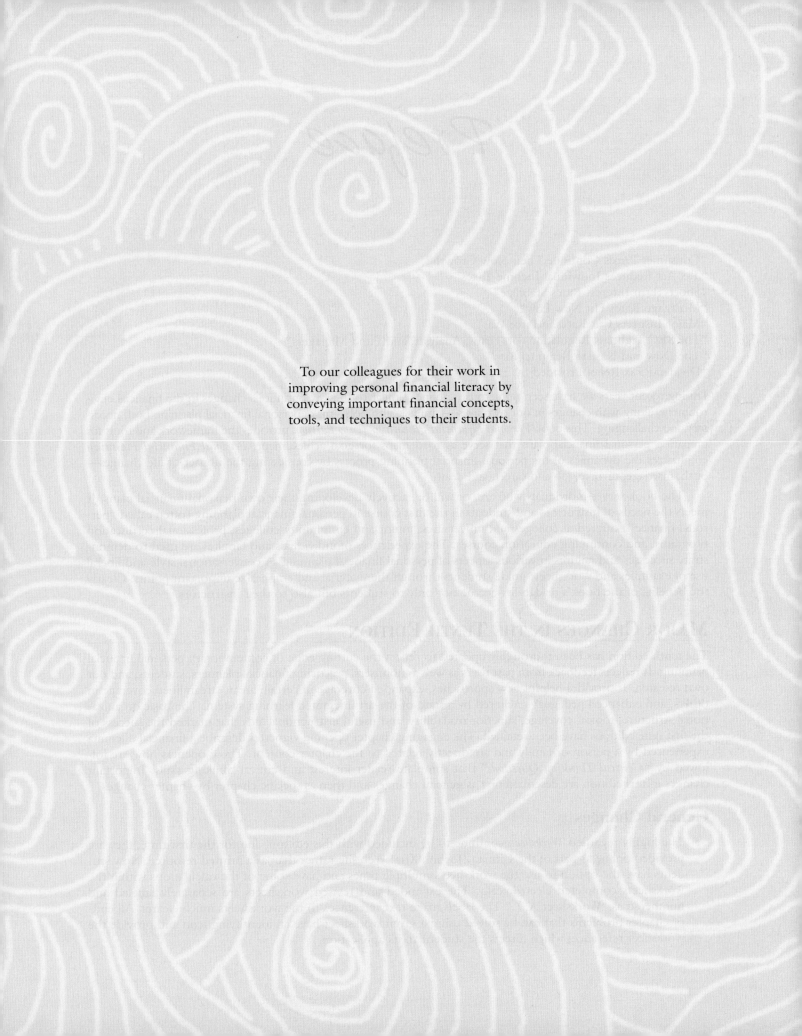

To our colleagues for their work in improving personal financial literacy by conveying important financial concepts, tools, and techniques to their students.

Preface

"Consumer Prices Continue Their Slow Growth"
"Tax Act Reduces Individual Income Taxes"
"Short-Term Interest Rates Stabilize"
"Mortgage Rates Hit New Low"
"Major Insurers Cut Rates in Price War"
"The SEC Tightens Regulations on Firms, Analysts, and Fund Managers"
"The Dow and Nasdaq Begin to Rise"
"Dividend Tax Relief Provided by Tax Act"

During recent years we have seen numerous headlines similar to these. Continuous changes in the financial environment, along with changes in our own lives—family, health, job—make personal financial planning both necessary and challenging. This book *Personal Financial Planning, Tenth Edition,* provides the framework and tools for preparing personal financial plans that serve as road maps for goal achievement. *Personal Financial Planning* emphasizes the dynamics of the personal financial planning process by considering the impact of life changes—birth, marriage, divorce, job and career, and death.

The book serves individuals who are, or will be, actively developing their own personal financial plans. It meets the needs of instructors and students in the first course in personal financial planning (often called "personal finance") offered at colleges and universities, junior and community colleges, professional certification programs, and continuing education courses. The experiences of individuals and families are used to demonstrate successes and failures in various aspects of personal financial planning. A conversational style and liberal use of examples and worksheets guide students through the material and emphasize important points. Clearly the benefits of the book's readability accrue not only to students but also to their instructors.

Major Changes in the Tenth Edition

The tenth edition has been thoroughly updated to reflect the cutting edge of contemporary personal financial planning. It reflects feedback from past users as well as nonusers, practicing financial planners, students, and our own research. It provides helpful new approaches, expanded coverage in certain areas, streamlined coverage in others, and enhanced pedagogy anchored by a state-of-the-art integrated learning system. The basic organizational structure, topical coverage, superior readability, and useful instructional aids that marked the success of the first nine editions have been retained. The engaging chapter opening vignettes describe a financial dilemma experienced by a person or family and are directly related to the chapter content. These openers now are followed by "*Critical Thinking Questions*" that stimulate reader interest and critical thinking skills. Important changes in this edition are described first as general changes and then as specific chapter-by-chapter changes.

General Changes

- The highly regarded *Worksheets* continue to be included with this edition, and for the first time, they are provided online as part of the Gitman/Joehnk Xtra! Web site rather than as a printed resource. Now students have the option to use the worksheets multiple times and have some of the calculations within the worksheets completed electronically. The expanded and revised worksheets are separately labeled and numbered as "Worksheet *X.Y.*" The labels make text references to the worksheets much clearer. All end-of-chapter problems that can be solved using a given worksheet have an identifying icon and provide the worksheet reference, which directs the student to its application.

- In addition to the worksheets, *Personal Financial Planning Software* also accompanies each new text as part of the Gitman/Joehnk Xtra! Web site. Students will find that the chapter concepts, worksheets, problems, and cases that are accompanied by this symbol can be solved with the use of the software. We feel that students using the *Personal Financial Planning Software* will be more inclined to begin and continue their own financial planning given the ease of using this program.
- New to this edition are *Web-based part-ending cases*, one for each of the six major parts of the text. These cases are also provided online as part of the Gitman/Joehnk Xtra! Web site. They have been developed to challenge readers to integrate and develop plans with regard to the major topics covered in the corresponding part.
- New to this edition are *CFP® Exam Questions* also provided online as part of the Gitman/Joehnk Xtra! Web site. For each Part, 12 to 15 actual exam questions are included from previous years' exams. These questions should help students gain insight into the CFP® program and the level of study required to earn this widely respected certification.
- The *book has been completely updated and redesigned* to allow improved presentation of each of the text's numerous pedagogical features. Additionally, the new design is expected to increase the interest of readers, most of whom are a product of today's highly visual media environment.
- This edition *places more emphasis on the use of the Internet.* A number of features that either link students to relevant Internet sites or describe how the Internet can be incorporated into the personal financial planning process are included in the tenth edition. The Internet feature, *Money Online,* has been refined, revised, and included at the end of each chapter of this edition. Each of these elements has two parts. The first part includes eight to ten Web addresses, each followed by a brief paragraph that in an interesting fashion challenges the reader to go to the site and either research specific information or merely review the resources that are available there. All of the Web topics presented within the chapter are intended to reinforce as well as expand the reader's practical grasp of the key concepts, tools, and techniques presented in the chapter. The second part of *Money Online,* titled "Just for Fun!", includes one to three Web addresses followed by brief paragraphs that direct the reader to interesting sites to obtain information, perform an activity, or answer specific questions. These sites, while expanding the reader's knowledge, tend to entertain a bit more than do the sites in the first part. Each chapter also includes a number of *Smart Sites,* brief boxes within the chapter that direct the reader to specific sites closely related to the topics under discussion. This element helps keep the reader in touch with the Web while reading and studying the chapter. In addition, many Web addresses are embedded in the text and exhibits. These Web links are included when referencing a specific company, information provider, or organization and provide the reader with a convenient way to learn more about the topic, obtain information, or make inquiries or transactions. Another source of additional Internet insights is the *Money in Action* boxes (described in detail below); some of these boxes are focused on technology and include descriptions and links to useful sites on the Internet. In summary, this edition's emphasis on the Internet is significant and widely present both in the chapter and in the end-of-chapter materials.
- The *focus of the text has been improved* by eliminating certain noncritical discussions and elements, tightening and streamlining wherever possible, and moving material to the text's Web site. Clearer focus on the dynamics of the personal financial planning process and the concepts, tools, and techniques used to implement this process are embodied in the tenth edition. Specific changes include new opening vignettes that describe a financial dilemma and are followed by *Critical Thinking Questions*; more concise *Money in Action* boxes that now include *Critical Thinking Questions*; revised and redesigned *Concept Check* questions at the end of each major chapter section; revised and redesigned *Financial Road Signs* that add interesting and useful sidebar information; and the refining of certain discussions by tightening the writing. In addition, many excessively detailed discussions have been eliminated on the basis of user and reviewer suggestions. Some of the discussions have been restructured to eliminate the need to reintroduce topics that were presented in previous chapters. All of these changes are believed to clarify and enhance reader understanding and comprehension of the text's content.
- Step-by-step *use of a financial calculator keystrokes* to make time value of money calculations is integrated into relevant discussions in this edition. To improve understanding, a calculator keyboard that highlights the relevant keystrokes now accompanies each of these demonstrations. The basics of time value of money are introduced in Chapter 2, *Your Financial Statements and Plans*, and an explanation of how to use financial

calculators to conveniently make time value calculations now appears in text Appendix E. The use of a financial calculator is reinforced in later chapters where time value techniques are applied. For example, the use of a calculator to find the future value of a deposit given various compounding periods is shown in Chapter 4, *Managing Your Cash and Savings,* and in Chapter 5, *Making Automobile and Housing Decisions,* the use of a calculator to find mortgage payments is explained. The inclusion of calculator keystrokes should help the reader learn how to more effectively develop financial plans using an important tool of the trade.

- This edition includes two *Money in Action* boxes in each chapter. A fresh box design with greater visual appeal appears in the tenth edition to stimulate greater reader interest. Most of these boxes are new to this edition; some have been revised and updated from the ninth edition. The use of a broad descriptor for all boxes allows us to better link the interesting and informative sidebar material contained in each box to the text discussions. These boxes address a variety of informative topics that help to ground many of the text discussions to actual financial planning ideas, experiences, practices, and events—all intended to fully engage readers in the personal financial planning process. Examples of the *Money in Action* boxes include those on financial portal Web sites (Chapter 1), researching and buying a car online (Chapter 5), bridging your health insurance coverage after graduation (Chapter 9), and choosing between individual securities and mutual funds (Chapter 13). Each box is followed by *Critical Thinking Questions* that can be used to improve reader understanding. The thirty boxes included in the text are drawn from recent articles in the popular press, thereby providing both relevant and timely information.
- The *integrated learning system* has been refined in this edition to help students better anchor their study to a set of chapter learning goals. Each chapter begins with a list of six numbered learning goals, LG1 through LG6. The learning goal numbers are tied to first-level chapter headings and restated and reviewed point by point in the end-of-chapter summary. Another element of this system is the *Concept Check* questions that appear at the end of each section of the chapter (located ahead of the next first-level heading). As students read through the chapters, they can test their understanding of the material in each section. The most effective advanced pedagogical features from the ninth edition—marginal glossary , exhibit and worksheet captions, and end-of-chapter questions, problems, and cases have also been retained and improved as part of the integrated learning system. Also included at the end of each chapter is *Applying Personal Finance*—a titled element appearing before the cases that presents a challenging outside exercise dealing with the main topic(s) presented in the chapter.
- *Each chapter opens with an engaging financial dilemma* experienced by an individual or family. Each dilemma is related to an important financial planning issue tied to the chapter content. The financial dilemmas emphasize the dynamic and often challenging nature of personal financial planning. The dilemmas involve both traditional and nontraditional family situations and focus attention on the text's "change" theme by describing how families and individuals adapt to change. In addition, these chapter openers are expected to pique the reader's interest and cause her or him to think critically about the issue and appreciate the importance of the chapter content.

Specific Chapter-by-Chapter Changes

Because users often like to know where new material appears, the significant but less sweeping changes that have been made in the tenth edition are summarized below, on a chapter-by-chapter basis.

Chapter 1 on understanding the financial planning process has been reorganized for better flow and streamlined to enhance readability. The addition of examples of personal financial planning in action throughout the chapter increases the material's relevance and applicability. An overview of the book now appears at the beginning of the chapter and serves as an introduction to the chapter. New exhibits include "Does Money Equal Happiness?" about money attitudes and a "Financial Planning Checkup" to help readers set their goals. We now also include practical discussions of evaluating your personal wealth, assessing out-of-town job offers, and avoiding online job-search mistakes.

Chapter 2 on your financial statements and plans is more streamlined and cohesive, with more anecdotal examples. The time value of money section has been restructured and subdivided to make it easier to follow. The section on financial calculators now appears in a new *Appendix E.* Condensing the balance sheet discussion now makes it easier to follow and apply. A new exhibit describes the different financial planning credentials, and other new exhibits streamline and clarify text discussions by displaying the key ideas for organizing your financial records and ratio analysis that were included in text discussions in the ninth edition. We now also provide sidebar discussions of Web sites that offer online financial planning, show how even the smallest expenses can lead to big savings, and provide tips to tame the paper tiger and get started with budgeting.

Chapter 3 on managing your taxes has been completely updated to reflect the changes in tax laws (including those resulting from the *Jobs and Growth Tax Relief Reconciliation Act of 2003*), rates, procedures, and forms in effect at the time we revised the chapter. The material has been streamlined considerably to emphasize current tax practices and clarify discussions of progressive tax rates, average tax rates, itemized deductions, IRAs, and other types of taxes. The chapter continues to provide readers with advice on using the most popular tax preparation software, reducing taxes, and avoiding common filing errors.

Chapter 4 on managing your cash and savings has been further streamlined for improved clarity. The discussion of online banking has been expanded and updated. The chapter includes the latest return and institutional data that accurately reflects current market rates and structure. Several background discussions have been condensed to maintain better focus on the future. Practical sidebar discussions of electronic bill paying, the safety of online banking, renting a safe-deposit box, short-term savings strategies, and choosing a bank are included in the chapter.

Chapter 5 on making automobile and housing decisions has been reorganized to improve the flow of the material. The automobile buying process is now presented in two sections, one focusing on selection and the other on financing. The discussion of renting now precedes the discussion of buying a home, given that most students will rent before they buy. The information on using the Internet to shop for and buy a car has been expanded and updated, and a new *Money in Action* box discusses the increasing trend in home purchases among people in their twenties. The mortgage sections have been condensed to enhance understanding and eliminate redundancy with the banking discussions in Chapter 4. Demonstrations of the use of a financial calculator to find both an auto loan payment and a mortgage payment are included in the chapter. New links and checklists have been added to help readers make wise car and housing purchasing decisions.

Chapter 6 on borrowing on open account has been revised and updated to reflect the impact that 40-year lows in interest rates have had on consumer borrowing. A new worksheet was added to help readers keep track of and manage their consumer credit, with emphasis on the debt safety ratio. Additionally, a new *Money in Action* box that addresses the costs and benefits of rebate credit cards was added, along with two new *Financial Road Sign* boxes, one that identifies the "5 C's of Credit," and another that deals with switching credit cards. Further, the discussion of home equity credit lines was tightened up considerably, and we added new discussion on student credit cards and balance transfer programs.

Chapter 7 on using consumer loans has been streamlined to provide better focus on the key issues surrounding the decision to use these types of loans. Dropped from the text was all the detailed discussion on the features and provisions contained in an installment purchase contract, although an example of an actual contract was moved to the IM and as a PowerPoint Slide. Added to this edition is a discussion of what to do when offered either a low rate of interest on a loan or a rebate on a high-ticket purchase (such as a car), including a step-by-step procedure to use when figuring which is the better deal. Also included is a *Money in Action* box dealing with the availability and use of 529 College Savings Plans as a way to finance a college education; finally, calculator keystroke demonstrations were added to show how financial calculators can be used to find both the monthly payment and the APR on an installment loan.

Chapter 8 on insuring your life has been reorganized for improved readability and comprehension. The needs assessment section and related worksheet have been restructured to make the process easier to follow. The material on underwriting and other types of insurance have been streamlined, and some coverage of Social Security has been eliminated because it is covered in Chapter 14. The coverage of other types of life insurance has been condensed. A new *Money in Action* box helps readers decide whether it is better to use an agent or to use the Internet to buy life insurance. Other new practical sidebar material appearing in this chapter includes questions to ask before buying insurance, expectations for a life insurance medical exam, and how to understand an insurance illustration. Descriptions of Internet resources and advice on buying life insurance online have been updated.

Chapter 9 on insuring your health includes the latest industry and policy data, with an increased focus on the growing cost of health insurance and how to minimize healthcare costs. The chapter restructuring results in a major new section on "Health Insurance Decisions" that appears ahead of the discussions of medical expense coverage and policy provisions and focuses on evaluating healthcare cost risk, determining available coverages and resources, and choosing a health insurance plan. New material includes a discussion of the *Health Insurance Portability Accountability Act* and the 2003 Medicare provisions such as prescription drug benefits. New exhibits provide a clear summary and comparison of the common types of health insurance plans and a list of the most widely offered employee health benefits. Practical sidebar material includes key questions for choosing a health-care plan, filling the health insurance gap when changing group carriers or starting a new job, dealing with health insurers that deny coverage, standards for a good long-term care policy, and tips for reducing the cost of disability income insurance.

Chapter 10 on protecting your property has been streamlined for greater readability. The guide to homeowner's policies in Exhibit 10.2 has been redesigned and simplified to make it easier to follow, and a new exhibit illustrates the calculation of replacement cost. The sample auto policy in Exhibit 10.5 has been updated. Material on no fault auto insurance and other types of property insurance has been condensed. New practical sidebar discussions offer tips for lowering property and liability insurance premiums and strategies for avoiding liability. We continue to emphasize practical advice for reducing homeowner's insurance premiums, filing auto insurance claims, preventing auto theft, buying an umbrella liability policy, and using the Internet to select and purchase property insurance.

Chapter 11 on investment planning was thoroughly updated to reflect the impact that the bear market of 2000-2002 had on investor returns and investment planning. In addition, calculator keystroke demonstrations were added to show how financial calculators can be used to find the terminal value of an investment program, and the payments needed to fund a given (target) amount in the future. All the discussion of the securities markets and the market infrastructure were updated to reflect the latest market statistics; also new is a *Financial Road Sign* that discusses Electronic Communications Networks and the impact that these ECN's will have on trade executions in the market. A new *Money in Action* box was added to provide an in-depth discussion of the market meltdown that occurred in 2000-2002—what led to the meltdown, and who some of the key players were; as part of this theme, we also added a brief discussion of the *Sarbanes-Oxley Act of 2002* and some of the key provisions that apply to accounting firms, corporate financial officers, and security analysts.

Chapter 12 on investing in stocks and bonds has been further streamlined and now focuses on just common stocks and bonds—the discussion of preferred stocks has been dropped due to the marginal role that these securities play in the investment community. On the other hand, considerable discussion was added on recent developments in the stock market (that is, the tech stock bubble that culminated in one of the worst bear markets in the past 70 years) and the bond market (particularly with regard to the near 40-year lows in interest rates and their impact on bond returns); at the same time, all relevant return and security performance data were updated through mid-to-late 2003. Also updated was the discussion of dividends to include the new (2002) preferential tax rates and their implications for investors; likewise, we updated the effects that the new federal tax rates have on the taxable equivalent yields of municipal bonds. The bond material was restructured to include a highly streamlined discussion of convertible bonds, while several calculator keystroke demonstrations were added to illustrate how financial calculators can be used to find the expected return on a stock and the yield to maturity on a bond.

Chapter 13 on investing in mutual funds has been revised and updated to reflect recent developments in this segment of the market, including the comparative performance of different types of mutual funds (through mid-2003). Also added was a discussion on how the new preferential tax rates on dividends apply to real estate investment trusts (REITs) and mutual funds, with particular emphasis on where the new preferential rates do *not* apply. Additional material found in this edition includes a new *Money in Action* box that takes a look at stable-value funds and how they can be expected to perform in good as well as bad markets, a new *Financial Road Sign* that relates different types of fund shares (A shares, B shares, C shares) to the typical fee structures that accompany them and notes which one(s) are best for investors, and a new calculator keystrokes demonstration that shows how financial calculators can be used to find the fully compounded return on a long-term mutual fund investment.

Chapter 14 on planning for retirement has been thoroughly updated and streamlined for improved clarity; in particular, the material on Social Security and annuities was tightened up to provide more focus on the major issues and key concepts embedded in these two retirement products. At the same time, the discussions of the various retirement/pension programs were updated across the board to reflect the latest guidelines, limitations, and requirements. In addition, new material was added on the growing use of cash balance plans in employer-sponsored retirement programs, and what such a shift holds for both employees and employers. Also, a new *Money in Action* box was added to show the very serious problems that can arise when individuals load up on company stock as the only, or principal, asset in their retirement programs. Finally, another calculator keystroke demonstration was added to show how financial calculators can be used in retirement planning.

Chapter 15 on preserving your estate has been updated to reflect the most recent estate tax laws and tax rates. The coverage has been streamlined to make this important technical subject more accessible. A new exhibit provides a useful checklist for survivors, and a discussion of ethical wills has been added. Valuable links include a comprehensive guide on what to do when a loved one dies and additional information on wills, living wills, and trusts. Practical sidebar material covers the excuses people use to avoid estate planning, tips for choosing a guardian for children, will-writing advice, and how to use trusts effectively.

Organization of the Book

Personal Financial Planning addresses all of the major personal financial planning problems that individuals and families encounter. It is built around a model that links together all of the major elements of effective money management. All of the latest financial planning tools and techniques are discussed. Most of the chapter opening vignettes and widely used examples involve relatively young people so that the student reader may more easily identify with each situation.

This comprehensive text is written in a low-key, personal style and uses state-of-the-art pedagogy to present the key concepts and procedures used in sound personal financial planning and effective money management. The roles of various financial decisions in the overall personal financial planning process are clearly delineated.

The book is divided into six parts. Part One presents the foundations of personal financial planning, beginning with the financial planning process and then covering financial statements and plans, and taxes. Part Two concerns the management of basic assets, including cash and savings instruments, automobiles, and housing. Part Three covers credit management, including the various types of open account borrowing and consumer loans. Part Four deals with managing insurance needs, and considers life insurance, healthcare insurance, and property insurance. Part Five concerns investments, including stocks, bonds, and mutual funds, and how to make transactions in securities markets. Part Six is devoted to retirement and estate planning. Web-based part cases and CFP® exam questions are available online as part of the Gitman/Joehnk Xtra! Web site.

Pedagogy

Each chapter opens with an engaging financial dilemma that describes some sort of financial planning situation being faced by a person or family, and which relates to the key issues being discussed in the chapter. *Critical Thinking Questions* follow each dilemma. Along with the opening financial dilemma are six learning goals that link the material covered to specific learning outcomes and, as noted earlier, anchor the text's *integrated learning system*. Then, at the end of each of the major sections are *Concept Check* questions that allow readers to confirm their understanding of the material before moving on to the next section.

Each chapter contains two *Money in Action* boxes set off from the text material and containing brief discussions of relevant personal financial planning material that serve to enrich the topical coverage. At the end of each of these boxes are *Critical Thinking Questions.* Also found in each chapter are two or three *Financial Road Signs,* which are set off from the text at various points throughout the chapter and provide important hints or suggestions to consider when implementing certain parts of a financial plan, such as "Avoiding Online Job-Search Mistakes," "Should You Buy or Lease Your Next Car," and "Tips for Successful Online Trades." *Worksheets,* which are typically filled out and discussed, are included to simplify demonstration of various calculations and procedures and to provide students with helpful materials they can use in managing their own personal finances. The worksheets are numbered to provide convenient reference to them in the end-of-chapter problems, and they include descriptive captions. Numerous exhibits, each containing descriptive captions, are used throughout to more fully illustrate key points in the text. Also included in each chapter is a *running glossary* that appears in the margin and that provides brief definitions of all highlighted terms that appear in the accompanying text.

Most chapters contain discussions and illustrations of how both the Internet and the personal computer can be used in various phases of personal financial planning. In addition, each chapter contains as many as six to eight *Smart Sites*, each of which directs the reader to specific Internet sites that deal with the topic(s) being discussed at that point, and that enable the reader to broaden his or her understanding of key financial planning concepts. End-of-chapter material includes a *Summary* that restates each learning goal and follows it with a brief paragraph that summarizes the material related to it. The next element is *Financial Planning Exercises*, which include questions and problems that students can use to test their grasp of the material. And that's followed by *Applying Personal Finance*, which generally involves some type of outside project or exercise. Two *Contemporary Case Applications* highlighting the important analytical topics and concepts are also supplied. Following the cases is the new and improved *Money Online* element that includes helpful Web addresses, home page descriptions, and a series of Web-related interactive exercises.

SUPPLEMENTARY MATERIALS

Recognizing the importance of outstanding support materials to the instructor and the student, we have continued to improve and expand our supplements package.

Instructor Supplements

Instructor's Manual and Test Bank

A comprehensive *Instructor's Manual* has been prepared to assist the instructor. For each chapter, the manual includes

- An outline
- Discussion of major topics
- A list of key concepts
- Solutions to all *Concept Check* questions, end-of-chapter financial planning exercises, and cases

The *Test Bank* has been revised, updated, and expanded. It includes true-false and multiple-choice questions, as well as four to six short problems for nearly every chapter.

Computerized Test Bank

A computerized version of the printed test bank is available in Windows Microsoft Word featuring Thomson Learning's computerized test bank program, ExamView, which has many features that allow the instructor to modify test questions, select items by key words, scramble tests for multiple class sections, and test completely online.

PowerPoint®

For instructors who enjoy working with computerized presentations, we have a complete lecture presentation in PowerPoint. Available to instructors on the free product support Web site and to students through the Gitman/Joehnk Xtra! Web site, each chapter's file includes an outline, appropriate numerical concepts, and key topics. Instructors can easily modify the presentations using PowerPoint's many features.

Workbook

The *Workbook* now includes more resources than ever for both the student and the instructor! It has been newly revised by Marilynn E. Hood of Texas A&M University, an experienced personal finance classroom instructor who has developed numerous instructional materials and holds the Certified Financial Planner® designation.

- *Workbook* features include:
  - Extensive study materials, including chapter outlines and extra practice problems (solutions included)
  - Exercises appropriate for use in classroom discussion
  - Worksheets that can be handed in for homework assignments (answers available for instructors)
  - Projects and case studies to aid students in their own financial planning and decision making
  - References to various Internet resources that can be used in assignments or for further information or outside study

Student Supplements

Gitman/Joehnk Xtra! Web site—http://gitmanxtra.swlearning.com

Access to the Gitman/Joehnk Xtra! Web site is included via a unique serial number with each new copy of the textbook. The Gitman/Joehnk Xtra! Web site provides a wealth of study tools using some of the most advanced technology features available in the personal financial planning course area, integrated in one location and organized by chapter. It includes the Personal Financial Planning Software, electronic Worksheets, PowerPoint, End of Part Cases, CFP® Exam Questions, and Xtra! Quizzing (interactive quizzing with feedback). Used book buyers may purchase access to the Gitman/Joehnk Xtra! Web site online.

Personal Financial Planning Software

The Personal Financial Planning software, now available online as part of the Gitman/Joehnk Xtra! Web site, performs like many of the widely used commercially available software packages and is completely interactive; best of all, being user-friendly, it streamlines the record-keeping and problem-solving activities presented in the text. An icon is used in the margin to identify sections of the book to which the software is applicable. End-of-chapter problems and cases that can be solved with the software are keyed with the same logo. Most of the worksheets used in the text correspond to the software to provide assistance in applying some of the more complex procedures, ranging from financial statement and budget preparation to investment management and retirement planning. In addition to various interactive calculations performed by the software, it also contains cutting-edge applications that differentiate it from more generic personal financial planning software. These applications include *graphing capabilities* (with several of the time value and asset valuation computations) that allow the user to immediately see the impact of changes to the input variables.

Worksheets

Blank worksheets identical to those presented and used in the text are now available online electronically on the Gitman/Joehnk Xtra! Web site. Access to Gitman/Joehnk Xtra! (at **http://gitmanxtra.swlearning.com**) is included free of charge with each new copy of the book. Each worksheet provides a logical format for dealing with some aspect of personal financial planning such as preparation of a cash budget, home affordability analysis, or an automobile lease versus purchase analysis. Providing worksheets electronically allows students to complete them multiple times for mastery, and many of the worksheets can actually be used to calculate figures needed to make financial decisions.

Product Support Web Site

The product support Web site, available at **http://gitman.swlearning.com**, includes relevant Internet exercises and URLs presented in the text, along with supplements available for download for qualified instructors. It also contains links to a wealth of finance resources available from South-Western, such as NewsWire: Finance in the News and the Thomson Financial Network.

Finance Resource Center

In order to provide the most current information and resources available related to financial planning we have developed a comprehensive resource center devoted to all course areas in finance. Instructors and students can access up-to-date teaching and learning aids through **http://finance.swlearning.com**.

Acknowledgments

In addition to the many individuals who made significant contributions to this book by their expertise, classroom experience, guidance, general advice, and reassurance, we also appreciate the students and faculty who used the book and provided valuable feedback on it, confirming our conviction that a truly teachable personal financial planning text could be developed.

Of course, we are indebted to all the academicians and practitioners who have created the body of knowledge contained in this text. We particularly wish to thank several people who gave the most significant help in developing and revising it. They include Marilynn E. Hood of Texas A&M and Vickie L. Hampton of Texas Tech. Thanks is also due attorney Robert J. Wright of Wright & Wright, CPAs, for his assistance in the chapter on taxes, and John C. Bost Esq., of San Diego State University, for his help in revising and updating the estate planning chapter. Last, but certainly not least, special thanks are due to Professor Edward Nelling of Drexel University for his invaluable help in revising credit chapters (6 and 7) and the retirement chapter (14).

Thomson Learning shared our objective of producing a truly teachable text and relied on the experience and advice of numerous excellent reviewers for the tenth edition: Eric W. Hayden, University of Massachusetts, Boston; Ray Jackson, University of Massachusetts, Dartmouth; Paul J. Maloney, Providence College; Armand Picou, University of Central Arkansas; Thomas M. Springer, Florida Atlantic University; and Janet Bear Wolverton, Oregon Institute of Technology.

We also appreciate the many suggestions from previous reviewers, all of whom have had a significant impact on the earlier editions of this book. Our thanks go to the following: Linda Afdahl, Micheal J. Ahern III, Robert J. Angell, H. Kent Baker, Harold David Barr, Catherine L. Bertelson, Steve Blank, Kathleen K. Bromley, D. Gary Carman, Dan Casey, P. R. Chandy, Tony Cherin, Larry A. Cox, Maurice L. Crawford, Carlene Creviston, Rosa Lea Danielson, William B. Dillon, David Durst, Jeanette A. Eberle, Mary Ellen Edmundson, Ronald Ehresman, Jim Farris, Stephen Ferris, Sharon Hatten Garrison, Alan Goldfarb, Carol Zirnheld Green, Joseph D. Greene, C. R. Griffen, John L. Grimm, Chris Hajdas, James Haltman, Vickie L. Hampton, Forest Harlow, Kendall B. Hill, Darrell D. Hilliker, Arlene Holyoak, Marilynn E. Hood, Frank Inciardi, Kenneth Jacques, Dixie Porter Johnson, Ted Jones, William W. Jones, Judy Kamm, Peggy Keck, Gary L. Killion, Earnest W. King, Karol Kitt, George Klander, Xymena S. Kulsrud, Carole J. Makela, David Manifold, Charles E. Maxwell, Charles W. McKinney, Robert W. McLeod, George Muscal, Robert Nash, Ed Nelling, Charles O'Conner, Albert Pender, Franklin Potts, Fred Power, Alan Raedels, Charles F. Richardson, Arnold M. Rieger, Vivian Rippentrop, Gayle M. Ross, Kenneth H. St. Clair, Brent T. Sjaardema, Rosemary Walker, Tom Warschauer, Gary Watts, Grant J. Wells, Betty Wright, and R. R. Zilkowski.

Because of the wide variety of topics covered in this book, we called on many experts for whose insight on recent developments we are deeply grateful. We would like to thank them and their firms for allowing us to draw on their knowledge and resources, particularly Bill Bachrach, Bachrach & Associates; Mark D. Erwin, LINSCO/Private Ledger; Robin Gitman, Willis M. Allen Co. Realtors; Craig Gussin, CLU, Auerbach & Gussin; John Markese, President of the American Association of Individual Investors; Mark Nussbaum, CFP®, UBS Financial Services, Inc.; Patt Rupp, CFP®, IDS, Inc.; Michael J. Steelman, Wachovia Securities; Sherri Tobin, Farmers Insurance Group; Fred Weaver, Washington Mutual; Karen Weston, Coldwell Banker Realtors; Keith Wibel, CFA, Foothills Asset Management; and Lynn Yturri, CFA, Bank One Investment Management. We would like to thank our colleagues at San Diego State University and Arizona State University for their expertise, encouragement, and support. Also, we want to thank Marlene G. Bellamy of Writeline Associates, La Jolla, California and her associates, Carolyn Z. Lawrence, Linda Ravden, and Renee Barnow, for revising the chapter opening scenarios and preparing the *Money in Action*, *Smart Sites*, and *Financial Road Sign* features, and their outstanding assistance in research and writing.

The editorial staff of Thomson Learning has been most cooperative. We wish to thank Starratt Alexander, Production Editor; John Barans, Technology Project Editor; Heather MacMaster, Marketing Manager, and Joe Squance, Editorial Assistant. Special thanks go to Mike Reynolds, Executive Editor, and Elizabeth Thomson, Senior Developmental Editor, without whose support this revision would not have been as lively and contemporary in approach as we believe it is and whose expert management of the writing and reviewing of the text proved invaluable. We are also grateful to Marissa Mathieson of GEX Publishing Services, who ably assured the book's timely and accurate production.

Finally, our wives, Robin and Charlene, have provided needed support and understanding during the writing of this book. We are forever grateful to them.

Lawrence J. Gitman, CFP®
La Jolla, California
Michael D. Joehnk, CFA
Flagstaff, Arizona
February 2004

About the Authors

Lawrence J. Gitman is a professor of finance at San Diego State University. He received his bachelor's degree from Purdue University, his M.B.A. from the University of Dayton, and his Ph.D. from the University of Cincinnati. Professor Gitman is a prolific textbook author and has more than fifty articles appearing in *Financial Management,* the *Financial Review,* the *Journal of Financial Planning,* the *Journal of Risk and Insurance,* the *Financial Services Review,* the *Journal of Financial Research, Financial Practice and Education,* the *Journal of Financial Education,* and other scholarly publications. He currently serves as an associate editor of the *Journal of Financial Education.*

His major textbooks include *The Future of Business,* Fifth Edition, which is coauthored with Carl McDaniel; *Fundamentals of Investing,* ninth Edition, which is coauthored with Michael D. Joehnk. Gitman and Joehnk also wrote *Investment Fundamentals: A Guide to Becoming a Knowledgeable Investor,* which was selected as one of 1988's ten best personal finance books by *Money* magazine; *Corporate Finance,* which is coauthored with Scott B. Smart and William L. Megginson; *Principles of Managerial Finance,* third brief edition; *Principles of Managerial Finance,* tenth edition; *Foundations of Managerial Finance,* fourth edition; and *Introduction to Finance,* which is coauthored with Jeff Madura.

An active member of numerous professional organizations, Professor Gitman is past president of the Academy of Financial Services, the San Diego Chapter of the Financial Executives Institute, the Midwest Finance Association, and the FMA National Honor Society. In addition, he is a Certified Financial Planner® (CFP®). Gitman recently served as a Director on the CFP® Board of Governors, as vice-president–Financial Education for the Financial Management Association, and as director of the San Diego MIT Enterprise Forum. He has two grown children and lives with his wife in La Jolla, California, where he is an avid bicyclist.

Michael D. Joehnk is an emeritus professor of finance at Arizona State University. In addition to his academic appointments at A.S.U., Professor Joehnk spent a year (1999) as a visiting professor of finance at the University of Otago in New Zealand. He received his bachelor's and Ph.D. degrees from the University of Arizona and his M.B.A. from Arizona State University. A Chartered Financial Analyst (CFA), he has served as a member of the Candidate Curriculum Committee and of the Council of Examiners of the Institute of Chartered Financial Analysts—now the Association for Investment Management and Research (AIMR). He has also served as a director of the Phoenix Society of Financial Analysts, secretary-treasurer of the Western Finance Association, and was elected to two terms as a vice-president of the Financial Management Association. Professor Joehnk is the author or coauthor of some fifty articles, five books, and numerous monographs. His articles have appeared in *Financial Management,* the *Journal of Finance,* the *Journal of Bank Research,* the *Journal of Portfolio Management,* the *Journal of Consumer Affairs,* the *Journal of Financial and Quantitative Analysis,* the *AAII Journal,* the *Journal of Financial Research,* the *Bell Journal of Economics,* the *Daily Bond Buyer, Financial Planner,* and other publications.

In addition to coauthoring several books with Lawrence J. Gitman, Professor Joehnk was the author of a highly successful paperback trade book, *Investing for Safety's Sake.* In addition, Dr. Joehnk was the editor of *Institutional Asset Allocation,* which was sponsored by the Institute of Chartered Financial Analysts and published by Dow Jones-Irwin. He also was a contributor to the *Handbook for Fixed Income Securities,* and *Investing and Risk Management*—Vol. 1 of the Library of Investment Banking. In addition, he served a 6-year term as executive co-editor of the *Journal of Financial Research.* He and his wife live in Flagstaff, Arizona, where they enjoy hiking and other activities in the nearby mountains and canyons.

Brief Contents

Contents

PART ONE

Foundations of Financial Planning

CHAPTER 1

Understanding the Financial Planning Process

Learning Goals

LG1. Identify the benefits of using personal financial planning techniques to manage your finances.

LG2. Describe the personal financial planning process and define your financial goals.

LG3. Explain why personal financial plans should be flexible and responsive to your life situation.

LG4. Examine the external factors that can influence personal financial planning.

LG5. Evaluate the impact of age, marital status, education, and geographic location on personal income.

LG6. Understand the importance of career choices and their relationship to personal financial planning.

Down But Not Out

Brian Scott worked for a software firm, the dominant employer in his small rural town. When it was acquired by a large Internet company, the new owner closed the local office and laid off half the employees, forcing Brian to put his carefully laid plans for the future on hold. Although demand was high nationally for workers with Brian's technical skills, he did not want to relocate to another city and leave his sickly mother behind. Friends encouraged him to start his own software consulting business—with the town's only local software company gone, there might be an opportunity for Brian to fill the gap it left behind. But Brian wondered if this was the right time to go out on his own. He still owed $16,000 in student loans, $7,000 on a car loan, and $3,000 in credit card debt. Another factor to consider was employee benefits; he wouldn't have any for a while if he were self-employed. And he was young and inexperienced in managing a business. But he could work from home, and if he started small, it might work out.

He contacted some former clients and local businesses to see if there was a demand for his consulting services. He needed to justify the risk of going out on his own. The response he received was overwhelmingly positive, and suddenly the possibility of owning his own company began to look like a reality.

But what really tipped the scales in Brian's favor was financial planning. He had wisely been putting money aside for a rainy day, funding an emergency savings account with 3 months' living expenses. The several months' severance pay he received, combined with his savings, would now cover his basic living costs, and carry him until consulting fees started coming in. Planning ahead had paid off, buying him the luxury of considering his options, without his being forced to leave a town he loved just to survive. The personal financial planning course he had taken in college had given him the tools to make informed choices and plan for his future. Now, he would need to review those plans and develop a new financial strategy to help him succeed with his new venture.

CRITICAL THINKING QUESTIONS

- What did Brian Scott's financial contingency plans provide for him? Explain.
- Without an emergency savings account, what might some of Brian Scott's options have been?
- Is funding an emergency savings account important to you? Explain how this might have an impact on your life choices in the future.

THE REWARDS OF SOUND FINANCIAL PLANNING

LG1

What does living "the good life" mean to you? Is it owning a home in a certain part of town, starting a company, being debt free, driving a particular type of car, taking luxury vacations, or having a large investment portfolio? Seventy-one percent of Americans say being debt free is their number one priority, while 52 percent say owning their own home is a top goal. But no matter how you define it, the good life requires sound planning to turn your financial goals into reality.

In today's complex, fast-paced world, there is a bewildering array of choices—where to live, what career path to follow, what car to buy, when to change jobs, how much to save or invest. Add to this a rapidly changing economic, political, technological, and social environment, and it is easy to see why developing solid financial strategies, guaranteed to improve your lifestyle, is becoming increasingly difficult. Many of the financial rewards our parents took for granted—home ownership, a college education, job security, and retiring at age 65—are becoming harder for today's young adults to achieve. A couple may need two incomes just to maintain an acceptable standard of living, and they may have to wait longer to buy a home.

Even if we're managing our personal finances pretty well today, we worry about the future. We want to improve our lifestyle, send our children to college, and have the funds to retire comfortably. Eighty-five percent of affluent Americans wish they had a bigger financial cushion. The estimated cost to raise a child born in 2000 to age 18 is more than $300,000. Add to that four years of college (tuition only), at an estimated cost of $51,364 for a public college, $110,708 for a private college, and $146,416 for Ivy League universities, and the need to plan ahead becomes very clear.

The best way to achieve your financial objectives is through *personal financial planning*. It helps us define our financial goals and develop appropriate strategies to reach them. We can no longer depend on employee or government benefits such as steady salary increases, or adequate funding from employer-paid pensions or Social Security, to retire comfortably. We must plan for our own future financial security, a daunting task if we don't know where to begin. And many people find the volatile economy and financial environment intimidating, even though we now have direct access to financial tools and research materials once reserved solely for stockbrokers. But we need to know how to use them effectively.

Financial needs and goals must be adjusted along with changes in personal circumstances, so personal financial planning is a lifelong activity. As you will learn, creating flexible plans and revising them on a regular basis is the key to building a sound financial future. And successful financial planning brings rewards, such as an improved standard of living, wise spending habits, and increased wealth. Of course, planning alone does not guarantee success, but if used effectively and consistently, it can help you use your resources wisely.

The goal of this book is to remove the mystery from the personal financial planning process and replace it with the tools you need to take charge of your personal finances and your life. The text is divided into six parts:

- **Part 1:** Foundations of Financial Planning
- **Part 2:** Managing Basic Assets
- **Part 3:** Managing Credit

Financial Road Sign

Evaluate Your Personal Wealth

Use the following seven steps to assess your current wealth and monitor it in the future.

1. Calculate your net worth (see Chapter 2).
2. Compare your net worth with others in your age and income bracket.
3. Compare your earnings with others in your field.
4. Compare your investment assets.
5. Examine your spending habits.
6. Total up your debt.
7. Review your results and adjust your financial plan accordingly.

Source: Adapted from Walter Updegrave, "How Are You Doing?" *Money*, July 1999, pp. 63–73.

- **Part 4:** Managing Insurance Needs
- **Part 5:** Managing Investments
- **Part 6:** Retirement and Estate Planning

Each part explains a different aspect of personal financial planning as shown in Exhibit 1.1. This organizational scheme revolves around financial decision-making that is firmly established on an operational set of financial plans. We believe that through sound financial planning, individuals can make decisions that will produce their desired results. Therefore, starting with Part 1, where we look at personal financial statements, plans, and taxes, we move successively through the various types of decisions individuals make when implementing a financial plan. To allow you to gain some hands-on financial planning experience, we include an integrative case at the end of each part.

EXHIBIT 1.1

Organizational Planning Model

This text emphasizes making financial decisions regarding assets, credit, insurance, investments, and retirement and estates.

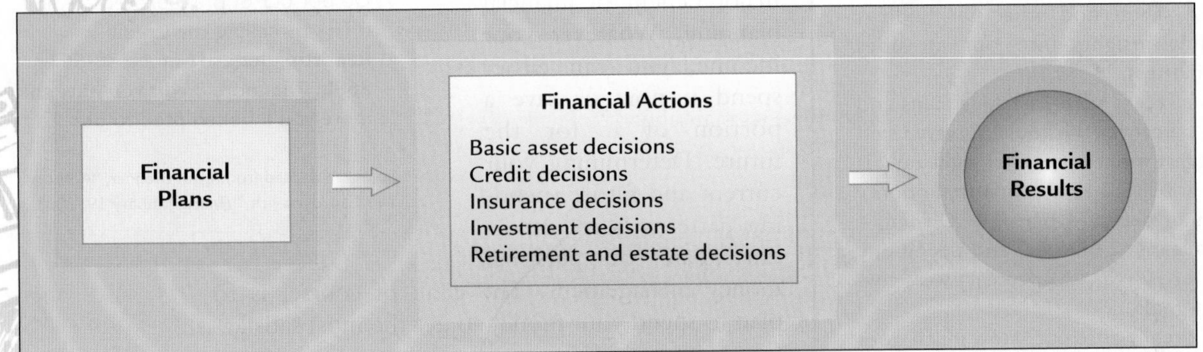

IMPROVING YOUR STANDARD OF LIVING

With personal financial planning we learn to acquire, use, and control our financial resources more efficiently. It allows us to gain more enjoyment from our income and thus improve our **standard of living**—the necessities, comforts, and luxuries we have or desire.

standard of living
The necessities, comforts, and luxuries enjoyed or desired by an individual or group.

Americans view standards of living and what constitutes necessities and luxuries differently depending on their level of affluence. For example, 45 percent of Americans consider a second or vacation home the ultimate symbol of affluence, while others see taking two or more annual vacations or living in an exclusive neighborhood as an indicator of wealth.

So our quality of life is closely tied to our standard of living. Although other factors—geographic location, public facilities, local cost of living, pollution, traffic, and population density—also affect quality of life, wealth is commonly viewed as its primary determinant. The presence or absence of material items, such as a house, car, and clothing, and having money available for healthcare, education, art, music, travel, and entertainment, contribute to our quality of life. Of course, many so-called wealthy people live "plain" lives, choosing to save or invest or support philanthropic organizations with their money, rather than indulge themselves with luxuries.

One trend with a profound effect on our standard of living is the *two-income family.* What was relatively rare in the early 1970s has become commonplace today, and the

Money in Action

How Americans Feel about Money

As the twenty-first century began, Americans were in the midst of an era of unprecedented prosperity. Yet despite the economic boom, people still had financial concerns. The median net worth of households headed by 18–34 year olds was only $11,600, with 50 percent of these carrying average credit card balances of $2,000. Only 45 percent of these households had retirement accounts (average balance $6,600), 17 percent owned stock (average balance $5,700), and 6 percent had CDs (average balance $4,000). These and other poll findings provide revealing insights into our attitudes toward money matters.

According to a recent survey on Americans and their money, 54 percent of the adults surveyed said one of their biggest money pressures right now is just meeting their bills. Their top financial priority was getting out of debt (71 percent). Owning a home free and clear (52 percent) and taking one luxury vacation every year (33 percent) were two other important goals.

So are the rich really different? How much does it take for Americans to feel rich? As mentioned, for 45 percent of affluent Americans—average age 47—$2.5 million was enough. Their most pressing financial concerns were retirement planning (34 percent), wealth accumulation (19 percent), and supporting their families (18 percent). A bigger financial cushion was important to 85 percent, and 42 percent said they are spending less so they can pay off their bills. As for the best way to get rich? The top three ways to increase wealth were to invest in real estate, start a business, and invest in stocks.

Gender differences are also a factor in the way Americans think about money. Although 75 percent of married adults say they and their mate share all their money, 60 percent of women say they manage money better, while 50 percent of men say they do. Women tend to be more conservative and less confident than male investors, but more married men (59 percent) trust their wives with managing money than women trust their

...continued on next page

incomes of millions of families have risen sharply as a result. Seventy-five percent of married adults say they and their mate share all their money, while some partners admit to having a secret stash of cash. Two incomes buy more but also require greater responsibility to manage the money wisely and coordinate the partners' financial and career goals.

Spending Money Wisely

Using money wisely is a major benefit of financial planning. Whatever your income, you can either spend it now or save a portion of it for the future. Determining your current and future spending patterns is an important part of personal money management. The goal, of course, is to plan to spend your money to get the most satisfaction from each dollar.

Financial Road Sign

Saving 101

1. Do have an emergency account big enough to cover your core expenses for 3 months.
2. Don't buy in response to unsolicited sales pitches.
3. Do use your own bank's ATM.
4. Don't put off paying your credit card bills! Late fees account for almost one-third of credit-card issuers profits.
5. Do save for retirement through automatic payroll deductions—and add half of every bonus or raise to your savings.
6. Don't make impulse purchases.
7. Do opt out of preapproved credit offers by calling the Credit Reporting Industry at 1-888-567-8688. The more credit you have the more you'll be tempted to use.

Source: Adapted from Lynn Brenner, "A Budget You Can Live With," *Parade*, January 19, 2003.

Current Needs

Your current spending level is based on the necessities of life and your average propensity to consume. A minimum level of spending would allow you to obtain only the necessities of life: food, clothing, and shelter. Although the quantity and type of food, clothing, and shelter purchased may differ among individuals depending on their wealth, we all need these items to survive.

Average propensity to consume refers to the percentage of each dollar of income, on average, that is spent for current needs rather than savings. Some people with high average propensities to consume earn low incomes and spend a large portion of it for basic necessities. On the other hand, many "ultraconsumers" choose to splurge on a few items and scrimp elsewhere. These people also exhibit high average propensities to consume. Conversely, individuals earning large amounts

average propensity to consume The percentage of each dollar of income, on average, that a person spends for current consumption.

quite often have low average propensities to consume, because the cost of necessities represents only a small proportion of their income.

Still, it is not unusual to find two people with significantly different incomes but the same average propensity to consume due to differences in their standard of living. The person making more money may believe it is essential to buy better-quality items or more items, and will thus, on average, spend the same percentage of each dollar of income as the person making far less. The *Money in Action* box on page 8 reveals some of our attitudes toward getting and keeping wealth.

husbands (41 percent). And women worry more about money, 64 percent compared to 51 percent of men.

Critical Thinking Questions

1. What is the top money pressure that adult Americans face?
2. What are some common financial concerns of Americans today?
3. Why do gender influences affect the way that Americans think about money? Explain.

Sources: "Gender Gaps," *Money.com*, downloaded from **http://cgi.money.com/cgibin/money/polls/womenpoll/womenpoll.plx**; Marion Asnes with Andy Borinstein and Douglas King, "The Changing Face of Affluence," *Money*, September 2002, p. 42; Gini Kopecky Wallace, "Can Money Buy Happiness?" *Family Circle*, April 15, 2003, pp. 64–68; Dori R. Perrucci, "Talking 'Bout My Generation," *Newsweek*, March 24, 2003; Suzanne Woolley, "Beating the Gender Rap," *Money for Women* (Special Bonus Issue), May–June 2000, downloaded from **http://www.money.com**.

Future Needs

In any carefully developed financial plan, you should set aside a portion of current income for deferred, or future, spending. Placing these funds in various savings and investment vehicles allows you to generate a return on your funds until you need them. For example, you may want to build up a retirement fund to maintain a desirable standard of living in your later years. Instead of spending the money now, you defer actual spending until the future when you retire. Thirty-four percent of Americans say retirement planning is their most pressing financial concern. Other examples of deferred spending include saving for a child's education, a primary residence or vacation home, a major acquisition (such as a car or home entertainment center), or even a vacation.

The portion of current income we commit to future needs is a function of how much we earn and our level of current spending. Forty-five percent of affluent Americans say they need at least $2.5 million to feel rich. The more we earn and the less we devote to current spending, the more we can commit to meeting future needs. In any case, some portion of current income should be set aside regularly for future use. This practice creates good saving habits.

wealth
The total value of all items owned by an individual, such as savings accounts, stocks, bonds, home, and automobiles.

financial assets
Intangible assets, such as savings accounts and securities, that are acquired for some promised future return.

tangible assets
Physical assets, such as real estate and automobiles, that can be held for either consumption or investment purposes.

Accumulating Wealth

In addition to using current income to pay the everyday expenses of living, we also spend it to acquire assets, such as cars, a home, or stocks and bonds. For the most part, our assets determine how wealthy we are. Personal financial planning plays a critical role in the accumulation of wealth by helping to direct our financial resources to the most productive areas.

As a rule, a person's **wealth** at any point in time is a function of the total value of all the items he or she owns. Wealth consists of financial and tangible assets. **Financial assets** are intangible, paper assets, such as savings accounts and securities (stocks, bonds, mutual funds, and so forth). They are *earning assets* that are held for the returns they promise. **Tangible assets**, in contrast, are physical assets, such as real estate, that can

Concept ✓

1-1. What is a *standard of living?* What factors affect the quality of life?
1-2. Are consumption patterns related to quality of life? Explain.
1-3. What is *average propensity to consume?* Is it possible for two people with very different incomes to have the same average propensity to consume? Why?
1-4. Discuss the various forms in which wealth can be accumulated.

be held for either consumption (like your home, car, artwork, or jewelry) or investment purposes (like the duplex you bought for rental purposes). In general, the goal of most people is to accumulate as much wealth as possible while maintaining current consumption at a level that provides a desired standard of living. To see how you compare with the typical American in financial terms, check out the statistics in Exhibit 1.2.

EXHIBIT 1.2

The Average American, Financially Speaking

This financial snapshot of the "Average American" gives you an idea of where you stand in terms of income, net worth, and other measures. This should help you set some goals for the future.

	Income and Assets
What Do We Earn? ***(average)***	
All households	$ 68,000
Self-employed	138,300
Retired	36,400
What Are We Worth? ***(median)***	
All households	$ 86,100
Self-employed	352,100
Retired	113,700
Home and Hearth ***(median)***	
Value of primary residence	$122,000
Equity in home	58,100
Mortgage amount	70,000
How Much Do We Save? ***(average)***	
Mutual funds	$12,200
Individual stocks	21,600
Bank accounts	11,500
Retirement accounts	28,400

Source: Adapted from Ana M. Aizcorbe, Arthur B. Lennickell, and Kevin B. Moore, "Recent Changes in U.S. Family Finances: Evidence from the 1998 and 2001 Survey of Consumer Finances," *Federal Reserve Bulletin,* Board of Governors of the Federal Reserve System, Washington, D.C., January 2003, **http://www.federalreserve.gov/pubs/bulletin/2003/0103lead.pdf**.

personal financial planning Planning that covers the important elements of an individual's financial affairs and is aimed at fulfilling his or her financial goals.

THE PERSONAL FINANCIAL PLANNING PROCESS

LG2

Many people erroneously assume that personal financial planning is only for the wealthy when nothing could be farther from the truth. Whether you have too much money or too little you still need personal financial planning. If you have enough money, planning can help you spend and invest it wisely. If your income seems inadequate, taking steps to control your financial situation will lead to an improved lifestyle. This is what **personal financial planning** is all about: taking conscientious and systematic steps toward fulfilling your financial goals.

No one is exempt from the need to develop a personal financial plan, whether you are a recent college graduate, single professional, young married couple, single parent, mid-career married breadwinner, or senior corporate executive. Knowing what you need to accomplish financially, and how you intend to do it, gives you an edge over someone who merely reacts to financial events as they unfold.

For example, purchasing a new car immediately after graduation may be an important goal for you. But buying a car is a major expenditure involving a substantial initial cash outlay and additional consumer debt that must be repaid over time. Therefore it warrants careful planning. Evaluating, and possibly even arranging, financing before your shopping trip, as opposed to simply accepting the financing arrangements offered by an auto dealer, might save you a considerable amount of money. Moreover, some dealers advertise low-interest loans but charge higher prices for their cars, so knowing all your costs in advance can help you identify the best deal. Using personal financial planning concepts to reach all your financial goals will bring similar positive benefits.

Steps in the Financial Planning Process

Take a closer look at financial planning and you will see that the process translates personal financial goals into specific financial plans, and then helps you implement those plans through financial strategies. The financial planning process involves the six steps shown in Exhibit 1.3.

In effect, the financial planning process runs full circle. You start with financial goals, formulate and implement financial plans and strategies to reach them, monitor and control progress toward goals through budgets, and use financial statements to evaluate the plan and budget results. This leads you back to redefining your goals to better meet your current needs, and to revising your financial plans and strategies accordingly.

Let's now look at how goal setting fits into the planning process. In Chapters 2 and 3, we will provide other tools essential to creating your financial plans: personal financial statements, budgets, and taxes.

EXHIBIT 1.3

The Six-Step Financial Planning Process

The financial planning process translates personal financial goals into specific financial plans and strategies, implements them, and then uses budgets and financial statements to monitor, evaluate, and revise plans and strategies as needed. This process typically involves the six steps shown in sequence here.

1. Define financial goals.
2. Develop financial plans and strategies to achieve goals.
3. Implement financial plans and strategies.
4. Periodically develop and implement budgets to monitor and control progress toward goals.
5. Use financial statements to evaluate results of plans and budgets, taking corrective action as required.
6. Redefine goals and revise plans and strategies as personal circumstances change.

DEFINING YOUR FINANCIAL GOALS

What are your **financial goals**? Have you spelled them out? Without financial goals it is impossible to effectively manage your financial resources. We need to know where we are going, in a financial sense, to effectively direct the major financial events in our lives. Perhaps achieving financial independence at a relatively early age is important to you. If so, then activities such as saving, investing, and retirement planning will be an important part of your financial life. Your financial goals or preferences must be stated in monetary terms because money, and the *utility* (defined later) it buys, is an integral part of financial planning.

financial goals
Short-, intermediate-, and long-term results that an individual wants to attain, such as controlling living expenses, managing one's tax burden, establishing savings and investment programs, and meeting retirement needs.

The Role of Money

Eighty-one percent of Americans believe that money is power, and 76 percent say that it is freedom. **Money** is also the common denominator by which all financial transactions are gauged. It is the medium of exchange used as a measure of value in financial transactions. Without the standard unit of exchange provided by the dollar, it would be difficult to set specific personal financial goals and measure progress toward achieving them. Money, as we know it today, is the key consideration in establishing financial goals, yet it is not money as such that most people want. Rather, we want the **utility**, the amount of satisfaction a person receives from purchasing certain types or quantities of goods and services, that money makes possible. Often, the utility or satisfaction provided, rather than the cost, is the overriding factor in the choice between two items of differing price. People may choose one item over another because of a special feature that provides additional utility. For example, many people will pay more for a car with a CD player than one with only a cassette player. The added utility may result from the actual usefulness of the special feature, or from the "status" it is expected to provide, or both. Regardless, people receive varying levels of satisfaction from similar items that is not necessarily related to the cost of the items. When evaluating alternative qualities of life, spending patterns, and forms of wealth accumulation, we need to consider utility along with cost.

money
The medium of exchange used as a measure of value in financial transactions.

utility
The amount of satisfaction an individual receives from purchasing certain types or quantities of goods and services.

The Psychology of Money

Money and its utility are not only economic concepts; they are also closely linked to the psychological concepts of values, emotion, and personality. Your personal value system—the ideals and beliefs you hold important and use to guide your life—will also shape your attitude toward money and wealth accumulation. If status and image are important to you, you may spend a high proportion of your current income to acquire luxuries. If you place a high value on family life, you may choose a career that offers regular hours and less stress, or an employer who offers "flextime" rather than a higher-paying position requiring travel and lots of overtime. You may have plenty of money but choose to live a frugal lifestyle and do things yourself rather than hire someone to do them for you. Clearly then, financial goals and decisions are consistent with your personal values. Identifying your values allows you to formulate financial plans that provide the greatest personal satisfaction and quality of life.

smart.sites

Is getting the lowest price important to you? Web sites such as **http://www.onsale.com**, **http://www.mysimon.com**, and **http://www.pricescan.com** search for the best prices, both online and off.

Financial Road Sign

Getting Your Financial Act Together

Will this be the year you finally straighten out your finances? Here are five important things you can do to get your financial act together:

1. Start keeping good financial records.
2. Put together a realistic budget you can live with.
3. Save for a specific goal by paying yourself first.
4. Begin saving seriously for retirement.
5. Set up an emergency fund.

People react differently to similar situations involving money. Depending on timing and circumstances, emotional responses to money may be positive—such as love, happiness, and security—or negative—such as fear, greed, and insecurity. For every 76 Americans who believe that money can't buy happiness, one believes that it does. Most Americans know that they must prepare for their financial futures. However, a recent survey about financial planning and security found that we are very unsure of how to make informed decisions about financial planning.

Because it has a strong effect on one's self-image, money is a primary motivator of personal behavior. Each individual's unique personality and emotional makeup determine the importance and role of money in his or her life. For example, some people, on receipt of a paycheck, feel satisfaction in their work. Others feel relief in knowing that they can pay past-due bills. Still others worry over what to do with the money. You should become aware of your own attitudes towards money because they are the basis of your "money personality" and management style. Exhibit 1.4 explores American attitudes towards money.

EXHIBIT 1.4

Does Money Equal Happiness?

Money. Would life be sweeter if we had more of it? The answer is . . . maybe.

- 77 percent of adults believe that America is the land of financial opportunity.
- 85 percent agree that the rich get richer and the poor get poorer.
- 94 percent believe that corporate greed is out of control.
- 76 percent of Americans believe that money can't buy happiness.
- 84 percent of adults believe that Americans worship money.
- 70 percent say the love of money is the root of all evil.
- 29 percent chose being healthy over being rich (14 percent).
- 70 percent of adults say it's as easy to love a rich person as a poor one.
- 69 percent say they are doing better than their parents did.
- 40 percent of seniors say they feel financially secure.

Source: Reprinted with permission of FAMILY CIRCLE magazine.

Some questions to ask yourself are: How important is money to you? Why? What types of spending give you satisfaction? Are you a risk taker? Do you need large financial reserves to feel secure? Knowing the answers to these questions is a prerequisite to developing realistic and effective financial goals and plans. For example, if you prefer immediate satisfaction, you will find it more difficult to achieve long-term net worth or savings goals than if you are highly disciplined and primarily concerned with achieving a comfortable retirement at an early age. Clearly, tradeoffs between current and future benefits are strongly affected by values, emotions, and personality.

While this book emphasizes a rational, unemotional approach to personal financial planning, we also recognize that universally applicable financial plans do not exist. In all cases, the key to effective personal financial planning is a realistic understanding of the role of money and its utility in the individual's life. Effective financial plans are both economically and psychologically sound. They must not only consider the individual's wants, needs, and financial resources, but must also realistically reflect his or her personality and emotional reactions to money.

You must resolve conflicts between your goals and your values, emotions, and personality early in the planning process. If you like to spend most of what you earn, you will find it hard to stick to a plan requiring high levels of annual savings to achieve future goals. You'll have to moderate your goals to achieve an acceptable balance between current and future needs.

Money and Relationships

With all the hoopla surrounding the wedding day—the average bride spends between 250 and 700 hours planning her wedding, and spends an average of $19,000 on the big day—many couples overlook one of the most important aspects of marriage—financial compatibility. Money can be one of the most emotional issues in any relationship, whether with a partner, your parents, or children. Most people are uncomfortable talking about money matters and avoid such discussions, even with their partners. However, differing opinions of how to spend money may threaten the stability of a marriage, or cause arguments between parents and children. Learning to communicate with your partner about money is a critical step in developing effective financial plans.

Your parents will play an important role in your financial planning. As they age, you may have to assume greater responsibility for their care. Do you know what healthcare coverage and financial plans they have in place? Where do they keep important financial and legal documents? What preferences do they have for healthcare should they become incapacitated? Asking these questions may be difficult, but having the answers will save you many headaches.

As we noted earlier, there are many distinct money personality types. One person may be analytical and see money as a means of control, while another may view it as a way to express affection, and yet another may use it to boost his or her self-esteem. When couples have very different attitudes towards money—for example, if one person likes to prepare detailed budgets but the other is an impulse shopper—conflicts are bound to arise.

The best way to resolve money disputes is to be aware of your partner's financial style, keep the lines of communication open, and be willing to compromise. It's highly unlikely that you can change your partner's style—or your own, for that matter—but you can work out your differences. Financial planning is an especially important part of the conflict resolution process.

You will gain a better understanding of your differences by working together to establish a set of financial goals that takes into account each person's needs and values. For instance, you may be a risk taker who likes to speculate in the stock market, while your more cautious partner wants to put all your money into a savings account in case one of you loses your job. If you can agree on the amount of money you should have readily available in low-risk investments and savings accounts, you can then allocate a specific portion of your funds to riskier investments.

Types of Financial Goals

Financial goals cover a wide range of financial desires—from controlling living expenses to meeting retirement needs, from setting up a savings and investment program to minimizing the amount of taxes you pay. Other important financial goals include having enough money to live as well as possible now, being financially independent, sending children to college, and providing for retirement.

Financial goals should be defined as specifically as possible. Saying that you want to save money next year is not a specific goal. How much do you want to save, and for what purpose? A goal such as "save 10 percent of my take-home pay each month to start an investment program" states clearly what you want to do and why.

Because they form the basis for your financial plans, your goals should be realistic and attainable. If you set your savings goals too high—for example, 25 percent of your take-home pay when your basic living expenses already account for 85 percent of your take-home pay—your goal is unattainable and there is no way to meet it. But if savings goals are set too low you may not accumulate enough for a meaningful investment program. If your goals are "pipe dreams," they will put the basic integrity of your financial plan at risk and be a source of ongoing financial frustration. You must also use realistic assumptions when setting goals. Exhibit 1.5 will help you do a reality checkup.

EXHIBIT 1.5

Financial Planning Checkup

How realistic are your assumptions about your financial future? Take this reality checkup and see:

Assumption 1: You only need 75 percent of your preretirement income to maintain a comfortable lifestyle after you retire.
Reality: That figure is more likely to be 100 percent, because health costs are increasing, outpacing any savings gained by eliminating work-related expenses.

Assumption 2: You'll cover 50 percent or more of your living expenses with your pension and Social Security.
Reality: Social Security and company pension plan payments are decreasing, so anticipate using your 401(k) and other retirement savings for living expenses.

Assumption 3: You can retire at 60.
Reality: You'll need more savings than you think to stretch your retirement nest egg over your life expectancy. If you can't save more, you'll need to retire later or work part-time after retirement.

Assumption 4: It takes a few thousand dollars a year to accumulate enough to finance your child's college education.
Reality: College costs are climbing faster than inflation. You'll need to save at least $260,000 to fund your newborn's private college education. Investigate state-sponsored 529 college savings plans or expect to use loans.

Assumption 5: A 3-month emergency fund provides enough financial cushion.
Reality: Six months is the minimum, and a year is better, especially if your industry is prone to lay-offs. It takes more than 4 months on average to find a new job.

Source: Adapted from Janice Revell, "Your Financial Reality Checkup," *Fortune*, June 16, 2003, pp. 90–96.

It is important to involve your immediate family in the goal-setting process. When family members "buy into" the goals, it eliminates the potential for future conflicts and improves the family's chances for financial success. Once you define and approve your goals, you can prepare appropriate cash budgets. Finally, you should assign priorities and a time frame to financial goals. Are they short-term goals for the next year, or intermediate or long-term goals, not to be realized for many more years? For example, saving for a vacation might be a medium-priority short-term goal, whereas buying a larger home may be a high-priority intermediate-term goal, and purchasing a vacation home a low-priority long-term goal. Normally, long-term financial goals are set first, followed by a series of corresponding short- and intermediate-term goals. Your goals will continue to change with your life situation, as Exhibit 1.6 demonstrates.

EXHIBIT 1.6

How Financial Goals Change with a Person's Life Situation

Financial goals are not static, but change continually over a lifetime. Here are some typical long-, intermediate-, and short-term goals for a number of different personal situations.

Personal Situation	Long-Term Goals (6+ years)	Intermediate-Term Goals (2–5 years)	Short-Term Goals (1 year)
College senior	Begin an investment program	Repay college loans	Find a job
	Buy a condominium	Trade in car and upgrade to nicer model	Rent an apartment
	Earn a master's degree	Buy new furniture	Get a bank credit card
			Buy new stereo
Single, mid-20s	Begin law school	Begin regular savings program	Prepare a budget
	Build an investment portfolio	Take a Caribbean vacation	Buy a new television and VCR
	Save enough for a down payment on a home	Buy life insurance	Get additional job training
		Start a retirement fund	Build an emergency fund
			Reduce expenses 10%
Married couple with children, late 30s	Diversify investment portfolio	Buy a second car	Repaint house
	Buy a larger home	Increase college fund contributions	Get braces for children
		Increase second income: from part-time to full-time	Review life and disability insurance
Married couple with grown children, mid-50s	Decide whether to relocate when retired	Take cruise vacation	Buy new furniture
	Retire at age 62	Shift investment portfolio into income-producing securities	Review skills for possible career change
	Travel to Europe and the Orient	Sell house and buy smaller residence	

Putting Target Dates on Financial Goals

Financial goals are most effective when set with goal dates. Goal dates are target points in the future when you expect to achieve or complete certain financial objectives. They may serve as progress checkpoints toward some longer-term financial goals, or as deadlines for others. One goal may be to purchase a boat in 2009 (the goal date), another to accumulate a net worth of $200,000 by 2020—goal dates of 2010 and 2015 could be set for the attainment of net worth of $10,000 and $110,000, respectively.

Long-Term Goals

Long-term financial goals should indicate wants and desires for a time period covering about 6 years out to the next 30 or 40 years. Although it's difficult to pinpoint exactly what you will want 30 years from now, it is useful to establish some tentative long-term financial goals. Recognize, though, that long-term goals will change over time, and you'll need to revise them accordingly. If the goals appear to be too high, you'll want to make them more realistic. If they are too low, you'll want to adjust them to a level that will encourage you to make financially responsible decisions rather than squander surplus funds.

Short- and Intermediate-Term Goals

Short-term financial goals are set each year and cover a 12-month period. They include making substantial, regular contributions to savings or investments to accumulate your desired net worth. Intermediate-term goals bridge the gap between short- and long-term goals. Both should be consistent with established long-term goals. Short-term goals become the key input for the cash budget, a tool used to plan for short-term income and expenses. To define your short-term goals, you should consider your immediate goals, expected income for the year, and long-term goals. Short-term planning should also include establishing an emergency fund with 3 to 6 months' worth of income. This special savings account serves as a safety valve in case of financial emergencies such as a temporary loss of income.

Unless you attain your short-term goals, you probably won't achieve your intermediate- or long-term goals. It's tempting to let our desire to spend now take priority over the need to save for the future. However, by making some short-term sacrifices now, we are more likely to have a comfortable future. If you don't realize this for another 10 or 20 years, you may discover that it is too late to attain some of your most important financial goals.

Worksheet 1.1 provides a convenient way to summarize your personal financial goals. It groups them by time frame (short-term, intermediate-term, or long-term) and lists a priority for each goal (high/medium/low), a target date to reach the goal, and estimated cost.

We have filled out the form showing the goals Tim and Andrea Shepard set in December 2004. The Shepards were married in 2001, own a condominium in a midwestern suburb, and have no children. Because Tim and Andrea are 28 and 26 years old, respectively, they have set their longest-term financial goal 33 years from now, when they want to retire. Tim has just completed his fifth year as a marketing representative for a large auto products manufacturer. Andrea, a former elementary school teacher, finished her MBA in May 2004 and began working at a local advertising agency. Tim and Andrea love to travel and ski. They plan to start a family in a few years, but for now they want to develop some degree of financial stability and independence. Their goals include purchasing assets (clothes, stereo, furniture, car), reducing debt, reviewing insurance, increasing savings, and planning for retirement.

Concept ✓

1-5. What is the role of money in setting financial goals? What is the relationship of money to utility?

1-6. Explain why financial plans must be psychologically as well as economically sound. What is the best way to resolve money disputes in a relationship?

1-7. Identify three financial goals that are important to you now. Why is it important to set realistically attainable financial goals? Explain using examples of realistic and unrealistic personal financial goals. Select one of your personal financial goals and develop a brief financial plan for achieving it.

1-8. Distinguish between long-term, intermediate-term, and short-term financial goals. Give examples of each.

LG3 FROM GOALS TO PLANS: A LIFETIME OF PLANNING

How will you achieve the financial goals you set for yourself? The answer, of course, lies in the financial plans you establish. Financial plans provide the roadmap to reach your financial destination. A six-step planning process results in separate yet interrelated components covering all the important financial elements in your life.

Some deal with the more immediate aspects of money management, such as preparing a budget to help manage spending. Others focus on acquiring major assets, such as a car or home. Liability plans control borrowing, while insurance plans reduce financial risk, and savings and investment plans provide emergency funds and future wealth accumulation. An employee benefit plan will help you take advantage of and manage employer-sponsored benefits, and coordinate them with

worksheet 1.1

Summary of Personal Financial Goals

Set financial goals carefully and realistically, as they form the basis for your personal financial plans. They should be defined in measurable, specific terms and have a priority and time frame.

Personal Financial Goals

Name(s) Tim and Andrea Shepard Date December 27, 2004

Short-Term Goals (1 year or less)

Goal	Priority	Target Date	Cost Estimate
Buy new tires and brakes for Ford Focus	High	Feb. 2005	$ 500
Buy career clothes for Andrea	High	May 2005	1,200
Take Colorado ski trip	Medium	Mar. 2005	1,800
Replace stereo components	Low	Sept. 2005	1,100
Buy new work clothes for Tim	Medium	June 2005	750

Intermediate-Term Goals (2 to 5 years)

Goal	Priority	Target Date	Cost Estimate
Start family	High	2007	–
Repay all loans except mortgage	High	2008	c. $ 7,500
Trade Focus and buy larger car	High	2008	c. 10,000
Buy new bedroom furniture	Low	2009	c. 4,000
Take 2-week Hawaiian vacation	Medium	2006/7	c. 5,000
Review insurance needs	High	2007	–
Accumulate $100,000 net worth	High	2009	–

Long-Term Goals (6+ years)

Goal	Priority	Target Date	Cost Estimate
Begin college fund	High	2010	?/year
Diversify/increase investment portfolio	High	2011	Varies
Buy larger home	High	2013	$250,000
Take European vacation	Low	2012	$ 10,000
Retire from jobs	High	2037	?
Increase college fund contributions	High	2012	–

the other components of your financial plan. A tax plan will allow you to defer and minimize your taxes. You will also need a retirement plan to provide financial security when you stop working, and an estate plan to ensure an orderly and cost-effective transfer of assets to your heirs. In the following sections, we'll take a closer look at six specific types of financial plans that combine to form a comprehensive personal financial plan.

As noted earlier, discussing your financial goals and attitudes toward money with your partner is important to successful personal financial planning. You must also allocate responsibility for money management tasks and decisions. Many couples make major decisions jointly and divide routine financial decision making on the basis of expertise and interest.

Anne and John North believed it was important for their entire family to work together as a team to manage the family finances. They held family financial meetings once every few months to help their children understand how the household money was spent. These meetings also served as a forum for their children to request a raise in allowance, a new bike, or funds for a school trip. The entire family was involved in the decision-making process on how surplus funds would be allocated.

Giving children an allowance is a good way to start teaching them to budget and save. By setting their own financial goals and taking steps to reach them, they will develop their own money management skills.

The Life Cycle of Financial Plans

Financial planning is a dynamic process. As you move through different stages of your life, your needs and goals will change. But certain financial goals are important regardless of age. Having extra resources to fall back on in an economic downturn or period of unemployment should be a priority whether you are 25, 45, or 65. Some changes—a new job, marriage, children, moving to a new area—may be part of your original plan.

However, more often than not, you will face unexpected "financial shocks" during your life: loss of a job, a car accident, divorce or death of a spouse, a long illness, or the need to support adult children or aging parents. With careful planning, you can get through tough times and prosper in good times. To weather life's financial storms, you need to plan ahead and take steps—for example, setting up an emergency fund or reducing monthly expenses—that will protect you and your family financially if a setback occurs.

As we move from childhood to retirement age, we traditionally go through different life stages. Exhibit 1.7 illustrates the various components of a typical *personal financial planning life cycle* as they relate to these different life stages. As we pass from one stage of maturation to the next, our patterns of income change simultaneously. From early childhood when we relied on our parents for support, to early adulthood when we held our first jobs and started our families, we can see a noticeable change in income patterns.

As we embark on our chosen career path, we replace negative income—in the form of reliance on our parents for money—with a rapidly increasing positive earnings stream. Then, as we move from career development to preretirement years, our income becomes more stable. Finally, our income begins to trail off (ideally, only a bit) as we enter our retirement years. Thus, as our emphasis in life changes, so do the kinds of financial plans we need to pursue.

Today, many young people wait to marry and have children, first focusing on their careers and building a financial base. Mary Padgett and Tim Connors met in college and completed their graduate degrees while continuing to date. When they both found jobs, they became engaged, and after two years of working and establishing themselves with their respective firms, they got married. Neither one regrets waiting. Not only did they have a chance to really get to know one another, they were able to develop financial goals and plans that worked for both of them.

Today new career strategies—planned and unplanned job changes, or several different careers over a lifetime, for example—are common and may require revising financial plans. The families of women who interrupt their careers to stay home with their children, whether for 6 months or 6 years, need to plan for periods of reduced income.

EXHIBIT 1.7

The Personal Financial Planning Life Cycle

As you move through life and your income patterns change, you'll typically have to pursue a variety of financial plans. For instance, when you graduate from college, you'll be focused on buying a car and a house, and you'll be concerned about health and automobile insurance to protect against loss.

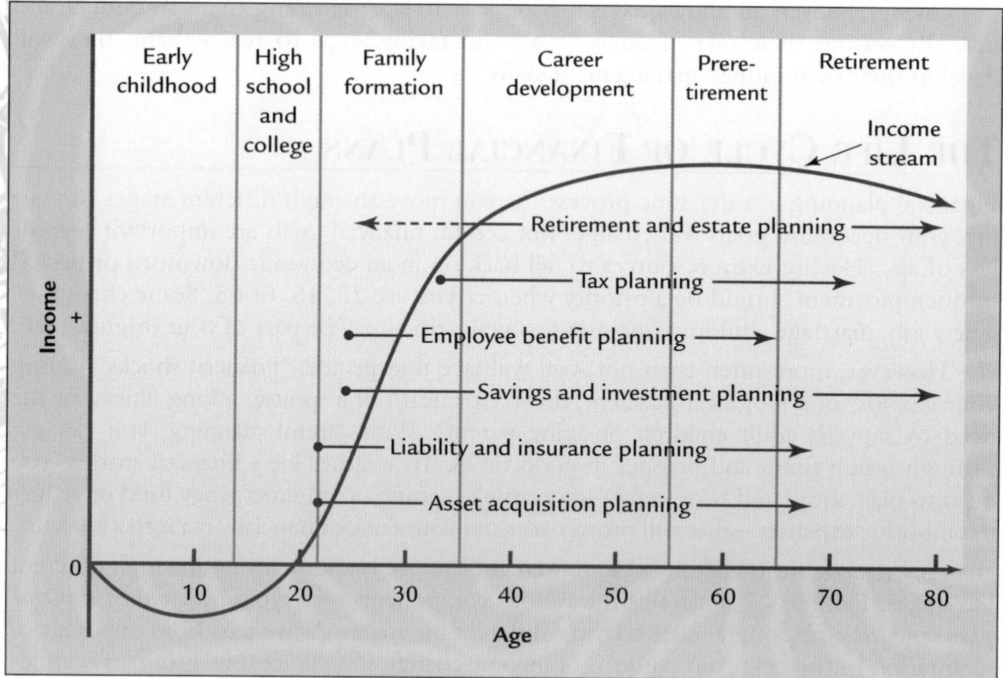

A divorce, the death of a spouse, and remarriage can drastically change one's financial circumstances. In addition, many people in their thirties, forties, and fifties find themselves in the "sandwich generation," supporting their elderly parents, while still raising their children and paying for college. And then there are those individuals who must cope with reduced income through lost jobs due to corporate downsizing or early retirement. We'll look at these and other special planning concerns in Chapter 2.

Finances of various age groups vary. Income tends to increase, then decline over the life cycle; home ownership and other assets tend to increase; debt tends to increase and then decline. Those in the 45–64 age range tend to have more income than those younger than age 45. Those aged 65–74 tend to have more nonmortgage debt than persons in other age groups.

Plans to Achieve Your Financial Goals

As discussed earlier, financial goals can range from short-term goals such as saving for a new stereo to long-term goals such as saving enough to start your own business. Reaching your particular goals requires different types of financial planning. Let's take a brief look at what each major plan category includes.

Asset Acquisition Planning

One of the first categories of financial planning we typically encounter is asset acquisition. We accumulate *assets*—things we own—throughout our lives. These include *liquid assets* (cash, savings accounts, and money market funds) used for everyday expenses, *investments* (stocks, bonds, and mutual funds) acquired to earn a return, *personal property* (movable property such as automobiles, household furnishings, appliances, clothing, jewelry, home electronics, and similar items), and *real property* (immovable property; land and anything fixed to it, such as a house). Chapters 4 and 5 focus on important considerations with regard to acquiring liquid assets and other major assets such as automobiles and housing.

Liability and Insurance Planning

Another category of financial planning is liability planning. A *liability* is something we owe and is represented by the amount of debt we incur. We create liabilities by borrowing money. By the time most of us graduate from college, we have debts of some sort: education loans, car loans, credit card balances, and so on. Our borrowing needs typically increase as we acquire other assets, such as a home, furnishings, and appliances. Regardless of the source of credit, such transactions have one thing in common: *the debt must be repaid at some future time.* The way we manage our debt burden is just as important as how we manage our assets. Using credit effectively requires careful planning and is the topic of Chapters 6 and 7.

Obtaining adequate *insurance coverage* is also essential. Like borrowing money, it is generally something that is introduced at a relatively early point in our life cycle (usually early in the family formation stage). Insurance is a means of reducing financial risk and protecting both income (life, health, and disability insurance) and assets (property and liability insurance). Most consumers regard insurance as absolutely essential, and for good reason. One serious illness or accident can wipe out everything one has accumulated over years of hard work. However, having the wrong amount of insurance can be costly, too. We'll examine the appropriate types and amounts of insurance coverage in Chapters 8, 9, and 10.

smart.sites

Go to the Learning Center at **http://www.insurance.com** for helpful information on insurance coverage.

Savings and Investment Planning

As your income begins to increase, so does the importance of savings and investment planning. Initially, people save to establish an emergency fund for meeting unexpected expenses. Eventually, however, they devote greater attention to investing excess income as a means of accumulating wealth, either for major expenditures, such as a child's college education, or for retirement. They acquire wealth through savings and subsequent investing of funds in various investment vehicles—common or preferred stocks, government or corporate bonds, mutual funds, real estate, and so on. The higher the returns on investments of excess funds, the greater wealth they accumulate.

The impact of alternative rates of return on accumulated wealth is illustrated in Exhibit 1.8. It shows that if you had $1,000 today and could keep it invested at 8 percent, you would accumulate a considerable sum of money over time. For example, at the end of 40 years, you would have $21,725 from your original $1,000. Earning a higher rate of return has even greater rewards. Some might assume that earning, say, 2 percentage points more—that is, 10 rather than 8 percent—would not matter a great deal. But it certainly would! Note that if you could earn 10 percent over the 40 years, you would accumulate $45,259, or more than twice as much as you would accumulate at 8 percent.

How long you invest for is just as important as how much you earn on your investments. With either rate of return, you can accumulate more than twice as much capital by investing for 40 rather than 30 years. This is the magic of compound interest, which explains why it's so important to create strong savings and investment habits early in life. We will more fully examine compounding in Chapter 2, savings in Chapter 4, and investments in Chapters 11, 12, and 13.

EXHIBIT 1.8

How a $1,000 Investment Grows Over Time

Eight percent, ten percent. What's the big deal? The deal is more than twice the money over a 40-year period! Because of the power of compound interest, a higher return means dramatically more money as time goes on.

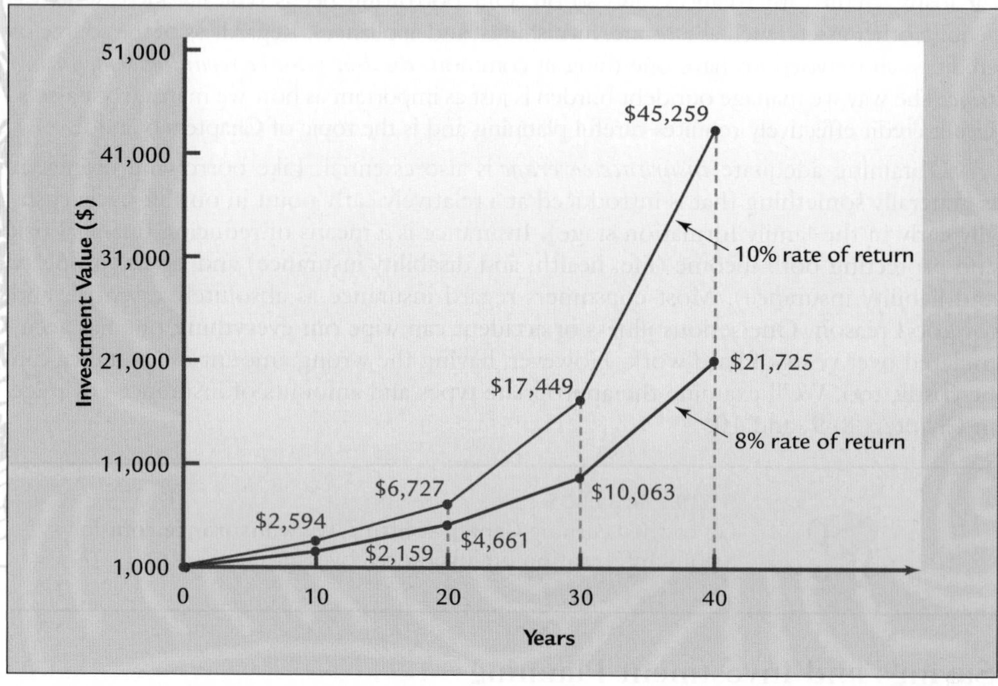

Employee Benefit Planning

Your employer may offer a wide variety of employee benefit plans, especially if you work for a large firm. These could include life, health, and disability insurance; tuition reimbursement programs for continuing education; pension and profit-sharing plans, and 401(k) retirement plans; flexible spending accounts for child care and healthcare expenses; stock options; sick leave, personal time, and vacation days; and miscellaneous benefits such as employee discounts and subsidized meals or parking. Many of these plans will be more fully described in later chapters.

Managing your employee benefit plans and coordinating them with your other plans is an important part of the overall financial planning process. For example, such benefits as tax-deferred retirement plans and flexible spending accounts offer tax advantages. Some retirement plans allow you to borrow against them. Employer-sponsored insurance programs may need to be supplemented with personal policies. In addition, in today's volatile labor market, you can no longer assume that you will be working at the same company for many years. If you change jobs, your new company may not offer the same benefits. Your personal financial plans should include contingency plans to replace employer-provided benefits as required. We will discuss employee benefits in greater detail in Chapters 2 (planning); 3 (taxes); 8, 9, and 10 (insurance); and 14 (retirement).

Tax Planning

In spite of all the talk about tax reform, our tax code remains highly complex. Income can be taxed as active (ordinary), portfolio (investment), passive, tax-free, or tax-deferred income. Then there are tax shelters, which use various aspects of the tax code (such as depreciation expenses) to legitimately reduce an investor's tax liability. Tax planning considers all these factors and more. It involves looking at an individual's current and projected earnings and developing strategies that will defer and minimize taxes. Tax plans are closely tied to investment plans and will often specify certain investment strategies. Although the use of tax planning is most common among individuals with high incomes, sizable savings can also result for people with lower levels of income. We will examine taxes and tax planning in Chapter 3.

Retirement and Estate Planning

While you are still working, you should be managing your finances to attain those goals you feel are important after you retire. These might include maintaining your standard of living, extensive travel, plans for visiting children, dining out frequently at better restaurants, and perhaps a vacation home or boat. Retirement planning actually begins long before you retire. As a rule, most people do not start thinking about retirement until well into their forties or fifties. This is unfortunate, because it usually results in a substantially reduced level of retirement income. The sooner you start, the better off you will be. Take, for instance, the IRA (individual retirement arrangement), in which certain wage earners are allowed to invest up to $2,000 per year. If you start investing for retirement at age 40, put $2,000 per year in an IRA for 25 years, and earn 10 percent, your account will grow to $196,694. However, if you start your retirement program 10 years earlier (at age 30), your IRA will grow to a whopping $542,049. Although you are investing a total of only $20,000 more ($2,000 per year for an extra 10 years), your IRA will nearly triple in size. We will look at IRAs and other aspects of retirement planning in Chapter 14.

Accumulating assets to enjoy in retirement is only part of the long-term planning process. As people grow older, they must also consider how they can most effectively pass their wealth on to their heirs, an activity called *estate planning*. We will examine this complex subject, which includes such topics as wills, trusts, and the effects of gift, estate, and inheritance taxes, in Chapter 15.

Concept ✓

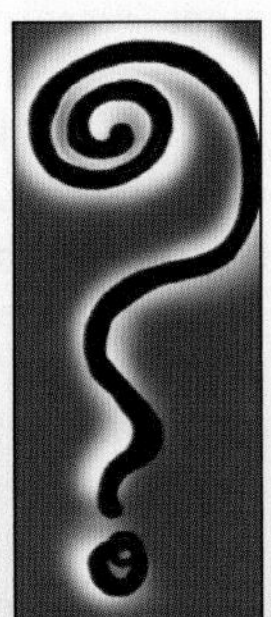

1-9. What types of financial planning concerns does a complete set of financial plans cover?

1-10. Discuss the relationship of life-cycle considerations to personal financial planning. What are some factors to consider when revising financial plans to reflect changes in the life cycle?

1-11. Mark Potter's investments over the past several years have not lived up to his full return expectations. He is not particularly concerned, however, because his return is only about 2 percentage points below his expectations. Do you have any advice for Mark?

1-12. Describe employee benefit and tax planning. How do they fit into the financial planning framework?

1-13. There's no sense in worrying about retirement until you reach "middle age." Discuss this point of view.

1-14. What role do the personal computer and the Internet play in personal financial planning?

Technology in Financial Planning

As they have in so many other aspects of our lives, personal computers (PCs) and the Internet have found their way into financial planning. Indeed, financial planning is a natural application of the PC. What better way is there to handle all the number crunching involved in

Money in Action

Financial Portals Open the Door to Online Information

With thousands of personal financial Web sites crowding the Internet, such an overabundance of online information can be intimidating. Don't let that stop you, however, because no matter how much you know—or don't know—about personal finance and investing, the Web is a research tool without equal, and many worthwhile sites are free.

Of the many sites competing to be your Web gateway to the Internet's educational riches, financial portals are an ideal starting place for the beginner. They are jam-packed with financial information—from personal-finance tasks such as paying bills online, shopping for a mortgage, or estimating taxes—to investment essentials such as stock quotes, online portfolio tracking, investment research, and news. Some also provide weather updates, a personal calendar, and an address book. Several comprehensive sites that consistently get rave reviews are Yahoo! Finance (**http://finance.yahoo.com**), Microsoft's MSN MoneyCentral (**http://moneycentral.msn.com**), and Intuit's Quicken.com (**http://www.quicken.com**). Each has a slightly different look, emphasis, and organizational scheme. Evaluate their unique features to find the one that best suits your needs.

Yahoo! Finance: This site provides fast access to financial data such as stock quotes, company profiles, and breaking news stories from the opening screen. An easily customized home page allows you to delete any content you don't want; other sites aren't as flexible. Among the options available for viewing the home page is one that calls up recent headlines for each of your stock holdings. Extensive message boards are available for investor discussions. Free online bill-paying services are also available, as are links to many personal finance resources, from online credit report agencies to tax preparation sites.

MSN MoneyCentral: This site places more emphasis on articles, tools, and step-by-step guides for investor education. It offers a wide range of sophisticated interactive tools such as stock

...continued on next page

budgeting, tax planning, and investment management? There are many reasonably priced, "user-friendly" programs available for personal financial planning and money management, including the popular *Quicken* and *Microsoft Money* packages.

The Internet puts a wealth of financial information literally at your fingertips. To help you find useful online resources, every chapter includes numerous "smart.sites," links to relevant financial planning Web sites. The *Money Online* feature at the end of each chapter describes related Web sites and includes companion exercises to help you effectively use the Web in financial planning. By bookmarking (saving) these sites, you will build up a valuable library of personal financial Web sites.

Where applicable, we will point out ways to use the computer and Internet to simplify and reduce the time required to manage your personal finances. As a start, check out the general personal finance sites described in the *Money in Action* box that follows. We also include a simple, menu-driven computer program to use with many of the analytical and computational procedures addressed in the text. This Financial Planning System (FPS) runs on IBM and IBM-compatible computers. Keyed to various sections of this book, it offers short programs that perform many of the routine financial calculations and procedures used in the text. FPS also automates the completion of the majority of the chapter worksheets. The following symbol identifies the major text headings and end-of-chapter problems that use FPS routines:

THE PLANNING ENVIRONMENT

LG4

Financial planning is not carried out in isolation, but in an economic environment created by the actions of business, government, and consumers. Your purchase, saving, investment, and retirement plans and decisions are influenced by both the present and future state of the economy. Understanding the economic environment will allow you to make better financial decisions.

For example, a strong economy can lead to big profits in the stock market, which can positively affect your investment and retirement programs. The economy can also affect the interest rates you pay on your mortgage and credit cards as well as those you earn on savings accounts and bonds. Periods of high inflation can lead to rapid price increases that make it difficult to make ends meet. This section briefly looks at two important aspects of the planning environment: the major financial planning players and the economy.

The Players

The financial planning environment contains various interrelated groups of players, each attempting to fulfill certain goals. Although their objectives are not necessarily incompatible, they do impose some constraints on one another. There are three vital groups: government, business, and consumers. Exhibit 1.9 depicts the relationship among these groups.

Government

The federal, state, and local governments provide us with many essential public goods and services, such as police and fire protection, national defense, highways, public education, and healthcare. The federal government also plays a major role in regulating the level of economic activity. Government is also a customer of business and an employer of consumers. As a result, it is a source of revenue for business and wages for consumers. The two principal constraints from the perspective of personal financial planning are taxes and government regulations.

screening and charting capabilities, plus investment research. It provides access to online brokers and a customizable portfolio you can synchronize with your e-brokerage account. The Research Wizard provides market data and explains why it's important. Other features include a bill paying capability, online tax preparation, and free e-mail.

Quicken.com: You'll find broad coverage and consistency of personal finance topics at this site. It is a fully customizable site with features for tracking personal spending and bill paying. Each area—brokerage, taxes, home mortgages, small business, banking, and insurance—has its own bulletin boards, reference materials, and advice. Using the latest version of Quicken, you can connect with more than 1,000 financial institutions for additional services.

Critical Thinking Questions

1. What is the most important function of the Internet in financial planning?
2. What makes financial Web sites unique and different from one another?
3. How would you use the Internet as a research tool? Explain.

Sources: "Best of the Web: Investing—Financial Portals," *Forbes Best of the Web*, Summer 2003, downloaded from **http://www.forbes.com/bow/**; MSN Moneycentral.com, **http://moneycentral.msn.com**; Quicken.com, **http://www.quicken.com**; and Yahoo! Finance, **http://finance.yahoo.com** (all accessed August 18, 2003).

Taxation

The federal government levies taxes on income, state governments levy taxes on sales and income, and local governments levy taxes primarily on real estate and personal property. The largest tax bite for consumers is federal income taxes, which are somewhat progressive, because (up to a point) the greater the taxable income, the higher the tax rate. Because changes in tax rates and procedures will increase or decrease the amount of income consumers have to spend, you should factor the effects of taxes into your personal money management activities. Due to the constraints of the tax structure and the potential magnitude of taxes, financial decisions should be evaluated on an "after-tax" basis. (Taxes are discussed in Chapter 3.)

Regulation

Federal, state, and local governments place many regulations on activities that affect consumers and businesses. Aimed at protecting the consumer from fraudulent and undesirable actions by sellers and lenders, these regulations require certain types of businesses to have licenses, maintain certain hygiene standards, adequately disclose financial charges, and warrant their goods and services. Other laws protect sellers from adverse activities by consumers—for example, shoplifting and nonpayment for services rendered. Certainly, any decisions relating to achieving personal financial goals should take into consideration the legal requirements that protect consumers and those that constrain their activities.

Business

As shown in Exhibit 1.9, business provides consumers with goods and services and in return receives payment in the form of money. To produce these goods and services, firms

EXHIBIT 1.9

The Financial Planning Environment

Government, business, and consumers are the major participants in our economic system. They all interact with one another to produce the environment in which we carry out our financial plans.

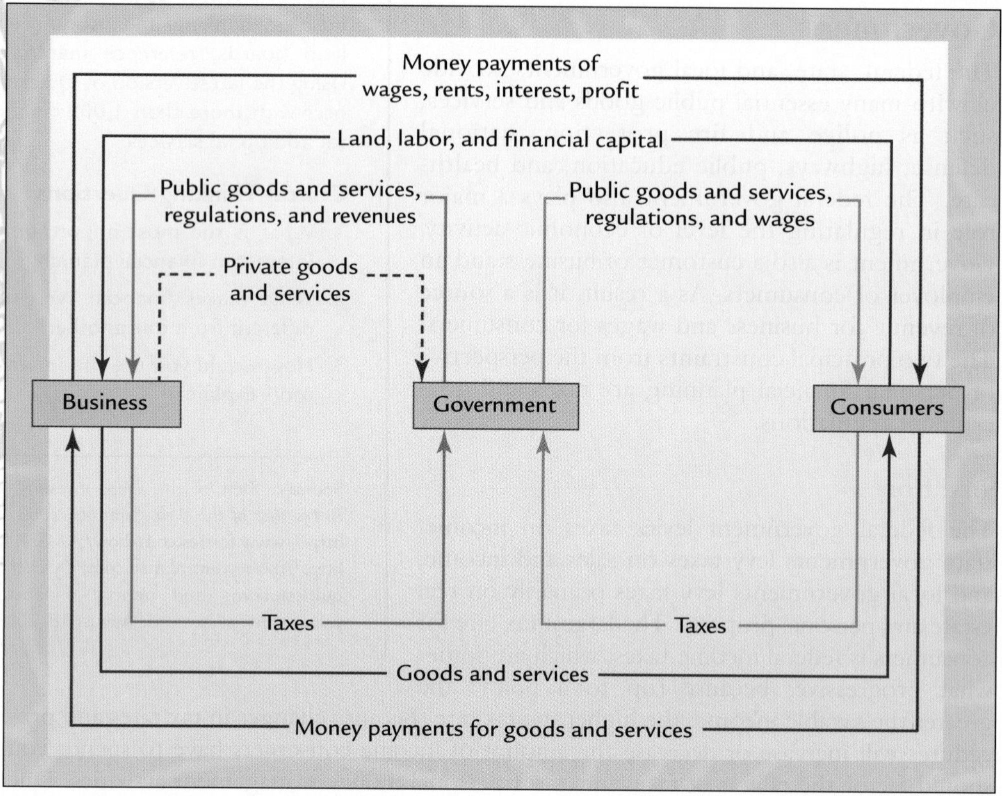

must hire labor and use land and capital (what economists refer to as *factors of production*). In return, firms pay out wages, rents, interest, and profits to the various factors of production. Thus, businesses are an important part of the circular flow of income that sustains our free enterprise system. In general, their presence creates a competitive environment in which consumers may select from an array of goods and services. There are, of course, certain industries, such as public utilities, in which the degree of competition or choice offered the consumer is limited for economic reasons by various regulatory bodies. As indicated in the preceding section, all businesses are limited in some way by federal, state, and local laws.

Consumers

The consumer is the central player in the financial planning environment. Consumer choices ultimately determine the kinds of goods and services businesses will provide. In addition, the consumer's choice of whether to spend or save has a direct impact on the present and future circular flows of money. Cutbacks in consumer spending are usually associated with a decline in economic activity, while an increase helps the economy to recover. Check out Exhibit 1.10 for how we are coping with tough economic times.

Consumers are often thought to have free choices in the marketplace, but they must operate within an environment that interacts with government and business. Although they can affect these parties through their elected officials and by their purchasing actions, lobbyists and consumer groups are necessary to create any real impact. The individual consumer should not expect to change government or business, but rather plan transactions within the existing financial environment.

EXHIBIT 1.10

How Are We Doing Financially?

In today's strained economy consumer debt is on the rise, and personal bankruptcies are skyrocketing.

- 98 percent of all recent bankruptcies are personal
- 64 percent of adults are living paycheck to paycheck
- 71 percent say getting out of debt is their top financial goal
- 26 percent listed insufficient salary as their main money complaint
- 75 percent have gone into debt

As many Americans struggle to make ends meet here are some examples of how they're reducing spending:

- 43 percent have curtailed doctor's visits
- 64 percent reduced spending on clothes
- 65 percent have cut back on restaurant meals
- 59 percent have stopped going to movies, plays, or other entertainment
- 60 percent have cut back on travel spending

Source: Lou Dobbs, "The Dobbs Report—In Hock to the Hilt," *U.S. News & World Report,* July 21, 2003, p. 36; Gini Kopecky Wallace, "Can Money Buy Happiness?" *Family Circle*, April 15, 2003, pp. 64–68.

THE ECONOMY

Our economy is influenced by interaction between government, business, and consumers, as well as world economic conditions. Through specific policy decisions, the government's goal is to regulate the economy and provide economic stability and high levels of employment. These government decisions have a major impact on the economic and financial planning environment. The federal government's ***monetary policy***, programs for controlling the amount of money in circulation (the money supply), is used to stimulate or contract economic growth. For example, increases in the money supply tend to lower interest rates. This typically leads to a higher level of consumer and business borrowing and spending that increases overall economic activity. The reverse is also true. Reducing the money supply raises interest rates, reducing consumer and business borrowing and spending and slowing economic activity.

The government's other principal tool for managing the economy is ***fiscal policy***, its programs of spending and taxation. Increased spending for social services, education, defense, and other programs stimulates the economy, while decreased spending slows economic activity. Increasing taxes, on the other hand, gives businesses and individuals less to spend and, as a result, negatively affects economic activity. Conversely, decreasing taxes stimulates the economy.

Economic Cycles

Although the government uses monetary and fiscal policy to regulate the economy and provide economic stability, the level of economic activity changes constantly. The upward and downward movement creates *economic cycles* (also called *business cycles*). These cycles vary in length and in how high or low the economy moves. An economic cycle typically contains four stages: *expansion, recession, depression,* and *recovery.*

Exhibit 1.11 shows how each of these stages relates to employment and production levels, two important indicators of economic activity. The stronger the economy, the higher the levels of employment and production. Eventually a period of economic **expansion** will peak and begin to move downward, becoming a **recession** when the decline lasts more than 6 months. A **depression** occurs when a recession worsens to the point where economic growth is almost at a standstill. The **recovery** phase, with increasing levels of employment and production, follows either a recession or a depression. For about 75 years, the government has been reasonably successful in keeping the economy out of a depression, although we have experienced periods of rapid expansion and high inflation followed by periods of deep recession.

expansion
The phase of the economic cycle during which the level of employment and growth of economic activity are both high; generally accompanied by rising prices for goods and services.

recession
The phase of the economic cycle during which the level of employment falls and growth of economic activity slows.

depression
The phase of the economic cycle during which the employment level is low and economic growth is at a virtual standstill.

recovery
The phase of the economic cycle during which the employment level is improving and the economy is experiencing increased activity and growth.

EXHIBIT 1.11

The Economic Cycle

The economy goes through various stages over time, although real depressions are extremely rare. These stages tend to be cyclical and directly affect the levels of employment and production.

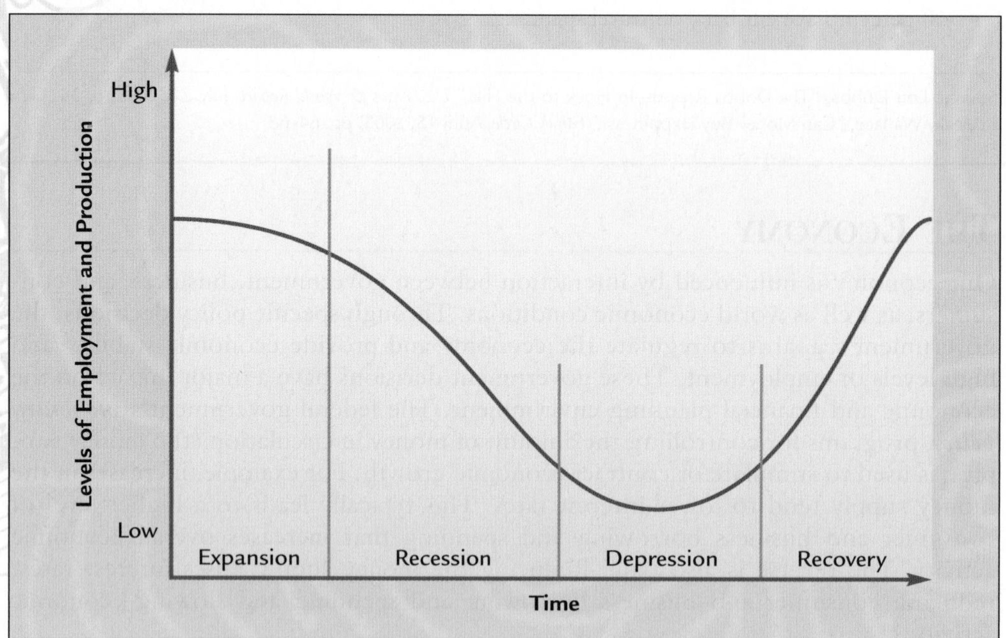

After the recession of the early 1990s, the economy went through a very long and drawn out expansion phase. Inflation and interest rates remained generally low, while the stock market soared to record levels. In early 2001, the stock market experienced some significant declines.

Economic growth is measured by changes in the **gross domestic product (GDP)**, the total of all goods and services produced by workers located within the country. The

gross domestic product (GDP)
The total of all goods and services produced by workers located within a country; used to monitor economic growth.

broadest measure of economic activity, GDP is reported quarterly and is used to compare trends in national output. A rising GDP means the economy is growing. The *rate* of GDP growth is also important. For example, although actual GDP rose year after year for much of the 1990s, the annual rate of GDP growth varied widely.

Another important yardstick of economic health is the *unemployment rate.* The swings in unemployment from one phase of the cycle to the next can be substantial. For example, during the Great Depression of the 1930s, U.S. unemployment reached a staggering 25 percent of the workforce. In contrast, during the expansion in 1968, unemployment dropped to slightly less than 4 percent. During the 1981–1982 recession, unemployment rose to over 10 percent. During the expansion that followed and lasted until late 1990, unemployment fell to 5.3 percent before rising to about 7.4 percent during the recessionary period of the early 1990s. By mid-2000, unemployment had dropped to 4.0 percent, from which it rose to 6.4 percent by June 2003.

Unemployment, inflation, interest rates, bank failures, corporate profits, taxes, and government deficits have a direct and profound impact on our financial well-being; these factors affect the very heart of our financial plans—our level of income, investment returns, interest earned and paid, taxes paid, and, in general, prices paid for goods and services consumed.

smart.sites

How is the U.S. Economy doing this month? Check out the Bureau of Labor Statistics "Economy at a Glance" page, **http://www.bls.gov/eag/eag.us.htm**.

Inflation, Prices, and Planning

inflation A state of the economy in which the general price level is rising due to excessive demand or rapidly rising production costs; usually occurs during the recovery and expansion phases of the economic cycle.

consumer price index (CPI) A measure of the cost of living and inflation based on changes in the cost of a market basket of consumer goods and services.

purchasing power The amount of goods and services each dollar buys at a given point in time.

As we have discussed, our economy is based on the exchange of goods and services between businesses and their customers—consumers, government, and other businesses—for a medium of exchange called money. The mechanism that facilitates this exchange is a system of *prices.* Technically speaking, the price of something is *the amount of money the seller is willing to accept in exchange for a given quantity of some good or service*—for instance, $3 for a pound of meat or $10 for an hour of work. When the general level of prices *increases* over time, the economy is said to be experiencing a period of **inflation**. The most common measure of inflation is the **consumer price index (CPI)**, which is based on the changes in the cost of a market basket of consumer goods and services. At times, the rate of inflation has been substantial. In 1980, for instance, prices went up by 13.5 percent. Fortunately, inflation has dropped dramatically in this country, and the annual rate of inflation has remained below 5 percent every year since 1983, except in 1990 when it was 5.4 percent. Recently the rate of inflation has been just over 2 percent.

Inflation is of vital concern to financial planning. It affects not only what we pay for the various goods and services we consume, but also what we earn in our jobs. Inflation tends to give an illusion of something that does not exist. That is, while we seem to be making more money, we really aren't. As prices rise, we need more income because our **purchasing power**—the amount of goods and services we can buy with our dollars—declines. For example, assume that you earned $30,000 in 2000 and received annual raises so that your salary was $34,000 by 2003. That represents an annual growth rate of 4.3 percent. If inflation averaged 5 percent per year, however, your purchasing power would have decreased, even though your income rose.

Concept ✓

1-15. Discuss the following statement: "It is the interaction among government, business, and consumers that determines the environment in which personal financial plans must be made."

1-16. What are the stages of an economic cycle? Explain their significance for your personal finances.

1-17. What is *inflation*, and why should it be a concern in financial planning?

You would require $34,729 just to keep pace with inflation. So be sure to look at what you earn in terms of its purchasing power, not just in absolute dollars.

Inflation also directly affects interest rates. High rates of inflation drive up the cost of borrowing money as lenders demand compensation for their eroding purchasing power. Higher interest rates mean higher mortgage payments, higher monthly car payments, and so on. High inflation rates also have a detrimental effect on stock and bond prices. Finally, sustained high rates of inflation can have devastating effects on retirement plans and other long-term financial goals. Indeed, for many people it can put such goals out of reach. Clearly, low inflation is good for the economy, for interest rates and stock and bond prices, and for financial planning in general.

smart.sites

Use the inflation calculator at **http://www.bls.gov/cgi-bin/cpicalc.htm** to check on the buying power of today's dollar.

WHAT DETERMINES YOUR PERSONAL INCOME?

LG5, LG6

An obvious and important factor in determining how well we live is the amount of income we earn. In the absence of any inheritance or similar financial windfall, your income will depend in large part on such factors as your age, marital status, education, geographic location, and choice of career. Making a lot of money is not easy, but it can be done! A high level of income—whether derived from your job, your own business, or your investments—is within your reach if you have the necessary dedication, commitment to hard work, and a well-thought-out set of financial plans. The data in Exhibit 1.12 shows how income changes with age and education.

Financial Road Sign

Calculate That Move

Before saying yes to that out-of-town job offer take a minute to consult the various online cost-of-living calculators at Homefair.com, **http://www.homefair.com/homefair/calc/salcalc.html**. It will give you a feel for how your dollar will stretch in your new city compared with your old one. The site also offers guides to housing, schools, and other useful information.

If you are a homeowner, or considering buying a home and want to know where you will get the most house for your money, go to **http://www.coldwellbanker.com**. Click on *homeowner* and *resource center* for their relocation price index covering hundreds of areas in the United States. You can use it to determine what it would cost to buy a home like the one you live in—or the one you want to own. It can also help you decide whether your standard of living will go up or down if you move.

Source: "How to Compare Housing Costs Across the USA," *USA Today*, August 9, 2002, p. B8.

DEMOGRAPHICS AND YOUR INCOME

Typically, people with low incomes fall into the very young or very old age groups, with the highest earnings generally occurring between the ages of 45 and 65. Those below age 45 are developing trades or beginning to move up in their jobs, and many over 65 are working only part-time or are completely retired. In the 35–44 age group, the average income of the heads of household is about $77,000, which jumps to over $93,000 for those in the 45–54 age group, and then falls sharply to about $58,000 in the 65–74 age group. Your own income will vary over time, too, so you need to incorporate anticipated shifts in earnings into your financial plans.

YOUR EDUCATION

Your level of formal education is a controllable factor that has a considerable effect on your income. As Exhibit 1.9 illustrates, heads of household who have more formal education earn higher annual incomes than those with lesser degrees. In a recent study of affluent Americans, defined as those earning $75,000 or more, 62 percent had college and/or postgraduate degrees, while only 11 percent had a high-school diploma or

EXHIBIT 1.12

How Age and Education Affect Annual Income

The amount of money you earn is closely tied to your age and education. Generally, the closer you are to middle age (45–65) and the more education you have, the greater your income will be.

Annual Income (Head of Household)	
Age	**Average Income**
35 and under	$44,200
35–44	77,100
45–54	93,200
55–64	86,900
65–74	58,100
75 and over	36,700
Education	**Average Income**
No high-school diploma	$ 25,100
High-school diploma	44,800
Some college	55,500
College graduate	116,600

Source: Adapted from Ana M. Aizcorbe, Arthur B. Lennickell, and Kevin B. Moore, "Recent Changes in U.S. Family Finances: Evidence from the 1998 and 2001 Survey of Consumer Finances," *Federal Reserve Bulletin,* Board of Governors of the Federal Reserve System, Washington, D.C., January 2003, downloaded from **http://www.federalreserve.gov/pubs/bulletin/2003/0103lead.pdf**.

less. According to recent census bureau data, the median salary of a high-school graduate is about $34,400, compared with $66,500 for a college graduate. Add a PhD or other professional degrees, and earnings rise substantially. Over a lifetime, these differences really add up! Although education alone cannot guarantee a high income, these statistics suggest that a solid formal education greatly enhances your earning power.

smart.sites

Use online calculators to help you save for college at **http://www.kiplinger.com/planning** and **http://www.money.com**.

WHERE YOU LIVE

Geographic factors can also affect your earning power. Salaries vary regionally tending to be higher in the Northeast and West than in the South. Typically, your salary will also be higher if you live in a large metropolitan area rather than a small town or rural area. Such factors as economic conditions, labor supply, and industrial base also affect salary levels in different areas.

In addition, living costs vary considerably throughout the country. You would earn more in Los Angeles than Boise, Idaho, but your salary would probably not go as far due to Los Angeles's much higher cost of living. Like many others you may decide that lifestyle considerations take priority over earning potential. Your local chamber of commerce or the Internet can provide an intercity cost of living index that compares living costs in major cities and serves as a useful resource for comparing jobs in different areas.

(See the Financial Road Sign "Calculate That Move" for more information.) The overall index is developed by tracking costs in six major categories: groceries, housing, utilities, transportation, healthcare, and miscellaneous goods and services.

Your Career

A critical factor in how much you earn over your lifetime depends very much on your career. The career you choose is closely related to your level of education and your particular skills, interests, lifestyle preferences, and personal values. Social, demographic, economic, and technological trends also influence your decision as to what fields offer the best opportunities for your future. Although not a prerequisite for many types of careers, such as sales, service, and certain types of manufacturing and clerical work, a formal education generally leads to greater decision-making responsibility—and consequently increased income potential—within a career. Exhibit 1.13 presents an alphabetical list of representative salaries for entry-level, midlevel, and managerial positions for a variety of careers.

EXHIBIT 1.13

Representative Salaries for Selected Professions

Professional and managerial workers, who typically have a college degree, tend to earn the highest salaries.

	Salary		
Profession	**Entry-Level**	**Midlevel**	**Managerial**
Accountant, public	$35,000	$ 67,000	$162,000
Computer programmer	35,000	50,000	95,000
Engineer	50,000	80,000	130,000
Family practice medical doctor	n/a	136,000	n/a
Financial manager	32,000	85,000	135,000
Human resources manager	28,000	60,000	104,000
Lawyer	52,000	88,000	146,000
Paralegal	24,000	38,000	56,000
Pharmacist	n/a	71,000	n/a
Police officer	31,000	40,000	79,000
Psychologist	33,000	49,000	73,000
Registered nurse	32,000	45,000	64,000
Teacher, K–12	28,000	42,000	65,000
Systems analyst	32,000	60,000	89,000

Sources: *CollegeJournal Salary Data*, **http://www.collegejournal.com/salaryinfo/**, downloaded August 18, 2003; *Occupational Outlook Handbook 2002–2003*, U.S. Bureau of Labor Statistics, **http://www.bls.gov/oco**; "Salary Wizard," *Business Week Online*, **http://swz-businessweek.salary.com**, downloaded August 18, 2003.

Planning Your Career

Career planning and personal financial planning are closely related activities, so the decisions you make in one area affect the other. Like financial planning, career planning is a lifelong process that includes short- and long-term goals. Since your career goals are likely to change several times, you should not expect to stay in one field, or remain with one company, your whole life.

Financial Road Sign

Avoiding Online Job-Search Mistakes

These tips will help you use online job-search resources wisely.

Format: Use ASCII format, not Word, to create an online résumé. Use only plain text (no bold, underlines) and keyboard symbols (asterisks, not bullets). Cut and paste your résumé into an e-mail; don't attach it.

Limit postings: Post your résumé on sites where employers browse for free, such as **http://hotjobs.yahoo.com** or **http://www.flipdog.com**, and on sites specializing in your field.

Follow up: If you use a service like **http://www.yourmissinglink.com** to send résumés to Human Resources (HR) departments, follow up by phone with companies that received it.

Avoid ads: If you post your résumé on a personal Web page, keep it simple and don't use a free Web-hosting site where employers see the site's ads as well.

Use other useful sites: Check out **http://www.monster.com** and **http://www.hotjobs.com** for job postings, as well as **http://www.careerjournal.com**, a career service offered by *The Wall Street Journal*.

Source: Adapted from Joellen Perry, "Avoid a Comedy of E-Errors," *U.S. News & World Report*, November 6, 2000, downloaded from **http://www.usnews.com**.

You might graduate with a computer science degree and accept a job with a software company. Your financial plan might include furnishing your apartment, saving for a vacation or new car, and starting an investment program. If 5 years later you decide to go to law school, your financial plan will have to be revised to include strategies to cover living expenses and finance your tuition. You may decide that you need to go to school at night while you earn a living during the day.

The average American starting his or her career today can expect to have at least 10 jobs with five or more employers, and many of us will have three, four, or even more careers during our lifetimes. Some of these changes will be based on personal decisions; others may result from lay-offs due to corporate downsizing. For example, a branch manager for a regional bank who feels that bank mergers have reduced her job prospects in banking may buy a quick-print franchise and become her own boss. Job security is practically a thing of the past, and corporate loyalty has given way to a more self-centered career approach, which requires new career strategies.

Through careful career planning, you can improve your work situation to gain greater personal and professional satisfaction. Some of the steps are similar to the financial planning process described earlier:

- Identify your interests, skills, needs, and values.
- Set specific long- and short-term career goals.
- Develop and implement an action plan to achieve those goals.
- Review and revise your career plans as your situation changes.

Your action plan will depend on your job situation. For example, if you are unemployed, it will focus on your job search. If you have a job but want to change careers, it might include researching career options, networking to develop a broad base of contacts, listing companies to contact for information, and getting special training to prepare for your chosen career.

smart.sites

One of the first steps in the job-search process is to assess your personality. Use this link to take the Keirsey Temperament Sorter as a starting point: **http://www.keirsey.com/cgi-bin/newkts.cgi**.

A personal portfolio of skills, both general and technical, will protect your earning power during economic downturns and advance it during prosperous times. Employers need flexible, adaptable workers as companies restructure and pare down their operations. It is important to continually upgrade your skills with on-the-job training programs and continuing education courses. Adding proficiency in technology or languages will help put you ahead of the pack in keeping up with changing workplace requirements. It is a good idea to broaden your contacts within your industry and among your professional colleagues, who know which industries have potential and which are in trouble, and know what skills are in demand in your field.

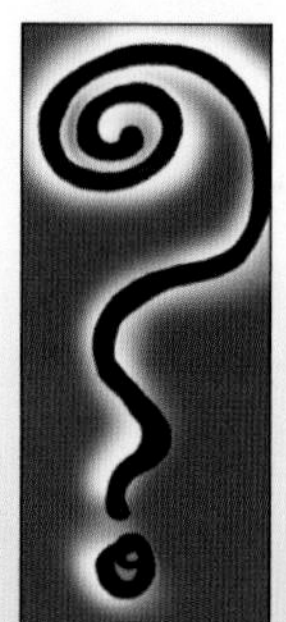

Concept ✓

1-18. "All people who have equivalent formal education earn similar incomes." Do you agree or disagree with this statement? Explain your position.

1-19. Discuss the need for career planning throughout the life cycle and its relationship to financial planning. What are some of your personal career goals?

Good job-hunting skills will serve you well throughout your career. Learn how to research new career opportunities and investigate potential jobs, taking advantage of online resources as well as traditional ones. Develop a broad base of career resources, starting with your college placement office, public library, and personal contacts such as family and friends. Know how to market your qualifications to your advantage in your résumé and cover letters, on the phone, and in person during a job interview.

smart.sites

The *U.S. News & World Report* Career Center has material on a variety of career topics, from internships and resumes to the hottest careers and benefits: **http://www.usnews.com/usnews/work/wohome.htm**.

SUMMARY

LG1. Identify the benefits of using personal financial planning techniques to manage your finances. Personal financial planning helps you marshal and control your financial resources. It should allow you to improve your standard of living, get more enjoyment from your money by spending it wisely, and accumulate wealth. By setting short- and long-term financial goals, you will enhance your quality of life both now and in the future. The ultimate result will be an increase in wealth.

LG2. Describe the personal financial planning process and define your financial goals. Personal financial planning is a six-step process that helps you achieve your financial goals. The six steps in the financial planning process are: (1) define financial goals; (2) develop financial plans and strategies to achieve goals; (3) implement financial plans and strategies; (4) periodically develop and implement budgets to monitor and control progress toward goals; (5) use financial statements to evaluate results of plans and budgets, taking corrective action as required; and (6) redefine goals and revise plans and strategies as personal circumstances change. Before you can manage your financial resources, you must realistically spell out your short-, intermediate-, and long-term financial goals. Goals, which reflect your values and circumstances, may change as personal circumstances dictate. They should also be specifically stated in terms of the desired results.

LG3. Explain why personal financial plans should be flexible and responsive to your life situation. As you move through various life-cycle stages, you must revise your financial plans to include goals and strategies appropriate to each stage. Income and expense patterns change with age. Changes in your life due to marriage, children, divorce, remarriage, and job status also necessitate adapting financial plans to meet current needs. Although these plans change over time, they are the roadmap that points you in the right direction to achieve your financial goals. Once you define your goals, you can develop and implement an appropriate personal financial plan. A complete set of financial plans covers asset acquisition, liability and insurance, savings and investments, employee benefits, taxes, and retirement and estate planning. These plans should be reviewed regularly and revised as necessary.

LG4. Examine the external factors that can influence personal financial planning. Financial planning occurs in an environment where the government, business, and consumers are all influential participants. Government provides certain essential services and the structure within which businesses and consumers function. Businesses provide goods and services to consumers, whose choices influence the products and services businesses offer. Personal financial decisions are affected by economic cycles (expansion, recession, depression, and recovery) and the impact of inflation on prices (purchasing power and personal income).

LG5. Evaluate the impact of age, marital status, education, and geographic location on personal income. Demographics, education, and career are all important factors that affect your income level. As a rule, people age 45 to 65 tend to earn more than others, as do those who are married. Equally important, statistics show a direct correlation between level of education and income. Where you live is an additional consideration—salaries and living costs are higher in some areas than in others. Career choices also affect your level of income—those in professional and managerial positions tend to earn the highest salaries.

LG6. Understand the importance of career choices and their relationship to personal financial planning. Career planning is a lifetime process that involves goal setting and career development strategies. A career plan should be flexible and able to adapt to new workplace requirements. Use continuing education and on-the-job training to facilitate changes in job, employer, and even career. When making career plans, you should identify your interests, skills, needs, and values; set specific long- and short-term career goals; develop and implement an action plan to achieve your goals; and review and revise your career plans as your situation changes. Most career decisions have monetary implications so you should coordinate your career plans with your personal financial plans.

Financial Planning Exercises

1. How can using personal financial planning tools help you improve your financial situation? Describe changes you can make in at least three areas.

2. *Use Worksheet 1.1.* Describe your current status based on the personal financial planning life cycle shown in Exhibit 1.3. Fill out Worksheet 1.1, "Summary of Personal Financial Goals," with goals that reflect your current situation and your expected life situation in 5 and 10 years. Discuss the reasons for the changes in your goals and how you will need to adapt your financial plans as a result. Which types of financial plans do you need for your current situation, and why?
3. Recommend three financial goals and related activities for someone in each of the following circumstances:
   a. Junior in college
   b. 25-year-old computer programmer who wants to get a master's degree in business administration
   c. Couple in their thirties with two children, ages three and six
   d. Divorced 45-year-old man with a 15-year-old child and a 75-year-old father who is ill
4. Summarize current and projected trends in the economy with regard to GDP growth, unemployment, and inflation. How should you use this information to make personal financial and career planning decisions?

5. Assume that you graduated from college with a major in marketing and took a job with a large consumer-products company. After 3 years, you are laid off when the company downsizes. Describe the steps you'd take to "repackage" yourself for another field.

Applying Personal Finance

Watch Your Attitude!

Many people's *attitude* toward money has as much or more to do with their ability to accumulate wealth than does the *amount* of money they earn. Attitude has an impact on the entire financial planning process and often determines whether financial goals become reality or end up being pipe dreams. The purpose of this project is to help you examine your attitude toward money and wealth so that you can formulate realistic goals and plans.

Use the questions below to stimulate your thought process. Does your attitude toward money help or hinder you? How can you better align your attitude so that you are more likely to accomplish your financial goals?

1. Am I a saver, or do I spend almost all the money I receive?
2. Does it make me feel good just to spend money, regardless of what it's for?
3. Is it important for me to have new clothes or a new car just for the sake of having new clothes or a new car?
4. Do I have clothes hanging in my closet with the price tags still on them?
5. Do I buy things because they are a bargain or because I need them?
6. Do I save for my vacations, or do I charge everything and take months paying off my charge card at high interest?
7. If I have a balance on my charge card, without looking at my statement can I recall what the charges were for?
8. Where do I want to be professionally and financially in 5 years? Ten years?
9. Will my attitude toward money help get me there? If not, what do I need to do?
10. If I dropped out of school today or lost my job, what would I do?

Contemporary Case Applications

1.1 Nathan's Need to Know: Personal Finance or Tennis?

During the Christmas break of his final year at Western State University, Nathan Strong planned to put together his résumé in order to seek full-time employment as a medical technician during the spring semester. To help Nathan prepare for the job interview process, his older brother arranged for him to meet with a friend, Alicia Nolan, who had worked as a medical technician since her graduation from Western State 2 years earlier. Alicia provided him with numerous pointers on résumé preparation, the interview process, and possible job opportunities.

After answering Nathan's many questions, Alicia asked Nathan to bring her up to date on Western State. As they discussed courses, Alicia indicated that of all the electives she had taken, she had found the personal financial planning course most useful. Nathan said that although he had considered personal financial planning for his last elective, he was currently leaning toward a beginning tennis course. He felt that because a number of his friends were taking tennis, it would be fun. He pointed out that he never expected to get rich and already knew how to balance his checkbook. Alicia told him that there is much more to personal financial planning than balancing a checkbook, and that the course was highly relevant regardless of income level. She strongly believed that the personal financial planning course would be more beneficial to Nathan than beginning tennis—a course that she had also taken while at Western State University.

Questions

1. Describe to Nathan the goals and rewards of the personal financial planning process.
2. Explain to Nathan what is meant by financial planning and why it is important regardless of income.
3. Describe the financial planning environment to Nathan. Explain the role of the consumer and the impact of economic conditions on financial planning.
4. What arguments would you present to convince Nathan that the personal financial planning course would be more beneficial for him than beginning tennis?

1.2 Tony's Dilemma: Finding a New Job

Anthony Como, a 47-year-old retail store manager earning $75,000 a year, had worked for the same company during his entire 28-year career. Then a major economic recession caused massive layoffs throughout the retail industry, and Tony was among the unlucky people who lost their jobs. Ten months later, he was still unemployed, and his 10 months' severance pay and 6 months' unemployment compensation had run out. Fortunately, when he first became a store manager he had taken a personal financial planning course offered by the local university. Because he then adopted careful financial planning practices, he had sufficient savings and investments to carry him through several more months of unemployment. His greatest financial need was to find a job.

Tony actively sought work but found himself overqualified for available lower-paying jobs and underqualified for higher-paying, more desirable positions. There were no openings for positions equivalent to the manager's job he had lost. Although Tony had attended college for 2 years after high school, he had not earned a degree. He had lost his wife several years earlier and is very close to his two grown children who live in the same city.

The options facing Tony are:

- Wait out the recession until another retail store manager position opens up.
- Move to another area of the country where store manager positions are still available.
- Accept a lower-paying job for 2 or 3 years and go back to school evenings to finish his college degree and qualify for a better position.
- Consider other types of jobs that could benefit from his managerial skills.

Questions

1. What important career factors should Tony consider when evaluating his options?
2. What important personal factors should Tony consider when deciding among his career options?
3. What recommendations would you give Tony in light of both the career and personal dimensions of his options noted in Questions 1 and 2?
4. What career strategies should today's workers employ in order to avoid Tony's dilemma?

MONEY ONLINE

Careers!

Note: Web addresses change frequently. If you have difficulty with the addresses below, consult our Web site at **http://gitman.swlearning.com** for updated site addresses or additional information.

1. **http://www.careerjournal.com**

Find *all* your career information at the Web site prepared by *The Wall Street Journal*! Salary and hiring information, job-hunting advice, tips on managing your career—it's all here along with their search features for jobs and articles. Use their tools or join in their discussions.

2. **http://stats.bls.gov**

Examine the employment outlook for the career you've chosen or learn what the average wage and benefits are for your area and occupation. Tap into the vital information on labor economics and statistics made available at the Web site of the Bureau of Labor Statistics. Search for publications such as the *Occupational Outlook Handbook* or the *Career Guide to Industries.* Research other topics as well, such as the nature of a given industry, working conditions, and training and advancement.

3. **http://www.jobstar.org/hidden**

Tap into the hidden job market! An estimated 80 percent of all positions are filled *without* employer advertising. Work through JobStar's step-by-step plan to find these jobs that are never advertised. Use their Web site to research various companies and find which are the best to work for.

4. **http://www.coolworks.com**

Vacation every day! Find a job at a resort, ski area, national park, ranch, or camp. Or maybe find a job on the water—perhaps river rafting or working aboard a yacht or cruise ship. Let the Cool Works Web site help you find a job at one of these great places so you can live and work where others only visit.

5. **http://www.monster.com**

Visit this great site to search for a job, post your resume, find out who's hiring or get tips on how to create either a traditional or scannable resume. Use Monster's resources to research companies and find out more about today's top employers. Explore their global network or let Monster e-mail you when suitable job openings arise.

6. **http://www.cfp-board.org**

What about a career in financial planning? Find out about the financial planning industry and what a financial planner does at the Web site of the Certified Financial Planner Board of Standards. Learn what the requirements are for becoming licensed as a CFP or search for one in your area.

7. **http://www.homefair.com**

Have you received job offers from around the country? Use "The Salary Calculator" provided by the National Association of Realtors to help you determine how far your paycheck will stretch. Compare where you live now with New York, Atlanta, Chicago, or Bowling Green.

Just for Fun!

8. **http://woodrow.mpls.frb.fed.us**

What's a dollar worth? Find the inflation calculator provided at the Web site of the Federal Reserve Bank of Minneapolis to determine today's equivalent of:

- A meal purchased in 1930 for $1
- A home purchased in 1970 for $40,000
- A car purchased in 1985 for $10,000

While you're there, compare the change in inflation from one decade to the next from 1950 to the present. Which decade saw the greatest amount of change? Or use the calculator at **http://www.westegg.com/inflation** to go all the way back to 1800!

9. **http://www.homefair.com**

Is there a community that you just love, but you must move somewhere else because of your job? Find a community with characteristics or demographics similar to one that you like using "The Community Calculator" provided at the Web site of the National Association of Realtors. Be sure to also use their "Lifestyle Optimizer" to create a list of the 10 best cities for you to live in.

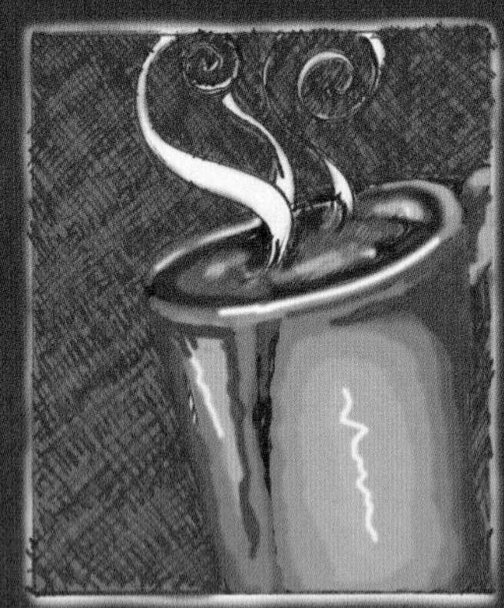

CHAPTER 2

Your Financial Statements and Plans

Learning Goals

LG1. Describe the role of financial statements, special planning concerns, and professional financial planners in the personal financial planning process.
LG2. Put a monetary value on financial goals using *time value of money* concepts.
LG3. Prepare a personal balance sheet.
LG4. Generate a personal income and expense statement.
LG5. Develop a good recordkeeping system and use ratios to interpret personal financial statements.
LG6. Construct a cash budget and use it to monitor and control spending.

Singing the Budgeting Blues

"Where does all the money go?" Tom and Mary Gibson wondered. "We never seem to have enough to save anything, no matter how hard we try." In their early thirties with two daughters ages 7 and 4, the Southern California couple struggles to live on Tom's $80,000 salary as a corporate accountant, plus any extra money he earns from his seasonal tax-return business. Because most of Mary's salary would go for day care, they agreed she would stay home with the girls for now. Compounding the problem, Mary's mother had died suddenly. She had been taking care of Mary's father, who has Parkinson's Disease, and now Mary must find either in-home care or a nursing home—both of which are expensive.

The Gibsons bought a home in the mid-1990s and also own 30 percent of a rental property that is just starting to earn a profit. The cost of living in their region is well above the national average, although their home has appreciated considerably in value. This pleases them, because they can borrow money through a home equity line. However, they are already heavily in debt—$20,000 in car loans and credit card spending—and they have only about $2,200 in cash to cover living expenses and emergencies. They want to save but never seem to have extra money at the month's end to put toward their financial goals, such as buying a second car, establishing a savings/emergency fund, and paying for the girls' college. Tom would also like to earn a graduate degree.

Although Tom and Mary track their expenses using a personal finance program on their computer, they had never actually prepared personal financial statements or a budget. Once they created a family budget, they could see exactly where all that money went! And some of what they learned came as a surprise, especially how the little expenses added up pretty quickly. By taking a closer look at their spending patterns, they saw how to make simple changes—for example, Tom now brings lunch from home several times a week instead of going out. With just this extra $15 a week, the Gibsons have been able to put about $60 a month into an automatic investment program. As they find other ways to trim expenses, both large and small, the amount of their monthly savings deposit is growing nicely.

Learning how to prepare and use budgets gave Tom and Mary greater control over their personal finances. In Chapter 2, you'll discover how personal financial statements and budgets work together to help you, like the Gibsons, reach your financial goals.

CRITICAL THINKING QUESTIONS

As you review the chapter, consider these questions in relation to the Gibsons' financial planning:

- How did preparing and analyzing their family budget help the Gibsons take control of their personal finances?
- What other financial statements should they prepare, and why?
- Would you recommend that the Gibsons use a financial planner, and why? Give them some advice for finding one and suggest several priorities to discuss.

MAPPING OUT YOUR FINANCIAL FUTURE

LG1

For the Gibsons, operating without a budget was like traveling through an unfamiliar state without a road map. On your journey to financial security, you need navigational tools to guide you to your destination: the fulfillment of your financial goals. Financial plans, financial statements, and budgets provide direction by helping you work toward specific financial goals. *Financial plans* are the roadmaps that show you the way, whereas *personal financial statements* let you know where you stand financially. *Budgets,* detailed short-term financial forecasts that compare estimated income with estimated expenses, allow you to monitor and control expenses and purchases consistent with your financial plans. All three are essential to sound personal financial management and the achievement of goals. They provide control by bringing the various dimensions of your personal financial affairs into focus.

As you learned in Chapter 1, the financial planning process includes six steps that translate personal financial goals into specific financial plans and the strategies to achieve these goals. In addition to clearly defining your financial goals in measurable terms, you need to put target dates and a monetary value on your short-, intermediate-, and long-term goals. In the first part of this chapter, we will discuss briefly some special planning concerns and the use of professional financial planners. Next, we will learn how to use time value of money concepts to calculate the value of a financial goal that occurs several years in the future. In the remainder of the chapter, we explain how to prepare and use your own personal financial statements and budgets.

The Role of Financial Statements in Financial Planning

Before you can set realistic goals, develop your financial plans, and effectively manage your money, you must take stock of your current financial situation. You also need tools to monitor your progress. Personal financial statements are planning tools that provide an up-to-date evaluation of your financial well-being, help you identify potential financial problems, and, in general, help you make better-informed financial decisions. They measure your financial condition so you can establish realistic financial goals and evaluate your progress toward those goals. Knowing how to prepare and interpret personal financial statements is therefore a cornerstone of personal financial planning.

Two types of personal financial statements—the *balance sheet* and *income and expense statement*—are essential to developing and monitoring personal financial plans. They show your financial position as it *actually* exists and report on financial transactions that have *really* occurred.

The **balance sheet** describes your financial position—the assets you hold, less the debts you owe, equal your net worth (general level of wealth)—at a *given point* in time. It helps you track the progress you're making in building up your assets and reducing your debt.

In contrast, the **income and expense statement** measures financial performance *over* time. It tracks income earned, as well as expenses made, during a given period (usually a month or a year). You use it to compare your actual expenses and purchases with the amounts budgeted and then make the necessary changes to correct discrepancies between the actual and budgeted amounts. This information helps you control your future expenses and purchases so you'll have the funds needed to carry out your financial plans.

Budgets, another type of financial report, are *forward* looking. Because they are based on expected income and expenses, budgets allow you to monitor and control spending.

Exhibit 2.1 summarizes the various financial statements and reports and their relationship to each other in the personal financial planning process. Note that *financial plans* provide direction to annual budgets. Budgets directly affect your balance sheet and income and expense statement. As you move from plans to budgets to actual

balance sheet
An important financial statement that describes a person's financial position—the assets held, less the debts owed, equal the net worth (general level of wealth)—at a *given point* in time.

income and expense statement
An important financial statement that measures financial performance *over* time by presenting income earned and expenses made during a given period.

budget
A detailed financial report looking *forward*, based on expected income and expenses, used to monitor and control spending.

statements, you can compare your actual results with your plans. This will show you how well you are meeting your financial goals and staying within your budget. Subsequent sections of this chapter take a detailed look at preparing and evaluating basic personal financial statements.

EXHIBIT 2.1

The Interlocking Network of Financial Plans and Statements

Personal financial planning involves a whole network of financial reports that link future goals and plans with actual results. Such a network provides direction, control, and feedback.

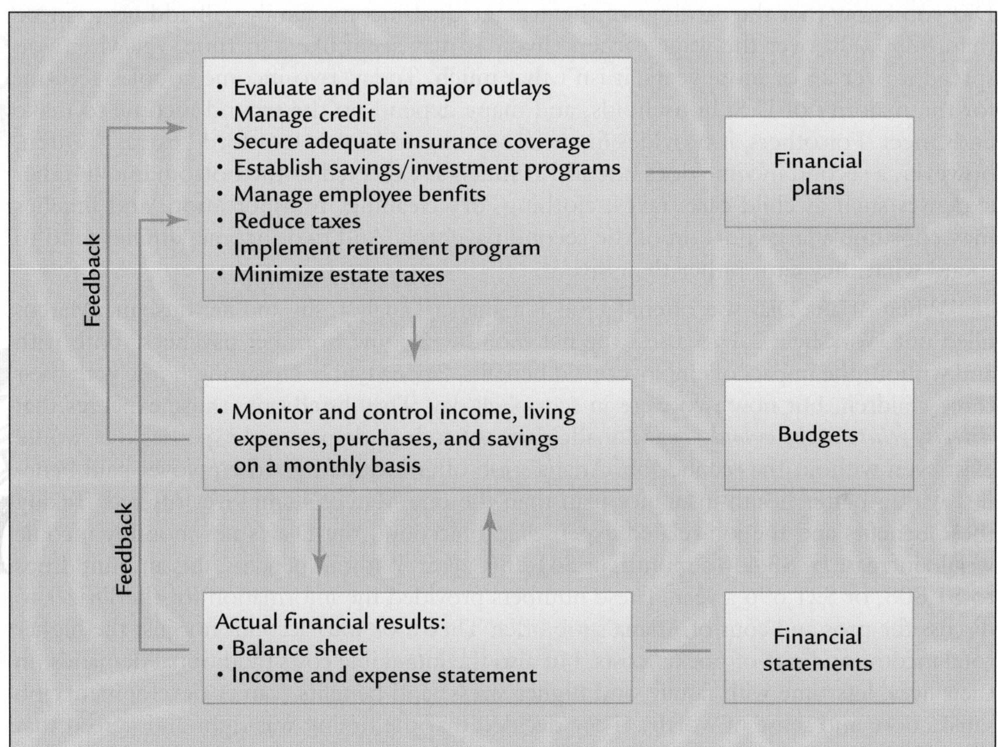

Special Planning Concerns

As a student, you may not think you need to spend much time on financial planning yet. The sooner you start, however, the better prepared you will be to adapt your plans to changing personal circumstances. Changing job status, relocating to a new state, getting married, having children, being in a serious car accident, getting a chronic illness, losing a spouse through divorce or death, retiring, taking responsibility for dependent parents—these and other stressful events are "financial shocks" that require reevaluation of your financial goals and plans.

However, don't rush to make major financial decisions at these times, when you are most vulnerable. Postpone any action until you have had time to recover from the event and evaluate all your options carefully. This can be difficult, because some financial salespeople will rush to contact you in these circumstances. For example, when you have a child, insurance agents, financial planners, and stockbrokers actively encourage you to buy insurance and start investing in a college fund. Although these are valid objectives, don't be pushed into any expensive decisions. People who get large sums of money—from severance packages, retirement benefits, or insurance policies when a loved one dies—are also likely to hear from financial salespeople eager to help them invest the funds. This is another time to wait. These brokers may have a greater interest in selling their own products than advising you on the best strategy for your needs.

smart.sites

The GE Center for Financial Learning will help you plan for changing life situations, with planning tools, online courses, and advice geared to different life stages: **http://www.financiallearning.com**.

Managing Two Incomes

Did you know that the earnings of the average dual-income family will add up to more than $750,000 over the wage earners' lives? It may seem like a fortune, yet when you spread it over 25 or more years, it isn't that much. Today, two-income couples account for the majority of U.S. households, and many depend on the second income to make ends meet. For others, it provides financial security and a way to afford "extras." Often, however, a second income does not add as much as expected to the bottom line. Higher expenses such as child care, taxes, clothing, dry cleaning, transportation, and lunches may consume a large portion of the second paycheck. And two-income families tend to spend what they earn rather than save it.

When Ariana Diaz was offered a job as a financial analyst, she and her husband Marcos filled out Worksheet 2.1 to assess the net monthly income from her paycheck, both with and without the impact of employer-paid benefits. Ariana had been staying home with their three children, but now two were in school all day. They listed only those expenses that *directly relate to the second job* and made sure not to include personal expenses that would exist even without the second job. Ariana's job offer included good employer-paid benefits, with a better health insurance plan than the one Marcos's employer offered. Taking these benefits and the job-related expenses into account, the Diaz's net monthly income would increase by $3,440 a month, or $41,280 a year. Without benefits, this amount drops to $1,808, or $21,696 a year. These numbers provided the information for the Diazes to discuss the pros and cons of Ariana's job offer. They took into account not just the higher total income and out-of-pocket costs, but also the intangible costs (additional demands on their lives, less time with family, and higher stress) and benefits (career development, job satisfaction, and sense of worth). They decided that the timing was right and agreed that they'd use the second income to increase their college savings accounts and build up their other investments. This would provide greater financial security in these uncertain times if Marcos were laid off from his research job at a biotechnology company.

smart.sites

Dollar Bank's Library of helpful articles on managing your personal finances includes a special section for two-income families. Check it out at: **http://www.dollarbank.com/dollarbankpersonal/INFO/2income.html**.

Like the Diazes, partners in double-income households need to approach discussions on financial matters with an open mind and be willing to compromise. Spouses need to decide together how to allocate income to household expenses, family financial goals, and personal spending goals. Will you use a second income to meet basic

worksheet 2.1

Analyzing the Benefit of a Second Income

Use this worksheet to estimate the contribution of a second paycheck. Without the employer-paid benefits of $1,632 (line 2) the Diazes would realize a net monthly income of $1,808 (line 1–line 3), and with them their net monthly income would be $3,440 (line 4).

Second Income Analysis

Name(s) *Ariana and Marcos Diaz* Date *December 31, 2004*

MONTHLY CASH INCOME	
Gross pay	$5,000
Pretax employer contributions (401(k) plans, dependent-care-reimbursement accounts)	400
Additional job-related income (bonuses, overtime, commissions)	0
(1) Total Cash Income	$5,400
EMPLOYER-PAID BENEFITS	
Health insurance	$550
Life insurance	100
Pension contributions	600
Thrift-plan contributions	0
Social Security	382
Profit sharing	0
Other deferred compensation	0
(2) Total Benefits	$1,632
MONTHLY JOB-RELATED EXPENSES	
Federal income tax	$1,500
Social Security tax	382
State income tax	250
Child care	640
Clothing; personal care; dry cleaning	400
Meals away from home	200
Public transportation	0
Auto-related expenses (gas, parking, mainteance)	220
Other	0
(3) Total Expenses	$3,592
(4) Net Income (Deficit) [(1) + (2) – (3)]	$3,440

Source: Adapted from Kevin McManus, "How to Get the Most from Two Incomes," *Changing Times*, July 1989, p. 24.

Money in Action

Planning on Online Financial Advice

Financial planning was once considered a luxury item, for those wealthy enough to pay high fees for personal advice from a financial professional. Today financial advice is just a click away for most Americans, courtesy of specialized Web sites that provide tools and advice ranging from retirement planning tools to advice on how to diversify your assets. Many sites have automated financial advisers. T. Rowe Price (**http://www.troweprice.com**), a mutual fund company, offers investors a variety of planning tools in its individual investor Tools and Calculators pages. These cover investment, retirement, college. Many other mutual fund Web sites have extensive online financial planning advice sections; the Vanguard Group (**http://www.vanguard.com**) and American Century Funds (**http://www.americancentury.com**) are two. You'll find broader planning capabilities at several independent advice sites, including Financial Engines (**http://www.financialengines.com**) and Morningstar.com's ClearFuture service (**http://www.morningstar.com/Cover/ClearFuture.html**). Because planning sites take different approaches, explore several to find one with the features you need.

Let's see how one of these sites approaches the financial planning process. Financial Engines is one of the most sophisticated online advisors, specializing in tax-deferred investment planning for retirement. It is available to individuals participating in employer-sponsored programs. A recent survey revealed that Financial Engines helped users increase their average savings from 6 percent to 10 percent of their income.

It offers a free forecast based on your financial profile—demographic information, current income, investments in your portfolio, savings rate, risk tolerance, retirement age, tax status, retirement income goals. Rather than asking you to make estimates about future inflation rates, interest rates, or investment returns, the planning model runs thousands of possible economic scenarios to simulate many different future financial climates. After taking into account your personal

...continued on next page

expenses, afford a more luxurious lifestyle, save for a special vacation, or invest in retirement accounts? You may need to try several money management strategies to find the one that works best for you. Some couples place all income into a single joint account. Others have each spouse contribute *equal* amounts into a joint account to pay bills, but retain individual discretion over remaining income. Still others contribute a *proportional* share of each income to finance joint expenses and goals. In any case, both spouses should have money of their own to spend without accountability.

Managing Employee Benefits

As discussed in Chapter 1, if you hold a full-time job, your employer probably provides a variety of employee benefits, ranging from health and life insurance to pension plans. As we saw in the Diaz's analysis, these can have a major financial impact on family income. The majority of American families depend solely on employer-sponsored group plans for their health insurance coverage and a big piece of their life insurance coverage and retirement needs.

Today's well-defined employee benefits packages cover a full spectrum of benefits that may include:

- Health and life insurance
- Disability insurance
- Long-term care insurance
- Pension and profit-sharing plans
- Supplemental retirement programs, such as 401(k) plans
- Dental and vision care
- Child care, elder care, and educational assistance programs
- Subsidized employee food services

Each company's benefit package is different. Some companies and industries are known for generous benefit plans, whereas others offer far less attractive packages. In general, large firms can afford more benefits than small ones. Because employee benefits can increase your total compensation by 30 percent or more, you should thoroughly investigate your employee benefits to choose those appropriate for your personal situation. Be sure to coordinate your benefits with your partners to avoid paying for duplicate coverage. Companies change their benefit packages often and today are shifting more costs to employees. Although an employer may pay for some benefits in full, typically employees pay for a portion of the cost of group health insurance, supplemental life insurance, long-term care insurance, and participation in voluntary retirement programs.

Because of the prevalence of two-income families and an increasingly diverse work force, many employers today are replacing traditional programs, where the company sets the type and amount of benefits, with **flexible-benefit (cafeteria) plans**. In flexible-benefit programs, the employer allocates a certain amount of money to each employee and then lets the employee "spend" that money for benefits that suit his or her age, marital status, number of dependent children, level of income, and so forth. These plans usually cover everything from child care to retirement benefits, offer several levels of health and life insurance coverage, and have some limits on the minimum and maximum amount of coverage. Within these constraints, you can select the benefits that do you the most good. In some plans, you can even take a portion of the benefits in the form of more take-home pay or extra vacation time!

flexible-benefit (cafeteria) plan A type of employee benefit plan wherein the employer allocates a certain amount of money, and the employee "spends" that money for benefits selected from a menu covering everything from child care to health and life insurance to retirement benefits.

Along with greater choice comes the responsibility to manage your benefits carefully. You should periodically assess the benefits package you have at work relative to your own individual/family needs, supplementing any shortfall in company benefits with personal coverage. Except perhaps for group medical coverage, don't rely on your employer as the sole source of financial security. Your coverage may disappear if you change jobs or become unemployed, and, especially with life insurance and retirement plans, most employee benefits fall short of your total financial needs.

variables such as savings rate, retirement age, and tax status, it charts the probability that you will achieve your goals. It suggests possible mutual funds to help you improve your results and even sends quarterly updates with new recommendations and reminders to review your plan.

You can view a demo, and if you decide to proceed, the advice costs $39.95 a quarter or $149.95 a year for individuals, which includes multiple accounts. (For $300 a year you receive more comprehensive portfolio advice.) You can experiment with your forecast and make changes to your portfolio or goals by adjusting portfolio risk, projected retirement age, ideal retirement income, or your annual contribution to a tax-deferred account. Financial Engines provides portfolio suggestions based on these variables. It's easy to run "what if" scenarios with different assumptions to quickly see a new portfolio with recommended changes. It also shows the tradeoffs between risk and reward.

Critical Thinking Questions

1. What advantages does a Web-based financial advising system provide? What are the drawbacks?
2. How does online planning compare to a traditional financial advisor?
3. Visit the Financial Engines (**http://www.financialengines.com**) and Morningstar.com's ClearFuture (**http://www.morningstar.com/Cover/ClearFuture.html**) sites. Compare the features and ease of use. Would you use an online advisor, and if so, which one?

Sources: Financial Engines Web site, **http://www.financialengines.com**, accessed June 15, 2003; Wayne Harris, "Plan on the Web," *Mutual Funds* (September 2000), pp. 60–63; and Kathy Yakal, "Investing in (Your) Futures," *Barron's Online*, March 24, 2003, downloaded from **http://online.wsj.com/barrons**.

Adapting to Other Major Life Changes

Other situations that require special consideration include changes in marital status and the need to support grown children or elderly relatives. The marriage, divorce, or death of a spouse results in the need to revise financial plans and money management strategies.

As mentioned earlier, couples should discuss their money attitudes and financial goals and decide how to manage joint financial affairs before they get married. Take an inventory of your financial assets and liabilities, including savings and checking accounts; credit card accounts and outstanding bills; auto, health, and life insurance policies; and investment portfolios. You may want to eliminate some credit cards if there is overlap. Too many cards can hurt your credit rating, and most people need only one or two. Each partner should have a card in his or her name to establish a credit record. Compare employee benefit plans to figure out the lowest-cost source of health insurance coverage and coordinate other benefits. Change the beneficiary on your life insurance policies. Adjust withholding amounts as necessary based on your new filing category.

In event of divorce, income may decrease because alimony and child support payments cause one salary to be divided between two households. Single parents may have to stretch limited financial resources farther to meet added expenses such as child care. Remarriage brings additional financial considerations, including decisions involving children from prior marriages and managing the assets that each spouse brings to the marriage. Some couples develop a prenuptial contract that outlines their agreement on financial matters, such as the control of assets, their disposition in event of death or divorce, and other important money issues.

Death of a spouse is another change that greatly affects financial planning. The surviving spouse is typically faced with decisions on how to receive and invest life insurance proceeds and manage other assets. In families where the deceased made most of the financial decisions with little or no involvement of the surviving spouse, the survivor may be overwhelmed by the need to take on financial responsibilities. Advance planning can minimize many of these problems.

Couples should regularly review all aspects of their finances. Each spouse should understand what is owned and owed, participate in formulating financial goals and investment strategies, and fully understand estate plans (covered in detail in Chapter 15).

Using Professional Financial Planners

Does developing your own financial plans seem like an overwhelming task? Help is at hand! **Professional financial planners** will guide you through establishing goals, plan preparation, and the increasingly complex maze of financial products and investment opportunities. This field has experienced tremendous growth, and there are now more than 250,000 financial planners in the United States.

professional financial planner
An individual or firm that helps clients establish financial goals and develop and implement financial plans to achieve those goals.

Financial planners provide a wide range of services, including preparing comprehensive financial plans that evaluate a client's total personal financial situation or abbreviated plans focusing on a specific concern, such as managing clients' assets and investments and retirement planning. Where once only the very wealthy used professional planners, now financial firms such as H&R Block's Financial Centers and American Express Financial Advisors compete for the business of middle-income people as well.

Why do people turn to financial advisers? A recent survey indicated that retirement needs motivated 50 percent, while 23 percent were unhappy with the results of trying to manage their own finances. Estate and inheritance planning caused another 13 percent to seek help, and saving for college and tax issues were also mentioned.

smart.sites

To find a financial planner in your area, use the Financial Planning Association's search feature, **http://www.fpanet.org/plannersearch/plannersearch.cfm**. Prefer a fee-only planner? Learn more about them at the National Association of Personal Financial Advisers Web site, **http://www.napfa.org**.

Types of Planners

Most financial planners fall into one of two categories based on how they get paid: commissions or fees. Commission-based planners earn commissions on the financial products they sell, whereas fee-only planners charge fees based on the complexity of the plan they prepare. Many financial planners take a hybrid approach and charge fees and collect commissions on products they sell, offering lower fees if you make product transactions through them.

Insurance salespeople and securities brokers who continue to sell the same financial products (life insurance, stocks, bonds, mutual funds, and annuities) often now call themselves "financial planners." Other planners work for large, established financial institutions that recognize the enormous potential in the field and train their planners to compete with the best financial planners. Still others work in small firms, promising high-quality advice for a flat fee or an hourly rate. Regardless of their affiliation, full-service financial planners help their clients articulate their long- and short-term financial goals, systematically plan for their financial needs, and help implement various aspects of the plans. Exhibit 2.2 provides a guide to some of the different planning designations.

EXHIBIT 2.2

Financial Planning Designations

Confused about what the letters after a financial adviser's name signifies? Here's a summary of the most common certifications so you can choose the one that best suits your needs.

Credential	Description
Chartered Financial Analyst (CFA)	Focuses primarily on securities analysis rather than comprehensive financial planning
Certified Financial Planner (CFP®)	Requires a comprehensive education in financial planning
Chartered Financial Consultant (ChFC)	Financial planning designation for insurance agents
Certified Public Accountant (CPA)	Accounting degree; when combined with PFS (see below) has training in comprehensive planning
Certified Trust & Financial Advisor (CTFA)	Estate planning and trusts expertise, found mostly in the banking industry
Personal Financial Specialist (PFS)	Comprehensive planning credential only for CPAs
Chartered Life Underwriter (CLU)	Insurance agent designation, often accompanied by the ChFC credential

Source: Adapted from "What the Titles Mean," *Business Week*, November 25, 2002, p. 148.

In addition to one-on-one financial planning services, some institutions offer computerized financial plans. Merrill Lynch, IDS/American Express, T. Rowe Price, and other major investment firms provide these computerized plans on the Internet to help clients develop plans to save for college or retirement, reduce taxes, or restructure investment portfolios. You can even turn to the Internet for financial planning help, as the *Money in Action* box on page 46 explains.

Personal finance programs such as Quicken and Microsoft Money also have a financial planning component that can help you set a path to your goals and do tax and retirement planning. As you'll see in later chapters, some Web sites provide planning advice on one topic, such as taxes, insurance, or estate planning. Although these plans are relatively inexpensive or even free, they tend to be somewhat impersonal. However, they are a good solution for those who need help getting started and for do-it-yourself planners who want some help.

The cost of financial planning services depends on the type of planner, the complexity of your financial situation, and the services you want. The cost may be well worth the benefits, especially for people who have neither the time, inclination, discipline, nor expertise to plan on their own. Remember, however, that the best advice is worthless if you are not willing to change your financial habits.

Choosing a Financial Planner

Planners who have completed the required course of study and earned the Certified Financial Planner (CFP) or Chartered Financial Consultant (ChFC) designation are often a better choice than the many self-proclaimed financial planners. Of course, CPAs, attorneys, investment managers, and other professionals without such certifications in many instances do provide sound financial planning advice.

Unlike accounting and law, the field is still largely unregulated, and almost anyone can call himself or herself a financial planner. Most financial planners are honest and reputable, but there have been cases of fraudulent practice. It is therefore critical to thoroughly check out a potential financial advisor—and preferably interview two or three—using the tips in Exhibit 2.3 and the checklist you'll find at the CFP Board Web site.

smart.sites

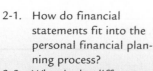

For "10 Questions to Ask When Choosing a Financial Planner," an interview checklist, and other advice on choosing and working with a financial planner, see the Certified Financial Planner Board Web site, **http://www.cfp.net/learn**.

Concept ✓

2-1. How do financial statements fit into the personal financial planning process?

2-2. What is the difference between a *budget* and a *financial plan?* Does a budget play any role in a financial plan?

2-3. Discuss briefly how the following situations affect personal financial planning:
a. Being part of a dual-income couple
b. Major life changes, such as marriage or divorce
c. Death of a spouse

2-4. What is a *professional financial planner?* Does it make any difference whether the financial planner earns money from commissions made on products sold as opposed to the fees he or she charges?

The way a planner is paid—fees, commissions, or both—should be one of your major concerns. Obviously, you need to be aware of potential conflicts of interest when using a planner with ties to a brokerage firm, insurance company, or bank. Many planners now provide clients with disclosure forms outlining fees and commissions for various transactions. In addition to asking questions of the planner, you should also check with your state securities department and the Securities and Exchange Commission (for planners registered to sell securities). Ask if the planner has any pending lawsuits, complaints by state or federal regulators, personal bankruptcies, or convictions

Financial Road Sign

Warning: Critical Life Events Ahead!

The following list summarizes major life situations that require extra attention to financial planning. You may want an outside opinion from a qualified financial planner to get through them:

1. *Death of a parent:* If you are named executor of the estate, you may not understand what is required. You'll also need help managing the inheritance.
2. *Marriage:* You need to carefully plan how to merge your finances and households.
3. *Divorce:* What are the tax and financial implications of the divorce?
4. *Complex financial products:* Do you need disability and long-term care insurance? An umbrella liability policy? Which policies are best for you?
5. *Buying and selling a house:* You'll face several big-dollar decisions with little time to think them through.
6. *Saving for college:* How can you save enough to send your children to college? How can you make the most of Junior's college fund?
7. *Estate planning:* Do you need a trust? Have you named a guardian for your kids?
8. *Retirement:* How do you calculate the amount you need to retire? What types of retirement plans make the most sense for you?

Source: Adapted from "When to Get Advice," *Motley Fool Advisor Center*, **http://www.fool.com**, accessed August 15, 2003.

for investment-related crimes. However, even these agencies may not have accurate or current information; simply being properly registered and without a record of disciplinary actions provides no guarantee that the planner's track record is good. You may also want to research the planner's reputation within the local financial community. Clearly, you should do your homework before engaging the services of a professional financial planner.

EXHIBIT 2.3

Finding and Using a Financial Planner

The following suggestions from the Certified Financial Planner Board of Standards will help you choose and work with a competent personal financial planner.

1. *Know what you want:* Determine your general financial goals and specific needs (insurance policy analysis, estate planning, investment advice, college tuition financing, etc.) to better focus your search for a suitable financial planner.
2. *Be prepared:* Read personal finance publications (*Worth*, *Money*, *Smart Money*, *Kiplinger's Personal Finance*, etc.) to maximize your familiarity with financial planning strategies and terminology.
3. *Talk to others:* Get referrals from advisors you trust, from business associates and friends, or one of the financial planning membership organizations.
4. *Look for competence:* Choose a financial planning professional who has met standards of financial planning competency required to earn the Certified Financial Planner (CFP) designation.
5. *Interview several planners:* Ask each about their credentials (education, experience, professional memberships), specialties, compensation, type of clients served, how often they communicate with clients, and whether an assistant handles client matters. Review a sample financial plan and contact several client references to evaluate the quality and completeness of the advice. You should feel comfortable discussing your finances with the planner you select.
6. *Check the planner's background:* Depending on the financial planner's area of expertise, call the securities or insurance departments in your state regarding each planner's complaint record. Check with the CFP Board (888-CFP-MARK) to ask if a planner is currently a licensed CFP or has ever been publicly disciplined by the CFP Board.
7. *Know what to expect:* Ask for a registration or disclosure statement (such as an ADV Form) detailing the planner's compensation methods, conflicts of interest, business affiliations, and personal qualifications.
8. *Get it in writing:* Request a written advisory contract or engagement letter to document the nature and scope of services the planner will provide. You should also understand whether compensation will be fee- or commission-based, or a combination of both.
9. *Receive regular statements:* If the advisor purchases insurance or securities for you, make sure you receive regular statements from the insurance company or investment broker as well as from the planner.
10. *Reassess the relationship regularly:* Financial planning engagements are often long-term relationships and require ongoing review. Make sure your financial planner understands your goals and needs as they develop and change over time. Question anything you don't understand until you are satisfied with the response. If you have questions regarding the conduct of your CFP certificant, call the CFP Board toll-free at 888-CFP-MARK and ask for a Complaint Package.

Source: Adapted from "Tips on Choosing a Financial Planner," Certified Financial Planner Board of Standards, Inc., downloaded from **http://www.cfp.net**.

THE TIME VALUE OF MONEY: PUTTING A DOLLAR VALUE ON FINANCIAL GOALS

LG2

Assume that one of your financial goals to buy your first home in 6 years. Then your first question is how much to spend. Let's say you have done some "window shopping" and feel that, taking future inflation into consideration, you can buy a townhouse condominium for about $150,000. Of course, you will not need the full amount, but assuming that you will make a 20 percent down payment of $30,000 (.20 × $150,000 = $30,000) and pay $5,000 in closing costs, you will need around $35,000. You now have a fairly well-defined long-term financial goal: *To accumulate $35,000 in 6 years to buy a home costing about $150,000.*

The next question is how to get all that money. You will probably accumulate it by saving or investing a set amount each month or year. You can easily estimate how much to save or invest each year if you know your goal and what you expect to earn on your savings or investments. In this case, if you have to start from scratch (that is, have nothing saved today) and estimate that you can earn about 10 percent on your money, you will have to save or invest about $4,540 per year for each of the next 6 years to accumulate $35,000 over that time period. Now you have another vital piece of information: *You know what you must do over the next 6 years to reach your financial goal.*

How did we arrive at the $4,540 figure? We used a concept called the **time value of money**, the idea that a dollar today is worth more than a dollar received in the future. With time value concepts, we can correctly compare dollar values occurring at different points in time. As long as you can earn a positive rate of return (interest rate) on your investments (ignoring taxes and other behavioral factors), in a strict financial sense you should always prefer to receive equal amounts of money sooner rather than later. The two key time value concepts, future value and present value, are discussed separately below. (*Note:* The following time value discussions and demonstrations initially rely on the use of financial tables. Appendix E explains how to use financial calculators, which have tables built into them, to conveniently make time value calculations.)

time value of money
The concept that a dollar today is worth more than a dollar received in the future; this is true as long as one can earn a positive rate of return (interest rate) on investments.

FUTURE VALUE

To calculate how much to save to buy the $150,000 condominium, we used **future value**, the value to which an amount today will grow if it earns a specific rate of interest over a given period. Assume, for example, that you make annual deposits of $2,000 into a savings account that pays 5 percent interest per year. At the end of 20 years, your deposits would total $40,000 (20 × $2,000). If you made no withdrawals, your account balance would have increased to $66,132! This growth in value occurs not only as a result of earning interest, but because of **compounding**—the interest earned each year is left in the account and becomes part of the balance (or principal) on which interest is earned in subsequent years.

future value
The value to which an amount today will grow if it earns a specific rate of interest over a given period; can be used to find the yearly savings needed to accumulate a given future amount of money.

compounding
When interest earned each year is left in the account and becomes part of the balance (or principal) on which interest is earned in subsequent years.

Future Value of a Single Amount

To demonstrate future value, let's return to the goal of accumulating $35,000 for a down payment to buy a home in 6 years. You might be tempted to solve this problem by simply dividing the $35,000 goal by the 6-year period: $35,000/6 = $5,833. Unfortunately, this procedure would be incorrect, because it would fail to take into account *the time value of money.* The correct way to approach this problem is to use the *future value* concept. For instance, if you can invest $100 today at 10 percent, you will have $110 in a year: You will earn $10 on your investment (.10 × $100 = $10), plus get your original $100 back. Once you know the length of time and rate of return involved, you can find the future value of any investment by using the following simple formula:

Future value = Amount invested × Future value factor

Tables of future value factors simplify the computations in this formula (see Appendix A). The table is very easy to use; simply find the factor that corresponds to a given year and interest rate. Referring to Appendix A, you will find the future value factor for a 6-year investment earning 10 percent is 1.772 (the factor that lies at the intersection of 6 years and 10 percent).

Returning to the problem at hand, let's say you already have accumulated $5,000 toward the purchase of a new home. To find the future value of that investment in 6 years earning 10 percent, you can use the above formula as follows:

$$\text{Future value} = \$5{,}000 \times 1.772 = \underline{\underline{\$8{,}860}}$$

In 6 years, then, you will have $8,860 if you invest the $5,000 at 10 percent. Because you feel you are going to need $35,000, you are still $26,140 short of your goal.

Future Value of an Annuity

How are you going to accumulate the additional $26,140? You will again use the future value concept, but this time you will employ the *future value annuity factor*. An **annuity** is a fixed sum of money that occurs annually; for example, a deposit of $1,000 per year for each of the next 5 years, with payment to be made at the end of each year. To find out how much you need to save each year to accumulate a given amount, use the following equation:

annuity
A fixed sum of money that occurs annually.

$$\text{Yearly savings} = \frac{\text{Amount of money desired}}{\text{Future value annuity factor}}$$

When dealing with an annuity you need to use a different table of factors, such as that in Appendix B. Note that it is very much like the table of future value factors and, in fact, is used in exactly the same way: The proper future value annuity factor is the one that corresponds to a given year *and* interest rate. For example, you'll find in Appendix B that the future value annuity factor for 6 years and 10 percent is 7.716. Using this factor in the above equation, you can find out how much to save each year to accumulate $26,140 in 6 years, given a 10 percent rate of return, as follows:

$$\text{Yearly savings} = \frac{\$26{,}140}{7.716} = \underline{\underline{\$3{,}387.77}}$$

You will need to save about $3,390 a year to reach your goal. Note in the example that you must add $3,390 each year to the $5,000 you initially invested to build up a pool of $35,000 in 6 years. At a 10 percent rate of return, the $3,390 per year will grow to $26,140 and the $5,000 will grow to $8,860, so in 6 years you will have $26,140 + $8,860 = $35,000.

How much, you may ask, would you need to save each year if you did not have the $5,000 to start with? In this case, your goal would still be the same (to accumulate $35,000 in 6 years), but because you would be starting from scratch, the full $35,000 would need to come from yearly savings. Assuming you can still earn 10 percent over the 6-year period, you can use the same future value annuity factor (7.716) and compute the amount of yearly savings as follows:

$$\text{Yearly savings} = \frac{\$35{,}000}{7.716} = \underline{\underline{\$4{,}536.03}}$$

or approximately $4,540. Note that this amount corresponds to the $4,540 figure cited earlier.

Using the future value concept, you can readily find either the future value to which an investment will grow over time or the amount that you must save each year to accumulate a given amount of money by a specified future date. In either case, the procedures allow you to put monetary values on long-term financial goals.

smart.sites

Still confused about time value concepts? Get another lesson at **http://www.teachmefinance.com/timevalueofmoney.html**.

THE RULE OF 72

Suppose that you don't have access to time value of money tables or a financial calculator but want to know how long it takes for your money to double. There is an easy way to approximate this using the **rule of 72**. Simply divide the number 72 by the percentage rate you are earning on your investment:

rule of 72 A useful approximation for estimating how long it will take to double a sum at a given interest rate. Dividing 72 by the annual compound interest rate results in a good estimate of the number of years it will take to double your money.

$$\text{Number of years to double money} = \frac{72}{\text{Annual compound interest rate}}$$

For example, assume that you recently opened a savings account with $1,000 that earns an annual compound rate of interest of 4.5 percent. Your money will double in 16 years (72 ÷ 4.5 = 16). If you can find a $1,000 investment that earns 6.25 percent, you will have $2,000 in about 11.5 years (72 ÷ 6.25 = 11.5).

The rule of 72 also applies to debts. Your debts can double very quickly with high interest rates, such as those charged on most credit card accounts. So keep the rule of 72 in mind whether you invest or borrow!

PRESENT VALUE

Lucky you! You've just won $100,000 in your state lottery. You want to spend part of it now, but because you are 30 years old you also want to use part of it for your retirement fund. Your goal is to accumulate $300,000 in the fund by the time you are age 55 (25 years from now). How much do you need to invest if you estimate that you can earn 7 percent annually on your investments during the next 25 years?

Using **present value**, the value today of an amount to be received in the future, you can calculate the answer. It represents the amount you would have to invest today at a given interest rate over the specified time period to accumulate the future amount. The process of finding present value is called **discounting**, which is the inverse of *compounding* to find future value.

present value The value today of an amount to be received in the future; it is the amount that would have to be invested today at a given interest rate over a specified time period to accumulate the future amount.

discounting The process of finding present value; the inverse of *compounding* to find future value.

Present Value of a Single Amount

Assuming you wish to create the retirement fund (future value) by making a single lump-sum deposit today, you can use the following formula to find the amount you need to deposit:

$$\text{Present value} = \text{Future value} \times \text{Present value factor}$$

Tables of present value factors make this calculation easy (see Appendix C). First, find the present value factor for a 25-year investment at a 7 percent discount rate (the factor that lies at the intersection of 25 years and 7 percent) in Appendix C; it is .184. Then, substitute the future value of $300,000 and the present value factor of .184 into the formula as follows:

$$\text{Present value} = \$300{,}000 \times .184 = \underline{\underline{\$55{,}200}}$$

The $55,200 is the amount you would have to deposit today into an account paying 7 percent annual interest to accumulate $300,000 at the end of 25 years.

Present Value of an Annuity

You can also use present value techniques to determine how much you can withdraw from your retirement fund each year over a specified time horizon. This calls for the *present value annuity factor*. Assume that at age 55 you wish to begin making equal annual withdrawals over the next 30 years from your $300,000 retirement fund. At first, you might think you could withdraw $10,000 per year ($300,000/30 years). However, the funds still on deposit would continue to earn 7 percent annual interest. To find the amount of the equal annual withdrawal, you again need to consider the time value of money. Specifically, you would use the following formula:

$$\text{Annual withdrawal} = \frac{\text{Initial deposit}}{\text{Present value annuity factor}}$$

Use the present value annuity factors in Appendix D at the end of this text for this calculation. Substituting the $300,000 initial deposit and the present value annuity factor for 30 years and 7 percent of 12.409 (from Appendix D) into the equation above, we get:

$$\text{Annual withdrawal} = \frac{\$300{,}000}{12.409} = \underline{\underline{\$24{,}176}}$$

Therefore, you can withdraw $24,176 each year for 30 years. This value is clearly much larger than the $10,000 annual withdrawal mentioned earlier.

Other Applications of Present Value

Furthermore, present value techniques can be used to analyze investments. Suppose that you have an opportunity to purchase an annuity investment that promises to pay you $700 per year for 5 years. You know that you will receive a total of $3,500 ($700 × 5 years) over the 5-year period. However, you wish to earn a minimum annual return of 8 percent on your investments. What is the most you should pay for this annuity today? You can answer this question by rearranging the terms in the equation above to get:

$$\text{Initial deposit} = \text{Annual withdrawal} \times \text{Present value annuity factor}$$

Adapting the equation to this situation, "initial deposit" represents the maximum price to pay for the annuity, and "annual withdrawal" represents the annual annuity payment of $700. The present value annuity factor for 5 years and 8 percent (found in Appendix D) is 3.993. Substituting this into the equation, we get:

$$\text{Initial deposit} = \$700 \times 3.993 = \underline{\$2{,}795.10}$$

The most you should pay for the $700, 5-year annuity, given your 8 percent annual return, is $2,795.10. At this price, you would earn exactly 8 percent on the investment.

Using the present value concept, you can easily determine the present value of a sum to be received in the future, equal annual future withdrawals available from an initial deposit, and the initial deposit that would generate a given stream of equal annual withdrawals. These procedures, like future value concepts, allow you to place monetary values on long-term financial goals.

Concept ✓

2-5. Why is it important to use time value of money concepts in setting personal financial goals?

2-6. What is *compounding?* Explain the *rule of 72*.

2-7. When might you use future value? Present value? Give specific examples.

THE BALANCE SHEET: HOW MUCH ARE YOU WORTH TODAY?

LG3

Because Tom and Mary Gibson want to track their progress toward their financial goals, they need a starting point that shows how much they are worth today. Preparing a personal *balance sheet,* or *statement of financial position,* will give them this important information. This financial statement represents a person's (or family's) financial condition at a certain *point in time.* Think of a balance sheet as a snapshot taken of a person's financial position on one day out of the year.

A balance sheet has three parts that, taken together, represent a summary of your financial picture:

- ***Assets:*** What you own
- ***Liabilities,* or debts:** What you owe
- ***Net worth:*** The difference between your assets and liabilities

The accounting relationship among these three categories is called the *balance sheet equation* and is expressed as follows:

Total assets = Total liabilities + Net worth

or

Net worth = Total assets − Total liabilities

Let's now look at the components of each section of the balance sheet.

ASSETS: THE THINGS YOU OWN

Assets are the items you own. An item is classified as an asset regardless of whether it was purchased for cash or financed with debt. In other words, even if you haven't fully paid for an asset, you should list it on the balance sheet. An item that is leased, in contrast, is not shown as an asset, because someone else actually owns it.

A useful way to group assets is on the basis of their underlying characteristics and uses. This results in four broad categories: liquid assets, investments, real property, and personal property.

- **Liquid assets:** Low-risk financial assets held in the form of cash or instruments that can readily be converted to cash with little or no loss in value. They help us meet the everyday needs of life and provide for emergencies and unexpected opportunities. Cash on hand or in a checking or savings account, money market deposit accounts, money market mutual funds, or certificates of deposit that mature within 1 year are all examples of liquid assets.
- **Investments:** Assets acquired to earn a return rather than provide a service. These assets are mostly intangible *financial assets* (stocks, bonds, mutual funds, and other types of securities), typically acquired to achieve long-term personal financial goals. Business ownership, the cash value of life insurance and pensions, retirement funds such as IRAs and 401(k) plans, and other investment vehicles such as commodities, financial futures, and options represent still other forms of investment assets. (With regard to retirement fund accounts, *only those balances that are eligible to be withdrawn should be shown as an asset on the balance sheet.*) They vary in marketability (the ability to sell quickly) from high (stocks and bonds) to low (real estate and business ownership investments).
- **Real and personal property:** Tangible assets that we use in our everyday lives. **Real property** refers to immovable property: land and anything fixed to it, such as a house. Real property generally has a relatively long life and high cost, and it may *appreciate*, or increase in value. **Personal property** is movable property, such as automobiles, recreational equipment, household furnishings and appliances,

assets
Items that one owns.

liquid assets
Assets that are held in the form of cash or can readily be converted to cash with little or no loss in value; help to meet everyday needs of life and provide for emergencies and unexpected opportunities.

investments
Assets such as stocks, bonds, mutual funds, and real estate that are acquired for the purpose of earning a return rather than providing a service.

real property
Tangible assets that are immovable, such as land and anything fixed to it, such as a house; generally has a relatively long life and high cost.

personal property
Tangible assets that are movable and used in everyday life; includes items such as automobiles, household furnishings, and jewelry.

clothing, jewelry, home electronics, and similar items. Most types of personal property *depreciate*, or decline in value, shortly after being put into use.

About 40 percent of the average household's assets consists of financial assets (liquid assets and investments); nearly half is real property (including housing); and the rest is other nonfinancial assets. The first section of Worksheet 2.2 lists some of the typical assets you'd find on a personal balance sheet.

All assets, regardless of category, are recorded on the balance sheet at their current **fair market value**, which may differ considerably from their original purchase price. Fair market value is either the actual value of the asset (such as money in a checking account) or the price that the asset can reasonably be expected to sell for in the open market (such as a used car or a home).

fair market value The actual value of an asset, or the price that it can reasonably be expected to sell for in the open market.

Those of you who have taken accounting will notice a difference between the way assets are recorded on a personal balance sheet and a business balance sheet. Under Generally Accepted Accounting Principles (GAAP), the accounting profession's guiding rules, assets appear on a company's balance sheet at *cost*, not *fair market value*. One reason for the disparity is that in business, an asset's value is often subject to debate and uncertainty. The user of the statements may be an investor, and accountants like to be conservative in their measurement. For purposes of personal financial planning, the user and the preparer of the statement are one and the same. Besides, most personal assets have market values that can be easily estimated.

liabilities Debts, such as credit card charges, installment loans, and real estate mortgages.

LIABILITIES: THE MONEY YOU OWE

current (short-term) liability Any debt due within 1 year of the date of the balance sheet.

open account credit obligations Current liabilities that represent the balances outstanding against established credit lines (usually through credit card purchases).

long-term liability Any debt due 1 year or more from the date of the balance sheet.

Liabilities represent an individual's or family's debts. They could result from department store charges, bank credit card charges, installment loans, or mortgages on housing and other real estate. A given liability, regardless of its source, is something that you owe and must repay in the future.

Liabilities are generally classified according to maturity:

- **Current**, or **short-term, liability:** Any debt currently owed and due within 1 year of the date of the balance sheet. Examples include charges for consumable goods, utility bills, rent, insurance premiums, taxes, medical bills, repair bills, and total **open account credit obligations**—the outstanding balances against established credit lines (usually through credit card purchases).
- **Long-term liability:** Debt due 1 year or more from the date of the balance sheet. They typically include real estate mortgages, most consumer installment loans, education loans, and margin loans used to purchase securities.

You must show all types of loans on your balance sheet. Although most loans will fall into the category of long-term liabilities, *any loans that come due within a year should be shown as current liabilities.* Examples of such short-term loans include a 6-month, single-payment bank loan and a 9-month consumer installment loan for a refrigerator.

Regardless of the type of loan, *only the latest outstanding loan balance should be shown as a liability on the balance sheet*, because at any given point in time it is the balance still due—not the initial loan balance—that matters. Another important and closely related point is that *only the principal portion of a loan or mortgage should be listed as a liability on the balance sheet.* In other words, you should not include the interest portion of your payments as part of your balance sheet debt. The principal actually defines the amount of debt you owe at a given point in time and does not include any future interest payments.

Lenders evaluate a prospective borrower's liabilities carefully. Very high levels of debt and overdue debts are both viewed with a great deal of disfavor. On Worksheet 2.2, you'll find the most common categories of liabilities.

worksheet 2.2

Balance Sheet for Tim and Andrea Shepard

A balance sheet is set up to show what you own on one side (your assets) and how you pay for them on the other (debt or net worth). As you can see, the Shepards have more assets than liabilities.

BALANCE SHEET

Name(s) Tim and Andrea Shepard Date December 31, 2004

ASSETS

Liquid Assets		
Cash on hand	$ 90	
In checking	575	
Savings accounts	760	
Money market funds and deposits	800	
Certificates of deposit (<1 yr. to maturity)		
Total Liquid Assets		$ 2,225
Investments		
Stocks	$ 1,250	
Bonds Corp.	1,000	
Certificates of deposit (>1 yr. to maturity)		
Mutual funds	1,500	
Real estate		
Retirement funds, IRA	2,000	
Other		
Total Investments		$ 5,750
Real Property		
Primary residence	$ 120,000	
Second home		
Other		
Total Real Property		$ 120,000
Personal Property		
Auto(s): '02 Toyota Corolla	$ 9,500	
Auto(s): '99 Ford Escort	4,500	
Recreational vehicles		
Household furnishing	3,700	
Jewelry and artwork	1,500	
Other		
Other		
Total Personal Property		$ 19,200
(I) Total Assets		$ 147,175

LIABILITIES AND NET WORTH

Current Liabilities		
Utilities	$ 120	
Rent		
Insurance premiums		
Taxes		
Medical/dental bills	75	
Repair bills		
Bank credit card balances	395	
Dept. store credit card balances	145	
Travel and entertainment card balances	125	
Gas and other credit card balances		
Bank line of credit balances		
Other current liabilities	45	
Total Current Liabilities		$ 905
Long-Term Liabilities		
Primary residence mortgage	$ 92,000	
Second home mortgage		
Real estate investment mortgage		
Auto loans	4,250	
Appliance/furniture loans	800	
Home improvement loans		
Single-payment loans		
Education loans	3,800	
Margin loans used to purchase securities		
Other long-term loans (from parents)	4,000	
Total Long-Term Liabilities		$ 104,850
(II) Total Liabilities		$ 105,755
Net Worth [(I) - (II)]		$ 41,420
Total Liabilities and Net Worth		$ 147,175

Net Worth: A Measure of Your Financial Worth

net worth
An individual's or family's actual wealth; determined by subtracting total liabilities from total assets.

equity
The actual ownership interest in a specific asset or group of assets.

insolvency
The financial state in which net worth is less than zero.

Now that you've listed what you own and what you owe, you can calculate your **net worth**, the amount of actual wealth or **equity** that an individual or family has in owned assets. It represents the amount of money you'd have left after selling all your owned assets at their estimated fair market values and paying off all your liabilities (assuming there are no transaction costs). As noted earlier, every balance sheet must "balance" so that total assets equal total liabilities plus net worth. Rearranging this equation, we see that net worth equals total assets minus total liabilities. Once you establish the fair market value of assets and the level of liabilities, you can easily calculate net worth by subtracting total liabilities from total assets. If net worth is less than zero, the family is *technically insolvent.* Although this form of **insolvency** does not mean that the family will end up in bankruptcy proceedings, it does reflect the absence of adequate financial planning.

Net worth typically increases over the life cycle of an individual or family, as Exhibit 2.4 illustrates. For example, the balance sheet of a college student will probably be fairly simple. Assets would include modest liquid assets (cash, checking, and savings accounts) and personal property, which may include a car. Liabilities might include utility bills, perhaps some open account credit obligations, and automobile and education loans. At this point in life, net worth would typically be very low, because assets are small in comparison with liabilities. A 29-year-old, single school teacher would have more liquid assets and personal property, may have started an investment program, and may have purchased a condominium. Net worth would be rising but may still be low due to the increased liabilities associated with real and personal property purchases. The higher net worth of a two-career couple in their late thirties with children would reflect a greater proportion of assets relative to liabilities as they save for college expenses and retirement.

In the long-term financial planning process, the level of net worth is important. Once you have established a goal of accumulating a certain level or type of wealth, you can track progress toward that goal by monitoring net worth.

Balance Sheet Format and Preparation

You should prepare your personal balance sheet at least once a year, preferably every 3 to 6 months. Here's how to do it, using the categories in Worksheet 2.2 as a guide:

1. *List your assets at their fair market value as of the date you are preparing the balance sheet.* You'll find the fair market value of liquid and investment assets on checking and savings account records and investment account statements. Estimate the values of homes and cars using published sources of information, such as advertisements for comparable homes and the *Kelley Blue Book* for used car values. Certain items—for example, homes, jewelry, and artwork—may appreciate, or increase in value, over time. The values of other assets, like cars and most other types of personal property, depreciate, or decrease in value, over time.

smart.sites
What's the fair market value of your car? The silver tea set you inherited from your grandmother? Find out at **http://www.bluebook.com**.

2. *List all current and long-term liabilities.* Show all outstanding charges, *even if you have not received the bill*, as current liabilities on the balance sheet. For example, assume that on June 23 you used your Visa card to charge $320 for a set of tires.

EXHIBIT 2.4

Median Net Worth by Age

Net worth starts to build in the 25–34 age bracket and continues to climb, peaking in the age 55–64 bracket. It declines once a person retires and begins to use assets to meet living expenses, usually at about age 65.

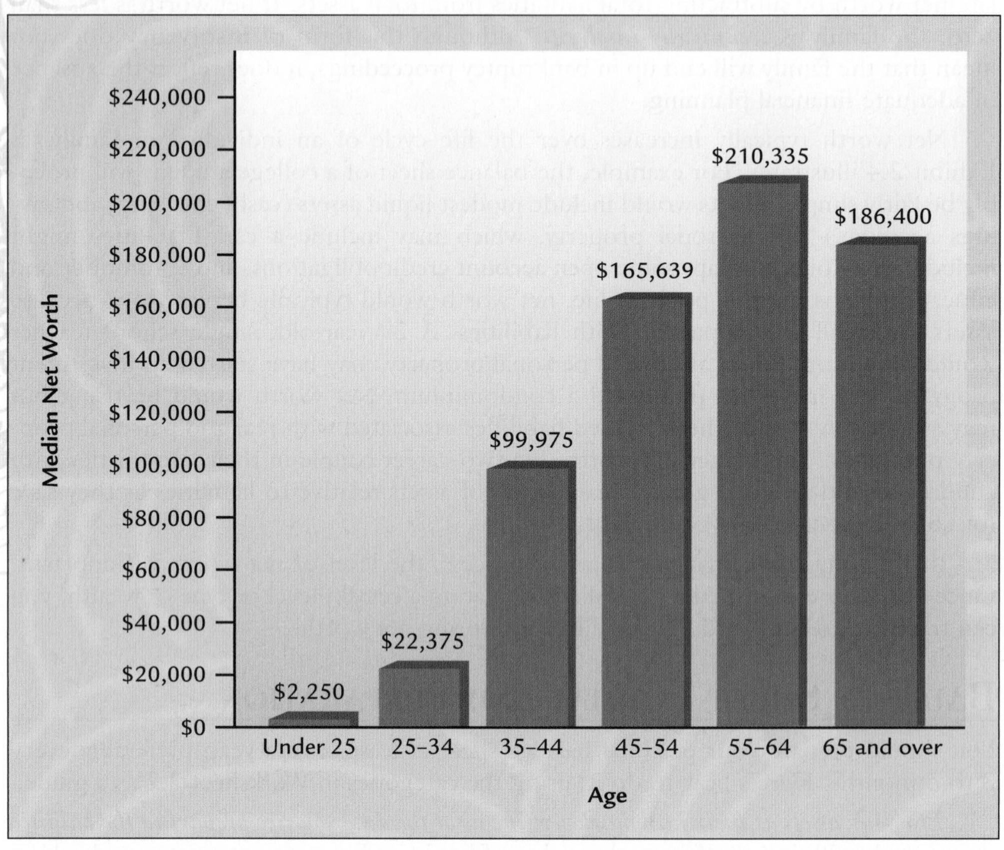

Source: Claritas Inc. Market Audit.

You typically receive your Visa bill around the 10th of the following month. If you were preparing a balance sheet dated June 30, you should include the $320 as a current liability, even though the bill won't arrive until July 10. Remember to list only the principal balance of any loan obligation.

3. *Calculate net worth.* Subtract your total liabilities from your total assets. This is your net worth, which reflects the equity you have in your total assets.

A Balance Sheet for Tim and Andrea Shepard

What can you learn from a balance sheet? Let's examine a hypothetical balance sheet as of December 31, 2004, prepared for Tim and Andrea Shepard, the young couple (ages 28 and 26, respectively) we met in Chapter 1, shown in Worksheet 2.2 on page 58. Assets are listed on the left side, the most liquid first, and liabilities on the right, starting with the most recent. The net worth entry is shown on the right side of the statement just below the liabilities. The statement should *balance*: total assets equal the sum of total liabilities and net worth, as shown in the balance sheet equation. Here's what this financial statement tells us about the Shepard's financial condition:

- **Assets:** Given their ages, the Shepards' asset position looks quite good. Their dominant asset is their condo. They also have $5,750 in investments, which include retirement funds, and appear to have adequate liquid assets to meet their bill payments and cover small, unexpected expenses.
- **Liabilities:** The Shepards' primary liability is the $92,000 mortgage on their condo. Their equity, or actual ownership interest, in the condo is approximately $28,000 ($120,000 market value minus $92,000 outstanding mortgage loan). Their current liabilities are $905, with other debts of $12,850 representing auto, furniture, and education loans, as well as a loan from their parents to help with the down payment on their home.
- **Net Worth:** The Shepards' net worth ($147,175 in total assets minus total liabilities of $105,755) is $41,420—considering their ages, a respectable amount that is well above the median shown in Exhibit 2.4.
- Comparing the Shepards' total liabilities to their total assets provides a more realistic view of their current wealth position than merely looking at just assets or just liabilities. By calculating their net worth at specified points in time, they can measure their progress toward achieving their financial goals.

Concept ✓

2-8. Describe the balance sheet, its components, and how you would use it in personal financial planning. Differentiate between investments and real and personal property.

2-9. What is the balance sheet equation? Explain when a family may be viewed as *technically insolvent*.

2-10. Explain two ways in which net worth could increase (or decrease) from one period to the next.

LG4

THE INCOME AND EXPENSE STATEMENT: WHAT WE EARN AND WHERE IT GOES

Remember the first question Tom and Mary Gibson asked themselves? "Where does all the money go?" Preparing an *income and expense statement* would provide this answer. Whereas the balance sheet describes a person's or family's financial position at a given point in time, the income and expense statement captures the various financial activities that have occurred over time—normally over the course of a year, although it technically can cover any time period (month, quarter, and so on). Think of this statement as a motion picture that not only shows actual results over time but also allows you to compare them with budgeted financial goals as well. Equally important, the statement allows you to evaluate the amount of saving and investing during the period it covers.

Like the balance sheet, the income and expense statement has three major parts: *income*, *expenses*, and *cash surplus* (or *deficit*). A cash surplus (or deficit) is merely the difference between income and expenses. The statement is prepared on a **cash basis**, which means that *only transactions involving actual cash receipts or actual cash outlays are recorded*. The term *cash* is used in this case to include not only coin and currency but also checks drawn against demand deposits and certain types of savings accounts.

cash basis
A method of preparing financial statements in which only cash income and cash expenses are recorded.

Income and expense patterns change over the individual's or family's life cycle. Income and spending levels rise steadily to a peak in the 45–54 age bracket. On average, persons in this age group, whose children are typically in college or no longer at home, generally have the highest level of income. They also spend more than other age groups on entertainment, dining out, transportation, education, insurance, and charitable contributions. Families in the 35–44 age bracket have slightly lower average levels of income and expenses but very different spending patterns. Because they tend to have school-age children, they spend more on groceries, housing, clothing, and other personal needs. The average percentage of income spent, however, is about the same: 85 to 87 percent for all age brackets through age 55, when it drops slightly to 82 percent. It rises sharply to 98 percent, however, for persons age 65 and over.

INCOME: CASH IN

Common sources of **income** include earnings received as wages, salaries, self-employment income, bonuses, and commissions; interest and dividends received from savings and investments; and proceeds from the sale of assets, such as stocks and bonds or an auto. Other income items include pension or annuity income; rent received from leased assets; alimony and child support; scholarships, grants, and Social Security received; tax refunds; and miscellaneous types of income. Worksheet 2.3 has general categories to record your income.

income Earnings received as wages, salaries, self-employment income, bonuses, and commissions; interest and dividends received from savings and investments; and proceeds from the sale of assets.

Note also that the proper figure to use is *gross* wages, salaries, and commissions, which constitute the amount of income you receive from your employer *before* taxes and other payroll deductions. The gross value is used because the taxes and payroll deductions will be itemized and deducted as expenses later in the income and expense statement. Therefore, you should not use *take-home* pay, because it will understate your income by the amount of these deductions.

EXPENSES: CASH OUT

expenses Money spent on living expenses and to purchase assets, pay taxes, or repay debt.

Expenses represent money used for outlays. Worksheet 2.3 categorizes them by the types of benefits they provide: (1) living expenses (such as housing, utilities, food, transportation, medical, clothing, and insurance), (2) tax payments, (3) asset purchases (such as autos, stereos, furniture, appliances, and loan payments on them), and (4) debt payments (on mortgages, installment loans, credit cards, and so on). Some are **fixed expenses**, which are usually contractual, predetermined, and involve equal payments each period (typically each month). Examples include mortgage and installment loan payments, insurance premiums, professional or union dues, club dues, monthly savings or investment programs, and cable television fees. Others (such as food, clothing, utilities, entertainment, and medical expenses) are **variable expenses**, because their amounts change from one time period to the next.

fixed expenses Contractual, predetermined expenses involving equal payments each period (typically each month).

variable expenses Expenses that involve payments that change from one time period to the next.

Exhibit 2.5 on page 64 shows the average annual expenses by major category as a percentage of after-tax income. It provides a useful benchmark to see how you compare with national averages. However, your own expenses will vary according to your age, lifestyle, and where you live. For example, it costs considerably more to buy a home in San Diego than in Indianapolis. If you live in the suburbs, your commuting expenses will be higher than those of city dwellers.

smart.sites

For current surveys and trends on consumer spending, check out the Consumer Expenditures Survey at the Department of Labor's Bureau of Labor Statistics site, **http://stats.bls.gov/cex/home.htm**.

worksheet 2.3

Income and Expense Statement for Tim and Andrea Shepard

The income and expense statement essentially shows what you earned, how you spent your money, and how much you were left with (or, if you spent more than you took in, how much you went "in the hole").

INCOME AND EXPENSE STATEMENT

Name(s) Tim and Andrea Shepard

For the Year Ended December 31, 2004

INCOME		
Wages and salaries	Name: Tim Shepard	$ 55,000
	Name: Andrea Shepard	15,450
	Name:	
Self-employment income		
Bonuses and commissions	Tim–sales commissions	2,275
Investment income	Interest received	
	Dividends received	195
	Rents received	120
	Sale of securities	
	Other	
Pensions and annuities		
Other income		
	(I) Total Income	$ 73,040
EXPENSES		
Housing	Rent/mortgage payment (include insurance and taxes, if applicable)	$ 16,864
	Repairs, maintenance, improvements	1,050
Utilities	Gas, electric, water	1,750
	Phone	480
	Cable TV and other	240
Food	Groceries	2,425
	Dining out	3,400
Transportation	Auto loan payments	2,520
	License plates, fees, etc.	250
	Gas, oil, repairs, tires, maintenance	2,015
Medical	Health, major medical, disability insurance (payroll deductions or not provided by employer)	1,200
	Doctor, dentist, hospital, medicines	305
Clothing	Clothes, shoes, and accessories	1,700
Insurance	Homeowner's (if not covered by mortgage payment)	425
	Life (not provided by employer)	260
	Auto	695
Taxes	Income and social security	15,430
	Property (if not included in mortgage)	1,000
Appliances, furniture, and other major purchases	Loan payments	800
	Purchases and repairs	450
Personal care	Laundry, cosmetics, hair care	700
Recreation and entertainment	Vacations	2,000
	Other recreation and entertainment	2,630
Other items	Tuition and books: Andrea	1,400
	Gifts	215
	Loan payments: Education loans	900
	Loan payments: Parents	600
	(II) Total Expenses	$ 61,704
	CASH SURPLUS (OR DEFICIT) [(I)-(II)]	$ 11,336

EXHIBIT 2.5

How We Spend Our Income

Just three categories account for almost two-thirds of spent after-tax income: food, housing, and transportation.

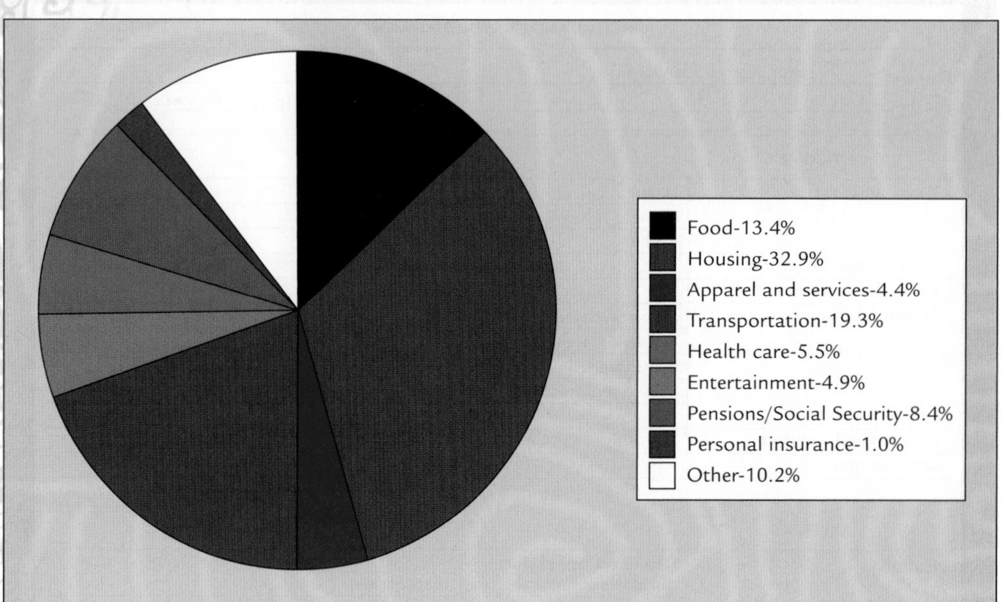

Source: "Consumer Expenditures in 2001," Washington D.C.: U.S. Department of Labor, Bureau of Labor Statistics Report 966, April 2003, p. 4.

Cash Surplus (or Deficit)

The third component of the income and expense statement shows the net result of the period's financial activities. Subtracting total expenses from total income gives you the cash surplus (or deficit) for the period. At a glance, you can see how you did financially over the period. A positive figure indicates that expenses were less than income, resulting in a **cash surplus**. A value of zero indicates that expenses were exactly equal to income for the period, while a negative value means that your expenses exceeded income and you have a **cash deficit**.

cash surplus An excess amount of income over expenses that can be used for savings or investments, to acquire assets, or to reduce debt; results in increased net worth.

cash deficit An excess amount of expenses over income resulting in insufficient funds that must be made up by drawing down savings or investments, reducing assets, or borrowing; results in decreased net worth.

You can use a cash surplus for savings or investment purposes, to acquire assets, or to reduce debt. Adding to savings or investments should increase your future income and net worth, and making payments on debt affects cash flow favorably by reducing future expenses. In contrast, when a cash deficit occurs, you must cover the shortfall from your savings or investments, reduce assets, or borrow. All of these strategies will reduce net worth and have undesirable effects on your financial future.

One final point: a cash surplus does not necessarily mean that funds are simply lying around waiting to be used. Because the income and expense statement reflects what has actually occurred, the disposition of the surplus (or deficit) is reflected in the asset, liability, and net worth accounts on the balance sheet. For example, if you used the surplus to make investments, this would increase the appropriate asset account. If it were used to pay off a loan, the payment would reduce that liability account. Of course, if you used the surplus to increase cash balances, you'd have the funds to use. In each case, your net worth *increases.* Whereas surpluses *add* to net worth, deficits *reduce* it, whether the shortfall is financed by reducing an asset (for example, drawing down a savings account) or by borrowing.

Preparing the Income and Expense Statement

As shown in Worksheet 2.3, the income and expense statement is dated to define the period covered. The steps to prepare the statement are:

1. *Record your income from all sources for the chosen period.* Use your salary check stubs to verify your gross pay for the period, and be sure to include bonuses, commission checks, and overtime pay. You'll find interest earned, securities bought and sold, interest and dividends received, and other investment matters on your bank and investment account statements. Keep a running list of other income sources, such as rents, tax refunds, and asset sales.
2. *Establish meaningful expense categories.* Those shown on Worksheet 2.3 provide a good starting point. Information on monthly house (or rent) payments, loan payments, and other fixed payments (such as insurance premiums and cable TV), is readily available from either the payment book or your checkbook (or, in the case of payroll deductions, your check stubs). (*Note:* Be careful with so-called *adjustable-rate loans,* because the amount of monthly loan payments will change when the interest rate changes.)
3. *Subtract total expenses from total income to get the cash surplus (a positive number) or deficit (a negative number).* This "bottom line" summarizes the *net cash flow* resulting from your financial activities during the designated period.

You will probably pay for most major variable expenses by check, debit card, or credit card, so it's easy to keep track of them. It's more difficult to keep tabs on all the items in a month that you pay with cash, such as parking, lunches, movies, and incidentals. Most of us don't care to write down every little expense to the penny. You might try counting the cash in your wallet at the beginning of the month, then count again after a week goes by to see how much money is missing. Try to reconstruct in your mind what you spent during the week, and write it down on your calendar to the nearest $5. If you can't remember, then try the exercise over shorter and shorter periods until you can.

Just as you show only the amounts of cash actually received as income, record only the amounts of money you actually pay out in cash as expenses. If you borrow to acquire an item, particularly an asset, include only the *actual cash payment—purchase price minus amount borrowed*—as an expense, as well as *payments on the loan* in the period you actually make them. You show credit purchases of this type as an asset and corresponding liability *on the balance sheet.* Record only the cash payments on loans, not the actual amounts of the loans themselves, on the income and expense statement.

For example, assume that you purchase a new car for $15,000 in September. You make a down payment of $3,000 and finance the remaining $12,000 with a 4-year, 10.5 percent installment loan. Your September 30 income statement would show a cash expenditure of $3,000, and each subsequent monthly income statement would include your monthly loan payment of $307. Your September 30 balance sheet would show the car as an asset valued at $15,000 and the loan balance as a $12,000 long-term liability. The market value of the car and the loan balance would be adjusted on future balance sheets.

Finally, when developing your list of expenses for the year, remember to include the amount of income tax and Social Security taxes withheld from your paycheck, and any other payroll deductions, such as health insurance, savings plans, retirement and pension contributions, and professional/union dues. These deductions (from gross wages, salaries, bonuses, and commissions) represent personal expenses, even if they do not involve the direct payment of cash.

You might be shocked when you make a list of what is taken out of your paycheck. Even if you're in a fairly low federal income tax bracket, your paycheck could easily be reduced by more than 25 percent for taxes alone. Your federal tax could be withheld at 15 percent, your state income tax could be withheld at 5 percent, and your Social Security tax could be withheld at 7 percent. That doesn't even count health and disability income insurance.

Preparing income and expense statements can involve a lot of number crunching. Fortunately, a number of good computer software packages, such as Quicken and Microsoft Money, can simplify the job of preparing personal financial statements and performing other personal financial planning tasks.

An Income and Expense Statement for Tim and Andrea Shepard

Tim and Andrea Shepard's balance sheet in Worksheet 2.2, showed us their financial condition as of December 31, 2004. Their income and expense statement for the year ended December 31, 2004, in Worksheet 2.3, was prepared using the background material presented earlier, along with the Shepards' balance sheet. This statement illustrates how cash flowed into and out of their "pockets":

- **Income:** Total income for the year ended December 31, 2004 is $73,040, with Tim's wages clearly representing the family's chief source of income, although Andrea has finished her MBA and will now be making a major contribution. Other sources of income include $195 in interest on their savings accounts and bond investments and $120 in dividends from their common stock holdings.
- **Expenses:** Total expenses for the year of $61,704 included their home mortgage, food, auto loan, clothing, and income and Social Security taxes. Other sizable expenses during the year include home repairs and improvements, gas and electricity, auto license and operating expenses, insurance, tuition, and education loan payments.
- **Cash surplus:** The Shepards end the year with a cash surplus of $11,336 (total income of $73,040 minus total expenses of $61,704).

The Shepards can use their surplus to increase savings, invest in stocks, bonds, or other vehicles, or make payments on some outstanding debts. The best strategy depends on their financial goals. If they had a cash deficit, the Shepards would have to withdraw savings, liquidate investments, or borrow an amount equal to

Concept ✓

2-11. What is an *income and expense statement?* What role does it serve in personal financial planning? Name its three components, some major sources of income, and the four basic categories of expenses.

2-12. Explain what *cash basis* means in the following statement: "An income and expense statement should be prepared on a cash basis." How and where are credit purchases shown when statements are prepared on a cash basis?

2-13. Distinguish between fixed and variable expenses, and give examples of each.

2-14. Is it possible to have a *cash deficit* on an income and expense statement? If so, how?

the deficit to meet their financial commitments (that is, "make ends meet"). With their surplus of $11,336, the Shepards have made a positive contribution to their net worth.

LG5 USING YOUR PERSONAL FINANCIAL STATEMENTS

Whether you are just starting out and have a minimal net worth or are further along the path toward achieving your goals, your balance sheet and income and expense statement provide insight into your current financial status. You now have the information you need to examine your financial position, monitor your financial activities, and track the progress you're making toward achieving your financial goals. Let's now look at ways to help you create better personal financial statements and analyze them to gain a more thorough understanding of your financial situation

Keeping Good Records

Although recordkeeping doesn't rank high on most "to do" lists, a good recordkeeping system helps you manage and control your personal financial affairs. With organized, up-to-date financial records, you'll prepare more accurate personal financial statements and budgets, pay less to your tax preparer, not miss any tax deductions, and save on taxes when you sell a house or securities or withdraw retirement funds. Also, good records make it easier for a spouse or relative to manage your financial affairs in an emergency. To that end, you should prepare a comprehensive list of these records, their locations, and your key advisors (financial planner, banker, accountant, attorney, doctors) for family members.

Prepare your personal financial statements at least once each year, ideally when you draw up your budget. Many people update their financial statements every 3 or 6 months. You may want to keep a *ledger*, or financial record book, to summarize all your financial transactions. The ledger has sections for assets, liabilities, sources of income, and expenses; these sections contain separate accounts for each item. Whenever any accounts change, make an appropriate ledger entry. For example, if you buy a DVD player for $300 cash, you'd show the DVD player on your balance sheet as an asset (at its fair market value) and as a $300 expenditure on your income and expense statement. If you borrowed to pay for the DVD player, the loan amount would be a liability on the balance sheet, and any loan payments made during the period would be shown on the income and expense statement. You'd keep similar records for asset sales, loan repayments, income sources, and so on.

Organizing Your Records

Your system doesn't have to be fancy to be effective. You'll need a bank safe-deposit box, the ledger book described earlier, and a set of files with general categories, such as banking and credit cards, taxes, home, insurance, investments, and retirement accounts. An expandable file, with a dozen or so compartments for incoming bills, receipts, pay stubs, or anything you might need later, works well.

Start by taking an inventory. Make a list of everything you own and owe. Check it at least once a year to make sure it's up to date and to review your financial progress. Then, record transactions manually in your ledger or with financial planning software. Exhibit 2.6 offers general guidelines for keeping and organizing your personal financial records.

smart.sites

Need help getting organized? You'll find advice for every area of your life at **http://www.organizedhome.com**.

EXHIBIT 2.6

Organizing Your Financial Records

Confused about what to keep, where to keep it, and when to toss it? Here are some general rules.

Permanent Papers: *Place in a fireproof box or safe deposit box at the bank*

Birth, marriage, and death certificates; separation or divorce agreements; adoption papers; passports; military service records; wills, healthcare proxy (giving someone legal right to make medical decisions if you become incapacitated), powers of attorney; copies of IRAs and 401(k)s; all current insurance policies and the names of the agents; securities certificates, deeds, and purchase and sale documents on all homes you've owned; other documents relating to property ownership such as a car title; retirement fund records (pension plans, IRAs, and so on) to know which portions of them are tax-deferred and therefore not subject to tax until funds are withdrawn.

Keep original wills, proxies, and powers of attorney at home because a safe deposit box may be sealed at your death.

Make copies of all other permanent papers to keep at home. Shred prior wills to avoid confusion.

Long-term papers: *Keep for 7 years in a file cabinet or file boxes*

Federal and state income tax returns and all supporting documentation (receipts, charitable contributions, canceled checks for tax deductible expenses, casualty losses); household papers such as receipts, instruction manuals and warranties, records of home capital improvements.

After 7 years transfer copies of tax returns to permanent storage—dispose of supporting documentation by shredding.

Keep the following at least 3 years after the due date of the tax return in which you report the sale, the period the IRS has to challenge your return: security purchase and sale confirmations, dividend reinvestment notices, and records of stock splits; home-related documents.

Keep product warranties until they expire.

Short-term papers: *Keep in a file cabinet or a file box at home*

Monthly bank, brokerage, mutual fund, 401(k) statements, pay stubs: *Shred when you receive your year-end statement and keep year-end statements for at least 3 years*

Credit card statements, utility, and telephone bills: *Shred when paid*

ATM receipts and deposit slips: *Shred when transaction appears on your bank statement*

Other papers worth keeping: In case of emergency, you should have photos and fingerprints of your children. Medical records are also good to keep.

You'll want to set up separate files for tax planning records, with one for income (paycheck stubs, interest on savings accounts, and so on) and another for deductions, as well as for individual mutual fund and brokerage account records. Once you set up your files, be sure to go through them at least once a year and throw out unnecessary items.

TRACKING FINANCIAL PROGRESS: RATIO ANALYSIS

Each time you prepare your financial statements, you should analyze them to see how well you are doing in light of your financial goals. For example, with an income and expense statement, you can compare actual financial results with budgeted figures to make sure that your spending is under control. Likewise, comparing a set of financial plans with a balance sheet will reveal whether you are meeting your savings and investment goals, reducing your debt, or building up a retirement reserve. You can compare current performance with historical performance to find out if your financial situation is improving or getting worse.

Calculating certain financial ratios can help you evaluate your financial performance over time. Moreover, if you apply for a loan, the lender probably will look at these ratios to judge your ability to carry additional debt. Four important money management ratios are the (1) solvency ratio, (2) liquidity ratio, (3) savings ratio, and (4) debt service ratio. The first two are associated primarily with the balance sheet, while the last two relate primarily to the income and expense statement. Exhibit 2.7 defines these ratios and illustrates their calculation for Tim and Andrea Shepard.

EXHIBIT 2.7

Ratios for Personal Financial Statement Analysis

Ratio	Formula	2004 Calculation for the Shepards
Solvency ratio	Total net worth / Total Assets	$41,420 / $147,175 = 0.281, or 28.1%
Liquidity ratio	Total liquid assets / Total current debts	$2,225 / $22,589(a) = 0.099, or 9.9%
Savings ratio	Cash surplus / Income after taxes	$11,336 / ($73,040 − $15,430) = $11,336 / $57,610 = 0.197, or 19.7%
Debt service ratio	Total monthly loan payments / Monthly gross (before tax) income	$1,807(b) / $6,807(c) = 0.266, or 26.6%

(a) You'll find the Shepards' total liquid assets ($2,225) and total current liabilities ($905) on Worksheet 2.2. The total current debt (from Worksheet 2.3) totals $22,589: current liabilities of $905 + loan payments due within 1 year of $21,684 – $16,864 in mortgage payments + $2,520 in auto loan payments + $800 in furniture loan payments + $900 in education loan payments + $600 in loan payments to parents.

(b) On an *annual* basis, the Shepards' debt obligations total $21,684 ($16,864 in mortgage payments, $2,520 in auto loan payments, $800 in furniture loan payments, $900 in education loan payments, and $600 in loan payments to parents, from Worksheet 2.3). The Shepards' total *monthly* loan payments are about $1,807 ($21,684 ÷ 12 months).

(c) Dividing the Shepards' *annual* gross income, also found in Worksheet 2.3, of $73,040 by 12 equals $6,087 monthly ($73,040 ÷ 12).

Balance Sheet Ratios

solvency ratio Total net worth divided by total assets; measures the degree of exposure to insolvency.

liquidity ratio Total liquid assets divided by total current debts; measures the ability to pay current debts.

When evaluating your balance sheet, you should be most concerned with your net worth at a given point in time. As explained earlier in this chapter, you are *technically insolvent* when your total liabilities exceed your total assets—that is, when you have a negative net worth. The **solvency ratio** shows, as a percentage, your degree of exposure to insolvency, or how much "cushion" you have as a protection against insolvency. Tim and Andrea's solvency ratio is 28.1 percent, which means that they could withstand only about a 28 percent decline in the market value of their assets before they would be insolvent. The low value for this ratio suggests they should consider improving it in the future.

Although the solvency ratio gives an indication of the potential to withstand financial problems, it does not deal directly with the ability to pay current debts. This issue is addressed with the **liquidity ratio**, which shows how long you could continue to pay current debts (any bills or charges that must be paid *within 1 year*) with existing liquid assets in the event of income loss.

This ratio indicates that the Shepards can cover only about 10 percent of their existing 1-year debt obligations with their current liquid assets. In other words, they have slightly over 1 month (1 month is 1⁄12, or 8.3 percent) of coverage. If an unexpected event curtailed their income, their liquid reserves would be exhausted very quickly. Although there is no hard and fast rule as to what this ratio should be, it seems low for the Shepards. They should consider strengthening it along with their solvency ratio. They should be able to add to their cash surpluses now that Andrea is working full time.

The amount of liquid reserves will vary with your personal circumstances and "comfort level." Another useful liquidity guideline is to have a reserve fund equal to 3 to 6 months of after-tax income available to cover living expenses. The Shepards' after-tax income for 2004 was $4,801 per month ([$73,040 total income − $15,430 income and social security taxes] ÷ 12). Therefore, this guideline suggests they should have between $14,403 and $28,806 in total liquid assets—considerably more than the $2,225 on their latest balance sheet. If you feel that your job is secure or you have other potential sources of income, you may be comfortable with 3 or 4 months in reserve. If you tend to be very cautious financially, you may want to build a larger fund. In troubled economic times, you may want to keep 6 months or more of income in this fund as protection should you lose your job.

Financial Road Sign

Declutter Your Life!

Too much paper in your house? Here are tips to eliminate what you don't need.

1. Be selective to avoid information overload; you don't need to know everything.
2. Set up a regular weekly time to read the key materials you select.
3. Sort mail daily into a mail basket for each person, tossing obvious junk immediately.
4. Don't procrastinate. Sort one pile at a time and take some action *now*.
5. Don't make copies "just in case."
6. File only the essentials. Eighty percent of paper filed is rarely used.
7. Purge files and other papers regularly to make room for new information.
8. Give away recent magazines, catalogs, or books when they're still useful.
9. Buy a shredder and use it to shred any paper with any personal identification and account numbers, including unsolicited credit card offers. This will minimize the risk of identity theft.

Income and Expense Statement Ratios

When evaluating your income and expense statement, you should be concerned with the bottom line, which shows the cash surplus (or deficit) resulting from the period's activities. You can relate it to income by calculating a **savings ratio**, which is done most effectively with after-tax income.

savings ratio Cash surplus divided by after-tax income; indicates relative amount of cash surplus achieved during a given period.

Tim and Andrea saved about 20 percent of their after-tax income, which is on the high side (American families, on average, normally save about 5 to 8 percent). How much to save is a personal choice. Some families would plan much higher levels, particularly if they are saving to achieve an important goal, such as buying a home.

While maintaining an adequate level of savings is obviously important to personal financial planning, so is the ability to pay debts promptly. In fact, debt payments have a higher priority. The **debt service ratio** allows you to make sure you can comfortably meet your debt obligations. This ratio excludes current liabilities and considers only mortgage, installment, and personal loan obligations.

debt service ratio Total monthly loan payments divided by monthly gross (before-tax) income; provides a measure of the ability to pay debts promptly.

Monthly loan payments account for about 27 percent of Tim and Andrea's gross income. This relatively low debt service ratio indicates that the Shepards

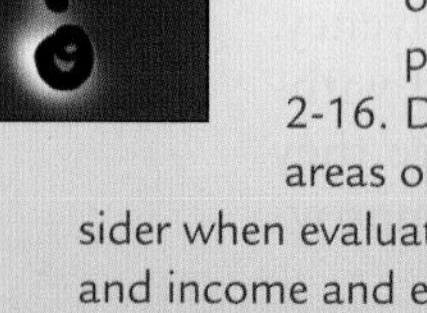

Concept ✓

2-15. How can accurate records and control procedures be used to ensure the effectiveness of the personal financial planning process?

2-16. Describe some of the areas or items you would consider when evaluating your balance sheet and income and expense statement. Cite several ratios that could help in this effort.

should have little difficulty in meeting their monthly loan payments. From a financial planning perspective, you should try to keep your debt service ratio somewhere under 35 percent or so, because that's generally viewed as a manageable level of debt—and, of course, the lower the debt service ratio, the easier it is to meet loan payments as they come due.

LG6 CASH IN/CASH OUT: PREPARING AND USING BUDGETS

Financial Road Sign

Budgeting Basics

No one likes to prepare budget, so here are some helpful hints to get you going:

1. Take the drudgery out of budgeting with special budgeting software or the budget-making tools in personal finance software such as Quicken or Microsoft Money.
2. Don't get bogged down by details. Concentrate on categories where you can cut spending.
3. Watch for cash leakage. Keep records of what happens to ATM withdrawals.
4. If you spend more than you make, you're probably buying luxuries that you consider necessities.
5. Spend no more than 90 percent of your income, and save the rest.
6. Don't count on windfalls to bail you out.
7. Beware of spending creep as your annual income climbs.
8. Budget preparation gets easier once you have a budget in place and fine-tune it over the first few months.

Source: Adapted from "Money 101: Making a Budget: Top 10 Things to Know," and "Money 101: The Dubious Joy of Budgets," *CNNMoney.com,* downloaded from **http://money.cnn.com.**

When we first met the Gibsons at the beginning of the chapter, they had never set up a family budget. They are certainly not alone! Many of us avoid budgeting like the plague. After all, do you really want to know that 30 percent of your take- home pay is going to restaurant meals? Yet preparing, analyzing, and monitoring your personal budget are essential steps for successful personal financial planning.

Once you define your short-term financial goals, you can prepare a cash budget for the coming year. Recall that a *budget* is a short-term financial planning report that helps you achieve your short-term financial goals. By taking the time to evaluate your current financial situation, spending patterns, and goals, you can develop a realistic budget consistent with your personal lifestyle, family situation, and values. A cash budget is a valuable money management tool that helps you:

1. Maintain the necessary information to monitor and control your finances
2. Decide how to allocate your income to reach your financial goals
3. Implement a system of disciplined spending—as opposed to just existing from one paycheck to the next
4. Reduce needless spending so you can increase the funds allocated to savings and investments
5. Achieve your long-term financial goals

Just as your goals change over your lifetime, so will your budget as your financial situation becomes more complex. Typically, the number of income and expense categories increases as you accumulate more assets and debts and have more family responsibilities. For example, the budget of a college student should be quite simple, with limited income from part-time jobs, parental contributions, and scholarships and grants. Expenses might include room and board, clothes, books, auto expenses, and entertainment. Once a student graduates and goes to work full time, his or her budget will include additional expenses, such as rent, insurance, work clothes, and commuting costs. Not until retirement can you expect this process to perhaps begin to simplify.

The Budgeting Process

Like the income and expense statement, *a budget should be prepared on a cash basis;* thus, we call this document a **cash budget** because it deals with estimated cash receipts and cash expenses, including savings and investments, that are expected to occur in the coming year. Because you receive and pay most bills monthly, you'll probably want to estimate income as well as expenses on a monthly basis.

cash budget
A budget that takes into account estimated monthly cash receipts and cash expenses for the coming year.

The cash budget preparation process has three stages: estimating income, estimating expenses, and finalizing the cash budget. When estimating income and expenses, you should take into account any anticipated changes in the cost of living and their impact on your budget components. If your income is fixed—not expected to change over the budgetary period—increases in various items of expense will probably cause the purchasing power of your income to deteriorate. Worksheet 2.4, "Annual Cash Budget by Month," has separate sections to record your income and expenses and lists the most common categories for each.

worksheet 2.4

The Shepards' Annual Cash Budget by Month

The Shepards' annual cash budget shows several months in which substantial cash deficits are expected to occur; they can use this information to develop plans for covering those monthly shortfalls.

ANNUAL CASH BUDGET BY MONTH

Name(s) Tim and Andrea Shepard

For the Year Ended December 31, 2005

INCOME	Jan.	Feb.	Mar.	April	May	June	July	Aug.	Sep.	Oct.	Nov.	Dec.	Total for the Year
Take-home pay	$ 4,775	$ 4,775	$ 4,775	$ 4,965	$ 4,965	$ 5,140	$ 5,140	$ 5,140	$ 5,140	$ 5,140	$ 5,140	$ 5,140	$ 60,235
Bonuses and commissions						1,350						1,300	2,650
Pensions and annuities													
Investment income			90			90			90			90	360
Other income													
(I) Total Income	$ 4,775	$ 4,775	$ 4,865	$ 4,965	$ 4,965	$ 6,580	$ 5,140	$ 5,140	$ 5,230	$ 5,140	$ 5,140	$ 6,530	$ 63,245
EXPENSES													
Housing (rent/mtge, repairs)	$ 1,506	$ 1,856	$ 1,506	$ 1,506	$ 1,505	$ 1,505	$ 1,505	$ 1,505	$ 1,505	$ 1,505	$ 1,505	$ 1,505	$ 18,414
Utilities (phone, elec., gas, water)	245	245	245	175	180	205	230	245	205	195	230	250	2,650
Food (home and away)	575	575	575	575	575	575	575	575	575	575	575	575	6,900
Transportation (auto/public)	370	620	370	540	370	370	575	370	370	450	370	370	5,145
Medical/dental, incl. insurance	30	30	30	30	30	45	30	30	30	30	30	30	375
Clothing	150	150	500	400	200	200	300	500	200	300	300	300	3,500
Insurance (life, auto, home)				225	370		300			225	370		1,490
Taxes (property)		550						550					1,100
Appliances, furniture, and other (purchases/loans)	60	60	30			750			300	300	300		1,800
Personal care	100	100	100	100	100	100	100	100	100	100	100	100	1,200
Recreation and entertainment	250	250	3,200	200	200	300	300	200	200	200	200	2,050	7,550
Savings and investments	375	375	375	375	375	375	375	375	375	375	375	375	4,500
Other expenses	135	250	235	135	610	180	135	285	245	135	605	385	3,335
Fun money	230	230	230	230	230	230	230	230	230	230	230	230	2,760
(II) Total Expenses	$ 4,026	$ 5,291	$ 7,396	$ 4,491	$ 4,745	$ 4,835	$ 4,655	$ 4,965	$ 4,335	$ 4,620	$ 5,190	$ 6,170	$ 60,719
CASH SURPLUS (OR DEFICIT) [(I)-(II)]	$ 749	$ (516)	$ (2,531)	$ 474	$ 220	$ 1,745	$ 485	$ 175	$ 895	$ 520	$ (50)	$ 360	$ 2,526
CUMULATIVE CASH SURPLUS (OR DEFICIT)	$ 749	$ 233	$ (2,298)	$ (1,824)	$ (1,604)	$ 141	$ 626	$ 801	$ 1,696	$ 2,216	$ 2,166	$ 2,526	$ 2,526

Estimating Income

The first step in the cash budget preparation process is to estimate your income for the coming year. Include all income expected for the year: the take-home pay of both spouses, expected bonuses or commissions, pension or annuity income, and investment income—interest, dividend, rental, and asset (particularly security) sale income. When estimating income, keep in mind that *any item you receive for which repayment is required is not considered income.* For instance, loan proceeds are treated not as a source of income but as a *liability* for which scheduled repayments are required.

Note also that, unlike the income and expense statement, you should use *take-home pay* (rather than gross income) in the cash budget. Your cash budget focuses on those areas over which you have control—and most people effectively have limited control over things like taxes withheld, contributions to company insurance and pension plans, and the like. In effect, take-home pay represents the amount of *disposable income* you receive from your employer.

Estimating Expenses

The second step in the cash budgeting process is by far the most difficult: preparing a schedule of estimated expenses for the coming year. This is usually done using actual expenses from previous years (as found on income and expense statements and in supporting information for those periods), along with predetermined short-term financial goals. Good financial records, as discussed earlier, make it easier to develop realistic expense estimates. If you do not have past expense data, you could reexamine old checkbook registers and credit card statements to approximate expenses, or take a "needs approach" and attach dollar values to projected expenses. Pay close attention to expenses associated with medical disabilities, divorce and child support, and similar special circumstances.

Regardless of whether you have historical information, as you prepare your budget *be aware of your expenditure patterns and how you spend money.* After tracking your expenses over several months, you can study your spending habits to see if you are doing things that should be eliminated (like going to the ATM too often or using credit cards too freely).

You will probably find it easier to budget expenses if you group them into several general categories, rather than trying to estimate each item. Worksheet 2.4 provides an example of one such grouping scheme, patterned after the categories used in the income and expense statement. You may also want to refer back to the average expense percentages given in Exhibit 2.5. Choose categories that reflect your priorities and allow you to monitor areas of concern.

Initially, your expense estimates should include the transactions necessary to achieve your short-term goals. You should also quantify any current or short-term contributions toward your long-term goals and schedule them into the budget. Equally important are scheduled additions to savings and investments, because planned savings should be high on everyone's list of goals. If your budget doesn't balance with all these items, you will have to make some adjustments in the final budget.

Base estimated expenses on current price levels and then increase them by a percentage that reflects the anticipated rate of inflation. For example, if you estimate the monthly food bill at $350 and expect 4 percent inflation, you should budget your monthly food expenditure at $364, or $350 + $14 (4 percent × $350).

Don't forget an allowance for "fun money," which family members spend as they wish. This gives each person a degree of financial independence and helps provide a healthy family budget relationship.

Finalizing the Cash Budget

After you estimate income and expenses, finalize your budget by comparing projected income to projected expenses. Show the difference in the third section as a surplus or deficit. In a *balanced budget*, the total income for the year equals or exceeds total expenses. If you

Money in Action

Small Savings Mean Big Bucks!

It should be obvious: Spend less than you earn so you'll have money to invest. Yet so many people don't recognize this simple fact. They run up large credit card bills and take out loans instead of building up a nest egg for the future.

Where to start? How about with the little stuff? You'd be amazed at how reducing even your smallest expenses can lead to big savings! Here are some examples of how reducing your discretionary spending now will yield big payoffs later, thanks to the large impact of compounding (future value):

- Instead of buying 40 $5 lottery tickets a year, invest the $200 at the end of each year at 8 percent. If you start at age 18, you'd have $106,068 by the time you reach age 67!
- Buy a used car instead of a new one and invest the amount you saved at 8 percent for 40 years. If you saved $9,000 buying a used car, you'd have more than $195,000 available for your retirement fund!
- Stop the money drain into vending machines, espresso stands, and restaurant or fast food lunches. Buy a regular cup of coffee rather than a latte or espresso, avoid the vending machines, and take a brown-bag lunch to work several days a week. If you save $22 a week for 50 weeks a year at 8 percent for 40 years, your savings will grow by more than $284,000!
- Use less of things like shampoo, detergent, and toothpaste. Try cutting the amount you use in half. Then look for other areas where this also applies.
- Pay attention to how you spend your loose change. Limit the amount of cash and coins you carry, and you'll plug one of the biggest financial leaks in most Americans' pockets.
- Learn to do it yourself instead of immediately hiring outside help. Use how-to videos, books, and magazines from your library to develop basic repair skills. Fixing one leaky faucet can save you $50 or more in plumbing bills. Such savings add up!

You'll soon find many other ways to "save small," such as taking public transportation, comparing

...continued on next page

find that you have a deficit at year end, you will have to *go back and adjust your expenses accordingly.* If you have several months of large surpluses, you should be able to cover any shortfall in a later month, as explained below. Budget preparation is complete once all monthly deficits are resolved and the total annual budget balances.

Admittedly, there is a lot of "number crunching" in personal cash budgeting. As discussed earlier, personal financial planning software can greatly streamline the budget preparation process.

smart.sites

Use the Family Budget Calculator at **http://www.epinet.org/content.cfm/datazone_fambud_budget** to compare how budgets vary by family type and area of the country.

Dealing with Deficits

Even if the annual budget balances, in certain months expenses may exceed income, causing a monthly budget deficit. Likewise, a budget surplus occurs when income in some months exceeds expenses. Two remedies exist:

- Shift expenses from months with budget deficits to months with surpluses (or, conversely, transfer income, if possible, from months with surpluses to those with deficits).
- Use savings, investments, or borrowing to cover temporary deficits.

Because the budget balances for the year, the need for funds to cover shortages is only temporary. In months with budget surpluses, you should return funds taken from savings or investments or repay loans. Either remedy is feasible for curing a monthly budget deficit in a balanced annual budget, although the second is probably more practical.

What can you do if your budget shows an annual budget deficit, even after you've made a few expense adjustments? You have three options:

- **Liquidate enough savings and investments or borrow enough to meet the total budget shortfall for the year:** Obviously, this action is not recommended, because it violates the objective of budgeting: To set expenses at a level that allows you to enjoy a reasonable standard of living *and* progress toward achieving your long-term goals. Reducing savings and investments or increasing debt to balance the budget reduces net worth. People who use this approach are *not* living within their means.

- **Cut low-priority expenses from the budget:** This method is clearly preferable to the preceding alternative! It balances the budget without using external funding sources by eliminating expenses associated with your least important short-term goals, such as flexible, or discretionary, expenses for nonessential items (such as recreation, entertainment, and some clothing). The *Money in Action* box on page 74 can help you find easy ways to spend less.
- **Increase income:** Finding a higher-paying job or perhaps a second, part-time job is the most difficult technique; it takes more planning and may result in lifestyle changes. However, individuals who cannot liquidate savings or investments or borrow funds to cover necessary expenses may have to choose this route to balance their budgets.

smart.sites
Find links to a variety of money saving resources at About.com's Frugal Living site, **http://frugalliving.about.com**.

prices before you buy, reading books and magazines from the library instead of buying them, and using coupons to buy groceries.

Then, make saving a given, not something you do when you have money left over. Pay yourself first. Have your employer deposit the maximum amount in your 401(k) plan each pay period. It will grow even faster if your employer matches your contributions. You can also authorize withdrawals from your checking account to an investment account or to a mutual fund.

Critical Thinking Questions

1. Explain how time value of money concepts apply to the examples in this box.
2. What is meant by "paying yourself first"? Why is it important?
3. List three small savings you can make and show how they will grow over time.

Sources: Scott Burns, "You Have A Fortune, You Just Have to Find It," *Dallas Morning News*, January 3, 1999, downloaded from **http://www.scottburns.com**; "Escape from Affluenza," *PBS*, downloaded from **http://www.pbs.org/kcts/affluenza/escape/action/index.html**.

A Cash Budget for Tim and Andrea Shepard

Using their short-term financial goals (Worksheet 1.1 in Chapter 1) and past financial statements (Worksheets 2.2 and 2.3), Tim and Andrea Shepard have prepared their cash budget for the 2005 calendar year. Worksheet 2.4 shows the Shepards' estimated total 2005 annual income and expenses by month, as well as the monthly and annual cash surplus or deficit.

The Shepards list their total 2005 income of $63,245 by source for each month. By using take-home pay, they eliminate the need to show income-based taxes, social security payments, and other payroll deductions as expenses. The take-home pay increases in April and June reflect Tim's and Andrea's expected salary increases, respectively.

In estimating annual expenses for 2005, the Shepards anticipate a small amount of inflation and have factored some price increases into their expense projections. They have also allocated $4,500 to savings and investments, a wise budgeting strategy, and included an amount for fun money, divided between them.

During their budgeting session, Tim and Andrea discovered that their first estimate resulted in expenses of $63,459, compared with their estimated income of $63,245. To eliminate the $214 deficit to balance their budget and allow for unexpected expenses, Tim and Andrea made the following decisions:

- Omit some low-priority goals: spend less on stereo components, take a shorter Hawaii vacation instead of the Colorado ski trip shown in Worksheet 1.1.
- Reschedule $200 of the loan repayment to their parents.
- Reduce their fun money slightly.

These reductions of $2,740 lower their total scheduled expenses to $60,719, giving them a surplus of $2,526 ($63,245 − $60,719), and more than balancing the budget on an annual basis. Of course, the Shepards can reduce other discretionary expenses to further increase the budget surplus and have a cushion for unexpected expenses.

The Shepards' final step is to analyze monthly surpluses and deficits and determine whether to use savings, investments, or borrowing to cover monthly shortfalls. The bottom line of their annual cash budget lists the cumulative, or running, totals of monthly cash surpluses and deficits. Despite their $2,526 year-end cumulative cash surplus, they have cumulative deficits in March, April, and May, primarily because of their March Hawaii vacation. To cover these deficits, Tim and Andrea have arranged an interest-free loan from their parents. If they had dipped into savings to finance the deficits, they would have lost some interest earnings, included as income. They could delay clothing and recreation and entertainment expenses until later in the year to reduce the deficits more quickly. If they were unable to obtain funds to cover the deficits, they would have to reduce expenses further or increase income. At year end, they should use their surplus to increase savings or investments or repay part of a loan.

Using Your Budgets

In the final analysis, a cash budget has value only if (1) you use it and (2) you keep careful records of actual income and expenses. These records show whether you are staying within budget limits. Record this information in a budget record book often enough so you don't overlook anything of significance, yet not so often that it becomes a nuisance. A loose-leaf binder with separate pages for each income and expense category works quite well. Rounding entries to the nearest dollar simplifies the arithmetic.

At the beginning of each month, record the budgeted amount for each category and enter income received and money spent on the appropriate pages. At month-end, total each account and calculate the surplus or deficit. With the exception of certain income accounts (such as salary) and fixed expense accounts such as mortgage or loan payments, most categories will end the month with a positive or negative variance, indicating a cash surplus or deficit. You can then transfer your total spending by category to a **budget control schedule** that compares actual income and expenses with the various budget categories and shows the variances.

budget control schedule
A summary that shows how actual income and expenses compare with the various budget categories and where surpluses or deficits exist.

This monthly comparison makes it easy to identify major budget categories where income falls far short or spending far exceeds desired levels (variances of 5 to 10 percent or more). Once you pinpoint these areas, you can take corrective action to keep your budget on course. Don't just look at the size of the variances. Analyze them, particularly the larger ones, to discover *why* they occurred. An account deficit that occurs in only one period is obviously less of a problem than one that occurs in several periods. If recurring deficits indicate that an account was underbudgeted, you may need to adjust the budget to cover the outlays, reducing overbudgeted or nonessential accounts. Only in exceptional situations should you finance budget adjustments with savings and investments or borrowing.

Concept ✓

2-17. Describe the *cash budget* and its three parts. How does a budget deficit differ from a budget surplus?

2-18. The Smith family has prepared their annual cash budget for 2002. They have divided it into 12 monthly budgets. Although only one monthly budget balances, they have managed to balance the overall budget for the year. What remedies are available to the Smith family for meeting the monthly budget deficits?

2-19. Why is it important to analyze actual budget surpluses or deficits at the end of each month?

Looking at the Shepards' budget control schedule for January, February, and March 2005, on Worksheet 2.5, you can see that actual income and expense levels are reasonably close to their targets and have a positive variance for the months shown (their surpluses exceed the budgeted surplus amounts). The biggest variances were in food and transportation expenses, but neither was far off the mark. Thus, for the first 3 months of the year, the Shepards seem to be doing a good job of controlling their income and expenses. They have, in fact, achieved a cumulative cash deficit of $419, smaller than the budgeted deficit (actual of −$1,879 versus budget of −$2,298) by cutting discretionary spending.

worksheet 2.5

The Shepards' Budget Control Schedule for January, February, and March 2005

The budget control schedule provides important feedback on how the actual cash flow is stacking up relative to the forecasted cash budget. If the variances are significant enough and/or continue month after month, the Shepards should consider altering either their spending habits or their cash budget.

BUDGET CONTROL SCHEDULE

Name(s) Tim and Andrea Shepard

For the 3 Months Ended March 31, 2005

	Month: January				Month: February				Month: March			
INCOME	Budgeted Amount (1)	Actual (2)	Monthly Variance (3)	Year-to-Date Variance (4)	Budgeted Amount (5)	Actual (6)	Monthly Variance (7)	Year-to-Date Variance (8)	Budgeted Amount (9)	Actual (10)	Monthly Variance (11)	Year-to-Date Variance (12)
Take-home pay	$4,775	$ 4,792	$ 17	$ 17	$ 4,775	$ 4,792	$ 17	$ 34	$ 4,775	$ 4,792	$ 17	$ 51
Bonuses and commissions												
Pensions and annuities												
Investment income									90	86	(4)	(4)
Other income												
(I) Total Income	$ 4,775	$ 4,792	$ 17	$ 17	$ 4,775	$ 4,792	$ 17	$ 34	$ 4,865	$ 4,878	$ 13	$ 47
EXPENSES												
Housing (rent/mtge, repairs)	$ 1,506	$ 1,506	$ 0	$ 0	$ 1,856	$ 1,856	$ 0	$ 0	$ 1,506	$ 1,506	$ 0	$ 0
Utilities (phone, elec., gas, water)	245	237	(8)	(8)	245	252	7	(1)	245	228	(17)	(18)
Food (home and away)	575	559	(16)	(16)	575	548	(27)	(43)	575	450	(125)	(168)
Transportation (auto/public)	370	385	15	15	620	601	(19)	(4)	370	310	(60)	(64)
Medical/dental, incl. insurance	30	0	(30)	(30)	30	45	15	(15)	30	0	(30)	(45)
Clothing	150	190	40	40	150	135	(15)	25	500	475	(25)	0
Insurance (life, auto, home)												
Taxes (property)					550	550	0	0				0
Appliances, furniture, and other (purchases/loans)	60	60	0	0	60	60	0	0	30	30	0	0
Personal care	100	85	(15)	(15)	100	120	20	5	100	75	(25)	(20)
Recreation and entertainment	250	210	(40)	(40)	250	240	(10)	(50)	3,200	3,285	85	35
Savings and investments	375	375	0	0	375	375	0	0	375	375	0	0
Other expenses	135	118	(17)	(17)	250	245	(5)	(22)	235	200	(35)	(57)
Fun money	230	200	(30)	(30)	230	225	(5)	(35)	230	230	0	(35)
(II) Total Expenses	$ 4,026	$ 3,925	$ (101)	$ (101)	$ 5,291	$ 5,252	$ (39)	$ (140)	$ 7,396	$ 7,164	$ (232)	$ (372)
CASH SURPLUS (OR DEFICIT) [(I)-(II)]	$ 749	$ 867	$ 118	$ 118	$ (516)	$ (460)	$ 56	$ 174	$(2,531)	$(2,286)	$ 245	$ 419
CUMULATIVE CASH SURPLUS (OR DEFICIT)	$ 749	$ 867	$	$	$ 233	$ 407	$	$	$(2,298)	$ (1,879)	$	$

Key: Col. (3) = Col. (2) – Col. (1); Col. (7) = Col. (6) – Col. (5); Col. (11) = Col. (10) – Col. (9); Col. (4) = Col. (3); Col. (8) = Col. (4) + Col. (7); Col. (12) = Col. (8) + Col. (11).

smart.sites

Get more budgeting advice from CNNMoney's budgeting tutorial, **http://money.cnn.com/pf/101/lessons/2/index.html**. Click on "Evaluating them [expenses]" for an interactive worksheet.

SUMMARY

LG1. Describe the role of financial statements, special planning concerns and professional financial planners, in the personal financial planning process. Preparing and using personal financial statements is important to personal financial planning, because they allow you to keep track of your current financial position and monitor your progress toward achieving your financial goals. Situations that require special attention include the timing of financial decisions (especially during periods of personal stress or major life changes), managing two incomes, managing employee benefits, and adapting to changes in your personal situation, such as marital status or taking responsibility for elderly relatives' care. Professional financial planners can help you with the planning process. Investigate a prospective financial planner's background carefully and understand how he or she is paid (fees, commissions, or both).

LG2. Put a monetary value on financial goals using *time value of money* concepts. When putting a dollar value on your financial goals, be sure to consider the time value of money and, if appropriate, use the notion of future value or present value when preparing your estimates. These techniques explicitly recognize that a dollar today is worth more than a dollar in the future.

LG3. Prepare a personal balance sheet. A balance sheet reports on your financial position at a given point in time. It provides a summary of the things you own (assets), the money you owe (liabilities), and your financial worth (net worth). Assets include liquid assets, investments, and real and personal property. Liabilities include current liabilities that are due in less than 1 year (unpaid bills, open account credit obligations) and long-term liabilities (real estate mortgages, consumer installment loans, education loans). Net worth represents your actual wealth and is the difference between your total assets and total liabilities.

LG4. Generate a personal income and expense statement. The income and expense statement summarizes the income you received and the money you spent over a given time period. It is prepared on a cash basis and, thus, reflects your actual cash flow. Expenses consist of cash outflows to (1) meet living expenses, (2) pay taxes, (3) purchase various kinds of assets, and (4) pay debts. A cash surplus (or deficit) is the difference between income and expenses. A cash surplus can be used to increase assets or reduce debts, and therefore has a positive effect on the balance sheet's net worth account. A cash deficit, in contrast, reduces assets or increases debts, acting to reduce net worth.

LG5. Develop a good recordkeeping system and use ratios to interpret personal financial statements. Good records facilitate the preparation of accurate personal financial statements. Organized records also simplify tax return preparation and provide the necessary documentation for tax deductions. Ratio analysis allows you to interpret your personal financial statements to assess how well you are doing relative to your past performance. Four important financial ratios are the solvency, liquidity, savings, and debt service ratios.

LG6. Construct a cash budget and use it to monitor and control spending. A cash budget will help you implement a system of disciplined spending. By curbing needless spending, it can increase the amount of funds allocated to savings and investments. Household budgets identify planned monthly cash income and cash expenses for the coming year. The objective is to take in more money than you spend, so you'll save money and add to your net worth over time. The final step in the budgeting process is to compare actual income and expenses with budgeted figures to learn whether, in fact, you are living within your budget and, if not, to take appropriate corrective actions.

Financial Planning Exercises

1. Use future or present value techniques to solve the following problems:
   a. Starting with $10,000, how much will you have in 10 years if you can earn 15 percent on your money? If you can earn only 8 percent?
   b. If you inherited $25,000 today and invested all of it in a security that paid a 10 percent rate of return, how much would you have in 25 years?
   c. If the average new home costs $125,000 today, how much will it cost in 10 years if the price increases by 5 percent each year?
   d. You feel that in 15 years it will cost $75,000 to give your child a college education. Will you have enough if you take $25,000 *today* and invest it for the next 15 years at 8 percent? If you start *from scratch,* how much will you have to save *each year* to have $75,000 in 15 years if you can earn an 8 percent rate of return on your investments?
   e. If you can earn 12 percent, how much will you have to save *each year* if you want to retire in 35 years with $1 million?
   f. You plan to have $750,000 in savings and investments when you retire at age 60. Assuming that you earn an average of 9 percent on this portfolio, what is the maximum annual withdrawal you can make over a 25-year period of retirement?

2. Over the past several years, Helen Chang has been able to save regularly. As a result, today she has $14,188 in savings and investments. She wants to establish her own business in 5 years and feels she will need $50,000 to do so.
   a. If she can earn 12 percent on her money, how much will her $14,188 savings/investments be worth in 5 years? Will Helen have the $50,000 she needs? If not, how much more money will she need?
   b. Given your answer to part **a**, how much will Helen have to save *each year* over the next 5 years to accumulate the additional money, assuming she can earn interest at a rate of 12 percent?
   c. If Helen can afford to save only $2,000 a year, given your answer to part a, will she have the $50,000 she needs to start her own business in 5 years?

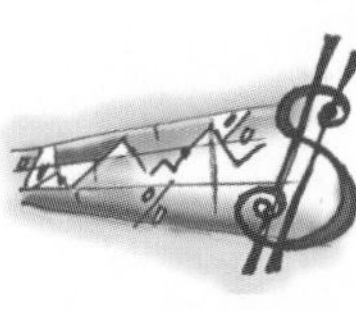

3. Bill Shaffer wishes to have $200,000 in a retirement fund 20 years from now. He can create the retirement fund by making a single lump-sum deposit today.
   a. If he can earn 10 percent on his investments, how much must Bill deposit today to create the retirement fund? If he can earn only 8 percent on his investments? Compare and discuss the results of your calculations.
   b. If upon retirement in 20 years Bill plans to invest the $200,000 in a fund that earns 11 percent, what is the maximum annual withdrawal he can make over the following 15 years?
   c. How much would Bill need to have on deposit at retirement to annually withdraw $35,000 over the 15 years if the retirement fund earns 11 percent?
   d. To achieve his annual withdrawal goal of $35,000 calculated in part **c,** how much more than the amount calculated in part **a** must Bill deposit today in an investment earning 10 percent annual interest?

4. Chris Jones is preparing his balance sheet and income and expense statement for the year ending June 30, 2004. He is having difficulty classifying six items and asks for your help. Which, if any, of the following transactions are assets, liabilities, income, or expense items?
   a. He rents a house for $950 a month.
   b. On June 21, 2004, he bought diamond earrings for his wife and charged them using his Visa card. The earrings cost $600, but he has not yet received the bill.
   c. He borrowed $2,000 from his parents last fall but so far has made no payments to them.
   d. He makes monthly payments of $120 on an installment loan, about half of which is interest and the balance is repayment of principal. He has 20 payments left totaling $2,400.
   e. He paid $2,800 in taxes during the year and is due a tax refund of $450, which he has not yet received.
   f. He invested $1,800 in some common stock.
5. Put yourself 10 years into the future. Construct a fairly detailed and realistic balance sheet and income and expense statement reflecting what you would like to achieve by that time.
6. *Use Worksheet 2.2.* Elizabeth Walker has been asked by her banker to submit a personal balance sheet as of June 30, 2004, in support of an application for a $3,000 home improvement loan. She has come to you for help in preparing it. So far, she has prepared the following list of her assets and liabilities at June 30, 2004:

Cash on hand		$70
Balance in checking account		180
Balance in money market deposit account with Mid-American Savings		650
Bills outstanding:		
Telephone	$ 20	
Electricity	70	
Charge account balance	190	
Visa	180	
MasterCard	220	
Taxes	400	
Insurance	220	1,300
Home and property		68,000
Home mortgage loan		52,000
Automobile: 2000 Honda Civic		10,000
Installment loan balances:		
Auto loans	3,000	
Furniture loan	500	3,500
Personal property:		
Furniture	1,050	
Clothing	900	1,950
Investments:		
U.S. government savings bonds	500	
Stock of WIMCO Corporation	3,000	3,500

From the data given, prepare Elizabeth Walker's balance sheet, dated June 30, 2004 (follow the balance sheet form shown in Worksheet 2.2). Then evaluate her balance sheet relative to the following factors: (a) solvency, (b) liquidity, and (c) equity in her dominant asset.

7. *Use Worksheet 2.3.* Chuck and Judy Schwartz are about to construct their income and expense statement for the year ending December 31, 2004. They have put together the following income and expense information for 2004:

Judy's salary	$37,000
Reimbursement for travel expenses	1,950
Interest on:	
Savings account	110
Bonds of Alpha Corporation	70
Groceries	4,150
Rent	9,600
Utilities	960
Gas and auto expenses	650
Chuck's tuition, books, and supplies	3,300
Books, magazines, and periodicals	280
Clothing and other miscellaneous expenses	2,700
Cost of photographic equipment purchased with charge card	2,200
Amount paid to date on photographic equipment	1,600
Judy's travel expenses	1,950
Purchase of a used car (cost)	9,750
Outstanding loan balance on car	7,300
Purchase of bonds in Alpha Corporation	4,900

Using the information provided, prepare an income and expense statement for the Schwartzes for the year ending December 31, 2004 (follow the form shown in Worksheet 2.3).

8. Dave and Betty Williamson are preparing their 2005 cash budget. Help the Williamsons reconcile the following differences, giving reasons to support your answers:
   a. Their only source of income is Dave's salary, which amounts to $3,000 a month before taxes. Betty wants to show the $3,000 as their monthly income, whereas Dave argues that his take-home pay of $2,350 is the correct value to show.
   b. Betty wants to make a provision for *fun money*, an idea that Dave cannot understand. He asks, "Why do we need fun money when everything is provided for in the budget?"

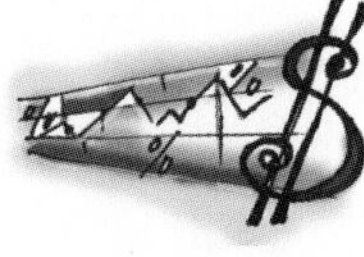

9. Below is a portion of Jeffrey Cook's budget record for April 2005. Fill in the blanks in columns 6 and 7.

Item (1)	Amount Budgeted (2)	Amount Spent (3)	Beginning Balance (4)	Monthly Surplus (Deficit) (5)	Cumulative Surplus (Deficit) (6)
Rent	$350	$360	$20	$____	$____
Utilities	150	145	15	____	____
Food	310	275	–15	____	____
Auto	25	38	–5	____	____
Recreation and entertainment	50	60	–50	____	____

10. *Use Worksheet 2.4.* Prepare a record of your income and expenses for the last 30 days; then prepare a personal cash budget for the next 3 months. (Use the format in Worksheet 2.4 but fill out only 3 months and the total column.) Use the cash budget to control and regulate your expenses during the next month. Discuss the impact of the budget on your spending behavior, as well as any differences between your expected and actual spending patterns.

Applying Personal Finance

What's Your Condition?

Financial statements reflect your financial condition. They help you measure where you are now. Then, as time passes and you prepare your financial statements periodically, you can use them to track your progress toward your financial goals. Good financial statements are also a must when you apply for a loan. The purpose of this project is to help you evaluate your current financial condition.

Look back at the discussion in this chapter on balance sheets and income and expense statements and prepare your own. If you're doing this for the first time, it may not be as easy as it sounds! Use the following questions to help you along:

1. Have you included all your assets at *fair market value* (not historical cost) on your balance sheet?
2. Have you included all your debt *balances* as liabilities on your balance sheet? (Do not take your monthly payment amounts multiplied by the number of payments you have left—this includes future interest as well.)
3. Have you included all items of income on your income and expense statement? (Remember, your paycheck is income and not an asset on your balance sheet.)
4. Have you included all debt payments as expenses on your income and expense statement? (Your phone bill is an expense for this month if you've already paid it. However, if the bill is still sitting on your desk staring you in the face, it is a liability on your balance sheet.)
5. Are there occasional expenses that you've forgotten about or hidden expenses such as entertainment that you have overlooked? Look back through your checkbook, spending diary, or any other financial records to find these occasional or infrequent expenses.
6. Remember that items go on either the balance sheet or income and expense statement, but not on both. For example, your $350 car payment that you made this month is an expense on your income and expense statement. The remaining $15,000 balance on your car loan is a liability on your balance sheet, while the fair market value of your car at $17,500 is listed as an asset.

Once you have completed your statements, calculate your solvency, liquidity, savings, and debt service ratios. Now, use your statements and ratios to assess your current financial condition. Do you like where you are? If not, how can you get where you want to be? Use your financial statements and ratios to help you formulate plans for the future.

Contemporary Case Applications

2.1 The Sullivans' Version of Financial Planning

John and Lisa Sullivan are a married couple in their mid-twenties. John is a financial analyst and Lisa works as a sales representative. Since their marriage 4 years ago, John and Lisa have been living comfortably. Their income has exceeded their expenses, and they have accumulated a net worth of nearly $45,000. This includes the $10,000 that they have built up in savings and investments. Because their income has always been more than adequate to allow them to live in the fashion they desire, the Sullivans have done no financial planning.

Lisa has just learned that she is 2 months pregnant and is concerned about how they will make ends meet if she quits work after their child is born. Each time she and John discuss the matter, John tells her not to worry because "we have always managed to pay our bills on time." Lisa cannot understand his attitude, because her income will be completely eliminated. To convince Lisa that there is no need for concern, John points out that their expenses for necessities last year were $24,885, which just about equaled his take-home pay of $26,480. With an anticipated promotion to a managerial position and an expected 10 percent pay raise, his income next year should exceed this amount. John also points out that they can reduce luxuries (trips, recreation, and entertainment) and can always draw down their savings or sell some for their stock if they get in a bind. Lisa asks about the long-run implications for their finances, John replies that there will be "no problems" because his boss has assured him that he has a bright future with the company. John also emphasizes that Lisa can go back to work in a few years if necessary.

In spite of John's somewhat convincing arguments, Lisa feels that they should carefully examine their financial condition in order to do some serious planning. She has gathered the following financial information for the year ending December 31, 2004:

Salaries	Take-home Pay	Gross Salary
John	$26,480	$38,350
Lisa	18,090	26,000

Item Amount	
Food	$ 4,200
Clothing	2,300
Mortgage payments, including property taxes of $1,400	9,400
Travel and entertainment card balances	2,000
Gas, electric, water expenses	1,990
Household furnishings	4,500
Telephone	640
Auto loan balance	2,650
Common stock investments	7,500
Bank credit card balances	675
Income taxes	16,940
Credit card loan payments	2,210
Cash on hand	85
2001 Nissan Sentra	7,000
Medical expenses (unreimbursed)	600
Homeowner's insurance premiums paid	400
Checking account balance	485
Auto insurance premiums paid	800
Transportation	2,800
Cable television	480
Estimated value of home	98,000
Trip to Europe	5,000
Recreation and entertainment	4,000
Auto loan payments	2,150
Money market account balance	2,500
Purchase of common stock	7,500
Addition to money market account	500
Mortgage on home	70,000

Questions

1. Using this information and Worksheets 2.2 and 2.3, construct the Sullivans' December 31, 2004, balance sheet and income and expense statement for the year ending December 31, 2004.
2. Comment on the Sullivans' financial condition with respect to (a) solvency, (b) liquidity, (c) savings, and (d) ability to pay debts promptly. If the Sullivans continue to manage their finances as described, what do you expect the long-run consequences to be? Discuss.
3. Critically evaluate the Sullivans' approach to financial planning. Point out any fallacies in John's arguments, and be sure to mention (a) implications for the long term, (b) the potential impact of inflation, and (c) the impact on their net worth. What procedures should they use to get their financial house in order? Be sure to discuss the role that long- and short-term financial plans and budgets might play.

2.2 Joe Garcia Learns to Budget

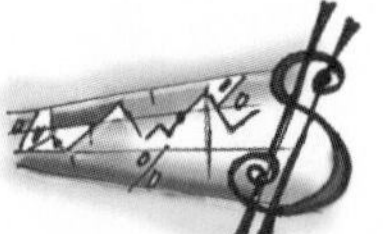

Joe Garcia graduated from college in 2003 and moved to Atlanta to take a job as a market research analyst. He was pleased to be financially independent and was sure that, with his $35,000 salary, he could cover his living expenses and also have plenty of money left over to furnish his studio apartment and enjoy the wide variety of social and recreational activities available in Atlanta. He opened several department store charge accounts and also obtained a bank credit card.

For awhile Joe managed pretty well on his monthly take-home pay of $2,250, but by the end of 2004 he was having trouble fully paying all his credit card charges each month. Concerned that his spending had gotten out of control and that he was barely making it from paycheck to paycheck, he decided to compile a list of his expenses for the past calendar year and develop a budget. He hoped not only to reduce his credit card debt but also to begin a regular savings program.

He prepared the following summary of expenses for 2004:

Item	Annual Expenditure
Rent	$9,600
Auto insurance	520
Auto loan payments	3,340
Clothing	2,200
Installment loan for stereo	540
Personal care	240
Phone	600
Cable TV	240
Gas and electricity	960
Medical care	120
Dentist	70
Groceries	2,500
Dining out	2,000
Car expenses (gas, repairs, fees, and so on)	1,560
Furniture purchases	900
Recreation and entertainment	1,900
Other expenses	600

After reviewing his 2004 expenses, Joe made the following assumptions about his expenses for 2005:

1. All expenses will remain at the same levels, with the following exceptions:
   a. Auto insurance, auto expenses, gas and electricity, and groceries will increase 5 percent.

b. Clothing purchases will decrease to $1,850.

c. Phone and cable TV will increase $5 per month.

d. Furniture purchases will decrease to $660, most of which is for a new television.

e. He will take a 1-week vacation to Lake Tahoe in July at a cost of $1,100.

2. All expenses will be budgeted in equal monthly installments except for the vacation and the following:

   a. Auto insurance is paid in two installments due in June and December.

   b. He plans to replace the brakes on his car in February at a cost of $120.

   c. Visits to the dentist will be made in March and September.

3. He will eliminate his bank credit card balance by making extra monthly payments of $75 during each of the first 6 months.

4. With regard to his income, he has just received a small raise, so his take-home pay will be $2,375 per month.

Questions

1. a. Prepare a preliminary cash budget for Joe for the year ending December 31, 2005, using the format shown in Worksheet 2.4.

   b. Compare Joe's estimated expenses with his expected income and make recommendations that will help him balance his budget.

2. Make any necessary adjustments to Joe's estimated monthly expenses and revise his annual cash budget for the year ending December 31, 2005, using Worksheet 2.4.

3. Analyze the budget and advise Joe on his financial situation. Suggest some long-, intermediate-, and short-term financial goals for Joe, and discuss some steps he can take to reach them.

MONEY ONLINE

1. **http://www.kiplinger.com/tools/budget.html**

What you *think* you're going to spend is one thing; what you *actually* spend may be another! Project your expenditures and then compare them with your actual expenses using Kiplinger's tool, "A Budget for Today and Tomorrow." Start today to get a handle on your expenditures.

2. **http://www.bhg.com**

Great articles, great tools and great tips are all assembled for you at *Better Homes and Garden's* Web site. Click on "Family" and then select "Money" from the drop-down box to find cost-cutting tips for managing your money, your home or raising your children.

3. **http://www.metlife.com**

Big events in your life present special needs. Met Life offers Life Advice to help you through the times and challenges of your life. Look for "Meeting Life," and under "Life Transitions" find coverage on topics such as marriage, divorce, remarriage, becoming a parent, coming to the United States, loss of a loved one, loss of a job, reentering the workforce, and leaving the military.

4. **http://www.financenter.com/consumertools**

How much of your paycheck will you get to bring home? The FinanCenter's Web site makes available to consumers the tools that they supply to professional institutions. Under "Calculators," look for "Paycheck Planning" for help with determining how much of your paycheck that you will be able to take home as either a salaried or an hourly employee, how much of your bonus you will be able to keep after taxes, or how your 401(k) contribution will affect your take-home pay. Note that many calculators are also available in Spanish.

5. **http://www.healthy.net/library/articles/cash/assessment/assessment.htm**
Your spending personality could be costing you big bucks every year! Take the Spending Personality Assessment Test to determine your dominant spending personality and obtain information on how best to deal with it. Explore other articles at the HealthyCash Web site **http://www.healthy.net/library/articles/cash** to help you develop a healthy attitude toward money and to learn to make better financial decisions.

6. **http://cbs.marketwatch.com**
Keep up to date with the latest news and developments in the personal finance arena at the CBS MarketWatch Web site. Click on "Personal Finance" and then on "Life & Money." Scroll down to see their many offerings or click on other topics of interest.

7. **http://moneycentral.msn.com**
Find articles and information on almost any personal finance topic imaginable at MoneyCentral. Click on "Planning" and choose from their many topics and tools. Search for a college or scholarship, evaluate your debt or your insurance needs, or start planning now for your retirement.

8. **http://www.pueblo.gsa.gov/cic_text/money/66ways/index.html**
How can you save more money? Browse through "66 Ways to Save Money" provided by the Consumer Literacy Consortium (in either Spanish or English). Find tips, ideas, and Web resources for saving on various items such as airline fares, auto leasing, prescription drugs, and even funeral arrangements!

Just for Fun!

9. **http://www.financenter.com/consumertools**
Want to become a millionaire? Once you get that million, what it will be worth in today's dollars? Find the answers to both these questions by clicking on "Calculators," and then "Savings," and then on "What will it take to become a millionaire?" Try the following scenarios:

- Give yourself a 10-year time frame, no current savings, and invest $200/month at 10 percent.
- Give yourself a 30-year time frame, $20,000 in current savings, and invest $500/month at 10 percent.

10. **http://www.consumerworld.org**
This one's all for you! A treasure trove of entries on shopping, bargains, consumer resources, consumer agencies, and much more await you at Consumer World. This site bills itself as a noncommercial guide with over 2,000 of the most useful consumer resources!

CHAPTER 3

Managing Your Taxes

Learning Goals

LG1. Discuss the basic principles of income taxes and determine your filing status.

LG2. Describe the various sources of gross income and adjustments to (gross) income, differentiate between standard and itemized deductions and exemptions, and calculate taxable income.

LG3. Prepare a basic tax return using the appropriate tax forms and rate schedules.

LG4. Explain who needs to pay estimated taxes, when to file or amend your return, and how to handle an audit.

LG5. Know where to get help with your taxes and how software can streamline tax return preparation.

LG6. Implement an effective tax planning strategy.

Audit Alert Taxes the Ashers

David Asher viewed the ominous-looking envelope from the Internal Revenue Service (IRS) with concern. He and his wife Mary had filed their taxes on time and had checked Form 1040 and the supporting schedules carefully before sending them to the IRS. When he opened the letter, his worst fear was confirmed: The IRS was auditing the Ashers' tax return from last year.

The Ashers were not alone: In 2003, the number of audits rose by about one-third. The IRS expanded its auditing forces and, in addition to returns selected for specific reasons, randomly chose 50,000 tax returns to audit.

After a momentary panic, David realized that in all probability the IRS was questioning some of their deductions. As a self-employed psychologist, he knew that small business owners and self-employed professionals were about twice as likely to be audited as other people. The potential to cross the line between business and personal expenses was much greater, for one thing. Because small business owners may be paid in cash or with personal checks, the IRS is also looking for hidden income. David's home office, for which he claimed certain deductions, raised another red flag for the IRS.

Over dinner that night, the Ashers discussed the best way to prepare for the upcoming audit. Mary pointed out that they were in very good shape because they made tax planning a priority throughout the year, not just at tax time. They stayed current on changing tax laws so that they could compute all appropriate deductions and exemptions correctly. They carefully separated personal and business expenses and, more importantly, kept detailed records for every deduction they claimed. This would help them document the legitimacy of any questioned items.

What could have been a financial disaster turned out to be only a minor problem, thanks to the Ashers' well-organized money management system and understanding of income tax basics. They were able to answer the IRS examiner's questions and avoid any tax penalties. After reading the material presented in Chapter 3, you will also be familiar with acceptable procedures for managing your income taxes.

CRITICAL THINKING QUESTIONS

As you review the chapter, consider these questions in relation to the Asher family's tax planning:

- Why should tax planning be a year-round process?
- Suggest several areas where the Ashers could use tax planning to reduce their tax liability.
- Discuss the advantages and disadvantages of using an outside tax preparer. Would you recommend this to the Ashers, and why?

UNDERSTANDING FEDERAL INCOME TAX PRINCIPLES

LG1

The Ashers are wise to make tax planning an important part of personal financial planning: A typical American family currently pays *about one-third of its gross income in taxes:* federal income and Social Security taxes and numerous state and local income, sales, and property taxes. Although you may think of tax planning as an activity to do between January, when tax forms arrive in the mail, and April 15, the filing deadline, like the Ashers you should make tax planning a year-round activity. You should always consider tax consequences when developing and revising your financial plans and making major financial decisions, such as purchasing a home and investing.

The overriding objective of tax planning is very simple: to maximize the amount of money you keep by minimizing the amount of taxes you pay. As long as it is done honestly and within the tax codes, there is nothing immoral, illegal, or unethical about trying to minimize your tax bill. Most tax planning centers on ways to minimize income and estate (see Chapter 15) taxes. This chapter concentrates on income taxes paid by individuals, particularly the federal income tax, the largest and most important tax for most taxpayers.

Taxes are dues we pay for membership in our society; they are the cost of living in this country. Federal, state, and local tax receipts fund government activities and a wide variety of public services, from national defense to local libraries. The administration and enforcement of federal tax laws is the responsibility of the IRS, a part of the U.S. Department of Treasury.

Although the largest tax a person will normally pay is federal income tax, there are other forms of taxes to contend with. For example, additional federal taxes may be levied on income and on certain types of transactions. At the state and local levels, sales transactions, income, property ownership, and licenses may be taxed. Because most individuals have to pay many of these other types of taxes, you should evaluate their impact on your financial decisions. Thus, a person saving to purchase a new automobile costing $18,000 should realize that the state and local sales taxes, as well as the cost of license plates and registration, may add another $1,500 or more to the total cost of the car.

smart.sites

How long does the average American have to work this year to pay federal, state, and local taxes? Get the answer at the Tax Foundation Web site, **http://www.taxfoundation.org**. You'll also find information there about tax policy, tax rates, tax collections, and the economics of taxation.

Because tax laws are complicated and subject to frequent revision, we will present key concepts and show how they apply to common tax situations. The provisions of the tax code may change annually with regard to tax rates, amounts and types of deductions and personal exemptions, and similar items. Often these changes are not finalized until late in the year. The tax tables, calculations, and sample tax returns presented in this chapter are based on the tax laws applicable to the calendar year 2003—those in effect at the time this book was being revised. *Although tax rates and other provisions will change, the basic procedures will remain the same.* Before preparing your tax returns, be sure to review the current regulations; IRS publications and other tax preparation guides should be helpful in this regard.

THE ECONOMICS OF INCOME TAXES

It should come as little surprise to learn that most people simply do not like to pay taxes. Some of this feeling undoubtedly stems from the widely held perception that a lot of government spending amounts to little more than bureaucratic waste. But a good deal of this feeling is probably also due to the fact that taxpayers get nothing tangible in return for their money. After all, paying taxes is not like spending $7,000 on furniture, a boat, or a European vacation. The fact is, we too often tend to overlook or take for granted the many services that are provided by the taxes we pay—public schools and state colleges, roads and highways, and parks and recreational facilities, not to mention police and fire protection, retirement benefits, and many other health and social services. In Exhibit 3.1 we can see where the government gets its tax dollars and how it uses them.

EXHIBIT 3.1

Major Categories of Federal Income and Outlays for Fiscal Year 2002

These pie charts show the relative sizes of the major categories of Federal income and outlays for fiscal year 2002.

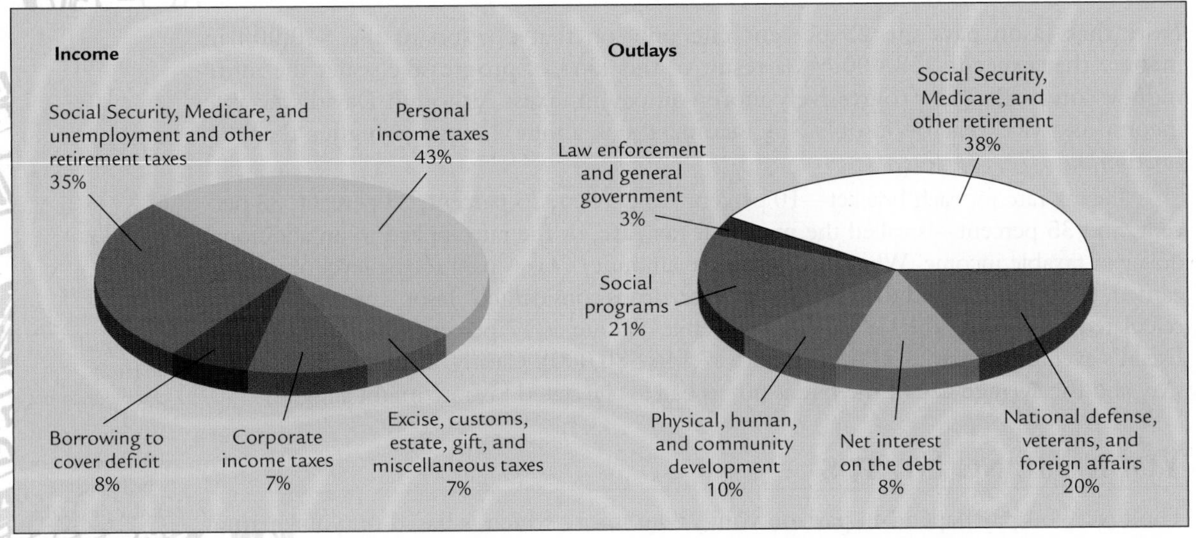

Source: Based on data from U.S. Office of Management and Budget, cited in *2003 Form 1040A Instructions*, Washington, DC: Internal Revenue Service, 2003, p. 56.

income taxes A type of tax levied on taxable income by the federal government and many state and local governments.

progressive tax structure A tax structure in which the larger the amount of taxable income, the higher the rate at which it is taxed.

Income taxes provide the major source of revenue for the federal government. Personal income taxes are scaled on progressive rates. To illustrate how this **progressive tax structure** works, we will use the following data for single taxpayers filing 2003 returns:

Taxable Income	Tax Rate
$1 to $7,000	10%
$7,001 to $28,400	15%
$28,401 to $68,800	25%
$68,801 to $143,500	28%
$143,501 to $311,950	33%
Over $311,950	35%

As income moves from a lower to a higher bracket, the higher rate applies *only to the additional income in that bracket* and not to the entire income. For example, consider two single brothers Jason and David, with taxable incomes of $40,000 and $80,000, respectively:

Name	Taxable Income	Tax Calculation	Tax Liability
Jason	$40,000	=[($40,000 − $28,400) × .25]	
		+ [($28,400 − $7,000) × .15]	
		+ [$7,000 × .10]	
		= $2,900 + $3,210 + $700 =	$6,810
David	$80,000	=[($80,000 − $68,800) × .28]	
		+ [($68,800 − $28,400) × .25]	
		+ [($28,400 − $7,000) × .15]	
		+ [$7,000 × .10]	
		=$3,136 + $10,100 + $3,210 + $700 =	$17,146

Note that Jason pays the 25 percent rate only on that portion of the $40,000 in income that exceeds $28,400. As a result of this kind of progressive scale, the more money you make, the progressively more you pay in taxes: Although David's taxable income is twice that of Jason's, his income tax is about 2.5 times higher than his brother's.

The tax rate for each bracket—10 percent, 15 percent, 25 percent, 28 percent, 33 percent, and 35 percent—is called the **marginal tax rate**, or the rate applied to an additional dollar of taxable income. When you relate the amount of taxes paid to the level of income earned, the tax rate, called the **average tax rate**, drops considerably. Jason's average tax rate, calculated by dividing the tax liability by taxable income, is 17 percent ($6,810/$40,000). David's average tax rate is 21.4 percent ($17,146/$80,000). Clearly, taxes are still progressive, and the average size of the bite is not as bad as the stated tax rate might suggest.

marginal tax rate The tax rate you pay on an additional dollar of taxable income.

average tax rate The rate at which each dollar of taxable income is taxed on average; calculated by dividing the tax liability by taxable income.

Your Filing Status

The taxes you pay depend in part on your *filing status*, which is based on your marital status and family situation on the last day of your tax year (usually December 31). Filing status affects whether you are required to file an income tax return, the amount of your standard deduction, and your tax rate. If you have a choice of filing status, you should calculate your taxes both ways and choose the status that results in the lower tax liability. There are five different filing status categories:

- **Single taxpayers:** Unmarried or legally separated from their spouses by either a separation or final divorce decree.
- **Married filing jointly:** Married couples who combine their income and allowable deductions and file one tax return.
- **Married filing separately:** Each spouse files his or her own return, reporting only his or her income, deductions, and exemptions.
- **Head of household:** A taxpayer who is unmarried or considered unmarried and pays more than half of the cost of keeping up a home for himself or herself and an eligible dependent child or relative.
- **Qualifying widow or widower with dependent child:** A person whose spouse died within 2 years of the tax year (for example, in 2001 or 2002 for the 2003 tax year) and who supports a dependent child may use joint return tax rates and is eligible for the highest standard deduction. (After the 2-year period, such a person may file under the head of household status if he or she qualifies.)

In general, married taxpayers who file jointly have a lower tax liability than if they file separately. However, sometimes these married couples pay more in total taxes than if they were single taxpayers. Combining the two incomes results in *bracket creep*—it pushes the couple into a higher tax bracket resulting in a "marriage tax." In an attempt to eliminate the marriage tax, recent (2003) tax legislation lowered taxes for married couples by making the standard deduction and the 15-percent bracket twice as large for couples compared with singles. There isn't too much you can do if you are in a situation where filing jointly results in paying a marriage penalty, because it is illegal for married individuals to use the single filing status. But a couple planning a December wedding may reap considerable tax savings by postponing their wedding until January!

The tax brackets (rates) and payments for married couples filing separately are typically higher than for joint filers because the spouses rarely account for equal amounts of taxable income. In some cases, however, it may be advantageous for spouses to file separate returns. For instance, if one spouse has a moderate income and substantial medical expenses, and the other has a low income and no medical expenses, filing separately may provide a tax savings. It's worth your time to calculate your taxes under both scenarios to see which results in the lower amount.

Every individual or married couple who earns a specified level of income is required to file a tax return. For example, for those under 65, a single person who earned more than $7,800, and a married couple with a combined income of more than $15,600 must file a tax return (for 2003). Like the personal tax rates, these minimums are adjusted annually based on the annual rate of inflation, and they are published in the instructions that accompany each year's tax forms. Note that if your income falls below the prevailing minimum levels, you are not required to file a tax return. However, if you had any tax withheld during the year, you must file a tax return—even if your income falls *below* minimum filing amounts—to receive a refund of these funds.

Your Take-Home Pay

Although many of us don't give much thought to taxes until April 15 approaches, we actually pay taxes as we earn income throughout the year. Under this *pay-as-you-go* system, your employer withholds (deducts) a portion of your income every pay period and periodically sends it to the IRS. Self-employed persons must likewise deduct and forward a portion of their income to the IRS each quarter. The amounts withheld are based on a taxpayer's estimated tax liability. After the close of the taxable year, you calculate the actual taxes you owe and file your tax return. When you file, you receive full credit for the amount of taxes withheld from your income during the year and either (1) receive a refund from the IRS (if too much tax was withheld from your paycheck), or (2) have to pay additional taxes (if the amount withheld did not cover your tax liability). Your employer normally withholds funds not only for federal income taxes, but also for FICA (or Social Security) taxes and, if applicable, state and local income taxes. In addition to taxes, you may have other deductions for items such as life and health insurance, savings plans, retirement programs, professional or union dues, or charitable contributions—all of which lower your take-home pay. Your *take-home pay* is what you are left with after subtracting the amount withheld from your *gross earnings*.

federal withholding taxes Taxes—based on the level of earnings and the number of withholding allowances claimed—that are deducted by an employer from the employee's gross earnings each pay period.

Federal Withholding Taxes

The amount of **federal withholding taxes** deducted from your gross earnings each pay period depends on both the level of your earnings and the number of withholding allowances you have claimed on a form called a *W-4*, which you must complete for your employer. Withholding allowances reduce the amount of taxes withheld from your income.

A taxpayer is entitled to one allowance for himself or herself, one for a spouse (if filing jointly), and one for each dependent claimed. In addition, you qualify for a *special allowance* if (1) you are single and have one job; (2) you are married, have only one job, and have a nonworking spouse; or (3) your wages from a second job or your spouse's wages (or the total of both) are $1,000 or less. *Additional withholding allowances* can be claimed by (1) heads of households, (2) those with at least $1,500 of child or dependent care expenses for which they plan to claim a credit, and (3) those with an unusually large amount of deductions. Of course, you can elect to have your employer withhold amounts greater than those prescribed by the withholding tables.

If you know you will work less than 8 months during a year—as you would if you are a college graduate starting your first job in the summer—you can ask your employer to calculate withholding using the part-year method. This method calculates withholding on what you actually earn in the tax year, rather than your annual salary. For example, if you began a $30,000 per year job on September 1, your withholding would be based not on the entire year's salary but rather on the $10,000 you'd earn during the remainder of that calendar year, resulting in substantially lower withholding.

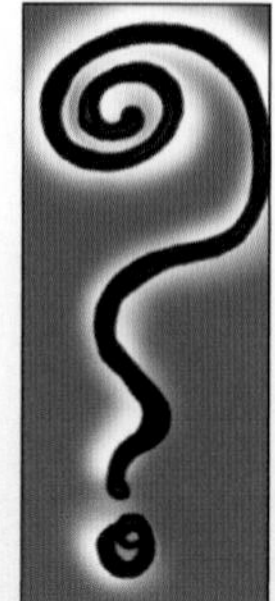

Concept ✓

3-1. What is a *progressive tax structure?* What is the economic rationale underlying the notion of progressive income taxes?

3-2. Carla Perez has an opportunity to earn $2,000 working overtime during the Christmas season. She thinks she will turn it down, however, because the extra income would put her in a higher tax bracket and the government would probably get most of it. Discuss Carla's reasoning.

3-3. Briefly define the five filing categories available to taxpayers. When might married taxpayers choose to file separately?

3-4. Distinguish between *gross earnings* and *take-home pay*. What does the employer do with the difference?

3-5. What two factors determine the amount of federal withholding taxes that will be deducted from gross earnings each pay period? Explain.

FICA and Other Withholding Taxes

In addition to withholding on earnings, all employed workers (except certain federal employees) have to pay a combined old-age, survivor's, disability, and hospital insurance tax under provisions of the **Federal Insurance Contributions Act (FICA)**. Known more commonly as the **Social Security tax**, it is paid equally by employer and employee. In 2003, the Social Security tax rate was 15.3 percent, allocated 12.4 percent to Social Security and 2.9 percent to Medicare. The 12.4 percent applies only to the first $87,000 of an employee's earnings (this number rises with national average wages), while the Medicare component is paid on all earnings. In 2003, the employer and employee each pay 7.65 percent—one-half of the 15.3 percent rate; self-employed persons pay the full 15.3 percent tax and can deduct 50 percent of it on their tax returns.

Federal Insurance Contributions Act (FICA), or **Social Security tax**
The law establishing the combined old-age, survivor's, disability, and hospital insurance tax levied on both employer and employee.

Most states have their own income taxes, which differ from state to state. Some cities assess income taxes as well. These state and local income taxes will also be withheld from earnings. They are deductible on federal returns, but deductibility of federal taxes on the state or local return depends on state and local laws.

IT'S TAXABLE INCOME THAT MATTERS

LG2

As you've no doubt gathered by now, paying your income taxes is a complex process involving several steps and many calculations. Exhibit 3.2 on page 96 depicts the procedure to compute your **taxable income** and subsequent tax liability. It looks simple enough—just subtract certain adjustments from your gross income to get your adjusted gross income, then subtract either the standard deduction or your itemized deductions and your total personal exemptions to get taxable income, and finally subtract your taxes and any tax credits from that amount and add any other taxes to it. This is not as easy as it sounds, however! Various sections of the Internal Revenue Code place numerous conditions and exceptions on the tax treatment and deductibility of

taxable income The amount of income that is subject to taxes, calculated by subtracting adjustments, the larger of itemized or standard deductions, and exemptions from gross income.

gross income The total of all of a taxpayer's income (before any adjustments, deductions, or exemptions) subject to federal taxes; it includes active, portfolio, and passive income.

certain income and expense items and define certain types of income as tax-exempt. As we will see, a number of problems can arise in defining what you may subtract.

Gross Income

Basically, **gross income** includes any and all income subject to federal taxes. Some of the more common forms of gross income include:

- Wages and salaries
- Bonuses, commissions, and tips
- Interest and dividends received
- Alimony received
- Business and farm income
- Gains from the sale of assets
- Income from pensions and annuities
- Income from rents and partnerships
- Prizes, lottery, and gambling winnings

In addition to these sources of income, some types of income are considered *tax exempt* and as such are excluded—totally or partially—from gross income. Tax-exempt income does not even have to be listed on the tax return. Common types of tax-exempt income include child support payments, certain types of employee fringe benefits, compensation from accident, health, and life insurance policies, federal income tax refunds, gifts, inheritances, scholarships and fellowships (limited as to amount and time), and veterans' benefits.

Three Kinds of Income

Individual income falls into one of three basic categories of income:

- **Active income:** Income *earned* on the job such as wages and salaries, bonuses and tips; most other forms of *noninvestment* income, including pension income and alimony
- **Portfolio income:** Earnings (interest, dividends, and capital gains [profits on the sale of investments]) generated from most types of investment holdings; includes savings accounts, stocks, bonds, mutual funds, options, and futures
- **Passive income:** A special category of income that includes income derived from real estate, limited partnerships, and other forms of tax shelters

These categories limit the amount of deductions and write-offs that taxpayers can take. Specifically, the amount of allowable, deductible expenses associated with portfolio and passive income *is limited to the amount of income derived from these two sources.* For example, if you had a total of $380 in portfolio income for the year, you could write off no more than $380 in portfolio-related interest expense. Note, however, that if you have more portfolio expenses than income, you can "accumulate" the difference and write it off in later years (when you have sufficient portfolio income) or when you finally sell the investment.

For deduction purposes, you cannot mix or combine portfolio and passive income with each other or with active income. *Investment-related expenses can be used only with portfolio income*, and with a few exceptions, *passive investment expenses can be used only to offset the income from passive investments.* All the other allowances and deductions we'll describe below are written off against the total amount of *active* income the taxpayer generates.

Capital Gains

Technically, a *capital gain* occurs whenever an asset (such as a stock, a bond, or real estate) is sold for more than its original cost. Thus, if you purchased stock for $50 per share and sold it for $60, you'd have a capital gain of $10 per share.

EXHIBIT 3.2

Calculating Your Taxable Income and Tax Liability

To find taxable income you must first subtract all adjustments to gross income and then subtract deductions and personal exemptions. Your total tax liability includes tax on this taxable income amount, less any tax credits plus other taxes owed.

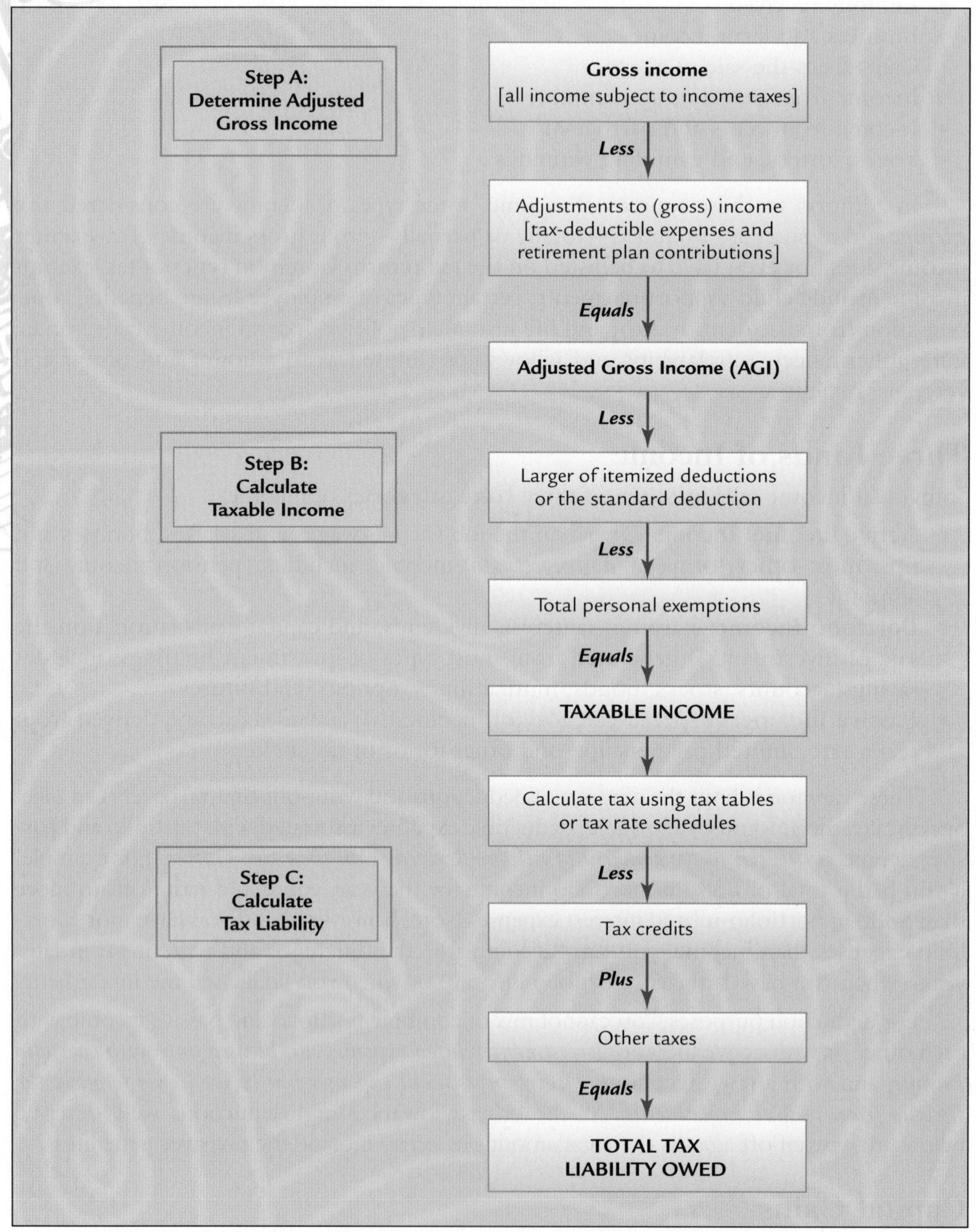

As of 2003, capital gains are taxed at different rates, depending on the holding period. Exhibit 3.3 shows the different holding periods and applicable tax rates based on the 2003 tax bracket. As a rule, taxpayers include most capital gains as part of *portfolio income.* They will add any capital gains to the amount of dividends, interest, and rents they generate to arrive at total investment income.

EXHIBIT 3.3

Capital Gains Tax Categories as of 2003

Capital gains tax rates have fallen recently to as low as 5 or 15 percent for holding periods over 12 months, depending on the tax bracket (year 2003).

Holding Period	Tax Bracket (2003)	Tax on Capital Gains
Less than 12 months	All (10%, 15%, 25%, 28%, 33%, and 35%)	Same as ordinary income
Over 12 months	10%, 15%	5%
	25%, 28%, 33%, 35%	15%

Although there are no limits on the amount of capital gains taxpayers can generate, the IRS imposes some restrictions on the amount of capital losses taxpayers can take in a given year. Specifically, a taxpayer can write off capital losses, dollar for dollar, against any capital gains. For example, a taxpayer with $10,000 in capital gains can write off up to $10,000 in capital losses. After that, he or she can write off a maximum of $3,000 in additional capital losses against other (active, earned) income. Thus, if the taxpayer in our example had $18,000 in capital losses in 2003, only $13,000 could be written off on 2003 taxes: $10,000 against the capital gains generated in 2003 and another $3,000 against active income. The remainder—$5,000 in this case—will have to be written off in later years, in the same order as indicated above: first against any capital gains and then up to $3,000 against active income. (*Note:* To qualify as a deductible item, the capital loss *must result from the sale of some income-producing asset*, such as stocks and bonds. The capital loss on a non–income producing asset, such as a car or TV set, does *not* qualify for tax relief.)

smart.sites

The *Guide to Capital Gains and Losses*, **http://www.fairmark.com/buystock/index.htm**, can help you understand the tax treatment of securities sales. It's just one of many tax guides you'll find at the site's *Tax Guide for Investors*.

Selling Your Home: A Special Case

Homeowners, for a variety of reasons, receive special treatment in the tax codes, including the taxation of capital gains on the sale of a home. The *Taxpayer Relief Act of 1997* made most home sales tax free. Under that law, single taxpayers can exclude from income the first $250,000 of gain on the sale of a principal residence. Married taxpayers can exclude the first $500,000. To get this favorable tax treatment, the taxpayer must own and occupy the residence as a principal residence for at least 2 of the 5 years prior to the sale. For example, the Greenmans (married taxpayers) just sold their principal residence for $475,000. They had purchased their home 4 years earlier for $325,000. They may exclude their $150,000 gain ($475,000 – $325,000) from their income because they occupied the residence for more than 2 years, and the gain is less than $500,000.

This exclusion is available on only one sale every 2 years. A loss on the sale of a principal residence is not deductible. Generally speaking, this law is quite favorable to homeowners.

Adjustments to (Gross) Income

Now that you have totaled up your gross income, you deduct your **adjustments to (gross) income**. These are allowable deductions from gross income, including certain employee, personal retirement, insurance, and support expenses. Most of these deductions are nonbusiness in nature. The following list, though not exhaustive, includes items that can be treated as adjustments to income:

- IRA contributions (limited)
- Self-employment taxes paid (limited to 50 percent of amount paid)
- Self-employed health insurance payments (up to 70 percent of amount paid)
- Keogh retirement plan and self-employed SEP contributions (limited)
- Penalty on early withdrawal of savings
- Alimony paid
- Moving expenses (some limits)

(*Note*: The limitations on deductions for self-directed retirement plans, such as IRAs and Keoghs, are discussed in Chapter 14.)

When the total of all allowable adjustments to income is subtracted from gross income, you are left with **adjusted gross income (AGI)**. AGI is in itself an important value, because AGI is used to calculate limits for certain itemized deductions.

adjustments to (gross) income Allowable deductions from gross income, including certain employee, personal retirement, insurance, and support expenses.

adjusted gross income (AGI) The amount of income remaining after subtracting all available adjustments to income from gross income.

Deductions: Standard or Itemized?

As we see from Exhibit 3.2, the next step in calculating your taxes is to subtract allowable deductions from your AGI. This is perhaps the most complex part of the tax preparation process. You have two options: take the *standard deduction*, a fixed amount that depends on your filing status or list your *itemized deductions* (specified tax-deductible personal expenses). Obviously, you should use the method that results in larger allowable deductions.

Standard Deduction

Instead of itemizing personal deductions, a taxpayer can take the **standard deduction**, a blanket deduction designed to capture the various deductible expenses that taxpayers normally incur. People who don't have sufficient itemized deductions take the stipulated standard deduction, which varies depending on the taxpayer's filing status (single, married filing jointly, and so on), age (65 or older), and vision (blind). In 2003, the standard deduction ranged from $4,750 to $13,300. For single filers, it was $4,750 and for married people filing jointly, $9,500. Those over 65 and those who are blind are eligible for a higher standard deduction. Each year the standard deduction amounts are adjusted in response to changes in the cost of living.

standard deduction A blanket deduction that depends on the taxpayer's filing status, age, and vision and can be taken by a taxpayer who doesn't have sufficient itemized deductions.

Itemized Deductions

Itemized deductions allow taxpayers to reduce their AGI by the amount of their allowable personal expenditures. The Internal Revenue Code defines the types of nonbusiness items that can be deducted from AGI. Some of the more common ones follow:

- Medical and dental expenses (in *excess* of 7.5 percent of AGI)
- State, local, and foreign income and property taxes; and state and local personal property taxes

itemized deductions Personal expenditures that can be deducted from AGI when determining taxable income.

- Residential mortgage interest and investment interest (limited)
- Charitable contributions (limited to 30 percent or 20 percent of AGI depending on certain factors)
- Casualty and theft losses (in excess of 10 percent of AGI; reduced by $100 per loss)
- Job and other expenses (in excess of 2 percent of AGI)
- Moving expenses (some restrictions; also deductible for those who don't itemize)

The instructions that accompany the tax forms provide detailed descriptions of allowable deductions in each category.

Taxpayers with AGI over a specified amount, adjusted upward annually, lose part of their itemized deductions. In 2003, the level of AGI at which the phase-out began was $69,750 for single taxpayers and $139,500 for married persons filing jointly. This limitation applies to certain categories of deductions, including other types of taxes, home mortgage interest, charitable contributions, unreimbursed employee expenses, moving expenses, and other miscellaneous deductions subject to the 2 percent limit. Medical expenses, casualty and theft losses, and investment interest are exempt from this limit on deductions, and the amount of the total reduction in itemized deductions cannot be more than 80 percent of the total deductions to which the limitation applies. These total itemized deductions are reduced by the smaller of 3 percent of AGI over $139,500 (or $69,750 for married taxpayers filing separately) or 80 percent of the deductions to which the limitation applies. Under the 2003 tax law, in 2006 this phase-out will itself begin to be phased out and be eliminated by 2010.

For example, assume that you are married, filing a joint return, and your AGI is $150,000. Your deductions (in excess of any specified percentages of AGI) affected by the income limitation total $45,000, and other deductions total $10,000. You must reduce deductions by $315 [($150,000 AGI − $139,500) × .03 = $315]. Therefore, you would subtract $315 from your $55,000 total itemized deductions, for an allowed deduction of $54,685. This loss of itemized deductions has the effect of raising the tax rate applied to your top bracket (in this case) from 28 percent to 28.84 percent [28.00 percent + (3 percent × 28 percent)]. Married taxpayers with combined income over the AGI deduction threshold and high itemized deductions that can be allocated to one spouse (such as medical expenses) may find that filing separately will allow them to avoid this limit on deductions.

smart.sites

About.com's Tax pages, **http://taxes.about.com/**, offer help on a variety of tax topics, including how to find all the possible deductions for which you qualify.

Choosing the Best Option

Your decision to take the standard deduction or itemize deductions may change from year to year, or even in the same year. Taxpayers who find they have chosen the wrong option and paid too much may recalculate their tax using the other method and claim a refund for the difference. For example, suppose that you computed and paid your taxes, which amounted to $2,450, using the standard deduction. A few months later you find that had you itemized your deductions, your taxes would have been only $1,950. Using the appropriate forms, you can file an *amended return (Form 1040X)* showing a $500 refund ($2,450 − $1,950). To avoid having to file an amended return as a result of using the wrong deduction technique, you should estimate your deductions using both the standard and itemized deduction amounts and then choose the alternative that results in lower taxes. Interestingly, most taxpayers use the standard deduction; generally homeowners who pay home mortgage interest and property taxes itemize because those expenses alone typically exceed the allowable standard deduction.

EXEMPTIONS

One more calculation remains in determining taxable income. Deductions from AGI based on the number of persons supported by the taxpayer's income are called **exemptions**. A taxpayer can claim an exemption for himself or herself, his or her spouse, and any *dependents*—which include children or other relatives earning less than a stipulated level of income ($3,050 in 2003) and for whom the taxpayer provides more than half of their total support. This income limitation is waived for children under the age of 24 (at the end of the calendar year) who are full-time students. Therefore, a college student, for example, could earn $8,000 and still be claimed as an exemption by his or her parents as long as all other dependency requirements are met. In 2003, each exemption claimed was worth $3,050. The personal exemption amount is tied to the cost of living and changes annually in line with the prevailing rate of inflation.

exemptions Deductions from AGI based on the number of persons supported by the taxpayer's income.

Exemptions are phased out and eliminated altogether for taxpayers with high levels of AGI. After adjustment for inflation, it applies to single taxpayers with 2003 AGI over $139,500 and married couples filing jointly with 2003 AGI over $209,250. As with itemized deductions, in 2006 the phase-out of exemptions will itself begin to be phased out and eliminated by 2010.

A personal exemption can be claimed only once. If a child is *eligible* to be claimed as an exemption by his or her parents, then the child does not have the choice of using a personal exemption on his or her own tax return regardless of whether the parents use the child's exemption.

In 2003, a family of four could take total exemptions of $12,200—that is, 4 × $3,050. Subtracting the amount claimed for itemized deductions (or the standard deduction) and exemptions from AGI results in the amount of your *taxable income*, which is the basis on which your taxes are calculated. A taxpayer who makes $40,000 a year may have only, say, $25,000 in taxable income after adjustments, deductions, and exemptions. It is the *lower*, taxable income figure that determines how much tax an individual must pay.

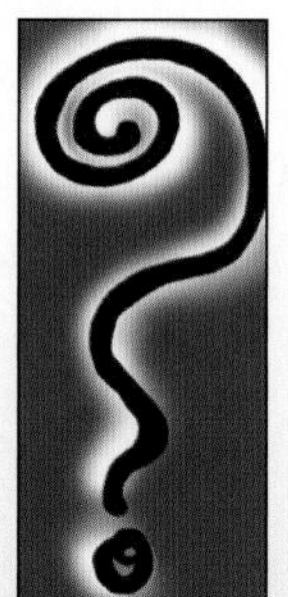

Concept ✓

3-6. Define and differentiate between *gross income* and *AGI*. Name several types of tax-exempt income. What is *passive income?*

3-7. What is a *capital gain*, and how is it treated for tax purposes?

3-8. If you itemize your deductions, you may include certain expenses as part of your itemized deductions. Discuss five types of itemized deductions and the general rules that apply to them.

3-9. Larry Torrelli was married on January 15, 2004. His wife, Rebecca, is a full-time student at the university and earns $125 a month working in the library. How many personal exemptions will Larry and Rebecca be able to claim on their joint return? Would it make any difference if Rebecca's parents paid for more than 50 percent of her support? Explain.

Financial Road Sign

Find Those Missing Deductions!

Often taxpayers miss deductions that would reduce their tax liability. Here are some you might overlook:

- Unused investment losses and charitable contributions carried over from prior years are sometimes forgotten.
- Doctor-prescribed weight loss or quit-smoking programs are medical expenses that count toward your total medical expenses, which are deductible if they are over 7.5 percent of AGI.
- Self-employed people can deduct 70 percent of health insurance premiums.
- Small business owners can depreciate equipment used in their business.
- Work expenses for which you aren't reimbursed count in miscellaneous deductions.
- Certain types of clean-fuel cars will give you a $2,000 tax break.
- You can deduct up to $3,000 in college tuition for a family member if your AGI falls within certain limits.

LG3 CALCULATING AND FILING YOUR TAXES

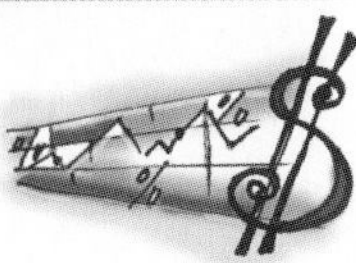

Now that we have reviewed the general principles of federal income taxes and the components of taxable income, we can direct our attention to calculating the amount of income tax due. To do this, we need to address several key aspects of measuring taxable income and taxes: (1) the tax rates applicable to various types of personal income, (2) tax credits, (3) the basic tax forms and schedules, and (4) the procedures for determining tax liability.

TAX RATES

As we saw earlier in this chapter, to find the amount of *taxable income* we subtract itemized deductions (or the standard deduction for nonitemizers) *and* personal exemptions from AGI. *Both itemizers and nonitemizers* use this procedure, which is a key calculation in determining your tax liability. It is *reported taxable income* that determines the amount of income subject to federal income taxes. Once you know the amount of your taxable income, you can refer to *tax rate tables* to find the amount of taxes you owe. (When actually filing a tax return, taxpayers with taxable income of more than $100,000 must use the tax rate schedules.)

Tax rates vary not only with the amount of reported taxable income, but also with filing status. Thus different tax rate schedules apply to each filing category, as shown in Exhibit 3.4. The vast majority of taxpayers fall into the first three brackets and are subject to tax rates of either 10, 15, or 25 percent.

To see how the tax rates in Exhibit 3.4 work, consider two single taxpayers: one has taxable income of $12,500, the other of $35,600. We would calculate their respective tax liabilities as follows:

- For taxable income of $12,500: $700 + [($12,500 − $7,000) × .15] = $700 + $825 = $1,525
- For taxable income of $35,600: $3,910 + [($35,600 − $28,400) × .25] = $3,910 + $1,800 = $5,710

The income of $12,500 is partially taxed at the 10 percent rate and partially taxed at the 15 percent rate. The first $7,000 of the $35,600 is taxed at 10 percent, the next $21,400 at 15 percent, and the remaining $7,200 at 25 percent. Keep in mind that taxpayers use the same procedures at this point whether they itemize or not. To show how the amount of tax liability will vary with the level of taxable income, Exhibit 3.5 lists the taxes due on a range of taxable incomes, from $1,500 to $350,000, for individual and joint returns.

Recall from our earlier discussions that the *average tax rate* is found by dividing your tax liability by the amount of reported taxable income. Returning to our example involving the taxpayer with an income of $35,600, we see that this individual had an average tax rate of 16.0 percent ($5,710 ÷ $35,600), which is considerably *less* than the stated tax rate of 25 percent. Actually, the 25 percent represents the taxpayer's **marginal tax rate**—the rate at which the next dollar of taxable income is taxed. Notice in our calculations that the marginal 25 percent tax rate applies only to that portion of the single person's income that exceeds $28,400, or $7,200, in the above example.

marginal tax rate
The tax rate you pay on an next dollar of taxable income.

Some taxpayers are subject to the *alternative minimum tax (AMT)*, currently 26 percent of the first $175,000 and 28 percent of the excess. A taxpayer's tax liability is the higher of the AMT or the regular tax. The AMT was originally designed to ensure that high-income taxpayers with many deductions and tax shelter investments that provide attractive tax write-offs pay their fair share of taxes. The AMT includes in taxable income certain types of deductions otherwise allowed, such as state and local income and property taxes, miscellaneous itemized deductions, unreimbursed

EXHIBIT 3.4

Sample Tax Rate Schedules

Tax rates levied on personal income vary with the amount of reported taxable income and the taxpayer's filing status.

2003 Tax Rate Schedules

Schedule X—Use if your filing status is **Single**

If the amount on Form 1040, line 40, is: *Over—*	*But not over—*	Enter on Form 1040, line 41	*of the amount over—*
$0	$7,000	---------- **10%**	**$0**
7,000	28,400	**$700.00 + 15%**	**7,000**
28,400	68,800	**3,910.00 + 25%**	**28,400**
68,800	143,500	**14,010.00 + 28%**	**68,800**
143,500	311,950	**34,926.00 + 33%**	**143,500**
311,950	----------	**90,514.50 + 35%**	**311,950**

Schedule Y-1—Use if your filing status is **Married filing jointly** or **Qualifying widow(er)**

If the amount on Form 1040, line 40, is: *Over—*	*But not over—*	Enter on Form 1040, line 41	*of the amount over—*
$0	$14,000	---------- **10%**	**$0**
14,000	56,800	**$1,400.00 + 15%**	**14,000**
56,800	114,650	**7,820.00 + 25%**	**56,800**
114,650	174,700	**22,282.50 + 28%**	**114,650**
174,700	311,950	**39,096.50 + 33%**	**174,700**
311,950	----------	**84,389.00 + 35%**	**311,950**

Schedule Y-2—Use if your filing status is **Married filing separately**

If the amount on Form 1040, line 40, is: *Over—*	*But not over—*	Enter on Form 1040, line 41	*of the amount over—*
$0	$7,000	---------- **10%**	**$0**
7,000	28,400	**$700.00 + 15%**	**7,000**
28,400	57,325	**3,910.00 + 25%**	**28,400**
57,325	87,350	**11,141.25 + 28%**	**57,325**
87,350	55,975	**19,548.25 + 33%**	**87,350**
155,975	----------	**42,194.50 + 35%**	**155,975**

Schedule Z—Use if your filing status is **Head of household**

If the amount on Form 1040, line 40, is: *Over—*	*But not over—*	Enter on Form 1040, line 41	*of the amount over—*
$0	$10,000	---------- **10%**	**$0**
10,000	38,050	**$1,000.00 + 15%**	**10,000**
38,050	98,250	**5,207.50 + 25%**	**38,050**
98,250	159,100	**20,257.50 + 28%**	**98,250**
159,100	311,950	**37,295.50 + 33%**	**159,100**
311,950	----------	**87,736.00 + 35%**	**311,950**

Source: Internal Revenue Service.

EXHIBIT 3.5

Taxable Income and the Amount of Income Taxes Due (2003)

Given the progressive tax structure that exists in this country, it follows that the larger your income, the more you can expect to pay in taxes.

	Taxes Due (rounded)	
Taxable Income	Individual Returns	Joint Returns
$ 1,500	$ 150[a]	$ 150[a]
8,000	850[b]	800
15,000	1,900	1,550[b]
30,000	4,310[c]	3,800
60,000	11,810	8,620[c]
100,000	22,746[d]	18,620
150,000	37,071[e]	32,181[d]
350,000	103,832[f]	97,707[f]

[a] Income is taxed at 10 percent.
[b] 15% tax rate now applies.
[c] 25% tax rate now applies.
[d] 28% tax rate now applies.
[e] 33% tax rate now applies
[f] 35% tax rate now applies

medical expenses, and depreciation. Therefore, taxpayers with moderate levels of taxable income, including those living in states with high tax rates and self-employed persons with depreciation deductions, may be subject to the AMT.

TAX CREDITS

tax credits Deductions from a taxpayer's tax liability that directly reduce his or her *taxes due* rather than *taxable income.*

Once you have determined your taxable income and calculated the *tax liability*, or amount of taxes you owe, you have one final step to determine the amount of taxes due. Some taxpayers are allowed to take certain deductions, known as **tax credits**, directly from their tax liability.

A tax credit is much more valuable than a deduction or an exemption, because it directly reduces, dollar for dollar, the amount of *taxes due*, whereas a deduction or an exemption merely reduces the amount of *taxable income*. In Exhibit 3.6 we see how this difference affects the tax liability of two single taxpayers with $34,000 of gross income and $6,000 of other deductions/exemptions (in the 15 percent tax bracket). One has $1,000 in deductions, and the other has a $1,000 tax credit. Look at what happens to the amount of taxes paid. In effect, the tax credit in this example has reduced taxes (and therefore *increased* after-tax income) by $850.

An often-used tax credit is for child and dependent care expenses. This credit is based on the amount spent for dependent care while a taxpayer (and spouse, if married) works or goes to school. The qualifying dependent must be less than 13 years old, except in the case of a disabled dependent or spouse. The amount of the credit is based

EXHIBIT 3.6

How Deductions and Tax Credits Affect Taxes Owed

As this example shows, a $1,000 tax credit reduces taxes due by far more than a $1,000 tax deduction.

Calculation		$1,000 Deduction	$1,000 Tax Credit
	Gross income	$34,000	$34,000
Less:	Other deductions/exemptions	6,000	6,000
Less:	$1,000 deduction	1,000	—
	Taxable income	$27,000	$28,000
	Tax liability*	$ 3,700	$ 3,850
Less:	$1,000 tax credit	—	1,000
	Taxes due	$ 3,700	$ 2,850

*The tax liability is figured as follows: the first $7,000 of taxable income is taxed at 10 percent, the balance at 15 percent.

on up to $3,000 in care expenses for one dependent and $6,000 for two or more dependents. The actual amount of the credit is a percentage of the amount spent or of the limit, whichever is less. The maximum possible credit for one child ranges from $600 to $1,050; for two or more children the range is $1,200 to $2,100. The percentages range from 20 to 35 percent, depending on the taxpayer's AGI. For example, a couple with AGI of $25,000 who spent $3,000 on child care expenses for their two young children would receive a dependent care credit of $750 (.25 × $3,000).

An important credit for lower-income workers is the *earned income credit.* In 2003, this credit is worth up to $2,547 for taxpayers with one qualifying child living with them in their home in the United States and $4,204 with two qualifying children. Taxpayers between 25 and 65 years old with no qualifying children receive a maximum credit of $382. The credit is gradually phased out for taxpayers with children, earned income (from wages), and AGI in excess of $13,750 ($6,250 for single taxpayers with no qualifying child; for married taxpayers this phase-out starts at $7,250). It is phased out completely when earned income or AGI reaches $29,650 for single taxpayers with one qualifying child, $33,852 for two or more qualifying children, or $11,200 for no children. The amounts for married taxpayers are slightly higher. These figures are adjusted annually based on inflation.

An ***adoption tax credit*** of up to $10,000 is available for the qualifying costs of adopting a child under age 18. Only taxpayers with AGI under $190,000 are eligible for the adoption tax credit. Beginning in 1998, taxpayers with dependent children under age 17 became entitled to a child tax credit which in 2003 was $1,000 per qualifying child. The credit is phased out for married couples with AGI above $110,000, $75,000 for single filers, and $55,000 for married persons filing separately. Other common tax credits include:

- Credit for the elderly or the disabled
- Foreign tax credit
- Credit for prior year minimum tax
- Mortgage interest credit
- Credit for qualified electric vehicle

To receive one of these credits, the taxpayer must file a return, along with a separate schedule in support of the tax credit claimed.

Tax Forms and Schedules

The IRS requires taxpayers to file their returns using certain specified tax forms. As noted earlier, these forms and a variety of instruction booklets on how to prepare them are available to taxpayers free of charge. Generally, all persons who filed tax returns in the previous year are automatically sent a booklet containing tax forms and instructions for preparing returns for the current year. Inside the booklet is a form that can be used to obtain additional tax forms for filing various tax-related returns and information. Exhibit 3.7 provides a list of some of the more commonly used tax forms and schedules.

smart.sites

Need a tax form or instructions on how to fill it out? Head for the IRS Digital Daily, **http://www.irs.gov**, where you can download tax forms, instructions, IRS publications, and regulations. You can also use the W-4 calculator to make sure you aren't having too much or too little withheld from your paycheck.

EXHIBIT 3.7

Commonly Used Tax Forms and Schedules

A number of types of 1040 tax return forms are available. If you use the standard Form 1040, you may need to include one or more schedules and forms with the tax return, depending on the amount and types of deductions claimed. Some of the more common ones are listed below the 1040s.

1040	Standard tax return, used with itemized deductions
1040A	Short-form tax return
1040EZ	Short-form tax return for single persons with no dependents
1040X	Amended U.S. individual tax return
1040-ES	Estimated tax for individuals
Schedule A	Itemized deductions
Schedule B	Interest and ordinary dividends
Schedule C	Profit or loss from business
Schedule D	Capital gains and losses
Schedule E	Supplemental income and losses from rents, royalties, partnerships, estates, trusts, etc.
Schedule EIC	Earned income credit
Schedule F	Profit and loss from farming
Schedule R	Credit for the elderly or disabled
Schedule SE	Social Security self-employment tax
2106	Employee business expenses
2119	Sale of your home
2441	Child and dependent care expenses
3903	Moving expenses
4562	Depreciation and amortization
4684	Casualties and thefts
4868	Application for automatic extension of time to file U.S. individual tax return
8829	Expenses for business use of your home
8839	Qualified adoption expenses

Variations of Form 1040

All individuals use some variation of Form 1040 to file their tax returns. *Form 1040EZ* is a simple, one-page form. You qualify to use this form if you are single or married filing a joint return; under age 65 (both if filing jointly); not blind; do not claim any dependents; have taxable income of less than $50,000 from only wages, salaries, tips, or taxable scholarships or grants; have interest income of less than $1,500; and do not itemize deductions or claim any tax credits. Worksheet 3.1 shows the Form 1040EZ filed in 2003 by Yoshio Ohno, a full-time graduate student at Anystate University. His sources of income include a $10,000 scholarship, of which $1,900 was used for room and board, $7,600 earned from part-time and summer jobs, and $50 interest earned on a savings account deposit. Because scholarships used for tuition and fees are not taxed, he must include as income only the portion used for room and board. He had a total of $465 withheld for federal income taxes during the year.

To use *Form 1040A*, a two-page form, your income must be less than $50,000 and derived only from specified sources. Using this form, you may deduct certain IRA contributions and claim certain tax credits, but you cannot itemize your deductions. If your income is over $50,000 or you itemize deductions, you must use the standard Form 1040 along with appropriate schedules, listed in Exhibit 3.7.

The use of these schedules, which provide detailed guidelines for calculating certain entries on the first two pages of *Form 1040*, varies among taxpayers depending on the relevance of these entries to their situations. Pages 1 and 2 of Form 1040, which summarize all items of income and deductions detailed on the accompanying schedules, are used to determine and report the taxable income and associated tax liability.

Despite detailed instructions that accompany the tax forms, taxpayers make many blunders when filling them out. Common errors include missing information and arithmetic errors. So check and recheck your forms before submitting them to the IRS.

> Financial Road Sign
>
> **Avoiding Common Tax Form Errors**
>
> Careful planning can save you from these common but unnecessary tax mistakes.
>
> **Identification mistakes:** Omitting or providing incorrect names, Social Security numbers, or tax-identification numbers for taxpayers or dependents.
>
> **Refund/amount due errors:** Calculating the refund or amount due incorrectly.
>
> **Tax amount:** Choosing the wrong tax amount from the tax tables.
>
> **Capital gains tax:** Miscalculating or incorrectly recording this tax.
>
> **Deductions and exemptions:** Miscalculating or incorrectly recording the standard deduction and personal exemptions.
>
> **Earned-income credit:** Omitting nontaxable earned income from W-2 form; miscalculating or incorrectly entering amounts used in calculations.

The 2003 Tax Return of Terry and Evelyn Becker

Let's now put all the pieces of the tax preparation puzzle together to see how Terry and Evelyn Becker calculate and file their income taxes. The Beckers own their own home and are both 35 years old. Married for 11 years, they have three children—Tom (age 9), Dick (age 7), and Jessica (age 3). Terry is a cost accountant for a major oil company headquartered in their hometown of Anytown, Anystate. Evelyn has 1½ years of college and works part-time as a sales clerk in a major department store. During 2003, Terry's salary totaled $45,415, while Evelyn earned $5,750. Terry's employer withheld taxes of $4,560, and Evelyn's, $650. During the year, the Beckers earned $500 interest on their joint savings account and realized $850 in capital gains on the sale of securities they had owned for 11 months. In addition, Terry kept the books for his brother's car dealership, from which he netted $4,800 during the year. Because no taxes were withheld from any of their outside income, during the year they made estimated tax payments totaling $500. The Beckers' records indicate they had $11,713 of

worksheet 3.1

2003 Tax Return (Form 1040EZ) for Yoshio Ohno

Form 1040EZ is very easy to use, and most of the instructions are printed right on the form itself. Yoshio Ohno qualifies to use it because he is single, under age 65, not blind, and meets its income and deduction restrictions.

Form **1040EZ** — Department of the Treasury—Internal Revenue Service — **Income Tax Return for Single and Joint Filers With No Dependents** (99) **2003** — OMB No. 1545-0675

Label (See page 12.) **Use the IRS label.** Otherwise, please print or type. — LABEL HERE

Your first name and initial	Yoshio
Last name	Ohno
Your social security number	978 : 76 : 1432
If a joint return, spouse's first name and initial	
Last name	
Spouse's social security number	
Home address (number and street). If you have a P.O. box, see page 12.	1000 State University Drive
Apt. no.	14A
City, town or post office, state, and ZIP code. If you have a foreign address, see page 12.	Anytown Anystate 10001

▲ Important! ▲ You **must** enter your SSN(s) above.

Presidential Election Campaign (page 12) — **Note.** Checking "Yes" will not change your tax or reduce your refund. Do you, or your spouse if a joint return, want $3 to go to this fund? — You: ☑ Yes ☐ No — Spouse: ☐ Yes ☐ No

Income — **Attach Form(s) W-2 here.** Enclose, but do not attach, any payment.	1	Wages, salaries, and tips. This should be shown in box 1 of your Form(s) W-2. Attach your Form(s) W-2.	1	9,500 00
	2	Taxable interest. If the total is over $1,500, you cannot use Form 1040EZ.	2	50 00
	3	Unemployment compensation and Alaska Permanent Fund dividends (see page 14).	3	
	4	Add lines 1, 2, and 3. This is your **adjusted gross income.**	4	9,550 00
Note. You **must** check Yes or No.	5	Can your parents (or someone else) claim you on their return? **Yes.** Enter amount from worksheet on back. ☐ **No.** ☑ If **single,** enter $7,800. If **married filing jointly,** enter $15,600. See back for explanation.	5	7,800 00
	6	Subtract line 5 from line 4. If line 5 is larger than line 4, enter -0-. This is your **taxable income.** ▶	6	1,750 00
Payments and tax	7	Federal income tax withheld from box 2 of your Form(s) W-2.	7	465 00
	8	**Earned income credit (EIC).**	8	0
	9	Add lines 7 and 8. These are your **total payments.** ▶	9	465 00
	10	**Tax.** Use the amount on **line 6 above** to find your tax in the tax table on pages 24–28 of the booklet. Then, enter the tax from the table on this line.	10	175 00
Refund — Have it directly deposited! See page 19 and fill in 11b, 11c, and 11d.	11a	If line 9 is larger than line 10, subtract line 10 from line 9. This is your **refund.** ▶	11a	290 00
	▶ b	Routing number ▶ c Type: ☐ Checking ☐ Savings		
	▶ d	Account number		
Amount you owe	12	If line 10 is larger than line 9, subtract line 9 from line 10. This is the **amount you owe.** For details on how to pay, see page 20. ▶	12	

Third party designee — Do you want to allow another person to discuss this return with the IRS (see page 20)? ☐ **Yes.** Complete the following. ☑ **No** — Designee's name ▶ — Phone no. ▶ ( ) — Personal identification number (PIN) ▶

Sign here — Joint return? See page 11. Keep a copy for your records. — Under penalties of perjury, I declare that I have examined this return, and to the best of my knowledge and belief, it is true, correct, and accurately lists all amounts and sources of income I received during the tax year. Declaration of preparer (other than the taxpayer) is based on all information of which the preparer has any knowledge.

Your signature	Date	Your occupation	Daytime phone number
Yoshio Ohno	4/1/04	student	(555) 555-1111
Spouse's signature. If a joint return, **both** must sign.	Date	Spouse's occupation	

Paid preparer's use only — Preparer's signature ▶ — Date — Check if self-employed ☐ — Preparer's SSN or PTIN — Firm's name (or yours if self-employed), address, and ZIP code ▶ — EIN — Phone no. ( )

For Disclosure, Privacy Act, and Paperwork Reduction Act Notice, see page 23. Cat. No. 11329W Form **1040EZ** (2003)

potential itemized deductions during the year. Finally, Terry Becker plans to contribute $2,000 to his traditional IRA account, something he's been doing for the past 6 years. He does this each year without fail, and, beginning in 2004, he plans to switch to a Roth IRA (see Chapter 14).

Finding the Beckers' Tax Liability: Form 1040

An examination of the Beckers' 2003 tax return (Worksheet 3.2) will show the basic calculations required in preparing Form 1040. Although we don't include the supporting schedules here, we illustrate the basic calculations they require. The Beckers have detailed records of their income and expenses, which they use not only for tax purposes but as an important input into their budgeting process. Using this information, the Beckers intend to prepare their 2003 tax return in a fashion that will allow them to reduce their tax liability as much as possible. Like most married couples, the Beckers file a *joint return.*

Gross Income

The Beckers' gross income in 2003 amounted to $ 57,315—the amount shown as "Total Income" on line 22 of their tax return. They have both active income and portfolio income, as follows:

Active Income		
Terry's earnings	$45,415	
Evelyn's earnings	5,750	
Terry's business income (net)	4,800	
Total active income		$55,965
Portfolio Income		
Interest from savings account	$ 500	
Capital gains realized*	850	
Total portfolio income		1,350
Total income		$57,315

*Because this gain was realized on stock held for less than 12 months, the full amount is taxable as ordinary income.

They have no investment expenses to offset their portfolio income, so they'll be liable for taxes on the full amount of portfolio income. Although they have interest income, the Beckers do not have to file Schedule B (for interest and dividend income) with the Form 1040 because the interest is less than $1,500 and they earned no dividends. (If they receive dividends on stock in the future, they will have to complete a Qualified Dividends and Capital Gains Worksheet, provided in the Form 1040 instruction booklet. As of 2003, qualified dividends are now taxed at the lower capital gains rates.) In addition, Terry will have to file Schedule C, detailing the income earned and expenses incurred in his bookkeeping business, and Schedule D to report capital gains income.

Adjustments to Gross Income

The Beckers have only two adjustments to income: Terry's IRA contribution and 50 percent of the self-employment tax on Terry's net business income. Because the Beckers fall below the $70,000 income ceiling, they can deduct their entire $2,000 contribution to an IRA account even if Terry and/or Evelyn are already covered by a company-sponsored retirement program (see Chapter 14). Even though they could put more money into the IRA, they have chosen to stick with Terry's $2,000 contribution (see line 24). Terry's self-employment tax will be 15.3 percent of his $4,800 net business income, and he will be able to deduct one-half that amount—$367.20 [(.153 × $4,800)/2]—on line 28.

Adjusted Gross Income

After deducting the $2,000 IRA contribution and the $367.20 self-employment tax from their gross income, the Beckers are left with an AGI of $54,947.80, as reported on lines 33 and 34.

worksheet 3.2

2003 Tax Return for the Beckers

Because they itemize deductions, the Beckers use standard Form 1040 to file their tax return. When filed with the IRS, their return will include not only Form 1040, but also other schedules and forms that provide details on many of their expenses and deductions.

Form **1040** Department of the Treasury—Internal Revenue Service **U.S. Individual Income Tax Return 2003** (99) IRS Use Only—Do not write or staple in this space.

For the year Jan. 1–Dec. 31, 2003, or other tax year beginning , 2003, ending , 20 OMB No. 1545-0074

Label (See instructions on page 19.) **Use the IRS label.** Otherwise, please print or type. LABEL HERE

Your first name and initial: **Terry B.**	Last name: **Becker**		Your social security number: **123 45 6789**
If a joint return, spouse's first name and initial: **Evelyn A.**	Last name: **Becker**		Spouse's social security number: **456 78 9012**
Home address (number and street). If you have a P.O. box, see page 19.: **125 Laughing Lane**		Apt. no.	**▲ Important! ▲** You **must** enter your SSN(s) above.
City, town or post office, state, and ZIP code. If you have a foreign address, see page 19.: **Anytown, Anystate, 10001**			

Presidential Election Campaign (See page 19.) **Note.** Checking "Yes" will not change your tax or reduce your refund. Do you, or your spouse if filing a joint return, want $3 to go to this fund? ▶ You: ☑ Yes ☐ No Spouse: ☑ Yes ☐ No

Filing Status Check only one box.

1 ☐ Single
2 ☑ Married filing jointly (even if only one had income)
3 ☐ Married filing separately. Enter spouse's SSN above and full name here. ▶
4 ☐ Head of household (with qualifying person). (See page 20.) If the qualifying person is a child but not your dependent, enter this child's name here. ▶
5 ☐ Qualifying widow(er) with dependent child. (See page 20.)

Exemptions

6a ☑ **Yourself.** If your parent (or someone else) can claim you as a dependent on his or her tax return, **do not** check box 6a
b ☑ **Spouse**
No. of boxes checked on 6a and 6b: **2**

c Dependents:

(1) First name Last name	(2) Dependent's social security number	(3) Dependent's relationship to you	(4) ✓ if qualifying child for child tax credit (see page 21)
Thomas T. Becker	065 01 2347	son	☑
Richard L. Becker	012 34 5678	son	☑
Jessica M. Becker	034 65 1234	daughter	☑
			☐
			☐

No. of children on 6c who: • lived with you **3** • did not live with you due to divorce or separation (see page 21) Dependents on 6c not entered above

If more than five dependents, see page 21.

d Total number of exemptions claimed — Add numbers on lines above ▶ **5**

Income

Attach Forms W-2 and W-2G here. Also attach Form(s) 1099-R if tax was withheld.

If you did not get a W-2, see page 22.

Enclose, but do not attach, any payment. Also, please use Form 1040-V.

7	Wages, salaries, tips, etc. Attach Form(s) W-2	7	51165 00
8a	**Taxable** interest. Attach Schedule B if required	8a	500 00
b	**Tax-exempt** interest. **Do not** include on line 8a — 8b		
9a	Ordinary dividends. Attach Schedule B if required	9a	
b	Qualified dividends (see page 23) — 9b		
10	Taxable refunds, credits, or offsets of state and local income taxes (see page 23)	10	
11	Alimony received	11	
12	Business income or (loss). Attach Schedule C or C-EZ	12	4,800 00
13a	Capital gain or (loss). Attach Schedule D if required. If not required, check here ▶ ☑	13a	850 00
b	If box on 13a is checked, enter post-May 5 capital gain distributions — 13b		
14	Other gains or (losses). Attach Form 4797	14	
15a	IRA distributions — 15a — b Taxable amount (see page 25)	15b	
16a	Pensions and annuities — 16a — b Taxable amount (see page 25)	16b	
17	Rental real estate, royalties, partnerships, S corporations, trusts, etc. Attach Schedule E	17	
18	Farm income or (loss). Attach Schedule F	18	
19	Unemployment compensation	19	
20a	Social security benefits — 20a — b Taxable amount (see page 27)	20b	
21	Other income. List type and amount (see page 27)	21	
22	Add the amounts in the far right column for lines 7 through 21. This is your **total income** ▶	22	57,315 00

Adjusted Gross Income

Line	Description		Amount		Amount
23	Educator expenses (see page 29)	23			
24	IRA deduction (see page 29)	24	2,000 00		
25	Student loan interest deduction (see page 31)	25			
26	Tuition and fees deduction (see page 32)	26			
27	Moving expenses. Attach Form 3903	27			
28	One-half of self-employment tax. Attach Schedule SE	28	367 20		
29	Self-employed health insurance deduction (see page 33)	29			
30	Self-employed SEP, SIMPLE, and qualified plans	30			
31	Penalty on early withdrawal of savings	31			
32a	Alimony paid b Recipient's SSN ▶	32a			
33	Add lines 23 through 32a			33	2,367 20
34	Subtract line 33 from line 22. This is your **adjusted gross income** ▶			34	54,947 80

For Disclosure, Privacy Act, and Paperwork Reduction Act Notice, see page 77. Cat. No. 11320B Form **1040** (2003)

worksheet 3.2 (continued)

Form 1040 (2003) Page 2

Tax and Credits

35	Amount from line 34 (adjusted gross income)			35	54,947 80
36a	Check if: ☐ You were born before January 2, 1939, ☐ Blind. ☐ Spouse was born before January 2, 1939, ☐ Blind. Total boxes checked ▶ 36a				
b	If you are married filing separately and your spouse itemizes deductions, or you were a dual-status alien, see page 34 and check here ▶ 36b ☐				
37	**Itemized deductions** (from Schedule A) **or** your **standard deduction** (see left margin)			37	$9,891 04
38	Subtract line 37 from line 35			38	45,056 76
39	If line 35 is $104,625 or less, multiply $3,050 by the total number of exemptions claimed on line 6d. If line 35 is over $104,625, see the worksheet on page 35			39	15,250 00
40	**Taxable income.** Subtract line 39 from line 38. If line 39 is more than line 38, enter -0-			40	29,806 76
41	**Tax** (see page 36). Check if any tax is from: a ☐ Form(s) 8814 b ☐ Form 4972			41	3,771 01
42	**Alternative minimum tax** (see page 38). Attach Form 6251			42	0
43	Add lines 41 and 42 ▶			43	3,771 01
44	Foreign tax credit. Attach Form 1116 if required	44			
45	Credit for child and dependent care expenses. Attach Form 2441	45			
46	Credit for the elderly or the disabled. Attach Schedule R	46			
47	Education credits. Attach Form 8863	47			
48	Retirement savings contributions credit. Attach Form 8880	48			
49	Child tax credit (see page 40)	49	3000 00		
50	Adoption credit. Attach Form 8839	50			
51	Credits from: a ☐ Form 8396 b ☐ Form 8859	51			
52	Other credits. Check applicable box(es): a ☐ Form 3800 b ☐ Form 8801 c ☐ Specify	52			
53	Add lines 44 through 52. These are your **total credits**			53	3,000 00
54	Subtract line 53 from line 43. If line 53 is more than line 43, enter -0- ▶			54	771 01

Standard Deduction for—

- People who checked any box on line 36a or 36b **or** who can be claimed as a dependent, see page 34.
- All others:

Single or Married filing separately, $4,750

Married filing jointly or Qualifying widow(er), $9,500

Head of household, $7,000

Other Taxes

55	Self-employment tax. Attach Schedule SE	55	734 40
56	Social security and Medicare tax on tip income not reported to employer. Attach Form 4137	56	
57	Tax on qualified plans, including IRAs, and other tax-favored accounts. Attach Form 5329 if required	57	
58	Advance earned income credit payments from Form(s) W-2	58	
59	Household employment taxes. Attach Schedule H	59	
60	Add lines 54 through 59. This is your **total tax** ▶	60	1,505 41

Payments

If you have a qualifying child, attach Schedule EIC.

61	Federal income tax withheld from Forms W-2 and 1099	61	5,210 00		
62	2003 estimated tax payments and amount applied from 2002 return	62	500 00		
63	**Earned income credit (EIC)**	63			
64	Excess social security and tier 1 RRTA tax withheld (see page 56)	64			
65	Additional child tax credit. Attach Form 8812	65			
66	Amount paid with request for extension to file (see page 56)	66			
67	Other payments from: a ☐ Form 2439 b ☐ Form 4136 c ☐ Form 8885	67			
68	Add lines 61 through 67. These are your **total payments** ▶			68	5710 00

Refund

Direct deposit? See page 56 and fill in 70b, 70c, and 70d.

69	If line 68 is more than line 60, subtract line 60 from line 68. This is the amount you **overpaid**	69	4,204 59
70a	Amount of line 69 you want **refunded to you** ▶	70a	4,204 59
b	Routing number ▶ c Type: ☐ Checking ☐ Savings		
d	Account number		
71	Amount of line 69 you want **applied to your 2004 estimated tax** ▶ 71		

Amount You Owe

72	**Amount you owe.** Subtract line 68 from line 60. For details on how to pay, see page 57 ▶	72	
73	Estimated tax penalty (see page 58) 73		

Third Party Designee

Do you want to allow another person to discuss this return with the IRS (see page 58)? ☐ **Yes.** Complete the following. ☐ **No**

Designee's name ▶ Phone no. ▶ ( ) Personal identification number (PIN) ▶

Sign Here

Joint return? See page 20. Keep a copy for your records.

Under penalties of perjury, I declare that I have examined this return and accompanying schedules and statements, and to the best of my knowledge and belief, they are true, correct, and complete. Declaration of preparer (other than taxpayer) is based on all information of which preparer has any knowledge.

Your signature	Date	Your occupation	Daytime phone number
Terry B. Becker	4-10-04	Cost accountant	(555) 555-1234
Spouse's signature. If a joint return, **both** must sign.	Date	Spouse's occupation	
Evelyn A. Becker	4-10-04	Sales clerk	

Paid Preparer's Use Only

Preparer's signature ▶ Date Check if self-employed ☐ Preparer's SSN or PTIN

Firm's name (or yours if self-employed), address, and ZIP code ▶ EIN Phone no. ( )

Form **1040** (2003)

Itemized Deductions or Standard Deduction?

The Beckers are filing a joint return and neither is over age 65 or blind, so according to the box on page two of Form 1040, they are entitled to a standard deduction of $9,500. However, they want to evaluate their itemized deductions before deciding which type of deduction to take—obviously they'll take the highest deduction, because it will result in the lowest amount of taxable income and keep their tax liability to a minimum. Their preliminary paperwork resulted in the following deductions:

Medical and dental expenses	$ 723
State income and property taxes paid	2,060
Mortgage interest	6,893
Charitable contributions	475
Job and other expenses	1,562
Total	$11,713

The taxes, mortgage interest, and charitable contributions are deductible in full; so at the minimum, the Beckers will have itemized deductions that amount to $9,428 ($2,060 + $6,893 + $475). However, to be deductible, the medical and dental expenses and job and other expenses must exceed stipulated minimum levels of AGI—only that portion which exceeds the specified minimum levels of AGI can be included as part of their itemized deductions. For medical and dental expenses, the minimum is 7.5 percent of AGI and for job and other expenses it is 2 percent of AGI. Because 7.5 percent of the Beckers' AGI is $4,121.09 (.075 × $54,947.80), they fall short of the minimum and cannot deduct any medical and dental expenses. In contrast, because 2 percent of the Beckers' AGI is $1,098.96 (.02 × $54,947.80), they can deduct any job and other expenses that exceed that amount, or $1,562 − $1,098.96 = $463.04. Adding that amount to their other allowable deductions ($9,428) results in total itemized deductions of $9,891.04. This amount exceeds the standard deduction of $9,500 by a slight margin, so the Beckers itemize their deductions. They would provide the details of these deductions on Schedule A and attach it to their Form 1040. (The total amount of the Beckers' itemized deductions is listed on line 37 of Form 1040.)

Personal Exemptions

The Beckers are entitled to claim two exemptions for themselves and another three exemptions for their three dependent children, for a total of five (see line 6d). Because each exemption is worth $3,050, they receive a total personal exemption of $15,250 (5 × $3,050), which is the amount listed on line 39 of their Form 1040.

The Beckers' Taxable Income and Tax Liability

Taxable income is found by subtracting itemized deductions and personal exemptions from AGI. Thus, in the Beckers' case, taxable income amounts to $54,947.80 − $9,891.04 − $15,250 = $29,806.76, as shown on line 40. Given this information, the Beckers can now refer to the tax rate schedule (like the one in Exhibit 3.4) to find their appropriate tax rate and, ultimately, the amount of taxes they'll have to pay. (Because the Beckers' taxable income is less than $100,000, they could use the *tax tables* [not shown] to find their tax. For clarity and convenience, we use the schedules here.) As we can see, the Beckers' $29,806.76 in taxable income places them in the 15 percent tax bracket. Using the schedule in Exhibit 3.4, they calculate their tax as follows: $1,400 + [.15 × ($29,806.76 − $14,000)] = $3,771.01. They enter this amount on line 41. (*Note:* Had the tax tables been used, the tax would have been $3,774.)

The Beckers also qualify for the child tax credit: $1,000 for each child under age 17. They enter $3,000 on lines 49 and 53 and subtract that amount from the tax on line 43, entering $771.01 on line 54. In addition, the Beckers owe self-employment (Social Security) tax on Terry's $4,800 net business income. This will increase their tax liability by $734.40 (.153 × $4,800) and would be reported on Schedule SE and entered on line 55 of Form 1040. (Remember, the Beckers deducted 50 percent of this amount—$367.20—on line 28 as an adjustment to income.) The Beckers enter their total tax liability on line 60: $1,505.41 ($771.01 + $734.40).

Do They Get a Tax Refund?

Because the total amount of taxes withheld of $5,210 ($4,560 from Terry's salary and $650 from Evelyn's wages) shown on line 61 plus estimated tax payments of $500 shown on line 62 total $5,710 as shown on line 68, the Beckers' total tax payments exceed their tax liability, and, as a result, they are entitled to a refund of $4,204.59: the $5,710 withholding less their $1,505.41 tax liability. (About 65 percent of all taxpayers receive refunds each year.) Instead of paying the IRS, they'll be getting money back. (Generally, it takes 1 to 2 months after a tax return has been filed to receive a refund check.)

All the Beckers have to do now is sign and date their completed Form 1040 and send it, along with any supporting forms and schedules, to the nearest IRS district office on or before April 15, 2004.

One reason for the Beckers' large refund was the child tax credit. With such a sizable refund, the Beckers may want to stop making estimated tax payments because their combined withholding more than covers the amount of taxes they owe. Another option is to change their withholding to reduce the amount withheld.

Note that if total tax payments had been less than the Beckers' tax liability, they would have owed the IRS money—the amount owed is found by subtracting total tax payments made from the tax liability. If they owed money, they would include a check in the amount due with Form 1040 when they filed their tax return.

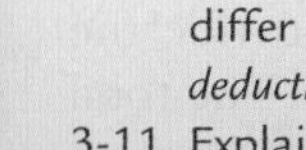

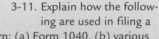

Concept ✓

3-10. Define and differentiate between the *average tax rate* and the *marginal tax rate*. How does a *tax credit* differ from an *itemized deduction?*

3-11. Explain how the following are used in filing a tax return: (a) Form 1040, (b) various schedules that accompany Form 1040, and (c) tax rate schedules.

Financial Road Sign

Time for Taxes

To minimize tax hassles, follow these tips:

1. File on time, even if you can't pay what you owe.
2. Don't overlook tax-free income, such as an inheritance, tuition, scholarships, and gifts of money (limited to $10,000 per year from any one person).
3. Don't forget to sign your return, even if you file online.
4. Use direct deposit to get your refund faster.
5. Pay in installments if you can't pay your whole tax bill (file Form 9465).
6. Pay what you think you will owe even if you get an extension.
7. Include receipts for all noncash charitable gifts valued at more than $500 with Form 8383.

OTHER FILING CONSIDERATIONS

LG4, LG5

The preparation and filing of tax returns does not merely involve filling out and filing a tax return on or before April 15. Other related considerations include the need to pay estimated taxes, file for extensions, or amend the return; the possibility of a tax audit; and whether to use a tax preparation service or computer software to assist you in preparing your return.

ESTIMATES, EXTENSIONS, AND AMENDMENTS

Like Terry Becker, who provided accounting services to his brother's business, you may have income that is not subject to withholding. You may need to file a declaration of estimated taxes with your return and to pay taxes on a quarterly basis. Or perhaps you are unable to meet the normal April 15 filing deadline or need to correct a previously filed return. Let's look at the procedures for handling these situations.

Estimated Taxes

Because federal withholding taxes are regularly taken only from employment income, such as that paid in the form of wages or salaries, the IRS requires certain people to pay **estimated taxes** on income earned from other sources. This requirement allows the principle of "pay as you go" to be applied not only to employment income subject to

estimated taxes
Quarterly tax payments required on income not subject to withholding.

withholding but also to other sources of income. The quarterly payment of estimated taxes is most commonly required of investors, consultants, lawyers, business owners, and various other professionals who are likely to receive income in a form that is not subject to withholding. Generally, if all your income is subject to withholding, you probably do not need to make estimated tax payments.

If you meet certain IRS requirements with regard to your tax liability and withholding, you must file a declaration of estimated taxes (Form 1040-ES) and make estimated tax payments. When the total of tax withheld and estimated payments does not meet IRS guidelines, you must pay estimated taxes consistent with the actual income earned in the immediately preceding quarter to avoid penalties. The estimated tax form packet includes a worksheet to calculate your estimated tax liability for the coming year. Each estimated tax payment equals the tax payable on income earned in the preceding quarter, or one-fourth of the total amount paid in taxes during the immediately preceding year, less the amount of tax withheld during the preceding quarter. After making a preliminary calculation, Terry Becker estimated that he would owe about $500 for the year 2003 on his additional income. Exhibit 3.8 shows the form that Terry Becker submitted on September 15, 2003 with his estimated tax payment for the preceding quarter—$125, or one-quarter of $500.

EXHIBIT 3.8

Terry Becker's Estimated Tax Payment

Because he has income from a second job on which taxes were not withheld, Terry Becker files and pays estimated tax payments each quarter.

Form **1040-ES**
Department of the Treasury
Internal Revenue Service

2003 Payment Voucher 3

OMB No. 1545-0087

File only if you are making a payment of estimated tax by check or money order. Mail this voucher with your check or money order payable to the "United States Treasury." Write your social security number and "2003 Form 1040-ES" on your check or money order. Do not send cash. Enclose, but do not staple or attach, your payment with this voucher.

Calendar year—Due Sept. 15, 2003

Amount of estimated tax you are paying by check or money order. Dollars 125 Cents 00

Type or print

Your first name and initial	Your last name	Your social security number
Terry B.	Becker	123-45-6789
If joint payment, complete for spouse		
Spouse's fist name and initial	Spouse's last name	Spouse's social security number

Address (number, street, and apt. no.)
125 Laughing Lane

City, state, and ZIP code (if a foreign address, enter city, providence or state, postal code, and country.)
Anytown, Anystate 10001

For Privacy Act and Paperwork Reduction Act Notice, see instructions on page 5.

Tear off here

The declaration of estimated taxes is normally filed with the tax return. Estimated taxes must be paid in four quarterly installments on April 15, June 15, and September 15 of the current year, and January 15 of the following year. Failure to estimate and pay these taxes in accordance with IRS guidelines can result in a penalty levied by the IRS.

April 15: Filing Deadline

As we've seen from the Becker family example, at the end of each tax year those taxpayers required to file a return must determine the amount of their tax *liability*—the amount of taxes that they owe as a result of the past year's activities. The tax year corresponds to the calendar year and covers the period January 1 through December 31. Taxpayers may file their returns any time after the end of the tax year and *must* file no later than April 15 of the year immediately following the tax year (or by the first business day after that date if it falls on a weekend or federal holiday). Taxpayers who file Form 1040EZ can file their returns by touch-tone phone using *TeleFile*. (Qualifying taxpayers receive special TeleFile tax packages.) If you have a computer, a modem, and tax preparation software, you can probably use the IRS's *e-file* and *e-pay* to file your return and pay your taxes electronically using either a credit card or authorizing an electronic withdrawal from your checking or savings account. You can use an "Authorized *e-file* Provider," who may charge a fee to file on your behalf, or do it yourself using commercial tax preparation software. (We'll discuss computer-based tax returns in greater detail later.)

Depending on whether the total of taxes withheld and any estimated tax payments is greater or less than the computed tax liability, the taxpayer either receives a refund or has to pay additional taxes. For example, assume that you had $2,000 withheld and paid estimated taxes of $1,200 during the year. After filling out the appropriate tax forms, you find your tax liability is only $2,800. In this case, you have overpaid your taxes by $400 ($2,000 + $1,200 − $2,800) and will receive a $400 refund from the IRS. On the other hand, if your tax liability had amounted to $4,000, you would owe the IRS an additional $800 ($4,000 − $2,000 − $1,200). Taxpayers can pay their taxes using a credit card; however, because the IRS cannot pay credit card companies an issuing fee, taxpayers must call a special provider and pay a service charge to arrange for the payment.

smart.sites

It's easy to file and pay your taxes online, as you'll learn when you visit Link2Gov's Pay 1040 Web site, **http://www.pay1040.com**.

Filing Extensions and Amended Returns

It is possible to receive an extension of time for filing your federal tax return. You can apply for an automatic 4-month **filing extension**, which makes the due date August 15, simply by submitting Form 4868. In filing for an extension, however, the taxpayer must estimate the taxes due and remit that amount with the application. The extension does *not* give taxpayers more time to pay their taxes. Taxpayers can also request additional extensions beyond the 4-month automatic extension, but the IRS will review reasons for the request to decide whether to grant the extension.

filing extension
An extension of time beyond the April 15 deadline during which taxpayers, with the approval of the IRS, can file their returns without incurring penalties.

After filing a return, you may discover that you overlooked some income or a major deduction or made a mistake, and, as a result, paid too little or too much in taxes. You can easily correct this by filing an **amended return** (Form 1040X) that shows the corrected amount of income or deductions and the amount of taxes you should have paid, along with the amount of any tax refund or additional taxes owed. You generally have 3 years from the date you file your original return or 2 years from the date you paid the taxes, whichever is later, to file an amended return. If you prepare and file your amended return properly and it reflects nothing out of the ordinary, it generally will not trigger an audit. By all means, do not "correct" an oversight in 1 year by "adjusting" next year's tax return—the IRS frowns on that.

amended return
A tax return filed to adjust for information received after the filing date of the taxpayer's original return or to correct errors.

Audited Returns

Because taxpayers themselves provide the key information and fill out the necessary tax forms, the IRS has no proof that taxes have been correctly calculated. In addition to returns

tax audit An examination by the IRS to validate the accuracy of a given tax return.

that stand out in some way that warrant further investigation, the IRS also randomly selects some returns for a **tax audit**—an examination to validate the return's accuracy. The odds of being audited are actually quite low; the IRS audits fewer than 1 percent of returns. However, higher-income earners tend to have a greater chance of audit. For example, those with incomes between $25,000 and $50,000 have less than a 1 percent chance of being audited, but the chance of audit jumps to nearly 5 percent for those with incomes over $100,000. The outcome of an audit is not always additional tax owed to the IRS. In fact, about 5 percent of all audits result in a refund to the taxpayer, and in 15 percent of all audits the IRS finds that returns are correctly prepared.

IRS audits attempt to confirm the validity of filed returns by carefully examining the data reported in them. You may receive a mail audit—a letter with questions requesting a written response with supporting documentation—or be asked to attend a face-to-face meeting at which the IRS examiner asks the you to explain and document some of the deductions taken. Even with documentation, the examiner may still question the legitimacy of the deductions. You may want to have a tax professional accompany you to an in-person audit meeting. If the taxpayer and the IRS examiner cannot informally agree on the disputed items, the taxpayer can meet with the examiner's supervisor to discuss the case further. If there is still disagreement, the taxpayer can appeal through the IRS Appeals Office. Finally, if the Appeals Office hearing does not resolve the issue to the taxpayer's satisfaction, the taxpayer can bring the case before the U.S. Tax Court, the U.S. Claims Court, or a U.S. District Court.

You can see why it is particularly important to keep satisfactory and thorough tax records, because some day you may be audited by the IRS. Keeping track of the source or use of all cash receipts and cash payments, along with notations about the purpose of the expenses are important, as well as proof that you actually made the expenses for which you have claimed deductions. Typically, audits question both (1) whether all income received has been properly reported and (2) if the deductions claimed are legitimate and the correct amount. The IRS can take as many as 3 years from the date of filing to audit your return—and in some cases an unlimited period of time—so you should retain records and receipts used in preparing returns for several years. Severe financial penalties—even prison sentences—can result from violating tax laws.

In sum, while you should take advantage of all legitimate deductions to minimize your tax liability, you must also be sure to properly report all items of income and expense as required by the Internal Revenue Code.

Financial Road Sign

Be Aware of these Audit Triggers

Despite the low risk of being audited, certain items are a red flag to the IRS. If any of these situations apply to you, your chances of being audited increase:

- An unusual increase in income
- Income that isn't properly documented
- Income that is lower than the amount reported on Forms 1099 submitted by financial institutions
- Returns that are missing signatures, Social Security numbers, or required forms,
- Math errors
- Owning a small business (Filing Schedule C significantly raises the chance of an audit)
- Itemized deductions that are much higher than the averages for your income bracket
- Taking the home-office deduction
- Casualty losses

While some of these are unavoidable, you can make sure that your numbers add up properly, you've included all required information and forms, and you're signed your returns.

Tax Preparation Services: Getting Help on Your Returns

Many people prepare their own tax returns. These "do-it-yourselfers" typically have fairly simple returns that can be prepared without a great deal of difficulty. Of course, some taxpayers with quite complicated financial affairs may also invest their time in preparing their own returns. The IRS offers many informational publications to help you prepare your tax return. You can order them directly from the IRS by mail, from the IRS

Money in Action

Which Tax Preparer Is Right for You?

If you've decided to use a professional tax preparer, as over half of all individual taxpayers do, you need to choose carefully. Bad or fraudulent advice can cost plenty, because *taxpayers themselves must accept primary responsibility for the accuracy of their returns*. As tax regulations become more complex, the number of errors that even the pros make increases.

First you must determine what type and level of professional advice you need. Someone who is basically a return preparer is not the best person to help you do complex tax planning. Although attorneys and CPAs are state-licensed, and Enrolled Agents have federal licenses, no license or certification is required to set up shop as a tax preparer. The number of so-called tax preparers has jumped since the IRS, began encouraging electronic filing. Many have minimal training and have other motives in helping with your return, such as offering a "refund anticipation loan" that allows you to spend anticipated tax refunds. These loans are usually very expensive.

In addition to nonlicensed tax preparers, you should consider a licensed tax professional if your situation calls for one:

- **CPAs:** CPAs provide ongoing tax advice and can suggest tax-saving strategies. Not all CPAs are tax specialists, though, so be sure to choose one who is! Check with the State Boards of Accountancy to make sure that he or she is licensed and hasn't been subject to any disciplinary actions. Membership in the American Institute of Certified Public Accountants (AICPA) offers some disciplinary oversight and requires continuing education.
- **Enrolled Agent (EA)**: The over 35,000 EAs licensed by the IRS must meet the IRS's criteria. They specialize in preparing returns and offering tax advice for individuals. Fees to use an EA are about one-third lower than CPA fees. Because there is no state regulation of EAs, you'll have to do your own background checks.
- **Tax Attorney:** Tax attorneys are best reserved for those who have complex tax situations that could result in legal issues, such as a complicated sale of a small business, not filing taxes in the past, or estate and trust tax issues. Otherwise using a tax attorney is overkill.

...continued on next page

Web site (**http://www.irs.gov**), or by calling the IRS's toll-free number (1-800-829-3676 or special local numbers in some areas). You can also download most of them from the IRS Web site. An excellent (and free) comprehensive tax preparation reference book is IRS *Publication 17, Your Federal Income Tax.* Other publications cover special topics, such as the earned income credit, self-employment taxes, and business use of your home. Each form and schedule comes with detailed instructions to guide you, step by step, in completing the form accurately. Other IRS information services are *TeleTax*, which provides recorded phone messages on selected tax topics via a toll free number (1-800-829-4477), and *TaxFax*, which will fax many forms and instructions to you when you call 1-703-368-9694.

Help from the IRS

The IRS, in addition to issuing various publications for use in preparing tax returns, also provides direct assistance to taxpayers. The IRS will compute taxes for those whose taxable is less than $100,000 and who do not itemize deductions. Persons who use this IRS service must fill in certain data, sign and date the return, and send it to the IRS on or before April 15 of the year immediately following the tax year. The IRS attempts to calculate taxes to result in the "smallest" tax bite. It then sends taxpayers a refund, if their withholding exceeds their tax liability, or a bill, if their tax liability is greater than the amount of withholding. People who either fail to qualify for or do not want to use this total tax preparation service can still obtain IRS assistance in preparing their returns from a toll-free service. Consult your telephone directory for the toll-free number of the IRS office closest to you.

Even the IRS sometimes makes mistakes, however. It may not always correctly answer your tax questions. To increase your chances of getting correct information, use *Publication 17* and other resources to research your question before calling. State your question as clearly as you can, and make sure that the IRS representative fully understands your question. Remember: *You are liable for any underpayment of taxes, including interest and penalties, that results from incorrect information provided by the IRS over the phone.* As an alternative, you may put the question in writing and receive a written response from the IRS. If the written answer is incorrect, and as a result you underpay your taxes, you will have to pay the additional taxes and interest due, but no penalties.

Private Tax Preparers

More than half of all taxpayers believe that the complexity of the tax forms makes preparation too difficult and time-consuming. They prefer to use professional *tax preparation services* to improve accuracy and minimize their tax liability as much as possible. The fees charged by professional tax preparers range from about $50 for very simple returns to $1,000 or more for complicated returns that include many itemized deductions, partnership income or losses, or self-employment income. You can select from several different types of tax preparation services:

- **National and local tax services:** These include national services such as H&R Block and independent local firms. These are best for taxpayers with relatively common types of income and expenditures.
- **Certified Public Accountants (CPAs):** Tax professionals who prepare returns and can advise taxpayers on planning.
- **Enrolled Agents (EAs):** Federally licensed individual tax practitioners who have passed a difficult, 2-day, IRS-administered exam. They are fully qualified to handle tax preparation at various levels of complexity.
- **Tax attorneys:** Lawyers who specialize in tax planning.

The services provided by CPAs, EAs, and tax attorneys can be expensive and are most suited to taxpayers with relatively complicated financial situations. The *Money in Action* box on page 116 will help you find the right preparer for your needs.

smart.sites

Use the tax section of H&R Block's Web site, **http://www.hrblock.com/tax_center/index.html**, to locate an H&R Block office near you, check the glossary of tax terms, take a quiz to decide the best way to file, and use many do-it-yourself tax tools.

Always check your own completed tax returns carefully before signing them. Remember that *taxpayers themselves must accept primary responsibility for the accuracy of their returns.* The IRS requires professional tax preparers to sign each return as the preparer, enter their own Social Security number and address, and provide the taxpayer with a copy of the return being filed. Tax preparers with the necessary hardware and software can electronically file their clients' tax returns, thereby permitting eligible taxpayers to more quickly receive refunds.

Once you've decided which type of tax advisor is right for you, ask for referrals from your lawyer, financial planner, and friends. Then interview your candidates before trusting anyone with your financial records. Among the areas to probe:

1. The tax and other services the firm offers
2. Training and experience of the firm's professionals
3. Who prepares your actual return
4. Whether the firm/person takes a conservative or aggressive approach to tax law
5. Audit experience
6. Fee structure
7. Amount of liability insurance
8. References of clients with similar tax situations

If you have a relatively simple return, a reputable tax preparer could be a cost-effective solution for you. You'd pay a tax preparer at H&R Block, on average, about $120 for your federal and state returns. Be sure the firm you select stands by its work and operates all year, not just at tax time, advises Brenda Schafer, H&R Block's senior tax-research coordinator.

A few other tips: make sure that you are getting objective advice and that your tax professional isn't also trying to sell you tax-sheltered investments. You must also be comfortable with the advisor's suggestions, especially with regard to strategies that involve gray areas of the tax law.

Critical Thinking Questions

1. Compare the qualifications, licensing requirements, and relative costs of a CPA, an EA, a tax attorney, and a tax preparer for a national or local tax preparation service.
2. You have decided to use a tax preparer to help you with your taxes. Which type would you choose, and why? What questions would be most important to you in selecting the tax professional?
3. Why is it important to understand your tax returns, even if they are prepared by a professional?

Sources: Stephanie AuWerter, "Looking for a Tax Pro?" *SmartMoney Tax Guide,* downloaded November 22, 2003, from **http://www.smartmoney.com**; Mary Dalrymple, "IRS Found Tolerating Poor Tax Preparers," *Newsday,* November 11, 2003, p. A46.

smart.sites
Looking for an enrolled agent (EA)? The National Association of Enrolled Agents, **http://www.naea.org/**, can help you find one in your area.

There is no guarantee that your professional tax preparer will correctly determine your tax liability. Even the best preparers may not have all the answers at their fingertips. In a recent *Money* magazine annual tax return test, none of the 45 experienced tax preparers they contacted prepared the tax return for a fictional family correctly, and only 24 percent of them calculated a tax liability that was within $1,000 of the correct amount of $42,336. To reduce the chance of error, you should become familiar with the basic tax principles and regulations, check all documents (such as W-2s and 1099s) for accuracy, maintain good communication with your tax preparer, and request an explanation of any entries on your tax return that you do not understand.

Computer-Based Tax Returns

Many people use their personal computers to help with tax planning and tax return preparation. Several good tax software packages will save hours when filling out the forms and schedules involved in filing tax returns. They often identify tax-saving opportunities you might otherwise miss. These computer programs are not for everyone, however. Very simple returns do not require them (although there are now Web sites like Online 1040EZ by H&R Block where you can prepare and file your return on paper or electronically free of charge). And for very complex returns, there is no substitute for the skill and expertise of a tax accountant or attorney. Tax preparation software will be most helpful for taxpayers who itemize deductions but do not need tax advice.

Basically there are two kinds of software: tax planning and tax preparation. Planning programs such as *Quicken* let you experiment with different strategies to see their effects on the amount of taxes you must pay. The other category of tax software focuses on helping you complete and file your tax return. These programs take much of the tedium out of tax preparation, reducing the time you spend from days to hours. If you file the long Form 1040 and some supporting forms, invest in the stock market, own real estate, or have foreign income or a home-based business, you'll probably benefit from using tax preparation programs. It's even easier and faster if you use a personal finance program to keep tabs on your income and expenses, because the tax software can extract the appropriate data. The programs automate much of the process; they know that *X* percent of the amount you entered on Line K has to be transferred to Line Q, saving you the agony of remembering to do it yourself. The programs are updated annually to include the hundreds of changes in tax laws. Another advantage is that the programs feed data to state tax returns, so you only have to enter it once.

The two major software players are Intuit's *TurboTax* and Block Financial Software's *TaxCut*, both available for either Windows or Macintosh. *TurboTax* even has a Web-based version that lets you work on your returns form any computer. Both major companies also offer an add-on program that assigns accurate, fair-market value to the household items most commonly donated to charity. Both programs feature a clean interface and guide you through the steps in preparing your return by asking you the questions that apply to your situation. In addition to the primary tax-form preparation section, they include extensive resources and links to additional Web references, video clips to make tricky concepts easier to understand, tax planning questionnaires, deduction finders, and more. They may warn you if a number you've typed looks out of line. Each program costs under $50 for the regular CD-ROM versions, including one electronically filed federal tax return. State tax return packages cost more.

Both *TurboTax* and *TaxCut* guarantee their calculations and will pay any penalties you incur because of program errors.

In certain situations, you should probably let a professional rather than a PC prepare your return. These include major life changes such as marriage, divorce, remarriage, and inheritance. The tax treatment of stock options, an increasingly common employee benefit, is tricky to figure out. Self-employed persons may want the advice of a tax professional when it comes to deciding where to draw the line between business and personal expenses.

smart.sites

Which version of *TaxCut* software is best for you? Find out at **http://www.taxcut.com**, where you will also find tax tips, a tax-withholding calculator, and more.

The IRS recently introduced "fill-in forms," which allow you to enter information while the form is displayed on your computer by Adobe *Acrobat Reader* (free software readily available on the Web). After entering the requested information, you can print out the completed form. Fill-in forms give you a cleaner, crisper printout for your records and for filing with the IRS. Unlike tax preparation software, these fill-in-forms have no computational capabilities, so you must do all your calculations before you start. In addition, you should be ready to enter all the data at once, because with just *Acrobat Reader* you can't save your completed forms. (If you purchase the complete Acrobat suite, you can save your forms to disk.) These forms are labeled "fill-in" at the IRS Web site.

Concept ✓

3-12. Define *estimated taxes,* and explain under what conditions such tax payments are required.

3-13. What is the purpose of a *tax audit*? Describe some things you can do to be prepared if your return is audited.

3-14. What types of assistance and tax preparation services does the IRS provide?

3-15. What are the advantages of using tax preparation software?

LG6

EFFECTIVE TAX PLANNING

As we saw in the chapter opener, the Ashers understood that there is more to taxes than filing returns annually. By keeping good records and thinking about tax implications of fiunancial transactions, they make *tax planning* a key ingredient of their overall personal financial planning. The overriding objective of effective tax planning is to maximize total after-tax income by reducing, shifting, and deferring taxes to as low a level as legally possible.

tax evasion
The illegal act of failing to accurately report income or deductions, and, in extreme cases, failing to pay taxes altogether.

tax avoidance
The act of reducing taxes in ways that are legal and compatible with the intent of Congress.

Keep in mind that *avoiding taxes* is one thing, but *evading* them is another matter altogether. By all means, don't confuse tax avoidance with tax evasion, which includes such illegal activities as omitting income or overstating deductions. **Tax evasion**, in effect, involves a failure to fairly and accurately report income or deductions, and, in extreme cases, a failure to pay taxes altogether. Persons found guilty of tax evasion are subject to severe financial penalties and even prison terms. **Tax avoidance**, in contrast, focuses on reducing taxes in ways that are legal and compatible with the intent of Congress.

FUNDAMENTAL OBJECTIVES OF TAX PLANNING

Tax planning basically involves the use of various investment vehicles, retirement programs, and estate distribution procedures to (1) reduce, (2) shift, and (3) defer taxes. You can *reduce* taxes, for instance, by using techniques that create tax deductions or credits, or that receive preferential tax treatment—such as investments that produce depreciation

Money in Action

Tax Planning Pays Off

Do you think that only the very rich can benefit from tax avoidance strategies? In fact, almost all taxpayers can avoid problems with the IRS and save money with the following tips for filing and year-round tax planning.

1. **File accurate and complete returns:** Although this may seem obvious, check your completed return carefully—names, Social Security numbers, filing status, arithmetic—before submitting it to the IRS. Errors can delay refunds and result in fines or penalties plus interest (compounded *daily*) for underpayment of taxes. Take all allowed exemptions. Put schedules and forms in the designated order (by sequence number, *not* form number, for numbered forms, alphabetically for schedules).
2. **Keep good records:** "The main reason that people miss deductions is because they are poor recordkeepers," says Ed Slott, a New York accountant. A good filing system for receipts of tax-deductible items will save you many headaches at tax time.
3. **Defer income until next year:** If you are self-employed, receive bonuses, or have income outside of a regular job (such as consulting), deferring income into the next tax year may keep you under the level where deduction and exemption phase-outs begin or prevent you from moving into a higher tax bracket. The amount you save depends on your current and anticipated income and tax bracket.
4. **Calculate tax credits carefully:** IRS rules for earned income and child tax credits are complicated, and it can be tricky to determine whether you qualify. Under the 2003 tax law, more people qualify for the earned income credit. It's important to take the time to calculate these correctly, because these credits can add up to substantial tax savings—in the case of the earned income credit, thousands of dollars in refunds even if a family doesn't have to pay any taxes. If you are in a qualifying tax bracket, don't forget two recently added credits: the Hope credit for college costs and the lifetime learning credit for college tuition.
5. **Make sure to keep up with changes in the tax laws:** For example, in 2003 taxes on capital

...continued on next page

(such as real estate) or that generate tax-free income (such as municipal bonds). You can *shift* taxes by using gifts or trusts to shift some of your income to other family members who are in lower tax brackets and to whom you intend to provide some level of support anyway, such as a retired, elderly parent.

The idea behind *deferring* taxes is to reduce or eliminate your taxes today by postponing them to some time in the future when you may be in a lower tax bracket. Perhaps more important, *deferring taxes gives you use of the money that would otherwise go to taxes*—thereby allowing you to invest it to make even more money. Deferring taxes is usually done through various types of retirement plans, such as IRAs, or by investing in certain types of annuities, variable life insurance policies, or even Series EE bonds (U.S. savings bonds).

The fundamentals of tax planning include making sure that you take all the deductions to which you are entitled and take full advantage of the various tax provisions that will minimize your tax liability. Thus comprehensive tax planning is an ongoing activity with both an immediate and a long-term perspective. *It plays a key role in personal financial planning*—in fact, one of the major components of a comprehensive personal financial plan is a summary of the potential tax impacts of various recommended financial strategies. Tax planning is closely interrelated with many financial planning activities, including investment, retirement, and estate planning.

smart.sites

To find the latest IRS Revenue rulings, search the database at TaxLinks, **http://www.taxlinks.com/**

Some Popular Tax Strategies

Managing your taxes is a year-round activity. Because Congress considers tax law changes throughout the year, you may not know all the applicable regulations until the middle of the year or later. For example, the *Jobs and Growth Tax Relief Reconciliation Act of 2003* became law at the end of May 2003 but its provisions applied to the whole year. Like other financial goals, tax strategies require review and adjustment when regulations and personal circumstances change.

Tax planning can become very complex at times and may involve rather sophisticated investment strategies. In such cases, especially those involving large amounts of money, you should seek professional help. Many tax strategies are fairly simple and straightforward and can be used by the average middle-income taxpayer. You certainly don't have to be in the top income bracket to enjoy the benefits of many tax-saving ideas and procedures. For example, the interest income on Series EE bonds is free from state income tax, and the holder can elect to delay payment of federal taxes until the earlier of the year the bonds are redeemed for cash or the year in which they finally mature. This feature makes Series EE bonds an excellent vehicle for earning tax-deferred income. Some other popular (and fairly simple) tax strategies follow. The *Money in Action* box on page 120 provides additional tips to help you reduce your tax liability.

There are other strategies that can cut your tax bill. Accelerating or bunching deductions into a single year may permit itemizing deductions. Shifting income from one year to another is one way to cut your tax liability. If you expect to be in the same or a higher income tax bracket this year than you will be next year, defer income until next year and shift expenses to this year so you can accelerate your deductions to reduce taxes this year.

Maximizing Deductions

Review a comprehensive list of possible deductions for ideas, because even small deductions can add up to big tax savings. Accelerate or bunch deductions into one tax year if it will allow you to itemize rather than take the standard deduction. For example, make your fourth quarter estimated state tax payment before December 31 rather than on January 15 to deduct it in the current taxable year. Group miscellaneous expenses and schedule non-reimbursed elective medical procedures to fall into one tax year to exceed the required "floor" for deductions (2 percent of AGI for miscellaneous expenses; 7.5 percent of AGI for medical expenses). Increase discretionary deductions such as charitable contributions.

Income Shifting

income shifting A technique used to reduce taxes in which a taxpayer shifts a portion of income to relatives in lower tax brackets.

One way of reducing income taxes is to use a technique known as **income shifting**. Here the taxpayer shifts a portion of his or her income—and thus taxes—to relatives in lower tax brackets. This can be done by creating trusts or custodial accounts or by making outright gifts of income-producing property to family members. For instance, parents with $125,000 of taxable income (28 percent marginal

gains were lowered, causing many investors to rethink their investment strategies. In addition, most stock dividends are now taxed at the same rates as capital gains rates instead of as ordinary income. Contributions to tax-deferred retirement accounts were raised for many taxpayers.

6. **Look at the tax implications of investment decisions:** Keep tax consequences in mind whenever you sell securities—but *never allow tax considerations to dictate investment decisions.* Consider waiting to sell a stock until it either qualifies for long-term capital gains treatment or you can use it to offset gains or losses. If you have securities in a company whose prospects aren't good, you may want to sell them to offset other gains or losses. If you don't have gains in the current tax year, you can carry over those losses until you do and also write off $3,000 a year against ordinary income. Report any changes in your mutual fund holdings, even if you just switch from one fund to another within the same fund family, because you incur a capital gain or loss. Failure to report such transfers and the resulting capital gains or losses could trigger an IRS audit.
7. **Plan ahead to avoid the alternative minimum tax if possible:** The AMT—which unlike many other tax provisions is not indexed for inflation—can kick in for people with AGI as low as $70,000. Year-end tax planning that runs counter to what you might otherwise do—for example, deferring certain deductions such as state and local tax payments until next year or accelerating income into this year—may help you avoid the tax.
8. **File electronically, if possible:** The error rate for electronically filed returns is under 1 percent, compared with 2 to 18 percent for paper returns. Using tax preparation software eliminates many common errors such as mathematical mistakes. An added benefit: if you are due a refund, you'll get it much sooner.

Critical Thinking Questions

1. Why are good tax records so important for tax planning?
2. Briefly discuss two of the strategies to minimize taxes.
3. Why should you avoid the AMT if possible?

Sources: Lynn Asinof, "Subtractions That Add Up," *The Wall Street Journal*, February 28, 2000, p. R8; Dinah Wisenberg Brin, "Oops!" *The Wall Street Journal*, February 28, 2000, p. R8; Tom Herman, "Tax Tip: Start Early This Year," *The Wall Street Journal*, September 18, 2003, pp. D1-2; Ann Perry, "Less-taxing Effort," *San Diego Union-Tribune*, March 23, 2003, pp. H1, H3; and Ann Perry, Year-Round Planning Offers Best Tax Breaks," *San Diego Union-Tribune*, March 23, 2003, pp. H1, H8.

tax rate) and $18,000 in corporate bonds paying $2,000 in annual interest might give the bonds to their 15-year-old child—with the understanding that such income is to be used ultimately for the child's college education. The $2,000 would then belong to the child, who would probably have to pay $125 (0.10 × [$2,000 − $750 minimum standard deduction for a dependent]) in taxes on this income, and the parents' taxable income would be reduced by $2,000, reducing their taxes by $560 (0.28 × $2,000).

Unfortunately, this strategy is not as simple as it might at first appear. Under current (2003) tax laws, investment income of a minor (under the age of 14) is taxed at the same rate as the parents *to the extent that it exceeds $1,500.* For example, if a 5-year-old girl received $2,500 from a trust set up for her by her parents, the first $1,500 of that income (subject to a minimum $750 standard deduction) would be taxed at the child's rate, and the remaining $1,000 would be subject to the parents' (higher) tax rate. These restrictions do not apply to children 14 and over, so it is possible to employ such techniques with older children (and presumably, with other older relatives, such as elderly parents).

Parents need to be aware that shifting assets into a child's name to save taxes could affect the amount of college financial aid for which the child qualifies. Most financial aid formulas expect students to spend 35 percent of assets held in their own name, compared with only 5.6 percent of the parents' nonretirement assets. Additional tax implications of gifts to dependents are discussed in Chapter 15.

Tax-Free and Tax-Deferred Income

There are some investments that provide tax-free income; in most cases, however, the tax on the income is only deferred (or delayed) to a later day. Although there aren't many forms of tax-free investments left today, probably the best example would be the *interest* income earned on *municipal bonds.* Such income is free from federal income tax. No matter how much municipal bond interest income you make, you don't have to pay any taxes on it. (Tax-free municipal bonds are discussed in Chapter 12.) Income that is **tax deferred**, in contrast, only delays the payment of taxes to a future date. Until that time arrives, however, tax-deferred investment vehicles allow you to *accumulate earnings* in a tax-free fashion. A good example of tax-deferred income would be income earned in a *traditional IRA.* See Chapter 14 for a detailed discussion of this and other similar arrangements.

tax deferred
Income that is not subject to taxes immediately but which will be subject to taxes at a later date.

Basically, any wage earner can open an IRA and contribute up to $3,000 a year to the account. This amount increases to $4,000 in 2005 and $5,000 in 2008. Of course, as noted earlier in this chapter, although any employed person can contribute to an IRA, only those people meeting certain pension and/or income constraints can deduct the annual contributions from their tax returns. If you fail to meet these restrictions, you can still have an IRA but you can't deduct the $3,000 annual contribution from your income. So why have an IRA? *Because all the income you earn in your IRA accumulates tax-free.* This is a *tax-deferred* investment, so you'll eventually have to pay taxes on these earnings, but not until you start drawing down your account. Roth IRAs, introduced in 1998, provide a way for people with AGI below a given level to contribute after-tax dollars. Not only do earnings grow tax-free, but so do withdrawals if the account has been open for five or more years and the individual is over 59½. In addition to IRAs, tax-deferred income can also be obtained from other types of pension and retirement plans and annuities. See Chapter 14 for more information on these financial products and strategies.

Concept ✓

3-16. Differentiate between *tax evasion* and *tax avoidance.*
3-17. Explain each of the following strategies for reducing current taxes: (a) maximizing deductions, (b) income shifting, (c) tax-free income, and (d) tax-deferred income.
3-18. Identify and briefly discuss at least six specific tax strategies that can be used by individuals to reduce their current taxes.

smart.sites

For still more tips and long-term tax planning strategies, head to SmartMoney's tax guide at **http://www.smartmoney.com/tax/**. This well-organized site also features a mini-course on tax basics and articles on a variety of tax topics.

SUMMARY

LG1. Discuss the basic principles of income taxes and determine your filing status. Because taxes have an impact on most individuals and families, understanding them is essential for effective personal financial planning and intelligent money management. The dominant tax in our country today is the federal income tax, a levy that provides the government with most of the funds it needs to cover its operating costs. Federal income tax rates are progressive, so that your tax rate increases as your income rises. Other types of taxes include state and local income taxes, sales taxes, and property taxes. The administration and enforcement of federal tax laws is the responsibility of the IRS, a part of the U.S. Department of the Treasury. The amount of taxes you owe depends on your filing status—single, married filing jointly, married filing separately, head of household, or qualifying widow(er) with dependent child—and the amount of taxable income you report. Because the government operates on a pay-as-you-go basis, employers are required to withhold taxes from their employees' paychecks.

LG2. Describe the various sources of gross income and adjustments to (gross) income, differentiate between standard and itemized deductions and exemptions, and calculate taxable income. Gross income includes active income (such as wages, bonuses, pensions, alimony), portfolio income (dividends, interest, and capital gains), and passive income (income derived from real estate, limited partnerships, and other tax shelters). You must decide whether to take the standard deduction or itemize your various deductions. Some allowable deductions for those who itemize include mortgage interest, medical expenses over 7.5 percent of AGI, and certain job-related expenses. To calculate taxable income, deduct allowable adjustments, such as IRA contributions and alimony paid, from gross income to get AGI, and subtract from AGI the amount of deductions and personal exemptions claimed.

LG3. Prepare a basic tax return using the appropriate tax forms and rate schedules. Once you determine your taxable income, you can find the amount of taxes owed using either the tax rate tables or, if your taxable income is over $100,000, the tax rate schedules. Tax rates vary with the level of reported income and filing status. Personal tax returns are filed using one of the following forms: 1040EZ, 1040A, or 1040. Certain taxpayers must include schedules with their Form 1040.

LG4. Explain who needs to pay estimated taxes, when to file or amend your return, and how to handle an audit. Persons with income not subject to withholding may need to file a declaration of estimated taxes and make estimated quarterly tax payments. Annual returns must be filed on or before April 15, unless the taxpayer requests an automatic 4-month filing extension. The IRS audits selected returns to confirm their validity by carefully examining the data reported in them.

LG5. Know where to get help with your taxes and how software can streamline tax return preparation. Assistance in preparing returns is available from the IRS and private tax preparers such as national and local tax firms, certified public accountants, enrolled agents, and tax attorneys. Computer programs can help do-it-yourselfers with both tax planning and tax preparation.

LG6. Implement an effective tax planning strategy. Effective tax planning is closely tied to other areas of personal financial planning. The objectives of tax planning are to reduce, shift, or defer taxes so the taxpayer gets maximum use of and benefits from the money he or she earns. Some of the more popular tax strategies include maximizing deductions, shifting income to relatives in lower tax brackets, investing in tax-exempt municipal bonds, setting up IRAs, and using other types of pension and retirement plans and annuities to generate tax-deferred income.

Financial Planning Exercises

1. Mary Parker is 24 years old, single, lives in an apartment, and has no dependents. Last year she earned $38,700 as a sales assistant for Texas Instruments; $3,150 of her wages were withheld for federal income taxes. In addition, she had interest income of $142. Estimate her taxable income, tax liability, and tax refund or tax owed.
2. Tina Marcelle received the following items and amounts of income during 2004. Help her calculate (a) her gross income and (b) that portion (dollar amount) of her income that is tax exempt.

Salary	$33,500
Dividends	800
Gift from mother	500
Child support from ex-husband	3,600
Interest on savings account	250
Rent	900
Loan from bank	2,000
Interest on state government bonds	300

3. If Jenny Perez is single and in the 28 percent tax bracket, calculate the tax associated with each of the following transactions using the tax schedules in Exhibit 3.4 and the IRS regulations for capital gains in effect in 2003:
   a. She sold stock for $1,200 that she purchased for $1,000 5 months earlier.
   b. She sold bonds for $4,000 that she purchased for $3,000 3 years earlier.
   c. She sold stock for $1,000 that she purchased for $1,500 15 months earlier.
4. Demonstrate the differences resulting from a $1,000 tax credit versus a $1,000 tax deduction for a single taxpayer in the 25 percent tax bracket with $40,000 of pre-tax income.

5. ***Use Worksheets 3.1 and 3.2.*** John Otsubo graduated from college in 2003 and began work as a systems analyst in July 2003. He is preparing to file his income tax return for 2003 and has collected the following financial information for calendar year 2003:

Tuition, scholarships, and grants	$ 5,750
Scholarship, room, and board	1,850
Salary	28,850

Interest income	185
Deductible expenses, total	3,000
Income taxes withheld	2,600

a. Prepare John's 2003 tax return, using a $4,750 standard deduction, a personal exemption of $3,050, and the tax rates given in Exhibit 3.4. Which tax form should John use, and why?

b. Prepare John's 2003 tax return using the data in part **a** along with the following information:

IRA contribution	$3,000
Cash dividends received	150

Which tax form should he use in this case? Why?

6. Ron and Lisa Ballard are married and have one child. Ron is putting together some figures so he can prepare the Ballard's joint 2003 tax return. He can claim three personal exemptions (including himself). So far, he's been able to determine the following with regard to income and possible deductions:

Total unreimbursed medical expenses incurred	$ 1,155
Gross wages and commissions earned	48,820
IRA contribution	3,000
Mortgage interest paid	5,200
Capital gains realized on assets held less than 12 months	1,450
Income from limited partnership	200
Job expenses and other allowable deductions	875
Interest paid on credit cards	380
Dividend and interest income earned	610
Sales taxes paid	2,470
Charitable contributions made	1,200
Capital losses realized	3,475
Interest paid on a car loan	570
Alimony paid by Ron to first wife	6,000
Social Security taxes paid	2,750
Property taxes paid	700
State income taxes paid	1,700

Given the above information, how much taxable income will the Ballards have in 2003? (*Note*: Assume that Ron is covered by a pension plan where he works, the standard deduction amount for married filing jointly ($9,500) applies, and each exemption claimed is worth $3,050.)

7. Maureen and Bob O'Flaherty have been notified that they are being audited. What should they do to prepare for the audit, and what steps can they take if they do not agree with the outcome of the audit?

Applying Personal Finance

Tax Relief!

Even though many were eliminated by the Tax Reform Act of 1986, tax shelters are still around. Beware, however, because some are legitimate, while others are not! American taxpayers have the right to lower their tax burdens, as long as they do it by legal means. The purpose of this project is to help you to learn about any tax shelters currently allowed by law.

Where can you go to find tax shelter opportunities? First, try the financial section of your newspaper. There may be advertisements or articles on tax shelters, such as tax-free bond funds. A bank is another source. Simply ask at "new accounts" if they can give you any tax shelter information. Another major source of new tax shelters are brokerage houses which sell stocks, bonds, and other securities to the investing public. If you have access to a brokerage house, ask them for tax shelter information. Also, you might want to search for "tax shelters" on the Internet.

List the tax shelters that you have found. Do any apply to you now, or are there any that you would like to use in the future? Finally, pull up the IRS's Web site at **http://www.irs.gov** and search for "abusive tax shelters" to determine if the tax shelters you have found are allowed by current tax laws.

Contemporary Case Applications

3.1 The Aggarwals Tackle Their Tax Return

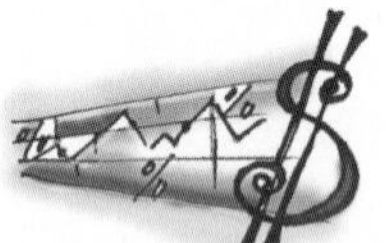

Sabash and Sue Aggarwal are a married couple in their early twenties living in Dallas. Sabash earned $30,600 in 2003 from his job as a sales assistant with Carson Corporation. During the year, his employer withheld $2,900 for income tax purposes. In addition, the Aggarwals received interest of $350 on a joint savings account, $750 interest on tax-exempt municipal bonds, and dividends of $400 on common stocks. At the end of 2003, the Aggarwals sold two stocks, A and B. Stock A was sold for $700 and had been purchased 4 months earlier for $800. Stock B was sold for $1,500 and had been purchased 3 years earlier for $1,100. Their only child, Rohn, age 2, received (as his sole source of income) dividends of $200 on stock of Kraft, Inc.

Although Sabash is covered by the Carson Corporation's pension plan, he plans to contribute $2,000 to a traditional deductible IRA for 2003. Following are the amounts of money paid out during the year by the Aggarwals:

Medical and dental expenses (unreimbursed)	$ 200
State and local property taxes	831
Interest paid on home mortgage	4,148
Charitable contributions	1,360
Total	$6,539

In addition, Sabash incurred some unreimbursed travel costs for an out-of-town business trip as follows:

Airline ticket	$250
Taxis	20
Lodging	60
Meals (as adjusted to 50% of cost)	36
Total	$366

Questions

1. Using the above information, determine the total amount of their itemized deductions. Assume that the Aggarwals will use the filing status of married filing jointly, the standard deduction for that status is $9,500, and each exemption claimed is worth $3,050. Should they itemize or take the standard deduction? Prepare a joint tax return for Sabash and Sue Aggarwal for the year ended December 31, 2003, to give them the smallest tax liability. Use the tax rate schedule provided in the text to calculate their taxes owed.

2. How much have you saved the Aggarwals as a result of your treatment of their deductions?
3. Discuss whether the Aggarwals need to file a tax return for their son.
4. Suggest some tax strategies the Aggarwals might use to reduce their tax liability for next year.

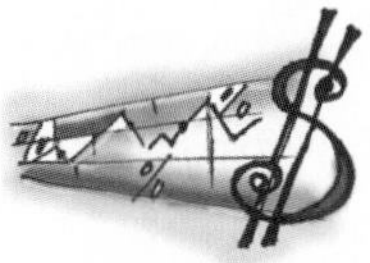

3.2 Joan Cavander: Bartender or Tax Expert?
Joan Cavander, who is single, goes to graduate school part-time and works as a bartender at the Twin Towers Supper Club in Atlanta. During the past year (2003), her gross income was $18,450 in wages and tips. She has decided to prepare her own tax return because she cannot afford the services of a tax expert. After preparing her return, she has come to you for advice. The following is a summary of the figures she has prepared thus far:

Gross income:	
Wages	$10,250
Tips	+ 8,200
Adjusted gross income (AGI)	$18,450
Less: Itemized deductions	− 2,300
	$16,150
Less: Standard deduction	− 4,750
Taxable income	$11,400

Joan believes that if an individual's income falls below $20,350, the federal government considers him or her "poor" and allows both itemized deductions and a standard deduction.

Questions

1. Calculate Joan Cavander's taxable income, being sure to consider her exemption. Assume that the standard deduction for a single taxpayer is $4,750 and that each exemption claimed is worth $3,050.
2. Discuss with Joan her errors in interpreting the tax laws, and explain the difference between itemized deductions and the standard deduction.
3. Joan has been dating Sam Haley for nearly 4 years, and they are seriously thinking about getting married. Sam has income and itemized deductions identical to Joan's. How much tax would they pay as a married couple (using the filing status of married filing jointly) versus the total amount the two would pay as single persons (each using the filing status of single)? Strictly from a tax perspective, does it make any difference whether Joan and Sam stay single or get married? Explain.

Money Online

Taxes, Taxes, and More Taxes!

1. **http://www.metlife.com**

How does a tax audit sound? Learn what an audit is, what to expect during an audit, and tips on surviving one. At MetLife's Web site, click on "Meeting Life" and then on "Financial" to find "About an IRS Audit."

2. **http://www.irs.gov/pub/irs-pdf/p1.pdf**

What are your rights as a taxpayer? Pull up Publication 1 from the IRS Web site to find out that among other rights, you are entitled to privacy and confidentiality, professional and courteous service, and representation.

3. **http://www.irs.gov/pub/irs-pdf/p5.pdf**
What if you disagree with the IRS's findings in your case? Refer to IRS Publication 5 entitled *Your Appeal Rights and How to Prepare a Protest if You Don't Agree.* For further information, search the main IRS Web site for "appeals" and "dispute resolution."

4. **http://www.irs.gov**
Become an enrolled agent and earn the privilege of representing taxpayers before the IRS. Find an overview of what an enrolled agent does and how to become one by clicking on "Tax Professionals" located under "Contents" and then on "Enrolled Agents."

5. **http://www.nolo.com**
Find legal self-help on taxing issues at Nolo's Web site. Search on "taxes" and discover hundreds of books and articles packed with legal information and resources.

6. **http://www.irs.gov/app/freeFile/welcome.jsp**
Reduce your tax preparation time and get your refund faster by e-filing. Find links to numerous tax preparation services at the IRS Web site. Maybe you'll even qualify to e-file for free!

7. **http://www.bhg.com**
Learn tax-lowering strategies, how to determine if you need a tax professional, or how to explain taxes to your teen at *Better Homes and Gardens*' Web site. Search on "taxes" to find numerous recent articles.

8. **http://www.turbotax.com**
Get organized with a "Tax Prep Checklist" or read through "Taxes 101." TurboTax provides plenty of educational material on taxes as well as information on the latest tax law changes and help with actually filing your taxes. Click on "Tax Planning" to get started.

9. **http://www.fairmark.com/estimate/est101.htm**
Should you be making estimated tax payments during the year? Read Fairmark's "Guide to Estimated Taxes" to learn who should make estimated payments, how much the payments should be, how to make the payments, and the penalty for underpayment.

10. **http://taxes.yahoo.com**
What do beginning investors need to know about taxes? Consult Yahoo's "Beginner's Guide" for help with managing the tax liability on investments, planning for capital gains, and purchasing and selling investments. While you're there, check out Yahoo's "Tools and Resources."

11. **http://www.taxadmin.org**
Federal income taxes are only *part* of your total tax burden! Click on "State Comparisons" at the Web site of the Federation of Tax Administrators to find information on state income taxes, state amnesty programs, state sales taxes, and state excise taxes. Click on "Link" to find your state's tax agency Web site.

Just for Fun!

12. **http://cbs.marketwatch.com**
Tax laws change faster than the weather! Keep up with the latest news on taxes at the CBS MarketWatch Web site. Click on "Personal Finance" and then on "Taxes" to find recent articles in their "Tax Library." Also check out the features "Taxing Times" and "Ask the Taxman."

PART TWO

Managing Basic Assets

CHAPTER 4 Managing Your Cash and Savings

Learning Goals

LG1. Understand the role of cash management in the personal financial planning process.
LG2. Describe today's financial services marketplace, both traditional and nondepository financial institutions.
LG3. Select the checking, savings, electronic banking, and other bank services that meet your needs.
LG4. Calculate the interest earned on your money using compound interest and future value techniques.
LG5. Develop a savings strategy that incorporates a variety of savings plans.
LG6. Open and use a checking account.

Breaking the Bank (Account)

Lisa Taylor's life was busy—too busy to check her current month's bank statement, which she tossed onto a pile with the others on her desk. She knew there was enough money in her account into cover her needs because her employer deposited her biweekly salary directly into her checking account. And she was pretty careful about keeping track of her spending. Or was she?

When an envelope marked "urgent" arrived from the bank the following week, Lisa discovered her account was overdrawn and the bank had bounced two of her checks. She immediately began reviewing her bank statements for the previous four months, and although she'd recorded each check she wrote, she'd been less diligent about recording ATM withdrawals and debit card purchases. Nor had she kept an accurate running balance in her checkbook, preferring to "guesstimate" her current balance based on her salary deposits and recollections of what she'd spent.

Compounding the problem was the bank's service charges. Jennifer had free checking—as long as she kept a minimum daily balance of $1,000. If she dipped below that amount, the bank charged a monthly service fee of $7.50 plus 25 cents for each check she wrote. Over several months the charges had added up! Lisa was even more upset when she realized that money she had in a savings account at the same bank could easily have been transferred to cover the shortfall in her checking account. The bank knew she had that money. Why hadn't someone called her to authorize a transfer of funds to cover her overdraft?

She put the question to the manager of her local branch the following day. He explained that handling thousands of customers and long lists of overdrawn accounts every day, the bank's staff did not have time to "hand-hold" its customers. "We expect our customers to be responsible in the way they manage their banking," he told Lisa.

Lisa realized that her poor cash management skills had almost cost her an otherwise clean credit record, and an up-to-then unblemished reputation with her bank. She vowed to pay closer attention to cash management in the future. The bank manager told her she should link her accounts and combine balances, and use online banking to monitor her account, pay bills, and make fund transfers as necessary. In addition, by getting a better handle on her bank balances she would be able to shift funds to higher interest-bearing accounts.

If, like Lisa, you need to get a better handle on your cash management practices, this chapter will show you how.

CRITICAL THINKING QUESTIONS

As you review the chapter, consider these questions in relation to Lisa Taylor's cash management practices:

- Why did Lisa Taylor believe that checking her monthly bank statement was unimportant?
- What factors contributed to Lisa finding herself overdrawn? Explain.
- What can Lisa Taylor do to protect herself from overdraft problems in the future?

THE ROLE OF CASH MANAGEMENT IN PERSONAL FINANCIAL PLANNING

LG1

As Lisa Taylor learned, establishing good financial habits applies to managing cash, as well as other areas of personal finance. In this chapter we'll focus on **cash management**—the routine, day-to-day administration of cash and near-cash resources, also known as *liquid assets*, by an individual or family. They are considered liquid because they are either held in cash or can be readily converted into cash with little or no loss in value.

cash management The routine, day-to-day administration of cash and near-cash resources, also known as *liquid assets*, by an individual or family.

In addition to cash, there are several other kinds of liquid assets, including checking accounts, savings accounts, money market deposit accounts, money market mutual funds, and other short-term investment vehicles. Exhibit 4.1 briefly describes some of the more popular types of liquid assets and the representative rates of return they earned in Fall 2003. As a rule, near-term needs are met using cash on hand, and unplanned or future needs are met using some type of savings or short-term investment vehicle.

EXHIBIT 4.1

Where to Stash the Cash

The wide variety of liquid assets available meets just about any savings or short-term investment need. Rates vary considerably, so shop around for the best interest rate.

Type	Representative Rates of Return (Fall 2003)	Description
Cash	0%	Pocket money; the coin and currency in one's possession.
Checking account	0–1%	A substitute for cash. Offered by commercial banks and other financial institutions such as savings and loans and credit unions.
Savings account	1%	Money is available at any time but cannot be withdrawn by check. Offered by banks and other financial institutions.
Money market deposit account (MMDA)	1–2%	Requires a fairly large (typically $1,000 or more) minimum deposit. Offers check-writing priveleges.
Money market mutual fund (MMMF)	1–2%	Savings vehicle that is actually a mutual fund (not offered by banks, S&Ls, and other depository institutions). Like an MMDA, it also offers check-writing privileges.
Certificate of deposit (CD)	1–3%	A savings instrument where funds are left on deposit for a stipulated period (1 week to 1 year or more); imposes a penalty for withdrawing funds early. Market yields vary by size and maturity; no check-writing privileges.
U.S. Treasury bill (T-bill)	1%	Short-term, highly marketable security issued by the U.S. Treasury (originally issued with maturities of 13 and 26 weeks); smallest denomination is $1,000.
U.S. Savings bond (EE)	2–3%	Issued by U.S. Treasury; rate of interest is tied to U.S. Treasury securities. Long a popular savings vehicle (widely used with payroll deduction plans). Matures in approximately 5 years; sold in denominations of $50 and more.

In personal financial planning, efficient cash management ensures adequate funds for both household use and an effective savings program. The success of your financial plans depends on your ability to establish and adhere to cash budgets.

An effective way to keep your spending in line is to make all household transactions (even the allocation of fun money or weekly cash allowances) using a tightly controlled *checking account*. In effect, you should write checks only at certain times of the week or month and, more important, you should avoid carrying your checkbook (or debit card) with you when you might be tempted to write checks (or make debits) for unplanned purchases. If you are going shopping, establish a maximum spending limit beforehand—an amount consistent with your cash budget. Such a system not only helps you avoid frivolous, impulsive expenditures, but also documents how and where you spend your money. Then, if your financial outcomes are not consistent with your plans, you can better identify causes and initiate appropriate corrective actions.

Another aspect of cash management is establishing an ongoing savings program, an important part of personal financial planning. Savings are not only a cushion against financial emergencies, but a way to accumulate funds to meet future financial goals. You may want to put money aside so you can go back to school in a few years to earn a graduate degree, or buy a new home, or perhaps take a vacation. Savings will help you meet these specific financial objectives.

Concept ✓

4-1. What is *cash management* and its major functions?

4-2. Give two reasons for holding liquid assets. Identify and briefly describe the popular types of liquid assets.

LG2 TODAY'S FINANCIAL SERVICES MARKETPLACE

Alison Green hadn't paid a visit to her bank for years. Her company paid her salary into her checking account each month by direct deposit, and she regularly did all her banking from her home computer—with the click of a mouse she could check her account balances, pay her bills, even search for the best rates on savings instruments. And by pushing a few buttons she was able to withdraw money in her U.S. bank account from an ATM in Paris!

The pace of change in the financial services industry is accelerating, thanks to advanced technology and less restrictive regulations. Consumers can now choose from many financial institutions competing for their business. No longer must you go to one place for your checking accounts, another for credit cards or loans, yet another for stock brokerage services. Today, you can choose an institution that provides "one-stop shopping," or have accounts with a variety of financial service providers, depending on what's best for your needs.

Before 1980 very little competition existed in the financial marketplace. The distinctions among various kinds of financial institutions were clear. Commercial banks offered checking accounts and short-term loans. Savings and loans offered savings accounts and real estate mortgage loans. Brokerage firms assisted in trading securities, and insurance companies offered life, disability, health, auto, and homeowner's insurance policies. This segmented marketplace changed in the early 1980s with passage of the *Depository Institutions Deregulation and Monetary Control Act of 1980*. This important law, together with additional legislation passed in 1982, removed many restrictions on banks and savings institutions, allowing them to compete with each other as well as nonbank financial institutions.

Deregulation has caused the differences among financial institutions to blur. Savings and loan associations and commercial banks now offer similar financial products and services. In addition, at many banks you can make securities transactions and buy mutual funds and insurance, while stockbrokers offer check-writing services, credit cards, loans, and access to ATMs. To compete with nonfinancial institutions, many banks and savings and loans now offer help with personal financial planning, take deposits across state lines, sell insurance, and offer securities brokerage services.

Thus the *financial services industry* as we know it today embraces all institutions that market various kinds of *financial products* (such as checking and savings accounts, credit cards, loans and mortgages, insurance, and mutual funds) and *financial services* (such as financial planning, securities brokerage, tax filing and planning, estate planning, real estate, trusts, retirement). In effect, what used to be several distinct (though somewhat related) industries is now, in essence, one industry whose firms are differentiated more by organizational structure than by name or product offerings.

Types of Financial Institutions

In spite of the growing number of firms in the financial services field, the vast majority of financial transactions continue to take place at traditional financial institutions—commercial banks, savings and loan associations, savings banks, and credit unions. They are commonly referred to as "banks" because of their similar products and services, although they are regulated by different agencies. What sets these institutions apart from their nonbank counterparts such as stock brokerages and mutual funds is their ability to accept deposits. These depository institutions are familiar and convenient, and most of us use them for our checking and savings account needs.

Commercial Banks

To millions of Americans, banking means doing business with a **commercial bank,** the most popular of the four types of traditional financial institutions. In addition to checking and savings accounts, commercial banks, also known as *full-service banks,* offer a full range of financial products and services, including a variety of savings vehicles, credit cards, consumer loans, trust services, as well as safe-deposit boxes, traveler's checks, and check-cashing privileges.

Commercial banks are also the only financial institutions that offer *non-interest-paying checking accounts (demand deposits)*—a feature that in today's deregulated financial market provides little competitive advantage. So commercial banks also offer checking accounts that combine check-writing privileges with the features of a savings account, and a selection of pure savings accounts. Most popular among these is the *regular savings account,* a basic savings account paying a minimum rate of interest.

Savings and Loan Associations.

Savings and loan associations (S&Ls) are found in most parts of the country. Savings and loans are important because they channel depositors' savings into mortgage loans for purchasing and improving homes. Since deregulation, S&Ls have greatly expanded their product and service offerings. Although they still cannot offer non-interest-paying checking accounts (demand deposits), they do offer many of the same checking, savings, and lending products and services as commercial banks—in fact, it has become more difficult to differentiate between the two institutions. Typically, savings deposits at S&Ls earn about .25 to .5 percent more than those at commercial banks. The availability of products and services at numerous branch offices, and their attractive rates of interest, contribute to the popularity of savings and loan associations.

Savings Banks

Savings banks are a special type of financial institution. They are similar to savings and loan associations, and are located primarily in the New England states. Like S&Ls, they offer various interest-paying checking and savings accounts on which they pay interest at a rate on par with that paid by savings and loans. Because most savings banks are

commercial bank
A financial institution that offers checking and savings accounts and a full range of financial products and services; the only institution that can offer *non-interest-paying checking accounts (demand deposits)*.

savings and loan association (S&L)
A financial institution that channels the savings of its depositors primarily into mortgage loans for purchasing and improving homes; due to deregulation, however, S&Ls now offer a competitive range of financial products and services.

savings bank
A type of financial institution, similar to an S&L and located primarily in the New England states, that is most often a *mutual* association owned by its depositors.

mutual associations, their depositors are their owners and thus receive a portion of the profits in the form of interest on their savings.

Credit Unions

credit union A member-owned financial cooperative that offers different types of interest-paying checking (share draft) accounts, savings accounts, and loans to its members (depositors).

share draft account An account offered by credit unions that is similar to interest-paying checking accounts offered by other financial institutions.

A **credit union** is a nonprofit, member-owned financial cooperative that provides a full range of financial products and services to specific groups of people who belong to a common occupation, religious or fraternal order, or residential area. Although credit unions are used by more than 76 million people, they are quite small when compared with commercial banks or S&Ls. A person who qualifies for membership in a credit union may buy a share by making a minimum deposit—often only $5 to $10. One *must* be a member—that is, have money on deposit—to borrow from a credit union. In addition to offering different types of interest-paying checking accounts—called **share draft accounts**—most credit unions also offer a variety of savings accounts to their members. Because the credit union is run to benefit its members, its fees and loan rates are lower and the interest it pays on savings is normally .5 to 1.5 percent higher than that paid by other savings institutions.

smart.sites
To learn more about credit unions and to find one in your area, visit the Credit Union National Association Web site, **http://www.cuna.org**.

Internet Banks

If you haven't set foot in your bank branch in months, you may be a prime candidate for an Internet bank. Because their operating expenses are so much lower than those of traditional brick-and-mortar banks, Internet banks can pass these savings along to their customers in the form of lower fees and higher yields. For example, twice as many online checking accounts as those at traditional banks carry no monthly service fees or per item charges. The average monthly service fee on interest-bearing Internet accounts is $8.24 versus $10.59 charged by traditional banks. And the average yield of 1.5 percent offered by Internet checking accounts beats that of 0.57 percent offered by traditional banks.

smart.sites
To help you decide if an Internet bank is for you, go to **http://www.kiplinger.com** to research Internet banks.

Nondepository Financial Institutions

With deregulation, other types of financial institutions began offering banking services. Because they do not accept deposits like traditional banks, they are considered "nondepository" institutions. Today you might hold a credit card issued by a stock brokerage firm or have an account with a mutual fund that allows you to write a limited number of checks.

- *Stock brokerage firms* offer several cash management options, including money market mutual funds that invest in short-term securities and earn a higher rate of interest than bank accounts, special "wrap" accounts, and credit cards.
- *Mutual funds*, discussed in detail in Chapter 13, provide yet another alternative to bank savings accounts. Like stockbrokers, mutual fund companies offer money market mutual funds.

Other nondepository financial institutions include life insurance and finance companies.

How Safe is Your Money?

The 1980s and early 1990s were tumultuous times in the banking industry. Large numbers of bank failures raised concerns about the strength of the deposit insurance system, and many banks merged. Understandably, depositors were concerned about the safety of their money. Fortunately, the booming economy of the 1990s contributed to a healthy U.S. banking industry. Today, the main reason that a bank goes out of business is its purchase by another bank.

Almost all commercial banks, S&Ls, savings banks, and credit unions are *federally insured* by U.S. government agencies. The few that are not federally insured usually obtain insurance through either a state-chartered or private insurance agency. Most experts believe that these so-called *privately insured* institutions have less protection against loss than those that are federally insured. Exhibit 4.2 lists the insuring agencies and maximum insurance amounts provided under the various federal deposit insurance programs.

EXHIBIT 4.2

Federal Deposit Insurance Programs

If you have your checking and savings accounts at a federally insured institution, you are covered up to $100,000.

Savings Institution	Insuring Agency	Amount of Insurance
Commercial bank	Federal Deposit Insurance Corporation (FDIC)	$100,000/depositor through the Bank Insurance Fund (BIF)
Savings and loan association	Federal Deposit Insurance Corporation (FDIC)	$100,000/depositor through the Savings Association Insurance Fund (SAIF)
Savings bank	Federal Deposit Insurance Corporation (FDIC)	$100,000/depositor through the Bank Insurance Fund (BIF)
Credit union	National Credit Union Administration (NCUA)	$100,000/depositor through the National Credit Union Share Insurance Fund (NCUSIF)

Deposit insurance protects the funds you have on deposit at banks and other depository institutions against institutional failure. In effect, the insuring agency stands behind the financial institution and guarantees the safety of your deposits up to a specified maximum amount ($100,000 per depositor in the case of federal insurance).

deposit insurance A type of insurance that protects funds on deposit against failure of the institution; insuring agencies include the Federal Deposit Insurance Corporation (FDIC) and the National Credit Union Administration (NCUA).

smart.sites

Look up your bank's deposit insurance status at the Federal Deposit Insurance Corp. Web site, **http://www.fdic.gov**.

Deposit insurance is provided to the *depositor* rather than a *deposit account.* Thus the checking *and* savings accounts of each depositor are insured and, *as long as the maximum insurable amount is not exceeded,* the depositor can have any number of accounts and still be fully protected. This is an important feature to keep in mind because many people mistakenly believe that the maximum insurance applies to *each* of their accounts. For example, a depositor with a checking account of $15,000 at a branch office of ABC bank, a MMDA of $35,000 at ABC bank's main office, and a $50,000 certificate of deposit

(CD) issued by ABC bank, is entirely covered by the FDIC's deposit insurance of $100,000 per depositor. If the CD was for $75,000. however, the total for this depositor would be $125,000 and therefore not entirely covered. Transferring the CD to another bank, which also provides $100,000 of deposit insurance, would fully protect all of this depositor's funds.

Now that banks are offering a greater variety of products, including mutual funds, it is important to remember that only deposit accounts, including certificates of deposit, are covered by deposit insurance. *Securities purchased through your bank are not subject to any form of deposit insurance protection.*

As a depositor, it is possible to increase your $100,000 of deposit insurance if the need arises by opening accounts in different depositor names at the same institution. For example, a married couple can obtain as much as $500,000 in coverage by setting up several accounts:

- One in the name of each spouse ($200,000 in coverage)
- A *joint* account in both names (good for another $100,000)
- *Separate trust or self-directed retirement (IRA, Keogh, etc.) accounts* in the name of each spouse (good for an additional $200,000).

Note that in this case each depositor name is treated as a separate legal entity, receiving full insurance coverage—the husband alone is considered one legal entity, the wife another, and the man and wife as a couple a third. The trust and self-directed retirement accounts are also viewed as separate legal entities.

Concept ✓

4-3. Discuss the effect that deregulation has had on financial institutions.

4-4. Briefly describe the basic operations and products and services offered by each of the following financial institutions: (a) commercial bank, (b) savings and loan association, (c) savings bank, (d) credit union, (e) stock brokerage firm, and (f) mutual fund.

4-5. What role does the FDIC play in insuring financial institutions? What other federal insurance program exists? Explain.

4-6. Would it be possible for an *individual* to have, say, six or seven checking and savings accounts at the same bank and still be fully protected under federal deposit insurance? Explain. Describe how it would be possible for a *married couple* to obtain as much as $500,000 in federal deposit insurance coverage at a single bank.

LG3 THE GROWING MENU OF CASH MANAGEMENT PRODUCTS

After meeting with an officer at his local bank, Ed Turner was confused. As a student on a tight budget, working to pay his way through college, he knew how important it was to plan his saving and spending, and he wanted to make the right decisions about managing his financial resources. A checking account comparison chart, similar to the one in Exhibit 4.3, provided Ed with information on daily balance requirements, services fees, and interest rates, and services available to college students and others, helping him understand the variety of checking programs offered by his bank. As Exhibit 4.3 demonstrates, banks offer a variety of convenient checking account services.

CHECKING AND SAVINGS ACCOUNTS

People hold cash and other forms of liquid assets, like checking and savings accounts, for the convenience they offer in making purchase transactions, meeting normal living expenses, and providing a safety net, or cushion, to meet unexpected expenses or take advantage of unanticipated opportunities. Deregulation has resulted in greater competition among financial institutions, which now offer a wide array of products to meet every liquid-asset need.

EXHIBIT 4.3

Checking Accounts Comparison Chart

Most banks offer a variety of checking account options, typically differentiated by minimum balances, fees, and other services.

ANYBANK USA

Features	College Checking	Custom Checking	Advantage Checking	Advantage Plus Checking
Minimum Daily Balance (to waive monthly service fee)	None	$1,000 in checking	$2,000 in checking, or $5,000 combined balance	$10,000 combined balance
Monthly Service Fee	$5 ($3.75 effective 9/1/03). No fee in summer (discontinued 9/1/03). $2 discount with a qualifying direct deposit of $100 or more.	$8 (No fee with direct deposit or direct debit)	$12 ($2 discount with direct deposit. No fee with Homeowner's Option)	$14 ($2 discount with direct deposit)
Interest	No	No	Yes	Yes
Online Statements	Free	Free	Free	Free
Check Safekeeping	Free	Free	Free	Free
Monthly Check Return	$3.00	$3.00	$3.00	Free
ATM & Check Card	Free	Free	Free	Free
Wells Fargo Phone Bank℠	Free automated calls	Free automated calls	Free automated calls	Free banker-assisted calls
Overdraft Protection	Credit card	Credit card	Credit card, line of credit account, and select deposit accounts	Credit card, line of credit account, and select deposit accounts
Direct Deposit Advance Service	Not available	Yes with a direct deposit of $100 a month or more	Yes with a direct deposit of $100 a month or more	Yes with a direct deposit of $100 a month or more

The federal *Truth-in-Savings Act of 1993* helps consumers evaluate the terms and costs of banking products. Commercial banks, savings institutions, and credit unions must clearly disclose fees, interest rates, and terms—of both checking and savings accounts. The act places strict controls on bank advertising and what constitutes a "free" account. For example, banks cannot advertise free checking if there are minimum balance requirements or per-check charges. Banks must use a standard *annual percentage yield (APY)* formula that takes compounding (discussed later) into account when stating the interest paid on accounts. This makes it easier for consumers to compare each bank's offerings. The law also requires banks to pay interest on a customer's full daily or monthly average deposit balance. No longer can banks pay interest only on the lowest daily balance or avoid paying any interest if the account balance falls below the minimum balance for 1 day. In addition, banks must notify customers 30 days before lowering rates on deposit accounts or certificates of deposit.

Checking Accounts

demand deposit An account held at a financial institution from which funds can be withdrawn (by check or in cash) on demand by the account holder; same as a *checking account.*

A checking account held at a financial institution is a **demand deposit**, meaning that the withdrawal of these funds must be permitted by the bank when demanded by the account holder. You put money into your checking account by *depositing* funds; you withdraw it by *writing a check using a debit card,* or *making a cash withdrawal.* As long as you have sufficient funds in your account, the bank, when presented with a valid check, or electronic debit, must immediately pay the amount indicated by deducting it from your account. Money held in checking accounts is liquid and therefore can easily be used to pay bills and make purchases.

Regular checking is the most common type of checking account. It pays no interest, and any service charges that exist can be waived if you maintain a minimum balance (usually between $750 and $1,500). Technically, non-interest-paying regular checking accounts can be offered only by commercial banks. S&Ls, savings banks, and credit unions also offer checking accounts, but these accounts, which must pay interest, are called *NOW (negotiable order of withdrawal) accounts* or, in the case of credit unions, *share draft accounts.* Demand deposit balances are an important type of cash balance, and using checks to pay bills or electronic debits to make purchases provide a convenient payment record.

smart.sites

Save money by ordering your checks online at **http://www. checksinthemail.com**. For interesting designs check out **http://www.designerchecks.com** or **http://www.artisticchecks.com**.

Savings Accounts

time deposit A savings deposit at a financial institution; so-called because it is expected to remain on deposit for a longer period of time than a demand deposit.

A savings account is another type of liquid asset serviced by commercial banks, savings and loan associations, savings banks, credit unions, and other types of financial institutions. Savings deposits are referred to as **time deposits** because they are expected to remain on deposit for longer periods of time than demand deposits. Because savings deposits earn higher rates of interest, savings accounts are typically preferable to checking accounts when the depositor's purpose is to accumulate money for a future expenditure, or maintain balances for meeting unexpected expenses. Most banks pay higher interest rates on larger savings account balances. For example, a bank might pay 2.50 percent on balances up to $2,500, 2.75 percent on balances between $2,500 and $10,000, and 3.00 percent on balances of more than $10,000.

Although financial institutions generally retain the right to require a savings account holder to wait a certain number of days before receiving payment of a withdrawal, most are willing to pay withdrawals immediately. In addition to withdrawal policies and deposit insurance, the stated interest rate and the method of calculating interest paid on savings accounts are important considerations in choosing the financial institution in which to place your savings.

Interest-Paying Checking Accounts

negotiable order of withdrawal (NOW) account A checking account on which the financial institution pays interest; NOWs have no legal minimum balance.

Depositors can choose from NOW accounts, money market deposit accounts, and money market mutual funds.

NOW Accounts

Negotiable order of withdrawal (NOW) accounts are checking accounts on which the financial institution pays interest. There is no legal minimum balance for a NOW, but many institutions impose their own requirement, often between $500 and $1,000.

Some pay interest on any balance in the account, but most institutions pay a higher rate of interest for balances above a specified amount.

Money Market Deposit Accounts

Money market deposit accounts (MMDAs) are a popular offering at banks and other depository institutions, and compete for deposits with money market mutual funds. MMDAs are popular with savers and investors due to their convenience and safety, because deposits in MMDAs, unlike those in money funds, are *federally insured.* Most banks require a minimum MMDA balance of $1,000 or more.

money market deposit account (MMDA)
A federally insured savings account, offered by banks and other depository institutions, that is meant to be competitive with a money market mutual fund.

Depositors can use check-writing privileges or ATMs to access MMDA accounts. They receive a limited number of free monthly checks and transfers—usually six—but pay a fee on additional transactions. Although this reduces the flexibility of these accounts, most depositors view MMDAs as savings rather than convenience accounts, and do not consider these restrictions a serious obstacle. Moreover, MMDAs pay the highest interest rate of any bank account on which checks can be written.

One of the major problems with the growing popularity of interest-paying checking accounts has been a rise in monthly bank charges, which can easily amount to more than the interest earned on all but the highest account balances. So the higher rates of interest offered by MMDAs can be misleading.

Money Market Mutual Funds

money market mutual fund (MMMF)
A mutual fund that pools the funds of many small investors and purchases high-return short-term marketable securities offered by the U.S. Treasury, major corporations, large commercial banks, and various government organizations.

Money market mutual funds have become the most successful type of mutual fund ever offered. A **money market mutual fund (MMMF)** pools the funds of many small investors to purchase high-return short-term marketable securities offered by the U.S. Treasury, major corporations, large commercial banks, and various government organizations. (Mutual funds are discussed in greater detail in Chapter 13.)

MMMFs generally pay interest at rates of 1 to 3 percent above those paid on regular savings accounts. Moreover, investors have instant access to their funds through check-writing privileges, although these must be written for a stipulated minimum amount (usually $500). The checks look and are treated like any other check drawn on a demand deposit account, and, as with all interest-bearing checking accounts, you continue to earn interest on your money while the checks make their way through the banking system.

Asset Management Accounts

asset management account (AMA)
A comprehensive deposit account, offered primarily by brokerage houses and mutual funds; combines checking, investing, and borrowing activities and automatically "sweeps" excess balances into a money market mutual fund and automatically provides loans when shortages exist.

Perhaps the best example of a banking service offered by a nondepository financial institution is the **asset management account (AMA)**, or *central asset account.* The AMA is a comprehensive deposit account that combines checking, investing, and borrowing activities, and is offered primarily by brokerage houses and mutual funds. AMAs appeal to investors because they can consolidate most of their financial transactions at one institution and on one account statement.

A typical AMA account includes a MMDA with unlimited free checking, a Visa or MasterCard debit card, use of ATMs, and brokerage and loan accounts. Annual fees and account charges, such as a per-transaction charge for ATM withdrawals, vary so it pays to shop around. AMAs have increased in popularity as more institutions have lowered minimum balance requirements to $5,000, and they pay higher interest rates on checking account deposits than banks. Their distinguishing feature is that they automatically "sweep" excess balances—for example, those more than $500—into a higher-return MMMF daily or weekly. When the account holder needs funds to purchase securities or cover checks written on the MMDA, the funds are transferred back to the MMDA. If the amount of securities purchased or checks presented for payment exceeds the account balance, the needed funds are supplied automatically through a loan.

Although AMAs are an attractive alternative to a traditional bank account, they have some drawbacks. Compared with banks there are fewer "branch" locations; however, AMAs are affiliated with ATM networks, making it easy to withdraw funds. ATM transactions are more costly, checks can take longer to clear, and some bank services, such as travelers' and certified checks, may not be offered. AMAs are not covered by deposit insurance, although these deposits are protected by the *Securities Investor Protection Corporation* (explained in Chapter 11) and the firm's private insurance.

Electronic Banking Services

The fastest changing area in cash management today is electronic banking services. Whether you are using an ATM or checking your account balance online, electronic banking services make managing your money easier and more convenient. No longer are you restricted to the hours that your bank is open. Electronic funds transfer systems allow you to conduct many types of banking business any hour of the day or night.

electronic funds transfer systems (EFTS) Systems that use the latest telecommunications and computer technology to electronically transfer funds into and out of customers' accounts.

debit cards Specially coded plastic cards used to transfer funds from a customer's bank account to the recipient's account to pay for goods or services. An ATM card is a debit card that also provides access to a variety of banking transactions through an ATM.

automated teller machine (ATM) A type of remote computer terminal at which customers of a bank or other depository institution can make basic transactions 24 hours a day, 7 days a week.

Electronic Funds Transfer Systems

Electronic funds transfer systems (EFTSs) use the latest telecommunications and computer technology to electronically transfer funds into and out of your account. For example, your employer may use an EFTS to electronically transfer your pay from its bank account directly into your personal bank account at the same or a different bank. This eliminates the employer's need to prepare and process checks and the employee's need to deposit them. Electronic transfer systems make possible such services as debit cards and ATMs, preauthorized deposits and payments, bank-by-phone accounts, and online banking.

Debit Cards and Automated Teller Machines

This form of EFTS uses specially coded plastic cards, called **debit cards**, to transfer funds from the customer's bank account (a debit) to the recipient's account. A debit card may be used to make purchases at any place of business set up with the point-of-sale terminals required to accept debit card payments. The personal identification number (PIN) issued with your debit card verifies that you are authorized to access the account.

Visa and MasterCard issue debit cards linked to your checking account that give you even more flexibility. In addition to using the card to purchase goods and services, it can be used at ATMs, which have become a popular way to make banking transactions. **Automated teller machines (ATMs)** are actually remote computer terminals that allow customers of a bank or other depository institution to make deposits, withdrawals, and other transactions such as loan payments or transfers between accounts, 24 hours a day, 7 days a week. Most banks have ATMs outside their offices, and some locate freestanding ATMs in shopping malls, airports, and grocery stores; at colleges and universities; and in other high-traffic areas to enhance their competitive position. If your bank belongs to an EFTS network, such as Cirrus, Star, or Interlink, you can get cash from the ATM of any bank in the United States or overseas that is a member of that network. (In fact, the easiest way to get foreign currency when you travel overseas is through an ATM on your bank's network! It also gives you the best exchange rate for your dollar.) Most banks charge a per-transaction fee of $1 to $4 for using the ATM of another bank, and some also charge when you use your ATM card to pay certain merchants.

Debit card use is increasing because these cards are convenient both for retailers, who don't have to worry about bounced checks, and for consumers, who don't have to write checks and can often get cash back when they make a purchase. First accepted by supermarkets, gas stations, and convenience stores, ATM and other debit cards are now accepted in most states and can be used at many retail and service outlets. The convenience of debit cards may, in fact, be their biggest drawback: It can be easy to overspend.

Money in Action

The Check's in the (E-)Mail

Do you hate writing checks and put off bill paying until the very last minute, then run out of stamps and have to dash to the post office? Discover how easy it is to stay on top of your bills with online bill payment. It may be the solution to your cash management problems. There are several ways to accomplish the move to Internet bill payment. Just turn on your computer and go to your bank's Web site. There, you can check your balance to make sure sufficient money is in your account, and pay your bills. It's fast and convenient, and you can schedule bills for payment when they arrive. Some banks offer free online bill paying if you open a checking account. Others require minimum balances for free online services.

In addition to your own bank's Web site, online bill paying is also available through independent services. The first type allows you to continue to receive your bills by mail and authorize a third party—your bank or a company such as Bills.com (**http://www.bills.com**) or the U.S. Postal Service (**http://www.usps.gov**)—to access your bank account and pay them. The initial setup can be time-consuming—you provide names, addresses, phone numbers, and account numbers for your payee list—although with payee lists already pre-programmed into many banks' systems, you just have to search for the right match. Once you've set it up, just select the recipient, fill in the amount, and click the "pay" button.

The second type, *electronic bill presentment and payment (EBPP),* offers a complete online bill management service, allowing you to avoid the clutter of paper entirely. It acts as a virtual mailbox, receiving your bills and notifying you via email that a bill has arrived. Then you go to the Web site to review it and arrange payment from any account with check-writing privileges. EBPP services will also confirm that the payment has been made, remind you that an unpaid bill is due, and let you view and print a report of bill payments by date or expense category. Companies that offer EBPP include CyberBill's StatusFactory (**http://www.statusfactory.com**), Bills.com (**http://www.bills.com**), and Paytrust (**http://www.paytrust.com**).

...continued on next page

To avoid problems, make sure to record all debit card purchases immediately in your checkbook ledger and deduct them from your checkbook balance. Also, if there is a problem with a purchase, you can't stop payment—an action you could take if you had paid by check or credit card.

Financial Road Sign

Small Savings Equal Large Gains

Think there are no other ways you can save money? When you're in a cash flow crunch and it's time for drastic action you *can* save more if you really put your mind to it. Here's how.

- **Use a crash budget:** A crash budget works just like a crash diet—cut out all unnecessary spending and don't buy on impulse. This works especially well for short periods.
- **The two-week rule:** Become an impulse saver, rather than an impulse buyer. If you want something, wait 2 weeks to get it.

Source: *A Working Woman's Guide to Financial Security*, "Planning for Financial Independence," downloaded from **http://www.urbanext.uiuc.edu**, August 29, 2003.

Preauthorized Deposits and Payments

Two related EFTS services are *preauthorized deposits and payments.* They allow you to receive automatic deposits or make payments that occur on a regular basis. For example, you can arrange to have your paycheck or monthly pension or Social Security benefits deposited directly into your account. Regular, fixed-amount payments, such as mortgage and consumer loan payments or monthly retirement fund contributions, can be preauthorized to be made automatically from your account. You can also preauthorize regular payments of varying amounts such as monthly utility bills. In this case, each month you would specify by phone the amount to be paid.

Charges for preauthorized payments vary from bank to bank. Typically, customers must maintain a specified minimum deposit balance and pay fees averaging 25 to 50 cents per transaction. Not only does this system better allow the customer to earn interest on deposits used to pay bills, it is also a convenient payment method that eliminates postage costs.

Bank-by-Phone Accounts

Bank customers can initiate a variety of banking transactions by telephone, either by calling a customer service operator who handles the transaction or by using the keypad on a touch-tone telephone to instruct the bank's computer. After the customer provides a secret code to access his or her accounts, the system provides the appropriate prompts to perform various transactions, such as obtaining an account balance, finding out what checks have cleared,

Financial Road Sign

How Safe Is Online Banking? To get the features and security you need from online banking, first check to see that your bank offers these important safety measures?

- 128-bit encryption, the industry standard, and a firewall to protect data from hackers.
- Written guarantees to protect you from losses in case of online fraud. Know in advance its policies for handling bills that don't get paid due to its error. Will it make up the money, pay a late fee, and help clear any blots on your credit record?
- Automatic lockout if you enter your password wrong more than three or four times.
- FDIC insurance.

Sources: Consumer Action, cited in Richard Newman, "Virtual Banking—A Growing Number of Americans Are Checking Out Online Services," *The Record* (Bergen County, NJ), December 3, 2000, p. B1; Hank Ezell, "Online Banking Growing Rapidly," *The Atlanta Journal and Constitution,* August 13, 2000, p. G3; "Some Tips for Choosing an Online Bill-Paying Service," *San Diego Union-Tribune ComputerLink,* October 17, 2000, p. 8.

transferring funds to other accounts, and dispatching payments to participating merchants. To encourage banking by telephone, many banks today charge no fee on basic account transactions or allow a limited number of free transactions per month.

Online Banking and Bill Payment Services

About 6 million households now use some form of *online banking* services, a number that has grown steadily as banks make online services easier to use and people become more comfortable using the Internet for financial transactions. Many individuals just check their balances, but more than half use the Internet to transfer funds as well. Thanks to improved Internet security procedures, most online bank services are delivered through the Internet although some may use direct dial-up connections with the customer's bank. Today about 800 banks compete for your online banking business. It's in their best financial interests to do so. A recent study showed that the cost of a full-service teller transaction is $1.07, an ATM transaction is 27 cents, and an Internet transaction is just 1 cent.

An online banking service lets you access your bank's Web site from your computer at any time. After logging on with your personal identification code and password, you can review your current statement to check your balance and recent transactions. Then, you can transfer funds from one account to another or pay bills electronically. You can also download account information to money management software such as Quicken or Microsoft Money.

Although a computer-based bank-at-home system doesn't replace the use of an ATM to obtain

"Although online bill paying seems convenient, there are issues people need to consider, such as privacy, security, and what happens when things go wrong," cautions Frank Torres of Consumers Union, publisher of *Consumer Reports.* Among the advantages are:

- **Convenience:** You can pay all your bills at once from one Web site, without writing checks or buying stamps. If you travel a lot, you can access your bill-paying site while you are on the road or schedule payments up to 1 year ahead. Some services will even pay people who don't normally send you bills, like your babysitter!
- **Organization:** EBPP services remind you if a payment due date is approaching and you haven't paid your bill. With credit card companies assessing $30 late-payment fees, this feature alone can save you a lot of money!
- **Recordkeeping:** Many services save your payments so you can retrieve and print a record for the year (some go back several years). This is especially helpful at tax time.
- **Customization:** You can arrange automatic payment for bills whose amounts do not change, such as mortgage or car loan payments, or if the amount is below a certain amount. With manual payments, you decide how much to pay and when.
- **Round-the-clock-help:** E-mail help lines are available at any time, or you can call for help during normal business hours.

The disadvantages are:

- **Start-up confusion:** With EBPP, there will be a lag time of several billing cycles while you change the address on all your bills to that of the service. This makes it difficult to try out the service first, and you will still have to pay some bills by hand.
- **Monthly fees:** Convenience isn't free. Most services charge $4 to $10 to pay from 10 to 30 bills per month, with a per-bill fee of up to 50 cents for additional bills.
- **Computer literacy:** If you are not comfortable using the Internet, wait until you master the basics.
- **Float:** Most bill-paying services immediately withdraw funds from your account when you hit the pay button, so you lose "float," the period between when you write a check and when the recipient cashes it, typically 3 to 10 days. Be sure the money is already in your account!
- **Privacy and security:** There is always a concern when you give a third party such valuable information as your Social Security number and bank and credit card numbers.

...continued on next page

Still interested in trying e-bill-payment? Use the checklist in Exhibit 4.4 to choose an online bill payment service wisely.

Critical Thinking Questions

1. What are the three main types of online bill paying services?
2. What are some advantages and disadvantages of paying your bills online?
3. How would you approach selecting an online bill-paying service? Explain.

Sources: Christine Dugas, "Virtual Banks Get Real, Offer Deals To Woo Customers," *USA Today*, April 13, 2000, p. 12B; Hank Ezell, "Online Banking Growing Rapidly," *The Atlanta Journal and Constitution,* August 13, 2000, p. G3; R. J. Ignelzi, "Online Bill Paying: Does It Make Good Cents for You?" *San Diego Union-Tribune ComputerLink,* October 17, 2000, pp. 6–8; Karen Thomas, "Millions Turn PCs into Personal Tellers", *USA Today,* October 3, 2000, p. 3D; "Weighing the Pros and Cons of Online Bill Paying," *San Diego Union-Tribune ComputerLink,* October 17, 2000, pp. 7–8; "What Is Online Banking?" **http://www.bankrate.com**, September 2, 2003; "Pay Your Bills Online," **http://www.kiplinger.com**, September 2, 2003.

cash or deposit money, it can save both time and postage when you are paying bills. Other benefits include convenience and the potential to earn higher interest rates and pay lower fees. Customers like the ability to check their account balances at any time of the day or night, not just when their printed statement comes once a month.

Online banking services charge between $5 and $10 per month, which typically includes some bill payments. Some banks do not charge their customers for viewing accounts and transferring funds. But online banking does not always live up to its promises. You can't make cash deposits, checks may get lost in the mail, and you don't know when the funds will reach your account. The *Money in Action* box that begins on page 144 provides more information to help you decide if online bill paying is right for you.

Most consumers prefer the security of a bank with a physical presence and a variety of other banking options such as branches, ATMs, and phone services. Your current "traditional" bank probably offers online banking services. Another option is to open an account at a ***virtual bank*** that exists only online and has few or no physical locations. Because they don't incur branch costs, Internet-only banks can offer high interest rates on checking and savings accounts and CDs, attractive loan rates, and low fees and charges. However, only 2 percent of all households that bank online choose these banks. Customers are concerned that virtual banks are less secure and find it inconvenient to have to deposit checks by mail. To counter these concerns, many Internet-only banks are moving to a "clicks-and-bricks" strategy, adding a physical presence such as ATM networks and staffed mini-branches with ATMs and videoconferencing stations.

EXHIBIT 4.4

Choosing an Online Bill Paying Service

Before signing up with any online bill paying service, use the following checklist to help you find the features you want and the security you need:

1. Check the Better Business Bureau for the company's reputation and any complaints that may have been lodged against it.
2. The service should provide you with written confirmation regarding its privacy policy, stating it will not share your personal information with anyone at any time.
3. Technological security is critical when handling sensitive financial information. Make sure the service offers secure data transmittal, as well as a firewall to protect information from hackers.
4. The company should perform background checks on its employees and guarantee your protection from losses due to fraud.
5. Be aware of the company's policy for handling bills not paid due to its error. Will it help clear your credit record, as well as pay any late fees and compensate you for any out-of-pocket costs?

smart.sites

Is an electronic bill presentment and payment (EBPP) service for you? Visit Paytrust's site, **http://www.paytrust.com**, to decide for yourself.

Regulation of EFTS Services

The federal *Electronic Fund Transfer Act of 1978* delineates your rights and responsibilities as an EFTS user. Under this law, you cannot stop payment on a defective or questionable purchase, although individual banks and state laws have more-lenient provisions. In the case of an error, you must notify the bank within 60 days of its occurrence. The bank must investigate and tell you the results within 10 days. The bank can then take up to 45 additional days to investigate the error but must return the disputed money to your account until the issue is resolved.

If you fail to notify the bank of the error within 60 days, the bank has no obligation under federal law to conduct an investigation or return your money. In addition, it is very important that you notify the bank immediately about the theft, loss, or unauthorized use of your EFTS card. Notification within 2 business days after you discover the card missing limits your loss to $50. After 2 business days, you may lose up to $500 (but never more than the amount that was withdrawn by the thief). If you do not report the loss within 60 days after your periodic statement was mailed, you can lose all the money in your account. When reporting errors or unauthorized transactions, it is best to notify your bank by telephone and follow up with a letter. Keep a copy of the letter in your file.

Many state regulations offer additional consumer protection regarding your use of EFTS. However, your best protection is to carefully guard the PIN used to access your accounts. Do not write the PIN on your EFTS card, and be sure to check your periodic statements regularly for possible errors or unauthorized transactions.

Financial Road Sign

Thinking Outside the (Safe-Deposit) Box

Some important factors to consider when deciding whether to rent a safe-deposit box from your bank:

- **Do** check with your homeowners insurance carrier to see if a safe-deposit box will reduce your insurance bill.
- **Don't** keep items in there that you may need in a hurry, such as passports or powers-of-attorney.
- **Do** prepare and update a list of the contents of the box and take a photograph of its contents at least once a year.
- **Don't** forget that although breaches are rare, safe-deposit boxes are not 100% safe and banks don't insure the contents.

Source: Adapted from Alex Frangos, "Think Inside the Safe Box," *The San Diego-Union Tribune,* February 23, 2003, p. H7.

Other Bank Services

In addition to the numerous services described earlier in this chapter, banks offer several other types of money management services: safe-deposit boxes, trust services, and mutual-fund sales.

- **Safe-deposit boxes:** A *safe-deposit box* is a rented drawer in a bank's vault. Boxes can be rented for between $40 and $85 per year, or more, depending on their size. When you rent a box, you receive one key to it, and the bank retains another key. The box can be opened only when both keys are used. This arrangement protects items in the box from theft and serves as an excellent storage place for jewelry, contracts, stock certificates, titles, and other important documents. Keeping valuables in a safe-deposit box may also reduce your homeowner's insurance by eliminating the "riders" that are often needed to cover such items.
- **Trust services:** Bank trust departments provide investment and estate planning advice. They manage and administer the investments in a trust account or from an estate.

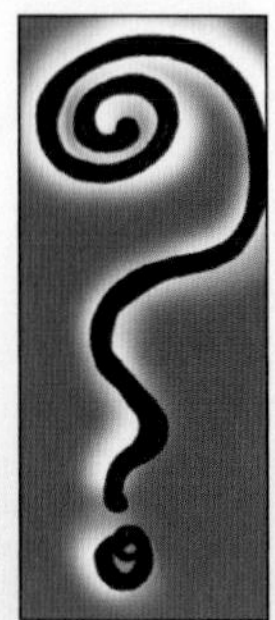

Concept ✓

4-7. Distinguish between a checking account and a savings account.

4-8. Define and discuss (a) demand deposits, (b) time deposits, (c) interest-paying checking accounts.

4-9. Briefly describe the key characteristics of each of the following forms of interest-paying checking accounts: (a) money market deposit account (MMDA), (b) NOW account, and (c) money market mutual fund (MMMF).

4-10. Describe the features of an asset management account (AMA), its advantages, and its disadvantages.

4-11. Briefly describe (a) debit cards, (b) banking at ATMs, (c) preauthorized deposits and payments, (d) bank-by-phone accounts, and (e) online banking and bill payment services.

4-12. What are your legal rights and responsibilities when using EFTS?

4-13. Describe briefly the following additional services that banks provide: (a) safe-deposit boxes, (b) trust services, and (c) mutual-fund sales.

- **Mutual-fund sales:** Most major commercial banks now offer mutual funds to their customers. Some of these mutual funds are from major mutual fund companies, whereas others are bank-sponsored funds. (Detailed discussion of mutual funds is the focus of Chapter 13.) Often bank representatives will suggest mutual funds to customers as an alternative to CDs. However convenient it may be to purchase these securities through your bank, be sure to evaluate these funds carefully. Investigate the fund's performance and all fees and sales expenses, and compare these with other mutual funds before making a purchase. Many bank mutual fund customers are novice investors who are not aware that, unlike CDs, the return on these investments is not guaranteed. Remember, too, that mutual funds are not deposits and are therefore not covered by federal deposit insurance.

ESTABLISHING A SAVINGS PROGRAM

LG4, LG5

Alan Wilson's father started a savings account for his son when he was born, and every birthday he would add $50 or $100, depending on his cash flow. He told Alan that when he was ready to quit work there would be a substantial sum available to help him retire. And there was. Alan now spends his days fishing and relaxing in the cabin he and his wife bought on Bluefish Lake, while most of his friends continue to work because they can't afford to retire.

An estimated 75 percent of American households have some money put away in savings, making it clear that most of us understand the value of saving for the future. The act of saving is a deliberate, well-thought-out activity designed to preserve the value of money, ensure liquidity, and earn a competitive rate of return. Almost by definition, *smart savers are smart investors.* They regard saving as more than putting loose change into a piggy bank; rather, they recognize the importance of saving and know that savings must be managed as astutely as any security.

After all, what we normally think of as "savings" is really a form of investment—a short-term, highly liquid investment—that is subject to minimum risk. Establishing and maintaining an ongoing savings program is a vital element of personal financial planning. To get the most from your savings, however, you must understand your savings options and how different savings vehicles pay interest.

STARTING YOUR SAVINGS PROGRAM

Careful financial planning dictates that you hold a portion of your assets to meet liquidity needs and accumulate wealth. Although opinions differ as to how much you should keep as liquid reserves, the consensus is that most families should have an amount equal to 3 to 6 months of after-tax income. Therefore, if you take home $2,000 a month, you should have between $6,000 and $12,000 in liquid reserves. If your employer has a strong salary continuation program covering extended periods of illness, or if you have a sizable line of credit available, the lower figure is probably adequate. If you lack one or both of these, however, the larger amount is more appropriate.

A specific savings plan must be developed to accumulate funds. Saving should be a priority item in your budget, not something that occurs only when income happens to exceed expenditures. Some people manage this by arranging to have savings directly withheld from their paychecks. Not only do direct deposit arrangements help your savings effort, they also enable your funds to earn interest sooner. Or you can transfer funds regularly to other financial institutions such as commercial banks, savings and loans, savings banks, credit unions, and even mutual funds. But the key to success is to establish a *regular* pattern of saving.

You should make it a practice to set aside an amount you can comfortably afford *each month,* even if it is only $50 to $100. (Keep in mind that $100 monthly deposits earning 4 percent interest will grow to more than $36,500 in 20 years.) Exhibit 4.5 lists 10 strategies you can use to increase your savings and build a nest egg.

EXHIBIT 4.5

Ten Strategies to Build Your Nest Egg

Having trouble getting your savings program started? Here are 10 strategies to begin building your nest egg:

1. *Make saving a priority* when you pay your bills. Write a check to yourself each month as if it were another invoice and deposit it in a savings account.
2. *Take a hard look at your spending habits* for places to cut back. Bring your lunch to work or school. Comparison shop. Carpool. Cut back on trips to the ATM.
3. *Set up a payroll deduction* and ask your employer to deduct money from your paycheck and have it deposited directly into your savings. It's painless because you never see the money in your checking account.
4. *Banking your raise* is a perfect way to save. Keep your lifestyle where it is and put the difference in your savings account.
5. *Work a little harder* and avoid wasting time watching too much TV. Spend another 5 hours a week working and deposit the cash into your savings account.
6. *Keep making those loan payments,* and you'll feel rich when those obligations finally end. But keep writing those checks—only now it's for your savings account.
7. *Keep an eye on your returns* and know what kind of return you are getting on your savings account. If your bank is only paying you 2 or 3 percent, you might be able to add another percentage point or two by moving your money to an asset management account at a brokerage firm.
8. *Reinvest interest and dividends*—you won't miss the money and your account will grow more rapidly. If you have a savings account, make sure the interest is reinvested rather than paid into your non-interest-bearing checking account. If you own stocks or mutual funds, virtually all offer dividend reinvestment plans.
9. *Set up a retirement plan* to make sure you contribute to your company's retirement program. Your contributions are tax deductible, and many employers match your contributions. Check out available individual retirement account options such as IRAs and 401(k)s (See Chapter 14).
10. *Splurge once in a while*—the boost you get will make saving money a little easier. All work and no play makes for a dull life so once you've reached a savings goal take some money and enjoy yourself.

You must also decide which savings products best meet your needs. Many savers prefer to keep their emergency funds in a regular savings or money market deposit account at an institution with federal deposit insurance. Although these accounts are safe, convenient,

Money in Action

There's Always a Place for Cash in Your Portfolio

If you're a college student just starting to build your savings you're most likely going to keep your money in a bank, perhaps one with a branch on campus, or the financial institution that provided your student loan. Right now, your choices for saving may seem limited, but in a few short years you may find yourself with a home, cars, paid-off student loans, and an investment portfolio of stocks, bonds, and mutual funds. Will there still be a place for cash savings? The answer is yes, although its role will be different.

You should, of course, continue to allocate 3 to 6 months' income to an "emergency fund" which is immediately accessible. But rather than put *all* your savings into a short-term certificate of deposit or money market mutual fund, you should increasingly allocate your money to investments with long-term growth potential, such as stocks and mutual funds. During a 20-year period, the stock market will provide you with a much higher return than any you could get from a bank. Remember, however, that stocks are volatile, and investment professionals recommend that money you invest in the stock market should remain there for many years.

If you need money for short-term needs, such as buying a house or car or paying for education, the money should be taken out of the stock market gradually and put into short-term savings. After all, you want to be sure the money will be there when you need it. Short-term savings, whether in the form of certificates of deposit, U.S. Treasury bills, or money market mutual funds, have a big advantage: They don't go down in value.

True, you won't make a fortune, but there are more options for short-term investments today. Take CDs, for instance. Chances are you can find better rates than those offered by your local bank. Because each percentage point means $100 a year on a $10,000 investment, you should do some research, but don't spend too much time searching for that extra fraction of a percent.

Keep in mind that if you're buying a CD and need to access your money in a matter of months,

...continued on next page

and highly liquid, they tend to pay relatively low rates of interest. Other important considerations include your risk preference, the length of time you can leave your money on deposit, and the level of current and anticipated interest rates.

Suppose that 1 year from now you plan to use $5,000 of your savings to make the down payment on a new car, and you expect interest rates to drop during that period. You should lock in today's higher rate by purchasing a 1-year certificate of deposit (CD). On the other hand, if you are unsure about when you will actually need the funds or believe that interest rates will rise, you are better off with an MMDA or MMMF because their rates change with market conditions, and you can access your funds at any time without penalty.

Short-term interest rates generally fluctuate more than long-term rates, so it pays to monitor interest rate movements, shop around for the best rates, and place your funds in savings vehicles consistent with your needs. If short-term interest rates drop, you won't be able to reinvest the proceeds from maturing CDs at comparable rates. You will need to reevaluate your savings plans and may choose to move funds into other savings vehicles with higher rates of interest, but greater risk.

Many financial planning experts recommend keeping a minimum of 10 to 25 percent of your investment portfolio in savings-type instruments in addition to the 3 to 6 months of liquid reserves noted earlier. Thus someone with $50,000 in investments should probably have a minimum of $5,000 to $10,000—and possibly more—in such short-term vehicles as MMDAs, MMMFs, or CDs. At times, the amount invested in short-term vehicles could far exceed the recommended minimum, approaching 50 percent or more of the portfolio. This generally depends on expected interest rate movements. If interest rates are relatively high, and you expect them to fall, you would invest in long-term vehicles in order to lock in the attractive interest rates. On the other hand, if rates are relatively low and you expect them to rise, you might invest in short-term vehicles so you can more quickly reinvest when rates do rise.

Earning Interest on Your Money

Interest earned is the reward for putting your money in a savings account or short-term investment vehicle, and it is important for you to understand how that interest is earned. But unfortunately, even in the relatively simple world of savings, all interest rates are not created equal.

The Effects of Compounding

Basically, interest can be earned in one of two ways. First, some short-term investments are sold on a *discount basis.* This means that the security is sold for a price that is lower than its redemption value; the difference is the amount of interest earned. Treasury bills, for instance, are issued on a discount basis. Another way to earn interest on short-term investments is by *direct payment,* which occurs when interest is applied to a regular savings account. Although this is a simple process, determining the actual rate of return can be complicated.

compound interest When interest earned in each subsequent period is determined by applying the nominal (stated) rate of interest to the sum of the initial deposit and the interest earned in each prior period.

simple interest Interest that is paid only on the initial amount of the deposit.

nominal (stated) rate of interest The promised rate of interest paid on a savings deposit or charged on a loan.

effective rate of interest The annual rate of return that is *actually earned* (or *charged*) during the period the funds are held (or borrowed).

The first complication relates to the method used to arrive at the amount and rate of **compound interest** earned annually: You have probably read or seen advertisements by banks or other depository institutions touting the fact that they pay daily, rather than annual, interest. To understand what this means, consider the following example. Assume that you invest $1,000 in a savings account advertised as paying annual **simple interest** at a rate of 5 percent. With simple interest, the interest is paid only on the initial amount of the deposit. This means that if you leave the $1,000 on deposit for 1 year, you will earn $50 in interest, and the account balance will total $1,050 at year end. Note that in this case the **nominal (stated) rate of interest** (the promised rate of interest paid on a savings deposit) is 5 percent.

it doesn't make sense to sign up for one with a 5-year maturity; 6 months would be a better choice. In addition, you can buy CDs through most big brokerage firms; unlike CDs sold through banks, they are negotiable so you can cash them in early without penalty. Because they originate at banks, they are insured. You can also buy CDs online through BankDirect.com (**http://www.bankdirect.com**) and eBank (**http://www.ebank.com**), which offer both CDs and money market deposit accounts.

As your net worth grows, a smaller and smaller percentage of your assets will be held in cash. The reason not to keep a big percentage of your net worth in cash savings is that you risk being left in the dust by inflation and taxes. Even if you can get 5 percent in a cash savings account, you'll lose up to 2 percent to taxes and the rest to inflation.

Critical Thinking Questions

1. Why is it important to keep some cash available?
2. How can you satisfy your liquidity needs while at the same time earning interest on your savings?
3. How do people's saving needs change over time?

Sources: Ken Brown, "The Best Short-Term Investments," *Smart Money,* August 1997, p. 79; Jonathan Burton, "Cash Ain't Trash," *Bloomberg Personal,* May/June 1997, p. 106; Kevin Demarrais, "T-Bills, CDs Are Wise Short-Term Investments," *The Record* (Bergen County, NJ), June 18, 2000, p. B1; Ann Coleman, "Why Short-Term Savings?" The Motley Fool at **http://www.fool.com**, September 2, 2003.

In contrast, the **effective rate of interest** is the annual rate of return that is *actually earned* (or *charged*) during the period the funds are held. You can calculate it with the following formula:

$$\text{Effective rate of interest} = \frac{\text{Amount of interest earned during the year}}{\text{Amount of money invested or deposited}}$$

In our example, because $50 was earned during the year on an investment of $1,000, the effective rate is $50/$1,000 or 5 percent, which is the same as the nominal rate of interest. (Note that in the above formula it is interest earned during the *year* that matters; if you wanted to calculate the effective rate of interest on an account held for 6 months, you would double the amount of interest earned.)

But suppose that you can invest your funds elsewhere at a 5 percent rate, *compounded semiannually.* Because interest is applied to your account at midyear, you will earn *interest on interest* for the last 6 months of the year, thereby increasing the total interest earned for the year. The actual dollar earnings are determined as follows:

$$\begin{aligned} &\text{First 6 months' interest} &&= \$1{,}000 \times 0.05 \times 6/12 = \$25.00 \\ &\text{Second 6 months' interest} &&= \$1{,}025 \times 0.05 \times 6/12 = \$25.63 \\ &\text{Total annual interest} &&= \underline{\underline{\$50.63}} \end{aligned}$$

Interest is generated on a larger investment in the second half of the year because the amount of money on deposit has increased by the amount of interest earned in the first half year ($25). Although the nominal rate on this account is still 5 percent, the effective rate is 5.06 percent ($50.63/$1,000). As you may have guessed, *the more frequently interest is compounded, the greater the effective rate for any given nominal rate.* These relationships are shown for a sample of interest rates and compounding periods in Exhibit 4.6. Note, for example, that with a 7 percent nominal rate, daily compounding adds one-fourth of a percent to the total return—not a trivial amount.

EXHIBIT 4.6

The Magic of Compounding

The effective rate of interest you earn on a savings account will exceed the nominal (stated) rate of interest if interest is compounded more than once a year (as are most savings and interest-paying accounts).

Nominal	Effective Rate				
Rate	Annually	Semiannually	Quarterly	Monthly	Daily
3%	3.00%	3.02%	3.03%	3.04%	3.05%
4	4.00	4.04	4.06	4.07	4.08
5	5.00	5.06	5.09	5.12	5.13
6	6.00	6.09	6.14	6.17	6.18
7	7.00	7.12	7.19	7.23	7.25
8	8.00	8.16	8.24	8.30	8.33
9	9.00	9.20	9.31	9.38	9.42
10	10.00	10.25	10.38	10.47	10.52
11	11.00	11.30	11.46	11.57	11.62
12	12.00	12.36	12.55	12.68	12.74

You can calculate the interest compounded daily by using a financial calculator similar to that described in Appendix E. Let's assume you want to invest $1,000 at 7 percent interest compounded daily. How much money will you have in the account at the end of the year? Exhibit 4.7 shows the steps to follow.

Compound Interest Equals Future Value

Compound interest is the same as the *future value* concept introduced in Chapter 2. You can use the procedures described there to find out how much an investment or deposit will grow over time at a compounded rate of interest. For example, using the future value formula and the future value factor from Appendix A (see Chapter 2), you can determine how much $1,000 will be worth in 4 years if it is deposited into a savings account that pays 5 percent interest per year compounded annually like this:

$$\text{Future value} = \text{Amount deposited} \times \text{Future value factor}$$
$$= \$1{,}000 \times 1.216$$
$$= \underline{\underline{\$1{,}216}}$$

EXHIBIT 4.7

Using a Financial Calculator to Find Interest Compounded Daily

How much will you have at the end of 1 year if you invest $1,000 at 7 percent, compounded daily?

Step 1: Enter 1000 and press **PV**.

Step 2: Enter the number of compounding periods, 365, and press **N**.

Step 3: Convert annual interest to a daily rate: press 7 divided by 365; then press **I** for the interest rate.

Step 4: Calculate the account value at the end of year 1: press **CPT** and then **FV**.

The result should be 1072.50 (that is, $1,072.50). This is clearly greater than the $1,070 that annual compounding would return. The effective interest rate would have been 7.25 percent ($72.50 interest earned/$1,000 initially invested), as noted in Exhibit 4.6.

You can use the same basic procedure to find the future value of an *annuity*, except you would use the future value annuity factor from Appendix B (see Chapter 2). For instance, if you put $1,000 a year into a savings account that pays 5 percent per year compounded annually, in 4 years you will have:

$$\begin{aligned} \text{Future value} &= \text{Amount deposited yearly} \times \text{Future value annuity factor} \\ &= \$1{,}000 \times 4.310 \\ &= \underline{\underline{\$4{,}310}} \end{aligned}$$

A Variety of Ways to Save

During the past decade or so there has been a tremendous proliferation of savings and short-term investment vehicles, particularly for the individual of modest means. As the *Money in Action* box on page 150 shows, there will always be a place in your portfolio for cash savings.

smart.sites

If you are not satisfied with the CD rate at your local bank, go to Bankrate.com (**http://www.bankrate.com**). You will find not only the highest rates on CDs and savings accounts nationwide but also the checking account and ATM fees at banks in your city.

certificate of deposit (CD) A type of savings instrument issued by certain financial institutions in exchange for a deposit; typically requires a minimum deposit and has a maturity ranging from 7 days to as long as 7 or more years.

Today, investors can choose from savings accounts, money market deposit accounts, money market mutual funds, NOW accounts, certificates of deposit, U.S. Treasury bills, Series EE bonds, and asset management accounts. We examined several of these savings vehicles earlier in this chapter. Now let's look at the three remaining types of deposits and securities.

Certificates of Deposit

Certificates of deposit (CDs) differ from the savings instruments discussed earlier in this chapter in that CD funds (except for CDs purchased through brokerage firms) must remain on deposit for a specified period, which can range from 7 days to as long as 7 or more years. Although it is possible to withdraw funds prior to maturity, an interest penalty usually makes withdrawal somewhat costly. Although the bank or other depository institution is free to charge whatever penalty it likes, most require forfeiture of some interest. Since October of 1983, banks, S&Ls, and other depository institutions have been free to offer any rate and maturity CD they wish. As a result, a wide variety of CDs are offered by most banks, depository institutions, and other financial institutions such as brokerage firms. Most pay higher rates for larger deposits and longer periods of time. CDs are convenient to buy and hold because they offer attractive and highly competitive yields plus federal deposit insurance protection.

U.S. Treasury bill (T-bill) A short-term (3-month or 6-month maturity) debt instrument issued by the U.S. Treasury in the ongoing process of funding the national debt.

U.S. Treasury Bills

The **U.S. Treasury bill (T-bill)** is considered the ultimate safe haven for savings and investments. T-bills are issued by the U.S. Treasury as part of its ongoing process of funding the national debt. They are sold on a discount basis in minimum denominations of $1,000 and are issued with 3-month (13-week) or 6-month (26-week) maturities. The bills are auctioned off every Monday. Backed by the full faith and credit of the U.S. government, T-bills pay an attractive and safe return that is free from state and local income taxes.

T-bills are almost as liquid as cash because they can be sold at any time (in a very active secondary market) without any interest penalty. However, should you have to sell before maturity, you may lose some money on your investment if interest rates have risen, and you will have to pay a broker's fee as well. Treasury bills pay interest on a *discount basis* and thus are different from other savings or short-term investment vehicles—that is, their interest is equal to the difference between the purchase price paid and their stated value at maturity. For example, if you paid $980 for a bill that will be worth $1,000 at maturity, you will earn $20 in interest ($1,000 − $980).

An individual investor may purchase T-bills directly by participating in the weekly Treasury auctions or indirectly through a commercial bank or a security dealer who buys bills for investors on a commission basis. In addition, T-bills may now be purchased over the Internet or by using a touch-tone phone (call 800-722-2678 and follow the interactive menu to complete transactions).

smart.sites

At the T-bill page of the Bureau of the Public Debt Online, **http://www.publicdebt.treas.gov/sec/sec.htm**, you can learn about T-bills and then buy them online.

Outstanding Treasury bills can also be purchased in the secondary market through banks or dealers. This approach gives the investor a much wider selection of maturities from which to choose, ranging from less than a week to as long as 6 months.

Financial Road Sign

How Much Interest Will You Earn?

Before you open a deposit account, you should investigate the factors that determine the amount of interest you will earn on your savings or interest-bearing checking account:

- **Frequency of compounding:** The more often interest is compounded, the higher your return.
- **Balance on which interest is paid:** For balances that qualify to earn interest, most banks now use the *actual balance,* or *day of deposit to day of withdrawal,* method. The actual balance method is the most accurate and fairest because it pays depositors interest on all funds on deposit for the actual amount of time they remain there.
- **Interest rate paid:** As mentioned earlier, the *Truth-in-Savings Act* standardized the way that banks calculate the rate of interest they pay on deposit accounts. This makes it easy to compare each bank's *annual percentage yield (APY)* and to choose the bank offering the highest APY.

Series EE Bonds

Series EE bond
A savings bond issued in various denominations by the U.S. Treasury.

Although issued by the U.S. Treasury on a discount basis, and free of state and local income taxes, **Series EE bonds** are quite different from T-bills. Savings bonds are *accrual-type securities,* which means that interest is paid when they are cashed in or before maturity, rather than periodically during their lives. The government does make Series HH bonds available through the exchange of Series E or Series EE bonds; they have a 10-year maturity and are available in denominations of $500 to $10,000. Unlike EE bonds, HH bonds are issued at their full face value and pay interest semiannually at the current fixed rate.

Series EE bonds are backed by the full faith and credit of the U.S. government and can be replaced without charge in case of loss, theft, or destruction. Now also designated as "Patriot Bonds," in honor of September 11, 2001, they present an opportunity for all Americans to contribute to the government's war effort and save for their own futures as well. You can purchase them at banks or other depository institutions, or through payroll deduction plans. Issued in denominations from $50 through $10,000, their purchase price is a uniform 50 percent of the face amount (thus a $100 bond will cost $50 and be worth $100 at maturity).

The actual maturity date on EE bonds is unspecified because the issues pay a variable rate of interest. The higher the rate of interest being paid, the shorter the time it takes for the bond to accrue from its discounted purchase price to its maturity value. Bonds can be redeemed any time after the first 6 months, although redeeming EE bonds in less than 5 years results in a penalty of the last 3 months of interest earned. Interest rates are calculated every 6 months (in May and November) and change with prevailing Treasury security market yields. To obtain current rates on Series EE bonds, call your bank, call 800-487-2663, or use the Web link for the savings bond site.

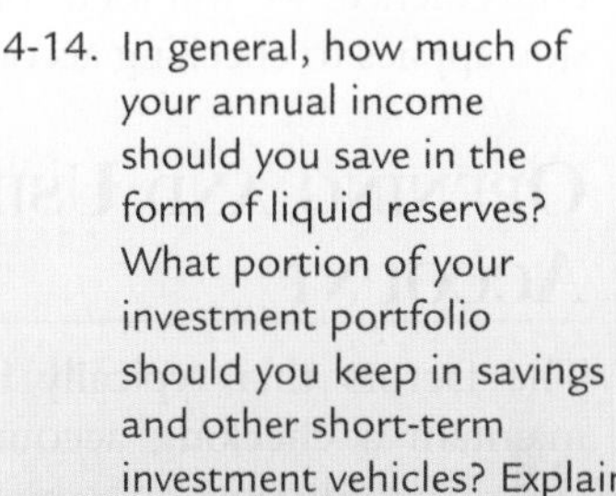

4-14. In general, how much of your annual income should you save in the form of liquid reserves? What portion of your investment portfolio should you keep in savings and other short-term investment vehicles? Explain.

4-15. Define and distinguish between the *nominal rate of interest* and the *effective rate of interest.* Explain why a savings and loan association that pays a nominal rate of 4.5 percent interest, compounded daily, actually pays an effective rate of 4.6 percent.

4-16. What factors determine the amount of interest you will earn on a deposit account? Which combination provides the best return?

4-17. Briefly describe the basic features of each of the following savings vehicles: (a) certificates of deposit, (b) U.S. Treasury bills, and (c) Series EE bonds.

smart.sites
Everything you always wanted to know about U.S. Savings Bonds—how to buy them, current rates, and a pricing calculator for bonds you own—is at **http://www.savingsbonds.gov**.

In addition to being exempt from state and local taxes, Series EE bonds provide their holders with an appealing tax twist: *Savers need not report interest earned on their federal tax returns until the bonds are redeemed.* Although interest can be reported annually (for example, when the bonds are held in the name of a child who has limited interest income), most investors choose to defer it. A second attractive tax feature allows partial or complete tax avoidance of EE bond earnings when proceeds are used to pay education expenses, such as college tuition, for the bond purchaser, a spouse, or an other IRS-defined dependent. To qualify, the purchaser must be age 24 or older, and for 2003, have adjusted gross income below $73,500 for single filers and $117,750 for married couples. (These maximum income levels are adjusted annually.)

MAINTAINING A CHECKING ACCOUNT

LG6

By the time Ben Adams started college he had a thriving car detailing business that earned him several hundred dollars per week. Sometimes his customers paid in advance, sometimes after the fact, and sometimes they forgot to pay him at all. But by depositing each check or cash payment into his checking account, Ben was able to keep track of his earnings without complicated bookkeeping. A checking account is one of the most useful cash management tools you can have, providing a safe and convenient way to hold money and streamlining point-of-sale purchases, debt payments, and other basic transactions. You can have regular or interest-paying checking accounts at commercial banks, S & Ls, savings banks, credit unions, and even brokerage houses through asset management accounts. For convenience, we will focus on commercial bank checking accounts, although our discussion applies to checking accounts maintained at other types of financial institutions as well.

Opening and Using Your Checking Account

The factors that typically influence the choice of where to maintain a checking account are convenience, services, and cost. Many people choose a bank solely on the basis of convenience factors: business hours, location, number of drive-in windows, and number and location of branch offices and ATMs. Ease of access is obviously an important consideration because most people prefer to bank near home or work. Although services differ from bank to bank, today most banks offer several types of accounts: debit, ATM, credit cards, and loans. Depending on its size, a bank may also offer online and telephone banking and bill-paying services, safe-deposit box rental, provision for direct deposits and withdrawals, and mutual-fund sales.

Once you determine the banking services you need, you should evaluate the offerings of conveniently located, federally insured financial institutions. In addition to convenience and safety, consider interest rates, types of accounts (including special accounts that combine such features as credit cards, free checks, and reduced fees), structure and level of fees and charges, and quality of customer service.

Financial Road Sign

Where Will You Bank?

It is a good idea to research what each bank offers before opening a checking account. Here are some important factors to consider before choosing a bank:

1. Convenience: bank location, disability access and services, hours
2. Minimum opening balance
3. Interest: Does it pay interest on the balance?
4. Minimum balance required before incurring fees
5. Electronic (Internet, ATM, pay-by-phone) services
6. Check-clearing policies
7. Pricing: account charges, fees for checks, services, or problems
8. Other useful services: ability to link with savings, charge cards, mutual-fund sales
9. Charges for statements and returned checks
10. Personal relationship: courtesy, support services

Things to ignore:

1. Advertising campaigns and promotional offers (forget the cookbook)
2. Interest-calculating methods on interest-bearing accounts (usually too insignificant to matter)
3. Prestige (image isn't important, service is)

Source: "Banking Basics: Checking Account Checklist," *Consumer Action*, **http://www.consumeraction.org**.

The Cost of a Checking Account

Bank service charges have increased sharply due to deregulation and the growth of interest-paying checking accounts. Today few, if any, banks and other depository institutions allow unlimited free check-writing privileges. Most banks levy monthly and per-check fees when your checking account balance drops below a stipulated minimum, and some may charge for checking no matter how large a balance you carry in your account.

Usually, you must maintain a minimum balance of $500 to $1,000 or more to avoid service charges. Although some banks use the *average monthly* balance in an account to determine whether to levy a service charge, most use the *daily* balance procedure. This means that if your account should happen to fall just $1 below the minimum balance *just once* during the month, you will be hit with the full service charge—even if you keep an average balance that is three times the minimum requirement.

Service charges take two forms: (1) a base service charge of, say, $7.50 a month, and (2) additional charges of, say, 25 cents for each check you write, and 10 cents for each ATM or bank-by-phone transaction. Using these fees as an illustration, assume you write 20 checks and make seven ATM transactions in a given month. If your balance falls below the minimum, you will have to pay a service charge of $7.50 + (20 × $.25) + (7 × $.10) = $13.20.

In addition to the service charges levied on checking accounts, banks have increased most other check-related charges and raised the minimum balances required for free checking and waivers of specified fees. The charge on a returned check can be as high as $15 to $20, and stop payment orders typically cost $10 to $25. Some banks charge fees for ATM or bank-by-phone transactions that exceed a specified number. Most also charge for using the ATM of another bank that is a member of the same network. It is not surprising that smart consumers use cost as the single most important variable in choosing where to set up a checking account.

Individual or Joint Account

Two people wishing to open a checking account may do so in one of three ways:

1. They can each open individual checking accounts (on which the other cannot write checks)
2. They can open a joint account that requires both signatures on all checks
3. They can open a joint account that allows either one to write checks (the most common type of joint account).

One advantage of the joint account over two individual accounts is lower service charges. In addition, the account has rights of survivorship, which, in the case of a married couple, means that if one spouse dies, the surviving spouse, after fulfilling a specified legal requirement, can draw checks on the account. If account owners are treated as tenants in common rather than having rights of survivorship, the survivor gets only his or her share of the account. Thus, when opening a joint account, it is important to specify the rights preferred.

General Checking Account Procedures

After you select the bank that meets your needs and the type of account you want, it's a simple matter to actually open the account. The application form is straightforward, asking for basic personal information such as name, date of birth, Social Security number, address, phone, and place of employment. You will also have to provide identification, sign signature cards, and make an initial deposit. The bank will give you a supply of checks to use until your personalized checks arrive.

Once you open a checking account, you should follow certain basic procedures:

- Always write checks in ink.
- Include the name of the person being paid, the date, and the amount of the check—written in both numerals and words for accuracy.
- Sign the check the same way as the signature card you filled out when you opened the account.
- Note the check's purpose on the check—usually on the line provided in the lower-left corner. This information is very helpful for both budgeting and tax purposes.

checkbook ledger
A ledger, provided with a supply of checks, used to maintain accurate records of all checking account transactions.

Make sure to enter all checking account transactions—checks written, deposits, point-of-sale debit purchases, ATM transactions, and preauthorized automatic payments and deposits—in the **checkbook ledger** provided with your supply of checks.

Then, subtract the amount of each check, debit card purchase, ATM cash withdrawal, or payment, and add the amount of each deposit to the previous balance to keep track of your current account balance. Good transaction records and an accurate balance prevent overdrawing the account.

Include with each deposit a deposit slip (generally included with your checks and also available at your bank) listing the currency, coins, and checks being deposited. List checks by the *transit I.D. number* printed on the check, usually at the top right. You should also properly endorse all checks that you are going to deposit. Federal regulations require your endorsement to be made in black or blue ink, within 1½ inches of the check's trailing edge (left end of the check when viewed from the front) so as not to interfere with bank endorsements. If you don't comply, you'll still get your money but it may take longer.

To protect against possible loss of endorsed checks, it is common practice to use a special endorsement, such as "Pay to the order of XYZ Bank," or a restrictive endorsement, such as "For deposit only." If the way your name is written on the check differs from the way that you signed the signature card, you should sign your correct signature below your endorsement. To further ensure that the deposit is properly entered into your account, write your account number below your endorsement.

When you deposit checks, you may encounter a delay in funds availability due to the time required for them to clear. To avoid overdrawing your account, you should know your bank's "hold" policy on deposits, which are capped by federal maximum funds-availability delays. It generally takes between 1 and 5 business days for funds to become available. For example, on a check drawn on another local bank, funds must be made available no later than the second business day after deposit. An out-of-town check, however, may take up to 5 business days to clear. Longer holds—up to 9 business days—can be applied by banks under special circumstances, such as larger amounts over $5,000 being deposited in a given account within 1 day, or when the depositor has repeatedly overdrawn his or her account within the immediately preceding 6 months.

Overdrafts

When a check is written for an amount greater than the current account balance, the result is an **overdraft**. If the overdraft is proven intentional, the bank can initiate legal proceedings against the account holder. The action taken by a bank on an overdraft depends on the strength of its relationship with the account holder and the amount involved. In many cases, the bank stamps the overdrawn check with the words "insufficient balance (or funds)" and returns it to the party to whom it was written. This is often called a "bounced check." The account holder is notified of this action, and the holder's bank deducts a penalty fee of as much as $15 to $20 or more from his or her checking account. In addition, the depositor of a "bad check" may be charged as much as $10 to $15 by his or her bank, which explains why merchants typically charge customers who give them bad checks $10 to $20 or more and often refuse to accept future checks from them.

overdraft The result of writing a check for an amount greater than the current account balance.

When you have a strong relationship with your bank or arrange **overdraft protection**, the bank will pay a check that overdraws the account. In cases where overdraft protection has not been prearranged but the bank pays the check, the account holder is usually notified by the bank and charged a penalty fee for the inconvenience. However, the check does not bounce, and the check writer's creditworthiness is not damaged.

overdraft protection An arrangement between the account holder and the depository institution wherein the institution automatically pays a check that overdraws the account.

There are several ways to arrange overdraft protection. Many banks offer an overdraft line of credit, which automatically extends a loan to cover the amount of an overdraft. In most cases, however, the loans are made only in specified increments, such as $50 or $100, and interest (or a fee) is levied against the loan amount, not the actual amount of the overdraft. This can be an expensive form of protection, particularly if you do not promptly repay such a loan.

For example, if you had a $110 overdraft and the bank made overdraft loans in $100 increments, it would automatically deposit $200 in your account. If the bank charged 12 percent annually (or 1 percent per month) and you repaid the loan within a month, you would incur total interest of $2 ([$200 × 12 percent]/12). But remember, you paid interest on $90 ($200 − $110) you didn't need, and the annualized rate of interest on this overdraft loan is *21.8 percent* ([$2/$110] × 12)!

Another way to cover overdrafts is with an *automatic transfer program,* which automatically transfers funds from your savings account into your checking account in the event of an overdraft. Under this program, some banks charge both an annual fee and a fee on each transfer. Of course, the best form of overdraft protection is to employ good cash management techniques and regularly balance your checking account.

Stopping Payment

stop payment An order made by an account holder instructing the depository institution to refuse payment on an already issued check.

Occasionally, it is necessary to **stop payment** on a check that has been issued because (1) checks or a checkbook has been either lost or stolen, (2) a good or service paid for by check is found to be faulty (some states prohibit you from stopping payment on faulty goods or services), or (3) a check is issued as part of a contract that is not carried out. (Note that if you lose your checkbook for any reason, you are probably better off closing the account and opening another rather than stopping payment on a large number of checks.)

To stop payment on a check, you must notify the bank and fill out a form indicating the check number and date, amount, and the name of the person to whom it was written. You can initiate stop payment orders online or by phone. Once you place a stop payment order, the bank refuses payment on the affected check, and the check will be rejected if another bank presents it in the check-clearing process. Banks typically charge a fee ranging from $10 to $25 to stop payment on a check.

Monthly Statements

Once a month, your bank will provide a statement containing an itemized listing of all transactions in your checking account (checks written, ATM transactions, debit purchases, automatic payments, and deposits made). Also included are bank service charges and interest earned (see James C. Morrison's May 2004 bank statement shown in Exhibit 4.8). Some banks include your original canceled checks with your bank statement, although as we move closer to a "paperless society" most are abandoning this practice. Banks that do not return canceled checks will provide photocopies of them on request, generally for a fee. Many banks now let you view canceled checks online, free of charge. It is important to review your monthly bank statement to verify the accuracy of your account records and reconcile differences between the statement balance and the balance shown in your checkbook ledger. The monthly statement is also a valuable source of information for your tax records.

account reconciliation The process of verifying the accuracy of one's checking account records in light of the bank's records as reflected in the bank statement, which contains an itemized listing of all transactions within the checking account.

Account Reconciliation

You should reconcile your bank account as soon as possible after receiving your monthly statement. The **account reconciliation** process, or *balancing the checkbook,* can uncover errors in recording checks or deposits, in addition or subtraction, and, occasionally, in the bank's processing of a check. It can also help you avoid overdrafts by forcing you to verify your account balance monthly. Assuming that neither you nor the bank has made any errors, discrepancies between your checkbook ledger account balance and your bank statement can be attributed to one of four factors.

1. Checks that you have written, ATM withdrawals, debit purchases, or other automatic payments subtracted from your checkbook balance have not yet been received and processed by your bank and therefore remain outstanding.

EXHIBIT 4.8

A Bank Statement

Each month you receive a statement from your bank or depository financial institution that summarizes the month's transactions and shows your latest account balance. This sample statement for May 2004 for James C. Morrison not only shows the checks that have been paid but also lists all ATM transactions, point-of-sale transactions using his ATM card (the Interlink payments at Lucky Stores), and direct payroll deposits.

YOUR BANK #240
P.O. BOX 516 ANY CITY, USA 90000-0000

JAMES C. MORRISON
1765 SHERIDAN DRIVE N
YOUR CITY, STATE 12091 21

CALL (800) 222-0000
24 HOURS/DAY, 7 DAYS/WEEK
FOR ASSISTANCE WITH
YOUR ACCOUNT.

PAGE 1 OF 1 THIS STATEMENT COVERS: 4/30/04 THROUGH 5/29/04

PREMIUM ACCOUNT 0123-45678

SUMMARY

PREVIOUS BALANCE	473.68	MINIMUM BALANCE	21.78
DEPOSITS	1,302.83+		
WITHDRAWALS	1,689.02-		
SERVICE CHARGES	7.50-		
DIRECT DEPOSIT DISCOUNT	1.00+		
NEW BALANCE	80.99		

CHECKS AND WITHDRAWALS

CHECK	DATE PAID	AMOUNT	CHECK	DATE PAID	AMOUNT
203	5/01	10.00	213	5/08	40.00
204	4/30	15.00	214	5/09	9.58
205	5/10	635.00	215	5/20	66.18
206	5/08	25.00	216	5/20	64.92
207	5/07	19.00	217	5/21	25.03
208	5/07	50.00	218	5/21	37.98
209	5/08	15.00	219	5/22	35.00
210	5/10	83.00	220	5/22	105.00
211	5/10	10.00	222*	5/22	100.00
212	5/08	70.00	223	5/21	40.00
			224	5/29	40.82

	PREMIUM ACCOUNT FEE LESS $1.00 DISCOUNT	4/30	6.50
ATM TRANSACTIONS	INTERLINK PURCHASE #572921 ON 04/30 AT LUCKY STORE NO 043	5/01	50.00
	WITHDRAWAL #08108 AT 00165A ON 05/04	5/06	20.00
	INTERLINK PURCHASE #807409 ON 05/11 AT LUCKY STORE NO 056	5/13	12.51
	WITHDRAWAL #01015 AT 00240C ON 05/17	5/17	20.00
	WITHDRAWAL #04792 AT 00167C ON 05/20	5/20	20.00
	WITHDRAWAL #04386 AT 00240D ON 05/21	5/21	40.00
	INTERLINK PURCHASE #880318 ON 05/28 AT LUCKY STORE #043	5/29	30.00

DEPOSITS		DATE POSTED	AMOUNT
	AVS RNT CAR SYST PAYROLL 62 000000035382	5/03	618.69
	AVS RNT CAR SYST PAYROLL 62 000000035382	5/17	83.39
	AVS RNT CAR SYST PAYROLL 62 000000035382	5/17	600.75

ATM LOCATIONS USED

00165A: 249 PRIMROSE RD, ANY CITY, USA
00240C: 490 BROADWAY, ANY CITY, USA
00167C: 1145 BROADWAY, ANY CITY, USA
00240D: 490 BROADWAY, ANY CITY, USA

2. Deposits that you have made and added to your checkbook balance have not yet been credited to your account.
3. Any service (activity) charges levied on your account by the bank have not yet been deducted from your checkbook balance.
4. Interest earned on your account (if it is a NOW or an MMDA account) has not yet been added to your checkbook balance.

Exhibit 4.9 lists the steps to reconcile your checkbook each month.

The reverse side of your bank statement usually provides a form for reconciling your account along with step-by-step instructions. Worksheet 4.1 includes an account reconciliation form that James Morrison completed for the month of May 2004 using the reconciliation procedures we have described. You can use the form to reconcile either regular or interest-paying checking accounts such as NOWs or MMDAs.

EXHIBIT 4.9

Make that Checkbook Balance!

Take the following steps to reconcile your account:

1. On receipt of your bank statement, arrange all canceled checks in ascending numerical order based on their sequence numbers or issuance dates. (Skip this step if your bank does not return canceled checks.)
2. Compare each check or its bank statement information with the corresponding entry in your checkbook ledger to make sure that no recording errors exist. Check off in your checkbook ledger each check and any other withdrawals such as from ATMs, point-of-sale debit transactions, or automatic payments.
3. List the checks and other deductions (ATM withdrawals or debit purchases) still *outstanding*—that is, those deducted in your checkbook but not returned with your bank statement (see Step 2). Total their amount.
4. Compare the deposits indicated on the statement with deposits shown in your checkbook ledger. Total the amount of deposits still outstanding—that is, those shown in your checkbook ledger but not yet received by the bank. Be sure to include all automatic deposits and deposits made at ATMs in your calculations.
5. *Subtract* the total amount of checks outstanding (from Step 3) from your bank statement balance, and *add* to this balance the amount of outstanding deposits (from Step 4). The resulting amount is your *adjusted bank balance.*
6. Deduct the amount of any bank service charges from your checkbook ledger balance, and add any interest earned to that balance. Make sure that you include all service charges for the period, including those for any returned checks, stop payments, or new checks ordered. The resulting amount is your *new checkbook balance.* This amount should equal your adjusted bank balance (from Step 5). If it does not, you should check all addition and subtraction in your checkbook ledger because you have probably made an error.

SPECIAL TYPES OF CHECKS

In some circumstances sellers of goods or services may not accept personal checks because they can't be absolutely sure that the check is good. This is common for large purchases or when the buyer's bank is not located in the same area where the purchase is being made. A form of check that guarantees payment may be required instead: cashier's checks, traveler's checks, or certified checks.

worksheet 4.1

An Account Reconciliation Form—James Morrison's May 2004 Statement

James Morrison used this form to reconcile his checking account for the month of May 2004. Because line A equals line B, he has fully reconciled the difference between the $80.99 bank statement balance and his $339.44 checkbook balance. Accounts should be reconciled each month—as soon as possible after receipt of the bank statement.

CHECKING ACCOUNT RECONCILIATION

For the Month of May, 20 04

Accountholder Name(s) James Morrison

Type of Account Regular Checking

1. Ending balance shown on bank statement — $ 80.99

Add up checks and withdrawals still outstanding:

Check Number or Date	Amount	Check Number or Date	Amount
221	$ 81.55		$
225	196.50		
Lucky—5/28	25.00		
ATM—5/29	40.00		
		TOTAL	$ 343.05

2. Deduct total checks/withdrawals still outstanding from bank balance — – $ 343.05

Add up deposits still outstanding:

Date	Amount	Date	Amount
5/29	595.00		
		TOTAL	$ 595.00

3. *Add* total deposits still outstanding to bank balance — + $ 595.00

A Adjusted Bank Balance (1 – 2 + 3) — $ 332.94

4. Ending balance shown in checkbook — $ 339.44

5. Deduct any bank service charges for the period (–$7.50 + $1.00) — – $ 6.50

6. Add interest earned for the period — + $ 0

B New Checkbook Balance (4 – 5 + 6) — $ 332.94

Note: Your account is reconciled when line A equals line B.

cashier's check
A check payable to a third party that is drawn by a bank on itself in exchange for the amount specified plus, in most cases, a service fee (of about $5).

traveler's check
A check sold (for a fee of about 1.5 percent) by many large financial institutions, in denominations ranging from $20 to $100, that can be used for making purchases and exchanged for local currencies in most parts of the world.

certified check
A personal check that is guaranteed (for a fee of $10 to $15 or more) by the bank on which it is drawn.

- **Cashier's Check:** Anyone can buy a **cashier's check** from a bank. These checks are often used by people who do not have checking accounts. They can be purchased for the face amount of the check plus a service fee of about $5, although occasionally they are issued at no charge to bank customers. The bank issues a check payable to a third party and drawn on itself, not you—the best assurance you can give that the check is good.
- **Traveler's Check:** A number of large financial organizations—such as Citibank, American Express, MasterCard, Visa, and Bank of America—issue **traveler's checks**, which can be purchased at commercial banks and most other financial institutions, in denominations ranging from $20 to $100. A fee of about 1.5 percent is charged on their purchase. Properly endorsed and countersigned traveler's checks are accepted by most U.S. businesses and can be exchanged for local currencies in most parts of the world. Because they are insured against loss or theft by the issuing agency, they provide a safe, convenient, and popular form of money for travel.
- **Certified Check:** A **certified check** is a personal check that the bank certifies, with a stamp, to guarantee that the funds are available. The bank immediately deducts the amount of the check from your account. There is normally a charge of $10 to $15 or more for this service.

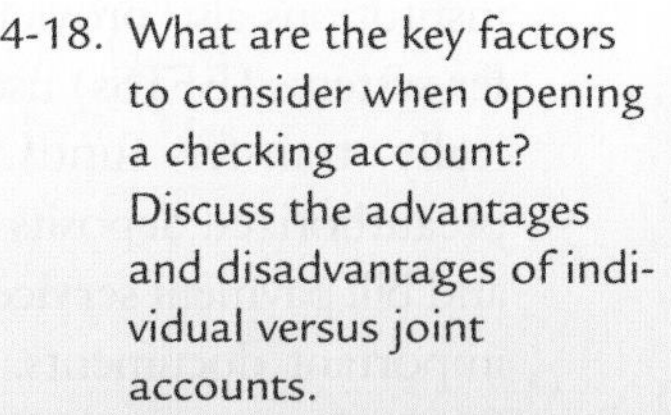

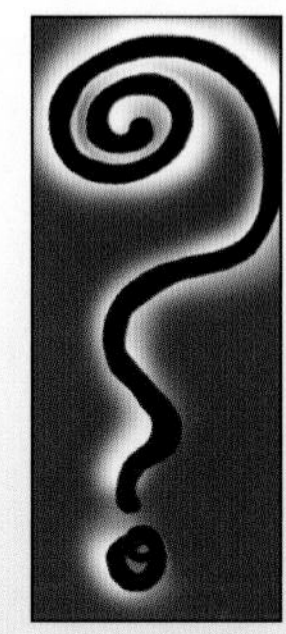

4-18. What are the key factors to consider when opening a checking account? Discuss the advantages and disadvantages of individual versus joint accounts.

4-19. Is it possible to bounce a check due to insufficient funds when the checkbook ledger shows a balance available to cover it? Explain what happens when a check bounces. Is it possible to obtain protection against overdrafts?

4-20. Describe the procedure used to stop payment on a check. Why might one wish to initiate this process?

4-21. What type of information is found in the monthly bank statement, and how is it used? Explain the basic steps involved in the account reconciliation process.

4-22. Briefly describe each of the following special types of checks:
a. Cashier's check
b. Traveler's check
c. Certified check

SUMMARY

LG1. Understand the role of cash management in the personal financial planning process. Cash management plays a vital role in personal financial planning. It involves the administration and control of liquid assets—cash, checking accounts, savings, and other short-term investment vehicles. With good cash management practices, you will have the necessary funds available to cover your expenses and establish a regular savings program.

LG2. Describe today's financial services marketplace, both traditional and nondepository financial institutions. Financial deregulation has changed the financial marketplace by increasing the number and types of firms providing financial services. Individuals and families continue to rely heavily on traditional depository financial institutions such as commercial banks, savings and loans, savings banks, and credit unions, for most of their financial services needs. Nondepository financial institutions also offer some banking services such as credit cards and money market fund accounts with check-writing privileges. You should make sure your bank has federal deposit insurance and is financially sound. Most traditional depository institutions are federally insured for up to $100,000 per depositor name.

LG3. Select the checking, savings, electronic banking, and other bank services that meet your needs. Financial institutions provide a variety of accounts to help you manage your cash: regular checking accounts, savings accounts, and interest-paying checking accounts, such as NOW accounts, money market deposit accounts, and money market mutual funds. Asset management accounts offered by brokerage firms and mutual funds combine checking, investment, and borrowing activities, and pay higher interest on deposits than other more traditional checking accounts. Financial institutions also provide other money management services. Electronic funds transfer systems (EFTSs) use telecommunications and computer technology to electronically transfer funds. Popular EFTS services include debit cards, ATMs, preauthorized deposits and payments, bank-by-phone accounts, and online banking and bill payment services. Safe-deposit boxes serve as a storage place for valuables and important documents. Today many banks also provide trust services and mutual-fund sales.

LG4. Calculate the interest earned on your money using compound interest and future value techniques. Once you know the interest rate, frequency of compounding, and how the bank determines the balance on which interest is paid, you can calculate how much interest you will earn on your money. Compound interest is the same as future value. Future value and future value of an annuity formulas can be used to find out how your savings will grow. The more frequently interest is compounded, the greater the effective rate for a given nominal rate of interest. Most banks use the actual balance, or day of deposit to day of withdrawl, method to determine which balances qualify to earn interest; this is the most accurate and fairest method for depositors.

LG5. Develop a savings strategy that incorporates a variety of savings plans. Your savings strategy should include establishing a regular pattern of saving with liquid reserves of 3 to 6 months of after-tax income. The choice of savings products depends on your needs, your risk preference, the length of time you can leave money on deposit, and current and expected rates of interest. You may wish to put some of your savings into vehicles that pay a higher rate of interest than savings or NOW accounts, such as certificates of deposit, U.S. Treasury bills, and Series EE bonds.

LG6. Open and use a checking account. A checking account provides a convenient way to hold cash and pay for goods and services. The sharp increase in bank service charges makes it important to evaluate different types of checking accounts and their service charges, minimum balance requirements, and other fees. You should understand how to write and endorse checks, make deposits, keep good checking account records, prevent overdrafts, and stop payment on checks. The account reconciliation, or balancing the checkbook, process confirms the accuracy of your account records and monthly bank statement. Other special types of checks you may use occasionally include cashiers', traveler's, and certified checks.

Financial Planning Exercises

1. What type of bank serves your needs best? Visit the Web sites of the following institutions and prepare a chart comparing the services offered, such as traditional and online banking, investment services, and personal financial advice. Which one would you choose to patronize, and why?
   a. Bank of America (**http://www.bankofamerica.com**)—a nationwide full-service bank
   b. A leading local commercial bank in your area
   c. A local savings institution
   d. A local credit union

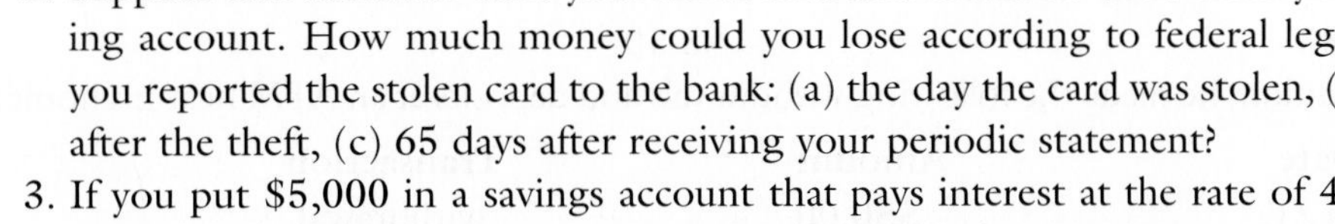

2. Suppose that someone stole your ATM card and withdrew $650 from your checking account. How much money could you lose according to federal legislation if you reported the stolen card to the bank: (a) the day the card was stolen, (b) 6 days after the theft, (c) 65 days after receiving your periodic statement?

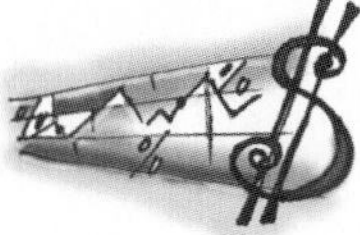

3. If you put $5,000 in a savings account that pays interest at the rate of 4 percent, compounded annually, how much will you have in 5 years? (*Hint:* Use the *future value* formula.) How much interest will you earn during the 5 years? If you put $5,000 *each* year into a savings account that pays interest at the rate of 4 percent a year, how much would you have after 5 years?
4. Bill and Betty Jacobs together earn approximately $42,000 a year after taxes. Through an inheritance and some wise investing, they also have an investment portfolio with a value of almost $90,000.
   a. How much of their annual income do you recommend they hold in some form of liquid savings as reserves? Explain.
   b. How much of their investment portfolio do you recommend they hold in savings and other short-term investment vehicles? Explain.
   c. How much, in total, should they hold in short-term liquid assets?
5. You are getting married and are unhappy with your present bank. Discuss your strategy for choosing a new bank and opening an account. Consider the factors that are important to you in selecting a bank such as the type and ownership of new accounts and bank fees and charges.
6. Determine the annual net cost of the following checking accounts:
   a. Monthly fee $5, check processing fee of 25 cents, average of 19 checks written per month
   b. Annual interest of 2.5 percent paid if balance exceeds $750, $8 monthly fee if account falls below minimum balance, average monthly balance $815, account falls below $750 during 4 months

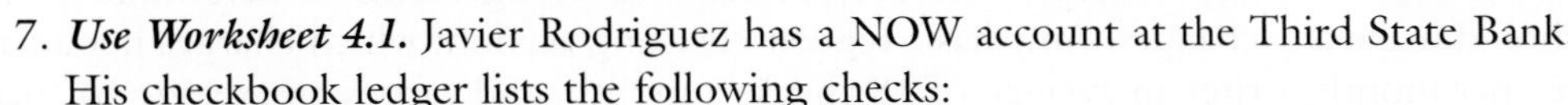

7. ***Use Worksheet 4.1.*** Javier Rodriguez has a NOW account at the Third State Bank. His checkbook ledger lists the following checks:

Check Number	Amount
654	$206.05
658	55.22
662	103.00
668	99.00
670	6.10
671	50.25
672	24.90
673	32.45
674	44.50
675	30.00
676	30.00
677	111.23
678	38.04
679	97.99
680	486.70
681	43.50

682	75.00
683	98.50

In addition, he made the following withdrawals and deposits at an ATM near his home:

Date	Amount	Transaction
11/1	$50.00	withdrawal
11/2	$525.60	deposit
11/6	$100.00	deposit
11/14	$75.00	withdrawal
11/21	$525.60	deposit
11/24	$150.00	withdrawal
11/27	$225.00	withdrawal
11/30	$400.00	deposit

Javier's checkbook ledger shows an ending balance of $286.54. He has just received his bank statement for the month of November. It shows an ending balance of $622.44; it also shows that he had earned interest for November of $3.28, a check service charge of $8 for the month, and another $12 charge for a returned check. His bank statement indicates the following checks have cleared: 654, 662, 672, 674, 675, 676, 677, 678, 679, and 681. ATM withdrawals on 11/1 and 11/14 and deposits on 11/2 and 11/6 have cleared; no other checks or ATM activities are listed on his statement, so anything remaining should be treated as outstanding. Use a checking account reconciliation form like the one in Worksheet 4.1 to reconcile Javier's checking account.

CONTEMPORARY CASE APPLICATIONS

4.1 Amy Chan's Savings and Banking Plans

Amy Chan is a registered nurse who earns $3,250 per month after taxes. She has been reviewing her savings strategies and current banking arrangements to determine if she should make any changes. Amy has a regular checking account which charges her a flat fee per month, writes an average of 18 checks a month, and carries an average balance of $795 (although it has fallen below $750 during 3 months of the past year). Her only other account is a money market deposit account with a balance of $4,250. She tries to make regular monthly deposits of $50 to $100 into her money market account but has only done so about every other month.

Of the many checking accounts Amy's bank offers, the three that best suit her needs are:

- *Regular Checking, per item plan:* $3 per month service charge plus 35 cents per check.
- *Regular Checking, flat fee plan (the one Amy currently has):* Monthly fee of $7 regardless of the number of checks written. With either of these Regular Checking accounts, she can avoid any charges by keeping a minimum daily balance of $750.
- *Interest Checking:* Monthly service charge of $7; interest of 3 percent, compounded daily (refer to Exhibits 4.6 and 4.7). With a minimum balance of $1,500, the monthly charge is waived.

Her bank also offers certificates of deposit for a minimum deposit of $500; the current interest rates are 3.5 percent for 6 months, 3.75 percent for 1 year, and 4 percent for 2 years.

Questions

1. Calculate the annual cost of each of the three accounts, assuming that Amy's banking habits remain the same. Which plan would you recommend and why?
2. Should Amy consider opening the interest checking account and increasing her minimum balance to at least $1,500 to avoid service charges? Explain your answer.
3. What other advice would you give Amy about her checking account and savings strategy?

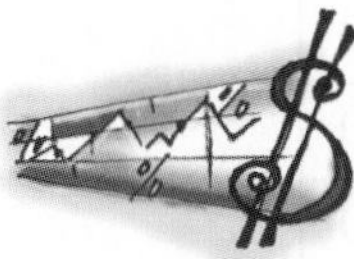

4.2. Reconciling the Pattersons' Checking Account

Mike and Jennifer Patterson opened their first checking account at The American Bank on September 14, 2004. They have just received their first bank statement for the period ending October 5, 2004. The statement and checkbook ledger are shown in the following table.

Questions

1. From this information, prepare a bank reconciliation for the Pattersons as of October 5, 2004, using a form like the one in Worksheet 4.1.
2. Given your answer to Question 1, what, if any, adjustments will the Pattersons need to make in their checkbook ledger? Comment on the procedures used to reconcile their checking account and their findings.
3. If the Pattersons earned interest on their idle balances as a result of the account being a money market deposit account, what impact would this have on the reconciliation process? Explain.

Bank Statement

MIKE & JENNIFER PATTERSON 2128 E. 51ST ST. DETROIT, MICHIGAN			THE AMERICAN BANK 800-000-0000 STATEMENT PERIOD SEPT. 6 – OCT. 5, 2004		
	Opening Balance	**Total Deposits for Period**		**Total Checks/Withdrawals for Period**	**Ending Balance**
	$0	**$569.25**		**$473.86**	**$95.39**
Date	**Withdrawals (Debits)**			**Deposits (Credits)**	**Balance**
Sept. 14				$360.00	$360.00
Sept. 15				97.00	457.00
Sept. 25	$45.20			9.25	421.05
Oct. 1				103.00	524.05
Oct. 1	3.00 BC				521.05
Oct. 4	65.90	$49.76	$45.00		360.39
Oct. 5	265.00				95.39

RT = Returned Check DM = Debit Memo BC = Bank Charges
FC = Finance Charges CM = Credit Memo

Checkbook Ledger

Check Number	Date 2003	Details	✔	Check Amount	Deposit Amount	Account Balance
—	Sept. 14	Cash—gift from wedding			$360.00	$360.00
—	Sept. 15	Mike's wages from library			97.00	457.00
101	Sept. 24	Kroger's—groceries		$45.20		411.80
102	Sept. 27	Mich. Bell Telephone bill		28.40		383.40
—	Oct. 1	Mike's wages from library			103.00	486.40
103	Oct. 1	Univ. Bk. Sto.—college books		65.90		420.50
104	Oct. 1	Kmart—sewing material		16.75		403.75
105	Oct. 1	G. Heller—apartment rent		265.00		138.75
106	Oct. 2	Blue Cross—health insurance		17.25		121.50
107	Oct. 3	Kroger's—groceries		49.76		71.74
108	Oct. 4	Cash: gas, entertain., laundry		45.00		26.74
—	Oct. 5	Jennifer's salary—BDM Corp.			450.00	476.74

Applying Personal Finance

Manage Your Cash!
What difference does it make where you keep your money? The returns are so low on checking and savings accounts that you certainly won't grow rich on their earnings! It's no wonder that many people tend to overlook the importance of managing their cash and liquid assets. The purpose of this project is to help you evaluate your cash management needs and the various financial service providers available so that you can select the one best suited to your needs.

First of all, spend some time making a list of your needs and preferences. Do you like to visit your banking institution in person, or would you just as soon do your banking electronically or by mail? Is a high yield important to you, or is your typical balance usually pretty low such that any earnings would be minimal? What other services might you need, such as a safe-deposit box, brokerage account, trust services, or financial and estate planning?

Next, go back through this chapter and review all the types of financial institutions and the services they provide. Then beside each need on your list, write down the institutions that would best meet that need. Is there one banking institution that would meet all your needs, or do you feel that you would need several? After you have identified the type or types that are appropriate for you, survey your community via the phone book, interviews with finance professionals, and other methods in order to identify the various financial institutions in your area. Look beyond your area as well and consider what services are available over the Internet or from other regions of the country. Make a list of your top choices and find out more information concerning their services, products, and fees charged to help you decide where you would like to do business. Bring your findings to class to compare and discuss with your classmates.

Money Online

Stash Your Cash!

1. **http://www.fdic.gov**
Want to bank online? Find out from the FDIC if your online bank has a legitimate charter and FDIC insurance. Click on "Consumer Protection" and then on "Consumer Resources" to find their informative article, "Safe Internet Banking."

2. **http://gomez.com**
How do online banks rank? Gomez's "Benchmarks" rate firms that are tops at online service. Under "Scorecards," select "Bankers." Resort the list by clicking on the various items to the right. Read the "Reviews" on banks that interest you, and then scroll down to find banks that were also evaluated.

3. **http://www.bankrate.com/brm/safesound/ss_home.asp**
How financially sound is your bank? Research your bank, thrift or credit union using Bankrate's "Safe and Sound" rating system to obtain an evaluation of your institution.

4. **http://www.imoneynet.com**
Need to find a money fund? Consult iMoneyNet, Inc., a leading provider of money market mutual fund data. Search through the various categories of funds to find what money funds are averaging and names of the top-yielding money funds.

5. **http://www.bankrate.com**
What are the best rates in your area? Select your state at Bankrate's Web site to find the rate offerings on auto loans, home equity loans, home mortgages, personal loans, and savings and CDs. While you're at their site, scroll down to find information on almost anything to do with banking or finances.

6. **http://www.dallasfed.org/fed/district.html**
There are 12 Federal Reserve Districts—which one are you in? Pull up this map provided at the Web site of the Federal Reserve Bank of Dallas and find out. Click on your district to pull up its Web site and learn more about your Federal Reserve district and its bank.

7. **http://www.bankrate.com/brm/news/checkup/savings.asp**
How are you doing with your savings? Work step by step through Bankate's "Savings Check-Up." When you've completed the exercise, look through the other financial check-ups also available at their Web site or browse their articles of interest.

8. **http://smartmoney.com/bonds**
What shape is the yield curve today? Look at the current chart and then click on "Living Yield Curve" to learn more about how interest rates affect the economy. Play the "Charting the Curve" graph of interest rates both backwards and forwards in time. Learn the different shapes of the yield curve and what they tell us about the future of our economy.

9. **http://www.bankrate.com**
What is a CD ladder and who would want one? Let Bankrate.com explain all about laddering bank CDs in order to increase the interest you receive. Search on "CD ladder" for articles and advice so you can start building your own!

Just for Fun!

10. **http://www.dallasfed.org/educate/pubs/comic.html**
Free comics! The Federal Reserve System provides a series of comic books to explain and illustrate various financial and economic concepts. Learn about the importance of savings, the development of the banking system, the purpose of money in a modern

economy, or the basic principals of foreign trade and exchange. Designed for younger students, these lively, well-written books make economic concepts understandable for everyone.

11. **http://www.xe.com/ucc**

Convert your currency! Pull up the Universal Currency Converter and plug in any amount of money to find the current conversion value from one country's currency to another. Convert one U.S. dollar into euros, Canadian dollars, German Deutsche marks, French francs and Japanese yen. Then convert one unit of each of these currencies into U.S. dollars.

CHAPTER 5
Making Automobile and Housing Decisions

Learning Goals

LG1. Implement a plan to research and select a new or used automobile.
LG2. Decide whether to buy or lease a car
LG3. Identify housing alternatives, assess the rental option, and perform a rent-or-buy analysis.
LG4. Evaluate the benefits and costs of home ownership and estimate how much you can afford for a home.
LG5. Describe the home-buying process.
LG6. Choose mortgage financing that meets your needs.

To Buy or Not To Buy—That is the Question

Steve and Rachel Adams were newly married and building their careers. Buying a house was something they looked forward to in the future. That was until Joe, a realtor friend, convinced them that they couldn't afford not to buy—and soon. House prices were steadily increasing, and he urged them to get into the housing market before they found themselves priced out of the kind of home they wanted to buy. It might require some sacrifice initially, he told the couple, but it would be well worth it in the long term.

He found the perfect "starter home" for them, a well-kept, reasonably priced house, in a good school district. Since they planned to start a family within the next few years, they took Joe's advice and made an offer for the property. Because Joe represented both the buyer and the seller in the transaction, he was able to reduce his commission and help seal the deal at a very favorable price for the Adams. A combination of their own savings and parental loans provided the down payment, and special mortgage financing assured them of low monthly payments. In fact, their mortgage payment wasn't much higher than their rent had been, and now they were able to enjoy the tax and other benefits of being homeowners.

Several years and two children later the Adamses were ready to look for a larger home. When Rachel saw a For Sale sign in the yard of her dream house, she rushed home to tell Steve. He was skeptical; the asking price was four times what they had paid for their present house. Although he knew that their home had increased in value, he felt the other house was out of their reach.

Once again their friend Joe came to their assistance. First he appraised their existing home. They were pleasantly surprised to discover that it had doubled in value in the 5 years they had owned it, providing them with a considerable chunk of equity to use as a down payment for a new home. And because the property they wanted to buy needed work, Joe was able to negotiate a more favorable purchase price for the house. Finally, based on Steve's burgeoning medical practice and the couple's excellent credit rating, they were candidates for very attractive mortgage financing. Joe reminded them that their decision to purchase their first home had played an important part in enabling them to own the home of their dreams. This chapter provides information and advice to help you have a positive experience like Rachel and Steve Adams when you make a major purchase such as an automobile or a home.

CRITICAL THINKING QUESTIONS

As you review the chapter, consider these questions in relation to the Adams' home purchases:

- How were Steve and Rachel Adams able to purchase their first home?
- How did that decision impact their ability to later purchase their dream home? Explain.
- Is homeownership important to you? Give your reasons as to why or why not.

BUYING AN AUTOMOBILE

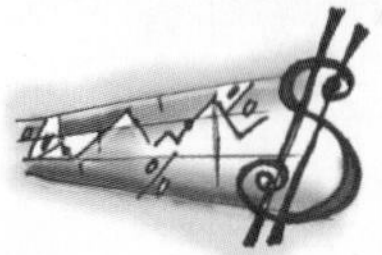

Buying an automobile is probably the first major expenditure many of us make. The car purchase is second only to housing in terms of the amount of money the typical consumer spends. Because you will buy an automobile many times during your life—most people purchase a car every 2 to 5 years—a systematic approach to selecting and financing a vehicle can mean significant savings. Before you make any major purchase, whether a car, house, or large appliance, you should follow some basic guidelines to enable you to make a wise purchase decision.

- *Research* your purchase thoroughly, considering not only the market but also your personal needs.
- *Select* the best item for your needs.
- *Buy* the item after negotiating the best price and arranging financing on favorable terms. Be sure you understand all the terms of the sale before you sign any contracts.
- *Maintain* your purchase and make necessary repairs promptly.

Exhibit 5.1 summarizes the steps in the car buying process.

EXHIBIT 5.1

10 Steps to Buying a Car

These 10 steps summarize the car-buying process discussed in this chapter.

1. Analyze how much car can you afford.
2. Choose the best way to pay for your new car—cash, financing, or lease.
3. Select the right car for you in terms of size, performance, safety, and styling. Choose at least three "target cars" to consider buying.
4. Decide on a price based on dealer's cost for the car and options, plus a markup for the dealer's profit, minus rebates and incentives.
5. Test-drive the car at least once, on both local streets and highways.
6. Get a used car inspected by a qualified independent mechanic.
7. Decide whether to trade in your used car or sell it yourself.
8. Begin negotiations with three or more dealers as necessary. Hold firm on your target price before closing the deal.
9. Review and sign contracts with the dealer's finance manager, avoiding pressure to buy unnecessary extras.
10. Consider alternate buying strategies such as Internet buying services, or faxing your offer to local dealerships for competitive bids.

Source: Adapted from Phil Read, "10 Steps To Buying A New Car: What Everyone Should Know," Edmunds.com, **http://www.edmunds.com/edweb/advice**.

CHOOSING A CAR

Sport utility vehicle (SUV) or pickup truck? Sedan, convertible, or coupe? Car buyers today have more choices than ever before so more than one category of vehicle may be of interest. A good way to start your research is by tapping into the many available sources of information about cars, their prices, features, and reliability. Industry resources include manufacturers' brochures and dealer personnel. Car magazines, such as *Car and Driver, Motor Trend,* and *Road and Track,* and consumer magazines, such as *Consumer Reports* and *Consumer Guide,* regularly compare and rate cars. In addition, *Consumer Reports* and

Kiplinger's Personal Finance magazine publish annual buying guides that include comparative statistics and ratings on most domestic and foreign cars. *Consumer Reports* includes information on used cars in its guide, and offers a fee-based service called *Consumer Reports* Auto Price Service, that provides the list price and dealer cost on a new car, and the available options.

The Internet has made it especially easy to do your homework before ever setting foot in a dealer's showroom. In addition to finding online versions of automotive magazines, you can visit one of the many comprehensive Web sites for car shoppers, offering pricing and model information, and links to other useful sites. Don't forget the Web sites of the automobile companies themselves; for example, General Motors is online at **http://www.gm.com**, and so on. Once you've done the research, you will be in a better position to negotiate with the dealer. (The *Money in Action* box on page 178 explores the online world of car buying.)

Although the primary motivation for automobile ownership is to provide transportation, automobiles can also be viewed as status symbols, or purchased as part of a hobby, or as an investment. Regardless of your motive, it's important to evaluate all of the following areas before buying a car. Knowing what you want and can afford before purchasing either a new or used car will prevent a slick auto salesperson from talking you into buying a car you do not need.

Affordability

Before you shop for a car, you should determine how much you can afford to spend. You will need to calculate two numbers unless you can pay cash for the entire cost of the car:

- **Amount of down payment:** This money will come from savings, so be sure not to deplete your emergency fund.
- **How much you can pay for the monthly loan payment:** Analyze your available resources—for example, your other expenses, including housing—and your transportation requirements. Don't forget to include insurance. Your monthly car payment should be no more than 20 percent of your monthly net income.

You can also use the down payment and monthly payment amount to back into the total amount you can afford for a car. For example, suppose that you have \$2,500 for a down payment, can pay \$450 a month, and your bank is offering 3-year car loans at 9 percent annual interest. How much of a loan can you afford? Using a financial calculator and the steps shown in Exhibit 5.2, you will find that you can pay off a loan of about \$14,150. Add that to the \$2,500 down payment, and you'll be able to afford a car costing \$16,650. It pays to shop around for loans because their rates can differ by as much as 2 percent!

EXHIBIT 5.2

Using a Financial Calculator to Find an Auto Loan Amount

How large a loan can you pay off in 3 years at 9 percent annual interest with a \$450 monthly payment?

Step 1: Multiply years by 12 to find total number of payments: 3 × 12 = 36. Press **N** to enter 36 as the number of payment periods.

Step 2: Divide annual interest by 12 to get monthly rate: 9 percent/12 = .75 monthly rate. Press **I** to enter the monthly rate.

Step 3: Enter the monthly payment, 450, and press **PMT**.

Step 4: Press **CPT** then **PV** to find the beginning loan amount: \$14,151.

smart.sites

With Bankrate.com's (**http://www.bankrate.com**) Auto Loan calculators, you can evaluate auto-financing options, then go to the rate page to find the lowest auto loan rates in your area.

Operating Costs

The out-of-pocket cost of operating an automobile consists of not only car payments, but also insurance, license, fuel, oil, tires, and other operating and maintenance outlays. Certain of these costs are *fixed* regardless of how much you drive; others are *variable*, depending on the number of miles you drive. The biggest fixed cost is likely to be the *installment payments* associated with the loan or lease used to acquire the car; the biggest variable cost will probably be fuel.

Another purchase cost is **depreciation**, which is the loss in value that occurs over its period of ownership. In effect, depreciation is the difference between the price you paid for the car and what you can sell it for. If you paid $15,000 for an automobile that can be sold 3 years later for $9,000, the car will cost you $6,000 in depreciation. Although depreciation may not be a recurring out-of-pocket cost, it is nonetheless an important operating expense that should not be overlooked.

depreciation The loss in the value of an asset such as an automobile that occurs over its period of ownership; calculated as the difference between the price initially paid and the subsequent sale price.

New, Used, or "Nearly New"?

One decision you must make is whether to buy a new, used, or "nearly new" car. If you cannot afford to buy a new car, the decision is made for you. Some people who

EXHIBIT 5.3

Don't Get Taken for a Ride

Thinking of buying a used car? Consider both advantages and disadvantages.
Some *advantages* are:

1. It is less expensive than a comparable new car, and the recent popularity of short-term car leases has increased the availability of late-model, attractively priced used cars.
2. It will not depreciate in value as quickly as a new car—purchasing a used car less than 18 months old often means saving the 20 to 25 percent depreciation in value typically experienced during the first 12 to 18 months of a car's life.
3. Because it is less expensive, the purchaser does not have to put down as much money as is required for a new car.
4. Today's used cars are more reliable. The quality and durability of well-maintained 2- to 4-year-old cars makes them more reliable and less expensive to maintain than the new cars of 10 years ago.
5. The *federal odometer disclosure law,* requiring sellers to give buyers a signed statement attesting to the mileage shown on the odometer of their used cars as being accurate, protects consumers. Penalties for violating this law are quite stringent.

The main *disadvantage* of buying a used car is uncertainty about its mechanical condition. It might look good and have low mileage but it could still have mechanical problems, requiring future maintenance and repair expenditure. Having your prospective used car purchase checked by a reputable mechanic or independent inspection service is money well spent and could save you hundreds of dollars and much aggravation later on.

can afford to buy a new car choose to buy a used car so they can have a better model—a used luxury car such as a BMW, Lexus, or Mercedes—rather than a less-expensive brand of new car such as a Chevrolet. With the increasing popularity of used cars, car dealers are trying to dispel the negative image associated with buying a used, or "preowned," car. You'll find used cars advertised in local or nearby city newspapers, publications like *AutoTrader*, and their Web sites. These provide an excellent source of information on used cars for sale. Exhibits 5.3 and 5.4 offer advice for buying a used car.

smart.sites

Looking for a 2004 Toyota Camry? At Internet classified service AutoTrader.com, **http://www.autotrader.com**, you can see ads from local sellers, some with pictures. Checking the ads is also a good way to learn the value of the car you want to sell or trade.

Once you know what you want, shop at the following places:

- **Franchise dealerships:** Offer the latest model used cars, provide financing, and will negotiate on price. Be sure to research values before shopping.
- **Superstores:** AutoNation USA, CarMax, and similar dealers offer no-haggle pricing and a large selection. They certify cars and may offer a limited short-term warranty. May cost slightly more than at a dealer who will negotiate.
- **Independent used car lots:** Usually offer older (4 to 6 years) cars and have lower overhead than franchise dealers. No industry standards, so be sure to check with the Better Business Bureau before buying.
- **Private individuals:** Generally cost less because there is no dealer overhead; may have maintenance records. Be sure seller has title to car.

EXHIBIT 5.4

Finding Your Used Car

In addition to trade-ins and privately sold vehicles, check out these other sources for used cars.

Type	Pros	Cons
Certified used car	"Near-new" cars; dealer inspects and reconditions car; generally includes warranty	
Off-lease cars	Single driver; usually fully equipped; inspected on return	Lessee may not do scheduled maintenance
Rental cars ("program cars")	Price. Also may still be under factory warranty or have limited warranty	Fewer features; multiple drivers; heavy mileage
Corporate fleet cars	Well maintained	High mileage—60,000+ miles in 2 or 3 years

Money in Action

Clicking the Tires

Getting a new car is exciting—once you have finished with the hassles of the car-buying process. It can be fun to research different types of cars and test drive the ones you like. Deciding how much you can afford to pay, figuring out how to finance the car, and negotiating the interest rate may be more of a hassle. But now you can do much of your searching online and perhaps even buy the car from an online dealer.

Online research is increasingly popular with today's car buyers—about 64 percent do at least some research on the Internet before heading to the showroom, and 49 percent of new-car buyers said the Internet helped them decide which make and model to buy, according to the J.D. Power and Associates 2003 New Autoshopper.com Study. Another 49 percent said that online price research was as big part of their buying process.

Comprehensive sites such as Edmunds (**http://www.edmunds.com**), Kelley Blue Book (**http://www.kbb.com**), and AutoSite (**http://www.autosite.com**) provide comparative new and used car prices, reviews, incentives and rebates, and advice on buying and selling, financing, and insurance. If safety is a priority, you'll find government crash-test ratings at the National Highway Traffic Safety Association site (**http://www.nhtsa.gov**).

After you've chosen several models, it is time to visit a dealer and test drive the cars, then head back to the Internet to compare prices. Only about 3 percent of car buyers actually buy online because many car-buying services don't deliver on their promises. You may not get a quote, and the price may change when you go to the dealer to finalize the transaction. Although it may be easy to contact various online dealers to get price quotes, there is no guarantee you will get the lowest price. One study showed that people buying their vehicle online actually paid 6.5 percent more than those negotiating in person.

Not all car-buying sites operate in the same manner. Autobytel (**http://www.autobytel.com**) and Autoweb (**http://www.autoweb.com**) are referral services that connect customers to dealers in their geographical area—who pay for the leads. AutoNationDirect (**http://www.autonation.com**)

...continued on next page

smart.sites

Which auto dealers have the best used car certification programs? IntelliChoice (**http://www.intellichoice.com**) rates the programs of 23 dealers according to their inspection lists, warranties, roadside assistance benefits, and return and exchange policies.

Size, Body Style, and Features

Your first consideration should be what type of car you need. More than one style category may work for you. For example, a family of five can buy a mid-size or full-size sedan, station wagon, minivan, or compact or full-size SUV. When considering size, body style, and features, give some thought to your needs, likes and dislikes, and also the cost. In most instances, there is a direct relationship between size and cost: In general, the larger the car, the more expensive it will be to purchase and to operate. Also consider performance, handling, appearance, fuel economy, reliability, repair problems, and the resale value of the car. And don't try to adapt your needs to fit the car you want—a two-passenger sports car may not be appropriate if you need the car for business or if you have children.

By listing all options you want before shopping for a new car, you can avoid paying for features you really do not need. There are literally hundreds of options available, ranging in price from a few dollars up to $1,500 or more, including automatic transmission, a bigger engine, air conditioning, high-performance brakes, a CD player, clock, power windows, power seats, electric door locks, leather seats, navigation systems, a rear window defroster, and special suspension. Some appearance-related options are two-tone or metallic paint, electric sunroof, special tires, sport wheels, and various interior and exterior trim packages.

Most cars have at least some options, but you can select additional optional features that provide a broad range of conveniences and luxuries—for a price. On new cars, a window sticker details each option and its price, but on a used car only close observation serves to determine the options. Window stickers quite often list standard features that might be considered optional on other models, and vice versa. When shopping for a new car, it is important to make certain that you are comparing comparably equipped models.

Reliability and Warranties

Assess the *reliability* of a car by talking with friends who own similar cars and reading objective assessments published by consumer magazines and buying guides such as *Consumer Reports.* Study the *warranty* offered by new car manufacturers, comparing those for cars that interest you. Significant differences may exist. Be sure to read the warranty booklet included with a new car to understand the terms of the warranty. Most warranties are void if the owner has not performed routine maintenance or has somehow abused the car.

On new cars, the manufacturer guarantees the general reliability and quality of construction for the vehicle for a specified period in a written warranty, obligating it to repair or replace, at little or no cost to the owner, any defective parts and/or flaws in workmanship. Today, most new car warranties cover a minimum of the first 3 years of ownership or 36,000 miles, whichever comes first, and many provide coverage for as long as 7 years or 70,000 miles. However, most warranties have limitations; for example, longer warranty periods may apply to only the engine and drive train. Auto manufacturers and private insurers also sell extended warranties and service contracts, sometimes called "buyer protection plans." Most experts consider these unnecessary and not worth their price, given the relatively long initial warranty periods now being offered by most manufacturers.

actually owns dealerships and sells vehicles from its own inventory, while CarsDirect (**http://www.carsdirect.com**) has agreements with dealers for guaranteed price quotes.

Getting the best deal means visiting as many Web sites as you can to gather information. In a test by *Kiplinger's Personal Finance* magazine to find the best deal on a Toyota Land Cruiser, price quotes varied by as much as $3,000. You shouldn't overlook your local dealers, however. In today's competitive market they often match Internet offers.

Critical Thinking Questions

1. How has the Internet changed the way people buy cars? What are the key benefits it offers?
2. Outline the steps you would take to research a car online.
3. Would you consider purchasing your car from an online dealer? Explain your reasons.

Sources: Roger Harris ,"More Car Buyers Browse Web, Survey Shows," *Ventura County Star*, October 2, 2003, downloaded from Big Chalk Library, **http://library.bigchalk.com**; Darrell Proctor, "Web Sites Offer Resources for Buying Vehicle," *Denver Rocky Mountain News*, June 16, 2003, p. 2B; and Bob Tedeschi, "The World Wide Web Is Emerging as a Powerful Force in Car Sales, with Benefits for Manufacturers and Buyers," *The New York Times*, September 16, 2002, p. C.5.

Other Considerations

Several other considerations you should take into account include:

- **Trading in or selling your existing car:** Although trading in is convenient, it is generally more financially advantageous to sell your old car outright. If you are willing to take the time, you can usually sell your car for more than the wholesale price typically offered by a dealer on a trade-in.
- **Fuel economy:** The *Environmental Protection Agency (EPA) mileage ratings* are especially useful on new vehicles, which carry a sticker indicating the number of miles per gallon each model is expected to get (as determined through EPA tests) for both city and highway driving.
- **Safety features:** These features are likely to be similar in new cars as a result of government regulations, but older used cars may not have some features such as side-impact airbags. Don't forget to include *auto insurance costs,* which vary depending on make, model, safety features, and other factors (and are discussed in detail in Chapter 10).

The Purchase Transaction

Once you have determined the amount you can afford to spend and the features you desire, you are ready to begin car shopping. If you plan to purchase a new car, visit all dealers with cars that meet your requirements. Look the cars over and ask questions—but don't make any offers until you have isolated two or three cars with the desired features that are priced within your budget. Also, if you can be flexible about the model and options you want, you can sometimes negotiate a better deal than if you have your heart set on a particular model and options. Make an appointment to test-drive the cars you are interested in. Drive—then leave! You need time to evaluate the car yourself, without pressure to buy from the salesperson.

Comparison shopping is essential, because a dealer selling the same brand as another may give you a better deal. Be aware of the sales technique called *low-balling*, where the salesperson quotes a low price for the car to get you to make an offer, and then negotiates the price upward prior to your signing the sales contract. Exhibit 5.5 lists some other factors to consider once you begin looking at cars.

EXHIBIT 5.5

Kicking the Tires

Start your examination of a car with an inspection of key points. Don't overlook the obvious:

- *How easy is it to get people and things into and out of the car?*
  Do the doors open easily?
  Is the trunk large enough for your needs?
  Does the car offer a pass-through or fold-down rear seat for larger items?
- *Comfort and visibility:*
  Are the seats comfortable?
  Can you adjust the driver's seat and steering wheel properly?
  What are the car's blind spots for a person of your height?
  Can you see all the gauges clearly?
  Can you reach the controls for the radio, CD player, heater, air conditioner, and other features easily while driving?
  Does it have the options you want?

Then take the car for a test drive.

- Set aside at least 20 minutes and drive it on highways and local roads.
- Merge into traffic getting onto the highway to test acceleration to safely merge with freeway traffic or to pass another car.
- If possible, drive home and make sure the car fits into your garage—especially if you're interested in a larger SUV or truck!
- For a used car, test the heater and air conditioner. Then turn the fan off and listen for any unusual engine noises.
- Check out overall handling. Parallel park, make a U-turn, brake hard, and so on. Do the gears shift smoothly? If testing a standard transmission, try to determine if the clutch is engaging too high or too low, which might indicate excessive wear or a problem.

As soon as you return to the car lot, take notes on how well the car handled and how comfortable you felt driving it. This is especially important if you are testing several cars.

Because low-balling, price haggling, and other high-pressure sales tactics can make car buying an unpleasant experience, many dealers have refocused their sales practices to emphasize customer satisfaction. Some manufacturers offer firm prices, so if you buy today, you can be sure that no one will get a better deal tomorrow. However, you should still research prices, as described in the next section, because a firm selling price does not guarantee the lowest cost.

Negotiating Price

Choosing among various makes, models, and options can make comparisons difficult, so the price you pay for a car, whether new or used, can vary widely. The more you narrow your choices to a particular car, the easier it is to get price quotes from dealers to make an "apples to apples" comparison.

The "sticker price" posted on a new car represents the manufacturer's *suggested retail price* for that particular car with its listed options. This price means very little. The key to negotiating a good price is knowing the *dealer's cost* for the car. The easiest and quickest way to find the dealer's invoice cost is going to the Edmunds and Kelley Blue Book Web sites mentioned earlier, or by checking car-buying guides available at your library or bookstore.

Before making an offer, prepare a worksheet with the cost versus the list price for the exact car you want. This will help you avoid high-pressure salesmanship and paying for options you don't want or need. Try to negotiate the lowest acceptable markup (3 to 4 percent for cars priced under $20,000; 6 to 7 percent for higher-priced models), push for a firm quote, and make it clear that you are comparison shopping. Don't let the salesperson pressure you into signing a sales contract or leaving a deposit until you are sure that you have negotiated the best deal. Good cost information will improve your bargaining position and possibly allow you to negotiate a price that is only several hundred dollars above the dealer's cost.

To research used car prices, you can check one of the popular price guides—the National Automobile Dealers Association (NADA) *Official Used Car Guide,* the *Kelley Blue Book,* or *Edmund's Used Car Prices*—available on the Internet or at your library or bank, and in the classified ads in your local newspaper.

If you want to avoid negotiating entirely, you can buy your car through a buying service, either by phone or over the Internet. These include independent companies, such as AutoVantage, Autobytel, AutoWeb, and Nationwide Auto Brokers, or services offered through credit unions, motor clubs, and discount warehouses such as Costco. Buying services work in a variety of ways. They may have an arrangement with a network of dealers to sell cars at a predetermined price above invoice, provide you with competitive bids from several local dealers, find the car you want and negotiate the price with the dealer, or place an order with the factory for a made-to-order car. The price for these services ranges from about $45 for a Costco membership to as much as $600, and results vary. You will get a good price through a service—although you can't assume that it will be the best price.

Indifferent to race and gender, the Internet is leveling the car-buying playing field for women and minorities. A new study of 672,000 new car purchases nationwide compares purchases made through dealerships and those made using an Internet referral service. The study found that online buyers saved at least 2 percent of the purchase price, with women and minorities benefiting the most—they tend not to haggle as much with salespeople. The Internet's primary advantage for buyers is that subtle clues that might tip off the dealer to inflate the price—such as how much jewelry you wear, or what your body language is like—aren't visible. The *Money in Action* box on page 178 tells you how to use the Internet to your advantage when buying a car.

It is best not to discuss your plan to finance the purchase or the value of your trade-in until you have settled the question of price. These should be separate issues. Salespeople will typically want to find out how much you can afford monthly and then offer financing deals with payments close to that amount. In the case of trade-ins, the dealer might offer you a good price for your old car and raise the price of the new car to compensate. The dealer may offer financing terms that sound attractive, but be sure to compare them with the cost of bank loans. Sometimes dealers increase the price of the car to make up for a low interest rate, or attractive financing may apply only to certain models. If you are interested in dealer financing, make sure the monthly payment quoted by the dealer's finance manager is just for the loan. Learn and compare the annual percentage rate (APR) with the rate quoted on a bank loan. Often financing charges include unneeded extras such as credit life insurance, accident insurance, an extended warranty, or a service package.

Manufacturers and dealers often offer buyers special incentives, such as rebates and cut-rate financing, particularly when car sales are slow. (Deduct rebates from the dealer's cost when you negotiate price.) You may have a choice between a rebate and low-cost financing. To determine which is the better deal, calculate the difference between the monthly payments on a market-rate bank loan and the special dealer loan for the same term. Multiply the payment difference by the loan maturity, in months, and compare it with the rebate. For example, assume the dealer offers either a $1,000 rebate or a 5 percent interest rate on a $10,000, 4-year loan. Your monthly payments would be $230 with dealer financing and $254 on a 10 percent bank loan with similar terms. The payment savings over the life of the loan are $1,152 ($24 per month × 48 months), which is greater than the $1,000 rebate. In this case you would be better off with the 5 percent loan. For more tips on getting the best price on your car purchase, check out the ideas in Exhibit 5.6.

EXHIBIT 5.6

Are You in the Driver's Seat?

Want a great deal on your next car? Do your homework and shop around—you could save $2,000 or more. Here's how:

- **Shop at the end of the month** when dealers try to meet quotas. Fall brings good deals but instant depreciation.
- **Research thoroughly** at car research Web sites like **http://www.consumerreports.com** or **http://www.carbuyingtips.com** to evaluate the latest models and options.
- **Leave your checkbook at home** so you won't be tempted to succumb to sales pressure and make an instant decision.
- **Know your car's value** by comparing prices at Kelley Blue Book (**http://www.kbb.com**).
- **Negotiate from dealer cost up** not sticker price down—treat the deal as though buying for cash to focus on the actual value not the monthly payments.
- **Arrange financing** before you begin negotiations. You'll probably get a better rate from a bank or credit union.
- **Do the math** after settling on a price. Bring a calculator. If you have a trade-in, buy your new car first, then negotiate the price for your old one.
- **Double-check the paperwork** for items you didn't request such as an extended warranty.
- **Be willing to walk away.** You sometime get the best price when you're in your car ready to drive away.

Sources: "AutoTrader.com Provides Simple Car Shopping Tips for Women," *PR Newswire*, March 31, 2003, downloaded from Find Articles, **http://www.findarticles.com**; Diane Hales, "Shop Smart," *Parade Magazine*, August 10, 2003, p. 18.

Closing the Deal

Whether you are buying a new or used car, to make a legally binding offer you must sign a **sales contract** that specifies the offering price and all the conditions of your offer.

sales contract
An agreement to purchase an automobile that states the offering price and all conditions of the offer; when signed by the buyer and seller, the contract legally binds them to its terms.

The sales contract also specifies whether the offer includes a trade-in. If it does, the offering price will include both the additional amount and the trade-in price. Because this agreement contractually binds you to purchase the car at the offering price, be certain that you want and can afford the car before you sign this agreement. To show that you are making an offer in good faith, you may be required to include a deposit of $100 or more with the contract.

Once the dealer accepts your offer, you complete the purchase transaction and take delivery of the car. If you are not paying cash for the car, you can arrange financing through the dealer, at your bank, a credit union, or a consumer finance company. The key aspects of these types of installment loans, which can be quickly negotiated if your credit is good, are discussed in Chapter 7. Prior to delivery, the dealer is responsible for cleaning the car and installing any optional equipment. It is a good idea to make sure that all equipment you are paying for has been installed and that the car is ready for use before paying the dealer. When you pay, you should receive a title or appropriate evidence that you own the car.

Trade in Your Loan

With interest rates at all time lows, should you still be paying the same high rates at which you financed your car a couple of years ago? Refinancing can pay off—but only under particular circumstances.

First, you need to have enough equity in the car to serve as collateral for what is essentially a used car loan. If you made large down payment, or are well into a loan, you may be a candidate for refinancing. If you can cut your interest rate by at least two percentage points, without stretching the payback period of your current loan, you could enjoy substantial savings.

Banks generally aren't interested in refinancing car loans so online lenders such as E-Loan (**http://www.eloan.com**) and PeopleFirst (**http://www.peoplefirst.com**) get most of the business. If you're a member of a credit union you may see what it can do for you. Consider tapping a home equity line of credit if you own a home to pay off a high interest auto loan. Unlike consumer loans, the interest paid on a home equity loan is tax deductible. Wherever you choose to refinance, you will probably have to pay $5 to $50 for a title change listing the new lien holder. And forget about refinancing your auto loan if you have bad credit.

Traditionally, car loans extended 3 or 4 years, but loan terms are lengthening as buyers stretch to afford cars and SUVs that can top $30,000 or even $40,000. These loans typically carry higher interest rates—the average rate for a 4-year loan is 5.5 percent compared with 8 to 9 percent for a 96-month loan—than shorter maturities, but lower monthly payments. So far only a handful of banks and credit unions are offering 8-year loans, but many now offer 7-year loans. Six-year loans already account for 28 percent of all new car loans, up from 19 percent just two years ago. Long-term loans are most commonly used to buy high-end luxury vehicles, and are not available for all vehicles. By the end of the loan term, you will still be making payments on a vehicle that has used up most of its life and is practically worthless, a major downside of longer-term car loans.

Concept ✓

5-1. Briefly discuss how each of the following purchase considerations would affect your choice of a car:
   a. Affordability
   b. Operating costs
   c. New, used, or "nearly new" car
   d. Model and feature selection
   e. Reliability and warranty protection

5-2. Describe the purchase transaction process, including shopping, price negotiation, and closing the deal on a car.

LEASING YOUR CAR

LG 2

Don't worry about temperamental engines or transmissions—just get a new car. Put nothing down, make easy payments. No wonder leasing is popular, accounting for about 25 percent of all vehicles sold today. When you **lease**, you (the lessee) receive the use of a car in exchange for monthly lease payments over a specified period, usually 2 to 5 years. Leasing appeals to a wide range of car buyers, even though the total cost of leasing is generally more expensive than buying a car with a loan, and at the end of the lease you have nothing. The car—and the money you paid to rent it—is gone. So why do so many car buyers lease their cars? Reasons include rising new car prices, the nondeductibility of consumer loan interest, lower monthly payments, getting a more expensive car for the same monthly payment, and minimizing the down payment to preserve cash.

lease
An arrangement in which the lessee receives the use of a car (or other asset) in exchange for making monthly lease payments over a specified period.

With all the advertisements promising low monthly lease payments, it's easy to focus on only the payment. Unlike a loan purchase, with a lease you're not paying for the whole car, only its use during a specified period. Leasing is a more complex arrangement than borrowing money to buy a car, and until you understand how leasing works, and compare lease terms with bank financing, you won't know if leasing is the right choice for you.

The Leasing Process

The initial step is the same for leasing and purchasing: Research car types and brands, comparison shop at several dealers, and find the car you want at the best price. Don't ask the dealer about leasing or any financing incentives until *after* you've negotiated the final price. Then compare the terms offered by at least one independent leasing firm. As with a purchase, try to negotiate lower lease payments—a payment reduction of $20 a month saves nearly $1,000 on a 4-year lease. And don't reveal what you can afford to pay per month; such a disclosure can lead you to a poor lease deal. Once you agree on leasing terms, be sure to get everything in writing.

Nearly 80 percent of car lessees choose the **closed-end lease**, often called the *walk-away lease,* because at the end of its term you simply turn in the car, assuming that you have neither exceeded the preset mileage limit nor abused the car. Under the less-popular **open-end (or finance) lease,** if the car is worth less than the estimated **residual value**—the remaining value of the car at the end of the lease term—you have to pay the difference.

closed-end lease
The most popular form of automobile lease, often called a *walk-away lease* because at the end of its term the lessee simply turns in the car, assuming the preset mileage limit has not been exceeded and the car hasn't been abused.

open-end lease
An automobile lease under which the estimated *residual value* of the car is used to determine lease payments; if the car is actually worth less than this value at the end of the lease, the lessee must pay the difference.

residual value
The remaining value of a leased car at the end of the lease term.

One of the commonly cited benefits of leasing is the absence of a down payment. However, today most leases require a "capital cost reduction," which is a down payment that lowers the potential depreciation and therefore your monthly lease payments. You may be able to negotiate a lower capital cost reduction or find a lease that doesn't require one.

The lease payment calculation is based on four variables:

1. The **capitalized cost** of the car (the price of the car you are leasing)
2. The forecast *residual value* of the car at the end of the lease
3. The **money factor**, or financing rate on the lease (similar to the interest rate on a loan)
4. The *lease term.*

capitalized cost
The price of a car that is being leased.

money factor
The financing rate on a lease; similar to the interest rate on a loan.

The *depreciation* during the lease term (which is what you are financing) is the capitalized cost minus the residual value. Dividing the sum of the depreciation and the sales tax (on the financed portion only) by the number of months in the lease term and adding the lessor's required monthly return (at the money factor) results in the monthly payment. (To convert the money factor to an annual percentage rate, multiply it by 2400. For example, a money factor of .00450 is the equivalent of paying interest at 10.8 percent on a loan.)

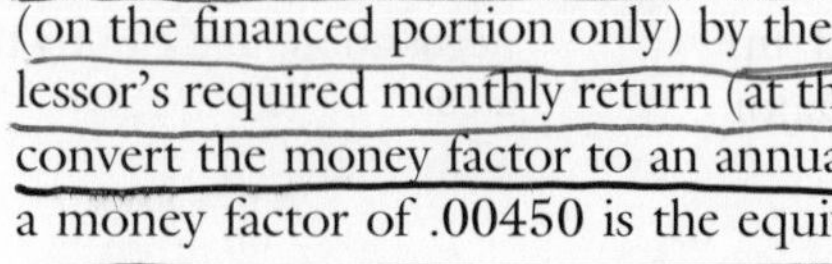

The lower the cost and higher the residual value, the lower your payment. Residual values quoted by different dealers can vary, so check several sources to find the highest residual value to minimize depreciation.

Lease terms typically run 2 to 5 years. Terminating a lease early is often difficult and costly, so be reasonably certain that you can keep the car for the full lease term. The lease contract should outline any costs and additional fees associated with early termination. Early termination clauses also apply to cars that are stolen or totaled in an accident. Some leases require "gap insurance" to cover the lost lease payments that would result from early termination caused by one of these events.

Under most leases, you are responsible for insuring and maintaining the car. At the end of the lease, you are obligated to pay for any "unreasonable wear and tear." A good lease contract should clearly define what is considered unreasonable. In addition, most leases require the lessee to pay a disposition fee of about $150 to $250 when the car is returned.

purchase option A price specified in a lease at which the lessee can buy the car at the end of the lease term.

Most auto leases include a **purchase option** (either a fixed price, the market price at the end of the lease term, or the residual value of the car) that specifies the price at which the lessee can buy the car at the end of the lease term. A lower residual results in a lower purchase price but raises monthly payments. Experts recommend negotiating a fixed-price purchase option, if possible.

The annual mileage allowance—typically, about 10,000 to 15,000 miles per year for the lease term—is another important lease consideration. Usually the lessee must pay between 10 and 20 cents per mile for additional miles. If you expect to exceed the allowable mileage, you would be wise to negotiate a more favorable rate for extra miles before signing the lease contract.

Financial Road Sign

Auto Leasing Checklist

Smart car buyers should insist on knowing the following eight figures before negotiating a lease:

1. The list price for the car and options
2. The capitalized cost (the value on which monthly payments are based)
3. The money factor (interest rate assumption)
4. The total interest paid
5. The total sales tax
6. The residual value for which the car can be purchased at the lease's end
7. The depreciation (the capitalized cost minus the residual value)
8. The lease term

The Lease versus Purchase Analysis

To decide whether it is less costly to lease rather than purchase a car, you need to perform a *lease versus purchase analysis* to compare the total cost of leasing to the total cost of purchasing a car over equal periods. In this analysis, the purchase is assumed to be financed with an installment loan with the same term as the lease.

For example, assume that Mary Dixon is considering either leasing or purchasing a new Ford Focus sedan costing $15,000. The 3-year, closed-end lease she is considering requires a $1,500 down payment (capital cost reduction), a $300 security deposit, and monthly payments of $300, including sales tax. If she purchases the car, she will make a $2,500 down payment and finance the balance with a 3-year, 8 percent loan requiring monthly payments of $392. In addition, she will have to pay 5 percent sales tax ($750) on the purchase, and she expects the car to have a residual value of $8,000 at the end of 3 years. Mary can earn 4 percent interest on her savings with short-term CDs. After filling in Worksheet 5.1, Mary concludes that purchasing is better because its *total cost* of $9,662 is $2,854 less than the $12,516 total cost of leasing—even though the monthly lease payment is $92 lower. Clearly, all else being equal, the least costly alternative is preferred.

Some Web sites can help you with your analysis. Intellichoice's lease area, **http://www.intellichoice.com**, has descriptions of current manufacturer lease deals. Or click on the "calculate" page of FinanCenter, **http://www.financenter.com**, and go to the auto section for several calculators to analyze a car purchase, including lease versus purchase. You can quickly run several "what if" scenarios to compare costs. The average cost per year of either owning or leasing is the highest in the first 2 years. Note also that the average cost of ownership is usually much lower if you own a vehicle for 4 years or more.

If you are fortunate enough to be able to pay cash for your car, you may still want to investigate leasing. Sometimes dealers offer such advantageous lease terms that you can come out ahead by leasing and then investing the money you would pay for the car. To compare the total cost of a cash purchase, simply take the cost of the car, including sales tax, add to it the opportunity cost of using all cash, and deduct the car's value at the end of the lease or loan term. At 4 percent per year on her savings, Mary's total cost of the car is as follows: \$15,750 cost + \$1,890 lost interest (3 × .04 × \$15,750) − \$8,000 residual value = \$9,640. In this case the cost of purchasing the car for cash is about the same as its purchase cost with financing, so Mary could do either.

Financial Road Sign

Should You Buy or Lease Your Next Car?

Leasing is tempting: little or no money up front and lower monthly payments. But when the lease ends, you need to get another car. It's more expensive initially to buy, but at the end of the loan period, you own the car. Other key factors to consider:

Advantages of Leasing
- Better car for less money
- A new car every few years
- No trade-in hassles at the end of the lease

Advantages of Buying
- When interest rates are low, owning makes more financial sense than leasing
- No mileage penalty
- Increased flexibility—you can sell the car whenever you want

smart.sites

If you are still unsure whether to lease or buy, try letting the numbers help you make the right decision. Go to **http://www.edmunds.com** "Decision Calculator" and see how much leasing or buying will cost for the same car.

When the Lease Ends

At the expiration of the lease, you will be faced with a major decision. Should you return the car and walk away, or should you buy the car? If you turn in the car and move on to a new model, you may be hit with "excess wear and damage" and "excess mileage" charges and disposition fees. To minimize these, replace worn tires, get repairs done yourself, and document the car's condition before returning it. You may be able to negotiate a lower disposition fee. If you can't return the car without high repair charges or greatly exceeded mileage allowances, you may come out ahead by buying the car.

Concept ✓

5-3. What are the advantages and disadvantages of leasing a car?

5-4. Given your personal financial circumstances, if you were buying a car today, would you probably pay cash, lease, or finance it, and why? Which factors were most important to you in making this decision?

Whether the purchase option makes sense depends on the residual value. Sometimes, with popular cars, the residual value in your lease agreement is below the car's market value. Buying the car then makes sense. Even if you want a different car, you can exercise the purchase option and sell the car on the open market and net \$1,000 or more. If the reverse is true, and the residual is higher than the price of a comparable used car, just let the lease expire. Find

worksheet 5.1

Comparing Mary Dixon's Automobile Lease versus Purchase Costs

This worksheet illustrates Mary Dixon's lease versus purchase analysis for a new car costing $15,000. The 3-year closed-end lease requires an initial payment of $1,800 ($1,500 down payment + $300 security deposit) and monthly payments of $300. Purchasing requires a $2,500 down payment, sales tax of 5 percent ($750), and 36 monthly payments of $392. *Because the total cost of leasing of $12,516 is greater than the $9,662 total cost of purchasing, Mary should purchase rather than lease the car.*

AUTOMOBILE LEASE VERSUS PURCHASE ANALYSIS*

Name Mary Dixon Date March 4, 2005

Item	Description		Amount
LEASE			
1	Initial payment:		
	a. Down payment (capital cost reduction):	$ 1,500	
	b. Security deposit:	300	$ 1,800
2	Term of lease and loan (years)*		3
3	Term of lease and loan (months) (Item 2 × 12)		36
4	Monthly lease payment		$ 300
5	Total payments over term of lease (Item 3 × Item 4)		$ 10,800
6	Interest rate earned on savings (in decimal form)		.04
7	Opportunity cost of initial payment (Item 1 × Item 2 × Item 6)		$ 216
8	Payment/refund for market value adjustment at end of lease ($0 for closed-end leases) and/or estimated end-of-term charges		$ 0
9	**Total cost of leasing (Item 1a + Item 5 + Item 7 + Item 8)**		$ 12,516
PURCHASE			
10	Purchase price		$ 15,000
11	Down payment		$ 2,500
12	Sales tax rate (in decimal form)		.05
13	Sales tax (Item 10 × Item 12)		$ 750
14	Monthly loan payment (Terms: 12,500, 36 months, 8 %)		$ 392
15	Total payments over term of loan (Item 3 × Item 14)		$ 14,112
16	Opportunity cost of down payment (Item 2 × Item 6 × Item 11)		$ 300
17	Estimated value of car at end of loan		$ 8,000
18	**Total cost of purchasing (Item 11 + Item 13 + Item 15 + Item 16 − Item 17)**		$ 9,662

DECISION

If the value of Item 9 is less than the value of Item 18, leasing is preferred; otherwise the *purchase alternative is preferred.*

**Note:* This form is based on assumed equal terms for the lease and the installment loan, which is assumed to be used to finance the purchase.

your car's market value by looking in used-car price guides and newspaper ads and compare it with the residual value of your car.

MEETING HOUSING NEEDS: BUY OR RENT?

LG3

As Steve and Rachel Adams discovered, knowing when to buy your first home is not always clear-cut. There are many factors to consider before taking on such a large financial responsibility. In the remainder of this chapter we will explore some of these, and how to approach the home buying process.

Because you have your own unique set of likes and dislikes, the best way to start your search for housing is to list your preferences and classify them according to whether their satisfaction is essential, desirable, or merely a "plus." This exercise is important for three reasons. First, it serves to screen out housing that will not meet your minimum requirements. Second, it helps you recognize that you may have to make tradeoffs because seldom will you find a single home that meets all your needs. Third, it will help you focus on those needs for which you are willing and able to pay.

Housing in America is diverse, and everybody's housing needs differ. Some people prefer quiet and privacy; others like the hustle and bustle of big-city life. The features you prefer vary as well, from gourmet kitchens to an extra bedroom for a home office. You'll find single-family homes, townhouses, condominiums, cooperative apartments, or numerous types of rental units that meet your needs.

Rising home prices have provided a bright spot in an otherwise sluggish economy. Nationally, home sales in 2003 were forecast to nearly match 2002, a record-smashing year. According to the National Association of Realtors, first time buyers almost anywhere can purchase a starter home for $137,500 with 10 percent or less down, and monthly payments of $795. When tax deductions for mortgage interest and property taxes are factored in, the real cost of owning is below the median monthly rent of $633 as reported by the U.S. Census bureau. It is no wonder the home-ownership rate has reached a new record, exceeding 58 percent of the population. However, as shown in Exhibit 5.7, prices vary widely from one part of the country to another.

WHAT TYPE OF HOUSING FITS YOUR NEEDS?

One of the first decisions you'll have to make is the type of housing unit that meets your needs. Several of the following may be suitable:

- **Single-family homes:** These are the most popular choice. They can be stand-alone homes on their own legally defined lots or *row houses* or *townhouses* that share a common wall. As a rule, single-family homes offer buyers privacy, prestige, pride of ownership, and maximum property control.
- **Condominiums:** The term **condominium**, or **condo**, describes a form of ownership rather than a type of building. Condominiums can be apartments, townhouses, or cluster housing. The condominium buyer receives title to an individual residential unit and joint ownership of common areas and facilities such as lobbies, swimming pools, lakes, and tennis courts. Buyers arrange their own mortgages and pay their own taxes for their units. They are assessed a monthly *homeowner's fee* for their proportionate share of common facility maintenance costs. The *homeowners' association* elects a board of managers to supervise the buildings and grounds. Condominiums generally cost less than single-family, detached homes because they are designed for more efficient land use and lower construction costs. Many home buyers are attracted to condominiums because they do not want the responsibility of maintaining and caring for a large property. Exhibit 5.8 on page 190 lists some of the key things to check before buying a condominium.

condominium (condo)
A form of direct ownership of an individual unit in a multiunit project in which lobbies, swimming pools, and other common areas and facilities are jointly owned by all property owners in the project.

EXHIBIT 5.7

Going Through the Roof? Home Prices in Selected Cities

The median sales price of existing single-family homes varies widely from one part of the country to another—$90,600 in Buffalo, New York, $237,3000 in Miami, Florida, and $436.500 in San Diego, California. Here are some other home prices in selected cities.

Location	Average Price
Albuquerque, NM	$142,200
Atlanta, GA	$157,500
Austin, TX	$157,900
Baltimore, MD	$220,200
Baton Rouge, LA	$124,500
Boston, MA	$432,700
Charlotte, NC	$161,600
Chicago, IL	$249,100
Cincinnati, OH	$142,800
Columbia, SC	$129,100
Dallas, TX	$142,600
Denver, CO	$250,800
Des Moines, IA	$138,500
Honolulu, HI	$392,500
Houston, TX	$139,200
Indianapolis, IN	$127,600
Las Vegas, NV	$184,300
Los Angeles CA	$365,300
Minneapolis-St. Paul, MN	$208,200
New Orleans, LA	$136,90
New York, NY	$367,400
Oklahoma City, OK	$107,100
Orlando, FL	$154,000
Philadelphia, PA	$181,800
Phoenix, AZ	$156,100
Portland, OR	$196,200
Richmond, VA	$159,400
Saint Louis, MO	$130,700
San Francisco, CA	$568,200
Seattle, WA	$276,100
Syracuse, NY	$104,700
Toledo, OH	$117,600
Tucson, AZ	$159,700
Washington DC	$296,200
Wilmington, DE	$176,400

Source: National Association of Realtors®, Metropolitan Area Prices–3rd quarter 2003, downloaded from **http://www.realtor.org** January 7, 2004.

- **Cooperative apartments:** In a **cooperative apartment**, or **co-op**, building, each tenant owns a share of the nonprofit corporation that owns the building. Residents lease their units from the corporation and pay a monthly assessment in proportion to ownership shares, based on the space they occupy. These assessments cover the cost of service, maintenance, taxes, and the mortgage on the entire building and are subject to change, depending on the actual costs of operating the building and the actions of the board of directors, which determines the corporation's policies. The cooperative owner receives the tax benefits resulting from interest and property taxes attributable to his or her proportionate ownership interest. Drawbacks of co-op ownership include difficulty in obtaining a mortgage (because many financial institutions don't like taking shares of a corporation rather than property as collateral), rent increases to cover maintenance costs of vacant units, and the need to abide by the capital improvement decisions of the co-op board of directors, which increases the monthly assessment.
- **Rental units:** Some individuals and families choose to *rent* or *lease* their place of residence rather than own it. They may be just starting out and have limited funds for housing, or they may be uncertain where they want to live. Perhaps they like the short-term commitment and limited maintenance. The cost and availability of rental units varies from one geographic area to another. Rental units range from duplexes, four-plexes, and even single-family homes, to large, high-rise apartment complexes containing several hundred units. Renting does come with restrictions, however. You may not be allowed to have a pet or make changes to the unit's appearance.

cooperative apartment (co-op)
An apartment in a building in which each tenant owns a share of the corporation that owns the building.

EXHIBIT 5.8

Condo Buyers Checklist

It pays to carefully check out the various operating and occupancy features of a condo before you buy.

- Thoroughly investigate the reputation of the developer—through local real estate brokers, banks, or the Better Business Bureau—whether the building is brand new, under construction, or being converted.
- Read the rules of the organization.
- Investigate the condo homeowners' association, the restrictions on condo owners, and the quality of the property management.
- Check the construction of the building and its physical condition. If the building is being converted to condos, ask to see an independent inspection firm's report on the building's condition.
- Insist that any planned changes in the property be detailed in writing.
- Talk to the occupants to see if they are satisfied with the living conditions.
- Determine how many units are rented; generally, owner-occupied units are better maintained.
- Determine if there is sufficient parking space.
- Watch for unusually low maintenance fees that may have to be increased soon.
- Consider the resale value.

For new developments, compare the projected monthly homeowner's fees with those of similar buildings already in operation. For older developments, check to see when capital improvements such as exterior painting and roof replacement were last made. Special assessments are usually levied on all unit owners for major costly improvements.

The Rental Option

Many people choose to rent rather than buy their home. For example, young adults usually rent for one or more of the following reasons: (1) They do not have the funds for a down payment and closing costs, (2) they are unsettled in their jobs and family status, (3) they do not want the additional responsibilities associated with home ownership, or (4) they believe they can afford a nicer home later by renting now because housing market conditions or mortgage rates are currently unattractive. A big drawback of renting is that the payments are *not* tax deductible.

The Rental Contract/Lease Agreement

rental contract (lease agreement) A legal instrument that protects both the lessor and the lessee from an adverse action by the other party; it specifies the *amount* of the monthly payment, the payment *due date, penalties* for late payment, the *length* of the lease agreement, *deposit* requirements, *fair wear and tear* definitions and provisions, the distribution of *expenses, renewal* options and *early termination penalties,* and any *restrictions* on children, pets, subleasing or using the facilities.

When you rent an apartment, duplex, house, or any other type of residence, you will be required to sign a **rental contract** or **lease agreement**. Although oral agreements are generally binding, a written contract is a legal instrument that better protects both the *lessor* (the person who owns the property) and the *lessee* (the person who leases the property). Because the rental contract binds you, the lessee, to various actions, you should make certain that you fully understand it before signing it. As a rule, the contract specifies the *amount* of the monthly payment, the payment *due date, penalties* for late payment, the *length* of the lease agreement, security and/or advance rent (*deposit*) requirements, *fair wear and tear* definitions and provisions, the distribution of *expenses, lease renewal* options and *early termination penalties,* and any *restrictions* on children, pets, subleasing, or using the facilities.

Most leases have a minimum term of either 6 months or 1 year and require payments at the beginning of each month. They may initially require a security deposit, and/or payment of the last month's rent in advance as security against damages or violation of the lease agreement. In the absence of any serious damage, most of the deposit should be refunded to the lessee shortly after the lease expires; a portion of the deposit is sometimes retained by the lessor to cover the cost of cleaning and minor repairs, regardless of how clean and well kept the unit was. Because the landlord has control over the deposit, a written statement describing any preexisting damage, *prior* to occupancy, may help the lessee avoid losing their entire deposit. Renters should also clarify who bears expenses such as utilities and trash collection and exactly what, if any, restrictions are placed on the use of the property. It's also a good idea for renters to check the renter-landlord laws in their state to fully understand their *rights* and responsibilities.

The Rent-or-Buy Decision

As the Adams discovered, owning a home is not always more costly on a monthly basis than renting, although there are many other factors to consider before making this important decision. The economics of renting or buying a place to live depends on three main factors: (1) housing prices and mortgage interest rates, (2) tax write-offs for homeowners, and (3) the increase or decrease in home values over time.

To choose the lowest-cost alternative, compare the cost of renting with the cost of buying, as illustrated by the rent-or-buy analysis in Worksheet 5.2. Note that because the interest deduction nearly always exceeds the amount of the standard deduction ($4,750 for single and $9,500 for married filing jointly in 2003), the form assumes that the taxpayer will itemize deductions. Assume that you must decide between renting an apartment for $700 a month or buying a similar-sized, $100,000 condominium. Purchasing the condo involves a $15,000 down payment, an $85,000, 9-percent, 30-year mortgage with monthly mortgage payments of $684, $4,500 in closing costs, and property taxes, insurance, and maintenance. With renting, the only costs are the $700 monthly rental payment, an annual renter's insurance premium of $300, and the opportunity cost of interest lost on the security deposit. Assume that you are in the 25 percent ordinary income tax bracket and that you will itemize deductions if you purchase the home. Substituting the appropriate values into Worksheet 5.2 and making the required calculations results in the total cost of each alternative.

The cost of renting in part A of Worksheet 5.2 is simply the annual rent (monthly rent multiplied by 12) plus the annual renter's insurance premium of $300 plus the opportunity cost of interest lost on the security deposit. This results in a total annual cost of $8,732. The annual cost of buying in part B includes: mortgage payments, property taxes, homeowner's insurance, annual maintenance, lost interest on the down payment, and closing costs to arrive at $12,386.

Then, subtract the portion of the mortgage payment going to pay off the loan balance because it is not part of the interest cost. Subtract the tax benefits derived from interest and property taxes to arrive at Item 11, the out-of-pocket, after-tax cost of home ownership, $9,415. If you stop there, it looks like renting is the way to go.

But as a homeowner, you also enjoy the benefits of appreciation. Assuming a modest 3 percent inflation in the value of the home reduces the annual cost to $6,415. Buying appears better than renting because the total cost of renting is $2,317 ($8,732 − $6,415) a year more than the total cost of buying.

However, don't make the rent-or-buy decision solely on the basis of numbers. Your personal needs and the general condition of the housing market are also important considerations. If you think you may want to move to a different city in a few years or if you are worried about job security, renting may make sense, even if the numbers favor buying. For some people, factors such as the need for privacy, the desire to personalize one's home, and the psychic satisfaction gained from home ownership outweigh the financial considerations. In some housing markets a relative surplus of rental properties causes the cost of renting to be lower than the cost of owning a comparable house or condominium. You should look at the rent-or-buy decision over a time line of several years, using different assumptions regarding rent increases, mortgage rates, home appreciation rates in the area, and the rate of return you can earn on the funds you can invest (if you rent) rather than use them toward a down payment on a house (if you buy).

Concept ✓

5-5. In addition to single-family homes, what other forms of housing are available in the United States? Briefly describe the advantages and disadvantages of each.

5-6. Differentiate between a *condominium* and a *cooperative apartment*.

5-7. What type of housing would you choose for yourself now, and why? Why might you choose to rent instead of buy?

5-8. Why is it important to have a written lease? What should a rental contract include?

HOW MUCH HOUSING CAN YOU AFFORD?

LG 4

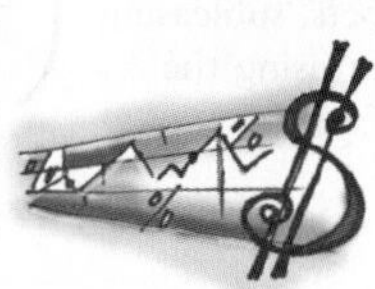

Buying a home obviously involves a good deal of careful planning and analysis. Not only must you decide on the kind of home you want (its location, number of bedrooms, and other features), you must also consider its cost, what kind of mortgage to get, how large a monthly payment you can afford, what kind of homeowner's insurance coverage to have, and so forth.

Buying a home (or any other major, big-ticket item) touches on many of the elements of personal financial planning. The money you use for a down payment will likely be drawn from your *savings program;* the homeowner's policy you choose is a part of your *insurance planning;* and your monthly mortgage payments undoubtedly will have an enormous impact on your *cash budget* and *tax plans.*

Sound financial planning dictates caution when buying a home or any other major item. Spending too much for a home or automobile can have a detrimental effect, not only on your budget and lifestyle, but also on your savings and investment plans, and possibly even your retirement plans. Knowing how much housing you can afford will go a long way toward helping you achieve balanced financial goals.

worksheet 5.2

Rent-or-Buy Cost Comparison

Using this procedure to make the rent-or-buy decision, you should *rent* if the total cost of renting is less than the total cost of buying, and *buy* if the total cost of renting is more than the total cost of buying. In this illustration, the rental option requires monthly payments of $700. The purchase option is a $100,000 condo, financed with a $15,000 down payment and an $85,000, 9-percent, 30-year mortgage, with additional closing costs of $4,500.

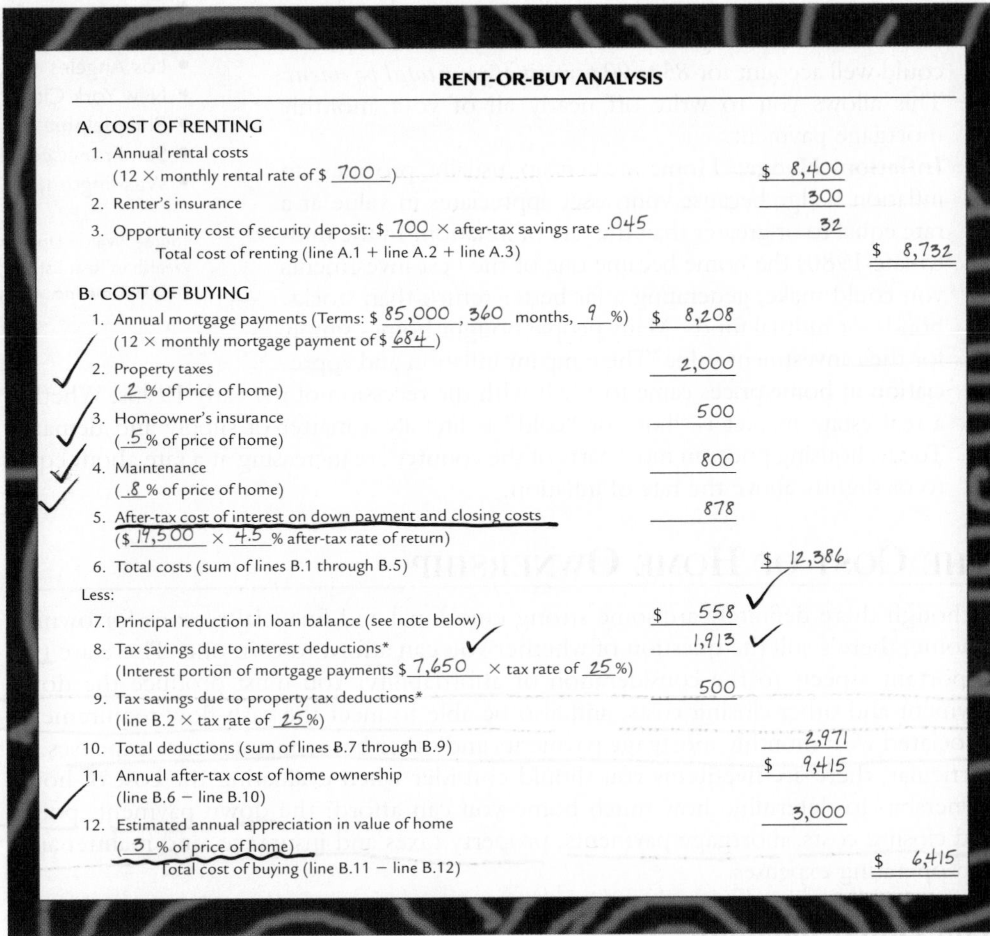

RENT-OR-BUY ANALYSIS

A. COST OF RENTING		
1. Annual rental costs (12 × monthly rental rate of $ 700)		$ 8,400
2. Renter's insurance		300
3. Opportunity cost of security deposit: $ 700 × after-tax savings rate .045		32
Total cost of renting (line A.1 + line A.2 + line A.3)		$ 8,732
B. COST OF BUYING		
1. Annual mortgage payments (Terms: $ 85,000 , 360 months, 9 %) (12 × monthly mortgage payment of $ 684)	$ 8,208	
2. Property taxes (2 % of price of home)	2,000	
3. Homeowner's insurance (.5 % of price of home)	500	
4. Maintenance (.8 % of price of home)	800	
5. After-tax cost of interest on down payment and closing costs ($ 19,500 × 4.5 % after-tax rate of return)	878	
6. Total costs (sum of lines B.1 through B.5)		$ 12,386
Less:		
7. Principal reduction in loan balance (see note below)	$ 558	
8. Tax savings due to interest deductions* (Interest portion of mortgage payments $ 7,650 × tax rate of 25 %)	1,913	
9. Tax savings due to property tax deductions* (line B.2 × tax rate of 25 %)	500	
10. Total deductions (sum of lines B.7 through B.9)		2,971
11. Annual after-tax cost of home ownership (line B.6 − line B.10)		$ 9,415
12. Estimated annual appreciation in value of home (3 % of price of home)		3,000
Total cost of buying (line B.11 − line B.12)		$ 6,415

Note: Find monthly mortgage payments from Exhibit 5.11. An easy way to approximate the portion of the annual loan payment that goes to interest (line B.8) is to multiply the interest rate by the size of the loan (in this case, $85,000 × .09 = $7,650). To find the principal reduction in the loan balance (line B.7), simply subtract the amount that goes to interest from total annual mortgage payments ($8,208 − $7,650 = $558).
*Tax-shelter items.

Benefits of Owning a Home

Home ownership is important to most people, whether they own a detached home or a condominium. It offers the security and peace of mind derived from living in one's own home and the feeling of permanence and sense of stability that ownership brings. This so-called "psychic reward" is not the only reason people enjoy owning their home. There are also financial payoffs from home ownership:

- **Tax shelter:** As noted in Chapter 3, you can deduct both mortgage interest and property taxes when calculating your federal and, in most states, state income taxes, reducing your taxable income and thus your tax liability. The only requirement is that you itemize your deductions. This tax break is so good that people who have never itemized usually begin doing so after they buy their first house. Also, keep in mind that for the first 15 to 20 years of ownership (assuming a 30-year mortgage), most of your monthly mortgage payment is made up of interest and property taxes—in fact, during the first 5 to 10 years or so, these could well account for *85 to 90 percent of your total payment.* This allows you to write off nearly all of your monthly mortgage payment.
- **Inflation Hedge:** Home ownership usually provides an inflation hedge because your asset appreciates in value at a rate equal to or greater than the rate of inflation. In the mid-to-late 1980s the home became one of the best investments you could make, generating a far better return than stocks, bonds, or mutual funds. Many people bought homes simply for their investment value. The rampant inflation and appreciation in home prices came to a halt with the recession of the early 1990s. Whether a real estate market is "hot" or "cold" is literally a matter of supply and demand. Today, housing prices in most parts of the country are increasing at a rate about equal to or slightly above the rate of inflation.

> **Financial Road Sign**
>
> **The Hottest Hoods**
>
> Want to see where your house or town stands in the ranks? Here are the eight largest metro regions where median home prices rose the most in the past 5 years.
>
> - Boston
> - Chicago
> - Detroit
> - Los Angeles
> - New York City
> - Philadelphia
> - San Francisco
> - Washington, D.C.
>
> Source: Walter Updegrave, "How to Build Wealth in Real Estate," *Money* Magazine, ©2003 Time Inc. All rights reserved.

The Cost of Home Ownership

Although there definitely are some strong emotional and financial reasons for owning a home, there's still the question of whether you can afford to own one. There are two important aspects to the consideration of affordability: You must produce the down payment and other closing costs, and also be able to meet the cash-flow requirements associated with monthly mortgage payments and other home maintenance expenses. In particular, there are five items you should consider when evaluating the cost of home ownership to determine how much home you can afford: the down payment, points and closing costs, mortgage payments, property taxes and insurance, and maintenance and operating expenses.

The Down Payment

The first major hurdle is the **down payment**. Most buyers finance a major part of the purchase price of the home, but they are required by lenders to invest money of their own, called *equity.* The actual amount of down payment required varies among lenders, mortgage types, and properties. To determine the amount of down payment that will be required in specific instances, lenders use the **loan-to-value ratio**, which specifies the maximum percentage of the value of a property that the lender is willing to loan. For example, if the loan-to-value ratio is 80 percent, the buyer will have to come up with a down payment equal to the remaining 20 percent.

down payment A portion of the full purchase price provided by the purchaser when a house or other major asset is purchased; often called *equity.*

loan-to-value ratio The maximum percentage of the value of a property that the lender is willing to loan.

Generally, first-time home buyers must spend a number of years accumulating enough money to afford the down payment and other costs associated with a home purchase. You can best accumulate these funds if you plan ahead, using future value techniques (presented in Chapters 2, 4, 11, and 14) to determine the monthly or annual savings necessary to have a stated amount by a specified future date. A detailed demonstration of this process is included in Chapter 11 (see Worksheet 11.1B). A disciplined savings program is the best way to obtain the funds needed to purchase a home or any other big-ticket item requiring a sizable down payment or cash outlay.

If you do not have enough savings to cover the down payment and closing costs, you can consider several other sources. You may be able to obtain some funds by withdrawing (subject to legal limitations) your contributions from your company's profit-sharing or thrift plan. Your IRA is another option. The *Taxpayer Relief Act of 1997* permits first-time homebuyers to withdraw $10,000 without penalty before age 59½. However, using retirement money should be a last resort because you must still pay income tax on retirement distributions. Thus, if you're in the 25 percent income-tax bracket, your $10,000 IRA withdrawal would net you only $7,500 ($10,000 − $2,500) for your down payment.

The Federal National Mortgage Association (known as "Fannie Mae") has several programs to help buyers who have limited cash for the down payment and closing costs. The "Fannie 3/2" program is available from local lenders. Borrowers who meet certain income criteria may qualify for a 95 percent loan-to-value mortgage, and may obtain up to 2 percent of their 5 percent down payment from a public or nonprofit agency or relative. "Fannie 97" helps the homebuyer who can handle monthly mortgage payments but doesn't have cash for the down payment. It requires only a 3 percent down payment from the borrower's own funds, and the borrower needs to have only 1 month's mortgage payment in cash savings, or reserves, after closing.

private mortgage insurance (PMI) An insurance policy that protects the mortgage lender from loss in the event the borrower defaults on the loan; typically required by lenders when the down payment is less than 20 percent.

As a rule, when the down payment is less than 20 percent, the lender will require the buyer to obtain **private mortgage insurance (PMI)**, which protects the lender from loss if the borrower defaults on the loan. Usually PMI covers the lender's risk above 80 percent of the price of the house. Thus, with a 10 percent down payment, the mortgage will be a 90 percent loan, and mortgage insurance will cover 10 percent of the home's price. The cost of mortgage insurance varies from about 0.5 percent to 1.0 percent of the loan balance each year, depending on the size of your down payment. It can be included in your monthly payment, and the average cost ranges from about $40 to $70 per month. You should contact your lender to cancel the mortgage insurance once the equity in your home reaches 20 to 25 percent. Under federal law, private mortgage insurance on most loans made on or after July 29, 1999, ends automatically once the mortgage is paid down to 78 percent of the original value of the house.

smart.sites

To find out how much more house you could afford with private mortgage insurance, visit the Mortgage Insurance Companies of America site on this subject: **http://www.privatemi.com**.

mortgage points Fees (one point equals 1 percent of the amount borrowed) charged by lenders at the time they grant a mortgage loan; they are related to the lender's supply of loanable funds and the demand for mortgages.

Points and Closing Costs

A second hurdle to home ownership relates to mortgage points and closing costs. **Mortgage points** are fees charged by lenders at the time they grant a mortgage loan. In appearance, points are like interest in that they are a charge for borrowing money. They are related to the lender's supply of loanable funds and the demand for mortgages; the greater the demand relative to the supply, the more points you can expect to pay. One point equals 1 percent of the amount borrowed. If you borrow $100,000 and loan fees equal 3 points, the amount of money you will pay in points will be $100,000 × .03 = $3,000.

Lenders typically use points as a way of charging interest on their loans. They can vary the interest rate along with the number of points they charge to create loans with comparable effective rates. For example, a lender might be willing to give you a 7 percent rather than an 8 percent mortgage if you are willing to pay more points; that is, you choose between an 8 percent mortgage rate with 1 point or a 7 percent mortgage rate with 3 points. If you choose the 7 percent loan, you will end up paying a lot more *at closing* (although the amount of interest paid *over the life of the mortgage* may be considerably less).

Points increase the *effective rate of interest* on a mortgage. The amount you pay in points and the length of time you hold a mortgage determine the increase in the effective interest rate. For example, on an 8 percent, 30-year, fixed-rate mortgage, each point increases the annual percentage rate by about .11 percent if the loan is held for 30 years, .17 percent if held for 15 years, .32 percent if held 7 years, and .70 percent if held 3 years. You pay the same amount in points regardless of how long you keep your home. Therefore the longer you hold the mortgage, the longer the period over which you amortize the points and the smaller the effect of the points on the effective annual interest rate.

According to recent IRS rulings, the points paid on a mortgage at the time a home is originally purchased are usually considered immediately tax deductible. The same points are *not* considered immediately tax deductible if they are incurred when *refinancing* a mortgage; rather, the amount paid in points must be written off (*amortized*) over the life of the new mortgage loan.

Closing costs are all expenses that borrowers ordinarily pay at the time a mortgage loan is closed and title to the purchased property is conveyed to them. Closing costs are like down payments: They represent money you must come up with *at the time you buy the house*. Closing costs are made up of such items as loan application and loan origination fees paid to the lender, mortgage points, title search and insurance fees, attorneys' fees, appraisal fees, and other miscellaneous fees for things such as mortgage taxes, filing fees, inspections, credit reports, and so on. As Exhibit 5.9 shows, these costs can amount to 50 percent or more of the down payment. For example, with a 10 percent down payment on a $100,000 home, the closing costs, as shown in Exhibit 5.9, are nearly 70 percent of the down payment, or $6,625. Simple arithmetic indicates that this buyer will need nearly $17,000 to buy the house (the $10,000 down payment plus another $6,625 in closing costs).

closing costs All expenses (including mortgage points) that borrowers ordinarily pay at the time a mortgage loan is closed and title to the purchased property is conveyed to them.

Mortgage Payments

A monthly mortgage payment is determined using a fairly complex formula. Each mortgage payment is made up partly of principal repayment on the loan and partly of interest charges on the loan. However, as Exhibit 5.10 on page 198 shows, for most of the life of the mortgage the vast majority of each monthly payment goes to *interest*. The loan illustrated in the exhibit is a $100,000, 30-year, 7 percent mortgage with monthly payments of $655.30, for a total of $7,983.60 per year. Note that it is not until after the 21st year of this 30-year mortgage that the principal portion of the monthly loan payment exceeds the amount that goes to interest.

In practice, mortgage lenders and realtors use *comprehensive mortgage payment tables* to obtain monthly payments. These tables provide monthly payments for virtually every combination of loan size, interest rate, and maturity. Exhibit 5.11 on page 199 provides an excerpt from one such comprehensive mortgage payment table (with values rounded to the nearest cent). It lists the *monthly payments* associated with a $10,000, fixed-rate loan for selected maturities of 10 to 30 years, and various interest rates ranging from 5 to 11 percent. This table can be used to find the monthly payment for any size loan. Alternately, you can purchase a relatively inexpensive business calculator and quickly and precisely calculate your monthly mortgage payments.

Suppose that you wish to use the mortgage payment tables to find the monthly loan payment on a $90,000, 6 percent, 30-year mortgage. To do this, simply divide the amount of the loan ($90,000) by $10,000 and then multiply this factor (9.0) by the payment amount shown in Exhibit 5.11 for a 6 percent, 30-year loan ($59.96):

$$\$90{,}000/\$10{,}000 = 9.0 \times \$59.96 = \$539.64$$

The resulting monthly mortgage payment would be $539.64.

EXHIBIT 5.9

Home Truths: The Hidden Costs of Buying a Home—Closing Costs

The closing costs on a home mortgage loan can be substantial—as much as 5 to 7 percent of the price of the home. Except for the real estate commission (which is generally paid by the seller), the buyer incurs the biggest share of the closing costs and must pay them—in addition to the down payment—at the time the loan is closed and title to the property is conveyed.

	Size of Down Payment	
Item	**20%**	**10%**
Loan application fee	$200	$200
Loan origination fee	800	900
Points	1,600	2,700
Mortgage insurance	—	675
Title search and insurance	500	550
Attorneys' fees	400	400
Appraisal fees	150	150
Home inspection	250	250
Mortgage tax	575	650
Filing fees	25	25
Credit reports	25	25
Miscellaneous	100	100
Total closing costs	$4,625	$6,625

Note: Typical closing costs for a $100,000 home—2 points charged with 20 percent down, 3 points with 10 percent down. Actual amounts will vary by lender and location.

Using Your Calculator

You can use a handheld business calculator to easily calculate mortgage payments. Before using your calculator, be sure that you've reviewed the instructions given in Appendix E. To find the mortgage payment on the $90,000, 6 percent, 30-year mortgage, we must first convert the number of years to months and the annual interest rate to a monthly rate, as follows:

$$\text{Number of months} = 12 \times \text{Number of years} = 12 \times 30 = 360$$

$$\text{Monthly interest rate} = \text{Annual interest rate}/12 = 6\%/12 = 0.5\%$$

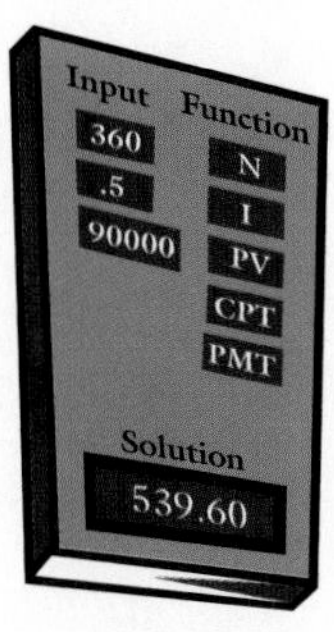

Having made these transformations, we can input the values into our calculator using the following steps:

1. Punch in 360 and press **N**.
2. Punch in .5 and press **I**.
3. Punch in 90000 and press **PV**.
4. To calculate the monthly mortgage payment, press **CPT** and then **PMT**. The payment value of $539.60 should appear on the calculator display. This slightly more precise value agrees with the value calculated earlier using the table of monthly mortgage payments.

EXHIBIT 5.10

Typical Principal and Interest Payment Patterns on a Mortgage Loan

For most of the life of a mortgage loan, the vast majority of each monthly payment goes to interest and only a small portion goes toward principal repayment. Over the 30-year life of the 7 percent, $100,000 mortgage illustrated here, the homeowner will pay almost $140,000 in interest.

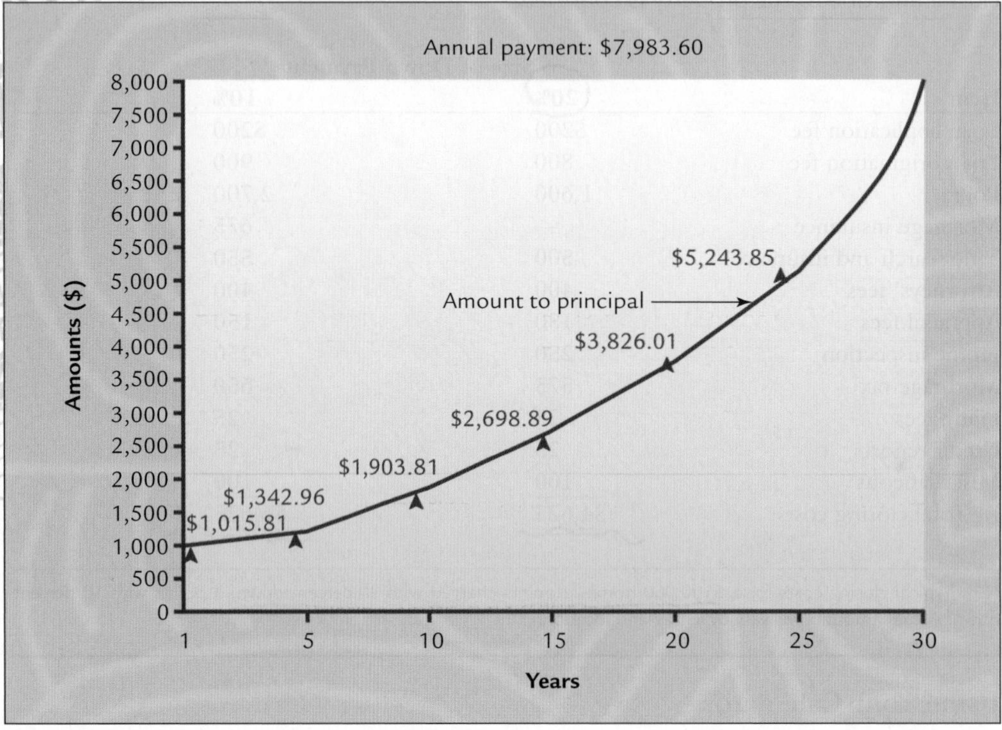

Note: Dollar amounts noted on the graph represent the total amount of principal repaid from the $7,983.60 annual payment made during the given year

Affordability Ratios

The key issue with respect to mortgage payments is *affordability*: How large a monthly mortgage payment can you afford, given your budget? This, in turn, will determine how much you can borrow to finance the purchase of a home.

To obtain a mortgage, a potential borrower must be "qualified"—demonstrate that he or she has adequate income and an acceptable credit record to reliably make scheduled loan payments. Federal and private mortgage insurers and institutional mortgage investors have certain standards they expect borrowers to meet to reduce their risk of default.

The most important affordability guidelines relate both *monthly mortgage payments and total monthly installment loan payments* (including the monthly mortgage payment

EXHIBIT 5.11

A Table of Monthly Mortgage Payments (Monthly Payments Necessary to Repay a $10,000 Loan)

The monthly loan payments on a mortgage vary not only by the amount of the loan, but also by the rate of interest and loan maturity.

	Loan Maturity				
Rate of Interest	10 Years	15 Years	20 Years	25 Years	30 Years
5.0%	$106.07	$ 79.08	$ 66.00	$ 58.46	$ 53.68
5.5	108.53	81.71	68.79	61.41	56.79
6.0	111.02	84.39	71.64	64.43	59.96
6.5	113.55	87.11	74.56	67.52	63.21
7.0	116.11	89.88	77.53	70.68	66.53
7.5	118.71	92.71	80.56	73.90	69.93
8.0	121.33	95.57	83.65	77.19	73.38
8.5	123.99	98.48	86.79	80.53	76.90
9.0	126.68	101.43	89.98	83.92	80.47
9.5	129.40	104.43	93.22	87.37	84.09
10.0	132.16	107.47	96.51	90.88	87.76
10.5	134.94	110.54	99.84	94.42	91.48
11.0	137.76	113.66	103.22	98.02	95.24

Note: **To use:** (1) Divide amount of the loan by $10,000, (2) find the loan payment amount in the table for the specific interest rate and maturity, and (3)multiply the amount from Step 1 by the amount from Step 2.

Example: The monthly payment for a $98,000, 7.5 percent, 30-year loan would be (1) $98,000/$10,000 = 9.8; (2) the payment associated with a 7.5 percent, 30-year loan, from the table, is *$69.93*; (3) the monthly payment required to repay a $98,000, 7.5 percent, 30-year loan is 9.8 × $69.93 = $685.31.

and monthly payments on auto, furniture, and other consumer installment loans) *to monthly borrower gross income.* Customary ratios for a *conventional mortgage* stipulate that monthly mortgage payments cannot exceed 25 to 30 percent of the borrower's monthly *gross* (before-tax) income, and the borrower's total monthly installment loan payments (including the mortgage payment) cannot exceed 33 to 38 percent of monthly gross income. Because both conditions stipulate a range, the lender has some leeway in choosing the most appropriate ratio for a particular loan applicant.

Let's look at how these affordability ratios work. Assume that your monthly gross income is $4,500. Applying the lower end of the ranges (that is, 25 percent and 33 percent), we see that this income level supports mortgage payments of $1,125 a month ($4,500 × .25 = $1,125) *so long as total monthly installment loan payments do not exceed $1,500* ($4,500 × .33 = $1,500). If your non-mortgage monthly installment loan payments exceeded $375 (the difference between $1,500 and $1,125), your mortgage payment would have to be reduced accordingly, or the other installment loan payments reduced or paid off. For instance, if you had $500 in other installment payments, your maximum monthly mortgage payment would be $1,500 − $500 = $1,000.

Determining the largest mortgage for which you qualify is just the first step. You also need to consider your lifestyle needs. Will taking on the responsibility of a mortgage require you to forgo luxuries or radically change your spending habits? To see how buying a house affects your cash flow, revise your personal budget to include the costs of buying a home—monthly mortgage payments, utilities, maintenance, insurance—and so on. Only you can decide how much of your income you are willing to allocate to a mortgage. You may have to make some tradeoffs, like choosing a lower-priced house with a smaller mortgage, to maintain greater financial flexibility.

Property Taxes and Insurance

Aside from loan costs, mortgage payments often include property tax and insurance payments. The mortgage payment therefore consists of *p*rincipal, *i*nterest, property *t*axes, and homeowner's *i*nsurance (or **PITI** for short). Actually, that portion of the loan payment that goes for taxes and insurance is paid into an *escrow account*, where it accumulates until the lender pays property taxes and homeowner insurance premiums as due. Some lenders pay interest—typically at no higher than the regular savings rate—on escrow account balances. However, it's preferable to pay insurance and taxes yourself, if you have the financial discipline. This strategy provides greater cash flexibility and an opportunity to earn a higher rate of return on funds than the escrow account pays.

Because they are local taxes levied to fund schools, law enforcement, and other local services, the level of **property taxes** differs from one community to another. In addition, within a given community, individual property taxes will vary according to the *assessed value* of the real estate—the larger and/or more expensive the home, the higher the property taxes, and vice versa. As a rule, annual property taxes vary from less than .5 percent to more than 2 percent of a home's approximate market value. Thus the property taxes on a $100,000 home could vary from about $500 to more than $2,000 a year, depending on location and geographic area.

Financial Road Sign

Keeping Your House in Order

Keeping up with basic home maintenance is a cost-effective way to save dollars in the future.

- **Have the furnace inspected and cleaned** every year to avoid the leading cause of home fires—faulty heating equipment. Change air filters of forced air systems annually.
- **Get a chimney sweep** to check your fireplace or woodstove for flammable creosote build-up.
- **Check your smoke alarms'** batteries every January and June and replace the detector every 10 years.
- **Install a carbon-monoxide detector** outside every sleeping area in the house if you use *any* gas appliances. Choose a model that offers a digital read-out of carbon-monoxide levels, and replace detectors every five to seven years.
- **Clean the clothes dryer vent** to prevent it clogging with flammable lint. Dryers are the third most common type of equipment to cause house fires, after stoves and heaters.
- **Schedule termite inspections** at regular intervals.

Sources: "Home Inspection Tips," *Better Homes & Gardens*, September 2001, downloaded from FindArticles, **http://www.findarticles.com**. Elizabeth Razzi "Cold Comfort," *Kiplinger's Magazine,* November 2002, p. 101.

The other component of the monthly mortgage payment is **homeowner's insurance**. Its cost varies with such factors as the age of the house, location, materials used in construction, and geographic area. Homeowner's insurance is required by mortgage lenders and covers only the replacement value of the home and its contents and not the land. Annual insurance costs usually amount to approximately .25 to .5 percent of the home's market value, or from $250 to $500 for a $100,000 house. The types, characteristics, and features of homeowner's insurance policies are discussed in more detail in Chapter 10.

PITI
Notation used to refer to a mortgage payment that includes stipulated portions of *p*rincipal, *i*nterest, property *t*axes, and homeowner's *i*nsurance.

Maintenance and Operating Expenses

In addition to the monthly mortgage payments, homeowners incur maintenance and operating expenses. Maintenance costs should be anticipated even on new homes. Painting, mechanical and plumbing repairs, and lawn maintenance, for example, are inescapable facts of home ownership. Such costs are likely to be greater for larger, older homes. Thus, although a large, established home may have an attractive purchase price, a new, smaller home may be a better buy in view of its lower maintenance and operating costs. Also consider the cost of operating the home, specifically the cost of utilities such as electricity, gas, water, and sewage. These costs have skyrocketed in the past 10 to 15 years and today represent a sizable component of home ownership costs, so get estimates of utilities when you evaluate a particular home for purchase.

Financial Road Sign

Are You Ready to buy a Home?

If you can answer yes to the following questions, you are probably ready for home ownership:

1. Have you worked consistently for at least the last 2 years, demonstrating a steady income and job history? If not, can you explain any gaps?
2. Have you established a favorable credit profile with a track record of debts owed and repaid on time?
3. Have you saved money for a cash down payment and closing costs?
4. Are the monthly mortgage payments for the house you want within the lender's limits for both your gross monthly income and your total monthly installment debt?

Source: Reprinted with permission of Homestore, Inc.

Performing a Home Affordability Analysis

Worksheet 5.3 helps you determine your maximum home-purchase price, using your monthly income and down payment amount after meeting estimated closing costs. In our example, the Renée and Edward Miller family has a combined annual income of $48,400, and savings of $22,500 for a down payment and closing costs. They estimate monthly property taxes and homeowner's insurance at $150 and expect the mortgage lender to use a 28 percent monthly mortgage-payment affordability ratio, to lend at an average interest rate of 7 percent on a 30-year mortgage, and to require a 10 percent minimum down payment. The Millers' analysis shows they can afford to purchase a home for about $150,000.

Worksheet 5.3 walks us through the steps the Miller family took to reach this conclusion. Based on their monthly income and the 28 percent affordability ratio, their monthly payment could be $1,130 ($4,033 × .28), shown as Item 4. After deducting taxes and insurance, the maximum monthly mortgage payment amount is $980 (Item 6). Using the table in Exhibit 5.11, a $10,000 loan for 30 years at 7 percent would result in a monthly payment of $66.53, as indicated in Item 9. Now, find out how much of a loan would a payment of $980 support:

$$\$10{,}000 \times \$980/\$66.53 = \$147{,}302 \text{ (Item 10)}$$

With a down payment of $15,000 and monthly income of $4,033, the Miller family can afford a home costing $162,302 (Item 13). The Millers then look at the maximum purchase price based on their $15,000 down payment , or $150,000 (Item 15). Their maximum home purchase price is the lower of Items 13 and 15, or $150,000 (Item 16) and is limited by the amount available for a down payment.

You can use Exhibit 5.12 to quickly estimate the size of mortgage you can afford, based on various monthly mortgage payment and interest rate assumptions. First determine the maximum monthly mortgage payment you can handle, then follow that line across to find the

property taxes Taxes levied by local governments on the *assessed value* of real estate for the purpose of funding schools, law enforcement, and other local services.

homeowner's insurance Insurance that is required by mortgage lenders and covers the replacement value of a home and its contents.

Concept ✓

5-9. Briefly describe the various benefits for owning a home. Which one is most important to you? Which is least important?

5-10. What does the *loan-to-value ratio* on a home represent? Is the down payment on a home related to its loan-to-value ratio? Explain.

5-11. What are *mortgage points?* How much would a homebuyer have to pay if the lender wanted to charge 2.5 points on an $85,000 mortgage? When would this amount have to be paid? What effect do points have on the mortgage's rate of interest?

5-12. What are *closing costs,* and what items do they include? Who pays these costs, and when?

5-13. What are the most common guidelines used to determine the monthly mortgage payment one can afford?

5-14. Why is it advisable for the prospective home buyer to investigate property taxes?

worksheet 5.3

Home Affordability Analysis for the Reneé and Edward Miller Family

By using the following variables in the home affordability analysis form, the Millers' estimate a maximum home purchase price of $150,000: their combined annual income of $48,400; the $22,500 available for a down payment and paying all closing costs; estimated monthly property taxes and homeowner's insurance of $150; the lender's 28 percent monthly mortgage-payment affordability ratio; an average interest rate of 7 percent and expected loan maturity of 30 years; and a minimum down payment of 10 percent.

HOME AFFORDABILITY ANALYSIS*

Name Renée and Edward Miller Date July 12, 2005

Item	Description	Amount
1	Amount of annual income	$ 48,400
2	Monthly income (Item 1 ÷ 12)	$ 4,033
3	Lender's affordability ratio (in decimal form)	.28
4	Maximum monthly mortgage payment (PITI) (Item 2 × Item 3)	$ 1,130
5	Estimated monthly property tax and homeowner's insurance payment	$ 150
6	Maximum monthly loan payment (Item 4 − Item 5)	$ 980
7	Approximate average interest rate on loan	7%
8	Planned loan maturity (years)	30
9	Mortgage payment per $10,000 (using Item 7 and Item 8 and Table of Monthly Mortgage Payments in Exhibit 5.11)	$ 66.53
10	Maximum loan based on monthly income ($10,000 × Item 6 ÷ Item 9)	$ 147,302
11	Funds available for making a down payment and paying closing costs	$ 22,500
12	Funds available for making a down payment (Item 11 × .67)	$ 15,000
13	Maximum purchase price based on available monthly income (Item 10 + Item 12)	$ 162,302
14	Minimum acceptable down payment (in decimal form)	.10
15	Maximum purchase price based on down payment (Item 12 ÷ Item 14)	$150,000
16	Maximum home purchase price (lower of Item 13 and Item 15)	$150,000

**Note:* This analysis assumes that ⅓ of the funds available for making the down payment and paying closing costs are used to meet closing costs while the remaining ⅔ are available for a down payment. This assumption means that closing costs will represent an amount equal to 50 percent of the down payment.

EXHIBIT 5.12

How Much Mortgage Will Your Payment Buy?

This table provides a quick way to estimate the size of the mortgage you can afford based on the monthly mortgage payment and mortgage interest rate. It assumes a 30-year, fixed-rate loan. Remember that this amount is only for mortgage principal and interest; you must have funds available for paying property taxes and homeowner's insurance as well.

Monthly Mortgage Payment	Mortgage Interest Rate 5%	6%	7%	8%	9%	10%	11%
$ 500	$93,141	$ 83,396	$ 75,154	$ 68,142	$ 62,141	$ 56,975	$ 52,503
600	111,769	100,075	90,185	81,770	74,569	68,370	63,004
700	130,397	116,754	105,215	95,398	86,997	79,766	73,504
800	149,025	133,433	120,246	109,027	99,425	91,161	84,005
900	167,653	150,112	135,277	122,655	111,854	102,556	94,506
1,000	186,282	166,792	150,308	136,283	124,282	113,951	105,006
1,100	204,910	183,471	165,338	149,912	136,710	125,346	115,507
1,200	223,538	200,150	180,369	163,540	149,138	136,741	126,008
1,300	242,166	216,829	195,400	177,169	161,566	148,136	136,508
1,400	260,794	233,508	210,431	190,797	173,995	159,531	147,009
1,500	279,422	250,187	225,461	204,425	186,423	170,926	157,510

Note: **To use:** (1) Find the amount of monthly mortgage payment you can afford, to the nearest $100. Then find the current mortgage interest rate to the nearest percent. The approximate mortgage amount will be at the intersection of the two columns. (2) To estimate the mortgage size if the interest rate ends in .5 percent, add the mortgage amounts for the lower and higher mortgage interest rates and divide by 2. (3) To estimate the mortgage size for a payment ending in 50, add the mortgage amounts for the lower and higher monthly mortgage payments and divide by 2.

Examples: (1) The estimated mortgage size if you have a monthly mortgage payment of $900 on a 30-year, 10 percent loan is $102,556. (2) To find the estimated mortgage size if you have a monthly mortgage payment of $900 and the mortgage interest rate is 9.5 percent, add the mortgage sizes for $900 at 9 percent and at 10 percent and divide by 2: ($111,854 + $102,556) ÷ 2 = $214,410 ÷ 2 = $107,205. (3) To find the estimated mortgage size if you have a monthly mortgage payment of $950 and the mortgage interest rate is 9 percent, add the mortgage sizes for $900 and $1,000 at 9 percent and divide by 2: ($111,854 + $124,282) ÷ 2 = $236,136 ÷ 2 = $118,068.

approximate size of the mortgage your payment will buy at each mortgage interest rate. (This figure assumes a 30-year, fixed-rate loan and does *not* include property taxes and homeowner's insurance.) For example, if you estimate that you have $1,000 available per month and the prevailing mortgage interest rate is 8 percent, you can afford a mortgage of about $136,000.

LG5 THE HOME-BUYING PROCESS

Are you in the market for your first home, like the buyers profiled in the *Money in Action* box on page 204. Buying a home requires time, effort, and money. You'll want to educate yourself about available properties and prevailing prices by doing a systematic search and careful analysis. You'll also need a basic understanding of the role of a real estate agent, the mortgage application process, the real estate sales contract, and other documents required to close a deal.

Money in Action

New Kids on the Block

Justin Townsend, a computer consultant in Allen, Texas, lives in a house on a cul-de-sac with a swimming pool and a big backyard. When friends visit they often ask where his parents are, but there are no parents living there. At 22 years old, Townsend is the homeowner. Tired of renting, he got a 100 percent loan to purchase the $152,500 three-bedroom home so he could have a living room large enough to accommodate his pool table—not possible in a condo.

In the past, homebuyers under 30 typically waited to buy a home until they get married, but today many successful young gen-Xers are choosing to put down roots, married or not. Many of the young and the restless are settling down, enticed by a shaky stock market, easier mortgage financing, and ultra-low interest rates. The number of homeowners under 25 doubled to 1.5 million (23 percent) in 2002, up from 792,000 (15 percent) in 1993, according to U. S. census data.

Too young to remember the housing bust of the late 1980s and early 1990s, today's young buyers consider real estate a promising investment compared with the ups and downs of the stock market. Helped by better mortgage terms, like those offered by Wells Fargo Home Mortgage, a unit of Wells Fargo & Co.—young homebuyers can finance the entire cost of a home—without a down payment. And the lowest interest rates in decades often make owning more affordable than renting.

Twenty-five-year-old Adam Mitchell, a commercial real estate advisor, bought a $240,000 condo in Chicago and found his mortgage only cost him $900 per month, less that the $1,100 per month he was paying in rent. Colleen Scavone, 24, a Chicago high-school teacher, says the $262,000 one-bedroom loft she bought in April wiped out most of her savings but only costs her $900 per month in mortgage overhead.

With the majority of homeowners still in their forties, homebuyers under 25 represent a mere 2 percent of all homeowners. But is this youthful nesting instinct a growing trend? While it may seem surprising for people barely out of college to be making such a large financial commitment, many of today's young adults are focused on

...continued on next page

Shop the Market First

Most people who shop the housing market rely on real estate agents for information, access to properties, and advice. Other sources of information, such as newspaper ads, are also used widely to identify available properties. Occasionally a person seeking to buy or rent property will advertise his or her needs and wait for sellers to initiate contact. Today the Internet is a valuable resource for homebuyers. You can search an online real estate database, specify preferences such as location, price, and size, and obtain descriptions and color pictures of all properties that meet your needs. Other systems allow buyers to use a touch-tone phone to get recorded descriptions of homes listed by a particular agency, or see and print descriptions and color pictures of homes for sale using an electronic kiosk.

smart.sites

A great place to begin your home search is at Realtor.com (**http://www.realtor.com**). This site has it all—from a Real Estate 101 course to lists of local realtors, homes for sale in a particular area, and financing information.

Buying a home involves many factors, both financial and emotional, and the emotional factors often carry the greatest weight. As noted earlier, you must begin your home search project by figuring out what *you* require for your particular lifestyle needs—in terms of living space, style, and other special features. The property's location, neighborhood, and school district are usually important considerations as well. It is helpful to divide your list into *necessary* features, such as the number of bedrooms and baths, and *optional*—but desirable—features, such as fireplaces, whirlpool tubs, and so on. And of course, an affordability analysis is a critical component of the housing search.

Keep an open mind as you start looking. You may find that you like a house that is far different from what you initially you thought you wanted. For example, you may begin your search looking for a one-story, contemporary ranch house with a pool, but fall in love with a two-story colonial with wonderful landscaping, no pool, and all the other features you want. Be flexible and look at a variety of homes in your price range. This can be invaluable in helping you define your wants and needs more clearly.

If you already own a house but want or need a larger or different type of home, you can either trade up or remodel it. You may choose to remodel it if you like your neighborhood and can make the desired changes to your current home. In some cases, the cost to remodel will be less than the transaction costs of buying another house. The best remodeling projects are those whose costs you can recover when you sell the house. Kitchen improvements, additional bathrooms, and family rooms tend to best enhance a home's market value. Although a swimming pool may give you pleasure, you may not recover its cost when you sell the house. Exhibit 5.13 demonstrates some effective ways to enhance your property's value.

success and lifestyle. And changes in their spending patterns prove they are serious in their commitment to homeownership—with less spent on clothes, cars, and entertainment, and more on housing and household furnishings.

Critical Thinking Questions

1. What emotional factors motivate people in their early twenties looking to buy homes now, instead of waiting until they are older and more settled?
2. How are young buyers able to afford to buy a home rather than rent?
3. Do you agree with the purchase decisions of new homeowners profiled in the article? Explain your answer.

Sources: Shirley Leung, "New Kids on the Block," *The Wall Street Journal,* July 18, 2003, p. B1; Walter Updegrave, "How to Build Wealth in Real Estate," *Money*, June 2003, pp. 77–81.

You are unlikely to find the "perfect" home at the "perfect" price so you will need to make some compromises, and the greater your research and advance preparation, the better off you will be. This should also help to reduce the *buyer's remorse* that can accompany a major purchase. Soon after signing the sales contract, homebuyers often question whether they did the right thing: Did I pay too much? Should I have negotiated harder? Is the location as good as I thought? Can I really afford the monthly payments? Can I manage without a pool, playroom, or workshop? These feelings are normal, and usually disappear once you move in. One way to reduce buyer's remorse is to shorten the time that elapses between signing the sales contract and closing the deal.

EXHIBIT 5.13

Home Sweet Investment

According to a survey of real estate agents by HomeGain.com, even seemingly small presale improvements generate a significant return on investment as measured by a higher selling price.

Project	Return on Investment
Lighten and brighten home, wash windows	769%
Clean and de-clutter	594%
Landscape and trim yard	266%
Repair electrical and plumbing problems	196%
Spruce up décor, including flowers	169%
Update kitchen and bathroom	138%

Source: Thomas Fogerty, "Value of Home Improvements," *Chicago Sun Times*, May 12, 2002, p. 4C; Real Estate, *Money*, June 2003, p.106.

Using an Agent

Most homebuyers rely on real estate agents because they are professionals who are in daily contact with the housing market. Once you describe your needs to an agent, he or she can begin to search for appropriate properties. Your agent will also help you negotiate with the seller, obtain satisfactory financing, and, although not empowered to give explicit legal advice, prepare the real estate sales contract.

Most real estate firms belong to a local **Multiple Listing Service (MLS)**, a comprehensive listing, updated daily, of properties for sale in a given community or metropolitan area. A brief description of each property and its asking price are included, with a photo of the property. Only realtors who work for an MLS member firm have access to this major segment of the market.

Multiple Listing Service (MLS) A comprehensive listing, updated daily, of properties for sale in a given community or metropolitan area that includes a brief description of each property and its asking price with a photo and can be accessed only by realtors who work for a MLS member firm.

Buyers should remember that *agents typically are employed by sellers.* Unless you have agreed to pay a fee to a sales agent to act as a *buyer's agent*, a realtor's primary responsibility, by law, is to sell listed properties at the highest possible prices. Agents are paid only if they make a sale, so some might try and pressure you to "sign now or miss the chance of a lifetime." But most agents will listen to your needs and work to match you with the right property, under terms that will benefit both you and the seller. Good agents recognize that their interests are best served when all parties to a transaction are satisfied.

Real estate commissions generally range from 5 to 6 percent for new homes and 6 to 7 percent for previously occupied homes or *resales.* It may be possible to negotiate a lower commission with your agent, or to find a discount broker, or one who charges a flat fee. Commissions are paid only by the seller, but because the price of a home is often inflated by the size of the real estate commission—many builders are believed to factor commission costs into the prices of their new homes—the buyer probably absorbs some or even all of the commission.

Whereas traditional agents represent the seller's interests, *buyer's brokers,* as the term implies, are hired by buyers to negotiate on their behalf. Commissions to buyer's brokers are negotiated, and may ultimately be paid by the seller. A *facilitator,* on the other hand, represents neither the buyer nor the seller but is typically paid by both parties to serve as a neutral intermediary between them.

Prequalifying and Applying for a Mortgage

Before beginning your home search, it may be helpful to meet with one or more mortgage lenders to prearrange a mortgage loan. **Prequalification** can work to your advantage in several ways. You will know ahead of time the specific mortgage amount that you qualify for, subject, of course, to changes in rates and terms, and can focus your search on homes within an affordable price range.

prequalification The process of arranging with a mortgage lender, in advance of buying a home, to obtain the amount of mortgage financing the lender deems affordable to the home buyer.

Prequalification also provides estimates of the required down payment and closing costs for different types of mortgages. It identifies in advance any problems, such as credit report errors, that might arise as a result of your application, and allows you time to correct them. Finally, prequalification enhances your bargaining power with the seller of a house you want by letting her or him know that the deal won't fall through because you can't afford the property or obtain suitable financing. And without the need to go through the entire mortgage application process, the time required to close the sale should be relatively short.

There are many sources of mortgage loans, and you should begin investigating them while you are looking for a house. When you actually apply for a mortgage loan on a particular home, you will need to give the lender information on your income, assets, and outstanding debts. Documents the lender may request include proof of your monthly income (paycheck stubs, W-2 forms, and so on), statements showing all debt balances (credit cards, car and education loans, bank lines of credit, and so on), lists of financial assets such as savings accounts and securities, several months' bank account statements, and at least 2 years' income tax returns. Financing your home will be covered in detail later in this chapter.

The Real Estate Sales Contract

Once you select a home to buy, you must enter into a sales contract. State laws generally specify that to be enforceable in court, real estate buy-sell agreements must be in writing and contain certain information, including (1) names of buyers and sellers, (2) a description of the property sufficient to provide positive identification, (3) specific price and other terms, and (4) usually the signatures of the buyers and sellers. Real estate sales transactions often take weeks and sometimes months to complete. They involve a fair amount of legal work and therefore require expert assistance in preparation. Contract requirements help keep the facts straight and reduce the chance for misunderstanding, misrepresentation, or fraud.

Although these requirements fulfill the minimums necessary for court enforcement, in practice real estate sales contracts usually contain several other contractual clauses relating to earnest money deposits, contingencies, personal property, and closing costs. An **earnest money deposit** is the money you pledge to show good faith when you make an offer. If, after you sign a sales contract, you withdraw from the transaction without a valid reason, you may forfeit this deposit. A valid reason for withdrawal would be stated in the contract as a contingency clause. With a **contingency clause**, you can condition your agreement to buy on such factors as the availability of financing, a satisfactory termite or other physical inspection of the property, or the advice of a lawyer or real estate expert. Generally speaking, your lawyer should review and approve all agreements before you sign them.

earnest money deposit
Money pledged by a buyer to show good faith when making an offer to buy a home.

contingency clause
A clause in a real estate sales contract that makes the agreement conditional on such factors as the availability of financing, property inspections, or obtaining expert advice.

Closing the Deal

After you obtain financing and your loan is approved, the closing process begins. Although closing expenses may climb into the thousands of dollars, homebuyers can often save significant amounts if they shop for financing, insurance, and other closing items rather than merely accepting the costs quoted by any one lender or provider of closing services.

The **Real Estate Settlement Procedures Act (RESPA)** governs closings on owner-occupied houses, condominiums, and apartment buildings of four units or fewer. This act reduced closing costs by prohibiting kickbacks made to real estate agents and others from lenders or title insurance companies. It also requires clear, advance disclosure of all closing costs to homebuyers. Lenders must give potential borrowers a U.S. Department of Housing and Urban Development booklet entitled *Settlement Costs and You: A HUD Guide for Homebuyers.* The booklet sets forth the specific requirements of RESPA, and can take much of the mystery out of the closing process. Exhibit 5.14 provides some tips to help you sail smoothly through the closing process.

Real Estate Settlement Procedures Act (RESPA)
A federal law that requires mortgage lenders to give potential borrowers a government publication that describes the closing process and provide clear, advance disclosure of all closing costs to homebuyers.

Concept ✓

5-15. Describe some of the steps homebuyers can take to improve the home-buying process and increase their overall satisfaction with their purchases.

5-16. What role does a real estate agent play in the purchase of a house? What is the benefit of the *Multiple Listing Service?* How is the real estate agent compensated, and by whom?

5-17. Why should you investigate mortgage loans and prequalify for a mortgage early in the home-buying process?

5-18. What information is normally included in a real estate sales contract? What is an *earnest money deposit?* What is a *contingency clause?*

5-19. Describe the steps involved in closing a home-purchase transaction.

Title Check

Numerous legal interests can exist in real estate simultaneously: for example, those of the owners, lenders, lien-holders (such as an unpaid roofing contractor), and easement holders. Before taking title to a property, you should make sure that the seller (who is conveying title to you) actually has the legal interest he or she claims, and that the title is free of all liens and encumbrances (except those specifically referred to in the sales contract).

Although it is up to you to question the integrity of the title to the property you are buying, in most cases an attorney or title insurance company performs a **title check**, which consists of the necessary research of legal documents and courthouse records. The customary practices and procedures and costs vary widely throughout the country. Regardless of the specific custom in your area, you should make some form of title check an essential part of your closing process.

title check
The research of legal documents and courthouse records to verify that the seller conveying title actually has the legal interest he or she claims, and that the title is free of all liens and encumbrances.

Closing Statement

A *closing statement*, provided to both buyer and seller at or before the actual closing, accounts for monies that change hands during the transaction. The statement reconciles the borrower's and seller's costs, and shows how much the borrower owes and the seller receives from the transaction. Before closing a home purchase, you should be given an opportunity to review the closing statement and have your questions answered. You should carefully and critically review the statement to make sure that it is accurate and consistent with the contractual terms of the transaction; if not, have the statement corrected before closing the deal.

EXHIBIT 5.14

10 Things You Should Not Do Before Closing

The seller has accepted your offer to purchase, and your new home is officially under contract. Here are some tips to help you sail smoothly through the closing.

1. **Don't make another major purchase** even if you think your new house needs a new car in the driveway. Talk to your mortgage loan officer before making a major purchase.
2. **Don't deplete your cash reserves** because banks consider available cash when approving a loan.
3. **Don't change jobs** because banks like to see a consistent employment history.
4. **Don't let your emotions take over** by letting the seller's refusal to make a small repair kill the deal. Be realistic because no home is perfect, especially older homes.
5. **Don't forget to switch utilities** and apply for service at your new home. Do so as soon as you know your closing date.
6. **Don't forget about homeowner's insurance** because your lender will require an insurance binder for the new home prior to closing.
7. **Don't become best friends with the seller** because personality conflicts can cloud your judgement.
8. **Don't panic if the appraisal comes in low** because there are things you and your agent can do to correct the problem. Study your options.
9. **Don't go it alone** because it is the agent's duty to help you make it to the closing. Their commission depends on it.
10. **Don't ignore the requirements**—make sure you know what is expected and take care of it. If your lender asks you for something, provide it immediately.

Source: Downloaded from **http://www.realestate.com**, October 4, 2003.

FINANCING THE TRANSACTION

LG6

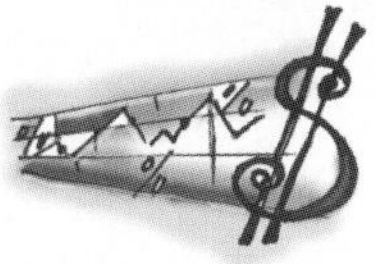

Earlier in the chapter, we saw that mortgage terms can have a dramatic effect on the amount you can afford to spend on a home. The success of a real estate transaction often

mortgage loan A loan secured by the property: In the event of default by the borrower, the lender has the legal right to liquidate the property to recover the funds it is owed.

mortgage banker A firm that solicits borrowers, originates primarily government-insured and government-guaranteed loans, and places them with mortgage lenders; often uses its own money to initially fund mortgages it later resells.

mortgage broker A firm that solicits borrowers, originates primarily conventional loans, and places them with mortgage lenders; the broker merely takes loan applications and then finds lenders willing to grant the mortgage loans under the desired terms.

hinges on obtaining a mortgage with favorable terms. A **mortgage loan** is secured by the property: in the event of default by the borrower, the lender has the legal right to liquidate the property to recover the funds it is owed. Before you obtain such a loan it is helpful to understand the sources and types of mortgages and their underlying economics.

Sources of Mortgage Loans

The major sources of home mortgages today are commercial banks, thrift institutions, and mortgage bankers or brokers; also, some credit unions make mortgage loans available to their members. Commercial banks are also an important source of *interim construction loans,* providing short-term financing during the construction process for individuals who are building or remodeling a home. After the home is completed, the homeowner obtains *permanent financing* in the form of a standard mortgage loan, and uses the proceeds from it to repay the construction loan.

Another way to obtain a mortgage loan is through a mortgage banker or mortgage broker. Both solicit borrowers, originate loans, and place them with traditional mortgage lenders as well as life insurance companies and pension funds. Whereas **mortgage bankers** often use their own money to initially fund mortgages they later resell, **mortgage brokers** take loan applications and then seek lenders willing to grant the mortgage loans under the desired terms. Mortgage bankers deal primarily in government-insured and government-guaranteed loans, whereas mortgage brokers concentrate on finding conventional loans for consumers. Most brokers also have ongoing relationships with different lenders, thereby increasing your chances of finding a loan even if you would not qualify at a commercial bank or thrift institution. They can often simplify the financing process by cutting through red tape, negotiating more favorable terms, and reducing the amount of time to close the loan. Mortgage brokers earn their income from commissions and origination fees paid by the lender, costs which are typically passed on to the borrower in the points charged on a loan. The borrower must often pay application, processing, and document preparation fees to the lender at closing. Exhibit 5.15 offers advice for working with a mortgage broker. You may prefer to shop for a mortgage on your own or with the assistance of your realtor, who is knowledgeable about various lenders and legally prohibited from collecting fees or kickbacks for helping to arrange financing.

Online Mortgage Resources

Shopping for the best mortgage rate and terms has become easier thanks to the Internet. Many sites allow you to search for the best fixed-rate or adjustable-rate mortgage in your area. HSH associates, a mortgage consulting firm with a Web site at **http://www.hsh.com**, lists mortgages offered by banks, mortgage companies, and brokerage firms across the country, along with information on prevailing interest rates, terms, and points. Bankrate, **http://www.bankrate.com**, and similar sites also offer mortgage comparisons. Shopping via the Internet gives you tremendous leverage when dealing with a lender. For example, if a local mortgage lender offers a 3-year adjustable-rate mortgage (ARM) with 1.20 points and a 6.75 percent rate, but a lender in a different state offers the same term with the same rate and only 1 point, you can negotiate with your local lender to get a better deal.

Although the Internet is still primarily a source of comparative information, online lenders such as E-Loan, **http://www.eloan.com**, a large online-only mortgage bank, hopes that homebuyers will choose to apply for and close a loan online. Or submit your information to LendingTree at **http://www.lendingtree.com**, and within 24 hours you'll receive bids from four lenders interested in making your loan. Visit House and Home at **http://www.houseandhome.msn.com** for loan and general home buying information.

EXHIBIT 5.15

Finding A Good Mortgage Broker

You've contracted to buy a property, and you have decided to use a mortgage broker to obtain a mortgage loan. Here are some tips to help you find a good mortgage broker.

- Get referrals from realtors, bankers, and other buyers.
- To help you get the best rate and terms, the broker should represent 10 or more lenders from around the United States.
- Investigate the firm and its reputation. Ask how many of their loan applications are actually funded; about 70 percent or more should result in closings.
- If your state licenses mortgage brokers, choose one who is licensed and has been in business for several years. Many brokers are certified by the National Association of Mortgage Brokers, although this is not a requirement.
- Request a written estimate of closing costs and explanation of each cost.
- Avoid a broker who asks for up-front fees and promises to find you a loan.

TYPES OF MORTGAGE LOANS

There is no single way to classify mortgages. For our purposes, we will group them in two ways: (1) terms of payment and (2) whether they are conventional, insured, or guaranteed.

There are literally dozens of different types of home mortgages from which to choose. The most common types of mortgage loans made today are fixed-rate and adjustable-rate mortgages. We now will take a closer look at their features, advantages, and disadvantages.

smart.sites

American Loan Search, **http://www.americanloansearch.com**, will provide a list of online mortgage lenders in your area when you enter your state. The site also has a rate search engine to help you find a lender with the rate you want.

Fixed-Rate Mortgages

The **fixed-rate mortgage** still accounts for a large portion of all home mortgages. Both the rate of interest and the monthly mortgage payment are fixed over the full term of the loan. The most common type of fixed-rate mortgage is the *30-year fixed-rate* loan, although *10- and 15-year loans* are becoming more popular as homeowners recognize the advantages of paying off their loan over a shorter period of time. Because of the risks the lender assumes with a 30-year loan, it is usually the most expensive form of home financing.

fixed-rate mortgage The traditional type of mortgage in which both the rate of interest and the monthly mortgage payment are fixed over the full term of the loan.

Gaining in popularity is the *15-year fixed-rate* loan. Its chief appeal is that it is repaid twice as fast (15 years versus 30) and yet the monthly payments don't increase significantly. To pay off a loan in less time the homeowner must pay more each month, but it does not take twice as large monthly payments to pay off the loan in half the time; rather, the monthly payment on a 15-year loan is generally only about 20 percent larger than the payment on a 30-year loan. The following table shows the difference in monthly payment and total interest paid for 30- and 15-year fixed-rate mortgages. In both cases the purchaser borrows $80,000 at a 9 percent fixed rate of interest:

Term of Loan	Regular Payment	Total Interest Paid over Life of Loan
30 years	$643.76 per month	$151,754
15 years	$811.44 per month	$ 66,059

Perhaps the most startling feature is the substantial difference in the total amount of interest paid over the term of the loan. In effect, you can save *about $85,000* just by financing your home with a 15-year mortgage rather than over the traditional 30 years. Note that this amount of savings is possible even though monthly payments differ by only $168. In practice, the difference in the monthly payment would be even less because 15-year mortgages are usually available at interest rates that are about half a percentage point below comparable 30-year loans.

Although the idea of paying off a mortgage in 15 years instead of 30 may seem like a good one, you should consider how long you plan to stay in the house. If you plan to sell the house in a few years, paying off the loan faster may not make much sense. In addition, the tax deductibility of mortgage interest makes a mortgage one of the least expensive sources of borrowing. If you can earn a higher rate of return than the rate of interest on a 30-year loan, you would be better off taking the 30-year loan and investing the difference in the payment between it and the comparable 15-year loan. Another way to shorten the mortgage term without committing to an initially shorter term is by making extra principal payments on a regular basis, or at times when you have extra funds.

balloon-payment mortgage A mortgage with a single large principal payment due at a specified future date.

Some lenders offer other types of fixed-rate loans. **Balloon-payment mortgages** offer terms of 5, 7, or 10 years where the interest rate is fixed, typically at .25 to .5 percent below the 30-year fixed rate. The monthly payments are the same as for a 30-year loan at the given rate. When the loan matures, the remaining principal balance comes due and must be refinanced. Although the lower rate results in lower monthly payments, these loans do carry some risk because refinancing may be difficult, particularly if rates have risen.

Adjustable-Rate Mortgages (ARMs)

adjustable-rate mortgage (ARM) A mortgage on which the rate of interest, and therefore the size of the monthly payment, is adjusted in accordance with market interest rate movements.

Another popular form of home loan is the **adjustable-rate mortgage (ARM)**. The rate of interest, and therefore the size of the monthly payment, is adjusted in accordance with market interest rate movements. The mortgage interest rate is linked to a specific *interest rate index* and is adjusted at specific time intervals (usually once or twice a year) in line with changes in the index. When the index moves up, so does the interest rate on the mortgage and, in turn, the size of the monthly mortgage payment increases. The new interest rate and monthly mortgage payment remain in effect until the next adjustment date.

The term of an ARM can be 15 or 30 years. Because the size of the monthly payments will vary with interest rates, there is no way to tell what your future payments will be. However, because the borrower assumes most or all of the interest rate risk in these mortgages, the *initial rate of interest* on an adjustable-rate mortgage is normally well below—typically by 2 to 3 percentage points—the rate of a standard 30-year fixed-rate loan. Of course, whether or not the borrower actually will end up paying less interest depends on the behavior of market interest rates during the term of the loan.

Features of ARMs

It is important that homebuyers understand the basic features of an adjustable rate mortgage:

- **Adjustment period:** Although the period of time between rate or payment changes is typically 6 months to 1 year, adjustment periods can range from 3 months to 3 or 5 years.
- **Index rate:** A baseline rate that captures the movement in interest rates, tied to 6-month U.S. Treasury securities, 6-month CDs, or the average cost of funds to savings institutions, commonly measured by the 11th Federal Home Loan Bank District Cost of Funds.
- **Margin:** The percentage points a lender adds to the index to determine the rate of interest on an ARM, usually a fixed amount over the life of the loan. Thus the rate of interest on an ARM equals the index rate plus the margin.
- **Interest rate caps:** Limits on the amount the interest rate can increase over a given period. *Periodic caps* limit interest rate increases from one adjustment to the next (typically lenders cap annual rate adjustments at 1 to 2 percentage points), and *overall caps* limit the interest rate increase over the life of the loan (lifetime interest rate caps are set at 5 to 8 percentage points). Many ARMs have both periodic and overall interest rate caps.
- **Payment caps:** Limits on monthly payment increases that may result from a rate adjustment—usually a percentage of the previous payment. If your ARM has a 5 percent payment cap, your monthly payments can increase no more than 5 percent from 1 year to the next—regardless of what happens to interest rates.

Because most ARMs are 30-year loans, you can determine the initial monthly payment in the same manner as for any other 30-year mortgage. For example, for an $80,000 loan at 7.5 percent (5.5 percent index rate + 2 percent margin), we can use Exhibit 5.11 to find the first-year monthly payments of $559.44. Assuming a 1-year adjustment period, if the index rate rises to 7 percent, the interest rate for the second year will be 9 percent (7 percent + 2 percent = 9 percent). The size of the monthly payment for the next 12 months will then be adjusted upward to about $642.34. This process is repeated each year thereafter until the loan matures.

adjustment period
On an adjustable-rate mortgage, the period of time between rate or payment changes.

index rate
On an adjustable-rate mortgage, the baseline index rate that captures interest rate movements.

margin
On an adjustable-rate mortgage, the percentage points a lender adds to the *index rate* to determine the rate of interest.

interest rate cap
On an adjustable-rate mortgage, the limit on the amount that the interest rate can increase each adjustment period and over the life of the loan.

payment cap
On an adjustable-rate mortgage, the limit on the monthly payment increase that may result from a rate adjustment.

Beware of Negative Amortization

Some ARMs are subject to **negative amortization**—an increase in the principal balance resulting from monthly loan payments that are lower than the amount of monthly interest being charged. In other words, you could end up with a larger mortgage balance on the next anniversary of your loan than on the previous one. This occurs when the payment is intentionally set below the interest charge, or when the ARM has interest rates that are adjusted monthly—with monthly payments that adjust annually. In the latter case, when rates are rising on these loans, the current monthly payment can be less than the interest being charged, and the difference is added to the principal, thereby increasing the size of the loan.

ARMs with a cap on the dollar amount of monthly payments can also lead to negative amortization. For example, assume that the monthly payment on a 7.5 percent, 30-year, $80,000 loan is $560 with its next annual adjustment in 10 months. If, as a result of rising interest rates, the applicable rate increases to 9 percent, increasing the monthly payment to $640, negative amortization in the amount of $80 per month would occur. If no other interest rate change was to occur over the remaining 10 months until its next adjustment, the mortgage balance would be $80,800—the increase of $800 attributable to an $80 per month negative amortization over 10 months.

negative amortization When the principal balance on a mortgage loan increases because the monthly loan payment is lower than the amount of monthly interest being charged; some ARMs are subject to this undesirable situation.

convertible ARM An adjustable-rate mortgage loan that allows borrowers to convert from an adjustable-rate to a fixed-rate loan, usually at any time between the 13th and the 60th month.

two-step ARM An adjustable-rate mortgage with just two interest rates: one for the first 5 to 7 years of the loan, and a higher one for the remaining term of the loan.

When considering an ARM, be sure to learn whether negative amortization could occur. Generally, loans without the potential for negative amortization are available although they tend to have slightly higher initial rates and interest rate caps.

Other types of ARMs lenders may offer include:

- **Convertible ARMs** allow borrowers to convert from an adjustable-rate to a fixed-rate loan during a specified time period, usually any time between the 13th and 60th month. Although these loans seldom provide the lowest initial rate, they allow the borrower to convert to a fixed-rate loan if interest rates decline. A conversion fee of around $500 is typical, and the fixed rate is normally set at .25 to .5 percent above the going rate on fixed-rate loans at the time you convert.
- **Two-step ARMs** have just two interest rates, the first for an initial period of 5 to 7 years and a higher one for the remaining term of the loan.

Choosing an Index

The index on your ARM significantly affects the level and stability of your mortgage payments over the term of your loan. Lenders use short-term indexes such as the Six-Month Treasury Bill, LIBOR, the *London Inter Bank Offering Rate,* a base rate similar to the prime rate and used in the international marketplace, CD-based indexes, and the 11th Federal Home Loan Bank District Cost of Funds.

The most important difference between the indexes is their volatility. LIBOR and CD rates are quite volatile because they quickly respond to changes in the financial markets. The 11th Federal Home Loan Bank District Cost of Funds index is less volatile because it represents an average of the cost of funds to S&Ls in the District. It tends to lag other short-term rate movements, both up and down, and exhibits a fairly smooth pattern over time. To more fully understand how one particular index behaves relative to another, you may want to compare index rates over the past several years.

smart.sites

HSH Associates offers current and historical information on the most popular ARM indexes. Visit **http://www.hsh.com/idxhst.html** to track how they have moved in recent years.

So what does this mean for the homebuyer considering an ARM? If your mortgage is tied to a LIBOR or CD index, you can expect sharper and more frequent upward and downward interest rate movements, while cost of funds indexes move more slowly in both directions. To choose which is better for you, consider the annual rate cap on the mortgage, the level of interest rates, and future interest rate expectations. If you have a low rate cap of 1 to 2 percentage points, and you think rates might go down, you may be comfortable with a more volatile index.

Some lenders offer special first-year "teaser" rates that are below the index rate on the loan. Be wary of lenders with very low rates. Ask them if the first-year rate is based on the index and verify the rate yourself. Be sure you can comfortably make the monthly mortgage payment when the interest rate steps up to the indexed rate.

Monitoring Your Mortgage Payments

You should carefully monitor your mortgage over its life. Always verify the calculation of your loan payment when rate or payment adjustments are made. To verify your payment amount, you need to know the index rate, the margin, and the formula used to adjust the loan; all are found in the loan agreement. The interest rates for the most commonly used indexes are readily available in the financial press, and are published weekly in the real estate section of most newspapers. The loan formula tells you when the rate is set—for example, 45 days before the adjustment date—and the margin on the loan. You can use a hand-held business calculator (as described earlier) to calculate the payment once you know the new rate, the number of years until the loan is paid off, and the current principal balance.

If you suspect you are being overcharged, call your lender and ask for an explanation of the rate and payment calculations. Special mortgage-checking services will review your ARM for a fee of about $70 to $100.

Fixed Rate or Adjustable Rate?

Fixed-rate mortgages are popular with homebuyers who plan to stay in their homes for at least 5 to 7 years and want to know what their payments will be. Of course, the current level of interest rates and your expectation about future interest rates will influence your choice of a fixed-rate or adjustable-rate mortgage. During periods when the average interest rate on a 30-year mortgage loan was high, people chose adjustable-rate mortgages to avoid being locked in to prevailing high rates. With current interest rates near all-time lows, many homebuyers are opting for fixed-rate mortgages to lock in these attractive rates. Homeowners with existing adjustable-rate mortgages are refinancing them with fixed-rate loans to take advantage of favorable current fixed rates.

Other Mortgage Payment Options

In addition to standard fixed-rate and adjustable-rate mortgage loans, some lenders offer variations designed to help first-time homebuyers:

- **Graduated-payment mortgages** are loans offering low payments for the first few years, gradually increasing until year three or five, then remaining fixed. The low initial payments appeal to people who are just starting out and expect their income to rise. If this does not occur, however, it could result in a higher debt load than the borrower can handle.
- **Growing-equity mortgages** are fixed-rate mortgages with payments that increase over a specific period. The extra funds are applied to the principal, so a conventional 30-year loan is paid off in about 20 years. However, you can accomplish the same thing without locking yourself into a set schedule by taking a fixed-rate mortgage that allows prepayments.
- **Shared-appreciation mortgages** are loans that have a below-market interest rate because the lender or other party shares from 30 to 50 percent of the appreciated value when the home is sold. This can be a useful tool if you absolutely cannot afford the higher rates of a conventional loan, but keep in mind that with appreciation of only 2 percent per year for just 5 years, such a loan could cost you up to $5,000 in shared equity on a $100,000 property.
- **Biweekly mortgages** are loans on which payments equal to half of a regular monthly payment are made every 2 weeks rather than once a month. Because you make 26 payments (52 weeks/2), which is the equivalent of 13 monthly payments, the principal balance declines at a faster rate, and you pay less interest over the life of the loan. Once again, with most 30-year mortgages you can make extra principal payments at any time, without penalty. This may be preferable to committing to a biweekly loan that can charge an additional processing fee.
- **Buy-downs** are a type of seller financing sometimes offered on new homes. A builder or seller arranges for mortgage financing with a financial institution at interest rates well below market rates—8 percent financing when the market rate of interest is around 9 or 9.5 percent. Typically the builder or seller subsidizes the loan for the buyer at a special low interest rate. However, the reduced interest rate may be for only a short period, or the buyer will pay for the reduced interest in the form of a higher purchase price.

graduated-payment mortgage
A mortgage that starts with unusually low payments that rise over several years to a fixed payment.

growing-equity mortgage
Fixed-rate mortgage with payments that increase over a specific period. The extra funds are applied to the principal so the loan is paid off more quickly.

shared-appreciation mortgage
A loan that allows a lender or other party to share in the appreciated value when the home is sold.

biweekly mortgage
A loan on which payments equal to half the regular monthly payment are made every 2 weeks.

buy-down
Financing made available by a builder or seller to a potential new-home buyer at well below-market interest rates, often only for a short period.

Conventional, Insured, and Guaranteed Loans

conventional mortgage A mortgage offered by a lender who assumes all the risk of loss; typically requires a down payment of at least 20 percent of the value of the mortgaged property.

FHA mortgage insurance A program under which the Federal Housing Administration (FHA) offers lenders mortgage insurance on loans having a high loan-to-value ratio; its intent is to encourage loans to homebuyers who have very little money available for a down payment and closing costs.

VA loan guarantee A guarantee offered by the U.S. Veterans Administration to lenders who make qualified mortgage loans to eligible veterans of the U.S. Armed Forces and their unmarried surviving spouses.

A **conventional mortgage** is a mortgage offered by a lender who assumes all the risk of loss. To protect themselves, lenders usually require a down payment of at least 20 percent of the value of the mortgaged property. For lower down payments, the lender usually requires *private mortgage insurance (PMI)* described earlier in the chapter. High borrower equity greatly reduces the likelihood of default on a mortgage, and subsequent loss to the lender. However, a high down payment requirement makes home buying more difficult for many families and individuals.

To promote home ownership, the federal government, through the Federal Housing Administration (FHA), offers lenders mortgage insurance on high loan-to-value ratio loans. These loans usually feature low down payments, below-market interest rates, few if any points, and relaxed income or debt ratio qualifications.

The **FHA mortgage insurance** program helps people buy homes even when they have very little money available for a down payment and closing costs. As of fall 2003, the up-front mortgage insurance premium for a 15- or 30-year mortgage was 1.5 percent of the loan amount—paid by the borrower at closing or included in the mortgage—plus another .5 percent annual renewal fee, paid monthly. Homebuyers who want a 15-year mortgage and make a down payment greater than 10 percent of the purchase price only pay the up-front fee. The FHA agrees to reimburse lenders for losses up to a specified maximum amount if the buyer defaults. The minimum required down payment on an FHA loan is 3 percent on the sales price. The interest rate on an FHA loan is generally about .5 percent to 1 percent lower than the rate on conventional fixed-rate loans. Affordability ratios used to qualify applicants for these loans are typically less stringent than those used for conventional loans. The maximum mortgage amount the FHA can insure is based on the national *median* price of homes and varies depending on location. To learn more about FHA mortgages, visit **http://www.fhalibrary.com**.

Guaranteed loans are similar to insured loans but better—if you qualify. **VA loan guarantees** are provided by the U.S. Veterans Administration to lenders who make qualified mortgage loans to eligible veterans of the U.S. Armed Forces and their unmarried surviving spouses. This program, however, does not require lenders or veterans to pay a premium for the guarantee. In many instances, an eligible veteran must pay only closing costs; in effect, under such a program, a veteran can buy a home with no down payment. (This can be done *only once* with a VA loan.) The mortgage loan—subject to a maximum of about $240,000 (as of fall 2003)—can amount to as much as 100 percent of a purchased property's appraised value. VA loans include a 2 percent funding fee (which is lower if the down payment is 5 percent or more). The VA sets the maximum interest rate, which, like FHA loans, is usually about .5 percent below the rate on conventional fixed-rate loans. To qualify, the veteran must meet VA credit guidelines. You'll find more information at **http://www.homeloans.va.gov/lgyinfo.htm**.

Refinancing Your Mortgage

After you've purchased a home and closed the transaction, interest rates on similar loans may drop. If rates drop by 1 to 2 percent or more, you should consider the economics of refinancing after carefully comparing the terms of the old and new mortgages, the anticipated number of years you expect to remain in the home, any prepayment penalty on the old mortgage, and the closing costs associated with the new mortgage.

Worksheet 5.4 presents a form to use when analyzing the impact of refinancing. The data for the Philipatos family's analysis is shown. Their original $80,000, 10-year-old, 10 percent mortgage, has a current balance of $72,750 and monthly payments of

$702 for 20 more years. If they refinance the $72,750 balance at the prevailing rate of 7 percent, over the remaining 20-year life of the current mortgage, the monthly payment would drop to $564. The Philipatoses plan to live in their house for at least 5 more years. They will not have to pay a penalty for prepaying their current mortgage, and closing and other costs associated with the new mortgage are $2,400 after taxes. Substituting these values into Worksheet 5.4 reveals (in Item 7) that it will take the Philipatoses 23 months to break even with the new mortgage. Because 23 months is considerably less than their anticipated minimum 5 years (60 months) in the home, the economics easily support refinancing their mortgage under the specified terms.

worksheet 5.4

Mortgage Refinancing Analysis for the Philipatos Family

Using the form below, the Philipatoses find that by refinancing the $72,750 balance on their 10-year-old, $80,000, 10-percent, 30-year mortgage (which has no prepayment penalty and requires payments of $702 per month) with a 7-percent, 20-year mortgage requiring $564 monthly payments and $2,400 in total after-tax closing costs, it will take 23 months to break even. Because the Philipatoses plan to stay in their home for at least 60 more months, the refinancing is easily justified.

MORTGAGE REFINANCING ANALYSIS

Name *Demi and Nicholas Philipatos* Date *September 6, 2005*

Item	Description		Amount
1	Current monthly payment (Terms: *$80,000, 10%, 30 years*)		$ *702*
2	New monthly payment (Terms: *$72,750, 7%, 20 years*)		*564*
3	Monthly savings, pretax (Item 1 − Item 2)		$ *138*
4	Tax on monthly savings [Item 3 × tax rate (*25* %)]		*35*
5	Monthly savings, after-tax (Item 3 − Item 4)		$ *103*
6	Costs to refinance:		
	a. Prepayment penalty	$ *0*	
	b. Total closing costs (after-tax)	*2,400*	
	c. Total refinancing costs (Item 6a + Item 6b)		$ *2,400*
7	Months to break even (Item 6c ÷ Item 5)		*23*

There are two basic reasons to refinance—to reduce the monthly payment or to reduce the total interest cost over the term of the loan. If a lower monthly payment is the objective, the analysis is relatively simple: Determine how long it will take for the monthly savings to equal your closing costs (see Worksheet 5.4).

If your objective is to reduce the total interest cost over the life of the loan, the analysis is more complex. The term of the new loan versus the existing loan is a critical element. If you refinance a 30-year loan that is already 10 years old, with another 30-year loan, you are extending the total loan maturity to 40 years. Consequently, even with a lower interest rate, you may pay more interest over the life of the newly extended loan. Therefore you should refinance with a shorter-term loan, ideally one that matures no later than the original loan maturity date. (The example in Worksheet 5.4 is prepared on this basis.)

Many homeowners want to pay their loans off more quickly to free up funds for their children's college education or for their own retirement. By refinancing at a lower rate and continuing to make the same monthly payment, a larger portion of each payment will go toward reducing the principal so the loan will be paid off more quickly. Alternately, the borrower can make extra principal payments whenever possible. Paying only an additional $25 per month on a 30-year, 9 percent, $80,000 mortgage reduces the term to about 25 years and saves about $30,000 in interest.

Some people consider the reduced tax deduction associated with a smaller mortgage interest deduction as a disadvantage of refinancing. Although the interest deduction may indeed be reduced as a result of refinancing, the more important concern is the amount of the actual after-tax cash payments. In this regard, refinancing with a lower-interest-rate mortgage (with all other terms assumed unchanged) will always result in lower after-tax cash outflows and is therefore economically appealing. Of course, as demonstrated in Worksheet 5.4, the monthly savings should be compared with the refinancing costs to make the final refinancing decision.

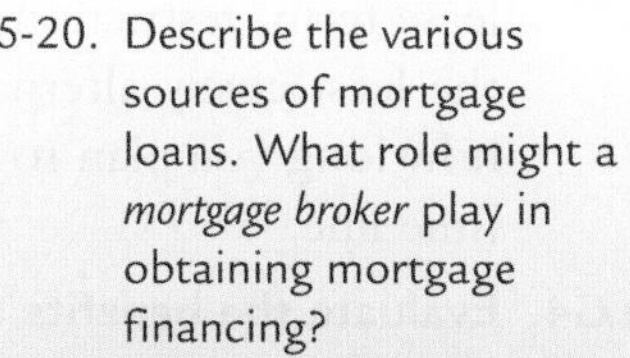

5-20. Describe the various sources of mortgage loans. What role might a *mortgage broker* play in obtaining mortgage financing?

5-21. Briefly describe the two basic types of mortgage loans. Which has the lowest initial rate of interest? What is *negative amortization,* and which type of mortgage can experience it? Discuss the advantages and disadvantages of each mortgage type.

5-22. Differentiate between conventional, insured, and guaranteed mortgage loans.

5-23. What factors should you take into account when deciding whether to refinance your mortgage to reduce the monthly payment? How can the refinancing decision be made?

Because lenders offer new mortgage products regularly, you should carefully check all your options before refinancing. Remember that when you refinance, most lenders require that you have at least 20 percent equity in your home, based on a current market appraisal. Many financial institutions are willing to refinance their existing loans, often charging fewer points and lower closing costs than a new lender would charge, so be sure to check with your existing lender first.

SUMMARY

LG1. Implement a plan to research and select a new or used automobile. The purchase of an automobile, usually the second largest expenditure a person will make, should be based on thorough market research and comparison shopping. Important purchase considerations include affordability, operating costs, whether to buy a new versus a used or nearly new car, the type of car and its features, reliability, and warranties. Knowing the dealer's cost is the key to negotiating a good price.

LG2. Decide whether to buy or lease a car. Before leasing a vehicle you should consider all the terms of the lease, including the annual mileage allowance and early termination penalties. The economics of leasing versus purchasing a car with an installment loan should only be considered once the price is set. The four components of the lease payment are the capitalized cost, residual value, money factor, and lease term.

LG3. Identify housing alternatives, assess the rental option, and perform a rent-or-buy analysis. A family can meet its housing needs in many different ways. In addition to single-family homes, there are condominiums, cooperative apartments, and rental units. You should evaluate the advantages and disadvantages of each for your current lifestyle. Many people rent because they cannot afford to buy a home; others choose to rent because it is more convenient for their lifestyle and economic situation. The rental contract, or lease agreement, describes the terms under which you can rent the property, including the monthly rental amount, lease term, restrictions, and so forth. A rent-or-buy analysis can help you choose the least costly alternative. You should also consider qualitative factors, such as how long you plan to stay in an area, and perform the analysis over a several-year time line.

LG4. Evaluate the benefits and costs of home ownership and estimate how much you can afford for a home. In addition to the emotional rewards, other benefits of home ownership are the tax shelter and inflation hedge it provides. Home ownership costs include the down payment, points and closing costs, monthly mortgage payments, property taxes and insurance, and normal home maintenance and operating expenses. Any of these can amount to a considerable sum of money. All of them should be carefully considered to estimate how much you can afford to spend on a home.

LG5. Describe the home-buying process. Most people shopping for a home seek the help of a real estate agent to obtain access to properties and provide needed information and advice. The agents involved in the transaction split a 5 to 7 percent commission, paid by the seller, when the transaction is closed. It's a good idea to prequalify yourself for a mortgage before starting to house hunt. A real estate sales contract is used to confirm all terms of the transaction between buyer and seller in writing. After a mortgage loan is approved, the loan is closed. A closing statement shows how much the borrower owes and the seller receives from the transaction.

LG6. Choose mortgage financing that meets your needs. Mortgage loans can be obtained from commercial banks, thrift institutions, or through a mortgage banker or mortgage broker. Although there are many types of mortgage loans available, the most widely used are 30- and 15-year fixed-rate mortgages and adjustable-rate mortgages (ARMs). Sometimes interest rates will drop a number of years after closing, and mortgage refinancing will become attractive. The refinancing analysis takes into account the difference in terms between the old and new mortgages, any prepayment penalty on the old mortgage, closing costs, and the number of years you plan to stay in the home.

Financial Planning Exercises

1. Janet Forrester has just graduated from college and needs to buy a car to commute to work. She estimates that she can afford to pay about $300 per month for a loan or lease and has about $1,500 in savings to use for a down payment. Develop a plan to guide her through her first car-buying experience, including researching car type, deciding whether to buy a new or used car, negotiating the price and terms, and financing the transaction.

2. *Use Worksheet 5.1.* Chris Svenson is trying to decide whether to lease or purchase a new car costing $12,000. If he leases, he will have to pay a $400 security deposit and monthly payments of $285 over the 36-month term of the closed-end lease. If, on the other hand, he purchases the car, he will have to make an $1,800 down payment and will finance the balance with a 36-month loan requiring monthly payments of $340; in addition, he will have to pay a 6 percent sales tax ($720) on the

purchase price, and he expects the car to have a residual value of $4,300 at the end of 3 years. Chris can earn 4 percent interest on his savings. Use the automobile lease versus purchase analysis form in Worksheet 5.1 to find the total cost of both the lease and the purchase and recommend the best strategy to Chris.

3. How much would you have to put down on a house costing $100,000 if the house had an appraised value of $105,000 and the lender required an 80 percent loan-to-value ratio?
4. Using the maximum ratios for a conventional mortgage, how big a monthly payment could the Bacon family afford if their gross (before-tax) monthly income amounted to $4,000? Would it make any difference if they were already making monthly installment loan payments totaling $750 on two car loans?
5. How much might a homebuyer expect to pay in closing costs on a $95,000 house with a 10 percent down payment? How much would the homebuyer have to pay at the time of closing, taking into account closing costs, down payment, and a loan fee of 3 points?
6. Find the *monthly* mortgage payments on the following mortgage loans using the table in Exhibit 5.11:
   a. $80,000/6.5 percent/30 years
   b. $105,000/8 percent/20 years
   c. $95,000/10.5 percent/15 years

7. ***Use Worksheet 5.2.*** Rebecca Serra is currently renting an apartment for $625 per month and paying $275 annually for renter's insurance. She just found a townhouse she can buy for $85,000. She has enough cash for a $10,000 down payment and $4,000 in closing costs. Her bank is offering 30-year mortgages at 9 percent per year. Rebecca estimated the following costs as a percentage of the home's price: property taxes, 2.5 percent; homeowner's insurance, .5 percent; and maintenance, .7 percent. She is in the 25 percent tax bracket. Using Worksheet 5.2, calculate the cost of each alternative and recommend the less costly option—rent or buy—to Rebecca.

8. ***Use Worksheet 5.3.*** Selena and Rodney Jackson need to calculate the amount they can afford to spend on their first home. They have a combined annual income of $47,500 and have $27,000 available for a down payment and closing costs. The Jacksons estimate that homeowner's insurance and property taxes will be $125 per month. They expect the mortgage lender to use a 30 percent (of monthly gross income) mortgage-payment affordability ratio, to lend at an interest rate of 8 percent on a 30-year mortgage, and to require a 15 percent down payment. Based on this information, use the home affordability analysis form in Worksheet 5.3 to determine the maximum-priced home the Jacksons can afford.
9. What would the monthly payments be on a $75,000 loan if the mortgage were set up as:
   a. A 15-year, 7 percent fixed-rate loan
   b. A 30-year adjustable-rate mortgage in which the lender added a margin of 2.5 to the index rate which presently stands at 4.5 percent

   Find the monthly mortgage payments for the first year only.

10. ***Use Worksheet 5.4.*** Lee Yang purchased a condominium 4 years ago for $70,000, paying $504 per month on her $60,000, 9 percent, 25-year mortgage. The current loan balance is $56,920. Recently, interest rates dropped sharply, causing Lee to

consider refinancing her condo at the prevailing rate of 6.5 percent. She expects to remain in the condo for at least 4 more years and has found a lender that will make a 6.5 percent, 21-year, $56,920 loan, requiring monthly payments of $415. Although there is no prepayment penalty on her current mortgage, Lee will have to pay $1,500 in closing costs on the new mortgage. She is in the 15 percent tax bracket. Based on this information, use the mortgage refinancing analysis form in Worksheet 5.4 to determine whether she should refinance her mortgage under the specified terms.

Applying Personal Finance

How's Your Local Housing Market?

What is the best source of information about available housing in your community? The answer is a well-informed professional real estate agent whose business is helping buyers find and negotiate the purchase of the most suitable property at the best price. However, there is another readily available source of information: the local newspaper. Almost anything you want to know about the local housing scene can be found in the real estate section of the paper. The purpose of this project is to for you to gather information concerning your local housing market.

Review recent issues of your local newspaper and describe the market for both purchased homes and rental units. Look for useful information such as location, size of property, price or rent, lease requirements and so forth. You should observe that the housing market is very fragmented, making good purchase and rent decisions more difficult. See if you can answer questions such as: What is the average size of a house or apartment in your community? What is the typical sales price or monthly rent per square foot? Is the purchase market competitive? How about the rental market? How great a difference exists in prices and rents between the most and least desirable areas of the community? Also check online for other sources of information, such as the county tax office, to try to find out how much property taxes and homeowner's insurance premiums average in your area. From your study of the local market, summarize its conditions and be prepared to participate in a class discussion of the local real estate market.

Contemporary Case Applications

5.1 The McNeils' New Car Decision: Lease versus Purchase

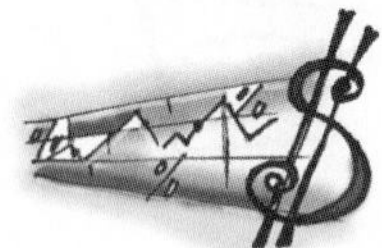

Kevin and Brigit McNeil, a dual-income couple in their late twenties want to replace their 7-year-old car, which has 90,000 miles on it and needs some expensive repairs. After reviewing their budget, the McNeils conclude that they can afford auto payments of not more than $350 per month and a down payment of $2,000. They enthusiastically decide to visit a local dealer after reading its newspaper ad offering a closed-end lease on a new car for a monthly payment of $245. After visiting with the dealer, test driving the car, and discussing the lease terms with the salesperson, they remain excited about leasing the car, but decide to wait until the following day to finalize the deal. Later that day the McNeils begin to question their approach to the new car acquisition process and decide to carefully reevaluate their decision.

Questions

1. What are some of the basic purchase considerations the McNeils should take into account when choosing which new car to buy or lease? How can they get the information they need?

2. How would you advise the McNeils to research the lease versus purchase decision before visiting the dealer? What are the advantages and disadvantages of each alternative?
3. Assume the McNeils can get the following terms on a lease or a bank loan for the car, which they could buy for $17,000. This amount includes tax, title, and license fees.
   - **Lease:** 48 months, $245 monthly payment, 1 month's payment required as a security deposit, $350 end-of-lease charges; a residual value of $6,775 is the purchase option price at the end of the lease.
   - **Loan:** $2,000 down payment, $15,000, 48-month loan at 5 percent interest requiring a monthly payment of $346.44. They assume that the car's value at the end of 48 months will be the same as the residual value. Sales tax is 6 percent.

   They can currently earn interest of 3 percent annually on their savings. They expect to drive about the same number of miles per year as they do now.

   a. Use the format given in Worksheet 5.1 to determine which deal is better for the McNeils.

   b. What other costs and terms of the lease option might affect their decision?

   c. Based on the available information, should the McNeils lease or purchase the car? Why?

5.2 Evaluating a Mortgage Loan for the Schmidts

Elisa and Dominic Schmidt, both in their mid-twenties, have been married for 4 years and have two preschool age children. Dominic has an accounting degree and is presently employed as a cost accountant at an annual salary of $42,000. At present, they are renting a duplex but wish to buy a home in the suburbs of their rapidly developing city. They have decided they can afford a $115,000 house and hope to find one with the features they desire in a good neighborhood.

The insurance costs on such a home are expected to be $800 per year, taxes are expected to be $2,500 per year, and annual utility bills are estimated at $1,440—an increase of $500 over those they pay in the duplex. The Schmidts are considering financing their home with a fixed-rate, 30-year, 7 percent mortgage. The lender charges 2 points on mortgages with 20 percent down and three points if less than 20 percent is put down (the commercial bank with which the Schmidts will deal requires a minimum of 10 percent down). Other closing costs are estimated at 5 percent of the purchase price of the home. Because of their excellent credit record, the bank will probably be willing to let the Schmidts' monthly mortgage payments (principal and interest portions) equal as much as 28 percent of their monthly gross income. Since getting married, the Schmidts have been saving for the purchase of a home and now have $24,000 in their savings account.

Questions

1. How much would the Schmidts have to put down if the lender required a minimum 20 percent down payment? Could they afford it?
2. Given that the Schmidts want to put only $15,000 down, how much would closing costs be? Considering only principal and interest, how much would their monthly mortgage payments be? Would they qualify for a loan using a 28 percent affordability ratio?
3. Using a $15,000 down payment on a $115,000 home, what would the Schmidt's loan-to-value ratio be? Calculate the monthly mortgage payments on a PITI basis.
4. What recommendations would you make to the Schmidts? Explain.

5.3 Julie's Rent-or-Buy Decision

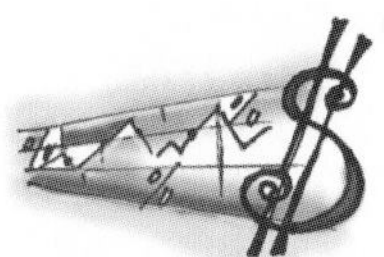

Julie Brown is a single woman in her late twenties. She currently rents an apartment in the fashionable part of town for $900 a month. After considerable deliberation, she is seriously considering the purchase of a condominium for $125,000. She intends to put 20 percent down and expects that closing costs will amount to another $5,000; a commercial bank has agreed to lend her money at the fixed rate of 7 percent on a 15-year mortgage. Julie would have to pay an annual condominium owner's insurance premium of $600 and property taxes of $1,200 a year (she is presently paying renter's insurance of $550 per year). In addition, she estimates that annual maintenance and upkeep expenses will be about 0.5 percent of the price of the condo (which includes a $30 monthly fee to the property owners' association). Julie's income puts her in the 25 percent tax bracket (she itemizes her deductions on her tax returns), and she earns an after-tax rate of return on her investments of around 4 percent.

Questions

1. Given the information provided above, evaluate and compare Julie's alternatives of remaining in the apartment or purchasing the condo, using Worksheet 5.3.
2. Working with a friend who is a realtor, Julie has learned that condos like the one she is thinking of buying are appreciating in value at the rate of 3.5 percent a year and are expected to continue doing so. Would such information affect the rent-or-buy decision made in Question 1? Explain.
3. Discuss any other factors that should be considered when making a rent-or-buy decision.
4. Which alternative would you recommend for Julie in light of your analysis?

MONEY ONLINE

Home, Sweet Home!

1. **http://bluecollardollar.com/loan.html**

Want to pay off your loan early? You can by paying extra each month. Use BlueCollarDollar's handy calculator to find out "How Long Will It Take?" While you're at their Web site, read through their common-sense approach to finance and debt, including their "Buyer's Guide" under "Mortgages."

2. **http://www.a-mortgage-home-loan.com**

Need a home mortgage? Use American Mortgage and Home Loan's free service designed to help you locate the best financing programs nationwide. Learn the mortgage lingo, use their calculators or find out the current mortgage rates.

3. **http://interest.com/calculators/discount.shtml**

Should you pay points and buy down the interest rate on your home mortgage? Use Interest.com's handy calculator to see how long it would take you to recoup the cost of paying discount points. Enter a rate of 7.5 percent with no points and 7.25 percent with 1 discount point on a 30-year loan for $100,000 to see that you would need to own the home at least 59 months before it would be worthwhile to pay the extra discount point, given this scenario.

4. **http://www.federalreserve.gov/pubs/homeline**

What is a home equity line of credit? Should you get a line of credit or a traditional second mortgage? Find out the facts from the Federal Reserve Board before putting your home on the line with either.

5. **http://www.relibrary.com**

Do you have questions concerning buying a home? Click "Enter" at The Real Estate Library for the answers! For starters, click on "Buyer and Seller Tools" for help with

6

Borrowing on Open Account

7

Using Consumer Loans

CHAPTER 6

Borrowing On Open Account

Learning Goals

LG1. Describe the reasons for using consumer credit, and identify its benefits and problems.
LG2. Develop a plan to establish a strong credit history.
LG3. Distinguish among the different forms of open account credit.
LG4. Apply for, obtain, and manage open account credit.
LG5. Choose the right credit cards and recognize their advantages and disadvantages.
LG6. Avoid credit problems, protect yourself against credit card fraud, and understand the personal bankruptcy process.

The House of Credit Cards Falls

"It's amazing how many banks will extend a $10,000 credit line to you when you buy a house," notes Josh Wallace. "When a new furnace, air conditioning unit, and roof ate up our available credit, we just added more credit cards and kept on buying." His wife Carol decided to stay home when their first daughter was born, and then Josh was unemployed for eight weeks. "That really put us in a tail-spin," he recalls. "I had been earning $60,000 a year with a monthly mortgage payment of $1,500, a car payment, and hardly any savings." It was easy to be tempted by the many credit card offers they received weekly. They signed the preapproved credit form, and in a few weeks a new card arrived. Soon they had over 12 cards with total available credit of $75,000.

Before long, the Wallaces, who live in a suburb of Minneapolis, could barely cover the credit card monthly interest charges. "Our budget was so tight that even buying groceries was hard," Carol says. "We ignored the warning signs and continued using credit to get by. We were by no means disciplined in our spending." By paying only the minimum monthly amount, which was less than the interest they owed, they were paying interest on the interest, and their credit card debts continued to rise.

After weighing their options, they consulted an attorney and filed for bankruptcy. Because Josh didn't expect much salary growth, they filed Chapter 7 (liquidation) instead of Chapter 13 (debt restructuring). "Knowing what we do now, we should have tried everything possible—like low interest loans from relatives or credit counseling—to resolve our situation before filing," Josh says. "If someone had asked, 'Do you really know what you're getting into?' we might have taken another route." Although the bankruptcy court permitted them to keep their house, car, and other personal effects, the stigma attached to bankruptcy caused them emotional scars. For one thing, they must answer "yes" when forms ranging from credit to employment ask: Have you ever declared bankruptcy?

When they were discharged from bankruptcy, the Wallaces took firm control of their personal finances. With almost no credit available for three years, they had to manage their cash better; Josh even worked a second job for a while. They used their few retail credit cards to reestablish their credit, charging small amounts that they paid off religiously. "But that black cloud of bankruptcy hung over us for what seemed like forever," Josh says. By studying the following chapter, you will learn how to manage your credit wisely and not get into trouble like the Wallaces did.

CRITICAL THINKING QUESTIONS

As you review the chapter, consider these questions in relation to the Wallaces' financial planning:

- What steps should the Wallaces have taken to limit their credit card and other open account debts?
- The Wallaces come to you for credit counseling before they file for bankruptcy. What other options would you discuss with them?
- Provide the Wallaces with at least four ways to control their spending.

THE BASIC CONCEPTS OF CREDIT

LG1, LG2

Just say "Charge it." With those two little words and a piece of plastic, you can buy gas for your car, have a gourmet meal at an expensive restaurant, or furnish an apartment. It happens *several hundred million times a day* across the United States. Credit, in fact, has become an entrenched part of our everyday lives, and we as consumers use it in one form or another to purchase just about every type of good or service imaginable. Indeed, because of the ready availability and widespread use of credit, our economy is often called a "credit economy." And for good reason: by early 2003, individuals in this country had run up almost *$1.7 trillion dollars* in consumer debt—and that *excludes* home mortgages.

Consumer credit is important in the personal financial planning process because of the impact it can have on (1) the attainment of financial goals, and (2) cash budgets. For one thing, various forms of consumer credit can help you reach your financial objectives by enabling you to acquire some of the more expensive items in a systematic fashion, without throwing your whole budget into disarray. But there's another side to consumer credit: It has to be paid back! Unless credit is used intelligently, the "buy-now-pay-later" attitude can quickly turn an otherwise orderly budget into a budgetary nightmare and lead to some serious problems—even bankruptcy! So, really, the issue is one of moderation and affordability.

In today's economy, consumers, businesses, and governments alike use credit to make transactions. Credit helps businesses supply the goods and services needed to satisfy consumer demand. In addition, business credit provides higher levels of employment and helps raise our overall standard of living. Local, state, and federal governments borrow for various projects and programs that also increase our standard of living and create additional employment opportunities. Clearly, borrowing helps fuel our economy and enhance the overall quality of our lives. Consequently, *consumers in a credit economy need to know how to establish credit and how to avoid the dangers of using it improperly.*

WHY BORROW?

People typically use credit as a way to pay for goods and services that cost more than they can afford to take from their current income. This is particularly true for those in the 25 to 44 age group, who simply have not had time to accumulate the liquid assets required to pay cash outright for major purchases and expenditures. As people begin to approach their mid-forties, however, their savings and investments start to build up, and their debt loads tend to decline, which is really not too surprising when you consider that the median household net worth for those in the 45 to 54 age group is *80 percent more* than those aged 35 to 44.

Whatever their age group, people tend to borrow for several major reasons:

- **To avoid paying cash for large outlays:** Rather than pay cash for large purchases, such as houses and cars, most people borrow a portion of the purchase price and then repay the loan on some scheduled basis. Spreading payments over time makes big-ticket items more affordable, and consumers get the use of an expensive asset right away. Most people consider the cost of such borrowing a small price to pay for the immediate satisfaction they get from owning the house, car, or whatever it happens to be. In their minds, at least, the benefits of current consumption outweigh the interest costs on the loan. Unfortunately, while the initial euphoria of the purchase may wear off over time, the loan payments remain—and perhaps for many more years to come.
- **To meet a financial emergency:** For example, people may need to borrow to cover living expenses during a period of unemployment, or to purchase plane tickets to visit a sick relative. As indicated in Chapter 4, however, use of savings (not credit) is a more preferred way to provide for financial emergencies.
- **For convenience:** Merchants as well as banks offer a variety of charge accounts and credit cards that allow consumers to charge just about anything—from gas and oil or clothes and stereos to doctor and dental bills and even college tuition. Further,

in many places—restaurants, for instance—using a credit card is far easier than writing a check. Although such transactions usually incur no interest (at least initially), these credit card purchases are still a form of borrowing, because payment is not made at the time of the transaction.

- **For investment purposes:** As we'll see in Chapter 11, it's relatively easy for an investor to partially finance the purchase of many different kinds of investment vehicles with borrowed funds. In fact, *margin loans,* as they're called, amounted to nearly $150 billion in mid-2003—a tidy sum, but down substantially from the $280 billion reached when the stock market peaked in March 2000.

Improper Uses of Credit

Many people use consumer credit to live beyond their means. Overspending is the biggest danger in borrowing, especially because it's so easy to do. Once hooked on "plastic," people may use their credit cards to make even routine purchases and don't realize they have overextended themselves until it's too late. Overspenders simply won't admit that they're spending too much. As far as they're concerned, they can afford to buy all those things because, after all, they still have their credit cards and can still afford to pay the minimum amounts each month.

Unfortunately, such spending eventually leads to mounting bills. And by making only the minimum payment, borrowers pay a huge price in the long run. Look at Exhibit 6.1, which shows the amount of time and interest charges required to repay credit card balances if you make only a minimum payment of 3 percent of the outstanding balance. For example, if you carry a $3,000 balance—which is about *one-third* the national average—on a card that charges 15.0 percent annually, it would take you 14 years to retire the debt, and your interest charges would total *some $2,000—or more than 66 percent of the original balance!* Incredibly, some cards offer even lower minimum payments of just 2 to 2½ percent of the outstanding balance. While such small payments may seem like a good deal, clearly they do not work to your advantage and only increase the time and amount of interest required to repay the debt!

To avoid the possibility of future repayment shock, you should keep in mind the following types of transactions for which you should *not* (routinely, at least) use credit: (1) to meet basic living expenses; (2) to make impulse purchases, especially expensive

EXHIBIT 6.1

Minimum Payments Mean Maximum Years

Paying off credit card balances at the minimum monthly amount required by the card issuer will take a long time and cost you a great deal of interest, as the following table demonstrates. The calculations here are based on a minimum 3 percent payment and 15.0 percent annual interest rate.

Original Balance	Years to Repay	Interest Paid	Total Interest Paid as Percent of Original Balance
$5,000	16.4	$3,434	68.7%
4,000	15.4	2,720	68.0
3,000	14.0	2,005	66.8
2,000	12.1	1,291	64.5
1,000	8.8	577	57.7

EXHIBIT 6.2

Some Credit Danger Signs

If one or more of these signs exist, you should take them as an indication that it is time to proceed with caution in your credit spending. Be prepared to revise and update your spending patterns, cut back on the use of credit, and be alert for other signs of overspending.

You may be headed for serious trouble if:

- You regularly use credit cards to buy on impulse.
- You postdate checks to keep them from bouncing.
- You regularly exceed the borrowing limit on your credit cards.
- You never add up all your bills, to avoid facing grim realities.
- You now take 60 or 90 days to pay bills you once paid in 30.
- You have to borrow just to meet normal living expenses.
- You often use one form of credit—such as a cash advance from a credit card—to make payments on other debt.
- You can barely make the minimum required payments on bills.
- You are using more than 20 percent of your take-home income to pay credit card bills and personal loans (excluding mortgage payments).
- You have no savings.
- You are so far behind on credit payments that collection agencies are after you.

ones; and (3) to purchase nondurable (short-lived) goods and services. Except in situations where credit cards are used occasionally for the sake of convenience (such as for gasoline and entertainment) or payments on recurring credit purchases are built into the monthly budget, a good rule to remember when considering the use of credit is that *the product purchased on credit should outlive the payments.*

Unfortunately, people who overspend eventually arrive at the point where they must choose to either become delinquent in their payments or sacrifice necessities, such as food and clothing. If payment obligations are not met, the consequences are likely to be a damaged credit rating, lawsuits, or even personal bankruptcy. Exhibit 6.2 lists some common signals that indicate it may be time to stop buying on credit. *Ignoring the telltale signs that you are overspending can only lead to more serious problems.*

ESTABLISHING CREDIT

The willingness of lenders to extend credit depends on their assessment of your creditworthiness—that is, your ability to repay the debt on a timely basis. They look at a number of factors in making this decision, such as your present earnings and net worth. Equally important, they look at your current debt position and your credit history. Thus it's worth your while to do what you can to build a strong credit rating.

First Steps in Establishing Credit

First, open checking and savings accounts. They signal stability to lenders and also indicate that you handle your financial affairs in a businesslike fashion. Second, use credit—open one or two charge accounts and use them periodically, even if you prefer paying cash. For example, get a Visa card and make a few credit purchases each month (don't overdo it, of course). You might pay an annual fee or interest on some (or all) of your account balances, but in the process, you'll become identified as a reliable credit customer. Third, obtain a small loan, even if you don't need one. If you don't actually need the money, put it in a liquid investment, such as a money market account or certificate of deposit. The interest you earn should offset some of the interest expense on the loan; you can view the difference as a cost of building good credit. (It goes without saying that you should repay the loan promptly, perhaps even a little ahead of schedule, to minimize the difference in interest rates—don't pay off the loan too quickly, though, as lenders like to see how you perform over an extended period of time.) Keep in mind, your ability to obtain a large loan in the future will depend in part on how you managed smaller ones in the past.

Build a Strong Credit History

From a financial perspective, maintaining a strong credit history is just as important as developing a solid employment record! Don't take credit lightly, and don't assume that getting the loan or the credit card is the toughest part. It's not. That's just the first step; servicing it (i.e., making payments) in a prompt and timely fashion—month in and month out—is the really tough part of the consumer credit process. And in many respects, it's the most important element of consumer credit, as it determines your creditworthiness. By using credit wisely and repaying it on time, you're establishing a *credit history* that tells lenders you're a dependable, reliable, and responsible borrower.

Financial Road Sign

The 5 Cs of Credit

Lenders often look to the "5 Cs of Credit" as a way to assess the willingness and ability of a borrower to repay a loan; they are:

1. **Character:** A key factor in defining the borrower's willingness to live up to the terms of the loan
2. **Capacity:** The ability of the borrower, financially, to service the loan in a prompt and timely fashion.
3. **Collateral:** Something of value that's used to secure a loan and which the lender can claim in case of default
4. **Capital:** The amount of unencumbered assets owned by the borrower, used as another indicator of the borrower's ability to repay the loan.
5. **Condition:** The extent to which prevailing economic conditions could affect the borrower's ability to service a loan.

The consumer credit industry keeps very close tabs on your credit and your past payment performance (more on this when we discuss *credit bureaus* later in the chapter). So the better job you do in being a responsible borrower, the easier it will be to get credit when and where you want it. The best way to build up a strong credit history and maintain your creditworthiness is to *consistently* make payments *on time,* month after month. Being late occasionally—say, two or three times a year—might label you a "late payer." When you take on credit, you have an *obligation* to live up to the terms of the loan, including how and when the credit will be repaid.

If you foresee difficulty in meeting a monthly payment, let the lender know and usually some sort of arrangements can be made to help you through the situation. This is especially true with installment loans that require fixed monthly payments. If you have one or two of these loans and, for some reason or another, you encounter a month that's going to be really tight, the first thing you should try to do (other than trying to borrow some money from a member of the family) is get an extension on your loan. Don't just skip a payment, because that's going to put your account into a *late status until you make up the missed payment*—in other words, until you make a *double* payment, your account/loan will remain in a late status, subject to a monthly late penalty. The alternative of trying to work out an extension with your lender obviously makes a lot more sense.

Here's what you do. Explain the situation to the loan officer and ask for an extension of one (or two) months on your loan. In most cases, so long as this hasn't occurred before, the extension is almost automatically granted. The maturity of the loan is formally extended for a month (or two), and the extra interest of carrying the loan for another month (or two) is either added to the loan balance or, more commonly, paid at the time the extension is granted (such an extension fee generally amounts to a fraction of the normal monthly payment). Then, in a month (or two), you pick up where you left off and resume your normal monthly payments on the loan. This is the most sensible way of making it through those rough times because it doesn't harm your credit record. Just don't do it too often.

To summarize, here are some things you can do to build a strong credit history:

- Use credit only when you can afford it and only when the repayment schedule fits comfortably into the family budget—in short, don't overextend yourself.
- Fulfill all the terms of the credit.
- Be *consistent* in making payments *promptly.*
- Consult creditors immediately if you cannot meet payments as agreed.
- Be truthful when applying for credit. Lies are not likely to go undetected.

smart.sites

The American Banker's Association provides helpful information about shopping for credit and managing debt at its consumer education site, **http://www.aba.com/Consumer+Connection/default.htm**.

How Much Credit Can You Stand?

Sound financial planning dictates that if you are going to use credit, you should have a good idea of how much you can comfortably tolerate. The easiest way to avoid repayment problems and ensure that your borrowing will not place an undue strain on your monthly budget is to *limit the use of credit to your ability to repay the debt!* A useful *credit guideline* (and one widely used by lenders) is to make sure your monthly repayment burden does not exceed 20 percent of your monthly *take-home pay.* Most experts, however, regard the 20 percent figure as the *maximum* debt burden and strongly recommend **debt safety ratios** closer to 10 to 15 percent—perhaps even lower if you plan on applying for a new mortgage in the near future. Note that the monthly repayment burden here does *include* payments on your credit cards, but *excludes* your monthly mortgage obligation.

debt safety ratio The proportion of total monthly consumer credit obligations to monthly take-home pay.

To illustrate, consider someone who takes home \$2,500 a month. Using a 20 percent ratio, she should have monthly consumer credit payments of no more than \$500—that is, \$2,500 × .20 = \$500. This is the maximum amount of her monthly disposable income she should have to use to pay off both personal loans and other forms of consumer credit (such as credit cards and education loans). This, of course, is not the maximum amount of consumer credit she can have outstanding—in fact, her total consumer indebtedness can, and likely would, be considerably larger. The key factor is that with her income level, her *payments* on this type of debt should not exceed \$500 a month. (*Caution:* This is not to say that credit terms should be lengthened just to accommodate this guideline; rather, in all cases, it is assumed that standard credit terms apply.)

Exhibit 6.3 provides a summary of low (10 percent), manageable (15 percent), and maximum (20 percent) monthly credit payments for a number of income levels. Obviously, the closer your total monthly payments are to your desired debt safety ratio, the less future borrowing you can undertake. Conversely, *the lower the debt safety ratio, the better shape you're in, creditwise, and the easier it should be for you to service your outstanding consumer debt.*

You can compute the debt safety ratio as follows:

$$\text{Debt safety ratio} = \frac{\text{Total monthly consumer credit payments}}{\text{Monthly take-home pay}}$$

EXHIBIT 6.3

Alternative Consumer Credit Guidelines Based on Ability to Repay

Using this credit guideline, the amount of consumer credit you should have outstanding depends on the montly payment you can afford to make.

	Monthly Consumer Credit Payments		
Monthly Take-Home Pay	*Low* Debt Safety Ratio (10%)	*Manageable* Debt Safety Ratio (15%)	*Maximum* Debt Safety Ratio (20%)
$1,000	$100	$150	$ 200
$1,250	$125	$188	$ 250
$1,500	$150	$225	$ 300
$2,000	$200	$300	$ 400
$2,500	$250	$375	$ 500
$3,000	$300	$450	$ 600
$3,500	$350	$525	$ 700
$4,000	$400	$600	$ 800
$5,000	$500	$750	$1,000

This measure is the focus of *Worksheet 6.1*, which provides a vehicle for keeping close tabs on your own debt safety ratio. It shows the impact that each new loan you take out, or credit card you sign up for, has on this important measure of creditworthiness. Consider, for example, Jack and Sally Bicman. As seen in Worksheet 6.1, they have five outstanding consumer loans, plus they're carrying balances on three credit cards. All totaled, these eight obligations require monthly payments of almost $740, which accounts for about ⅕ of their combined take-home pay and gives them a debt safety ratio of 18 percent. And note toward the bottom of the worksheet that if the Bicmans want to lower this ratio to, say, 15 percent, they're going to either have to get their monthly payments down to $615, or increase their take-home pay to over $4,900 a month.

The Special Credit Problems of Women

At one time, a woman stood very little chance of getting credit on her own. In most lenders' minds, she was too much of a risk; even if she was gainfully employed, she might become pregnant and lose her job. Today, the Equal Credit Opportunity Act (ECOA) has removed most of these credit obstacles. Creditors cannot check into a woman's marital status or childbearing plans and, with two-income families, must consider the woman's income on the same basis as the man's, even if it's part-time employment.

Even with these and other protections, however, some women—especially those who are divorced or widowed—still have difficulty getting credit if they do not have their own credit history. The following steps can help overcome this problem:

- **Use your own name when filing a credit application:** Use your legal name, not a social title, such as Mrs. Thomas Watkins. A married woman can choose from several legal names; for example, if your maiden name is Joan Brown and you take your husband's name of Watkins, you can choose Joan Watkins or Joan Brown Watkins. Use your legal name consistently to build your own credit history.

worksheet 6.1

How's My Credit?

A worksheet like this one will help a household stay on top of their monthly credit card and consumer loan payments, as well as their debt safety ratio—an important measure of one's creditworthiness. The key here is to keep the debt safety ratio as low as (reasonably) possible; something that can be done by keeping monthly loan payments in line with monthly take-home pay.

MONTHLY CONSUMER LOAN PAYMENTS & DEBT SAFETY RATIO

Name Jack & Sally Bicman **Date** June 21, 2004

Type of Loan*	Lender	Current Monthly (or Min.) Payment
• *Auto and Personal loans*	1. GMAC	$360.
	2. Bank One	115.
	3.	
• *Education loans*	1. U.S. Dept. of Education	75
	2.	31.
• *Overdraft Protection Line*	1. Bank One	30.
• *Personal line of credit*		
• *Credit Cards*	1. MBNA Visa	28.
	2. Fidelity MC	31.
	3. Dillard's	28.
	4.	
• *Home Equity Line*	1. Wash. Mutual	72.
	TOTAL MONTHLY PAYMENTS	$739.

***Note:** List only those loans that require regular monthly payments.

Monthly Take-Home Pay		
	1. Jack	$1,855
	2. Sally	2,250.
	TOTAL MONTHLY TAKE HOME PAY	$4,105.

Debt Safety Ratio:

$$\frac{\text{Total monthly payments}}{\text{Total monthly take-home pay}} \times 100 = \frac{\$\ 739.}{\$\ 4,105.} \times 100 = 18.0\%$$

• *Changes needed to reach a new debt safety ratio*

1. New (Target) debt safety ratio: 15.0%

2. At current take - home pay of $4,105. , total monthly payments must equal:

Total monthly take-home pay × Target debt safty ratio**

$\$\ 4,105. \times 0.15 = \$\ 615.75$ **New Monthly Payments**

OR

3. With current monthly payments of $ 739. , total take-home pay must equal:

$$\frac{\text{Total monthly payments}}{\text{New (target) debt safety ratio}} \times 100 = \frac{\$\ 739.}{\$\ 0.15} = \$\ 4,926.67$$

New take-home pay

****Note:** Enter debt safety ratio as a decimal (e.g., 15%=0.15).

- **Make sure any information reported to the credit bureau is in your name as well as your husband's.**
- **Consider retaining a credit file separate from your husband's when you marry:** This is true particularly if you have already established a good credit rating. You should notify creditors of your name change and intention to maintain your own file.

A Final Word of Caution

One of the real dangers of credit cards and other forms of open account credit is that they are so easy to use. Too many people tend to overlook the fact that they must eventually pay for the merchandise that's been charged with their cards; yet each time they make a transaction this way, they are incurring a liability to the issuer. The bottom line is, if credit is used properly, it can go a long way in helping you manage your personal finances; misuse it and you're just asking for trouble.

Concept ✓

6-1. Why do people borrow? What are some of the improper uses of credit? Are there any dangers associated with borrowing? Explain.

6-2. Describe the general guidelines lenders use to calculate an applicant's maximum debt burden. How can you use the *debt safety ratio* to determine whether your debt obligations are within reasonable limits?

6-3. What steps can you take to establish a good credit rating? What extra steps might be necessary for a woman?

LG3

TYPES OF OPEN ACCOUNT CREDIT

open account credit A form of credit extended to a consumer in advance of any transaction; type of credit that accompanies charge accounts and credit cards.

credit limit A specified amount beyond which a customer may not borrow or purchase on credit.

credit statement A monthly statement that summarizes the transactions, interest charges, fees, and payments in a consumer credit account.

Open account credit is a form of credit extended to a consumer in advance of any transactions. Typically, a retail outlet or bank agrees to allow the consumer to buy or borrow up to a specified amount on open account. Credit is extended as long as the consumer does not exceed the established **credit limit,** and makes payments in accordance with the specified terms. Open account credit issued by a retail outlet, such as a department store or oil company, is usually applicable only in that establishment or one of its locations. In contrast, open account credit issued by banks, such as *MasterCard* and *Visa* accounts, can be used to make purchases at a wide variety of businesses. In the remainder of this chapter, we will direct our attention to the various types and characteristics of open account credit; in Chapter 7, we will look at various forms of single-payment and installment loans.

Having open account credit is a lot like having your own personal line of credit—it's there when you need it. But unlike most other forms of debt, consumers who use open account credit can often avoid paying interest charges *if they promptly pay the full amount of their account balance.* For example, assume that in a given month you charge $75.58 on an open account at a department store. Sometime within the next month or so, you will receive a **credit statement** from the store that summarizes recent transactions on your account. Now, if there are no other charges and the total account balance is $75.58, you can (usually) avoid any finance charges by paying the account in full before the next billing date.

Open account credit generally is available from two broadly defined sources: (1) financial institutions and (2) retail stores/merchants. *Financial institutions* issue general-purpose credit cards as well as secured and unsecured revolving lines of credit and overdraft protection lines. Commercial banks have long been a major provider of consumer credit; and since deregulation, so have S&Ls and credit unions. Deregulation has also brought other financial institutions into this market—most notably, major stock-brokerage firms, consumer finance companies, and a growing list of commercial banks that have gone *interstate* to market their credit cards and other consumer credit products. *Retail stores and merchants* make up the other major source of open account credit. They provide credit to promote the sales of their products. Their principal forms of credit include open charge accounts and credit cards.

Of the various types of open account credit, the two biggest are *bank credit cards* and *retail charge cards*. Together, there are nearly 2 billion of these cards outstanding today. Let's now take a closer look at the many forms of open account credit: bank credit cards, retail charge cards, 30-day charge accounts, travel and entertainment cards, prestige cards, affinity cards, secured and prepaid credit cards, student credit cards, *debit cards*, and several kinds of *revolving lines of credit*, including overdraft protection lines, unsecured lines of credit, and home equity credit lines—all of which are available from banks and other financial services institutions.

Bank Credit Cards

Probably the most popular form of open account credit is the **bank credit card** issued by commercial banks and other financial institutions—Visa and MasterCard are the two dominant types. These cards allow their holders to charge purchases worldwide at literally millions of stores, restaurants, shops, and gas stations, as well as at state and municipal governments, colleges and universities, medical groups, and mail-order houses—not to mention the Internet, where they have become the currency of choice. They can be used to pay for almost anything—groceries, doctor bills, college tuition, airline tickets, and car rentals. Thousands of banks, S&Ls, credit unions, brokerage houses, and other financial services institutions issue Visa and MasterCard, and each issuer, within reasonable limits, can set its own credit terms and conditions. In recent years, several more big-league players have entered the field. Sears, for example, introduced the *Discover Card* (now a part of Morgan Stanley Dean Witter), American Express its *Blue Card,* and AT&T its *Universal Card* (which is actually just a special Visa or Mastercard).

bank credit card
A credit card issued by a bank or other financial institution that allows the holder to charge purchases at any establishment that accepts it; can also be used to obtain cash advances.

Features of Bank Credit Cards

Bank credit cards can be used to borrow money as well as buy goods and services on credit. Because of their potential for use in thousands of businesses and banks, they can be of great convenience and value to consumers. Individuals who use them, however, should be thoroughly familiar with their basic features.

Line of Credit

The **line of credit** provided to the holder of a bank credit card is set by the issuer for each card. It is the maximum amount that the cardholder can owe at any point in time. The size of the credit line depends on both the applicant's request and the results of the issuer's investigation of the applicant's credit and financial status. Lines of credit offered by issuers of bank cards can reach $50,000 or more, but for the most part they range from about $500 to $2,500. Although card issuers fully expect you to keep your credit within the specified limits, most won't take any real action unless you extend your account balance a certain percentage beyond the account's stated maximum. For example, if you had a $1,000 credit limit, you probably wouldn't hear a thing from the card issuer until your outstanding account balance exceeded, say, $1,200; that is, 20 percent above the $1,000 line of credit. On the other hand, don't count on getting off scot-free, because most card issuers assess *over-the-limit* fees whenever you go over your credit limit (more on this later).

line of credit
The maximum amount of credit a customer is allowed to have outstanding at any point in time.

cash advance
A loan that can be obtained by a bank credit cardholder at any participating bank or financial institution; it begins to accrue interest immediately and requires no formal application.

Cash Advances

In addition to purchasing merchandise and services, the holder of a bank credit card can also obtain a **cash advance** from any participating bank. Cash advances are loans on which interest begins to accrue immediately. They are transacted in the same fashion as merchandise purchases except that they take place at a commercial bank or some other financial institution and involve the receipt of cash (or a check) instead of goods and services. Another way to get a cash advance is to use the "convenience checks" you receive from the card issuer to pay for purchases. You can even use your credit card to draw cash from an ATM, any time of the day or night. Usually, the size of the cash advance from an ATM is limited to some nominal amount (perhaps $300), though the amount you can obtain from the teller window at a bank is limited only by the unused credit in your account. Thus, if you've used only $1,000 of a $5,000 credit limit, you can take out a cash advance of up to $4,000.

Balance Transfers

balance transfer
A program that enables cardholders to readily transfer credit balances from one card to another.

A relatively new feature of bank credit cards is the ability to transfer balances from one card to another. Known as **balance transfers**, they have become a hot promotional feature in the ongoing credit card wars. That is, the card issuers make a big deal out of allowing you to transfer the balances from one or more (old) cards to their (new) card. The idea is to dump the old card(s) by putting everything, including current balances, on the issuer's (new) card. There are two potential advantages to these balance transfer programs. First, there's the convenience of being able to consolidate your credit card payments. And there's also the potential savings in interest that accompanies the transfer, as these deals usually come with very low (introductory) rates. But these transfers have their drawbacks, too. For starters, although you may benefit (initially) from a low rate on all transferred funds, the issuer will often charge a much higher rate on new purchases. On top of that, your monthly payment is usually applied first to the transferred balance, and not the *new purchases*, which face the higher rate. In addition, some banks will also charge a flat fee on all transferred funds. For example, suppose that you transfer a balance of $5,000 to a card that imposes a 4% fee for the transfer. This would result in a charge of $200, and that's on top of any other interest charges! Finally, while many balance transfer programs may offer relatively low introductory rates, those low rates usually don't last very long.

Other Features

Bank credit cards sure aren't what they used to be! The fact is, credit cards today offer a lot more than just a convenient way of getting credit. Because the market has become so competitive, card issuers have had to offer all sorts of services and features (some would call them "gimmicks") in an attempt to get you to use their cards. One popular feature is the so-called *buyer protection plan,* which automatically protects most items of merchandise purchased with your credit card against loss, theft, or damage for up to 90 days. For example, if the purchased item breaks during the 90-day period, the card issuer will see that the item is replaced for free.

Here's a list of some of the other services offered:

- High-value travel accident insurance
- Full-value auto rental insurance coverage
- 24-hour toll-free travelers' emergency message service
- Lost card registration
- Discounts on long-distance phone calls
- Price protection plans
- 24-hour toll-free customer service lines
- Extended warranties on products purchased with the card
- 100% reimbursement protection against fraud or theft of card
- Year-end summaries breaking down purchases by groups (e.g., airline tickets, entertainment, transactions at gas stations, etc.)

Although it is not clear just how valuable the above mentioned services really are, one thing is sure: they do act to keep interest costs on credit cards high. For make no mistake about it, one way or another, cardholders end up paying for all these services!

Rebate (Co-branded) Credit Cards

One of the fastest growing segments of the bank card market is the **rebate (co-branded) credit card**, which combines features of a traditional bank credit card with an incentive: either cash, merchandise rebates, airline tickets, or even investments. Over 50 million cardholders carry Visa or MasterCard rebate cards, and new types are introduced regularly. Among the many incentive programs are:

rebate (co-branded) credit card A bank credit card that combines features of a traditional bank credit card with an additional incentive, such as rebates and airline mileage.

- **Frequent flyer programs.** In this program, the cardholder earns free frequent flyer miles for each dollar charged on his or her credit card. These frequent flyer miles can then be used with airline-affiliated programs for free tickets, first-class upgrades, and other travel-related benefits. Examples include Delta Sky Miles, American Airlines Visa or MasterCard, United Airlines Mileage Plus Visa or MasterCard, and American Express and Diners Club programs, with miles that can be used on one of several airlines.
- **Automobile rebate programs.** General Motors offers a bank credit card that allows the cardholder to earn annual rebates of 5 percent for new car purchases or leases, up to specified limits. While the amount of the GM rebate depends on the model of car purchased (or leased), Citibank's Drivers Edge rebates 1 percent of your charges, up to $500 annually, for almost any new car bought.
- **Other merchandise rebates.** An increasing number of companies are participating in bank card rebate programs, including, for example, Carnival Cruise Lines (4 percent, up to $500 per cruise). Some major oil companies also offer rebate cards, where the cardholder earns credit that can be applied to the purchase of the company's gasoline. Several regional phone companies even offer rebates on phone calls. (A good site for finding information about these and other rebate card offers is **http://www.cardtrak.com.**)

Are rebate cards a good deal? Well, yes and no. You should evaluate these cards carefully by looking at your usage patterns and working out the annual cost of the cards before and after the rebate, to see if they make sense for you. Don't get so carried away with the gimmick that you lose sight of the total costs. Most incentive cards carry higher interest rates than regular bank cards. As the *Money in Action* box on pages 240–241 explains, these cards work best for those who can use the rebates, charge a lot, and who don't carry high monthly balances.

Interest Rates on Bank Card Charges

With few exceptions, the *annual* rate of interest charged on bank credit cards in 2003 ranged from about 5 percent to over 20 percent (these exclude introductory rates). Keep in mind, however, that interest rates on credit cards were abnormally low in 2003, in large part because market interest rates were at 40-year lows. That is, whereas rates on 2003 ranged from 5 to 20 percent, in the late 1990s, the range was more like 14 or 15 percent to over 23 percent. Also, you'll find that most bankcards have one rate for merchandise purchases and a much higher rate for cash advances. For example, the rate on merchandise purchases might be, say, 12%, while the rate on cash advances could be 19½ or 20 percent. And when shopping for a credit card, watch out for those *special low introductory rates* that many banks offer. Known as "teaser rates," they're usually only good for the first 6 to 12 months. Then, just as soon as the introductory period ends, so do the low interest rates.

smart.sites

Which credit cards are best? The Citizens for Fair Credit Card Terms, a nonprofit consumer organization, offers free independent ratings at **http://www.cardratings.com** that evaluate interest rates, fees, and benefits of leading cards.

base rate
The rate of interest a bank uses as a base for loans to individuals and small to midsize businesses.

Most of these cards have variable interest rates that are tied to an index that moves with market rates. The most popular is the prime or **base rate**, the rate a bank uses as a base for loans to individuals and small or midsize businesses. These cards adjust their interest rate monthly or quarterly, and usually have minimum and maximum rates. To illustrate, consider a bankcard whose terms are *prime plus 7.5 percent*, with a minimum of 10% and a maximum of 15½ percent. If the prime rate is 3½ percent, then the rate of interest charged on this card would be: 3.5 + 7.5 = *11.0 percent*. Given the widespread use of variable interest rates, bank cardholders should be aware that just as falling rates have brought down interest rates on credit cards; rising market rates are guaranteed to lead (and probably very quickly) to much higher interest charges!

Generally speaking, *the interest rates on credit cards are higher than any other form of consumer credit*. In fact, the average rate on standard bankcards was 13.8% in 2003, which is low compared to what they're been in the past (they were more than 17% in mid-2000). But more and more banks—even the bigger ones—are now offering more competitive rates, especially to their better customers. Indeed, because competition has become so intense, a growing number of banks today are actually willing to negotiate their fees as a way to retain their customers. Whether this trend will have any significant impact on permanently reducing interest rates and fees remains to be seen, but at least most consumers would agree it is a step in the right direction.

grace period
A short period of time, usually 20 to 30 days, during which you can pay your credit card bill in full and not incur any interest charges.

Bank credit card issuers must disclose interest costs and related information to consumers *before* extending credit. In the case of purchases of merchandise and services, the specified interest rate may not apply to charges until after the **grace period**. During this short period, usually 20 to 30 days, you can pay your credit card bill in full and avoid any interest charges. Once you carry a balance—that is, when you don't pay your card in full during the grace period—the interest rate is usually applied to any unpaid balances carried from previous periods, as well as any new purchases made. Interest on cash advances, however, *begins the day the advance is taken out*.

Other Fees

In addition to the interest charged on bank credit cards, there are a few other fees you should be aware of. To begin with, many—though not all—bank cards charge *annual fees* just for the "privilege" of being able to use the card. In most cases, the fee is around $25 to $40 a year, though it can amount to much more for prestige cards. Sometimes, this annual fee will be waived in the first year, but you'll be stuck with it for the second and every other year you hold the card. As a rule, the larger the bank or S&L, the more likely it is to charge an annual fee for its credit cards. What's more, many issuers also charge a *transaction fee* for each cash advance; this fee usually amounts to about $5 per cash advance *or* 3 percent of the amount obtained in the transaction, whichever is more.

And now, more and more card issuers are coming up with new ways to sock it to you. These include: late-payment fees, over-the-limit charges, foreign transaction fees, and balance transfer fees. For example, if you're a bit late in making your payment, at some banks you'll be hit with a late-payment fee—which is really a redundant charge because you're already paying interest on the unpaid balance. In a similar fashion, if you happen to go over your credit limit, you'll get hit with a charge for that, too (again, this is on top of the interest you're already paying). Critics really dislike this fee because they maintain it's very difficult for cardholders to know when they've hit their credit ceilings. Some card issuers today are even going so far as to slap you with a fee for *not using your credit card*—one bank, for example, charges a $15 fee to customers (cardholders) who don't use their credit cards in a 6-month period. The card issuers justify these charges by saying it costs money to issue and administer these cards, so they have a right to charge these fees if you don't use their cards. Of course, you have the right to let the issuer know what you think of these charges

Money in Action

Get Your Just Rewards

Considering one of the more than 700 credit cards that offer rewards, from plane tickets, hotel rooms, or gasoline to cash rebates? It's easy to get so carried away with the gimmick that you lose sight of the total costs.

For example, suppose you charge $2,200 a year on a General Motors rebate card and carry a monthly balance of $1,100. If the interest rate is 18 percent, the annual interest cost is about $198. You'll earn a $110 rebate ($2,200 × .05), so the cost to you drops to $88 if you use the rebate towards your purchase of a GM car.

Frequent flier cards, in contrast, are best for high-volume chargers who do not carry balances. Most airline programs require $25,000 in charges to earn one domestic coach ticket. If you pay your balance in full each month and assume the ticket is worth $350, the net benefit after the $60 annual fee is $290. But if you charge only $2,200 and carry a $1,100 balance, the card costs $248 per year (assuming interest at 18 percent and a $50 annual fee) and earns less than 10 percent of a ticket. In that case, you would be better off with a low-rate card.

Several card-related Web sites have search engines to help you choose an appropriate rewards card. Check at least two or three, because they will give you different results. The best ones are Bankrate.com, **http://www.bankrate.com**, and Cardratings.com, **http://www.cardratings.com**. Bankrate's site summarizes the features of about 80 reward cards, while Cardratings has thousands of card reviews as well as consumer reviews. You may also want to try Card Web, **http://www.cardweb.com**; Card Offers, **http://www.cardoffers.com**; Expertcredit.com., **http://www.expertcredit.com** and others. Be sure to note which cards are linked to advertisers at the site.

Here are more tips to consider when choosing (and using) a rewards card:

1. **What's the real deal?** Read the fine print to be sure you understand how the rewards work. Many cash back cards tie the rebate percent to your annual spending levels or require you to carry a balance to get higher rebates, so you may not earn the amount the ads offer.

...continued on next page

by canceling your card! Regardless of when or why any of these fees are levied, the net effect is that *they add to the true cost of using bank credit cards.*

Other Credit Cards and Charge Accounts

In addition to bank cards, credit cards are also issued by most large retailers. You should be aware of these and several other kinds of credit cards and charge accounts, including 30-day charge accounts, travel and entertainment cards, prestige cards, affinity cards, secured credit cards, and student credit cards.

Retail Charge Cards

Retail charge cards are the second largest category of credit card and are issued by department stores, oil companies, airlines, car rental agencies, and so on. These cards are popular with merchants because they build consumer loyalty and enhance sales; consumers like them because they offer a convenient way to shop. These cards carry a preset credit limit—a line of credit—that varies with the creditworthiness of the cardholder.

retail charge card
A type of credit card issued by retailers, airlines, and so on, that allows customers to charge goods and services up to a preestablished amount.

This form of credit is most common in department and clothing stores and other high-volume outlets, where customers are likely to make several purchases each month. Most large oil companies offer charge cards that allow customers to buy gas and oil products, but they're expected to pay for such purchases in full upon receipt of the monthly bill. To promote the sale of their more expensive products, oil companies frequently offer revolving credit for use in purchasing items such as tires, batteries, and accessories. Many families have—and regularly use—five or six different retail charge cards. Interest on most retail charge cards is fixed at 1.5 to 1.85 percent monthly, or 18 to 22 percent per year. These cards are generally more expensive than bank credit cards.

30-Day Charge Accounts

Commonly offered by certain types of businesses for the general convenience of their customers, the **30-day**, or **regular**, **charge account** requires the customer to pay the full amount billed within 10 to 20 days after the billing date. If payment is made within the specified period, no interest is charged; if received after the due date, however, an interest penalty is usually tacked on to the account

30-day (regular) charge account
A charge account that requires customers to pay the full amount billed within 10 to 20 days after the billing date.

balance. These accounts generally do not involve the use of a charge card. They are offered by various types of public utilities (such as gas and electric companies, telephone companies, and so on), as well as some doctors and dentists, drugstores, and repair services. But due to the widespread availability of credit cards, these types of charge accounts are slowly disappearing—pretty soon, public utilities will probably be the only ones offering them.

Travel and Entertainment Cards

travel and entertainment (T&E) card A credit card, such as American Express or Diners Club, accepted by travel and entertainment-related establishments, as well as a growing number of other businesses and stores.

Travel and entertainment (T&E) cards are similar to bank credit cards in that they enable holders to charge purchases at a variety of locations. Although these cards used to be accepted primarily at travel- and entertainment-related businesses—such as hotels, airlines, and restaurants—they have now found their way into all sorts of establishments, from upscale department and clothing stores to gas stations and drugstores. Like most bank cards, T&E cards today offer a full array of services, including frequent flyer miles, collision coverage (for car rentals), and luggage insurance. T&E cards have annual fees of up to $1,000 just for the privilege of using them. In sharp contrast to retail and bank credit cards, however, most T&E cards do *not* carry an extended line of credit. Instead, the outstanding balances must be *paid in full* within either one or two billing periods for the account to remain current. *American Express* is, by far, the biggest issuer of this type of card (with over 35 million cardholders worldwide), followed by *Diners Club* (around 7 million). However, these numbers are minute compared with the number of bank credit cards outstanding—in 2003, there were some 260 million Visa cards and another 250 million or so MasterCards in circulation (and that's just in the United States; worldwide, the numbers are much higher).

In 1994, American Express added a new twist to this segment of the market by introducing the *Optima card*. Like the regular American Express card, the Optima card is aimed at affluent cardholders who want not only convenience, but also a regular revolving charge account that carries with it a line of credit. Because the Optima card's outstanding balance does not have to be paid in full each month, it is, for all practical purposes, just another type of *bank credit card!* Its special feature is a 25-day interest-free grace period for all new purchases, *whether or not you carry a balance.* Most credit

Financial Road Sign

Credit Card Checklist

Before choosing a credit card, ask yourself these questions.

1. What is the interest rate? Is it fixed or variable?
2. Is this an introductory interest rate that will go up after a (short) period of time?
3. What is the annual fee?
4. What late fee is charged if I don't pay on time? When will a late fee be charged?
5. What is the grace period before interest is applied?
6. How and when will I be informed of changes in my contract?

What purchases count towards the rebates? Is there a limit on the rebate? Do reward points expire? Check terms and conditions often; they may change.

2. **What is the interest rate?** Rewards cards work best if you pay off your balance every month. Because rewards cards have a higher rate than regular cards—up to 6 percent more!—check the interest rate before signing up. You never know when you may have to carry a balance for a month.
3. **Is it worth paying a higher annual fee?** Be sure you can earn rewards in a reasonable period of time, and that you can use those rewards.
4. **Resist the urge to spend more to earn rewards.** Often rewards cardholders make unnecessary purchases to earn rewards. Evaluate your spending habits *before* you select a rewards card.

Critical Thinking Questions:

1. What type of rewards card would work best for you? Explain the reasons behind your choice.
2. List the steps you would use to evaluate the true cost or benefit of any reward card and apply them to the card you chose in question 1.
3. Visit two of the card comparison sites mentioned in the box and search for the category of card you chose. What card best meets your needs? Which site was easier to use, and why?

Sources: Betty Lin-Fisher, "Reward Yourself," *San Diego Union-Tribune*, March 2, 2003, p. H5; Betty Lin-Fisher, "5 Tips for Finding, Using a Reward Card Wisely," *San Diego Union-Tribune*, March 2, 2003, p. H5; Jeanne Sahadi, "The Best Credit Card Perks for You," *Money.com*, October 16, 2002, downloaded from **http://money.cnn.com**.

cards immediately charge interest on new purchases if the cardholder has an outstanding balance. Then, in 1999, American Express launched its *Blue card,* aimed at Generation Xers. This product allows the holder to carry balances, with their own line of credit. But what makes this card so unusual is that it's a *total Internet-functional product,* from start (applications are taken on line) to finish (payments are also made on line). In addition, it is the first major card issued in the United States with a smart chip built in.

Prestige Cards

Not all credit cards are created alike. Some offer many more advantages and features than others. That's precisely what **prestige cards** are; they offer higher credit limits (up to $100,000 or more), worldwide travel services, and other features meant to attract the upscale cardholder. Such cards impose higher credit standards for qualification, and sometimes charge higher annual fees. MasterCard, Visa, American Express, and Optima all offer prestige cards—in either gold or platinum, or in the color of some other precious metal. Indeed, platinum (generally considered to be the "ultimate" in credit cards) and other prestige cards now make up the fastest growing segment of the credit card market.

prestige card
A type of bank or T&E card that offers higher credit limits, has stricter requirements for qualification, and generally offers more features than its "regular" counterpart.

Exhibit 6.4 on pages 244–245 compares some of the major features of different bank and T&E cards. Most of these cards are fully interchangeable, because they perform many of the same functions. Together, these cards account for about 80 to 85 percent of all credit card activity, the balance of the transactions being made with retail charge cards.

Affinity Cards

Credit cards with a cause—that's the way to describe **affinity cards**. These cards are nothing more than standard Visa or MasterCards that are issued in conjunction with a sponsoring group—most commonly, some type of charitable, political, or professional organization. So named because of the bond between the sponsoring group and its members, affinity cards are sponsored by such nonprofit organizations as MADD, the American Association of Individual Investors, the American Wildlife Fund, AARP, and Special Olympics. In addition, they are issued by college and university alumni groups, labor organizations, religious and fraternal groups, and professional societies. In many cases, all you have to do is support the cause to obtain one of these cards (as in the case of MADD). In other cases, you'll have to belong to a certain group in order to get one of their cards (for example, be a graduate of the school or member of a particular professional group to qualify).

affinity cards
A standard bank credit card issued in conjunction with some charitable, political, or other sponsoring nonprofit organization.

Why even bother to carry one of these cards? Unlike traditional bank cards, affinity cards make money for the group backing the card, as well as for the bank, because the sponsoring groups receive a share of the profits (usually ½ to 1 percent of retail purchases made with the card). So, for the credit cardholder, it's a form of "painless philanthropy." But to cover the money that goes to the sponsoring organization, the cardholder usually pays higher fees or higher interest costs. In spite of this, some may view these cards as a great way to contribute to a worthy cause. Others, however, may feel it makes more sense to use a traditional credit card and then write a check to their favorite charity.

Secured Credit Cards

You may have seen the ad on TV where the announcer says that no matter how bad your credit, you can still qualify for one of their credit cards. The pitch may sound too good to be true; and in some respects it is because there's a catch. Namely, the credit

secured (collateralized) credit cards A type of credit card that's secured with some form of collateral, like a bank CD.

is "secured"—meaning you have to put up *collateral* in order to get the card! These are so-called **secured**, or **collateralized credit cards** where the amount of credit is determined by the amount of liquid collateral you're able to put up. These cards are targeted at people with no credit or bad credit histories, who don't qualify for conventional credit cards. Issued as Visa or MasterCard, except for the collateral, they're like any other credit card. To qualify, a customer must deposit a certain amount (usually $500 or more) into a 12- to 18-month certificate of deposit that the issuing bank holds as collateral. The cardholder then gets a credit line equal to the deposit. If the customer defaults, the bank has the CD to cover its losses. By making payments on time, it's hoped that these cardholders will establish (or reestablish) a credit history that may qualify them for a conventional (unsecured) credit card. Even though fully secured, these cards still carry annual fees and finance charges that are equal to, or greater than, those of regular credit cards.

Student Credit Cards

student credit card A credit card marketed specifically to college students.

A number of large banks, through their Visa and MasterCard programs, have special credit cards that target college students (and in some cases, even high school students). These **student credit cards** often come packaged with special promotional programs that are meant to appeal to this segment of the market—such as free music CDs, movie tickets, and the like. Some even offer special discounts on pizzas, clothing, computer software, and so on. Except for these features, there's really nothing out of the ordinary about these cards or their terms. Most simply require that you be enrolled in a 2- or 4-year college or university, and have some source of income, whatever that may be. In contrast, they usually *do not require* any parental or guardian guarantees, nor do they require that you hold a full-time (or even part-time) job.

So what's in it for the card issuers? While they know that most college students don't earn much money, they also know that's likely to change after they graduate—which is why they are so willing to offer the cards. Their logic seems to be that you (students) obviously have some source of income and you're going to be spending money anyway, so why not spend it with one of their credit cards. From the student's perspective, these cards not only offer convenience, but are also great for building up a solid credit history. Just *remember to use them responsibly*—that's the way to get the most from these cards or any other form of credit, for that matter!

smart.sites
Looking for the best rates on credit cards? CardWeb.com (**http://www.cardweb.com**) lets you compare credit card offers from major providers.

Debit Cards

debit card A card used to make transactions for *cash* rather than credit; replaces the need for cash or checks by initiating charges against one's *checking* account.

It looks like a credit card, it works like a credit card, it even has the familiar MasterCard and Visa credit card markings. But it's not a *credit* card—rather, it is a *debit* card. Simply put, a **debit card** provides direct access to your checking account and, thus, *works like writing a check*. For example, when you use a debit card to make a purchase, the amount of the transaction is charged directly to your checking account. Thus, using a debit card is not the same thing as buying on credit; it may appear that you are charging it, but actually you are paying with cash. Accordingly, there are no finance charges to pay.

Debit cards are becoming very popular, especially with consumers who want the convenience of a credit card but not the high cost of interest that comes with them.

EXHIBIT 6.4

Major Credit Card Features

There are some important differences among the major credit cards, including the annual fee, maximum amount of credit available, required minimum monthly payment, and the credit criteria used.

BANK CARDS	Standard MasterCard*	Gold MasterCard*	Platinum MasterCard*	VISA* Classic
Annual fee	$0–$50, as set by issuing bank	$0–$75, as set by issuing bank	$0–$100 or more, as set by issuing bank	$0–$75, as set by issuing banks
Criteria	Set by issuing bank	Set by issuing bank	Set by issuing bank	Set by issuing bank
Minimum credit	$200	$5,000	$10,000	$200
Maximum credit	$10,000	$25,000	$100,000	$10,000
Minimum payment	Bank sets according to state regulations; expressed as a percentage of amount owed.			
Cash machine link	Yes	Yes	Yes	Yes
Cash advances available	Yes	Yes	Yes	Yes

T&E CARDS	American Express (Green/Gold)
1. Annual fee	$65/$90
2. Criteria	Minimum income of $15,000/$20,000
3. Minimum credit	None/$10,000
4. Maximum credit	None
5. Minimum payment	Balance
6. Cash machine link	Yes (bank checking)
7. Cash advances available	No/Yes

*Data for MasterCard and Visa are meant to reflect the features typically found on the vast majority of these cards; unfortunately, more exact information is not available because the cards are issued by thousands of financial institutions worldwide, and these institutions are mostly free to set their own standards.

EXHIBIT 6.4 (continued)

VISA Gold*	VISA Platinum*	Discover Card	American Express Optima	Amex Blue
\$0–\$75, as set by issuing bank	\$0–\$100 or more, as set by issuing bank	\$0	\$0	\$0
Set by issuing bank	Set by issuing bank	Varies by state	Minimum income of \$20,000	Determined by credit department
\$5,000	\$10,000	\$1,000	Determined by credit department	Determined by credit department
\$25,000	\$100,000	None	Determined by credit department	Determined by credit department
*Bank sets according to state regulations; expressed as a percentage of amount owed.		Percentage of amount owed	Set by state law; expressed as percentage of amount owed	Determined by credit department
Yes	Yes	Yes	Yes	Yes
Yes	Yes	Yes	Yes	Yes

American Express (Platinum)	Citicorp Diners Club
1. \$395	\$95
2. Minimum charged must be \$10,000 annually	Minimum income of \$25,000
3. \$10,000	None
4. None	None
5. Balance	Balance
6. Yes	Yes
7. Yes	Yes

There are over 200 million debit cards in the U.S. today, which together account for about 22 percent of all credit/debit card transactions. They are accepted at most establishments displaying the Visa or MasterCard logo but function as an alternative to writing checks. If you use a debit card to make a purchase at a department store or restaurant, the transaction will show up on your next monthly *checking account* statement. Needless to say, to keep your records straight, you should enter debit card transactions directly into your checkbook ledger as they occur and treat them as withdrawals, or checks, by subtracting them from your checking account balance. Debit cards can also be used to gain access to your account through 24-hour teller machines or ATMs—which is the closest thing to a cash advance that these cards have to offer.

A big disadvantage of a debit card, of course, is that it does not provide a line of credit. In addition, it can cause overdraft problems if you fail to make the proper entries to your checking account or inadvertently use it when you think you are using a credit card. Also, some debit card issuers charge a transaction fee or a flat annual fee; and even some *merchants* may charge you for using your debit card. On the plus side, a debit card does not carry with it the potential credit problems and high costs that credit cards do. Further, it is every bit as convenient to use as a credit card—in fact, if convenience is the major reason you use a credit card, you might want to consider switching to a debit card for at least some transactions, especially at outlets such as gas stations that give discounts for cash purchases and consider a debit card to be as good as cash.

There's one more (very important) difference between debit and credit cards that every cardholder should be aware of, and that is the level of protection for the user when a card is lost or stolen. When a credit card is lost or stolen, federal banking laws state that the cardholder is not liable for fraudulent charges if the loss or theft is reported before that card is used. If reported after the card is used, the cardholder's maximum liability is $50. Unfortunately, *this protection does not extend to debit cards. Indeed, there are no limits at all on your loss exposure.* As a result, if your debit card is stolen, the thief could wipe out your entire checking account! As noted above, debit cards can be useful, but check with your bank regarding policies on lost or stolen cards.

Prepaid Cards

Tired of fumbling for change to buy a candy bar from a vending machine or to use a pay phone? Buy a **prepaid card** and your pockets won't jingle with coins anymore. These "smart cards" can now be used to purchase a variety of items—phone calls, meals in some employee cafeterias, vending machine snacks—and their use is increasing. You pay a fixed amount, which is then stored on either a magnetic strip or rechargeable microchip on the card. Each time you make a purchase, the amount is electronically deducted from the card. First used for public transportation fares in large cities, prepaid cards are now used by many companies. In fact, you might be carrying one yourself, as they have become very popular on college campuses, where they're used to purchase meals, books, long-distance phone calls, and other items. The popularity of these "electronic purses" is increasing, as consumers and merchants alike find them convenient. And they're likely to become even more popular as the microchips that are being embedded in these smart cards today can be used to not only execute transactions, but also store such things as electronic plane tickets or theater tickets. In addition, it is easier to control Internet fraud with them, as they have electronic readers which plug easily into your computer for authenticity verification.

prepaid card
A plastic card with a magnetic strip or microchip that stores the amount of money the purchaser has to spend and deducts the value of each purchase; eliminates the need to use cash.

Prepaid cards are a lot like *debit cards*, in that each time you use one you are actually debiting the amount purchased to what you have stored on the card (or in your checking account). They should *not*, however, be confused with prepaid *credit cards*, which you can use over and over again. With prepaid cards, once the card is used up, you either toss it or get it recharged—there's no line of credit here, no monthly bills with their minimum monthly payments, none of that.

Revolving Credit Lines

revolving line of credit
A type of open account credit offered by banks and other financial institutions that can be accessed by writing checks against demand deposit or specially designated credit line accounts.

Revolving lines of credit are offered by banks, brokerage houses, and other financial institutions. These credit lines normally do not involve the use of credit cards. Rather, they are accessed by simply writing checks on regular checking accounts or specially designated credit line accounts. They are a form of open account credit and often represent a far better deal than credit cards, not only because they offer more credit but also because they can be a lot less expensive. And, according to the latest tax laws, there may even be a tax advantage to using one of these other kinds of credit!

These lines basically provide their users with ready access to borrowed money (that is, cash advances) through revolving lines of credit. They are every bit as convenient as credit cards, since access is gained by simply writing a check. The three major forms of open (non-credit card) credit are: overdraft protection lines, unsecured personal lines of credit, and home equity credit lines.

Overdraft Protection

overdraft protection line A line of credit linked to a checking account that allows a depositor to overdraw the account up to a specified amount.

An **overdraft protection line** is simply a line of credit linked to a checking account that enables a depositor to overdraw his or her checking account up to a predetermined limit. These lines are usually set up with credit limits of $500 to $1,000, but they can be for as much as $10,000 or more. The consumer taps this line of credit by simply writing a check. If that particular check happens to overdraw the account, the overdraft protection line will automatically advance funds in an amount necessary to put the account back in the black. In some cases, overdraft protection is provided by *linking the bank's credit card to your checking account.* These arrangements act like regular overdraft lines, except when the account is overdrawn, the bank automatically taps your credit card line and transfers the money into your checking account. It's treated as a cash advance from your credit card, but the result is the same as a regular overdraft protection line; it automatically covers overdrawn checks.

Unfortunately, you never know for sure just how much a given check will overdraw your account (if in fact it does). The reason is that unless you write very few checks, the balance shown on your checkbook ledger will seldom be the same as the amount shown by the bank. The way to handle this is to simply record the check in your checkbook ledger as you normally would, including the new balance after the check is written. If this overdraws your account—at least as far as your checkbook ledger is concerned—this will not be a problem, because you have an overdraft protection line to cover it. If it does, in fact, overdraw your account, the bank will notify you of this in a matter of days and inform you that it has advanced funds to your checking account. The amount of the advance will be shown on the notice and should immediately be entered into your checkbook ledger as a *deposit.* Once an advance is made, a monthly repayment schedule is set up for systematically repaying the loan, along with all interest charges—generally with monthly payments being spread out over a period of 18 to 36 months.

It should be clear that if you are not careful, you can quickly exhaust this type of credit by writing a lot of overdraft checks. As with any line of credit, there is a limit to how much you can obtain. You should be extremely careful with such a credit line and *under no circumstances take it as a license to routinely overdraw your account!* Doing so on a regular basis is a signal that you are probably mismanaging your cash and/or living beyond your budget. It is best to view an overdraft protection line strictly as an *emergency* source of credit—and any funds advanced should be repaid as quickly as possible.

Unsecured Personal Lines

unsecured personal credit line A line of credit made available to an individual on an as-needed basis.

Another form of revolving credit is the **unsecured personal credit line**, which basically makes a line of credit available to an individual on an as-needed basis. In essence, it is a way of borrowing money from a bank, S&L, credit union, savings bank, or brokerage firm any time you wish, without going through all the hassle of setting up a new loan.

Here is how it works. Suppose you submit a loan application for a personal line of credit at your bank. Once you have been approved and the credit line established, you will be issued *checks* that you can write against it. Thus, if you need a cash advance, all you need to do is write a check (against your credit line account) and deposit it into your checking account. Alternatively, if you need the money to buy some high-ticket item—say, an expensive stereo system—you can just make the credit line check out to the dealer and, when it clears, it will be charged against your unsecured personal credit line as an advance. (These credit line checks look and "spend" just like regular checks and thus do not have to be channeled through your normal checking account.) Personal lines of credit are usually set up for minimums of $2,000 to $5,000 and often amount to $25,000 or more. As with an overdraft protection line, once an advance is made, repayment is set up on a monthly installment basis. Depending on the amount outstanding, repayment is normally structured over a period of 2 to 5 years; to keep the monthly payments low, larger amounts of debt are usually given longer repayment periods.

Although these credit lines do offer attractive terms to the consumer, they do not come without their share of problems, perhaps the biggest of which is the ease with which cash advances can be obtained. In addition, these lines normally involve *substantial* credit limits and are about as easy to use as credit cards. This combination can have devastating effects on a family's budget if it leads to overspending or excessive reliance on credit. To be safe, these lines should be used only for emergency purposes or to make *planned credit expenditures*. In addition, systematic repayment of the debt should be built into the budget, and every effort should be made to ensure that the use of this kind of credit will not place an undue strain on the family finances.

Home Equity Credit Lines

Here is a familiar situation. A couple buys a home for $85,000; some 10 years later, it is worth $165,000. The couple now has an asset worth $165,000 on which all they owe is the original mortgage, which may now have a balance of, say, $45,000. The couple clearly has built up a substantial amount of equity in their home: $165,000 − $45,000 = $120,000. But how can they tap that equity without having to sell their home? The answer is to obtain a **home equity credit line**. Such lines are much like unsecured personal credit lines except that they are *secured* with a second mortgage on the home. Offered by most banks, S&Ls, major brokerage firms, and a growing number of credit unions, these lines of credit allow you to tap up to 100 percent (or more) of the equity in your home by merely writing a check. Although there are banks and financial institutions that do allow their customers to borrow up to 100 percent of the *equity* in their homes—or, in some cases, even more—the majority of the lenders set their maximum credit lines at 75 to 80 percent of the *market value* of the home, which reduces the amount of money they'll lend. For a variety of reasons, including attractive tax features (which we'll examine later), the popularity of home equity credit lines has grown almost exponentially. Indeed, the amount of home equity loans outstanding today actually *exceeds* the amount of credit card debt outstanding!

home equity credit line
A line of credit issued against the existing equity in a home.

Here's how these lines work. Recall the couple in our example has built up an equity of $120,000 in their home—equity against which they can borrow through a home equity credit line. Assuming they have a good credit record and using a 75 percent loan-to-market-value ratio, a bank would be willing to lend up to $123,750; that is, 75 percent of the value of the house is .75 × $165,000 = $123,750. Subtracting the $45,000 still due on the first mortgage, we see that our couple could qualify for a home equity credit line of a whopping $78,750. Note, in this case, that if the bank had been willing to lend the couple *100 percent of the equity* in their home, it would have given them a (much higher) credit line of $120,000, which is the difference between what the house is worth and what they still owe on it. Most lenders don't like to do this because it results in very large credit lines and, perhaps more important, it doesn't provide the lender with much of a cushion should the borrower default.

smart.sites

If you need a home equity line of credit but your credit is not the best, Bankrate.com can point you to the best rates in your own state or suggest a more distant bank with a good deal: **http://www.bankrate.com/brm/bcd/creditpage.asp**.

Home equity lines also have an interesting tax feature that you should be aware of—that is, the annual interest charges on such lines may be fully deductible for those who itemize. This is the only type of consumer loan that still qualifies for such tax treatment. According to the latest provisions of the tax code, a homeowner is allowed to *fully deduct the interest charges on home equity loans of up to $100,000*, regardless of the original cost of the house or use of the proceeds. Indeed, the only restriction is that *the amount of total indebtedness on the house cannot exceed its fair market value*—which is highly unlikely, because homeowners usually cannot borrow more than 75 to 80 percent of the market value of the house anyway. (Effectively, the interest on that portion of the loan that exceeds $100,000, or 100 percent of the market value of the house—whichever is lower—*cannot* be treated as a tax-deductible expense.) In our preceding example, the homeowners could take out the full amount of their credit line ($78,750), and every dime they paid in interest would be tax deductible. If they paid, say, $7,400 in interest, and if they were in the 28 percent tax bracket, this feature would reduce their tax liability by some $2,070—(i.e., $7,400 × .28)—given, of course, that they itemize their deductions.

Not only do home equity credit lines offer shelter from taxes, they're also among *the cheapest forms of consumer credit.* For example, while the average rate on standard credit cards in mid-2003 was 13.8 percent, the average rate on home equity credit lines was less than half that, or 6.2 percent. To see what that can mean to you as a borrower, assume you have $10,000 in consumer debt outstanding. If you had borrowed that money through a standard consumer loan at, say, 9.5 percent, you'd pay interest of $950 per year—none of which would be tax deductible. But borrow the same amount through a home equity credit line at 6.2 percent, and you'll pay only $620 in interest. That's all tax deductible though, so if you're in the 28 percent tax bracket, the after-tax cost to you would be $620 × (1 − .28) = $446. This is less than half the cost of the other loan! So, which would you rather pay for a $10,000 loan, $950 or $446? That's really not a tough decision, but it does explain, in large part, why these lines have become so popular and are today one of the fastest growing forms of consumer credit.

Home equity credit lines are offered by a variety of financial institutions, from banks and S&Ls to major brokerage houses. All sorts of credit terms and credit lines are available, and most of them carry repayment periods of 10 to 15 years, or longer. What is perhaps most startling, however, is the maximum amount of credit available under these lines—indeed, $100,000 figures are not at all unusual. And it's precisely because of the enormous amount of money available that this form of credit should be used with caution. *The fact that you have equity in your home does not mean that you have the cash flow necessary to service the debt that such a credit line imposes.* Remember that your house is the collateral. If you can't repay the loan, you could lose it! At the minimum, paying for major expenditures through a home equity credit line should be

Concept ✓

6-4. What is *open account credit?* Who are the main providers and what are the main categories of this form of credit?

6-5. What is a *line of credit?* Does a line of credit come with all types of credit cards?

6-6. How do bank credit cards and *travel and entertainment* cards differ? Comment on the following statement: "If used intelligently, bank credit cards can be quite useful."

6-7. What is the attraction of *rebate cards?* List and briefly describe some of the more popular services and features that are now being offered on bank credit cards.

6-8. Explain how you could use your credit card to obtain a *cash advance*. Does it make any difference whether you obtain the cash advance from an ATM or the bank's teller window?

6-9. How is the interest rate typically set on bank credit cards? In terms of interest rate, does it matter if you use your credit card to purchase merchandise or obtain a cash advance?

6-10. Many bank card issuers impose different types of fees; briefly describe three of these fees. Do these fees have any impact on the true (effective) cost of using credit cards? Explain.

6-11. Explain the difference between a *retail charge card* and a *30-day charge account*. What's a *secured credit card* and how does it differ from a *prestige card?*

6-12. What is a *debit card?* How is it similar to a credit card? How does it differ?

6-13. Describe how *revolving credit lines* provide open account credit. How would you obtain an advance from an *overdraft protection line?* What are the basic features of a *home equity credit line?*

done only after you have determined that you can afford the purchase and the required monthly payments will fit comfortably within your budget.

OBTAINING AND MANAGING OPEN ACCOUNT CREDIT

LG4

Americans love to use their charge cards. In the year 2002 alone, they bought nearly *$1.5 trillion* in goods and services on credit. And this figure is rising as more places accept "plastic," consumers find credit and debit cards more convenient than cash or checks, and the number of other benefits, like rebates and frequent flyer miles, continues to grow.

For the sake of convenience, people often maintain a variety of open accounts. Nearly every household, for example, uses 30-day charge accounts to pay their utility bills, phone bills, and so on. In addition, most families have one or more retail charge cards, a couple of bank cards, and possibly a T&E card; some people, in fact, may have as many as 15 to 20 cards, or more. And that's not all—families can also have one or more revolving credit lines in the form of overdraft protection, an unsecured personal line, or a home equity line. When all these cards and lines are totaled together, a family conceivably can have tens of thousands of dollars of readily available credit. It is easy to see why consumer credit has become such a popular way of making relatively routine purchases. Although open account credit can increase the risk of budgetary overload, these accounts can serve as a useful way of keeping track of expenditures.

Opening an Account

Unlike many 30-day charge accounts, retail charge cards, bank credit cards, T&E cards, and revolving lines of credit all require *formal application procedures.* Let's look now at how you'd go about obtaining open account credit, including the normal credit application, investigation, and decision process. We'll couch our discussion in terms of credit cards, but keep in mind that similar procedures apply to other revolving lines of credit as well.

The Credit Application

With over a billion credit cards in the hands of American consumers, one would think that consumer credit is readily available. And it is—but you must apply for it. Applications are usually available at the store or bank involved. Sometimes they can be found at the businesses that accept these cards or obtained on request from the issuing companies. Exhibit 6.5 provides an example of a bank credit card application. In this case, it is for the Bank of America Visa Platinum Card. As can be seen, the type of information requested in a typical credit application concerns personal/family matters, housing, employment and income, existing charge accounts, and credit references. Such information is intended to provide the lender with insight about the applicant's creditworthiness. In essence, the lender is trying to determine whether the applicant has the *character* and *capacity* to handle the debt in a prompt and timely manner.

The Credit Investigation

credit investigation An investigation that involves contacting credit references or corresponding with a credit bureau to verify information on a credit application.

Once the credit application has been completed and returned to the establishment issuing the card, it is subject to a **credit investigation**. The purpose is to evaluate the kind of credit risk you pose to the lender (the party issuing the credit or charge card). So be sure to fill out your credit application carefully. Believe it or not, they really do look at those things. The key items lenders look at are how much money you make, how much debt you presently have outstanding and how well you handle it, and how stable you are (for example, your age, employment history, whether you own or rent a home, and so on). Obviously, the higher your income and the better your credit history, the greater the chances of having your credit application approved.

As a part of the investigation process, the lender will attempt to verify much of the information provided by you on the credit application—for obvious reasons, false or misleading information will almost certainly result in outright rejection of your application. For example, the lender may verify your place of employment, level of income, current debt load, debt service history, and so forth. Often, this can be done through one or two quick phone calls. If you've lived in the area for a number of years and have established relations with a local bank, a call to your banker may be all it takes to confirm your creditworthiness. If you haven't established such bank relations—and most young people have not—the lender is likely to turn to the local credit bureau for a *credit report* on you.

The Credit Bureau

credit bureau An organization that collects and stores credit information about individual borrowers.

Basically a **credit bureau** is a type of reporting agency that gathers and sells information about individual borrowers. If, as is often the case, the lender does not know you personally, it must rely on a cost-effective way of verifying your employment and credit history. It would be far too expensive and time-consuming for individual creditors to confirm your credit application on their own, so they turn to credit bureaus that maintain fairly detailed credit files about you. Information in your file comes from one of three sources: creditors who subscribe to the bureau, other creditors who supply information at your request, and publicly recorded court documents (such as tax liens or bankruptcy records).

Contrary to popular opinion, your credit file does *not* contain everything anyone would ever want to know about you—there's nothing on your lifestyle, friends, habits, or religious or political affiliations. Instead, most of the information is pretty dull stuff, and covers such things as:

- Your name, Social Security number, age, number of dependents, and current and previous addresses
- Your employment record, including current and past employers and salary data, if available
- Your credit history, including the number of loans and credit lines you have, number of credit cards issued in your name, your payment record, and account balances
- Public records data involving bankruptcies, tax liens, foreclosures, civil suits, and criminal convictions
- The names of firms and financial institutions that have recently requested copies of your file

While one late MasterCard payment probably won't make much of a difference on an otherwise clean credit file, a definite pattern of delinquencies (consistently being 30 to 60 days late with your payments) or a personal bankruptcy certainly will. Unfortunately, poor credit traits will stick with you for a long time, because delinquencies will remain on

EXHIBIT 6.5

An Online Credit Card Application

You can apply for many credit cards today right on the Internet, which is the case with the *Bank of America Visa Platinum Card* application shown here (actually the first page of the application). This credit app, like most, seeks information about the applicant's place of employment, monthly income, place of residence, credit history, and other financial matters that are intended to help the lender decide whether or not to extend credit.

Bank of America Higher Standards

Credit Card Application

Bank of America Visa Platinum

Step 3: General Information

Pursuant tor equirements of law, including the USA PATRIOT Act, Bank of America is obtaining information and will take necessary actions to verify your identity.

Personal Information

An asterisk (*) indicates a required field.

* First Name (Do not use nicknames):
Middle Initial:
* Last Name:
Suffix:
* Social Security Number (format: xxx-xx-xxxx):
* Date of Birth (format: mm/dd/yyyy):
* Mother's Maiden Name (Required for security verification):
* Are you a Bank of America customer?: Yes No
* Are you a U.S. citizen or permanent resident of the U.S.?: Yes No

Residence Information

Indicate your physical address.
An asterisk (*) indicates a required field.

* Physical Address (No P.O. Boxes):
Apartment/Room Number:
* City:
* State: New Hampshire
* ZIP Code:
Time at Address: Years Months
Housing Status: Other
Monthly Housing Payment: $ .00

Contact Information

Indicate your mailing address.
An asterisk (*) indicates a required field.

* Is your mailing address the same as your physical address? (If yes, skip the next 4 address fields): Yes No
Mailing Address:
City:
State: New Hampshire
ZIP Code:
* Home Phone Number (format: xxx-xxx-xxxx):
* E-mail Address:

(Providing your current e-mail address enables you to check the status of your application online and to send yourself terms and conditions for the card you're applying for. Bank of America does not sell or share any customer information with marketers outside Bank of America who may want to offer you their own products and services.)

Employment Information

Income from alimony, child support or separate maintenance payments need not be revealed if you do not choose to disclose it as income.
An asterisk (*) indicates a required field.

* Gross Annual Household Income: $ .00
Employer:
Work Phone Number (format: xxx-xxx-xxxx):
Time with Employer: Years Months

Continue Cancel

Secure Area

Bank of America, N.A. Member FDIC. Equal Housing Lender

Source: Courtesy of Bank of America, **http://www.bankofamerica.com**.

your credit file for as long as 7 years and bankruptcies for 10 years. An example of an actual credit bureau report (or at least a part of one) is provided in Exhibit 6.6. It demonstrates the kind of information you can expect to find in one of these reports.

Local credit bureaus (there are about a thousand of them) are established and mutually owned by local merchants and banks. They collect and store credit information on people living within the community and make it available, for a fee, to members who request it. Local bureaus are linked together nationally through one of the "big three" national bureaus—Trans-Union, Equifax Credit Information Services, and Experian—each of which provides the mechanism for obtaining credit information from almost any place in the United States. It's important to understand that credit bureaus merely collect and provide credit information. They do not analyze it, they do not rate it (or at least they're not supposed to), and they certainly do not make the final credit decision.

Credit bureaus have been heavily criticized because of the large numbers of reporting errors and their poor record in correcting these errors on a timely and efficient basis. And consumers have been frustrated by the time-consuming process and credit bureaus' apparent "care less" attitude about their mistakes—as far as they are concerned, you are guilty until proven innocent. Fortunately, things have changed in recent years as the major credit bureaus have taken a more consumer-oriented approach, greatly improving their customer service and dispute resolution procedures and making reports easier to read. Many of these changes were formalized by a 1995 amendment to the Fair Credit Reporting Act that established industry guidelines for credit reporting procedures. According to this legislation, credit bureaus must provide you with low-cost copies of your own credit report, and they must have toll-free phone numbers. Disputes must be resolved in 30 days and take the consumer's documentation into account, not just the creditor's.

Financial Road Sign

What to Look for in Your Credit Report

1. Verify your name, address, Social Security number, driver's license number, spouse's name, and address.
2. Review your credit history. Note errors such as late payments you believe were made on time or disputed bill amounts.
3. Some credit reports use payment codes ranging from 1 to 9. An R1 or I1 indicates a good payment history.
4. Check the public records section for inaccuracies about bankruptcies, judgments, and tax liens.
5. If you find a mistake, follow the report's instructions. It may take as long as 30 days to have disputed information removed from your credit report.

Source: Bankrate, Inc., N. Palm Beach, FL, 2003, **http://www.bankrate.com**.

Even with these changes, though, credit bureaus still make mistakes. Unfortunately, when they do, it can mean *big* problems for you, because a credit report can affect whether or not you get credit. Millions of Americans have learned the hard way that their credit records are riddled with errors. You should ensure that your credit report accurately reflects your credit history. The best way to do that is to obtain a copy of your own credit report, and then go through it very carefully. If you do find a mistake, let the credit bureau know immediately—and by all means, put it writing; *then request a copy of the corrected file to make sure that the mistake has been eliminated.* Most consumer advisors recommend that you review your credit files annually. It's easy to get a copy of your credit report. Just go online to the Web sites listed here, or call the listed toll-free number. The addresses, Web sites, and toll-free phone numbers for the three national credit bureaus are provided below:

- Equifax Credit Information Services
  P.O. Box 105873
  Atlanta, GA 30348
  http://www.equifax.com or phone 1-800-997-2493
- Trans-Union Corporation
  Consumer Disclosure Center
  P.O. Box 1000
  Chester, PA 19022
  http://www.transunion.com or phone 1-800-888-4213
- Experian (formerly TRW)
  http://www.experian.com or phone 1-888-397-3742

credit scoring
A method of evaluating an applicant's creditworthiness by assigning values to such factors as income, existing debts, and credit references.

The Credit Decision

Using the data provided by the credit applicant, along with any information obtained from the credit bureau, the store or bank must decide whether or not to grant credit. Very likely, some type of **credit scoring** scheme will be used to make the credit decision. By assigning values to such factors as your age, annual income, number of years on your present job,

EXHIBIT 6.6

An Example of a Credit Bureau Report

Displayed here is an actual credit report from a major credit reporting bureau. These reports have been revised and are easier to understand. Notice that in addition to some basic information, the report deals strictly with credit information—including payment records, past due status, and types of credit.

Your Credit Report as of 04/09/2001

This Credit Report is available for you to view for 30 days. If you would like a current Credit Report, you may order another from MyEquifax.

ID # XXXXXXXXXXXXX

• *Personal Data*

John Q. Public
2351 N 85th Ave
Phoenix, AZ 85037

Social Security Number: 022-22-2222
Date of Birth: 1/11/1960

• *Previous Address(es):*

133 Third Avenue
Phoenix, AZ 85037

• *Employment History*

	Location:	Employment Date:	Verified Date:
Cendant Hospitality FR	Phoenix, AZ	2/1/1989	1/3/2001

Previous Employment(s):

	Location:	Employment Date:	Verified Date:
SOFTWARE Support Hospitality Franch	Atlanta, GA	1/3/2001	1/3/2001

• *Public Records*

No bankruptcies on file
No liens on file
No foreclosures on file

• *Collection Accounts*

No collections on file.

• *Credit Information*

Company Name	Account Number and Whose Account	Date Opened	Last Activity	Type of Account and Status	High Credit	Items as of Date Reported Terms	Balance	Past Due	Date Reported
Americredit Financial Services	40404XXXX JOINT ACCOUNT	03/1999	03/2000	Installment REPOSSESSION	$16933	$430	$9077	$128	2/2000

Prior Paying History
30 days past due 07 times; 60 days past due 05 times; 90+ days past due 03 times
INVOLUNTARY REPOSSESION AUTO

Company Name	Account Number and Whose Account	Date Opened	Last Activity	Type of Account and Status	High Credit	Items as of Date Reported Terms	Balance	Past Due	Date Reported
Capital One	412174147128XXXX INDIVIDUAL ACCOUNT	10/1997	01/2001	Revolving PAYS AS AGREED	$777	15	$514		01/2001

Prior Paying History
30 days past due 02 times; 60 days past due 1 times; 90+ days past due 00 times
CREDIT CARD

Company Name	Account Number and Whose Account	Date Opened	Last Activity	Type of Account and Status	High Credit	Items as of Date Reported Terms	Balance	Past Due	Date Reported
Desert Schools FCU	423325003406XXXX INDIVIDUAL ACCOUNT	07/1997	06/1998	Revolving PAYS AS AGREED	$500		$0		07/1999

Prior Paying History
30 days past due 02 times; 60 days past due 00 times; 90+ days past due 00 times
ACCOUNT PAID CLOSED ACCOUNT

• *Credit Inquiries*

Companies that Requested your Credit File

04/09/2001 EFX Credit Profile Online
06/30/2001 Automotive
01/18/2000 Desert Schools Federal C.U.
07/02/1999 Time Life, Inc.

whether you rent or own your home and how long you have lived there, age of your cars, number and type of credit cards you hold, level of your existing debts, whether you have savings accounts, whether you have a phone, and general credit references, an overall credit score for you can be developed. There may be 10 or 15 different factors or characteristics that are considered, and each characteristic will receive a score based on some predetermined standard. For example, if you're 26 years old, single, earn $32,500 a year (on a job that you've had for only 2 years), and rent an apartment, you might receive the following scores:

1. Age (25–30)	5 points
2. Marital status (single)	–2 points
3. Annual income ($30—35 thousand)	12 points
4. Length of employment (2 yrs. or less)	4 points
5. Rent or own a home (rent)	0 points
	19 points

Based on information obtained from your credit application, similar scores would be assigned to another 7 to 10 factors.

In all cases, the stronger your personal traits or characteristics, the higher the score you'll receive. For instance, if you had been 46 years old (rather than 26), you might have received 18 points for your age factor, being married rather than single would have given you 9 points, and earning $75,000 a year would obviously have been worth a lot more than earning $32,500! The idea is that the more stable you are *perceived* to be, the more income you make, the better your credit record, and so on, the higher the score you should receive. In essence, statistical studies have shown that certain personal and financial traits can be used to determine your creditworthiness. Indeed, the whole credit scoring system is based on extensive statistical studies, which identify the characteristics to look at and the scores to assign. It's all very mechanical: assign a score to each characteristic, add up the scores, and, based on that total score, determine the creditworthiness of the applicant. While it may sound simple, credit scoring has, in fact, come under criticism because very few people really know the specifics of what determines credit scores. To alleviate some of the mystery, Fair, Isaac—the firm that produces the widely used *FICO Scores*—has defined the five major components (along with their respective weights) that go into their credit scores. They are as follows: payment history (35%), outstanding debt (30%), credit history (15%), number of new credit inquiries (10%), and types of credit (10%).

Generally, if your score equals or exceeds a predetermined minimum, you will be given credit; if not, credit will be refused. Sometimes borderline cases are granted credit on a limited basis. For example, a large department store that normally limits the outstanding balance on its revolving charge accounts to $1,000 might give a customer with a marginal credit score a revolving charge account with a $250 credit limit. Even when a formal credit scoring scheme is used, the credit manager or loan officer is normally empowered to offer credit if such action seems appropriate. Applicants who are granted credit are notified and sent a charge card and/or checks, along with material describing the credit terms and procedures.

smart.sites

To learn more about FICO Scores, including what's in your FICO score, what's not in them, and what you can do to improve your FICO score, go to: **http://www.myfico.com**.

annual percentage rate (APR) The actual or true rate of interest paid over the life of a loan.

Computing Finance Charges

Because card issuers do not know in advance how much you will charge on your account, they cannot specify the dollar amount of interest you will be charged. But they can—and must, according to the Truth in Lending Act—disclose the *rate of interest* they charge and their method of computing finance charges. This is the **annual percentage rate (APR)**, the true rate of interest paid over the life of the loan, which must be calculated in the manner outlined by law. Remember, it is your right as a consumer to know—and the obligation of the lender to tell you—the dollar amount of charges (where applicable) and the APR on any financing you consider.

The amount of interest you pay for open account credit depends in part on the method the lender uses to calculate the balances on which they apply finance charges. Most bank and retail charge card issuers use one of four variations of the **average daily balance (ADB) method**, which applies the interest rate to the average daily balance of the account over the billing period. According to Bankcard Holders of America, a nonprofit consumer education organization, the most common method (used by an estimated 95 percent of bank card issuers) is the *average daily balance including new purchases*. The other techniques are average daily balance excluding new purchases, two-cycle average daily balance including new purchases, and two-cycle average daily balance excluding new purchases. Balance calculations under each method are as follows:

average daily balance (ADB) method
A method of computing finance charges by applying interest charges to the average daily balance of the account over the billing period.

- **ADB including new purchases.** For each day in the billing cycle, add the outstanding balance, including new purchases, and subtract payments and credits, then divide by the number of days in the billing cycle.
- **ADB excluding new purchases.** Same as first method, *excluding* new purchases.
- **Two-cycle ADB including new purchases.** Calculated like the first method, but using the average daily balance for both the current and previous billing cycles.
- **Two-cycle ADB excluding new purchases.** Same as the two-cycle method, but *excluding* new purchases.

These different calculations can obviously have an impact on a card's credit balance, and therefore on the amount of finance charges you'll have to pay. You should also be aware that the finance charges on two cards with the same APR but different methods of calculating balances may differ dramatically. It's very important to know the method your card issuer uses. Most banks compute finance charges for a 1-month period, though some issuers (among them Discover Card) still use the *two-cycle average daily balance method*. As we can see from the comparisons in Exhibit 6.7, carrying a balance on a credit card can turn out to be very expensive.

Let's look at an example of how to calculate balances and finance charges under the most popular method, *the average daily balance including new purchases*. Assume that you have a LastBank Visa card with a monthly interest rate of 1.5 percent. Your statement for the billing period extending from October 10, 2004, through November 10, 2004—a total of 31 days—shows that your beginning balance was \$582, you made purchases of \$350 on October 15 and \$54 on October 22, and you made a \$25 payment on November 6. Therefore, the outstanding balance for the first 5 days of the period (October 11 through 15) was \$582; for the next 7 (October 16 through 22), it was \$932 (\$582 + \$350); for the next 15 days (October 23 through November 6) it was \$986 (\$932 + \$54); and the last 4 days, it was \$961 (\$986 less the \$25 payment). We can now calculate the average daily balance using the procedure shown in Exhibit 6.8. Note that the outstanding balances are weighted by the number of days that the balance existed and then averaged (divided) by the number of days in the billing period. By multiplying the average daily balance of \$905.42 by the 1.5 percent interest rate, we get a finance charge of \$13.58.

MANAGING YOUR CREDIT CARDS

Congratulations! You have applied for and been granted a bank credit card, as well as a retail charge card from your favorite department store. You carefully reviewed the terms of the credit agreement and have at least a basic understanding of how finance charges are computed for each account. Now you must manage your accounts efficiently, using

EXHIBIT 6.7

Finance Charges for Different Balance Calculation Methods

The way a credit card issuer calculates the average daily balance on which the consumer pays finance charges has a big effect on the amount of interest you actually pay, as the following table demonstrates.

Example: A consumer starts the first month with a zero balance and charges $1,000, of which he pays off only the minimum amount due (1/36 of balance due). The next month, he charges another $1,000. He then pays off the entire balance due. This same pattern is repeated three more times during the year. The interest rate is 19.8 percent.

	Finance Charges
Average Daily balance (including new purchases):	$132.00
Average Daily Balance (excluding new purchases):	$ 66.00
Two-cycle Average Daily Balance (including new purchases):	$196.20
Two-cycle Average Daily Balance (excluding new purchases):	$131.20

Source: Based on data from Bankcard Holders of America, Salem, Virginia.

the monthly statement to help you make the required payments on time, and to track purchases and returned items.

The Statement

If you use a credit card, you will receive monthly statements similar to the sample bank card statement in Exhibit 6.9, showing billing cycle and payment due dates, interest rate, minimum payment, and all account activity during the current period. Retail charge cards have similar monthly statements, but without a section for cash advances. (Revolving line of credit lenders will also send you a monthly statement showing the amount borrowed, payments, and finance charges.) The statement summarizes your account activity: the previous balance (the amount of credit outstanding at the beginning of the month, not to be confused with past-due, or late, payments); new charges made during the past month (four in this case); any finance charges (interest) on the unpaid balance; the preceding period's payment; any other credits (such as those for returns); and the new balance (previous balance plus new purchases and finance charges, less any payments and credits).

Although merchandise and cash transactions are separated on the statement, the finance charge in each case is calculated at the rate of 1.5 percent per month (18 percent annually). While this procedure works fine for this illustration, it is a bit out of the ordinary, because most card issuers charge a higher rate for cash advances than for purchases. Note that the average daily balance method is used to compute the finance charge in this statement.

You should review your statements promptly each month. Save your receipts and use them to verify statement entries for purchases and returns *before* paying. If you find any errors or suspect fraudulent use of your card, first use the issuer's toll-free number to report any problems. Then always follow up *in writing* within 60 days of the postmark on the bill.

EXHIBIT 6.8

Finding the Average Daily Balance and Finance Charge

The average daily balance including new purchases is the method most widely used by credit card issuers to determine the monthly finance charge on an account:

	Number of Days (1)	Balance (2)	(1) × (2) (3)
	5	$582	$2,910
	7	$932	6,524
	15	$986	14,790
	4	$961	3,844
Total	31		$28,068

Average daily balance $= \frac{\$28,068}{31} = \$905.42$

Finance Charge: $\$905.42 \times .015 = \$13.58$

Concept ✓

6-14. Briefly describe the basic steps involved in opening a charge account; provide your answer from the customer's point of view. Describe *credit scoring* and explain how it's used (by lenders) in making a credit decision.

6-15. Describe the basic operations and functions of a *credit bureau*. What kind of information do they gather about you? Is there anything you can do if the information they have on file is wrong?

6-16. What is the *annual percentage rate (APR)*? Describe the most common method used to compute finance charges. What are the legal requirements with respect to disclosure of interest rates and charges?

6-17. The monthly statement is a key feature of bank and retail credit cards. What does this statement typically disclose? Why are merchandise and cash-advance transactions often separated on bank card statements?

Payments

Credit card users can avoid *future* finance charges by paying the total new balance shown on their statement each month. For example, if the $534.08 total new balance shown in Exhibit 6.9 is paid by the September 21, 2004 due date, no additional finance charges will be incurred. (The cardholder, however, will still be liable for the $4.40 in finance charges incurred to date.) If cardholders cannot pay the total new balance, they can pay any amount that is equal to or greater than the **minimum monthly payment** specified on the statement. If they do that, however, they will incur additional finance charges in the following month. Note that the account in Exhibit 6.9 has a minimum payment of 5 percent of the new balance, rounded to the nearest full dollar. As shown at the bottom of the statement, this month's minimum payment is $27.00; i.e.: $\$534.08 \times .05 = \$26.70 = \$27.00$. If the new balance had been less than $200, the bank would have required a payment of $10 (which is the absolute minimum dollar payment), or of the total new balance, if less than $10. Cardholders who fail to make the minimum payment are considered in default on their account, and the bank issuing the card can take whatever action it deems necessary.

minimum monthly payment
In open account credit, a minimum specified percentage of the new account balance that must be paid in order to remain current.

Returning Merchandise

When you return merchandise purchased with a credit card, the merchant will issue a *credit* to your account.

EXHIBIT 6.9

A Bank Credit Card Monthly Statement

Each month, a bank credit cardholder receives a statement that provides an itemized list of charges and credits, as well as a summary of previous activity and finance charges.

Please detach the above portion and return it with your payment to insure proper credit.

Bank Card Statement

Retain this statement for your records.

Account Number	Name(s)	Statement Date	Payment Due Date
123-XYZ-45678	Mr. Bill A. Bitshort Mrs. Bonnie R. Bitshort	8-24-04	09-21-04

ACCOUNT ACTIVITY

Previous Balance	203.64	Credit Status
Payments −	119.89	Your Credit Limit is:
Credits −	.00	
Subtotal	83.75	
New Transaction +	445.93	2000.00
Finance Charge +	4.40	Your Available Credit is:
Late Charge +	.00	
NEW BALANCE	534.08	1465.92

FINANCE CHARGE CALCULATION

Amounts Subject to Finance Charge		This Month's Charge	ENTIRE BAL.	
A. *Average Daily Balance	293.25	4.40	1.5%	18.00%
B. *Cash Advance	.00	.00	Monthly Periodic Rate	Nominal Annual Rate
C. *Loan Advance	.00	.00		
		4.40	18.00%	
*Finance Charges explained on reverse side		Finance Charge	Annual Percentage Rate	

Mail Billing Inquiries to: Post Office Box 7890, Van Niles, California, 85258, or call 800/000-0000
For Inquiries on Past Due Accounts, Overlimits or Credit Line Increase, call 800/000-0000

Posted Mo./Day	Transaction Description or Merchant Name and Location		Purchase Mo./Day	Bank Reference Number	Purchases/ Advances/Debits	Payments Credits
8-08	AMERICA WEST AIRLINES	LOS ANGELES	07-25	850000008823395192	42.00	
8-13	HACIENDA MOTORS	COSTA MESA	08-05	015400018537022316	166.86	
8-15	RICOS RESTAURANT	PALM SPRG	08-10	114500018856161722	132.47	
8-12	PAYMENT—THANK YOU		08-11	4501000182MD02139		119.89
8-24	RENEES RESTAURANT	NEWPORT	08-13	114500068201632483	104.60	

Notice See reverse side for important information

MIN. PAYMENT:	27.00	NEW BALANCE:	534.08	Total Debits 445.93	Total Credits 119.89

The credit is transacted in the same fashion as a purchase and will appear on your statement as a *deduction* from the balance. If you purchase an item and have problems with it, you may not have to pay that part of your credit card bill if you have attempted in good faith to resolve the problem with the merchant. This protection is provided by the Fair Credit Billing Act. Of course, if the problem is resolved in the merchant's favor, you will ultimately have to pay.

smart.sites

Use Financenter's Credit Card Calculators, **http://www.financenter.com/consumertools/calculators/** to find out how interest rate changes affect your balance, if debt consolidation makes sense, and answers to similar questions.

USING CREDIT WISELY

LG5, LG6

Does it seem that every week there's at least one new credit card application in your mailbox? Well, there's a very good reason for that, because each year, the 20,000 or so institutions and organizations that issue these cards mail out *over 3 billion* credit card applications! Every one of these unsolicited pieces of junk mail tries to give the impression that their offer is better than all the rest. It's very easy to be overwhelmed by all these choices. And although we've discussed how credit cards and revolving lines of credit can simplify your life financially, you can get into trouble unless you use them wisely. That's why you should carefully shop around to choose the right credit cards for your personal situation, understand the advantages and disadvantages that credit cards present, know how to resolve credit problems, and how to avoid the ultimate cost of credit abuse—bankruptcy.

Shop Around for the Best Deal

They say it pays to shop around, and when it comes to credit cards, that adage certainly holds true. With all the fees and high interest costs, it pays to get the best deal possible. So, where do you start? Most credit experts suggest the first thing you should do is step back and take a look at yourself. What kind of "spender" are you, and how do you pay your bills? The fact is, no single credit card is right for everyone. If you pay off your card balance each month, you'll want a card that's different from the one that's right for someone who carries a credit balance from month to month and may only pay the minimum due.

Regardless of which category you fall into, there are basically four card features to look for:

- Annual fees
- Rate of interest charged on account balance
- Length of the grace period
- Method of calculating balances

Now, if you normally pay your account balance in full each month, get a card with *no annual fees and a long grace period.* The rate of interest on the card is really irrelevant, since you don't carry account balances from month to month anyway.

In sharp contrast, if you don't pay your account in full, then look for cards that charge *a low rate of interest on unpaid balances.* The length of the grace period isn't all that important here, but obviously, other things being equal, you're better off with low (or no) annual fees. Sometimes, however, "other things aren't equal," in which case you have to decide between interest rates and annual fees. If you're not a big spender and don't build up big balances on your credit card (i.e., the card balance rarely goes above $400 or $500), then *avoid* cards with annual fees and get one with as *low* a rate of interest as possible. (*Note*: The above situation would probably apply to most college students—or at

Financial Road Sign

Should You Switch?

Shopping for a better deal on a credit card can be confusing because card issuers frequently change their offers. Here's how to figure out if it's time to switch.

1. Review your card terms about every six months. Visit the Web site of the card issuer to learn of current offers for new customers. If it's better than what you have, call the company and ask for the better deal. It may be willing to offer you the same terms to keep your business.

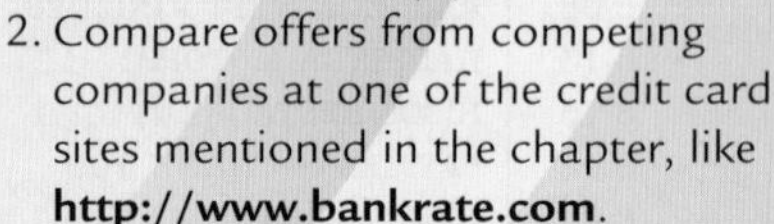

2. Compare offers from competing companies at one of the credit card sites mentioned in the chapter, like **http://www.bankrate.com**.
3. Know what you need. If you carry balances, you'll want a lower introductory rate. If you pay in full each month, look for ways to reduce fees or earn rewards.

Financial Road Signs

Advantages and Disadvantages of Credit Cards

Credit cards can sure make your life easier, as long as they are used properly. Here are some *ADVANTAGES* they offer:

- **Interest free loans:** They provide short-term, interest-free loans on the purchase of goods and services, as long as you pay your bill in full before the end of the (20–30 day) grace period.
- **Defer payments:** Customers can delay payments until the end of the billing period and even then, the bill does not have to be paid in full; instead, a series of smaller payments can be made over time.
- **Simplify record keeping:** Monthly credit card statements provide detailed records of all transactions, payments, and returned merchandise.
- **Resolution of disputes:** Its much easier to resolve disputed and returned merchandise if you haven't paid for it yet, especially if the card issuer takes your side.
- **Convenience and security:** It's easier to use a credit card to buy goods and services than it is to write a check for each transaction; plus, if your card is lost or stolen, your loss is limited.

But they do have their *DISADVANTAGES*:

- **High interest rates:** If you don't pay your bill in full each month, expect to pay a very high rate of interest (as much as 18 to 20 percent) on the unpaid balance.
- **Tendency to overspend:** They're so easy to use, you start buying things without really thinking about it. It's an easy trap to fall into, so be alert!

least it should.) On the other hand, if you do carry big balances (say, $1,000 or more), then you'll probably be better off *paying an annual fee* (even a relatively high one) *to keep the rate of interest on the card as low as possible.* For example, with a $2,000 average balance, your total yearly finance charges (including annual fees) will be *less* with a card that has, say, a $50 annual fee and an interest rate of 15 percent than one which has no annual fee but charges a higher (19 percent) rate of interest.

The bottom line is—don't take the first credit card that comes along. Instead, get the one that's right for you. To do that, learn as much as you can about the credit cards you've been offered or are considering. Be sure to read the credit agreement carefully and look for information about annual fees, grace periods, interest rates, and how finance charges are calculated. And don't overlook all those other charges and fees you may get socked with if you're ever late with a payment or go over your credit limit; not that you're going to make it a habit of doing these things, but just in case. Also, if the local deals aren't all that great, you might want to consider cards that are offered nationally. Many banks market their cards throughout the United States, and it may pay to check them out. To help you do that, look to publications like *Money* magazine and *Kiplinger's Personal Finance* magazine. They have Internet sites located at **http://www.money.com** and **http://www.kiplinger.com**, respectively. These magazines and Internet sites regularly publish information about banks and other financial institutions that offer low-cost credit cards nationally, an example of which is provided in Exhibit 6.10.

One final point: Some people, it seems, spend a lot of time and energy shopping for deals, jumping from one card to another to take advantage of low introductory rates. Although a strategy like this may result in lower internet payments, it can backfire if the low rates rise significantly after the introductory period, or if you miss a payment. A wiser approach is to shop around, check for better deals from time to time, and then *direct the rest of your energy toward working to reduce (or even eliminate) any monthly balances.*

AVOIDING CREDIT PROBLEMS

As more places accept credit cards, and as shopping online becomes more widely accepted, the volume of credit card purchases has grown tremendously—and so has the level of credit card debt. It's not unusual to find people using credit cards to solve cash flow problems; even the most careful consumers can occasionally find themselves with mounting credit card debt, especially after the year-end holiday buying season. The real problems occur when the situation is no longer temporary and the debt continues to increase. If overspending is not curtailed, the size of the unpaid balance may place a real strain on the budget. Essentially, individuals who let their credit balances build up are *mortgaging their future.* By using credit, they are actually committing a part of their future income to

EXHIBIT 6.10

Published Information About Bank Credit Card Terms

Information about low-cost credit cards is readily available in the financial media. Here's an example of what you can find in *Kiplinger's Personal Finance*. Notice the report lists the *cards with the lowest rates* (which are probably best for people who regularly carry an account balance), and *no-fee cards with the lowest rates* (which are probably best for people who pay their accounts in full each month), and the *best rebate cards*. The rates and fees shown here are for premium (silver and gold) cards, but similar rates and fees apply to the issuer's standard cards as well.

Low-interest premium cards Best if you carry a balance

Issuer	Recent Rate	Cash-Advance Rate/Fee	Annual fee	Late/Over Limit	Telephone Number
Pulaski Bank & Trust (G)	5.50%	5.50%/none	$50	$29/$29	800-980-2265
Amalgamated Bank of Chicago (G)	6.75%	6.75/2.5%	45	25/20	800-723-0303
Branch Banking & Trust (G)	8.15	19.90/3	29	29/29	800-476-4228

No-Fee Cards With the Lowest Rates Best if you usually pay the balance each month

Issuer	Recent Rate	Cash-Advance Rate/Fee	Grace Period	Late/Over Limit	Telephone Number
Chase Manhattan Bank (G, P)	5.65%	15.55%/3%	22 days	$29/$29	800-413-5661
Branch Banking & Trust (P)	8.15	19.90/3	25 days	29/29	800-476-4228
Associated Card Services (P)	8.24	19.99/3	20 days	35*/29	800-472-7708

Rebate cards Best of the cash-back cards

Issuer	Recent Rate	Cash-Advance Rate/Fee	Annual Fee	Rebate Terms	Telephone Number
Citibank Dividend Platinum Select (P)	9.74%	19.99%/3%	none	1%†	800-950-5114
Motley Fool Visa (P)	9.90	9.90/3	none	1#	800-932-2775
Principal Bank Platinum Visa (P)	10.00	10.00/none	none	1.25††	800-253-0938

As of July 3, 2003; rates are adjustable. (G) gold card (P) platinum card * varies according to balance †$300 annual maximum #expires after 90 days ††$600 annual maximum, deposited to a Principal account. Source: Bankrate.com, N. Palm Beach, Fla. Banks sometimes offer lower introductory rates.

Source: Bankrate, Inc., N. Palm Beach, FL, 2003, **http://www.bankrate.com**.

make payments on the debt. Unfortunately, the more income that has to go just to make payments on charge cards (and other forms of consumer credit), the less there is available for other purposes.

The best way to avoid credit problems is to be disciplined when using credit. Reduce the number of cards you carry, and don't rush to accept all of the tempting preapproved credit card offers that fill your mailbox. A wallet full of cards can work against you in two ways. Obviously, the ready availability of credit could tempt you to overspend and incur too much credit card debt. But there's another, less obvious, danger: When you apply for a loan, lenders look at the *total amount* of credit you have available as well as at the outstanding balances on your credit cards. If you have a lot of unused credit capacity, it may be harder to get a major loan because of lender concerns that you could become overextended. So think twice before accepting a new credit card. You really don't need three or four bank cards. Two is the most financial advisors suggest you carry: perhaps one rebate card, if you charge enough to make the benefit worthwhile, and a low-rate card for purchases you want to repay over time. And should you decide to start using a new card (because their offer was just too good to pass up), then *get rid of one of your old cards*—physically cut up the old card and inform the issuer in writing that you're canceling your account.

Suppose that, despite all your efforts, you find that your credit card balances are higher than you'd like and you anticipate having problems reducing them to a more manageable level. The first step is to stop making any new charges until you pay off (or pay down) the existing balances. Then, commit to a repayment plan. One good strategy is to pay off the highest-interest cards first, keeping the original payment rather than reducing it as your balance drops, or, even better, pay more than the minimum—even if it's just $10 more. You'd be surprised how much difference this makes.

smart.sites

Safeguard your identity with the help of The Identity Theft Resource Center, **http://www.idtheftcenter.org**, where you'll find scam and consumer alerts, resources, information on current legislation, and more.

You may also want to consider transferring your balances to a card with a low introductory rate and paying off as much as possible before the rate increases. Another option is to consolidate all your credit card debt and pay it off as quickly as possible using a lower-rate loan, such as a home equity line of credit. This can be a risky strategy, however. If you continue to be undisciplined about repaying your debts, you could lose your home. And clearing up your credit card balances may tempt you to start the credit card borrowing cycle all over again.

Important Consumer Credit Legislation

Just as you have an obligation to repay your debt in a prompt and timely fashion, lenders also have certain legal obligations they're expected to fulfill when they extend credit. Accordingly, when you apply for credit, it's in your best interest to be aware of the legal obligations of the issuing establishment.

A number of important consumer protection laws, pertaining to the extension of credit, have been passed nationally. The major pieces of legislation and their principle concerns have been:

- The *prohibition of credit discrimination* based on sex, marital status, race, religion, or national origin, as set forth in the **Equal Credit Opportunity Act** of 1975 and 1977
- The *full and accurate disclosure of credit information*, as well as the creation of limits as to how information can be disseminated, provisions for the resolution of errors and disputes, and the rights of consumers to view their files, all of which is contained in the **Consumer Credit Reporting Reform Act** of 1996
- The *establishment of acceptable billing procedures*, including the resolution of billing errors, complaints, and recourse on unsatisfactory purchases, as mandated by the **Fair Credit Billing Act** of 1975
- The *full and accurate disclosure of all finance charges*, as well as stipulation of the annual percentage rate (APR) being charged, any other fees and charges, credit terms, and liability limitations for lost or stolen credit cards, as set forth in the **Consumer Credit Protection (Truth in Lending) Act** of 1969, '71, and '82
- *Protection against collector harassment*, as stipulated in the **Fair Debt Collection Practices Act** of 1978 and '96

Protect Yourself from Identity Theft

When Shon Boulden, 22, applied for his first credit card, he received a nasty shock: his credit report showed there were already dozens of credit card accounts open in his name with thousands of dollars of delinquent bills. Boulden was a victim of identity theft. Likewise, the man who stole John Harrison's identity opened 60 accounts and charged more than $250,000 in Harrison's name before he was caught.

According to the Federal Trade Commission (FTC), identity theft is the top consumer complaint in the United States, affecting almost 10 million people in 2002 alone. These victims suffered losses of $5 billion, while losses to financial institutions and businesses totaled a staggering $48 billion. Identity thieves obtain personal data such as social security, driver's license, and credit card numbers and then use the information to open credit and bank accounts in the victim's name. Once the accounts are set up, the thieves spend freely—and the delinquent payments go on the victim's credit report. Most victims don't discover the theft until their checks bounce or their real credit cards are rejected.

It can take months, even years, to untangle the mess. Although victims usually aren't held responsible for more than $50 in fraudulent credit card charges, the damage to their good names and credit history can be long-lasting. They can have trouble getting mortgages, car loans, and even jobs. Harrison took prompt action and placed a fraud alert on his account with the three major credit bureaus. Even so, it took him two years to clear his name.

Experts say the best defense is a good offense, so protect your personal information:

- Shred all credit card receipts, cancelled checks, preapproved offers of credit or any other papers that contain identifying information before discarding them.
- Keep your personal records in a safe place. Many victims of identity theft find out the culprit was someone they knew.
- Be careful about giving out personal identification to businesses, Web sites, and others whom you do not know. Do not give credit card numbers, account passwords, or other

...continued on next page

Credit Card Fraud

Despite all the legislation, there are still people out there who are doing their very best to rip you off! In fact, plastic has become the vehicle of choice among crooks as a way of defrauding and stealing from both you and the merchants that honor credit cards. No doubt about it—credit card crime is big business, with estimated losses of between $4 billion and $8 billion a year! Stolen account numbers (obtained by dishonest employees or even by thieves going through the trash to find discarded receipts) are the biggest source of credit card fraud. Not surprisingly, the latest methods of credit card fraud revolve around the Internet. Be especially careful where you use your credit card in cyberspace. Most, if not all, of the major, big-name sites are about as secure as they can get, but when you go to one of the less-reputable sites, you may well be asking for trouble by giving them your credit card number! Remember, all the bad guys need to order merchandise or services over the phone or on the Internet is your account number. Even worse, a crook who also has your bank account number or home address may be able to get a credit card or open other types of charge accounts—*all in your name!* Unfortunately, as the accompanying *Money in Action* box explains, when that happens, you've just become another victim of *identity theft.*

Basically, "it's us against them," and the first thing you have to understand is that the credit card you're carrying around is a very powerful piece of plastic. Be careful with it. And don't count on retail merchants to protect you—for example, in a test conducted by *Money* magazine, only 5 percent of merchants checked signatures against the card and most accepted purchases made with borrowed cards. To reduce your chances of being defrauded, here are some suggestions you should follow:

- Never, ever, give your account number to people or organizations *who call you*—no matter how legitimate it sounds, if you didn't initiate the call, don't give out the information!
- It's okay to give your account number over the phone (if you initiated the call) when ordering or purchasing something from a major catalog house, airline, hotel, and so on, but don't do it for any other reason.
- Now, the same precautions should be exercised *when purchasing something over the Internet* with your credit card—don't do it *unless* you're dealing at the site of a major

retailer who uses state-of-the-art protection against fraud and thievery.

- When paying for something *by check*, don't put your credit card account number on the check and don't let the store clerk do it—show the clerk a check guarantee card (if you have one), a driver's license, or some other form of identification—but *not* your Social Security number.
- Don't put your phone number or address (and certainly not your Social Security number) on credit/charge slips, even if the merchant asks for it—they're *not* entitled to it anyway; but if the clerk insists, just scribble down any number you want.
- When using your card to make a purchase, *always keep your eye on it* (so the clerk can't make an extra imprint); and if the clerk makes a mistake and wants to make another imprint, ask for the first imprint, and tear it up on the spot.
- Always draw a line on the credit slip through any blank spaces above the total, so the amount can't be altered.
- *Destroy* all carbons and old credit slips; and when you receive your monthly statement, be sure to *go over it promptly* to make sure there are no errors (if you find a mistake, call or send a letter immediately, detailing the error).
- If you lose a card or it's stolen, *report it to the card issuer immediately*—the most you're ever liable for with a lost or stolen card is $50 (per card), but if you report the loss *before* the card can be used, you won't be liable for any unauthorized charges (the phone number to call is listed on the back of your statement).
- Destroy old cards or those you no longer use.

Bankruptcy: Paying The Ultimate Price for Credit Abuse

It certainly wouldn't be an overstatement to say that during the 1980s and 1990s, *debt was in!* In fact, the explosion of debt that has occurred since 1980 is almost incomprehensible. The national debt rose from less than a trillion dollars when the 1980s began to about $6.8 trillion by mid-2003. Businesses also took on debt at a rapid pace. And, not to be outdone, consumers were using credit like there was no tomorrow. So it shouldn't be too surprising that when you couple this heavy debt load with a serious economic recession (like the

sensitive data in response to unsolicited e-mails or phone calls, even if they claim to be from a business you know. Although giving your social security number to an employer is unavoidable, you can ask your employer what they will do to protect the information.

- Don't carry your Social Security Card or PIN numbers in your wallet or checked luggage or write your Social Security or driver's license number on your checks.
- Don't carry all your credit cards, just take the ones you need.
- Be wary of someone trying to crowd you as you use an ATM; a thief may be trying to learn your PIN before stealing your wallet.
- Make sure your bills arrive on time. If they don't, someone may have changed your address on the account or stolen the bill from your mailbox.
- Consider buying a mailbox that locks and send bill payments directly from the post office to reduce the chances of mail theft.
- Review your bank, telephone, and credit card statements carefully every month to see if there are any unauthorized charges or transactions.
- Request a credit report from one of the major credit bureaus once a year to look for suspicious activity conducted under your name.

If you are a victim of identity theft, take action immediately. Report the crime to the Federal Trade Commission's Identity Theft Hotline at 877-438-4338. Next, contact all creditors listed on your credit report to inform them of the problem. Let your local police know about the crime and, if you suspect the mail was used, notify your local postmaster.

Critical Thinking Questions

1. What factors in today's society have contributed to the current rise in identity theft?
2. List four specific actions that apply to you right now that will guard against identity theft.
3. Upon reviewing your bank credit card bill, you discover four unauthorized charges totaling $8,000. What steps will you take to investigate this situation and prevent further charges?

Sources: Sandra Block, "Don't Fall Prey to Identity Thieves," *USA Today*, September 12, 2000, p. 3B; Robert Moritz, "When Someone Steals Your Identity," *Parade*, July 6, 2003, pp. 12–13; Ann Perry, "Vacation Time a Picnic for Busy Identity Thieves," *San Diego Union-Tribune*, June 22, 2003, pp. H1, J8; The Identity Theft Resource Center, **http://www.idtheftcenter.org**, accessed October 25, 2003; and "USA Today Snapshots: ID Theft Costs Victims, Businesses," *USA Today*, September 19, 2003, p. 1A.

one we had in 1990 to 1991) and a very slow economic recovery (from 1992 to 1993), you have all the ingredients of a real financial crisis. And that's just what happened, as personal bankruptcies soared—indeed, nearly a million people a year filed for **personal bankruptcy** during that period. Even during the strong economic expansion from 1994 to 1997, the number of bankruptcies continued to climb; and during the economic recession in 2002, they reached a record of more than 1.5 million.

personal bankruptcy
A form of legal recourse open to insolvent debtors in which they may petition a court for protection from creditors and arrange for the orderly liquidation and distribution of their assets.

When too many people are too heavily in debt, a recession (or some other economic reversal) can come along and push many of them over the edge. But let's face it, the recession is not the main culprit here, because the only way a recession can push you over the edge is if you're already sitting on it! The real culprit is excess debt. Some people simply abuse credit by taking on more than they can afford. Maybe they're pursuing a lifestyle beyond their means, or an unfortunate event—like the loss of a job—takes place.

Whatever the cause, sooner or later, they start missing payments and their credit rating begins to deteriorate. Unless some corrective actions are taken, this is followed by repossession of property and, eventually, even bankruptcy. These people basically have reached the end of a long line of deteriorating financial affairs. Households that cannot resolve serious credit problems on their own need help from the courts. Two legal remedies that are widely used under such circumstances include (1) the Wage Earner Plan and (2) straight bankruptcy.

Wage Earner Plan

The **Wage Earner Plan** (as defined in *Chapter 13* of the U.S. Bankruptcy Code) is a workout procedure that involves some type of debt restructuring—usually by establishing a debt repayment schedule that's more compatible to the person's income. It may be a viable alternative for someone who has a steady source of income, not more than $750,000 in secured debt and $250,000 in unsecured debt, and a reasonably good chance of being able to repay the debts in 3 to 5 years. A majority of creditors must agree to the plan, and interest charges, along with late-payment penalties, are waived for the repayment period. Creditors usually will go along with this plan because they stand to lose more in a straight bankruptcy. After the plan is approved, the individual makes periodic payments to the court, which then pays off the creditors. Throughout the process, the individual retains the use of, and keeps title to, all of his or her assets. Chapter 13 filings account for less than 30 percent of all personal bankruptcies.

Wage Earner Plan
An arrangement for scheduled debt repayment over future years that is an alternative to straight bankruptcy; used when a person has a steady source of income and there is a reasonable chance of repayment within 3 to 5 years.

Straight Bankruptcy

Straight bankruptcy, which is allowed under *Chapter 7* of the bankruptcy code, can be viewed as a legal procedure that results in "wiping the slate clean and starting anew." *About 70 percent of those filing personal bankruptcy choose this route.* However, straight bankruptcy does not eliminate all the debtor's obligations, nor does the debtor necessarily lose all of his or her assets. For example, the debtor must make certain tax payments and keep up alimony and child-support payments but is allowed to retain certain payments from Social Security, retirement, veterans', and disability benefits. In addition, the debtor may retain the equity in a home (up to $17,425), a car (up to $2,775), and other personal assets, such as clothing, books, and tools of his or her trade. These are minimums as established by federal regulations; generally, state laws are much more generous with regard to the amount the debtor is allowed to keep. The choice of federal or state regulations would depend on the debtor's assets.

straight bankruptcy
A legal proceeding that results in "wiping the slate clean and starting anew"; most of a debtor's obligations are eliminated in an attempt to put the debtor's financial affairs in order.

Other Bankruptcy Options

Although most individual bankruptcies involve either straight liquidations or Wage Earner Plans, several other options have been added recently. To begin with, the

U.S. Supreme Court ruled that individuals can now file for reorganization under *Chapter 11* of the bankruptcy code—a type of bankruptcy that had previously been reserved mostly for businesses. Chapter 11 bankruptcy is for individuals who don't qualify for Chapter 13 reorganization—either because they exceed the debt limitations or do not have a regular source of income—but who want to try to restructure their debt. For these people, Chapter 11 is really the only alternative to straight bankruptcy. Like the Wage Earner Plan discussed above, Chapter 11 filers can restructure their debts, or a portion of them, to be repaid over time. The big difference is that in Chapter 11 bankruptcy, the creditors vote on—and can possibly block—the restructuring plan. This, of course, means the reorganization process can drag on for years and involve hefty legal fees, which probably explains why Chapter 11 is used in only about 1 percent of all personal bankruptcies.

The second alternative now available is a so-called *Chapter 20* bankruptcy—it's labeled as such because it combines parts of both Chapters 7 and 13. Although not actually a part of the bankruptcy code, this procedure allows individuals to wipe out their unsecured debt, as per Chapter 7, *and* then use Chapter 13 to restructure their secured debt, including mortgages, home equity loans, and nondischargeable debts, such as certain tax and child support payments.

Using the Services of a Credit Counselor

Filing for bankruptcy is a serious matter and should only be taken as a last resort. For one thing, it's going to stick with you for a long time (it will remain in your credit file for up to 10 years) and certainly won't help your chances of getting credit in the future. It often makes a lot more sense to try to work problems out before they get so bad that bankruptcy is the only workable alternative. Some people can do that on their own but, in many cases, it may be a good idea to seek the help of a qualified *credit counselor.*

credit counselor A professional financial advisor who assists overextended consumers in repairing budgets for both spending and debt repayment.

Credit counselors work with a family to set up a budget and may even negotiate with creditors to establish workable schedules for repaying outstanding debts. The counseling service will often go so far as to collect money from the debtor and distribute it to creditors. There are private firms that, for a fee, will act as intermediaries between borrowers and creditors and provide counseling services. These counselors generally attempt to reduce the size of payments, the size of outstanding debt, or both. However, their fees can run as much as 20 percent of the amount owed.

Another option is a nonprofit agency, such as those affiliated with the nationwide network of *Consumer Credit Counseling Services* (CCCS) (800-388-2227). You'll get many of the services that private agencies provide, at a lower cost. Of course, as with any financial advisor, you should check out a credit counselor's credentials, fees, services provided, and track record *before* using his or her services. Be cautious; sometimes these organizations aren't all

Concept ✓

6-18. What are some of the key factors you should consider when choosing a credit card? Given your current spending habits, what types of cards would be best for you and why?

6-19. Describe briefly the advantages and disadvantages of using credit cards.

6-20. How does consumer credit legislation relate to (a) credit discrimination, (b) disclosure of credit information, (c) disclosure of finance charges, (d) loss of credit cards, (e) errors, complaints, and recourse on unsatisfactory purchases, (f) protection against collector harassment, and (g) credit card renewal notices?

6-21. Discuss the steps you would take to avoid and/or resolve credit problems.

6-22. What's the biggest source of credit card fraud? List at least five things you can do to reduce your chances of being a victim of credit card fraud.

6-23. Explain the conditions that might make bankruptcy necessary. Distinguish between a *Wage Earner Plan* and *straight bankruptcy*. How might you use the services of a credit counselor?

they appear to be. For example, nonprofit groups like CCCS often advertise themselves as charitable organizations, although they are mostly funded by creditors. Unfortunately, there have been cases where these counselors were encouraging debtors to get into repayment plans they couldn't afford and ultimately couldn't pay. Plus these groups sometimes neglect to discuss the option of bankruptcy—even when it is in the consumer's best interest.

smart.sites

In over your head with credit card debt? The National Foundation for Consumer Credit (**http://www.nfcc.org**) has links to credit counseling agencies, free budgeting calculators, and helpful tips on getting out of debt.

To avoid falling into such a trap, debtors should explore all their options before seeking the help of a credit counselor. First, advisors suggest, try contacting your creditors yourself; you can probably work out a deal on your own if you have few lenders and need only 2 to 3 months to catch up. If, however, you have six or more creditors, you should probably see a credit counselor. Make sure to ask your counselor for *several debt-reduction options* appropriate for your financial situation. More importantly, face up to credit and debt problems as soon as they occur, and do everything possible to avoid ruining your credit record.

SUMMARY

LG1. Describe the reasons for using consumer credit, and identify its benefits and problems. Families and individuals use credit as a way to pay for relatively expensive items and, occasionally, to deal with a financial emergency. Consumer credit is also used simply because it is so convenient. Finally, it is used to partially finance the purchase of various types of investments. Unfortunately, while there are some definite positive aspects to the use of consumer credit, there are also some negatives, the most important being that it can be misused to the point where people live beyond their means by purchasing goods and services they simply can't afford. Such overspending can get so bad that it eventually leads to bankruptcy.

LG2. Develop a plan to establish a strong credit history. Establishing a strong credit history is an important part of personal financial planning. Opening checking and savings accounts, obtaining one or two credit cards and using them judiciously, and taking out a small loan and repaying it on schedule are ways to show potential lenders that you can handle credit wisely. Be sure to use credit only when you are sure you can repay the obligation, make payments promptly, and notify a lender immediately if you cannot meet payments as agreed. Using the debt safety ratio, you can calculate how much of your monthly take-home pay is going to consumer credit payments. One widely used credit capacity guideline is that total monthly consumer credit payments (exclusive of your mortgage payment) should not exceed 20 percent of your monthly take-home pay.

LG3. Distinguish among the different forms of open account credit. Open account credit is one of the most popular forms of consumer credit; it is available from various types of financial institutions and from all sorts of retail stores and merchants. The major types of open account credit include bank credit cards, retail charge cards, 30-day charge accounts, travel and entertainment cards, and various forms of revolving lines of credit. Many bank cards offer an incentive such as rebates or merchandise discounts. Be sure to calculate the total cost of the card, based on your spending patterns, to determine whether these special cards make sense for you. Although credit cards account for a significant portion of consumer transactions, revolving lines of credit also provide their users with ready access to borrowed money (by simply writing checks). Basically, there are three types of revolving credit lines: overdraft protection lines, unsecured personal lines of credit, and home equity credit lines.

LG4. Apply for, obtain, and manage open account credit. Most types of open account credit require formal application, which generally involves an extensive investigation of your credit background and an evaluation of your creditworthiness. This usually includes checking credit bureau reports. You should verify the accuracy of these reports regularly and promptly correct any errors. The amount of finance charges, if any, due on consumer credit depends in large part on the technique used to compute the account balance; the average daily balance method is the most common today. Managing your accounts involves understanding the monthly statement and making payments on a timely basis.

LG5. Choose the right credit cards and recognize their advantages and disadvantages. With so many different types of credit cards available, it pays to shop around to choose the best credit card for your needs. You should consider your spending habits and then compare the fees, interest rates, grace period, and any incentives. If you pay your balance off each month, you will want a card with low annual fees; if you carry a balance, a low interest rate is your best bet. Advantages of credit cards include interest-free loans, simplified recordkeeping, ease of making returns and resolving unsatisfactory purchase disputes, convenience and security, and use in emergencies. The disadvantages are the tendency to overspend and high interest costs on unpaid balances.

LG6. Avoid credit problems, protect yourself against credit card fraud, and understand the personal bankruptcy process. Avoiding credit problems requires self-discipline. Keep the number of cards you use to a minimum and be sure you can repay any balances quickly. When credit card debt gets out of control, adopt a payment strategy to pay off the debt in as short a time as possible by looking for a low-rate card, paying more than the minimum payment, and not charging any additional purchases until the debt is repaid or substantially paid down. Another option is a consolidation loan. To protect yourself against credit card fraud, don't give out your card number unnecessarily, destroy old cards and receipts, verify your credit card transactions, and report a lost card or suspicious activity immediately. A solution to credit abuse, albeit a drastic one, is personal bankruptcy. Those who file for bankruptcy work out a debt restructuring program under Chapter 13's Wage Earner Plan or Chapter 7's straight bankruptcy. If you have serious problems managing personal credit, a credit counselor may be able to help you learn to control spending and work out a repayment strategy.

Financial Planning Exercises

1. After graduating from college last fall, Janet Price took a job as a consumer credit analyst at a local bank. From her work reviewing credit applications, she realizes that she should begin establishing her own credit history. Describe for Janet several steps she could take to begin building a strong credit record. Does the fact that she took out a student loan for her college education help or hurt her credit record?

2. Brett Willard has a monthly take-home pay of $1,685; he makes payments of $410 a month on his outstanding consumer credit (excluding the mortgage on his home). How would you characterize Brett's debt burden? What if his take-home pay were $850 a month, and he had monthly credit payments of $150?
3. Calculate your own debt-safety ratio. What does it tell you about your current credit situation and your debt capacity? Does this information indicate a need to make any changes in your credit use patterns, and, if so, what steps should you take?
4. *Use Worksheet 6.1.* Sandra Adams is evaluating her debt safety ratio. Her monthly take-home pay is $3,320. Each month, she pays $380 for an auto loan, $120 on a home-equity line of credit, $60 on a department store charge card, and $85 on her bank credit card. Complete Worksheet 6.1 by listing Sandra's outstanding debts, and then calculate her debt safety ratio. Given her current take-home pay, what is the maximum amount of monthly debt payments that Sandra can have if she wants her debt safety ratio to be 12½ percent? Given her current monthly debt payment load, what would Sandra's take-home pay have to be if she wanted a 12½ percent debt safety ratio?
5. Mary Maffeo has an overdraft protection line. Assume that her October 2004 statement showed a latest (new) balance of $862. If the line had a minimum monthly payment requirement of 5 percent of the latest balance (rounded to the nearest $5 figure), what would be the minimum amount she would have to pay on her overdraft protection line?
6. Don and Judy Nesbit have a home with an appraised value of $180,000 and a mortgage balance of only $90,000. Given that an S&L is willing to lend money at a loan-to-value ratio of 75 percent, how big a home equity credit line can Don and Judy obtain? How much, if any, of this line would qualify as tax deductible interest if their house originally cost $100,000?
7. Sylvia Galano, a student at City Community College, has a balance of $380 on her retail charge card; if the store levies a finance charge of 21 percent per annum, how much monthly interest will be added to her account?
8. Sanjiv Patel recently graduated from college and is evaluating two credits cards. Card A has an annual fee of $75 and an interest rate of 9 percent. Card B has no annual fee and an interest rate of 16 percent. Assuming that Sanjiv intends to carry no balance and pay off his charges in full each month, which card represents the better deal? If Sanjiv expected to carry a significant balance from one month to the next, which card would be better? Explain.
9. Donna Wilson has several credit cards, on which she is carrying a total current balance of $12,500. She is considering transferring this balance to a new card issued by a local bank. The bank advertises that for a 2 percent fee, she can transfer her balance to a card that charges a 0 percent interest rate on transferred balances for the first nine months. Calculate the fee that Donna would pay to transfer the balance, and describe the benefits and drawbacks of balance transfer cards.
10. Alan Bell recently received his monthly MasterCard bill for the period June 1–30, 2004, and wants to verify the monthly finance charge calculation, which is assessed at a rate of 15 percent per year and based on average daily balances including new purchases. His outstanding balance, purchases, and payments are as follows:

Previous balance:	$386		
Purchases:		Payments:	
June 4	$137	June 21	$35
June 12	78		
June 20	98		
June 26	75		

What is his average daily balance and the finance charge for the period? (Use a table like the one in Exhibit 6.8 for your calculations.)

11. Mark Strom is trying to decide whether to apply for a credit card or a debit card. He has $7,500 in a savings account at the bank and spends his money frugally. What advice would you have for Mark? Describe the benefits and drawbacks of each type of card.
12. Jean Wong was reviewing her credit card statement and noticed several charges that did not look familiar to her. Jean is unsure as to whether she should pay the bill in full and forget about the unfamiliar charges, or "make some noise." If some of these are not hers, is she still liable for the full amount of the charges? Is she liable for any part of these charges, even if they are fraudulent?
13. Rhett Weaver recently graduated from college and wants to borrow $50,000 to start a business which he believes will produce a cash flow of at least $10,000 per year. As a student, Rhett was very active in clubs, held many leadership positions, and performed a considerable amount of community service. He currently has no other debts. He owns a car worth about $8,000, and has $4,000 in a savings account. Although the economy is currently in a recession, economic forecasters expect the recession to end soon. If you were a bank loan officer, how would you evaluate Rhett's loan request within the context of the "5 Cs of Credit"? Briefly describe each characteristics and indicate whether that characteristic has *favorable* or *unfavorable* implications for Rhett's loan request.

Applying Personal Finance

How's Your Credit?

Establishing credit and maintaining your creditworthiness are essential to your financial well being. With good credit, you will be able to obtain loans and acquire assets that you otherwise might not be able to. The purpose of this project is to help you examine your credit.

If you have already established credit, get a copy of your credit report from one of the credit bureaus mentioned in this chapter. (If you have applied for a loan recently, you may have already received a copy of your credit report from your lender.) Carefully examine your report for any inaccuracies and take the necessary steps to correct them. Then look over your report and evaluate your creditworthiness. If you feel you need to improve your creditworthiness, what steps do you need to take?

If you have not yet established credit, find an application for a card such as Visa, MasterCard, American Express, Optima, Discover, or a department store or gasoline company credit card. Places to look might be at a department store, banking institution, gas station, or the Internet. Take it home and fill it out. Then look over your application and try to do a self-evaluation of your own creditworthiness. Based on the information you have provided, do you think you would qualify for the credit card? What do you see as your major strengths? What are your major weaknesses? Is there anything you can do about them?

Contemporary Case Applications

6.1 The Alvarados Seek Some Credit Card Information

Alberto and Sabina Alvarado are a newly married couple in their mid-twenties. Alberto is a senior at a state university and expects to graduate in the summer of 2005. Sabina graduated last spring with a degree in marketing and recently started working as a sales rep for the Alhambra Corporation. She supports both of them on her monthly salary of $2,500 after taxes. At present, the Alvarados pay all their expenses by cash or check. They would, however, like to use a bank credit card for some of their transactions. Because neither Alberto nor Sabina is familiar with how to go about applying for a credit card, they approach you for help.

Questions

1. Advise the Alvarados on how they should go about filling out a credit application.
2. Explain to them the procedure the bank will probably follow in processing their application.
3. Tell them about credit scoring and how the bank will arrive at a credit decision.
4. What kind of advice would you offer the Alvarados on the "correct" use of their card? What would you tell them about building a strong credit record?

6.2 Michelle Starts over after Bankruptcy

A year after declaring bankruptcy and moving, with her daughter, back into her parents' home, Michelle Lamphere is about to get a degree in nursing. As she starts out in a new career, she also wants to begin a new life—one built on a solid financial base. Michelle will be starting out as a full-time nurse at a salary of $42,000 a year, and plans to continue working at a second (part-time) nursing job that provides an annual income of $10,500. She will be paying back $24,000 in bankruptcy debts and wants to be able to move into an apartment within a year, then buy a condo or house in 5 years.

Michelle will not have to pay rent for the time she lives with her parents. She also will have child care at no cost, which will continue after she and her daughter are able to move out on their own. While the living arrangement with her parents is great financially, the accommodations are "tight," and Michelle's work hours interfere with her parents' routines. Everyone agrees that one more year of this is about all the family can take. However, before Michelle is able to make a move, even into a rented apartment, she will have to reestablish credit over and above paying off her bankruptcy debts. To rent the kind of place she'd like, she will need to have a good credit record for a year, and to buy a home she will need to sustain that credit standing for at least 3 to 5 years.

Questions

1. In addition to opening checking and savings accounts, what else might Michelle do to begin establishing credit with a bank?
2. Although Michelle is unlikely to be able to obtain a major bank credit card for at least a year, how might she begin establishing credit with local merchants?
3. What's one way she might be able to obtain a bank credit card? Explain.
4. How often should Michelle monitor her credit standing with credit reporting services?
5. What general advice would you offer with regard to getting Michelle back on track to a new life financially?

Money Online

Give Us Credit!

1. **http://www.cardweb.com**

Learn the whole story behind those credit card offers. Pull up CardWeb's site and click on "CardLocator." Select three cards of your choice and search until you find the terms of their offers. Look for words such as "Disclosure" or "Terms and Conditions." Compare the cards on the following points:

a. Annual percentage rate for purchases
b. Variable rate information
c. Grace period for purchases
d. Annual fee
e. Method of computing the balance for purchases

f. Minimum finance charge
g. Late payment fee
h. Over-the-limit fee
i. Transaction fee for cash advances
j. Annual percentage rate for cash advances

2. **http://www.powersource.com/cccs**

Overdosed on debt? Consumer Credit Counseling Service provides budget counseling, educational programs, debt management assistance, and housing counseling. Their counseling services are available online, by telephone or in person in either Spanish or English. Perhaps you've already dug your way out of debt using the services CCCS provides. Share your story by clicking on "Client Profile," and maybe you will inspire someone else to turn his or her life around!

3. **http://www.consumer.gov/sentinel/**

What's the latest trend in consumer fraud? Pull up the Consumer Sentinel's site and click on "Fraud Trends" to learn the most reported consumer complaint categories. Use this site to get the facts on consumer fraud, report your fraud complaints, and learn how law enforcers worldwide work together with the private sector to combat fraud.

4. **http://www.privacyrights.org**

Protect your identity. Learn about identity theft and the many other issues affecting your privacy at the Web site of the Privacy Rights Clearinghouse.

5. **http://www.ftc.gov**

Have a complaint against a business? File it online with the Federal Trade Commission, the agency in charge of enforcing a variety of federal antitrust and consumer protection laws. Among its many offerings, the FTC's Web site also provides information on consumer protection, the FTC's investigative and law enforcement authority, business guidance, and economic issues.

6. **http://www.ftc.gov/foia**

What's on your record? You have the right to know, thanks to the Freedom of Information Act (FOIA), a federal law that requires agencies to make public certain types of records. To learn more about the FOIA, pull up the "FOIA Handbook." Browse their "Reading Room" for records that are already available, or find the "On-Line Request Form" to obtain records about you.

7. **http://www.abiworld.org**

What are the alternatives to bankruptcy? What are the statistics on both business and personal bankruptcies? Visit the "Public Library" of the American Bankruptcy Institute to find bankruptcy filings, articles, reports, statutes and laws, and most anything else to do with bankruptcy.

Just for Fun!

8. **http://home4.americanexpress.com/blue/student/blue_student_home.asp**

What effect will paying an extra $10 per month have on your credit card debt? Use American Express' Debt Reduction Calculator to find out. Under "Student Services," click on "Money Management Tools." While you're there, also click on "Managing Your Credit" to get useful information on credit management and how to maintain a good credit record.

9. **http://www.fool.com/ccc/ccc.htm**

Get in on the secret! You can use credit wisely and to your advantage—let the Motley Fool show you how. Visit the Credit Center and click on "Industry Secrets."

CHAPTER 7

Using Consumer Loans

Learning Goals

LG1. Know when to use consumer loans, and be able to differentiate between the major types.
LG2. Identify the various sources of consumer loans.
LG3. Choose the best loans by comparing finance charges, maturity, collateral, and other loan terms.
LG4. Describe the features of, and calculate the finance charges on, single-payment loans.
LG5. Evaluate the benefits of an installment loan.
LG6. Determine the costs of installment loans, and analyze whether it is better to pay cash or take out a loan.

College Financing by Degrees

"Looking back on the past 10 years, I wonder how I managed it all!" exclaims Gwen Thomas, a 42-year-old psychotherapist who lives near Portland, Maine. Widowed in 1997, when sons David and Jeffrey were 13 and 11, the family was emotionally and financially devastated. "It was really touch and go for a while," she recalls. "My income was small, and my husband's life insurance was inadequate. My main concern was taking care of the kids, pulling us together as a family." She resisted taking out loans because basically she is "debt-averse," rarely carrying a balance on her credit cards—maybe for school clothes, Christmas shopping—and then repaying it in a few months.

However, she realized she'd have to start saving whatever she could and prepare to borrow to send her sons to college. At the same time, her car was on its last leg and the house needed a new roof. "It was truly terrifying to think about sending two boys to college. I had no one to fall back on; I was it! But for me, education was the top priority, so I used every possible financial resource." As she researched the various loan options, she also learned about 529 college savings plans, tax-exempt investments that could help ease the loan burden. She opened one for each son and in so doing, was able to qualify for tax-free earnings on each account.

Both boys are attending the University of Maine and were able to finance about half of their college expenses with federal and college-sponsored grants. The other half was split among federal, college-sponsored, and home equity loans and personal funds—part-time and summer jobs and family savings. Gwen was able to take advantage of lower mortgage rates to refinance her home. She put the $120 she saved on her monthly payments into her sons' 529 accounts and used a home equity loan to buy a car and fix the roof. She thought about cashing in part of her retirement fund, but decided not to when she realized that it was her only source of retirement savings. "Funding our education was a family effort. We cut expenses drastically and took no vacations; the boys had no cars or computers. My aim was to keep our loans as small as possible," Gwen explains.

Through sound personal financial planning and wise use of consumer loans, Gwen and her sons have improved their lives. Chapter 7 tells you what to look for if you, too, need to borrow to reach financial goals.

CRITICAL THINKING QUESTIONS

As you review the chapter, consider these questions in relation to the Thomas family's financial planning:

- What financial planning steps should a family take to protect itself from a tragedy such as the death of a wage-earning spouse?
- What loan options were available to Gwen to finance her car and home repair? Was a home equity loan a good choice, and why?
- Describe the different types of student loans David and Jeffrey could apply for and compare their features.

BASIC FEATURES OF CONSUMER LOANS

LG1, LG2

At several points in this book, we have discussed the different types of financial goals that individuals and families can set for themselves. These goals often involve substantial sums of money and may include such things as a college education or the purchase of a new car. One way to reach these goals is to systematically save the money. Another is to use a loan to at least partially finance the transaction. Consumer loans are important to the personal financial planning process because of the help they provide in reaching certain types of financial goals. Working a major expenditure or purchase into a financial plan can be done just as easily with a consumer loan as it can by saving. The key, of course, is to successfully manage the credit by keeping the amount of debt used and debt-repayment burden *well within your budget*!

USING CONSUMER LOANS

As we saw in Chapter 6, the use of open account credit can prove helpful to those who plan and live within their personal financial budgets. More important to the long-run achievement of personal financial goals, however, are single-payment and installment consumer loans. These long-term liabilities are widely used to finance goods that are too expensive to buy from current income, to help with a college education, or to pay for certain types of nondurable items, such as expensive vacations. Of course, the extent to which this type of borrowing is used must be governed by personal financial plans and budgets.

These loans differ from open account credit in a number of ways, including the formality of their lending arrangements. That is, while open account credit results from a rather informal process, **consumer loans** are *formal, negotiated contracts* that specify both the terms for borrowing and the repayment schedule. In addition, whereas an open account credit line can be used over and over again, consumer loans are one-shot transactions that are made for specific purposes. Because there is no revolving credit with a consumer loan, there is no more credit available (from that particular loan) once it is paid off. Further, there are no credit cards or checks issued with this form of credit. Finally, while open account credit is used chiefly to make repeated purchases of relatively low-cost *goods and services*, consumer loans are used mainly to *borrow money* to pay for big-ticket items.

consumer loans
Loans made for specific purposes using formally negotiated contracts that specify the borrowing terms and repayment.

DIFFERENT TYPES OF LOANS

Although they can be used for just about any purpose imaginable, most consumer loans fall into one of the five following categories:

- **Auto loans**. Financing a new car, truck, SUV, or minivan is the single most common reason for borrowing money through a consumer loan. Indeed, auto loans account for about 35 percent of all consumer credit outstanding. Generally speaking, about 80 to 90 percent of the cost of a new vehicle (somewhat less with used cars) can be financed with credit; the buyer must provide the rest through a *down payment*. The loan is *secured* with the auto, meaning that the vehicle serves as **collateral** for the loan and can be repossessed by the lender should the buyer fail to make payments. These loans generally have maturities that run from 36 to 60 months.
- **Loans for other durable goods**. Consumer loans can also be used to finance other kinds of *costly durable goods,* such as furniture, home appliances, TVs, home computers, recreational vehicles, and even small airplanes and mobile homes. These loans are also secured by the items purchased and generally require some down payment. Maturities vary with the type of asset purchased: 9- to 12-month loans are common for less costly items, such as TVs and stereos, whereas 10- to 15-year loans (or even longer) are normal with mobile homes.

collateral
An item of value used to secure the principal portion of a loan.

- **Education loans**. Getting a college education is another very important reason for taking out a consumer loan. Such loans can be used to finance either undergraduate or graduate studies, and there are special government-subsidized loan programs available to students and parents; we'll discuss student loans in more detail in the following section.
- **Personal loans**. These loans are typically used for nondurable expenditures, such as an expensive European vacation or to cover temporary cash shortfalls. Many personal loans are made on an *unsecured* basis—that is, there is no collateral with the loan other than the borrower's good name.
- **Consolidation loans**. This type of loan is used to straighten out an unhealthy credit situation. When consumers overuse credit cards, credit lines, or consumer loans, and can no longer service the debt in a prompt and timely fashion, a consolidation loan may help control this deteriorating credit situation. By borrowing money from one source to pay off other forms of credit, borrowers can replace, say, five or six monthly payments that total $400 with one payment amounting to $250. *Consolidation loans are usually expensive, and people who use them must be careful to stop using credit cards and other forms of credit until they repay the loans. Otherwise, they may end up right back where they started.*

Student Loans

Today, the annual cost of a college education ranges from about $10,000 at a state school to well over $35,000 at many private colleges—and the cost is rising at about 4 or 5 percent a year, well above the inflation rate. Many families, even those who started saving for college when their children were young, are faced with higher than expected bills. Fortunately, many different types of financial aid programs exist, including some federal programs described below, as well as state, private, and college-sponsored programs.

Certainly paying for a college education is one of the most legitimate reasons for going into debt. Although you could borrow money for college through normal channels—that is, take out a regular consumer loan from your bank and use the proceeds to finance an education—there are better ways to go about getting education loans. That's because the federal government (and some state governments) have available several different types of subsidized educational loan programs. The four federally sponsored programs are:

- Stafford loans (Direct and Federal Family Education Loans—FFEL)
- Perkins loans
- Supplemental Loans for Students (SLS)
- Parent Loans (PLUS)

The Stafford and Perkins loans have the best terms and are the foundation of the government's student loan program. SLS and PLUS are *supplemental loans* for students who demonstrate a need but, for one reason or another, do not qualify for Stafford or Perkins loans, or whose total need is not being met by the other types of aid they are receiving. Whereas Stafford, Perkins, and SLS loans are made directly to students, PLUS loans are made to the parents or legal guardians of college students. Probably the best place to look for information about these and other programs is the Internet; for example, look up

Financial Road Sign

How to Get the Best Auto Loan Deal

You're ready to buy the car of your dreams. To find the best financing deal, follow these tips:

1. Don't be fooled by "low monthly payments," which may mean longer loan terms and paying more in interest.
2. Shop for a loan *before* you go to the dealer's showroom to have the most negotiation power. Dealer financing can cost more than bank and credit union auto loans. If you do finance through the dealer, ask about add-on costs or loan processing fees.
3. Consider applying a rebate to your down payment and financing a smaller amount rather than taking the low interest rate option.

Source: Lucy Lazarony, "Auto Loans Negotiations Salted with Landmines," *Bankrate.com,* February 8, 2001, **http://www.bankrate.com**.

FASTWEB (which stands for *F*inancial *A*id *S*earch *T*hrough the *WEB*). This site, which is free, not only provides details on all the major, and some of the not-so-major, student loan programs, but also has a service that matches individuals with scholarships and loans, and even goes so far as to provide form letters to use in requesting more information (the address for this Web site is: **http://www.fastweb.com**).

To see how student loans work, let's take a look at the Stafford loan program (except where noted, the other three federally subsidized programs have much the same standards and follow the same procedures as discussed here). Stafford loans carry low, government-subsidized interest rates; most major banks as well as some of the bigger S&Ls and credit unions participate in the program. Actually, the loans are made directly by one of the participating banks or financial institutions (in the case of the Stafford FFEL loan program), although the student has no direct contact with the lending institution. Instead, the whole process—and it really is quite simple—begins with a visit to the school's financial aid office, where a financial aid counselor will help you determine your eligibility. To be eligible, you have to demonstrate a *financial need*, where the amount of your financial need is defined as the cost of attending school *LESS* the amount that can be paid by you or your family (in these programs, students are expected to contribute something to their educational expense, regardless of their income). In addition, you have to be making *satisfactory progress in your academic program*, and you cannot be in default on any other student loans. (Each academic year, you will have to fill out a Free Application for Federal Student Aid [FAFSA] statement that shows these qualifications are being met. The financial aid office will have the forms available in hard copy, or you can complete and submit the form on the Web at **http://www.fafsa.ed.gov**). In effect, so long as you can demonstrate a financial need, are making satisfactory academic progress, and are not a deadbeat, you'll probably qualify for a Stafford loan.

Obtaining a Student Loan

All you have to do to obtain a loan is complete a simple application form, which is then submitted to *your school's financial aid office*. You do *not* have to deal with the bank (your school will submit all the necessary papers to the institution actually making the loan in the case of a FFEL loan, or directly to the federal government in the case of a Stafford Direct loan), and you will not be subject to any credit checks (although with SLS or PLUS loans, you may be subject to a credit judgment by the lender). The latest innovation in this procedure involves transmitting the application, like the one in Exhibit 7.1, electronically to the necessary parties, thus reducing paperwork and speeding up the processing. Most schools are converting to this method, if they haven't already done so.

There are specific loan limits with each of the four programs. For example, with Stafford loans, you can borrow up to $2,625 per academic year for first-year studies, $3,500 for the second year, and $5,500 per academic year thereafter, up to a maximum of $23,000 for undergraduate studies—you can obtain even more if you can show that you are no longer a dependent of your parents; that is, that you're an *independent* undergraduate student paying for your college education on your own. Graduate students can qualify for up to $8,500 per academic year. The maximum for both undergraduate and graduate loans combined is $138,500. Should you require even more money—that is, if your financial need exceeds the maximum amount of a Stafford loan—you can also apply for an SLS loan. There's no limit on the *number* of loans you can have, only on the maximum dollar amount that you can receive annually from each program.

Each year, right on through graduate school, a student can take out a loan from one or more of these government programs. Over time, that can add up to a lot of loans and

EXHIBIT 7.1

A Student Loan Application Form for a Stafford Loan

This is a standard application form for Stafford loans, and requests only the most basic information about the student borrower. It does not require information about a student's credit history, income level, and so on. Indeed, the student only has to fill out the top (shaded) part of the application, which includes the actual promissory note that the student is expected to sign.

Application and Promissory Note for Federal Stafford Loans *(subsidized and unsubsidized)*

OMB No. 1840-0717 Form Approved Exp. Date 03/31/99

WARNING: Any person who knowingly makes a false statement or misrepresentation on this form is subject to penalties which may include fines or imprisonment under the United States Criminal Code and 20 U.S.C. 1097.

Guarantor or Program Identification
UNITED STUDENT AID FUNDS, INC. 94
US

Borrower Section — *Please print neatly or type. Read the instructions carefully.*

1. Last Name	First Name	MI	2. Social Security Number
3. Permanent Street Address (If P.O. Box, see instructions.)		4. Telephone Number ( )	5. Loan Period (Month/Year) From: To:
City	State	Zip Code	6. Driver's License Number (List state abbreviation first.)
7. Lender Name City	State	Zip Code	8. Lender Code, if known	9. Date of Birth (Month/Day/Year)

10. **References:** You must provide two separate references with different U.S. addresses. The first reference should be a parent or legal guardian (if living). Both references must be completed fully.

	1.	2.
Name		
Permanent Address		
City, State, Zip Code		
Area Code/Telephone	( )	( )
Relationship to Borrower		

Loan Assistance Requested

11. I request the following loan type(s), to the extent I am eligible (see instructions): ❒ a. Subsidized Federal Stafford ❒ b. Unsubsidized Federal Stafford

12. I request a total amount under these loan types not to exceed (see instructions for loan maximums): My school will certify my eligibility for each loan type for which I am applying. The amount and other details of my loan(s) will be described to me in a disclosure statement. $ .00

13. If I check yes, I am requesting postponement (deferment) of repayment for my Stafford and prior SLS loan(s) during the in-school and grace periods. If I check no, I do not want to defer repayment. ❒ a. Yes, I want a deferment ❒ b. No, I do not want a deferment

14. If I check yes, I am requesting that the lender add the interest on my unsubsidized Stafford and prior SLS loan(s) which accrues during the in-school and deferment periods, to my loan principal (capitalization). If I check no, I prefer to pay the interest. ❒ a. Yes, I want my interest capitalized ❒ b. No, I prefer to pay the interest

15. If my school participates in electronic funds transfer (EFT), I authorize the school to transfer the loan proceeds received by EFT to my student account. ❒ a. Yes, transfer funds ❒ b. No, do not transfer funds

Promissory Note — *Continued on the reverse side.*

Promise to Pay: I promise to pay to the lender, or a subsequent holder of this Promissory Note, all sums disbursed (hereafter "loan" or "loans") under the terms of this Note, plus interest and other fees which may become due as provided in this Note. If I fail to make payments on this Note when due, I will also pay reasonable collection costs, including attorney's fees, court costs, and collection fees. I understand I may cancel or reduce the size of any loan by refusing to accept any disbursement that is issued. I understand that this is a Promissory Note. I will not sign this Note before reading it, including the writing on the reverse side, even if otherwise advised. I am entitled to an exact copy of this Promissory Note and the Borrower's Rights and Responsibilities. My signature certifies I have read, understand, and agree to the terms and conditions of this Application and Promissory Note, including the Borrower Certification and Authorization printed on the reverse side and the accompanying Borrower's Rights and Responsibilities statement.

THIS IS A LOAN(S) THAT MUST BE REPAID.

16. Borrower's Signature ______________ Today's Date *(Month/Day/Year)* ______________

School Section — *To be completed by an authorized school official.*

17. School Name	23. School Code/Branch	28. Telephone Number ( )
18. Street Address	24. Cost of Attendance $ .00	29. Recommended Disbursement Date(s) (Month/Day/Year) 1st 2nd
City State Zip Code	25. Federal Expected Family Contribution $ .00	3rd 4th
19. Loan Period (Month/Day/Year) From: To:	26. Estimated Financial Aid $ .00	30. School Certification (See box on the reverse side.)
20. Grade Level	27. Certified Loan Amounts a. Subsidized $ .00	Signature of Authorized School Official
21. Enrollment Status (Check one.) ❒ Full Time ❒ At Least Half Time	b. Unsubsidized $ .00	Print or Type Name and Title
22. Anticipated Completion (Graduation) Date (Month/Day/Year)		Date. Check box if electronically transmitted to guarantor: ❒

Lender Section — *To be completed by an authorized lending official.*

31. Lender Name	32. Lender Code/Branch	33. Telephone Number ( )	34. Lender Use Only
Street Address	35. Amount(s) Approved a. Subsidized $ .00	b. Unsubsidized $ .00	
City State Zip Code	36. Signature of Authorized Lending Official	Print or Type Name, Title, and Date	

1/31/94 LENDER COPY

Source: Downloaded from **http://www.loans4students.org/Login/DownloadApplication.asp**.

Money in Action

Saving for College with a 529 Plan

Financing their children's education ranks high on most parents' list of financial priorities. *Qualified tuition programs*, or *529 plans*, offer another way to help families reach this goal at a time when these costs are rising much faster than inflation. Named after the section of the tax code that defines them, 529 plans are state-sponsored tax-exempt investments similar to IRAs. Contributions to 529 plans has skyrocketed from about $2.6 billion in 2000 to more than $25 billion in 2002.

Each state offers at least one 529 plan, which may take one of two forms:

- Prepaid plans that lock in a student's future tuition at today's rates. These typically cover tuition at eligible schools within the state that offers the program. Some private colleges and universities also offer prepaid plans for either the sponsoring school or group of schools.
- College savings plans for qualified higher education expenses at any eligible educational institution, such as tuition, fees, books, and room and board.

Although contributions to the plans are made with after-tax dollars, the account's earnings and distributions to the student beneficiary are tax free. Under current tax regulations, the tax free status of distributions ends in 2010 unless Congress extends this tax benefit. Many states allow contributions of $200,000 or more per beneficiary, with no income limitations or age restrictions. Tax treatment at the state level–deductions for contributions and tax exemptions for earnings used in accordance with the plan guidelines–and other guidelines vary by state. Another state's plan may be better for you than your own, so investigate several plans before investing any money.

Some basic features are common to all 529 plans. Contributions to a 529 plan remain under the donor's control, and cannot be touched by the beneficiary without the donor's approval. If you move, you can roll over your plan assets tax-free into your new state's 529 plan or leave it as is (although the treatment for state taxes may change). If your child decides not to go to college, you may transfer plan

...continued on next page

a substantial amount of debt—all of which has to be repaid. But here's another nice feature: in addition to carrying low (government-subsidized) interest rates, loan repayment does not begin until after you're out of school (for the Stafford and Perkins programs only—repayment on SLS and PLUS loans normally begins within 60 days of loan disbursement). In addition, interest does not begin accruing until you get out of school (except, of course, with SLS or PLUS loans, where interest starts accumulating with the first disbursement). Of course, while you're in school, the lenders will receive interest on their loans, but it's paid by the federal government! Once repayment begins, you start paying interest on the loans, which may be tax deductible, depending on your income.

As a rule, student loans are amortized with monthly (principal and interest) payments over a period of 5 to 10 years. To help you service the debt, if you have a number of student loans outstanding, you can *consolidate* the loans, at a single blended rate, and extend the repayment period to as far as 20 years. In addition, you can ask for either an *extended repayment* for a longer term of up to 30 years; a *graduated repayment schedule*, which will give you low payments in the early years and then higher payments later on; or an *income-contingent repayment plan*, with payments that fluctuate annually according to your income and debt levels. But no matter what you do, *take the repayment provisions seriously, because defaults will be reported to credit bureaus and become a part of your credit file*! What's more, due to recent legislation, you cannot get out of repaying your student loans by filing for bankruptcy—no matter which Chapter you file under (7 or 13), *student loans are no longer dischargeable in a bankruptcy proceeding*.

In summary, here are some things about student loans to keep in mind:

- Check with your school's financial aid office to see what programs are available and then apply early.
- Register on FASTWEB (**http://www.fastweb.com**) for scholarships, grants, and loans that will be matched to your background.
- Borrow no more than you need—remember, these loans are eventually going to have to be repaid.
- Consider work-study as an alternative to borrowing.
- Become aware of loan forgiveness programs for selected occupations (military, law enforcement, Peace Corps, and so on).

- Take the loan repayment provisions seriously—defaults aren't taken lightly and can cause serious credit problems for you.
- Once you begin repaying the loans, take the interest deduction, up to the maximum allowed, on your (itemized) tax return.
- If you're having problems servicing the loans, contact the lender and see if some arrangements can be worked out (most lenders would rather work with you than have you default).

In addition to the government programs described above, there are other ways to pay for a college education. One of the most innovative is the so-called **529 College Savings Plan**. As explained in the accompanying *Money in Action* box, these plans aren't based on borrowing money to pay for college, but rather on using a special tax-sheltered *savings and investment program*.

529 College Savings Plan
A government-sponsored investment vehicle that allows earnings to grow free from federal taxes as long as they are used to meet college education expenses.

smart.sites
To find advice on financing college (loans and scholarships) and helpful online calculators, check out The Princeton Review's financing section, **http://www.princetonreview.com/college/finance/**.

Single Payment or Installment Payments

Consumer loans can also be broken into categories based on the type of repayment arrangement—single-payment or installment. **Single-payment loans** are made for a specified period of time, at the end of which payment in full (principal plus interest) is due. They generally have maturities ranging from 30 days to a year; rarely do these loans run for more than a year. Sometimes single-payment loans are made to finance purchases or pay bills when the cash to be used for repayment is known to be forthcoming in the near future; in this case, they serve as a form of **interim financing**. In other situations, single-payment loans are used by consumers who want to avoid being strapped with monthly installment payments and choose instead to make one large payment at the end of the loan.

single-payment loan
A loan made for a specified period of time, at the end of which payment is due in full.

interim financing
The use of a single-payment loan to finance a purchase or pay bills in situations where the funds to be used for repayment are known to be forthcoming in the near future.

installment loan
A loan that is repaid in a series of fixed, scheduled payments rather than a lump sum.

Installment loans, in contrast, are repaid in a series of fixed, scheduled payments rather than in one lump sum. The payments are almost always set up on a monthly basis, with each installment being made up partly of principal and partly of interest. For example, out of a $75 monthly payment, $50

assets to another beneficiary or request a refund of all of your principal and 90 percent of the earnings.

As attractive as these plans are, families need to be aware of their drawbacks such as the possible impact on qualifying for financial aid. These rules are complex and depend on the beneficiary family's income, type of plan (prepaid plan assets offset aid dollar for dollar, while savings plans are considered assets of the plan owner; however, distributions could be considered student income the following year), household income levels, and other considerations. Current rules may change by the time the beneficiary reaches college, so parents need to stay current on these rules and also investigate individual college rules for 529 plans.

How can you decide if 529 plans are suitable for your family and if so, choose the best plan for your needs? The key factors include amount of time the money will be invested, initial investment required, tax considerations such as your tax bracket and deductibility of contributions, costs of the plan (fees and sales charges vary by plan; look for total fees under 1 percent a year to preserve returns), and whether you think you will qualify for financial aid. Equally important are the plan's investment options. These also vary by style of investment and performance. Plan funds are professionally managed according to the style of the plan, which may be based on beneficiary's age, desired risk level, guaranteed return, or other parameters.

Clearly, 529 plans can be confusing to understand, and we've only skimmed the surface in this box. To learn more about 529 plans, visit one of the many Web sites dedicated to these plans, including: **http://www.529solutions.com**; **http://www.collegesavings101.com**; **http://www.savingforcollege.com**; and **http://www.finaid.org/savings**. In addition to these sites, many personal finance sites offer rankings based on plan performance, fees, tax treatment, and so forth.

...continued on next page

Critical Thinking Questions

1. What factors have contributed to the growing popularity of 529 college plans?
2. Differentiate between prepaid tuition plans and college savings plans. Which offers the greater flexibility, and why?
3. Visit two of the Web sites mentioned in the box and compare two 529 plans, including your own state's offerings and one other, on such factors as cost, investment style, initial investment, performance, tax implications, impact on financial aid, and any other considerations important to you. Which would you choose, and why?

Sources: Sarah Breckinridge, "Getting Schooled," *Smart Money*, August 2003, pp. 75–80; "A Guide to Understanding 529 Plans," *College Plans Savings Network*, downloaded from **http://www.collegesavings.org**, October 5, 2003; "Is a 529 Plan the best college savings vehicle for every family?" College Savings 101.com, downloaded from **http://www.collegesavings101.com**, November 6, 2003, "Rating the State Section 529 Plans," FinAid.com, downloaded from **http://www.finaid.org/savings/529ratings.phtml**, November 6, 2003.

might be credited to principal and the balance to interest. These loans are typically made to finance the purchase of a good or service for which current resources are inadequate. The repayment period can run from 6 months to 6 years or more. Installment loans have become a way of life for many consumers. They are popular because they provide a convenient way to "buy now and pay later" in fixed monthly installments that can be readily incorporated into a family budget.

smart.sites

Which state's 529 plan is the best for you? FinAid, a guide to student financial aid, rates the plans on its site: **http://www.finaid.org/savings/529ratings.phtml**.

Fixed or Variable Rate Loans

The majority of consumer loans are made at fixed rates of interest—that is, the interest rate charged (as well as the monthly payment) remains the same over the life of the obligation. However, variable rate loans are also being made with increasing frequency, especially on *longer-term installment loans*. As with an adjustable-rate home mortgage, the rate of interest charged on such credit changes periodically, in keeping with prevailing market conditions. If market interest rates go up, the rate of interest on the loan goes up accordingly, as does the monthly loan payment. These loans have periodic adjustment dates (for example, monthly, quarterly, or semiannually), at which time the interest rate and monthly payment are adjusted as necessary. Once an adjustment is made, the new rate remains in effect until the next adjustment date (sometimes the payment amount remains the same, but the number of payments changes). Many variable rate loans have caps on the maximum increase per adjustment period, and also over the life of the loan.

Variable rates can also be used with single-payment loans, but the mechanics are a bit different. That is, the rate charged is usually pegged to the *prime rate*, or some other "base" rate. Such rates are meant to be reflective of the bank's cost of funds, and moves in response to fundamental credit conditions in the market. Changes in the prime rate are widely reported in the media because of the widespread impact the prime has on the cost of borrowing. Here's how the prime rate is used to set the interest rate on a single-payment loan. Instead of putting a single, specific rate on a loan, it might be quoted at, say, prime plus 3 points; under these conditions, if prime is 4 percent, the borrower starts with a rate of interest of 4 + 3 = 7 percent. If the prime rate changes, the rate of interest on the loan changes automatically, except in this case the adjustment is made *immediately* (there are usually no adjustment dates with single-payment, variable rate loans). The loan will then carry a new rate of interest that will remain in effect until the next change. At maturity, interest charges at the different rates will be totaled and added to the principal to determine the size of the (single) loan payment. Generally speaking, variable rate loans are desirable *if interest rates are expected to fall* over the course of the loan; in contrast, fixed rate loans are preferable *if interest rates are expected to rise.*

Regardless of whether the loans are fixed or variable, their cost tends to vary with market conditions. As a rule, when interest rates move up or down in the market, so will the cost of consumer loans. Inevitably, there are going to be times when *the cost of credit simply becomes too high to justify borrowing* as a way of making major purchases. So when market rates start climbing, you should ask yourself whether the cost is really worth it. Financially, you may be far better off delaying the purchase until rates come down.

Where Can You Get Consumer Loans?

Consumer loans can be obtained from a number of sources, including commercial banks, consumer finance companies, credit unions, savings and loan associations, sales finance companies, and life insurance companies—even brokerage firms, pawnshops, or friends and relatives. *Commercial banks* dominate the field and provide nearly half of all consumer loans. Second to banks are *consumer finance companies* and then *credit unions*; together, about 75 percent of all consumer loans are originated by these three financial institutions! Interestingly, S&Ls are not much of a force in this market, as they tend to focus on mortgage loans rather than consumer loans. The selection of a lender often depends on both the rate of interest being charged and the ease with which the loan can be negotiated. Exhibit 7.2 provides a summary of the types of loans, lending policies, costs, and services *offered by the major providers of consumer loans.* Of course, today, it's becoming easier than ever to obtain consumer loans online. Just go to Yahoo! and search for "installment loans" and you'll end up with literally hundreds of Web sites. Some of these sites will actually accept applications online, whereas others offer a brief listing of their services, along with a toll-free phone number.

Commercial Banks

Because they offer various types of loans at attractive rates of interest, commercial banks are a popular source of consumer loans. One nice thing about commercial banks is that they typically charge lower rates than most other lenders, in large part because they take only the best credit risks and are able to obtain relatively inexpensive funds from their depositors. The demand for their loans is generally high, and they can be selective in making consumer loans. Commercial banks usually lend only to customers with good credit ratings who can readily demonstrate an ability to make repayment in accordance with the specified terms. They also give preference to loan applicants who are account holders. The fact that an applicant is already a good customer of the bank enhances his or her chances of being approved for the requested financing. Although banks prefer to make loans secured by some type of collateral, they also make unsecured loans to their better customers. The interest rate charged on a bank loan may be affected by the loan's size, terms, and whether it is secured by some type of collateral.

Consumer Finance Companies

consumer finance company
A firm that makes secured and unsecured personal loans to qualified individuals; also called a *small loan company.*

Sometimes called *small loan companies*, **consumer finance companies** make secured and unsecured (signature) loans to qualified individuals. These companies do not accept deposits but obtain funds from their stockholders and through open market borrowing. Because they do not have the inexpensive sources of funds that banks and other deposit-type institutions do, their interest rates are generally quite high. The actual rates charged by consumer finance companies are regulated by interest rate ceilings (or usury laws) set by the states in which they operate. The maximum allowable interest rate may vary with the size of the loan, and the state regulatory authorities may also limit the length of the repayment period. Loans made by consumer finance companies typically are for $5,000 or less and are secured by some type of collateral. Repayment is required on an installment basis, usually over a period of 5 years or less.

EXHIBIT 7.2

The Major Sources of Consumer Loans

Banks, finance companies, and other financial institutions provide a full range of consumer credit products to their customers. These institutions follow a variety of lending policies and lend money at different rates of interest.

	Commercial Banks	Consumer Finance Companies
Types of Loans	• Single-payment loans • Installment loans • Savings account loans • Check-credit plans • Credit card loans • Second mortgages (aka, home equity loans) • Education loans	• Installment loans • Second mortgages
Lending Policies	• Seek customers with established credit history • Often require collateral or security • Prefer to deal in large loans, such as auto, home improvement, and modernization, with the exception of credit card and check-credit plans • Determine repayment schedules according to purpose of loan • Vary credit rates according to the type of credit, time period, customers' credit history, and security offered • May require several days to process a new credit application	• Often lend to consumers without established credit history • Often make unsecured loans • Often vary rates according to size of loan balance • Offer a variety of repayment schedules • Make a higher percentage of small loans than other lenders • Maximum loan size limited by law • Process applications quickly, often the same day as application is made
Costs	• Lower than some lenders, because they: — Take fewer credit risks — Lend depositors' money, a relatively inexpensive source of funds — Deal primarily in large loans, which yield larger dollar income without raising administration costs	• Higher than most because they: — Take greater risks — Must borrow and pay interest on money to lend — Often deal in small loans, which are costly to make and yield a small income
Services	• Offer several different types of consumer credit plans • May offer financial counseling • Handle credit transactions confidentially	• Provide credit promptly • Make loans to pay off accumulated debts willingly • Design repayment schedules to fit the borrower's income • Usually offer financial counseling • Handle credit transactions confidentially

EXHIBIT 7.2 (continued)

Credit Unions	Savings and Loan Associations	Life Insurance Companies
• Installment loans • Share draft credit plans • Credit card loans • Second mortgages • Education loans	• Installment loans • Home improvement loans • Education loans • Savings account loans • Second mortgages	• Single- or partial-payment loans
• Lend to members only • Make unsecured loans • May require collateral or cosigner for loans over a specified amount • May require payroll deductions to payoff loan • May submit large loan applications to a committee for approval • Offer a variety of repayment schedules	• Will lend to all creditworthy individuals • Often require collateral • Loan rates vary depending on loan, length of payment, and security involved	• Lend on cash value of certain types of life insurance policies • No date or penalty on repayment • Deduct amount owed from value of policy benefit if death or other maturity occurs before repayment
• Lower than most because they: — Take fewer credit risks — Lend money deposited by members, which is less expensive than borrowed money — Often receive free office space and supplies from sponsoring organization — Are managed by members whose services in most cases are donated — Enjoy federal income tax exemptions	• Lower than some lenders because they: — Lend depositors' money, a relatively inexpensive source of funds — Secure most loans by savings accounts, real estate, or some other asset	• Lower than many because they: — Take no risk — Pay no collection costs — Secure loans by cash value of policy (and are thus lending the policy holders their own money)
• Design repayment schedules to fit borrowers' income • May offer financial counseling • Handle credit transactions confidentially	• Often offer financial counseling • Specialize in mortgages and other housing-related loans • Handle credit transactions confidentially	• Permit repayment at any time or not at all, if borrower chooses to use the cash value of the policy as a source of repayment • Handle credit transactions confidentially

Consumer finance companies specialize in small loans to high-risk borrowers. While these loans are quite costly, they may be the only alternative for people with poor credit ratings. Because of the high rates of interest charged, individuals should consider this source only after exhausting other alternatives.

smart.sites

What does a consumer finance company like Household Finance offer its customers? Visit the site, **http://www.household.com**, to check out the company's different credit cards and loans, as well as its consumer education sections.

Credit Unions

As it now stands, only members can obtain installment and single-payment loans from credit unions (*Note*: Although you still have to be a member of a credit union to obtain loans and other services, Congress has recently passed legislation enabling credit unions, if they so choose, to offer membership to just about anybody they want, rather than just a certain group of people.) Because they are nonprofit organizations with minimal operating costs, credit unions charge relatively low rates on their loans. They make either unsecured or secured loans, depending on the size and type of loan being requested. Generally speaking, membership in a credit union provides the most attractive borrowing opportunities available, because their interest rates and borrowing requirements are usually more favorable than other source of consumer loans. An added convenience of a credit union loan is that loan payments can often be deducted directly from payroll checks.

Savings and Loan Associations

Savings and loan associations (as well as savings banks) primarily make mortgage loans. Even so, although they are not major players in the consumer loan field, S&Ls are permitted to make loans on such consumer durables as automobiles, televisions, refrigerators, and other appliances. In addition, they can make certain types of home improvement and mobile-home loans, as well as some personal and educational loans. As a rule, the rates of interest on consumer loans at S&Ls are fairly close to the rates charged by commercial banks; if anything, they tend to be a bit more expensive. Like their banking counterparts, the rates charged on specific loans will, in the final analysis, depend on such factors as the type and purpose of the loan, the duration and type of repayment, and the overall creditworthiness of the borrower.

Sales Finance Companies

Businesses that sell relatively expensive items—such as automobiles, furniture, and appliances—often provide installment financing to purchasers of their products. Because dealers cannot afford to tie up their funds in installment contracts, they sell them to a **sales finance company** for cash. This procedure is often referred to as "selling paper," because the merchants, in effect, are selling their loans to a third party. When the sales finance company purchases these notes, customers are usually notified to make payments directly to it.

sales finance company
A firm that purchases notes drawn up by sellers of certain types of merchandise, typically big-ticket items.

captive finance company
A sales finance company that is owned by a manufacturer of big-ticket merchandise. GMAC is a captive finance company.

The largest sales finance organizations are the **captive finance companies** owned by manufacturers of big-ticket items—automobiles and appliances. General Motors Acceptance Corporation (GMAC) and General Electric Credit Corporation (GECC) are just two examples of captive finance companies that purchase the installment loans made by the dealers of their products. Also, most commercial banks act as sales finance companies by buying paper from auto dealers and other businesses. The cost of financing through a sales finance company is generally higher than the rates charged by banks and S&Ls, particularly when you let the dealer do all the work in arranging the financing (dealers normally get a cut of the finance income, so it's obviously in their best interest to secure as high a rate as possible). That's certainly not true in all cases, however, as automakers today will frequently use interest rates on new-car loans (or leases) as a marketing tool. They do this by dropping the rate of interest (*usually for selected models*) to levels that are well below the market—even 0 percent financing! Auto manufacturers use these loan rates (along with rebates) to stimulate sales by keeping the cost of buying a new car down. Clearly, cutting the cost of borrowing for a new car can result in big savings.

smart.sites

Do you think General Motors Acceptance Corporation just finances cars? Discover the full range of its services, from auto loans to home mortgages and insurance products, at **http://www.gmacfs.com**.

Life Insurance Companies

Life insurance policyholders may be able to obtain loans from their insurance companies. That's because certain types of policies not only provide death benefits but also have a savings function, in which case they can be used as collateral for loans. (*Be careful with these loans, however, as they could involve a tax penalty if certain conditions are not met.* A detailed discussion of life insurance is presented in Chapter 8.) Life insurance companies are required by law to make loans against the **cash value**—the amount of accumulated savings—of certain types of life insurance policies. The rate of interest in this type of loan is stated in the policy, and it used to be set as low as 5 or 6 percent. *The newer policies, however, carry loan rates that aren't set until the loans are made*, which usually means borrowing money at or near prevailing market rates. Although you will be charged interest for as long as the policy loan is outstanding, these loans do not have repayment dates—in other words, *you do not have to pay them back.* When you take out a loan against the cash value of your life insurance policy, you are really borrowing from yourself. Therefore, the amount of the loan outstanding, plus any accrued interest, will be deducted from the amount of coverage provided by the policy—effectively lowering your insurance coverage and endangering your beneficiaries with a lower pay-out should you die before repayment. The chief danger in life insurance loans is that they do not have a firm maturity date; consequently, borrowers may lack the motivation to repay them.

cash value (of life insurance) An accumulation of savings in an insurance policy that can be used as a source of loan collateral.

In addition to life insurance companies, many other *financial services organizations* have entered the consumer loan field. Indeed, it's now possible to get home equity lines and other consumer loan products from most of the major brokerage firms, like Merrill Lynch or Prudential Securities. And in 1999, another major financial services organization—American Express—launched its *Membership Banking* product, which provides a full menu of banking services, from money market and checking accounts to CDs, electronic bill payments, and lines of credit that are linked to their credit and charge card services. While it's true that banks, credit unions, and consumer finance companies dominate the consumer loan field, other players are entering the market and, in the process, offering borrowers options and choices they never had before.

Friends and Relatives

Sometimes, rather than going to a bank or some other financial institution, there may be a close friend or relative who is willing to lend you money. In many cases, such loans are attractive because little or no interest is charged. The terms will, of course, vary depending on the financial needs of the borrower, but they should be specified in some type of loan agreement that states the costs, conditions, and maturity date of the loan, as well as the obligations of both borrower and lender. Not only does a written loan agreement reduce opportunities for disagreement and unhappiness, it also protects both borrower and lender should either of them die or if other unexpected events occur. *Still, given the potential for disagreement and conflict, borrowing from friends or relatives is not advisable*, and should be seriously considered only when there are no other viable alternatives, or perhaps if the terms of credit are so much better than those available from the more traditional sources. Remember, a loan to or from a friend or family member is far more than a run-of-the-mill banking transaction: the interest is emotional, and the risks are the relationship itself!

As a last resort, you might even want to consider a *pawnshop*—if you have some sort of valuable asset (like a piece of jewelry, a musical instrument, or a CD player) you can leave as collateral. Such establishments tend to proliferate during economically tough times, as an increasing number of people turn to them as a source of "financing." As long as you have an asset to pawn, you may be able to obtain a short-term, single payment loan from one of these shops. But bear in mind that the amount of money you receive is likely to be only a small fraction of the perceived resale value of the asset you pawn. Moreover, the rate of interest charged on the loan can be extremely high, and the pawned asset can be sold if you do not repay the loan within the designated period of time.

Concept ✓

7-1. Discuss the difference between consumer loans and open-account credit.

7-2. List and briefly discuss the five major reasons for borrowing money through a consumer loan.

7-3. Identify several different types of federally sponsored student loan programs. Briefly note some of the basic features of these programs and how they differ from regular consumer loans. As a college student, what aspects of these student loan programs appeal to you the most?

7-4. Define and differentiate between (a) fixed and variable rate loans and (b) a *single-payment loan* and an *installment loan*.

7-5. Compare the consumer lending activities of (a) *consumer finance companies* and (b) *sales finance companies*. Describe a *captive finance company*.

7-6. Discuss the role of (a) credit unions and (b) savings and loan associations in consumer lending. Point out any similarities or differences in their lending activities. How do they compare to commercial banks?

Financial Road Sign

A Potential for Disaster

If you're faced with little or no alternative and must either lend or borrow money from a friend or family member, then do it carefully; here are some guidelines to follow.

- **Lend only money you can afford to give away:** Around 20 to 50 percent of these loans are never repaid.
- **Do it in a businesslike fashion:** Draw up a formal promissory note with specific terms.
- **Charge interest if the loan is not to be quickly repaid:** Make it around what you'd get in a savings account, but less than prevailing loan rates.
- **Both parties must understand this is a loan, not a gift:** Be specific about repayment terms.

MANAGING YOUR CREDIT

LG3

Borrowing money to make major acquisitions—and, in general, using consumer loans—is a sound and perfectly legitimate way to conduct your financial affairs. Meeting a major financial goal by buying on credit can be worked into your network of financial plans, and servicing the debt can be factored into your monthly cash budget. Doing it this way certainly is far superior to borrowing in a haphazard manner, giving little or no consideration to debt repayment. When borrowing is well thought out in advance and *full consideration is given not only to the need for the asset or item in question but also to the repayment of the ensuing debt*, sound credit management is the result. And sound credit management underlies effective personal financial planning.

From a financial planning perspective, you should ask yourself two questions when considering the use of a consumer loan: (1) Does making this acquisition fit into your financial plans, and (2) does the required debt service on the loan fit into your monthly cash budget? If the expenditure in question will seriously jeopardize your financial plans or if the repayment of the loan is likely to place an undue strain on your cash budget, you should definitely reconsider the purchase! Perhaps it can be postponed, or you can liquidate some assets in order to come up with more down payment. You may even have to alter some other area of your financial plan in order to work the expenditure in. Whatever route you choose, the key point is to make sure that the debt will be fully compatible with your financial plans and cash budget *before* the loan is taken out and the money spent.

SHOPPING FOR LOANS

Once you have decided to use credit, it is equally important that you shop around and evaluate the various costs and terms available. You may think the only thing you need do to make a sound credit decision is determine which source offers the lowest finance charge. But this could not be farther from the truth—for as we'll see below, finance charges are just one of the factors to consider when shopping for a loan.

Finance Charges

What's it going to cost me? For a lot of people, that's one of the first things they want to know when taking out a loan. And that's appropriate, because borrowers should know what they're going to have to pay to get the money. Lenders are required by law to clearly state all finance charges and other loan fees. Find out the effective (or true) *rate* of interest you're going to have to pay on the loan, and whether the loan carries a fixed or variable rate. Obviously, *as long as everything else is equal*, it's in your best interest to secure the least expensive loan. In this regard, ask the lender what the *annual rate of interest* on the loan will be, because it's easier (and far more relevant) to compare percentage rates on alternative borrowing arrangements than the dollar amount of the loan charges. This rate of interest is known as the *APR* (annual percentage rate) and includes not only the basic cost of money, but also any additional fees that might be required on the loan (APR will be more fully discussed later). Also, if it's a variable rate loan, find out what the interest rate is pegged to, how many "points" are added to the base rate, how often the loan rate can be changed, and if rate caps exist. Just as important, how will the lender make the periodic adjustments—will the *size* of the monthly payment change, or the *number* of monthly payments? To avoid any future shock, it's best to find these things out before the loan is made.

Low Rate or a Rebate?

Sometimes the question of what's the best finance charge can become a bit of a challenge. Case in point: What do you do when you're offered *either* a low rate of interest, *or* a cash rebate on your purchase. Sound familiar? It should, as this is a common tactic used by auto dealers today. The problem is, you can have one or the other, but not both. So which is bet, the low rate or the rebate?

Actually, there's a relatively straightforward way of figuring which is the better deal. *All you need is a good hand held financial calculator, and then just follow the three steps as described below.* Here's a simple, albeit very realistic example: You're shopping for a new car and the dealer offers you a choice of either a low, 1.9 percent rate of interest to finance the car, or a cash rebate of $2,500 (in which case you'll have to pay the market rate of interest to finance the car). For purposes of our discussion here, let's assume the car costs $20,000, and you plan to borrow the full amount. Also, if you take the rebate, we'll assume that you'll finance the car at your bank, which is offering new car loans at an annual rate of 10 percent. Finally, we'll assume that both loans will be paid off over a period of 5 years (or 60 monthly payments). Given this information, we can determine which alternative (the low rate or the rebate) is better, as follows:

Step 1. *Compute the monthly payments you'd have to make if you take out the low rate loan (through the dealer).* Here you want to find the monthly payments on a $20,000 loan

Money in Action

Borrowers Who Ask Questions Get the Best Deals

For decades, the average borrower had just three questions: How much money can I borrow? What's my monthly payment? And when can I have the money? That mind-set allowed lenders to charge 18 percent and more for credit card interest. Now, however, many consumers are wising up. They're asking questions about high interest costs and lending fees and comparing competitive offers from lenders before committing.

Why have so many borrowers become so much more sophisticated? One reason is increased media attention on financial issues. Magazines, newspapers, radio, and television are filled with personal finance advice articles and programs. The Internet is also making it easier to comparison shop for everything from credit cards to auto loans. Another factor: the huge volume of direct mail offers from competing lenders promising low interest rates and minimum fees.

Unfortunately, not all consumers are yet savvy enough about shopping for loans and credit cards. Because they don't know how to ask the right questions, they may fall victim to predatory lenders—lenders who use unfair credit practices to suck unwary consumers into higher interest rates and poor credit terms. For example, with equity stripping, lenders look for people who have almost paid off or recently paid off their mortgages. They promise them cash in exchange for a high-interest second mortgage.

Seniors are especially prone to these tactics. Atlanta resident Johnnie Edge, 76, was talked into taking out one of these second mortgage loans. Even after five years and $45,000 in payments, his principal dropped only $1,200.

Likewise, Helen Ferguson, a 78-year-old widow, saw a television advertisement for a loan company that would consolidate payments on the two mortgages she had taken out for home repairs by refinancing the loans. What she didn't know, however, was that signing the loan papers gave the company the right to charge lender fees totaling more than 10 percent of the loan balance. The loan also carried terms that prevented Ferguson from refinancing

...continued on next page

to be repaid in 60 monthly payments, where the loan carries an annual interest rate of 1.9 percent. In this case, because the loan is to be paid off in monthly installments, you'll have to set the *payments per year (P/Y)* key to 12 to put the calculator in a *monthly payment mode.* You can do that with the following keystrokes: hit **2nd**, then **I/Y**, then **12**, then **enter**; the screen should show P/Y = 12.00. Once that's done just enter the keystrokes as shown in the adjacent calculator, where:

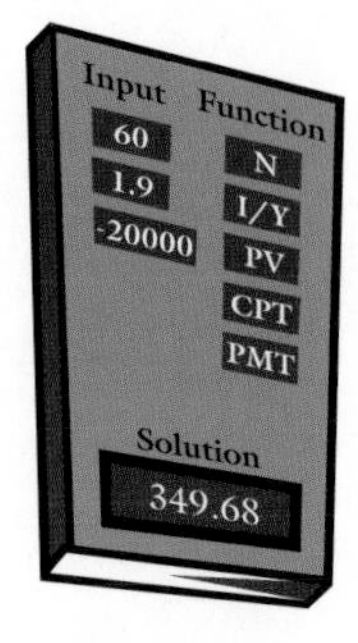

N = the number of *monthly* payments to be made on the loan,

I/Y = the *annual* rate of interest on the loan,

PV = the amount of the loan, entered as a *negative.*

As indicated, you'd have to make 60 monthly payments of *$349.68* to pay off this loan.

Step 2. *Find the present value of those monthly payments using the rate of interest offered by the alternative financing source (in this case, a bank).* Here we want to find the present value of 60 payments of $349.68 per month using a 10 percent discount rate, which is the rate of interest on new car loans being offered by your bank. To do that, make the keystrokes as shown in the adjacent calculator, where:

N = the number of *monthly* payments,

I/Y = the *annual* rate of interest offered by the bank,

PMT = the monthly payments to be made on the low-rate loan offered by the dealer, entered as a *negative.*

As can be seen, the present value of the low-rate loan payment works out to be $16,458. That figure represents *the amount of money you could borrow, at a 10 percent rate of interest, given you're willing to make 60 monthly payments of $349.68.* Essentially, this shows what $350 a month, for 60 months, will buy at 10 percent—that is, a loan in the amount of $16,458. Remember, at a 1.9 percent rate of interest, the same monthly payment will enable you to obtain a loan of $20,000—or some $3,542 more. (As you might have guessed, the alternative cost of financing plays a key role in this analysis—that is, other things being equal, the *higher* the alternative cost of funds, the *more attractive* the low-rate option becomes.)

Step 3. *Compare the present value found in Step 2 to the cost of the new car purchase, after the rebate, and select the lowest one.* In our example, the cost of the car *after the $2,500 rebate* would be: $20,000 − $2,500 = $17,500. In contrast, the "computed cost" of the car (financed at the *dealer's low rate*) would be equal to the present value of the monthly payments, or $16,458. So, if you take the rebate, the car will cost $17,500 (net), but if you take the low-rate loan, the car will have an equivalent cost of $16,458. Clearly, the dealer's low-rate loan is a less expensive route than the rebate, and therefore *represents the best deal*—in this case. Indeed, given an alternative cost of funds of 10 percent, a low-rate loan (of 1.9 percent) will *always be the better deal* so long as the rebate is less than: $20,000 − $16,458 = $3,542. Thus, in our example, for any rebate less than this amount, take the dealer's offer of low-rate financing. If the dealer offers a rebate of more than $3,542, then take it and finance the balance elsewhere (e.g., at your local bank).

Loan Maturity

Try to make sure that the size and number of payments will fit comfortably into your spending and savings plans. As a rule, the cost of credit increases with the length of the repayment period. Thus, to lower your cost, you should consider shortening the loan maturity—but only to the point where doing so will not place an unnecessary strain on your cash flow. For although a shorter maturity may reduce the cost of the loan, it will also increase the size of the monthly loan payment. Indeed, finding a monthly loan payment you will be comfortable with is a critical dimension of sound credit management. Fortunately, the personal computer provides an effective way of evaluating different loan configurations. Altering the loan maturity is just one way of coming up with an affordable monthly payment; with the aid of a personal computer (through either a piece of software or a site on the Internet), you can quickly run through all sorts of alternatives to find the one that will best fit your monthly budget. (The "tools" section of most major financial services sites on the Internet have "calculators" that enable you to quickly and easily figure interest rates and monthly loan payments for all sorts of different types of loans; generally, all you have to do is plug in a few key pieces of information, hit "calculate," and the computer does the rest. For example, go to **http://www.kiplinger.com/tools** and try out their calculators.)

Total Cost of the Transaction

When comparison shopping for credit, always look at the total cost of both the price of the item purchased *and* the price of the credit. Retailers often

with another bank without paying hefty prepayment penalties first. When Ferguson had trouble meeting the payments, she was forced to refinance again and again with the same lender—taking on a larger debt each time to cover all of the extra fees—until she almost lost her house.

Many other borrowers, most often with low or moderate income levels and limited knowledge of personal finance, have also learned the hard way about the dangers of not reading the fine print. Using deceptive sales practices, lenders pressure them into taking high interest loans that carry high levels of hidden fees.

Congress, the Federal Trade Commission, state governments, and organizations like the American Association of Retired Persons are all pushing for legislative changes that would make it harder for predatory lenders to operate. However, smart borrowers won't wait for those changes. To protect yourself, get all the facts before you sign on the dotted line for any loan. Ask if this is the lowest priced loan you qualify for and shop around to compare rates from other lenders. Don't let yourself be talked into borrowing more than you need; unscrupulous lenders may push you to consolidate loans to increase the loan size and hence, their fees. Always read the loan documents carefully, paying special attention to fees, terms, and conditions. Ask for explanations of any items you don't fully understand and then find out if this is standard lending practice. Seek advice before you sign, especially when a mortgage on your home is involved. Get a copy of the lender's Notice of Right to Cancel or Notice of Rescission, which spells out your rights about canceling the loan, usually within three days. Finally, remember the old adage: if it sounds too good to be true, it probably is.

Critical Thinking Questions:

1. Why should you compare loan terms with other lenders before signing a loan agreement?
2. List at least seven questions you should ask a lender before agreeing to its loan terms.
3. What are state and federal governments doing to protect consumers against predatory lenders? Use the Web to find and summarize the latest regulations for your state and the nation.

Sources: Michael D. Larson, "Predatory Lending: One Victim's Story," *Bankrate.com*, April 14, 2000, **http://www.bankrate.com**; Richard Newman, "Predatory Lenders Can Leave You Without Your Money or Home," *The Record* (Hackensack, N.J.), January 7, 2002, downloaded from Find Articles, **http://www.findarticles.com**; Shelly K. Schwartz, "Don't Fall Prey to Lenders," CNNfn, March 15, 2000, **http://cnnfn.cnn.com**; and Stacy Shelton, "Town Hall Meeting: Victims Urge Action to Stop Predatory Lending Practice," *The Atlanta Journal and Constitution*, February 3, 2002, p. E4.

manipulate both sticker prices and interest rates, so you really will not know what kind of deal you are getting until you look at the total cost of the transaction. Along this line, comparing *monthly payments* is a good way to get a handle on total cost. It is a simple matter to compare total costs: just add the amount put down on the purchase to the total of all the monthly loan payments; other things being equal, the one with the lowest total is the one you should pick.

smart.sites

To get the latest consumer loan rates, plus helpful guides on borrowing, visit Bankrate.com, **http://www.bankrate.com**.

Collateral

Make sure you know up front what collateral (if any) you will have to pledge on the loan and what you stand to lose in case you default on your payments. Actually, if it makes no difference to you and if it is not too inconvenient, using collateral often makes sense, because it may result in *lower* finance charges—perhaps half a percentage point or so.

Other Credit Considerations

In addition to the preceding guidelines, other questions you should ask include the following: Can you choose a *payment date* that will be compatible with your spending patterns? Can you obtain the loan *promptly and conveniently*? What are the charges for late payments, and are they reasonable? Will you receive a refund on credit charges if you prepay your loan? Or will you have to pay prepayment penalties? Taking the time to look around for the best credit deal will pay off, not only in reducing the cost of such debt but also in keeping the burden of credit in line with your cash budget and financial plans. In the long run, you are the one who has the most to gain (or lose). Thus *you should see to it that the consumer debt you undertake does in fact have the desired effects on your financial condition.* As suggested in the *Money in Action* box on pages 290–291, the lenders may not like the idea, but you're paying for the loan, so you might as well make the most of it!

Keeping Track of Your Credit

To stay abreast of your financial condition, it is a good idea to periodically take inventory of the consumer debt you have outstanding. You should do this a minimum of once a year, and ideally every 3 or 4 months. To take inventory of what you owe, simply prepare a list of all your outstanding consumer debt. Include *everything except your home mortgage*—installment loans, single-payment loans, credit cards, revolving credit lines, overdraft protection lines, and home equity credit lines.

Financial Road Sign

No Payments, No Interest—What a Deal!

Or is it? You've seen plenty of these offers, for everything from carpeting to cars. Buy now and don't pay a penny until a year or more in the future. Or maybe you've received an offer for a credit card with a 0 percent interest rate. Is there a catch?

Before you jump into one of these arrangements, make sure you fully understand the terms—including the fine print!

- *Do you have to make a minimum monthly payment for a specified period to avoid interest?* Even though the amount is small, if you miss a payment the seller may be able to charge interest *from your purchase date*. At the end of the payment period, the merchant may begin charging very high interest on the remaining balance—which might still be quite high.
- *Are no payments of either principal or interest required until a future date?* Be prepared to *pay the full purchase price* when this payment moratorium ends. If you can't pay in full, the merchant may be able to charge you interest starting from your purchase date.
- *When does the 0 percent interest rate period end?* Read the fine print in the terms that come with these deals. You're likely to discover that zero percent is a teaser rate that jumps after a short initial period. The real rate may be much higher, and the lender probably will not hesitate to bump up the rate if you make a late payment.

Sources: Ed Blitz, "If It Sounds too Good to Be True, It Probably Is," *San Diego Union-Tribune*, April 5, 2003, p. E3; "The Fine Print," *The Record* (Bergen County, NJ), December 16, 2002, p. L6; John Withum, Credit Card Companies Deceive, *University Wire*, January 24, 2003, downloaded from Big Chalk Library, **http://library.bigchalk.com**.

You might find Worksheet 7.1 helpful in preparing a list of your debts. To use it, simply list the current monthly payment and the latest balance due for each type of consumer credit outstanding; then, total both columns to see how much you are paying each month and how large a debt load you have built up. Hopefully, when all the numbers have been totaled up, you will not be surprised to learn just how much you really do owe.

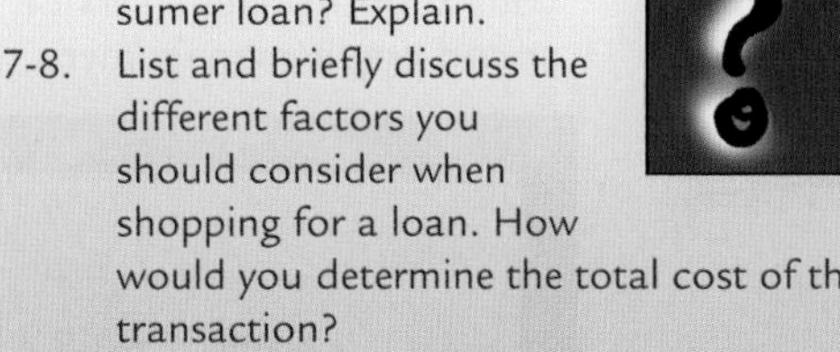

7-7. What two questions should be answered before taking out a consumer loan? Explain.

7-8. List and briefly discuss the different factors you should consider when shopping for a loan. How would you determine the total cost of the transaction?

A way to quickly assess your debt position is to compute your *debt safety ratio* (we looked at this ratio in Chapter 6) by dividing the total monthly payments (from the worksheet) by your monthly take-home pay. If 20 percent or more of your take-home pay is going to monthly credit payments, you are relying too heavily on credit; in contrast, if your debt safety ratio works out to 10 percent or less, you are in a strong credit position. *Keeping track of your credit and holding the amount of outstanding debt to a reasonable level is the surest way to maintain your creditworthiness.*

LG4

SINGLE-PAYMENT LOANS

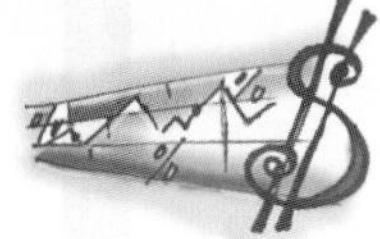

Unlike most types of consumer loans, a single-payment loan is repaid in full with a single payment on a given due date. The payment usually consists of principal and all interest charges. Sometimes, however, interim interest payments may have to be made (for example, every quarter), in which case the payment at maturity is made up of principal plus any unpaid interest. Although installment loans are far more popular, single-payment loans still have their place in the consumer loan market.

Single-payment loans can be secured or unsecured and can be taken out for just about any purpose, from buying a new car to paying for a vacation. They are perhaps most useful when the funds needed for a given purchase or transaction are temporarily unavailable but are expected to be forthcoming in the near future. By helping you cope with a temporary cash shortfall, these loans can serve as a form of interim financing until more-permanent arrangements can be made.

Single-payment loans can also be used to help establish or rebuild an individual's credit rating. Many times, a bank will agree to a single-payment loan for a higher credit risk customer if an equal amount is deposited into an account at the bank, with both the loan and deposit having the same maturity. In this manner, the bank has the principal of the loan fully secured and need only be concerned about the difference between the rate charged for the loan and the rate paid on the deposit.

IMPORTANT LOAN FEATURES

loan application
An application that provides a lender with information about the purpose of the loan, and the applicant's financial condition.

The first thing you have to do when applying for either a single-payment or installment loan is submit a **loan application**, an example of which is shown in Exhibit 7.3. Basically, the loan application provides the lending institution with information about the purpose of the loan, whether it will be secured or unsecured, and the financial condition of the borrower. The loan officer uses this document, along with other information (such as a credit report from the local credit bureau and income verification) to determine whether you should be granted the loan—here again, some type of *credit scoring* (as discussed in Chapter 6) may be used to make the decision. As part of the loan application process, you should also consider the various features of the debt, the three most important of which are loan collateral, loan maturity, and loan repayment.

worksheet 7.1

Tracking Your Consumer Debt

A worksheet like this one allows you to keep track of your outstanding credit, along with your monthly debt service requirements. Such information is a major component of sound credit management.

AN INVENTORY OF CONSUMER DEBT

Name *John & Mary Jergens* Date *June 14, 2004*

Type of Consumer Debt	Creditor	Current Monthly Payment*	Latest Balance Due
Auto loans	1. *GMAC*	$ 342.27	$ 13,796
	2.		
	3.		
Education loans	1. *U.S. Dept. of Education*	117.00	7,986
	2.		
Personal installment loans	1. *Bank One*	183.00	5,727
	2. *B of A*	92.85	2,474
Home improvement loan			
Other installment loans	1.		
	2.		
Single-payment loans	1.		
	2.		
Credit cards (retail charge cards, bank cards, T&E cards, etc.)	1. *MBNA Visa*	42.00	826.
	2. *Amex Blue*	35.00	600
	3. *Sears*	40.00	1,600
	4.		
	5.		
	6.		
	7.		
Overdraft protection line	*Hiland Schools Credit Union*	15.00	310
Personal line of credit			
Home equity credit line	*Wells Fargo*	97.00	9,700
Loan on life insurance			
Margin loan from broker			
Other loans	1. *Mom & Dad*	—	2,500
	2.		
	3.		
	Totals	$ 964.12	$ 45,519

$$\text{Debt safety ratio} = \frac{\text{Total monthly payments}}{\text{Monthly take-home pay}} \times 100 = \frac{\$\ 964.12}{\$5{,}200.00} \times 100 = 18.5\ \%$$

*Leave the space blank if there is *no* monthly payment required on a loan (e.g., as with a single-payment or education loan).

EXHIBIT 7.3

A Consumer Loan Credit Application

A typical loan application, like this one, contains information about the persons applying for the loan, including source(s) of income, current debt load, and a brief record of employment.

CONSUMER CREDIT APPLICATION

LOAN INFORMATION			COLLATERAL INFORMATION
Amount Requested $	Purpose	Application Type ❒Individual ❒Joint	❒Motor Vehicle: Year____Make________Model____________Miles______ ❒Personal Property ❒Other (Describe)

APPLICANT INFORMATION				CO-APPLICANT INFORMATION			
Name (Last, First, M.I.)		E-mail Address		Name (Last, First, M.I.)		E-mail Address	
Social Security # - -	Date of Birth / /	❒Married ❒Unmarried ❒Separated	# of Dependents	Social Security # - -	Date of Birth / /	❒Married ❒Unmarried ❒Separated	# of Dependents

APPLICANT RESIDENCE INFORMATION			CO-APPLICANT RESIDENCE INFORMATION		
Address (Number, St, and Apt. or Lot # if applicable)		Telephone #	Address (Number, St, and Apt. or Lot # if applicable)		Telephone #
City, State, Zip Code		Time At Residence Years / Months /	City, State, Zip Code		Time At Residence Years / Months /
Previous Address		Time At Residence Years / Months /	Previous Address		Time At Residence Years / Months /
❒Rent ❒Live with Parents ❒Own ❒Other________	Landlord or Mortgage Holder Name: Phone #:	Monthly Payment $	❒Rent ❒Live with Parents ❒Own ❒Other________	Landlord or Mortgage Holder Name: Phone #:	Monthly Payment $

APPLICANT EMPLOYMENT INFORMATION			CO-APPLICANT EMPLOYMENT		
Employer	Employer Telephone		Employer	Employer Telephone	
Employer Address	Position		Employer Address	Position	
Gross Income: $	❒Weekly ❒Bi-weekly ❒Monthly	Time At Job Years / Months /	Gross Income: $	❒Weekly ❒Bi-weekly ❒Monthly	Time At Job Years / Months /
Other Income: $ Source			Other Income: $ Source	Alimony, Child support, or separate maintenance income need not be revealed ifyou do not wish to have it considered as abasis for repaying this obligation.	
Previous Employer & location		Previous Emp. Phone #	Previous Employer & Location		Previous Emp. Phone #
Position		Time At Job Years / Months /	Position		Time At Job Years / Months /

APPLICANT CREDIT REFERENCES			CO-APPLICANT CREDIT REFERENCES		
Creditor	Payment	Balance	Creditor	Payment	Balance
❒Checking Bank Name________ Acct#________ ❒Savings Bank Name________ Acct#________			❒Checking Bank Name________ Acct#________ ❒Savings Bank Name________ Acct#________		

AUTHORIZATION AND SIGNATURES			
By signing this application, you promise that all information provided is true and complete. You also promise that you have revealed any pending lawsuits or unpaid judgements against you. You intend the lender and/or assignee to rely upon these promises in deciding whether to extend credit to you. You authorize a full investigation of your credit record and your employment history. You also authorize the seller and/or assignee to release information about your credit experience with them. You understand that the lender will retain this application whether or not it is approved. I understand that if the application is for a secured loan addit ional information may be required.			
Applicant Signature	Date	Co-Applicant Signature	Date

Loan Collateral

Most single-payment loans are secured by certain specified assets. For *collateral*, lenders prefer items they feel are readily marketable at a price sufficiently high to cover the principal portion of the loan—for example, an automobile, jewelry, or stocks and bonds. If a loan is obtained to purchase some personal asset, that asset may be used to secure it. In most cases, lenders do not take physical possession of the collateral but instead file a **lien**, which is a legal claim that permits them to liquidate the collateral to satisfy the loan in the event the borrower defaults. The lien is filed in the county courthouse and is a matter of public record. If the borrowers maintain possession or title to *movable* property—such as cars, TVs, and jewelry—the instrument that gives the lenders title to the property in event of default is called a **chattel mortgage**. If lenders hold title to the collateral—or actually take possession of it, as in the case of stocks and bonds—the agreement giving them the right to sell these items in case of default is a **collateral note**.

lien
A legal claim that permits the lender, in event the borrower defaults, to liquidate the items serving as collateral to satisfy the obligation.

chattel mortgage
A mortgage on personal property given as security for the payment of an obligation.

collateral note
A legal note that gives the lender the right to sell collateral in the event of the borrower's default on the obligation.

Loan Maturity

As indicated earlier, the maturity, or term, on a single-payment loan usually extends for a period of 1 year or less and very rarely goes out to 2 years or longer. When you request a single-payment loan, you should be sure the term is long enough to allow you to obtain the funds to repay the loans, but not any longer than necessary. Don't stretch the maturity out too far, since the amount of the finance charges paid normally increases with time. Because the loan is retired in a single payment, the lender must be assured that you will be able to repay it even if certain unexpected events occur in the future. The term of your single-payment loan therefore must be reconciled with your budget, as well as your ability to pay. If the money you plan to use for repayment will be received periodically over the term of the loan, an installment-type loan may be more suitable.

Loan Repayment

The repayment of a single-payment loan is expected to take place at a single point in time: on its maturity date. Occasionally the funds needed to repay this type of loan will be received prior to maturity. Depending on the lender, the borrower might be able to repay the loan early and thereby reduce the finance charges. Many credit unions actually permit early repayment of these loans with *reduced* finance charges. Commercial banks and other single-payment lenders, however, may not accept early repayments; or, if they do, they may charge a **prepayment penalty** on them. This penalty normally amounts to a set percentage of the interest that would have been paid over the remaining life of the loan. The Truth in Lending Act requires lenders to disclose in the loan agreement whether, and in what amount, prepayment penalties are charged on a single-payment loan. *A borrower should understand this information before signing a loan agreement.*

prepayment penalty
An additional charge you may owe if you decide to pay off your loan prior to maturity.

Occasionally an individual will borrow money using a single-payment loan, only to discover that he or she is short of money when the loan comes due—after all, making one big loan payment can cause a real strain on one's cash flow. Should this happen to you, don't just let the payment go past due; rather, *inform the lender in advance so a partial payment, loan extension, or some other arrangement can be made.* Under such circumstances, the lender will often agree to a **loan rollover**, in which case the original loan is paid off by taking out another loan. The lender will usually require that all the interest and at least part of the principal be paid at the time of the rollover. Thus, if you originally borrowed $5,000 for 12 months, the bank might be willing to lend you, say, $3,500 for another 6 to 9 months as part of a loan rollover. In this case, you'll have to "pay down" $1,500 of the original loan, along with all interest due. However, you can expect the interest rate on a rollover loan to go up a bit; that is the price you pay for falling short on the first loan. Also, you should not expect to get

loan rollover
The process of paying off a loan by taking out another loan.

more than one, or at the most two, loan rollovers—a bank's patience tends to grow somewhat short after a while!

Finance Charges and the Annual Percentage Rate

loan disclosure statement A document lenders are required to supply borrowers that states both the dollar amount of finance charges and the APR applicable to a loan.

As indicated in Chapter 6, the Consumer Credit Protection Act, or Truth in Lending Act, requires lenders to disclose both the dollar amount of finance charges and the annual percentage rate (APR) of interest. A sample **loan disclosure statement** applicable to either a single-payment or installment loan can be seen in Exhibit 7.4. Note that such a statement discloses not only interest costs, but also other fees and expenses that may be tacked on to the loan. Although disclosures like this one allow you to compare the various borrowing alternatives, you still need to understand the methods used to compute finance charges, because similar loans with the same *stated* interest rates may have different finance charges and APRs. The two basic procedures used to calculate the finance charges on single-payment loans are the *simple interest method* and the *discount method.*

Simple Interest Method

simple interest method A method of computing finance charges in which interest is charged on the actual loan balance outstanding.

Interest is charged only on the *actual loan balance outstanding* in the **simple interest method**. This method is commonly used on revolving credit lines by commercial banks, S&Ls, and credit unions. To see how it is applied to a single-payment loan, assume that you borrow $1,000 for two years at a 12 percent annual rate of interest. On a single-payment loan, the actual loan balance outstanding for the two years will be $1,000, because no principal payments will be made until this period ends. With simple interest, the finance charge, F_s, is obtained by multiplying the *principal* outstanding by the stated annual rate of interest and then multiplying this amount by the term of the loan:

$$F_s = \text{P} \times r \times t$$

where

F_s = *finance charge calculated using simple interest method*

P = principal amount of loan

r = stated annual rate of interest

t = term of loan, as stated in years (for example, t would equal 0.5 for a 6-month loan, 1.25 for a 15-month loan, and 2.0 for a 2-year loan)

Substituting $1,000 for *P*, .12 for *r*, and 2 for *t* in the equation, we see that the finance charge, F_s, on this loan equals some $240 ($1,000 × .12 per year × 2 years). Because the size of the loan payment with this type of credit arrangement is found by adding the finance charges to the principal amount of the loan, you would have to make a loan payment of $1,000 + $240 = $1,240 at maturity to retire this debt.

To calculate the true, or annual, percentage rate (APR) of interest on this loan, the average annual finance charge is divided by the average loan balance outstanding, as follows:

$$\text{APR} = \frac{\text{Average annual finance charge}}{\text{Average loan balance outstanding}}$$

The figure for the average annual finance charge is found by dividing the total finance charge by the life of the loan (in years). In our example, the result is $120 ($240/2). Because the loan

Financial Road Sign

What Do Lenders Look For?

What do lenders look for when reviewing loan applications and credit reports? Here are their top questions:

1. Do you pay your bills on time?
2. How much of your income is already committed to debt repayment?
3. How much available credit do you already have, even if it's not currently being used?
4. How stable and responsible are you? How long have you been with your employer and lived at the same address?
5. Are there many recent inquiries on your credit report? (Lenders see this as a sign that you may be applying for lots of credit.)

Source: Bankrate, Inc., N. Palm Beach FL, 2003, **http://www.bankrate.com**.

EXHIBIT 7.4

A Loan Disclosure Statement

The loan disclosure statement informs the borrower of all charges (finance and otherwise) associated with the loan and the annual percentage rate (APR). In addition, it specifies the payment terms as well as the existence of any balloon payments.

TRUTH IN LENDING DISCLOSURE STATEMENT

Creditor	Applicant(s)
Mailing Address	Property Address
Loan Number	Preparation Date

ANNUAL PERCENTAGE RATE	FINANCE CHARGE	Amount Financed	Total of Payments
The cost of your credit as a yearly rate.	The dollar amount the credit will cost you.	The amount of credit provided to you or on your behalf.	The amount you will have paid after you have made all payments as scheduled.
E %	E$	E$	E$

PAYMENT SCHEDULE:

NUMBER OF PAYMENTS	* AMOUNT OF PAYMENTS	MONTHLY PAYMENTS ARE DUE BEGINNING	NUMBER OF PAYMENTS	* AMOUNT OF PAYMENTS	MONTHLY PAYMENTS ARE DUE BEGINNING

* Includes mortgage insurance premiums, excludes taxes, hazard insurance or flood insurance.

DEMAND FEATURE: ☐ This loan does not have a Demand Feature ☐ This loan has a Demand Feature.

ITEMIZATION: You have a right at this time to an ITEMIZATION OF AMOUNT FINANCED.
I/We ☐ do ☐ do not want an itemization.

REQUIRED DEPOSIT:
☐ The annual percentage rate does not take into account your required deposit.

VARIABLE RATE FEATURE:
☐ This Loan has a Variable Rate Feature. Variable Rate Disclosures have been provided to you earlier.

SECURITY: You are giving a security interest in:

ASSUMPTION: Someone buying this property
☐ cannot assume the remaining balance due under original mortgage terms.
☐ may assume, subject to lender's conditions, the remaining balance due under original mortgage terms.

FILING / RECORDING FEES: $

PROPERTY INSURANCE:
☐ Property / hazard insurance is a required condition of this loan. Borrower may purchase this insurance from any insurance company acceptable to the lender.
Hazard insurance ☐ is ☐ is not available through the lender at an estimated cost of for a month term.

LATE CHARGES: If your payment is more than days late, you will be charged a late charge of % of the overdue payment.

PREPAYMENT: If you prepay this loan in full or in part, you
☐ may ☐ will not have to pay a penalty.
☐ may ☐ will not be entitled to a refund of part of the finance charge.

See your contract documents for any additional information regarding non-payment, default, required repayment in full before scheduled date, and payment refunds and penalties.
E means estimate.

I/We hereby acknowledge reading and receiving a complete copy of this disclosure. I/We understand there is no commitment for the creditor to make this loan and there is no obligation for me/us to accept this loan upon delivery or signing of this disclosure.

Date Date

Date Date

GENESIS 2000, INC. * V9.3/W11.0 * (818) 223-3260 Form RegZD (03/95)

Source: Ellie Mae, **http://www.prioritytitle.com/forms/truth%20in%20lending%20disclosure%20statement.pdf**, accessed 1/12/04.

balance outstanding remains at $1,000 over the life of the loan, the average loan balance outstanding is $1,000. Dividing the $120 average annual finance charge by the $1,000 average loan balance outstanding, we obtain an APR of 12 percent. Thus, the APR and the stated rate of interest are equivalent: They both equal 12 percent. *This is always the case when the simple interest method is used to calculate finance charges, regardless of whether loans are single-payment or installment.*

Concept ✓

7-9. What is a *lien*, and under what circumstances is it part of a consumer loan?

7-10. Briefly describe and differentiate between (a) a *chattel mortgage* and (b) a *collateral note*.

7-11. When might you request a *loan rollover?*

7-12. Describe the two methods used to calculate the finance charges on a single-payment loan. As a borrower, which method would you prefer? Explain.

Discount Method

discount method A method of calculating finance charges in which interest is computed, then subtracted from the principal, and the remainder is disbursed to the borrower.

The **discount method** calculates total finance charges on the full principal amount of the loan, which is then subtracted from the amount of the loan. The difference between the amount of the loan and the finance charge is then disbursed (paid) to the borrower—in other words, finance charges are paid in advance and represent a discount from the principal portion of the loan. The finance charge on a single-payment loan using the discount method, F_d, is calculated in exactly the same way as for a simple interest loan:

$$F_d = F_s = P \times r \times t$$

Using the above method, the finance charge, F_d, on the $1,000, 12 percent, 2-year, single-payment loan is, of course, the same $240 we calculated earlier. However, in sharp contrast to simple interest loans, the loan payment with a discount loan is the original principal amount of the loan, *P*, because the finance charges on the loan are deducted up front from the loan proceeds. Thus, for the $1,000 loan above, the borrower will receive $760—which is found by subtracting the interest charges from the loan principal ($1,000 less $240)—and in 2 years will be required to pay back $1,000.

To find the APR on this discount loan, substitute the appropriate values into the APR equation cited above. For this 2-year loan, the average annual finance charge is $120 ($240/2). However, as explained above, since this is a discount loan, the borrower will receive only $760. And because this is a single-payment loan, the average amount of money outstanding is also $760. When these figures are used in the APR equation, we find the true rate for this 12 percent discount loan is more like 15.8 percent ($120/$760). Clearly, the discount method yields a much higher APR on single-payment loans than does the simple interest method. Exhibit 7.5 contrasts the results from both methods for the single-payment loan example discussed here.

EXHIBIT 7.5

Finance Charges and APRs for a Single-Payment Loan ($1,000 Loan for Two Years at 12 Percent Interest)

Sometimes what you see is not what you get—such as when you borrow money through a discount loan and end up paying quite a bit more than the quoted rate.

Method	Stated Rate on Loan	Finance Charges	APR
Simple interest	12%	$240	12.0%
Discount	12	240	15.8

INSTALLMENT LOANS

LG5, LG6

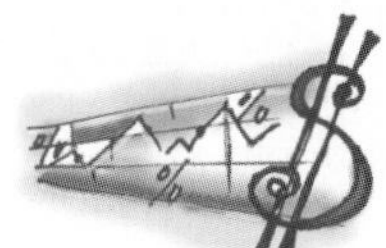

Installment loans (known as ILs for short) differ from single-payment loans in that they require the borrower to repay the debt in a series of installment payments (usually on a monthly basis) over the life of the loan. Installment loans have long been one of the most popular forms of consumer credit—right up there with credit cards! Much of this popularity is, of course, due to the convenient way in which the loan repayment is set up; not surprisingly, most people find it easier on their checkbooks to make a series of small payments rather than one big one.

A Real Consumer Credit Workhorse!

As a financing vehicle, there are few things installment loans can't do—which explains, in large part, why this form of consumer credit is so widely used. ILs, in fact, account for roughly two-thirds of all consumer debt outstanding (excluding home mortgages). Installment loans can be used to finance just about any type of big-ticket item imaginable. New car loans are, of course, the dominant type of IL, but this form of credit is also used to finance home furnishings, appliances and entertainment centers, camper trailers and other recreational vehicles, even expensive vacations; and, of course, more and more college students are turning to this type of credit as the way to finance their education.

Not only can they be used to finance all sorts of things, installment loans can also be obtained at many locations. You'll find them at banks and other financial institutions, as well as major department stores and merchants that sell relatively expensive products. Go into a home appliance store to buy a high-priced stereo and chances are you'll be able to arrange for IL financing right there on the spot. These loans can be taken out for just a few hundred dollars, or they can involve thousands of dollars—indeed, ILs of $25,000 or more are not uncommon. What's more, they can be set up with maturities as short as 6 months to as long as 7 to 10 years, even 15 years!

Most installment loans are secured with some kind of collateral—for example, the car or home entertainment center you purchased with the help of an IL will usually end up serving as collateral on the loan. Even personal loans used to finance things like expensive vacations can be secured—in this case, the collateral could be securities, CDs, or some other type of financial asset. One rapidly growing segment of this market is, in fact, ILs secured by second mortgages. These so-called *home equity loans* are similar to the home equity credit lines discussed in Chapter 6, except they involve a set amount of money loaned over a set period of time (often as long as 15 years), rather than a revolving credit line from which you can borrow, repay, and reborrow. Thus, if a borrower needs, say, $25,000 to help pay for an expensive new boat, he would simply take out a loan in that amount and secure it with a second mortgage on his home. For all practical purposes, this loan would be like any other IL in the sense that it's for a set amount of money and is to be repaid over a set period of time in monthly installments. In addition to their highly competitive interest rates, a big attraction of *home equity loans* is that the interest paid on them usually can be used as a tax deduction. So, borrowers get the double benefit of *low interest rates and tax deductibility*! As with home equity credit lines, however, failure to repay could result in the loss of your home.

smart.sites

Find out about federal protection laws for borrowers and get tips on financing consumer loans at the Federal Trade Commission site, **http://www.ftc.gov**.

Finance Charges, Monthly Payments, and APR

Earlier we discussed the simple interest and discount methods of determining finance charges on single-payment loans. In this section, we look at the use of simple and add-on interest to compute finance charges and monthly payments for installment loans (technically, discount interest can also be used with ILs, but because this is rare, we ignore it here). For purposes of illustration, we will use a 12 percent, $1,000 installment loan that is to be paid off in 12 monthly payments. As in the earlier illustration for single-payment loans, we assume interest is the only component of the finance charge; there are no other fees and charges.

Using Simple Interest

When simple interest is used with ILs—and most major banks and S&Ls use it on their installment loans—interest is charged only on the outstanding balance of the loan. Thus, as the loan principal declines with monthly payments, the amount of interest being charged decreases as well. Because finance charges change each month, the procedure used to find the interest expense is mathematically very complex. Fortunately, this is not much of a problem in practice due to the widespread use of desktop computers/computer terminals, hand-held financial calculators (which we'll illustrate below), and preprinted finance tables—an example of which is provided in Exhibit 7.6. Essentially, the tables provide the *monthly payment* that would be required to retire an installment loan that carries a given simple rate of interest and has a given term to maturity. Because these tables (which are sometimes referred to as *amortization schedules*) have interest charges built right into them, the monthly payments shown cover both principal and interest.

Note that the loan payments shown in Exhibit 7.6 cover a variety of interest rates (from 7½ to 18 percent) and loan maturities (from 6 to 60 months). The values in the table represent the monthly payments required to retire a $1,000 loan. Although it's assumed you're borrowing $1,000, the table can be used with any size loan. For example, if you're looking at a $5,000 loan, just multiply the monthly loan payment from the table by 5—that is, $5,000/$1,000 = 5; or, if you have, say, a $500 loan, multiply the loan payment by .5 ($500/$1,000 = .5). In many respects, this table is just like the mortgage loan payment schedule introduced in Chapter 5, except we use much shorter loan maturities here than with mortgages.

Here's how to use the table in Exhibit 7.6. Suppose we want to find the monthly payment required on our $1,000, 12 percent, 12-month loan. Looking under the 12-month column and across from the 12 percent rate of interest, we find a value of $88.85; that is the monthly payment it will take to pay off the $1,000 loan in 12 months. When the monthly payments ($88.85) are multiplied by the term of the loan in months (12), the result will be total payments of $88.85 × 12 = $1,066.20. The difference between the total payments on the loan and the principal portion represents the *finance charges on the loan*—in this case, $1,066.20 − $1,000 = interest charges of $66.20.

Calculator Keystrokes. Instead of using a table like the one in Exhibit 7.6, you could just as easily have used a handheld financial calculator to *find the monthly payments on an IL.* Here's what you'd do: First, set the payments per year (P/Y) key to 12 to put the calculator in a monthly payment mode. Now, to find the monthly payment needed to pay off a 12 percent, 12-month, $1,000 installment loan, use the keystrokes shown here, where:

N = length of the loan, *in months*,

I/Y = the *annual* rate of interest being charged on the loan,

P/V = the amount of the loan, entered as a *negative*.

As seen, to pay off this IL, you'll have to make payments of $88.85 per month for the next 12 months.

EXHIBIT 7.6

A Table of Monthly Installment Loan Payments (to Repay a $1,000/ Simple Interest Loan)

A table like this one can be used to find the monthly payments on a wide variety of simple interest installment loans. Although it's set up to reflect payments on a $1,000 loan, with a little modification it can easily be used with any size loan (the principal can be more or less than $1,000).

	Loan Maturity						
Rate of Interest	6 Months	12 Months	18 Months	24 Months	36 Months	48 Months	60 Months
7.5%	$170.33	$86.76	$58.92	$45.00	$31.11	$24.18	$20.05
8.0	170.58	86.99	59.15	45.23	31.34	24.42	20.28
8.5	170.82	87.22	59.37	45.46	31.57	24.65	20.52
9.0	171.07	87.46	59.60	45.69	31.80	24.89	20.76
9.5	171.32	87.69	59.83	45.92	32.04	25.13	21.01
10.0	171.56	87.92	60.06	46.15	32.27	25.37	21.25
10.5	171.81	88.15	60.29	46.38	32.51	25.61	21.50
11.0	172.05	88.50	60.64	46.73	32.86	25.97	21.87
11.5	173.30	88.62	60.76	46.85	32.98	26.09	22.00
12.0	172.50	88.85	60.99	47.08	33.22	26.34	22.25
12.5	172.80	89.09	61.22	47.31	33.46	26.58	22.50
13.0	173.04	89.32	61.45	47.55	33.70	26.83	22.76
14.0	173.54	89.79	61.92	48.02	34.18	27.33	23.27
15.0	174.03	90.26	62.39	48.49	34.67	27.84	23.79
16.0	174.53	90.74	62.86	48.97	35.16	28.35	24.32
17.0	175.03	91.21	63.34	49.45	35.66	28.86	24.86
18.0	175.53	91.68	63.81	49.93	36.16	29.38	25.40

From each monthly payment (of $88.85), a certain portion goes to interest and the balance is used to reduce the principal. Because the principal balance declines with each payment, the amount that goes to interest also *decreases* whereas the amount that goes to principal *increases.* Exhibit 7.7 illustrates this cash flow stream. Note that because *monthly* payments are used with the loan, the interest column in Exhibit 7.7 is also based on a *monthly* rate of interest—that is, the annual rate is divided by 12 to obtain a monthly rate (12 percent per year/12 = 1 percent per month). This monthly rate is then applied to the outstanding loan balance to find the monthly interest charges in column 3. Because interest is charged only on the outstanding balance, *the annual percentage rate (APR) on a simple interest IL will always equal the stated rate*—in this case, 12 percent.

smart.sites

LendingTree.com (**http://www.lendingtree.com**) lets you compare loan rates and fees from up to four lenders instantly.

Add-on Method

A number of installment loans, particularly those obtained directly from retail merchants or made at finance companies and the like, are made using the **add-on method**. Add-on

add-on method A method of calculating interest by computing finance charges on the original loan balance and then adding the interest to that balance.

EXHIBIT 7.7

Monthly Payment Analysis for a Simple Interest Installment Loan (Assumes a $1,000, 12 Percent, 12-Month Loan)

Part of each monthly payment on an installment loan goes to interest and part to principal. As the loan is paid down over time, less and less of each payment goes to interest, and more and more goes to principal.

Month	Outstanding Loan Balance (1)	Monthly Payment (2)	Interest Charges [(1) × 0.01] (3)	Principal [(2) − (3)] (4)
1	$1,000.00	$88.85	$10.00	$78.85
2	921.15	88.85	9.21	79.64
3	841.51	88.85	8.42	80.43
4	761.08	88.85	7.61	81.24
5	679.84	88.85	6.80	82.05
6	597.79	88.85	5.98	82.87
7	514.92	88.85	5.15	83.70
8	431.22	88.85	4.31	84.54
9	346.68	88.85	3.47	85.38
10	261.30	88.85	2.61	86.24
11	175.06	88.85	1.75	87.10
12	87.96	88.85	0.89	87.96
Total		$1,066.20	$66.20	$1,000.00

Note: Column 1 values for months 2 through 12 are obtained by subtracting the principal payment shown in column 4 for the preceding month from the outstanding loan balance shown in column 1 for the preceding month; thus, $1,000 − $78.85 = $921.15, which is the outstanding loan balance in month 2.

loans are very expensive; indeed, they generally rank as one of the most costly forms of consumer credit, with APRs that are often well above rates charged even on many credit cards. With add-on interest, the finance charges are calculated using the *original* balance of the loan; this amount (the total finance charges) is then added-on to the original loan balance to determine the total amount to be repaid. Thus, the amount of finance charges on an add-on loan can be found by using the familiar simple interest formula:

$$F = P \times r \times t$$

Given the $1,000 loan we have been using for illustrative purposes, the finance charges on a 12 percent, 1-year add-on loan would be

$$F = \$1{,}000 \times .12 \times 1 = \$120.$$

Compared with the finance charges for the same loan on a simple interest basis ($66.20), the add-on loan is a lot more expensive, a fact that will also show up in monthly payments and APR. Keep in mind that both of these loans would be quoted as "12 percent" loans; thus, you may think you are getting a 12 percent loan, but looks can be deceiving—especially when you are dealing with add-on interest! So, when taking out an installment loan, make sure you find out whether simple or add-on interest

EXHIBIT 7.8

Comparative Finance Charges and APRs (Assumes a $1,000, 12 Percent, 12-Month Installment Loan)

In sharp contrast to simple interest loans, the APR with add-on installment loans is much higher than the stated rate.

	Simple Interest	Add-on Interest
Stated rate on loan	12%	12%
Finance charges	$ 66.20	$120.00
Monthly payments	$ 88.25	$93.33
Total payments made	$1,066.20	$1,120.00
APR	12%	21.4%

is being used to compute finance charges. And if it's add-on you might want to consider looking elsewhere for the loan.

To find the monthly payments on an add-on loan, all you need to do is add the finance charge ($120) to the *original* principal amount of the loan ($1,000) and then divide this sum by the number of monthly payments to be made. In the case of our $1,000, one-year loan, this results in monthly payments of $93.33, found as follows:

$$\text{Monthly payments} = \frac{\$1{,}000 + \$120}{12} = \frac{\$1{,}120}{12} = \$93.33$$

As expected, these monthly payments are much higher than the ones with the simple interest loan ($88.85).

Because the actual rate of interest with an add-on loan is considerably higher than the stated rate, we must determine the loan's APR. That can easily be done with a financial calculator, as shown below. When all is said and done, we find that the APR on this 12 percent add-on-loan ends up to be more like 21.4 percent. Clearly, when viewed from an APR perspective, this add-on loan turns out to be a very expensive form of financing! (A rough but reasonably accurate rule of thumb is that the APR on an add-on loan is about *twice* the stated rate—thus, if the loan is quoted at an add-on rate of 9 percent, you're probably going to end up paying a true rate that's closer to 18 percent.) This is because when add-on interest is applied to an installment loan, the interest included in each payment is charged on the initial principal even though the outstanding loan balance is reduced as installment payments are made. A summary of comparative finance charges and APRs for the simple interest and add-on interest methods is presented in Exhibit 7.8, above.

Calculator Keystrokes. Here's how you *find the APR on an IL* using a financial calculator. First, make sure the payments per year (P/Y) key is set to 12, so the calculator is in the monthly payment mode. Then, to find the APR on a $1,000, 12-month, 12 percent add-on IL, use the following keystrokes, where:

N = length of the loan, *in months*,

PV = size of the loan, entered as a *negative*,

PMT = size of the *monthly* IL payments.

Thus, the APR on the 12 percent add-on loan is a whopping 21.45 percent!

Under the Truth in Lending Act, the exact APR (accurate to the nearest 0.25 percent) must be disclosed to borrowers. Note that not only interest but also any other fees required to obtain a loan are considered part of the finance charges and should be included in the computation of APR.

Prepayment Penalties

Another type of finance charge that's often found in installment loan contracts is the *prepayment penalty,* an additional charge you may owe if you decide to pay off your loan prior to maturity. When you pay off a loan early, you may find that you owe quite a bit more than you expected, especially if the lender uses the **Rule of 78s**, (or **sum-of-the-digits method**) to calculate the amount of interest paid and the principal balance to date. You might think that paying off a $1,000, 12 percent, 1-year loan at the end of 6 months would mean that you have paid about half of the principal and owe somewhere around $500 to the lender. Well, that's just not so with a loan that uses the rule of 78s! This method charges more interest in the early months of the loan, on the theory that the borrower has use of more money in the early stages of the IL and should pay more finance charges in the early months of the loan and progressively less later. There's nothing wrong with that, of course, as that's the way all loans operate. But what is wrong is the fact that the Rule of 78s front-loads an inordinate amount of interest charges to the early months of the loan, thereby producing a much higher principle balance than you would normally expect (remember: the more of the loan payment that goes to interest, the less that goes to repayment of principle).

Rule of 78s (sum-of-the-digits method) A method of calculating interest that has extra-heavy interest charges in the early months of the loan.

To see how this works, let's assume that we want to pay off the $1,000, 12 percent, 1-year add-on loan after 6 months. Using the Rule of 78s, of your $559.98 in total payments (that is, six payments at $93.33 each = 6 × $93.33 = $559.98), just $389.73 went to principal—all the rest went to interest. As a result, even though you have made payments for half of the life of the loan, you still owe more than 60 percent of the principal—the same loan under simple interest would have paid off $485 in principal after 6 months. So, before signing the loan agreement, be sure to ask how the interest will be calculated, just in case you decide to prepay the loan.

Credit Life Insurance

Sometimes, as a condition of receiving an installment loan, a borrower is required to buy **credit life insurance** and possibly **credit disability insurance**. Credit life (and disability) insurance is tied to a particular IL and basically provides insurance that the loan will be paid off if the borrower dies (or becomes disabled) before the loan matures. In essence, these policies insure the borrower for an amount sufficient to repay the outstanding loan balance. The seller's (or lender's) ability to dictate the terms of these insurance requirements is either banned or restricted by law in many states. If this type of insurance is required as a condition of the loan, its cost must be added in the finance charges and included as part of the APR. From the borrower's perspective, credit life and disability insurance is NOT a very good deal: *It's very costly and really does little more than provide lenders with a very lucrative source of income.* Not surprisingly, because it is so lucrative, some lenders aggressively push it on unsuspecting borrowers and, in some cases, even require it as a condition for granting a loan. The best advice is to avoid it if at all possible!

credit life (or disability) insurance A type of life (or disability) insurance in which the coverage decreases at the same rate as the loan balance.

smart.sites

Having trouble managing your debt? Find credit counselors and attorneys who can help at GotTrouble.com, **http://www.gottrouble.com**.

Buy on Time or Pay Cash?

Often when you buy a big-ticket item, you have little choice but to take out a loan to finance the purchase—the acquisition (perhaps it's a new car) is just so expensive that you cannot afford to pay cash. And even if you do have the money, you may still be better off using something like an IL *if the cash purchase would end up severely depleting your liquid reserves.* But don't just automatically take out a loan. Rather, take the time to find out if, in fact, that's the best thing to do. Such a decision can easily be made by using Worksheet 7.2. This worksheet considers the cost of the loan relative to the after-tax earnings generated from having your money in some type of short-term investment vehicle. A basic assumption here is that the consumer has an adequate level of liquid reserves, and that these reserves are being held in some type of savings account. (Obviously, if this is not the case, there's little reason to go through the exercise, because you have no choice but to borrow the money.) Essentially, it boils down to this: *If it costs more to borrow the money than you can earn in interest, then draw the money from your savings to pay cash for the purchase; if not, consider taking out a loan.*

To see how this works, consider the following situation: You're thinking about buying a second car (a nice, low-mileage used vehicle) and after the normal down payment, you still need to come up with $12,000. This balance can be taken care of in one of two ways: (1) You can take out a 36-month, 10 percent IL (such an IL would have a monthly payment of $387.24), or (2) you can pay cash for the car by drawing the money from a money fund (the fund currently pays 5 percent interest, and that's expected to hold for the foreseeable future). We can now run the numbers to decide whether to buy on time or pay cash—the complete details of which are provided in Worksheet 7.2. In this case, we assume the loan is a standard IL, where the interest does not qualify as a tax deduction, and that you're in the 28 percent tax bracket. Note in the worksheet that by borrowing the money, you'll end up paying nearly $1,941 in interest (line 4), none of which is tax deductible. In contrast, by leaving your money on deposit in the money fund, you'll receive only $1,296 in interest, after taxes (see line 11). Taken together, we see the net cost of borrowing (line 12) is nearly $650—in essence, you'll be paying over $1,900 to earn less than $1,300, which certainly doesn't make much sense! Clearly, it's far more cost-effective in this case to take the money from savings in order to pay cash for the car, for by doing so you will save nearly $650.

Although such a figure provides a pretty convincing reason for avoiding a loan, occasions might arise where the actual dollar spread between the cost of borrowing and interest earned is very small, perhaps only $100 or less. Being able to deduct the interest on a loan can lead to a relatively small spread, but it can also occur, for example, if the amount being financed is relatively small—say, you want $1,500 or $2,000 for a ski trip to Colorado. Under these circumstances, and so long as the spread stays sufficiently small, you may decide it's still worthwhile to borrow the money in order to maintain a higher level of liquidity. Although this course of action is perfectly legitimate when very small spreads exist, it makes less sense as the gap starts to widen.

Concept ✓

7-13. Briefly describe the basic features of an installment loan. What is a home equity loan and how are these loans similar to other installment loans? What are the major advantages and disadvantages of home equity loans?

7-14. Explain why a borrower is often required to purchase *credit life and disability insurance* as a condition for receiving an installment loan. Is this a good deal for the borrower?

7-15. Define simple interest as it relates to an installment loan.

7-16. Under what conditions does it make more sense to pay cash for a big-ticket item than to borrow the money to finance the purchase? Are there ever times when borrowing the money is the best course of action?

worksheet 7.2

To Borrow or Not to Borrow

Using a worksheet like the one shown here, you can decide whether to buy on time or pay cash by comparing the (after-tax) cost of interest paid on a loan with the after-tax interest income lost by taking the money out of savings and using it to pay cash for the purchase.

BUY ON TIME OR PAY CASH

Name John E. Jones Date February 28, 2004

Cost of Borrowing		
1. Terms of the loan		
a. Amount of the loan	$12,000.00	
b. Length of the loan (in years)	3 yrs.	
c. Monthly payment	$ 387.24	
2. Total loan payments made (monthly loan payment × length of loan in months) $ 387.24 per month × 36 months		$ 13,940.64
3. Less: Principal amount of the loan		$ 12,000
4. Total interest paid over life of loan (line 2 − 3)		$ 1,940.64
5. Tax considerations:		
• Is this a home equity loan (where interest expenses can be deducted from taxes)?	☐ yes ☒ no	
• Do you itemize deductions on your federal tax returns?.	☒ yes ☐ no	
• If you answered yes to BOTH questions, then proceed to line 6; if you answered no to *either one* or *both* of the questions, then proceed to *line 8* and use *line 4* as the after-tax interest cost of the loan.		
6. What federal tax bracket are you in? (use either 10, 15, 25, 28, 33, or 35%)	___%	
7. Taxes saved due to interest deductions (line 4 × tax rate, from line 6: $ ______ × ______%)		$ —
8. Total after-tax interest cost on the loan (line 4 − line 7)		$ 1,940.64
Cost of Paying Cash		
9. Annual interest earned on savings (annual rate of interest earned on savings × amount of loan: 5 % × 12,000.00)		$ 600.00
10. Annual after-tax interest earnings (line 9 × [1 − tax rate] − e.g., 1 − 28% = 72%: $ 600.00 × 72%)		$ 432.00
11. Total after-tax interest earnings over life of loan (line 10 × line 1b: $ 432.00 × 3 years)		$ 1,296.00
Net Cost of Borrowing		
12. Difference in cost of borrowing vs. cost of paying cash (line 8 minus line 11)		$ 644.64

BASIC DECISION RULE: *Pay cash* if line 12 is positive; *borrow the money* if line 12 is negative.

Note: For simplicity, compounding is ignored in calculating *both* the cost of interest and interest earnings.

Summary

LG1. Know when to use consumer loans, and be able to differentiate between the major types. Single-payment and installment loans are formally negotiated consumer loan arrangements used mainly to finance big-ticket items. Most of these consumer loans are taken out as auto loans, loans for other durable goods, education loans, personal loans, and consolidation loans.

LG2. Identify the various sources of consumer loans. Consumer loans can be obtained from a number of sources, including commercial banks (the biggest providers of such credit), consumer finance companies, credit unions, S&Ls, sales finance (and captive finance) companies, life insurance companies (and other financial services organizations), and, finally, as a last resort, your friends and relatives.

LG3. Choose the best loans by comparing finance charges, maturity, collateral, and other loan terms. Before taking out a consumer loan, you should be sure the purchase is compatible with your financial plans and that you can service the debt without straining your budget. When shopping for credit, it's in your best interest to compare such loan features as finance charges (APRs), loan maturities, monthly payments, and collateral requirements and choose the loan with terms that are fully compatible with your financial plans and cash budget.

LG4. Describe the features of, and calculate the finance charges on, single-payment loans. In a single-payment loan, the borrower is obligated to make just one principal payment (at the maturity of the loan), though he or she may be required to make one or more interim interest payments. Such loans are usually made for a period of 1 year or less, and are normally secured by some type of collateral. A major advantage of the single-payment loan is that it doesn't require monthly payments and therefore won't tie up the borrower's cash flow. Finance charges can be calculated using either the simple interest method, which applies the interest rate to the outstanding loan balance, or the discount method, where the interest is calculated the same way as simple interest, but then deducted from the loan principal, resulting in a higher APR.

LG5. Evaluate the benefits of an installment loan. In an installment loan, the borrower agrees to repay the loan through a series of equal installment payments (usually monthly) until the obligation is fully repaid; in this way, the borrower can come up with a loan-repayment schedule that fits neatly into his or her financial plans and cash budget. This highly popular form of consumer credit can be used to finance just about any type of big-ticket asset or expenditure, and many of them are taken out as home equity loans to capture tax advantages.

LG6. Determine the costs of installment loans, and analyze whether it is better to pay cash or take out a loan. Most single-payment loans are made with either simple or discount interest, whereas most ILs are made with either simple or add-on interest. So long as simple interest is used, the actual finance charge will always correspond to the stated rate of interest; in contrast, when add-on or discount rates are used, the APR will always be more than the stated rate. In the final analysis, whether it makes sense to borrow rather than pay cash comes down to a matter of which is the least costly alternative.

Financial Planning Exercises

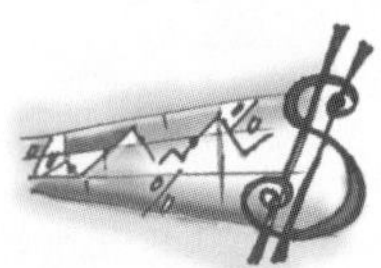

1. Assume that you have been shopping for a new car and intend to finance it, in part, through an installment loan. The car you are looking for has a sticker price

of $15,000. Big A Autos has offered to sell it to you for $2,500 down and finance the balance with a loan that will require 48 monthly payments of $329.17; Cars-Are-Us will sell you exactly the same vehicle for $3,000 down plus a 60-month loan for the balance, with monthly payments of $260.91. Which is the better deal? Explain.

2. ***Use Worksheet 7.1.*** Every 6 months, Neal Simone takes an inventory of the consumer debts he has outstanding. The latest tally showed the following list: he still owed $4,000 on a home improvement loan (monthly payments of $125); he was making $85 monthly payments on a personal loan that had a remaining balance of $750; he had a $2,000, secured single-payment loan that is due late next year; he had a $70,000 home mortgage on which he was making $750 monthly payments; he still owed $8,600 on a new-car loan (monthly payments of $375); he had a $960 balance on his Visa card (minimum payment of $40), a $70 balance on his Shell credit card (balance due in 30 days), and a $1,200 balance on a personal line of credit ($60 monthly payments). Use Worksheet 7.1 to prepare an inventory of Neal's consumer debt. Find his debt-safety ratio given that he has take-home pay of $2,500 per month; would you consider this ratio to be good or bad? Explain.
3. James Washington is thinking about buying a new car; he's negotiated a purchase price of $25,000 for a car that's loaded with all the options he wants, and plans to finance the entire amount. A local car dealer is offering a choice of a $3,000 rebate, or 3.9 percent financing on all vehicles in stock. The typical interest rate for a new car loan at the local bank is 9 percent. Based on comparative costs, should James finance the car at the low rate from the dealer, or take the rebate and obtain a loan for the balance from his bank? (*Note:* Use the simple interest method and assume all rates are stated as annual interest rates.)
4. Robert Martino plans to borrow $8,000 for five years. The loan will be *repaid with a single payment after five years*, and the interest on the loan will be computed using the simple interest method at an annual rate of 8 percent. How much will Robert have to pay in five years? How much will he have to pay at maturity if he's required to make *annual interest payments* at the end of each year?

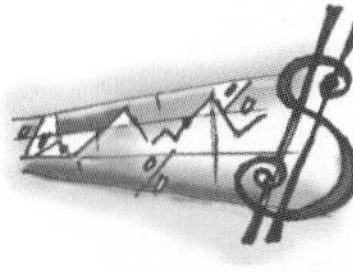

5. Using the simple interest method, find the monthly payments on a $3,000 installment loan, given the funds are borrowed for 24 months at an annual interest rate of 14 percent. How much interest will be paid during the first year of this loan? (Use a monthly payment analysis similar to the one in Exhibit 7.7.)

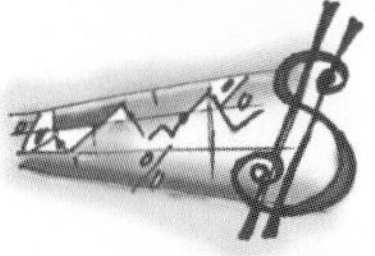

6. Find the finance charges on a 7½ percent, 18-month single-payment loan when interest is computed using the simple interest method. Find the finance charges on the same loan when interest is computed using the discount method. Determine the APR in each case.

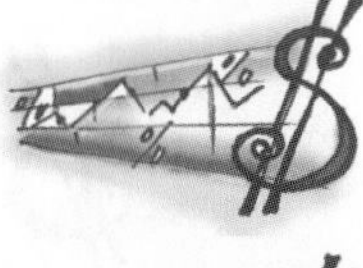

7. Sally Gibbs has to borrow $4,000. First State Bank will lend her the money for 12 months through a single-payment loan at 13.5 percent discount; Home Savings and Loan will make her a $4,000 single-payment, 12-month loan at 15 percent simple. Where should Sally borrow the money? Explain.

8. Assuming that interest is the only finance charge, how much interest would be paid on a $5,000 installment loan to be repaid in 36 monthly installments of $166.10? What is the APR on this loan?
9. After careful comparison shopping, Chris Jenkins decided to buy a new Nissan Maxima. With some options added, the car had a price of $29,500—including plates and taxes. Because he could not afford to pay cash for the car, he used some

savings and his old car as a trade-in to put $9,500 down and financed the rest with a $20,000, 60-month loan at a simple interest rate of 9½ percent.

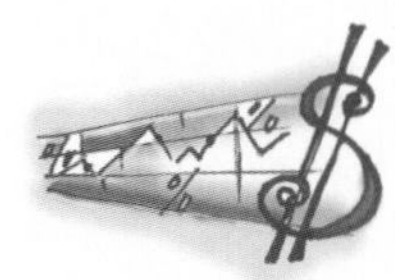

a. What will his monthly payments be?

b. How much total interest will Chris pay in the first year of the loan? (Use a monthly payment analysis procedure similar to the one in Exhibit 7.7.)

c. How much interest will Chris pay over the full (60-month) life of the loan?

d. What is the APR on this loan?

10. Justin Walton wants to buy a new high-end audio system for his car. The system is being sold by two dealers in town, both of whom sell the equipment for the same price: $2,000. Justin can buy the equipment from Dealer A, with no money down, by making payments of $119.20 a month for 18 months; in contrast, he can buy the same equipment from Dealer B by making 36 monthly payments of $69.34 (again, with no money down). Justin is considering purchasing the system from Dealer B due to the lower payment. Find the APR for each alternative. What do you recommend?

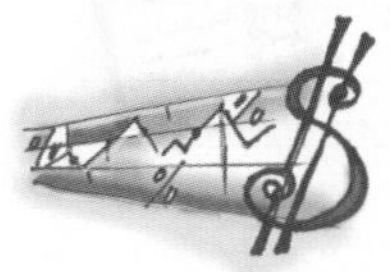

11. Joan Clark plans to borrow $5,000 and repay it in 36 monthly installments. This loan is being made at an annual add-on interest rate of 11½ percent.

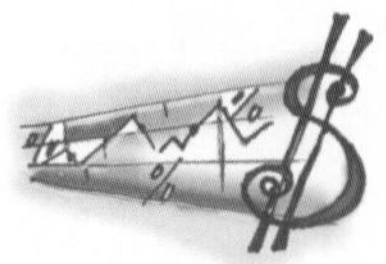

a. Calculate the finance charge on this loan, assuming that the only component of the finance charge is interest.

b. Use your finding in part **a** to calculate the monthly payment on the loan.

c. Using a financial calculator, determine the APR on this loan.

12. ***Use Worksheet 7.2 to help Grace make this credit decision:***

a. Consider the following situation: Grace Hesketh wants to buy a home entertainment center. Complete with a big-screen TV, VCR, and sound system, the unit would cost $4,500. Grace has over $15,000 in a money fund, so she can easily afford to pay cash for the whole thing (the fund is currently paying 5.5 percent interest, and Grace expects that yield to hold for the foreseeable future). To stimulate sales, the dealer is offering to finance the full cost of the unit with a 36-month installment loan at 9 percent, simple. Grace wants to know: Should she pay cash for this home entertainment center or buy it on time? (*Note:* assume Grace is in the 28 percent tax bracket and that she itemizes deductions on her tax returns.) Briefly explain your answer.

b. Rework the preceding problem, assuming Grace has the option of using a 48-month, 9.5 percent *home equity loan* to finance the full cost of this entertainment center. Again, use Worksheet 7.2 to determine if Grace should pay cash or buy on time. Does your answer change (from the one you came up with in part **a**)? Explain.

13. Due to a job change, Alex Rodriquez just relocated to the Pacific Northwest. He sold what furniture he had before he moved, so he's now shopping for new furnishings. He's found the perfect assortment of couches, chairs, tables, and beds at a local furniture store to fill his two-bedroom apartment; the total cost for everything is $6,400. Because of the cost of the move, Alex is a bit short of cash right now and has therefore decided to take out an installment loan in the amount of $6,400 to pay for the furniture. The furniture store has offered to lend him the money for 48 months at an add-on interest rate of 8½ percent. The credit union at Alex's place of employment has also offered to lend him the money—they said

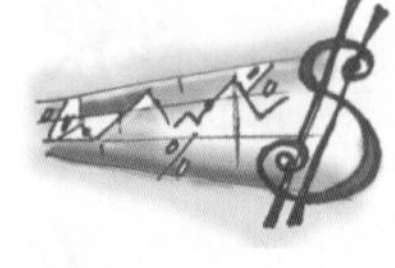

they'd give him the loan at an interest rate of 12 percent, simple, but only for a term of 24 months.

a. Compute the monthly payments for both of the loan offers.

b. Determine the APR for both loans.

c. Which is more important: low payments or a low APR? Explain.

14. Megan Myers is short of cash and is considering a short-term loan from Harry's Pawnshop. If she is willing to offer her grandmother's heirloom diamond necklace as collateral, Harry will lend her $500 for one month, after which she must pay back the $500 with an additional $50 in interest. (If she misses the payment, Harry is entitled to sell the necklace to cover his loss.) Compute the APR for this loan—keep in mind the term of the loan is *1 month.*

Applying Personal Finance

Making the Payments!

For many of us, new cars can be so appealing! We get bitten by the new car bug and think how great it would be to have a new car. Then we tell ourselves that we really *need* a new car because our old one is just a piece of junk waiting to fall apart in the middle of the road anyway. Of course, we don't have the money to purchase a new car outright, so we'll have to get a loan. That means car payments. Trouble is, car payments often turn out to be a lot less affordable *after* we actually get the loan than we thought they would be *before* we signed on the dotted line. And they tend to last way beyond the time when the new car smell wears off. This project is aimed at helping you understand how loan payments are determined and the obligation they place on you as the borrower.

Let's assume for the sake of this project that your parents have promised to make the down payment on a new car once you have your degree in hand. They have agreed to pay 30 percent of the cost of any car you choose as long as you are able to obtain a loan and make the payments on the remainder. Find the price of the vehicle you would like by visiting a car dealership or pulling up a Web site such as **http://www.edmunds.com**. Add another 4 percent to the price for tax, title, license, and so on, or ask a dealer to estimate these costs for you. Take 70 percent of the total to determine how much you will have to finance on your car loan. Then find out what the going rate is for car loans in your area by calling or visiting your bank or by consulting a Web site such as **http://www.bankrate.com**. Calculate what your monthly payments would be at this rate if you financed the loan for 3 years, 5 years, and 6 years. How well do you think these car payments would fit into your budget? What kind of income would you have to make to comfortably afford these payments? If the payments are more than you thought they would be, what can you do to bring them down?

Contemporary Case Applications

7.1 Financing Annette's Education

At age 19, Annette Peterson is in the middle of her second year of studies at a community college in San Diego. She has done well in her course work; majoring in pre-business studies, she currently has a 3.75 grade point average. Annette lives at home and works part-time as a filing clerk for a nearby electronics distributor. Her parents cannot afford to pay any of her tuition and college expenses, so she is virtually on her own as far as college goes. Annette hopes to transfer to the University of Texas at Austin next year. She has already been accepted and feels she would get an excellent education there. After talking with her counselor, Annette feels she will not be able to hold down a part-time job and still manage to complete her bachelor's degree program at Texas in

2 years. Knowing that on her 22nd birthday she will receive approximately $35,000 from a trust fund left her by her grandmother, Annette has decided to borrow against the trust fund to support herself during the next 2 years. She estimates she will need $25,000 to cover tuition, room and board, books and supplies, travel, personal expenditures, and so on during that period. Unable to qualify for any special loan programs, Annette has found two sources of single-payment loans, each requiring a security interest in the trust proceeds as collateral. The terms required by each potential lender are as follows:

a. California State Bank will lend $30,000 at 8 percent discount interest. The loan principal would be due at the end of 2 years.
b. National Bank of San Diego will lend $25,000 under a 2-year note. The note would carry a 10 percent simple interest rate and would also be due in a single payment at the end of 2 years.

Questions

1. How much would Annette (a) receive in initial loan proceeds and (b) be required to repay at maturity under the California State Bank loan?
2. Compute (a) the finance charges and (b) the APR on the loan offered by California State Bank.
3. Compute (a) the finance charges and (b) the APR on the loan offered by the National Bank of San Diego. How big a loan payment would be due at the end of 2 years?
4. Compare your findings in Questions 2 and 3, and recommend one of the loans to Annette. Explain your recommendation.
5. What other recommendations might you offer Annette relative to the disposition of the loan proceeds?

7.2 Rob Gets His 4-Runner

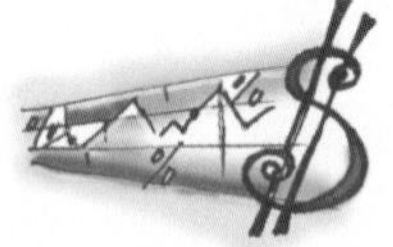

Rob Lewis, a 27-year-old bachelor living in Charlotte, North Carolina, has been a high-school teacher for 5 years. For the past 4 months, he has been thinking about buying a Toyota 4-Runner, but feels he is not able to afford a brand-new one. Recently, however, a friend, John McKenzie, has offered to sell him his fully loaded Toyota 4-Runner Ltd. John wants $22,500 for his SUV, which has been driven only 8,000 miles and is in very good condition. Rob is eager to buy the vehicle but has only $8,000 in his savings account at Tar Heel Bank. He expects to net $8,000 from the sale of his Chevrolet Camero, but this will still leave him about $6,500 short. He has two alternatives for obtaining the money:

a. Borrow $6,500 from the First National Bank of Charlotte at a fixed rate of 12 percent per annum, simple interest. The loan would be repaid in equal monthly installments over a 3-year (36-month) period.
b. Obtain a $6,500 installment loan requiring 36 monthly payments from the Charlotte Teacher's Credit Union at a 6.5 percent stated rate of interest. The add-on method would be used to calculate the finance charges on this loan.

Questions

1. Using Exhibit 7.6 or a financial calculator, determine the required monthly payments if the loan is taken out at First National Bank of Charlotte.
2. Compute (a) the finance charges and (b) the APR on the loan offered by First National Bank of Charlotte.
3. Determine the size of the monthly payment required on the loan from the Charlotte Teacher's Credit Union.

4. Compute (a) the finance charges and (b) the APR on the loan offered by the Charlotte Teacher's Credit Union.
5. Compare the two loans and recommend one of them to Rob. Explain your recommendation.

MONEY ONLINE

Loans, Loans, and More Loans!

Note: Web addresses change frequently, so you may need to determine the home page and do a site search to find the page or topic that's referenced.

1. **http://www.nelliemae.com**

What are your student loan options? Whether you're an undergraduate, graduate, or professional student, learn the basics of student loans from Nellie Mae, a leading national provider of higher education loans for students and parents. Receive entrance and exit counseling, apply online, check on your loan's status, and calculate your payments at this site as well.

2. **http://nces.ed.gov/ipeds/cool**

Find the college that best suits you. The National Center for Education Statistics in the U.S. Department of Education has prepared College Opportunities On-Line to help students and their parents compare over 7,000 colleges and the costs to attend them. Visit the Department of Education's main site at **http://www.ed.gov** for information concerning student financial aid.

3. **http://www.usaaedfoundation.org**

Find useful information on obtaining loans and managing debt at the USAA Educational Foundation's Web site. Click on "Financial" and scroll down to "Financing College" to search for scholarships, explore financial aid options, and find student loan information. Under "Personal Finance," find topics on identity theft and avoiding fraud, and under "Basic Investing," find out about managing debt.

4. **http://www.teri.org**

Don't qualify for financial aid? Find student loans based on your creditworthiness rather than your family's income. The Education Resources Institute (TERI), a private, not-for-profit institution, provides education financing and information services to students and their families. Their loan program is designed to meet the needs of students in all phases of their education—whether elementary, secondary, undergraduate, graduate, professional, or specialized programs of study.

5. **http://www.bankrate.com**

Find the best loan rates in your area! Select the product you're interested in and your state at Bankrate's Web site to comparison shop among the loan, credit, or savings offerings in your area. Learn basic loan information, calculate your loan payment, or research your bank's financial condition at this site as well.

6. **http://www.consumer.gov/idtheft**

What four things should you do immediately if someone tries to steal your identity? Find out at the Web site designed to provide consumer information on identity theft by the Federal Trade Commission. Learn about the federal and state laws concerning identity theft, how to file a complaint, and what you can do to minimize your risk of identity theft occurring to you.

7. **http://www.consumer.gov**

Explore the wealth of consumer information available from the federal government at FirstGov for Consumers prepared by the Federal Trade Commission. Listings here include the Consumer Action Handbook, Kidz Privacy, FDA Information for Consumers, and the Military Sentinel.

8. **http://www.quicken.com/planning/debt**
Create an action plan to reduce your debt using Quicken's interactive "Debt Reduction Planner." Determine how much of your savings to contribute toward your debt and how much of your expenses to cut out in order to pay off your debt sooner. Graphically view changes in the level of your debt as you work through various debt reduction scenarios.

Just for Fun!

9. **http://www.publicdebt.treas.gov**
Think you have a lot of debt? Check out the amount of the government's debt on this day. Scroll down to "Public Debt" and click on "Public Debt Outstanding" to find the amount down to the penny. Compare today's debt with that from a year ago. Also learn about savings bonds, Treasury securities, and the regulation of the government securities market at the Web site of the Bureau of the Public Debt.

10. **http://moneycentral.msn.com/investor/calcs/n_spend/main.asp**
Take the "Savvy Spending Quiz" to find out what kind of spender you are! While you're at MSN's MoneyCentral, scroll down to find other useful tools, such as the Debt Evaluator, Savings Calculator, and Debt Consolidator.

PART FOUR

Managing Insurance Needs

8
Insuring Your Life

9
Insuring Your Health

10
Protecting Your Property

CHAPTER 8

Insuring Your Life

Learning Goals

LG1. Explain the concept of risk and the basics of insurance underwriting.
LG2. Discuss the primary reasons for life insurance and identify those who need coverage.
LG3. Calculate how much life insurance you need.
LG4. Differentiate among the various types of life insurance policies and describe their advantages and disadvantages.
LG5. Choose the best life insurance policy for your needs at the lowest cost.
LG6. Become familiar with the key features of life insurance policies.

Lessons in Life

Imagine losing both of your parents when you are still dependent on them. That's exactly what happened to Shanna and Ebony Blanchard. Their father died when the girls were still in elementary school, leaving their mother, Jackie, responsible for raising them on her own. Jackie worked hard to make sure that the girls had everything they needed and dreamed of sending them to college. Then, when Shanna and Ebony were still in high school, Jackie was diagnosed with incurable lung cancer. Within a short time, she too was gone.

Although Shanna and Ebony were devastated, they did not have to worry about their financial future. Soon after her husband's death, Jackie had purchased a life insurance policy so that her children would be taken care of if anything happened to her. The policy had a terminal illness benefit that allowed Jackie to use some of the insurance proceeds before her death. Jackie purchased a new home for Shanna and Ebony to live in and set aside money for their education. Thanks to their mom's foresight, Ebony graduated from college with honors and Shanna will soon start college as well.

Life insurance also let Harvey Wood take care of his family after he died. Wood owned and operated an Arizona cotton and citrus farm that had been in his family for three generations. Over the years, as he and his wife, Sandy, expanded their family, Harvey increased his life insurance coverage. Then, disaster struck. Harvey died in a tractor accident at age 50.

Sandy was faced with a mountain of debt: farm loans, credit card bills, the mortgage—and college for her children. At first, she feared the worst. "We owed hundreds of thousands of dollars," says Sandy today. "I kept thinking, 'This farm has been in our family for generations, I can't lose it now.'"

Harvey's life insurance, however, came to the rescue. With it, Sandy was able to pay off all of the family's debts and send her children through college. Today, Sandy and her son, H. C., still manage the family farm. "Our life is forever different without Harvey," says Sandy, "but because he cared so much and bought the life insurance, our way of life hasn't changed."

CRITICAL THINKING QUESTIONS

As you review the chapter, consider these questions in relation to the Blanchard and Wood families:

- Based on the stories you've just read, what purposes does life insurance serve?
- Who should have life insurance, and why?
- When is the best time to purchase life insurance?

Source: Adapted from "Real Life Stories, 2003," *The Life and Health Insurance Foundation*, downloaded from **http://www.life-line.org/reallife/index.html**.

BASIC INSURANCE CONCEPTS

LG1

As the Blanchard and Wood families discovered, life is full of unexpected events that can have far-reaching consequences. Your car is sideswiped on the highway and damaged beyond repair. A family member falls ill and can no longer work. A fire or other disaster destroys your home. Your spouse dies suddenly. Although most people don't like to think about possibilities like this, protecting yourself and your family against unforeseen events like these is part of sound financial planning. Insurance plays a central role in providing that protection. *Auto and homeowner's insurance*, for example, reimburses you if your car or home are destroyed or damaged. *Life insurance* helps replace lost income if premature death occurs, providing funds so that your loved ones can keep their home, maintain an acceptable lifestyle, pay for education, and meet other special needs. *Hospitalization and health insurance* covers medical costs when you get sick and *disability insurance* protects your income during your illness.

The basic purpose of all of these types of insurance is *to protect you and your dependents from the financial consequences of losing assets or income when an accident, illness, or death occurs.* By anticipating the potential risks that your assets and income could be exposed to and weaving insurance protection into your financial plan, you lend a degree of certainty to your financial future. This chapter begins with an introduction to important insurance concepts such as risk and underwriting before focusing on how to make decisions regarding life insurance. The chapters that follow will discuss other important types of insurance including health insurance and property insurance.

THE CONCEPT OF RISK

An important concept in any discussion of insurance is *risk.* In insurance terms, risk is defined as uncertainty with respect to economic loss. Whenever you and your family have a financial interest in something—whether it's your life, health, home, car, or business—there's a risk that you will suffer financial loss if that item is lost or damaged. Because such losses can have a devastating effect on your financial security, you must devise strategies for anticipating and dealing with potential risks. These strategies include risk avoidance, loss prevention and control, risk assumption, and insurance.

Risk Avoidance

The simplest way to deal with risk is to avoid the act that creates it. As an example, people who are afraid they might lose everything they own because of a lawsuit resulting from an automobile accident could avoid driving. With respect to life and health risks, avid skydivers or bungee jumpers might want to choose another recreational activity!

Although **risk avoidance** can be an effective way to handle some risks, it is not without its costs. For instance, people who avoid driving suffer considerable inconvenience, and the retired skydiver may find he or she now suffers *more* stress, which can lead to different types of health risks. Risk avoidance is an attractive way to deal with risk only when the estimated cost of avoidance is less than the estimated cost of handling it in some other way.

risk avoidance
Avoidance of an act that would create a risk.

Loss Prevention and Control

In a broad sense, **loss prevention** can be defined as any activity that reduces the probability that a loss will occur (such as driving within the speed limit to lessen the chance of being in a car accident). **Loss control**, in contrast, is any activity that lessens the severity of loss once it occurs (such as wearing a safety belt or buying a car with air bags). Loss prevention and loss control should be important parts of the risk management program of every individual and family. In fact, insurance provides a reasonable

loss prevention
Any activity that reduces the probability that a loss will occur.

loss control
Any activity that lessens the severity of loss once it occurs.

means for handling risk only when people use effective loss prevention and control measures.

Risk Assumption

risk assumption The choice to accept and bear the risk of loss.

With **risk assumption**, you choose to accept and bear the risk of loss. Risk assumption can be an effective way to handle many types of potentially small exposures to loss when insurance would be too expensive. (For example, the risk of having your *Personal Financial Planning* text stolen probably doesn't justify buying insurance.) It's also a reasonable approach for dealing with very large risks that you can't ordinarily prevent or secure insurance for (nuclear holocaust, for example). Unfortunately, people often assume risks unknowingly. They may be unaware of various exposures to loss or think that their insurance policy offers adequate protection when, in fact, it doesn't.

Insurance

insurance policy A contract between the insured and the insurer under which the insurer agrees to reimburse the insured for any losses suffered according to specified terms.

An **insurance policy** is a contract between you (the insured) and an insurance company (the insurer) under which the insurance company agrees to reimburse you for any losses you suffer according to specified terms. From your perspective, *you are transferring your risk of loss to the insurance company.* You pay a relatively small amount (the insurance premium) in exchange for a promise from the insurance company that they'll reimburse you if you suffer a loss covered by the insurance policy.

Why are insurance companies willing to accept this risk? Simple. They combine the loss experiences of large numbers of people, and, by using statistical information known as *actuarial data*, they are able to estimate the risk of loss faced by the insured population. The losses of the entire group of policyholders are thus more predictable than for any one of the insureds individually. Insurance companies invest the amount they collect from premiums and, if the amount they pay out in losses and expenses is less than what they earn on those investments, they make a profit. Therefore, accurately estimating the number and size of insured losses that will occur is extremely critical for insurance companies.

Underwriting Basics

underwriting In insurance, the process used by insurers to decide who can be insured and to determine applicable rates they will charge for premiums.

Insurance companies take great pains to decide whom they will insure and the applicable rates they will charge for premiums. This function is called **underwriting**. Underwriters design rate-classification schedules so that people pay premiums equal with their chance of loss. Through underwriting, insurance companies try to guard against *adverse selection*, which happens when only high-risk clients apply for and get insurance coverage.

Underwriting directly impacts an insurance company's chances of success. If underwriting standards are too high, people will be unjustly denied insurance coverage, and insurance sales will drop. On the other hand, if standards are too low, many insureds will pay less than their fair share based upon their potential for losses, and the insurance company's solvency may be jeopardized.

A basic problem facing insurance underwriters is how to select the best criteria for classifying the people they insure. Because a perfect relationship between available criteria and loss experience does not exist, some people invariably believe they're being charged more than they should be for their insurance. Insurers are always trying to improve their underwriting capabilities

Concept ✓

8-1. Discuss the role insurance plays in the financial planning process. Why is it important to have enough life insurance?

8-2. Define (a) *risk avoidance*, (b) *loss prevention*, (c) *loss control*, (d) *risk assumption*, and (e) an *insurance policy*. Explain their interrelationships, if any.

8-3. Explain the purpose of underwriting. What are some of the factors underwriters consider when evaluating a life insurance application?

in order to set premium rates that will provide adequate protection against insolvency and yet be attractive and reasonable for policyholders.

Because underwriting practices and standards also vary between insurance companies, you can often save money by shopping around for the company that offers the most favorable underwriting policies for your specific characteristics and needs. To make an effective decision about any insurance product, therefore, you need to have a basic understanding of the different types of insurance available as well as insight into your own tolerance for risk when it comes to protecting your financial assets and your family. The discussion of life insurance that follows in this chapter, and succeeding chapters that discuss other types of insurance, will help you accomplish these goals.

WHY BUY LIFE INSURANCE?

LG2

Life insurance planning is an important part of every successful financial plan. Its primary purpose is to *protect your dependents from financial loss in the event of your untimely death.* In essence, it provides an umbrella of protection for your loved ones by protecting the assets you've built up during your life and providing funds to help your family reach important financial goals even after you die.

BENEFITS OF LIFE INSURANCE

In spite of its importance to sound financial planning, many people put off the decision to buy life insurance, in part because life insurance is associated with something unpleasant in many people's minds—namely, death. People don't like to talk about death or the things closely associated with it, so they often put off considering their life insurance needs. Life insurance is also intangible. You can't see, smell, touch, or taste its benefits—and those benefits mainly happen after you've died. However, life insurance does have very important benefits that should not be ignored in the financial planning process.

The benefits of life insurance include:

- **Financial Protection for Dependents:** If you have family or loved ones who depend on your income, what would happen to them after you die? Would they be able to maintain their current lifestyle, stay in your home, or afford a college education? Life insurance provides a financial cushion for your dependents, giving them a set amount of money after your death that they can use for many different purposes. For example, your spouse may use your life insurance proceeds to pay off the mortgage on your home so your family can continue to live there comfortably or set aside funds for your child's college education. In short, the most important benefit of life insurance is providing financial protection for your dependents after your death.
- **Protection from Creditors:** A life insurance policy can be structured so that death benefits are paid directly to a named beneficiary rather than being considered as part of your estate. This means that even if you have outstanding bills and debts at the time of your death, creditors cannot claim the cash benefits from your life insurance policy, providing further financial protection for your dependents.
- **Tax Benefits:** Life insurance proceeds paid to your heirs, as a rule, are not subject to state or federal income taxes. Further, if certain requirements are met, policy proceeds can pass to named beneficiaries free of any *estate* taxes.
- **Vehicle for Savings:** Some types of life insurance policies can serve as a savings vehicle, particularly for those who are looking for safety of principal. In particular, *variable life policies,* which we will discuss later in this chapter, are more investment vehicles than they are life insurance products. However, don't assume that all life insurance products can be considered savings instruments. As we'll see later in this chapter, the comparison is often inappropriate.

Just like other aspects of personal financial planning, life insurance decisions can be made easier by following a step-by-step approach to answer the following questions:

1. Do you need life insurance?
2. If so, how much life insurance do you need?
3. Which type of life insurance is best given your financial objectives?
4. What factors should be considered in making the final purchase decision?

Do You Need Life Insurance?

The first question to ask when considering the purchase of life insurance is if, in fact, you need it. Not everyone does. Many factors, including your personal situation and other financial resources, play a role in determining your need for life insurance. Remember, the major purpose of life insurance is to provide financial security for your dependents in the event of your death. As we've discussed, life insurance can also provide other benefits but they're all a distant second to this primary reason for buying life insurance.

Who needs life insurance? In general, life insurance should be considered if you have dependents counting on you for financial support. Therefore, a single adult who doesn't have children or other relatives to support may not need life insurance at all. Children also usually don't require insurance on their life.

Once you marry, your life insurance requirements should be reevaluated, depending on your spouse's earning potential and assets—such as a house—that you want to protect. The need for life insurance increases the most when children enter the picture, because young families stand to suffer the greatest financial hardship from the premature death of a parent. Even a non-wage-earning parent may require some life insurance to ensure that children will be adequately cared for if the parent died.

As families build assets, their life insurance requirements continue to change, both in terms of the amount of insurance needed and the type of policy necessary to meet their financial objectives and protect their assets. Other life changes will also affect your life insurance needs. For example, if you divorce or your spouse dies, you may require additional life insurance to protect your children. In contrast, once your children finish school and are on their own, the need for life insurance may drop. In later years, life insurance needs vary depending on the availability of other financial resources, such as pensions and investments, to provide for your dependents.

multiple-of-earnings method
A method of determining the amount of life insurance coverage needed by multiplying gross annual earnings by some selected (often arbitrary) number.

Concept ✓

8-4. Discuss some of the benefits of life insurance in addition to protecting family members financially after the primary wage earner's death

8-5. Explain the circumstances under which a single college graduate would or would not need life insurance. What life-cycle events would change this initial evaluation, and how might they affect his or her life insurance needs?

LG3 HOW MUCH LIFE INSURANCE IS RIGHT FOR YOU?

Once you've decided that life insurance makes sense for your particular situation, you need to make several other decisions to find the life insurance product that best fits your needs. First, you must determine how much life insurance will provide adequate coverage. Buying too much life insurance can be costly; buying too little may prove disastrous. To avoid these problems, you can use one of two methods to estimate how much insurance is necessary: the *multiple-of-earnings method* and the *needs analysis method.*

The **multiple-of-earnings method** takes your gross annual earnings and multiplies it by some selected (often arbitrary) number to arrive at an estimate of adequate life insurance coverage. The general rule of thumb used by many insurance agents is that your insurance coverage should be equal to five to ten times your current income. For example, if you currently earn $100,000 a year, using the multiple earnings method you'd need between $500,000 and $1 million worth of life insurance. Although simple to use, the multiple-of-earnings method fails to fully recognize the financial obligations and resources of the individual and his or her family. Therefore, the multiple-of-earnings method should be used only to get a very rough approximation of life insurance needs.

needs analysis method A method of determining the amount of life insurance coverage needed by considering the person's financial obligations and his or her available financial resources *in addition to life insurance.*

A more-detailed approach is the **needs analysis method**. The needs analysis method considers both the financial obligations and financial resources of the insured and his or her dependents. Essentially, this method involves three steps, as shown in Exhibit 8.1:

1. Estimate the total economic resources needed if the individual were to die
2. Determine all financial resources that would be available after death, including existing life insurance and pension plan death benefits
3. Subtract available resources from the amount needed to calculate how much additional life insurance is required.

EXHIBIT 8.1

How Much Life Insurance Do You Need?

The needs analysis method uses the following three steps to estimate life insurance needs.

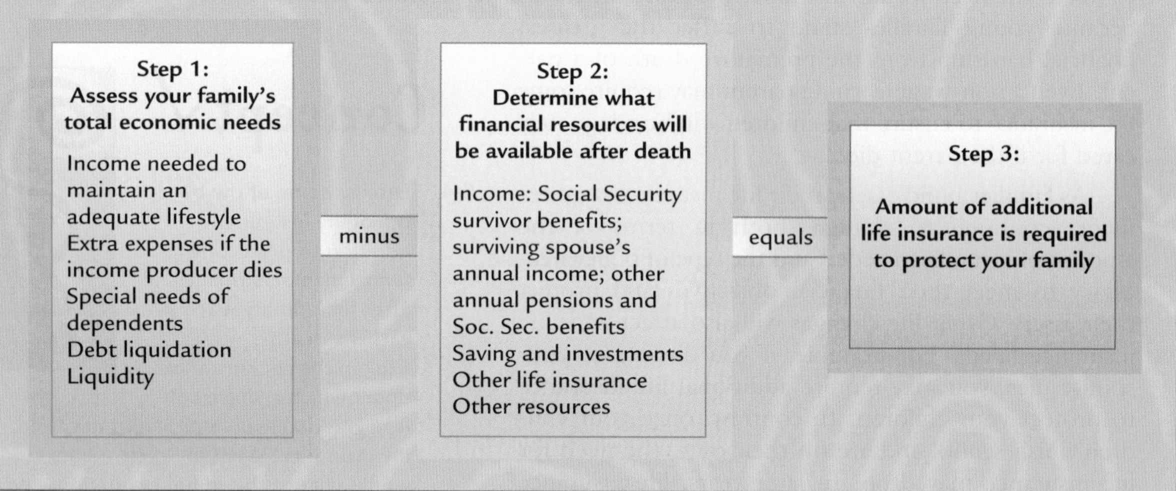

STEP 1: ASSESS YOUR FAMILY'S TOTAL ECONOMIC NEEDS

The first question the needs analysis method asks is: *What financial resources will my survivors need should I die tomorrow?* You should consider the following five items in answering this question:

1. **Income needed to maintain an adequate lifestyle:** If you died, how much money would your dependents need each month in order to live a comfortable life? Estimate this amount by looking at your family's current monthly budget, including expenses for housing costs, utilities, food, clothing, and medical and dental needs. Other expenses to consider include property taxes, insurance, recreation and travel, and savings. Try to take into account that the amount needed

may change over time. For example, once children are grown, monthly household expenses should decrease substantially but the surviving spouse may still need monthly support. Therefore, the survivor's life expectancy and the income they'll require may also need to be considered.

2. **Extra expenses if the income producer dies:** These expenses include funeral costs and any expenses that might be incurred to replace services you currently provide. For example, a mother who doesn't work outside of the home still provides childcare, cooking, cleaning, and other services. If she were to die or have to return to work, these services might have to be replaced using the family's income. Because such expenses can stretch a family budget to the breaking point, they should be included when you're estimating insurance needs.
3. **Special needs of dependents:** In addition to daily economic needs, you may want to provide for special needs of your dependents. These needs might include long-term nursing care for a disabled or chronically ill dependent, an emergency fund for unexpected financial burdens, or a college education fund for your children.
4. **Debt liquidation:** In the event of their death, most breadwinners prefer to leave their families relatively debt free. To accomplish this, it's necessary to calculate the average amount due for outstanding bills. This amount would include the balances on credit cards, department store accounts, and other similar obligations. In addition, some will want to leave enough money to allow their dependents to pay off the home mortgage.
5. **Liquidity:** After your death, it may take time for your dependents to be able to sell noncash assets. Real estate, for example, is difficult to convert to cash quickly. If you have a very high percentage of your wealth in nonliquid assets, the cash proceeds from life insurance can be used to pay the bills and maintain assets until they can be sold at a fair market value.

Step 2: Determine What Financial Resources Will Be Available after Death

After estimating the lifetime financial needs of dependents, the next step is to list all current resources that will be available for meeting those needs. For most families, money from savings, investments, and Social Security survivor's benefits make up the largest non-life-insurance financial resources. Additional resources include proceeds from employer-sponsored group life insurance policies and the death benefits payable from accumulated pension plans and profit-sharing programs. Another important source is income that can be earned by the surviving spouse or children. If the surviving spouse is skilled and readily employable, his or her earnings could be a family's largest available resource. In addition, many families have real estate (in addition to their homes), jewelry, stocks, bonds, and other assets that can be liquidated to meet financial needs. After developing a complete list of available resources, you should make some reasonable estimate of their value. Although this step can be difficult due to the changing values of many of the assets, coming up with a set of reasonably accurate estimates is certainly within reach.

Step 3: Subtract Resources from Needs to Calculate How Much Life Insurance You Require

Finally, subtract the total available resources from the total needed to satisfy all of the family's financial objectives. If available resources are greater than needs, no additional life insurance is required. If the resources are less than the needs—as is the case in most families with children—the difference is the amount of life insurance necessary to provide the family with its desired standard of living.

While the needs analysis method may seem complex, technology has made it simpler to use. Insurance companies now have computer software that can quickly determine the insurance needs of individuals and families. There are also many Internet sites and software programs that let you do your own analysis.

smart.sites

Estimate the amount of life insurance your family needs for financial security with the Life Insurance Coverage Needs Analyzer in the Tools section of InsWeb, **http://www.insweb.com**.

Regardless of which procedure you use, remember that *life insurance needs are not static*. The amount and type of life insurance you need today will probably differ from the amount and type suitable for you 10 or 20 years from now. As with other areas of your personal financial plan, you should review and adjust life insurance programs (as necessary) at least every 5 years, or after any major changes in the family (for example, the birth of a child, the purchase of a home, or a job change).

Needs Analysis in Action: The Benson Family

Let's take a closer look at how the Needs Analysis Method works by considering the hypothetical case of Bill and Joan Benson. Bill Benson is 37 and the primary breadwinner in the family; current earnings are $85,000. Bill and his wife Joan want to make certain that his life insurance policy would provide enough proceeds to take care of Joan and their two children, ages 6 and 8, if he should die. You can follow their analysis of needs and resources shown in Worksheet 8.1.

Estimating Family Economic Needs (Step 1)

Bill and Joan Benson review their budget and decide that monthly living expenses for Joan and the two children would be about $3,500 in current dollars while the children are still living at home, or $42,000 annually. After both children leave home, Joan, now 35, will need a monthly income of $3,000—or $36,000 a year-until she retires at age 65. At that point, the Bensons estimate Joan's living expenses would fall to $2,750 a month, or $33,000 annually. The life expectancy of a woman Joan's age is 87 years, so the Bensons calculate that Joan will spend about 22 years in retirement. Therefore, as shown in the first section of the worksheet, the total income necessary for the Bensons' living expenses over the next 52 years is $1,878,000.

Financial Road Sign

5 Questions to Ask Yourself before You Buy an Insurance Policy

1. Am I sure that buying this policy is a necessary addition to my financial plan?
2. Have I compared the features of several policies?
3. Do I fully understand the policy I'm considering, including fees and potential penalty costs?
4. Do I feel comfortable with the company, agent, and product?
5. Have I reviewed the financial stability of the insurance company?

Although Joan previously worked as a stockbroker, they planned for her to stay home until the children graduated from high school. The Bensons are concerned that her previous education may be somewhat out of date at that point, so they include $25,000 for Joan to update her education and skills. In addition, Bill and Joan want to fund their children's college educations. After researching the current cost of their state's public university, they decide to establish a college fund of $75,000 for this purpose. Finally, they estimate final expenses of $15,000.

The Bensons use credit sparingly, so their outstanding debts are limited to a mortgage (with a current balance of $150,000), an automobile loan ($4,000), and

worksheet 8.1

Determining the Benson's Need for Life Insurance

LIFE INSURANCE NEEDS ANALYSIS METHOD					
Insured's Name *Bill and Joan Benson*				Date *April 12, 2005*	
Step 1: Estimate the total economic resources needed					
1. Annual living expenses and other needs:					
		Period 1	**Period 2**	**Period 3**	
a.	Monthly living expenses	$3,500	$3,000	$2,750	
b.	Net yearly income needed (a × 12)	$42,000	$36,000	$33,000	
c.	Number of years in time period	12	18	22	
d.	Total living need per time period (b × c)	$504,000	$648,000	$726,000	
TOTAL LIVING EXPENSES (add line d for each period):					$1,878,000
2. Special needs					
a.	Spouse education fund				$25,000
b.	Children's college fund				$75,000
c.	Other needs				0
3. Final expenses (funeral, estate costs, etc.)					$15,000
4. Debt liquidation					
a.	House mortgage	$150,000			
b.	Other loans	5,000			
c.	Total debt (4 a + 4 b)				$155,000
5. Other financial needs					0
TOTAL INCOME NEEDS (add right column)					$2,148,000
Step 2: Financial resources available after death					
1. Income					
		Period 1	**Period 2**	**Period 3**	
a.	Annual Social Security survivor benefits	$38,400	0	0	
b.	Surviving spouse's annual income	0	$35,000	0	
c.	Other annual pensions and Soc. Sec benefits	0	0	$27,000	
b.	Annual income	$38,400	$35,000	$27,000	
e.	Number of years in time period	12	18	22	
f.	Total period income (d × e)	$460,800	$630,000	$594,000	
g. TOTAL INCOME					$1,684,800
2.	Savings and investments				$65,000
3.	Other life insurance				$100,000
4.	Other resources				0
TOTAL RESOURCES AVAILABLE (1g + 2 + 3 + 4)					$1,849,800
Step 3: Subtract available resources (Step 2) from the amount needed (Step 1)					
Step 1: Total income needs					$2,148,000
Step 2: Available resources					$1,849,800
ADDITIONAL LIFE INSURANCE NEEDED					$298,200

miscellaneous charge accounts ($1,000). Bill and Joan, therefore, estimate that $155,000 would pay off all of their existing debts. They also allow $15,000 to pay off estate administration expenses, taxes, and funeral costs.

All of these estimates are shown in the top half of Bill and Joan's insurance calculations in Worksheet 8.1. Note that the total amount they estimate will be necessary to meet their financial goals if Bill were to die is $2,148,000.

Financial Resources Available after Death (Step 2)

If Bill died, Joan would be eligible to receive **Social Security survivor's benefits** for both herself and her children. Social Security survivor benefits are intended to provide basic, minimum support to families faced with the loss of their principal wage earner. The benefits are paid to unmarried children until age 18 (or 19 if they are still in high school) and nonworking surviving spouses until their children reach age 16. The surviving spouse will also receive individual survivor benefits upon turning 65. There are limits placed on the total amount of survivor's benefits that can be paid to a household, and if the surviving spouse returns to work, the amount of benefits will be reduced if earnings exceed certain limits. We'll discuss Social Security and its benefits in more detail in Chapter 14.

Social Security survivor's benefits Benefits included under provision of social security that are intended to provide basic, minimum support to families faced with the loss of their principal wage earners.

Joan and Bill visit the Social Security Administration's Web site for an estimate of the survivor benefits Joan will receive. Based on the number of years Bill has worked, his income, and the number of children they have, the Bensons estimate that Joan will receive approximately $3,200 a month, or $38,400 a year, in Social Security survivor benefits for herself and the children until the youngest child graduates from high school in 12 years.

smart.sites

Want to know how much your spouse and children will receive in survivor benefits? The answers are at the Social Security Administration's Web site **http://www.ssa.gov**.

In the 18 years between the time the children leave home and Joan retires, the Bensons expect Joan to be employed full-time and earn about $35,000 after taxes. After Joan turns 65, she will receive approximately $2,250 a month ($27,000 a year) from Bill's survivor's benefits, her own Social Security benefits, and her own retirement benefits.

Joan will have some other resources available if Bill should die, however. The couple has saved $65,000 in a mutual fund and Bill's employer provides a $100,000 life insurance policy on his life. Adding these amounts to Joan's expected income means she will have $1,849,800 in total resources available.

Calculate Insurance Requirement (Step 3)

How much life insurance should the Bensons buy for Bill in order to make certain Joan and the children will be adequately cared for? To find out, the Bensons subtract the total amount of available resources—$1,849,800—from the total income needed—$2,148,000. The difference is $298,200. So the minimum life insurance Bill should buy to protect his family is about $300,000.

Of course, Bill and Joan will find that their insurance situation will need to be examined periodically as their children grow and the family's financial circumstances change. But, for now, they feel satisfied that they have a good estimate of the amount of insurance they need to buy for Bill. They can now begin to consider which type of policy is best.

Life Insurance Underwriting Considerations

As we discussed earlier, insurance companies use a process called underwriting to determine whom they will insure and what they will charge for insurance coverage. Underwriting policies are particularly important to understand when choosing life insurance products, so let's briefly examine some of the factors life insurance underwriters consider.

Life insurance underwriting begins by asking potential insureds to complete an application designed to gather information about their risk potential. In other words, underwriters consider the likelihood that the insured will die while the life insurance policy is in effect. Underwriters use life expectancy figures to look at overall longevity for various age groups. Specific factors related to the applicant's health are also considered. Someone who smokes, is obese, has a history of heart disease or has a dangerous job or hobby is considered a greater risk than someone who doesn't. An applicant who has been charged with driving under the influence of drugs or alcohol or has had their driver's license suspended may also have higher risk factors.

All these factors are then used to determine whether to accept you, and, based on your risk factors, what premium to charge. For example, someone in excellent health is usually considered "preferred" and pays the lowest premium. Other typical categories include standard, preferred smoker, and smoker. Those with special medical conditions—high cholesterol or diabetes, for example—fall into rated categories and pay considerably higher premiums if they are accepted.

The bottom line: if you have any of the risks commonly considered in life insurance underwriting—such as obesity, heart disease, or a high risk hobby or job—it is important to shop carefully and compare the cost implications of different types of insurance policies and the underwriting standards used by different companies.

smart.sites

What's your life expectancy? Northwestern Mutual, **http://www.northwesternmutual.com**, offers a quick and simple calculator that gives you a statistical estimate of how long you'll live. Click on "life insurance" and then "The Longevity Game."

Concept ✓

8-6. Discuss the two most commonly used ways to determine a person's life insurance needs.

8-7. Name and explain the most common economic needs that must be satisfied after the death of a family breadwinner.

8-8. What are some of the factors underwriters consider when evaluating a life insurance application? Which, if any, apply to you or your family members?

LG4 WHAT KIND OF POLICY IS RIGHT FOR YOU?

Once you've determined the amount of life insurance you need to cover your family's financial requirements and considered how various underwriting policies might affect you, the next step is to decide on the type of insurance policy. While there is a variety of life insurance products available, three major types account for 90 to 95 percent of life insurance sales: term life, whole life, and universal life.

smart.sites

At **http://www.life-line.org**, the site for the nonprofit Life and Health Insurance Foundation, an insurance education organization, you'll find information to help you sort out your life insurance options.

Term Life Insurance

term life insurance Insurance that provides only death benefits, for a specified period, and does not provide for the accumulation of cash value.

Term life insurance is the simplest type of insurance policy. You purchase a specified amount of insurance protection for a set time period. If you die during that time, your beneficiaries will receive the full amount specified in your policy. Term insurance can be bought for many different increments of time such as 5 years, 10 years, even 30 years. Depending on the policy, premiums can be paid annually, semiannually, or quarterly.

Types of Term Insurance

The most common types of term insurance are straight (or level) term and decreasing term.

Straight-Term

A straight-term life insurance policy is written for a set number of years, during which time the amount of life insurance coverage remains unchanged. The *annual premium* on a straight-term policy may increase each year, as with *annual renewable term policies,* or remain level throughout the policy period, as with *level-premium term policies.*

straight-term policy
A term insurance policy that is written for a given number of years, with coverage remaining unchanged throughout the effective period.

Exhibits 8.2 and 8.3 list representative annual premiums for annual renewable term and level-premium term life policies, respectively. Until recently, annual renewable term premiums were less expensive in the early years but increased rapidly over time. These policies, however, are not popular today. Because people now live longer, the rates for level-premium term have fallen sharply and are well below those on annual renewable term from year 1 on, thereby representing a better value.

EXHIBIT 8.2

Representative Annual Renewable Term Life Insurance Premiums; $100,000 Policy, Preferred Nonsmoker Rates

When you buy term life insurance, you are basically buying a product that provides life insurance coverage and nothing more. The following table shows representative rates for several age categories and selected policy years; actual premiums increase every year. As you can see, females pay less than males for coverage, and premiums increase sharply with age.

	Age 25		Age 40		Age 60	
Policy Year	**Male**	**Female**	**Male**	**Female**	**Male**	**Female**
1	$ 130	$ 119	$ 148	$ 139	$ 366	$ 252
5	$ 169	$ 147	$ 252	$ 219	$ 927	$ 562
10	$ 218	$ 187	$ 426	$ 368	$ 1,702	$ 1,080
15	$ 196	$ 176	$ 647	$ 507	$ 2,666	$ 1,313
20	$ 279	$ 259	$1,258	$1,054	$ 4,574	$ 2,989
Total Cost, 20 years	$3,777	$3,381	$9,871	$8,287	$38,457	$22,346

EXHIBIT 8.3

Representative Level-Premium Term Life Rates; $100,000 Preferred Nonsmoker Policy

This table shows annual, representative premiums for $100,000 of level-premium term life insurance. Although level premium costs less than annual renewable term for the same period, you must requalify at the end of each term to retain the low premium.

	5 year	10 year	15 year	20 year
Age	**Male/Female**	**Male/Female**	**Male/Female**	**Male/Female**
25	$102/$102	$ 81/$75	$ 89/$84	$103/$95
35	$102/$101	$ 81/$75	$ 90/$84	$103/$95
40	$121/$119	$ 96/$89	$111/$102	$132/$113
50	$176/$136	$183/$142	$237/$167	$259/$195
60	$358/$245	$380/$259	$475/$295	$555/$394

Decreasing Term

Because the death rate increases with each year of life, the premiums on annual renewable straight-term policies for each successive period of coverage will also increase. As an alternative, some term policies *maintain a level premium* throughout all periods of coverage, but *the amount of protection decreases.* Such a policy is called a **decreasing-term policy** because the amount of protection decreases over its life. Decreasing term is used when the amount of needed coverage declines over time. For example, decreasing-term policies are popular with homeowners who want a level of life insurance coverage that will decline at about the same rate as the balances on their home mortgages. Families with young children use these policies to ensure a sufficient level of family income while the kids are growing up. As they grow older, the amount of coverage needed decreases until the last child becomes independent and the need expires.

decreasing-term policy
A term insurance policy that *maintains a level premium* throughout all periods of coverage, but *the amount of protection decreases.*

Again, remember the type and length of term policy you choose will affect the amount of premiums you'll pay over time. Exhibit 8.4 shows the differences in total premiums that would be paid over a 20-year period for $250,000 in life insurance using a 20-year level term policy, a decreasing term policy, or a level term policy that is renewed annually. Note that in the 20th year, the death benefit from the decreasing term policy has dropped to $12,500.

EXHIBIT 8.4

Comparison of Term Life Premiums over 20 Years

The total premiums for a 20-year, $250,000 term life insurance policy differ considerably, depending on whether you buy a level term policy, decreasing term policy, or a level term policy that is renewed annually. Note that in the 20th year, the death benefit from the decreasing term policy has dropped to $12,500.

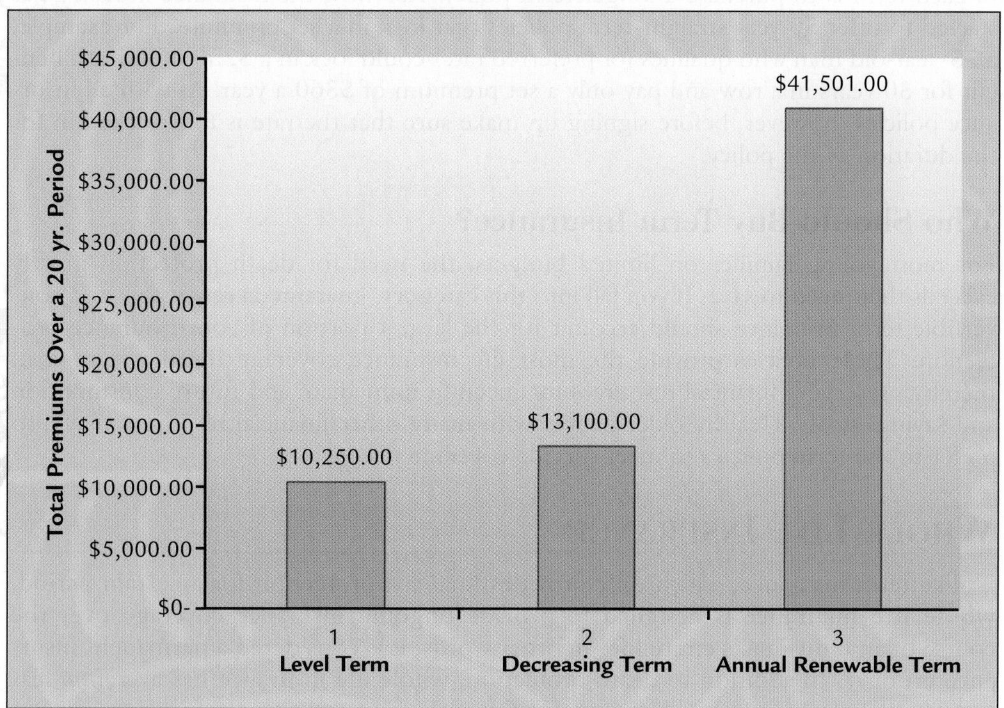

Source: QuickQuote.com, **http://www.quickquote.com/pix/litvswl_big.gif** (accessed September 28, 2003).

Advantages and Disadvantages of Term Life

One of the biggest advantages of term life is cost. Term life usually offers lower initial premiums than other types of insurance, especially for younger people. Term life is an economical way to buy a large amount of life insurance protection over a given, relatively short period, making it particularly advantageous for covering needs that will disappear over time. For example, a family with young children can use term insurance to provide coverage until the children are grown.

The main disadvantage, however, is that term insurance offers only temporary coverage. Once the policy term expires, you must renew the policy. This can be a problem if you develop underwriting factors in the future that make it difficult to qualify for insurance.

However, some term life policies overcome part of this drawback by offering a **renewability** provision that gives you the option of renewing your policy at the end of its term without having to show evidence of insurability. A guaranteed renewable provision allows you to renew the policy even if you have become uninsurable due to an accident or other illness during the original policy period. Generally, term policies are renewable at the end of each term until the insured reaches age 65 or 70. However, the premium will still increase to reflect the greater chance of death at older ages.

renewability
A term life policy provision that allows the insured to renew his or her policy at the end of its term without having to show evidence of insurability.

Another option that can help overcome some of the limitations of term insurance is a **convertability provision**. This lets you convert your term insurance policy to a comparable whole life policy at a future time. A whole life policy, as we will discuss below, provides lifelong protection, eliminating the need to continually renew your life insurance. Convertability is particularly useful if you need a large amount of relatively low cost, short-term protection immediately but in the future expect to have greater income that will allow you to purchase permanent insurance. Convertibility options are standard on most term policies today, but many place specific limits on when the conversion can take place.

convertibility
A term life policy provision that allows the insured to convert the policy to a comparable whole life policy.

One way to overcome the drawback of having to pay increased premiums at the end of each term is to purchase a longer term policy. Recently, the insurance industry has started to offer 30-year straight-term policies that lock in a set premium. For example, a 35-year-old man who qualifies for preferred rates could lock in a $250,000 death benefit for 30 years in a row and pay only a set premium of $360 a year. As with all insurance policies, however, before signing up make sure that the rate is fully locked in for the duration of the policy.

Who Should Buy Term Insurance?

For most young families on limited budgets, the need for death protection greatly exceeds their need to save. If you fall into this category, guaranteed renewable and convertible term insurance should account for the largest portion of your insurance protection. These policies provide the most life insurance coverage for the least cost, thereby preserving financial resources for meeting immediate and future consumption and savings goals. Healthy older people with many other financial resources may also prefer to use term policies to meet specific coverage needs.

whole life insurance
Life insurance designed to offer ongoing insurance coverage over the course of an insured's entire life; it provides stated death benefits and allows for the accumulation of *cash value*.

cash value
The accumulated refundable value of an insurance policy; results from the investment earnings on paid-in insurance premiums.

Whole Life Insurance

Unlike term insurance, which only provides financial protection for a certain period, **whole life insurance** is designed to provide ongoing insurance coverage over the course of an individual's entire life. In other words, it is considered a permanent insurance product. In addition to death protection, whole life insurance has a *savings* feature, called **cash value**, which results from the investment earnings on paid-in insurance premiums. Thus, *whole life provides not only insurance coverage but also a* *modest return on your investment.* The idea behind cash value is to provide the insurance buyer with a tangible return while he or she also receives insurance coverage—the savings rates on whole life policies are normally *fixed* and *guaranteed* to be more than a certain rate (say, 4 to 6 percent). Exhibit 8.5 illustrates how the cash value in a whole life policy builds up over time. Obviously, the longer the insured keeps the policy in force, the greater the cash value. Whole life can be purchased through several different payment plans, including continuous-premium, limited-payment, and single-premium, all providing for accumulation of cash values.

EXHIBIT 8.5

Illustration of the Cash Value and Pure Death Protection in a Whole Life Policy

Here is an example of the projected cash value for an actual $200,000 whole life policy issued by a major life insurer to a male, age 30. For each year of the illustration, the difference between the $200,000 death benefit and the projected cash value represents the *death protection* offered by the insurer.

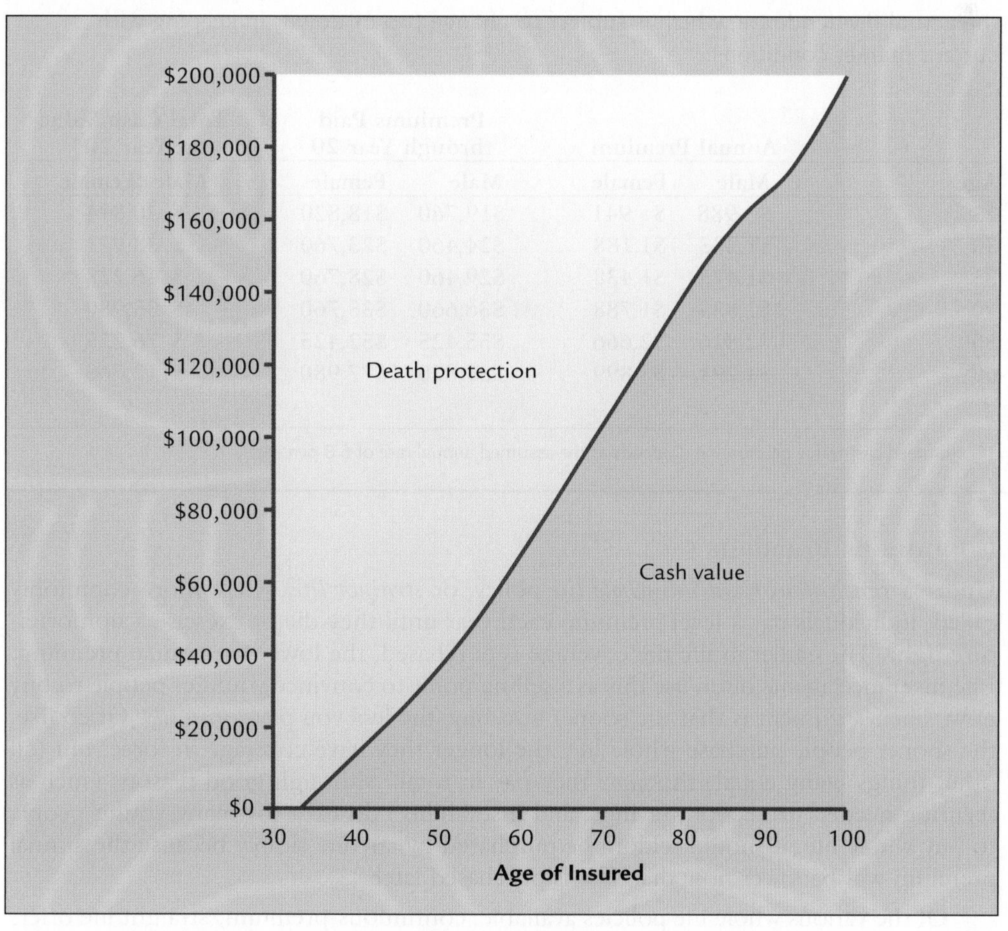

nonforfeiture right
A life insurance feature that gives the whole life policyholder, on policy cancellation, the portion of those assets that had been set aside to provide payment for the future death claim.

The cash value of a policy increases over time to reflect the greater chance of death that comes with age. If policyholders cancel their contracts prior to death, that portion of the assets set aside to provide payment for the death claim is available to them. This right to a cash value is termed the policyholder's **nonforfeiture right**. Policyholders, by terminating their insurance contracts, forfeit their rights to death benefits. Likewise, the company must forfeit its right to keep all the monies paid by these policyholders for the future death benefit it is no longer required to pay.

Types of Whole Life Policies

There are three major types of whole life policies available: continuous premium, limited payment, and single payment. To get a feel for the costs of these policies, look at the representative rates shown in Exhibit 8.6.

EXHIBIT 8.6

Representative Whole Life Insurance Annual Premiums; $100,000 Policy, Preferred Nonsmoker Rates

As with any life insurance product, the older you are, the more expensive it is to buy whole life. Also, whole life is more costly than term because you are getting an investment/savings account, represented by the cash value column, in addition to life insurance coverage. Of course, the actual amount of cash value will depend on the actual dividend rate, which is subject to change (up or down) in keeping with current market conditions.

	Annual Premium		Premiums Paid through Year 20		Total Cash Value at Year 20*
Age	Male	Female	Male	Female	Male/Female
25	$ 988	$ 941	$19,760	$18,820	$ 30,894
30	$1,233	$1,188	$24,460	$23,760	$ 38,971
35	$1,473	$1,438	$29,460	$28,760	$ 46,223
40	$1,833	$1,788	$36,660	$35,760	$ 55,980
50	$2,816	$2,666	$55,425	$52,425	$ 76,225
60	$4,291	$3,899	$85,820	$77,980	$112,765

*Guaranteed cash value plus annual dividends at the assumed annual rate of 6.8 percent.

Continuous Premium

Under a *continuous-premium whole life* policy, or *straight life,* as it's more commonly called, individuals pay a level premium each year until they die or exercise a nonforfeiture right. The earlier in life the coverage is purchased, the lower the annual premium. Life insurance agents often use this as a selling point to convince younger people to buy now. Their argument is that the sooner you buy, the less you pay *annually.* Of course, the sooner people purchase whole life, the longer they have coverage in force, but (all other things being equal) the *more* they pay in total. Although good reasons (such as securing needed protection, savings, and insurability) do exist for many young people to buy whole life, it should seldom be purchased by anyone simply because the annual premium will be lower now than if it is purchased later.

Of the various whole life policies available, continuous-premium/straight life offers the greatest amount of permanent death protection and the least amount of savings per premium dollar. This emphasis on *death protection* makes it the wisest choice to fill a permanent life insurance need.

Limited Payment

With a *limited-payment whole life* policy, you are covered for your entire life but the premium payment is based on a specified time period—for example, 20-pay life and 30-pay life require level premium payments for a period of 20 or 30 years, respectively. For stipulated-age policies such as those paid up at age 55 or 65, you pay premiums until you reach the stated age. In all of these cases, on completion of the scheduled payments, *the insurance remains in force at its face value for the remainder of the insured's life.*

Some insurance companies try to convince consumers to buy limited-payment policies by stressing the "large" savings element that will develop and the fact that the policyholder won't have to pay premiums for his or her entire life. This logic fails on two points. First, for most people the primary purpose of whole life insurance is permanent protection against financial loss resulting from death, not the accumulation of savings. Second, even if people buy continuous-premium whole life (straight life) policies, they need to pay the premium only as long as they wish to keep the policies in force for their full face value. If lifelong death protection is the primary aim of the life insurance policy, the insured should purchase continuous-premium whole life instead of a limited-payment policy. Because more continuous-premium whole life insurance can be purchased with the same number of dollars as limited-payment whole life, people who need whole life insurance are probably better off using continuous-premium (straight) life insurance to get the most from their life insurance dollars. Then, once their insurance needs are reduced, they can convert the policy to a smaller amount of paid-up life insurance. On the other hand, if people have life insurance already in force that is sufficient to protect against income loss, they can use limited-payment policies as part of their savings or retirement plans.

Single Premium

Continuous-premium and limited-payment whole life policies represent methods of acquiring life insurance on an installment basis. In contrast, a *single-premium whole life* policy is purchased with one cash premium payment at the inception of the contract, thus buying life insurance coverage for the rest of your life. The single-premium policy has only limited usefulness in the life insurance programs of most families. However, because of its investment attributes, single-premium life insurance, or *SPLI* for short, appeals to those looking for a *tax-sheltered investment vehicle.* Like any whole life insurance policy, interest/investment earnings within the policy are tax deferred. There is a catch, however: Any cash withdrawals or loans taken against the SPLI cash value before you reach age 59½ will both be taxed as capital gains and be subject to the 10 percent penalty for early withdrawal.

Advantages and Disadvantages of Whole Life

The most noteworthy advantage of whole life insurance is that premium payments contribute toward building an estate, regardless of how long the insured lives. The face value of the policy is paid on death, or alternately the insured can borrow against it or withdraw cash value—which can be significant, as the final column of Exhibit 8.6 shows—when the need for insurance protection has expired.

A corresponding benefit of whole life (except single-premium) is that individuals who need insurance for an entire lifetime can budget their premium payments over a relatively long period, thus eliminating the problems of affordability and uninsurability often encountered with term insurance in later years.

Some people like whole life because the periodic payments force them to save regularly. There is also the favorable tax treatment afforded to accumulated earnings—because your earnings build up on a tax-sheltered basis, the underlying cash value of the policy also increases at a much faster rate than it otherwise would. Insurance experts also point out that the whole life policy offers other potentially valuable options in addition to death protection and cash value. Some of these options include the continuation of coverage after allowing the policy to lapse because premiums were not paid (nonforfeiture option) and the ability to revive an older, favorably priced policy that has lapsed (policy reinstatement). These and other options will be discussed in a later section on insurance contract features.

One disadvantage of whole life insurance is its cost. It provides less death protection per premium dollar than term insurance. Contrast the premiums paid for various whole life products as shown with those paid for term insurance by comparing Exhibits 8.2, 8.3, and 8.6. You can readily see how much more expensive whole life is relative to term life. The reason for the difference? You pay extra for the savings/investment feature included with whole life.

Another frequently cited disadvantage of whole life is that it provides lower yields than many investment vehicles. Returns on most whole life insurance policies are just not very competitive. As with term insurance, the negative aspects of whole life often arise from misuse of the policy. In other words, a *whole life policy should not be used to obtain maximum return on investment.* However, if a person wishes to combine a given amount of death protection for the entire life of the insured (or until the policy is terminated) with a savings plan that provides a *moderate* tax-sheltered rate of return, whole life insurance may be a wise purchase.

One way to keep the cost of whole life down is to consider the purchase of *low-load* whole life insurance. Low-load products are sold directly by insurers to consumers, sometimes via a toll-free number or over the Internet, thereby eliminating sales agents from the transaction. With traditional whole life policies sold by an agent, sales commissions and marketing expenses account for between 100 and 150 percent of the first year's premium, and between 20 and 25 percent of total premiums paid over the life of the policy. In comparison, only about 5 to 10 percent of low-load policy premiums go to cover selling and marketing expenses. As a result, cash values grow much more quickly. In one case a 50-year-old male was able to purchase a low-load policy with a $500,000 death benefit for an annual premium of $7,500. Within 5 years his cash surrender value was projected to be more than $36,000, although a comparable, fully loaded policy was projected to produce only a $24,000 cash value.

Who Should Buy Whole Life Insurance?

Most families also need some amount of permanent insurance and savings, which a continuous-premium whole life policy can satisfy. Some financial advisors recommend that you use cash value insurance to cover your *permanent need for insurance*—the amount your dependents will need regardless of the age at which you die. (Although term insurance is less expensive, you may not be able to buy term insurance as you get older, or it may be too expensive.) Such needs may include final expenses—funeral costs and estate taxes—and either the survivor's retirement need (Period 3 in Worksheet 8.1) or additional insurance coverage, whichever is less. This amount is different for every person. Using these guidelines, the Bensons in our earlier example would need about $147,000 in whole life insurance (in Worksheet 8.1: $15,000 final expenses [Step 1, line 3] plus about $132,000 of Period 3 living expenses [Step 1, line 1d for Period 3 minus Step 2, line 1f for Period 3, i.e., $726,000 − $594,000]) and about another $151,000 in term life (in Worksheet 8.1: about $298,000 [Step 3] minus about $147,000 permanent insurance calculated above). Limited-payment whole life and single-premium whole life policies should be purchased only when the primary goal is savings or additional tax-deferred investments and not protection against financial loss resulting from death.

universal life insurance
A form of permanent cash value insurance that combines term insurance (death benefits) with a tax-sheltered savings/investment account that pays interest at competitive money market rates.

Whole life may make sense in several other situations as well. For example, a family history of heart disease, cancer, or similar conditions may increase your risk of developing health problems and make it hard to qualify for term insurance at a later date. If you are already over 50, term life insurance may be too expensive. Or, perhaps you've "maxed" out your other tax-deferred savings options and want to buy cash value insurance to accumulate additional retirement funds.

Universal Life Insurance

Universal life insurance is another form of permanent cash value insurance that combines term insurance, which provides death benefits, with a tax-sheltered savings/investment account that pays interest, usually at competitive money market rates. The death protection (or pure insurance) portion and the savings portion are identified separately in its premium. This is referred to as *unbundling*. Exhibit 8.7 shows representative premiums and cash values for a $100,000 universal life policy.

EXHIBIT 8.7

Representative Universal Life Insurance Annual Outlays; $100,000 Policy, Preferred Nonsmoker Rates

Universal life premiums are lower than whole life and can vary over the policy's life. After deducting the cost of the death benefit and any administrative fees from your annual contribution, the rest goes into an accumulation account and builds at a variable rate—in this example, the current rate is 7.4 percent. The guaranteed rate, however, is only 4 percent, so your actual cash value may be less.

	Annual Outlay		Premiums Paid through Year 20		Cash Surrender Value at Year 20*	
Age	Male	Female	Male	Female	Male	Female
25	$2,419	$2,358	$ 8,380	$ 7,160	$ 6,091	$ 5,048
30	$2,505	$2,425	$10,100	$ 8,500	$ 8,137	$ 6,176
35	$2,644	$2,534	$12,880	$10,680	$11,235	$ 8,453
40	$2,841	$2,682	$16,820	$13,640	$15,107	$11,399
50	$1,469	$1,146	$29,380	$22,920	$25,168	$20,074
60	$2,598	$1,992	$51,960	$39,840	$36,638	$32,633

*Based on an assumed annual rate of 7.4 percent.

Traditionally, for whole life insurance, you pay a premium to purchase a stated face amount of coverage in a policy with a *fixed cash-value schedule*. With universal life, part of your premium payment pays administrative fees and the remainder is put into the cash value, or savings portion of the policy, where it earns a certain rate of return. This rate of earnings varies with market yields, but is guaranteed to be more than some stipulated minimum rate (say, 3 percent). Then, each month the cost of 1 month's term insurance is withdrawn from the cash value to purchase the required death protection. As long as there's enough in the savings portion to buy death protection, the policy will stay in force. Should the cash value grow to an unusually large amount, the amount of insurance coverage has to be increased in order for the policy to retain its favorable tax treatment (tax laws require that the death benefits in a universal life policy *must always exceed the cash value* by a stipulated amount).

The clear separation of the protection and savings elements in the universal policy has raised the question of whether or not this type of insurance is in fact whole life insurance. This question is important because the accumulation of cash values in whole life policies arises partly from interest credited to them. Under present tax laws, *this accumulation occurs tax free as long as the cash value does not exceed the total premiums paid to the insurer.* However, if a whole life policy is surrendered for its cash value, and that cash value exceeds the premiums paid, then *the gain* is taxed. As a result of an Internal Revenue Service ruling and federal legislation, universal life policies enjoy the same favorable tax treatment as do other forms of whole life insurance—that is, death benefits are tax-free and, prior to the death of the insured, amounts credited to the cash value, including investment earnings, accumulate on a tax-deferred basis. The insurance company sends the insured an annual statement summarizing the monthly credits of interest and deductions of expenses.

Within the basic structure of a universal life insurance policy, there are two types of death protection. The first type, known as Option A, provides a level death benefit. As the cash value increases, the amount of pure insurance protection *decreases.* The second type, Option B, provides a stated amount of insurance plus the accumulated cash value. Therefore, the death benefit at any time varies with the rate of earnings on the savings plan and will increase along with the accumulated cash value.

Advantages and Disadvantages of Universal Life

As with any insurance policy, universal life has its pros and cons. Among the advantages:

- **Flexibility:** The annual premium you pay can be increased or decreased from year to year, because the cost of the death protection *may be covered from either the annual premium or the accumulation account* (that is, cash value). If the accumulation account is adequate, you can use it to pay the annual premium. In addition, the death benefit can be increased or decreased, and you can change from the level benefit type of policy to the cash value plus a stated amount of insurance. Note, however, that evidence of insurability is usually required if the death benefit is to be increased. This flexibility allows you to adapt the death benefit to your life-cycle needs—for example, increasing the death benefit when you have another child and decreasing it when your children are grown.
- **Savings feature:** A universal life insurance policy credits cash value at the "current" rate of interest. For example, the *current* rate of interest may be 4.5 percent, compared with a *guaranteed* minimum rate of 3 percent. Find out the benchmark used to determine the current rate of interest; the 90-day U.S. Treasury bill rate is often used.

Universal life's flexibility in making premium payments, although an attractive feature, is also one of its major drawbacks:

- **Changing premiums and protection levels:** A policyholder who economizes on premium payments in early years may find that he or she must pay higher premiums than originally planned in later policy years to keep the policy in force. Indeed, some policyholders buy universal life expecting their premiums to vanish once cash value builds to a certain level. All too often, however, the premiums never disappear altogether, or, if they do, they reappear when interest rates fall below the rate in effect at the time the policy was purchased.

- **Charges or fees:** Universal life carries heavy fees compared to other policy types: the front-end load or commission on the first premium, the expense charge on each annual premium, investment expense charged by the insurer in determining the "current" rate of return, and other charges. Most states require the insurance company to issue an annual disclosure statement that spells out premiums paid, expenses and mortality costs, interest earned, and beginning and ending cash values.

Who Should Buy Universal Life Insurance?

Universal life is a suitable choice if you're looking for a savings vehicle with greater potential returns than a whole life policy offers. Its flexible nature makes it particularly useful for people who anticipate changes in their current need for death protection. For example, if you're recently married and expect to have children in the future, a universal life policy will allow you to increase the death benefit as your family grows.

smart.sites

For more details about various life insurance products and policy types, turn to Insure.com's searchable database of over 3,000 articles on insurance topics at **http://www.insure.com**.

Other Types of Life Insurance

In addition to term, whole life, and universal life, you can buy several other types of life insurance products, including variable life insurance, group life, and other special-purpose life policies such as credit life, mortgage life, and industrial life insurance. These insurance products serve very diverse needs. Some may help you meet specific needs, while others are simply alternatives to traditional types of life insurance.

Variable Life Insurance

variable life insurance Life insurance in which the benefits are related to the returns being generated on the investments selected by the policy holder.

A **variable life insurance** policy goes further than whole and universal life policies in combining death benefits and savings. The policyholder decides how to invest the money in the savings (cash value) component. The investment accounts are set up just like *mutual funds,* and most firms that offer variable life policies let you choose from a full menu of different funds, ranging from money market accounts and bond funds to international investments or aggressively managed stock funds. Unlike whole or universal life policies, however, *no minimum return is guaranteed.* In addition, as the name implies, the amount of insurance coverage provided will vary with the profits (and losses) generated in the investment account. Thus, in variable life insurance policies, the amount of death benefits payable are, for the most part, related to the policies' investment returns. Exhibit 8.8 demonstrates how two possible investment return scenarios would affect the cash value and death benefits of a variable life insurance policy for a 45-year-old, nonsmoking male over a 20-year period.

Although all these features may sound great, it's important to keep in mind that variable life puts more emphasis on investments than any other life insurance product. Indeed, many observers view variable life more as an investment vehicle than a life insurance policy—it is an investment product wrapped around just enough life insurance coverage to make it legal. Thus, if you want the benefits of higher investment returns, you must also be willing to assume the risks of reduced insurance coverage. Clearly, *you should use extreme care when buying variable life insurance.*

EXHIBIT 8.8

Representative Variable Life Insurance Values; $100,000 Policy, Preferred Nonsmoker, Male, Age 45

Variable life insurance pays a death benefit related to the policy's investment returns. The cash value created over the life of the policy is also related to investment return. The illustration below shows the effects of 6 percent and 12 percent annual returns over a 20-year period. Lower returns will result in lower cash value and death benefits; higher returns will result in higher cash value and death benefits.

		6% return		12% return	
Policy Year	Total Premiums Paid	Cash value	Death benefit	Cash value	Death benefit
1	$ 1,575	$ 995	$100,995	$ 1,064	$101,064
5	$ 8,705	$ 5,244	$105,244	$ 5,705	$104,869
10	$19,810	$10,592	$110,592	$ 15,365	$115,365
15	$33,986	$15,093	$115,093	$ 27,688	$127,688
20	$52,079	$17,080	$117,080	$ 43,912	$143,913

smart.sites

Find out how well Prudential Insurance variable life policies are performing at **http://www.prudential.com/insurance**, where you will also find a variety of interactive tools to educate yourself about the company's products.

Group Life Insurance

Under **group life insurance**, one master policy is issued, and each eligible member of the group receives a certificate of insurance. Group life is nearly always term insurance, and the premium is based on the characteristics of the group as a whole, rather than related to any specific individual. Employers often provide group life insurance as a fringe benefit for their employees. However, just about any type of group (be it a labor union, a professional association, or an alumni organization) can secure a group life policy, as long as the insurance is only incidental to the reason for the group.

group life insurance
A type of life insurance that provides a master policy for a group and each eligible member of the group receives a certificate of insurance.

Accounting for about one-third of all life insurance in the United States, group life insurance is one of the fastest-growing areas of insurance. Many group life policies now offer coverage for dependents in addition to the group members. In addition, group life policies generally provide that if individual members leave the group, they may continue the coverage by converting their protection to individually issued whole life policies—such conversion normally does not require evidence of insurability as long as it occurs within a specified period. Of course, after conversion, the individual pays all premiums. Before buying additional coverage purchased through a group plan or converting a group policy to an individual one, it's important to compare rates. Often the premiums are more expensive than other readily available sources of term insurance.

As noted in Chapters 1 and 2, the availability of group coverage through employee benefit programs should be considered when developing a life insurance program. However, because of its potentially temporary nature and relatively low benefit amount (often equal to about 1 year's salary), it should fulfill only low-priority insurance needs. Only in rare cases should a family rely solely on group life insurance to fulfill its primary income-protection requirements.

Other Special-Purpose Life Policies

credit life insurance A type of life insurance sold in conjunction with installment loans; usually a term policy of less than 5 years, with a face value that corresponds to the outstanding balance on a loan.

mortgage life insurance A term policy designed to pay off the mortgage balance in the event of the borrower's death.

industrial life insurance (home service life) A type of whole life insurance issued in policies with relatively small face amounts, often $1,000 or less; agents call on policyholders weekly or monthly to collect premiums.

Use caution before buying one of the following types of life insurance:

- **Credit Life Insurance:** Banks, finance companies, and other lenders generally sell **credit life insurance** in conjunction with installment loans. Usually credit life is a term policy of less than 5 years, with a face value that corresponds to the outstanding balance on the loan. Although liquidating debts on the death of a family breadwinner is often desirable, it's usually preferable to do so through an individual's term or whole life insurance rather than buying a separate credit life insurance policy. This is because credit life is one of the most expensive forms of life insurance—and one you should therefore avoid.
- **Mortgage Life Insurance: Mortgage life insurance** is a term policy designed to pay off the mortgage balance on a home in the event of the borrower's death. As in the case of credit life, this need can usually be met less expensively by shopping the market for a suitable decreasing-term policy.
- **Industrial Life Insurance:** Now called **home service life**, this whole life insurance is issued in policies with small face amounts, often $1,000 or less. Agents call on policyholders weekly or monthly to collect the premiums. The term *industrial* became popular when they were first sold primarily to low-paid industrial wage earners. Industrial life insurance costs a good deal more per $1,000 of coverage than regular whole life policies, primarily because of its high marketing costs. Even so, some insurance authorities believe that industrial life insurance offers the only practical way to deliver coverage to low-income families.

Concept ✓

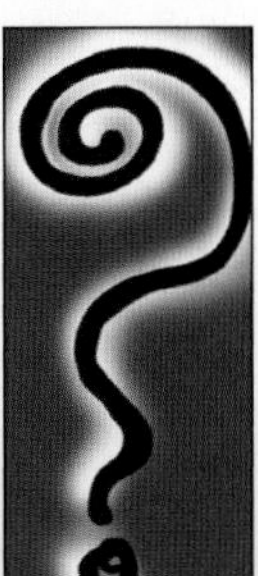

8-9. What is *term life insurance?* Describe some of the common types of term life insurance policies.

8-10. What are the advantages and disadvantages of term life insurance?

8-11. Explain how *whole life insurance* offers financial protection to an individual throughout his or her life.

8-12. Describe the different types of whole life policies. What are the advantages and disadvantages of whole life insurance?

8-13. What is *universal life insurance?* Explain how it differs from whole life and *variable life insurance*.

8-14. Explain how *group life insurance* differs from standard term life insurance. What do employees stand to gain from group life?

8-15. Why should the following types of life insurance contracts be avoided? (a) *credit life insurance*, (b) *mortgage life insurance*, (c) *industrial life insurance (home service life)*.

LG5 BUYING LIFE INSURANCE

Once you've evaluated your personal financial needs and become familiar with the basic life insurance options, you're ready to begin shopping for a life insurance policy. Exhibit 8.9 summarizes the major advantages and disadvantages of the most popular types of life insurance we've discussed in this chapter.

Several factors should be considered in making the final purchase decision: (1) a comparison of the costs and features of competitive products, (2) selecting a financially heathy insurance company, and (3) choosing a good agent.

EXHIBIT 8.9

Advantages and Disadvantages of the Most Popular Types of Life Insurance

The major advantages and disadvantages of the most popular types of life insurance are summarized below. They should be considered when shopping for life insurance.

Type of Policy	Advantages	Disadvantages
Term	Low initial premiums	Provides only temporary coverage for a set period
	Simple, easy to buy	May have to pay higher premiums when policy is renewed
Whole Life	Permanent coverage	Cost: provides less death protection per premium dollar than term
	Savings vehicle: cash value builds as premiums are paid	Often provides lower yields than other investment vehicles
	Some tax advantages on accumulated earnings	Sales commissions and marketing expenses can increase costs of fully loaded policy
Universal Life	Permanent coverage	Can be difficult to evaluate true cost at time of purchase; insurance carrier may levy costly fees and charges
	Flexible; lets insured adapt level of protection and cost of premiums	
	Savings vehicle: cash value builds at current rate of interest	
	Savings and death protection identified separately	
Variable Life	Investment vehicle: insured decides how cash value will be invested	Higher risk

Compare Costs and Features

The cost of a life insurance policy can vary considerably from company to company, even for the same amount and type of coverage. Comparison shopping, therefore, can save you thousands of dollars over the life of your policy. For example, the total cost for a 10-year, $250,000, term life policy at preferred rates for a 25-year-old can range from $1,170 to over $2,000. Exhibit 8.10 provides a quick overview of differences in the key features of various types of life insurance.

If you smoke or have a health problem, such as high cholesterol or high blood pressure, spending time to check out several companies can really pay off. Some companies

EXHIBIT 8.10

Key Features of Various Types of Life Insurance

Differences in the key features of various types of life insurance are noted below. It is important to compare both costs and features when shopping for life insurance.

Feature	Term	Whole Life	Universal Life
Death protection	High	Moderate	Low to high
Coverage period	Temporary for set period	Ongoing	Ongoing
Costs	Low fixed premiums, no fees	High fixed premiums, may also be charged fees	Can vary from high to low, may also be charged fees
Return on Investment?	None	Yes, moderate	Yes, return can vary
Tax Advantages	No	Yes	Yes

are more willing to accept these risks than others and they may even give you preferred rates if, within a certain period, you correct the problem. However, until you do your homework, you won't know which policy offers you the coverage you need at the lowest cost. Keep in mind that if you have an unusual health problem or some other type of complication, an agent-sold policy may actually be cheaper than the low-cost alternatives.

It's not enough, however, to look only at current rates. You'll also need to ask how long the rates are locked in and about guaranteed rates—the maximum you can be charged when you renew. Although a guaranteed policy may cost another $20 a year, you won't be hit with unexpected rate increases later. Know how long you need the coverage and find the best rates for the total period; low premiums for a 5-year policy may jump when you renew for additional coverage. In addition, be sure you are getting the features you need, like the convertibility of term policies.

Finally, be sure the policies you are comparing *are similar in terms of provisions and amounts.* In other words, you should not compare a $100,000 term life policy from one company with a $150,000 universal life policy from another. Instead, *you should first decide how much and what kind of policy you want and then compare costs.* For similar cash value policies, you may find it useful to compare interest-adjusted cost indexes that are often shown on policy illustrations. The *surrender cost index* measures the policy's cost if you surrender it at a certain point, typically 10 or 20 years, assuming that premiums and dividends earn 5 percent interest. The *net payment cost index* is calculated in a similar manner but assumes that the policy is kept in force.

Luckily, gathering the information that allows you to compare costs and features has never been easier. Term life quote services, available over the phone or on the Internet, can streamline the selection process by providing you, free of charge, with the names of several companies offering the lowest-cost policies based on your specifications. For example, *Quotesmith* (800-431-1147), *Life Quote* (800-521-7873), *TermQuote* (800-444-8376), and *SelectQuote* (800-343-1985) maintain databases of life insurance policy costs for

Money in Action

Agent or No Agent?

There's an old axiom in the insurance industry that life insurance is sold, not bought. Traditionally, most life insurance products have been sold through insurance agents who act as intermediaries between consumers and insurance companies. Today, however, life insurance shoppers have more options. How do you decide which purchasing method is best for your particular needs?

Agents are adept at helping consumers determine their life insurance needs and can be a valuable source of advice if you're considering complex insurance products, such as cash-value policies. Using an agent also makes sense for people who have health conditions or other risk factors that may make finding insurance coverage difficult. After your death, an agent can also help steer your beneficiaries through the process of filing an insurance claim.

Agents are licensed by their state insurance commission and are expected to meet certain standards of performance. However, just because an agent is licensed, don't automatically assume that he or she will always act in your best interests. Many insurance agents receive commissions from insurance carriers for selling certain life insurance products. Therefore, it's a smart idea to ask up front if they will be receiving a commission on any product they suggest.

If you already have a pretty good idea of your life insurance needs, consider other purchasing options. Most insurance companies now let consumers buy policies directly, either over the phone or through the Internet. Your bank or financial institution may also sell life insurance. The drawback of buying insurance directly, however, is that you will probably have to do your own research to pinpoint the best deal.

That's where Internet insurance sites come in. Once you answer a few basic questions, sites such as **http://quickquote.com**, **http://intelliquote.com**, or **http://yourlowestrate.com** give you a fast list of instant quotes from higher-rated insurance carriers. The side-by-side comparison makes it easy to compare insurance carriers, policies, and

...continued on next page

various companies and will also act as your agent to buy the policy if you wish. In addition, Quotesmith and TermQuote provide quotes for both whole life and term insurance. Also, don't overlook companies who sell directly to the public or offer low-load policies, such as John Alden, Ameritas, Lincoln Benefit, and USAA.

Probably the fastest growing source of life insurance quotes and policies in recent years is the Internet. Indeed, it's now easier than ever to not only obtain quick, real-time quotes, but also buy insurance electronically! Buying on the Internet allows you to avoid dealing with pesky insurance salespeople, plus you can purchase the policies (usually term insurance only) on very cost-effective terms. For example, one major life insurer offers discounts of up to 20 percent for term life policies purchased online. Of course, you'll still need a physical exam, but often the insurance company will send a qualified technician/nurse to your house or office to take a blood sample and other basic readings. The *Money in Action* box on this page will help you decide whether to use an agent or surf the Internet to buy life insurance.

Financial Road Sign

What to Expect from a Life Insurance Medical Exam

If you're buying life insurance—especially large policies—you'll often be asked to take a medical exam before the policy is approved by the insurance company. Here's what you should know before taking one:

- Don't fudge your medical history—insurance companies are able to track down your medical background through insurance industry information clearinghouses.
- A paramedical professional will conduct the exam, which can sometimes be done at your home or office.
- Samples of blood, urine, and even saliva may be taken to test for the presence of HIV antibodies, cholesterol, diabetes, and other medical issues. Blood pressure will also be taken.
- If you're buying larger policies or are older than 40, an EKG, x-rays, or even a treadmill test may be required.
- For best results, avoid drinking alcoholic beverages and caffeinated beverages as well as smoking or chewing tobacco in the hours before the exam. Don't engage in strenuous exercise for at least 24 hours.

Sources: Adapted from "Life Insurance Health Exam," *Life Insurance In-Depth*, **http://www.lifeinsuranceindepth.com/medical-exam.html**, downloaded October 4, 2003; and "The Lowdown on Life Insurance Medical Exams," Money Central, **http://moneycentral.msn.com**, downloaded October 1, 2003.

smart.sites

Discover how easy it is to get quotes on term and whole life policies at QuickQuote's life insurance center, **http://www.quickquote.com/lihome.html**.

prices. Although most online shopping sites provide quotes only for term insurance, some now offer quotes on other options, such as whole and variable life policies. Click on the option you're interested in and an application will pop up.

However, before you agree to buy via the Internet, bear in mind that life insurance decisions can be complex. If you're not confident of your knowledge and understanding of the options, you might feel more comfortable asking an agent to walk you through the final decision.

Critical Thinking Questions

1. When should you consider buying life insurance through an agent?
2. What questions should you ask when choosing an insurance agent?
3. What are some of the advantages and disadvantages of buying life insurance online?

Sources: Jim Freer, "It's Your Life: Decide How to Insure It," *The South Florida Business Journal*, September 1, 2003, downloaded from **http://www.bizjournals.com**; Niles Howard, "Locking in the Best Policy," *On Investing*, Summer 2002, pp. 21–25; Mark Wesson and Ken Kehrer, "How Banks Are Competing for Life Insurance Sales," *Birmingham Business Journal*, September 30, 2002, downloaded from **http://www.bizjournals.com**.

Select an Insurance Company

Selecting a life insurance company is an important part of shopping for life insurance. In addition to looking for a firm that provides reasonably priced products, attractive contract features, and good customer service, it is vital to consider the financial health of any insurance firm before buying a life insurance policy. You want to be certain that the company will be around and have the assets to pay your beneficiaries should you die. Even before you die, however, the financial stability of your insurance company is important. If the company fails, you may be forced to buy a new policy at less-favorable rates.

To narrow your choices, age and size are useful indicators. Unless a good reason exists to do otherwise, you should probably limit the companies you consider to those that have been doing business for 25 years or more and that have annual premium volume in excess of $50 million. Although these criteria will rule out a lot of smaller firms, there will still be plenty of companies left from which to choose. You may also find that one company is preferable for your term protection and another for your whole life needs.

Factors to consider before making the final choice include the firm's reputation, financial history, commissions and other fees, and the specifics of their policy provisions. If you're choosing a company for a cash value life insurance policy, the company's investment performance and dividend history is also an important consideration.

smart.sites

How satisfied are the customers of your prospective insurance company? The National Association of Insurance Commissioners site, **http://www.naic.org/cis**, lets you see how many consumer complaints have been filed against each company.

How do you find all of this information? Luckily, private rating agencies have done much of the work for you. These agencies use publicly available financial data from insurance companies to analyze their debt structure, pricing practices, and management strategies in an effort to assess their financial stability. The purpose is to evaluate the insurance company's ability to pay future claims made by policyholders, known as their *claims paying ability*. In most cases insurance firms pay ratings agencies a fee for this rating service. The ratings agencies then give each insurance firm a "grade" based on their analysis of the firm's financial data.

The three biggest rating agencies include A.M. Best Company, Moody's Investor Service, and Standard & Poor's Corporation (S&P). Two smaller, but growing, rating agencies are Fitch Inc. and Weiss Ratings, Inc. Weiss does not charge a fee to the insurance firms it examines. Exhibit 8.11 provides detailed contact information for each of the major rating agencies, including their Internet addresses. Basic rating information is usually free of charge at these sites. You can also usually find these ratings on the insurance company's Web site, or you can ask your agent how the company is rated by Best's, Moody's, and S&P.

smart.sites

A.M. Best's site, **http://www.ambest.com**, offers more than insurance company ratings. The site also has the latest insurance industry news and trends, an insurance products guide, and links to state insurance regulatory agencies.

Each rating agency uses its own grading system. When looking at these ratings, however, keep several things in mind. With the exception of Moody's and Weiss, the ratings agencies will not publish a firm's rating if the insurer requests that it be withheld. Obviously, an insurance firm receiving a low rating is more likely to suppress publication, something that should be viewed as a clear signal that it is an insurance company to avoid. Also, remember that a high rating doesn't ensure lasting financial stability. Even highly rated insurance firms can quickly encounter financial difficulties. In fact, in a recent report A.M. Best noted that fewer life insurers are receiving top ratings. It's a good idea, therefore, to check the ratings of your insurance carrier periodically even after you have purchased a policy.

Most experts agree that it's wise to purchase life insurance only from insurance companies that are assigned ratings by at least two of the major rating agencies and are consistently rated in the top two or three categories (say, Aaa, Aa1, or Aa2 by Moody's) by each of the major agencies from which they received ratings.

Financial Road Sign

Watch Out for Unethical Sales Practices

Although most insurance agents are helpful and professional, some may try to build their commissions with unethical sales practices. Here are four warning signs to watch for:

1. Suggestions to replace an existing policy that already has a large cash value with a new policy.
2. Promises that premiums will "vanish" in just 3 or 4 years.
3. Unrealistically high interest rates used to demonstrate how a policy value will grow.
4. Pressure to borrow from a whole life policy to buy a variable life annuity.

Source: Adapted from Ginger Applegarth, "How to Spot Unethical Sales Practices," *CNBC on MSN Money,* downloaded from **http://moneycentral.msn.com**.

EXHIBIT 8.11

Major Insurance Rating Agencies

The three biggest insurance rating agencies are A.M. Best Company, Moody's Investor Services, and Standard & Poor's Corporation; Fitch Inc. and Weiss Ratings, Inc. are smaller but growing rating agencies. Contact information for each of these agencies is given here.

A.M. Best Company
Internet address: **http://www.ambest.com**
Phone: 800-424-2378
Top three grades: A++, A+, and A

Moody's Investor Services
Internet address: **http://www.moodys.com**
Phone: 212-553-0377
Top three grades: Aaa, Aa1, and Aa2

Standard & Poor's Corporation
Internet address:
http://www.standardandpoors.com
Phone: 212-208-1527
Top three grades: AAA, AA+, and AA

Fitch Inc.
Internet address:
http://www.fitchratings.com
Phone: 212-908-0500
Top three grades: AAA, AA+, and AA

Weiss Ratings, Inc.
Internet address:
http://www.weissratings.com
Phone: 800-289-9222
Top three grades: A, A-, B

Choose an Agent

There's an old axiom in the life insurance business that life insurance is sold, not bought. Life insurance agents play a major role in most people's decision to buy life insurance. Unless you plan to buy all of your life insurance via the Internet, the selection of a good life insurance agent is important because you will be relying on him or her for guidance with respect to some very important financial decisions. Don't assume that just because agents are licensed they are competent and will serve your best interests. Consider an agent's formal and professional level of educational attainment. Does the agent have a college degree with a major in business or insurance? Does the agent have a professional designation, such as Chartered Life Underwriter (CLU), Chartered Financial Consultant (ChFC), or Certified Financial Planner (CFP®)? These designations are awarded only to those who meet certain experience requirements and pass comprehensive examinations in such fields as life and health insurance, estate and pension planning, investments, and federal income tax law.

In addition, observe how an agent reacts to your questions. Does he or she use fancy buzzwords and stock answers or instead listen attentively and, after a period of thought, logically answer your questions? These and other personal characteristics should be considered. In most instances, you should talk with several agents and discuss the pros and cons of each agent with your spouse before committing yourself. Then, when you have decided, call and ask that agent to return for another visit.

When seeking a good life insurance agent, try to obtain recommendations from other professionals who work with agents. For example, bankers in trust departments, attorneys, and accountants who are specialists in estate planning are usually good sources. In contrast, be a bit wary of selecting an agent simply because of the agent's aggressiveness in soliciting your patronage.

Financial Road Sign

How to Understand Insurance Illustrations

Life insurance agents and companies often use insurance policy illustrations to help sell life insurance products. These sales materials show financial projections for how a policy is expected to perform over time, but they can be difficult to use when comparing different policies. Here's what to look for:

- The Interest Adjusted Net Cost (IANC)—All illustrations must include this index which provides the cost per $1,000 for projected death benefits and policy cash value.
- Payoff projections—These numbers show the policy payout if current interest rates continue into the future. Always ask for a second illustration that shows what will happen if the rates drop by at least two percentage points.
- For a variable insurance product, an agent with a National Association of Securities Dealers (NASD) license—By law, only NASD-licensed agents can explain policy illustrations for these policies, because they are considered an investment product.

Sources: Adapted from Ginger Applegarth, "Avoid the Insurance Illustration Trap," available at Money Central, **http://moneycentral.msn.com**; and "Life Insurance Illustrations," *Life Insurance in Depth*, **http://www.lifeinsuranceindepth.com**, downloaded October 4, 2003.

Concept ✓

8-16. Briefly describe the steps to take when you shop for and buy life insurance.

8-17. Briefly describe the insurance company ratings assigned by A.M. Best, Moody's, and S&P's. Why is it important to know how a company is rated? What ratings would you look for when selecting a life insurance company? Explain.

8-18. What characteristics would be most important to you when choosing an insurance agent?

smart.sites

Looking for an insurance agent? Try **http://www.iiaa.org**, a site sponsored by the Independent Insurance Agents of America, Inc.

KEY FEATURES OF LIFE INSURANCE POLICIES

LG6

When you buy a life insurance policy, you will enter into a contract with the insurance company. The provisions in this contract spell out the policyholder's and the insurer's rights and obligations, and the features of the policy being purchased. Unfortunately, there's no such thing as a standard life insurance policy. Each insurance company uses its own wording. Policies can also vary from state to state, depending on the law of the state where the policy is sold. Nevertheless, certain elements are common in most life insurance contracts.

LIFE INSURANCE CONTRACT FEATURES

The key features found in most life insurance contracts include the beneficiary clause, settlement options, policy loans, premium payments, grace period, nonforfeiture options, policy reinstatement, and change of policy.

Beneficiary Clause

The **beneficiary** is the person who will receive the death benefits of the policy on the insured's death. All life insurance policies should have one or more beneficiaries. Otherwise, death benefits are paid to the estate of the deceased and are subject to the often lengthy and expensive legal procedure of going through probate. An insured person is able to name both a *primary beneficiary* and various *contingent beneficiaries.* The primary beneficiary will receive the entire death benefit if he or she is surviving when the insured dies. If the primary beneficiary does not survive the insured, the insurer will distribute the death benefits to the contingent beneficiary or beneficiaries. If neither primary nor contingent beneficiaries are living at the death of the insured, the death benefits pass to the estate of the insured and are distributed by the probate court according to the insured's will or, if no will exists, according to state law.

beneficiary
A person who receives the death benefits of a life insurance policy on the insured's death.

When naming the beneficiary, make sure the identification is clear. For example, a man could buy a policy and simply designate the beneficiary as "my wife." However, if he later divorces and remarries, there could be a controversy as to which "wife" was entitled to the benefits. Obviously, you should consider changing your named beneficiary if circumstances, such as marital status, change. The person you name as a beneficiary can be changed at any time as long as you did not indicate an *irrevocable beneficiary* when you took out the policy. Thus, if your wishes change, all you need to do is notify the insurance company—easy to do but also easy to forget.

Settlement Options

Insurance companies generally offer several ways of paying life insurance policy death proceeds. How the insurance benefits will be distributed can be permanently established by the policyholder before his or her death, or left up to the beneficiary when the policy matures on the insured's death.

- **Lump sum:** This is the most common settlement option, chosen by more than 95 percent of policyholders. The entire death benefit is paid in a single amount, allowing beneficiaries to use or invest the proceeds soon after death occurs.
- **Interest only:** The insurance company keeps policy proceeds for a specified time; the beneficiary receives interest payments, usually at some guaranteed rate. This option can be useful when there is no current need for the principal—for example, proceeds could be left on deposit until children go to college, with interest supplementing family income. Typically, however, interest rates paid by insurers are lower than those available on other savings vehicles.

- **Fixed-period:** The face amount of the policy, along with interest earned, is paid to the beneficiary over a fixed time period. For example, a 55-year-old beneficiary may need additional income until Social Security benefits start.
- **Fixed-amount:** The beneficiary receives policy proceeds in regular payments of a fixed amount until the proceeds run out.
- **Life income:** The insurer guarantees to pay the beneficiary a certain payment for the rest of his or her life, based on the beneficiary's sex, age when benefits start, life expectancy, the policy face value, and interest rate assumptions. This option appeals to beneficiaries who don't want to outlive the income from policy proceeds and be dependent on others for support. An interesting variation of this settlement option is the *life-income-with-period-certain option,* whereby the company guarantees a specified number of payments that pass to a secondary beneficiary if the original benificiary dies before the period ends.

The *Money in Action* box on pages 350–351 provides useful advice with regard to filing a life insurance claim when the insured dies.

Policy Loans

policy loan
An advance, secured by the cash value of a whole life insurance policy, made by an insurer to the policyholder.

An advance made by a life insurance company to a policyholder against a whole life policy is called a **policy loan**. These loans are secured by the cash value of the life insurance policy. Although these loans do *not* have to be repaid, any balance plus interest on the loan remaining at the death of the insured is *subtracted from the proceeds of the policy.* Typically policies offer either a fixed-rate loan or a rate that varies with market interest rates on high-quality bonds. Some policies let the insured choose whether the loans will be at fixed or variable rates. Only take out a policy loan if your estate is large enough to cover the accompanying loss of death proceeds if the loan is not repaid. Remember that life insurance is intended to provide basic financial protection for your dependents, and spending those proceeds prematurely definitely defeats the purpose of life insurance. A word of caution: *Be very careful with these loans because unless certain conditions are met, the IRS may treat them as withdrawals, meaning they could be subject to tax penalties.* If you're in any way unsure, consult your insurance agent or a tax advisor.

Premium Payments

All life insurance contracts have a provision that specifies when premiums, which are normally paid in advance, are due. With most insurers, the policyholder may elect to pay premiums annually, semiannually, quarterly, or monthly. In most cases, insurance companies charge a fee if you decide to pay more often than annually.

Grace Period

The *grace period* permits the policyholder to retain full death protection for a short period (usually 31 days) after missing a premium payment date. In other words, you won't lose your insurance protection just because you're a little late in making the premium payment. If the insured dies during the grace period, the face amount of the policy less the unpaid premium is paid to the beneficiary.

Nonforfeiture Options

As discussed earlier, a *nonforfeiture option* provides a cash value life insurance policyholder with some benefits even when a policy is terminated prior to its maturity. State laws require that all permanent whole, universal, or variable life policies (and term contracts that cover an extended period) contain a nonforfeiture provision. Instead of just

Money in Action

How to File a Life Insurance Claim

Although no one likes to deal with paperwork immediately after a loved one's death, filing a life insurance claim should not be delayed. Life insurance proceeds can provide surviving family members with access to cash quickly so they can meet pressing needs.

First, identify the existence of all life insurance policies. Ideally, every person should leave clear instructions for their heirs concerning their life insurance that includes the policy itself and contact information for the insured's insurance agent or insurance company. If this information is available, call your loved one's agent or broker immediately. They can help you sort through the required paperwork and act as an intermediary with the insurance company.

Never assume that the deceased didn't have life insurance. It's always a good idea to check with current and former employers to see if group life insurance was provided. Many banks, credit unions, and credit card companies also offer free life insurance to their customers, so contact your relative's financial institutions as well. The deceased's lawyer, banker, or accountant may also know where the insured had his or her life insurance policy. If all else fails, write to the Missing Policy Service at the American Council of Life Insurance, 1001 Pennsylvania Avenue, NW, Washington, DC 20004-2599. For a nominal fee, the Council will contact 100 large insurance companies in an effort to locate life insurance information.

Once each insurance policy has been identified, contact the issuing insurance companies for the necessary forms to file a claim. Most insurance companies will ask each adult beneficiary to file a "proof of death" form and require you to provide at least one certified copy of the insured's death certificate. If the insured didn't specify a payment option when the policy was purchased, the beneficiaries will also be asked to specify how they wish to receive payments.

After you submit the paperwork, the insurance company will confirm that the policy is valid and

...continued on next page

taking a check in the amount of the cash value of the policy, insurance companies usually offer the two options—*paid-up insurance* and *extended-term insurance*—described below.

- **Paid-Up Insurance:** The policyholder receives a policy exactly like the terminated one, except with a lower face value. In effect, the policyholder uses the cash value to buy a new, single-premium policy. For example, a policy canceled after 10 years might have a cash value of $90.84 per $1,000 of face value, which will buy $236 of paid-up whole life insurance. The cash value continues to grow because of future interest earnings, even though the policyholder makes no further premium payments. This option is useful when a person's income and need for death protection declines—when he or she reaches age 60 or 65, for example—yet that person still wants some coverage.
- **Extended-Term Insurance:** The insured uses the accumulated cash value to buy a term life policy for the same face value as the lapsed policy. The coverage period is based on the amount of term protection a single-premium payment (equal to the total cash value) buys at the insured's present age. This option usually goes into effect automatically if the policyholder quits paying premiums and gives no instructions to the insurer.

Policy Reinstatement

As long as a whole life policy is under the reduced paid-up insurance option or the extended-term insurance option, the policyholder may reinstate the original policy by paying all back premiums plus interest at a stated rate, and providing evidence that he or she can pass a physical examination and meet any other insurability requirements. *Reinstatement* basically revives the original contractual relationship between the company and the policyholder. Most often, the policyholder must reinstate the policy within a specified period (3 to 5 years) after the policy has lapsed. However, before exercising a reinstatement option, a policyholder should determine whether buying a new policy (from the same or a different company) might be less costly.

Change of Policy

Many life insurance contracts contain a provision that permits the insured to switch from one policy form to another. For instance, policyholders may decide that they would rather have paid-up at age 65 policies as opposed to their current continuous-premium whole life policies. A change of policy provision would allow this change without penalty. When policyholders change from high- to lower-premium policies, they may need to prove insurability. This requirement reduces the possibility of adverse selection against the insurance company.

process the settlement. If everything is in order, the beneficiaries should receive payment within a few weeks.

Critical Thinking Questions

1. Why is it important to file life insurance claims as soon as possible?
2. What are three approaches for finding out about a deceased loved one's insurance coverage?
3. What information is needed when filing an insurance claim?

Sources: Michelle Martin, "Making a Claim—How the Process Works," Insweb.com, **http://www.insweb.com**, downloaded September 28, 2003; Charles K. Plotnick and Stephan R. Leimberg, *How to Settle an Estate,* (New York: Penguin Putnam Inc.), 1998, pp.100–104, "Life Insurance Claims—Here's What to Do," Illinois Association of Insurance and Financial Advisors, **http://www.iaifa.com**, downloaded September 20, 2003.

Other Policy Features

In addition to the key contractual features described in the preceding section, here are some other policy features to consider:

multiple indemnity clause
A clause in a life insurance policy that typically doubles or triples the policy's face amount in the event the insured dies in an accident.

disability clause
A clause in a life insurance contract containing a waiver-of-premium benefit alone or coupled with disability income.

guaranteed purchase option
An option in a life insurance contract giving the policyholder the right to purchase additional coverage at stipulated intervals without providing evidence of insurability.

- **Multiple Indemnity Clause: Multiple indemnity clauses** increase the face amount of the policy, most often doubling or tripling it, if the insured dies in an accident. This benefit is usually offered to the policyholder at a small additional cost. Many insurance authorities dismiss the use of a multiple indemnity benefit as irrational. This coverage should be ignored as a source of funds when programming insurance needs because it provides no protection in the event of death due to illness.
- **Disability Clause**: A **disability clause** may contain a waiver-of-premium benefit alone or coupled with disability income. A *waiver-of-premium benefit* excuses the payment of premiums on the life insurance policy if the insured becomes totally and permanently disabled prior to age 60 (or sometimes age 65). Under the *disability income portion,* the insured is granted not only a waiver of premium, but also receives a monthly income equal to $5 or $10 per $1,000 of policy face value. Some insurers will continue these payments for the life of the insured, whereas others terminate them at age 65. Disability riders for a waiver of premium and disability income protection are relatively inexpensive and can be added to most whole life policies, but generally not to term policies.
- **Guaranteed Purchase Option:** The policyholder who has a **guaranteed purchase option** may purchase additional coverage at stipulated intervals without providing evidence of insurability. This option is frequently offered to buyers of a whole life policy who are under age 40. The increases in coverage usually can be purchased every 3, 4, or 5 years in amounts equal to the amount of the original policy or $10,000, whichever is lower. This option should be quite attractive to individuals whose life insurance needs and ability to pay are expected to increase over a 5- to 15-year period.
- **Suicide Clause:** Nearly all life insurance policies have a *suicide clause* that voids the contract if an insured commits suicide within a certain period, normally 2 years after the policy's inception. In these cases, the company simply returns the premiums that have been paid. If an insured takes his or her own life after this initial period has elapsed, the policy proceeds are paid without question.
- **Exclusions:** Although all private insurance policies exclude some types of losses, life policies offer very broad protection. In addition to the suicide clause, the only other common exclusions are aviation, war, and hazardous occupation or hobby. However, seldom, if ever, would a company be able to modify the premium charged or coverage offered should the insured take up, say, Formula One racing or hang gliding *after* a policy is issued.

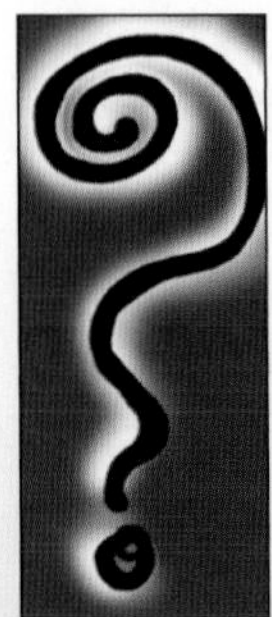

Concept ✓

8-19. What is a *beneficiary?* A *contingent beneficiary?* Explain why it is essential to designate a beneficiary.

8-20. Explain the basic settlement options available for the payment of life insurance proceeds on a person's death.

8-21. What do *nonforfeiture options* accomplish? Differentiate between *paid-up insurance* and *extended-term insurance.*

8-22. Explain the following clauses often found in life insurance policies: (a) *multiple indemnity clause,* (b) *disability clause,* and (c) *suicide clause.* Give some examples of common exclusions.

8-23. Describe what is meant by a *participating policy,* and explain the role of *policy dividends* in these policies.

- **Participation:** In a **participating policy**, the policyholder is entitled to receive *policy dividends* that reflect the difference between the premiums that are charged and the amount of premium necessary to fund the actual mortality experience of the company. When the base premium schedule for participating policies is established, a company estimates what it believes its mortality and investment experience will be, and then adds a generous margin of safety to these figures. The premiums charged the policyholder are based on these overly conservative estimates.

participating policy
A life insurance policy that pays *policy dividends* that reflect the difference between the premiums that are charged and the amount of premium necessary to fund the actual mortality experience of the company.

- **Living Benefits:** Also called *accelerated benefits*, this feature allows the insured to receive a percentage of his or her death benefits from a whole or universal life policy prior to death. Some insurers offer this option free of charge to established policyholders if the insured suffers a terminal illness expected to result in death within a specified period, such as 6 months to a year, or needs an expensive treatment, such as an organ transplant, to survive. These benefits can also be added as a *living benefit rider* that pays a portion of a policy's death benefit in advance, usually about 2 percent per month, for long-term healthcare, such as nursing home expenses. This rider can add an extra 5 to 15 percent to the normal life insurance premium, and benefits are capped as a percentage of the death benefit.
- **Viatical Settlement:** Like a living benefits feature, this option allows a terminally ill insurance holder to get a percentage of the insurance policy for immediate use. However, unlike the living benefits feature, this is not done through the insurance company but rather through a third-party investor. The insured sells an interest in the life insurance policy to the investor, who then becomes the policy's beneficiary, and the insured receives a cash amount from the investor—most commonly 60 percent of the value of the policy; after the insured dies, the investor receives the balance from the policy. Approach viatical settlements carefully, because it means giving up all future claims on the life insurance policy and can also affect a patient's medicare eligibility in some cases. Additionally, some viatical settlement companies—the firms that arrange the transfer between insured and investors—have been scrutinized by government agencies for unethical practices.

SUMMARY

LG1. Explain the concept of risk and the basics of insurance underwriting. Adequate life insurance coverage is vital to sound personal financial planning because it not only protects that which you have already acquired, but also helps ensure the attainment of unfulfilled financial goals. The whole notion of insurance is based on the concept of risk and the different methods of handling it, including risk avoidance, loss prevention and control, risk assumption, and insurance (a cost-effective procedure that allows families to reduce financial risks by sharing losses). Through the underwriting process, insurance companies decide whom they consider an acceptable risk and the premiums to charge for coverage.

LG2. Discuss the primary reasons for life insurance and identify those who need coverage. Life insurance fills the gap between the financial resources available to your dependents if you should die prematurely and what they need to maintain a given lifestyle. Some policies provide only a death benefit, whereas others also have a savings component. If you have children or elderly relatives who count on your income to support them, you should include life insurance as one of several financial resources to meet their requirements. If you have no dependents, however, you probably don't need life insurance. Your life insurance needs change over your life cycle and should be reviewed regularly.

LG3. Calculate how much life insurance you need. There are a number of ways to determine the amount of life insurance a family should have. Although the multiple-of-earnings method is simple to use, most experts agree that the needs analysis method is the best procedure. It systematically considers such variables as family income, household and other expenses, special needs, final expanses, debt liquidation, and other financial needs, which are then compared with the financial resources available to meet these needs.

LG4. Differentiate among the various types of life insurance policies and describe their advantages and disadvantages. The three basic types of life insurance policies are term life, whole life, and universal life. Term life insurance basically provides a stipulated amount of death benefits, whereas whole life combines death benefits with a modest savings program, and universal life packages term insurance with a tax-deferred investment account that pays competitive money market returns. Other types of life insurance include variable life, group life, credit life, mortgage life, and industrial life.

LG5. Choose the best life insurance policy for your needs at the lowest cost. To get as much coverage as possible from your insurance dollar, it is important that you not only compare costs but also buy the proper amount of life insurance and pick the right type of insurance policy. Beyond the cost and features of the insurance policy, you should also carefully consider the financial stability of the insurer offering the policy, paying special attention to the ratings assigned by major rating agencies. The Internet has become an excellent resource for comparison shopping. In addition to selecting a company, you must also choose an agent who understands your needs.

LG6. Become familiar with the key features of life insurance policies. Some important contract features of life insurance policies you should become familiar with are the beneficiary clause, settlement options, policy loans, premium payments, grace period, nonforfeiture options, policy reinstatement, and change of policy. Other policy features include multiple indemnity and disability clauses, guaranteed purchase options, suicide clause, exclusions, participation, living benefits, and viatical settlements.

Financial Planning Exercises

1. ***Use Worksheet 8.1.*** Mildred Meyers is a 72-year-old widow who has recently been diagnosed with Alzheimer's disease. She has limited financial assets of her own and has been living with her daughter Janna for 2 years. Her only income is $850 a month in Social Security survivor's benefits. Janna wants to make sure her mother will be taken care of if Janna should die. Janna, 40, is single and earns $55,000 a year as a human resource manager for a small manufacturing firm. She

owns a condo with a current market value of $100,000 and has a $70,000 mortgage. Other debts include a $5,000 auto loan and $500 in various credit card balances. Her 401(k) plan has a current balance of $24,500, and she keeps $7,500 in a money market account for emergencies. After talking with her mother's doctor, Janna believes that her mother will be able to continue to live independently for another 2 to 3 years. She estimates that her mother would need about $2,000 a month to cover her living expenses and medical costs during this time. After that, Janna's mother will probably need nursing home care. Janna calls several local nursing homes and finds that it will cost about $5,000 a month when her mother enters a nursing home. Her mother's doctor says it is difficult to estimate her mother's life expectancy but indicates that with proper care some Alzheimer's patients can live 10 or more years after diagnosis. Janna also estimates that her personal final expenses would be around $5,000, and she'd like to provide a $25,000 contingency fund that would be used to pay a trusted friend to supervise her mother's care if Janna was no longer alive. Use Worksheet 8.1 to calculate Janna's total life insurance requirements and recommend the type of policy she should buy.

2. ***Use Worksheet 8.1.*** Given your current personal financial situation, do you feel you need life insurance coverage? Why or why not? Use Worksheet 8.1 to confirm your answer and calculate how much additional insurance (if any) you might need to purchase.

3. ***Use Worksheet 8.1.*** Jim Henderson, 43, is a recently divorced father of two children, ages 9 and 7. He currently earns $95,000 a year as an operations manager for a utility company. The divorce settlement requires him to pay $1,500 a month in child support and $400 a month in alimony to his ex-wife. She currently earns $25,000 a year as a preschool teacher. Jim is currently renting an apartment and the divorce settlement left him with approximately $100,000 in savings and retirement benefits. His employer provides a $75,000 life insurance policy. Jim's ex-wife is currently the beneficiary listed on the policy. What advice would you give to Jim? What factors should he consider in deciding whether to buy additional life insurance at this point in his life? If he does need additional life insurance, what type of policy or policies should he buy? Use Worksheet 8.1 to help answer these questions for Jim.

4. Using the premium schedules provided in Exhibits 8.2, 8.3, and 8.6, how much in *annual* premiums would a 25-year-old male have to pay for $100,000 of annual renewable term, level-premium term, and whole life insurance (assume a 5-year term or period of coverage)? How much would a 25-year-old woman have to pay for the same coverage? Consider a 40-year-old male (or female): Using annual premiums, compare the cost of 10 years of coverage under annual renewable and level-premium term options and whole life insurance coverage. Compare the pluses and minuses of each type of policy in relation to their price differences.

5. Monica and Manuel Juarez are a dual-career couple who just had their first child. Manuel, age 29, already has a group life insurance policy, but Monica's employer does not offer life insurance. A financial planner is recommending that the 25-year-old Monica buy a $250,000 whole life policy with an annual premium of $1,670—the policy has an assumed rate of earnings of 8 percent a year. Help Monica evaluate this advice and decide on an appropriate course of action.

6. While at lunch with a group of coworkers, one of your friends mentions that he plans to buy a variable life insurance policy because it provides a good annual return and is a good way to build savings for his 5-year-old's college education. Another colleague says that she is adding coverage through the group plan's additional insurance option. What advice would you give them?

Applying Personal Finance

Insure Your Life!

Providing for our loved ones in the event of our death is a serious concern for most of us. Trouble is, planning for such an event is not particularly pleasant, and most of us would just as soon put off thinking about it. The purpose of this project is to help you determine your life insurance needs both for now and in the future.

Life insurance can be put in place to provide income for your family, educate your children, or pay off debt obligations. Life insurance can also be used in estate planning or to benefit a cause that is important to you. Make a list of your present life insurance needs and another list of what you expect your needs to be 10 years down the road. Estimate the dollar amount for each of your needs. Using the worksheet provided in this chapter, determine the amount of life insurance you need both for now and in the future. Consider the features of the different types of life insurance available. Which type of life insurance would be most appropriate for you? What would the cost be to provide these amounts of life insurance? You may use the premium schedules in this chapter or get actual quotes from an agent or off the Internet. Use these estimates to help you with your personal financial planning.

Contemporary Case Applications

8.1 Lee Hsiah's Insurance Decision: Whole Life, Variable Life, or Term Life?

Lee Hsiah, a 38-year-old widowed mother of three children, ages 12, 10, and 4, works as a product analyst for Ralston Purina. Although she is covered by a group life insurance policy at work, she feels, based on some rough calculations, that she needs additional protection. David Dustimer, an insurance agent from Siegfried Insurance, has been trying to persuade Lee to buy a $150,000, 25-year, limited-payment whole life policy. However, Lee favors a variable life policy. To further complicate matters, Lee's father feels that term life insurance is more suitable to the needs of her young family. To resolve the issue, Lee has decided to consult Terry Patrick, a childhood friend who is now a professor of insurance at a nearby university.

Questions

1. Explain to Lee the differences between a (a) whole life policy, (b) variable life policy, and (c) term life policy.
2. What are the major advantages and disadvantages of each type of policy?
3. In what way is a whole life policy superior to either a variable life or term life policy? In what way is a variable life policy superior? How about term life insurance?
4. Given the limited information in the case, which type of policy would you recommend for Ms. Hsiah? Defend and explain your recommendations.

8.2 The Kings Want to Know When Enough Is Enough

Dave and Karen King are a two-income couple in their early thirties. They have two children, ages 6 and 3. Dave's monthly take-home pay is $1,800, and Karen's is $2,100. The Kings feel that because they are a two-income family, they both should have adequate life insurance coverage. Accordingly, they are presently trying to decide how much life insurance *each one of them* needs.

To begin with, they would like to set up an education fund for their children in the amount of $80,000 to provide college funds of $10,000 a year—in today's dollars—for 4 years for each child. Moreover, in the event of either one of their deaths, they want the surviving spouse to have the funds to pay off all outstanding debts, including the $140,000 mortgage on their house. They estimate that they have $15,000 in consumer installment loans and credit cards. They also project that if either of them dies, the other probably will be left with about $10,000 in final estate and burial expenses.

As far as their annual income needs are concerned, Dave and Karen both feel very strongly that each should have enough insurance to replace their respective current income levels until the youngest child turns 18 (a period of 15 years). Though neither Dave nor Karen would be eligible for social security survivor's benefits because they both intend to continue working, both children would qualify, in the (combined) amount of around $1,400 a month. The Kings have amassed about $75,000 in investments, and they have a decreasing-term life policy on each other in the amount of $85,000, which would be used to partially pay off the mortgage. Further, Dave has a $60,000 group policy at work and Karen a $90,000 group policy.

Questions

1. Assume that Dave's gross annual income is $30,000, and Karen's is $40,000. Their insurance agent has given them a multiple earnings table showing that the earnings multiple to replace 75 percent of their lost earnings is 8.7 for Dave and 7.4 for Karen. Use this approach to find the amount of life insurance each should have if they wanted to replace 75 percent of their lost earnings.
2. Use Worksheet 8.1 to find the additional insurance needed on both Dave's and Karen's lives. (Because Dave and Karen hold secure, well-paying jobs, both agree that they won't need any additional help once the kids are grown; both also agree that he or she will have plenty of income from Social Security and company pension benefits to take care of themselves in retirement. Thus, when preparing the worksheet, assume "funding needs" of zero in Periods 2 and 3.)
3. Is there a difference in your answers to Questions 1 and 2? If so, why? Which number do you think is more indicative of the King's life insurance needs? Using the amounts computed in Question 2 (employing the needs approach), what kind of life insurance policy would you recommend for Dave? For Karen? Briefly explain your answers.

MONEY ONLINE

Insure Your Life!

1. **http://www.usaaedfoundation.org**

Who needs life insurance? Click on "Insurance" at the USAA Educational Foundation's Web site, and scroll down to "Life Insurance" to find out. Other topics to explore include "How Insurable Are You," "Should You Replace an Existing Policy," and "Military Insurance Options."

2. **http://www.northwesternmutual.com**

How much life insurance do you need? Click on "Calculators" found at the "Learning Center" of Northwestern Mutual's Web site and scroll down to "Life Insurance." Work through this interactive calculator to determine the amount of protection you may need to provide for your loved ones.

3. **http://www.usaaedfoundation.org/insurance**
How do you compare life insurance policies? Click on "Life Insurance" and then on "Comparing Life Insurance Policies" at USAA Educational Foundation's Web site for a guide to help you comparison shop. Discover the two cost indexes adopted by the National Association of Insurance Commissioners that can help you compare similar policies and determine the better value.

4. **http://www.actuary.com**
Interested in a career as an actuary? Actuary.com's Web site serves as an excellent resource for anyone who is considering or is actually in the insurance business. Or you can use this site to find a link to your own insurance company's Web site by clicking on "Insurance Industry."

5. **http://financenter.com/consumertools**
Learn all about term life insurance. The FinanCenter provides information and calculators to help you with almost every aspect of insurance. Under "Educators," click on "Insurance." Scroll down to "Life Insurance" to find out how term life insurance works, the features of other types of life insurance, or to compare term insurance to permanent life insurance.

6. **http://www.insure.com**
Find the top-rated life insurance companies that sell policies in your state at Insure.com's Web site. Select "Insurance Company Guide," "Financial Ratings," and then "Standard and Poor's Ratings." Select "individual life," your state, and "AAA (extremely strong)" in the drop-down boxes. To learn more about a particular company, click on "Insurer Profile" for background information and a financial report.

7. **http://info.insure.com/ratings/define.cfm**
What do the Standard and Poor's ratings mean? Find a detailed explanation of the financial strength ratings assigned to insurance companies by Standard and Poor's at Insure.com's Web site.

8. **http://www.bls.gov/oco/ocos118.htm**
What is the difference between a captive and an independent agent? What training is needed to become an agent? If you are considering insurance as a career, read through "Insurance Sales Agent" from the Bureau of Labor Statistic's Occupational Outlook Handbook.

9. **http://info.insure.com/life**
How will health conditions, such as high blood pressure, asthma, alcohol use, cancer, or being overweight affect life insurance premiums? At Insure.com's Web site, scroll down to the section entitled "Buy Life Insurance Wisely" to find information concerning a variety of health issues.

10. **http://info.insure.com/life**
What happens when life insurance policies are lost? What if you're healthy but are denied life insurance? Scroll down to "Solve Life Insurance Problems" at Insure.com's Web site to find these topics addressed. Then browse through the "More Help" topics to find many other life insurance related articles.

Just for Fun!

11. **http://www.northwesternmutual.com**
Play the Longevity Game! Click on "Calculators" found at the "Learning Center" of Northwestern Mutual's Web site, and scroll down to "The Longevity Game." Work your way through this interactive quiz to get a general idea of how long you may live past retirement. Then work through the "Retirement Savings" calculator to make sure you'll have enough to retire in style!

CHAPTER 9

Insuring Your Health

Learning Goals

LG1. Discuss why having adequate health insurance is important and identify the factors contributing to the growing cost of health insurance.

LG2. Differentiate among the major types of health insurance plans and identify major public and private health insurance providers and their programs.

LG3. Analyze your own health insurance needs and explain how to shop for appropriate coverage.

LG4. Explain the basic types of medical expenses covered and policy provisions of health insurance plans.

LG5. Assess the need for and features of long-term care insurance.

LG6. Discuss the features of disability income insurance and how to determine your need for it.

Healthy Coverage

When Chris Stevens was laid off in a corporate reorganization, he lost more than his job; he also lost his employer-paid health insurance coverage. Chris and his wife Sidney were given the option of paying $600 a month to continue insurance coverage for themselves and their two children but decided doing so would be too much to handle while Chris was unemployed. The Stevens joined the ranks of the over 43 million Americans who do not have health insurance.

Their decision worked—until Sidney had to get her that she was due for her annual mammogram for breast cancer screening. Yearly mammograms were necessary after a suspicious lump had been found and removed from her breast the year before. When she had to admit to the doctor's receptionist that she no longer had health insurance, Sidney felt "ashamed, like a second class citizen." She had to pay $200 out-of-pocket for the exam. Luckily, her mammogram came back clean.

Clifford Wilson and his family never had to go without health insurance. In fact, Clifford had a very expensive health insurance plan that allowed his family to see any doctor they chose if they paid 20 percent of their medical bills.

When Clifford's wife was diagnosed with breast cancer in her fifth month of pregnancy, the Wilsons received discouraging news from their local doctor. The pregnancy would have to be terminated immediately so that Mrs. Wilson could begin chemotherapy. The Wilsons turned to cancer specialists at a major research hospital who used experimental drugs to treat Mrs. Wilson's cancer while she was still pregnant. The baby was born healthy, and Mrs. Wilson went into remission.

The total cost of Mrs. Wilson's treatment was $98,000—but Clifford soon discovered that his health insurance company refused to pay their share of the bill. The reason? The company argued that the "usual and customary" cost of such care should be $65,000. Although the Wilsons challenged the insurance company's ruling, in the end, they ended up paying the $33,000 difference, plus 20 percent of the remaining balance.

As these stories illustrate, understanding the provisions of different health insurance plans is an important part of your personal financial planning. Read on to learn how to choose the right coverage for you and your family.

CRITICAL THINKING QUESTIONS

As you read this chapter, consider these questions in relation to the Stevens and Wilson families' health insurance planning:

- If you were in the same situation as the Stevenses, would you go without health insurance?
- Based on these examples, what types of costs and limitations of health insurance coverage should you be familiar with?
- What should you look for when purchasing health insurance?

Sources: Barbara Martinez, "A Matter of Definition," *The Wall Street Journal*, April 22, 2003, p. R7; Sidney Stevens, "When Times Were Tough, We Went 'Bare'," *Newsweek*, July 29, 2003, p. 16.

THE IMPORTANCE OF HEALTH INSURANCE COVERAGE

LG1

The next best thing to good health is probably a good health insurance plan. In recent years, the price of medical treatment has risen dramatically. As a result, a serious illness or accident can involve not only physical pain from sickness and injury, but also economic pain. A major illness can easily cost tens of thousands of dollars once you consider hospitalization and medical expenses as well as the loss of income while you recover. Even routine medical care such as doctors' office visits and healthcare screenings can quickly add up. Health insurance helps you pay for the costs associated with both routine and major medical care so that your financial accomplishments and plans are not seriously damaged or even destroyed.

In spite of the financial importance of health insurance, however, many Americans remain underinsured or uninsured. According to the U.S. Census Bureau, 15 percent of the population—over 43 million people—do not have health insurance. Young adults between 18 and 24 are even less likely to have health insurance. Only about 30 percent of individuals in that age group are covered by health insurance.

Why are so many uninsured? As Exhibit 9.1 shows, the cost of adequate health insurance has skyrocketed in recent years, increasing an average of 13 percent annually since 1999—significantly faster than the overall inflation rate or the average worker's earnings. It now costs over $9,000 a year to insure an average family. While many employers pay for some of this cost, most employees are now paying almost 50 percent more towards their health insurance than they were just 3 years ago. Others do not get any help from their employers, or are unemployed, and have to foot the entire bill themselves.

EXHIBIT 9.1

Historical Trends in Health Insurance Costs

As the chart shows, the year-to-year percentage change for health insurance premiums has been much higher than both the inflation rate and average workers' earnings.

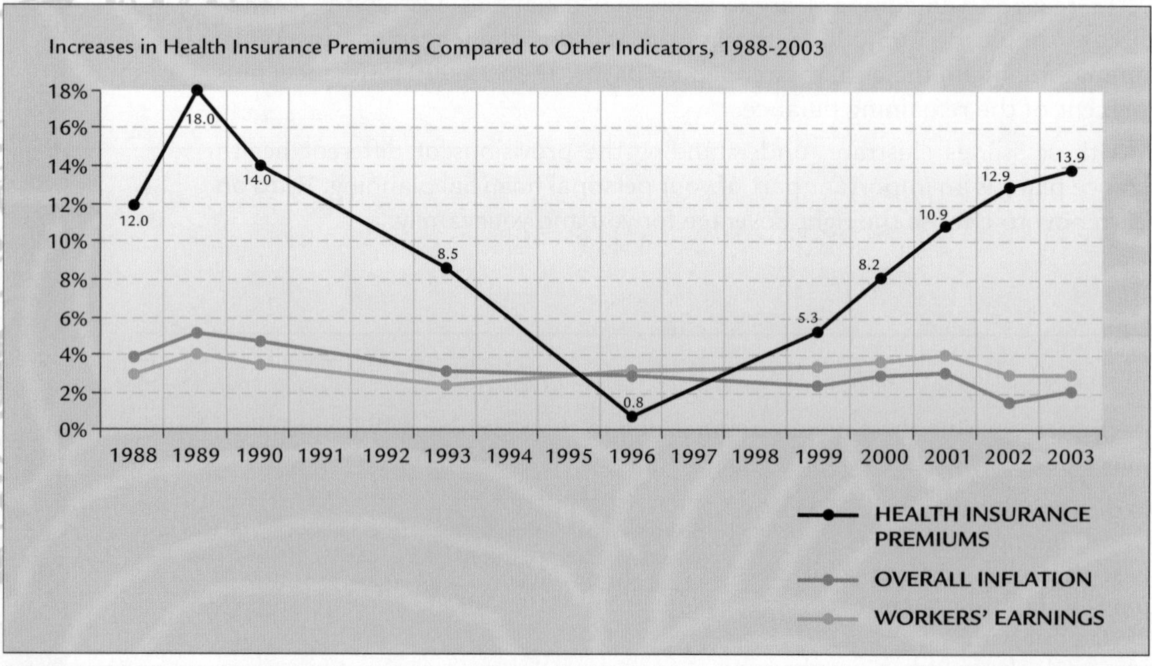

Source: "Employer Health Benefits 2003 Annual Survey," (#3369), The Henry J. Kaiser Family Foundation and Health Research and Educational Trust, September 2003. This information was reprinted with permission of the Henry J. Kaiser Family Foundation. The Kaiser Family Foundation, based in Menlo Park, California, is a nonprofit, independent national health care philantropy and is not associated with Kaiser Permanente or Kaiser Industries.

Several health-related trends are behind the rise in health insurance costs. First, recent advances in medical technology have resulted in advanced prescription drugs and new treatments. Although these advances are saving more lives than ever before, they also cost more to provide. The U.S. population is also aging, resulting in growing use of healthcare services. A poor demand-and-supply distribution of healthcare facilities and services may be yet another factor. Administrative costs, excessive paperwork, increased regulation, and insurance fraud are also contributing to rising healthcare costs. When all of these factors are added together, insurance companies are finding it necessary to pass along rising healthcare costs to consumers by charging more for health insurance.

Concept ✓

9-1. Why should health insurance planning be included in your personal financial plan?
9-2. What factors have contributed to today's high costs of healthcare and health insurance?

Still, as we've already noted, it can be very risky to go without adequate health insurance coverage. As with other types of insurance decisions, cost-effective health insurance depends on understanding the types of policies available and then matching them to your own specific medical needs.

smart.sites

You can learn more about the political, economic, and social factors affecting the cost and availability of health insurance from the American Association of Health Plans, **http://www.aahp.org**.

LG2

HEALTH INSURANCE PLANS

Health insurance coverage is available from two main sources: private and government-sponsored programs. Private health insurance pays for approximately 33 percent of all medical care expenditures in the United States, while government programs fund about 44 percent. Most of the remaining amount spent on medical care is paid for out of pocket by patients themselves.

Private Health Insurance Plans

group health insurance
A type of health insurance consisting of contracts written between a group (for example, employer, union, or other organization) and a private insurance company, Blue Cross/Blue Shield plan, or managed care organization.

Private companies sell a variety of health insurance plans to both groups and individuals. **Group health insurance** refers to health insurance contracts written between a group (such as an employer, union, credit union, or other organization) and the healthcare provider: a private insurance company, Blue Cross/Blue Shield plan, or a managed care organization. Typically, group plans provide comprehensive medical expense coverage and may also offer prescription drug, dental, and vision care service. The coverage provided by any given plan is subject to negotiation between the group and the insurer, and the group may offer several different options for health insurance coverage.

If you work for an employer that has more than just a few employees, you will probably have access to some type of group health plan. With the high cost of health insurance, most employers now require employees to pay a portion of the cost. Trade associations and professional groups may also offer group insurance to their members at attractive rates. Some groups choose to self-insure, which means that the employer or other group takes responsibility for full or partial payment of claims.

People who do not work for an employer who provides health insurance as well as those who require additional personal or family health insurance can purchase health coverage on an individual basis directly from providers.

At one time, group health insurance coverage was far superior to individual coverage, especially in terms of availability and cost to the employee. Today, however, the differences between group and individual coverage have narrowed, and many of the advantages of group coverage have disappeared. To control rising costs, many employers no longer provide universal coverage but merely underwrite employee applications much the way insurers do. Employers are also shifting a larger percentage of the cost to employees. As a result, you may want to compare group and individual policies before deciding which coverage to buy.

Most private health insurance plans fall into one of two categories: traditional *indemnity (fee-for-service) plans* and *managed care plans*, which include health maintenance organizations (HMOs), preferred provider organizations (PPOs), and similar plans. Both types of plans provide financial aid for the cost of medical care arising from illness or accidents, but do so in somewhat different ways. Exhibit 9.2 compares some of the features of the three most common types of health plans.

indemnity (fee-for-service) plan Health insurance plan in which the person or organization from which you get the healthcare services is separate from the insurer, who pays the provider or reimburses you for a specified percentage of eligible expenses after payment of a deductible. These plans usually provide unlimited choice of doctors and hospitals.

Traditional Indemnity (Fee-for-Service) Plans

With a traditional **indemnity (fee-for-service) plan**, the person or organization from which you obtain healthcare services is separate from your insurer. Your insurer either pays the health service provider directly or reimburses you for your expenses when you submit claims for medical treatment. Typically, indemnity plans pay 80 percent of the eligible healthcare expenses, while the insured pays the other 20 percent. The health insurance company will begin paying its share after you pay a deductible amount of expenses. The deductible can range from $100 to over $2,000. The lower your deductible, the higher your premium.

The amount the insurance company pays is commonly based on the usual, customary, and reasonable (UCR) charges—what the insurer considers to be the prevailing fees within your area, not what your doctor or hospital actually charges. If your doctor charges more than the UCR, you may be responsible for the full amount of the excess. UCR charges vary significantly among insurers, so you should compare your doctor's fees with what a plan pays. Some carriers offer indemnity plans wherein physicians who accept the insurance agree to accept the UCR payments set by the insurer.

EXHIBIT 9.2

How the Most Common Types of Health Plans Compare

This table highlights one of the key differences between the three most common types of health plans.

Type	Choice of Service Providers	Premium Cost	Out-of-Pocket Costs	Annual Deductible
Indemnity	Yes	Low if high deductible plan, high if low deductible	Usually 20 percent of medical expenses plus deductible	Yes
HMO	No	Low	Low co-pay	No
PPO	Some	Higher than HMO	Low if using network providers, higher if provider is outside the network	No

Managed Care Plans

managed care plan
A healthcare plan in which subscribers/users contract directly with the provider organization, which uses a designated group of providers meeting specific selection standards to furnish comprehensive healthcare services for a fixed fee. These plans emphasize cost control and preventive treatment.

health maintenance organization (HMO)
An organization consisting of hospitals, physicians, and other healthcare providers who have joined to provide comprehensive healthcare services to its members.

In a **managed care plan**, subscribers/users contract with and make monthly payments directly to the organization that provides the healthcare service. An insurance company may not even be involved, although today most major health insurance companies offer both indemnity and managed care plans. Managed care plan members receive comprehensive healthcare services from a designated group of doctors, hospitals, and other providers, who must meet the managed care provider's specific selection standards. Managed care plans use various strategies to provide cost-efficient medical care, such as controlling the amount of care provided and emphasizing prevention of illness.

With a managed care plan, the insured pays no deductibles and only a small fee, or co-payment, for office visits and medications. Most medical services—including preventive and routine care that indemnity plans may not cover—are fully covered when obtained from plan providers. Managed care plans include health maintenance organizations (HMOs), preferred provider organizations (PPOs), exclusive provider organizations (EPOs) and point-of-service plans (POS).

Health Maintenance Organizations (HMO)

A **health maintenance organization (HMO)** is an organization of hospitals, physicians, and other healthcare providers who have joined to provide comprehensive healthcare services to its members. As an HMO member, you pay a monthly fee that varies according to the number of people in your family. You may also pay a co-payment of $5 to $20 each time you use some of the services provided by the HMO or fill a prescription. The services provided to HMO members include doctors' office visits, x-ray and laboratory services, preventive care, health screenings, hospital inpatient care and surgery, maternity care, mental health, and drug prescriptions. The advantages of HMO membership include a lack of deductibles, few or no exclusions, and not having to file insurance claims. The primary disadvantage is that HMO members are not always able to choose their physicians and may face limitations if they need care outside of the geographic area of their HMO. Exhibit 9.3 shows the HMOs that receive the highest satisfaction ratings from their members.

There are two main types of HMOs: group and individual practice association. A **group HMO** employs a group of doctors to provide healthcare services to members *from a central facility*. Group HMO members obtain medical care from the doctors and other

EXHIBIT 9.3

Top 10 HMOs for Customer Satisfaction

1. Kaiser Permanente Northwest (OR, WA)
2. Capital District Physicians' Health Plan (NY)
3. Group Health Cooperative (ID, WA)
4. Independent Health (Western NY)
5. Harvard Pilgrim Health Care (Northeast)
6. Kaiser Permanente Southern California
7. Tufts Health Plan (CT, MA, NH, RI, VT)
8. Kaiser Permanente Northern California
9. John Deere Health Plan (IA, IL, TN, VA)
10. Blue Choice (Rochester NY area)

Source: Copyright 2003 by Consumers Union of U.S., Inc. Yonkers, NY 10703-1057, a nonprofit organization. Reprinted with permission from the October 2003 issue of CONSUMER REPORTS(r) for educational purposes only. No commercial use or reproduction permitted. Full article also available at **http://www.ConsumerReports.org**.

medical personnel who practice in this facility. Often, the group HMO's hospital facilities are located in the same facility. Group HMOs are most prevalent in larger cities.

An **individual practice association (IPA)** is the most popular type of HMO. IPA members receive medical care from individual physicians practicing *from their own offices and from community* hospitals that are affiliated with the IPA. As a member of an IPA, you have some choice of which doctors and hospitals to use.

group HMO
An HMO that provides health-care services *from a central facility;* most prevalent in larger cities.

individual practice association (IPA)
A form of HMO in which subscribers receive services from physicians practicing from *their own offices and from community hospitals* that are affiliated with the IFA.

Preferred Provider Organization

A **preferred provider organization (PPO)** is a managed care plan that has the characteristics of both an IPA and an insurance plan. An insurance company or provider group contracts with a network of physicians and hospitals that agree to accept a negotiated fee for medical services provided to the PPO customers. Unlike the HMO, however, a PPO also provides insurance coverage for medical services not provided by the PPO network so you can choose to go to other doctors or hospitals. You will, however, pay a lower price for medical services provided by network doctors and hospitals.

preferred provider organization (PPO)
A health provider that combines the characteristics of the IPA form of HMO with an insurance plan to provide comprehensive health-care services to its subscribers within a network of physicians and hospitals.

Other Managed Care Plans

In addition to the plans described above, you may encounter two other forms of managed care plans. An **exclusive provider organization (EPO)** contracts with medical providers to offer services to members at reduced costs, but reimburses members only when affiliated providers are used. Plan members who use a nonaffiliated provider must bear the entire cost. The **point-of-service (POS) plan** is a hybrid form of HMO that allows members to go outside of the HMO network for care. Payment for nonaffiliated physician services is similar to indemnity plan payments: the plan pays a specified percentage of the cost after your medical costs reach an annual deductible.

Blue Cross/Blue Shield Plans

In a technical sense, **Blue Cross/Blue Shield plans** are not insurance policies but rather prepaid hospital and medical expense plans. Although originally a nonprofit healthcare service organization, in 1994 the 47 independent local Blue Cross/Blue Shield organizations became for-profit corporations.

Blue Cross contracts with hospitals which agree to provide specified hospital services to members of groups covered by Blue Cross in exchange for a specified fee or payment. Blue Cross also contracts for surgical and medical services. Blue Cross serves as the intermediary between the groups that want these services and the physicians who contractually agree to provide them. Today, many Blue Cross and Blue Shield plans have combined to form one provider, and they compete for business with other private insurance companies. Because Blue Cross/Blue Shield is a producer cooperative, payments for healthcare services are seldom made to the subscriber but rather directly to the participating hospital or physician.

smart.sites
To learn more about the services covered under Blue Cross/Blue Shield and for contact information for your local Blue Cross organization, go to **http://www.bcbs.org**.

Financial Road Sign

Key Questions for Choosing a Health Insurance Plan

1. How much will it cost on a monthly basis?
2. Are there deductibles I must pay before the insurance begins to help cover my costs?
3. What doctors, hospitals, and other medical providers are part of the plan?
4. Are there enough of the kinds of doctors I want to see?
5. If I use doctors outside a plan's network, how much more will I pay to get care?
6. Are there any limits to how much I must pay in case of major illness?

Government Health Insurance Plans

exclusive provider organization (EPO) A managed care plan that is similar to a PPO, but reimburses members only when affiliated providers are used.

point-of-service (POS) plan A hybrid form of HMO that allows members to go outside the HMO network for care; the plan reimburses members for unaffiliated services at a specified percentage of the cost after satisfaction of an annual deductible.

Blue Cross/Blue Shield plans Prepaid hospital and medical expense plans under which healthcare services are provided to plan participants by member hospitals and physicians.

Medicare A health insurance plan administered by the federal government to help persons age 65 and over, and others receiving monthly Social Security disability benefits, meet their healthcare costs.

In addition to health insurance coverage provided by private sources, federal and state agencies also provide healthcare coverage to eligible individuals. About 25 percent of the U.S. population is covered by some form of government health insurance program.

Medicare

Medicare is a health insurance program administered under the Social Security Administration. It is primarily designed to help persons 65 and over meet their healthcare costs, but it also covers many people under 65 who are recipients of monthly Social Security disability benefits. Funds for Medicare benefits come from Social Security taxes paid by covered workers and their employers. Traditionally, Medicare has provided two primary healthcare components: basic hospital insurance and supplementary medical insurance:

- **Basic hospital insurance**. This coverage (commonly called *Part A*) provides inpatient hospital services such as room, board, and other customary inpatient service for the first 90 days of illness. A deductible is applied during the first 60 days of illness. Coinsurance provisions, applicable to days 61 to 90 of the hospital stay, can further reduce benefits. Medicare also covers all or part of the cost of up to 100 days in post-hospital extended-care facilities that provide skilled care, such as nursing homes. However, it does not cover the most common types of nursing home care—intermediate and custodial care. Medicare basic hospital insurance also covers some post-hospital medical services such as intermittent nursing care, therapy, rehabilitation, and home healthcare. Medicare deductibles and coinsurance amounts are revised annually to reflect changing medical costs.
- **Supplementary medical insurance.** The **supplementary medical insurance (SMI)** program (commonly called *Part B*) covers the services of physicians and surgeons, as well as the costs of medical and health services such as x-rays, laboratory tests, prosthetic devices, rental of medical equipment, and ambulance transportation. It also covers some home health services (such as in-home visits by a registered nurse) and limited psychiatric care. Unlike the basic Medicare hospital plan, SMI is a *voluntary program* for which participants pay premiums, which are then matched with government funds. Anyone age 65 or over can enroll in SMI.

In late 2003, Federal legislators approved sweeping changes to Medicare. Although Medicare did not cover the cost of prescription drugs in the past, as of 2006 Medicare beneficiaries will have the option of signing up for drug coverage. Under Medicare, they will pay additional premiums of about $425 a year for prescription coverage. After paying a $250 deductible towards drug costs, Medicare will cover up to 75 percent of drug costs up to $2,250. After $2,250 in total drug costs have accumulated, Medicare will pay nothing more until the beneficiary pays a total of $3,600 out of pocket, at which point Medicare will pay 95 percent of prescription costs. Beyond adding prescription coverage, beginning in 2006, people with incomes over $80,000 a year will be asked to pay larger premiums for the Medicare Part B which covers doctors' services and other outpatient care.

Although Medicare pays for many healthcare expenses for the disabled and those over 65, there are still gaps in its coverage. About 70 percent of Medicare enrollees buy private insurance policies to fill in these gaps.

Medicaid

Medicaid is a state-run public assistance program that provides health insurance benefits only to those who are unable to pay for healthcare. Each state has its own regulations about who is eligible for Medicaid coverage and the types of medical services that are covered.

Concept ✓

9-3. What are the two main sources of health insurance coverage in the United States?
9-4. What is *group health insurance*? Differentiate between group and individual health insurance.
9-5. Describe the features of traditional *indemnity (fee-for-service) plans* and explain the differences between them and *managed care plans*.
9-6. Briefly explain how an *HMO* works. Contrast *group HMOs, IPAs,* and *PPOs*.
9-7. Discuss the basics of the *Blue Cross/Blue Shield plans*.
9-8. Who is eligible for *Medicare* and *Medicaid* benefits? What do those benefits encompass?
9-9. What is the objective of *workers' compensation insurance*? Explain its benefits for employees who are injured on the job or become ill through work-related causes.

Although Medicaid is primarily funded by each individual state, the federal government also contributes funds. Just over 14 million people receive Medicaid health benefits.

Workers' Compensation Insurance

Workers' compensation insurance is designed to compensate workers who are injured on the job or become ill through work-related causes. Although mandated by the federal government, each state is responsible for setting workers' compensation legislation and regulating its own program. Although specifics vary from state to state, typical workers' compensation benefits include medical and rehabilitation expenses, disability income, and scheduled lump-sum amounts for death and certain injuries, such as dismemberment. Employers bear nearly the entire cost of workers' compensation insurance in most states. Premiums are based on merit; employers who file the most claims pay the highest rates. People who are self-employed are required to contribute to workers' compensation for themselves and their employees.

supplementary medical insurance (SMI) A *voluntary program* under Medicare (commonly called *Part B*) that provides payments for services not covered under *basic hospital insurance (Part A)*, such as physicians' and surgeons' services, x-ray and laboratory services, and home health services for which participants pay premiums.

smart.sites
What does Medicaid cover in your state? The Kaiser Family Foundation offers an online state-by-state explanation of these and other healthcare benefits at **http://www.statehealthfacts.org**.

HEALTH INSURANCE DECISIONS

LG3

Given all these options, how can you systematically plan your purchases of health insurance? As with other insurance decisions, you'll need to consider potential areas of loss, types of coverage and other resources available to you and your family, and any gaps in protection. Once you have done all three, you can structure a health insurance plan that is best for you.

Evaluate Your Healthcare Cost Risk

Most people need protection against two types of losses that can result from illness or accidents: (1) expenses for medical care and rehabilitation and (2) loss of income or household services caused by an inability to work. The cost of medical care cannot be easily estimated, but in cases of long-term, serious illness, medical bills and related expenses can easily run into the hundreds of thousands of dollars. An adequate amount of protection against these costs for most people would be at least $250,000 and, with a protracted disability, as high as $1 million. In contrast, lost income is relatively easy to calculate: it is simply a percentage of your (or your spouse's) current monthly earnings. Most people believe that 60 to 75 percent is sufficient.

However, a good health insurance plan considers more than financing medical expenses, lost income, and replacement services. It should also incorporate other means of risk reduction. Recall from Chapter 8 that you can deal with risk in four ways: risk avoidance, loss prevention and control, risk assumption, and insurance. Therefore, in

Medicaid A state-run public assistance program that provides health insurance benefits only to those who are unable to pay for healthcare.

workers' compensation insurance A type of health insurance, required by state and federal governments and nearly paid in full by employers in most states, that compensates workers for job-related illness or injury.

making a decision about health insurance, you should also consider these other ways of minimizing your risk:

- **Risk Avoidance:** Look for ways to avoid exposure to healthcare loss before it occurs. For example, people who do not take illegal drugs never have to worry about disability from overdose, people who refuse to ride on motorcycles avoid the risk of injury from this relatively dangerous means of transportation, and people who do not smoke in bed will never doze off and start a fire in their house.
- **Loss Prevention and Control:** People who accept responsibility for their own well-being and live healthier lifestyles can prevent illness and reduce high medical costs. Smoking, alcohol and drug dependency, improper diet, inadequate sleep, and a lack of regular exercise contribute to more than 60 percent of all diagnosed illnesses. Eliminating some or all of these factors from your lifestyle can reduce your chances of becoming ill. Similarly, following highway safety laws, not driving while intoxicated, and wearing a seat belt helps prevent injury from car accidents.
- **Risk Assumption:** Consider the risks you are willing to retain as you deal with health insurance decisions. Some risks pose relatively small loss potential; you can budget for them rather than insure against them. For example, choosing insurance plans with deductibles and waiting periods is a form of risk assumption because it's more economical to pay small losses from savings than to pay higher premiums to insure them.

Determine Available Coverage and Resources

As noted earlier, many employers offer some form of health insurance as an employee benefit. In some cases, the employer only offers one plan and pays for it either entirely or partially. If you work for an employer who provides health insurance this way, you should evaluate the plan's benefits and costs in order to determine if additional coverage—either for yourself or your dependents—will be necessary. Exhibit 9.4 shows the healthcare benefits most commonly offered to employees by employers who provide them. Other employers offer their employees a choice among several different types of plans. During an open-enrollment period each year, employees sign up for the type of health insurance plan they feel best suits their needs.

EXHIBIT 9.4

Healthcare Benefits Most Commonly Offered by Employers

Although not all employers offer employee healthcare benefits, among those who do, prescription drug coverage is the most common benefit.

Benefit	Percent of employees providing the benefit
Prescription drug benefits	98%
Dental Insurance	96
PPO (Preferred Provider Organization)	87
Mail order prescriptions	87
Mental health services	76
Vision insurance	71

Source: Society for Human Resource Management (SHRM), *2003 Benefits Survey*, available at **http://www.shrm.org**.

Money in Action

Health Insurance: Don't Leave School without It

After months of going to employer recruiting sessions on campus, senior Jennifer Carter was offered an entry-level job after graduation at a small publishing company. The job offered a chance to learn about the publishing field, as well as opportunities for advancement—but her employee health insurance benefits wouldn't start until she had been with the firm for 6 months.

Like Jennifer, many recent college graduates find themselves without health insurance as they search for their first job. Others accept lower-level jobs that don't provide health benefits, or take jobs that have a waiting period before health coverage begins. While they like to think of themselves as invincible, the truth is they're just as likely as anyone else to get sick or injured. What can you do to fill in the gap if you find yourself without a group plan at work or in a waiting period for health insurance eligibility? Luckily, health insurance providers offer short-term bridge policies that typically provide up to 6 months of major medical coverage. Premiums for a plan with a $250 deductible run about $40 to $60 a month, depending on your age, sex, and health. Signing up is usually as simple as filling out a brief form and mailing a check; these plans often don't require a physical or waiting period. A search for "short-term insurance" or "temporary insurance" on the Internet will turn up a host of policy offerings.

However, these policies are best viewed as temporary measures because they have limitations. Typical plans cover hospitalization and doctor's visits but not pregnancy, mental disorders, preventive care, or dentistry. They also exclude pregnant women, people with preexisting health conditions, and people seeking coverage during international travel. Most insurance companies will not write a second short-term policy if you don't get other health coverage by the time your policy expires and they require you to pay the premiums for the entire coverage period in advance. Best bet: seek out a plan that offers prorated refunds if you cancel your policy before the coverage period is over or one that allows premiums to be paid monthly.

...continued on next page

Some employers offer employees a *flexible-benefit ("cafeteria") plan* that provides a choice of fringe benefits. Typically, the menu of benefits includes more than one health insurance option as well as life insurance, disability income insurance, and other benefits. As we discussed in Chapter 2, the employer specifies a set dollar amount they will provide and employees choose a combination from these benefits, depending on their preferences and circumstances. If, after choosing your benefits from the menu offered, you decide you want or need additional insurance benefits, most employers will deduct the additional cost of providing them from your paycheck. However, before you make this decision, compare the cost and service offerings of coverage through your employer with that available through other sources.

Some employers offer consumer-driven health plans that go one step beyond a flexible-benefit plan. Typically, these plans combine a high-deductible health insurance policy with a **medical reimbursement account**. Your employer contributes to the medical reimbursement account, and you can use the money to pay for your health-care needs. If you don't use the money by the end of the year, you can "roll over" the amount. After several years of rolling over, you can accumulate quite a bit of cash to pay for medical expenses. The Internal Revenue Service considers employer-made contributions to medical reimbursement accounts to be tax-free income.

medical reimbursement account
An account into which employers place contributions that employees can use to pay for medical expenses. Usually combined with a high-deductible health insurance policy.

If your spouse is employed, then you should also evaluate his or her benefit package before making any decisions. You may, for example, already be covered under your spouse's group health insurance plan or be able to purchase coverage for yourself and family members at a cheaper rate than through your own employer's plan.

If you are laid off from or leave a job where you have had health benefits, you are legally eligible to continue your coverage for a period of 18 months under federal COBRA regulations (discussed later in the chapter). You will be responsible for paying the full cost of the insurance if you decide to continue your coverage during this time, but you will still pay group insurance rates that are frequently less expensive than buying individual insurance. However, you must arrange to continue your coverage before you leave your former employer.

Another important area of group coverage to consider is retiree benefits. Because the number of companies providing health insurance to retirees has decreased sharply, you may not be able to count on receiving employer-paid benefits once you retire. Know what your options are to ensure continued coverage for both you and your family after you retire. Medicare will cover basic medical expenses, but you will probably want to supplement this coverage with one of the 10 standard Medigap plans. These plans will cost from $600 to $2,500 per year for the typical 65-year-old, depending on coverage.

Supplementing traditional health insurance plans are several other possible sources of funds or services. As we'll discuss in Chapter 10, homeowner's and automobile insurance policies often contain limited amounts of medical expense protections. Your automobile policy, for example, may cover you if you are involved in an automobile accident regardless of whether you are in a car, on foot, or on a bicycle when the accident occurs. In addition to Social Security's Medicare program, various other government programs help pay medical expenses as well. For instance, medical care is provided for people who've served in the armed services and were honorably discharged. Public health programs exist to treat communicable diseases, handicapped children, and mental health disorders.

Of course, you may still need or want to purchase additional medical insurance coverage on an individual basis. Private insurance companies sell a variety of indemnity and managed care plans to individuals. Well-known health insurance carriers are Aetna, CIGNA, and Prudential, among others. When buying health insurance—as with all types of insurance—you should buy plans from an insurance agent who will listen to your needs and answer your questions with well-thought-out responses. You should also research the carrier that will be providing your insurance. Look for a carrier that is rated highly by at least two of the major ratings agencies and that has a reputation for settling claims fairly and promptly. Avoid companies that have narrow and unusual legalistic claims practices. The National Committee on Quality Assurance (NCQA) is another source of information. This nonprofit, unbiased organization issues annual "report cards" that rate the service quality of various health plans.

If you think your job search may take more than a year, or you accept a job that doesn't provide health insurance benefits, it's wise to investigate standard long-term coverage. Individual plans are typically more expensive than group coverage, with minimum premiums of $100 to $200 a month. Additionally, individual plans usually require that you take a physical exam or prove "evidence of insurability." If you're shopping for individual insurance, be careful of plans that seem to offer unusually low rates and require little or no medical prescreening. In recent years, there's been a spate of unlicensed companies offering bogus deals to unsuspecting health insurance shoppers. If a plan sounds too good to be true, protect yourself by contacting your state insurance commission office to verify that the company is legitimate before you buy.

Beware of "catastrophic health insurance" that cover only major hospital and medical expenses, such as treatment in intensive care after an auto accident. Although premiums are attractively low, the deductible on these plans is typically very high, often as much as $5,000. Could you afford such a high deductible if you were seriously injured or needed major treatment?

Even without a group plan through work, you may find group coverage through college alumni groups, religious and social organizations, trade or professional associations, and state business associations. Students covered under a parent's group plan can extend their coverage after they graduate under COBRA legislation for up to 26 months if they pay the full premium. However, to qualify, you must act fast: The deadline for signing up under COBRA is 60 days from the existing policy's expiration date.

Critical Thinking Questions

1. What are the advantages and disadvantages of the various types of health insurance options available to recent graduates?
2. If you were graduating today and didn't have access to employer-sponsored health insurance, what option would be most attractive to you? Why?
3. Do you think most recent college graduates need health insurance? Why or why not?

Sources: "Finding Affordable Health Insurance After the Apron Strings Are Cut," *Insure.com*, downloaded from **http://www.insure.com**, November 21, 2003; Brian Gerard, "The Basics of Short-Term Health Insurance," *Insure.com*, downloaded from **http://www.insure.com**, November 22, 2003; Chad Terhune, "Fast-Growing Health Plan Has a Catch: $1,000-a-Year Cap," *The Wall Street Journal*, May 14, 2003, p. A1; Kyung M. Song, "Individual Health Insurance Market Tricky for Consumers," *The Seattle Times*, December 12, 2002; Christopher Windham, "Bogus Health Insurance Is Growing," *The Wall Street Journal*, August 28, 2003, p. D15.

Choose a Health Insurance Plan

Once you have familiarized yourself with the different health insurance plans and providers and reviewed your needs, you must choose one or more plans to provide coverage for you and your dependents. If you are employed, first review the various health insurance plans your company offers. If you can't get coverage from an employer, get plan descriptions and policy costs from several providers, including a group plan from a professional or trade organization, if available, for both indemnity and managed care plans. Then take your time and carefully read the plan materials to understand exactly what is covered, and at what cost. Next, add up what you have spent on medical costs over the past few years and what you might expect to spend in the future, so you can see what your costs would be under various plans.

> **Financial Road Sign**
>
> **Five Ways to Save on Health Insurance**
>
> 1. Opt for a managed care plan.
> 2. If you're buying an indemnity plan, choose a higher deductible.
> 3. Buy group health insurance.
> 4. Buy while you're healthy.
> 5. Negotiate. If your health plan covers services you won't use, ask if you can eliminate them from your policy to lower your cost.

How do you find health insurance if you have just graduated from college, don't yet have a job, and can no longer be covered by your parents' policy? Or maybe you are between jobs or need time to search out the best policy but don't want to be without protection. The *Money in Action* box on pages 368–369 will help you with these situations.

You'll have to ask yourself some difficult questions to decide whether you want an indemnity or a managed care plan, and then to choose the particular plan:

- **How important is cost compared with having freedom of choice?** You may have to pay more to stay with your current doctor if he or she is not part of a managed care plan you are considering. Also, you have to decide if you can live with the managed care plan's approach to healthcare.
- **Will you be reimbursed if you choose a managed care plan and want to see an out-of-network provider?** For most people, the managed care route is cheaper, even if you visit a doctor only once a year, because of indemnity plan "reasonable charge" provisions.
- **What types of coverage do you need?** Everyone has different needs; one person may want a plan with good maternity and pediatric care, whereas another wants outpatient mental health benefits. Make sure the plans you consider offer what you want.
- **How good is the managed care network?** Look at the participating doctors and hospitals to see how many of your providers are part of the plan. Check out the credentials of participating providers; a good sign is accreditation from the National Committee for Quality Assurance (NCQA). Are the providers' locations convenient for you? What preventive medical programs does it provide? Has membership grown? Talk to friends and associates to see what their experiences have been with the plan.
- **How old are you and how is your health?** Many financial advisors recommend buying the lowest-cost plan—which may be an indemnity plan with a high deductible—if you're young and healthy.

Once you've considered all of the coverage and resources that are available to you, consider where gaps in your health insurance coverage potentially lie and

> **Concept ✓**
>
> 9-10. Explain four methods for controlling the risks associated with healthcare expenses.
> 9-11. Explain what factors should be considered in evaluating available employer-sponsored health insurance plans.
> 9-12. Discuss possible sources of health insurance available to supplement employer-sponsored health insurance plans.
> 9-13. Answer the five questions posed to help you choose a plan, based on your current situation. What type of plan do you think will best suit your needs?

how best to fill them. Doing this requires an understanding of the features, policy provisions, and coverage provided by various insurance carriers and policies. We will discuss these in detail in the next section.

smart.sites

What grade did your health plan get on its quality "report card" this year? The National Committee on Quality Assurance (NCQA) can tell you: **http://www.ncqa.org**.

LG4

MEDICAL EXPENSE COVERAGE AND POLICY PROVISIONS

Thus far, we have discussed the major types of health insurance plans, their providers, and the factors that should be considered in evaluating the need for health insurance. To evaluate different insurance plan options, however, you must be able to compare and contrast what they cover and how each plan's policy provisions may affect you and your family. By doing so, you can decide which health plan offers the best protection at the most reasonable cost. Worksheet 9.1 provides a convenient checklist for comparing the costs and benefits of competing health insurance plans. You may want to refer to it as you read the following sections.

TYPES OF MEDICAL EXPENSE COVERAGE

The type of medical services covered varies from health plan to health plan. You can purchase narrowly defined plans that cover only what you consider the most important medical services or, if you can afford it and want the comfort of broader coverage, you can purchase insurance coverage to help you pay for most or all of your healthcare needs. Here are the medical expenses that are most commonly covered by health insurance.

Hospitalization

If you must spend time in the hospital, a *hospitalization insurance policy* will reimburse you for the cost of your stay. Hospitalization policies usually pay for a portion of (1) the hospital's daily semiprivate room rate, which typically includes meals, nursing care, and other routine services; and (2) the cost of ancillary services such as laboratory tests, x-rays, and medications you receive while hospitalized. Many hospitalization plans also cover some outpatient and out-of-hospital services once you are discharged, such as in-home rehabilitation, diagnostic treatment, and preadmission testing. Some hospitalization plans simply pay a flat daily amount for each day the insured is in the hospital, regardless of actual charges. Most policies set a limit on the number of days of hospitalization and the maximum dollar amount for ancillary services they will reimburse.

Surgical Expenses

Surgical expense insurance covers the cost of surgery in or out of the hospital. Usually, surgical expense coverage is provided as part of a hospitalization insurance policy or as a rider to such a policy. Most plans reimburse *reasonable and customary* surgical expenses based on a survey of surgical costs during the previous year. They may also cover anesthesia, nonemergency treatment using x-rays, and a limited allowance for diagnostic tests. Some plans still pay according to a *schedule of benefits,* reimbursing up to a fixed maximum for a particular surgical procedure. For example, the policy might state that you would receive no more than $1,000 for an appendectomy or $900 for diagnostic arthroscopic surgery on a knee. Scheduled benefits are often inadequate when compared with typical surgical costs. Most elective cosmetic surgeries, such as the proverbial "nose job" or "tummy tuck," are typically excluded from reimbursement unless they are deemed a medical necessity.

worksheet 9.1

Health Insurance Checklist

This worksheet provides a convenient checklist that can be used to compare the costs and benefits of competing healthcare plans:

	Company 1	Company 2	Company 3
PLAN TYPE (HMO, PPO, etc.)			
COSTS			
Premium per month			
Annual deductible: Per person/Per family			
Co-payment percent after deductible			
Co-pay or % coinsurance per office visit			
Co-pay or % coinsurance for "wellness" care			
COVERED MEDICAL SERVICES WITHIN NETWORK			
Inpatient hospital services			
Outpatient surgery			
Physician visits (in the hospital)			
Office visits (provider)			
Skilled nursing care			
Medical tests and x-rays			
Prescription drugs			
Mental healthcare			
Drug and alcohol abuse treatment			
Home healthcare visits			
Rehabilitation facility care			
Physical therapy			
Speech therapy			
Hospice care			
Maternity care			
Chiropractic treatment			
Preventive care and checkups			
Well-baby care			
Dental care			
Other covered services			
OTHER PROVISIONS			
Out-of-network coverage			
Medical service limits, exclusions, or preexisting conditions			
Requirements for utilization review, preauthorization, or certification procedures			

Source: Developed from information in *HIAA Guide To Health Insurance,* **http://www.hiaa.org/consumer/guidehi.html**.

Physician Expenses

Physicians expense insurance, previously called *regular medical expense*, covers the cost of physician fees for nonsurgical care in a hospital, including consultation with a specialist. Also covered are x-rays and laboratory tests performed outside of a hospital. Home, clinic, or doctor's office visits normally are not covered except through special provisions. Plans are offered on either a reasonable and customary or scheduled benefit basis. Often, the first few visits with the physician for any single cause will be excluded. This exclusion serves the same purpose as the deductible and waiting period features found in other types of insurance.

Major Medical Insurance

major medical plan
An insurance plan designed to supplement the basic coverage of hospitalization, surgical, and physicians expenses; used to finance medical costs of a more catastrophic nature.

comprehensive major medical insurance
A health insurance plan that combines, into a single policy, basic hospitalization, surgical, and physicians expense coverage with major medical protection.

Major medical plans provide broad coverage for nearly all types of medical expenses resulting from either illnesses or accidents. As the name implies, the amounts that can be collected under this coverage are relatively large. Lifetime limits of $500,000, $1,000,000, or higher are common, and some policies have no limits at all. Because hospitalization, surgical, and physicians expense coverage meets the smaller medical costs, major medical is used to finance medical costs of a more catastrophic nature. Many people use major medical with a high deductible to protect them in case they have a catastrophic illness.

Comprehensive Major Medical Insurance

A **comprehensive major medical insurance plan** combines basic hospitalization, surgical, and physicians expense coverage with major medical protection into a single policy, usually with a low deductible. Comprehensive major medical insurance is often written under a group contract. However, some efforts have been made to make this type of coverage available on an individual basis.

Dental Services

Dental insurance covers necessary dental care and some dental injuries sustained through accidents. (Expenses for accidental damage to natural teeth are normally covered under standard surgical expense and major medical policies.) Depending on the policy, covered services may include examinations, x-rays, dental cleanings, fillings, extractions, dentures, root canal therapy, orthodontics, and oral surgery. The maximum limit on most dental policies is often low—$1,000 to $2,500 per patient—so these plans do not fully protect against unusually high costs for dental work.

An examination of every type of health insurance coverage available would fill a book twice the size of this one. The types of health plans already discussed are sufficient to meet the protection needs of most individuals and families. However, there are other options offered by insurance companies that provide limited protection against certain types of perils. These include:

- *Accident policies* that pay a specified sum to an insured injured in a certain type of accident.
- *Sickness policies*, sometimes called *dread disease policies*, that pay a specified sum for a named disease, such as cancer.
- *Hospital income policies* which promise to guarantee a specific daily, weekly, or monthly amount as long as the insured remains hospitalized.

Before purchasing any of these or similar options, however, you should remember that sound insurance planning seldom dictates the purchase of these types of policies. Also, bear in mind that the extra cost of purchasing these insurance options typically outweighs the limited coverage they provide. Accident and sickness policies, for instance, usually only cover one type of accident or illness, while hospital income policies generally exclude illnesses that could result in extended hospitalization or health conditions that exist at the time of purchase.

The basic problem with buying policies that cover only a certain type of accident, illness, or financial need is that major gaps in coverage will occur. Clearly, the financial loss can be just as great regardless of whether the insured falls down a flight of stairs or contracts cancer, lung disease, or heart disease. Most limited-peril policies should be used only to supplement a comprehensive insurance program if the coverage is not overlapping.

Policy Provisions of Medical Expense Plans

To compare the health insurance plans offered by different insurers, evaluate whether they contain liberal or restrictive provisions. Generally, policy provisions can be divided into two groups: terms of payment and terms of coverage.

Terms of Payment

Four provisions govern how much your health insurance plan will pay: (1) deductibles, (2) the participation (coinsurance) clause, (3) the policy's internal limits, and (4) the coordination of benefits clause, if any.

Deductibles

Because major medical insurance plans are designed to supplement basic hospitalization, surgical, and physicians expense plans, those offered under an indemnity (fee-for-service) plan often have a relatively large *deductible,* typically $500 or $1,000. The **deductible** represents the initial amount *not* covered by the policy and therefore the responsibility of the insured. Comprehensive major medical plans tend to offer lower deductibles, sometimes $100 or less. Most plans offer a calendar-year, all-inclusive deductible. In effect, this allows a person to accumulate the deductible from more than one incident of use. Some plans also include a *carryover provision* whereby any part of the deductible that occurs during the final 3 months of the year (October, November, and December) can be applied to the current year's deductible and can *also* be applied to the following calendar year's deductible. In a few plans the deductible is on a per-illness or per-accident basis. If you were covered by this type of policy with a $1,000 deductible and suffered three separate accidents in the course of a year, each requiring $1,000 of medical expenses, you would not be eligible to collect any benefits from the major medical plan.

deductible
The initial amount *not* covered by an insurance policy and therefore the responsibility of the insured; it is usually determined on a calendar-year or on a per-illness or per-accident basis.

participation (coinsurance) clause
A provision in many health insurance policies stipulating that the insurer will pay some portion—say, 80 or 90 percent—of the amount of the covered loss in excess of the deductible.

internal limits
A feature commonly found in health insurance policies that places a constraint on the amounts that will be paid for certain specified expenses—even if the overall policy limits are *not* exceeded by the claim.

Participation (Coinsurance)

A **participation**, or **coinsurance**, **clause** stipulates that the company will pay some portion—say, 80 or 90 percent—of the amount of the covered loss in excess of the deductible rather than the entire amount. Coinsurance helps reduce the possibility that policyholders will fake illness and discourages them from incurring unnecessary medical expenses. Many major medical plans also have a *stop-loss provision* that places a cap on the amount of participation required. Without a stop-loss provision, a $1 million medical bill could leave the insured with, say, $200,000 of costs. Often such provisions limit the insured's participation to less than $10,000, and sometimes as little as $2,000.

Internal Limits

Most major medical plans are written with **internal limits** that limit the amounts paid for certain specified expenses—even if the overall policy limits are *not* exceeded by the claim. Charges that are commonly subject to internal limits are hospital room and board, surgical fees, mental and nervous conditions, and nursing services. If an insured elects a highly expensive physician or medical facility, he or she will be responsible for paying the portion of the charges that are above a "reasonable and customary" level or beyond a specified maximum amount. The example in the following section illustrates how deductibles, coinsurance, and internal limits constrain the amount a company is obligated to pay under a major medical plan.

Major Medical Policy: An Example

Assume that Frank Payne, a graduate student, has coverage under a major medical insurance policy that specifies a $500,000 lifetime limit of protection, a $1,000 deductible, an 80 percent coinsurance clause, internal limits of $350 per day on hospital room and board, and $2,000 as the maximum payable surgical fee. Recently he was hospitalized for 5 days to remove a small tumor. He incurred the following costs:

Hospitalization: 5 days at $500 a day	$2,500
Surgical expense	1,800
Other covered medical expenses	1,800
Total medical expenses	$6,100

Because of the coinsurance clause in the policy, however, the maximum the company has to pay is 80 percent of the covered loss in excess of the deductible. In the absence of internal limits the company would pay $4,080 (.80 × [$6,100 − $1,000]). The internal limits further restrict the payment. Even though 80 percent of the $500-per-day hospitalization charge is $400, the most the company would have to pay is $350 per day. Therefore the insured becomes liable for $50 per day for 5 days, or $250. The surgical expense is below the $2,000 internal limit, so the 80 percent coinsurance clause applies and the insurer will pay $1,440 (.80 × $1,800). The company's total obligation is reduced to $3,830 ($4,080 − $250), whereas the insured must pay a total of $2,270 ($1,000 deductible + .20[$6,100 − $1,000] coinsurance + $250 excess hospital charges). This example shows that, although major medical insurance can offer very large amounts of reimbursement, you may still be left responsible for substantial payments.

Coordination of Benefits

Health insurance policies are not contracts of *indemnity*. This means that those insured can collect multiple payments for the same illness or accident unless health insurance policies include a **coordination of benefits provision**. This clause prevents you from collecting more than 100 percent of covered charges by collecting benefits from more than one policy. For example, many private health insurance policies coordinate benefit provisions with medical benefits paid under workers' compensation. In contrast, some companies widely advertise that their policies will pay claims regardless of other coverage the policyholder has. Of course, these latter types of insurance policies often cost more per dollar of protection. From the standpoint of insurance planning, the use of policies with coordination of benefits clauses can help you prevent coverage overlaps and, ideally, reduce your premiums.

coordination of benefits provision
A provision often included in health insurance policies to prevent the insured from collecting more than 100 percent of covered charges; it requires that benefit payments be coordinated in the event the insured is eligible for benefits under more than one policy.

Considering the complexity of medical expense contracts, the various clauses limiting payments, and coordination of benefits with other policies, one might expect that insurers often pay only partial claims and sometimes completely deny claims. If you make a claim and do not receive the payment you expected, do not give up. Exhibit 9.5 provides some guidelines on how you might go about getting your health insurance claims paid.

Terms of Coverage

A number of contract provisions affect the value of a health insurance plan to you. Some of the more important provisions address (1) the persons and places covered, (2) cancellation, (3) preexisting conditions, (4) pregnancy and abortion, (5) mental illness, (6) rehabilitation coverage, and (7) continuation of group coverage.

EXHIBIT 9.5

How to Get Your Health Insurance Claims Paid

The following guidelines will help you cut through red tape to get your health insurance claims paid:

1. *Treat your insurance claims almost like tax records.* Keep them, along with any supporting documentation, and keep them up to date. Set up a good filing system.
2. *List every claim, including the doctor's name, the date of the treatment, the type of treatment, the charge, and the date the claim was filed.* Photocopy it along with the bills or other supporting documents you submit and keep the copies in your file folder.
3. *Double-check your claim form for accuracy before filing it.* Make sure that all the information is complete and correct; with computer processing, a typographic error or missing item could delay your claim or even cause it to be rejected.
4. *File all claims promptly, even if you don't think you are covered.* You need to file claims, usually within 6 to 12 months of the date of service, to meet your annual deductible.
5. *Review the company's Explanation of Benefits statement.* Within 30 days, you should receive a statement from your insurer that tells you how much the insurance company will pay on the claim. If 30 days pass, and you haven't heard from the carrier, call or write.
6. *If a claim is rejected, don't take "no" for an answer.* Find out why the claim was denied and provide additional information if required. The reason may be a misspelled name or transposed numbers or an incorrect diagnostic code. Properly documented appeals for covered services have a high likelihood of success.
7. *If your claim is not handled to your satisfaction, go directly to the company's claims supervisor or home office.* Sometimes a letter to the company president breaks the logjam. As a last resort, tell the company that you will file a complaint with the state insurance department—and do it if necessary.
8. *Keep good records of utilization review approvals for hospital admissions or medical procedures.* You are ultimately responsible for getting these approvals, so be sure to allow enough time before your hospitalization and request written confirmation. If you have a chronic or life-threatening disease, it may be worth it to hire a private claims advocate to help you sort through your medical bills and insurance claims to figure out what you owe. Find one through the Alliance of Claims Assistance Professionals Web site, **http://www.claims.org**.

Sources: Michelle Andrews, "Don't Get Killed by Bills," *U.S. News & World Report*, August 25, 2003, p. 52; Josh Fischman, "Who'll Pay for the Doc You Want?," *U.S. News & World Report*, August 25, 2003, p. 50.

Persons and Places Covered

Some health insurance policies cover only the named insured, whereas others offer protection to all family members. Of those that offer family coverage, some terminate benefits payable on behalf of children at age 18 and others continue them to age 24 as long as the child remains in school or is single. *If you are in this age group, you or your parents should check to see if you are covered under your parents' policy.* If not, sometimes by paying an additional premium, you can add such coverage. Some policies protect you only while you are in the United States or Canada; others offer worldwide coverage but exclude certain named countries.

Cancellation

Many health insurance policies are written to permit *cancellation* at any time at the option of the insurer. Some policies explicitly state this; others do not. To protect yourself against premature cancellation, you should buy policies that specifically state that the insurer will not cancel coverage as long as premiums are paid.

Preexisting Conditions

Most health insurance policies sold to individuals (as opposed to group/employer-sponsored plans) contain a **preexisting condition clause**. This means the policy might exclude coverage for any physical or mental problems you had at the time you bought it. In some policies, the exclusion is permanent; in others, it lasts only for the first year or two that the coverage is in force. Group insurance plans may also have preexisting condition clauses, but these tend to be less restrictive than those in individually written policies.

preexisting condition clause A clause included in most individual health insurance policies that permits permanent or temporary exclusion of coverage for any physical or mental problems the insured had at the time the policy was purchased; this clause, if included at all, is much less restrictive in group policies.

Health Insurance Portability and Accountability Act (HIPAA) Federal law that protects the ability of people to get and continue health insurance after they leave a job or retire, even if they have a serious health problem.

However, employees who have recently left a job or retired are covered by the **Health Insurance Portability and Accountability Act**, or **HIPAA**. This federal law, implemented in 1996, is designed to protect the ability of people to get and continue health insurance after they leave a job or retire, even if they have a serious health problem. Under HIPAA, if you have already been covered by a health plan and you apply for new insurance, insurers cannot turn you down, charge you higher premiums, or enforce an exclusionary period because of your health status. While HIPAA does not guarantee you group coverage, it does protect your ability to buy individual health insurance even if you have a preexisting health condition.

smart.sites

For an online primer that explains your rights under the Health Insurance Portability and Accountability Act (HIPAA), visit: **http://www.aarp.org/hcchoices**

Pregnancy and Abortion

Many individual and group health insurance plans include special clauses for medical expenses incurred through pregnancy or abortion. Some liberal policies pay for all related expenses, including sick-leave pay during the final months of pregnancy, whereas others pay for medical expenses that result from pregnancy or abortion complications but not for routine procedure expenses. In the most restrictive cases, the policy offers no coverage for any costs of pregnancy or abortion.

Mental Illness

Many health insurance plans omit or offer reduced benefits for treatment of mental disorders. For example, a health insurance policy may offer hospitalization benefits that continue to pay as long as you remain hospitalized—except for mental illness. It may restrict payment for mental illness to one-half the normally provided payment amounts and for a period not to exceed 30 days. Unfortunately, mental illness is the

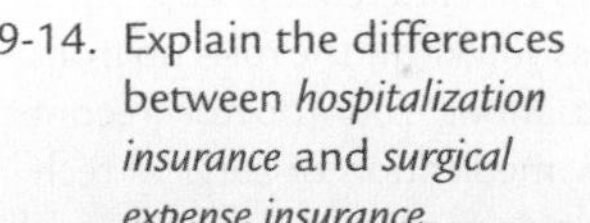

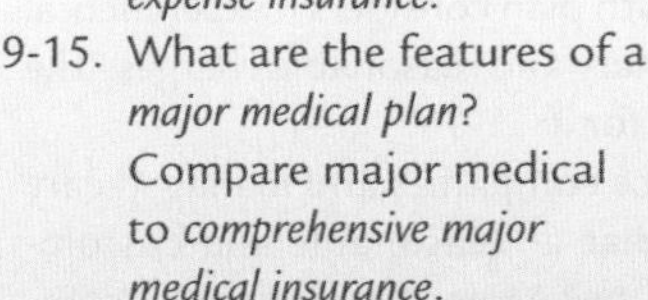

9-14. Explain the differences between *hospitalization insurance* and *surgical expense insurance.*

9-15. What are the features of a *major medical plan?* Compare major medical to *comprehensive major medical insurance*.

9-16. Describe the following policy provisions commonly found in medical expense plans: (a) deductibles, (b) coinsurance, (c) coordination of benefits, and (d) preexisting conditions.

9-17. What are the key provisions of the *Consolidated Omnibus Budget Reconciliation Act (COBRA)*? How do they relate to continuation of group coverage when an employee voluntarily or involuntarily leaves the group?

9-18. Explain the cost containment provisions commonly found in medical expense plans. How might the provision for second surgical opinions help an insurer contain its costs?

Money in Action

When Your Insurance Company Says No

If you or a loved-one is facing the need for expensive medical treatment, don't assume that your health plan will automatically pay for it. Most insurance companies and managed care plans are reluctant to pay for treatment beyond what they have decided is "reasonable and customary." Unfortunately, many patients are stuck paying medical bills out of pocket when they discover that a treatment recommended by their doctor was not fully covered by their health plan.

To prevent unexpected medical bills, start by learning the rules of your health plan. Every insurance and managed care plan has a different set of rules. Even doctors, many of whom participate in several plans, have trouble keeping the rules straight. Let's say you're referred to a specialist and wind up visiting that specialist several times. However, your managed care rules say you're only allowed three visits. You may have to pay the difference in cost out of your own pocket, unless you know the rules up front. Another common situation: Your doctor recommends a relatively new medication or surgical technique, but your health plan considers it experimental and beyond customary and reasonable charges. The plan refuses to pay for it.

How do insurance companies and managed care plans determine what a "reasonable and customary" charge should be? Most large insurance companies use a tool called the Prevailing Healthcare Charges System, a giant database containing billions of records of what doctors have charged for similar procedures. Insurance firms use this information to determine what a particular medical service should cost. If you have indemnity insurance or belong to a preferred provider organization and are seeking treatment beyond the plan's participating physician network, your insurance plan will use that cost estimate to determine how much of the actual cost they will reimburse.

Therefore, before you agree to major surgery or complex medical treatment, it's wise to get an estimate of the cost from your doctor. Call your insurance company and ask whether the charge is within the range it considers reasonable and

...continued on next page

number one sickness requiring long-term hospital care. Because coverage for mental illness is an important insurance protection, check your policies to learn how liberal—or how restrictive—they are with respect to this feature.

Rehabilitation Coverage

In the past, health insurance plans focused almost exclusively on reasonable and necessary medical expenses. If an illness or accident left an insured partially or totally disabled, no funds normally would be available to help the person retrain for employment and a more productive life. Now, though, many policies include *rehabilitation coverage* for counseling, occupational therapy, and even some educational or job-training programs. This is a good feature to look for in major medical and disability income policies.

Continuation of Group Coverage

Under the *Consolidated Omnibus Budget Reconciliation Act (COBRA)*, passed by Congress in 1986, an employee who leaves the group voluntarily or involuntarily (except in the case of "gross misconduct") may elect to continue coverage for up to 18 months by paying premiums to his or her former employer on time (up to 102 percent of the company cost). The employee retains all benefits previously available, except for disability income coverage.

Similar continuation coverage is available for retirees and their families for up to 18 months or until they become eligible for Medicare, whichever occurs first. The dependents of an employee may be covered for up to 36 months under COBRA under special circumstances, such as divorce or death of the employee. After COBRA coverage expires, most states provide for conversion of the group coverage to an individual policy regardless of the current health of the insured and without evidence of insurability. Premium charges and benefits of the converted policy are determined at the time of conversion.

Cost Containment Provisions for Medical Expense Plans

Considering the continued inflation in medical costs, it's hardly surprising that insurers, along with employers that sponsor medical expense plans, are looking for ways to limit the costs incurred. During the past decade, various cost containment provisions have been added to almost all medical expense plans, both indemnity and managed care policies. Although the success of such provisions has been limited, you are likely to find them in your own health insurance policy. These cost containment provisions include:

- **Preadmission Certification.** Requires you to receive approval from your insurer before entering the hospital for a scheduled stay. Such approval is not normally required for emergency stays.
- **Continued Stay Review.** To receive normal reimbursement, the insured must secure approval from the insurer for any stay that exceeds the originally approved limits.
- **Second Surgical Opinions.** Many plans require second opinions on specific, nonemergency procedures and, in their absence, may reduce the surgical benefits paid. Most surgical expense plans now provide for full reimbursement of the cost of second opinions.
- **Waiver of Coinsurance.** Because insurers can save money on hospital room and board charges by encouraging outpatient surgery, many now agree to waive the coinsurance clause and pay 100 percent of surgical costs for outpatient procedures. A similar waiver is sometimes applied to generic pharmaceuticals. For example, the patient may choose between an 80 percent payment for a brand-name pharmaceutical that cost $35 or 100 percent reimbursement for its $15 generic equivalent.
- **Limitation of Insurer's Responsibility.** Many policies also contain provisions that limit the insurer's financial responsibility to reimbursing only for costs that are considered "reasonable and customary." This provision can sometimes place limitations on the type and place of medical care for which the insurer will pay. As the *Money in Action* box on pages 378–379 discusses, there are ways to work with your health plan to insure that your medical treatment costs are fully covered.

customary. If it isn't, find out how much higher it is: The difference is what you will likely be expected to pay out of your own pocket.

Negotiation can help. For example, a PPO may agree to foot a higher bill if you can demonstrate that none of the plan's network physicians can provide a needed specialized treatment. Another tip: Call your insurance company and ask to have your situation reviewed by a "case manager." Usually, case managers are nurses who may be more understanding of your medical needs. If you still don't get satisfaction, most states allow you to take your dispute to a neutral party for an external review. This type of external review can take up to 60 days. One study found that 42 percent of all appeals for additional services are eventually decided in favor of the patient.

Critical Thinking Questions:

1. How does the Prevailing Healthcare Charges System affect what your insurance company pays?
2. What steps should you take if your health plan refuses to pay for medical treatment recommended by your doctor?
3. Do you think that health insurance carriers have an ethical and legal responsibility to cover all treatment costs of beneficiaries? Why or why not?

Sources: Michelle Andrews, "Don't Get Killed by Bills," *U.S. News & World Report*, August 25, 2003, p. 52; Josh Fischman, "Who'll Pay for the Doc You Want?," *U.S. News & World Report*, August 25, 2003, p. 50; Barbara Martinez, "A Matter of Definition," *The Wall Street Journal*, April 23, 2003, p. R7, "If your Plan Gives You a Pain," *AOL Finance/Consumer Reports*, downloaded from **http://aolsvc.aol.consumerreports.org**, November 4, 2003.

smart.sites

Which health insurance policy is best for your needs? How much will it cost? Search for the best deal at Ehealthinsurance.com, **http://www.ehealthinsurance.com**.

long-term care The delivery of medical and personal care, other than hospital care, to persons with chronic medical conditions resulting from either illness or frailty.

LG5 LONG-TERM CARE INSURANCE

The need for **long-term care**—whether in a nursing home, in an assisted-living community, or through care provided in the patient's home—can have major financial impact. A year's stay in a nursing home, for example, averages $57,000, according to GE Financial's Long-Term Care Insurance unit.

According to research conducted by the Healthcare Policy Institute, consumers pay 25 percent of long-term care costs—over $40 billion annually—out of their own pockets. Government programs such as Medicare and Medicaid shoulder only 16 percent of the total cost, and eligibility for their benefits is strictly defined. Major medical insurance plans also exclude most of the costs related to long-term care. When a person receiving nursing home care cannot afford to cover such a large personal expense out of pocket, it is often the younger generation that ends up footing the bill.

Fortunately, special insurance policies are available to cover long-term care. Most are indemnity policies that pay a fixed dollar amount for each day you receive specified care either in a nursing home or at home. The decision to buy long-term care insurance is an important part of health insurance and retirement financial planning. Today, more than 6.3 million individuals have made the decision to purchase this type of insurance.

Most people purchase individual long-term care products either through organizations like the American Association of Retired People (AARP) or directly from the more than 100 insurance companies that offer them. Employer-sponsored long-term care insurance is also growing in popularity. More than 5,000 businesses now offer some type of long-term care insurance to their employees. Usually, however, employees pay the full cost of premiums, although employer-sponsored plans can often be less costly than purchasing long-term care on an individual basis. Whether you purchase long-term care insurance as an individual or through an employer-sponsored plan, however, it is important to evaluate policy provisions and costs.

Do You Need Long-Term Care Insurance?

The odds of needing more than one year of nursing home care before you reach age 65 are 1 in 33. On the other hand, the expense of a prolonged nursing home stay can cause severe financial hardship. How do you decide if you need long-term care insurance? Answer these questions:

- **Do you have a lot of assets to preserve for your dependents?** Because you must deplete most of your assets before Medicaid will pay for nursing home care, some financial advisors recommend that people over 65 whose net worth is more than $100,000 and income exceeds $50,000 a year consider long-term care insurance—*if* they can afford the premiums. The very wealthy, however, may prefer to self-insure.
- **Can you afford the premiums?** Premiums of many good-quality policies can be 5 to 7 percent of annual income or more. Such high premiums may cause more financial hardship than the cost of a potential nursing home stay. You may be better off investing the amount you would spend in premiums; it would then be available for *any* future need, including long-term healthcare.
- **Is there a family history of disabling disease?** This factor increases your odds of needing long-term care. If there's a history of Alzheimer's, neurological disorders, or

Financial Road Sign

Standards for a Good Long-Term Care Policy:

1. At least 1 year of nursing home or home healthcare coverage, including intermediate and custodial care, and coverage for Alzheimer's disease.
2. Inflation protection.
3. A detailed "outline of coverage" describing the policy's benefits, limitations, and exclusions.
4. A long-term care insurance shopper's guide that helps you decide whether long-term care insurance is appropriate for you.
5. A guarantee against cancellation or nonrenewal because of age or deteriorating physical or mental health.
6. The right to return the policy for a refund within 30 days of purchase.
7. No requirement that policyholders first be hospitalized to receive nursing home or home healthcare benefits, or first receive a higher level of care before receiving lower care levels.

Source: The National Association of Insurance Commissioners, cited in *HIAA Guide to Long-Term Care Insurance,* p. 16–17, downloaded November 25, 2003, from **http://www.hiaa.org/consumer/guideltc.htm**.

other potentially debilitating diseases, the need for long-term care insurance may increase.

- **Are you male or female?** Women tend to live longer and thus are more likely to require long-term care. They are also the primary caregivers for other family members, which may mean that when they need care help will not be available.
- **Do you have family who can care for you?** The availability of relatives or home health services to provide care can reduce the cost of long-term care.

Long-Term Care Insurance Provisions and Costs

Whether you purchase long-term care insurance as an individual or through an employer-sponsored plan, it's important to understand what you are buying. Substantial variation exists between product offerings, so you must be especially careful to evaluate the provisions of each policy. Exhibit 9.6 summarizes the typical provisions of policies offered by leading insurers. Of course, policy provisions are important factors in determining the premium for each policy. Let's take a closer look at the most important policy provisions to consider in purchasing long-term care insurance:

EXHIBIT 9.6

Typical Provisions in Long-Term Care Insurance Policies

Long-term care insurers offer a wide range of provisions in their policies. A typical policy includes the following:

Services covered	Skilled, intermediate, and custodial care; home healthcare; adult day care (often)
Benefit eligibility	Physician certification/medically necessary
Daily benefit	\$50–\$300/day, nursing home \$25–\$150/day, home healthcare
Benefit period	3–4 years
Maximum benefit period	5 years; unlimited
Waiting period	0–100 days
Renewability	Guaranteed
Preexisting conditions	Conditions existing 6 months prior to policy coverage
Inflation protection	Yes, for an additional premium
Deductibility periods	0, 20, 30, 90, 100 days
Alzheimer's disease coverage	Yes
Age limits for purchasing	40–84

- **Type of Care.** Some long-term care policies offer benefits only for nursing home care, whereas others pay only for services in the insured's home, such as skilled or unskilled nursing care, physical therapy, homemakers, and home health aides. Because you cannot easily predict whether a person might need to be in a nursing home, most financial planners recommend policies that cover both. Many of these policies focus on nursing home care, and any expenses for healthcare in the insured's home are covered in a rider to the basic policy. Many policies also cover assisted-living, adult daycare and other community-care programs, alternative care, and respite care for the caregiver.
- **Eligibility Requirements.** Some very important provisions determine whether the insured will receive payment for claims. These are known as *gatekeeper* provisions. The most liberal policies state that the insured will qualify for benefits as long as his

or her physician orders the care. A common and much more restrictive provision pays only for long-term care that is medically necessary due to sickness or injury.

One common gatekeeper provision requires the insured's inability to perform a given number of *activities of daily living (ADLs)* such as bathing, dressing, or eating. Some policies also provide care for cognitive impairment or when medically necessary and prescribed by the patient's physician. In the case of an Alzheimer's patient who remains physically healthy, inclusion of cognitive abilities as ADLs would be extremely important. Newer policies no longer require a certain period of nursing home care before covering home healthcare services.

- **Services Covered.** Most policies today cover several levels of service in state-licensed nursing homes; specifically skilled, intermediate, and custodial care. *Skilled care* is needed when a patient requires constant attention from a medical professional, such as a physician or registered nurse. *Intermediate care* is provided when the patient needs medical attention or supervision but not the constant attention of a medical professional. *Custodial care* provides assistance in the normal activities of daily living, but no medical attention or supervision; a physician or nurse may be on call, however. Most long-term care policies also cover home care services, such as skilled or unskilled nursing care, physical therapy, homemakers, and home health aides provided by state-licensed or Medicare-certified home health agencies. Newer policies no longer require a certain period of nursing home care before covering home healthcare services.
- **Daily Benefits.** Long-term care policies reimburse the insured for services incurred up to a daily maximum. For nursing home care policies, the daily maximums generally range from $50 to $300, depending on the amount of premium the insured is willing to pay. For combination nursing home and home care policies, the maximum home care benefit is normally half the nursing home maximum.
- **Benefit Duration.** The maximum duration of benefits ranges from 1 year to the insured's lifetime. Lifetime coverage is very expensive, however. The consumer should realize that the average stay in a nursing home is now about 2½ years. Most financial planners recommend the purchase of a policy with a duration of 3 to 6 years to provide the insured with protection for a longer-than-average period of care.
- **Waiting Period.** Even if the insured meets the eligibility requirements of his or her policy, he or she must pay long-term care expenses during the **waiting**, or **elimination, period**. Typical waiting periods are 90 to 100 days. Although premiums are much lower for policies with longer waiting periods, the insured must have liquid assets to cover his or her expenses during that period. If the insured is still receiving care after the waiting period expires, he or she will begin to receive benefits for the duration of the policy as long as its eligibility requirements continue to be met.
- **Renewability.** Most long-term care insurance policies now include a **guaranteed renewability** provision to ensure continued coverage for your lifetime as long as you continue to pay the premiums. This clause does not ensure a level premium over time, however. Nearly all policies allow the insurer to raise premiums if the claims experience for your peer group of policyholders is unfavorable. Watch out for policies with an **optional renewability** clause. These policies are renewable *only at the option of the insurer.*
- **Preexisting Conditions.** Many policies include a *preexisting conditions clause,* similar to those explained earlier, ranging from 6 to 12 months. On the other hand, many policies have no such clause, which effectively eliminates one important source of possible claim disputes.
- **Inflation Protection.** Many policies offer riders that, for an additional premium, allow you to increase your benefits over time so that benefits roughly match the

waiting (elimination) period
The period, after the insured meets the policy's eligibility requirements, during which he or she must pay long-term care expenses; after the waiting period expires, the insured will begin to receive benefits for the duration of the policy as long as its eligibility requirements continue to be met.

guaranteed renewability
Policy provision ensuring continued insurance coverage for the insured's lifetime as long as he or she continues to pay the premiums. The insurer may raise premiums in the future, however, if the claims experience for the insured's peer group of policyholders is unfavorable.

optional renewability
Contractual clause allowing the insured to continue insurance *only at the option of the insurer.*

rising cost of nursing home and home healthcare. Most inflation protection riders allow you to increase benefits by a flat amount, often 5 percent, per year. Others offer benefits linked to the rise in the CPI. Most policies discontinue inflation adjustments after either 10 or 20 years. Inflation protection riders can add between 25 and 40 percent to the basic premium for a long-term care insurance policy.

- **Premium Levels.** Long-term care insurance is not inexpensive, and premiums vary widely among insurance companies. For example, a healthy 65-year-old may pay about $2,000 per year for a policy that pays for 4 years' care at $100 per day for nursing home care and $50 per day for home care, with a 100-day waiting period and a 5 percent inflation rider. The same coverage may cost a 50-year-old $850 per year, and a 79-year-old, $5,900 per year. Because of this marked rise in premium with age, some financial planners recommend buying long-term care insurance when you are fairly young.

smart.sites

Confused about long-term care insurance coverage? The *Guide to Long-Term Health Care* at the Health Insurance Association of America site, **http://www.hiaa.org/consumer/guideltc.html**, will provide the answers.

How to Buy Long-Term Care Insurance

If you decide that you or a relative should have long-term care insurance, be sure to buy from a financially sound company (based on ratings from the major ratings agencies) that has experience in this market segment. Here are some additional guidelines to help you choose the right policy.

- **Buy the policy while you're healthy.** Once you have a disease, such as Alzheimer's or multiple sclerosis, or have a stroke, you become uninsurable. The best time to buy is when you're in your mid-fifties or sixties.
- **Buy the right types of coverage—but don't buy more coverage than you need.** Your policy should cover skilled, intermediate, and custodial care, and also adult daycare centers and assisted living facilities. If you have access to family caregivers or home health services, opt for only nursing home coverage; if not, select a policy with generous home healthcare benefits. To reduce costs, increase the waiting period before benefits start; the longer you can cover the costs yourself, the lower your premiums. You may also choose a shorter benefit payment period; 3 years is a popular choice, but the average nursing home stay is about 2½ years. Lifetime coverage increases the premium for a 65-year-old by as much as 40 percent.
- **Understand what the policy covers and when it pays benefits.** The amounts paid, benefit periods, and services covered vary among insurers. One rule of thumb is to buy a policy that covers 80 to 100 percent of current nursing home costs in your area. Some policies pay only for licensed healthcare providers, whereas others include assistance with household chores. Know how the policy defines benefit eligibility.

Concept ✓

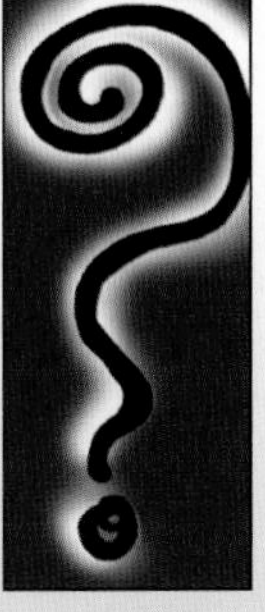

9-19. Why should a consumer consider purchasing a long-term care insurance policy?

9-20. Describe the differences among long-term care policies with respect to (a) type of care, (b) eligibility requirements, and (c) services covered. List and discuss some other important policy provisions.

9-21. Discuss some of the questions one should ask before buying long-term care insurance. What guidelines can be used to choose the right policy?

DISABILITY INCOME INSURANCE

LG6

When a family member becomes sick for an extended period, the effect on the family goes beyond medical bills. The average chance of a person age 35 becoming disabled for 90 days or longer before age 65 is about 50 percent; this chance drops to about 32 percent—2.5 times greater than the chance of death at that age—at age 55. These percentages are far higher than the chance of dying, but although most Americans have life insurance, few have taken steps to protect their family should a serious illness or accident prevent them from working for an extended period.

The best way to protect against the potentially devastating financial consequences of a health-related disability is with disability income insurance. **Disability income insurance** provides families with weekly or monthly payments to replace income when the insured is unable to work as a result of a covered illness, injury, or disease. Some companies also offer disability income protection for a homemaker-spouse; such coverage helps pay for the services that the spouse would normally provide.

disability income insurance
Insurance that provides families with weekly or monthly payments to replace income when the insured is unable to work as a result of a covered illness, injury, or disease.

Almost all employers offer disability income insurance at advantageous rates. However, coverage is often voluntary, and you may have to pay the entire premium yourself. Group coverage is usually a good buy, however: Premiums for employer-sponsored group coverage average $175 to $300 a year—about one-third the cost of comparable private coverage. A disadvantage is that if you change jobs, you may lose the coverage. The benefits from a group plan in which you pay the premiums are tax-free (unless paid through a flexible spending account). Be sure to run a needs analysis, as described in the instructions for Worksheet 9.2, to ensure that you have enough coverage for your needs.

Social Security offers disability income benefits, but you must be unable to do *any* job whatever to receive benefits. Benefits are payable only if your disability is expected to last at least 1 year (or to be fatal), and do not begin until you have been disabled for at least 5 months. The actual amount paid is a percentage of your previous monthly earnings, with some statistical adjustments. The percentage is higher for people with low earnings. A 35-year-old who earns $20,000 and has dependents would receive $1,261 per month (about 76 percent of earnings); if he or she earned $50,000, the amount rises to $2,215 per month (53 percent of earnings).

The need for disability income coverage is great, yet generally ignored by the public. Although most workers receive some disability insurance benefits from their employer, in many cases the group plan falls short and pays only about 60 percent of salary for a limited period. The first step in considering disability income insurance is to determine the dollar amount your family would need (typically monthly) in the event an earner becomes disabled. Then you can buy the coverage you need or supplement existing coverage if necessary.

ESTIMATING YOUR DISABILITY INSURANCE NEEDS

The overriding purpose of disability income insurance is to replace all (or most) of the income—that is, earnings—that would be lost if you became disabled and physically unable to hold a job. In essence, it should enable you to maintain a standard of living at or near your present level. To help decide how much disability income insurance is right for you, use Worksheet 9.2 to estimate your monthly disability benefit needs. Here is all you have to do:

1. **Calculate take-home pay.** Disability benefits are generally, but not always, tax-free, so you typically need to replace only your *take-home* (after-tax) pay. Benefits from employer-paid policies are fully or partially taxable. To estimate take-home pay,

worksheet 9.2

Estimating Disability Income Insurance Needs

Using a worksheet like this makes the job of estimating disability benefit needs a lot easier.

DISABILITY BENEFIT NEEDS

Name(s) ______________________ Date ______________

1. Estimate current monthly *take-home* pay		$ ______
2. Estimate existing monthly benefits:		
a. Social Security benefits	$ ______	
b. Other government benefits	______	
c. Company benefits	______	
d. Group disability policy benefits	______	
3. Total existing monthly disability benefits (2a + 2b + 2c + 2d)		$ ______
4. Estimated monthly disability benefits needed ([1]–[3])		$ ______

subtract income and Social Security taxes paid from your gross earned income (salary only). Divide this total by 12 to get your monthly take-home pay.

2. **Estimate the monthly amounts of disability benefits from government or employer programs:**
   a. *Social Security benefits.* Get an estimate of your benefits by calling 1-800-772-1213 for a *Personal Earnings and Benefit Estimate Statement.* An insurance agent may also have a computer program that can easily calculate it. As of 2003, the average Social Security disability benefit ranged from $1,261 to $2,600 per month for a wage earner with dependents, depending on age and income.
   b. *Other government programs* with disability benefits for which you qualify (armed services, Veterans Administration, civil service, the Federal Employees Compensation Act, state workers' compensation systems). There are also special programs for railroad workers, longshoremen, and people with black-lung disease.
   c. *Company disability benefits.* Ask your company benefits supervisor to help you calculate company-provided benefits, including sick pay or wage continuation plans (for all practical purposes, these are short-term disability income insurance) and plans formally designated as disability insurance. For each benefit your employer offers, check on its tax treatment.
   d. *Group disability policy benefits.* A private insurer provides the coverage, and you pay for it, often through payroll deduction.
3. **Add up your existing monthly disability benefits.**
4. **Subtract your existing monthly disability benefits from your current monthly take-home pay.** The result will show the estimated monthly disability benefits you will need to maintain your present after-tax income. Note that investment income and spousal income (if he or she is presently employed) are ignored because it is assumed this income will continue and is necessary to maintain your current standard of living. If your spouse is presently unemployed but would enter the workforce in the event you ever became disabled, his or her estimated monthly income (take-home pay) could be subtracted from item 4 of Worksheet 9.2 to determine your net monthly disability benefit needs.

Disability Income Insurance Provisions and Costs

The scope and cost of your disability income coverage depends on its contractual provisions. Although disability income insurance policies can be very complex, certain features are important, including (1) definition of disability, (2) benefit amount and duration, (3) probationary period, (4) waiting period, (5) renewability, and (6) other provisions.

Definition of Disability

Disability policies vary in the standards you must meet to receive benefits. Some pay benefits if you are unable to perform the duties of your customary occupation—the *own occupation* (or "Own Occ") definition—whereas others pay only if you can engage in no gainful employment at all—the *any occupation* (or "Any Occ") definition. Under the "Own Occ" definition, a professor who lost his voice, but still could get paid to write or do research, would receive full benefits because he could not lecture, a primary function of his occupation. With a *residual benefit option,* you would be paid partial benefits if you can only work part-time or at a lower salary. The "Any Occ" definition is considerably less expensive because it gives the insurer more leeway in determining whether the insured should receive benefits.

Individual disability policies may contain a *presumptive disability* clause that supersedes the previously discussed definition of disability when certain types of losses occur. Loss of both hands, sight in both eyes, and hearing in both ears are examples where the insured may be *presumed* totally disabled and may receive full benefits even though he or she still can be employed in some capacity.

Benefit Amount and Duration

Most individual disability income policies pay a flat monthly benefit, which is stated in the policy, whereas group plans pay a fixed percentage of gross income. In either case, insurers normally will not agree to amounts in excess of 60 to 70 percent of the insured's gross income. Insurers will not issue policies for the full amount of gross income because this would give some people an incentive to fake a disability (for example, "bad back") and collect more in insurance benefits than they normally would receive as take-home pay.

Monthly benefits can be paid for a few months or for a lifetime. If you are ensured substantial pension, Social Security, or other benefits at retirement, a policy that pays benefits until age 65 is adequate. Most people, however, will need to continue their occupations for many more years and should consider a policy offering lifetime benefits. Many policies offer benefits for periods as short as 2 or 5 years. Although these policies may be better than nothing, they do not protect against the major financial losses associated with long-term disabilities.

Probationary Period

Both group and individual disability income policies are likely to include a probationary period, usually 7 to 30 days, which is a time delay from the date the

Financial Road Sign

7 Tips for Reducing the Cost of Disability Income Insurance

1. See if your employer offers disability insurance as an employee benefit. Group rates are usually 15–35 percent below individual rates.
2. Consider buying a small policy now with a rider that will let you buy more later.
3. Get several price quotes; rates vary considerably.
4. Lengthen waiting periods to reduce premiums but still get adequate coverage.
5. A policy with benefits to age 65, not lifetime, saves on premiums.
6. Ask about discounted premiums. Some companies offer 10 percent off if you provide copies of tax returns or prepay premiums.
7. Ask to have a recurring medical problem excluded. You can reduce your premium if you exclude problems such as a bad back or knee.

policy is issued until benefit privileges are available. Any disability stemming from an illness, injury, or disease that occurs during the probationary period is *not* covered—even if it continues beyond this period. This feature keeps costs down.

Waiting Period

The waiting, or elimination, period provisions in a disability income policy are similar to those discussed for long-term care insurance. Typical waiting periods range from 30 days to 1 year. If you have an adequate emergency fund to provide family income during the early months of disability, you can choose a longer waiting period and substantially reduce your premiums, as shown in Exhibit 9.7.

EXHIBIT 9.7

Disability Income Insurance Premium Costs

The cost of disability income insurance varies with the terms of payment as well as the length of the waiting period. Because they have longer life expectancies, women pay substantially higher rates than men. This table shows premiums for basic disability income coverage for a 35-year-old that pays $2,000 per month in benefits, with guaranteed premiums to age 65. Any additional features, such as inflation riders, cost more.

Benefit Period	2 Years		5 Years		To Age 65		Lifetime	
Waiting Period	**Male**	**Female**	**Male**	**Female**	**Male**	**Female**	**Male**	**Female**
30 days	$698	$1,192	$922	$1,601	$1,284	$2,327	$1,402	$2,508
60 days	539	983	715	1,145	986	1,674	1,086	1,821
90 days	427	587	559	809	746	1,163	829	1,281
6 months	386	514	514	728	692	1,067	774	1,183
One year	358	464	475	660	638	972	718	1,086

With most insurers, you effectively can trade off an increase in the waiting period from, say, 30 days to 90 days for an increase in the duration of benefits from 5 years to age 65. In fact, as Exhibit 9.7 shows, the premium charged by this insurer for a policy covering a 35-year-old male with a 30-day waiting period and 2-year benefit period ($698) is about the same as one charged for benefits payable to age 65 with a 6-month waiting period ($692). Accepting this type of trade-off usually makes sense because the primary purpose of insurance is to protect the insured against a catastrophic loss, rather than smaller losses that are better handled through proper budgeting and saving.

Renewability

Most individual disability income insurance is either *guaranteed renewable* or *noncancelable*. As with long-term care policies, guaranteed renewability ensures that you can renew the policy until you reach the age stated in the clause, usually age 65. Premiums can be raised over time if justified by the loss experience of all those in the same class (usually based on age, sex, and occupational category). Noncancelable policies offer guaranteed renewability, but also guarantee that future premiums will remain the same as those stated in the policy at issuance. Because of this stable premium guarantee, noncancelable policies generally are more expensive than those with only a guaranteed renewability provision.

9-22. What is *disability income insurance?* Explain the waiting period provisions found in such policies.

9-23. Describe both the liberal and strict definitions used to establish whether an insured is disabled. Why is benefit duration an important consideration when shopping for disability income coverage?

Other Provisions

The purchasing power of income from a long-term disability policy that pays, say, $2,000 per month could be severely affected by inflation. In fact, a 3 percent inflation rate would reduce the purchasing power of this $2,000 benefit to less than $1,500 in 10 years. To counteract such a reduction, many insurers offer a *cost-of-living adjustment (COLA)*. With a COLA provision, the monthly benefit is adjusted upward each year, often in line with the CPI, although these annual adjustments are often capped at a given rate, say 8 percent. Although some financial advisors suggest buying COLA riders, others feel the 10 to 25 percent additional premium is not worth it with today's low inflation rate.

Although the COLA provision applies only once the insured is disabled, the *guaranteed insurability option (GIO)* can allow you to purchase additional disability income insurance in line with inflation increases while you are still healthy. Under the GIO, the price of this additional insurance is fixed at the inception of the contract, and you do not have to prove insurability.

A *waiver of premium* is standard in disability income policies. If you are disabled for a minimum period, normally 60 or 90 days, the insurer will waive any future premiums that come due while you remain disabled. In essence, the waiver of premium provides you with additional disability income insurance in the amount of your regular premium payment.

Remember that disability income insurance is just one part of your overall personal financial plan. You'll need to find your own balance between cost and coverage.

smart.sites

Shopping for disability insurance? The Health Insurance Association of America offers a directory of insurance carriers that sell disability policies at **http://www.hiaa.org/consumer/disability_dir.cfm**

Summary

LG1. Discuss why having adequate health insurance is important and identify the factors contributing to the growing cost of health insurance. A serious illness or major injury can have devastating financial consequences, easily ringing up a bill of tens of thousands of dollars in medical care and lost income. Even routine medical care can be costly. Adequate health insurance protects you from having to pay all of these costs out of pocket. However, many Americans are uninsured or underinsured because the cost of health insurance has skyrocketed. Trends pushing medical expenses and health insurance higher include the growth of new drugs and treatments that save lives but also cost more to provide. Administrative costs, excessive paperwork, increased regulation, and insurance fraud are also contributing to rising costs.

LG2. Differentiate among the major types of health insurance plans and identify major public and private health insurance providers and their programs. Health insurance is available from both private and government-sponsored programs. Private health insurance plans include indemnity (fee-for-service) plans and managed care plans. Indemnity plans pay a share of healthcare costs directly to a medical provider, who is usually separate from the insurer. The insured pays the remaining amount. In a managed care plan, subscribers contract with and make monthly payments directly to the organization providing the health services. Examples of managed care plans include health maintenance organizations (HMOs) and preferred provider organizations (PPOs). Blue Cross/Blue Shield plans are prepaid hospital and medical expense plans. Federal and state agencies also provide health insurance coverage to eligible individuals. Medicare, Medicaid, and workers' compensation insurance are all forms of government health insurance plans.

LG3. Analyze your own health insurance needs and explain how to shop for appropriate coverage. From a health insurance perspective, most people need protection from two types of losses: (1) the cost of medical bills and other associated expenses and (2) loss of income or household services caused by an inability to work. A good healthcare plan should use risk avoidance, loss prevention and control, and risk assumption strategies to reduce risk and the associated need and cost of insurance. The best way to buy health insurance is to determine your current coverage and resources and then match your needs with the various types of coverage available. When shopping for health insurance, consider the cost of coverage, its availability as an employee benefit, the quality of both the agent and the insurer or managed care provider, and your own medical needs and care preferences.

LG4. Explain the basic types of medical expenses covered and policy provisions of health insurance plans. The basic types of medical expenses covered by insurance are hospitalization, surgical expenses, physicians expenses (nonsurgical medical care), and major medical insurance (which covers all types of medical expenses). Some health insurers offer comprehensive major medical policies that combine basic hospitalization, surgical, and physicians expense coverage with a major medical plan to form a single policy.

The most important provisions in medical insurance policies pertain to terms of payment, terms of coverage, and cost containment. How much your plan will pay depends on deductibles, participation (coinsurance), internal limits, and coordination of benefits. Terms of coverage encompass the persons and places covered, cancellation, preexisting conditions, pregnancy and abortion, mental illness, rehabilitation, and group coverage continuation. The most common cost containment provisions are preadmission certification, continued stay review, second surgical opinions, and waiver of coinsurance.

LG5. Assess the need for and features of long-term care insurance. Long-term care insurance covers nonhospital expenses, such as nursing home care or home healthcare, caused by chronic illness or frailty. Coverage availability depends on provisions addressing type of care, eligibility requirements, services covered, renewability, and preexisting conditions. Terms-of-payment provisions include daily benefits, benefit duration, waiting period, and inflation protection. Premium levels result from differences in coverage and payment provisions, and vary widely among insurance companies.

LG6. Discuss the features of disability income insurance and how to determine your need for it. The loss of family income caused by the disability of a principal wage earner can be at least partially replaced by disability income insurance. Disability insurance needs can be estimated by subtracting the amount of existing monthly disability benefits from current monthly take-home pay. Important coverage terms include the definition of disability, probationary period, renewability, guaranteed insurability, and waiver of premium. Provisions pertaining to benefit amount and duration, waiting period, and cost-of-living adjustments define the terms of payment. Because these policies are expensive, you should choose as long a waiting period as possible given your other available financial resources.

FINANCIAL PLANNING EXERCISES

1. John and Linda Carter have two children, ages 6 years and 5 months. Their younger child, Caleb, was born with a congenital heart defect that will require several major surgeries in the next few years to fully correct. John is employed as a salesperson for a major pharmaceutical firm and Linda is a stay-at-home mother. John's employer offers employees a choice between two health benefit plans:
   - An indemnity plan that will allow the Carters to choose health services from a wide range of doctors and hospitals. The plan will pay 80 percent of all medical costs and the Carters will be responsible for the other 20 percent. There is a $500 per person deductible. John's employer will pay 100 percent of the cost of this plan for John, but the Carter's will be responsible for paying $380 a month to cover Linda and the children under this plan.
   - A group HMO. If the Carters choose this plan, the company will still pay 100 percent of the plan's cost for John but insurance for Linda and the children will cost $295 a month. They will also have to pay a $20 co-payment for doctor's office visits and prescription drugs. They will be restricted to using the HMO's doctors and hospital for medical services.

   Which plan would you recommend that the Carters choose? Why? What other health coverage options should the Carters consider?
2. David Chang was seriously injured in a snowboarding accident that broke both his legs and an arm. His medical expenses included: 5 days of hospitalization at $900 a day, $6,200 in surgical fees, $4,300 in physician's fees (including time in the hospital and eight follow-up office visits), $520 in prescription medications, and $2,100 for physical therapy treatments. All of these charges fall within customary and reasonable payment amounts.
   a. If David has an indemnity plan with a $500 deductible that pays 80 percent of his charges and has a $5,000 stop-loss provision, how much will he have to pay out of pocket?
   b. What would David's out-of-pocket expenses be if he belonged to an HMO with a $20 co-pay for office visits?
   c. Monthly premiums are $155 for the indemnity plan and $250 for the HMO. If he has no other medical expenses this year, which plan provides more cost-effective coverage for David? What other factors should he consider in deciding between the two plans?

3. *Use Worksheet 9.1.* Sarah Connelly, a recent college graduate, has decided to accept a job offer from a nonprofit organization. She will earn $28,000 a year but will not receive any employee health benefits. She estimates that her monthly living expenses will be about $1,800 a month, including rent, food, transportation, and clothing. She doesn't have any health problems and expects to remain in good health in the near future. Using the Internet or other resources, gather information about three health insurance policies that Sarah could purchase on her own. Include at least one HMO. Use Worksheet 9.1 to compare the policies' features. Should Sarah buy

health insurance? Why or why not? Assuming that she does decide to purchase health insurance, which of the three policies would you recommend and why?

4. Discuss the pros and cons of long-term care insurance. Does it make sense for anyone in your family at the present time? Why or why not? What factors might change this assessment in the future?
5. *Use **Worksheet 9.2.*** John Fitzmorris, a 35-year-old computer programmer, earns $72,000 a year. His monthly take-home pay is $3,750. His wife, Linda, works part-time at their children's elementary school but receives no benefits. Under state law, John's employer contributes to a worker's compensation insurance fund that would provide $2,250 per month for 6 months if John were disabled and unable to work.
    a. Use Worksheet 9.2 to calculate John's disability insurance needs assuming that he will not qualify for Medicare under his Social Security benefits.
    b. Based on your answer in part **a**, what would you advise John about his need for additional disability income insurance? Discuss the type and size of disability income insurance coverage he should consider, including possible provisions he might want to include. What other factors should he take into account if he decides to purchase a policy?

6. *Use **Worksheet 9.2.*** Do you need disability income insurance? Calculate your need using Worksheet 9.2. Discuss how you would go about purchasing this coverage.
7. Assess your current health insurance situation. Do you have any health insurance at present? What does your policy cover? What is excluded? Are there any gaps that you think need to be filled? Are there any risks in your current lifestyle or situation that might make additional coverage necessary? If you were to purchase health insurance for yourself in the near future, what type of plan would you select, and why? What steps can you take to keep your health costs down?

Applying Personal Finance

Insure Your Health!

Health care costs have increased dramatically in recent years, and many insurance providers have reduced their coverage, leaving the individual to foot more of the bill. The purpose of this project is to examine your health insurance needs and determine the coverage that is appropriate for you.

First of all, make a list of the possible healthcare needs you are likely to have during the year. Be sure to include the potential accident risks to which you are typically exposed as a result of your lifestyle activities. Then, if you currently have health insurance, make a list of the coverages it provides, including deductibles, coinsurance amounts, prescription coverage, policy limits and exclusions, and so forth. Is your coverage adequate in light of your needs? Are there ways you can reduce your costs? If you do not currently have health insurance, research possible providers. Can you obtain insurance through your place of employment or through an organization to which you belong? Do you qualify for insurance that may be provided by your state? Consider all of your feasible alternatives, the coverages that would be provided, and the cost of each.

Contemporary Case Applications

9.1 Evaluating Rick's Health Care Coverage

Rick Lannefeld was a self-employed window washer earning approximately $500 per week. One day, while cleaning windows on the eighth floor of the First National Bank Building, he tripped and fell from the scaffolding to the pavement below. He sustained severe multiple injuries but miraculously survived the accident. He was immediately rushed to Mt. Sinai Hospital for surgery. He remained there for 60 days of treatment, after which he was allowed to go home for further recuperation. During his hospital stay, he incurred the following expenses: surgeon, $2,500; physician, $1,000; hospital bill, room, and board, $250 per day; nursing services, $1,200; anesthetics, $300; wheelchair rental, $70; ambulance, $60; and drugs, $350. Rick has a major medical policy with LIC Corporation that has a $3,000 deductible clause, an 80 percent coinsurance clause, internal limits of $180 per day on hospital room and board, and $1,500 as a maximum surgical fee. The policy provides no disability income benefits.

Questions

1. Explain the policy provisions as they relate to deductibles, coinsurance, and internal limits.
2. How much should Rick recover from the insurance company? How much must he pay out of his pocket?
3. Would any other policies have offered Rick additional protection? What about his inability to work while recovering from his injury?
4. Based on the information presented, how would you assess Rick's healthcare insurance coverage? Explain.

9.2 Benito and Teresa Get a Handle on Their Disability Income Needs

Benito Fernandez and his wife, Teresa, have been married for 2 years and have a 1-year-old son. They live in Michigan, where Benito works for Ford Motor Company. He earns $3,200 per month, of which he takes home $2,300. As an employee of Ford, he and his family are entitled to receive the benefits provided by the company's group health insurance policy. In addition to major medical coverage, the policy provides a monthly disability income benefit amounting to 20 percent of the employee's average monthly take-home pay for the most recent 12 months prior to incurring the disability. (*Note*: Benito's average monthly take-home pay for the most recent year is equal to his current monthly take-home pay.) In the instance of complete disability, Benito would also be eligible for Social Security payments of $700 per month.

Teresa is also employed. She earns $700 per month after taxes working part-time at a nearby grocery store. The store provides her with no benefits other than Social Security. Should Benito become disabled, Teresa would continue to work at her part-time job. If she became disabled, Social Security would provide monthly income of $300. Benito and Teresa spend 90 percent of their combined take-home pay to meet their bills and provide for a variety of necessary items. They use the remaining 10 percent to fulfill their entertainment and savings goals.

Questions

1. How much, if any, additional disability income insurance does Benito require to ensure adequate protection against his becoming completely disabled? Use Worksheet 9.1 to assess his needs.
2. Does Teresa need any disability income coverage? Explain.
3. What specific recommendations with respect to disability income insurance would you give Benito and Teresa to provide adequate protection for themselves and their child?

Money Online

Insure Your Health!

1. **http://www.healthinsuranceinfo.net**

What are your rights and protections concerning health insurance? What if you lose your job or have a serious health condition? Laws concerning health insurance vary from state to state. Find a *Consumer Guide for Getting and Keeping Health Insurance* for each state at this site presented by the Georgetown University Health Policy Institute.

2. **http://www.insure.com/health**

How do you judge the quality of a health insurance plan? What if your insurance claim is denied? How does divorce affect your health insurance coverage? Insure.com's Web site provides help, advice, and an abundance of important information concerning health insurance.

3. **http://hprc.ncqa.org**

How does your health plan rate? Look at your company's "Health Plan Report Card" prepared by the National Committee for Quality Assurance. View the specifics on your company or find a list of all NCQA-Accredited Plans.

4. **http://cms.hhs.gov/schip**

Are your children currently uninsured? Learn more about the State Children's Health Insurance Plan (SCHIP) at the Centers for Medicare and Medicaid Services Web site. The Children's Defense Fund also provides another helpful site concerning services for children at **http://www.childrensdefense.org**.

5. **http://www.actuary.com**

Need to find your health insurance company's Web site? The Actuary.com Web site provides an extensive listing of links to various health insurance companies. Under "Insurance Industry," click on "Health Insurance Companies," and search for your company.

6. **http://www.northwesternmutual.com**

How likely are you to be affected by a long-term disability? Is your current disability insurance plan adequate? Find information on disability insurance at Northwestern Mutual's Web site by clicking on "Insurance Products" and then on "Disability Insurance." Use their calculators to find the odds that you will become disabled before age 65 or to see if you have a gap in your coverage.

7. **http://www.ssa.gov/disability**

Learn about Social Security's two disability programs at the Web site of the Social Security Administration. Find the eligibility requirements, read up on the services and benefits provided, or use their "Benefits Eligibility Screening Tool" to find out which programs may be able to pay you benefits.

8. **http://www.medicare.gov**

Learn all about Medicare at the official U.S. government site for Medicare information. Find information on coverage, eligibility, and enrollment. Use their search tools to help you compare health plan options or to find prescription drug or other assistance programs.

9. **http://www.medicare.gov/nursing/overview.asp**

Need information on a nursing home? Visit Medicare's Web site for a checklist to use in selecting a nursing home or to find a Medicare and Medicaid certified nursing home in your area at "Nursing Home Compare." Learn the "Alternatives to Nursing Home Care" and read through "Resident Rights."

10. **http://www.pueblo.gsa.gov/crh/insurance.htm**

Need to find the office responsible for enforcing your state's insurance laws? Scroll through the list of state insurance regulators at the Web site of the Federal Consumer Information Center. Find information to help you choose an insurance policy or learn how to file an insurance-related complaint.

Just for Fun!

11. **http://www.nia.nih.gov**

What are the latest developments in health and aging research? Search the Web site of the National Institute on Aging to keep up with the exciting discoveries being made which will ultimately work to improve the health and longevity of all people!

CHAPTER 10

Protecting Your Property

Learning Goals

LG1. Discuss the importance and basic principles of property insurance, including types of exposure, indemnity, and coinsurance.
LG2. Identify the types of coverage provided by homeowner's insurance.
LG3. Select the right homeowner's insurance policy for your needs.
LG4. Analyze the coverage in a personal automobile policy (PAP) and choose the most cost-effective policy.
LG5. Describe other types of property and liability insurance.
LG6. Choose a property and liability insurance agent and company, and settle claims.

Caution! Protecting Your Possessions Can Be Perilous

When Ken and Alice Bacon inquired about homeowner's insurance for their weekend cottage at the lake, their insurance agent advised them to install an alarm system and reduce their annual homeowner's insurance premium by almost $350. Although the cottage was located close to a small village, a security system would afford them peace of mind while the property stood empty all week as the Bacons pursued their lives and jobs in the city.

They contacted a company advertising a complete home security system for $750, but when its representative came to call she convinced the Bacons that such a basic system would be of limited value in securing their property. Although the system they finally bought cost them over $2,000, they were happy to invest in state-of-the-art home protection, especially as they were the proud owners of an extensive "revolving" art collection—frequently switching paintings back and forth between their home in the city and the cottage.

Then the midnight call came from the police, reporting that their cottage had been broken into. It seemed the thieves knew what they were after—the Bacons' art collection. The Bacons heaved a sigh of relief. Thankfully their alarm system had alerted the police, who would have arrived in time to disturb the burglars and prevent them from getting away with their precious paintings.

But the police had been called by a concerned neighbor who had seen lights on there and knew the Bacons were still in town. By the time the police arrived, the thieves had cleared out the house. But why hadn't the alarm signaled trouble? Ken and Alice had left the cottage late the previous Sunday night for the 2-hour drive back to the city. In their rush to get away, each thought the other had set the alarm. In the end, neither one had done it. Even if their insurance company covered their loss, the stolen art was irreplaceable.

CRITICAL THINKING QUESTIONS

As you read this chapter, consider the following questions about the Bacon family's property coverage:

- Should the Bacons' insurance company cover their loss in full, or should the Bacons be held responsible for a portion of the loss due to their carelessness?
- Because the Bacons moved their paintings from one property to the other what kind of additional personal property insurance might they have purchased to cover them?
- What other steps could the Bacons have taken to secure their cottage and art collection during the week while they lived in town 2 hours away?

BASIC PRINCIPLES OF PROPERTY INSURANCE

LG 1

Suppose that a severe storm destroyed your home. Could you afford to replace it? Most people could not. To protect yourself from this and other similar types of property loss, you need property insurance. In addition, every day you face some type of risk of negligence. For example, you might be distraught over a personal problem and unintentionally run a red light, seriously injuring a pedestrian. Could you pay for the medical and other costs? Because consequences like this and other potentially negligent acts could cause financial ruin, appropriate liability insurance is essential.

Accordingly, property and liability insurance should be as much a part of your personal financial plans as life and health insurance. Such coverage protects the assets you have already acquired and safeguards your progress towards your financial goals. **Property insurance** guards against catastrophic losses of real and personal property caused by such perils as fire, theft, vandalism, windstorms, and other calamities. **Liability insurance** offers protection against the financial consequences that may arise from the insured's responsibility for property loss or injuries to others.

property insurance
Insurance coverage that protects real and personal property from catastrophic losses caused by a variety of perils, such as fire, theft, vandalism, and windstorms.

liability insurance
Insurance that protects against the financial consequences that may arise from the insured's responsibility for property loss or injuries to others.

People spend a lot of money for insurance coverage, but few really understand what they are getting for their premium dollars. Even worse, the vast majority of people are totally unaware of any gaps, overinsurance, or underinsurance in their property and liability insurance policies. Inefficient or inadequate insurance protection is at odds with the objectives of personal financial planning, so it is important to become familiar with the principles of property and liability insurance.

The basic principles of property and liability insurance pertain to types of exposure, the principle of indemnity, and coinsurance. Each of these principles is discussed in the following sections.

TYPES OF EXPOSURE

Most individuals face two basic types of exposure: physical loss of property and loss through liability.

Exposure to Property Loss

The vast majority of property insurance contracts define the property covered and name the **perils**—the causes of loss—for which the insured will be compensated in the event of a claim against their policy. As a rule, most property insurance contracts impose two obligations on the property owner: (1) developing a complete inventory of the property being insured and (2) identifying the perils against which protection is desired. Some property contracts limit coverage by excluding certain types of property and perils, while others offer protection on a more comprehensive basis.

peril
A cause of loss.

Property Inventory

Do you know the value of all the property you own? If you are like most people, you don't, nor do you have an itemized property list for insurance purposes. This is especially important in the case of a total loss—if your home is burned by fire, for example. All property insurance companies require you to show proof of loss when making a claim, and your personal property inventory, along with corresponding values at the time of inventory, can serve as evidence to satisfy the company. A comprehensive property inventory will not only help you settle a claim when a loss occurs, but it also serves as a useful guide for selecting the most appropriate coverage for your particular needs.

Most families have a home, household furnishings, clothing and personal belongings, lawn and garden equipment, and motor vehicles, all of which need to be insured.

Fortunately, most homeowner's and automobile insurance policies provide coverage for these types of belongings. But many families also own such items as motorboats and trailers, various types of off-road vehicles, business property and inventories, jewelry, stamp or coin collections, furs, musical instruments, antiques, paintings, bonds, securities, and other items of special value, such as cameras, golf clubs, electronic equipment, and personal computers. Coverage for these belongings (and those that accompany you when you travel) often require special types of insurance.

To help policyholders prepare inventories, many insurance companies have easy-to-complete personal property inventory forms available. A partial sample of one such form is shown in Exhibit 10.1. These inventory forms can be supplemented with photographs or videos of household contents and belongings. For insurance purposes, a picture may truly be worth a thousand words. Regardless of whether inventory forms are supplemented with photographs or videotapes, *every effort should be made to keep these documents in a safe place,* where they can't be destroyed—such as a bank safe-deposit box. You might also consider keeping a *duplicate copy* with a parent or trusted relative. Remember, you may need these photographs and inventories if something serious does happen and you have to come up with an authenticated list of property losses.

Identifying Perils

Many people feel a false sense of security after buying insurance because they believe they are safeguarded against all contingencies. The fact is, however, that certain *perils* cannot be reasonably insured. For example, most homeowner's or automobile insurance policies limit or exclude damage or loss caused by flood, earthquake, mudslides, mysterious disappearance, war, nuclear radiation, and wear and tear. In addition, property insurance contracts routinely limit coverage on the basis of location of the property, time of loss, persons involved, and the types of hazards to which the property is exposed. These limitations are explained further in later sections of this chapter.

Liability Exposures

We all encounter a variety of liability exposures daily. Driving a car, entertaining guests at home, or being careless in performing professional duties are some of the more common liability risks. Loss exposures that result from these activities are examples of **negligence**—the failure to act in a reasonable manner or take necessary steps to protect others from harm. However, even if you are never negligent and always prudent, someone might *think* you are the cause of a loss and bring a costly lawsuit against you. Losing the judgment could cost you thousands—or even millions—of dollars. A debt that size could force you into bankruptcy or financial ruin.

negligence The failure to act in a reasonable manner or take necessary steps to protect others from harm.

Fortunately, *liability insurance* coverage will protect you against losses resulting from these risks, *including the high legal fees* required to defend yourself against suits that may, or may not, have merit. It's important to include adequate liability insurance in your overall insurance program, either through your homeowner's and automobile policies or through a separate umbrella policy.

principle of indemnity An insurance principle stating that an insured may not be compensated by the insurance company in an amount exceeding the insured's economic loss.

Principle of Indemnity

The **principle of indemnity** states that the insured may not be compensated by the insurance company in an amount exceeding the insured's economic loss. Most property and liability insurance contracts are based on this principle—although, as noted in Chapters 8 and 9, this *principle does not apply to life and health insurance.* Several important concepts related to the principle of indemnity include actual cash value, subrogation, and other insurance.

EXHIBIT 10.1

A Personal Property Inventory Form

Using a form like this will help you keep track of your personal property, including date of purchase, original price, and replacement cost.

Living Room

Stereo System

Brand	
Model	
Serial #	Date purchased
Purchase price $	Replacement cost $

Large Screen TV

Brand	
Model	
Serial #	Date purchased
Purchase price $	Replacement cost $

Compact Disc Player

Brand	
Model	
Serial #	Date purchased
Purchase price $	Replacement cost $

Home Theater System

Brand	
Model	
Serial #	Date purchased
Purchase price $	Replacement cost $

DVD Player

Brand	
Model	
Serial #	Date purchased
Purchase price $	Replacement cost $

Living Room

Article	Qty.	Date Purchase	Purchase Price	Replacement Cost
Air conditioners (window)				
Blinds/shades				
Bookcases				
Books				
Cabinets				
Carpets/rugs				
Chairs				
Chests				
Clocks				
Couches/sofas				
Curtains/draperies				
Fireplace fixtures				
Lamps/lighting fixtures				
Mirrors				
Pictures/paintings				
CDs				
Planters				
Stereo equipment				
Tables				
Television sets				
Other				
Other				

Actual Cash Value versus Replacement Cost

actual cash value A value assigned to an insured property that is determined by subtracting the amount of physical depreciation from its replacement cost.

The principle of indemnity limits the amount an insured may collect to the **actual cash value** of the property: the replacement cost less the amount of physical depreciation. Some insurers guarantee replacement cost without taking depreciation into account—for example, most homeowner's policies will settle building losses on a replacement cost basis, if the proper type and amount of insurance is purchased. Without a replacement-cost provision, it is common practice to deduct the amount of depreciation to obtain the actual cash value. If an insured property is damaged, the insurer is obligated to pay no more than the property would cost new today (its replacement cost) less the amount of depreciation from wear and tear.

For example, assume that fire destroys two rooms of furniture that was 6 years old, with an estimated useful life of 10 years. Replacement cost is $5,000. Therefore, at the time of loss, the furniture was subject to an assumed physical depreciation of 60 percent (6 years ÷ 10 years)—in this case, $3,000. Because the actual cash value is estimated at $2,000 ($5,000 replacement cost minus $3,000 of depreciation), the maximum the insurer would have to pay is $2,000. Note: the original cost of the property has no bearing on the settlement.

Subrogation

right of subrogation The right of an insurer, who has paid an insured's claim, to request reimbursement from the person who caused the loss or that person's insurer.

After an insurance company pays a claim, its **right of subrogation** allows it to request reimbursement from the person who caused the loss or that person's insurance company. For example, assume that you are in an automobile accident in which the other party damages your car. You may collect from your insurer or the at-fault party's insurer, but not from both (not for the same loss). Clearly, to collect the full amount of the loss from both parties would leave you better off after the loss than before it. This violates the principle of indemnity. Because the party who caused the accident (or loss) is ultimately responsible for paying the damages, your insurance company can go after the responsible party to collect its loss (the amount it paid out to you).

Other Insurance

Nearly all property and liability insurance contracts have an *other-insurance clause*, prohibiting insured persons from insuring their property with two or more insurance companies and collecting from multiple companies for the same loss. The other-insurance clause normally states that if a person has more than one insurance policy on a property, each company is liable for only a prorated amount of the loss based on its proportion of the total insurance covering the property. Without this provision, insured persons could use duplicate property insurance policies to actually profit from their losses.

coinsurance In property insurance, a provision that requires a policyholder to buy insurance in an amount equal to a specified percentage of the replacement value of their property; if not, the *policyholder* is required to pay for a proportional share of losses.

COINSURANCE

Coinsurance, a provision commonly found in property insurance contracts, requires policyholders to buy insurance in an amount equal to a specified percentage of the replacement value of their property, or the *policyholder* is required to pay for a proportional share of the loss. In essence, the coinsurance provision stipulates that if a property isn't properly covered, the property owner will become the "coinsurer" and bear part of the loss. If the policyholder has the stipulated amount of coverage (usually 80 percent of the value of the property), then the insurance company will reimburse him or her for covered losses, dollar for dollar, up to the amount of the policy limits. Assume, for example, that John and Mary have a fire insurance policy on their $200,000 home with an 80 percent coinsurance clause. The policy limits must equal or exceed 80 percent of the replacement value of their home. Further, assume that they ran short of money and decided to save by buying a $120,000 policy instead of $160,000 (80 percent of $200,000) as

10-1. Briefly explain the fundamental concepts related to property and liability insurance.
10-2. Explain the *principle of indemnity.* Are any limits imposed on the amount an insured may collect under this principle?
10-3. Explain the *right of subrogation.* How does this feature help lower insurance costs?
10-4. Describe how the *coinsurance* feature functions.

required by the coinsurance clause. If a loss occurred, the company would be obligated to pay only 75 percent ($120,000/$160,000) of the loss, up to the amount of the policy limit. Thus, on damages of $40,000, the insurer would pay only $30,000 (75 percent of $40,000). Obviously, you should closely evaluate the coinsurance clause of any property insurance policy so you will not have an unexpected additional burden in event of loss.

smart.sites
For assistance on evaluating your insurance needs go to **http://www.insurance.com** and click on Insurance 101—home insurance—for quotes and other useful information.

HOMEOWNER'S INSURANCE

LG2, LG3

Although homeowner's insurance is often thought of as a single type of insurance policy, homeowners can choose from four different forms (HO-1, HO-2, HO-3, and HO-8). Two other forms (HO-4 and HO-6) meet the needs of renters and owners of condominiums (See Exhibit 10.2). An HO-4 renter's policy offers essentially the same broad protection as an HO-2 homeowner's policy, except that the coverage does not apply to the rented dwelling unit because tenants usually do not have a financial interest in the real property.

All HO forms are divided into two sections. Section I applies to the dwelling, accompanying structures, and personal property of the insured. Section II deals with comprehensive coverage for personal liability and for medical payments to others. The scope of coverage under Section I is least with an HO-1 policy and greatest with an HO-3 policy. HO-8 is a modified coverage policy for older homes, used to insure houses that have market values well below the cost to rebuild. The coverage in Section II is the same for all forms.

In the following paragraphs, we'll explain the important features of homeowner's forms HO-2 and HO-3, the most commonly sold policies. (As Exhibit 10.2 shows, HO-1 is a very basic, seldom used policy with relatively narrow coverage.) The coverage offered under the HO-2 and HO-3 forms is basically the same; the differences lie only in the number of perils against which protection applies.

PERILS COVERED

Some property and liability insurance agreements, called **comprehensive policies**, cover all perils except those specifically excluded, whereas **named peril policies** name individual perils covered.

comprehensive policy
Property and liability insurance policy that covers all perils unless they are specifically excluded.

named peril policy
Property and liability insurance policy that names the perils covered individually.

Section I Perils

The perils against which the home and its contents are insured are shown in Exhibit 10.2. The coverage on household belongings is the same for the HO-2 and HO-3 forms, but coverage on the house itself and other structures (for example, a detached garage) is comprehensive under HO-3 and a named peril in HO-2. Whether homeowners should buy an HO-2 or an HO-3 form depends primarily on the amount they are willing to spend to secure the additional protection. The size of premiums for HO-2 and HO-3 policies can differ substantially among insurance companies, and in some states an HO-3 policy is the

EXHIBIT 10.2

A Guide to Homeowner's Policies

The amount of insurance coverage you receive depends on the type of homeowner's (HO) policy you select. You can also obtain coverage if you live in a rental unit or own a condominium.

Form	Coverages*	Covered perils
Basic Form (HO-1)	A-$15,000 minimum; B-10% of A; C-50% of A D-10% of A; E-$100,000 F-$1,000 per person	Fire, smoke, lightning, windstorm, hail, volcanic eruption, explosion, glass breakage, aircraft, vehicles, riot or civil commotion, theft, vandalism or malicious mischief
Broad Form (HO-2)	Minimum varies; other coverages in same percentages or amounts except D-20% of A	Covers all basic-form risks plus: Weight of ice, snow, sleet; freezing; accidental discharge of water or steam; falling objects; accidental tearing, cracking, or burning of heating/cooling/sprinkler system or appliance; damage from electrical current
Special Form (HO-3)	Minimum varies; other coverages in same percentages or amounts except D-20% of A	Dwelling and other structures covered against risks of direct physical loss to property except losses specifically excluded Personal property covered by same perils as HO-2 plus damage by glass or safety glazing material, which is part of a building, storm door, or storm window
Renter's Form (HO-4)	Coverages A and B-Not applicable C-Minimum varies by company D-20% of C E-$100,000 F-$1,000 per person	Covers same perils covered by HO-2 for personal property
Condominium Form (HO-6)	Coverage A-Minimum $1,000 B-Not applicable C-Minimum varies by company D-40% of C E-$100,000 F-$1,000 per person	Covers same perils covered by HO-2 for personal property
Modified Coverage Form (HO-8)	Same as HO-1, except losses are paid based on the amount required to repair or replace the property using common construction materials and methods	Same perils as HO-1, except theft coverage applies only to losses on the residence premises up to a maximum of $1,000; certain other coverage restrictions also apply

*Coverages:

A. Dwelling
B. Other structures
C. Personal property
D. Loss of use
E. Personal liability
F. Medical payments to others

better buy, because the premium differential is small. In other states, the HO-2 form has a substantially lower premium. Because of its more limited coverage, the purchase of an HO-1 is not recommended.

Note in Exhibit 10.2 that the types of Section I perils covered include just about everything from fire and explosions to lightning and wind damage, and theft and vandalism; unfortunately, these are all perils to which any homeowner is exposed. Although the list of perils is quite extensive, some are specifically excluded from most homeowner's contracts—in particular, *most policies (even HO-2 and HO-3 forms) exclude earthquakes and floods.* Many areas of the country are not susceptible to earthquakes and floods, and homeowners in those areas shouldn't have to pay premiums for coverage they don't need. But even if you live in an area where the risk of an earthquake or a flood is relatively high, you'll find that *standard homeowner's policies do not provide protection against these perils* because the catastrophic nature of such events causes widespread and costly damage. As we'll see later in this chapter, you can obtain coverage for earthquakes and floods under a separate policy or a rider.

Section II Perils

The perils insured against under Section II of the homeowner's contract are the (alleged) negligence of an insured. The coverage is called *comprehensive personal liability coverage* because it offers protection against nearly any source of liability (major exclusions are noted later) resulting from negligence. It does not insure against other losses for which one may become liable, such as libel, slander, defamation of character, and contractual or intentional wrongdoing. For example, coverage would apply if you carelessly, but unintentionally, knocked someone down your stairs. If you purposely struck and injured another person, however, or harmed someone's reputation either orally or in writing, homeowner's liability coverage would not protect you.

Section II also provides a limited amount of medical coverage for persons other than the homeowner's family in certain types of minor accidents on or off the insured's premises. The basic purpose of this coverage is to help homeowners meet their moral obligations and help deter possible lawsuits. The limited medical payment coverage pays irrespective of negligence or fault.

Factors That Affect Home Insurance Costs

Several influences have an impact on premiums for home and property insurance:

- **Type of structure.** Do you live in a home made from wood or brick? The type of construction materials used in your home affect the cost of insuring it. A home built from brick costs less to insure than a similar home of wood, yet the reverse is true when it comes to earthquake insurance—brick homes are more expensive to insure. The style and age of the house also contribute to its potential insurance risk, thereby affecting insurance costs.
- **Location of home.** Local crime rates, weather, and proximity to a fire hydrant all have an impact on your home's insurance premium costs. If many claims are filed from your area, insurance premiums for all the homeowners there will be higher. Hailstorms and hurricanes will affect them, too.
- **Other factors.** If you have a swimming pool, trampoline, large dog, or other potentially hazardous risk factors on your property, your homeowner's premiums will be higher. Deductibles and the type and amount of coverage also affects the cost.

Property Covered

The homeowner's policy offers property protection under Section I for the dwelling unit, accompanying structures, and personal property of homeowners and their families.

Coverage for certain types of loss also applies to lawns, trees, plants, and shrubs. However, the policy excludes structures on the premises used for business purposes (except incidentally), animals (pets or otherwise), and motorized vehicles not used in the maintenance of the premises (such as autos, motorcycles, golf carts, or snowmobiles). *Business inventory* (for example, goods held by an insured who is a traveling salesperson, or other goods held for sale) is not covered. Although the policy does not cover business inventory, it does cover *business property* (such as books, computers, copiers, office furniture, and supplies), up to a maximum of $2,500, while it is on the insured premises.

If you work at home, either full- or part-time, you may need to increase your policy's limits to protect your home office. This insurance is critical because damage to your home affects not only where you live, but your source of income as well. In many cases, adding a rider to your homeowner's policy can increase your home business limits to adequate levels for your computer and office equipment, and also provide additional limited liability coverage. The cost for these riders is low, about $50 per year, depending on what coverage you include. If you need greater protection, you should investigate a separate business owner's policy that offers broader coverage for business liability, all-risk protection for equipment, and business income protection if damage to your home results in lost income.

Personal Property Floater

As we will see later in the chapter, policies limit the type and amount of coverage provided. Your homeowner's policy may offer inadequate protection for your items of expensive personal property. To overcome this deficiency, you can add the **personal property floater (PPF)** as an endorsement to your homeowner's policy, or take out a separate floater policy. *The PPF provides either blanket or scheduled coverage of items not adequately covered in a standard homeowner's policy.*

personal property floater (PPF) An insurance endorsement or policy that provides either blanket or scheduled coverage of expensive personal property not adequately covered in a standard homeowner's policy.

A *blanket*, or *unscheduled*, *PPF* provides the maximum protection available for virtually all the insured's personal property. *Scheduled PPFs* list the items to be covered and provide supplemental coverage under a homeowner's contract. This coverage is especially useful for property valued at more than Schedule C limits, and includes loss, damage, and theft. Some of the more popular uses of PPFs are for furs, jewelry, personal computers and peripheral equipment, photographic equipment, silverware, fine art and antiques, musical instruments, and stamp and coin collections. For example, you should itemize a diamond ring valued at $7,500 because it is worth more than the standard $1,000 Schedule C allowance for jewelry theft. Generally, insurance companies require appraisals to determine value before scheduling items.

Renter's Insurance: Don't Move In Without It

If you live in an apartment (or some other type of rental unit), you should be aware that although the building you live in is very likely fully insured, *your furnishings and other personal belongings are not.* As a renter (or even the owner of a condominium unit), you need a special type of HO policy to obtain insurance coverage on your personal possessions.

Consider, for example, the predicament of Lois Weaver. She never got around to insuring her personal possessions in the apartment she rented in Denver. One wintry night, a water pipe ruptured, and escaping water damaged her furniture, rugs, and other belongings. When the building owner refused to pay for the loss, Ms. Weaver hauled him into court—and lost. Why did she lose her case? Simple: *Unless a landlord can be proven negligent—and this one wasn't—he or she isn't responsible for a tenant's property.*

The moral of this story is clear: Once you've accumulated personal belongings of value (from clothing and home furnishings to stereo equipment, TVs, computers, and DVD players), make sure they are adequately covered by insurance, even if you're only renting a place to live! Otherwise, you could risk losing everything you own.

Apparently many tenants don't realize this, because surveys show most of them are without insurance—although renter's insurance is available at very reasonable rates. The policy, called Renter's Form HO-4, is a scaled-down version of homeowner's insurance; it covers the contents of a house, apartment, or cooperative unit, but not the structure itself. Owners of condominium units need Form HO-6; it's similar but includes a minimum of $1,000 in protection for any building alterations, additions, and decorations paid for by the policyholder. Like regular homeowner's insurance, HO-4 and HO-6 policies include liability coverage and protect you at home and away. For example, if somebody is injured and sues you, the policy would pay for damages up to a specified limit, generally $100,000, although some insurers go as high as $500,000.

A standard renter's insurance policy covers furniture, carpets, appliances, clothing, and most other personal items, for their cash value at the time of loss. Expect to pay around $200 to $250 a year for about $15,000 in coverage, depending on where you live. For maximum protection, you can buy *replacement-cost insurance* (discussed again later in this chapter), which pays the actual cost of replacing articles with comparable ones, though some policies limit the payout to four times the cash value. You'll pay more for this—perhaps as little as another 10 percent—perhaps much more, depending on the insurer. Also, the standard renter's policy provides limited coverage of such valuables as jewelry, furs, and silverware. Coverage varies, although some insurers pay up to $1,000 for the loss of watches, gems, and furs, and up to $2,500 for silverware. For larger amounts, you need an endorsement or a separate policy, called a PPF, as discussed earlier.

Renter's insurance pays for losses caused by fire or lightning, explosion, windstorms, hail, theft, civil commotion, aircraft, vehicles, smoke, vandalism and malicious mischief, falling objects, building collapse, and the weight of ice and snow. Certain damages caused by water, steam, electricity, appliances, and frozen pipes are covered as well. Plus, if your residence can't be occupied because of damage from any of those perils, the insurer will pay for any increase in living expenses resulting from staying at a hotel and eating in restaurants. The liability coverage also pays for damages and legal costs arising from injuries or damage caused by you, a member of your family, or a pet, on or off your premises.

smart.sites

Not sure where to find earthquake insurance? Go to **http://www.westernmutual.com** for an instant Internet quote.

Coverage: What Type, Who, and Where?

We've discussed what types of property homeowner's policies cover. These policies also define the types of losses they cover and the persons and locations covered.

Types of Losses Covered

There are three different types of property-related losses when misfortune occurs:

1. Direct loss of property
2. Indirect loss occurring as a result of loss of damaged property
3. Additional expenses resulting from direct and indirect losses

Homeowner's insurance contracts offer compensation for each type of loss.

Section I Coverage

When a house is damaged by an insured peril, the insurance company will pay reasonable living expenses a family might incur. One such covered expense would be the cost of renting alternative lodgings or accommodation while the insured's home is being repaired or rebuilt. Also, in many instances the insurer will pay for damages caused by perils other than those mentioned in the policy if a named peril is determined to be the underlying cause of the loss. Assume, for instance, that lightning (a covered peril) strikes a house while a family is away and knocks out power, causing $400 worth of food in the freezer and refrigerator to spoil. Insurance will pay for the loss even though temperature change (the direct cause) is not mentioned in the policy.

Section II Coverage

In addition to paying successfully pursued liability claims against an insured, a homeowner's policy includes coverage for (1) the cost of defending the insured, (2) reasonable expenses incurred by an insured in helping the insurance company's defense, and (3) the payment of court costs. Because these costs apply even in cases in which the liability suit is found to be without merit, insurance coverage for this can save you thousands of dollars in attorney fees.

Persons Covered

A homeowner's policy covers the persons named in the policy and members of their families who are residents of the household. A person can be a resident of the household even while temporarily living away from home. For example, college students who live at school part of the year and at home during vacations are normally classified as household residents. Their parents' homeowner's policy may cover their belongings at school—including such items as stereo equipment, TVs, personal computers, and microwave ovens. But there could be limits and exceptions to the coverage, so check the policy to make sure what is covered. For example, some companies may consider a student living off-campus to be independent, and therefore ineligible for coverage under his or her parents' insurance. The standard homeowner's contract also extends limited coverage to guests of the insured.

Locations Covered

Although some insurance contracts have territorial exclusions, most homeowner's policies offer coverage worldwide. Consequently, an insured's personal property is fully covered even if it is lent to the next-door neighbor or kept in a hotel room in Outer Mongolia. The only exception is property left at a second home, such as a beach house or resort condominium—in which case coverage is reduced to 10 percent of the policy limit on personal property—unless the loss occurs while the insured is residing there.

Homeowners and their families have liability protection for their negligent acts wherever they occur. This liability protection, however, does not include negligent acts involving certain types of motorized vehicles (such as large boats and aircraft), or those that occur in the course of employment or professional practice. It does include golf carts (when used for golfing purposes), and recreational vehicles such as snowmobiles and minibikes, provided that they are used on the insured's premises.

LIMITATIONS ON PAYMENT

In addition to the principle of indemnity, actual cash value, subrogation, and other insurance features that restrict the amount paid out under a property and liability insurance contract, replacement-cost provisions, policy limits, and deductibles also influence the amount an insurance company will pay for a loss.

Replacement Cost

The amount necessary to repair, rebuild, or replace an asset at today's prices is the **replacement cost**. When replacement-cost coverage is in effect, a homeowner's reimbursement for damage to a house or accompanying structures is based on the cost of repairing or replacing those structures. This means the insurer will repair or replace damaged items without taking any deductions for depreciation. Exhibit 10.3 provides an illustration of a replacement-cost calculation for a 2,400-square-foot home with a two-car garage.

replacement cost The amount necessary to repair, rebuild, or replace an asset at today's prices.

EXHIBIT 10.3

Calculating Replacement Cost

This is a typical example of how an insurance company calculates replacement cost. It would take $210,400 to fully replace the home in question today.

Dwelling Cost: 2,400 sq. ft. at $72 per sq. ft.	$172,800
Extra features: built-in appliances, mahogany cabinets, 3 ceiling fans	8,600
Porches, patios: screened and trellised patio	2,700
Two-car garage: 900 sq. ft. at $24 per sq. ft.	21,600
Other site improvements: driveway, storage, landscaping	4,700
Total replacement cost	$210,400

Keep in mind, however, that for homeowners to be eligible for reimbursement on a full replacement-cost basis, they must keep their homes insured for at least 80 percent of the amount it would cost to build them today, exclusive of the value of the land. In periods of inflation, homeowners must either increase their coverage limits on the dwelling unit every year or take a chance on falling below the 80 percent requirement. Alternatively, for a nominal cost homeowners can purchase an inflation protection rider that automatically adjusts the amount of coverage in keeping with prevailing inflation rates. The inflation protection rider basically eliminates the chance of a coinsurance penalty. Without the rider, if the 80 percent condition is not met, the coinsurance penalty kicks in; the maximum compensation for total or partial losses would therefore be based on a specified percentage of loss. With the inflation protection rider, this would not happen.

Contrary to popular opinion, replacement cost and actual cash value may not bear any relationship to a home's market value. Because replacement cost and actual cash value relate only to the physical structure and do not consider the influence of location, a home's market value can be in excess of its replacement cost or below its actual cash value. Even if a home is in an excellent state of repair, its market value may be lessened due to functional obsolescence within the structure. The HO-8 homeowner's form (for older homes) was adopted in partial response to this problem. A 2,200-square-foot home in an older neighborhood might have a market value, excluding land, of $95,000—although the replacement cost might be $160,000. The HO-8 policy solves this problem so homeowners don't have to buy more expensive coverage based on replacement value. This policy covers property in full, up to the amount of the loss, or up to the property's market value, whichever is less.

Although coverage on a house is often on a *replacement-cost basis,* standard coverage on its contents may be on an *actual cash-value basis,* which deducts depreciation

Financial Road Sign

Tips to Lower Premiums
Looking for ways to lower your insurance premiums? Because insurance companies base insurance premiums on the risks involved and the potential for losses, the steps you take to lower those risks can save you money.

- Maintain adequate lighting around your property.
- Keep swimming pools secured.
- Keep electrical wiring, stairways, carpeting, and flooring in good repair.
- Install smoke, fire, and security alarms.
- Keep limited cash or valuables at home. Use bank safe-deposit boxes for your valuables and important documents.
- Keep detailed records of insured items—with photos where possible.

Raising your deductible where appropriate will also contribute to lower premiums.

from the *current replacement cost* for claims involving furniture, clothing, and other belongings. Some policies offer, for a slight increase in premium, replacement-cost coverage on contents. For an additional premium of only about 5 to 15 percent more, you should seriously consider this option—and an inflation protection rider on the dwelling—when buying homeowner's insurance.

Policy Limits

In Section I of the homeowner's policy the amount of coverage on the dwelling unit (coverage A) establishes the amounts applicable to the accompanying structures (coverage B), the unscheduled personal property (coverage C), and the temporary living expenses (coverage D). Generally, the limits under coverage B, C, and D are 10, 50, and 10 to 20 percent, respectively, of the amount of coverage under A.

For example, if a house is insured for $150,000, the limits for coverage B, C, and D would be $15,000, $75,000, and $30,000, respectively (that is, 10 percent of $150,000, 50 percent of $150,000, and 20 percent of $150,000). Each of these limits can be increased if it is insufficient to cover the exposure. Also, for a small reduction in premium, some companies will permit a homeowner to reduce coverage on unscheduled personal property to 40 percent of the amount on the dwelling unit.

Remember that homeowner's policies usually specify limits for certain types of personal property included under the coverage C category. These coverage limits are *within the total dollar amount* of coverage C, and in no way act to increase that total. For example, the dollar limit for losses of money, bank notes, bullion, and related items is $200, and securities, accounts, deeds, evidences of debt, manuscripts, passports, tickets, and stamps have a $1,000 limit. As mentioned earlier, loss from jewelry theft is limited to $1,000, and payment for theft of silverware, goldware, and pewterware has a $2,500 limit. Some policies also offer $5,000 coverage for home computer equipment. You can increase these limits by increasing your Schedule C coverage.

In Section II the personal liability coverage (in part E) often tops out at $100,000, and the medical payments portion (part F) normally has a limit of $1,000 per person. Additional coverage included in Section II consists of claim expenses, such as court costs and attorney fees, first aid and medical expenses, including ambulance costs, and damage to others' property of up to $500 per occurrence.

Although these are the most common limits, most homeowners need additional protection, especially liability coverage. In these days of high damage awards by juries, a $100,000 liability limit may not be adequate. The cost to increase the liability limit with most companies is nominal. For example, the annual premium difference between a $100,000 personal liability limit and a $300,000 limit is likely to be only $40 to $50. You can also increase personal liability coverage with a personal liability umbrella policy, discussed later in the chapter.

Deductibles

Each of the preceding limits on recovery constrains the maximum amount an insurance company must pay under the policy. In contrast, *deductibles* limit what a company must pay for small losses. Deductibles help reduce insurance premiums because they do away with the frequent small loss claims that are proportionately more expensive to administer. The standard deductible in most states is $250 on the physical damage protection covered in Section I. However, choosing higher deductible amounts of $500 or $1,000 results in considerable premium savings—as much as 10 percent in some states. Deductibles do not apply to liability and medical payments coverage because insurers want to be notified of all claims, no matter how trivial. Otherwise, they could be notified too late to properly investigate and prepare adequate defenses for resulting lawsuits.

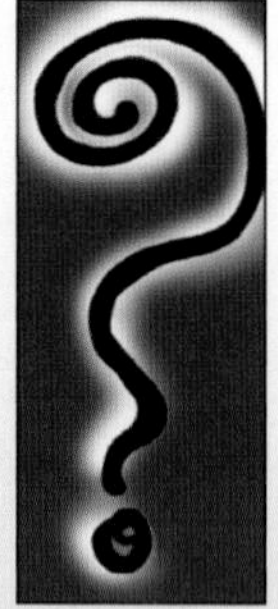

Concept ✓

10-5. What are the *perils* most properties are insured for under various types of homeowner's policies?

10-6. What types of property are covered under a homeowner's policy? When should you consider adding a *PPF* to your policy? Are the following included in the coverage of a standard policy: (a) an African parrot, (b) a motorbike, (c) Avon cosmetics held for sale, and (d) Tupperware® for home use?

10-7. Describe (a) types of losses, (b) persons, and (c) locations that are covered under a homeowner's policy.

10-8. Describe *replacement-cost coverage* and compare this coverage to *actual cash value.* Which is preferable?

10-9. What are *deductibles?* Do they apply to either liability or medical payments coverage under the homeowner's policy?

Homeowner's Premiums

For a basic package of protection—physical damage protection up to 80 percent of today's cost to rebuild, related coverage on other structures and personal property, personal liability ($100,000), and medical payments to others ($1,000 per person)—an insurer will quote you a premium. As you might expect, the size of insurance premiums vary widely depending on the insurance provider (company) and the location of the property (neighborhood/city/state). It pays to shop around! When you're shopping, use a checksheet like the one in Exhibit 10.4 to help you compare insurers and policies. And remember, each type of property damage coverage is subject to a deductible of $250 or more.

Most people need to modify the basic package of coverage by adding an inflation rider and increasing the coverage on their homes to 100 percent of the replacement cost. Also, changing the contents protection from actual cash value to replacement cost and scheduling some items of expensive personal property may be desirable. Most insurance professionals also advise homeowners to increase their liability and medical payments limits. Each of these changes will result in an additional premium charge.

At the same time, you can reduce your total premium by increasing the amount of your deductible. Because it is better to budget for, rather than insure, small losses, larger deductibles are becoming more popular. You may also qualify for discounts for deadbolt locks, monitored security systems, and other safety features, such as smoke alarms and sprinkler systems. Indeed, as explained in the *Money in Action* box on pages 410–411, there are many steps you can take to keep your homeowner's insurance premiums in check.

AUTOMOBILE INSURANCE

LG4

Another asset that involves major exposure to loss is the automobile. Damage to this asset, or negligence in its use, can result in significant loss. In addition, indirect monetary losses to society result from police and legal costs, and from the lost productive capacity of capital and human resources. Fortunately, insurance can protect individuals against a big part of these costs.

Automobile insurance is actually a group of several types of coverage packaged together. You can adjust any coverage to suit your needs. Here we describe the major features of automobile insurance, starting with typical coverage of a private passenger automobile policy. We'll also explain how no-fault laws, in force

EXHIBIT 10.4

Homeowner's Insurance Comparison Checksheet

Here's a convenient checksheet to use when shopping for homeowner's insurance; notice that this checksheet lists not only information that you should give to your insurance agent (key items about your dwelling, types of coverage you're looking for, etc.), but also the cost of the insurance, net of any discounts. In effect, this checksheet enables you to clearly spell out the type of insurance you're looking for and for the agent to tell you how much that's going to cost.

INFORMATION TO GIVE AGENTS OR INSURANCE COMPANIES

Address of property to be insured: ________
Number of losses in the past three years if covered by homeowner's or fire insurance: ________
Description of dwelling:
Number of apartments or households in building ________
Construction (frame, brick, etc.) ________
Number of stories ________
Number of rooms ________
Total square feet ________
Age of dwelling ________
Age of roof ________
Age/type of furnace ________
Number of smoke detectors ________
Security devices ________
Owner occupant? ________
Inside city limits? ________
Name of fire department ________
Distance from fire hydrant/fire station ________
Business in the home? ________
Current dwelling replacement cost $________
Current market value of dwelling and land $________
Purchase price of dwelling $________
Property coverage:
Dwelling (100% of replacement cost) ________
Other structures (detached garages, sheds, fences) ________
Unscheduled personal property (contents of home) ________
Additional living expense (usually 20% of dwelling coverage) ________
Deductible for property coverage *($500 or $1,000 recommended)*: $________
Liability coverage:
Personal liability (bodily injury and property damage) $________
Medical payments to others $________
Riders:
Business activities ________
Earthquake ________
Flood ________
Scheduled personal property (antiques, computer equipment, jewelry, silverware, etc.) ________
Secondary residence (vacation home) ________
Windstorm (not included in basic coverage in some coastal areas) ________

INFORMATION TO GET FROM AGENTS OR INSURANCE COMPANIES

	Insurer (current)	*(#2)*	*(#3)*
Policy forms (perils included)			
Coverage exclusions			
Inflation guard included?			
Discounts available:			
Auto policy with same insurer			
New home/renovation			
Nonsmoker			
Renewal/longtime policyholder			
Security devices			
Senior citizen			
Smoke detectors/fire extinguishers/fire-retardant roof			
Storm shutters			
Other			
Annual premium:	$	$	$
Installment charges (if applicable):	$	$	$

Source: *Kiplinger's Smart Ways to Save on Insurance*, Winter 1997, p. 19.

Money in Action

Keep Your Homeowner's Premiums from Going through the Roof

Everyone who pays monthly premiums for homeowner's insurance will tell you it's not cheap. But because most people can't afford to bear the risk of a catastrophic loss, it is an absolute necessity. Fortunately, the industry is competitive so prices vary. The first step to keeping premiums down is to shop around. Major insurance companies are easily accessible by telephone and the Internet, sources that will provide an idea of price ranges. Some companies offer a 5 percent to 15 percent discount on a homeowner's policy if you use the same companies for auto insurance.

But there are factors other than cost to consider when selecting a policy. Ask friends or colleagues about companies they have done business with and their reputations for good service. If a claim is filed, do they pay right away or do they stall? Do they have a local office and an agent with whom you can meet personally, or does the company operate from a distant city?

Once you've chosen a company, you can reduce your premiums even more by making certain decisions. If you have to choose between buying a new home or an older one, be aware that the older home, although quaint, may cost more to insure because of antiquated heating and plumbing systems. Statistically, newer homes are less susceptible to fire and other hazards, and therefore are less costly to insure. The closer your home is to a fire station, the lower your premium will be. A house near a fault line in California is going to cost more to insure than the same home in Montana. Frame and brick homes, because of their resistance to earthquake and wind damage, respectively, also reduce premiums. Avoiding areas prone to flooding will save several hundred dollars in flood insurance–a risk that homeowner's insurance doesn't cover.

Some insurers offer discounts if you install a sprinkler system or a burglar alarm. Other ways to reduce the risk of loss include installing multiple smoke detectors and fire extinguishers, and using

...continued on next page

in many states, typically affect reimbursement for losses caused by automobile accidents. Finally, we will discuss auto insurance premiums and financial responsibility laws.

smart.sites
For online auto insurance quotes and premium price comparisons go to **http://www.autoinsuranceindepth.com** and punch in your zip code. A brief online questionnaire is the first step to helping you assess your auto insurance options.

Types of Auto Insurance Coverage

The **personal automobile policy (PAP)** is a comprehensive automobile insurance policy designed to be easily understood by the "typical" insurance purchaser. Made up of six parts, the first four parts identify the coverage provided in the policy:

- Part A: Liability coverage
- Part B: Medical payments coverage
- Part C: Uninsured motorists coverage
- Part D: Coverage for damage to your vehicle

personal automobile policy (PAP) A comprehensive automobile insurance policy designed to be easily understood by the "typical" insurance purchaser; it is made up of six parts.

Part E pertains to your duties and responsibilities should you be involved in an accident, and Part F defines basic provisions of the policy, including the policy coverage period and the right of termination. We'll focus mostly on the types of coverage in Parts A through D of the policy.

You are almost sure to purchase liability, medical payments, and uninsured motorists protection. You may, however, choose *not* to buy protection against damage to your automobile if it is an older vehicle and of relatively little value. On the other hand, if you have a loan against your car, you will probably be required to have physical damage coverage—part D—at least equal to the amount of the loan.

Let's take a closer look at the coverage provided by parts A through D. Exhibit 10.5 (on page 412) illustrates how the four basic parts of a PAP (Part A: Liability coverage; Part B: Medical payments coverage; Part C: Uninsured motorists coverage; and Part D: Collision and comprehensive coverage) might be displayed in a typical automobile insurance policy. Note that the premiums shown are for a 6-month period.

deadbolt locks to increase your security. Some companies offer lower premiums if none of the residents in the house smoke, because smoking accounts for more than 23,000 residential fires per year.

One way *not* to save money is to underinsure. It's imperative to get "guaranteed replacement-cost" coverage, not just actual cash value. Your insurance agent should be able to help you come up with the right figure. Make sure a company representative visits your home to measure and photograph it. Otherwise, it will be difficult to set appropriate replacement-cost amounts. You could find yourself overinsured or underinsured, either paying too much in premiums, or underprotected.

It's likely that replacement cost will be higher than actual cash value because the cost to build is usually higher than the cost to buy. Don't scrimp on liability coverage either—it's important to be covered for damages if someone who's injured on your property sues you.

As a general rule, you should review your homeowner's insurance coverage every other year to establish that your premium is still competitive and ensure that your coverage is adequate to completely rebuild your home in the event of a catastrophe.

Critical Thinking Questions

1. What should you look for when selecting a homeowner's insurance policy?
2. When purchasing a home, what factors should you consider in order to reduce the cost of your homeowner's insurance premiums? What improvements can you make to an existing home to take advantage of premium reduction programs?
3. Why is it not cost-effective to underinsure your property?

Sources: "Lowering Your Homeowner's Insurance Premiums—Twelve Ways to Lower Your Homeowner's Insurance Cost," *Claiminformation.com,* **http://www.claiminformation.com/homeownerpremiums.htm**, downloaded December 2, 2003; Bobbie Sage, "Homeowner's Insurance Savings Checklist," *PersonalInsure.com,* **http://www.personalinsure.about.com**, downloaded December 2, 2003.

Part A: Liability Coverage

Most states require that you buy at least a minimum amount of liability insurance. As part of the liability provisions of a PAP, the insurer agrees to:

1. Pay damages for bodily injury and/or property damage for which you are legally responsible due to an automobile accident
2. Settle or defend any claim or suit asking for such damages

The provision for legal defense is important and could mean savings of thousands of dollars. Even a person who is not at fault in an automobile accident may be compelled to prove his or her innocence in court, incurring expensive legal fees. Note, though, that the coverage is for a defense in civil cases only. It provides no defense against criminal charges against the insured as a result of an accident (such as a drunk driver who's involved in an accident).

In addition to providing reimbursement for bodily injury and property damage, the automobile liability portion of your insurance policy includes certain supplemental payments for items such as expenses incurred in settling the claim, reimbursement of premiums for appeal bonds, bonds to release attachments of the insured's property, and bail bonds required as a result of an accident. These supplemental payments are not restricted by the applicable policy limits.

Policy Limits

Although the insurance company provides both bodily injury and property damage liability insurance under part A, it typically sets *a dollar limit up to which it will pay for damages from any one accident.* Typical limits are $50,000, $100,000, $300,000, and $500,000. You'd be well advised to consider nothing less than $300,000 coverage in today's legal liability environment. Damage awards are increasing, and the insurer's duty to defend you *ends when the coverage limit has been exhausted.* It is very easy to "exhaust" $50,000 or $100,000, leaving you to pay any additional costs above the policy limit. So be sure to purchase adequate coverage—*regardless of the minimum requirements in your state.* Otherwise, you place your personal assets at risk. As Exhibit 10.5 shows, the Jones family obtained fairly high limits.

Some insurers make so-called *split limits* of liability coverage available, with the first amount in each combination the per-individual limit and the

EXHIBIT 10.5

The Four Parts of an Automobile Insurance Policy

This automobile insurance statement for 6 months of coverage illustrates how the four major parts (A through D) of a personal automobile policy (PAP) might be incorporated into a typical auto policy. Note in this case that the premium for comprehensive/collision damage is relatively low due to the age and type of car (a 1999 Ford Taurus); also note that these drivers enjoyed a premium reduction of more than $130 for the 6 months due to a good driving record, the car's alarm system, and having other insurance with the same provider.

ANYSTATE INSURANCE COMPANIES **AUTO RENEWAL**

Anystate Automobile Insurance Company
1665 West Anywhere Drive
Yourtown, CA 91001

1999 Ford Taurus

POLICY NUMBER	PERIOD COVERED	DATE DUE	PLEASE PAY THIS AMOUNT
ABC-123-XYZ-456	MAY 26 2004 to NOV 26 2004	MAY 26 2004	$392

1 H -1582 A

Jones, Drew E. & Linda S.
240 E. Hazelwood St. # 50
Yourtown, CA 91004-0003

Coverages and Limits			Premiums
Part A	A	Liability	
		Bodily Injury 250,000/500,000 Property Damage 100,000	$219
Part B	M	Medical 5,000	14
Part C	U	Uninsured Motor Vehicle	
		Bodily Injury 100,000/300,000	27
Part D	D-WG	500 Deductible Comprehensive	24
	G	500 Deductible Collision	102
	H	Emergency Road Service	6
Amount Due			$392

Your premium has already been adjusted by the following:

Premium Reductions	
Multiple Line	22
Antitheft devices	40
Good driver	70

Your premium is based on the following . . .
If not correct, contact your agent.

1999 Ford Taurus GL 4DR Sedan
Serial number: 4 ABCD12M3NP456789

Drivers of vehicle in your household...
There are no male or unmarried female drivers under age 25.
Younger drivers included if rated on another car insured with us.

Ordinary use of vehicle...
To and from work or school, more than 100 miles weekly.
Driven more than 7,500 miles annually.
(National average is 10,000 miles annually.)

Source: Adapted from a major automobile insurance company quote.

second the per-accident limit. Some policy limit combinations for protecting individuals against claims made for **bodily injury liability losses** are $25,000/$50,000, $50,000/$100,000, $100,000/$300,000, $250,000/$500,000, and $500,000/$1,000,000. Because the Joneses purchased the $250,000/$500,000 policy limits, the maximum amount any one person negligently injured in an accident could receive from the insurance company would be $250,000. Further, the total amount that the insurer would pay to all injured victims in one accident would not exceed $500,000. If a jury awarded a claimant $80,000, the defendant whose insurance policy limits were $50,000/$100,000 could be required to pay $30,000 out of his or her pocket ($80,000 award – $50,000 paid by insurance). For the defendant, this could mean loss of home, cars, bank accounts, and other assets. In many states, if the value of these assets is too little to satisfy a claim, the defendant's wages may be garnished (taken by the court and used to satisfy the outstanding debt).

bodily injury liability losses A provision in a PAP that protects the insured against claims made for bodily injury; may specify coverage as a combination of per-individual and per-accident limits.

The policy limits available to cover **property damage liability losses** are typically $10,000, $25,000, $50,000, and $100,000. In contrast to bodily injury liability limits, property damage limits are stated as a per-accident limit, without specifying limits applicable on a per-item or per-person basis.

property damage liability losses A provision in a PAP that protects the insured against claims made for damage to property; specified on a per-accident basis.

Persons Insured

Two basic definitions in the PAP determine who is covered under the liability coverage: insured person and covered auto. Essentially, an *insured person* includes you (the named insured) and any family member, any person using a covered auto, and any person or organization that may be held responsible for your actions. The *named insured* is the person named in the declarations page of the policy. The spouse of the person named is considered a named insured if he or she resides in the same household. Family members are persons related by blood, marriage, or adoption who reside in the same household. An unmarried college student living away from home usually would be considered a family member. *Covered autos* are the vehicles shown in the declarations page of your PAP, autos acquired during the policy period, any trailer owned, and any auto or trailer used as a temporary substitute while your auto or trailer is being repaired or serviced. An automobile that you lease for an extended time can be included as a covered automobile.

The named insured and family members have Part A liability coverage regardless of the automobile they are driving. However, for persons other than the named insured and family members to have liability coverage, they must be driving a covered auto.

When a motorist who is involved in an automobile accident is covered under two or more liability insurance contracts, the coverage *on the automobile* is primary and the other coverage is secondary. For example, if Dan Slater, a named insured in his own right, was involved in an accident while driving Diana Bauer's automobile (with permission), a claim settlement in excess of the limits of Diana's liability policy would be necessary before Dan's liability insurance would apply. If Diana's insurance had lapsed, Dan's policy would then offer primary protection (but it would apply to Dan only and not to Diana).

Part B: Medical Payments Coverage

Medical payments coverage provides payment to a covered individual for reasonable and necessary medical expenses incurred within 3 years of an automobile accident, in an amount not to exceed policy limits. It provides for reimbursement even if other sources of recovery, such as health or accident insurance, also make payments. In addition, in most states the insurer reimburses the insured for medical payments even if the insured proves that another person was negligent in the accident and receives compensation from that party's liability insurer.

As with liability insurance, discussed in the previous section, and uninsured motorists insurance, detailed in the following section, a person need not be occupying an automobile when the accidental injury occurs to be eligible for benefits. Injuries sustained as a pedestrian, or on a bicycle in a traffic accident, are covered, too. (Motorcycle accidents are normally not covered.) This insurance also pays on an excess basis. For instance, if you are a passenger in a friend's automobile during an accident and suffer $8,000 in medical expenses, you can collect under your friend's medical payments insurance up to his or her policy limits. Further, you can collect (up to the amount of your policy limits) from your insurer the amount in excess of what the other medical payments provide. Of course, you may also collect from the liability insurance of another person involved in the accident if that person can be shown to have been at fault. In addition, you may also be able to collect from your health insurance policy.

Policy Limits

Medical payments insurance usually has per-person limits of $1,000, $2,000, $3,000, $5,000, or $10,000. Thus an insurer could conceivably pay $60,000 or more in medical payments benefits for one accident involving a named insured and five passengers. Most families are advised to buy the $5,000 or $10,000 limit because although they may have an ample amount of other health insurance available, they cannot be certain that their passengers are equally well protected. Having automobile medical payments insurance also reduces the probability that a passenger in your auto will sue you and attempt to collect under your liability insurance coverage (in those states that permit it).

Persons Insured

Coverage under an automobile medical payments insurance policy applies to the named insured and family members who are injured while occupying an automobile (whether owned by the named insured or not) or when struck by an automobile or trailer of any type. It also applies to any other person occupying a covered automobile.

Part C: Uninsured Motorists Coverage

Uninsured motorists coverage is available to meet the needs of "innocent" victims of accidents who are negligently injured by uninsured, underinsured, or hit-and-run motorists. Nearly all states require uninsured motorists insurance to be included in each liability insurance policy issued. The insured is allowed, however, to reject this coverage in most of these states. Because there are about 25 million uninsured drivers, and many others who meet only minimum insurance coverage requirements, rejecting uninsured motorists coverage is not a good idea. In many states a person may also collect if the negligent motorist's insurance company is insolvent. With uninsured motorists insurance, an insured is legally entitled to collect an amount equal to the sum that could have been collected from the negligent motorist's liability insurance, had such coverage been available, up to a maximum amount equal to the policy's stated *uninsured motorists limit.*

uninsured motorists coverage Automobile insurance designed to meet the needs of "innocent" victims of accidents who are negligently injured by uninsured, underinsured, or hit-and-run motorists.

Three points must be proven to receive payment through uninsured motorists insurance: (1) another motorist must be at fault, (2) the motorist has no available insurance or is underinsured, and (3) damages were incurred. As property damage is not included in this coverage in most states, with uninsured motorists coverage, you can generally only collect for losses arising from bodily injury. If the motorist and insurer cannot agree on the terms of the settlement of a claim under uninsured motorists coverage, the motorist can seek an attorney to negotiate the claim. If a mutually agreeable settlement still cannot be worked out, the insured has the right to have the case arbitrated by a neutral third party. In most cases, the accident victim and the insurer are then bound to accept the decision of the arbitrator. (In addition to *uninsured* motorists, for a nominal premium you can also obtain protection for *underinsured* motorists—that is, for coverage when you're involved in an accident where the driver at fault has a liability limit much lower than your claim. Under such coverage, your insurance company makes up the difference and then goes after the negligent driver for any deficiency.)

Policy Limits

Uninsured motorists insurance is available at a fairly low cost (usually around $50 to $75 per year). Because the cost of this coverage is very small compared to the amount of protection it provides, drivers should purchase at least the minimum available limits of uninsured motorists insurance. The Joneses purchased $100,000/$300,000 coverage for just $54 per year ($27 per 6 months).

Persons Insured

Uninsured motorists protection covers the named insured, family members, and any other person occupying a covered auto.

Part D: Coverage for Physical Damage to a Vehicle

This part of the PAP provides coverage for damage to your auto. The two basic types of coverage provided are collision and comprehensive (or "other than collision").

Collision Insurance

collision insurance Automobile insurance that pays for collision damage to an insured automobile *regardless of who is at fault.*

Collision insurance is automobile insurance that pays for collision damage to an insured automobile *regardless of who is at fault.* The amount of insurance payable is the actual cash value of the loss in excess of your deductible. Remember that *actual cash value is defined as replacement cost less depreciation.* Therefore, if a car is demolished, the insured will be paid an amount equal to the car's depreciated value minus any deductible.

Lenders typically require collision insurance on cars they finance. In some cases, especially when the auto dealer is handling the financing, it will attempt to sell you this insurance. *Avoid buying automobile insurance from car dealers or finance companies.* Buy such insurance from your regular insurance agent and include collision insurance as part of your full auto insurance policy (PAP). A full-time insurance agent is better able to assess and meet your insurance needs. The collision provision of your insurance policy will often fully protect you, even in a rental car, so you may not need to purchase expensive supplemental collision insurance when renting a car. Be sure to check what rental car coverage your PAP provides. In addition, when you charge your car rental to your credit card, collision insurance may be offered.

When purchasing collision insurance, deductibles between $50 and $1,000 may be available. Selecting a higher deductible, as did the Joneses, will reduce your premium.

---

smart.sites

It's important to know what to do if you have a car accident. CarAccidents.com, **http://www.car-accidents.com**, outlines your legal rights and responsibilities in the event of an accident.

---

comprehensive automobile insurance Coverage that protects against loss to an insured automobile caused by any peril (with a few exceptions) *other than collision.*

Comprehensive Automobile Insurance

Comprehensive automobile insurance protects against loss to an insured automobile caused by any peril (with a few exceptions) *other than collision.* The maximum compensation provided under this coverage is the actual cash value of the automobile. This broad coverage includes, but is not limited to, damage caused by fire, theft, glass breakage, falling objects, malicious mischief, vandalism, riot, and earthquake. Contrary to popular belief, the automobile insurance policy normally does *not* cover theft of personal property left in the insured vehicle. The off-premises coverage of the homeowner's policy may cover such a loss if the auto was locked when the theft occurred.

no-fault automobile insurance A concept of automobile insurance that favors reimbursement without regard to negligence. Under *pure* no-fault, each insured party is compensated by his or her own company, regardless of which party caused the accident.

No-Fault Automobile Insurance

The concept of **no-fault automobile insurance** is a system that reimburses the parties involved in an accident without regard to negligence. Each insured party is compensated by his or her own company, regardless of which party caused the accident. In return, legal remedies and payments for pain and suffering are restricted. Under the concept of *pure* no-fault insurance, the driver, passengers, and injured pedestrians are reimbursed by the insurer of the car for economic losses stemming from bodily injury. The insurer does not have to cover claims for losses to other motorists who are covered by their own policies.

Unfortunately, advocates of no-fault forgot that liability insurance is not intended to serve as the primary system for compensating injured parties. Its sole purpose is to protect the assets of the insured, not to pay losses, *per se*, a concept that applies to all liability insurance. State laws governing no-fault insurance vary substantially as to both the amount of no-fault benefits provided and the degree to which restrictions for legal actions apply. Most states provide from $2,000 to $10,000 in personal injury protection and restrict legal recovery for pain and suffering to cases where medical or economic losses exceed some threshold level, such as $500 or $1,000. In all states recovery based on negligence is permitted for economic loss in excess of the amount payable by no-fault insurance.

Automobile Insurance Premiums

The cost of car insurance depends on many things, including your age, where you live, what kind of car you drive, your driving record, what kind of coverage you have, the amount of your deductible, and so forth. Consequently, car insurance premiums—even for basically the same coverage—vary all over the map. If you're fortunate enough to live in a low-premium state, such as North Dakota, Iowa, Maine, or Wyoming, you're probably relatively satisfied with the cost of your car insurance; if on the other hand you're in one of the more expensive states, like New Jersey, California, Rhode Island, or Massachusetts, you may well be feeling the pinch of rapidly increasing auto insurance rates.

After several years of declining rates, auto insurance premiums began to climb again in many states, including New York, Florida, and Texas. Insurers cite higher healthcare and vehicle repair costs, and larger liability payouts, as justification for the rate increases. Many residents in high-premium states are protesting these rates and demanding through state legislators and the ballot box, a return to more reasonable premiums.

Factors Affecting Premiums

Among the factors that influence how auto insurance premiums are set are (1) rating territory, (2) the amount of use

Financial Road Sign

Do You Drive a High Risk Car?

There are many factors that influence auto insurance costs, including where we live and what we drive. Another factor is whether that make of car is frequently stolen. The National Insurance Crime Bureau (NICB) tracks the most stolen vehicles in America by tallying all cars that are reported stolen. If your car is on the list insurance companies will charge you a higher rate to insure it.You may want to use the NICB's current top ten list of most stolen vehicles nationwide as a guide if you are considering purchasing a vehicle.

1. Toyota Camry
2. Honda Accord
3. Honda Civic
4. Oldsmobile Cutlass
5. Jeep Cherokee/Grand Cherokee
6. Chevrolet Full-Size Pickup
7. Toyota Corolla
8. Ford Taurus
9. Chevrolet Caprice
10. Ford F-150 Pickup

Source: Abbey Wagner, "Is Your Car on the "Most Stolen" List?" downloaded from **http://www.insweb.com/learningcenter**, February 8, 2004.

the automobile receives, (3) the personal characteristics of the driver, (4) the type of automobile, and (5) the insured's driving record.

- **Rating Territory**: Rates are higher in geographic areas where accident rates, number of claims filed, and average cost of claims paid are higher. Rates reflect auto repair costs, hospital and medical expenses, jury awards, and theft and vandalism in the area. Even someone with a perfect driving record will be charged the going rate for the area where the automobile is garaged. Exhibit 10.6 provides some helpful tips on protecting your vehicle wherever you live. Some jurisdictions prohibit the use of rating territories, age, and sex factors because they believe these factors unfairly discriminate against the urban, the young, and the male.

EXHIBIT 10.6

Top 10 Ways to Prevent Auto Theft

1. Invest in and install a good anti-theft device.
2. Take any packages that are in plain sight with you.
3. Turn off the car and remove keys from the ignition when leaving the car unattended.
4. Close windows and lock your doors.
5. Park in well-lit, heavily traveled areas, and keep your driveway light on all night when at home.
6. Etch the VIN (vehicle identification number) in the windows and other major parts of your car, thereby making the car more difficult to resell on the black market.
7. Keep any spare keys on your person, not in your car.
8. Remove any portable electronics, such as cell phones, car stereos, and PDAs when you park.
9. Park your car in a garage and lock the garage door, if one is available to you.
10. Make your car harder to tow by parking between other cars, turning the wheels toward the curb, and putting on the emergency brake.

Sources: Adapted from "Top 10 Ways to Prevent Auto Theft," *Insurance.com*, **http://auto.insurance.com/profiles_insights/hot_topics/article_0902_3.asp**, accessed February 6, 2004 and "10 Tips to Avoid Auto Crime," Insurance Corporation of British Columbia, **http://www.icbc.com/Crime-Fraud/autocr_thefta_tentip.html**, accessed February 12, 2004.

- **Use of the automobile.** Drive less, pay less! Low annual miles translate into a smaller probability of being in an accident, so you pay lower rates. Rates are also lower if the insured automobile is not usually driven to work, or is driven less than 3 miles one way to your job site. Premiums rise slightly if you drive more than 3 but fewer than 15 miles to work, and increase if your commute exceeds 15 miles each way.
- **Drivers' personal characteristics.** The age, sex, and marital status of the insured can also affect automobile insurance premiums. Insurance companies base the premium differentials on the number of accidents involving certain age groups. For example, drivers aged 25 and under make up only 15 percent of the total driving population but are involved in nearly 30 percent of auto accidents, and 26 percent of all fatal accidents. Male drivers are involved in a larger percentage of fatal crashes, so unmarried males age 29 or under, and married males under age 25, pay higher premiums than older individuals. Females over age 24, and married females of any age, are exempt from the youthful operator classification and pay lower premiums.
- **Type of automobile.** Insurance companies charge higher rates for automobiles classified as intermediate-performance, high-performance, and sports vehicles, and

for rear-engine models. Some states even rate four-door cars differently from two-door models. If you are thinking of buying, say, a Corvette or a Porsche, you'd better be prepared for some pretty hefty insurance rates.

- **Driving record.** The driving records—traffic violations and accidents—of those insured and the people who live with them affect premium levels. More severe traffic convictions—driving under the influence of alcohol or drugs, leaving the scene of an accident, homicide or assault arising from the operation of a motor vehicle, and driving with a revoked or suspended driver's license—result in higher insurance premiums. In addition, any conviction for a moving traffic violation that results in the accumulation of points under a state point system may result in a premium surcharge. In most states, accidents determined to be the fault of the insured also incur points and a premium surcharge.

Many states place drivers with multiple traffic violations in an **automobile insurance plan** (formerly called an *assigned-risk plan*), providing automobile insurance to those refused regular coverage. The automobile insurance plan generally offers less coverage for a higher premium. Even with high premiums, however, insurers lost billions of dollars on this type of business in a recent 5-year period.

automobile insurance plan An arrangement that provides automobile insurance to drivers who have been refused regular coverage under normal procedures; formerly called an *assigned-risk plan*.

smart.sites

Can you save money on your insurance by using a direct underwriter? Get a quote from Geico Direct, at **http://www.geico.com**, and compare it with your current policies and premiums.

Driving Down the Cost of Car Insurance

Comparison shopping for car insurance can really pay off, yet only one-third of car owners shop around for auto coverage. One of the best ways to reduce the cost of car insurance is to take advantage of the discounts auto insurers offer. Taken together, such discounts can knock 5 to 50 percent off your annual premium. Exhibit 10.7 summarizes some of the discounts offered by top auto insurance companies. Some give overall *safe-driving* (accident-free) discounts, and most give youthful operators lower rates if they have had *driver's training*. Some states have laws requiring insurers to offer lower premiums to any driver, young or old, who has taken driver's training. High-school and college students may also receive *good-student* discounts for maintaining a B average or making the dean's list at their school.

Nearly all insurance companies provide discounts to families with two or more automobiles insured by the same company (the *multicar* discount). Most insurers also offer discounts to owners who install *antitheft devices* in their cars. Likewise, a number of insurers offer *nonsmoker* and *nondrinker* discounts. There are even companies that specialize in insuring only certain portions of the population. For example, some insurers accept only persons who are educators, or executives, and others accept only government employees. Although not offering discounts in the normal sense, through more selective underwriting these companies are able to reduce losses and operating expenses, resulting in lower premiums.

Clearly, it's to your advantage to look for and use as many of these discounts as you can. Take another look at the auto insurance statement in Exhibit 10.5, and you'll see that the insured reduced his overall cost of coverage by 25 percent by qualifying for just three of the discounts. Another very effective way to drive down the cost of car insurance is to *raise your deductibles* (as discussed earlier in this chapter). This frequently overlooked tactic can have a dramatic impact on the amount of insurance premium you pay. For example, the difference between a $100 deductible and a $500 deductible may

EXHIBIT 10.7

Are You a Good Auto Insurance Risk?

Many insurance companies offer discounts for auto safety equipment and good driving habits. Here are some of the items that will buy you insurance discounts:

Anti-Theft Devices. Many insurance companies will only offer a discount if you have an active or passive disabling alarm system or alarm-only system. Check with your insurer for the specific types they will discount for.

Anti-Lock Brakes (ABS). Anti-lock braking systems can help prevent the loss of control in sudden braking situations.

Restraint Systems. Air bags, dual air bags, and seat belts are now common in most late-model vehicles. Having all three may qualify you for the highest level of discount.

Driver Training. For teenage drivers who successfully complete training with a certified instructor.

Good Student Discount. Awarded to teenagers with a "B" average or better.

Accident Prevention Course. Discounts for approved accident prevention courses with presentation of a completion certificate.

Good Driver. A good driver has a license for more than 3 years in the United States, and not more than 2 violation points on his or her driving record for either an accident and/or moving violation. Also no DWI, DUI, manslaughter, or gross negligence in an accident within the past 7 years.

Multiple Policies: Discounts offered for having more than one vehicle and/or a homeowner's insurance policy with the same company.

Carpool: Discount for participating in a shared-vehicle car pool.

Electronic Fund Transfer (EFT). Pay your policy in full through EFT.

Sources: Adapted from "Discounts," at **http://www.cheap-auto-car-insurance-quotes.com/discounts.htm**, downloaded February 9, 2004: "Discounts" at **http://www.4-insuraance-auto.com/discounts/discounts.php**, downloaded February 9, 2004.

be as much as 30 percent on comprehensive coverage and 25 percent on collision coverage; request a $1,000 deductible and you may save as much as 45 to 50 percent on both comprehensive and collision coverage.

smart.sites

Fill out an online questionnaire with Progressive Insurance Company (**http://www.progressive.com**) to get quotes on its insurance, and prices for up to three of its competitors.

Financial Responsibility Laws

financial responsibility laws
Laws that *require motorists to buy a specified minimum amount of automobile liability insurance*, or provide other proof of financial responsibility. They attempt to force motorists to be financially responsible for the damage they cause as a result of automobile accidents.

The annual losses from automobile accidents in the United States run into billions of dollars. For this reason, **financial responsibility laws** have been enacted in most states, whereby motorists *must buy a specified minimum amount of automobile liability insurance*, or provide other proof of comparable financial responsibility. These laws attempt to force motorists to be financially responsible for the damage they cause as a result of automobile accidents although the required limits are very low in most states—well below what you should carry.

Concept ✓

10-10. Briefly explain the major types of coverage available under the *personal auto policy (PAP)*. Which persons are insured under (a) automobile medical payments coverage and (b) uninsured motorists coverage?

10-11. Explain the nature of (a) automobile collision insurance and (b) automobile comprehensive insurance.

10-12. Define *no-fault insurance* and discuss its pros and cons.

10-13. Describe the important factors that influence the availability and cost of auto insurance.

10-14. Discuss the role of *financial responsibility laws* and describe the two basic types currently employed.

Financial responsibility laws fall into two categories. *Compulsory auto insurance laws* require motorists to show evidence of insurance coverage *before* receiving their license plates. Penalties for not having liability insurance include fines and suspension of your driver's license. The second type requires motorists to show evidence of their insurance coverage only *after* they are involved in an accident. If they then fail to demonstrate compliance with the law, their registrations and driver's licenses are suspended. This law has been criticized on the grounds that it allows negligent motorists to have one "free" accident. Although motorists who are not able to fulfill their financial responsibility lose their driving privileges, victims may never recover their losses.

OTHER PROPERTY AND LIABILITY INSURANCE

LG5

Although homeowner's and automobile insurance policies represent the basic protection needed by most families, other types of insurance, such as property and liability coverage, may be appropriate for some people. Among those discussed here are popular forms of supplemental property insurance coverage—earthquake insurance, flood insurance, and other forms of transportation insurance—as well as the personal liability umbrella policy.

SUPPLEMENTAL PROPERTY INSURANCE COVERAGE

Because homeowner's policies exclude certain types of damage, you may want to consider some of the following types of supplemental coverage.

- **Earthquake Insurance:** Although most people think of California when earthquakes are mentioned, areas in other states are also subject to this type of loss. Very few homeowners buy this coverage because these policies typically carry a 15 percent deductible on the replacement cost of a home damaged or destroyed by earthquake. So even though the premiums are relatively inexpensive you have to pay a lot out of pocket before you can collect on the policy.
- **Flood Insurance:** Before 1968, most private insurers regarded floods as an uninsurable peril because the risk could not be spread among people not located in flood-prone areas. But in 1968, the federal government established a subsidized flood insurance program in cooperation with private insurance agents, who can now sell this low-cost coverage to homeowners and tenants living in designated communities. In addition, the flood insurance program encourages communities to initiate land-use controls to reduce future flood losses.
- **Other Forms of Transportation Insurance.** In addition to automobile insurance, you may wish to insure other types of vehicles, such as mobile homes, recreational vehicles, or boats.

PERSONAL LIABILITY UMBRELLA POLICY

Persons with moderate to high levels of income and net worth may want to take out a **personal liability umbrella policy**. It provides added liability coverage for both homeowner's and automobile insurance, and additional coverage not provided by either of those

personal liability umbrella policy
An insurance policy that provides excess liability coverage for both homeowner's and automobile insurance, and additional coverage not provided by either of those policies.

policies. Umbrella policies often include limits of $1 million or more. In addition, some provide added amounts of coverage for a family's major medical insurance.

Because middle- and upper-income individuals are logical targets for liability claims, umbrella protection provides a desirable, added layer of coverage. The premiums are usually quite reasonable for the broad coverage offered—$150 to $300 a year for as much as $1 million in coverage. Although the protection is comprehensive, it does contain some exclusions. In addition, the insured party must already have relatively high liability limits ($100,000 to $300,000) on their auto and homeowner's coverage in order to purchase a personal liability umbrella policy.

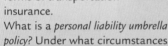

Concept ✓

10-15. Briefly describe the following supplemental property insurance coverage: (a) earthquake insurance (b) flood insurance, and (c) other forms of transportation insurance.

10-16. What is a *personal liability umbrella policy?* Under what circumstances might it be a wise purchase?

Do you need the extra protection a personal liability umbrella policy provides? As discussed in the *Money in Action* box on pages 422–423, the answer is yes if you have sizable assets that could be seized to pay a judgment against you, not fully covered by your homeowner's and automobile policies. But you may also need this coverage if you rent your home to others, have house sitters, or unbonded hired help such as gardeners or babysitters, because you're responsible for any injuries they incur or cause. Or you may need this coverage if you work from home and clients visit you at your home office.

BUYING INSURANCE AND SETTLING CLAIMS

If you're thinking about buying property and liability insurance, the first step is to develop an inventory of exposures to loss and arrange them from highest to lowest priority. Losses that lend themselves to insurance protection are those that seldom occur but have potential for being substantial—for example damage to a home and its contents, or liability arising from a negligence claim. Somewhat less important, but nevertheless desirable, is insurance to cover losses that could be disruptive to the financial plans of a family, even though they might not result in insolvency. Such risks include physical damage to automobiles, boats, and other personal property of moderate value. Lowest-priority exposures can be covered by savings or from current income, and some personal property of minor value, such as an old auto, may not merit coverage—at least as far as collision insurance is concerned.

captive agent
An insurance agent who represents only one insurance company and is more or less an employee of that company.

independent agent
An insurance agent who may place coverage with any company with which he or she has an agency relationship, as long as the insured meets that company's underwriting standards.

Property and Liability Insurance Agents

There is more to the purchase of property insurance than simply signing applications for homeowner's and automobile insurance, and a good agent can make the process much easier. Most property insurance agents fall into either the captive or independent category. A **captive agent** is one who represents only one insurance company and is more or less an employee of that company. Allstate, Nationwide, and State Farm are major insurance companies that market their products through captive agents. In contrast, **independent agents** typically represent between two and ten different insurance companies. These agents may place your coverage with any of the companies they have an agency relationship with, as long as you meet the underwriting standards of that company. Some well-known companies that operate through independent agents include Hartford, Kemper, Chubb, and Travelers. Either type can serve your needs well and should take the time to:

- Review your total property and liability insurance exposures
- Inventory property and identify exposures
- Determine appropriate covered perils, limits, deductibles, and floater policies

Because of large variations in premiums and services, it pays to comparison shop.

Money in Action

Buy an Umbrella before You Get Soaked

When a 16-year-old dove into a pool, hit his head on the bottom, and became paralyzed from the neck down, it resulted in a $1.5 million settlement against the homeowner. A 22-year-old who suffered permanent eye damage after being struck by a golf ball won a judgment of $160,000 against the golfer. In both these cases, had the homeowner and golfer had an umbrella policy that picked up excess liability, they would have been spared great financial distress.

In today's litigious society a $1 million judgment for such accidents is all too common. Although the odds of being involved in such an accident are small, it only takes one brush with tragedy to ruin you financially. The vast majority of claims arise from car accidents, but they also arise from a myriad of other causes: a visitor who slips on your stairs, a babysitter who's poked in the eye by your kids, a neighbor bitten by your dog, a bicyclist with whom you collide, a so-called friend who sues you for slander. The possibilities are endless, making an umbrella policy costing $150 to $300 per year (cost depends on geographical location—big cities tend to cost more) very desirable. People with homes, swimming pools, boats, golf clubs, dogs, and other sources of potential liability are particularly at risk.

Umbrella policies supplement homeowner's, auto, and boat policies, and typically cover liability beyond $300,000. The smallest policies pay $1 million per incident beyond what's covered by the underlying policy, although many companies, such as Nationwide Insurance, offer up to $2 million in coverage. So if your auto policy provides $300,000 of personal liability protection and you have a $2 million umbrella, you would have a total of $2.3 million worth of insurance.

The easiest way to buy an umbrella policy is through the same company that provides your basic coverage. Note that most umbrella policies do not cover business liability or your liability as a board member of a nonprofit organization. Small businesses and home-based businesses need separate liability insurance to cover suits against the

...continued on next page

Property insurance agents who meet various experiential and educational requirements, including passing a series of written examinations, qualify for the *Chartered Property and Casualty Underwriter (CPCU)* or *Certified Insurance Counselor (CIC)* designation. Another alternative to consider is companies that sell directly to the consumer through an 800 number or online. Generally, their premiums are lower. Examples of direct sellers are Amica Mutual, Erie, Geico, and USAA.

Property and Liability Insurance Companies

Although selecting an agent is an important step when purchasing property and liability insurance, you should ask questions about the company, including its financial soundness, its claims-settlement practices, and the geographic extent of its operations (this could be important if you are involved in an accident 1,000 miles from home). As with any form of insurance, you should check the company's ratings (see Chapter 8) and stick with those rated in the top categories. The agent should be a good source of information about the technical aspects of a company's operations, whereas friends and acquaintances often can provide insight into its claims-settlement policy. The Internet also offers a wealth of information about various property and liability insurance products. Indeed, many insurance companies now have elaborate home pages on the Web that provide basic information about the provider and its products, directions to local agents, or calculators to crunch the numbers and generate sample premiums.

smart.sites

What is your insurance carrier's financial strength rating? Go to the Standard & Poor's Web site at **http://www.standardandpoors.com**, click Credit Ratings, then Financials/Insurance, and then Credit Ratings Lists to search for the company.

Settling Property and Liability Claims

Generally speaking, insurance companies settle claims promptly and fairly, especially life and healthcare claims. However, in settling property and liability claims, some claimant–insurer disagreement does exist. The following discussion reviews the claims-settlement process and the people who participate in it. First, however, let's consider what you should do immediately following an accident.

Financial Road Sign

Strategies to Avoid Liability
Understanding liability can help you avoid it. Here are some practical strategies to put into practice.

- **Understand what causes liability:** Educate yourself through books and seminars or by consulting with those in a position to advise you.
- **Develop your own personal safety program:** A dedication to the safety of yourself and others for whom you are responsible will reduce the risk of injuries and, consequently, liability. Regular auto or equipment inspections will keep you a step ahead.
- **Carry adequate liability insurance:** It does not prevent liability but may protect your home, your savings, and your property, in the event a claim or lawsuit is brought against you. At the very least, insurance could spare you the enormous cost of a legal defense.

First Steps Following an Accident

After an accident, record the names, addresses, and telephone numbers of all witnesses, drivers, occupants, and injured parties, along with the license numbers of the automobiles involved. Immediately notify law enforcement officers and your insurance agent of the accident. Never discuss liability at the scene of an accident, or with anyone other than the police and your insurer. Before it can be determined whom, if anyone, is legally liable for an accident, the requisites of liability must be established. The duties of the police are to assess the probability of a law violation and maintain order at the scene of an accident—not to make judgments with respect to liability.

Steps in Claims Settlement

If you're involved in an accident, one of the first things you're going to decide is whether you want to file a claim. Should you opt to file a claim—and most experts agree that unless it's a very minor or insignificant accident, the best course of action is to file a claim—it'll probably involve the following steps.

1. **Notice to your insurance company.** You must notify your insurance company that a loss (or potential for loss) has occurred. Timely notice is extremely important.

business. Home-based business people risk huge potential financial losses because standard homeowner's policies do not cover losses to a business located inside a home. If the UPS person trips over your children's toys while delivering a business package, your liability insurance won't apply. Director's and officer's insurance will cover board members. Professionals such as doctors, dentists, lawyers, architects, engineers, and anyone else who could be sued as a result of their work should consider having professional liability insurance to cover malpractice suits.

Some excess liability policies cover the cost of legal defense and others do not. You should determine whether your coverage includes this feature and if there are limits on legal costs in the policy. Some policies will exclude swimming pools, or pools that have diving boards. Others won't insure young drivers. As with any insurance policy, comparing the price of one umbrella to another means comparing apples with apples.

If paying the premium for an umbrella policy is a hardship, consider boosting the deductibles on your basic policies from $100 to $500, or from $500 to $1,000. The reduction in premiums will likely pay for the umbrella policies, thus protecting you against financial calamity.

Critical Thinking Questions

1. Based on an analysis of your lifestyle and activities, would you would benefit from carrying an umbrella liability policy, and why?
2. From where do the majority of claims arise under umbrella liability policies? Who is most at risk and would benefit most from carrying such insurance?
3. If you already carry homeowner's, auto, and boat insurance, why do you need an umbrella policy? Explain.

Sources: Bobbie Sage, "Why Every Policyholder Needs Umbrella Insurance," *PersonalInsure.com,* **http://www.personalinsure.about.com**, downloaded December 2, 2003, and "Common Questions About Umbrella Insurance," *MundusInsurance.com,* **http://www.mundusinsurance.com**, downloaded December 2, 2003.

2. **Investigation.** Insurance company personnel may talk to witnesses or law enforcement officers and gather physical evidence to determine whether the claimed loss is covered by the policy, and check to make sure that the date of the loss falls within the policy period. If you delay filing your claim, you hinder the insurer's ability to check the facts. All policies specify the time period within which you must give notice. Failure to report can result in your loss of the right to collect.
3. **Proof of loss.** This requires you to give a sworn statement. You may be required to show medical bills, an inventory, and certify the value of lost property (for example, a written inventory, photographs, and purchase receipts), an employer statement of lost wages, and, if possible, physical evidence of damage (x-rays if you claim a back injury, a broken window or pried door if you claim a break-in and theft at your home). After you submit proof of loss, the insurer may (1) pay you the amount you asked for, (2) offer you a lesser amount, or (3) deny that the company has any legal responsibility under the terms of your policy.

If the amount is disputed, most policies provide for some form of claims arbitration. You hire a third party, the company hires a third party, and these two arbitrators jointly select one more person. When any two of the three arbitrators reach agreement, their decision binds you and the company to their solution. When a company denies responsibility, you do not get the right of arbitration. In such an instance the company is saying the loss does not fall under the policy coverage. You must then either forget the claim or bring in an attorney or, perhaps, a public adjustor (discussed next).

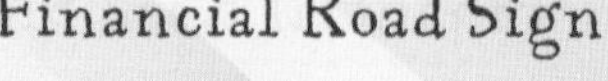

Financial Road Sign

What to Do When a Claim Is Denied

Fight back if your homeowner's or automobile insurance company refuses to pay all or part of a claim.

1. *Document everything.* Get written copies of police or fire department reports and outside appraisals, and take photos.
2. *Don't accept "no" for an answer.* Complain to your insurer and ask for another review.
3. *File and follow up on your appeal promptly.* Some companies have a 1-year limit on challenges, starting with the date of the first decision.
4. *Go to your state's insurance department.* Insurers then have about 6 weeks to resolve a dispute.
5. *Don't bother filing a lawsuit for small claims.* State regulators can't force a solution, but most lawyers won't handle lawsuits for relatively small amounts.

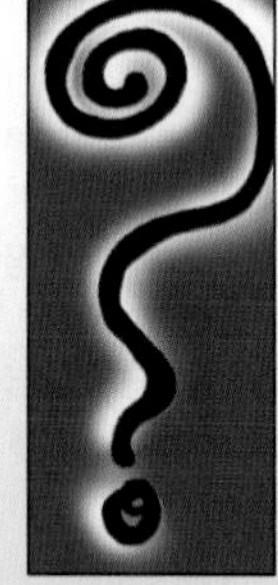

Concept ✓

10-17. Differentiate between *captive* and *independent insurance agents.* What characteristics should you look for when choosing an insurance agent and an insurance company when buying property or liability insurance?

10-18. Briefly describe key aspects of the claims-settlement process, explaining what to do after an accident, the steps in claim settlement, and the role of *claims adjustors.*

Claims Adjustment

Usually the first person to call when you need to file a claim is your insurance agent. If your loss is relatively minor, the agent can quickly process it and, in fact, will often give you a check right on the spot. If your loss is more complex, your company will probably assign a claims adjustor to the case. A **claims adjustor** is an insurance specialist who works for the insurance company as an independent adjustor, or for an adjustment bureau. The adjustor investigates claims, looking out for the interests of the company—which might very well be to keep you, its customer, satisfied. However, many claimants are out to collect all they can from insurance companies, which they think have "deep pockets." Thus the adjustor walks a fine line: He or she must diligently question and investigate, while at the same time offering service to minimize settlement delays and financial hardship. To promote your own interest in the claim, you should cooperate with the adjustor and answer inquiries honestly—keeping in mind that the company writes the adjustor's paycheck.

claims adjustor An insurance specialist who works for the insurance company as an independent adjustor, or for an adjustment bureau. He or she investigates claims, looking out for the interests of the company.

SUMMARY

LG1. Discuss the importance and basic principles of property insurance, including types of exposure, indemnity, and coinsurance. Property and liability insurance protects against the loss of real and personal property that can occur from exposure to various types of perils. In addition, such insurance protects against loss from lawsuits based on alleged negligence by the insured. The principle of indemnity limits the insured's compensation to the amount of economic loss. The coinsurance provision requires that the policyholder buy insurance coverage that equals a set percentage of the property's value to receive full compensation under the policy's terms.

LG2. Identify the types of coverage provided by homeowner's insurance. Most homeowner's insurance policies are divided into two major sections. Section I covers the dwelling unit, accompanying structures, and personal property of the insured. Section II pertains mainly to comprehensive coverage for personal liability and medical payments to others. The most commonly sold homeowner's policies (Forms HO-2 and HO-3) cover a broad range of perils, including damage from such occurrences as fire or lightning, windstorms, explosions, aircraft, vehicles, smoke, vandalism, theft, freezing, and so on. Personal property coverage is typically set at 50 percent of the coverage on the dwelling.

LG3. Select the right homeowner's insurance policy for your needs. Everyone should have some form of homeowner's insurance, whether you own a single-family house or a condominium, or rent an apartment. Renter's insurance covers your personal possessions. Except for the house and garage, which are covered on a replacement-cost basis, homeowner's or renter's insurance normally reimburses all losses on an actual cash-value basis, subject to applicable deductibles and policy limits. However, for an additional premium, you can usually obtain replacement-cost coverage on personal belongings. Within Section I, internal limits are set for various classes of property. You may wish to increase these limits if you have valuable property. One way to do so is with a personal property floater (PPF). Because the standard Section II liability limit is only $100,000, it's a good idea to buy additional liability coverage, generally available at minimal cost. To reduce premiums, choose a policy with a higher deductible.

LG4. Analyze the coverage in a personal automobile policy (PAP) and choose the most cost-effective policy. Automobile insurance policies usually contain provisions that protect the insured from loss due to personal liability, medical payments, uninsured motorists, collision (property damage to the vehicle), and comprehensive coverage (which applies to nearly any other type of noncollision damage a car might suffer, such as theft or vandalism). Where you live, type of car, driving record, how much you drive, and your personal characteristics influence the policy premium cost. Most automobile insurers offer discounts for good driving records, safety and antitheft devices, driver's training courses, and similar factors. Other ways to reduce premiums are through higher deductibles and eliminating collision coverage if your car is old.

LG5. Describe other types of property and liability insurance. In addition to the major forms of homeowner's and automobile insurance, a variety of other property and liability coverage is available, including supplemental property insurance coverage—earthquake insurance, flood insurance, and other forms of transportation insurance (mobile-home, recreational vehicle, and boat insurance)—and personal liability umbrella policies.

LG6. Choose a property and liability insurance agent and company, and settle claims. Before buying property and liability coverage, evaluate your exposure to loss and determine the coverage needed. You should also carefully select your insurance agent and insurance company to obtain appropriate coverage at a reasonable price. Equally important—make sure the agent and company you deal with have reputations for fair claims-settlement practices. Before filing a claim, you should decide whether the amount of damage warrants a claim. Document all claims properly and file promptly. In the event of a complex loss claim, expect your insurer to assign a claims adjustor to the case.

Financial Planning Exercises

1. Assume Marcus Browning had a homeowner's insurance policy with $100,000 of coverage on the dwelling. Would a 90 percent coinsurance clause be better than an 80 percent clause in such a policy? Give reasons to support your answer.
2. Last year Steve and Jessica Morgan bought a home with a dwelling replacement value of $250,000 and insured it (via an HO-3 policy) for $210,000. The policy reimburses for actual cash value and has a $500 deductible, standard limits for Schedule C items, and no scheduled property. Recently, burglars broke into the house and stole a 2-year-old television set with a current replacement value of $600 and an estimated life of 8 years. They also took jewelry valued at $1,850 and silver flatware valued at $3,000.
   a. If the Morgans' policy has an 80 percent coinsurance clause, do they have enough insurance?
   b. Assuming a 50 percent Schedule C limit, calculate how much the Morgans would receive if they filed a claim for the stolen items.
   c. What advice would you give the Morgans about their homeowner's coverage?
3. Vickie Korte's luxurious home in the suburb of Broken Arrow, Oklahoma, was recently gutted in a fire. Her living and dining rooms were completely destroyed, and the damaged personal property had a replacement price of $27,000. The average age of the damaged personal property was 5 years, and its useful life was estimated to be 15 years. What is the maximum amount the insurance company would pay Vickie, assuming that it reimburses losses on an actual cash-value basis?
4. Doris and Ed Barnow, both graduate students, moved into an apartment near the university. Doris wants to buy renter's insurance, but Ed thinks they don't need it because their furniture isn't worth much. Doris points out that, among other things, they do have some expensive computer and stereo equipment. To help the Barnows resolve their dilemma, suggest a plan for deciding how much insurance to buy, and give them some ideas for finding a policy.
5. Robert Taylor has a personal automobile policy (PAP) with coverage of $25,000/$50,000 for bodily injury liability, $25,000 for property damage liability, $5,000 for medical payments, and a $500 deductible for collision insurance. How much will his insurance cover in each of the following situations? Will he have any out-of-pocket costs?
   a. He loses control and skids on ice, running into a parked car and causing $3,785 damage to the unoccupied vehicle and $2,350 damage to his own car.
   b. He runs a stop sign and causes a serious auto accident, badly injuring two people. The injured parties win lawsuits against him for $30,000 each.
   c. Taylor's wife borrows his car while hers is being repaired. She backs into a telephone pole and causes $450 damage to the car.

Applying Personal Finance

Insure Your Property!

Adequate property insurance is a vital part of financial planning. It helps protect our hard-earned investments in a home, car, or other property. The purpose of this project is to help you determine your property insurance needs.

List your property for which you would need insurance coverage. Your list may include such things as a home, car, boat, motorcycle, or household items. Beside each entry, list the insurance you currently have in place on each. Then examine the depth of coverage of your policies. Is this coverage adequate? What are its exclusions and limits? What are the costs? Can you do something to lower these costs? If you do not have coverage, or if your coverage is inadequate, research various policies. If you rent a place to live, do you have renter's insurance? If not, tally up what it would cost you to replace all your household items and then find several quotes for renter's insurance.

Contemporary Case Applications

10.1 The Salvatis' Homeowner's Insurance Decision

Rodrigo and Anita Salvati, ages 30 and 28, respectively, were recently married in Chicago. Rodrigo is an electrical engineer with Geophysical Century, an oil exploration company. Anita has a master's degree in special education and teaches at a local junior high school. After living in an apartment for 6 months, the Salvatis have negotiated the purchase of a new home in a rapidly growing Chicago suburb. Republic Savings and Loan Association has approved their loan request for $108,000, which represents 90 percent of the $120,000 purchase price. Prior to closing the loan, the Salvatis must obtain homeowner's insurance for the home. The Salvatis currently have an HO-4 renter's insurance policy, which they purchased from Rodrigo's tennis partner, Kelly Duvall, who is an agent with Kramer's Insurance Company. To learn about the types of available homeowner's insurance, Rodrigo has discussed their situation with Kelly, who has offered them a variety of homeowner's policies for their consideration. He has recommended that the Salvatis purchase an HO-3 policy because it would provide them with comprehensive coverage.

Questions

1. What forms of homeowner's insurance are available? Which forms should the Salvatis consider?
2. What are the perils against which the home and its contents should be insured?
3. Discuss the types of loss protection provided by the homeowner's policies under consideration.
4. What advice would you give the Salvatis regarding Kelly's suggestion? What coverage should they buy?

10.2 Auto Insurance for Cheryl Weisbach

Cheryl Weisbach of Phoenix, Arizona, is a divorced 40-year-old loan officer at the Frontier National Bank of Arizona and has a 16-year-old son. She has decided to use her annual bonus as a down payment on a new car. One Saturday afternoon in late December, she visited Chuck Thomas's Auto Mall and purchased a new car for $23,000. To obtain insurance on the car, Cheryl called her agent, Jane Cunningham, who represents Farmers Insurance Company, and explained her auto insurance needs. Jane said she would investigate the various options for her. Three days later, Cheryl and Jane got together to review her coverage options. Jane offered several proposals, including various combinations of the following coverages: (a) basic automobile liability insurance, (b) uninsured motorists coverage, (c) automobile medical payments insurance, (d) automobile collision insurance, and (e) comprehensive automobile insurance.

Questions

1. Describe the key features of these insurance coverages.
2. Are there any limitations on these coverages? Explain.
3. Indicate the persons who would be protected under each type of coverage.
4. What kind of insurance coverages would you recommend that Ms. Weisbach purchase? Explain your recommendation.

MONEY ONLINE

Protect Your Property!

1. **http://www.financenter.com/consumertools**

What do you need to know about insurance? The FinanCenter has information and calculators for all types of property insurance, whether for auto, homeowners, or renters. Click on "Insurance" under "Educators" for help with all your insurance questions.

2. **http://www.usaaedfoundation.org**

Buying a home? Read up on homeowner's insurance at the USAA Educational Foundation's Web site. Click on "Insurance" and then on "Homeowner's Insurance" for an extensive primer on the subject. Interested in building a home or remodeling? Look under "Other Insurance" to find "Builder's Risk Insurance" to learn what insurance concerns you will encounter during the process.

3. **http://www.statefarm.com/insuranc/renters/renters.htm**

Should you buy renter's insurance? How much do you need? State Farm's Web site helps you make informed choices concerning renter's insurance and other types of insurance as well.

4. **http://www.fema.gov/nfip**

Do you need flood insurance? Visit the Web site of the Federal Emergency Management Association to learn about the National Flood Insurance Program. Find many flood-related topics at "Select a Quick Link."

5. **http://www.redcross.org**

What disaster services does the Red Cross provide? What services does the organization provide for members of the military and their families? How can you prepare for a disaster? Learn the answers to these questions and many more at the Web site of the American Red Cross.

6. **http://info.insure.com/auto**

What options do you have when your insurance company totals your car? What should you do in the event of an auto accident? Should you buy a salvaged vehicle? Browse through Insure.com's offerings at "Auto" to find the answers to these and many, many other frequently asked questions concerning autos and auto insurance.

7. **http://www.nicb.org**

Where are the hot spots for vehicle theft? Visit the National Insurance Crime Bureau's Web site to view the top ten cities. Find out how your city ranks and what you can do to combat vehicle theft and insurance fraud. Also find links to numerous organizations, agencies, and government offices which deal with vehicle insurance, theft, and fraud.

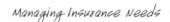

8. **http://nhtsa.gov/ncap**
Buy a safer car! Find your car or browse through lists of cars you are considering buying to find how they rate on various safety features at the Web site of the National Highway Traffic Safety Administration.

9. **http://www.wellsfargo.com/biz/products/insurance/insurance.jhtml**
Do you have a business of your own? Visit Wells Fargo's "Small Business Insurance" center for information on insuring your business from property damage, theft, and the liability that you may face as a business owner. Click on "FAQ" for answers to questions concerning umbrella insurance, commercial auto insurance, worker's compensation, and the insurance needed when you have a home-based business.

Just for Fun!

10. **http://www.actuarialjokes.com**
Do insurance actuaries have a sense of humor? You be the judge. Read through Actuarial Jokes for a glimpse at the lighter side of the number crunching business. If you're interested in a career as an actuary, explore the main Web site of **http://www.actuary.com**.

PART FIVE

Managing Investments

Chapter 11
Investment Planning

Chapter 12
Investing in Stocks and Bonds

Chapter 13
Investing in Mutual Funds

CHAPTER 11

Investment Planning

Learning Goals

LG1. Discuss the role that investing plays in the personal financial planning process and identify several different investment objectives.

LG2. Distinguish between primary and secondary markets, as well as listed exchanges and the over-the-counter market.

LG3. Explain the process of buying and selling securities and recognize the different types of orders.

LG4. Develop an appreciation of how various forms of investment information can lead to better investing skills and returns.

LG5. Gain a basic understanding of the growing impact that the computer and the Internet are having on the field of investments.

LG6. Describe an investment portfolio and how you'd go about developing and managing a portfolio of securities.

Riding the Market's Roller Coaster

In the spring of 2000, Michael Janson began to panic as technology stocks tumbled, and the value of his small portfolio fell. Was this the beginning of a bear market, or just a temporary correction? He and his wife Karen, an elementary school teacher, had started investing in 1997, as soon as Michael finished medical school. They were able to catch the end of the phenomenal stock market surge in the late 1990s, when annual returns on equities were averaging more than 25 percent. Because Michael loves technology and follows the latest trends, he had allocated a sizable percentage of their investment funds to the tech sector, especially to new, fast-growing dot-com companies that were making their stockholders very wealthy.

Karen was more conservative and decided to invest her 401(k) plan in a mutual fund that covered a wider range of growth stocks and one that focused on blue chip, well-known companies. She, too, was uneasy as the broader markets also took a dive. As novice investors they didn't know what to do. Should they sell their stocks before they incurred greater losses, or was the market going through one of its periodic corrections?

Michael searched various financial Web sites to gain some insight into what more experienced investors were doing. Because he and Karen were investing for the long term—their goals include buying a home and starting a college fund for baby Sarah and any future children—Michael realized that panic selling was a bad move. Markets go through many up and down cycles over time and therefore, he decided that the most important thing was to stay invested to earn a fully-compounded return on his funds. However, he decided to sell some of his tech stocks to reinvest in a wider range of market sectors. This proved to be a wise move. Even though the market took a huge nosedive, he picked solid companies and monitored his portfolio regularly. He also implemented a strategy of selling stocks that fell below a certain percentage of purchase price to minimize his losses. Karen's more balanced portfolio was more successful in riding out the market dips without too many changes. As the markets finally rallied in 2003, the Jansons' foresight and patience paid off as their respective portfolios began to grow once again.

In this chapter, you'll learn about investment planning, securities markets, brokers, securities transactions, information sources, and portfolio strategies so, like the Jansons, you too can build your own portfolio.

CRITICAL THINKING QUESTIONS

As you review the chapter, consider these questions in relation to the Jansons' financial planning:

- Summarize the Janson's investment objectives. Does their investment strategy match their goals?
- Why, even though they were investing for the long term, did the Jansons monitor their portfolios on a regular basis?
- Recommend at least five different specific sources of investment information that would help the Jansons to both track their investments and educate themselves about securities. Explain how they would use these resources.

THE OBJECTIVES AND REWARDS OF INVESTING

LG1

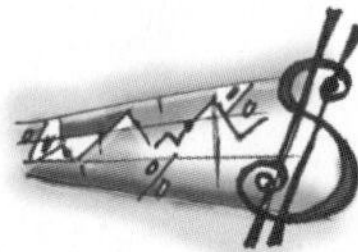

People invest their money for all sorts of reasons. Some do it as a way to accumulate the down payment on a new home; others do it as a way to supplement their income; still others invest to build up a nest egg for retirement. Actually, the term *investment* means different things to different people. That is, while millions of people *invest* regularly in securities like stocks, bonds, and mutual funds, others *speculate* in commodities or options. **Investing** is generally considered to take more of a long-term perspective and is viewed as a process of purchasing securities wherein stability of value and level of return are somewhat predictable. **Speculating**, on the other hand, is viewed as a short-term activity that involves the buying and selling of securities in which future value and expected return are highly uncertain. Obviously, speculation is far more risky than investing.

investing
The process of placing money in some medium such as stocks or bonds in the expectation of receiving some future benefit.

speculating
A form of investing in which future value and expected returns are highly uncertain.

If you're like most investors, at first you'll probably keep your funds in some form of savings vehicle (as described in Chapter 4). Once you have *sufficient savings*—for emergencies and other purposes—you can begin to build up a *pool of investable capital.* This often means making sacrifices and doing what you can to *live within your budget.* Granted, it's far easier to spend money than to save it, but if you're really serious about getting into investments, you're going to have to accumulate the necessary capital! In addition to a savings and capital accumulation program, it's also important to have adequate *insurance coverage* to provide protection against the unexpected (we discussed different kinds of insurance in Chapters 8, 9, and 10). For our purposes here, we will assume you are adequately insured and that the cost of insurance coverage is built into your family's monthly cash budget. Ample insurance and liquidity (cash and savings) with which to meet life's emergencies are two *investment prerequisites* that are absolutely essential for the development of a successful investment program. Once these conditions are met, you are ready to start investing.

smart.sites
With so many investing Web sites, how can you find what you need? Start with An Opinionated Guide to the Web's Best Investing Sites, **http://www.winninginvesting.com**, for links to useful Web sites listed by category. An added benefit: most are free.

BUT HOW DO I GET STARTED?

Contrary to what you may believe, there is really nothing magical about the topic of investments—in fact, as long as you have the capital to do so, it's really quite easy to get started in investing. The terminology may seem baffling at times and some of the procedures and techniques quite complicated. But don't let that mislead you into thinking there is no room for the small, individual investor. Nothing could be farther from the truth! For as we will see in this and the next two chapters, individual investors have a wide array of securities and investment vehicles to choose from. Further, opening an investment account is no more difficult than opening a checking account.

How, then, do you get started? To begin with, you need some money—not a lot; $500 to $1,000 will do, although $4,000 or $5,000 would be better (and remember, this is *investment capital* we're talking about here—money you've accumulated above and beyond any basic emergency savings). In addition to money, you need knowledge and know-how. You should never invest in something you are not sure about—that is the quickest way to lose money. Learn as much as you can about the market, different types of securities, and various trading strategies. This course you're taking on personal finance is a good start, but you may want to do more. For one thing, you can become a regular reader of publications such as *Money*, *The Wall Street Journal*, *Barron's*, and *Forbes* (these and other sources of information are reviewed later in this chapter). Also, try to stay current with major developments as they occur in the market; start following the stock market, interest rates, and developments in the bond market.

We strongly suggest that, after you've learned a few things about stocks and bonds, you set up a portfolio of securities on paper and make *paper trades* in and out of your portfolio, for 6 months to a year, to get a feel for what it is like to make (and lose) money in the market. Start out with an imaginary sum of, say, $50,000 (as long as you are going to dream, you might as well make it worthwhile). Then keep track of the stocks and bonds you hold, record the number of shares bought and sold, dividends received, and so on. Throughout this exercise, be sure to use actual prices (as obtained from *The Wall Street Journal* or your local newspaper) and keep it as realistic as possible. If you have access to a computer, you might want to use one of the *portfolio tracking* programs offered at such sites as **http://www.quicken.com** or **http://moneycentral.msn.com**; there are some powerful Internet sites out there that make it very easy to track the behavior of a portfolio of securities. The advantage to creating a paper portfolio is clear: If you're going to make mistakes in the market, you're much better off doing so on paper. Also, if your parents, relatives, or friends have done a lot of investing, talk to them! Find out what they have to say about investing, pick up some pointers and possibly even learn from their mistakes. Eventually, you will gain a familiarity with the market and become comfortable with the way things are done there. When that happens, you will be ready to take the plunge.

At that point, you will also need a way to invest—more specifically, a broker and some investment vehicle in which to invest. As we will see later in this chapter, the stockbroker is the party through whom you will be buying and selling stocks, bonds, and other securities. If your relatives or friends have a broker they like and trust, have them introduce you to him or her. Alternatively, visit several of the brokerage firms in your community; talk to one of their brokers about your available investment funds and your investment objectives.

As a beginning investor with limited funds, it is probably best to confine your investment activity to the basics. Stick to stocks, bonds, and mutual funds. Avoid getting fancy, and certainly don't try to make a killing each and every time you invest—that will only lead to frustration, disappointment, and very possibly, heavy losses. Further, *be patient*! Don't expect the price of the stock to double overnight, and don't panic when things fail to work out as expected in the short run (after all, security prices do occasionally go down). Finally, remember that you do not need spectacular returns in order to make a lot of money in the market. Instead, be consistent and let the concept of compound interest work for you. Do that and you'll find that just $2,000 a year invested at the fairly conservative rate of 10 percent will grow to well over $100,000 in 20 years! While the type of security in which you invest is a highly personal decision, you might want to give serious consideration to some sort of mutual fund as your first investment (see Chapter 13). Mutual funds provide professional management and diversification that individual investors—especially those with limited resources—can rarely obtain on their own.

smart.sites

Zacks Investment Research (**http://www.zacks.com**) offers a comprehensive "Investing 101" tutorial and a glossary of financial terms.

The Role of Investing in Personal Financial Planning

Buy a car, build a house, enjoy a comfortable retirement—these are goals we would all like to attain some day and are, in many cases, the centerpieces of well-developed financial plans. As a rule, a financial goal such as building a house is not something we pay for out of our cash reserves; the cost (in most cases, even the down payment) is simply too great to allow for that. Instead, we must accumulate the funds over time—which is where investment planning and the act of investing enter into the personal financial planning process. By investing our money, we are letting it work for us.

It all starts with an objective—a particular financial goal we would like to achieve within a certain period of time. Take the case of the Thompsons. Shortly after the birth of their first child, they decided to start building a college education fund. After performing some rough calculations, they concluded they'd need to accumulate about $60,000 over the next 18 years to have the kind of money they feel they'll need for their daughter's education. Simply by setting that objective, the Thompsons created a well-defined, specific financial goal. The purpose is to meet the educational needs of their child, and the amount of money involved is $60,000 in 18 years. But how do they reach their goal? The first thing they must decide is where the money will come from. While part of it will come from the return (profit) on their investments, they still have to come up with the *investment capital.*

Coming Up with the Capital

So far, the Thompsons know how much money they want to accumulate, and how long they have to accumulate it. The only other thing they need to determine at this point is the *rate of return* they feel they can earn on their money. Having taken a financial planning course in college, the Thompsons know that the amount of money they'll have to put into their investment program depends in large part on *how much they can earn from their investments*—the higher their rate of return, the less they'll have to put up. Let's say they feel comfortable using a 9 percent rate of return. That's a fairly conservative number—one that won't require them to put all or most of their money into a bunch of high-risk investments—and they're reasonably certain they'll be able to reach that level of return, *on average*, over the long haul. It's important to use some care in coming up with a projected rate of return. Don't saddle yourself with an unreasonably high rate, as that will simply reduce the chance of reaching your targeted financial goal.

Probably the best way of arriving at a reasonable projection is to look at what the market has done over the past 10 to 15 years, and then use the average return performance over that period as your estimate—or, if you want to be a bit more conservative, knock a point or two off the market's return. To help you in this regard, take a look at the statistics that appear on the next page; they show the average annual returns on stocks, bonds, and U.S. Treasury bills over various holding periods of from 5 to 25 years.

One of the first things you'll notice is the abnormally low returns generated by stocks over the 5-year period from 1998 to 2002. This was the result of a very nasty bear market that started in 2000 and ran until late 2002. Fortunately, 5-year stock returns of less than 3 percent just don't happen very often; the last time it did was in the early 1970s. Thus, it wouldn't seem to make much sense to use such low returns as the basis for forecasting future returns. Instead, consider using one of the other holding periods—they all produce returns that are within a point or two of each other, and are more representative of long-term returns in the market. To be on the conservative side, let's use the 10- to 15-year returns as viable standards of market performance. Using those benchmarks, it's clear that unless you had put just about everything into short-term U.S. Treasury bills, generating an average return of around 8 to 10 percent (or even more) was well within the reach of most investors. Of course, there's no guarantee these returns will happen again in the next 10 to 20 years, but at least the past does provide us with a basis—or "handle"—for making projections into the future.

Now, returning to our problem at hand, there are two ways of coming up with the capital needed to reach a targeted sum of money: (1) you can make a lump-sum investment right up front and let that amount grow over time, or (2) you can set up a systematic savings plan and put away a certain amount of money each year. Worksheet 11.1 is designed to help you find the amount of investment capital you'll need to reach a given financial goal. It employs the *compound value* concept discussed in Chapter 2, and is based on a given financial target (line 1), and a projected average rate of return on your investments (line 2). Note that you can use the worksheet to find either a required lump-sum investment (part A), or an amount that will have to be put away each year in a savings plan (part B). For our purposes here, we'll assume that the Thompsons have $7,500 to start with (this comes mostly from gifts their daughter received from her grandparents). Since they know they'll need a lot more than that to reach their target, the Thompsons decide to use part B of the worksheet to find out how much they'll have to save annually.

Holding Periods	Stocks (as measured by the DJIA)	High-grade Corp. Bond Returns	Stocks and Bonds Together (50/50)	Returns on Short-Term U.S. Treasury Bills	Stocks, Bonds, and T-Bills Combined (⅓-⅓-⅓)
5 years: 1998–'02	2.9%	7.1%	5.0%	4.2%	4.7%
10 years: 1993–'02	11.8	8.4	10.1	4.5	8.2
15 years: 1988–'02	12.8	9.7	11.2	5.1	9.2
20 years: 1983–'02	13.9	10.5	12.2	5.7	10.0
25 years: 1978–'02	13.2	9.5	11.4	6.7	9.8

The first thing to do is find the future value of the $7,500 initial investment—the question here is: How much will that initial lump-sum investment grow to over an 18-year period of time? Using the compound value concept and the appropriate "future value factor" (from Appendix A), we see, in line 7, that this deposit will grow to some $35,400. That's nearly 60 percent of the targeted $60,000 that we already have covered. Thus, by subtracting the terminal value of the initial investment (line 7) from our target (line 1), we come up with the amount that must be generated from some sort of annual savings plan—see line 8. (*Note*: If you were starting from scratch, you'd enter a zero in line 5, and the amount in line 8 would be equal to the amount in line 1.) Again, using the appropriate future value factor (this time from Appendix B), we find the Thompsons will have to put away/invest just $600 a year (actually $596) to reach their target of $60,000 in 18 years. That is, the $596 a year will grow to $24,600, which, when added to the $35,400 that the initial $7,500 will grow to, equals the Thompsons' targeted financial goal of $60,000. (By the way, they can also reach their target by making a lump-sum investment right up front of $12,712—try working out part A of the worksheet on your own, and see if you can come up with that number.) As you might have suspected, the last few steps in the worksheet can just as easily be done on a good hand-held calculator. That is, once the size of the nest egg has been determined (as in Step 8, for example), a financial calculator can be used to find the amount of money that must be put away each year to fund the nest egg.

worksheet 11.1

Finding the Amount of Investment Capital

A worksheet like this one can be used to find out how much money you must come up with to reach a given financial goal. Note that this worksheet is based on the same future value concepts we first introduced in Chapter 2.

DETERMINING AMOUNT OF INVESTMENT CAPITAL

Financial goal: To accumulate $60,000 in 18 years for the purpose of meeting the cost of daughter's college education.

1. Targeted Financial Goal (see Note 1)	$ 60,000
2. Projected Average Return on Investments	9.0%
A. Finding a Lump Sum Investment:	
3. Future Value Factor, from Appendix A ■ based on ________ years to target date and a projected average return on investment of ________	
4. Required Lump Sum Investment ■ line 1 ÷ line 3	$
B. Making a Series of Investments over Time:	
5. Amount of Initial Investment, if any (see Note 2)	$ 7,500
6. Future Value Factor, from Appendix A ■ based on 18 years of target date and a projected average return on investment of 9%	4.72
7. Terminal Value of Initial Investment ■ line 5 × line 6	$ 35,400
8. Balance to Come from Savings Plan ■ line 1 − line 7	$ 24,600
9. Future Value Annuity Factor, from Appendix B ■ based on 18 years to target date and a projected average return on investment of 9%	41.3
10. Series of Annual Investments Required over Time ■ line 8 ÷ line 9	$ 596

Note 1: The "targeted financial goal" is the amount of money you want to accumulate by some target date in the future.

Note 2: If you're starting from scratch—i.e., there is *no* initial investment—enter zero on line 5, *skip* lines 6 and 7, and then use the total targeted financial goal (from line 1) as the amount to be funded from a savings plan; now proceed with the rest of the worksheet.

Calculator Keystrokes. You can use a financial calculator to *find the annual payments necessary to fund a target amount* by first putting the calculator in the *annual compounding* mode. Then, to determine the amount of money that must be put away each year, at a 9 percent rate of return, to accumulate $24,600 in 18 years, make the keystrokes shown here, where:

N = number of *years* in investment horizon,

I/Y = expected average *annual* rate of return on investments,

FV = the targeted amount of money you want to accumulate, entered as a *negative.*

A value of $595.62 should appear in the calculator display, which is the amount of money that must be put away each year to reach the targeted amount of $24,600 in 18 years. (*Note:* The calculator keystrokes shown above basically takes you from Steps 8 to 10 in Worksheet 11.1. You can also do Steps 5 to 7 on the calculator by letting: **N** = 18; **I/Y** = 9.0; **PV** = -7,500; and then solve for **(CPT)FV**. Try it—you should come up with a number fairly close to the amount shown on line 7 of Worksheet 11.1).

An Investment Plan Provides Direction

Now that the Thompsons know how much they have to save each year, their next step is to decide how they will save it. Probably the best thing to do in this regard is to follow some type of *systematic routine*—for example, build a set amount of savings each month or quarter into the household budget, and then stick with it. But whatever procedure is followed, keep in mind that all we are doing here is accumulating the required investment capital. That money still has to be put to work in some kind of investment program, and that's where an investment plan comes into the picture. Basically, an **investment plan** is nothing more than a simple, preferably written, statement that explains how the accumulated investment capital will be invested for the purpose of reaching the targeted goal. In the example we've been using, the Thompsons' capital accumulation plan calls for a 9 percent rate of return as a target they feel they can achieve. Now they need to come up with a way of obtaining that 9 percent return on their money—meaning they have to specify, in general terms at least, the kinds of investment vehicles they intend to use. *When completed, an investment plan is a way of translating an abstract investment target* (in this case, a 9 percent return) *into a specific investment program.*

investment plan A statement, preferably written, that specifies how investment capital will be invested for the purpose of achieving a specified goal.

What Are Your Investment Objectives?

Some people buy securities for the protection they provide from taxes (that's what tax shelters are all about). Others want to have money put aside for that proverbial rainy day or, perhaps, to build up a nice retirement nest egg. *Your goals tend to set the tone for your investment program, and they play a major role in determining how conservative (or aggressive) you're likely to be in making investment decisions.* In a very real way, they provide a purpose for your investments. Given that you have adequate savings and insurance to cover any emergencies, the most frequent investment objectives are to (1) enhance current income, (2) save for a major purchase, (3) accumulate funds for retirement, and (4) seek shelter from taxes.

Current Income

The idea here is to put your money into investments that will enable you to supplement your income. In other words, it's for people who want to live off their investment income. A secure source of high current income, from dividends or interest, is the principal concern of such investors. Retired people, for example, often choose investments offering high current income—at low risk. Another common reason for seeking supplemental income is that a family member requires extended costly medical care. Even after insurance, such recurring costs can heavily burden a family budget without this vital income supplement.

Major Expenditures

People often put money aside, sometimes for years, to save up enough to make just one major expenditure, the most common ones being:

- The down payment on a home
- Money for a child's college education
- Some capital for going into business
- An expensive (perhaps once-in-a-lifetime) vacation
- The purchase of a very special, expensive item
- Funds for retirement (discussed in the following section)

Whatever your goal, the idea is to set your sights on something and then go about building your capital with that objective in mind. It sure makes the act of investing more pleasurable. Once you have a handle on how much money you're going to need to attain one of these goals (following a procedure like the one illustrated with Worksheet 11.1), you can specify the types of investment vehicles you intend to use. For example, you might follow a low-risk approach by making a single lump-sum investment in a bond that matures in the year in which you need the funds; or you could follow a more risky investment plan that calls for investing a set amount of money over time in something like a growth-oriented mutual fund (where there is little or no assurance of what the terminal value of the investment will be). Of course, for some purposes—such as the down payment on a home or a child's education—you will probably want to accept a lot less risk than for others, as the attainment of these goals should not be jeopardized by the types of investment vehicles you choose to employ.

Retirement

Accumulating funds for retirement is *the single most important reason for investing.* Too often, though, retirement planning occupies only a small amount of our time, because we tend to rely very heavily on employers and Social Security for our retirement needs. As many people learn too late in life, that can be a serious mistake. A much better approach is to review the amounts of income you can realistically expect to receive from Social Security and your employee pension plan, and then decide, based on your retirement goals, *whether or not they will be adequate to meet your needs.* You'll probably find that you'll have to supplement them through personal investing. Obviously, the earlier in life you make this assessment, the greater your opportunity to accumulate the needed funds. (Retirement plans are discussed in Chapter 14.)

smart.sites

Will your investment portfolio provide adequate retirement income? Use Quicken's retirement planner to find out. Go to the brokerage section on Quicken's home page, **http://www.quicken.com**, select Planning & Tax, and then click on Retirement Planner.

Shelter from Taxes

As Chapter 3 explained, federal income tax law does not treat all sources of income equally. For example, if you own real estate—either directly or through some pooling arrangement—you may be able to take depreciation deductions against certain other sources of income, thereby reducing the amount of your final taxable income. This tax write-off feature can make real estate an attractive investment vehicle for some investors, even though its pretax rate of return may not appear very high. The goal of sheltering income from taxes is a legitimate one and, for some investors, often goes hand in hand with the goals of saving for a major outlay or for retirement. Clearly, if you can avoid paying taxes on the income from an investment, you will, all other things considered, have more funds available for reinvestment during the period.

Different Ways to Invest

Once you've established your investment objectives, there are a variety of investment vehicles you can use to fulfill those goals. Various types of investment vehicles are briefly described in the following paragraphs; *most of these securities will be more fully examined in the next two chapters.*

Common Stock

Common stocks are basically a form of *equity*—meaning that, as an investment, they represent an ownership interest in a corporation. Each share of stock symbolizes a fractional ownership position in a firm; for example, one share of common stock in a corporation that has 10,000 shares outstanding would denote a 1/10,000 ownership interest in the firm. A share of stock entitles the holder to equal participation in the corporation's earnings and dividends, an equal vote, and an equal voice in management. From the investor's perspective, the return to stockholders comes from dividends and/or appreciation in share price. Common stock has no maturity date and, as a result, remains outstanding indefinitely (*discussed in Chapter 12*).

Bonds

In contrast to stocks, *bonds* are *liabilities*—they're IOUs of the issuer. The bondholder actually loans money to the issuer. Governments and corporations issue bonds that pay a stated return, called *interest.* When an individual invests in a bond, he or she receives a stipulated interest return, typically paid every 6 months, plus the return of the principal (face) value of the bond at maturity. For example, if you purchased a $1,000 bond that paid 10 percent interest in semiannual installments, you could expect to receive $50 every 6 months (that is, 10% × $1,000 × .5 years) and at maturity recover the $1,000 face value of the bond. Of course, a bond can be bought or sold prior to maturity at a price that can differ from its face value because bond prices, like common stock prices, do fluctuate in the marketplace (*discussed in Chapter 12*).

Preferreds and Convertibles

These are forms of *hybrid securities* in that each has the characteristics of both stocks and bonds; in essence, they are a cross between the two. *Preferred securities* are issued as stock and, as such, represent an equity position in a corporation. Unlike common stock, however, preferreds have a stated (fixed) dividend rate, payment of which is given preference over dividends to holders of common stock. Like bonds, preferred stocks are usually purchased for the current income (dividends) they pay. A *convertible security*, in contrast, is a special type of fixed-income obligation (usually a bond, but sometimes a preferred stock) that carries a conversion feature permitting the investor to convert it into a specified number of shares of common stock. Convertible securities, therefore, provide the fixed-income benefits of a bond (interest) while offering the price appreciation (capital gains) potential of common stock. (*Convertibles are briefly discussed in Chapter 12.*)

Mutual Funds

An organization that invests in and professionally manages a diversified portfolio of securities is called a *mutual fund.* A mutual fund sells shares to investors, who then become part owners of the fund's securities portfolio. Most mutual funds issue and repurchase shares at a price that reflects the underlying value of the portfolio at the time the transaction is made. Mutual funds have become very popular with individual investors because they offer not only a wide variety of investment opportunities but also a full array of services that many investors find particularly appealing (*discussed in Chapter 13*).

Real Estate

Investments in *real estate* can take many forms, ranging from raw land speculation to limited-partnership shares in commercial property. The returns on real estate can come from rents, capital gains, and certain tax benefits. Unfortunately, estimating both the risk and the return in a real estate venture can be difficult and usually requires expert advice, particularly with respect to income tax implications. (*A type of publicly traded real estate investment—known as a real estate investment trust, or REIT for short—is discussed in Chapter 13.*)

Commodities, Financial Futures, and Options

Commodities are contracts to buy/sell such things as cotton, corn, wheat, coffee, and cocoa, as well as raw materials (like copper, silver, and oil), at some future date. *Financial futures* are just like commodities, except they apply to certain types of financial instruments, like stock prices, bond interest rates, even foreign currencies. Commodities and financial futures are actively traded in what is known as the *futures markets.* Because they do not pay interest or dividends, the returns on commodities and financial futures contracts are derived solely from the change in the price of the underlying commodity or financial instrument. These are very risky investments, because losses can mount up quickly and, in a short period of time, far exceed the amount invested.

Concept ✓

11-1. Briefly discuss the relationship between *investing* and personal financial planning. Do these two activities complement each other?

11-2. What's the difference between an *investment plan* and a capital accumulation plan? Are they in any way related?

11-3. Identify four major investment objectives. Why is it important to have one or more investment objective(s) when embarking on an investment program? Of the various investment objectives, which two would *you* consider most important? Explain.

In a similar fashion, *options* give the holder the right to buy or sell common stocks (and other financial instruments) at a set price, over a specified period of time. Again, to earn a positive return one must correctly anticipate future price movements in the underlying financial asset. In contrast to futures contracts, the price paid for an option is the maximum amount that can be lost; however, options have very short maturities, and consistent losses can quickly exhaust one's investment capital. Futures and options are often referred to as **derivative securities** to the extent that they derive their value from the price behavior of some underlying real or financial asset.

derivative securities
Securities such as futures and options, whose value is derived from (or linked to) the price behavior of an underlying real or financial asset.

SECURITIES MARKETS

LG2

It takes more than money to be a successful investor. Indeed, as anyone who's found success in the market will tell you, *there is no substitute for being an informed investor!* Among other things, that means you must understand the institutions, mechanisms, and procedures involved in making security transactions. We looked at some investment fundamentals above; in the balance of this chapter, we will examine different securities markets and market transactions, sources of investment information, online investing, and ways to manage your investment holdings.

securities markets The marketplace in which stocks, bonds, and other financial instruments are traded.

The term **securities markets** is generally used to describe the place where stocks, bonds, and other financial instruments are traded. The securities markets can be broken into two parts: capital markets and money markets. The *capital market* is where long-term securities (those with maturities of more than a year) are traded, while the *money market* is the marketplace for short-term, low-risk credit instruments with maturities of 1 year or less, like U.S. Treasury bills, commercial paper, negotiable certificates of deposit, and so on. Both types of markets provide a vital mechanism for bringing the buyers and sellers of securities together. Some of the more popular money market securities were discussed in Chapter 4, where we looked at short-term investment vehicles. *This chapter considers the capital markets.*

Primary or Secondary Markets

The securities markets can also be divided into primary and secondary segments. The *primary market* is the market where new securities are sold to the public—where one party to the transaction is always the issuer. The *secondary market*, in contrast, is where old (outstanding) securities are bought and sold—here the securities are "traded" between investors. A security is sold in the primary market just once, when it is originally issued by the corporation or some governmental body, like a state or municipality. Subsequent transactions, in which securities are sold by one investor to another, take place in the secondary market. As a rule, when people speak of the securities markets, they are referring to the secondary market, because that is where the vast majority of security transactions take place.

Primary Markets

When a corporation sells a new issue to the public, several financial institutions participate in the transaction. To begin with, the corporation will probably use an *investment banking firm*, which specializes in *underwriting* (selling) new security issues. The investment banker will give the corporation advice on pricing and other aspects of the issue and will either sell the new security itself or arrange for a *selling group* to do so. The selling group is normally made up of a number of brokerage firms, each of which accepts the responsibility for selling a certain portion of the new issue. On very large issues, the originating investment banker will bring in other underwriting firms as partners and form an *underwriting syndicate* in an attempt to spread the risks associated with underwriting and selling the new securities.

prospectus A document made available to prospective security buyers that describes the firm and a new security issue.

A potential investor in a new issue must be provided with a **prospectus**, which is a document describing the firm and the issue. Certain federal agencies have the responsibility of ensuring that all the information included in a prospectus is an accurate representation of the facts. Many times investors have trouble purchasing new security issues because all shares have been sold—often before the official sale date. Also, if the new shares are sold using rights or warrants, the ability to purchase the new securities will be somewhat restricted, because only the holders of these rights or warrants can buy the stock.

Secondary Markets

The secondary markets permit investors to execute transactions among themselves—it's the marketplace where an investor can easily sell his or her holdings to someone else. Included among the secondary markets are the various *securities exchanges*, in which the buyers and sellers of securities are brought together for the purpose of executing trades.

Money in Action

Anatomy of a Market Meltdown

It seemed like the bull market that would never end. Between August 1982 and January 2000, the Dow Jones Industrial Average (DJIA) rose an average of 17 percent a year. When the U.S. economy really took off in 1995, the stock markets of the late 1990s carried investors on a wild ride. Share prices moved sharply upward as the DJIA broke through successive 1000-point barriers, peaking at 11,723 on January 14, 2000. Annual returns from 1995 to 1999 averaged about 26 percent. Technology stocks led the way, and investors cheered as they made impressive gains, on paper at least—while Alan Greenspan, chairman of the Federal Reserve Board, cautioned against the "irrational exuberance" in the markets.

Throughout the five year run-up, naysayers warned that this market euphoria couldn't last much longer. Each year investors wondered when the bull would stumble, and each year it continued to surge ahead, carried by a strong economy and a relatively peaceful world situation. Excited investors bought stock in young technology and internet companies, many with no track record, products, or profits. Novices and pros alike ignored warning signs along the way. "In the '90s, the public got sucked into that vortex of speculation where they thought that 'this time is different' and that we would never have another recession," commented Ned Riley, chief investment strategist at State Street Global Advisors, Boston.

In 2000 the DJIA and Nasdaq Composite reached all-time highs in January and March, respectively. When the market peaked, tech stocks made up more than 40 percent of the S&P 500's value. But under Wall Street's slick surface were rumblings that all was not well. In March the Fed raised interest rates to curb inflation, and businesses reported decreasing investment in technology.

In the following weeks, the Nasdaq Composite lost one-third of its value. Even the best dot-coms suffered; Yahoo lost 40 percent of its market value in just three weeks. But blue chips held firm, leading market strategists to speculate whether this was a warning sign or another brief setback.

...continued on next page

In addition, there is the **over-the-counter (OTC) market**, made up of a nationwide network of brokers and dealers who execute transactions in securities that are not listed on one of the exchanges. The **organized securities exchanges** typically handle securities of larger, better-known companies, and the over-the-counter market handles many of the smaller, lesser-known firms—though, as we'll see later, there are a lot of big, well-known firms that trade in the OTC market. The organized exchanges are well-structured institutions that bring together the market forces of supply and demand; the over-the-counter market is basically a mass telecommunications network linking buyers and sellers. Most of the transactions of small investors are made in the secondary market; as such, we will focus on it throughout this chapter.

over-the-counter (OTC) market
The market in which securities not listed on one of the organized exchanges are traded.

organized securities exchanges
Exchanges where various types of securities are traded by exchange members for their own accounts and the accounts of their customers.

Organized Securities Exchanges

The market forces of supply and demand are brought together in organized securities exchanges. So-called **listed securities** are traded on organized exchanges and account for about 60% of the *total dollar volume* of all shares traded in the U.S. stock market—the Nasdaq/OTC market accounts for the rest. All trading in listed securities is carried out in one place (such as the New York Stock Exchange on Wall Street) and under a broad set of rules by people who are *members* of the exchange. Members are said to "own a seat" on the exchange, a privilege obtained by meeting certain financial requirements. Only the securities of companies that have met established listing requirements are traded on the exchanges, and those firms must comply with various regulations to ensure they will not make financial or legal misrepresentations to their stockholders. Firms must not only comply with the rules of the specific exchange, but also must fulfill certain requirements as established by the Securities and Exchange Commission (SEC), which will be discussed later.

listed security
A security that has met the prerequisites for, and thus is traded on, one of the organized securities exchanges.

New York Stock Exchange

The *New York Stock Exchange (NYSE)* is the largest and most prestigious organized securities exchange in the world. Known as "the big board," it lists over *350 billion* shares of stock that, at mid-year 2003, had a market value of some *$10.7 trillion.* Membership on the NYSE is limited to 1,366 seats. Most seats are owned by brokerage firms, the largest of which—Merrill Lynch—owns more than 20.

The NYSE has the most stringent listing requirements of all the organized exchanges. For example, in order to be listed, a firm must have at least 2,200 stockholders, each owning 100 shares or more. It must also have a minimum of 1.1 million shares of publicly held stock outstanding; demonstrated pretax earning power of $2.5 million (or $25 million in cash flow) at the time of listing; a market value (of publicly held shares) of $60 million for new stocks, or $100 million for stocks that transfer from another market or stock exchange; and pay a listing fee. Firms that fail to continue to meet listing requirements can be *delisted*. More than 3,200 firms from around the world list their shares on the NYSE.

American Stock Exchange

The *American Stock Exchange (AMEX)* is the second largest organized stock exchange in terms of the number of listed companies; when it comes to the dollar volume of trading, however, the AMEX is actually smaller than the largest *regional* exchange (the Midwest in Chicago). Its organization and procedures are similar to those of the NYSE, though its membership costs and listing requirements are not as stringent. There are approximately 850 seats on the AMEX, and it is home to around 800 listed stocks and a handful of listed corporate bonds. The AMEX handles only about 4 percent of the total annual dollar volume of shares traded on *organized* security exchanges. In contrast, the NYSE handles around 90 percent of all common shares traded on organized exchanges, so the AMEX is nowhere near the New York exchange in terms of size or stature. Further, whereas the NYSE is home for many of the biggest and best-known companies in the world, firms traded on the AMEX are much smaller and, with few exceptions, would hardly qualify as "household names."

All this is changing, however, as the stock market landscape was altered dramatically in 1998, when *Nasdaq* (see below)—a major market force in the U.S. market—took over the American Stock Exchange and shortly thereafter, the Philadelphia Stock Exchange (a major regional exchange). Thus, the AMEX today functions as a subsidiary of the Nasdaq—the principle market maker in the OTC market. A number of major changes have been made to enable the AMEX to create its own market niche and, in so doing, become more competitive with the NYSE. One area where the AMEX has really become the dominant player is in

Money continued to flow into stocks as a rebound followed each sharp drop. This up and down pattern continued for the next three years. For example, the DJIA took a record 499.19 point (4.9 percent) leap in mid-March 2000, but then resumed its downward spiral.

Just as tech stocks led the market to new heights, they pulled it down when the dot-com bubble burst. A comeback in spring and summer 2000 drew investors back to tech mainstays. But news such as lower sales at Dell Computer and the antitrust suit against Microsoft made investors reconsider their tech stock positions. By year-end, shares of Oracle and Cisco dropped 40 percent, and Intel plunged 60 percent.

Once again the blue chips rallied, and the DJIA ended the year down just 8 percent from its high, although the more tech-heavy S&P 500 was down 14 percent and the Nasdaq, 51 percent. Investors began to abandon tech companies that offered promises rather than earnings, turning to sectors that seemed safer—for example, financial institutions and utilities. One exciting new area was energy, where natural gas trading companies like Enron and Dynegy were revitalizing the utility industry.

The first of a series of Federal Reserve rate cuts in January 2001 sent the markets soaring. Subsequent cuts, however, did little to stimulate the economy, and the country entered a recession. Unable to revive sales, companies cut costs to keep earnings from falling further. A spring rally was again short-lived; even blue chips provided no haven. The markets continued to bounce investors around through the summer months.

On September 11, 2001, the financial markets suffered another blow—literally a physical one—as terrorists struck the World Trade Center towers in the heart of the financial district. A stunned country and world went into shock. The markets closed for about a week, amidst great uncertainty and insecurity. When they reopened, the Dow dropped another 14 percent. By September 2001, investors had lost more than $6 trillion since the January 2000 market peak.

To bolster the financial markets, the Fed again poured money into the system, sparking a rally that amazed everyone in light of the shocking terrorist attacks. The Nasdaq jumped 45 percent between September 2001 and January 2002, and the DJIA and S&P 500 were also up considerably. Was the market finally going to turn bullish again?

...continued on next page

A Crisis in Ethics

Investors had little time to enjoy the latest rebound, however. The battered markets faced a very different setback: corporate scandals that severely undermined investor trust. The first to erupt was Enron, the new-breed energy company. As word of Enron's manipulation of accounting rules to create the illusion of earnings growth and enhance its financial statements became public in late 2001, its financial house of cards tumbled down. Along with it came its once prestigious auditor Arthur Andersen, and other financial institutions found themselves under investigation for involvement in its off-balance sheet deals.

Alarmed at how Enron had obscured financial information in its published financial reports, investors now questioned the overall reliability of corporate financial reporting. Before long executives from Adelphia, Qwest, Tyco, WorldCom, Xerox and other companies joined the rogue's gallery for corporate financial wrongdoing. A crackdown on stock analyst malfeasance by New York State's attorney general further damaged investor confidence. Money drained out of the equity markets into bonds and other investment vehicles.

It was downhill from there, as the DJIA slid to 7,286 on October 9, 2002—a 38 percent decline. Likewise, the S&P 500 and Nasdaq, with their larger numbers of technology stocks, dropped 49 percent and 77 percent from their peaks.

What or who is to blame for this bear market, which ranks among the worst in market history? Fingers point in many directions, as events unrelated to fiscal or monetary policy—among them 9/11 and subsequent terrorist threats, corporate scandals, and the 2003 war in Iraq—joined with the more traditional causes to create a sense of financial insecurity that weakened investor faith in the financial system. From 1999 through 2002, the DJIA closed lower at year end—the first time since 1941 it had declined in three successive years. Total return on investment for stocks in the DJIA plummeted from 27.2 percent in 1999 to 15 percent in 2002. Every sector, including the most solid blue chips, suffered greatly from the weak economy, corporate scandals, and lower earnings. About 70 percent of stocks on major exchanges closed down for the year. Jaded investors looked to companies that paid dividends, not those promising astronomical growth rates.

In March 2003, after a few more false starts, the markets appeared to be moving steadily upward. By mid-November, the S&P 500 posted an 18 percent gain and the Nasdaq composite, almost 42 percent. However, experts were divided on whether the bear

...continued on next page

so-called *index shares*, or *exchange traded funds (ETFs)*, which we'll examine in Chapter 13 when we discuss mutual funds.

Regional Stock Exchanges

In addition to the NYSE and AMEX, there are a handful of so-called **regional exchanges**. The number of securities listed on each of these exchanges is typically in the range of 100 to 500 companies. As a group they handle around 6 percent of all shares traded on organized exchanges. The best known of these are the Midwest, Pacific, Philadelphia, Boston, and Cincinnati exchanges. These exchanges deal primarily in securities with local and regional appeal. Most are modeled after the NYSE, but their membership and listing requirements are considerably more lenient. To enhance their trading activity, regional exchanges will often list securities that are also listed on the NYSE or AMEX.

regional exchanges Organized securities exchanges (other than the NYSE and AMEX) that deal primarily in securities having a local or regional appeal.

smart.sites

What are the stock markets doing today? Get the latest market summary and other statistics at the New York Stock Exchange site, **http://www.nyse.com/marketinfo/marketinfo.html**.

The Over-the-Counter Market

Unlike an organized exchange, the over-the-counter (OTC) market is not a specific institution but, instead, exists as an intangible relationship between the buyers and sellers of securities. Securities traded in this market are sometimes called **unlisted securities**. It accounts for about 40 percent of the total dollar volume of domestic shares traded, and today trades close to *35,000* issues. The market is linked by a mass telecommunications network. Unlike those in the organized securities exchanges, trades in the OTC market represent *direct* transactions between investors and securities dealers—that is, the investors buy from and sell to the securities dealers, whereas on the listed securities exchanges the broker acts as a middleman between buyers and sellers. All municipal bonds, along with most government

unlisted security A security that is traded in the over-the-counter market; such a trade is made directly between the investor and the security dealer.

and corporate bonds and a numerical majority of common stocks, are traded in the OTC market. Dealers make markets in certain OTC securities by offering to either buy or sell them at stated prices.

Financial Road Sign

ECNs Lead the Way

One of the fastest and least costly ways of executing trades is through electronic communications networks, or ECN's. These privately owned trading networks execute transactions directly between the buyers and sellers of securities. Unlike the auction process of the organized exchanges, ECN's bypass the dealer/broker, and automatically match customer's electronic buy and sell orders in less than a second, without any human intervention. If there is no immediate match, the ECN acts like a broker and posts the order under its own name; the open order is then filled as soon as an offsetting trade comes in. ECN's are cheap, costing less than 1 percent of the trade; in addition, traders get the best price quickly and at very narrow spreads. And, of course, the electronic order handling system is also far less prone to human errors. So don't be surprised if ECN's start showing up in your investing future.

Nasdaq

A part of the OTC market is made up of a select list of stocks that trade on the *National Association of Securities Dealers Automated Quotation System (Nasdaq)*, which provides up-to-the-minute quotes and bid/ask prices on several thousand securities. (The **bid** and **ask prices** represent, respectively, the highest price offered to purchase a given security and the lowest price at which the security is offered for sale. In effect, an investor pays the ask price when *buying* securities and receives the bid price when *selling* them.)

bid price
The price at which one can sell a security.

ask price
The price at which one can purchase a security.

There are about 7,000 actively traded issues in the Nasdaq portion of the OTC market, and, of these, about 2,700 are part of the so-called *National Market System (NMS)*. The National Market System is reserved for the biggest and most actively traded stocks, and, in general, for those stocks that have a *national following*. These securities are widely quoted, and the trades are executed about as efficiently here as they are on the floor of the NYSE. A number of large and well-known firms are found on the Nasdaq National Market System, including companies like Intel, Oracle, Dell, Microsoft, Starbucks, Northwest Airlines, Petsmart, Cisco Systems, Herman Miller, and Hollywood Entertainment. Generally speaking, the big-name stocks traded on the Nasdaq/NMS receive about as much national visibility and are about as liquid as those traded on the NYSE.

The situation is considerably different, however, for OTC stocks that are not part of Nasdaq—which applies to the vast majority of the firms traded in the OTC market. These include the very small firms that may not even have much of a regional following, let alone a national constituency. These stocks are *thinly traded*, meaning there's not much of a market for them, and they often lack any measurable degree of liquidity. Many of these stocks appear in the so-called *pink sheets*. So named because

market was over or this represented a short-lived correction.

While investor mania is nothing new—in the 17th century, for example, Dutch investors speculated on tulips, not tech stocks—the recent boom and bust cycle underlies important shifts in the workings of the economy and the capital markets. The stock market's meteoric rise brought individual investors, many of whom previously shunned equities as too risky, into the picture. Everyone wanted a piece of the tech stock action as young companies such as VA Linux Systems went public and saw its share price rise an unbelievable 698 percent on its first day of trading. Have investors now learned their lessons, to look for a solid track record and not empty promises? Only time will tell.

Critical Thinking Questions

1. Describe the basic pattern of stock market cycles between the late 1990s and the present day.
2. What factors contributed to the bear market that began in 2000?
3. Why did corporate ethics became a factor in the market meltdown?

Sources: Ken Brown, "Company Blowups Abound, Rebounds Rare," *The Wall Street Journal*, January 2, 2003, p. R2; E.S. Browning, "Investors Seek Ray of Hope," *The Wall Street Journal*, January 2, 2003, p. R1; E.S. Browning, "Stocks, Bonds Slip on Fed Move," *The Wall Street Journal*, June 26, 2003, p. C1; E.S. Browning and Ianthe Jeanne Dugan, "Aftermath of a Market Mania," *The Wall Street Journal*, December 16, 2002, pp. C1, C13; James M. Pethokoukis, "Is the Rally Real?" *Newsweek*, July 7, 2003, pp. 16–17; "2001 investment Scoreboard," *The Wall Street Journal*, January 2, 2002, p. R2; "2002 Investment Scoreboard, *The Wall Street Journal*, January 2, 2003, p. R2; Penelope Wang, Amy Feldman, Jon Birger, Aravind Adiga, "How Bad Is It?" *Money*, September 2002, p. 78.1

of the color of paper used, the pink sheets are published daily and are available from brokers. The companies who use pink-sheet listings are either unable or unwilling to meet the financial reporting requirements of the SEC. They cover the full spectrum of securities, including new, rapidly growing firms, obscure but well-established firms that are closely held, companies on the verge of bankruptcy, and penny stocks peddled by shady brokers. Although quotes on pink-sheet companies today are available electronically, prices are updated only when there's significant trading or when requested by traders making markets in pink-sheet stocks, so quotes may not be current. Nor do they necessarily reflect the market, as these prices are set solely by the market makers and reflect the price(s) at which they're willing to buy and sell these securities—usually after a big dealer spread has been tacked on!

FOREIGN SECURITIES MARKETS

In addition to those in the United States, there are organized securities exchanges in more than 100 other countries worldwide. Indeed, actively traded markets can be found not only in the major industrialized nations like Japan, Great Britain, Germany, and Canada, but also in emerging economies as well. In terms of market capitalization (total market value of all shares traded), the New York Stock Exchange is the biggest stock market in the world, followed by the Nasdaq market. After these two U.S. markets comes the Tokyo stock market, followed by the London market, then Paris, Frankfurt, and Toronto. Other major exchanges are located in Sydney, Zurich, Hong Kong, Singapore, Rome, and Amsterdam. In addition to these markets, you'll also find developing markets all over the globe—from Argentina and Armenia to Egypt and Fiji, from Iceland, Israel, and Malaysia to New Zealand, Russia, and Zimbabwe. Surely, as these and other markets begin to develop, they'll open up opportunities not only for investors in those countries, but also for U.S. investors willing to go off-shore in search of returns.

REGULATING THE SECURITIES MARKETS

A number of laws have been enacted to regulate the activities of various participants in the securities markets and provide for adequate and accurate disclosure of information to potential and existing investors. State laws, which regulate the sale of securities within state borders, typically establish procedures that apply to the sellers of securities doing business within the state. The most important and far-reaching securities laws, however, are those enacted by the federal government:

- **Securities Act of 1933.** This act was passed by Congress to ensure full disclosure of information with respect to new security issues and to prevent a stock market collapse similar to the one that occurred during 1929–1932. It requires the issuer of a new security to file a registration statement containing information about the new issue with the **Securities and Exchange Commission (SEC)**, an agency of the U.S. government established to enforce federal securities laws.
- **Securities Exchange Act of 1934.** One of the most important pieces of securities legislation ever passed, it expanded the scope of federal regulation and formally established the SEC as the agency in charge of the administration of federal securities laws. The act gives the SEC power to regulate organized securities exchanges and the over-the-counter market by extending disclosure requirements to outstanding securities. It requires the stock exchanges and the stocks traded on them to be registered with the SEC.
- **Investment Company Act of 1940.** This act protects those purchasing investment company (mutual fund) shares. It established rules and regulations for investment companies and formally authorized the SEC to regulate their practices and procedures.

Securities and Exchange Commission (SEC)
An agency of the federal government that regulates the disclosure of information about securities and generally oversees the operation of the securities exchanges and markets.

It requires the investment companies to register with the SEC and to fulfill certain disclosure requirements. The act was amended in 1970 to prohibit investment companies from paying excessive fees to their advisors as well as charging excessive commissions to purchasers of company shares.

- **The Sarbanes-Oxley Act of 2002.** This act (known as "SOX") is viewed as the most sweeping piece of securities legislation in decades. Its purpose is to eliminate corporate fraud as related to accounting practices and other information released to investors. Among other things, SOX requires an annual evaluation of internal controls and procedures for financial reporting, and requires the top executives of the corporation, as well as its auditors, to certify the accuracy of its financial statements and disclosures. In addition, it prohibits audit/accounting firms from engaging in consulting activities with its clients, and establishes ethical guidelines for financial officers and security analysts. The law also establishes a five-member oversight board to monitor the accounting industry and its standards of performance.
- **Other Significant Federal Legislation.** The *Maloney Act of 1938* provides for the establishment of trade associations for the purpose of self-regulation within the securities industry; this act led to the creation of the **National Association of Securities Dealers (NASD)**, which is made up of all brokers and dealers who participate in the OTC market. The NASD is a self-regulatory organization that polices the activities of brokers and dealers to ensure that its standards are upheld. The SEC supervises the activities of NASD, thus providing investors with further protection from fraudulent activities. The *Investment Advisors Act of 1940* was passed to protect investors against potential abuses by investment advisors who sell their services to the investing public. The *Securities Investor Protection Act of 1970* created the SIPC (Securities Investor Protection Corp.), an organization that protects investors against the financial failure of brokerage firms, much as the FDIC protects depositors against bank failures (we'll examine the SIPC later in this chapter). The *Insider Trading and Securities Fraud Enforcement Act of 1988* toughened penalties for securities fraud and required brokerage firms to establish written policies to prevent trading abuses by their employees; it also made it easier for investors to bring legal action against brokers.

National Association of Securities Dealers (NASD) An agency made up of brokers and dealers in over-the-counter securities that regulates the operations of the OTC market.

Concept ✓

11-4. Explain what is meant by the *securities markets* and briefly describe the difference between the money market and the capital market. Give some examples of the types of securities found in the money market; in the capital market.
11-5. How does a primary market differ from a secondary market? Where are most securities traded—in the primary or secondary market?
11-6. What are *organized securities exchanges?* What is the difference between the New York Stock Exchange and the American Stock Exchange? What are *regional exchanges,* and what role do they play?
11-7. Describe the operations of the *over-the-counter market;* compare and contrast it with organized securities exchanges. What are Nasdaq and the National Market System?
11-8. Explain the difference between a *bull market* and a *bear market.* How would you characterize the current state of the stock market? Are we in a bull market or a bear market?
11-9. Briefly summarize the key provisions of major securities legislation.

Bull Market or Bear?

The general condition of the market is termed *bullish* or *bearish*, depending on whether security prices are rising or falling over extended periods of time. Changing market conditions generally stem from changing investor attitudes, changes in economic activity, and certain governmental actions aimed at stimulating or slowing down the economy. Prices go *up* in **bull markets**; these favorable markets are normally associated with investor optimism, economic recovery,

bull market A condition of the market normally associated with investor optimism, economic recovery and expansion; characterized by generally rising securities prices.

and growth. In contrast, prices go *down* in **bear markets**, which are normally associated with investor pessimism and economic slowdowns. These terms are used to describe conditions in the bond and other securities markets as well as the stock market. For example, the bond market is considered bullish when interest rates fall, causing bond prices to rise; on the other hand, a bear market in bonds exists when bond prices fall (which occurs when rates rise). As a rule, investors are able to earn attractive rates of return during bull markets and only low (or negative) returns during bear markets. Market conditions are difficult to predict and usually cannot be identified until after they exist.

bear market
A condition of the market typically associated with investor pessimism and economic slowdown; characterized by generally falling securities prices.

EXHIBIT 11.1

The Five Biggest Bull Markets Since the Second World War (as Measured by Changes in the DJIA)

The prices of most stocks will go up in a bull market. Thus it is hard to lose money—though not impossible, because not all stocks will appreciate in value during such markets. The most recent bull market started in November 1990 and ended in March 2000, with one of the worst bear markets on record.

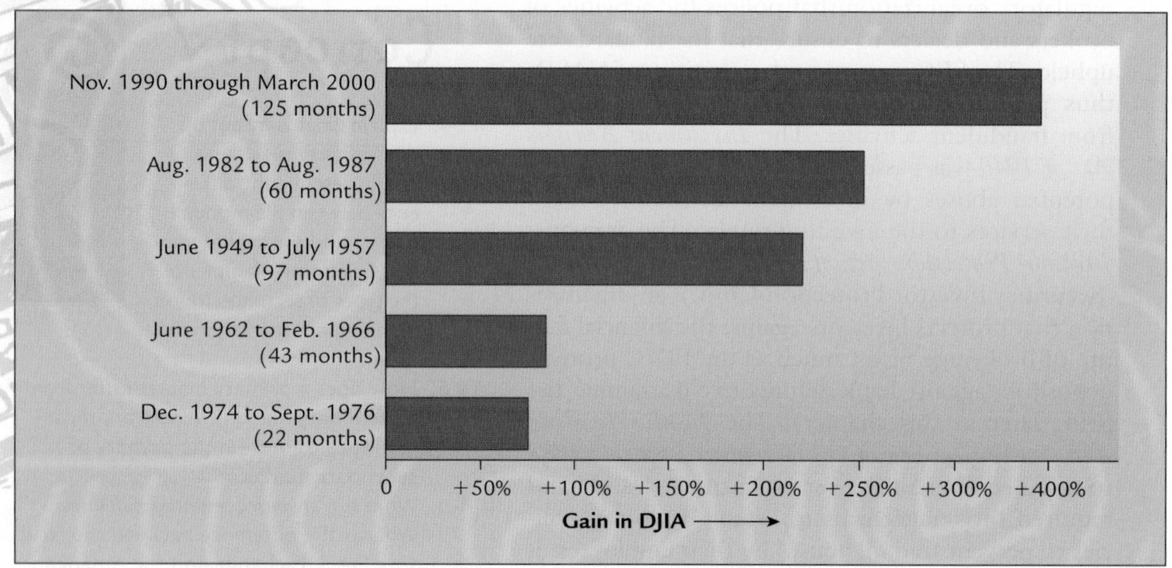

Over the past 50 or so years, the behavior of the stock market has been generally bullish, reflecting the growth and prosperity of the economy. Exhibit 11.1 shows the five biggest bull markets since the Second World War, the longest of which lasted 125 months—from November 1990 through March 2000. Interestingly, the 1990–2000 bull market is probably as well known for *how it ended* as it is for the returns it generated! For that record-breaking bull market ended abruptly in the spring of 2000 when a near-record-breaking bear market took over. Indeed, after increasing nearly fourfold over the decade of the nineties, the market (as measured by the Dow Jones Industrial Average) gave back nearly 40 percent of those gains over the course of the next 3 years. As it turned out, this bear market (which ran from early-2000 to late-2002) was one of the worst in the last 75 years and only the fourth time in the 108-year history of the DJIA that the index fell three years in a row. But as explained in the *Money in Action* box on pages 444–447, this market was dealing with far more than old fashioned speculation and overenthusiasm;

it also had to cope with the 9/11 attack on America, terrorism, war, and various accounting and corporate scandals, not to mention a weak economy. No wonder this bear of a market lasted for nearly 3 years!

LG3

MAKING TRANSACTIONS IN THE SECURITIES MARKETS

In many respects, dealing in the securities markets almost seems like you are operating in another world—one with all kinds of unusual orders and strange-sounding transactions. Actually, making securities transactions is relatively simple once you understand the basics—in fact, you will probably find it is no more difficult than using a checking account! Indeed, while making money in the market isn't all that easy, making transactions is.

STOCKBROKERS

stockbroker (account executive, financial consultant) A person who buys and sells securities on behalf of clients and provides them with investment advice and information.

Stockbrokers, or **account executives** and **financial consultants**, as they're also called, purchase and sell securities for their customers. Although deeply ingrained in our language, the term *stockbroker* is really somewhat of a misnomer, because such an individual assists you in the purchase and sale of not only stocks but also bonds, convertibles, mutual funds, options, and many other types of securities. Brokers must be licensed by the exchanges and must abide by the strict ethical guidelines of the exchanges and the SEC. They work for brokerage firms and in essence are there to execute the orders placed. The largest stockbrokerage firm, Merrill Lynch, has brokerage offices in virtually every major U.S. city (and many foreign countries). Orders from these offices are transmitted by brokers to the main office of Merrill Lynch and then to the floor of one of the stock exchanges, or to the OTC market, where they are executed. Although the procedure for executing orders on organized exchanges differs a bit from that in the OTC market, you as an investor would never know the difference, because you would place your order with the broker in exactly the same fashion.

Selecting a Broker

If you decide to start investing with a so-called *full-service broker*, it's important to select someone *who understands your investment objectives, and who can effectively help you pursue them.* If you choose a broker whose own disposition toward investing is similar to yours, you should be able to avoid conflict and establish a solid working relationship. A good place to start the search is to ask friends, relatives, or business associates to recommend a broker. It is not important—and often not even advisable—to know your stockbroker socially because most, if not all, of your transactions/ orders will probably be placed by phone. In addition, a strict business relationship eliminates the possibility of social concerns interfering with the achievement of your investment objectives. This does not mean, of course, that your broker's sole interest should be commissions. Indeed, a broker should be far more than just a salesperson; *a good broker is someone who's more interested in your investments than his or her commissions.* Should you find you're dealing with someone who's always trying to get you to trade your stocks, or who's pushing new investments on you, then by all means, dump that broker and find a new one!

Full-Service, Discount, and Online Brokers

Just a few years ago, there were three distinct types of brokers—full-service, discount, and online—and each occupied a well-defined market niche. Today, the lines between these three types of brokers are no longer clear cut. Most brokerage firms, even the most traditional ones, now offer online services to compete with the increasingly popular online firms. And many discount brokers now offer services once available only from a full-service broker, like research reports for clients. The traditional **full-service broker** offers investors a full array of brokerage services, including investment advice and information, execution of securities transactions, holding securities in safekeeping, online brokerage services, and margin loans. Such services are fine for those investors who want such help—and are willing to pay for them! In contrast, those investors who simply want to execute trades and aren't interested in obtaining all those brokerage services should consider either a *discount broker* or *online broker.* **Discount brokers** tend to have low overhead operations and offer fewer customer services than full-service brokers. Those with the very lowest commissions and who offer hardly any of the normal broker services, other than executing trades, are called *deep discounters.* Many discount brokers, however, do provide research and other services, but charge higher commissions. Transactions are initiated by calling a toll-free number—or visiting the broker's Web site—and placing the desired buy or sell order. The brokerage firm then executes the order at the best possible price and confirms the details of the transaction by phone, e-mail, or regular mail. Depending on the size of the transaction, *discount brokers can save investors from 30 to 80 percent of the commissions charged by full-service brokers.* The investor who does not need the research and advisory help available from full-service brokers may find discount brokers especially attractive.

full-service broker
A broker who, in addition to executing clients' transactions, provides them with a full array of brokerage services.

discount broker
A broker with low overhead who charges low commissions and offers little or no services to investors.

With the technology that's available to almost anyone today, it's not surprising that investors can just as easily trade securities online as on the phone. All you need is an **online broker** (also called *Internet* or *electronic brokers*) and you, too, can execute trades electronically. The investor merely accesses the online broker's Web site to open an account, review the commission schedule, or see a demonstration of the available transactional services and procedures. Confirmation of electronic trades can take as little as 10 seconds and most occur within one minute. Online investing is becoming increasingly popular, particularly among affluent, young investors who enjoy surfing the Web—so much so, in fact, that it has prompted virtually every traditional full service broker (and many discount brokers) to offer online trading to their clients. The rapidly growing volume of business done by discount and online brokers attests to their success. Today, many banks and savings institutions are making discount and online brokerage services available to depositors who wish to buy stocks, bonds, mutual funds, and other investment vehicles. Some of the major full-service, discount, and online brokers are listed across the bottom of this page.

online broker
Typically a discount broker through which investors can execute trades electronically/online through a commercial service or on the Internet; Also called Internet broker or electronic broker.

Type of Broker		
Full-Service	**Discount**	**Online**
A.G. Edwards	American Express Brokerage	AccuTrade
Morgan Stanley Dean Witter	Charles Schwab	Ameritrade
Merrill Lynch	J.D. Seibert	E*Trade
Paine Webber	Muriel Siebert	Fidelity Brokerage Services
Prudential Securities	T. Rowe Price Brokerage	Net Investor
Salomon Smith Barney	York Securities	TD Waterhouse

smart.sites
Confused about which broker is right for you? Use The Motley Fool's checklist, 10 Ways to Size Up a Broker, at the Fool's Discount Brokerage section, **http://www.fool.com/dbc**.

Brokerage Services

While discount or online brokers offer little more than execution of trades, that's certainly not the case with full-service brokers. Indeed, these brokers offer their clients a wide variety of brokerage services. For that reason, selecting a good *brokerage firm* is often just as important as choosing a good broker, because not all brokerage firms provide the same services. Try to select a broker with whom you can work and who is affiliated with a firm that provides the types of services you are looking for. Many brokerage firms, for example, provide all sorts of free information, ranging from stock and bond guides to research reports on specific securities or industries. Some have a research staff that periodically issues analyses of economic, market, industry, or company behavior and events, and relates them to its recommendations for buying or selling certain securities. As a brokerage firm client, you can expect to receive monthly bulletins discussing market activity and possibly even a recommended investment list. You will also receive an *account statement* describing all your transactions for the period, commission charges, interest charges, dividends and interest received, the securities you currently hold, and your account balances.

Most brokerage offices provide up-to-the-minute stock price quotations and world news. Stock price information can be obtained either from the quotation board (a large screen that electronically displays security transactions within minutes of their occurrence) or from the computerized telequote system. World news, which can significantly affect the stock market, is obtained from a news wire service. Most offices also have a reference library the firm's clients can use. Another valuable service offered by most major brokerage firms is the automatic transfer of surplus cash left in a customer's account into one of the firm's money funds, thereby allowing the customer to earn a return on temporarily idle funds. Brokerage houses will also hold your securities for you, as protection against their loss; the securities kept in this way are said to be held in *street name*. Some of these services are also offered by discount brokerages.

Securities Investor Protection Corporation (SIPC)
A nonprofit corporation, created by Congress and subject to SEC and congressional oversight, that insures customer accounts against the financial failure of a brokerage firm.

arbitration
A procedure used to settle disputes between a brokerage firm and its clients; both sides of the "story" are presented to a board of arbitration, which makes a final and often binding decision on the matter.

Investor Protection

As a client, you are protected against the loss of securities or cash held by your broker by the **Securities Investor Protection Corporation (SIPC)**—a nonprofit corporation authorized by the Securities Investor Protection Act of 1970 to protect customer accounts against the financial failure of a brokerage firm. Although subject to SEC and congressional oversight, the SIPC is *not* an agency of the U.S. government.

SIPC insurance covers each account for up to $500,000 (of which up to $100,000 may be in cash balances held by the firm). Note, however, that SIPC insurance does not guarantee that the dollar value of the securities will be recovered. It only ensures that *the securities themselves will be returned.* So, what happens if your broker gives you bad advice, and, as a result, you lose a lot of money on an investment? SIPC won't help you, as it's not intended to insure you against bad investment advice. Instead, if you have a dispute with your broker, first discuss the situation with the managing officer at the branch where you do your business. If that doesn't do any good, then write or talk to the firm's compliance officer and contact the securities office in your home state. If you still don't get any satisfaction, you may have to take the case to **arbitration**, a process whereby you and your broker present the two sides to the argument before an arbitration panel, which then makes a decision about how the case will be resolved. If it's *binding* arbitration, and it usually is, you have no choice but to accept the decision—you cannot go to court to appeal your case. Many brokerage firms, in fact, require you to resolve disputes by going to binding arbitration. Thus, before you open an account, check the brokerage agreement to see if it contains a binding arbitration clause.

Odd or Round Lots

Security transactions can be made in either odd or round lots. An **odd lot** consists of fewer than 100 shares of stock, while a **round lot** represents a 100-share unit or multiples thereof. The sale of 400 shares of stock would be considered a round-lot transaction, but the purchase of 75 shares would be an odd-lot transaction; trading 250 shares of stock would involve two round lots and an odd lot. Because the purchase or sale of odd lots requires additional processing and the assistance of a specialist (an *odd-lot dealer*), an added fee—known as an *odd-lot differential*—is often tacked on to the normal commission charge, driving up the costs of these small trades. Indeed, the relatively high cost of an odd-lot trade is why it's best to deal in round lots whenever possible.

odd lot
A quantity of fewer than 100 shares of a stock.

round lot
A quantity of 100 shares of stock, or multiples thereof.

Brokerage Fees

Brokerage firms receive commissions for executing buy and sell orders for their clients. Brokerage commissions are said to be *negotiated*, which means that they are not fixed. In practice, however, most firms have *established fee schedules* that they use with small transactions (on larger, mostly institutional trades, negotiation of commissions actually does take place). Although these fees are not really negotiated, they do differ from one brokerage firm to another; thus it pays to shop around. Also if you're an "active trader," generating a couple thousand dollars (or more) in annual commissions, then by all means try to negotiate a reduced commission schedule with your broker. Chances are, they'll probably cut a deal with you—the fact is, brokers much prefer traders to buy-and-hold investors, because traders generate a lot more commissions. Generally speaking, brokerage fees on a round lot of common stock will amount to approximately 2 to 4 percent of the transaction value. (As a rule, at full-service brokerage firms, the broker gets to keep about 40 percent of the commission and the brokerage firm gets the rest.)

As the number of discount brokerage firms grows, there is greater variation in fees charged and services offered. The way commissions are calculated also varies; some firms base them on the dollar value of the transaction, some on the number of shares, and some use both. Exhibit 11.2 provides a list of representative commissions at eight discount and online brokerage firms. *(Note:* Many *discount* brokers, especially the larger ones, also offer online brokerage services, so there is a good deal of overlap here.) The firms with higher commissions generally offer more services; moreover, many discounters charge clients extra for research services.

Brokerage commissions on bond transactions differ from those on stock transactions. Brokerage firms typically charge a minimum fee of $25 to $30, regardless of the number of bonds involved. For multiple bond transactions, the brokerage cost per $1,000 corporate bond typically amounts to around $10 (which is decidedly lower than that on a stock transaction). The commission schedules for other securities, such as mutual funds and options, differ from those used with stocks and bonds (we will look at some of these in the next two chapters). The magnitude of brokerage commissions is obviously an important consideration when making security transactions, because these fees tend to raise the overall cost of purchasing securities and lower the overall proceeds from their sale.

EXECUTING TRADES

For most individual investors, a securities transaction involves placing a buy or sell order, usually by phone or on the Net, and later getting a confirmation that it has been completed. They have no idea what happens to their orders. In fact, a lot goes on—and very quickly—once the order is placed. It has to, because on a typical day, the NYSE alone executes more than 2.8 *million* trades, and many more occur on the Nasdaq, the AMEX, and the other exchanges. In most cases, if the investor places a market order (which we will explain below), it should take *less than two minutes* to place, execute, and confirm a trade.

EXHIBIT 11.2

Comparison of Discount and Online Brokers' Commissions

They say it pays to shop around, and that advice certainly applies when it comes to selecting a broker. Just look at the different commissions these brokers charge to execute essentially the same trade—to trade 500 shares of a $50 stock, for example, the commission ranges from $9 to $195 at the listed discount and online brokers, and as high as $399 at one of the major full-service brokers.

	Broker-Assisted Commissions		Online Commissions
Firm*	**100 shares at $50/share ($5,000)**	**500 shares at $50/share ($25,000)**	**500 shares at $50/share ($25,000)**
A.B. Watley (OLB)	$17.95	$17.95	$9.95
AccuTrade (OLB)	30.00	38.00	29.95
Brown & Co. (OLB)	17.00	17.00	5.00
Charles Schwab (DB)	55.00	155.00	29.95
Fidelity Brokerage Services (OLB)	55.00	111.00	29.95
Muriel Siebert (DB)	45.00	75.00	14.95
T. Rowe Price Brokerage (DB)	50.00	150.00	19.95
Vanguard Brokerage Serv. (DB)	48.00	60.00	20.00
Avg. of 76 Discount (DB) and Online (OLB) brokerage firms	$36.20	$62.64	$20.09
Highest broker	$75.00	$195.00	$156.00
Lowest broker	9.00	9.00	2.50
Major full-service firm	$99.90	$399.00	—

Note*: **DB after the firm name indicates fees & commissions as a "Discount Broker"; **OLB** indicates fees & commissions as an "Online Broker."

Source: Adapted from Jean Henrich, "The 2003 Discount Broker Survey: A Guide to Commissions and Services," *AAII Journal*, January 2003; and a major full-service stock brokerage firm.

The process starts with a phone call to the broker, who then transmits the order via sophisticated telecommunications equipment to the stock exchange floor, or to the OTC market, where it is promptly executed. Confirmation that the order has been executed is transmitted back to the original broker and then to the customer. Once the trade takes place, the investor has three (business) days to "settle" his or her account with the broker—that is, to pay for the securities.

As we noted earlier, investors can also use their PCs to execute online securities trades. There are more than 75 online brokers, including AccuTrade, Net Investor, Trading Direct, and Charles Schwab, all of whom are there to execute investor trades in a prompt, efficient, and low-cost manner. In an online trade, your order goes by modem from your computer to the brokerage computer, which checks the type of order and confirms that it is in compliance with regulations. It is then transmitted to the exchange floor or an OTC dealer for execution. The time for the whole process, including a confirmation that is sent back to your computer, is usually one minute or less.

TYPES OF ORDERS

Investors may choose from several different kinds of orders when buying or selling securities. The type of order chosen normally depends on the investor's goals and expectations with respect to the given transaction. The three basic types of orders are the market order, limit order, and stop-loss order.

Market Order

An order to buy or sell a security at the best price available at the time it is placed is a **market order**. It is usually the quickest way to have orders filled, because market orders are executed as soon as they reach the trading floor. In fact, on small trades of less than a few thousand shares, it takes only about 15 to 20 seconds to fill a market order once it hits the trading floor! These orders are executed through a process that attempts to allow *buy orders* to be filled at the lowest price and *sell orders* at the highest, thereby providing the best possible deal to both the buyers and sellers of a security. Because of the speed with which market orders are transacted, the investor can be sure that the price at which the order is completed will be very close to the market price that existed at the time it was placed.

market order
An order to buy or sell a security at the best price available at the time it is placed.

Limit Order

An order to buy at a specified price (or lower), or sell at a specified price (or higher) is known as a **limit order**. The broker transmits a limit order to a *specialist* dealing in the given security on the floor of the exchange. The order is executed as soon as the specified market price is reached and all other such orders with precedence have been filled. The order can be placed to remain in effect until a certain date or until canceled; such an instruction is called a **good 'til canceled (GTC) order**. For example, assume you place a limit order to buy 100 shares of a stock at a price of $20, even though the stock is currently selling at $20.50. Once the specialist has cleared all similar orders received before yours, and the market price of the stock is still at $20 or less, he or she will execute the order. Although a limit order can be quite effective, it can also cost you money! If, for instance, you wish to buy at 20 or less and the stock price moves from its current $20.50 to $32 while you are waiting, your limit order will have caused you to forgo an opportunity to make a profit of $11.50 ($32.00−$20.50) per share. Had you placed a market order, this profit would have been yours.

limit order
An order to either buy a security at a specified or lower price, or to sell a security at or above a specified price.

good 'til canceled (GTC) order
A limit order placed with instructions that it remain in effect indefinitely or until canceled.

Stop-Loss Order

An order to *sell a stock* when the market price reaches or drops below a specified level is called a **stop-loss**, or **stop order**. Used to protect the investor against rapid declines in stock prices, the stop order is placed on the specialist's book and activated when the stop price is reached. At that point, the stop order becomes a *market order* to sell. This means that the stock is offered for sale at the prevailing market price, which could be less than the price at which the order was initiated by the stop. For example, imagine that you own 100 shares of DEF, which is currently selling for $25. Because of the high uncertainty associated with the price movements of the stock, you decide to place a stop order to sell at $21. If the stock price drops to $21, your stop order is activated and the specialist will sell all your DEF stock at the best price available, which may be $18 or $19 a share. Of course, if the market price increases, or stays at or about $25 a share, nothing will have been lost by placing the stop-loss order.

stop-loss (stop order)
An order to sell a stock when the market price reaches or drops below a specified level.

MARGIN TRADES: BUYING SECURITIES ON CREDIT

When you're ready to buy securities, you can do so by putting up your own money, or by borrowing some of the money. *Buying on margin*, as it is called, is a common practice that allows investors to use borrowed money to make security transactions. Margin trading is closely regulated and is carried out under strict *margin requirements* set by the Federal Reserve Board. These requirements specify the amount of *equity* an investor must put up when buying stocks, bonds, and other securities. The most recent requirement is 50 percent for common stock, which means that at least 50 percent of each dollar invested must be the investor's own; the remaining 50 percent may be borrowed. For example, with a 50 percent margin requirement, you could purchase $5,000 worth of stock by putting up only $2,500 of your own money and borrowing the remaining $2,500. Other securities besides stocks can be margined, and these have their own margin requirements; Treasury bonds, for example, can be purchased with a margin as low as 10 percent.

margin purchase The purchase of securities with borrowed funds, the allowable amount of which is limited by the Federal Reserve.

To make **margin purchases**, you must open a *margin account* and have a minimum of $2,000 in cash (or *equity* in securities) on deposit with your broker. Once you meet these requirements, the brokerage firm will loan you the needed funds and retain the securities purchased as collateral. You can also obtain loans to purchase securities from your commercial bank, but the Fed's margin requirements still apply. To see how margin trading works, assume the margin requirement is 50 percent and that your brokerage firm charges 9 percent interest on margin loans (brokerage firms usually set the rate on margin loans at 1 to 3 points above prime). If you want to purchase a round lot (100 shares) of Engulf & Devour, which is currently trading at $50 per share, you can either make the purchase entirely with your own money or borrow a portion of the purchase price. The cost of the transaction will be $5,000 ($50/ share × 100 shares). If you margin, you will put up only $2,500 of your own money (50 percent × $5,000) and borrow the $2,500 balance. Exhibit 11.3 compares the rates of return you would receive with and without the 50 percent margin. This is done for two cases: (1) a $20 per share increase in the stock price, to $70 per share, and (2) a $20 per share decrease in the stock price, to $30 per share. It is assumed that the stock will be held for one year and all broker commissions are ignored.

As indicated in Exhibit 11.3, the use of margin allows you to increase the return on your investment when stock prices increase. Indeed, one of the major attributes of margin trading is that it allows you to *magnify your returns*—that is, you can use margin to reduce your equity in an investment and thereby magnify the returns from invested capital when security prices go up. As seen in Exhibit 11.3, the return on your investment when the stock price increases from $50 to $70 a share is 40 percent *without* margin and 71 percent *with* margin. However, when the stock price declines from $50 to $30 per share, the return on your investment will be a *negative* 40 percent without margin and a whopping *89 percent loss* with margin. Clearly, the use of margin magnifies losses as well as profits! If the price of the stock in our example continues to drop, you will eventually reach the point at which your equity in the investment will be so low that the brokerage house will require you to either provide more collateral or liquidate the investment. The risks inherent in buying on margin make it imperative that you thoroughly acquaint yourself with the risk-return tradeoffs involved *before* using margin in your investment program.

short sale A transaction that involves selling borrowed securities with the expectation that they can be replaced at a lower price at some future date; generally made in anticipation of a decline in the security's price.

Short Selling: The Practice of Selling Borrowed Securities

Most security transactions are *long transactions;* they are made in anticipation of increasing security prices in order to profit by buying low and selling high. A **short sale** transaction, in contrast, is made in anticipation of a decline in the price of a security. Although not nearly as common as long transactions, short selling is often done by the more sophisticated investor as a way to profit during a period of declining prices. When used by individual investors, most short sales are made with common stocks. When an investor sells a security short, the broker borrows the security and then sells it on behalf of the short seller's account—short sellers actually *sell securities they don't own.* The borrowed shares must, of course, be replaced in the future. If the investor can repurchase the shares at a lower price, a profit will result. In effect, the objective of a short sale is to take advantage of a drop in price by first selling high and then buying low (which, of course, is nothing more than the old "buy low, sell high" adage in reverse).

EXHIBIT 11.3

The Impact of Margin Trading on Investment Returns

The rate of return an individual earns on his or her investment is affected by, among other things, the amount of margin being used; unfortunately, although margin trading can magnify profits, it will also magnify losses.

Transaction	Without Margin	With Margin
The Initial Investment		
Amount invested	$5,000	$2,500
Amount borrowed	0	2,500
Total purchase (100 shares @ $50)	$5,000	$5,000
Price *Increases*: Sell Stock for $70/Share One Year Later		
Gross proceeds (100 shares @ $70)	$7,000	$7,000
Less: Interest @ 9% of amount borrowed	0	225
Net proceeds	$7,000	$6,775
Less: Total investment	5,000	5,000
Net profit (loss)	$2,000	$1,775
Return on your investment (net profit ÷ amount invested)	$\frac{\$2,000}{\$5,000} = 40\%$	$\frac{\$1,775}{\$2,500} = 71\%$
Price *Decreases*: Sell Stock for $30/Share One Year Later		
Gross proceeds (100 shares @ $30)	$3,000	$3,000
Less: Interest @ 9% of amount borrowed	0	225
Net proceeds	$3,000	$2,775
Less: Total investment	5,000	5,000
Net profit (loss)	($2,000)	($2,225)
Return on your investment (net profit ÷ amount invested)	$\frac{(\$2,000)}{\$5,000} = (40\%)$	$\frac{(\$2,225)}{\$2,500} = 89\%$

Short selling is perfectly legitimate; there's nothing illegal or unethical about it. Indeed, because the shares sold are *borrowed securities*, numerous rules and regulations protect the party that lends the securities and govern the short-sale process. One regulation, for example, permits stocks to be sold short only when the last change in the market price of the stock has been upward. Another safeguard is the requirement that all proceeds from the short sale of the borrowed securities be held by the brokerage firm—the short seller never sees any of this money! In addition, the short seller must deposit with the broker a certain amount of money (equivalent to the prevailing initial margin requirement) when the transaction is executed—so even a short-sale transaction involves an investment of capital.

A short-sale transaction can be illustrated with a simple example (one that ignores brokerage fees). Assume that Patrick O'Sullivan wishes to sell short 100 shares of Advanced Buggy-Whips, Inc. at \$52.50 per share. After Pat has met the necessary requirements (including making a margin deposit of \$52.50 × 100 × 50% = \$2,625), his broker borrows the shares and sells them, obtaining proceeds of \$5,250 (100 shares × \$52.50/share). If the stock price goes down as Pat expects, he will be able to repurchase the shares at the lower price. Now suppose the price drops to \$40 per share, and he repurchases the 100 shares. Pat will make a profit, because he will have been able to replace the shares for \$4,000 (100 shares × \$40/share), which is below the \$5,250 received when he sold the stock. His profit will be \$1,250 (\$5,250 − \$4,000). If, on the other hand, the stock price rose to, say, \$60 per share, and Pat repurchased the stocks at that price, he would sustain a loss of \$750 (\$52.50 − \$60.00 = −\$7.50 × 100 = −\$750.00). Because of the high risk involved in short sales, you should thoroughly familiarize yourself with this technique and all its pitfalls *before* attempting to short sell any security.

Concept ✓

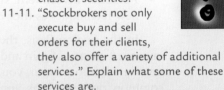

11-10. What is a *stockbroker*? Why does the selection of a broker play such an important role in the purchase of securities?
11-11. "Stockbrokers not only execute buy and sell orders for their clients, they also offer a variety of additional services." Explain what some of these services are.
11-12. Describe the role that *discount brokers* play in carrying out security transactions. To whom are their services especially appealing? What are *online brokers* and what kind of investors are most likely to use them?
11-13. What is the SIPC, and how does it protect investors? Does the SIPC protect investors against loss? Explain.
11-14. What is *arbitration*? Does SIPC require the use of arbitration in investor disputes? Explain.
11-15. Name and describe three basic types of orders.
11-16. What are *margin* requirements? Why might an investor buy securities on margin?
11-17. What is a *short sale*? Explain the logic behind it.

LG4 BECOMING AN INFORMED INVESTOR

Face it: Some people are more knowledgeable about investing than others. As a result, they may use certain investment vehicles or tactics that are not even in the vocabulary of others. Investor know-how, in short, defines the playing field. It helps determine how well you'll meet your investment objectives. Being knowledgeable about investments is important, because one of the key elements in successful investing is ***knowing how to achieve decent rates of return without taking unnecessary risks.***

Basing investment decisions on sound information lies at the very heart of any successful investment program. Indeed, there is simply no substitute for being informed when it comes to making investment decisions. While it can't guarantee success, it can help you avoid unnecessary losses—like the ones that happen all too often when people put their money into investment vehicles they don't fully understand. Such results aren't too surprising, because these investors violate the first rule of investing: *Never start an investment program, or buy an investment vehicle, unless you're thoroughly familiar with what you're getting into!* Before making any major investment decision, you should thoroughly investigate the security and its merits. Formulate some basic expectations about its future performance, and gain an understanding of the sources of risk and return. This can usually be done by reading the popular financial press and referring to other print or Internet sources of investment information.

There are four basic types of investment information you should try to follow; they are:

- **Economic developments and current events:** To help you evaluate the underlying investment environment
- **Alternative investment vehicles:** To keep you abreast of market developments
- **Current interest rates and price quotations:** To monitor your investments and also stay alert for developing investment opportunities
- **Personal investment strategies:** To help you hone your skills and stay alert for new techniques as they develop

In the final analysis, the payoff of an informed approach to investing is both an improved chance of gain and a reduced chance of loss. While there are many sources of investment information, you, as a beginning investor, should concentrate on the more common ones, such as annual stockholders' reports, the financial press, brokerage reports, advisory services, investment advisors, and of course, as we'll see, the Internet.

Annual Stockholders' Reports

Every publicly traded corporation is required to provide its stockholders and other interested parties with **annual stockholders' reports**. These documents provide a wealth of information about the companies, including balance sheets, income statements, and other summarized statements for the latest fiscal year, plus a number of prior years. Annual reports usually describe the firm's business activities, recent developments, and future plans and outlook. Financial ratios describing past performance are also included, along with other relevant statistics. In fact, annual reports provide a great deal of insight into the company's past, present, and future operations. You can obtain them for free directly from the companies, through a brokerage firm, or at most large libraries; and with today's technology, most companies are also posting their annual reports on the Internet, so now you can obtain them online.

annual stockholders' report A report made available to stockholders and other interested parties that includes a variety of financial and descriptive information about a firm's operations over the recent past.

Here are some suggestions to help you get the most information when reading an annual report:

- **Start with the Highlights or Selected Financial Data sections:** These provide a quick overview of performance by summarizing key information, such as the past two years' revenues, net income, assets, earnings per share (EPS), and dividends. EPS have the most effect on the stock's price, so watch them closely.
- **Read the chief executive's letter:** But read it with a careful eye, looking for euphemisms like "a slowing of growth" for drop in earnings.
- **Move on to the discussion of operations in Management's Discussion and Analysis:** This section provides information on sales, earnings, debt, inventory levels, litigation, taxes, and so on.
- **Review the financial statements, including the notes:** These will tell you about the company's financial condition and performance. Look for trends in sales, costs, profit, cash position, inventory, and net working capital.
- **Read the auditor's report:** This statement from the independent accountants who review the numbers has two paragraphs when everything is fine; a third paragraph or terms like "except for" or "subject to" means there may be problems you need to understand.

smart.sites

If annual reports confuse you, the *Guide to Understanding Financial Reports* at the IBM Investor site, **http://www.ibm.com/investor/financialguide**, will help you understand these valuable information sources.

The Financial Press

The most common source of financial news is the local newspaper. The newspapers in many larger cities often devote several pages to business and information and, of course, big-city papers, like *The New York Times*, provide even more information. Other, more specific sources of financial news include *The Wall Street Journal*, *Barron's*, *Investor's Business Daily*, and the "Money" section of *USA Today*. These are all national publications that include articles on the behavior of the economy, the market, various industries, and individual companies. The most comprehensive and up-to-date coverage of financial news is provided Monday through Friday by *The Wall Street Journal*, whereas *Barron's* concentrates on the week's activities as they relate to the financial markets and individual security prices. Other excellent sources of investment information include magazine-type publications, such as *Money*, *Forbes*, *Fortune*, *Business Week*, *Smart Money*, and *Kiplinger's Personal Finance*. (Today, of course, the Internet is rapidly becoming a major source of information for investors; we will discuss this source in more detail later in this chapter.)

Economic Data

Summaries and analyses of economic events can be found in all the above sources. Economic data include news items related to government actions and their effects on the economy; political and international events as they pertain to the economy; and statistics related to price levels, interest rates, the federal budget, and taxes.

Market Data

Usually presented in the form of averages, or indexes, *market data* describe the general behavior of the securities markets. The averages and indexes are based on the price movements of a select group of securities over an extended period of time. They are used to capture the overall performance of the market as a whole. You would want to follow one or more of these measures *to get a feel for how the market is doing over time* and, perhaps, an indication of what lies ahead. The absolute level of the index at a given point in time (or on a given day) is far less important than *what's been happening to that index over a given period of time*. The most commonly cited market measures are those calculated by Dow Jones, Standard & Poor's, the New York Stock Exchange, the American Stock Exchange, and Nasdaq (for the OTC market). These measures are all intended to keep track of the behavior in the stock market, particularly stocks on the NYSE (the Dow, S&P, and NYSE averages all follow stocks on the big board). In addition, several averages and indexes follow the action in other markets, including the bond, commodities, and options markets, and even the markets for mutual funds, real estate, and collectibles. However, because all these other averages and indexes are not followed nearly as much as those of stocks, we will concentrate here on stock market performance measures.

Dow Jones Averages

Dow Jones Industrial Average (DJIA) The most widely followed measure of stock market performance; consists of 30 blue-chip stocks listed mostly on the NYSE.

The granddaddy of them all and probably the most widely followed measure of stock market performance is the **Dow Jones Industrial Average (DJIA)**. Actually, the Dow Jones averages, which began in 1896, are made up of four parts: (1) an industrial average based on 30 stocks, (2) a transportation average based on 20 stocks, (3) a utility average based on 15 stocks, and (4) a composite average based on all 65 industrial, transportation, and utility stocks. (Dow Jones recently added several more market indexes to their lineup, including: the DJ U.S. Total Market index and the DJ World index, which excludes the U.S.) The makeup of the 30 stocks in the DJIA does change a bit over time as companies go private, are acquired by other firms, or become less of a force in the marketplace. For example, in the past few years, Allied Signal, Chevron, Goodyear, Sears, Travelers, and Union Carbide were dropped from the DJIA and replaced with Citigroup, Home Depot,

Honeywell, Intel, Microsoft, and SBC Communications. Most of the stocks are picked from the NYSE, but there are a few Nasdaq shares in there, such as Intel and Microsoft. Although these stocks are intended to represent a cross-section of companies, there is a strong bias toward blue chips, which is one of the major criticisms of the Dow Jones Industrial Average. Critics also claim that an average made up of only 30 blue-chip stocks—out of some 5 or 6 thousand issues—is hardly representative of the market. However, the facts show that as a rule, the behavior of the DJIA closely reflects that of other broadly based stock market measures—with the possible exception of the Nasdaq. Exhibit 11.4 lists the 30 stocks in the DJIA, along with some important dates in its life.

EXHIBIT 11.4

The Dow Jones Industrial Average

The DJIA is made up of 30 of the bluest of blue-chip stocks and has been closely followed by investors for the past 100 years or so.

The 30 Stocks in the DJIA:

Aluminum Co. of Amer.	Exxon Mobil	Johnson & Johnson
Altria Group	General Electric	McDonald's
American Express	General Motors	Merck
AT&T	Hewlett-Packard	Minnesota M&M
Boeing	Home Depot	Microsoft
Caterpillar	Honeywell	Procter & Gamble
Citigroup	IBM	SBC Communications
Coca-Cola	Intel	United Technologies
DuPont	International Paper	Wal-Mart
Eastman Kodak	J.P. Morgan	Walt Disney

Some Important Dates for the Dow:

May 26, 1896	The Dow Jones Industrial Average makes its debut; originally made up of just 12 stocks (of the 12 stocks that originally made up the DJIA, only GE is still on the list).
January 12, 1906	Closes above 100 for the first time.
October 28, 1929	The infamous "1929 crash"; Dow drops 38.33 points in one day.
November 14, 1972	Closes above 1000 for the first time.
August 12, 1982	Closes at 776.92, as the market bottoms out and the Great Bull Market of the 1980s and 1990s is born.
October 19, 1987	The market crashes; the DJIA closes at 1,738.74, for a record 1-day drop of 508 points (23%).
November 21, 1995	Closes above 5,000 for the first time.
October 27, 1997	Stocks plunge as the market falls 554 points (a new record) to 7,161.15.
March 29, 1999	Closes above 10,000 for the first time.
January 14, 2000	Closes at all-time high of 11,722.98, as the bull market that started in 1982 reaches the end of the road; a couple months later, the worst bear market since the Depression begins.
September 10, 2001	Closes the day before 9/11 at 9605.51; the market closes after 9/11 for the rest of the week. Opens the following Monday to a 700 point loss.
October 9, 2002	Closes at 7286.27 as the bear market that started 2½ years earlier bottoms out; over the course of those 2½ years, the Dow drops 4,436.71 points (or 37.8%).
September 11, 2003	Closes at 9459.76—up more than 2,100 points from the low reached on October 9, 2002.

Standard & Poor's Indexes

Standard & Poor's (S&P) indexes
Indexes compiled by Standard & Poor's that are similar to the DJIA but employ different computational methods and consist of far more stocks.

The **Standard & Poor's (S&P) indexes** are similar to the Dow Jones averages to the extent that they both are used to capture the overall performance of the market. However, some important differences exist between the two measures. For one thing, the S&P uses a lot more stocks; the popular S&P 500 composite index is based on 500 different stocks, whereas the DJIA uses only 30 stocks. What's more, the S&P index is made up of all large NYSE stocks, as well as some major AMEX and OTC stocks, so there's not only more issues in the S&P sample, but also a greater breadth of representation. And, finally, there are some technical differences in the mathematical procedures used to compute the two measures; the Dow Jones is an *average*, whereas the S&P is an *index*. Yet in spite of these technical differences, movements in these two measures are, in fact, *very highly correlated* and as a result, they are used in much the same way.

There are eight basic S&P indexes: (1) an industrial index based on 400 stocks; (2) a transportation index of 20 stocks; (3) a public utility index of 40 stocks; (4) a financial index of 40 stocks; (5) a composite index for all 500 of the stocks used in the first four indexes; (6) the *MidCap 400*; (7) the *SmallCap 600*; and (8) the composite *S&P 1500* made up of the S&P 500, 400, and 600 indexes. The MidCap index is made up of 400 medium-sized companies—those with market values that, for the most part, range from about $500 million to $3 billion, or more, while the SmallCap index consists of small companies, with market caps of around $500 million or less.

The S&P 500, like the DJIA, is widely followed by the financial media, and is reported not only in publications like *The Wall Street Journal* and *Barron's*, but also in most of the major newspapers around the country and other market outlets. The S&P has a much lower value than the DJIA—for example, in September 2003, the Dow stood at over 9,500, whereas the S&P index of 500 stocks was just over 1,030. Now this does not mean that the S&P consists of less valuable stocks; rather, the disparity is due solely to the different methods used to compute the measures.

The NYSE, AMEX, and Nasdaq Indexes

NYSE index
An index of the performance of all stocks listed on the New York Stock Exchange.

AMEX index
An index of the performance of all stocks listed on the American Stock Exchange.

Nasdaq index
An index, supplied by the National Association of Securities Dealers, that tracks the performance of stocks traded in the OTC market.

The most widely followed exchange-based indexes are those of the New York Stock Exchange (NYSE), the American Stock Exchange (AMEX), and the Nasdaq (for the OTC market). The **NYSE index** includes all the stocks listed on the "big board." In addition to the composite index, the NYSE publishes indexes for industrials, utilities, transportation, and finance subgroups. The behavior of the NYSE Industrial index closely mimics that of the DJIA and the S&P 500.

The **AMEX index** reflects share prices on the American Stock Exchange. Made up of all stocks on the AMEX, it is set up in such a way that it directly captures the actual *percentage change* in share prices. For example, if the price change in AMEX stocks from one day to the next were +3 percent, the AMEX index would likewise increase by 3 percent over the previous day's value. Like the NYSE indexes, the AMEX index is often cited in the financial news.

Activity in the OTC market is captured by the **Nasdaq indexes**, which are calculated like the S&P and NYSE indexes. The most comprehensive of these indexes is the *Nasdaq composite index*, which is calculated using virtually all the stocks traded on the Nasdaq system. The other Nasdaq indexes are the industrial, insurance, bank, computers, and telecommunications indexes. In addition, there is the *Nasdaq 100 Index*, which tracks the price behavior of the biggest 100 (nonfinancial) firms traded on the Nasdaq—companies like Microsoft, Intel, Oracle, Cisco, Staples, and Dell. The Nasdaq Composite is often used today as a benchmark in assessing the price behavior of *high-tech* stocks. This index is far more volatile than either the Dow or the S&P and way outperformed other market measures from 1995 to 1999—before taking a big dive in 2000, 2001, and 2002.

In addition to the major indexes described above, another measure of market performance is the **Wilshire 5000 Index**, which is also known as the *Wilshire Total Market Index.* Published by Wilshire Associates, Inc., the Wilshire 5000 is reported daily in *The Wall Street Journal* and many other major publications. Although this index originally covered some 5,000 stocks, today that number is up to more like 6,000 or 7,000 stocks (clearly, the number of stocks covered has changed but the name hasn't). Whatever the number, it's estimated that the Wilshire index reflects the *total market value of 98–99 percent of all publicly-traded stocks in this country.* In essence, it shows what's happening in the stock market as a whole—the dollar amount of market value added or lost as the market moves up and down. In this index, one point is worth $1 *billion* (vs. about 1 cent in the DJIA). Thus, the Wilshire can be used to not only track the behavior of the U.S. stock market, but also give you a pretty accurate reading as to the size of our market on any given day. For example, in September 2003, the Wilshire index stood at just over 10,000. Because this index is in billions of dollars, a measure of 10,000 translates into a total market value of some $10 *trillion!!*

Wilshire 5000 index
An index of the total market value of the 6,000 to 7,000 (originally 5,000) or so most actively traded stocks in this country.

In addition, the Frank Russell Co., a pension advisory firm, produces three indexes that are also widely followed by market participants. Probably the most popular is the *Russell 2000,* which tracks the behavior of 2,000 relatively small companies and is widely felt to provide a fairly accurate measure of the small-cap segment of the market. There is also the *Russell 1000,* which follows the price behavior of the 1,000 largest companies in this country, and the *Russell 3000,* which is a combination of the two previously mentioned indexes.

Industry Data

Local newspapers, *The Wall Street Journal, Barron's,* and various financial publications regularly contain articles and data about different industries. For example, Standard & Poor's *Industry Surveys* provides detailed descriptions and statistics for all the major industries; on a smaller scale, *Business Week* and other magazines regularly include indexes of industry performance and price levels. Other industry-related data can be obtained from industry trade associations, one example of which is the American Petroleum Institute.

Company Data

Articles about new developments and the performance of companies are included in local newspapers, *The Wall Street Journal, Barron's,* and most investment magazines. The prices of the securities of all listed companies and the most active over-the-counter stocks are quoted daily in *The Wall Street Journal, Investor's Business Daily,* and *USA Today,* and weekly in *Barron's.* Many daily newspapers also contain stock price quotations, though in the smaller ones the listing may be selective; in some cases, only stocks of local interest are included.

Stock Quotes

To see how price quotations work and what they mean, consider the quotes that appear daily (M–F) in *The Wall Street Journal.* As we'll see, the quotations provide not only current prices, but a great deal of additional information as well. A portion of the NYSE stock quotations from *The Wall Street Journal* is presented in Exhibit 11.5 on page 466. (Here we look at *stock quotes;* in chapter 12, we'll look at *bond quotes.*) Let's use the ***Disney*** quotations for purposes of illustration. These quotes were published on July 8, 2003, and are for trades that occurred the day before, on July 7th. A glance at the quotations shows that stocks, like most other securities, are quoted in dollars and cents.

Looking at the Disney quotes, the first column (YTD % CHG) gives the stock's year-to-date change in price; note that Disney's stock has gone up a whopping 26.2 percent since the first of the year. The two columns labeled "HI" and "LO" show the highest and lowest prices at which the stock sold during the past 52 weeks. You can see that Disney has traded between $21.55 and $13.48 per share during the preceding 52-week period. Listed to the right of the company's name is its *stock symbol* (Disney goes by the three-letter initial **"DIS"**). These stock symbols are the abbreviations used on the *market tapes* seen in brokerage offices and on television, as well as on Internet sites such as Quicken to identify specific securities. The figure listed right after the stock symbol is the annual cash dividend paid on each share of stock. This is followed by the dividend yield. (*Note*: Because Disney paid a cash dividend of $.21 per share, its dividend yield is just 1.0 percent, which is found by dividing the 21 cents in dividends by the closing price of $20.58.) The next entry is the P/E ratio, which is the current market price divided by the per share earnings for the most recent 12-month period. Because it is believed to reflect investor expectations concerning the firm's future prospects, the P/E ratio is closely followed by investors as part of the stock valuation process. Note that Disney was trading at 39 times its earnings, a pretty high multiple.

The daily volume follows the P/E ratio. Here, the sales numbers are listed in round lots (of 100 shares), so a figure of 66186 for Disney indicates that 6,618,600 *shares* of Disney stock were traded on July 7th. The next entry, labeled "CLOSE", shows the closing (final) price of $20.58, at which the stock sold on the day in question. Finally, as the last (NET CHG) column shows, Disney closed up $0.51. This means the stock closed 51 cents higher than the day before (which in this case was Thursday, July 3), when it closed at $20.07.

The same quotation system is used for Nasdaq *National Market* stocks. However, a slightly different procedure is used with AMEX and OTC securities that are not part of the National Market system—that is, for many AMEX and OTC stocks, only the stock name, symbol, volume, closing price, and change in price are included in the quotes.

Brokerage Reports

The reports produced by the research staffs of the major (full-service) brokerage firms provide still another important source of investor information. These reports cover a wide variety of topics, from economic and market analyses to industry and company reports, news of special situations, and reports on interest rates and the bond market. Reports on certain industries or securities prepared by the house's backoffice research staff may be issued on a regular basis and contain lists of securities within certain industries classified as to the type of market behavior they are expected to exhibit. Brokerage houses also regularly issue reports, prepared by their security analysts, on specific securities, which include among other things their recommendations as to the type of investment returns expected and whether to buy, hold, or sell the securities in question.

Advisory Services

A number of subscription advisory services—available both in print and online—provide information and recommendations on various industries and specific securities. The services normally cost from $50 to several hundred dollars a year. Although these costs may be tax deductible, only the most active investors will find them worthwhile, because you can usually review such materials (for free) at your broker's office, at university and public libraries, or online. Probably the best known financial services are those provided by Standard & Poor's, Moody's Investors Service, and Value Line

EXHIBIT 11.5

Listed Stock Quotes

This list summarizes 1 day's trading activity and price quotes for a group of stocks traded on the New York Stock Exchange. Note that in addition to the latest stock prices, a typical stock quote conveys an array of other information.

YTD % CHG	52-WEEKS HI	52-WEEKS LO	STOCK (SYM)	DIV	YLD %	PE	VOL 100s	CLOSE	NET CHG
16.4	13.86	7.75♣	DnbryRes DNR		...	12	2530	13.15	-0.29
19.9	15.69	8.95	Dept56 DFS		...	7	741	15.47	0.31
-3.3	10.11	5.21	DescSA ADR DES	.56e	8.6	...	25	6.53	0.14
45.7	72.23	35.26	DtscheBK DB	1.53e	2.3	...	540	66.18	0.60
18.8	15.64	8.10♣	DtscheTel ADS DT		...	...	5203	15.09	0.09
35 .1	29.62	17.25	DevDivRlty DDR	1.64	5.5	24	2779	29.70	0.32
47.9	26.38	12.10	DeVry DV		...	26	2205	24.57	0.72
-0.5	53	37.55	Diageo ADS DEO	1.69e	3.9	...	7071	43.59	-1.21
4.9	47.64	30	DiagnstPdt DP	.24	.6	24	1208	40.50	-0.05
-3.0	22.45	17.12	DialCp DL	.16	.8	29	4377	19.75	0.14
-5.7	28.70	17.30	DmndOffshr DO	.50	2.4	cc	16969	20.60	-0.93
99.4	38.83	12.15	DicksSprtgGds DKS n		...	20	3509	38.28	0.99
10.6	45.90	30.30	Diebold DBD	.68	1.5	25	4706	45.60	1.00
-13.2	28.14	12.32	Dillards DDS	.16	1.2	11	5716	13.76	0.09
21.7	7.50	5.35♣	Dimon DMN	.30	4.1	12	1050	7.30	0.18
26.2	21.55	13.48	Disney DIS	.21	1.0	39	66186	20.58	0.51
8.9	27.48	23.70	Disney 6.875Corts KVJ n	1.72	6.3	...	14	27.18	0.23
27.0	13.05	7.50	Dist&Srv ADS DYS	.21e	1.7	...	540	12.70	-0.20
211.2	**11.40**	**2.70**	**djOrthopedics DJO**		**...**	**dd**	**1703**	**11.70**	**0.69**
58.4	19.95	9.50	DirGenl DG	.14	.7	23	13925	18.93	0.27
-7.1	26.60	14.35♣	DlrThrfty DTG		...	14	575	19.65	0.15
24.9	27.30	17.55	DomResBlkWar DOM	2.56e	9.5	...	196	27.05	-0.01
15.5	66.15	35.40♣	DominRes D	2.58	4.1	13	8587	63.43	-0.19
11.0	55	36.77♣	Domin un	4.38	8.1	...	95	53.90	-0.07
8.8	11.73	8.60	Domtar DTC	.17fg	...	...	840	10.95	-0.07
27.8	45.68	29.91♣	Donaldson DCI	.36	.8	22	924	46.01	0.57
23.2	28.40	16.94	Donnelly DNY	1.00	3.7	24	5762	26.83	0.78

Year-to-date change in price, in percentages

High and low prices for previous 52 weeks

Company name and stock symbol

Annual dividends per share for past 12 months

Dividend yield (dividends as percent of share price)

Price/earnings ratio: $\left(\frac{\text{market price}}{\text{earnings per share}}\right)$

Net change in price from previous day

Closing (final) price for the day—this is also the price used to compute dividend yield and the P/E ratio

Share volume, in hundreds

Source: *The Wall Street Journal,* July 8, 2003.

Investment Survey. Each offers an array of services. Both Standard & Poor's and Moody's publish manuals containing historical facts and financial data on thousands of corporations, broken down by industry groups. Standard & Poor's publishes a monthly stock guide and bond guide, each of which summarizes the financial conditions of a few thousand issues; Moody's also publishes stock and bond guides. And a number of reports are also prepared weekly, like Standard & Poor's *Outlook*.

Separate reports on specific companies are another valuable type of subscription service. An example of one such stock report is given in Exhibit 11.6 on pages 468 and 469.

Financial Road Sign

Let the Buyer Beware!!!
For better or worse, analysts' reports are widely used by investors. Most of them provide investors with valuable insights, but some are really bad!! In particular, beware of an analyst who:

- Downplays bad news
- Claims a company is unaffected by the economy
- Shrugs it off when a major customer leaves a company
- Insists the departure of a top executive won't hurt the company
- Declares the cost to launch a new product will be low
- Gives instant approval of a merger
- Insists that a company that has struggled for years will have a bright future.

Source: USA TODAY. Copyright May 27, 2003. Reprinted with permission.

This report, prepared by Standard & Poor's, presents a concise summary of a company's financial history, current finances, and future prospects; a similar type of report, with even more emphasis given to the security's investment merits and future prospects, is also available from *Value Line*. Recommended lists of securities, broken down into groups on the basis of investment objectives, constitute still another type of service. In addition to these popular subscription services, numerous *investment letters*, which periodically advise subscribers on the purchase and sale of securities, are available. Finally, by subscribing to weekly chart books, investors may also obtain graphs showing stock prices and volume over extended periods of time. (We'll discuss online services a little later in this chapter.)

Investment Advisors

Successful investors often establish themselves as professional investment advisors. In this capacity, they attempt to develop investment plans consistent with the financial objectives of their clients. You can obtain the services of a professional money manager in several ways: (1) you can hire an *independent investment advisor* (but they're usually pretty expensive and prefer to deal with well-heeled clients); (2) you can go to the *trust department of a major bank* (many offer their investment services to the general public at very reasonable costs, and you don't have to die or have a trust account to obtain such services—all you have to do is enter into a simple *agency agreement*); (3) if you deal with a full-service brokerage firm, you can check with your broker to see if they offer fee-based *wrap accounts* (in these portfolio management accounts, your brokerage firm takes over the full-time management of your investments, in return for a flat annual fee—but watch out, that annual fee can get pretty hefty); or (4) you might consider the services of a *financial planner* (preferably a *fee-based* planner who has a strong track record in the field of *investments*).

If you're thinking of using a professional money manager, the best thing to do is shop around—look at the kind of returns he or she has been able to generate (in good markets and bad), and don't overlook the matter of cost—find out up front how much you'll have to pay and what the fee is based on. Annual fees for advisory services, which may involve the complete management of the client's money, are likely to range from about 1 percent to as much as 2 or 3 percent of assets under management. Equally important, find out if the advisor has a specialty and, if so, make sure it's compatible with your investment objectives; for example, don't go to a financial planner who specializes in high-risk limited partnerships or high-cost variable annuities if you're not interested in those kinds of investment.

Concept ✓

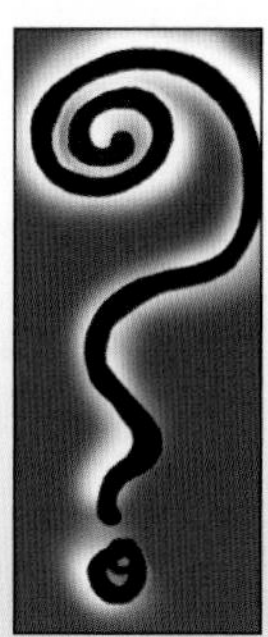

11-18. Identify and briefly discuss the four basic types of information that you, as an investor, should try to follow.

11-19. Describe some of the major sources of investment information.

11-20. What role do market averages and indexes play in the investment process?

11-21. Briefly describe the *DJIA*, *S&P 500*, *S&P 600*, *Nasdaq Composite*, *Nasdaq 100*, *Russell 2000*, and *Wilshire 5000* indexes; which segments of the market does each track?

EXHIBIT 11.6

An S&P Stock Report

An S&P report like this one provides a wealth of information about the operating results and financial condition of the company and is an invaluable source of information to investors.

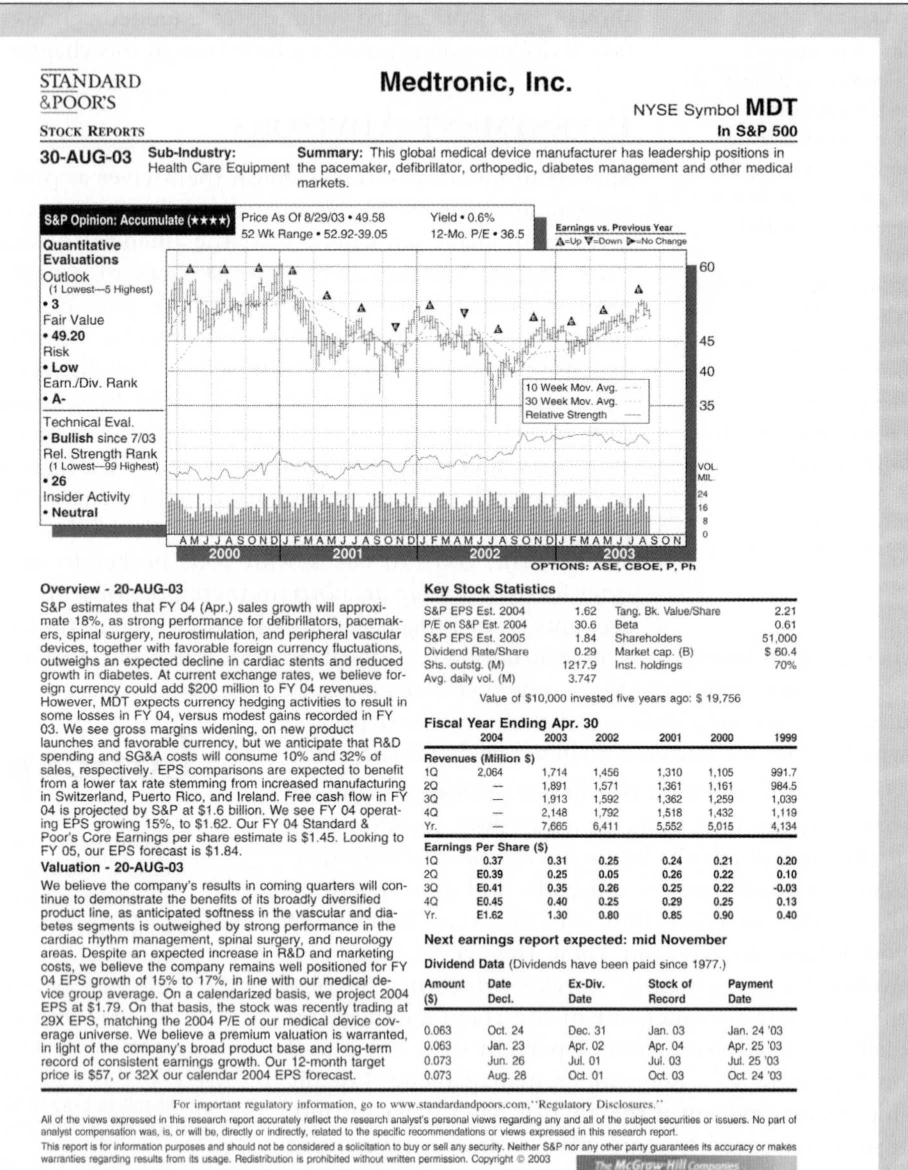

STANDARD
&POOR'S
STOCK REPORTS

Medtronic, Inc.

NYSE Symbol **MDT**
In S&P 500

30-AUG-03 **Sub-Industry:** Health Care Equipment **Summary:** This global medical device manufacturer has leadership positions in the pacemaker, defibrillator, orthopedic, diabetes management and other medical markets.

S&P Opinion: Accumulate (★★★★) Price As Of 8/29/03 • 49.58 52 Wk Range • 52.92-39.05 Yield • 0.6% 12-Mo. P/E • 36.5

Quantitative Evaluations
Outlook (1 Lowest—5 Highest) • **3**
Fair Value • **49.20**
Risk • **Low**
Earn./Div. Rank • **A-**
Technical Eval. • **Bullish** since 7/03
Rel. Strength Rank (1 Lowest—99 Highest) • **26**
Insider Activity • **Neutral**

Overview - 20-AUG-03

S&P estimates that FY 04 (Apr.) sales growth will approximate 18%, as strong performance for defibrillators, pacemakers, spinal surgery, neurostimulation, and peripheral vascular devices, together with favorable foreign currency fluctuations, outweighs an expected decline in cardiac stents and reduced growth in diabetes. At current exchange rates, we believe foreign currency could add $200 million to FY 04 revenues. However, MDT expects currency hedging activities to result in some losses in FY 04, versus modest gains recorded in FY 03. We see gross margins widening, on new product launches and favorable currency, but we anticipate that R&D spending and SG&A costs will consume 10% and 32% of sales, respectively. EPS comparisons are expected to benefit from a lower tax rate stemming from increased manufacturing in Switzerland, Puerto Rico, and Ireland. Free cash flow in FY 04 is projected by S&P at $1.6 billion. We see FY 04 operating EPS growing 15%, to $1.62. Our FY 04 Standard & Poor's Core Earnings per share estimate is $1.45. Looking to FY 05, our EPS forecast is $1.84.

Valuation - 20-AUG-03

We believe the company's results in coming quarters will continue to demonstrate the benefits of its broadly diversified product line, as anticipated softness in the vascular and diabetes segments is outweighed by strong performance in the cardiac rhythm management, spinal surgery, and neurology areas. Despite an expected increase in R&D and marketing costs, we believe the company remains well positioned for FY 04 EPS growth of 15% to 17%, in line with our medical device group average. On a calendarized basis, we project 2004 EPS at $1.79. On that basis, the stock was recently trading at 29X EPS, matching the 2004 P/E of our medical device coverage universe. We believe a premium valuation is warranted, in light of the company's broad product base and long-term record of consistent earnings growth. Our 12-month target price is $57, or 32X our calendar 2004 EPS forecast.

Key Stock Statistics

S&P EPS Est. 2004	1.62	Tang. Bk. Value/Share	2.21
P/E on S&P Est. 2004	30.6	Beta	0.61
S&P EPS Est. 2005	1.84	Shareholders	51,000
Dividend Rate/Share	0.29	Market cap. (B)	$ 60.4
Shs. outstg. (M)	1217.9	Inst. holdings	70%
Avg. daily vol. (M)	3.747		

Value of $10,000 invested five years ago: $ 19,756

Fiscal Year Ending Apr. 30

	2004	2003	2002	2001	2000	1999
Revenues (Million $)						
1Q	2,064	1,714	1,456	1,310	1,105	991.7
2Q	—	1,891	1,571	1,361	1,161	984.5
3Q	—	1,913	1,592	1,362	1,259	1,039
4Q	—	2,148	1,792	1,518	1,432	1,119
Yr.	—	7,665	6,411	5,552	5,015	4,134
Earnings Per Share ($)						
1Q	0.37	0.31	0.25	0.24	0.21	0.20
2Q	E0.39	0.25	0.05	0.26	0.22	0.10
3Q	E0.41	0.35	0.26	0.25	0.22	-0.03
4Q	E0.45	0.40	0.25	0.29	0.25	0.13
Yr.	E1.62	1.30	0.80	0.85	0.90	0.40

Next earnings report expected: mid November

Dividend Data (Dividends have been paid since 1977.)

Amount ($)	Date Decl.	Ex-Div. Date	Stock of Record	Payment Date
0.063	Oct. 24	Dec. 31	Jan. 03	Jan. 24 '03
0.063	Jan. 23	Apr. 02	Apr. 04	Apr. 25 '03
0.073	Jun. 26	Jul. 01	Jul. 03	Jul. 25 '03
0.073	Aug. 28	Oct. 01	Oct. 03	Oct. 24 '03

For important regulatory information, go to www.standardandpoors.com, "Regulatory Disclosures."

All of the views expressed in this research report accurately reflect the research analyst's personal views regarding any and all of the subject securities or issuers. No part of analyst compensation was, is, or will be, directly or indirectly, related to the specific recommendations or views expressed in this research report.

EXHIBIT 11.6 (continued)

STANDARD &POOR'S

Medtronic, Inc.

STOCK REPORTS 30-AUG-03

Business Summary - 20-AUG-03

Formed in 1949, Medtronic has leading positions in many medical device categories including cardiac rhythm management, neurological/spinal, vascular and cardiac surgery markets. About 30% of net sales in FY 03 (Apr.) were derived outside of the U.S.

Cardiac rhythm management products (47% of FY 03 revenues) include implantable pacemakers to treat bradycardia (slow or irregular heartbeats). Bradycardia systems include pacemakers, leads and accessories. Some models are noninvasively programmed by a physician to adjust sensing, electrical pulse intensity, duration, rate and other factors, as well as pacers that can sense in both upper and lower heart chambers and produce appropriate impulses.

Implantable cardioverter defibrillators (ICDs) treat tachyarrhythmia (abnormally fast heart beats) by monitoring the heart; when very rapid heart rhythm is detected, they send electrical impulses or an electrical shock to restore normal rhythm. Within the cardiac resynchronization therapy (CRT), devices synchronize contractions of multiple heart chambers. In mid-2002, the FDA approved Medtronic's InSynch ICD, which offers CRT for heart failure plus advanced defibrillation capabilities for patients also at risk for potentially lethal tachyarrythmias that may lead to sudden cardiac arrest. In March 2003, FDA approval was received for the Insynch Marquis system, which combines the cardiac resynchronization of InSynch devices with state-of-the-art defibrillation therapies of the Marquis ICD platform. MDT also sells external defibrillators.

Neurological and diabetes products (18%) include implantable neurostimulation systems, external and implantable drug administration devices, continuous glucose monitoring systems, hydrocephalic shunts and drainage devices, surgical instruments and diagnostic equipment.

Spinal, ear, nose and throat, and surgical navigation technologies (18%) products, which are used in surgical procedures of the head and spine, include thoracolumbar, cervical and interbody spinal devices, surgical navigation tools and surgical products. In July 2002, the FDA approved MDT's InFuse Bone Graft, a product containing a recombinant human bone morphogenetic protein that induces bone growth after spinal fusions.

Vascular products (10%) include coronary and peripheral stents and related delivery systems, stent grafts for minimally invasive abdominal aortic aneurysm repair, distal embolic protection systems, and a line of catheters, guidewires and accessories.

Cardiac surgery products (7%) include positioning and stabilizing systems for beating heart surgery, perfusion systems, products for the repair and replacement of heart valves, and surgical accessories.

Per Share Data ($) (Year Ended Apr. 30)	2003	2002	2001	2000	1999	1998	1997	1996	1995	1994
Tangible Bk. Val.	2.21	1.10	3.53	2.61	1.99	1.68	1.34	1.41	1.45	1.13
Cash Flow	1.64	1.07	1.10	1.10	0.58	0.63	0.68	0.59	0.43	0.32
Earnings	1.30	0.80	0.85	0.90	0.40	0.48	0.56	0.47	0.32	0.25
S&P Core Earnings	1.10	0.76	0.91	NA	NA	NA	NA	NA	NA	NA
Dividends	0.25	0.20	0.12	0.15	0.12	0.11	0.10	0.08	0.05	0.04
Payout Ratio	19%	25%	14%	16%	30%	23%	17%	17%	16%	17%
Cal. Yrs.	2002	2001	2000	1999	1998	1997	1996	1995	1994	1993
Prices - High	50.69	60.81	62.00	44.62	38.37	26.37	17.46	15.00	6.98	5.96
- Low	32.50	36.64	32.75	29.93	22.71	14.40	11.12	6.54	4.32	3.22
P/E Ratio - High	39	72	61	50	97	55	31	32	22	24
- Low	25	43	32	33	58	30	20	14	14	13
Income Statement Analysis (Million $)										
Revs.	7,665	6,411	5,552	5,015	4,134	2,605	2,438	2,169	1,742	1,391
Oper. Inc.	3,062	2,479	2,176	1,871	1,535	1,017	901	759	543	396
Depr.	408	330	297	243	213	138	117	112	107	63.0
Int. Exp.	7.20	Nil	74.0	13.0	28.8	8.16	9.38	7.96	9.00	8.20
Pretax Inc.	2,341	1,524	1,549	1,630	822	702	809	668	442	347
Eff. Tax Rate	31.7%	35.4%	32.5%	32.6%	43.0%	34.8%	34.5%	34.4%	33.5%	33.0%
Net Inc.	1,600	984	1,046	1,099	468	457	530	438	294	232
S&P Core Earnings	1,347	936	1,121	NA	NA	NA	NA	NA	NA	NA
Balance Sheet & Other Fin. Data (Million $)										
Cash	1,470	411	1,030	448	376	383	251	461	324	181
Curr. Assets	4,606	3,488	3,757	3,013	2,395	1,552	1,238	1,343	1,104	846
Total Assets	12,321	10,905	7,039	5,669	4,870	2,775	2,409	2,503	1,947	1,623
Curr. Liab.	1,813	3,985	1,359	992	990	572	519	525	456	439
LT Debt	1,980	9.50	13.0	14.0	17.6	16.2	13.9	15.3	14.2	20.2
Common Equity	7,906	6,431	5,510	4,491	3,655	2,044	1,746	1,789	1,335	1,053
Total Cap.	10,191	6,674	5,523	4,520	3,703	2,074	1,762	1,850	1,385	1,090
Cap. Exp.	380	386	440	342	226	148	171	164	96.9	86.0
Cash Flow	2,008	1,314	1,343	1,342	681	595	647	549	401	295
Curr. Ratio	2.5	0.9	2.8	3.0	2.4	2.7	2.4	2.6	2.4	1.9
% LT Debt of Cap.	19.4	0.1	0.2	0.3	0.5	0.8	0.7	1.0	1.0	1.9
% Net Inc.of Revs.	20.9	15.3	18.8	21.9	11.3	17.6	21.7	20.1	16.9	16.7
% Ret. on Assets	13.8	11.0	16.5	20.6	11.0	17.6	21.3	19.7	16.5	15.9
% Ret. on Equity	22.3	16.5	20.9	26.6	14.8	24.1	29.5	28.0	24.7	24.5

Data as orig reptd.; bef. results of disc opers/spec. items. Per share data adj. for stk. divs. Bold denotes diluted EPS (FASB 128)-prior periods restated. E-Estimated. NA-Not Available. NM-Not Meaningful. NR-Not Ranked.

Office—710 Medtronic Pkwy., N.E., Minneapolis, MN 55432.**Tel**—(763) 514-4000. **Website**—http://www.medtronic.com **Chrmn & CEO**—A. D. Collins Jr.**Vice Chrmn**—G. D. Nelson. **SVP & CFO**—R. L. Ryan. **Investor Contact**—Tracy Burns (763-505-2692). **Dirs**—R. H. Anderson, M. R. Bonsignore, W. R. Brody, A. D. Collins Jr., A. M. Gotto Jr., B. P. Healy, S. A. Jackson, D. M. O'Leary, J.-P. Rosso, J. W. Schuler, G. M. Sprenger. **Transfer Agent & Registrar**—Wells Fargo Minnesota, N.A., St. Paul. **Incorporated**—in Minnesota in 1957. **Empl**— 30,000. **S&P Analyst:** Robert M. Gold/PMW/BK

LG5 ONLINE INVESTING

Not that many years ago, online investing focused on finding the lowest transaction cost at one of the few discount brokers offering cheap electronic trades. Today, the Internet is a major force in the investing environment. It has opened the world of investing to individual investors, creating a more level playing field and providing access to tools and market information formerly restricted to professionals. Not only can you trade many types of securities online, you can also find a wealth of information, from real-time stock quotes to securities analysts' research reports. Instead of weeding through mounds of paper, investors can quickly sort through vast databases to find appropriate investments, monitor their current investments, and make securities transactions—all without leaving their computers. Even if you prefer to use a human broker, the Internet provides an abundance of resources to help you become a more informed investor.

How can you successfully navigate through the cyberinvesting universe? You probably already have the technology you need: a computer, modem, and an Internet service provider (or ISP, as they are more commonly known). Open your Web browser and you are ready to explore the multitude of investing sites. Typically one site includes a combination of resources for novice and sophisticated investors alike. For example, take a look at Exhibit 11.7, which shows the home page for *E*Trade*, a major online brokerage firm (**http://www.etrade.com**). With a few clicks of the mouse, you can learn about E*Trade's services, open an account, or place an order to trade securities. In addition, you can get a quick overview of recent market activity, obtain price quotes and research reports, or use their services to track a whole portfolio of securities. You can use their site to select stocks, bonds, and mutual funds, get advice on retirement planning and saving for college, go to their Knowledge Center to learn about the markets, even do your banking at their *E*Trade Bank*.

> Financial Road Sign
>
> **Tips for Successful Online Trades**
>
> Before submitting an online stock trade, do the following to protect yourself from common problems:
>
> - Know how to place and confirm your order before your begin trading.
> - Verify the stock symbol of the security you wish to buy (or sell).
> - Use limit orders.
> - Don't get carried away with the ease of online trading. It's easy to churn your account.
> - Double-check orders for accuracy. Review the confirmation notice to make sure each trade was completed according to your instructions.

Online Investor Services

As the E*Trade Web site reveals, the Internet offers a full array of online investor services, from up-to-the-minute stock quotes and research reports to charting services and portfolio tracking. When it comes to investing, you name it and you can probably find it online! Unfortunately, although many of these are truly high-quality sites that offer valuable information, many others are pure garbage, so you have to use care when entering the world of online investing. But even if you confine yourself to the quality sites, the fact is all this information can be overwhelming and even intimidating. It takes time and effort to use the net wisely. Let's take some time here to review the kinds of investor services you can find online, starting with investor education sites.

Investor Education

The Internet offers a wide array of tutorials, online classes, and articles to educate the novice investor. Even experienced investors will find sites that expand their investing knowledge. Although most good investment-oriented Web sites include many educational resources, here are a few good sites that feature *investment fundamentals:*

- *The Motley Fool* (**http://www.fool.com**) *Fool's School* has sections on fundamentals of investing, mutual fund investing, choosing a broker, investment strategies and styles, lively discussion boards and more.
- America Online's (AOL) *Money Basics* (developed with *Smart Money* magazine and for subscribers only) offers Investing 101, which covers basic investment theory, risk management, asset categories, and taxes. Other departments include building and managing your portfolio, investment strategies, and personal finance topics.

EXHIBIT 11.7

Investor Resources Available Online

There's a wealth of investor information and services available online. Here, for example, we see the Investing page for *E*Trade*. By going to this one Web site, you can check the day's market news, get research reports, look up stock quotes, obtain information about specific mutual funds, and more.

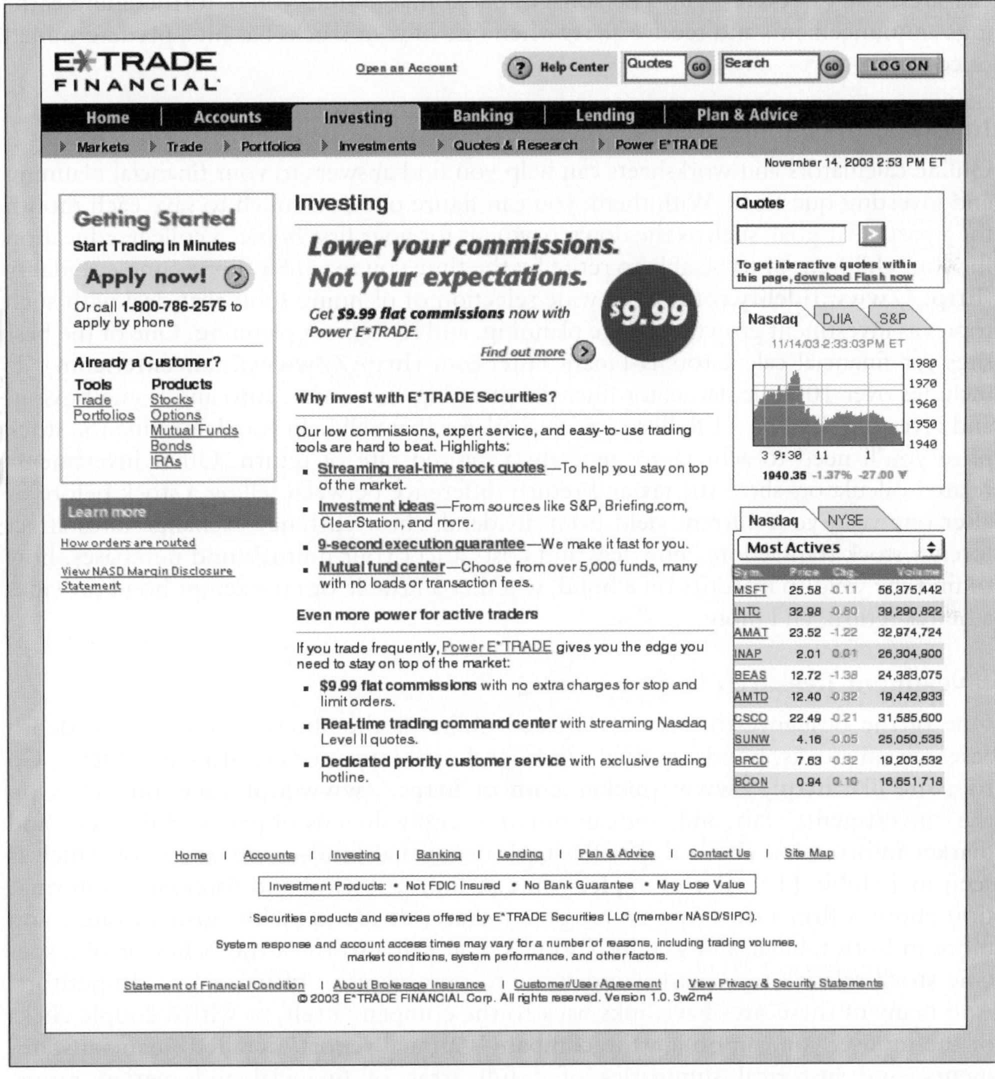

Source: **http://www.etrade.com** (accessed 9/15/03).

- Zacks Investment Research (**http://www.zacks.com**), a free site from *The Wall Street Journal,* is an excellent starting place to learn what the Internet can offer investors.
- Nasdaq (**http://www.nasdaq.com**) has an Investor Resource section that helps with financial planning and choosing a broker.

Other good educational sites include leading personal finance magazines like *Money* (**http://money.cnn.com**), *Kiplinger's Personal Finance Magazine* (**http://www.kiplinger.com**), and *Smart Money* (**http://www.smartmoney.com**).

Investment Tools

Once you're familiar with the basics of investing, you can use the Internet to develop financial plans and set investment goals, find securities that meet your investment objectives, analyze potential investments, and organize your portfolio. Many of these tools, once used only by professional money managers, are free to anyone who wants to go online. You'll find financial calculators and worksheets, screening and charting tools, and portfolio trackers at the Web sites of large brokerage firms, as well as other financial sites. You can even set up a personal calendar that notifies you of forthcoming earnings announcements and receive alerts when one of your stocks has hit a predetermined price target.

Investment Planning

Online calculators and worksheets can help you find answers to your financial planning and investing questions. With them, you can figure out how much to save each month for a particular goal, such as the down payment for your first home, a college education for your children, or to be able to retire by the time you reach 55. For example, Fidelity (**http://www.fidelity.com**) has a wide selection of planning tools that deal with such topics as investment growth, college planning, and retirement planning. One of the best sites for financial calculators is FinanCenter.com (**http://www.financenter.com**). It includes over 100 calculators for financial planning, insurance, auto and home buying, and investing. Exhibit 11.8 illustrates a calculator that will help you determine the stock price you'll need to achieve to generate a desired rate of return. Other investment-related calculators show the tax and return difference between selling a stock before or after one year, your current yield from dividends, how currency exchange rates affect foreign stock transactions, how fees and costs affect your mutual fund purchases, how to find the yield to maturity on a bond, whether a taxable or tax-exempt bond provides a better return, and more.

Investment Research and Screening

One of the best investor services offered online is the ability to conduct in-depth research on stocks, bonds, mutual funds, and other types of investment vehicles. Go to a site like **http://www.quicken.com** or **http://www.kiplinger.com**, click on the "investments" tab, and you can obtain literally dozens of pages of financial and market information about a specific stock or mutual fund—an example of which is seen in Exhibit 11.9. For example, you can find historical and forecasted information about a firm's earnings, earnings per share, dividend yields, growth rates, and more in both tabular and graphic formats; you can also track the behavior of a specific stock relative to a market index, or to one or more of its major competitors. And many of these sites have links back to the company itself, so with a couple clicks of the mouse, you can obtain the company's annual report, detailed financial statements, and historical summaries of a full array of financial and market ratios. Moreover, you'll find sites that offer detailed reports produced by major brokerage firms (some of which require a nominal charge).

In addition to the types of research information described above, investors can also use various *online screening tools* to identify attractive and potentially rewarding investment vehicles. Most major sites, like Quicken, Morningstar, or MSN Money Central, offer screening tools. Basically, these tools enable you to quickly sort through huge databases of stocks and mutual funds to find those that meet specific characteristics, such as

EXHIBIT 11.8

Online Financial Calculators

At sites like **http://www.kiplinger.com**, you'll find calculators, similar to the one shown here, to help you with your investment planning. In this particular case, just input the variables for your situation and the calculator will show you the selling price at which you will earn your desired rate of return.

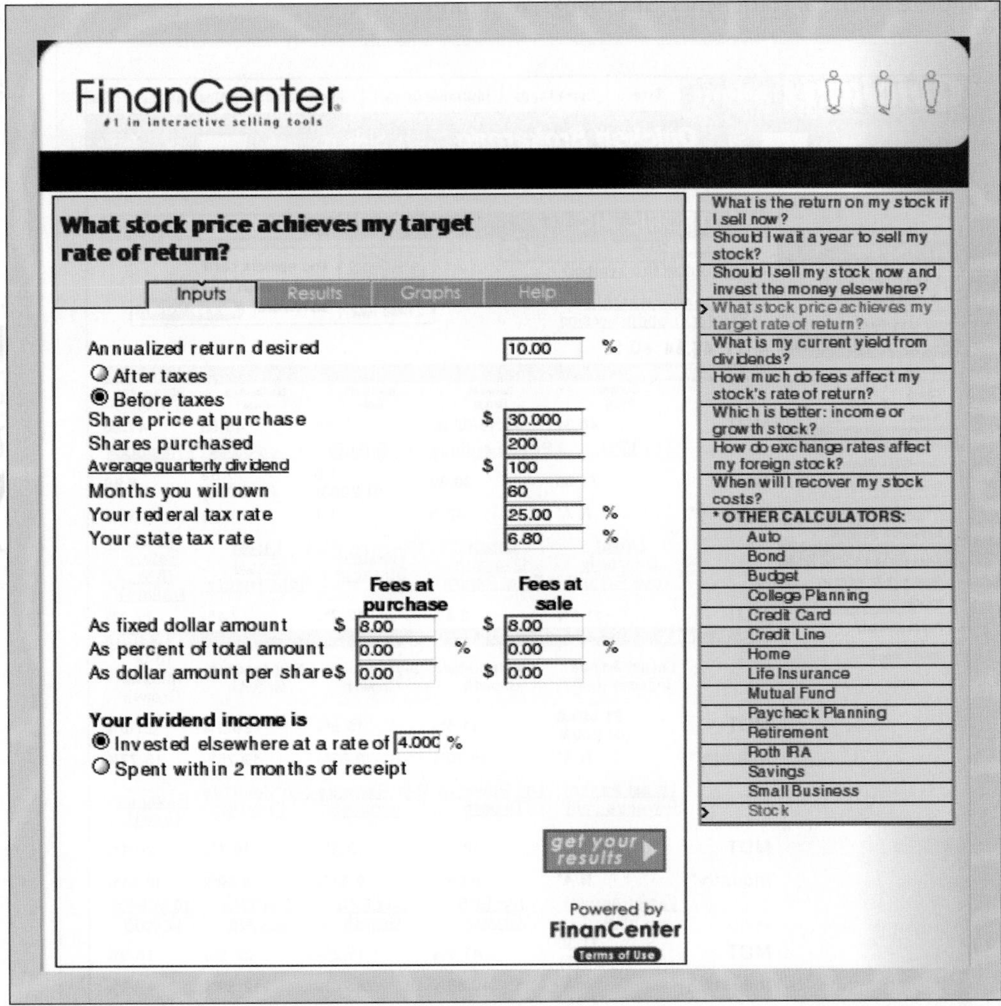

Source: **http://www.financenter.com/consumer/calculate** (accessed 9/15/03).

stocks with low or high P/E multiples, small market capitalizations, high dividend yields, specific revenue growth, and low debt to equity ratios. For mutual funds you might specify a certain type of fund, a particular industry or geographical sector, and low fees. Each screening tool uses a different method to sort. You answer a series of questions to specify the type of stock or fund you're looking for, performance criteria you desire, cost parameters, and so on. The screen then provides a list of stocks (or funds) that have met the standards you've set. You can then do more research (as described above) on the listed stocks (or mutual funds) to decide which ones you want to further pursue.

EXHIBIT 11.9

An Example of Online Investment Research

Here's just a small sample of the type of investment research available online; this Quicken report provides information about the price, valuation, growth, and financial strength of Medtronic, Inc. At this site, you can also obtain stock price and return charts, analysts' ratings, comparative performance, insider trading activity, complete financial statements, SEC filings, and more.

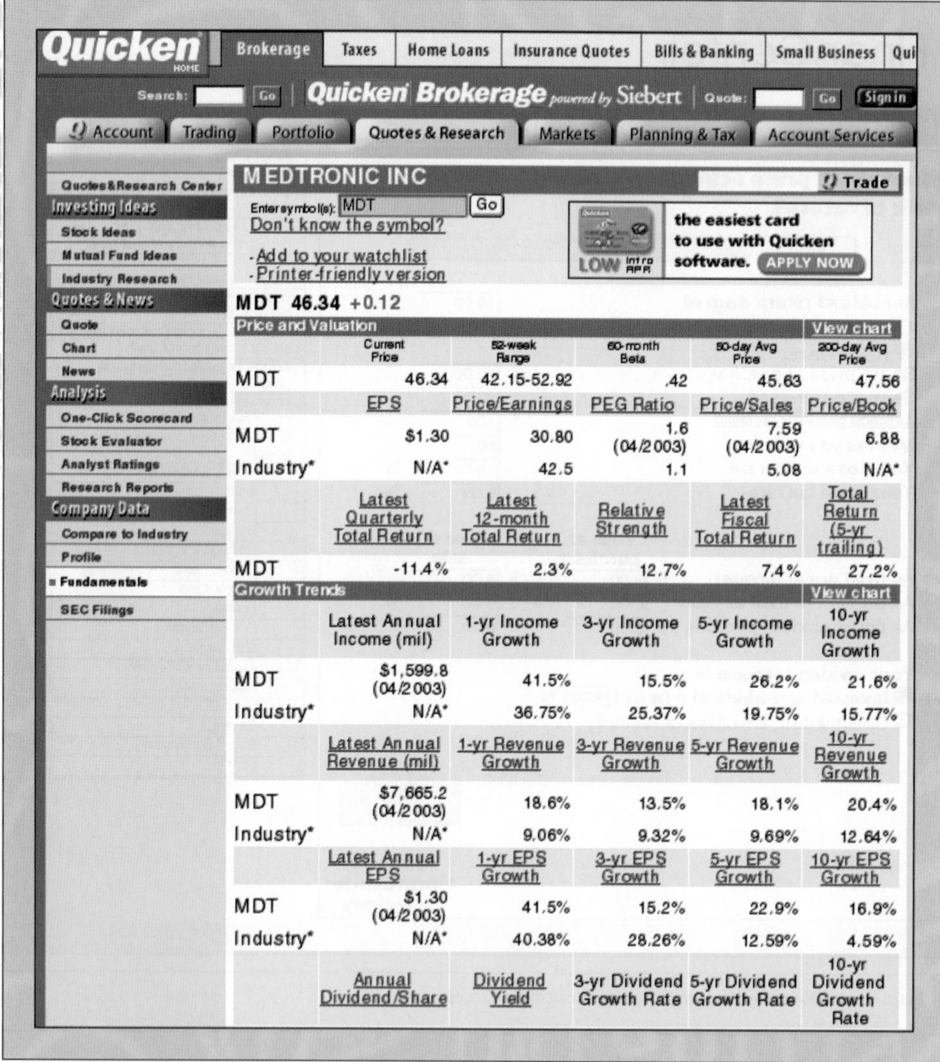

Price and Valuation

	Current Price	52-week Range	60-month Beta	50-day Avg Price	200-day Avg Price
MDT	46.34	42.15-52.92	.42	45.63	47.56

	EPS	Price/Earnings	PEG Ratio	Price/Sales	Price/Book
MDT	$1.30	30.80	1.6 (04/2003)	7.59 (04/2003)	6.88
Industry*	N/A*	42.5	1.1	5.08	N/A*

	Latest Quarterly Total Return	Latest 12-month Total Return	Relative Strength	Latest Fiscal Total Return	Total Return (5-yr trailing)
MDT	-11.4%	2.3%	12.7%	7.4%	27.2%

Growth Trends

	Latest Annual Income (mil)	1-yr Income Growth	3-yr Income Growth	5-yr Income Growth	10-yr Income Growth
MDT	$1,599.8 (04/2003)	41.5%	15.5%	26.2%	21.6%
Industry*	N/A*	36.75%	25.37%	19.75%	15.77%

	Latest Annual Revenue (mil)	1-yr Revenue Growth	3-yr Revenue Growth	5-yr Revenue Growth	10-yr Revenue Growth
MDT	$7,665.2 (04/2003)	18.6%	13.5%	18.1%	20.4%
Industry*	N/A*	9.06%	9.32%	9.69%	12.64%

	Latest Annual EPS	1-yr EPS Growth	3-yr EPS Growth	5-yr EPS Growth	10-yr EPS Growth
MDT	$1.30 (04/2003)	41.5%	15.2%	22.9%	16.9%
Industry*	N/A*	40.38%	28.26%	12.59%	4.59%

	Annual Dividend/Share	Dividend Yield	3-yr Dividend Growth Rate	5-yr Dividend Growth Rate	10-yr Dividend Growth Rate

Source: Intuit, **http://www.quicken.com/investments** (accessed 9/15/03).

Portfolio Tracking

Almost every investment-oriented Web site includes *portfolio-tracking tools*. Simply enter the number of shares held and the symbol for those stocks or mutual funds you wish to follow and the tracker automatically updates the value of your portfolio every time you check. You can usually link to more detailed information about each stock or mutual fund. The features, quality, and ease of use of stock trackers varies, so check several to find the one that meets your needs. Quicken.com, MSN MoneyCentral (**http://investor.msn.com**) and E*Trade (**http://www.etrade.com**) all have portfolio trackers that are easy to set up and use. Quicken's tracker, also available on Excite and AOL, alerts you whenever an analyst changes the rating on one of your stocks or funds and tells you how well you are diversified among the major asset classes or sectors you hold.

smart.sites

For a one-stop financial portal, head to MSN MoneyCentral Investor (**http://moneycentral.msn.com**). You'll find good educational articles, research, interactive tools like Research Wizard, and a portfolio tracker. (Many tools don't run on Macintosh.)

Day Trading

day trader An investor who buys and sells stocks (and other securities) rapidly throughout the day in the hopes of making quick profits.

As discussed earlier, trading stocks (and other securities) online has become very popular among investors—if for no other reason than the rock-bottom cost of executing such trades. Face it, it's an easy, convenient, and low-cost way of trading securities. But for some investors, the attraction of trading stocks online is so compelling that they become day traders. The opposite of buy-and-hold investors with a long-term perspective, **day traders** buy and sell stocks quickly throughout the day. They hope their stocks will continue to rise in value for the very short time they own them—sometimes just seconds or minutes—so they can make quick profits. True day traders do not own any stocks overnight—hence the term *day trader*—because they believe the chance of prices changing radically overnight (from the close on one day to the open on the next) can lead to large losses. While day trading is not illegal or unethical, *it is highly risky.* To compound their risk, day traders usually buy on margin to earn even higher returns. But as we've seen, margin trading also increases the risk of larger losses. Day traders typically incur major financial losses when they start trading. Some never reach profitability. Day traders also have high expenses for brokerage commissions, training, and computer equipment. By some estimates, they must make a 50 to 60 percent profit just to break even on fees and commissions.

USING THE INTERNET WISELY

The power of the Internet as an investing tool is alluring. Do-it-yourself investing is now possible for the average investor, even novices who have never before bought stock. However, online investing also carries risks. The Internet requires investors to exercise the same—and possibly more—caution than they would if they were getting information from and placing orders with a human broker. You don't have the safety net of a live broker suggesting that you rethink your trade. The ease of point-and-click investing can be the financial downfall of inexperienced investors. Drawn by stories of others who have made lots of money, many novice investors take the plunge before they acquire the necessary skills and knowledge—often with disastrous results. Online or off, the basic rules for smart investing are still the same: ***know what you are buying, from whom, and at what level of risk.***

Here are a couple other guidelines you might want to consider when investing online:

- *Do your own research*: Don't take somebody else's word that the security's a good one.

- *Don't let the speed and ease of making online transactions blind you to the realities of online trading*: More frequent trades mean high transaction costs. Although some brokers advertise per-trade costs as low as $2 or $3, the average online transaction fee is higher (just over $20 in January 2003). Studies reveal that the more often you trade, the harder it is to beat the market. Plus, on short-term trades of less than a year, you'll pay taxes on profits at the higher ordinary income tax rates, not the lower capital gains rate.
- *Don't believe everything you read on the Internet*: It's easy to be impressed with a screen full of data touting a stock's prospects or to act on a hot tip you find on a discussion board or online chat room. Stick to the sites of major brokerage firms, mutual funds, academic sites, and well-known business and financial publications.

The bottom line is just be careful and exercise due care. Be skeptical—if it sounds too good to be true, it probably is!

Avoid Online Scams

Before leaving our discussion of online investing, we should say a few words about *online scams*. The fact is, just as the Internet increases the amount of information available to all investors, it also makes it easier for scam artists and others to spread false news and manipulate information. Anyone can sound like an investment expert online, posting stock tips with no underlying substance. The problem is you may not know the real identity of the person touting or panning a hot stock on message boards. The person panning a stock could be a disgruntled former employee or a short seller. In the fast-paced online environment, two types of scams seem to turn up the most: *pump-and-dump* schemes—where promoters hype stocks, quickly send the prices sky-high, and then dump them at inflated prices, and *get-rich-quick scams*—where promoters sell worthless investments to naïve buyers. One well-publicized pump-and-dump scheme demonstrates how easy it is to use the Internet to promote stocks. In September 2000, the SEC caught a 15-year-old boy who made more than $270,000 by promoting small company stocks. The self-taught young investor would buy a block of a company's shares and then send out a barrage of false and misleading e-mail messages and message board posts singing the praises of that stock and the company's prospects. Once this misinformation pushed up the stock price, he sold and moved on to a new target company.

To crack down on cyberfraud, the SEC created the Office of Internet Enforcement. The agency can quickly take action against reports of suspected hoaxes and prosecute the offenders. Former SEC chairman Arthur Levitt cautions investors to remember that the Internet is basically another way to send and receive information, one which has no controls for accuracy or truthfulness. The SEC Web site (**http://www.sec.gov/investor/pubs/cyberfraud.htm**) includes some valuable tips on how to avoid investment scams. Here are three questions every investor should ask:

- *Is the stock registered?* Check the SEC's EDGAR database and with your state securities regulator (**http://www.nasaa.org**).
- *Who is making the sales pitch?* Make sure that the seller is licensed in your state. Check with the NASD to see if they have a record of complaints or fraud.
- *Is it too good to be true?* Then it probably is. Just because it's on the Web doesn't mean it's legitimate.

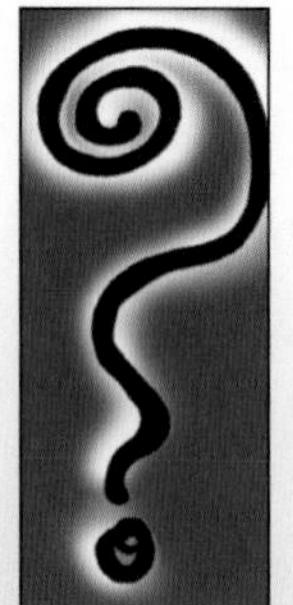

Concept ✓

11.22. Describe the impact the Internet has had on the world of investing. What are some of the products and services that you, as an individual investor, can now obtain online?

11.23. Briefly describe several different types of online investment tools and note how they can help you become a better investor.

11.24. What is *day trading* and how does it differ from the more traditional approach to investing?

11.25. What are some common types of online investment scams and hoaxes? How can you protect yourself from them?

LG6 MANAGING YOUR INVESTMENT HOLDINGS

As noted previously, buying and selling securities is not difficult; the hard part is finding securities that will provide the kind of return you're looking for. Like most individual investors, in time you too will be buying, selling, and trading securities with ease. Eventually, your investment holdings will increase to the point where you are managing a whole portfolio of securities. In essence, a **portfolio** is a collection of investment vehicles assembled to meet a common investment goal. For instance, Bill Hansen's investment portfolio is made up of 150 shares of Cisco Systems, 200 shares of The Home Depot, 100 shares of Wal-Mart Stores, 300 shares of Medtronic, 400 shares of P. F. Chang's China Bistro, and 20 American Greetings convertible bonds. But a portfolio is far more than a collection of investments! For a portfolio breathes life into your investment program; *it's an investment philosophy that provides guidelines for carrying out your investment program.* A portfolio, in effect, combines your personal and financial traits with your investment objectives to give some structure to your investments.

portfolio
A collection of securities assembled for the purpose of meeting common investment goals.

Seasoned investors often devote a good deal of attention to constructing diversified portfolios of securities. Such portfolios consist of stocks and bonds selected not only for their returns but also for their combined risk-return behavior. The idea behind **diversification** is that by combining securities with dissimilar risk-return characteristics, you can produce a portfolio of reduced risk and more predictable levels of return. In recent years, investment researchers have shown that you can achieve a noticeable reduction in risk simply by diversifying your investment holdings. For the small investor with a moderate amount of money to invest, this means that *investing in a number of securities rather than a single one should be beneficial.* The payoff from diversification comes in the form of reduced risk without a significant impact on return. For example, Joan Rainer, who has all of her $30,000 portfolio invested in just one stock (Stock A), might find that by selling two-thirds of her holdings and using the proceeds to buy equal amounts of Stocks B and C, she will continue to earn the same level of return—say, 12 percent—while greatly decreasing the associated risk. Professional money managers emphasize the point that investors should not put all their eggs in one basket but instead should hold portfolios that are diversified across a broad segment of businesses.

diversification
The process of choosing securities having dissimilar risk-return characteristics in order to create a portfolio that will provide an acceptable level of return and an acceptable exposure to risk.

BUILDING A PORTFOLIO OF SECURITIES

Developing a portfolio of investment holdings is predicated on the assumption that diversification is a desirable investment attribute that leads to improved return and/or reduced risk. Again, as emphasized previously, holding a variety of investments is far more desirable than concentrating all your investments in a single security or industry (for example, a portfolio made up of nothing but auto stocks, such as GM, Ford, and Daimler Chrysler, would hardly be well diversified). Of course, when you first start investing, you probably will not be able to do much, if any, diversifying because of insufficient investment capital. However, as you build up your investment funds, your opportunities (and need) for diversification will increase dramatically. Certainly, by the time you have $10,000 to $15,000 to invest, you should start to diversify your holdings. To give you an idea of the kind of portfolio diversification employed by investors, take a look at the following numbers; they show the types of investments held by *average individual investors:*

Type of Investment Product	Percent of Portfolio (August, 2003)
Stocks and stock funds	61.4%
Bonds and bond funds	11.2%
Short-term investments	
(CDs, money mkt. dep. accts., etc.)	27.4%
Total	100.0%

This portfolio reflects the results of a monthly asset allocation survey conducted by the *American Association of Individual Investors*, and shows the portfolio holdings of a typical individual investor. Whether this is what your portfolio should look like depends on a number of factors, including your own needs and objectives.

Investor Characteristics

To formulate an effective portfolio strategy, begin with an honest evaluation of your own financial condition and family situation. Pay particular attention to such variables as:

- Level and stability of income
- Family factors
- Investment horizon
- Net worth
- Investment experience and age
- Disposition toward risk

These are the variables that set the tone for your investments. They determine the kinds of investments you should consider and how long you can tie up your money. For your portfolio to work, it must be tailored to meet your personal financial needs. Your income, family responsibilities, relative financial security, experience, and age all enter into the delicate equation that yields a sound portfolio strategy. For example, a married investor with young children probably would not be interested in high-risk investments until some measure of financial security has been provided for the family. Once that investor has ample savings and insurance protection for the family, he or she may be ready to undertake more risky ventures. On the other hand, a single investor with no family responsibilities would probably be better able to handle risk than one who has such concerns. Simply stated, an *investor's risk exposure should not exceed his or her ability to bear risk.*

The size and certainty of an investor's employment income also has a significant bearing on portfolio strategy. An investor with a secure job is more likely to embark on a more risk-oriented investment program than one with a less secure position. Income taxes bear on the investment decision as well. The higher an investor's income, the more important the tax ramifications of an investment program become. For example, municipal bonds normally yield about 25 to 30 percent less in annual interest than corporate bonds, because the interest income on municipal bonds is tax-free. On an after-tax basis, however, municipal bonds may provide a superior return only if an investor is in a tax bracket of 28 percent or higher.

An individual's investment experience also influences the appropriateness of an investment strategy. Normally, investors assume higher levels of investment risk gradually over time. It is best to "get one's feet wet" in the investment market by slipping into it slowly rather than leaping in head first. Investors who make risky initial investments very often suffer heavy losses, damaging the long-run potential of the entire investment program. A cautiously developed investment program will likely provide more favorable long-run results than an impulsive, risky one. Finally, investors should carefully consider risk. High-risk investments not only have high return potential but also a high risk of loss. Remember, by going for the home run (via a high-risk, high-return investment), the odds of striking out are much higher than by going for a base hit (a more conservative investment posture).

Investor Objectives

Once an investor has developed a personal financial profile, the next question is: "What do I want from my portfolio?" This seems like an easy question to answer. Ideally, we would all like to double our money every year by making low-risk investments. However, the realities of the highly competitive investment environment make this

Financial Road Sign

Some Portfolio Pitfalls

Avoiding these *common mistakes* will make you a better and more successful investor:

- Not defining objectives and priorities for each investment and reviewing them regularly
- Not rebalancing your portfolio every year or so, to keep asset allocation percentages in line
- Owning too many different stocks, bonds, and mutual funds
- Inefficient use of tax strategies
- Paying too much in mutual fund fees
- Excessive stock overlap in various 401(k) and mutual fund holdings

Source: Sue Stevens, "Top 10 Portfolio Pitfalls," *Morningstar.com*, June 15, 2000, downloaded from **http://www.morningstar.com**.

outcome unlikely, so the question must be answered more realistically. There generally is a tradeoff between earning a high current income from an investment and obtaining significant capital appreciation from it. An investor must choose one or the other; it is difficult to obtain both from a single investment vehicle. It is possible, of course, in a *portfolio*, to have a *balance* of both income and growth (capital gains), but more often than not, that involves "tilting" the portfolio one direction (e.g., toward income) or the other (toward growth). The price of having high appreciation potential in the portfolio is low current income potential. One must balance the certainty of high current income and limited price appreciation with the uncertainty of high future price appreciation.

The investor's needs may determine which avenue to choose. For instance, a retired investor whose income depends in part on his or her portfolio will probably choose a lower-risk, current income-oriented approach out of the need for financial survival. In contrast, a high-income, financially secure investor may be much more willing to take on risky investments in the hope of improving his or her net worth. Likewise, a young investor with a secure job may be less concerned about current income and more able to bear risk. This type of investor will likely be more capital-gains oriented and may choose speculative investments. As an investor approaches age 60, the desired level of income likely rises as retirement approaches. The more senior investor will be less willing to bear risk and will want to keep what he or she has, because these investments will soon be needed as a source of retirement income.

Asset Allocation and Portfolio Management

A portfolio must be built around an individual's needs, which, in turn, depend on income, family responsibilities, financial resources, age, retirement plans, and ability to bear risk. These needs shape one's financial goals. But to create a portfolio geared to those goals, you need to develop an **asset allocation** strategy. Basically, all that asset allocation involves is a decision on *how to divide your portfolio among different types of securities.* For example, what portion of your portfolio is going to be devoted to short-term securities, longer bonds and bond funds, and common stocks and equity funds? In asset allocation, emphasis is placed on *preservation of capital.* The idea is to position your assets in such a way that you can protect your portfolio from potential negative developments in the market, while still taking advantage of potential positive developments. Asset allocation is one of the most overlooked yet most important aspects of investing. Indeed, there's overwhelming evidence that, over the long run, *the total return on a portfolio is influenced far more by its asset allocation plan than by specific security selections.*

asset allocation
A plan for dividing a portfolio among different classes of securities in order to preserve capital by protecting the portfolio against negative market development.

Asset allocation deals in broad categories and *does not tell you which individual securities to buy or sell.* It might look something like this:

Type of Investment	Asset Mix
Short-term securities	5%
Longer bonds	
(7- to 10-year maturities)	20%
Equity funds	75%
Total portfolio	100%

Money in *Action*

How to Build a Portfolio When You're Just Starting Out

You've set aside funds for emergencies, developed long-term goals and an investment strategy including an asset allocation plan to reach them, and are ready to start investing. But where do you go from here? The following framework will help you invest wisely so you don't end up with an assortment of investments that do not meet your needs. If your funds are limited at first, start with your largest asset category and add the others as more money becomes available. No matter what asset allocation strategy you choose, you have several ways to make your portfolio grow. You can use mutual funds, individual stocks, or both.

A balanced or asset allocation mutual fund with an asset mix of stock and bonds matching your plan is a conservative approach. It appeals to many novice investors and provides instant diversification among asset classes with just one investment. You can add to this fund regularly until you have enough money—and investment experience—to move into specific fund categories or individual stocks. The main disadvantage to this approach is that you don't control the asset mix.

If you are more daring, you can use a stock index fund which invests in the Standard and Poor 500 as the core of your portfolio. This requires more risk tolerance, because you're starting with just common stocks, but the core fund itself is fairly conservative. Over time, you should be able to ride the market's ups and downs, particularly if you have a long time horizon.

With either strategy, you then diversify into other investment categories to meet allocation goals. If you want to stay with funds, you'd increase your equity percent with a stock fund. Or you may decide to branch out to individual stocks to emphasize a certain sector in your portfolio, although you can also select a sector fund. With the core (index) approach, adding an intermediate bond fund creates your own balanced fund. Or you might buy small-cap or international funds. Don't agonize if you are a few percentage points from your plan; use the target percents as a general guide.

...continued on next page

As you can see, all you're really doing here is deciding how to cut up the pie. You still have to decide which particular securities to invest in. Once you've decided that you want to put, say, 20 percent of your money into intermediate-term (7- to 10-year) bonds, your next step is to select those specific securities. For ideas on how to start your own portfolio, even if you don't have a lot of money, see the *Money in Action* box on this and the next page.

Once you establish your asset allocation strategy, you should check it regularly for two reasons: first, to make sure that your portfolio is in fact in line with your desired asset mix, and, second, to see if that mix is still appropriate for your investment objectives. Here are some reasons to reevaluate your asset allocations:

- A major change in personal circumstances—marriage, birth of a child, loss of a spouse from divorce or death, child graduating from college, loss of job, or family illness, for example—that changes your investment goals.
- The proportion of an asset rises or falls considerably, changing your target allocation for that class by more than, say, 5 percent.
- You're close to reaching a certain goal (such as saving for your child's college or for your retirement).

Periodically, you may find it necessary to *rebalance* your portfolio—that is to reallocate the assets within your portfolio. For example, suppose that your asset allocation plan calls for 75 percent equities and the stock market falls so that stocks represent only 65 percent of your total portfolio. If you are still bullish on the market and stocks are still appropriate for your portfolio, you may view this as a good time to buy stocks and, in so doing, bring your portfolio back up to 75 percent in equities. If your personal goals change, or if you think the market may not recover in the near future, you may decide to change your percentages so as to hold fewer stocks. However, don't be too quick to rebalance every time your portfolio gets a little out of whack; you must allow for some variation in the percentages, as market fluctuations may make it impossible to constantly maintain exact percentages. And don't forget the costs from commissions or sales charges and tax considerations.

Security selection and portfolio management are recurring activities that become an almost routine part of your investment program. You receive an interest or dividend check, and you have to find a place to put it; you add new capital to your investment program, or one of the Treasury notes you're holding matures, and you have to decide what to do with the money. These events occur with considerable regularity, so you're likely to be faced with a series of little (and sometimes not so little) investment decisions over time. This, in short, is portfolio management: the initial construction and ongoing administration of a collection of securities and investments.

Portfolio management involves the buying, selling, and holding of various securities for the purpose of meeting a set of predetermined investment needs and objectives. To give you an idea of portfolio management in action, Exhibit 11.10 provides examples of four different portfolios, each developed with a particular financial situation in mind. Note that in each case the asset allocation strategies and portfolio structures change with the different financial objectives. The first one is the *newlywed couple;* in their late twenties, they earn $58,000 a year and spend just about every cent. They have managed to put away some money, however, and are quickly beginning to appreciate the need to develop a savings program. Next there is the *two-income couple*; in their early forties, they earn $115,000 a year and are concerned about college costs for their children, ages 17 and 12. Next is the *divorced mother;* she is 34, has custody of her children, ages 7 and 4, and receives $40,000 a year in salary and child support. Finally, we have the *older couple;* in their mid-fifties, they are planning for retirement in 10 years, when the husband will retire from his $95,000-a-year job.

Keeping Track of Your Investments

Keeping track of your investment holdings is essential to a well-managed securities portfolio. Just as you need investment objectives to provide direction for your portfolio, so too do you need to *monitor* it by keeping informed about what your investment holdings consist of, how they have performed over time, and whether they have lived up to your expectations. Sometimes investments fail to perform the way you thought they would. Their return may be well below what you would like, or perhaps you may even have suffered a loss. In either case, it may be time to sell the investments and put the money elsewhere. A monitoring system for keeping track of your investments should allow you to identify such securities in

Building a portfolio of individual stocks takes more time and discipline than the fund route. Dividend reinvestment plans (DRPs), offered by about 1,000 companies, are a way for an investor with limited funds to buy stocks and also keep expenses down. After you own at least one share of stock, you can reinvest dividends in more shares and buy stock directly from the company, usually without a fee. Be sure to study the shareholder information packages and DRP prospectuses from companies that interest you.

Diversify with shares in a variety of industries and economic sectors, and include growth, value, and income stocks. Include both U.S. and foreign stocks. Your goal should be about 10 to 15 companies, but focus on quality, not quantity; four good stocks are better than 10 bad ones. Know whether you can buy more shares monthly or quarterly.

Remember to invest regularly in your funds or stocks, every month or pay period if possible. Be patient and stick with your investment strategy, even if returns aren't as high as you'd like. Unless you hold your investments for a while, transaction costs and taxes will wipe out profits. With the market's volatility, you're bound to have down periods. Remember you chose this plan for the long term, so being consistent should pay off over time. Stick with your target asset allocation percentages, reviewing your holdings regularly and rebalancing your portfolio as needed. Rebalancing controls risk by preventing overinvestment in one sector. You'll be surprised how quickly your investments grow.

Critical Thinking Questions:

1. Why should you develop an investment strategy before you make your first securities purchase?
2. Which of the strategies suggested in the box would you choose for yourself, and why?
3. Describe your plan for researching potential mutual funds or stocks you'd like to buy for your portfolio.

Sources: Adapted from Jonathan Clements, "Make Sure to Stay the Course," *San Diego Union-Tribune*, September 21, 2003, p. H7; Karen Hube et al., "Time to Check Your Investment Strategy," *The Wall Street Journal*, January 6, 2000, pp. C1, C18; John A. Prestbo, "We Have a Winner," *SmartMoney.com*, August 12, 2003, downloaded from **http://www.smartmoney.com**; and Maria Crawford Scott, "How to Implement Your Strategy If You Are Starting from Scratch," *AAII Journal*, February 1995, pp. 18–20.

your portfolio. In addition, it should enable you to stay on top of the holdings that are performing to your satisfaction. Knowing when to sell and when to hold can have a significant impact on the amount of return you are able to generate from your investments—certainly it will help you keep your money fully invested.

EXHIBIT 11.10

Four Model Portfolios

The type of portfolio you put together will depend on your financial and family situation as well as on your investment objectives. Clearly, what is right for one family may be totally inappropriate for another.

Family Situation	Portfolio
Newlywed couple:	80 to 90 percent in common stocks, with three-quarters of that in mutual funds aiming for maximum capital gains and the rest in growth-and-income or equity-income funds 10 to 20 percent in a money market fund or other short-term money market securities
Two-income couple:	60 to 70 percent in common stocks, with three-quarters of that in blue chips or growth mutual funds and the remainder in more aggressive issues or mutual funds aiming for maximum capital gains 25 to 30 percent in discount Treasury notes whose maturities correspond with the bills for college tuition 5 to 10 percent in money market funds or other short-term money market securities
Divorced mother:	40 to 50 percent in money market funds or other short-term money market securities 50 to 60 percent in growth and income mutual funds
Older couple:	60 to 70 percent in blue-chip common stocks, growth funds, or value funds 25 to 30 percent in municipal bonds or short- and intermediate-term discount bonds that will mature as they start to need the money to live on 5 to 10 percent in CDs and money market funds

You can use something like Worksheet 11.2 to keep an inventory of your investment holdings. All types of investments can be included on this worksheet—from stocks, bonds, and mutual funds to real estate and savings accounts. To see how it works, consider the investment portfolio that has been built up over the last 15 years or so by John and Mary Maffeo, a two-income couple in their early fifties. As the figures in Worksheet 11.2 reveal, John and Mary hold common and preferred stock in five companies, three bond issues, two mutual funds, some real estate, and two savings accounts. In addition to the type and description of the investment vehicles, the worksheet contains the dates the investments were made (the purchase date is needed for tax purposes), the original amount of the investment, the amount of annual income currently being earned from it, and its latest market value. (Using such a worksheet in conjunction with an online portfolio tracker would provide an investor with plenty of information about the performance of his or her portfolio—the *worksheet* providing long-term information from the date of purchase of an asset, and the *online portfolio trackers* providing year-to-date or annual returns.)

Concept ✓

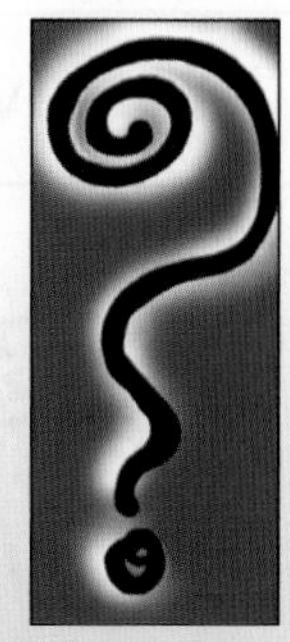

11-26. Explain why it might be preferable for a person to invest in a *portfolio* of securities rather than in a single security. Be sure to mention risk and return in your response.

11-27. Briefly describe the concept of *asset allocation* and note how it works. Give an example of an asset allocation scheme. Discuss the role that asset allocation plays in the management of a portfolio.

11-28. What, if anything, can be gained from keeping track of your investment holdings?

Worksheet 11.2 lists all the investments John and Mary held as of December 2004, regardless of when they were purchased. In contrast, any securities/investments sold during the year (2004) would not be included. A report like this should be prepared at least once a year; when completed, it will provide a quick overview of your investment holdings and let you know where you stand at a given point in time. Note that the Maffeos earn almost $4,500 a year from their investments and that—thanks, in large part, to their investments in a couple of stocks and stock funds—their holdings have grown from around $100,000 to more than $460,000! In fact, they have only one security that is not doing too well—Pall Corp. All the rest are quite profitable.

smart.sites

One of the best portfolio trackers is in the Investing section of MSN Money's offering, **http://moneycentral.msn.com/investor/home.asp**. It's free with registration and provides maximum flexibility is setting up your reporting options.

worksheet 11.2

Keeping Tabs on Your Investment Holdings

A worksheet like this one will enable you to keep track of your investment holdings and identify investments that are not performing up to expectations.

AN INVENTORY OF INVESTMENT HOLDINGS

Name(s): John & Mary Maffeo Date: December 2004

Type of Investment	Description of Investment Vehicle	Date Purchased	Amount of Investment (Quote—$ Amount)	Amount of Annual Income from Dividends, Interest, etc.	Latest Market Value (Quote—$ Amount)	Comments/ Planned Actions
Common stock	250 shares-McDonald's	12/8/90	8.25-$2,062	$230	23.50 (now 1,000 shs.)-$23,500	A keeper
Common stock	300 shares-Disney	10/20/92	15-$4,500	$190	20.00 (now 900 shs.)-$18,000	Another keeper
Common stock	400 shares-Pall Corp.	4/10/93	23.50-$9,400	$145	22.60 (now 400 shs.)-$9,040	DUMP IT!
Common stock	150 shares-Intel	8/11/95	8.50-$1,275	$96	28.00 (now 1,200 shs.)-$33,600	Doing great...
Preferred stock	100 shares-Dupont pf 4.50	1/26/89	50.75-$5,075	$450	62.25-$6,225	
Corporate bond	$5,000-Pacific Telephone 7 1/4-17	8/19/92	75 1/2-$3,775	$363	94 3/4-$4,738	
Corporate bond	$7,000-Texaco 5 3/4-17	2/27/87	39 1/4-$2,748	$402	94 1/2-$6,615	
Treasury bond	$6,000-U.S. Treasury 7 1/2-15	10/4/95	62-$3,720	$450	102-$6,120	
Mutual fund	1,300 shares-Vanguard Health Care	6/16/89	9.08-$11,800	$120	108.50-$141,050	A great fund!!
Mutual fund	725 shares-Clipper Fund	12/12/92	17.72-$12,850	$994	79.80-$57,855	Stay with it...
Real estate	Four-plex at 1802 N. 75 Ave.	9/16/87	$140,000-$28,000	N/A	(est.) $250,000-$138,000	Time to sell?
Savings	1-year/6.5% CD at First National Bank	6/10/00	N/A-$10,000	$650	N/A-$10,000	
Savings	Money Fund at Paine Webber	3/13/95	N/A-$7,200	$340	N/A-$7,200	
	Totals		$102,369	$4,430	$461,943	

Instructions: List number of shares of *common and preferred stock* purchased as part of the description of securities held; then put the price paid *per share* under the "Quote" column and total amount invested (number of shares × price per share) under the "$ Amount" column. Enter the principal (par) value of all bonds held in place of number of shares: "$ Amount" column for bonds = principal value of bonds purchased × quote (for example, $5,000 × .755 = $3,775). List *mutual funds* as you did for stock. For *real estate*, enter total market value of property under "Quote" column and amount actually invested (down payment and closing costs) under "$ Amount." Ignore the "Quote" column for *savings* vehicles. For "Amount of Income" column, list total amount received from dividends, interest, and so on (for example, dividends per share × number of shares held). Under "Latest Market Value," enter market price as of the date of this report (for instance, in December 2001, Pall Corp. was trading at 18.50). The latest market value for real estate is entered as an estimate of what the property would likely sell for (under "Quote") and the estimated amount of equity the investor has in the property (under "$ Amount").

SUMMARY

LG1. Discuss the role that investing plays in the personal financial planning process and identify several different investment objectives. Investing plays an important part in personal financial planning, as it is the vehicle through which many of your financial goals can be reached. Your investment activities should be based on a sound investment plan that is linked to an ongoing savings plan. Most people invest their money to enhance their current income, accumulate funds for a major expenditure, save for retirement, or shelter some of their income from taxes.

LG2. Distinguish between primary and secondary markets, as well as listed exchanges and the over-the-counter market. Stocks, bonds, and other long-term securities are traded in the capital, or long-term, markets. Newly issued securities are sold in the primary markets, whereas transactions between investors occur in the secondary markets. Listed securities are traded on organized exchanges, such as the New York and American stock exchanges, as well as on a number of smaller regional exchanges. In contrast, the over-the-counter (OTC) market handles thousands of unlisted securities.

LG3. Explain the process of buying and selling securities and recognize the different types of orders. The securities transaction process starts when you call and place an order with your broker, who then transmits it via sophisticated telecommunications equipment to the floor of the stock exchange or the OTC market, where it is promptly executed and confirmed. Investors can buy or sell securities in odd or round lots by simply placing one of the three basic types of orders: a market order, limit order, or stop-loss order.

LG4. Develop an appreciation of how various forms of investment information can lead to better investing skills and returns. Becoming an informed investor is essential to developing a sound investment program. Vital information about specific companies and industries, the securities markets, the economy, and different investment vehicles and strategies can be obtained from such sources as annual stockholders' reports, brokerage and advisory service reports, and the financial press. In addition, the personal computer is rapidly becoming a popular source of investment information.

Various averages and indexes, such as the Dow Jones Industrial Average, the Standard & Poor's Indexes, and the NYSE, AMEX, and Nasdaq indexes, provide information about daily market performance. These averages and indexes not only measure performance in the overall market, they also provide standards of performance for specific types of stocks, such as transportation issues, banks, insurance companies, and public utilities.

LG5. Gain a basic understanding of the growing impact that the computer and the Internet are having on the field of investments. The computer and the Internet have empowered individual investors by providing information and tools formerly available only to investing professionals, thereby greatly simplifying the investing process. The savings they provide in terms of time and money are huge. Investors get the most current information, including real-time stock price quotes, market activity data, research reports, educational articles, and discussion forums. Tools such as financial planning calculators, stock screening programs, and portfolio tracking are free at many sites. Buying and selling securities online is convenient, simple, inexpensive, and fast.

LG6. Describe an investment portfolio and how you'd go about developing and managing a portfolio of securities. While an investment portfolio represents a collection of the securities/investments you hold, it also provides a focus and purpose to your investing activities. Developing a well-diversified portfolio of investment holdings enables an investor to not only achieve given investment objectives, but also enjoy reduced exposure to risk and a more predictable level of return. To develop such a portfolio, the investor must carefully consider his or her level and stability of income, family factors, financial condition, experience and age, and disposition toward risk. Designing an asset allocation strategy, or mix of securities, that's based on these personal needs and objectives is also an important part of portfolio management. You should monitor your investment portfolio regularly to measure its performance and make changes as required by return data and lifecycle factors.

FINANCIAL PLANNING EXERCISES

1. ***Use Worksheet 11.1*** Erin Coates is a young career woman who's presently employed as the managing editor of a well-known business journal. While she thoroughly enjoys her job and the people she works with, what she would really like to do is open a bookstore of her own. In particular, she would like to open her store in about 8 years, and she figures she'll need about $50,000 in capital to do so. Given that she thinks she can make about 10 percent on her money, use Worksheet 11.1 to find the following:
   a. How much would Erin have to invest today, in one lump sum, to end up with $50,000 in 8 years?
   b. If she's starting from scratch, how much would she have to put away annually to accumulate the needed capital in 8 years?
   c. How about if she already has $10,000 socked away; how much would she have to put away annually to accumulate the required capital in 8 years?
   d. Given Erin now has an idea of how much she has to save, briefly explain how she could use an *investment plan* to help her reach her objective.
2. Assume that the following quote for Financial Learning Systems (a NYSE stock) appeared in the Thursday, August 10th issue of *The Wall Street Journal*:

   16.4 29.62 17.75 FinLrnSys FLS 1.64 5.5 24 2779 29.70 0.32

   Given this information, answer the following questions:
   a. On what day did the trading activity occur?
   b. At what price did the stock sell at the end of the day on Wednesday, August 9?
   c. How much (in percentage terms) has the price of this stock gone up or down since the first of the year?
   d. What is the stock's price/earnings ratio? What does that indicate?
   e. What is the last price at which the stock traded on the date quoted?
   f. How large a dividend is expected in the current year?
   g. What are the highest and lowest prices at which the stock traded during the latest 52-week period?
   h. How many shares of stock were traded on the day quoted?
   i. How much, if any, of a change in price took place between the day quoted and the immediately preceding day? At what price did the stock close on the immediately preceding day?

3. Listed below are three pairs of stocks. Look at each pair and select the security you would like to own, given that you want to *select the one that's worth more money.* Then, *after* you make all three of your selections, use *The Wall Street Journal* or some other source the find the latest market value of the two securities in each pair.
   a. 50 shares of Berkshire Hathaway (stock symbol BRKA) or 150 shares of Coca-Cola (stock symbol KO). (Both are listed on the NYSE.)
   b. 100 shares of WD-40 (symbol WDFC—a Nasdaq National Market issue) or 100 shares of Nike (symbol NKE—a NYSE stock).
   c. 150 shares of Wal-Mart (symbol WMT) or 50 shares of Sears (symbol S). (Both are listed on the NYSE.)

   How many times did you pick the one that was worth more money? Did the price of any of these stocks surprise you? If so, which one(s)? Does the price of a stock represent its value? Explain.
4. Assume that Cecile Higgins places an order to buy 100 shares of Kodak; explain how the order will be processed if it is a market order. Would it have made any difference if it had been a limit order? Explain.
5. Sarah Jordan wants to buy 300 shares of PepsiCo, which is currently selling in the market for $45 a share. Rather than liquidate all her savings, she decides to borrow through her broker. Assume the margin requirement on common stock is 50 percent and the brokerage firm charges 9 percent interest on margin loans. What would be the interest cost on the transaction if Sarah sold the stocks at the end of 1 year? If the stock rises to $60 a share by the end of the year, show the kind of profit (in dollars) and return (in percentages) Sarah would earn if she makes the investment with 50 percent margin; contrast this to what she would make if she uses no margin.
6. Which of the following would offer the best return on investment? Assume that you buy $5,000 in stock in all three cases; also, ignore interest costs in all your calculations.
   a. Buy a stock at $80 without margin, and sell it at $120 one year later.
   b. Buy a stock at $32 with 50 percent margin, and sell it one year later at $41.
   c. Buy a stock at $50 with 75 percent margin, and sell it in one year at $65.
7. How much profit (if any) would Buster Summers make if he short sold 300 shares of stock at $75 a share and the price of the stock suddenly tumbled to $60?
8. Given that Humphrey Dog Toys Inc.'s stock is currently selling for $50 a share, calculate the amount of money that Elmer D. will make, or lose, on each of the following transactions (assume that all transactions involve 100 shares of stock, and ignore brokerage commissions).
   a. He short sells and then repurchases the borrowed shares at $60.
   b. He buys the stock and then sells it some time later at $60.
   c. He short sells and then repurchases the borrowed shares at $35.
9. Assume that an investor short sells 500 shares of stock at a price of $65 a share, using 50 percent margin. A year later, she repurchases the borrowed shares at $45 a share.
   a. How much of her own money did the short seller have to put up to make this transaction?
   b. How much money did the investor make, or lose, on this transaction?
   c. What rate of return did she make on her invested capital?

10. Why do you suppose that large, well-known companies such as Oracle, Starbucks, and JDS Uniphase prefer to have their shares traded on the Nasdaq National Market, rather than on one of the major organized exchanges, such as the NYSE (for which they'd easily meet all listing requirements)? What's in it for them? What would they gain by switching over to the NYSE?
11. Using a resource like *The Wall Street Journal* or *Barron's* (either in print or online), find the latest values for each of the following market averages and indexes, and indicate how each has performed over the past 6 months:
    a. DJIA
    b. Dow Jones U.S. Total Market
    c. S&P 500
    d. NYSE Composite
    e. AMEX index
    f. Nasdaq Composite
    g. MidCap 400
    h. Wilshire 5000
    i. Russell 2000
12. Using the stock quotations in Exhibit 11.5, find the 52-week high and low for *Dillards Department Stores* common stock (stock symbol: DDS). How much does the stock pay annually in dividends, and what is its latest dividend yield? How many shares of Dillards changed hands (were traded), what was the closing price, and at what P/E ratio was the stock trading? There are 27 stocks listed in Exhibit 11.5; which one has had the largest year-to-date increase in price? The largest drop in price? Which three stocks had the highest dividend yields, and which three had the highest closing prices?
13. Using the S&P report in Exhibit 11.6, find the following information as it pertains to Medtronic:
    a. What was the amount of revenues (that is, sales) the company generated in 2003?
    b. What were the latest annual dividends per share and dividend yield?
    c. What were the earnings (per share) projections for 2004?
    d. What were the number of common shares outstanding?
    e. What was the book value per share and earnings per share in 2003?
    f. Where is the stock traded?
    g. How much long-term debt did the company have in 2003?
    h. When was the company formed and who is the chairman and CEO?
    i. What was the company's effective tax rate in 2003?
14. The following is an *Online Investing* question and requires access to the Internet. First, go to the Quicken Web site at **http://www.quicken.com**, click on the "Brokerage" tab from the menu along the top, then enter the stock symbol MDT (for Medtronic) in the "Quotes & Research" box and hit "Go." Now, from the menu on the left, click on "Compare to Industry"; this site will enable you to compare the performance of Medtronic, Inc. to some of its close competitors. Select any three companies from the list provided (e.g., St. Jude Medical), then choose

"Fundamentals" and press the "Compare" key. Briefly review the comparative information provided and answer the following questions:

a. Of the four stocks shown (Medtronic and the three firms you selected), which one has the best 12-month return? Which one has the poorest?
b. Which stock has the best total 5-year return?
c. Rank the four stocks (from best to worst) in terms of their 1-year income growth rates (%).
d. Which stock has the highest annual EPS (earnings per share)?
e. Which stock pays the most in annual dividends?
f. Which stock has the highest market cap? Which has the lowest?
g. Which stock is currently trading at the highest market price; which is trading at the lowest price?
h. Based on the information shown, if you had to select ONE of these four stocks, which would it be? Briefly explain why.

15. ***Use Worksheet 11.2*** to help Rebecca and Andrew Cook, a married couple in their early 30s, evaluate their securities portfolio, which includes the following holdings:

a. *Adams Express* (NYSE—stock symbol: ADX): 100 shares bought in December 1994 for $18 per share (stock had a 3 for 2 split in 2000, so the Cooks now own 150 shares of ADX).
b. *Fannie Mae* (NYSE—stock symbol: FNM): 250 shares purchased in December 1995 for $24.25 per share (stock had a 4 for 1 stock split in 1996, so the Cooks now own 1000 shares of FNM).
c. *Bed Bath and Beyond* (Nasdaq—stock symbol: BBBY): 150 shares purchased in 1997 at $8.75 per share (stock has since had *two* 2 for 1 stock splits, so the Cooks now own 600 shares of BBBY).
d. *Starbucks* (Nasdaq—stock symbol: SBUX): 200 shares purchased in 1998 at $15.25 per share (stock split 2 for 1 in 1999, so the Cooks now own 400 shares of SBUX).
e. The Cooks also have $8,000 in a 3-year *bank CD* that pays 6.15 percent annual interest.

   1. Based on the latest quotes obtained from *The Wall Street Journal*, or elsewhere, complete Worksheet 11.2.
   2. What's the total amount the Cooks invested in these securities, the annual income they now receive, and the latest market value of their investments?

Applying Personal Finance

Research Your Investments!

Investing involves making informed decisions and researching companies and industries ahead of time, before you plunk down your hard-earned money! An excellent source of information about a company is from the company itself, particularly its annual report to stockholders. The purpose of this project is to examine the annual stockholders' report of a company in which you are interested.

The annual report is a document that provides financial and operating information about a company to its owners, the stockholders. Obtain a copy of the latest annual report of the company you are researching. Copies can be found in many public and college libraries, local brokerage offices, or the company's Web site. Carefully study the annual report and prepare a *Corporate Profile* of the firm you selected. Include the following:

a. Name of the company, its ticker symbol, and the exchange on which it trades.
b. Current market price of the stock and its percentage change from 1, 3, and 5 years ago. Try to find a chart of its stock price.
c. Location of its corporate headquarters, names of its officers, and percentage of inside ownership.
d. Brief description of the company, including its major products or services.
e. Brief history of the company
f. Major competitors
g. Sales and profit summaries
h. Other relevant financial ratios and measures
i. Recent developments and future plans

Based on your findings, would you consider this company for a potential investment? Why or why not?

CONTEMPORARY CASE APPLICATIONS

11.1 The Thomsons Struggle with Two Investment Goals

Like a lot of married couples, Steve and Barbara Thomson are trying their best to save for two very important investment objectives: (1) an education fund to put their two children through college and (2) a retirement nest egg for themselves. They want to have set aside $40,000 per child by the time each one starts college. Given that their children are now 10 and 12 years old, Steve and Barbara have 6 years remaining for one child and 8 with the other. As far as their retirement plans are concerned, the Thomsons both hope to retire in 20 years when they reach age 65. Both Steve and Barbara work, and together they currently earn about $90,000 a year.

Six years ago, the Thomsons started a college fund by investing $6,000 a year in bank CDs. That fund is now worth $45,000—enough to put one child through an in-state college. In addition, they have $50,000 which they received from an inheritance invested in several mutual funds and another $20,000 in a tax-sheltered retirement account. Steve and Barbara feel they'll easily be able to continue to put away $6,000 a year for the next 20 years. In fact, Barbara thinks they'll be able to put away even more, particularly after the children are out of school. The Thomsons are fairly conservative investors and feel they can probably earn about 8 percent on their money. (Ignore taxes for the purpose of this exercise.)

Questions

1. *Use **Worksheet 11.1*** to determine whether the Thomsons have enough money right now to meet the educational needs of their children. That is, will the $45,000 they've accumulated so far be enough to put their children through school, given they can invest their money at 8 percent? Remember, they want to have $40,000 set aside for each child by the time each one starts college.
2. Regarding their retirement nest egg, assuming that no additions are made to either the $50,000 they now have in mutual funds or the $20,000 in the retirement account, how much would these investments be worth in 20 years, given they can earn 8 percent?

3. Now, if they can invest $6,000 a year for the next 20 years and apply all of that to their retirement nest egg, how much would they be able to accumulate given their 8 percent rate of return?
4. How do you think the Thomsons are doing with regard to meeting their twin investment objectives? Explain.

11.2 Col Takes Stock of His Securities

Col Thomas is 32 years old, single, and works as a designer for a major architectural firm. He is well paid and over time has built up a sizable portfolio of investments. He considers himself an aggressive investor and, because he has no dependents to worry about, likes to invest in high-risk/high-return securities. His records show the following:

1. In 1997, Col bought 400 shares of eBay (Nasdaq; symbol: EBAY) at $4 a share—the stock has since spilt 2 for 1 *three times*, so he now owns 800 shares of the stock.
2. In 1998 he bought 250 shares of WD-40 Co. (Nasdaq; symbol: WDFC) at $30 a share.
3. In 1997, Col bought 200 shares of Franklin Resources (NYSE; symbol: BEN) at $52 a share—Col now owns 400 shares, because the stock has since split 2 for 1.
4. In early 1999, he bought 450 shares of Fisher Scientific (NYSE; symbol: FSH) at $17.50 a share.
5. Also in 1999, Col bought 400 shares of P.F. Chang's China Bistro (Nasdaq; symbol: PFCB) at $18.75 a share—Col now owns 800 shares of the stock, because it split 2 for 1 in 2002.
6. He has $12,000 in a 3-percent money market mutual fund.

Every 3 months or so, Col prepares a complete, up-to-date inventory of his investment holdings.

Questions

1. Use a form like Worksheet 11.2 to prepare a complete inventory of Col's investment holdings. (*Note:* Look in the latest issue of *The Wall Street Journal* or pull up an online source such as **http://finance.yahoo.com** to find the most recent closing price of the five stocks in Col's portfolio.)
2. What is your overall assessment of Col's investment portfolio? Does it appear that his personal net worth is improving as a result of his investments?
3. Based on the worksheet you prepared in Question 1, do you see any securities that you think Col should consider selling? What other investment advice might you give Col?

Money Online

Master the Markets!

1. **http://www.ftc.gov/bcp/conline/edcams/investment/index.html**

Does that investment offer sound too good to be true? Then it probably is! Search the Federal Trade Commission's site for investment alerts, scams, and frauds. Then click the links to other Investment Information Resources. While you're there, scroll down to Online Quiz, and click on "Test Your Investment I.Q."

2. **http://www.smartmoney.com/marketmap**

What color is the market today? Pull up SmartMoney's fantastic "Map of the Market" to view the performance of over 600 companies at once! Click on the map's Control Panel to see the top five market gainers or losers for various time periods. Use this wonderful tool to create a map of your own portfolio. (Be patient while map loads!)

3. **http://www.nyse.com**
Become an educated investor! The New York Stock Exchange presents *A Guide to the World's Leading Securities Market*, seven chapters of informative material on the markets and investing. To find the guide, look under "About the NYSE." Click on "Education" and then on "Educational Publications." For other great educational material, click on "Other Resources" and browse through the many offerings.

4. **http://www.gomez.com**
Find the broker that's right for you. Choose "Benchmarks" at the Gomez Web site to see how online financial services firms rank in key areas. Under "Scorecards," choose "Broker-Discount" to see the top firms. You may sort the list according to your needs. Read the reviews and find the broker that best suits your investing style.

5. **http://www.investorguide.com**
Take charge of your own investing! The InvestorGuide Web site was designed specifically to provide a one-stop site for the needs of Internet investors. Find the latest news, research your investments, or link to the home pages of thousands of companies. Be sure to check out their university!

6. **http://www.investorguide.com/womensites.html**
Find sites designed with women in mind. InvestorGuide provides numerous links to sites that cover great topics such as personal finance, investing, and starting your own business.

7. **http://www.ino.com**
Interested in options? Visit INO.com, the site that specializes in the futures and options markets, serving traders worldwide with a continuous information service of quotes, charts, and news. INO also offers a storefront for trading tools, charts, publications, educational courses, and other resources.

8. **http://www.fool.com**
Learn investing wisdom from the Fool. Go to Fool's School and work your way through the "13 Steps to Investing Foolishly." Tap into the Fool's stock research information or learn more about investing strategies, retirement, or personal finance.

9. **http://personal.fidelity.com**
Learn from the investing master! Find the "Planning Center" located under "Planning & Retirement" at Fidelity's Web site. Then read through *Peter Lynch on Investing* to learn more about the market and long-term financial planning.

Just for Fun!

10. **http://www.fantasystockmarket.com**
Play trade with $100,000 Fantasy Dollars! Let Fantasy Stock Market track your portfolio and rank you against the other players. Even better, create a league for your class. See how your returns compare to the others in your league, and then see how your league stacks up against the other leagues.

11. **http://www.nyse.com**
Experience the excitement! Visit "The Trading Floor" at the Web site of the New York Stock Exchange. Click on "Anatomy of a Trade" for a step-by-step account of how trades are executed or "On the Floor" for a panorama of the trading floor. Which NYSE company has been listed the longest? Check the FAQs under "Listed Companies."

CHAPTER 12 Investing in Stocks and Bonds

Learning Goals

LG1. Describe the various types of risks to which investors are exposed, as well as the sources of return.

LG2. Know how to search for an acceptable investment, based on risk, return, and yield.

LG3. Discuss the merits of investing in common stock and be able to distinguish among the different types of stocks.

LG4. Become familiar with the various measures of performance and how to use them in putting a value on stocks.

LG5. Describe the basic issue characteristics of bonds and note how these securities are used as investment vehicles.

LG6. Distinguish between the different types of bonds, gain an understanding of how bond prices behave, and know how to compute different measures of yield.

The Seven Year Itch

Lifelong friends Allen Stockman and Benjamin Bonder had a history of doing things the same way at the same time. Now in their late 20s, married, and with one child, each started a college fund with $25,000 on their children's first birthdays. Despite frequent get-togethers, investment strategies had never been a topic of conversation. When Allen asked Ben how he planned to invest his portfolio, the pair discovered that they had different investment philosophies and tolerances for risk.

Allen loved the thrill of investing in stocks and focused on growth rather than income. He quickly became enamored with the extensive reach of technology and e-commerce companies. In 1996, he invested the $25,000 exclusively in stocks, almost all of which were in the telecommunications sector. Using the standard rule of 72 to determine how quickly his money would double at current average investment rates, Allen expected the portfolio to be worth $200,000, if he didn't withdraw funds, when his oldest child would turn 21. Over the first four years he saw the college fund, as well as his other investments, also all in stocks, grow at exponential rates averaging almost 25 percent per year.

Benjamin, while fascinated with new technology and Internet transactions, didn't feel comfortable investing in them. He looked more for the steady yield from fixed income vehicles and put 60 percent of the $25,000 college funds in bonds—two government-issued municipals and one corporate-issued zero-coupon. With the remaining 40 percent, Benjamin invested in common stocks from large, well established companies he remembered his grandfather talking about, such as General Electric and Ford Motor Company, as well as some financial institutions like Citigroup. He knew that someone his age would usually have a larger percentage of growth stocks than income securities, but he wisely recognized he couldn't handle the uncertainty on which Allen seemed to thrive. He also wanted a more diversified portfolio—not just in terms of security types but also industry exposure.

After the first seven years, when Allen expected his $25,000 to be worth $50,000, the college fund was worth less than $7,000 while Benjamin's fund was worth approximately $37,500. Allen learned the hard way that he needed to do more homework on his stocks and monitor his portfolio more closely. In Chapter 12 you'll learn how to evaluate stocks and bonds so that you, too, can be an informed investor.

CRITICAL THINKING QUESTIONS

As you review the chapter, consider these questions in relation to Allen's and Benjamin's college fund investing:

- How would you describe Allen's risk tolerance and why is assessing an investor's risk tolerance so important?
- Discuss reasons for allocating common stock investments across several industry sectors.
- What role do bonds play in portfolios focused on the long term?

THE RISKS AND REWARDS OF INVESTING

LG1, LG2

Most rational investors are motivated to buy or sell securities based on the security's expected (or anticipated) return—buy if the return looks good, sell if it doesn't. Of course, it's a lot more complex than that, but this statement pretty much describes the role that *return* plays in the investment decision-making process. A security's return, however, is just part of the story, for you cannot consider the return on an investment without also looking at its *risk*—the chance that the actual return from an investment may differ from (i.e., fall short of) what was expected. Generally speaking, you'd expect riskier investments to provide higher levels of return. Otherwise, what incentive is there for an investor to risk his or her capital? These two concepts of risk and return are of vital concern to investors and as such, before we take up the issue of investing in stocks and bonds, we'll look more closely at the risks of investing and the various components of return. Equally important, we'll see how these two components (risk and return) can be used together to find potentially attractive investment vehicles.

THE RISKS OF INVESTING

As noted previously, when selecting investments, you should look at potential returns and the level of perceived risk to which the investment is exposed. The fact is, just about any type of investment is subject to one type of risk or another—some more than others. The basic types of investment risk are business risk, financial risk, market risk, purchasing power risk, interest rate risk, liquidity risk, and event risk. Obviously, other things being equal, you'd like to reduce your exposure to these risks as much as possible.

Business Risk

When you invest in a company, you may have to face up to the possibility that the firm will fail to maintain sales and profits, or even stay in business. Such failure is due either to economic or industry factors or, as is more often the case, to poor decisions on the part of management. In a general sense, this is **business risk**; it may be thought of as the degree of uncertainty surrounding the firm's earnings and subsequent ability to meet principal and interest payments on time. Companies that are subject to high degrees of business risk generally experience wide fluctuations in sales, have widely erratic earnings, and can, in fact, experience substantial operating losses every now and then.

business risk
The degree of uncertainty associated with a firm's earnings and subsequent ability to pay interest and dividends.

Financial Risk

Financial risk relates to the amount of debt used to finance the firm. Look to the company's balance sheet to get a handle on a firm's financial risk. As a rule, companies that have little or no long-term debt are fairly low in financial risk. This is particularly so if a company has a healthy earnings picture as well. The problem with debt financing is that it creates principal and interest obligations that have to be met regardless of how much profit the company is generating. As with business risk, financial risk can lead to failure (as in the case of bankruptcy), or a rate of return that is sharply below your expectations.

financial risk
A type of investment risk associated with the mix of debt and equity financing used by the issuing firm.

smart.sites
What's your investment risk tolerance? Take a few quizzes at the Investor Education Fund site, **http://www.investored.ca/en/interactive/games_quizzes_risk.htm** and find out more about your risk profile and investing style.

Market Risk

market risk A type of investment risk associated with the price volatility of a security.

Market risk results from the behavior of investors in the securities markets. The fact is, prices of stocks and bonds will sometimes change even though business and financial risks, and other intrinsic factors, stay about the same. Such changes may have little to do with the securities themselves but instead are due to changes in political, economic, and social conditions or in investor tastes and preferences. Essentially, market risk is reflected in the *price volatility* of a security—the more volatile the price of a security, the greater its perceived market risk.

Purchasing Power Risk

purchasing power risk A type of risk, resulting from possible changes in price levels, that can have a significant effect on investment returns.

Possible changes in price levels within the economy also result in risk. In periods of rising prices (inflation), the purchasing power of the dollar declines. This means that a smaller quantity of goods and services can be purchased with a given number of dollars. An awareness of **purchasing power risk** and changes in purchasing power allows investors to select investments that are best suited for a given price level environment. In general, investments whose values tend to move with general price levels (like stocks or real estate) are most profitable during periods of rising prices, whereas those providing fixed returns (like bonds) are preferred during periods of low or declining price levels/inflation.

Interest Rate Risk

fixed-income securities Securities such as bonds, notes, and preferred stocks that offer purchasers fixed periodic returns.

interest rate risk A type of risk, resulting from changing market interest rates, that mainly affects fixed-income securities.

Fixed-income securities, which include notes, bonds, and preferred stocks, offer investors a fixed periodic return and, as such, are most affected by **interest rate risk**. As interest rates change, the prices of these securities fluctuate, decreasing with rising interest rates and increasing with falling rates. For example, the prices of fixed-income securities drop when interest rates increase, in order to provide investors with rates of return that are more competitive with those securities offering higher levels of interest income. Changes in interest rates are the result of fluctuations in the supply of or demand for money. These fluctuations are caused by various economic actions of the government or the interactions of business firms, consumers, and financial institutions.

Liquidity Risk

liquidity (or **marketability**) **risk** A type of risk associated with the inability to liquidate an investment conveniently and at a reasonable price.

The risk of not being able to liquidate (i.e., sell) an investment conveniently and at a reasonable price is called **liquidity** (or **marketability**) **risk**. The liquidity of a given investment vehicle is important because it provides investors with a safety valve in case they ever have to get out. In general, investment vehicles traded in *thin markets*, in which supply and demand are small, tend to be less liquid than those traded in *broad markets*. However, to be liquid, an investment must not only be easily salable, but also must be so *at a reasonable price*. One can generally enhance the liquidity of an investment merely by cutting its price. For example, a security recently purchased for $1,000 would not be viewed as highly liquid if it could be sold only at a significantly reduced price, such as $500. Vehicles such as mutual funds, or the stocks and bonds of major companies listed on the New York Stock Exchange, are generally highly liquid; others, such as an isolated parcel of raw land in rural Georgia, are not.

Event Risk

More than just a buzz word used by the financial media, **event risk** is real, and it can have a direct and dramatic impact on investment return. Basically, it occurs when something substantial happens to a company and that event, in itself, has a sudden impact on the company's financial condition. Event risk goes beyond business and financial risk, and it doesn't necessarily mean the company or market is doing poorly. Instead, it involves an event that is largely (or totally) unexpected, and that which has a significant and usually immediate effect on the underlying value of an investment. A good example of event risk was the action by the Food and Drug Administration several years ago to halt the use of silicone breast implants. The share price of Dow Chemical—the dominant producer of this product—was quickly affected (in a negative fashion) as a result of this single event! Event risk can take many forms, although fortunately its impact tends to be confined to specific companies, securities, or segments of the market.

event risk The risk that some major, unexpected event will occur, leading to a sudden, substantial change in the value of an investment.

smart.sites
At RiskGrades (**http://www.riskgrades.com**) you can compare the risk of a particular stock or your portfolio with the overall market.

The Returns from Investing

Any investment vehicle—be it a share of stock, a bond, a piece of real estate, or a stock option—has just two basic sources of return: *current income* and *capital gains.* Some investments offer only one source of return (for example, options provide only capital gains), but many offer both income and capital gains, which together make up what is known as the *total return* from an investment. Of course, where both elements of return are present, the relative importance of each will vary among investments. For example, whereas current income is more important with bonds, capital gains usually make up a larger portion of total return in the case of common stocks.

Current Income

Current income is generally received with some degree of regularity over the course of a year, and may take the form of dividends on stock, interest from bonds, or rents from real estate. People who invest to obtain income look for investment vehicles that will provide regular and predictable patterns of income. Preferred stocks and bonds, which are expected to pay known amounts at specified times (quarterly or semiannually, for example), are usually viewed as good income investments.

Capital Gains

The other type of return available from investments is capital appreciation (or growth), which is reflected in an increase in the market value of an investment vehicle. Capital gains occur when you're able to sell a security for more than you paid for it, or when your security holdings go up in value. Investments that provide greater growth potential through capital appreciation normally have lower levels of current income, because the firm achieves its growth by reinvesting its earnings instead of paying dividends out to the owners. Many common stocks, for example, are acquired for their capital gains potential.

Interest-on-Interest: An Important Element of Return

Question: When does an 8 percent investment end up yielding only 5 percent? Answer: Probably more often than you think! Of course, it can happen when investment performance fails to live up to expectations. But it can also happen even when everything goes right. That is, so long as at least part of the return from an investment involves the periodic receipt of current income (such as dividends or interest payments), that income has to be *reinvested* at a given rate of return in order to achieve the yield you thought you had going into the investment. To see why that's so, consider an investor who buys an 8 percent U.S. Treasury bond and holds it to maturity, a period of 20 years. Each year the bondholder receives $80 in interest, and at maturity, the $1,000 in principal is repaid. There is no loss in capital, no default; everything is paid right on time. Yet this sure-fire investment ends up yielding only 5 percent. Why? Because the investor failed to reinvest the annual interest payments he was receiving. By not plowing back all the investment earnings, the bondholder failed to earn any *interest-on-interest.*

Take a look at Exhibit 12.1. It shows the three elements of return for an 8 percent, 20-year bond: (1) the recovery of principal, or capital gain, if any is earned; (2) periodic interest income; and (3) the interest-on-interest earned from reinvesting the periodic interest payments. Observe that because the bond was originally bought at par ($1,000), you start off with an 8 percent investment. Where you end up depends on what you do with the profits (interest earnings) from this investment. If you don't reinvest the interest income, you'll end up on the 5 percent line.

EXHIBIT 12.1

Three Elements of Return for an 8 Percent, 20-Year Bond

As seen here, the long-term return from an investment (in this case, a bond) is made up of three parts: recovery of capital, current income, and interest-on-interest; of the three components, interest-on-interest is particularly important, especially for long-term investments.

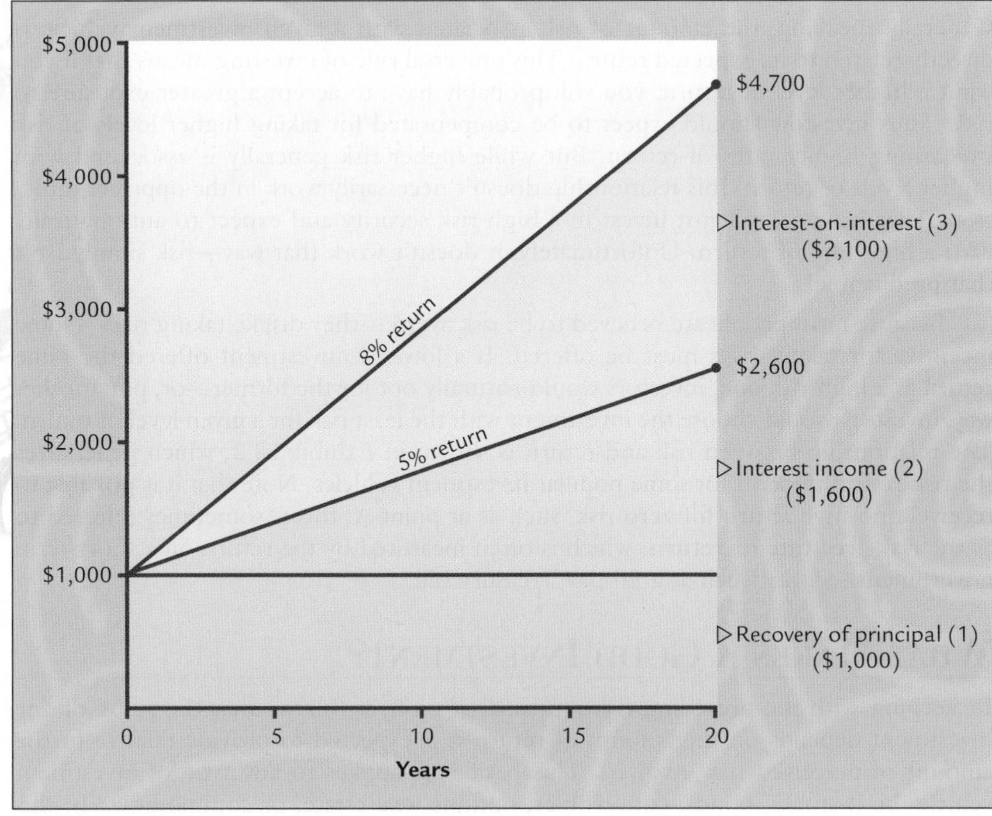

To move to the 8 percent line, you have to earn interest-on-interest from your investments. Specifically, because you started out with an 8 percent investment, that's the rate of return you have to earn when reinvesting your income. The rate of return you start with, in effect, is the required, or minimum, reinvestment rate. Put your investment profits to work at that rate and you'll earn the rate of return you set out to; fail to do so and your return will decline accordingly. And keep in mind that even though we used a bond in our illustration, as long as current income is part of an investment's return, *this same principle applies to any type of long-term investment vehicle.* It's just as relevant to common stocks and mutual funds as it is to long-term bond instruments. This notion of earning interest-on-interest is what the market refers to as a *fully compounded rate of return.* It's an important concept because you can't start reaping the full potential from your investments until you start earning a fully compounded return on your money.

Thus, if periodic investment income is a part of your investment return, the reinvestment of that income and interest-on-interest are matters you're going to have to deal with. In fact, *interest-on-interest is a particularly important element of return for investment programs that involve a lot of current income.* This is so because, in contrast to capital gains, current income has to be reinvested by the individual investor. (With capital gains, the investment vehicle itself is doing the reinvesting, all automatically.) It follows, therefore, that if your investment program tends to lean toward income-oriented securities, then interest-on-interest—and the continued reinvestment of income—will play an important role in defining the amount of investment success you have.

The Risk-Return Tradeoff

Generally speaking, the amount of risk associated with a given investment vehicle is directly related to its expected return. This universal rule of investing means that if you want a higher level of return, you will probably have to accept a greater exposure to risk. Thus investors should expect to be compensated for taking higher levels of risk by earning higher rates of return. But while higher risk generally is associated with higher levels of return, this relationship doesn't necessarily work in the opposite direction. That is, you can't just invest in a high-risk security and expect to automatically earn a high rate of return. Unfortunately, it doesn't work that way—risk simply isn't that predictable!

Because most people are believed to be risk averse—they dislike taking risks—some incentive for taking risks must be offered. If a low-risk investment offered the same return as a high-risk one, investors would naturally opt for the former—or, put another way, investors would choose the investment with the least risk for a given level of return. The relationship between risk and return is shown in Exhibit 12.2, which generalizes the risk-return tradeoff for some popular investment vehicles. Note that it is possible to receive a positive return for zero risk, such as at point A; this is sometimes referred to as the **risk-free rate of return**, which is often measured by the return on a short-term government security, such as a 90-day Treasury bill.

risk-free rate of return
The rate of return on short-term government securities, such as Treasury bills, that is free from any type of risk.

What Makes a Good Investment?

In keeping with the preceding risk-return discussion, it follows that the value of any investment depends on the amount of return it is expected to provide relative to the amount of perceived risk involved. This basic rule applies to any type of investment vehicle, be it stocks, bonds, convertibles, options, real estate, or commodities. In this respect, they should all be treated the same.

EXHIBIT 12.2

The Risk-Return Relationship

In the field of investments, there generally is a direct relationship between risk and return: the more risk you face, the greater the return you should expect to generate from the investment.

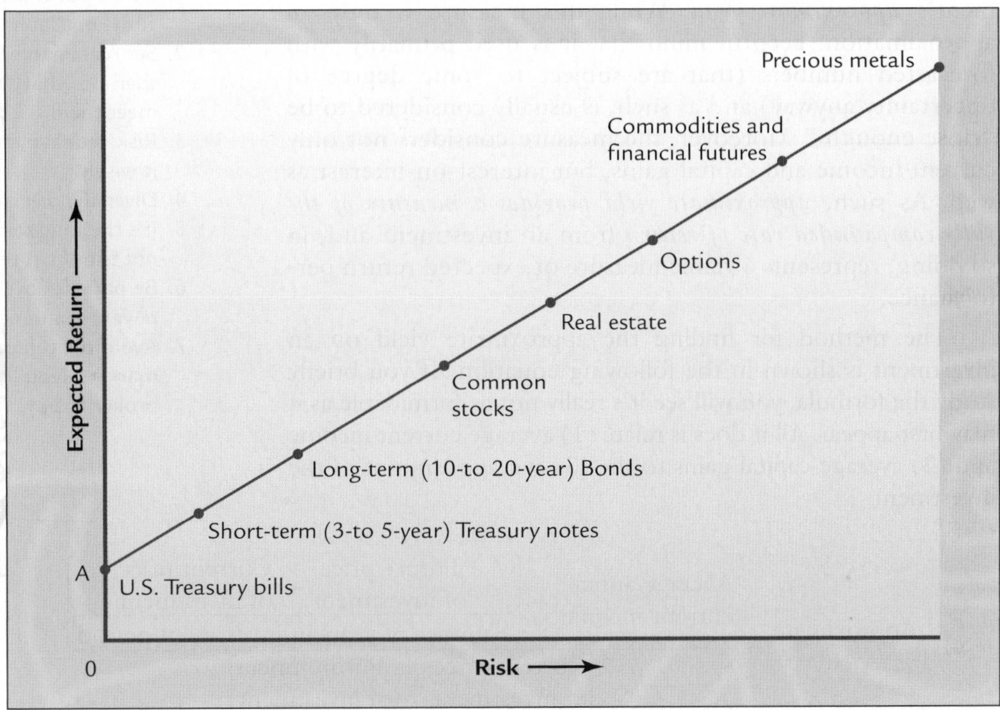

Future Return

In the field of investments, the only return that matters is *the expected future return.* Aside from the help they can provide in getting a handle on future income, past returns are of little value to investors—after all, it is not what the security did last year that matters, but, rather, what it is expected to do next year.

Earlier, we defined returns as being made up of current income and capital gains. To get an idea of the future return on an investment, we must formulate expectations of its future current income and future capital appreciation. To illustrate, assume you are thinking of buying some stock in Rose Colored Glasses, Inc. (RCG). By reviewing several financial reports, you have come up with an estimate of the future dividends and price behavior of RCG as follows:

Expected average annual dividends, 2004–06	\$2.15 a share
Expected market price of the stock, 2006	\$95.00 a share

Because the stock is now selling for \$60 a share, the difference between its current and expected future market price (\$95 − \$60) represents the amount of *capital gains* you can expect to receive over the next three years—in this case, \$35 a share. The projected future price, along with expected average annual dividends, provides you with an estimate of the *stock's future income stream;* what you need now is a way to measure *expected return.*

Approximate Yield

Finding the exact rate of return on an investment involves a highly complex mathematical procedure—one that's very difficult to determine without the aid of a hand-held financial calculator (which we'll demonstrate below). There is, however, a fairly easy way to obtain a reasonably close estimation of expected return, and that is to compute an investment's *approximate yield.* While this measure is only an approximation, keep in mind that it is used primarily with forecasted numbers (that are subject to some degree of uncertainty anyway) and as such, is usually considered to be "close enough." Moreover, the measure considers not only current income and capital gains, but interest-on-interest as well. As such, *approximate yield provides a measure of the fully compounded rate of return* from an investment and, in so doing, represents a viable measure of expected return performance.

The method for finding the approximate yield on an investment is shown in the following equation. If you briefly study the formula, you will see it's really not as formidable as it may first appear. All it does is relate (1) average current income and (2) average capital gains to the (3) average amount of the investment.

Financial Road Sign

The 7 Pillars of Effective Investing

Here are some guidelines to follow if you want to get the most from your investment capital:

1. Don't put it off—start investing early, not later.
2. Set reasonable savings goals and then do what's necessary to meet them.
3. Risk is unavoidable, so manage it wisely.
4. Diversify, diversify, diversify.
5. It's the long term that matters, not the short term.
6. Be patient—over time, the market rewards patience.
7. Avoid the temptation to time the markets—you'll only make your broker happy.

$$\text{Approximate yield} = \frac{\text{Average annual current income} + \left[\dfrac{\text{Future price of investment} - \text{Current price of investment}}{\text{Number of years in investment period}}\right]}{\left[\dfrac{\text{Current price of investment} + \text{Future price of investment}}{2}\right]}$$

$$= \frac{CI + \left[\dfrac{FP - CP}{N}\right]}{\left[\dfrac{CP + FP}{2}\right]}$$

where

CI = *average* annual current income (amount you expect to receive annually from dividends, interest, or rent)

FP = expected future price of investment

CP = current market price of investment

N = investment period (length of time, in years, that you expect to hold the investment)

To illustrate, let's use the Rose Colored Glasses example again. Given the average annual dividends (CI) of \$2.15, current stock price (CP) of \$60, future stock price (FP) of \$95, and an investment period (N) of 3 years (you expect to hold the stock from

2004 through 2006), you can use this equation to find the expected approximate yield on RCG as follows:

$$\text{Approximate yield} = \frac{\$2.15 + \left[\frac{\$95 - \$60}{3}\right]}{\left[\frac{\$60 + \$95}{2}\right]} = \frac{\$2.15 + \left[\frac{\$35}{3}\right]}{\left[\frac{\$155}{2}\right]} = \frac{\$2.15 + \$11.67}{\$77.50} = \frac{\$13.82}{\$77.50} = \underline{\underline{17.8\%}}$$

In this case, if your forecasts of annual dividends and capital gains hold up, an investment in Rose Colored Glasses should provide a return of around 17.8 percent per year.

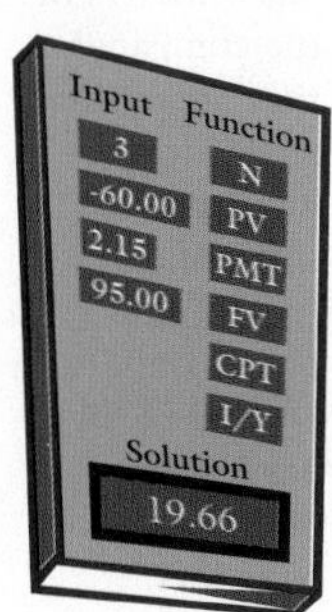

Calculator Keystrokes. You can easily find the *exact* return on this investment with the help of a hand held financial calculator. Here's what you do: First, put the calculator in the *annual compounding* mode. Then, to find the expected return on a stock that you buy at $60 a share, hold for 3 years (during which time you receive average annual dividends of $2.15 a share), and then sell at $95, use the keystrokes shown in the margin, where:

N = number of *years* you hold the stock,

PV = the price you pay for the stock (entered a *negative* number),

PMT = *average* amount of dividends received *each year*,

FV = the price you expect to receive when you *sell* the stock (in 3 years).

You'll notice there's a difference in the computed yield measures (17.8 percent with the approximate procedure vs. 19.7 percent here); that's to be expected, since one is only an approximate measure of performance, whereas this is an exact, and more accurate, measure.

Whether you should consider RCG a viable investment candidate depends on how this level of expected return stacks up to the amount of risk you must assume. Suppose that you have decided the stock is moderately risky. To determine whether the expected rate of return on this investment will be satisfactory, you can compare it to some benchmark. One of the best is the rate of return you can expect from a *risk-free* security, such as a *U.S. Treasury bill.* The idea is that the return on a *risky* security should be greater than that available on a risk-free security (this is the concept underlying the graph in Exhibit 12.2). If, for example, U.S. T-bills are yielding, say, 5 or 6 percent, then you'd want to receive considerably more—perhaps 12 to 15 percent—to justify your investment in a moderately risky security like RCG. In

Concept ✓

12-1. Describe the various types of risk to which investors are exposed. What is meant by the risk-return tradeoff? What is the *risk-free rate of return?*

12-2. Briefly describe the two basic sources of return to investors. What is interest-on-interest, and why is it such an important element of return?

12-3. What is the *approximate yield* measure and how would it be used to make an investment decision? What is the *desired rate of return* and how would it be used to make an investment decision?

essence, the 12 to 15 percent is your **desired rate of return**—it is the minimum rate of return you feel you should receive in compensation for the amount of risk you must assume. *An investment should be considered acceptable only if it's expected to generate a rate of return that meets (or exceeds) your desired rate of return.* In the case of RCG, the stock *should be considered a viable investment candidate*, because it more than provides the minimum or desired rate of return. In short, even after factoring in the perceived exposure to risk, the stock still generates a sufficiently attractive expected return—one that comfortably *exceeds* the amount you desire, based on the risks involved.

desired rate of return The minimum rate of return an investor feels should be earned in compensation for the amount of risk assumed.

INVESTING IN COMMON STOCK

LG3, LG4

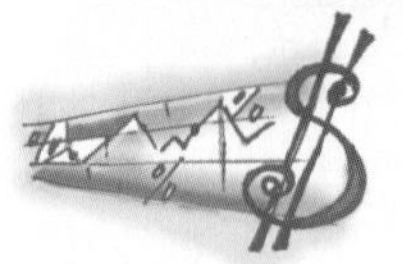

Common stocks appeal to investors for a variety of reasons. To some, investing in stocks is a way to hit it big if the issue shoots up in price; to others, it is the level of current income they offer. In fact, given the size and diversity of the stock market, it is safe to say that no matter what the investment objective, there are common stocks available to fit the bill. Not surprisingly, common stocks are a popular form of investing, used by literally millions of individuals and a variety of financial institutions.

The basic investment attribute of a share of common stock is that it enables the investor to participate in the profits of the firm, which is how it derives its value. Every shareholder is, in effect, a part owner of the firm and, as such, is entitled to a piece of its profit. However, this claim on income is not without its limitations, for common stockholders are really the **residual owners** of the company, meaning they are entitled to dividend income and a prorated share of the company's earnings only after all the other obligations of the firm have been met. Equally important, as residual owners, *holders of common stock have no guarantee that they will ever receive any return on their investment.*

residual owners Shareholders of the company, they are entitled to dividend income and a share of the company's profits only after all of the firm's other obligations have been met.

smart.sites

At StarMine Investor, **http://investor.starmine.com**, a free service for individual investors, you'll discover which securities analysts have been the most accurate in estimating a company's earnings and see StarMine's own earnings forecasts.

COMMON STOCKS AS A FORM OF INVESTING

Given the underlying nature of common stocks, when the market is strong, investors can generally expect to benefit from steady price appreciation. A good example is the performance in 1999, when the market, as measured by the Dow Jones Industrial Average (DJIA) went up more than 25 percent. Unfortunately, when markets falter, so do investor returns. Just look what happened over the 3-year period from early 2000 through late 2002, when the market (again, as measured by the DJIA) fell some 38 percent. Excluding dividends, that means a $100,000 investment would have declined in value to a little over $60,000.

Make no mistake about it: The market does have its bad days, and sometimes those bad days seem to go on for months. Even though it may not always appear to be so, those bad days *really are the exception rather than the rule.* That was certainly the case over the 50-year period from 1953 through 2003, when the Dow went down (for the year) just 16 times. That's 30 percent of the time; the other 70 percent, the market was up—anywhere from around 2 percent on the year to over 40 percent! True, there is some risk and price volatility (even in good markets), but that's the price you have to pay for all that upside potential. Consider, for example, the behavior of the market from 1982 through early 2000. Starting in August 1982, when the Dow stood at 777, this market saw the DJIA climb nearly 11,000 points to a high of 11,723, reached in January 2000. This turned out to be one of the longest bull markets in history, as the DJIA grew (over 18 years) at an annual rate of nearly 17 percent. Yet, even in this market, there were some off days, and even a few off years. But, clearly, they were the exception rather than the rule.

A Tech Stock Bubble

The bull market that started in 1982 continued on through the 1980s and into the early 1990s. Except for the length of this market, it didn't appear to be out of the ordinary in any other way—at least through the first half of the nineties. Indeed, the average rate of growth in share prices through 1994 was just 12 percent. But then in 1995, 1996, and 1997, things began to heat up, and the average rate of growth in share prices jumped to over 27 percent. And by 1998, *the tech stock bubble* was in full bloom. This is readily apparent in Exhibit 12.3, which tracks the behavior of the DJIA and the Nasdaq Composite over the 10-year period ending mid-2003.

As can be seen, in August 1998, the tech-heavy Nasdaq Composite began to skyrocket and over the next 18 months, went up an incredible 240 percent. Outright speculation was in firm control of the market—price/earnings multiples (a widely used measure of market sentiment) went through the roof and, in fact, it really didn't seem to matter whether companies were generating earnings or not. These kinds of details, we were told, really weren't important any more; the only thing that seemed to matter was whether the stock had a technology or internet connection! That, of course, all come to a screeching halt in early 2000. The three major market indexes—the DJIA, the Nasdaq Composite, and the S&P 500—all peaked in early 2000; the Dow at 11,722.98, the Nasdaq at 5048.62, and the S&P500 at 1527.46. Over the course of the next 32 months, through September 2002, these market measures fell flat on their collective faces; that is:

- The Dow fell 38 percent.
- The S&P dropped percent.
- The Nasdaq fell percent.

This turned out to be one of the worst bear markets in recent history and clearly had a devastating effect on investor returns. All the excesses that had built up over the last half of the 1990s were eliminated in a little over 2½ years.

Issuers of Common Stock

Shares of common stock can be issued by any corporation in any line of business. Even so, although all corporations have stockholders, not all of them have publicly traded shares. The stocks of interest to us in this book are the so-called *publicly traded issues*—the shares that are readily available to the general public and that are bought and sold in the open market. Just about every facet of American industry is represented in the stock market. You can buy shares in public utilities, airlines, mining concerns, manufacturing firms, online companies and retail organizations, or financial institutions such as banks and insurance companies.

Aside from the initial distribution of common stock when the corporation is formed, subsequent sales of additional shares may be made through a procedure known as a *public offering*. In a public offering, the corporation, working with its underwriter, simply offers the investing public a certain number of shares of its stock at a certain price. Exhibit 12.4 depicts the announcement for such an offering. Note in this case that *White Electronic Designs* is offering 5,175,000 shares of stock at a price of $10 per share. The new issue of common stock will provide this Nasdaq-traded company with some $50 million in new capital. When issued, the new shares will be commingled with

EXHIBIT 12.3

A Bull, A Bubble, and A Bear

One of the greatest bull markets in history began on August 12, 1982, with the Dow at 777. It continued on through the 1980s and into the 1990s. But in late 1998, the bull turned into a bubble that lasted for about 18 months before it burst in early 2000, at which time the market went from a bubble to a full-fledged bear.

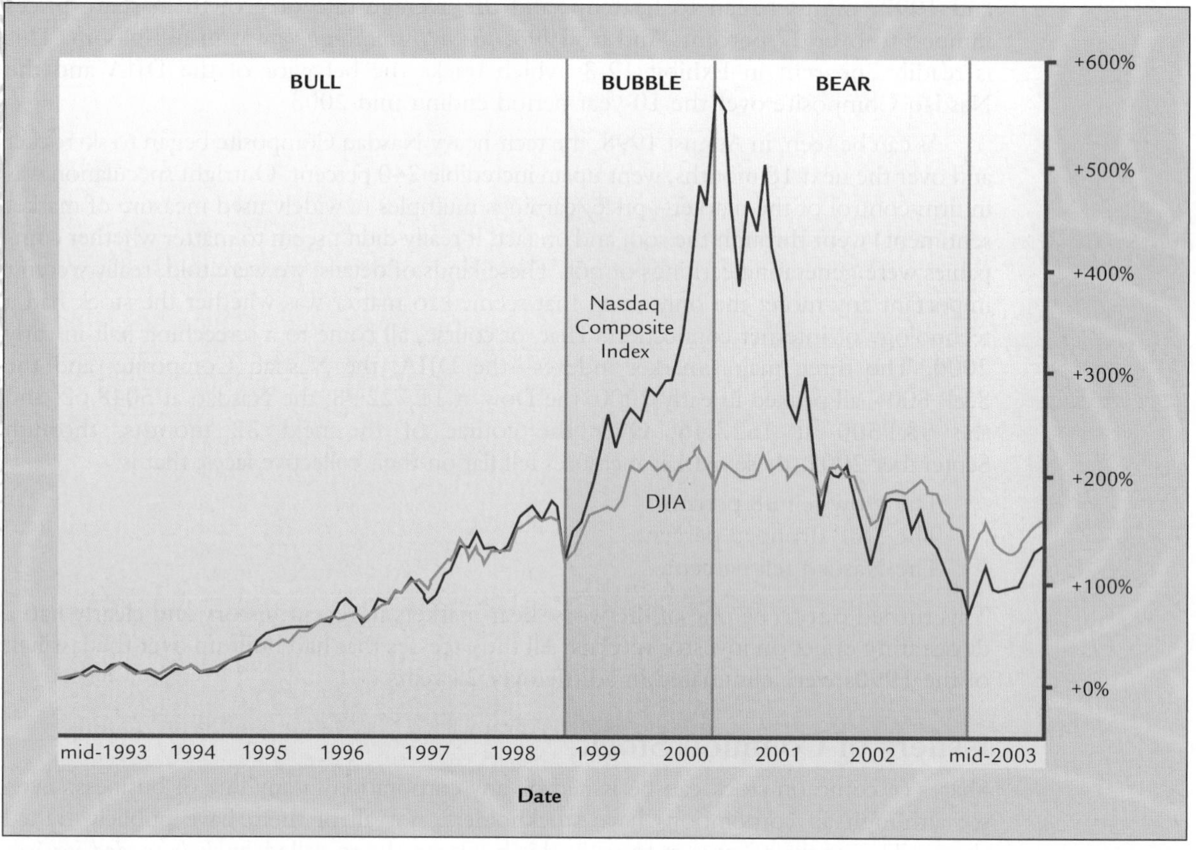

Source: Based on data from Business Week online: **http://www.businessweek.com**. Accessed 8/29/03.

the outstanding shares (they are all the same class of stock), and the net result will be an increase in the number of shares outstanding—after the new stocks are issued, the company will have about 23.9 million shares of stock outstanding.

Voting Rights

The holders of common stock normally receive *voting rights*, which means that for each share of stock held, they receive one vote. In certain instances, common stock may be designated as nonvoting at the time of issue, but this is the exception rather than the rule. Although different voting systems exist, the small stockholders need not concern themselves with them because, regardless of the system used, the chance they will be able to affect corporate control with their votes is quite slim.

EXHIBIT 12.4

An Announcement of a New Common Stock Issue

Here the company—White Electronic Designs—is issuing over 5 million shares of stock at a price of $10 per share. For this manufacturer of specialty microelectronic memory products, the new issue will mean some $50,000,000 in new captial.

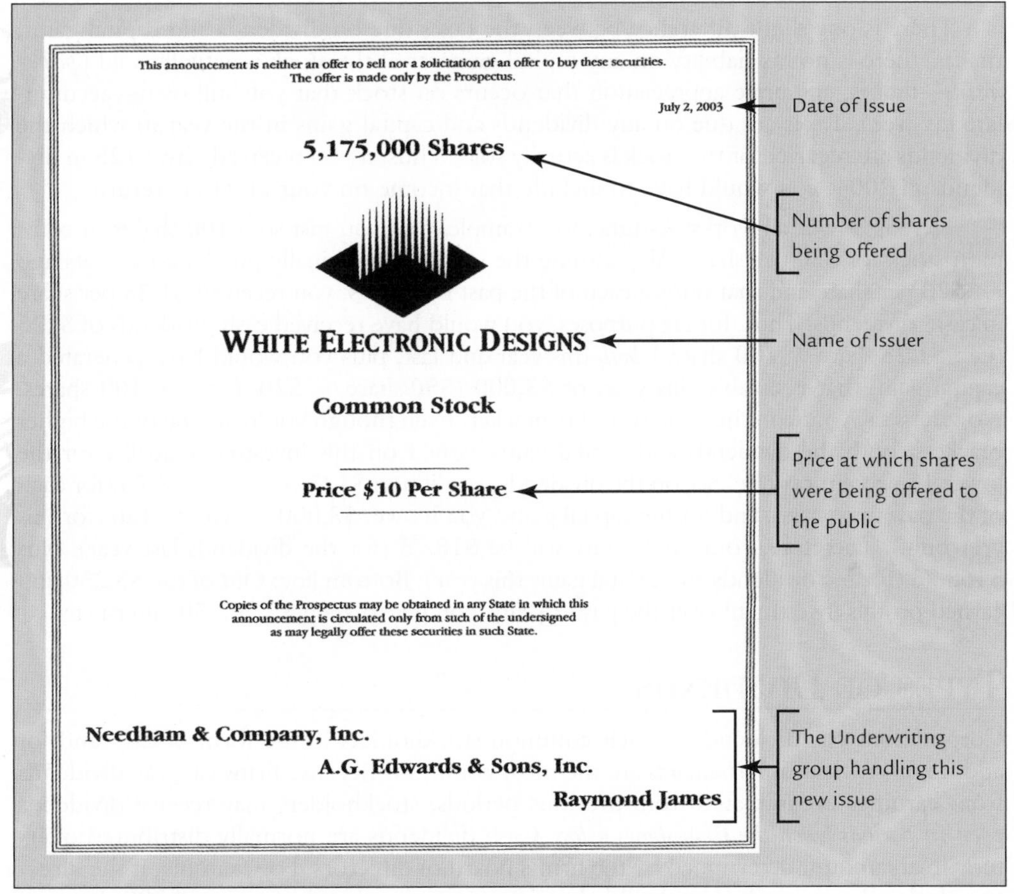
This announcement is neither an offer to sell nor a solicitation of an offer to buy these securities.
The offer is made only by the Prospectus.

July 2, 2003

5,175,000 Shares

WHITE ELECTRONIC DESIGNS

Common Stock

Price $10 Per Share

Copies of the Prospectus may be obtained in any State in which this announcement is circulated only from such of the undersigned as may legally offer these securities in such State.

Needham & Company, Inc.
A.G. Edwards & Sons, Inc.
Raymond James

Source: *The Wall Street Journal*, August 14, 2003.

Corporations have annual stockholders' meetings, at which time new directors are elected and special issues are voted on. Because most small stockholders are unable to attend these meetings, they can use a proxy to assign their votes to another person, who will vote their stock for them. A **proxy** is merely a written statement assigning voting rights to another party.

proxy A written statement used to assign a stockholder's voting rights to another person, typically one of the directors.

Basic Tax Considerations

Common stocks provide income in the form of dividends, usually paid quarterly, and/or capital gains, which occurs when the price of the stock goes up over time. From a tax *rate* perspective, it really doesn't make any difference whether the investment return comes in the form of dividends or long-term capital gains—today, they're both taxed at the same rate of 15 percent, or less (it's 5 percent for those filers in the 10 percent and 15 percent tax brackets). Actually, the appeal of cash dividends took a giant leap forward in 2003, when the federal tax code was changed to reduce the tax on dividends. Prior to this time, cash dividends were taxed as ordinary income, meaning they could be taxed at rates as high as 39 percent. For that reason, many investors viewed cash dividends as a highly unattractive source of income, especially since capital gains (when realized) were taxed at much lower preferential rates. Now, *both dividends and capital gains are taxed at the same low, preferential rate.* That, of course, makes dividend-paying stocks far more attractive, even to those investors in the higher tax brackets. (See Chapter 3 for details on taxes and tax rates.)

There is one slight difference between the taxes due on dividends and capital gains; that is, there is no tax liability on any capital gains until the stock is actually sold (*paper gains*—that is, any price appreciation that occurs on stock that you still own—accumulate tax-free). Taxes are due on any dividends and capital gains in the year in which the dividends are received or the stock is actually sold. Thus, if you received, say, $125 in dividends in 2004, you would have to include that income on your 2004 tax return.

Here is how it all works: Assume, for example, that you just sold 100 shares of common stock for $50 per share. Also assume the stock was originally purchased 2 years ago for $20 per share and that during each of the past two years, you received $1.25 per share in cash dividends. Thus, for tax purposes, you would have received cash dividends of $125 (i.e., $1.25/share × 100 shares) *both* this year and last, plus you would have generated a capital gain, that is taxable this year, of $3,000 ($50/share − $20/share) × 100 shares. Now, let's say you're in the 33 percent tax bracket. Even though you're in one of the higher brackets, both the dividends and capital gains earned on this investment qualify for the lower 15 percent tax rate. So, on the dividends, you'll pay: $125 × .15 = $18.75 (for each of the past two years), and for the capital gains, you'll owe: $3,000 × .15 = $450 (for this year only). Therefore, your tax liability will be $18.75 (for the dividends last year), plus $468.75 (for the dividends and capital gains this year). Bottom line: Out of the $3,250 you earned on this investment over the past 2 years, you get to keep $2,762.50, after taxes.

Types of Dividends

Corporations pay dividends to their common stockholders in the form of cash and/or additional stock. *Cash dividends* are the most common. Because firms can pay dividends from earnings accumulated from previous periods, stockholders may receive dividends *even in periods when the firm shows a loss.* Cash dividends are normally distributed quarterly in an amount determined by the firm's board of directors. For example, if the directors declared a quarterly cash dividend of 50 cents a share, and you owned 200 shares of stock, you would receive a check for $100.

A popular way of assessing the amount of dividends received is to measure the stock's dividend yield. Basically, **dividend yield** is a measure of common stock dividends on a relative (percent), rather than absolute (dollar), basis—that is, the dollar amount of dividends received is related to the market price of the stock. As such, dividend yield is an indication of the rate of current income being earned on the investment. It is computed as follows:

dividend yield The percentage return provided by the dividends paid on common stock; calculated by dividing the cash dividends paid during the year by the stock's market price.

$$\text{Dividend yield} = \frac{\text{Annual dividend received per share}}{\text{Market price per share of stock}}$$

Thus, a company that annually pays $2 per share in dividends and whose stock is trading at $50 a share will have a dividend yield of 4 percent ($2/$50 = .04). Dividend yield is widely used by income-oriented investors looking for (reasonably priced) stocks that have a long and sustained record of regularly paying higher-than-average dividends.

stock dividends New shares of stock distributed to existing stock holders as a supplement to or substitute for cash dividends.

Occasionally the directors may declare a stock dividend as a supplement to or in place of cash dividends. **Stock dividends** are paid in the form of additional shares of stock. That is, rather than receiving cash, shareholders receive additional shares of the company's stock—say, 1/10 of a share of new stock for each share owned (as in a *10 percent stock dividend*). Although they often satisfy the needs of some investors, stock dividends really have no value, because they represent the receipt of something already owned. For example, if you owned 100 shares of stock in a company that declared a 10 percent stock dividend, you'd receive 10 new shares of stock. Unfortunately, you'll be no better off after the stock dividend than you were before. That's because all stockholders will receive a 10 percent increase in the number of shares they own, so the relative ownership position of all shareholders will remain the same.

Moreover, the total market value of the shares owned is (roughly) the same after the stock dividend as before. Why is that so? Because the price of the stock will usually fall in direct proportion to the size of a stock dividend. Thus, in our example above, a drop in price will bring the total market value of 110 shares (after the stock dividend) to about the same as the total market value of the 100 shares that existed before the dividend. Clearly, under such circumstances, the investor is right back where he started from: He's received nothing of value. The shareholder who has received a stock dividend can, of course, sell the new shares to cash out the dividend. But then the value of the stocks owned by that shareholder will be reduced—granted, he'll then own the same number of shares as before the stock dividend, but they'll be worth less.

Some Key Measures of Performance

Professional money managers and seasoned investors use a variety of financial ratios and measures when making common stock investment decisions. They look at such things as dividend yield (mentioned earlier), book value, return on equity, earnings per share, and price/earning multiples to get a feel for the investment merits of a particular stock. In short, they use these and other ratios to help them decide whether to invest in a particular stock. Fortunately, most of the widely followed ratios can be found in published reports (like *Value Line*—an example of which is shown in Exhibit 12.5), so you don't have to compute them yourself. Even so, if you're thinking about buying a stock, or already have a position in common stock, there are a few measures of performance you'll want to keep track of. These would include book value (or book value per share), net profit margin, return on equity, earnings per share, price/earnings ratio, and beta. (Note in Exhibit 12.5 that all these ratios are reported by *Value Line*, in this case for Medtronic, Inc.)

Book Value

book value The amount of stockholders' equity in a firm; determined by subtracting the company's liabilities and preferred stock value from its assets.

The amount of stockholders' equity in a firm is measured by **book value**. This accounting measure is determined by subtracting the firm's liabilities and preferred stocks from the value of its assets. Book value indicates the amount of stockholder funds used to finance the firm. For example, assume Rose Colored Glasses (RCG) had assets of $5 million, liabilities of $2 million, and preferred stock valued at $1 million. The book value of the firm's common stock would be $2 million ($5 million − $2 million − $1 million). If the book value is divided by the number of shares outstanding, the result is *book value per share*. If RCG had 100,000 shares of common stock outstanding, its book value per share would be $20 ($2,000,000/100,000 shares). Because of the positive impact it can have

EXHIBIT 12.5

A Value Line Report for Medtronic, Inc.

A variety of information about a company's performance and financial condition is widely available in published reports, like the *Value Line* Report shown here for Medtronic, Inc. Note that the highlighted data (covering everything from a stock's dividend yield to its beta) represent just a small sample of what's available in these reports.

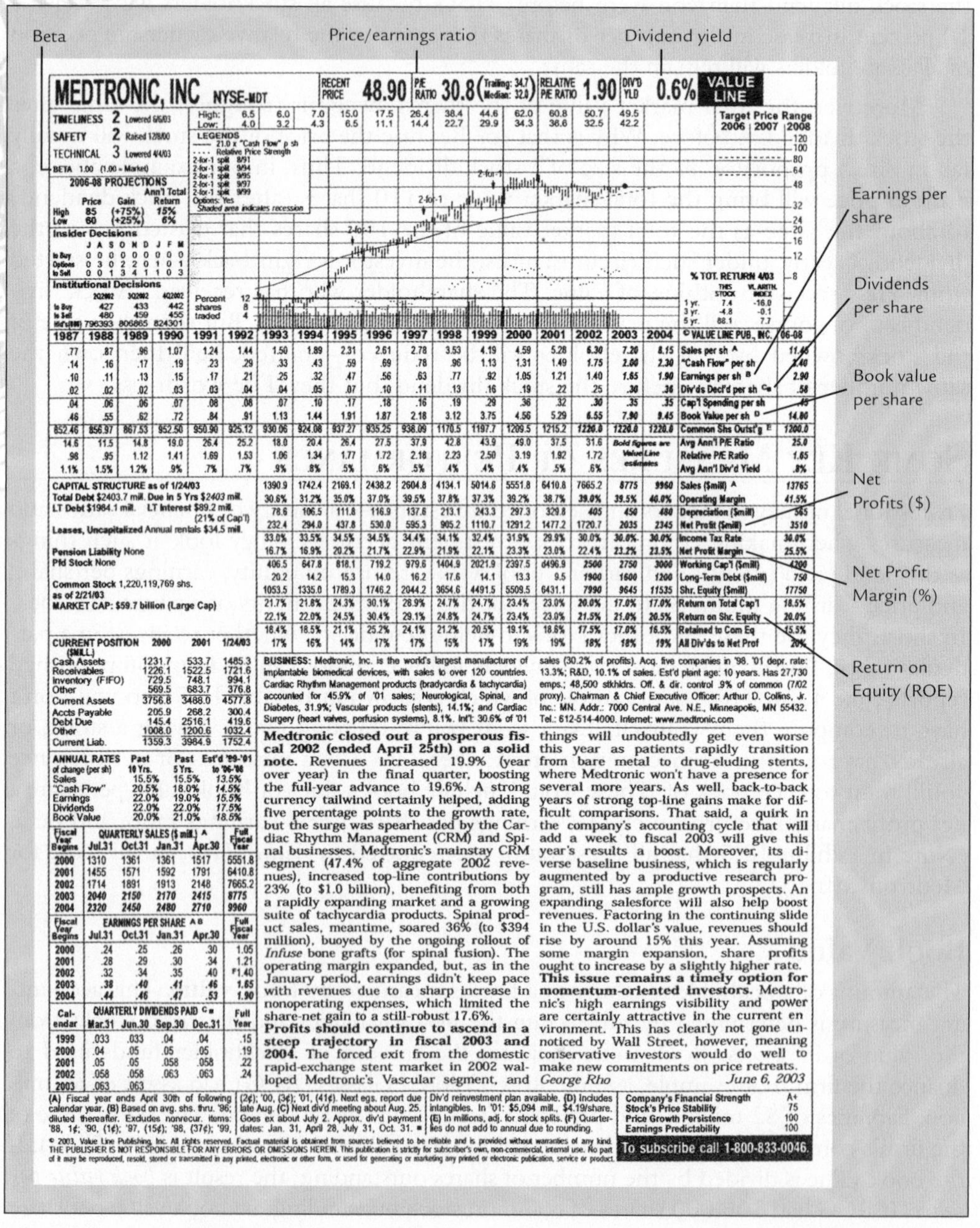

MEDTRONIC, INC NYSE-MDT | RECENT PRICE 48.90 | P/E RATIO 30.8 (Trailing: 34.7 / Median: 32.0) | RELATIVE P/E RATIO 1.90 | DIV'D YLD 0.6% | VALUE LINE

TIMELINESS 2 Lowered 6/6/03
SAFETY 2 Raised 12/8/00
TECHNICAL 3 Lowered 4/4/03
BETA 1.00 (1.00 = Market)

BUSINESS: Medtronic, Inc. is the world's largest manufacturer of implantable biomedical devices, with sales to over 120 countries. Cardiac Rhythm Management products (bradycardia & tachycardia) accounted for 45.9% of '01 sales; Neurological, Spinal, and Diabetes, 31.9%; Vascular products (stents), 14.1%; and Cardiac Surgery (heart valves, perfusion systems), 8.1%. Int'l: 30.6% of '01 sales (30.2% of profits). Acq. five companies in '98. '01 depr. rate: 13.3%; R&D, 10.1% of sales. Est'd plant age: 10 years. Has 27,730 emps.; 48,500 stkhldrs. Off. & dir. control .9% of common (7/02 proxy). Chairman & Chief Executive Officer: Arthur D. Collins, Jr. Inc.: MN. Addr.: 7000 Central Ave. N.E., Minneapolis, MN 55432. Tel.: 612-514-4000. Internet: www.medtronic.com

Medtronic closed out a prosperous fiscal 2002 (ended April 25th) on a solid note. Revenues increased 19.9% (year over year) in the final quarter, boosting the full-year advance to 19.6%. A strong currency tailwind certainly helped, adding five percentage points to the growth rate, but the surge was spearheaded by the Cardiac Rhythm Management (CRM) and Spinal businesses. Medtronic's mainstay CRM segment (47.4% of aggregate 2002 revenues), increased top-line contributions by 23% (to $1.0 billion), benefiting from both a rapidly expanding market and a growing suite of tachycardia products. Spinal product sales, meantime, soared 36% (to $394 million), buoyed by the ongoing rollout of *Infuse* bone grafts (for spinal fusion). The operating margin expanded, but, as in the January period, earnings didn't keep pace with revenues due to a sharp increase in nonoperating expenses, which limited the share-net gain to a still-robust 17.6%.

Profits should continue to ascend in a steep trajectory in fiscal 2003 and 2004. The forced exit from the domestic rapid-exchange stent market in 2002 walloped Medtronic's Vascular segment, and things will undoubtedly get even worse this year as patients rapidly transition from bare metal to drug-eluding stents, where Medtronic won't have a presence for several more years. As well, back-to-back years of strong top-line gains make for difficult comparisons. That said, a quirk in the company's accounting cycle that will add a week to fiscal 2003 will give this year's results a boost. Moreover, its diverse baseline business, which is regularly augmented by a productive research program, still has ample growth prospects. An expanding salesforce will also help boost revenues. Factoring in the continuing slide in the U.S. dollar's value, revenues should rise by around 15% this year. Assuming some margin expansion, share profits ought to increase by a slightly higher rate.

This issue remains a timely option for momentum-oriented investors. Medtronic's high earnings visibility and power are certainly attractive in the current environment. This has clearly not gone unnoticed by Wall Street, however, meaning conservative investors would do well to make new commitments on price retreats.

George Rho *June 6, 2003*

Company's Financial Strength	A+
Stock's Price Stability	75
Price Growth Persistence	100
Earnings Predictability	100

To subscribe call 1-800-833-0046.

Source: *The Value Line Investment Survey*, Value Line Publishing, Inc. June 6, 2003.

on the growth of the firm, you'd like to see book value per share steadily increasing over time; also, look for stocks whose market prices are comfortably above their book values.

Net Profit Margin

net profit margin A key measure of profitability that relates the net profits of a firm to its sales; shows the rate of return the company is earning on its sales.

As a yardstick of profitability, **net profit margin** is one of the most widely followed measures of corporate performance. Basically, this ratio relates the net profits of the firm to its sales, providing an indication of how well the company is controlling its cost structure. The higher the net profit margin, the more money the company earns. Look for a relatively stable—or even better, an increasing—net profit margin.

Return on Equity

return on equity (ROE) ROE captures the overall profitability of the firm; it is important because of its impact on the growth, profits, and dividends of the firm.

Another very important and widely followed measure, **return on equity** (or **ROE**, for short) reflects the overall profitability of the firm. It captures, in a single ratio, the amount of success the firm is having in managing its assets, operations, and capital structure. Return on equity is important because it has a direct and significant impact on the profits, growth, and dividends of the firm. The better the ROE, the better the financial condition and competitive position of the company. Look for a stable or increasing ROE, and watch out for a falling ROE, as that could spell trouble.

Earnings per Share

earnings per share (EPS) The return earned on behalf of each share of common stock; calculated by dividing all earnings remaining after paying preferred dividends by the number of common shares outstanding.

With stocks, the firm's annual earnings are usually measured and reported in terms of **earnings per share (EPS)**. Basically, EPS translates total corporate profits into profits on a per-share basis and provides a convenient measure of the amount of earnings available to stockholders. Earnings per share is found by using the following simple formula:

$$\text{EPS} = \frac{\text{Net profit after taxes} - \text{Preferred dividends paid}}{\text{Number of shares of common stock outstanding}}$$

For example, if RCG reported a net profit of $350,000, paid $100,000 in dividends to preferred stockholders, and had 100,000 shares of common outstanding, it would have an EPS of $2.50 [($350,000 − $100,000)/100,000]. Note that preferred dividends are *subtracted* from profits because they have to be paid before any monies can be made available to common stockholders. Earnings per share are closely followed by stockholders because it represents the amount the firm has earned on behalf of each outstanding share of common stock. Here, too, look for a steady rate of growth in EPS.

Price/Earnings Ratio

price/earnings (P/E) ratio A measure of investors' confidence in a given security; calculated by dividing market price per share by earnings per share.

When the prevailing market price of a share of common stock is divided by the annual earnings per share, the result is the **price/earnings (P/E) ratio**, which is viewed as an indication of investor confidence and expectations. The higher the price/earnings multiple, the more confidence investors are presumed to have in a given security. In the case of RCG, whose shares are currently selling for $30, the price/earnings ratio is 12 ($30 per share/$2.50 per share). This means that RCG stock is selling for 12 times its earnings. P/E ratios are important to investors because they reveal how aggressively the stock is being priced in the market. Watch out for very high P/Es—that is, P/Es that are way out of line with the market—because that could indicate the stock is being overpriced (and thus might be headed for a big drop in price). P/E ratios are not static, but tend to move with the market: When the market's soft, a stock's P/E will be low, and when things heat up in the market, so will the stock's P/E.

Beta

A stock's **beta** is an indication of its *price volatility*; it shows how responsive the stock is to the market. In recent years, the use of betas to measure the *market risk* of common stock has become a widely accepted practice, and as a result, published betas are now available from most brokerage firms and investment services. The beta for a given stock is determined by a statistical technique that relates the stock's historical returns to the market. The market (as measured by something like the S&P index of 500 stocks) is used as a benchmark of performance, and it always has a beta of 1.0. From there, everything is relative: low-beta stocks—those with betas of less than 1.0—have low price volatility (they're relatively price-stable), while high-beta stocks—those with betas of more than 1.0—are considered to be highly volatile. In short, the higher a stock's beta, the more risky it is considered to be. Stock betas can be either positive or negative, though the vast majority are positive, meaning the stocks move in the same general direction as the market (that is, if the market is going up, so will the price of the stock).

beta
An index of the price volatility imbedded in a share of common stock; provides a reflection of how the price of the stock responds to market forces.

Actually, beta is an *index* of price performance and is interpreted as a percentage response to the market. Thus, if RCG has a beta of, say, 0.8, it should rise (or fall) only 80 percent as fast as the market—if the market goes up by 10 percent, RCG should go up only 8 percent (10 percent × .8). In contrast, if the stock had a beta of 1.8, it would go up or down 1.8 times as fast—the price of the stock would rise higher and fall lower than the market. Clearly, other things being equal, if you're looking for a relatively conservative investment, you should stick with low-beta stocks; on the other hand, if it's capital gains and price volatility you're after, then go with high-beta securities.

smart.sites

Enter a stock's ticker symbol or the company name and 411 Stocks, **http://www.411stocks.com**, pulls together a complete page of stock data: price, news, discussion groups, charts, and fundamentals.

Putting a Value on Stock

No matter what kind of investor you are or what your investment objectives happen to be, sooner or later you will have to face one of the most difficult questions in the field of investments: *How much are you willing to pay for the stock?* To answer this question, you have to put a value on the stock. Such measures as book value, earnings per share, P/E multiples, and betas are a part of the *fundamental analysis* used to determine the underlying value of a share of stock.

Basically, the notion of fundamental analysis is that the value of a stock depends on its expected stream of future earnings. Once you have a handle on the expected stream of future earnings, you can use that information in the *approximate yield* formula (Equation 12.1)—or input it to a hand-held calculator—to find the *expected rate of return on the investment*. If the expected return from the investment exceeds your desired or minimum rate of return, you should make the investment—in effect, you should be willing to pay the current or prevailing market price. Put another way, with fundamental analysis you are trying to determine whether or not you should pay the current or prevailing market price for the stock. If the return you expect from the investment (via the approximate yield equation) is less than your desired rate of return, you should not buy the stock (at its current market price), because it is currently "overpriced" and, therefore, you will not be able to earn your desired rate of return. (*Note*: We'll work through this valuation process with a real-world example later in this chapter.)

smart.sites

When you come across an investing term you don't understand, head over to InvestorWords.com, **http://www.investorwords.com**, for an extensive online glossary.

Types of Common Stock

Common stocks are often classified on the basis of their dividends or their rate of growth in EPS. Among the more popular types of common stock are blue-chip, growth, tech stocks, income, speculative, cyclical, defensive, mid-cap, and small-cap stocks.

Blue-Chip Stocks

blue-chip stock A stock generally issued by companies expected to provide an uninterrupted stream of dividends and good long-term growth prospects.

These are the cream of the common stock crop; **blue chips** are stocks that are unsurpassed in quality and have a long and stable record of earnings and dividends. They are issued by large, well-established firms that have impeccable financial credentials—firms like GE, Wal-Mart, Citigroup, Microsoft, 3M Co., United Parcel Service, and Pfizer. These companies hold important, if not leading, positions in their industries and often determine the standards by which other firms are measured. Blue chips are particularly attractive to investors who seek high-quality investment outlets that offer decent dividend yields and respectable growth potential. Many use them for long-term investment purposes, and, because of their relatively low-risk exposure, as a way of obtaining modest but dependable rates of return on their investment dollars. They are popular with a large segment of the investing public and, as a result, are often relatively high priced, especially when the market is unsettled and investors become more quality-conscious.

Growth Stocks

growth stock A stock whose earnings and market price have increased over time at a rate well above average.

Stocks that have experienced, and are expected to continue experiencing, consistently high rates of growth in operations and earnings are known as **growth stocks**. A good growth stock might exhibit a *sustained* rate of growth in earnings of 15 to 20 percent (or more) over a period during which common stocks are averaging only 6 to 8 percent. Starbucks, Lowe's, Medtronic, Harley-Davidson, Kohl's, and Boston Scientific are all prime examples of growth stocks. These stocks normally pay little or nothing in dividends, because the firm's rapid growth potential requires that its earnings be retained and reinvested. The high growth expectations for these stocks usually cause them to sell at relatively high P/E ratios, and they typically have betas in excess of 1.0. Because of their potential for dramatic price appreciation, they appeal mostly to investors who are seeking capital gains rather than dividend income.

Tech Stocks

tech stock A stock that represents the technology sector of the market.

Over the past 10 to 15 years, *tech stocks* have become such a dominant force in the market that they deserve to be put in a class all their own. **Tech stocks** basically represent the technology sector of the market, and include all those companies that produce or provide technology-based products and services such as computers, semiconductors, data storage devices, computer software and hardware, peripherals, Internet services, content providers, networking, and wireless communications. These companies provide high-tech equipment, networking systems, and online services to all lines of businesses, schools, healthcare facilities, communications firms, governmental agencies, and home users. Although some of these stocks are listed on the NYSE and AMEX, the vast majority are traded on the Nasdaq. These stocks, in fact, dominate the Nasdaq market and as such, the Nasdaq Composite Index and other Nasdaq measures of market performance. They were the ones that were hammered especially hard during the market fall of

2000–02, when the tech-heavy Nasdaq Composite fell nearly 80 percent! Indeed, many tech stocks fell to just pennies a share, as literally hundreds of these firms simply went out of business. But the strongest did survive, and some even thrived.

There are literally thousands of companies that fall into the tech stock category, including everything from very small firms providing some service on the Internet to huge multinational companies. These stocks would likely fall into either the *growth stock* category (see above) or the *speculative stock* class (see below), though some of them are legitimate *blue chips.* Although tech stocks may offer the potential for attractive (and in some cases, phenomenal) returns, they also involve considerable risk, and (for the most part anyway) are probably most suitable for the more risk-tolerant investor. Included in the tech stock category you'll find some big names, such as Microsoft, Cisco Systems, Applied Materials, and Dell, as well as many not-so-big names such as BEA Systems, NVIDIA, Invitrogen, KLA-Tencor, and Rambus.

Income Stocks Versus Speculative Stocks

Stocks whose appeal is based primarily on the dividends they pay out are known as **income stocks**. They have a fairly stable stream of earnings, a large portion of which is distributed in the form of dividends. Income shares have relatively high dividend yields and, thus, are ideally suited for investors who are seeking a relatively safe and high level of current income from their investment capital. An added (and often overlooked) feature of these stocks is that, unlike bonds and preferred stock, holders of income stock can expect *the amount of dividends paid to increase over time.* Examples of income stock include J.P. Morgan Chase, Hershey Foods, Pitney Bowes, R.R. Donnelly, AT&T, Bank of America, and PPG Industries. Because of their low risk, these stocks commonly have betas of less than 1.0.

income stock
A stock whose chief appeal is the dividends it pays out; typically offers dividend payments that can be expected to increase over time.

Rather than basing their investment decisions on a proven record of earnings, investors in **speculative stocks** gamble that some new information, discovery, or production technique will favorably affect the growth of the firm and inflate the price of its stock. For example, a company whose stock is considered speculative may have recently discovered a new drug or located a valuable resource, such as oil. The value of speculative stocks and their P/E ratios tend to fluctuate widely as additional information with respect to the firm's future is received. The betas for speculative stocks are nearly always well in excess of 1.0. Investors in speculative stocks should be prepared to experience losses as well as gains, since *these are high-risk securities.* They include companies like P. F. Chang's China Bistro, Quicksilver, K-Swiss, Indexx Labs, Serena Software, and Dollar General.

speculative stock
Stock that is purchased on little more than the hope that its price per share will increase.

Cyclical Stocks or Defensive Stocks

Stocks whose price movements tend to follow the business cycle are called **cyclical stocks**. This means that when the economy is in an expansionary stage (recovery or expansion), the prices of cyclical stocks increase, and during a contractionary stage (recession or depression), they decline. Most cyclical stocks are found in the basic industries—automobiles, steel, and lumber, for example; these industries are sensitive to changes in economic activity. Investors try to purchase cyclical stocks just prior to an expansionary phase and sell just before the contraction occurs. Because they tend to move with the market, these stocks always have positive betas. Caterpillar, Genuine Parts, Maytag Corp., Rohm & Haas, Alcoa, and Timken are examples of cyclical stocks.

cyclical stock
Stock whose price movements tend to parallel the various stages of the business cycle.

The prices and returns from **defensive stocks**, unlike those of cyclical stocks, are expected to remain stable during periods of contraction in business activity. For this reason, they are often called *countercyclical.* The shares of consumer goods companies, certain public utilities, and gold mining companies are good examples of defensive stocks. Because they are basically income stocks, their earnings and dividends tend to hold their market prices up during periods of economic decline. Betas on these stocks are quite

defensive stock
Stock that tends to exhibit price movements contrary to movements in the business cycle; often called countercyclical stock.

low and occasionally even negative. Bandag, Checkpoint Systems, Union Corp., and WD-40 are all examples of defensive stocks.

Mid-Caps and Small-Caps

In the stock market, a stock's size is based on its market value—or, more commonly, on what is known as its *market capitalization* or *market cap*. A stock's market cap is found by multiplying its market price by the number of shares outstanding. Generally speaking, the market can be broken into three major segments, as measured by a stock's market "cap":

Small-cap—Stocks with market caps of less than $1 billion
Mid-cap—Market caps of $1 billion to $4 or $5 billion
Large-cap—Market caps of more than $4 or $5 billion

In addition to these three segments, another is reserved for the *really small* stocks, known as *micro-caps*. Many of these stocks have market caps well below $100 million (some as low as $10–$15 million), and should only be used by investors who fully understand the risks involved and can tolerate such risk exposure.

Of the three major categories above, the large-cap stocks are the real biggies—the Wal-Marts, GEs, and Microsofts of the world. Many of these are considered to be blue-chip stocks, and, although there are far fewer large-cap stocks than any of the other market cap categories, these companies account for about 80 to 90 percent of the total value of all U.S. equity markets. Just because they're big, however, doesn't mean they're better. Indeed, both the small- and mid-cap segments of the market tend to hold their own with, or even outperform, large stocks over time.

mid-cap stock
A stock whose total market value—that is, number of shares outstanding × market price per share—falls somewhere between $1 billion and $4 or $5 billion; these mid-sized companies offer attractive return potential without lots of price volatility.

Mid-cap stocks are a special breed unto themselves and offer investors some very attractive return opportunities. They provide much of the sizzle of small-stock returns, but without all the price volatility. At the same time, because these are fairly good-sized companies, and many of them have been around for a long time, they offer some of the safety of the big, established stocks. Among the ranks of the mid-caps are such well-known companies as Tootsie Roll, Wendy's International, Barnes & Noble, Petsmart, Pall Corp., and the Cheesecake Factory, in addition to some not-so-well-known names. For the most part, although these securities offer a nice alternative to large stocks without all the drawbacks and uncertainties of small-caps, they probably are most appropriate for investors who are willing to tolerate a bit more risk and price volatility.

small-cap stock
A stock with a total market value of less than $1 billion that offers high growth and above average returns but at the cost of high risk.

Some investors consider small companies to be in a class by themselves. They believe these firms' stocks hold especially attractive return opportunities, which in many cases, has turned out to be true. Known as **small-cap stocks**, these companies generally have *annual revenues* of less than $250 million, and, because of their size, spurts of growth can have dramatic effects on their earnings and stock prices. Green Mountain Power, Hancock Fabrics, Hot Topic, JoAnn Stores, and Sonic Corp. are just some of the better-known small-cap stocks. Now although some small-scaps (like Sonic, for example) are solid companies with equally solid financials, that's definitely not the case with most of them! Indeed, because many of these companies are so small, they don't have a lot of stock outstanding, and their shares are not widely traded. In addition, small company stocks have a tendency to be "here today and gone tomorrow." Although some of these stocks may hold the potential for high returns, investors should also be aware of the very high risk exposure that comes with many of them.

Market Globalization and the Allure of Foreign Stocks

In addition to all the different types of stocks mentioned above, a growing number of American investors are turning to foreign markets as a way to earn attractive returns.

Such securities became increasingly popular during the 1980s and 1990s, and many investment advisors today recommend that investors put at least part of their capital into foreign stocks. A good deal of this interest has come about as advances in technology and communications, together with the gradual elimination of political and regulatory barriers, have allowed investors to make cross-border securities transactions with relative ease. Because of these changes, not only are more and more Americans beginning to invest in foreign securities, but foreign investors are becoming major players in U.S. markets as well. The net result is a rapidly growing trend toward market globalization, whereby investing is practiced on an international scale rather than confined to a single (domestic) market.

Ironically, as our world is becoming smaller, our universe of investment opportunities is growing by leaps and bounds! Consider, for example, that in 1970 the U.S. stock market accounted for fully *two-thirds of the world market.* In essence, our stock market was twice as big as all the rest of the world's stock markets *combined.* That's no longer true, for in 2002 the U.S. share of the world equity market had dropped to less than 50 percent. Today, the world equity markets are dominated by just six countries, which together account for about 80 percent of the total market. The United States, by far, has the biggest equity market, which in mid-2003 had a total market value of around $10 *trillion.* In a distant second place was Japan (at about ⅓ the size of the U.S. market), closely followed by the United Kingdom. Rounding out the list was Germany, France, and Canada.

In addition to these six, another dozen or so markets, such as Switzerland, Australia, Italy, Singapore, and Hong Kong, are also regarded as major world players—not to mention a number of relatively small, emerging markets, such as Mexico, South Korea, Thailand, and Russia. Thus, investors who confine all their investing to the U.S. markets are missing out on a big chunk of the worldwide investment opportunities. Not only that, they're missing out on some very attractive returns as well! Over the 23-year period from 1980 through 2002, the U.S. stock market provided the highest annual return just *once*—in 1982. And that statistic pertains to just the 8 largest (major) markets of the world—it doesn't include the smaller (emerging) markets that, in recent years, have provided some spectacular returns. Of course, it also ignores some spectacular crashes that have occurred recently in these same emerging markets—like the major meltdowns that took place in 1997–98 in Thailand, Indonesia, Malaysia, Korea, and the Philippines.

Financial Road Sign

Investing Myths

As appealing as these well-known "rules" may be, don't accept them as the absolute truth:

1. *Stocks outperform bonds over the long term.* The historical annualized return on stocks may be 10 to 12 percent, but over rolling 10-year periods you may earn less than 10 percent about half the time. Over 30 years, you have a 77 percent chance of topping 10 percent.
2. *Small-cap stocks beat large-cap stocks.* While small-cap stocks tend to outperform large caps over the long run, since the mid-1980s, the Russell 2000 index has lagged the S&P 500.
3. *Value stocks outperform growth stock*: Not always. In one study of large-cap companies, the difference between growth and value stocks was insignificant.
4. *Asset allocation accounts for 90 percent of your returns.* Although asset allocation is indeed important, don't overlook *security selection*; it also plays a key role.

Source: Walter Updegrave, "Everything You Think You Know about Investing is Wrong," *Money* magazine, ©2003 Time Inc. All rights reserved.

So, if you're looking for better returns, you might want to give some thought to investing in foreign stocks. There are several different ways of doing that. Without a doubt, from the perspective of an individual investor, the best and easiest way is through *international mutual funds* (we'll discuss such funds in Chapter 13). Mutual funds aside, you could, of course, buy securities directly in the foreign markets. *Investing directly* is not for the uninitiated, however. For although most major U.S. brokerage houses are set up to accommodate investors interested in buying foreign shares, many *logistical* problems still have to be faced. Fortunately, there is an easier way, and that is to buy *foreign securities that are denominated in dollars and traded directly on U.S. exchanges.* One such investment vehicle is the American Depositary

Financial Road Sign

Market Muscle
The total market value of a company, defined as the price of the stock multiplied by the number of shares outstanding, is a measure of what investors think a company is worth. In March of 2003, Microsoft topped the list with a market value of $266 billion, followed by General Electric at $255 billion and Exxon Mobil at $231 billion. Some other big-cap companies are Wal-Mart ($217 billion), Merck ($114 billion), Intel ($112 billion), and Coca-Cola ($99 billion). Interestingly, these were not necessarily the companies with the most assets or profits—for example, Microsoft ranked 59th in terms of assets, while Coca-Cola was 29th in terms of profits. Rather, what made these companies special as far as investors were concerned was their promise for the future!

Receipt (ADR). ADRs are just like common stock, except that each ADR represents a specific number of shares in a specific foreign company. Indeed, the shares of more than 1,000 companies from some 50 foreign countries are traded on U.S. exchanges as ADRs—companies like Sony, Nestlé, Ericsson Telephone, Nokia, Vadafone Airtouch, Shanghai Petro-chemicals, and Grupo Televisa, to mention just a few. ADRs are a great way to invest in foreign stocks because they are bought and sold, on American markets, just like stocks in U.S. companies—and their prices are quoted in dollars, not British pounds, Swiss francs, or Euros. Furthermore, all dividends are paid in dollars.

smart.sites
Everything you ever wanted to know about ADRs is at J.P. Morgan's ADR Site, **http://www.adr.com**, where you'll find general information about the ADR market and can search by company, region, or industry.

Whereas the temptation to go after higher returns may be compelling, keep one thing in mind when investing in foreign stocks—that is, whether investing in foreign securities directly or through something like ADRs, the whole process of investing involves a lot more risk. That's because *the behavior of foreign currency exchange rates plays a vital role in defining returns to U.S. investors.* As the U.S. dollar becomes weaker (or stronger) relative to the currency in which the foreign security is denominated, the returns to U.S. investors, from investing in foreign securities, will increase (or decrease) accordingly. Currency exchange rates can, in fact, have a dramatic impact on investor returns and quite often can convert mediocre returns, or even losses, into very attractive returns—and vice versa. Only one thing really determines whether the impact is going to be positive or negative, and that's the behavior of the U.S. dollar relative to the currency in which the foreign security is denominated. In effect, *a stronger dollar has a negative impact on total returns to U.S. investors, and a weaker dollar has a positive impact.* Thus, other things being equal, the best time to be in foreign securities is when the dollar is *falling*, because that increases returns to U.S. investors.

smart.sites
A good source for overseas business news and research on stocks not listed on U.S. exchanges is the *Financial Times* Web site, FT.com (**http://www.ft.com**).

Investing in Common Stock

The first step in investing is to know *where* to put your money; the second is to know *when* to make your moves. The first question basically involves matching your risk and return objectives with the available investment vehicles. As noted earlier, *a stock (or any investment vehicle for that matter) should be considered a viable investment candidate only as long as it promises to generate a sufficiently attractive rate of return* and, in particular, one that fully compensates you for any risks you have to take. Thus, if you're considering the purchase of a stock, you should expect to earn more than what you can get from

T-bills or high-grade corporate bonds. The reason: Stocks are riskier than bills or bonds, so you deserve more return. Indeed, if you can't get enough return from the security to offset the risk, then you shouldn't invest in the stock!

Selecting a Stock

Granted, you want an investment that provides an attractive rate of return—one that meets or exceeds your required return. So, how do you go about selecting such a stock? The answer is by doing a little digging and crunching a few numbers. Here's what you'd want to do: To begin with, find a company you like and then take a look at how it has performed over the past 3 to 5 years. Find out what kind of growth rate (in sales) it has experienced, if it has a strong ROE and has been able to maintain or improve its profit margin, how much it has been paying out to stockholders in the form of dividends, and so forth. This kind of information is readily available in publications like *Value Line* and *S&P Stock Reports* (which we discussed in Chapter 11), or online, at a number of sites. The idea is to find stocks that are financially strong, have done well in the past, and continue to be market leaders or hold prominent positions in a given industry or market segment. Looking at the past is only the beginning, however; what's really important to stock valuation is the *FUTURE!* That is, as we discussed earlier in this chapter (see the section "What Makes a Good Investment?"), *the value of a share of stock at any point in time is a function of future returns, not past performance.*

So, let's turn our attention to the expected future performance of a stock. The idea is to assess the *outlook* for the stock, thereby *gaining some insight about the benefits to be derived from investing in it.* Of particular concern are future dividends and share price behavior. As a rule, it doesn't make much sense to go out more than 2 or 3 years because the accuracy of most forecasts begins to deteriorate rapidly after that point. Thus, using a 3-year investment horizon, you'd want to forecast annual dividends per share for each of the next 3 years, *plus* the future price of the stock at the end of the 3-year holding period (obviously, if the price of the stock is projected to go up over time, you'll have some capital gains). You can try to generate these forecasts yourself, or you can look to a publication like *Value Line* to obtain projections (*Value Line* projects dividends and share prices 3 to 5 years into the future). Once you have projected dividends and share price, you can use the approximate yield equation, or a hand-held calculator, to determine the expected return from the investment.

To see how that can be done, consider the common shares of Medtronic, Inc., the world's largest manufacturer of implantable biomedical devices. According to *Value Line* (refer back to Exhibit 12.5), the company has very strong financials; its sales have been growing at around 15 or 16 percent per year for the past 5 years, it has a net profit margin of more than 20 percent, and an ROE of around 20 percent.

Financial Road Sign

Reading between the Lines of an Annual Report

How do you make sense of all the information in an annual report? Here are some pointers:

1. **Fancy isn't better:** Don't let all the glossy pages, wonderful updates, and lovely photos color your thinking. They mean little or nothing if the financial statements reflect declining performance.
2. **Start at the end:** The financial information is the heart of the annual report, so begin there. Check the auditor's opinion to see if the report conforms with "generally accepted accounting principles."
3. **Read the footnotes:** Do this *before* you look at the financial statements themselves. They reveal key information about the financial statements, such as whether an increase or decrease in profits was largely due to an accounting change or a one-time event. Are there any lawsuits pending?
4. **Focus on the Management Discussion and Analysis:** This in-depth discussion, financial results, and other factors within the business precedes the financial statements and should provide a clear and candid explanation of significant financial trends. How much is disclosed? Cross-reference it with the financial statements themselves; they should be consistent.
5. **Dear Stockholder...:** The chairman's letter to stockholders should summarize key events of the past year and underlying reasons, what's changed or changing, success in meeting goals, and what lies ahead. Watch out for phrases like "except for" or "in spite of," which could signal problems.
6. **Number, please:** Now delve into the financial statements

...continued on next page

Financial Road Sign (continued)

themselves, looking at trends in sales, profits, expenses, inventory and debt levels, cash flow, and more. Compare your company to industry norms.

7. **What's left?** The narrative sections will fill in the picture, telling you about the company's products, marketing, and operations in general.

Sources: Jeff Fischer, "5 Investing Don'ts," *Motley Fool*, October 23, 2003, downloaded from **http://www.fool.com**; "Intro to Fundamental Analysis: The Quarterly and Annual Reports," Investopedia.com, **http://www.investopedia.com/university/fundamentalanalysis/annualreport.asp**; and Jane Bryant Quinn, "How to Read an Annual Report" (free reprint from International Paper Company), downloaded December 1, 2003 from **http://shamino.quincy.edu/~jschlepp/anrpread.html**.

Thus, historically, the company has performed very well and is definitely a market leader in its field. In June of 2003, the stock was trading at around $49 a share and was paying annual dividends at the rate of about 30 cents a share. *Value Line* was projecting dividends to go up to about 58 cents a share within the next 3 to 5 years; they were also estimating the price of the stock could rise to as high as $80 a share within 3 years.

Using these *Value Line* projections and given current dividends (in 2003) of 30 cents a share, we could expect dividends of, say, 36 cents a share next year (2004), 47 cents a share the year after (2005), and 58 cents a share in 2006—assuming, of course, that dividends do in fact grow as estimated by *Value Line*. Now, because the approximate yield equation uses "average annual current income" as one of the inputs, let's use the midpoint of our projected dividends (47 cents a share) as a proxy for average annual dividends. In addition, given this stock is currently trading at $49 a share, has a projected future price of $80 a share, and we have a 3-year investment horizon, we can find our expected return as follows:

$$\text{Approximate yield (Expected return)} = \frac{\$0.47 + \left[\dfrac{\$80 - \$49}{3}\right]}{\left[\dfrac{\$80 + \$49}{2}\right]}$$

$$= \frac{\$0.47 + \$10.35}{\$64.50} = \underline{\underline{16.78\%}}$$

Calculator Keystrokes. Using a hand-held financial calculator—set in the *annual compounding mode*—to find the expected return on a stock that you purchase at $49 a share, hold for 3 years (during which time you receive average annual dividends of 47 cents a share), and then sell at $80 per share, use the keystrokes shown in the margin below, where

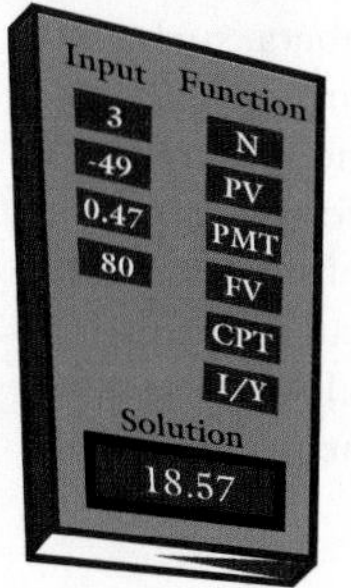

N = number of *years* you hold the stock,

PV = the price you pay for the stock (entered as a *negative* value),

PMT = average amount of dividends received each *year*,

FV = the price you expect to receive when you sell the stock (in 3 years).

The expected return (of 18.6 percent) is a bit higher here, but even so, it's still close to the return we computed using the approximate yield method (of 16.8 percent).

Thus, if Medtronic stock performs as expected, it should provide us with a return of around 17 or 18 percent. In today's market, that would be a very attractive return, and one that very likely will *exceed* our required rate of return (which probably should be around 12 to 15 percent). If that is the case, then this stock very definitely *SHOULD* be considered a viable investment candidate. According to our standards, the stock is currently undervalued and thus, should be given serious consideration as a possible addition to our portfolio.

Timing Your Investments

Once you find a stock you think will give you the kind of return you're looking for, you're ready to deal with the matter of timing your investment. As long as the prospects for the market and the economy are positive, the time may be right to invest in stocks.

On the other hand, there are a couple of conditions when investing in stocks doesn't make any sense at all. In particular, *don't* invest in stocks if:

- You feel *very strongly* that the market is headed down in the short run. If you're absolutely certain the market's in for a big fall (or will continue to fall, if it's already doing so), then wait until the market drops, and buy the stock when it's cheaper.
- You feel uncomfortable with the general tone of the market—it lacks direction, or there's way too much price volatility to suit you. For example, this became a problem prior to and after the October 1987 crash, when computer-assisted trading started taking over the market. The result was a stock market that behaved more like a commodities market, with an intolerable amount of price volatility. When this happens, fundamentals go out the window, and the market simply becomes too risky. Do what the pros do, and wait it out on the sidelines. (See the *Money in Action* box on pages 524–525 for suggestions on deciding when to *sell* a stock.)

Why Invest in Stocks?

There are three basic reasons for investing in common stock: (1) to use the stock as a warehouse of value, (2) to accumulate capital, and (3) to provide a source of income. Storage of value is important to all investors, because nobody likes to lose money. However, some investors are more concerned about it than others and therefore put safety of principal first in their stock selection process. These investors are more quality-conscious and tend to gravitate toward blue chips and other nonspeculative shares. Accumulation of capital generally is an important goal to individuals with long-term investment horizons. These investors use the capital gains and dividends that stocks provide to build up their wealth. Some use growth stocks for such purposes; others do it with income shares; still others use a little of both. Finally, some people use stocks as a source of income; to them, a dependable flow of dividends is essential. High-yielding, good-quality income shares are usually their preferred investment vehicle.

Advantages and Disadvantages of Stock Ownership

Ownership of common stock has both advantages and disadvantages. Its advantages are threefold. First, the potential returns, in the form of both dividend income and price appreciation, can be quite substantial—the recent bear market of 2000–02 notwithstanding, of course. Second, many stocks are actively traded (there are literally thousands of such actively traded stocks); thus they are a highly liquid form of investment—meaning they can be quickly bought and sold. Finally, they don't involve any direct management (or unusual management problems) and market/company information is usually widely published and readily available.

Risk, the problem of timing purchases and sales, and the uncertainty of dividends are all disadvantages of common stock ownership. Although potential common stock returns may be high, the risk and uncertainty associated with the actual receipt of that

Financial Road Sign

Clubbing Your Way to Better Investing

An investment club can teach you to become a more successful investor. These small groups of investors pool their resources and jointly decide what securities to buy. To start your own club:

- Invite 10–20 people to an organizational meeting.
- Discuss which investing goals potential members share.
- Agree on an investment strategy for the club.
- Write a mission statement that describes the group's investment philosophy.
- Determine the organizational structure and develop a framework for investment decisions.
- Decide on the amount of each member's initial investment and monthly contributions.
- Remember that the club is a business with your money at risk, and operate it accordingly.
- Make meetings fun as well as educational.

It's important to outline clearly the expectations for members, such as active participation and regular attendance at meetings, and researching stocks thoroughly before recommending them. For more information on starting and running an investment club, visit the National Association of Investment Clubs at **http://www.better-investing.org**.

Sources: "Investment Clubs," *Investor Guide.com*, downloaded December 1, 2003, from **http://www.investorguide.com/iguinvestclub.html**; and Lynn Ostrem, "So You Want To Start An Investment Club?" *NAIC Online*, January 2003, downloaded from **http://www.better-investing.org**.

return is also great. Even though careful selection of stocks may reduce the amount of risk to which the investor is exposed, the risk-return tradeoff cannot be completely eliminated. In other words, high returns on common stock are not guaranteed; they may or may not occur depending on numerous economic, industry, and company factors. The timing of purchases and sales is closely related to risk. Many investors purchase a stock, hold it for a period of time during which the price drops, and then sell it below the original purchase price—that is, at a loss. The proper strategy, of course, is to buy low and sell high, but the problem of predicting price movements makes it difficult to implement such a plan.

Be Sure to Plow Back Your Earnings

dividend reinvestment plan (DRP) A program whereby stockholders can choose to take their cash dividends in the form of more shares of the company's stock.

Unless you're living off the income, the basic investment objective with stocks is the same as it is with any other security: to earn an attractive, fully compounded rate of return. This requires regular reinvestment of dividend income. And there's no better way to accomplish such reinvestment than through a **dividend reinvestment plan (DRP)**. The basic investment philosophy at work here is that if the company is good enough to invest in, it's good enough to reinvest in. In a dividend reinvestment plan, shareholders can sign up to have their cash dividends automatically reinvested in additional shares of the company's common stock—in essence, it's like taking your cash dividends in the form of more shares of common stock. The idea is to put your money to work by building up your investment in the stock. Such an approach can have a tremendous impact on your investment position over time, as seen in Exhibit 12.6.

EXHIBIT 12.6

Cash or Reinvested Dividends

Participating in a dividend reinvestment plan is a simple yet highly effective way of building up capital over time. Over the long haul, it can prove to be a great way of earning a fully compounded rate of return on your money.

Situation: Buy 100 shares of stock at $25 a share (total investment $2,500); stock currently pays $1 a share in annual dividends. Price of the stock increases at 8 percent per year; dividends grow at 5 percent per year.

Investment Period	Number of Shares Held	Market Value of Stock Holdings	Total Cash Dividends Received
Take Dividends in Cash			
5 years	100	$ 3,672	$ 552
10 years	100	$ 5,397	$1,258
15 years	100	$ 7,930	$2,158
20 years	100	$11,652	$3,307
Participate in a DRP			
5 years	115.59	$ 4,245	$0
10 years	135.66	$ 7,322	$0
15 years	155.92	$12,364	$0
20 years	176.00	$20,508	$0

Today, over 1,000 companies (including most major corporations) have DRPs, and each one provides investors with a convenient and inexpensive way to accumulate capital. Stocks in most DRPs are acquired free of any brokerage commissions, and

Concept ✓

12.4. From a tax perspective, would it make any difference to an investor whether the return on a stock took the form of dividends or capital gains? Explain.

12.5. What's the difference between a cash dividend and a *stock dividend?* Which would you rather receive?

12.6. Define and briefly discuss each of the following common stock measures: (a) *book value*, (b) ROE, (c) *earnings per share* (EPS), (d) *price/earnings (P/E) ratio*, and (e) *beta*.

12.7. Briefly discuss some of the different types of common stock. Which types would be most appealing to you, and why?

12.8. With so many different types of stocks to choose from in the United States, why would an American investor even want to consider investing in foreign markets? Identify two or three different ways of investing in foreign stocks. As an individual investor, which approach would you find most appealing? Why are currency exchange rates so important to investors in foreign markets.

12.9. Under what conditions would a stock be considered a viable investment candidate? What are *dividend reinvestment plans*, and how do they fit into a stock investment program?

most plans allow *partial participation*. That is, rather than committing all their cash dividends to these plans, participants may specify a portion of their shares for dividend reinvestment and receive cash dividends on the rest. Some plans even sell stocks to their DRP investors at below-market prices—often at discounts of 3 to 5 percent. In addition, most plans credit fractional shares to the investors' accounts. Shareholders can join these plans simply by sending in a completed authorization form to the company. Once in the plan, the number of shares you hold will begin to accumulate with each dividend date. There is a catch, however—even though these dividends take the form of additional shares of stock, *reinvested dividends are taxable, in the year they're received, just as if they had been received in cash.*

INVESTING IN BONDS

LG5, LG6

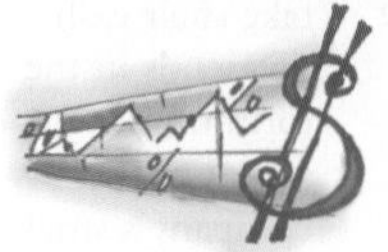

In contrast to stocks, *bonds are liabilities*—they're nothing more than publicly traded IOUs where the bondholders are actually *lending money* to the issuer. They represent borrowed funds and as such are a form of *debt capital.* Bonds are often referred to as *fixed-income securities* because the debt service obligations of the issuer are fixed—that is, the issuing organization agrees to pay a *fixed amount of interest periodically and to repay a fixed amount of principal* at or before maturity. Bonds normally have face values of $1,000 or $5,000, and maturities of 10 to 30 years or more.

WHY INVEST IN BONDS?

Like many other types of investment vehicles, bonds provide investors with two kinds of income: (1) They provide a generous amount of current income, and (2) they can often be used to generate substantial amounts of capital gains. The current income, of course, is derived from the interest payments received periodically over the life of the issue. Indeed, this regular and highly predictable source of income is one of the key factors that draws investors to bonds. But these securities can also produce capital gains, which occurs whenever market interest rates fall. A basic trading rule in the bond market is that *interest rates and bond prices move in opposite directions*: when interest rates rise, bond prices fall; and when they drop, bond prices rise. Thus, it is possible to buy bonds at one price and, if interest rate conditions are right, to sell them some time later at a higher price. Of course, it is also possible to incur a capital loss should market rates move against the investor. Taken together, the current income and capital gains earned from bonds can lead to highly competitive investor returns.

Bonds are also a highly versatile investment outlet. They can be used conservatively by those who seek high current income, or aggressively by those who actively go after capital gains. Although bonds have long been considered as attractive investments by those going after high levels of current income, it's only been since the advent of volatile interest rates that they've also become recognized for their capital gains potential and as trading vehicles. Indeed, given the relationship between bond prices to interest rates, investors found that the number of profitable trading opportunities increased substantially as wider and more frequent swings in interest rates began to occur.

Finally, because of the general high quality of many bond issues, they can also be used for the preservation and long-term accumulation of capital. In fact, some individuals, regularly and over the long haul, commit all or a good deal of their investment funds to bonds because of this single attribute.

BONDS VS. STOCKS

Although bonds definitely do have their good points—low risk and high levels of current income, along with *desirable diversification properties*—they also have a significant downside: their *comparative* returns. The fact is, *relative to stocks*, there's a big sacrifice in returns when investing in bonds—which, of course, is the price you pay for the even bigger reduction in risk! But just because there's a deficit in long-term returns, doesn't mean that bonds are always the underachievers. Consider, for example, what's happened over the past 20 years or so: Starting in the 1980s, fixed-income securities held their own and continued to do so through the early 1990s, only to fall far behind for the rest of the decade. But then along came a nasty bear market in stocks (2000–02) and the impact was nothing short of spectacular. The net results of all this can be seen in Exhibit 12.7, which tracks the comparative returns of stocks (via the S&P 500) and bonds (using the Lehman Bros. Long Bond Index) over the 1990s and through mid-2003. Note that for the first half of the period, bonds held up very well, pretty much matching the returns in the stock market. But things started to change in 1995, as stock returns shot up, while bond returns began to level off. For the decade as a whole (i.e., from January 1990 through December 1999), long-term bonds produced average annual returns of 8.7 percent, whereas stocks turned in average returns of 18.2 percent. That difference meant that a $10,000 investment in bonds would have led to a terminal value of some $23,000, versus more than $53,000 for stocks.

EXHIBIT 12.7

Comparative Performance of Stocks and Bonds—1990 Through Mid-2003

This graph shows what happened to $10,000 invested in bonds over the 13½-year period from January 1990 through June 2003, versus the same amount invested in stocks. Clearly, while stocks held a commanding lead through early 2000, the ensuing bear market erased virtually all of that. As a result, stocks and bonds finished the period at almost the same ending (or "terminal") values.

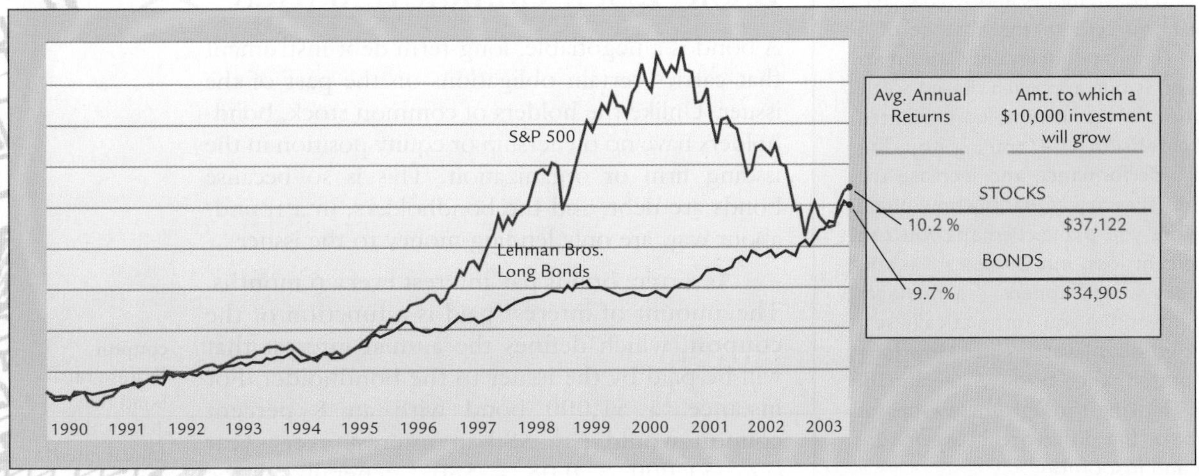

Source: *Morningstar Principia Pro for Mutual Funds*, June 30, 2003.

Money in Action

Swim, Sink or Bail: When is it Time to Sell Your Stocks?

Unless you are a buy-and-hold-forever investor, you will one day change your mind about a stock's prospects and need to sell it. This is easier said than done in the investment world where uncertainty reigns and emotions run high. Buying a stock is easier than deciding if or when to sell it, and it is the losers that we seem to have a particularly hard time getting rid of.

So why do investors cling to their portfolio duds? Numerous factors play into this, and understanding the behavioral biases that can inhibit wise financial decision-making can help overcome the "fear factor" when it's time to unload losing stocks.

There is more involved here than investors not wanting to admit an error. One reason we hold onto losing stocks is a perverse pride of ownership that binds us to our mistakes, making us overly attached to what we own. Another reason we stick with our losers is that we will do almost anything to avoid regret. Our greatest fear is selling a stock, then watching it climb back to great heights–without us. Yet another reason is plain, simple greed. Hesitant to take profits today and lose out on possible gains tomorrow, investor regret is not just tied to money loss, but also to money that could have been made if they hadn't sold. So rather than sell and redeploy their funds, they sit on dead money and avoid regret.

So when *should* you sell? In the absence of a magic formula to eliminate uncertainty, automating the sell decision is one approach. Based solely on stock price movements, it removes unwanted emotion from the decision. Use "trailing stops" to monitor a stock's performance and increase the stop (sell) price if necessary. Quantify how much you can lose before you panic. Perhaps you can live with a 15 percent loss, but 20 percent is too much. Think about what happens if a manager leaves a fund you own. Do you automatically sell, or does the fund go on a "watch" list? How long will you accept performance below a benchmark before you sell? Thinking through these types of questions can make the difference between successful investing and just drifting.

...continued on next page

That's a high opportunity cost to pay for holding bonds, and it prompted some market observers to question whether bonds should have *any place at all* in an investment portfolio. They reasoned that since market interest rates have dropped so low, bonds really don't have much to offer, other than relatively low returns. But the market experts overlooked one tiny detail: It wasn't bonds that would prove to be the problem, it was stocks! For, as can be seen in the Exhibit (12.7), the bear market had a devastating effect on stocks. So much so, in fact, that by mid-2003, the differential return between stocks and bonds had all but evaporated. Indeed, over the period from January 1990 through June 2003, stocks outperformed bonds by only half a percentage point (10.2 percent vs. 9.7 percent). The bottom line was a terminal value of slightly over $37,000 for stocks, compared to nearly $35,000 for bonds.

Most investors would agree that's a very low price to pay for *the level of stability that bonds bring to a portfolio!* The fact is bond returns are far more stable that stock returns, plus they possess *excellent portfolio diversification properties.* Thus, except for the most aggressive of investors, bonds have a lot to contribute from a portfolio perspective. Indeed, as a general rule, adding bonds to a portfolio will—*up to a point*—have a much bigger impact on (lowering) risk than it will on return! Face it: You don't buy bonds for their high returns (except when you think interest rates are heading down); rather, you buy them for their current income and the stability they bring to a portfolio. And that's still true, even today.

BASIC ISSUE CHARACTERISTICS

A bond is a negotiable, long-term debt instrument that carries certain obligations on the part of the issuer. Unlike the holders of common stock, bondholders have no ownership or equity position in the issuing firm or organization. This is so because bonds are debt, and the bondholders, in a roundabout way, are only lending money to the issuer.

As a rule, bonds pay interest every 6 months. The amount of interest paid is a function of the **coupon**, which defines the annual interest that will be paid by the issuer to the bondholder. For instance, a $1,000 bond with an 8 percent coupon would pay $80 in interest every year (i.e., $1,000 × 0.08 = $80), generally in the form of two $40 semiannual payments. The principal amount of a bond, also known as *par value*,

coupon
Feature on a bond that defines the annual interest income the issuer will pay the bondholder.

specifies the amount of capital that must be repaid at maturity—thus there is $1,000 of principal in a $1,000 bond.

Of course, debt securities regularly trade at market prices that differ from their principal (or par) values. This occurs whenever an issue's coupon differs from the prevailing market rate of interest; in essence, the price of an issue will change until its yield is compatible with prevailing market yields. Such behavior explains why a 7 percent issue will carry a market price of only $825 when the market yield is 9 percent; the drop in price is necessary to raise the yield on this bond from 7 percent to 9 percent. Issues with market values lower than par are known as *discount bonds* and carry coupons that are less than those on new issues. In contrast, issues with market value in excess of par are called *premium bonds* and have coupons greater than those currently being offered on new issues.

But if this approach seems too cut and dried for you, do your own quick and simple analysis to determine the market value of a stock you might sell in terms of cash-in-hand. Would you put it right back into the same stock? Would you buy a different stock? Would you buy a bond? Or would you hold onto the cash? Or profit from the pros at Zack's (**http://stockstosellprbw.zacks.com**) who know it is just as powerful to know what and when to sell, as buy.

Be aware of the mental minefield you need to negotiate when considering selling a stock, and know that fellow investors suffer the same angst. So quit sitting on your under-performers. Free up your cash for more promising opportunities by carefully reviewing your portfolio. Then sell, sell, sell.

Critical Thinking Questions

1. What critical factors can affect a stock's prospects, forcing an investor to re-evaluate its future in their portfolio?
2. What psychological issues come into play when an investor is confronted with the prospect of having to sell a stock? Explain.
3. What techniques would you use in determining whether or not to sell a stock?

Sources: Maggie Mahar, "Seller's Remorse," *Bloomberg Personal Finance*, July/August 2002, pp 72-75; Carl Sibilski, "When to Take a Profit," *Morningstar.com*, August 1, 2003, downloaded from **http://www.morningstar.com**; Dr. Robert Stepleman, "Investing Safely in Dangerous Times," *Sarasota Herald-Tribune,* November 16, 2003, p. D1; Jim Norris, "How to Take Your Emotions Out of the Sell Decision," *AA11 Journal*, August 2002, p. 15; Sue Stevens, "Top 10 Portfolio Pitfalls," *Morningstar.com*, August 21, 2003, downloaded from **http://www.morningstar.com**.

Types of Issues

A single issuer may have any number of bonds outstanding at a given point in time. In addition to their coupons and maturities, bonds can be differentiated from one another by the type of collateral behind them. In this regard, the issues can be viewed as having either junior or senior standing. *Senior bonds are secured obligations*, because they are backed by a legal claim on some specific property of the issuer that acts as *collateral* for the bonds. Such issues include **mortgage bonds**, which are secured by real estate, and **equipment trust certificates**, which are backed by certain types of equipment and are popular with railroads and airlines. *Junior bonds*, on the other hand, are backed only with a promise by the issuer to pay interest and principal on a timely basis. There are several classes of *unsecured* bonds, the most popular of which is known as a **debenture**. Issued as either notes (with maturities of 2 to 10 years) or bonds (maturities of more than 10 years), debentures are totally unsecured in the sense that there is no collateral backing them up—other than the good name of the issuer. But in the final analysis, even in the world of corporate finance, that's all that matters!

mortgage bond A bond secured by a claim on real assets, such as a manufacturing plant.

equipment trust certificate A bond secured by certain types of equipment, such as railroad cars and airplanes.

debenture An unsecured bond issued on the general credit of the firm.

sinking fund A provision in a bond that specifies the annual repayment schedule that will be used to pay off the issue.

Sinking Fund

Another provision that's important to investors is the **sinking fund**, which stipulates how a bond will be paid off over time. Not all bonds have these requirements, but for those that do, a sinking fund specifies the annual repayment schedule that will be used to pay off the issue and indicates how much principal will be retired each year. Sinking fund requirements generally begin 1 to 5 years after the date of issue and continue annually thereafter until all or most of the issue has been paid off. Any amount not repaid by maturity (which might equal 10 to 25 percent of the issue) is then retired with a single balloon payment.

Money in Action

These TIPS Can Really Pay!

Some people have the mistaken impression that they can't lose money in U.S. Treasury bonds. But they can—not because the government can't pay, but because bond prices fall in a rising inflationary environment (the higher inflation, of course, leads to higher interest rates, which ultimately lead to the lower bond prices). Now, the U.S. government wants investors to buy its bonds without fearing inflation. So, in 1997, Uncle Sam created TIPS, Treasury Inflation-Protection Securities. As direct obligations of the United States government, these debt securities offer high credit quality and pay interest semiannually. You can buy TIPS directly from the U.S. Treasury or from a broker. Several mutual fund companies now offer TIPS funds.

Here's how TIPS work: Suppose in January 2002 you bought a new 10-year inflation-indexed bond with a $1,000 face value paying 3 percent interest, or $30 per year. That rate stays fixed for the life of the issue, but interest is paid on the inflation-adjusted principal amount—that is, if the Consumer Price Index rises, *so does the face amount of the bond*. In December 2002, the Consumer Price Index indicated that inflation rose 2.4 percent during the year. Therefore your principal would be adjusted upward to $1,000 × .024 = $1,024 and your annual interest payment was $30.72 (3 percent of $1,024). (Because TIPS pay interest every 6 months, the principal is adjusted twice a year. Our illustration shows just an annual adjustment, for simplicity.) When the TIPS mature in 10 years, the investor gets the inflation-adjusted face value at that time, which could be as much as $2,000 if inflation takes off.

TIPS also protect you if *deflation* occurs. The bond's value will *not* fall below face value. Unfortunately, the IRS considers the increase in par value as taxable income, so the investor is going to have to pay taxes on it (just like he or she would have to pay taxes on the interest income). Thus, the IRS collects taxes on the increased value of the bond (the tax has to be paid in the year in which the increase in par value occurs), even though the increased par value isn't collected until the bond matures.

...continued on next page

Call Feature

Every bond has a **call feature**, which stipulates whether a bond can be called (that is, retired) prior to its regularly scheduled maturity date, and, if so, under what conditions. Often, a bond cannot be called until it has been outstanding for 5 years or more. Call features are normally used to replace an issue with one that carries a lower coupon; in this way, the issuer benefits by being able to realize a reduction in annual interest cost. In an attempt to compensate investors who have their bonds called out from under them, a *call premium* (usually equal to about a half to one year's interest) is tacked on to the par value of the bond and paid to investors, along with the issue's par value, at the time the bond is called. For example, if a company decides to call its 12 percent bonds some 15 years before they mature, it might have to pay $1,090 for every $1,000 bond outstanding (a call premium equal to 9 months' interest—$120 × .75 = $90—would be added to the par value of $1,000).

call feature
A feature included in bond (or preferred stock) issues that allows the issuer to retire the security prior to maturity at some specified, predetermined price.

Although this might sound like a good deal, it's really not. Indeed, the only party that benefits from a bond refunding is the issuer. The bondholder may indeed get a few extra bucks when the bond is called, but in turn, he or she loses a source of high current income—for example, the investor may have a 10 percent bond called away at a time when the best he or she can do in the market is maybe 7 or 8 percent. To avoid this, stick with bonds that are either *noncallable* (these issues cannot be called or retired prior to maturity, for any reason), or that have long *call-deferment periods*, meaning they can't be called for refunding (or any other purpose) until the call-deferment period ends.

The Bond Market

One thing that really stands out about the bond market is its size—the U.S. bond market is huge and getting bigger almost every day. Indeed, from a $250 billion dollar market in 1950, it has grown to the point where, in 2002, the amount of bonds outstanding in this country exceeded $17 *trillion!* Given such size, it's not surprising that today's bond market offers securities to meet just about any type of investment objective and suit virtually any type of investor, no matter how conservative or aggressive. As a matter of convenience, the bond market is usually divided into four segments, according to type of issuer: Treasury, agency, municipal, and corporate.

Treasury Bonds

Treasury bond A U.S. Treasury obligation that has a maturity of more than 10 years and pays interest semiannually.

Treasury bonds (sometimes called *Treasuries* or *governments*) are a dominant force in the bond market and, if not the most popular, certainly are the best known. The U.S. Treasury issues bonds, notes, and other types of debt securities (such as the Treasury bills discussed in Chapter 4) as a means of meeting the ever increasing needs of the federal government. All Treasury obligations are of the highest quality (backed by the full faith and credit of the U.S. government), a feature that, along with their liquidity, makes them extremely popular with individual and institutional investors, both here and abroad. U.S. Treasury securities are traded in all the major markets of the world, from New York to London to Tokyo.

Treasury notes are issued with maturities of 2, 3, 5, and 10 years, whereas *Treasury bonds* carry 20- and 30-year maturities. (Note that while the Treasury is authorized to issue these securities, *the last time they issued 20-year bonds was in January 1986 and the last 30-year bond was issued in August 2001.* Even so, many of these bonds are still outstanding and actively traded in the secondary market.) The Treasury issues its securities at regularly scheduled auctions, the results of which are widely reported by the financial media. It's through this auction process that the Treasury establishes the initial yields and coupons on the securities it issues. All Treasury notes and bonds are sold in minimum denominations of $1,000, and although interest income is subject to normal federal income tax, *it is exempt from state and local taxes.* Also, the Treasury today issues only *noncallable* securities—the last time the U.S. Treasury issued callable debt was in 1984.

Treasury inflation-indexed bond (TIPS) A type of Treasury security that provides protection against inflation by adjusting investor returns for the annual rate of inflation.

In 1997, the Treasury began issuing its newest security, the **Treasury inflation-indexed bond—or TIPS** as they're also known, which stands for "Treasury Inflation-Protection Securities." Basically, these securities—which are issued as notes with 10-year maturities, and until 2001, as bonds with 30-year maturities—provide investors with the opportunity to stay ahead of inflation by periodically adjusting their returns for any inflation that has occurred. That is, if inflation is running at an annual rate of, say, 3 percent, then at the end of the year the par (or maturity) value of your bond will increase by 3 percent (actually, the adjustments to par value are done every 6 months). Thus, the $1,000 par value will grow to $1,030 at the end of the first year and, if the 3 percent inflation rate continues for the second year, the par value will once again move up, this time from $1,030 to $1,061 (or $1,030 × 1.03). Unfortunately, the coupons on these securities are set very low, as they're meant to provide investors with so-called *real (inflation-adjusted) returns.* Thus, one of these bonds might carry a coupon of only 3½ percent (at a time when regular T-bonds are paying, say, 6½ or 7 percent). But there's an upside even to this: The actual *size of the coupon payment*

Take a look at what happens to a conventional bond offering 5 percent interest if inflation is rekindled. Investors get 5 percent per year, or $50, no matter what happens to the level of prices. In 10 years, that $1,000 principal will certainly have less purchasing power than it does today. It might be able to buy just $700 worth of goods. In addition, rising inflation generally means rising interest rates. In the marketplace, conventional bond prices fall when interest rates rise. Therefore, an investor who wishes to sell a conventional bond prior to maturity will probably take a loss if interest rates are higher than when the bond was purchased.

TIPS protect investors from such bond price erosion. TIPS are not so great, however, if inflation stays dormant, because the investor is getting a very low rate on his or her money. In fact the coupon for the July 2003 10-year TIPS was a mere 1.875 percent, compared to 4.25 for a regular 10-year Treasury note in August 2003. You may be able to get similar returns from other investments which don't require you to lock up your money nearly as long as you do with a TIP. Of course, inflation looks pretty tame these days. So, as one professional investor puts it, buying TIPS today is like buying flood insurance during a drought.

Critical Thinking Questions

1. What features of TIPS are especially appealing to investors?
2. Summarize the advantages and disadvantages of buying TIPS.
3. Do they appeal to you as an investor, and why?

Sources: Robert Barker, "A Bond Anybody Can Love," *Business Week*, June 19, 2000, p. 260; Iris L. Blasi and Frank Byrt, "TIPS Are Finally Getting Respect," *The Wall Street Journal*, July 11, 2002, p. D.9; James Grant, "An Inflation Tip," *Forbes*, October 30, 2000, p. 402; and "Treasury Inflation Protected Securities: What You Should Know," InvestinginBonds.com, downloaded from **http://www.investinginbonds.com**, accessed September 30, 2003.

will increase over time as the par value on the bond goes up. For investors who are concerned about inflation protection, these securities may be just the ticket. But as the *Money in Action* box on pages 526–527 suggests, these securities are a lot more complex than your normal Treasury bond.

Agency Bonds

Agency bonds are an important segment of the U.S. bond market. Though issued by political subdivisions of the U.S. government, *these securities are not obligations of the U.S. Treasury.* An important feature of these securities is that they customarily provide yields comfortably above the market rates for Treasuries and, therefore, offer investors a way to increase returns with little or no real difference in risk. Some of the more actively traded and widely quoted agency issues include those sold by the Federal Farm Credit Bank, the Federal National Mortgage Association (or "Fannie Maes," as they are more commonly known), the Federal Land Bank, the Student Loan Marketing Association, and the Federal Home Loan Bank. Although these issues are not the direct obligations of the U.S. government, a number of them actually do carry government guarantees and thus effectively represent the full faith and credit of the U.S. Treasury. Moreover, some have unusual interest-payment provisions (interest is paid monthly in a few instances and yearly in one case), and, in some cases, the interest is exempt from state and local taxes.

agency bond
An obligation of a political subdivision of the U.S. government; typically provides yields above the market rates for Treasury securities.

smart.sites
If bonds are still a mystery to you, the Bond Market Association's "Investing in Bonds" site (**http://www.investinginbonds.com**) has a wealth of practical and educational tools and useful links.

Municipal Bonds

Municipal bonds are the issues of states, counties, cities, and other political subdivisions, such as school districts and water and sewer districts. They are unlike other bonds in that their interest income is usually free from federal income tax (which is why these issues are known as *tax-free bonds*). Note, however, that the same tax-free status does not apply to any capital gains that may be earned on these securities—that is, such gains are subject to the usual federal taxes. A tax-free yield is probably the most important feature of municipal bonds and is certainly a major reason why individuals invest in them. Exhibit 12.8 shows what a taxable bond (like a Treasury issue) would have to yield to equal the take-home yield of a tax-free municipal bond. It demonstrates how the yield attractiveness of municipal bonds varies with an investor's income level; clearly, the higher the individual's tax bracket, the more attractive municipal bonds become.

municipal bond
A bond issued by state or local governments; interest income is usually exempt from federal taxes.

As a rule, the yields on municipal bonds are (almost always) lower than the returns available from fully taxable issues. Thus, unless the tax effect is sufficient to raise the yield on a municipal to a level that equals or exceeds the yields on taxable issues, it obviously doesn't make sense to buy municipal bonds. You can determine the return a fully taxable bond would have to provide in order to match the after-tax return on a lower-yielding tax-free issue by computing what is known as a municipal's *fully taxable equivalent yield:*

$$\text{Fully taxable equivalent yield} = \frac{\text{Yield on Municipal bond}}{1 - \text{Tax rate}}$$

For example, if a certain municipal bond offered a yield of 6 percent, an individual in the maximum 35 percent federal tax bracket would have to find a fully taxable

EXHIBIT 12.8

Table of Taxable Equivalent Yields

Tax-exempt securities generally yield less than fully taxable obligations, and, because of that, you have to be in a sufficiently high tax bracket (25 percent or more) to make up for the yield shortfall.

	To Match a Tax-Free Yield of:					
	5%	6%	7%	8%	9%	10%
Tax Bracket*	**You Must Earn This Yield on a Taxable Investment:**					
10 %	5.55%	6.66%	7.77%	8.88%	10.00%	11.11%
15	5.88	7.06	8.24	9.41	10.59	11.76
25	6.67	8.00	9.33	10.67	12.00	13.33
28	6.94	8.33	9.72	11.11	12.50	13.89
33	7.46	8.96	10.45	11.94	13.43	14.92
35	7.69	9.23	10.77	12.31	13.85	15.38

*Federal tax rates in effect on Jan. 1, 2004.

bond with a yield of more than 9 percent to reap the same after-tax return: that is, 6 percent ÷ (1 − .35) = 6 percent ÷ 0.65 = 9.23 percent.

serial obligation An issue, usually a municipal bond, that is broken down into a series of smaller bonds, each with its own maturity date and coupon rate.

revenue bond A municipal bond serviced from the income generated from a specific project.

general obligation bond A municipal bond backed by the full faith and credit of the issuing municipality.

Municipal bonds are generally issued as **serial obligations**, meaning that the issue is broken into a series of smaller bonds, each with its own maturity date and coupon rate. Thus, instead of the bond having just one maturity date 20 years from now, it will have a series of, say, 20 maturity dates over the 20-year time frame. Because such a diversity of municipal bonds is available, investors must also be careful to assess their quality to ensure that the issuer will not default. Although it may not seem that municipal issuers would default on either interest or principal payments, it does occur! Investors should be especially cautious when investing in **revenue bonds**, which are municipal bonds serviced from the income generated from specific income-producing projects, such as toll roads. Unlike issuers of so-called **general obligation bonds**—which are backed by the full faith and credit of the municipality—the issuer of a revenue bond is obligated to pay principal and interest *only if a sufficient level of revenue* is generated. General obligation municipal bonds, in contrast, are required to be serviced in a prompt and timely fashion regardless of the level of tax income generated by the municipality.

Caution should be used when buying municipal bonds because *some of these issues are tax-exempt and others are not.* One effect of the far-reaching Tax Reform Act of 1986 was to change the status of municipal bonds used to finance nonessential projects so their interest income is no longer exempt from federal taxes. Such bonds are known as *taxable munies*, and they offer yields considerably higher than normal tax-exempt securities. Buy one of these issues and you'll end up holding a bond whose interest income is *fully taxable* by the IRS.

Corporate Bonds

The major nongovernmental issuers of bonds are corporations. The market for **corporate bonds** is customarily subdivided into several segments, which include *industrials* (the most diverse of the group), *public utilities* (the dominant group in terms of volume of new issues), *rail and transportation bonds*, and *financial issues* (banks, finance companies, and so forth). The corporate bond market offers the widest range of issue types. There are *first mortgage bonds*, *convertible bonds* (discussed below), *debentures*, *subordinated debentures*, and *income bonds*, to mention just a few. Interest on corporate bonds is paid semiannually, and sinking funds are common. The bonds usually come in $1,000 denominations and are issued on a term basis with a single maturity date. Maturities usually range from 5 to 10 years, to 30 years or more. Many of the issues—particularly the longer-term bonds—carry call provisions that prohibit prepayment of the issue during the first 5 to 10 years. Corporate issues are popular with individuals because of their relatively high yields.

corporate bond A bond issued by a corporation; categories include industrials, public utilities, railroad and transportation bonds, and financial issues.

The Special Appeal of Zero Coupon Bonds

In addition to the standard bond vehicles described above, investors can also choose from several types of *specialty issues*—bonds that, for the most part, have unusual coupon or repayment provisions. That's certainly the case with **zero coupon bonds**, which, as the name implies, are bonds issued without coupons. To compensate for their lack of coupons, these bonds are sold at a deep discount from their par values and then increase in value over time, at a compound rate of return, so at maturity they are worth much more than their initial investment. Other things being equal, the cheaper the bond, the greater the return one can earn (for example, whereas a 10 percent bond might sell for $239, an issue with a 6 percent yield will cost a lot more—say, $417).

zero coupon bond A bond that pays no annual interest but sells at a deep discount to its par value.

Because they have no coupons, these bonds pay nothing to the investor until they mature. In this regard, zero coupon bonds are like the Series EE savings bonds we discussed in Chapter 4. Strange as it may seem, this is the main attraction of zero coupon bonds. Because there are no interest payments, investors need not worry about reinvesting coupon income twice a year; instead, the fully compounded rate of return on a zero coupon bond is virtually guaranteed at the rate that existed when the issue was purchased. For example, in mid-2003, good-grade (corporate) zero coupon bonds with 20-year maturities were available at yields of around 8 percent; thus, for just a little over $200, investors could buy a bond that would be worth five times that amount, or $1,000, when it matures in 20 years. Best of all, they would be *locking in* an 8 percent compound rate of return on their investment capital for the full 20-year life of the issue. Because of their unusual tax exposure (even though the bonds do not pay regular yearly interest, the IRS treats the annually accrued interest as taxable income), zeros should be used only in tax-sheltered investments, such as individual retirement accounts (IRAs), or be held by minor children who are likely to be taxed at low rates, if at all.

Zeros are issued by corporations, municipalities, and federal agencies; you can even buy U.S. Treasury notes and bonds in the form of zero coupon securities. During the eighties, major brokerage houses used to package U.S. Treasury securities as zeros and sell them to the investing public in the form of investment trusts. These unit trusts were marketed under such names as *TIGRS*, *CATS*, and *LIONS* and became enormously popular with investors. Seeing this, the Treasury decided to eliminate the middleman and "issue" their own form of zero coupon bond, known as *Treasury STRIPS*, or *STRIP-Ts*, for short. When that happened, the market for CATS and other felines all but dried up. (Some old issues are still out there, but the new issue market for these securities has virtually disappeared.) Actually, the Treasury does not issue zero coupon bonds, but instead, *they allow government securities dealers to take regular coupon-bearing notes and bonds in stripped form*, which can then be sold to the public as zero coupon securities. Essentially, the coupons are stripped from the bond, repackaged, and then sold separately as zero coupon bonds. For example, a 10-year Treasury bond has 20 semiannual coupon payments, plus one principal payment—each of these 21 cash flows can be repackaged and sold as 21 different zero coupon securities, with maturities that range from 6 months to 10 years.

Convertible Bonds

Another very popular type of specialty issue is the convertible bond. Found only in the corporate market, these issues are a type of *hybrid security* because they possess the features of both corporate bonds and common stocks. That is, they are initially issued as debentures (i.e., unsecured debt), but carry the provision that, within a stipulated time period, *they may be converted into a certain number of shares of the issuing company's common stock.*

Generally speaking, there is little or no cash involved at the time of conversion; the investor merely trades in the convertible bond for a stipulated number of shares of common stock. For example, assume that a certain convertible security recently came to the market, and it carried a provision that each $1,000 bond could be converted into shares of the issuing company's stock at $62.55 a share. Thus, *regardless of what happens to the market price of the stock*, the convertible investor can redeem each bond for 15.98 shares of the company's stock (i.e., $1,000 ÷ $62.55 = 15.98 shares). If at the time of conversion, the company's stock is trading in the market at, say, $125 a share, then the investor would have just converted a $1,000 debt obligation into $1,997.50 worth of stock (15.98 × $125 = $1,997.50).

conversion privilege The provision in a convertible issue that stipulates the conditions of the conversion feature, such as the conversion period and conversion ratio.

conversion ratio A ratio that specifies the number of shares of common stock into which a convertible bond can be converted.

conversion value A measure of what a convertible issue would trade for if it were priced to sell on the basis of its stock value.

conversion premium The difference between a convertible security's market price and its conversion value.

The key element of any convertible issue is its **conversion privilege**, which stipulates the conditions and specific nature of the conversion feature. First, it states exactly when the bond can be converted. Sometimes, there will be an initial waiting period of 6 months to perhaps 2 years after the date of issue, during which time the issue cannot be converted. The *conversion period* then begins, after which the issue can be converted at any time. Technically it is the *bondholder* who has the right to convert the bond into common stock, but more commonly the issuing firm will initiate the conversion by calling the issue. From the investor's point of view, the most important item of information is the **conversion ratio**, which specifies the number of shares of common stock that the bond can be converted into. For example, a $1,000 convertible bond might stipulate a conversion ratio of 20, meaning that you can "cash in" one convertible bond for 20 shares of the company's stock.

Given the significance of the price behavior of the underlying common stock to the value of a convertible security, one of the most important measures to a convertible bond investor is conversion value. In essence, **conversion value** is an indication of what a convertible issue would trade for *if it were priced to sell on the basis of its stock value*. Conversion value is easy to find: Simply multiply the conversion ratio of the issue by the current market price of the underlying common stock. For example, a convertible that carried a conversion ratio of 20 would have a conversion value of $1,200 if the firm's stock traded at a current market price of $60 per share (20 × $60 = $1,200). Unfortunately, convertible issues seldom trade precisely at their conversion value; rather, they invariably trade at **conversion premiums**, which means the convertibles are priced in the market at more than their conversion values. For example, a convertible that traded at $1,400 and had a conversion value of $1,200 would have a conversion premium of $200 (that is, $1,400 − $1,200 = $200). Convertible securities appeal to investors who want *the price potential of a common stock along with the downside risk protection of a corporate bond*. This two-sided feature is critical with convertibles and is virtually impossible to match with straight common stock or straight debt.

BOND RATINGS

Bond ratings are like grades: A letter grade is assigned to a bond, which designates its investment quality. Ratings are widely used and are an important part of the municipal and corporate bond markets. The two largest and best-known rating agencies are Moody's and Standard & Poor's. Every time a large, new corporate or municipal issue comes to the market, it is analyzed by a staff of professional bond analysts to determine its default risk exposure and investment quality. The financial records of the issuing organization are thoroughly examined and its future prospects assessed. The result of all this is the assignment of a bond rating at the time of issue that indicates *the ability of the issuing organization to service its debt in a prompt and timely manner*. Exhibit 12.9 lists the various ratings assigned to bonds by each of the two major agencies. Except for slight variations in designations (Aaa versus AAA, for example), the meanings and interpretations are basically the same. Note that the top four ratings (Aaa through Baa; or AAA through BBB) designate *investment-grade bonds*—such ratings are highly coveted by issuers because they indicate financially strong, well-run companies or municipalities. The next two ratings (Ba/B; or BB/B) are where you'll find most **junk bonds**; these ratings mean that although the principal and interest payments on the bonds are still being met, the risk of default is relatively high, as the issuers generally lack the financial strength found with investment-grade issues. While junk bonds—or *high-yield bonds*, as they're also known—are popular with some investors, it should be understood that these are highly speculative securities. They may offer high rates of return, but they also involve substantial amounts of risks; in particular, there's a very real likelihood that the issue may encounter some difficulties.

junk bond
Also known as *high-yield bonds*, these are highly speculative securities that have received low ratings from Moody's or Standard & Poor's; the low ratings mean the issuers could have difficulty meeting interest and principal payments as they come due.

EXHIBIT 12.9

Moody's and Standard & Poor's Bond Ratings

Agencies like Moody's and Standard & Poor's rate corporate and municipal bonds; the ratings provide an indication of the bonds' investment quality (particularly with respect to an issue's default risk exposure).

Bond Ratings*		
Moody's	S&P	Description
Aaa	AAA	*Prime-Quality Investment Bonds*—This is the highest rating assigned, denoting extremely strong capacity to pay.
AaA A	AA A	*High-Grade Investment Bonds*—These are also considered very safe bonds, though they're not quite as safe as Aaa/AAA issues; double-A-rated bonds (Aa/AA) are safer (have less risk of default) than single-A-rated issues.
Baa	BBB	*Medium-Grade Investment Bonds*—These are the lowest of the investment-grade issues; they're felt to lack certain protective elements against adverse economic conditions.
Ba B	BB B	*Junk Bonds*—With little protection against default, these are viewed as highly speculative securities.
Caa Ca C	CCC CC C D	*Poor-Quality Bonds*—These are either in default or very close to it; these are often referred to as "Zombie Bonds."

*Some ratings may be modified to show relative standing within a major rating category; for example, Moody's uses numerical modifiers (1, 2, 3), whereas S&P uses plus (+) or minus (−) signs.

Once a new issue is rated, the process doesn't stop there. Older, outstanding bonds are also regularly reviewed to ensure that their assigned ratings are still valid. Most issues will carry a single rating to maturity, but it is not uncommon for some to undergo revision.

Finally, although it may appear that the issuing firm or municipality is receiving the rating, it is actually the individual issue that is being rated. As a result, a firm (or municipality) can have different ratings assigned to its issues; the senior securities, for example, might carry one rating and the junior issues a slightly lower rating. Most bond investors pay careful attention to ratings, because they can affect comparative market yields—specifically, *the higher the rating, the lower the yield of an obligation*, other things being equal. Thus, whereas an A-rated bond might offer an 8 percent yield, a comparable AAA issue would probably yield something like 7.25 or 7.50 percent.

Bond Quotes

Exhibit 12.10 contains examples of corporate bond quotes; these quotes were reported in *The Wall Street Journal* and were for trades that occurred on July 31, 2003. To understand the system used with corporate bonds, look at the highlighted Sara Lee quote. Note that the name of the issuer is followed parenthetically by the company's ticker symbol (in this case, SLE). The following two items are pretty self-explanatory: this particular issue carries a coupon of 3.875 percent and will mature on June 15, 2013 (thus, it has 10 years to maturity). Next is the "last price" at which the issue traded on July 31; in other words, the last trade for the day was at 90.546 percent of par. Unless you're a big-time investor, this is probably *not* the price you'd pay to buy the bond, as these prices are for minimum *trades of $1 million or more.* Buy in smaller lots and a "dealer spread" will be tacked on, meaning that you'll buy at a higher price, or sell at a lower price than the one quoted here.

Following the last price is the "last yield" (of 5.106 percent), which represents the bond's closing *yield-to-maturity* (a fully compounded measure of return that captures both current income and capital gains or losses, and which will be discussed later in this chapter). The next two columns ("Est. Spread" and "UST") show the spread (or differential) between the yield on the Sara Lee bond and a comparable U.S. Treasury security. The spread is measured in "basis points," where 1 basis point = $\frac{1}{100}$ of 1 percent—in other words, there are 100 basis points in a percentage point. Note in Exhibit 12.10 that SLE's last yield was 63 basis points higher than a comparable 10-year Treasuries; the 10 in the "UST" column indicates that a 10-year Treasury is used as the benchmark issue in the yield spread measure. Finally, as can be seen in the last column, some $85 million worth of these SLE bonds changed hands on July 31, 2003. *All bonds are quoted as a percent of par*, meaning that a quote of, say, 85 translates into a price of 85 percent of the bond's par value. Because corporate bonds typically have par values of $1,000, a bond quote of 85 means the price is really $850 (85% × $1,000). Thus, Sara Lee's closing price for the day was $905.46, found by multiplying the quoted price by $1,000; that is, 90.546% of par = 0.90546 × $1,000 = $905.46.

In contrast to corporates, U.S. Treasury (and agency) bond quotes are listed in thirty-seconds of a point. With government bonds, the figures to the right of the colon (:) show the number of thirty-seconds in the fractional bid or ask price. For example, look at the bid price of the 9.25 percent U.S. Treasury issue highlighted in Exhibit 12.11; it's being quoted at 141:08 (ask). Translated, that means the bond is being quoted at 141$\frac{8}{32}$, or 141.25 percent of par. Thus, if you wanted to buy, say, 15 of these bonds (with a par value of $15,000), you'd have to pay $21,187.50 (i.e., $15,000 × 1.4125). Here again, these quotes are for minimum trades of $1 million or more, so the amount you'd actually pay would likely be more than that after dealer spreads and other transaction costs are tacked on. Take another look at Exhibit 12.11; you'll notice the quotes on these securities include not only the coupon (see the "Rate" column), but the month and year of maturity as well. Listed next are the price quotes on the bonds. Note that Treasuries are quoted in bid/ask terms; *bid* means what bond dealers are willing to pay (and how much you can sell them for) and *ask*

EXHIBIT 12.10

Price Quotes for Corporate Notes and Bonds

Like most fixed-income securities, corporate notes and bonds are quoted as a percent of their par values. Listed here are *The Wall Street Journal* quotes for the 40 most actively traded (fixed-rate) corporate bonds; the *Journal* doesn't devote any space to thinly-traded issues for the simple reason that there are just too many of them (there are literally hundreds of NYSE-listed bonds, for example, that trade just 5 or 10 bonds a day).

Corporate Bonds

Thursday, July 31, 2003
Forty most active fixed-coupon corporate bonds

Sara Lee Issue (note)

COMPANY (TICKER)	COUPON	MATURITY	LAST PRICE	LAST YIELD	*EST SPREAD	UST†	EST $ VOL (800's)
General Motors (GM)	8.375	Jul 15, 2033	93.455	9.008	365	30	340,425
Bank of America (BAC)	3.250	Aug 15, 2008	96.625	3.997	78	5	194,555
Bank of America (BAC)	4.750	Aug 15, 2013	95.398	5.348	94	10	146,190
General Motors (GM)	7.125	Jul 15, 2013	97.628	7.465	305	10	146,096
General Electric (GE)	5.000	Feb 01, 2013	98.037	5.265	85	10	144,634
Comcast Cable Communications Holdings(CMCSA)	8.375	Mar 15, 2013	118.129	5.878	147	10	135,940
General Motors (GM)	8.250	Jul 15, 2023	95.410	8.738	335	30	117,653
Ford Motor Credit (F)	7.250	Oct 25, 2011	98.903	7.428	301	10	117,617
Goldman Sachs Group (GS)	4.750	July 15, 2013	93.669	5.588	119	10	111,659
Citigroup (C)	3.500	Feb 01, 2008	98.772	3.800	58	5	104,746
DaimlerChrylser North America Holding (DCX)	4.050	Jun 04, 2008	96.129	4.960	168	5	99,620
Morgan Stanley (MWD)	5.300	Mar 01, 2013	97.882	5.588	118	10	93,529
Wal-Mart Stores (WMI)	4.558	May 02, 2013	96.497	5.008	54	10	88,705
Sara Lee (SLE)	3.875	Jun 15, 2013	90.546	5.106	63	10	85,019
American Express (AXP)	4.875	Jul 15, 2013	97.153	5.246	83	10	83,560
General Electric Capital (GE)	3.500	May 01, 2008	98.251	3.907	62	5	82,391
General Motors Acceptance (GMAC)	8.000	Nov 01, 2031	92.482	8.718	336	30	81,937
Comcast Holdings (CMCSA)	5.300	Jan 15, 2014	95.530	5.875	147	10	80,008
Houshold Finance (HSBC)	4.750	Jul 15, 2013	93.210	5.652	123	10	77,682
Ford Motor Credit (F)	7.375	Oct 28, 2009	102.108	6.949	373	5	74,962
General Dynamics (GD)	4.250	May 15, 2013	93.395	5.116	71	10	71,113
Houshold Finance (HSBC)	6.500	Jan 24, 2006	108.740	2.811	53	3	70,691
Sprint Capital (FON)	8.750	Mar 15, 2032	109.755	7.885	254	30	67,855
General Electric Capital (GE)	5.450	Jan 15, 2013	100.752	5.415	90	10	65,319
Citigroup (C)	5.625	Aug 27, 2012	102.275	5.305	80	10	64,782
DaimlerChrylser North America Holding (DCX)	8.500	Jan 18, 2031	110.332	7.598	225	30	62,075
Bank of America (BAC)	4.875	Jan 15, 2013	96.507	5.351	93	10	60,355
Lehman Brothers Holdings (LEH)	6.625	Jan 18, 2012	109.515	5.218	68	10	59,943
AT&T Wireless Services (AWE)	8.125	May 01, 2012	114.634	5.951	155	10	57,225
Wetts Fargo (WFC)	6.625	Jul 15, 2004	104.919	1.364	n.a.	n.a.	54,683
Citigroup (C)	6.000	Feb 21, 2012	106.012	5.122	69	10	54,483
Tenet Healthcare (THC)	7.375	Feb 01, 2013	94.500	8.221	372	10	51,310
Fod Motor Credit (F)	6.875	Feb 01, 2000	105.095	4.682	245	3	51,085
General Motors Acceptance (GMAC)	4.500	Jul 15, 2006	100.270	4.399	219	3	50,093
Bank of America (BAC)	7.400	Jan 15, 2011	114.869	4.984	50	10	50,048
Washington Mutual Bank (WM)	6.875	Jun 15, 2011	111.644	5.060	64	10	49,328

Source: The *Wall Street Journal*, August 1, 2003.

EXHIBIT 12.11

Price Quotes for U.S. Treasury Securities

Listed here are *The Wall Street Journal* quotes for some coupon-bearing and zero-coupon Treasury securities. Note that Treasuries are quoted in fractions of thirty-seconds of a point, rather in decimals (like corporate bonds). You can also see here that both coupon and maturity play vital roles in the quotation system. For example, look in the Treasury quotes (the ones on the left) and you'll find no less than five issues that mature in 2007, yet these bonds have five different (ask) prices—the reason: five different coupons.

TREASURIES

RATE	MATURITY MO/YR	BID	ASKED	CHG	ASK YLD	
5.625	Feb 06n	108:27	108:28	-10	2.02	
9.375	Feb 06	118:02	118:03	-12	2.03	
2.000	May 06n	99:15	99:16	-9	2.19	
4.625	May 06n	106:17	106:18	-10	2.18	
6.875	May 06n	112:17	112:18	-10	2.20	
7.000	Jul 06n	113:10	113:11	-10	2.30	
6.500	Oct 06n	112:12	112:13	-10	2.45	
3.500	Nov 06n	103:03	103:04	-10	2.50	
6.625	May 07n	113:27	113:28	-10	2.74	
4.375	May 07n	105:23	105:24	-11	2.76	
3.250	Aug 07n	101:10	101:11	-10	2.89	
6.125	Aug 07n	112:10	112:11	-11	2.87	
3.000	Nov 07n	99:29	99:30	-11	3.01	
6.500	Feb 10n	115:13	115:14	-22	3.81	← U.S. Treasury note
11.750	Feb 10	115:07	115:08	-9	1.67	
10.000	May 10	114:11	114:12	-10	1.78	
5.750	Aug 10n	110:28	110:29	-24	3.96	
12.750	Nov 10	123:26	123:27	-11	2.02	
5.000	Feb 11n	105:25	105:26	-26	4.09	
13.875	May 11	131:03	131:04	-16	2.28	
5.000	Aug 11n	105:11	105:12	-28	4.20	
14.000	Nov 11	136:15	136:16	-12	2.38	
12.000	Aug 13	140:06	140:07	-17	3.27	
13.250	May 14	150:25	150:26	-20	3.48	
12.500	Aug 14	148:02	148:03	-25	3.57	
11.750	Nov 14	144:26	144:27	-27	3.69	
11.250	Feb 15	158:11	158:12	-55	4.65	
10.625	Aug 15	153:21	153:22	-56	4.72	
8.875	Nov 15	146:29	146:30	-54	4.70	
9.250	Feb 16	141:07	141:08	-52	4.83	← U.S. Treasury bond
7.250	May 16	122:02	122:03	-49	4.90	
7.500	Nov 16	124:11	124:12	-53	4.97	
8.750	May 17	137:08	137:09	-55	4.98	
8.875	Aug 17	138:22	138:23	-56	5.00	
9.125	May 18	140:22	140:23	-87	5.15	
9.000	Nov 18	140:18	140:19	-74	5.13	
8.875	Feb 19	139:13	139:14	-73	5.15	
8.125	Aug 19	131:10	131:11	-73	5.22	
8.500	Feb 20	135:29	135:30	-75	5.23	
8.750	May 20	138:30	138:31	-75	5.23	
8.750	Aug 20	139:01	139:02	-75	5.25	
7.857	Feb 21	129:03	129:04	-74	5.30	
8.125	May 21	132:06	132:07	-76	5.30	
8.125	Aug 21	132:06	132:07	-77	5.32	
8.000	Nov 21	130:28	130:29	-76	5.33	
7.250	Aug 22	122:00	122:01	-74	5.39	
7.625	Nov 22	126:23	126:24	-76	5.38	
7.125	Feb 23	120:21	120:22	-73	5.40	
6.250	Aug 23	109:29	109:30	-69	5.43	
7.500	Nov 24	126:01	126:02	-78	5.42	
7.625	Feb 25	127:24	127:25	-79	5.42	
6.875	Aug 25	118:06	118:07	-73	5.44	
6.000	Feb 26	106:29	106:30	-68	5.46	

U.S. TREASURY STRIPS

	MATURITY	TYPE	BID	ASKED	CHG	ASK YLD
	Feb 06	bp	94:26	94:28	-10	2.10
	Feb 06	np	94:28	94:29	-10	2.08
	May 06	ci	93:30	93:31	-11	2.25
	May 06	np	93:27	93:28	-11	2.28
	Jul 06	ci	94:07	94:09	-12	2.01
	Jul 06	np	93:08	93:10	-12	2.36
	Aug 06	ci	93:04	93:06	-12	2.35
	Oct 06	np	92:05	92:07	-11	2.55
	Nov 06	ci	91:31	92:01	-13	2.55
	Nov 06	np	91:27	91:29	-16	2.59
	Feb 07	ci	90:20	90:22	-12	2.79
	Feb 07	np	90:27	90:29	-12	2.72
	May 07	ci	89:20	89:22	-13	2.90
	May 07	np	89:24	89:26	-13	2.87
	Aug 07	np	88:24	88:26	-13	2.96
	Aug 07	ci	88:23	88:25	-14	2.97
	Aug 07	np	88:20	88:23	-13	2.99
	Nov 07	ci	87:29	87:31	-14	3.02
	Nov 07	np	87:20	87:22	-14	3.09
	Feb 08	ci	86:16	86:18	-15	3.21
	Feb 08	np	86:14	86:17	-14	3.22
	May 08	ci	85:09	85:12	-15	3.34
	May 08	np	85:06	85:09	-15	3.36
	Aug 08	ci	84:18	84:21	-16	3.34
	Nov 08	ci	83:08	83:10	-16	3.48
	Nov 08	np	82:31	83:02	-16	3.55
	Feb 09	ci	81:15	81:18	-23	3.72
	May 09	ci	80:09	80:12	-23	3.82
	May 09	np	80:21	80:24	-24	3.73
	Aug 09	ci	79:17	79:20	-24	3.82
	Aug 09	np	79:10	79:13	-24	3.86
	Nov 09	ci	78:29	79:00	-25	3.79
	Nov 09	bp	77:17	77:20	-25	4.08
	Feb 10	ci	76:17	76:20	-27	4.12
Stripped (zero-coupon) Treasury →	Feb 10	np	76:28	76:31	-27	4.05
	May 10	ci	75:15	75:18	-27	4.18
	Aug 10	ci	74:18	74:22	-28	4.20
	Aug 10	np	74:18	74:22	-28	4.20
	Nov 10	ci	73:28	74:00	-29	4.18
	Feb 11	ci	72:02	72:06	-29	4.38
	Feb 11	np	72:13	72:17	-29	4.31

Source: *The Wall Street Journal*, August 1, 2003.

is what they will sell the bonds for (or what it will cost you to buy). Finally, the last two columns include the change ("CHG") in the ask price and the yield-to-maturity on the issue, based on the latest ask price ("ASK YLD").

Quotes on Zero-Coupon Bonds

Also included in Exhibit 12.11 are quotes for some zero-coupon bonds. You'll find these listed under the heading "U.S. Treasury Strips." As we discussed earlier in this chapter, these securities are created by "stripping" coupons from bond issues and selling them separately from the principal. Thus the principal and interest *cash flows* can be sold on their own. (Look at the quotes: A *ci* behind the maturity date means the issue is made up of coupon/interest cash flow, whereas an *np* or *bp* means it is made up of principle from a note or bond.) The prices of most zeros are quite low compared to regular coupon bonds. For example, note the highlighted Strip-T of February 2010. This issue is trading at an ask price of 76³¹⁄₃₂, or less than $770 for each $1,000 in par value. The same issue in coupon form is the highlighted 6½ percent U.S. Treasury note of February 2010, which is trading at an ask price of just under 115½. Thus, the strip-T version is selling at about ⅔ the price of the comparable coupon bearing security. Now keep in mind these quotes occurred at a time when market yields were at near-40 year lows. As a result, the market prices are abnormally high. Several years ago, in early 2000, when market yields were more like 6 or 7 percent, this same February 2010 strip-T was trading at something closer to $525.

Bond Prices and Yields

The price of a bond is a function of its coupon, maturity, and the movement of market interest rates. *When interest rates go down, bond prices go up, and vice versa.* The relationship of bond prices to market rates is captured in Exhibit 12.12. Basically, the graph serves to reinforce the *inverse* relationship between bond prices and market interest rates; note that *lower* rates lead to *higher* bond prices. The exhibit also shows the difference between premium and discount bonds. A **premium bond** is one that sells for more than its par value, which occurs whenever market interest rates drop below the coupon rate on the bond; a **discount bond**, in contrast, sells for less than par, and is the result of market rates being greater than the issue's coupon rate. Thus, the 10 percent bond in our illustration traded as a premium bond when market rates were at 8 percent but as a discount bond when rates stood at 12 percent.

premium bond
A bond that has a market value in excess of par; occurs when interest rates drop below the coupon rate.

discount bond
A bond with a market value lower than par; occurs when market rates are greater than the coupon rate.

When a bond is first issued, it is usually sold to the public at a price that equals, or is very close to, its par value. Likewise, when the bond matures—some 15, 20, or 30 years later—it will once again be priced at its par value. But what happens to the price of the bond in between is of considerable concern to most bond investors. In this regard, we know that the extent to which bond prices move depends not only on the *direction* of change in interest rates, but also on the *magnitude* of such changes; for the greater the moves in interest rates, the greater the swings in bond prices. But there's more, for bond prices will also vary according to the coupon and maturity of the issue—that is, bonds with *lower coupons* or *longer maturities* will respond more vigorously to changes in market rates and undergo *greater price swings.* It should be obvious, therefore, that if interest rates are moving up, the investor should seek high coupon bonds with short maturities, because this will cause minimal price variation and *preserve as much capital as possible.* In contrast, if rates are heading down, that's the time to be in long-term bonds—if you're a speculator looking for lots of capital gains, then go with long-term, *low coupon bonds*, whereas if you're trying to lock in a high level of coupon (interest) income, then stick with long-term, *high coupon* bonds that offer plenty of call protection (which you can get from issues that are noncallable or have extended call-deferment periods).

EXHIBIT 12.12

Price Behavior of a Bond with a 10 Percent Coupon

A bond will sell at its par value as long as the prevailing market interest rate remains the same as the bond's coupon (for example, when both coupon and market rates equal 10 percent). However, when market rates drop, bond prices rise, and vice versa; moreover, as a bond approaches its maturity, the price of the issue will always move toward its par value, no matter what happens to interest rates.

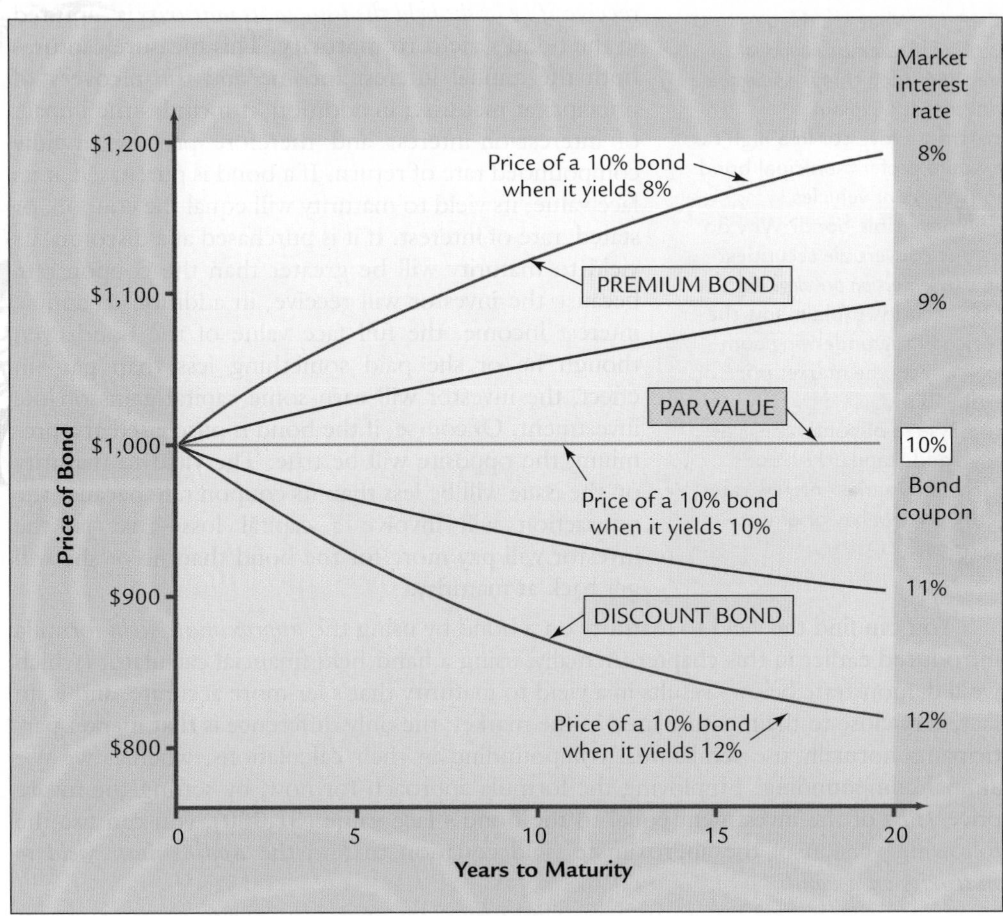

Current Yield and Yield to Maturity

The *yield* on a bond is the rate of return you would earn if you held the bond for a stated period of time. The two most commonly cited bond yields are current yield and yield to maturity. **Current yield** reflects the amount of annual interest income the bond provides relative to its current market price. The formula for current yield is:

current yield The amount of current income a bond provides relative to its market price.

$$\text{Current yield} = \frac{\text{Annual interest income}}{\text{Market price of bond}}$$

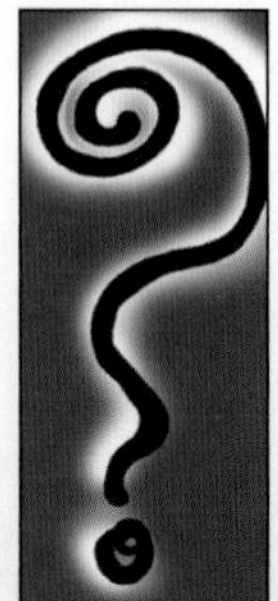

Concept✓

12-10. What is the difference between a secured bond and an unsecured bond? Give a few examples of each. Briefly describe the following bond features: (a) *sinking funds,* (b) *call features,* and (c) *coupon.*

12-11. Are *junk bonds* and *zero coupon bonds* the same? Explain. What are the basic tax features of a tax-exempt *municipal bond?* Are there such things as *taxable* municipal bonds? Explain.

12-12. Illustrate why an investor in a high tax bracket would prefer municipal bonds to other investment vehicles.

12-13. What is a convertible bond? Why do investors buy convertible securities?

12-14. Describe the *conversion privelege* on a convertible security. Explain how the market price of the underlying common stock affects the market price of a convertible bond.

12-15. Explain the system of bond ratings used by Moody's and Standard & Poor's.

12-16. What effects do market interest rates have on the price behavior of outstanding bonds?

As you can see, the current yield on a bond is basically the same as the dividend yield on a stock. Assume, for example, that a 9 percent bond with a $1,000 face value is currently selling for $910. Because annual interest income would amount to $90 (i.e., 0.09 × $1,000) and the current market price of the bond is $910, its current yield would be 9.89 percent ($90/$910). This measure of yield would be of interest to *investors seeking current income*; other things being equal, the higher the current yield, the more attractive a bond would be to such an investor.

The annual rate of return a bondholder would receive *if he or she held the issue to its maturity* is captured in the bond's **yield to maturity**. This measure captures both the annual interest income and the recovery of principal at maturity; in addition, it includes the impact of interest-on-interest and therefore provides a fully compounded rate of return. If a bond is purchased at its face value, its yield to maturity will equal the coupon, or stated, rate of interest. If it is purchased at a discount, its yield to maturity will be greater than the coupon rate because the investor will receive, in addition to annual interest income, the full face value of the bond even though he or she paid something less than par—in effect, the investor will earn some capital gains on the investment. Of course, if the bond is purchased at a premium, the opposite will be true: The yield to maturity on the issue will be less than its coupon rate because the transaction will involve a capital loss—that is, the investor will pay more for the bond than he or she will get back at maturity.

yield to maturity The fully compounded rate of return a bondholder would earn if he or she held it to maturity.

You can find the yield to maturity on a bond by using the *approximate yield* formula introduced earlier in this chapter. Actually, using a hand-held financial calculator (which we'll demonstrate below) results in a yield to maturity that's far more accurate, and is, in fact, very close to the measure used in the market; the only difference is that market participants normally use semiannual compounding in their calculations, whereas we use annual compounding. Employing the formula approach for now, by setting the future price *(FP)* of the investment equal to the bond's face value ($1,000), you can use the following version of the approximate yield equation to find the *approximate yield to maturity on a bond:*

$$\text{Approximate yield to maturity} = \frac{CI + \left[\dfrac{\$1{,}000 - CP}{N}\right]}{\left[\dfrac{CP + \$1{,}000}{2}\right]}$$

As you will recall, CI equals annual current income (or annual interest income, in the case of a bond), CP stands for current price (of the bond), and N is the investment period (the number of years to maturity). Assume, for example, you are contemplating the purchase of a $1,000, 9 percent bond with 15 years remaining to maturity, and that the bond currently trades at a price of $910. Given CI = $90, CP = $910, and N = 15 years, the approximate yield to maturity on this bond will be:

$$\text{Approximate yield to maturity} = \frac{\$90 + \left[\dfrac{\$1{,}000 - \$910}{15}\right]}{\left[\dfrac{\$910 + \$1{,}000}{2}\right]} = \frac{\$90 + \left[\dfrac{\$90}{15}\right]}{\left[\dfrac{\$1{,}910}{2}\right]} = \underline{\underline{10.05\%}}$$

This is above both the 9 percent stated (coupon) rate and the 9.89 percent current yield, because the bond is purchased at a discount from its face value. (Note that had the bond been selling at $1,090, it would have had a current yield of 8.26 percent and an approximate yield to maturity of 8.04 percent—both below the 9 percent coupon rate; such behavior would be due to the fact that the bond was selling at a premium price.)

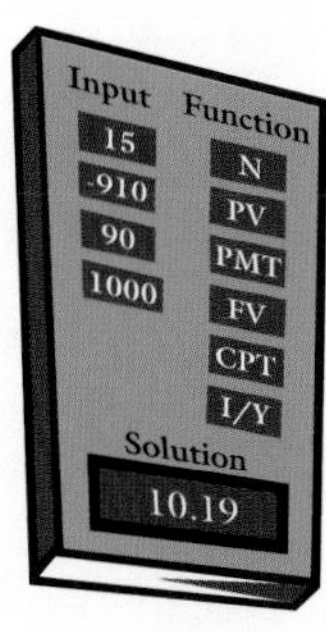

Calculator Keystrokes. You can also *find the yield to maturity on a bond* by using a financial calculator; here's what you'd do. With the calculator in the *annual mode*, to find the yield to maturity on our 9 percent (annual pay coupon), 15-year bond that's currently trading at $910, use the keystrokes shown here where:

N = number of *years* to maturity,

PV = the current market price of the bond, entered as a *negative*,

PMT = the size of the annual coupon payments, in *dollars*,

FV = the par value of the bond.

A value of 10.19 should appear in the calculator display—this is the yield to maturity on the bond in question (and it's a *more accurate* measure of yield than the 10.05 percent found by using the "approximate" procedure).

Yield to maturity measures are used by investors to assess the underlying attractiveness of a bond investment. The higher the yield to maturity, the more attractive the investment, other things being equal. *If a bond provided a yield to maturity that equaled or exceeded an investor's desired rate of return, it would be considered a worthwhile investment candidate*, because it would promise a yield that should adequately compensate the investor for the level of risk involved.

SUMMARY

LG1. Describe the various types of risks to which investors are exposed, as well as the sources of return. Although investing offers returns in the form of current income and/or capital gains, it also involves risk; the basic types of investment risk are business risk, financial risk, market risk, purchasing power risk, interest rate risk, liquidity risk, and event risk—all of which combine to affect the level of return from an investment.

LG2. Know how to search for an acceptable investment, based on risk, return, and yield. The value, and therefore the acceptability, of any investment is a function of the amount of return it's expected to produce relative to the amount of perceived risk involved in the investment. Investors are entitled to be compensated for the risks they must accept in an investment; therefore, the more risk there is in an investment, the more return you should expect to earn. This risk-return tradeoff is generally captured in the "desired rate of return," which is that rate of return you feel you should receive in compensation for the amount of risk you must assume. As long as the expected return on an investment (the return you *think* you'll earn) is greater than the desired rate of return (the return you *should* earn), it should be considered an acceptable investment candidate—one worthy of your attention.

LG3. Discuss the merits of investing in common stock and be able to distinguish among the different types of stocks. Common stocks are a popular form of investing that can be used to meet just about any investment objective—from capital gains or current income to some combination of both. Investors can choose from blue chips, growth, or tech stocks; income, speculative, cyclical, or defensive stocks; and small- or mid-cap stocks. If they're so inclined, they can even buy foreign stocks by investing in ADRs (American Depositary Receipts).

LG4. Become familiar with the various measures of performance and how to use them in putting a value on stocks. The value of a share of stock is based in large part on various performance measures such as dividend yield, book value, net profit margin, return on investment (ROE), earnings per share, price/earnings (P/E) ratio, beta, and approximate yield, which can be used to provide a measure of expected return. Investors look at these measures to gain insights about the financial condition and operating results of the company, and ultimately, to obtain the input needed to measure the expected return on the stock.

LG5. Describe the basic issue characteristics of bonds and note how these securities are used as investment vehicles. Bonds are another popular form of investing; they are often referred to as fixed-income securities because the debt service obligations of the issuer are fixed. The coupon that the bond carries defines the amount of annual interest income that the investor will receive over time, while the par value defines the amount of capital to be repaid at maturity. Bonds may be issued with or without collateral and most bonds allow the issuer to retire the issue prior to its maturity. As investment vehicles, bonds can be used to generate either current income or capital gains (which occur when market rates go down).

LG6. Distinguish between the different types of bonds, gain an understanding of how bond prices behave, and know how to compute different measures of yield. Bonds are the publicly issued debt of corporations and various levels of government (from the U.S. Treasury and various agencies of the U.S. government to state and local—municipal—governments). Regardless of the issuer, the price of a bond moves inversely with market interest rates—thus, the lower the market rate, the higher the price of the bond. There are basically two ways to measure the yield performance of a bond: one is current yield, which looks only at the coupon income on a bond, and the other is yield to maturity, which provides a full-compounded rate of return that considers not only interest income, but also any capital gains (or loss).

Financial Planning Exercises

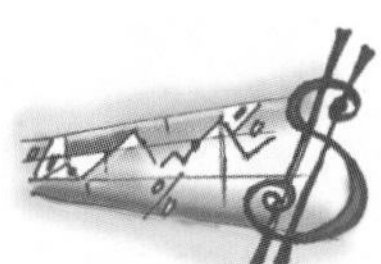

1. What makes for a good investment? Use the approximate yield formula, or a financial calculator, to rank the following investments according to their expected returns:
   a. Buy a stock for $45 a share, hold it for 3 years, then sell it for $75 a share (the stock pays annual dividends of $3 a share).

b. Buy a security for $25, hold it for 2 years, then sell it for $60 (current income on this security is zero).

c. Buy a 1-year, 12 percent note for $950 (assume that the note has a $1,000 par value and that it will be held to maturity).

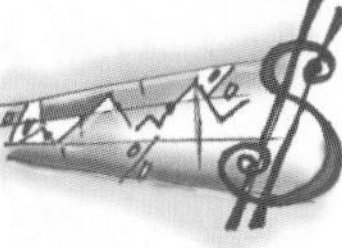

2. Selected financial information about Engulf and Devour, Inc. is provided as follows:

Total assets	$20,000,000
Total liabilities	$ 8,000,000
Total preferred stock	$ 3,000,000
Total annual preferred stock dividends	$ 240,000
Net profits after tax	$ 2,500,000
Number of shares of common stock outstanding	500,000 shares
Current market price of common stock	$50.00 a share
Annual common stock dividends	$ 2.50 a share

Using the above information, compute the following:

a. The stock's dividend yield

b. Book value per share

c. Earnings per share

d. P/E ratio

3. Assume that you've just inherited $350,000 and have decided to invest a big chunk of it ($250,000 to be exact) in common stocks. Your objective is to build up as much capital as you can over the next 15 to 20 years, and you're willing to tolerate a "good deal" of risk.

a. What *types* of stocks (for example, blue chips, income stocks, and so on) do you think you'd be most interested in and why? Come up with at least three different types of stocks and briefly explain the rationale for each.

b. Would your selections change if you were dealing with a smaller amount of money—say, only $50,000? What if you were a more risk-adverse investor?

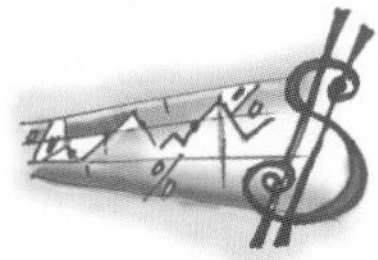

4. Using the resources available at your campus or public library, select a company from *Value Line* that would be of interest to you. (*Hint*: choose a company that's been publicly traded for at least 10 to 15 years, and *avoid* public utilities, banks, and other financial institutions.) Obtain a copy of the latest *Value Line* report on your chosen company. Using the forecasted data reported in *Value Line*, determine the following. (*Note:* Use a 3-year holding period throughout this exercise.)

a. What's the latest price of the stock you selected and how much is the stock currently paying in annual dividends?

b. According to *Value Line*, what are the (approximate) projected dividends per share for each of the next 3 years? Also, what's the (approximate) estimated price of the stock at the end of the 3-year holding period?

c. Use the approximate yield equation to find the expected return on this stock; repeat the calculation using a financial calculator.

d. If you were investing in this stock, what would you want to earn as a minimum/required rate of return? Briefly explain how you came up with that number.

e. Would you consider this stock to be a worthwhile investment candidate? Explain.

5. An investor is thinking about buying some shares of FinComm-I at $60 a share. She expects the price of the stock to rise to $100 a share over the next 3 years. During that time, she also expects to receive annual dividends of $3 per share. Given that the

investor's expectations (about the future price of the stock and the dividends it pays) hold up, what rate of return can the investor expect to earn on this investment? (*Hint*: Use either the approximate yield formula or a financial calculator to solve this problem.)

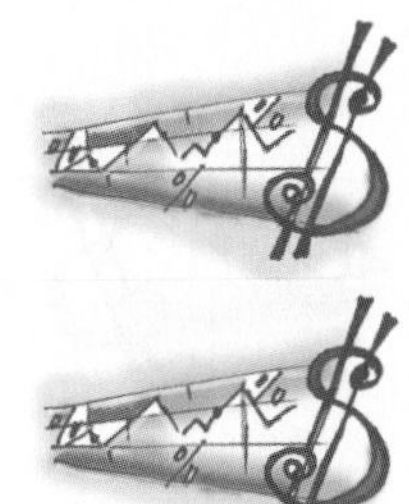

6. A company has total assets of $2.5 million, total liabilities of $1.8 million, and $200,000 worth of 8 percent preferred stock outstanding. What is the firm's total book value? What would its book value per share be if the firm had 50,000 shares of common stock outstanding?
7. The Med Online Co. recently reported net profits after taxes of $15.8 million. It has 2.5 million shares of common stock outstanding and pays preferred dividends of $1 million a year. The company's stock currently trades at $60 per share.
   a. Compute the stock's earnings per share (EPS).
   b. What's the stock's P/E ratio?
   c. Determine what the stock's dividend yield would be if it paid $1.75 per share to common stockholders.
8. The price of Consolidated Everything is now $65. The company pays no dividends. Mr. M. Bags expects the price 4 years from now to be $105 a share. Should Mr. B. buy Consolidated E. if he desires a 15 percent rate of return? Explain.
9. An investor in the 28 percent tax bracket is trying to decide which of two bonds to select: One is a 6.5 percent U.S. Treasury bond selling at par and the other is a municipal bond with a 5.25 percent coupon, which is also selling at par. Which of these two bonds should the investor select? Why?

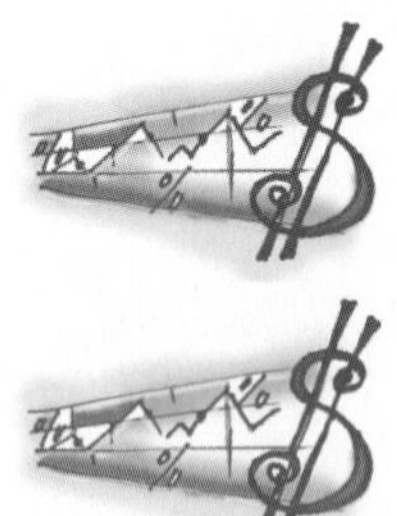

10. Describe and differentiate between a bond's (a) current yield and (b) yield to maturity. Why are these yield measures important to the bond investor? Find the yield to maturity of a 20-year, 9 percent, $1,000 par value bond trading at a price of $850. What's the current yield on this bond?
11. Which of the following three bonds offers the highest current yield? Which one has the highest yield to maturity?
    a. A 9.5 percent, 20-year bond quoted at 97.75
    b. A 16 percent, 15-year bond quoted at 164.625
    c. A 5.25 percent, 18-year bond quoted at 54
12. Using the bond quotes in Exhibits 12.10 and 12.11, how much would you have to pay for the following bonds? (Assume that all the bonds have $1,000 par values.)
    a. The 8¼ percent General Motors bond that matures in 2023
    b. The 3.5 percent Citigroup bond that matures in 2008
    c. The 8¾ percent Sprint Capital bond that matures in 2032
    d. The 12½ percent U.S. Treasury bond that matures in August 2014
    e. The Treasury Strip bond that matures in February 2011

    Also, according to the quotes, what's the latest yield on each of these five bonds?

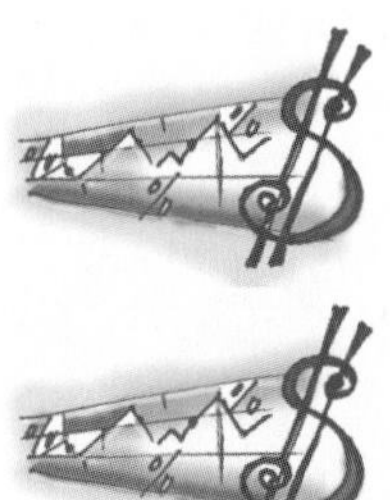

13. Find the current yield of a 10 percent, 25-year bond that is currently priced in the market at $1,250. Now, use a financial calculator to find the yield-to-maturity on this bond. What's the current yield and yield-to-maturity on this bond given that it trades at $1,000? How about if it's priced at $750? Comment on your findings.
14. A 25-year, zero coupon bond was recently quoted at 12.50. Find the current yield and yield to maturity of this issue, given the bond has a par value of $1,000. (Assume annual compounding for the yield-to-maturity measure.)

15. Assume that an investor pays $850 for a long-term bond that carries a 7½ percent coupon. Over the course of the next 12 months, interest rates drop sharply. As a result, the investor sells the bond at a price of $962.50.
    a. Find the current yield that existed on this bond at the beginning of the year. What was it by the end of the 1-year holding period?
    b. Compute the return on this investment using the approximate yield formula and a 1-year investment period.
16. Find the conversion value of a convertible bond that carries a conversion ratio of 24, given that the market price of the underlying common stock is $55 a share. Would there be any conversion premium if the convertible bond had a market price of $1,500? If so, how much?
17. A certain 6 percent convertible bond (maturing in 20 years) is convertible into 20 shares of the company's common stock. The bond has a par value of $1,000 and is currently trading at $800; the stock (which pays a dividend of 75 cents a share) is currently trading in the market at $35 a share. Use the above information to answer the following questions:
    a. What is the current yield on the convertible bond? What is the dividend yield on the company's common stock? Which provides more current income: the convertible bond or the common stock? Explain.
    b. What is the bond's conversion ratio? Its conversion price?
    c. What is the conversion value of this issue? Is there any conversion premium in this issue? How much?
    d. What is the (approximate) yield to maturity on the convertible bond?

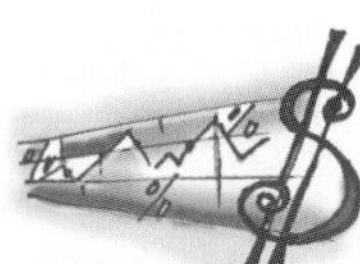

18. Using the resources available at your campus or public library, work the following problems. (*Note*: Show your work for all your calculations.)
    a. Select any two *common* stocks, and determine the dividend yield, earnings per share, and P/E ratio for each.
    b. Select any two *bonds*, and determine the current yield and yield to maturity of each.
    c. Select any two *convertible debentures*, and determine the conversion ratio, conversion value, and conversion premium for each.

APPLYING PERSONAL FINANCE

What's Your Type?

In this chapter, we learned that common stock is often classified into various categories, such as blue chip, growth, income, and so forth, and according to its size, such as large-, mid-, or small-cap. The purpose of this project is to examine and compare the returns on various types of common stock.

Common comparisons frequently include:

- Large-cap vs. mid- or small-cap
- Blue chip vs. speculative
- Growth vs. income
- Growth vs. value

Pick two combinations that interest you and select a stock to represent each of the categories included in your choices. For all four of your stocks, obtain information on:

- The company's growth in earnings (EPS)
- Growth in dividends per share
- Dividend yield

- Price/earnings ratio
- The stock's beta

In addition, use the formula given in this chapter to compute each stock's approximate yield for the past year, based on what the stock is trading for today versus the price it sold for a year ago. Be sure to include any dividends paid over the past 12 months. This information can be obtained from financial newspapers or from online sources, such as **http://finance.yahoo.com**.

Compare and contrast the performance and characteristics of the stocks you have chosen. Based on your findings, does the type of stock you own make a difference? Which type or types are the most suitable for your investment purposes?

CONTEMPORARY CASE APPLICATIONS

12.1 The Jordons' Problem: What to Do with All That Money?

A couple in their early thirties, Allen and Sandra Jordon recently inherited $90,000 from one of their relatives. Allen earns a comfortable income as a sales manager for Smith and Johnson, Inc., and Sandra does equally well as an attorney with a major law firm. Because they have no children and do not need the money, they have decided to invest all their inheritance in stocks, bonds, and perhaps even some money market instruments. However, because they are not very familiar with the market, they turn to you for help.

Questions

1. What kind of investment approach do you think the Jordons should adopt—that is, should they be conservative with their money or aggressive? Explain.
2. What kind of stocks do you think the Jordons should invest in? How important is current income to them (that is, dividends or interest income)? Should they be putting any of their money into bonds? Explain.
3. Construct an investment portfolio that you feel would be right for the Jordons; invest the full $90,000. Put actual stocks, bonds, and/or convertible securities in the portfolio; also, if you like, you may put up to one-third of the money into short-term securities such as CDs, Treasury bills, money funds, or MMDAs. Select any securities you want, so long as you feel they would be suitable for the Jordons. Make sure that the portfolio consists of six or more different securities; use the latest issue of *The Wall Street Journal* or an online source such as **http://finance.yahoo.com** to determine the market prices of the securities you select. Show the amount invested in each security along with the amount of current income (from dividends and/or interest) that will be generated from the investments. Briefly explain why you selected these particular securities for the Jordons' portfolio.

12.2 Kathy Decides to Try Her Hand at Investing

Kathy Karras is a 26-year-old management trainee at a large chemical company. She is single and has no plans for marriage. Her annual salary is $34,000 (placing her in the 15 percent tax bracket), and her monthly expenditures come to approximately $1,500. During the past year or so, Kathy has managed to save around $8,000, and she expects to continue to save at least that amount each year for the foreseeable future. Her company pays the premium on her $35,000 life insurance policy. Because Kathy's entire education was financed by scholarships, she was able to save money from the summer and part-time jobs she held as a student. Altogether, she has a nest egg of nearly $18,000, out of which she would like to invest about $15,000. She will keep the remaining $3,000 in a bank CD that pays 3 percent interest and will use this money only in the event of an emergency. Although Kathy can afford to take more risks than someone with family obligations, she does not wish to be a speculator; rather, she simply wants to earn an attractive rate of return on her investments.

Questions

1. What investment options are open to Kathy?
2. What chance does she have of earning a satisfactory return on her investments if she invests her $15,000 in (a) blue-chip stocks, (b) growth stocks, (c) speculative stocks, (d) corporate bonds, or (e) municipal bonds?
3. Discuss the factors you would consider when analyzing these alternate investment vehicles.
4. What recommendation would you make to Kathy with respect to her available investment alternatives? Explain.

Money Online

1. **http://finance.yahoo.com**
Find the ticker symbol for not only stocks and mutual funds, but also for indices and options at Yahoo's Lookup site. Enter any part of the name of the security and click on "Lookup" to bring up a listing of all the securities with those letters in their names. Type in "depot" for Home Depot to find that this company's ticker is HD and that it is listed as Home Depot, Inc.

2. **http://www.metlife.com**
When it comes to investing, one size does not fit all! Choose investments that are appropriate for you and your financial goals by determining your level of risk tolerance. At Met Life's Web site, click on "Meeting Life," "Financial," and then on "About Building Financial Freedom." Work your way through this excellent resource material or simply skip down to "Assess Your Level of Risk Tolerance." Continue through the material to learn more about the types of investments that meet your needs.

3. **http://www.zacks.com**
Profit from the pros! Scroll down to find free e-mail newsletters offered by Zacks, a premier investment research firm. Packed with insight and stock picks from leading investment experts, Zack's newsletters give the inside scoop on how the top professionals are making money in the market today.

4. **http://www.zacks.com/research**
Screen your stocks at Zacks. Design your own custom screen to find stocks that meet your criteria, or choose among several predefined screens used successfully by other investors. After you've found your stocks, be sure to research them at "Quotes & Research." Then create a portfolio of your favorite companies and track their performance.

5. **http://www.investors.com/learn**
What should you look for in stocks? How should you measure their performance? *Investor's Business Daily* presents the "IBD Learning Center," a series of lessons based on a half century of investment research. Sign up to receive two free weeks of their newspaper, a great resource for individual investors.

6. **http://www.bondsonline.com**
Don't know much about bonds? Want to know even more about all types of fixed income securities? Register with BondsOnline and then click on "Research Bonds" to find a world of information awaiting you! Browse through the Bond Professor's library or ask your own questions.

7. **http://www.nasd.com/Investor/choices**
Does the variety of investments confuse you? How do you know which ones are right for you? The Nasdaq Web site presents a tremendous collection of investor information.

Among their many offerings, read up on bonds and fixed-income investments, futures and options, or retirement accounts.

8. **http://www.investopedia.com**

What part about investing do you not understand? Whether you're a beginning investor, experienced investor, or active trader, Investopedia is geared to answer all your questions! Finding an investments dictionary, articles, tutorials, and even information concerning NASD exams for investment professionals.

9. **http://www.adrbny.com**

Invest internationally the convenient way with American Depositary Receipts. Visit the Web site of the Bank of New York, the world's largest depositary for American Depositary Receipts (ADRs) and Global Depositary Receipts (GDRs). Find up-to-date information about depositary receipts as well as site links to many companies that issue DRs. While you're there, you can also access news, pricing, analytical tools and financial data for depositary receipts.

Just for Fun!

10. **http://www.better-investing.org**

Start your own investment club and learn the ropes of investing with your friends! The National Association of Investment Clubs provides information on establishing and maintaining an investment club as well as guidance on becoming a successful long-term investor. While you're there, find out which stocks make up the *Better Investing* "Top 100 Index."

CHAPTER 13

Investing in Mutual Funds

Learning Goals

LG1. Describe the basic features and operating characteristics of a mutual fund.

LG2. Differentiate between open- and closed-end funds, as well as other types of professionally managed investment companies, and discuss the various types of fund loads and charges.

LG3. Discuss the types of funds available to investors, and the variety of investment objectives these funds seek to fulfill.

LG4. Identify and discuss the different kinds of investor services offered by mutual funds.

LG5. Gain an understanding of the variables that should be considered when selecting funds for investment purposes.

LG6. Identify the sources of return and calculate the rate of return earned on an investment in a mutual fund.

Not to Their Mutual Benefit . . .

Jay Rowan's retirement plans weren't flashy: He'd play a little more golf and take his wife out to dinner a little more frequently. Maybe they'd do the traveling they'd always dreamed about.

Like more than 95 million other Americans, the Rowans saw investing in mutual funds as a way to turn their dreams into reality. As the stock market boomed in the 1990s, mutual funds also grew at a phenomenal rate. By 2000, investors had poured $7 trillion into mutual fund shares in hopes of cashing in on that growth. Smaller investors like Rowan were particularly attracted to mutual funds, which pool investor's money in order to buy and manage a diversified portfolio of stocks or bonds. Seeking to maximize their returns, they placed money both in a fund tied to the Standard & Poor's 500 Index and a fund focused on riskier stocks.

As the bull market turned into a bear market, however, many investors discovered that mutual fund profits were not guaranteed. Overall, stock mutual funds lost 12 percent a year between 2000 and 2002. In mid-2003, after legal and ethical questions began surfacing about the trading practices of some funds, some investors began to question whether mutual funds should still be part of their investment strategy.

After seeing his investments decline, Rowan decided that the answer was "maybe." He sold his shares in the riskier Putnam mutual fund but held on to his Vanguard S&P 500 Index fund. "The Vanguard fund has lower operating costs and seems to be more consistent in performance," Rowan said. "I made more money in the Putnam fund but when the market went south, I also lost more. So I plan to stick with the safer bet. And unlike Putnam, there haven't been any questions about Vanguard's ethics or management."

Financial advisors say mutual funds can make good sense for people like Rowan—if they are chosen and managed wisely. Doing so requires an understanding of how mutual funds are organized and managed, their costs and restrictions, and their role in your overall investment strategy. In this chapter, we'll take a closer look at all of these issues to help you decide whether mutual funds make sense for you.

CRITICAL THINKING QUESTIONS

- Why did Rowan choose to invest in mutual funds instead of individual stocks?
- How are mutual funds managed and what factors should be considered in choosing one?
- What role should mutual funds play in an investment portfolio?

Sources: Julie Creswell, "Dirty Little Secrets," *Fortune*, September 1, 2003, p. 133; Ali Velshi, Pat Kiernan, and Gerri Willis, "Mutual Fund Scandal Hurts Investor Confidence," *The Money Gang*, CNNfn, November 13, 2003, downloaded from **http://www.elibrary.com**; Dustin Woodard, "The Mutual Fund Advantage," *About.com*, downloaded from **http://mutualfunds.about.com**, December 5, 2003.

MUTUAL FUNDS: SOME BASICS

LG1, LG2

For individual investors today, mutual funds are, without a doubt, the investment vehicle of choice. The fact is, more people invest in mutual funds than any other type of investment product. The reason they are so popular is that they offer not only a variety of interesting investment opportunities, but also a wide array of services that many investors find appealing. They provide an easy and convenient way to invest, and are especially suited to beginning investors and those with limited investment capital. A mutual fund is basically a financial services organization that receives money from its shareholders and invests those funds on their behalf in a diversified portfolio of securities. Thus, when investors buy shares in a mutual fund, they actually become *part owners of a widely diversified portfolio of securities.* In an abstract sense, a mutual fund can be thought of as the *financial product* that's sold to the public by an investment company. That is, the investment company builds and manages a portfolio of securities and sells ownership interests—shares of stock—in that portfolio through a vehicle known as a mutual fund. This concept underlies the whole mutual fund structure and is depicted in Exhibit 13.1.

EXHIBIT 13.1

The Basic Mutual Fund Structure

A mutual fund brings together the funds from a large number of individual investors and uses this pool of money to acquire a diversified portfolio of stocks, bonds, and other securities.

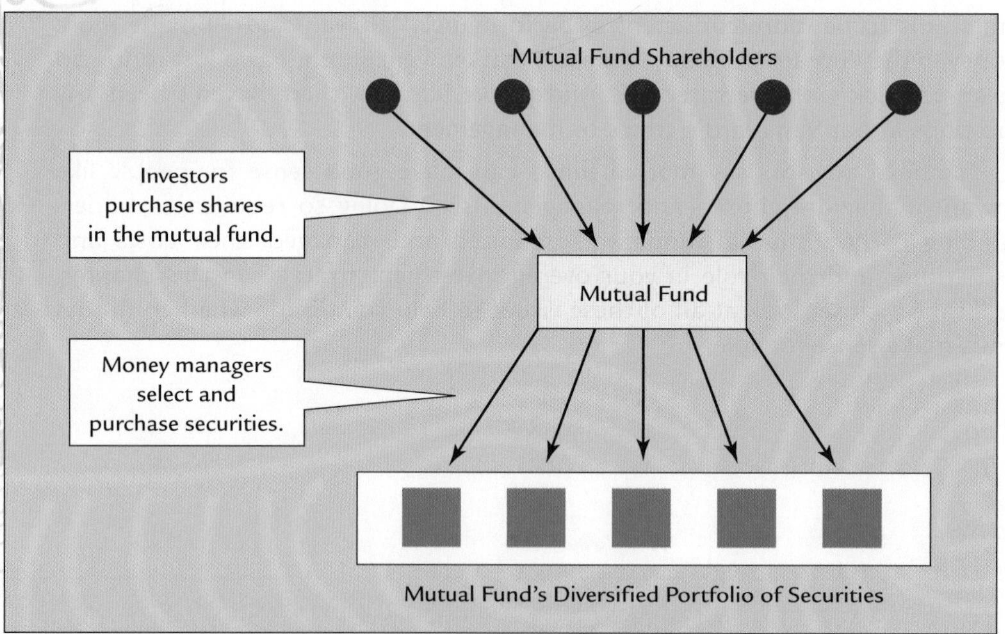

The Mutual Fund Concept

The first mutual fund in this country was started in Boston in 1924; by 1940, there were 68 mutual funds in operation, and by 1980 there were 564. But that was only the beginning, for the next 20 years saw unprecedented growth in the mutual fund industry, as assets under management grew to some $6.4 trillion in 2002. Indeed, by 2002, *there were nearly 8,300 publicly traded mutual funds.* (Actually, counting duplicate or multiple fund offerings from the same portfolio, there were more like *15,000 funds available*—such duplication occurs because sometimes two or three versions of the same fund will be offered, with each "fund" having a different type of load charge or fee structure.) To put that number in perspective, *there are more mutual funds in existence today than there are stocks listed on the New York and American exchanges combined!* The fund industry has grown so much, in fact, that it is now *the largest financial intermediary* in this country—ahead of even banks.

Mutual funds are big business in the United States and, indeed, all over the world. As the year 2003 began, an estimated 95 million individuals in 54 million U.S. households owned mutual funds. That's 49.6% of all U.S. households! Clearly, mutual funds appeal to a lot of investors—investors who come from all walks of life and all income levels. And they all share one common view: They've decided, for one reason or another, to turn the problems of security selection and portfolio management over to professional money managers. Questions of which stock or bond to select, when to buy, and when to sell have plagued investors for about as long as there have been organized securities markets. Such concerns lie at the very heart of the mutual fund concept and, in large part, are behind the growth in funds. The fact is, a lot of people simply lack the time, the know-how, or the commitment to manage their own securities. As a result, they turn to others. And more often than not, that means mutual funds.

smart.sites

Want to know more about the mutual fund industry, from the funds themselves to fund investors and legislation affecting funds? The Investment Company Institute Web site (**http://www.ici.org**) has all the answers.

Pooled Diversification

The mutual fund concept is based on the simple idea of turning the problems of security selection and portfolio management over to professional money managers. In essence, a mutual fund combines the investment capital of many people with similar investment goals, and invests the funds in a wide variety of securities. Investors receive shares of stock in the mutual fund and, through the fund, are able to enjoy much wider investment diversification than they could otherwise achieve. To appreciate the extent of such diversification, you need only look at Exhibit 13.2 on page 553. It provides a partial list of the securities held in the portfolio of a major mutual fund (actually, just two pages out of a 21-page list of security holdings). Observe that in June 2003, this fund owned anywhere from 800 shares of Maxim Integrated Products to just over *9.6 million* shares of First Data Corp. Furthermore, note that within each industry segment, the fund diversified its holdings across a number of different stocks. Clearly, except for all but the super-rich, this is far more diversification than most investors could ever hope to attain. Yet each investor who owns shares in this fund is, in effect, a part owner of this diversified portfolio of securities.

Of course, not all funds are as big or as diversified as the one depicted in Exhibit 13.2. Even so, no matter what the size of the fund, as the securities held by it move up and down in price, the market value of the mutual fund shares moves accordingly. And when dividend and interest payments are received by the fund, they too are passed on to the mutual fund shareholders and distributed on the basis of prorated ownership. For example, if you own 1,000 shares of stock in a mutual fund and that represents, say, 1 percent of all shares outstanding, you would receive 1 percent of the dividends paid by the fund. When a security held by the fund is sold for a profit, the capital gain is also passed on to fund shareholders. The whole mutual fund idea, in fact, rests on the concept of **pooled diversification**, and works very much like insurance, whereby individuals pool their resources for the collective benefit of all the contributors.

pooled diversification
A process whereby investors buy into a diversified portfolio of securities for the collective benefit of the individual investors.

Why Invest in Mutual Funds?

Mutual funds can be used by individual investors in a variety of ways. Thus, whereas one investor may buy a fund because of the substantial capital gains opportunities it provides, another may buy a totally different fund not for its capital gains, but for its current income. Regardless of the kind of income a fund provides, individuals tend to use these investment vehicles for one or more of the following reasons: (1) to achieve diversification in their investment holdings, (2) to obtain the services of professional money managers, (3) to generate an attractive rate of return on their investment capital, and (4) for the convenience they offer.

Diversification

Certainly, as we saw above, diversification is a primary motive for investing in mutual funds. This ability to diversify, in effect, allows investors to sharply reduce their exposure to risk by indirectly investing in a number of different types of securities and companies, rather than just one or two. If you have only $500 or $1,000 to invest, you obviously will not achieve much diversification on your own. However, if you invest that money in a mutual fund, you will end up owning part of a diversified portfolio made up perhaps of several hundred securities, or even more.

Professional Management

Another major appeal of a mutual fund is the professional management it offers. Of course, management is paid a fee from the fund's earnings, but the contributions of a full-time expert manager should be well worth the cost. These pros know where to look for return, and how to avoid unnecessary risk; at the minimum, their decisions should result in better returns than the average individual investor can achieve.

Financial Returns

Although professional managers *may* be able to achieve returns that are better than what small investors can generate, the relatively high purchase fees, coupled with the management and operating costs, tend to reduce the returns actually earned on mutual fund investments. However, the mutual fund industry has not attracted millions of investors because of the substandard returns they generate! Quite the contrary; over the long haul, mutual funds have been able to provide relatively attractive returns. Look at Exhibit 13.3 on page 554. It shows the average return performance on a variety of different types of mutual funds and is indicative of the kind of returns investors were able to achieve over the 10½-year period from January 1993 through mid-year 2003. With such return potential, it's easy to see why investors are so anxious to put their money into mutual funds.

Convenience

The fact that mutual fund shares can be purchased through a variety of sources is still another reason for their appeal. Mutual funds make it easy to invest, and most do not require a great deal of capital to get started. They are relatively easy to acquire, they handle all the paperwork and recordkeeping, their prices are widely quoted, and it is usually possible to deal in fractional shares. Opening a mutual fund account is about as easy as opening a checking account. Just fill in a few blank spaces, send in the minimum amount of money, and you're in business!

EXHIBIT 13.2

A Partial List of Portfolio Holdings

This list represents just *two pages* of security holdings for this particular fund; the total list of holdings goes on for another 19 pages and includes stocks in hundreds of different companies. Certainly, this is far more diversification than most individual investors could ever hope to achieve.

Common Stocks – continued

	Shares	Value (Note 1) (000s)
INFORMATION TECHNOLOGY – continued		
Internet Software & Services – 1.0%		
DoubleClick, Inc. (a)	333,968	$ 3,089
Expedia, Inc. (a)	253,200	19,339
FindWhat.com (a)	332,300	6,294
Open Text Corp. (a)	137,200	3,880
United Online, Inc. (a)	505,940	12,821
WebEx Communications, Inc. (a)	1,207,970	16,851
webMethods, Inc. (a)	674,550	5,484
Yahoo!, Inc. (a)	7,020,262	229,984
		297,742
IT Services – 2.1%		
Affiliated Computer Services, Inc. Class A (a)	1,034,200	47,294
Anteon International Corp. (a)	1,610,300	44,943
CheckFree Corp. (a)	7,800	217
Cognizant Technology Solutions Corp. Class A (a)	1,998,929	48,694
First Data Corp.	9,663,000	400,435
Iron Mountain, Inc. (a)	1,329,900	49,326
ManTech International Corp. Class A	391,500	7,509
Paychex, Inc.	431,300	12,641
SRA International, Inc. Class A (a)	780,500	24,976
The BISYS Group, Inc. (a)	548,600	10,078
		646,113
Office Electronics – 0.3%		
Canon, Inc.	659,000	30,083
Xerox Corp. (a)	2,246,000	23,785
Zebra Technologies Corp. Class A (a)	449,600	33,805
		87,673
Semiconductors & Semiconductor Equipment – 2.7%		
Analog Devices, Inc. (a)	4,157,700	144,771
ARM Holdings PLC sponsored ADR (a)	79,000	269
Broadcom Corp. Class A (a)	950,377	23,674
Cabot Microelectronics Corp. (a)	78,500	3,962
Cree, Inc. (a)	616,000	10,028
Infineon Technologies AG sponsored ADR (a)	730,500	7,005
Integrated Circuit Systems, Inc. (a)	1,584,800	49,810
Intersil Corp. Class A (a)	1,225,900	32,621
KLA-Tencor Corp. (a)	1,116,500	51,906
Lam Research Corp. (a)	1,301,400	23,698
Linear Technology Corp.	1,527,200	49,191
Marvell Technology Group Ltd. (a)	1,373,900	47,221

Common Stocks – continued

	Shares	Value (Note 1) (000s)
INFORMATION TECHNOLOGY – continued		
Semiconductors & Semiconductor Equipment – continued		
Maxim Integrated Products, Inc.	800	$ 27
Microchip Technology, Inc.	900	22
NVIDIA Corp. (a)	705,264	16,228
O2Micro International Ltd. (a)	416,400	6,708
Omnivision Technologies, Inc. (a)	237,800	7,419
Samsung Electronics Co. Ltd.	683,700	203,108
Silicon Laboratories, Inc. (a)	1,672,420	44,553
STMicroelectronics NV (NY Shares)	266,500	5,541
Taiwan Semiconductor Manufacturing Co. Ltd. sponsored ADR (a)	1,823,900	18,385
Teradyne, Inc. (a)	1,185,400	20,519
Texas Instruments, Inc.	39,200	690
Xilinx, Inc. (a)	1,426,200	36,097
		803,453
Software – 1.4%		
Adobe Systems, Inc.	3,843,295	123,254
Agile Software Corp. (a)	114,967	1,109
Altiris, Inc. (a)(c)	1,225,804	24,577
Amdocs Ltd. (a)	505,900	12,142
Autodesk, Inc.	235,200	3,801
BEA Systems, Inc. (a)	1,604,853	17,429
Business Objects SA sponsored ADR (a)	392,300	8,611
Citrix Systems, Inc. (a)	1,359,800	27,686
Computer Associates International, Inc.	234,900	5,234
Electronic Arts, Inc. (a)	195,800	14,487
Hyperion Solutions Corp. (a)	269,957	9,114
Intuit, Inc. (a)	78,300	3,487
Kronos, Inc. (a)	68,000	3,455
Mercury Interactive Corp. (a)	1,319,018	50,927
Network Associates, Inc. (a)	995,648	12,625
Red Hat, Inc. (a)	626,300	4,741
Symantec Corp. (a)	614,015	26,931
Synopsys, Inc. (a)	398,515	24,648
Vastera, Inc. (a)	5,700	34
Verint Systems, Inc. (a)	339,829	8,635

Source: *Fidelity Contrafund*, June 30, 2003.

How Mutual Funds Are Organized and Run

Although it's tempting to think of a mutual fund as a monolithic entity, that's really not accurate. Various functions—investing, recordkeeping, safekeeping, and others—are split among two or more companies. Besides the fund itself, which is organized as a separate corporation or trust and *is owned by the shareholders*, there are several other main players:

- The *management company* runs the fund's daily operations. These are the firms we know as Fidelity, Vanguard, T. Rowe Price, American Century, Dreyfus, and so forth; they are the ones that create the funds in the first place. Usually, the management firm also serves as investment advisor.
- The *investment advisor* buys and sells the stocks or bonds and otherwise oversees the portfolio. Usually, three parties participate in this phase of the operation: the

EXHIBIT 13.3

The Comparative Performance of Mutual Funds for the 10½-year period through June 2000

The type of fund you invest in has a lot to do with the kind of return you can expect. For example, had you put $10,000 in a typical health care fund in January 1993, that investment would have grown to nearly $37,000 by mid-year 2003; in contrast, had you invested the same $10,000 in a typical foreign stock fund, it would have grown to less than $18,000.

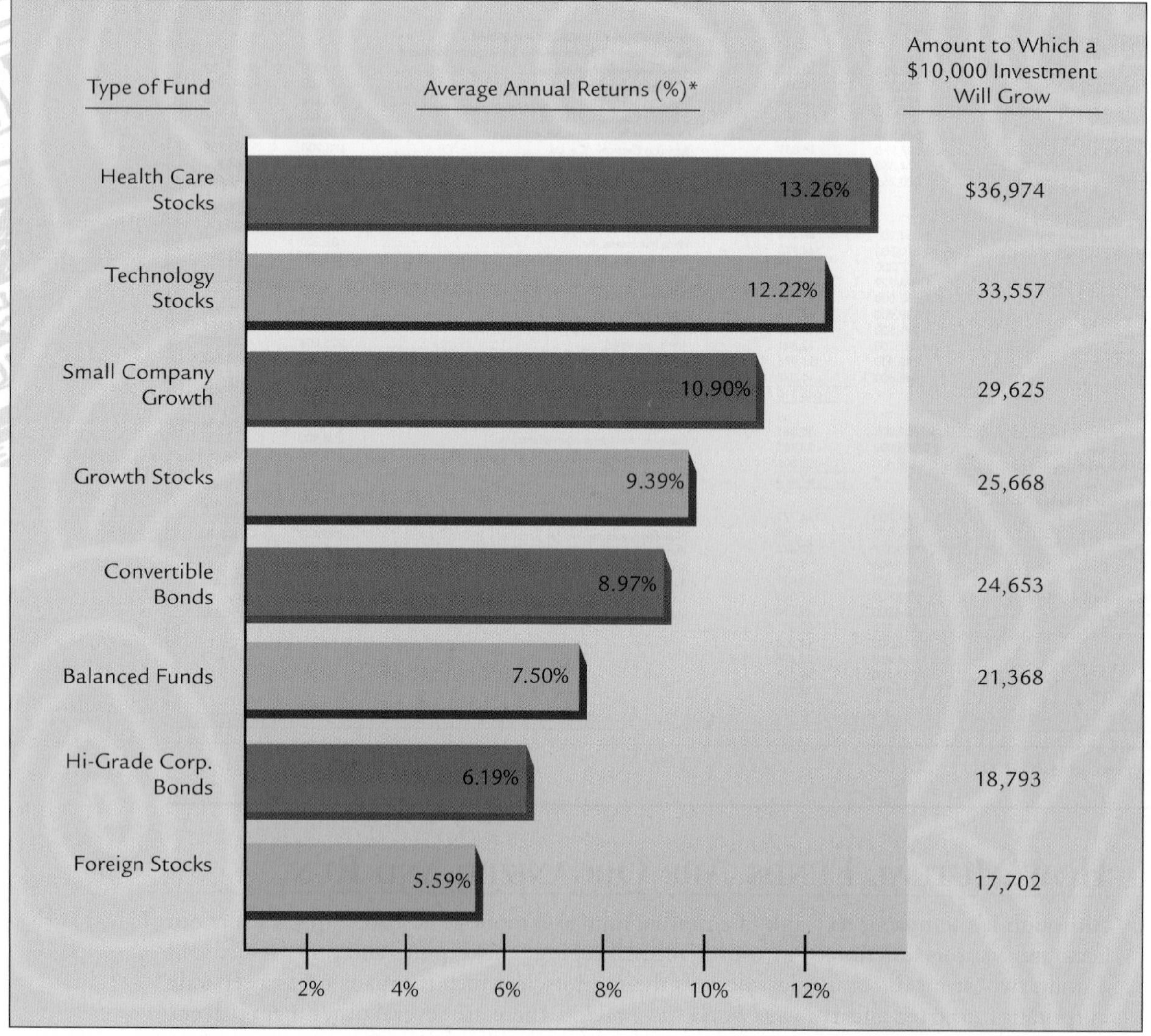

*Assumes reinvestment of all dividends and capital gains distributions.
Source: *Morningstar*, June 2003.

money manager, who actually runs the portfolio and makes the buy and sell decisions; *securities analysts*, who analyze securities and look for attractive investment candidates; and *traders*, who try to buy and sell big blocks of securities at the best possible price.

- The *distributor* sells the fund shares, either directly to the public or through certain authorized dealers (such as major brokerage houses and commercial banks). When you request a prospectus and sales literature, you deal with the distributor.
- The *custodian* physically safeguards the securities and other assets of a fund, without taking an active role in the investment decisions. To discourage foul play, an independent party (a bank, in most cases) serves in this capacity.
- The *transfer agent* executes transactions, keeps track of purchase and redemption requests from shareholders, and maintains other shareholder records.

All this separation of duties is designed for just one thing—to protect the mutual fund investor/shareholder. Obviously, you can always lose money if your fund's stock or bond holdings go down in value. But that's really the only risk of loss you face, because the chance of ever losing money from fraud or a mutual fund collapse is actually quite low—almost nonexistent. For in addition to the separation of duties noted earlier, the only formal link between the mutual fund and the company that manages it (i.e., the management company) is a contract that must be renewed—and approved by shareholders—on a regular basis. One provision of this contractual arrangement is that the fund's assets—stocks, bonds, cash, or other securities in the portfolio—*can never be in the hands of the management company.* As still another safeguard, each fund must have a board of directors, or trustees, elected by shareholders and charged with keeping tabs on the management company and renewing its contract. The bottom line is that in more than 75 years, there has never been a major crisis in the mutual fund industry, nor, with all the tight regulations and structural firewalls in place, is there ever likely to be one.

smart.sites

Who's managing your fund? Brill's Mutual Fund Interactive interviews a top mutual find portfolio manager each week and has archives of past profiles (**http://www.fundsinteractive.com/profiles.html**).

Open-End Versus Closed-End

Although all mutual funds may appear to be organized in pretty much the same way, investors should be aware of some major differences. One way that funds differ is with respect to how they are structured. That is, funds can be set up either as *open-end companies*, which can sell an unlimited number of ownership shares, or as *closed-end companies*, which can issue only a limited number of shares.

open-end investment company
A company that can issue an unlimited number of shares that it buys and sells at a price based on the current market value of the securities it owns; also called a mutual fund.

Open-End Investment Companies

The term *mutual fund* is commonly used to denote an open-end investment company. Such organizations are the dominant type of investment company and account for well over 95 percent of assets under management. In an **open-end investment company**, investors actually buy their shares from, and sell them back to, the mutual fund itself. When they buy shares in the fund, the fund issues new shares of stock and fills the purchase order with these new shares. There is no limit to the number of shares the fund can issue, other than investor demand. Further, all open-end mutual funds stand behind their shares and buy them back when investors decide to sell. Thus, there is never any trading among individuals. Many of these funds are very large and hold billions of dollars' worth of securities. Indeed, in mid-2003 the average stock or bond fund had about $560 million in assets under management, and there were nearly 600 billion-dollar funds in existence.

Buy and sell transactions in an open-end mutual fund are carried out at prices based on the current value of all the securities held in the fund's portfolio. This is known as the fund's **net asset value (NAV)**; it is calculated at least once a day and represents the underlying value of a share of stock in a particular fund. NAV is found by taking the total market value of all securities held by the fund, subtracting any liabilities, and dividing the result by the number of shares outstanding. For example, if on a given day, the market value of all the securities held by the XYZ mutual fund equaled some $10 million, and if XYZ on that day had 500,000 shares outstanding, the fund's net asset value per share would amount to $20 ($10,000,000/500,000 = $20). This figure would then be used to derive the price at which the fund shares could be bought and sold. (As we'll see later, NAV is generally included in the fund's quoted price, and indicates the price at which an investor can *sell* shares—or, the price an investor would pay to *buy no-load funds.*)

net asset value (NAV) The price at which a mutual fund will buy back its own shares; NAV represents the current market value of all the securities the fund owns, less any liabilities.

Closed-End Investment Companies

Although the term *mutual fund* is supposed to be used only with open-end funds, it is, as a practical matter, regularly used with closed-end investment companies as well. Basically, **closed-end investment companies** operate with a fixed number of shares outstanding and do *not* regularly issue new shares of stock. In effect, they have a capital structure like that of any other corporation, except that the corporation's business happens to be investing in marketable securities. Like open-end funds, closed-end investment companies have enjoyed remarkable growth in the past decade or so. That is, while there were only 34 of these funds in existence in 1980, by mid-year 2003, there were more than 560 closed-end funds, with total net assets of nearly $135 billion—still just a tiny fraction of the $6.4 trillion invested in open-end funds. Shares in closed-end investment companies are actively traded in the secondary market, just like any other common stock; but, unlike open-end funds, *all trading is done between investors in the open market.* The fund itself plays no role in either buy or sell transactions; once the shares are issued, the fund is out of the picture. By far, most closed-end investment companies are traded on the New York Stock Exchange, a few are on the American Exchange, and, occasionally, some are traded in the OTC market or on some other exchange.

closed-end investment company An investment company that issues a fixed number of shares, which are themselves listed and traded on an organized securities exchange or in the OTC market.

Many of the investment advisors that run closed-end funds (such as Putnam, Eaton Vance, Nuveen, MFS, and Franklin-Templeton) also manage open-end funds, often with similar investment objectives. So, why would they do that? The answer is, because these are two different animals. While it may not appear so, some major differences exist between open- and closed-end funds. To begin with, because closed-end funds have a fixed amount of capital to work with, they don't have to worry about stock redemptions or new money coming into the fund. As such, they don't have to be concerned about keeping cash on hand to meet redemptions.

Equally important, closed-end funds can be more aggressive in their investment styles and invest in obscure yet attractive securities, even if they are not actively traded (because there'll be no pressure on the portfolio manager to cash in these securities at inopportune times). And, because they don't have new money flowing in all the time, they don't have to worry about finding new investments. Instead, they can concentrate on a set portfolio of securities and do the best job they can in managing them. But that also puts added pressures on the money managers, because their investment styles and fund portfolios are closely monitored and judged by the market. That is, the share prices of closed-end companies are determined not only by their net asset values, but also by general supply and demand conditions in the market. As a result, depending on the market outlook and investor expectations, closed-end companies generally trade at a discount or premium to NAV. For example, a fund with a net asset value of $10 per share would be selling at a *discount* of $1 if it were trading at $9 and at a *premium* of $1 if it were quoted at a price of $11. Share price discounts can become quite large at times—for example, it is not unusual for discounts to amount to as much as 25 to 30 percent of net asset value. In contrast, price premiums occur less often and seldom exceed 10 to 15 percent.

Exchange-Traded Funds

exchange-traded fund (ETF) A type of mutual fund that trades as a listed security (principally on the AMEX); usually structured as an index fund that's set up to match the performance of a certain segment of the market.

Combine some of the operating characteristics of an open-end fund with some of the trading characteristics of a closed-end fund and what you'll end up with is something called an *exchange-traded fund*. While these securities are being promoted as the newest product to hit the fund world, they're really a recreation of an old product that's been around since the early 90s. Technically, an **exchange-traded fund (ETF)** is a type of mutual fund that trades as a listed security on one of the stock exchanges (mostly the AMEX). Actually, all ETFs thus far (through mid-year 2003) have been structured as *index funds*, set up to match the performance of a certain segment of the market; they do this by owning all or a representative sample of the stocks (or bonds) in a targeted market segment or index (we'll examine traditional index funds in more detail later in this chapter). Thus, ETFs offer the professional money management of traditional mutual funds and the liquidity of an exchange-traded stock.

Even though ETFs are like closed-end funds (in that they are traded on listed exchanges), *they are in reality open-end mutual funds*, where the number of shares outstanding can be increased or decreased in response to market demand. That is, while ETFs can be bought or sold like any stock on a listed exchange, *the ETF distributor can also create new shares or redeem old shares.* This is done to prevent the fund from trading at (much of) a premium or discount, thereby avoiding one of the big pitfalls of closed-end funds. By mid-year 2003, there were more than 100 ETFs listed on the American Stock Exchange, covering a wide range of domestic and international stock indexes, as well as a handful of U.S. Treasury and corporate bond indexes. The biggest and oldest (started in 1993) are based on the S&P 500, and are known as *Spiders.* In addition to spiders, there are *Diamonds* (which are based on the DJIA), *Qubes* (based on the NASDAQ 100 and so-named because of their QQQ ticker symbol), and ETFs based on 28 international markets (from Australia and Canada to Germany, Japan, and the United Kingdom). Just about every major U.S. Index, in fact, has its own ETF, along with a lot of minor indexes that cover very specialized segments of the market. The net asset values of ETFs are set at a fraction of the underlying index value at any given point in time. For example, if the S&P 500 index stands at, say, 1164.46, the ETF on that index will trade at around $116.50 (or about 1⁄10 of the index); likewise, the ETF on the Dow is set at 1⁄100 of the DJIA (thus, when it is at say, 10449.30, the ETF will trade at around 104.50).

ETFs combine many of the advantages of closed-end funds with those of traditional (open-end) index funds. That is, like closed-end funds, you can buy and sell ETFs at *any time of the day* by placing an order through your broker (and paying a standard commission just like you would with any other stock). In contrast, you *cannot* trade a traditional open-end fund on an intraday basis, because all buy and sell orders for these funds are filled at the end of the trading day, at closing prices. What's more, because ETFs are passively managed, they offer all the advantages of any index fund: low costs, low portfolio turnover, and low taxes. The fund's tax liability is kept low because ETFs rarely distribute any capital gains to shareholders; you could hold one of these things for decades and never pay a dime in capital-gains taxes (at least not until you sell the shares).

smart.sites

Before investing in ETFs, visit ETFConnect.com, **http://www.etfconnect.com**, to learn more about these funds, get price quotes, and find the right ETF for your portfolio, as well as links to other Web resources.

Two Other Types of Investment Companies

In addition to open-end, closed-end, and exchange-traded funds, there are two other types of investment companies that should be discussed at this point. They are: (1) unit investment trusts and (2) real estate investment trusts. The first type, a unit investment trust is similar to a mutual fund to the extent that it, too, invests primarily in marketable securities, like stocks and bonds; real estate investment trusts, in contrast, invest primarily in various types of real estate or real estate-related types of investments, such as mortgages.

Unit Investment Trust

A **unit investment trust (UIT)** represents little more than an interest in an *unmanaged* pool of investments. UITs are like mutual funds to the extent that both involve portfolios of securities. But that's where the similarity ends, because once a portfolio of securities is put together for a UIT, it is simply held in safekeeping for investors under conditions set down in a trust agreement. Traditionally, these portfolios were made up of various types of fixed-income securities, with long-term municipal bonds being, by far, the most popular type of investment vehicle. Because there is no trading in the portfolios, the returns, or yields, are fixed and fairly predictable—at least for the short term. Not surprisingly, these unit investment trusts appeal mainly to income-oriented investors looking for a safe, steady stream of income.

unit investment trust (UIT) A type of investment vehicle whereby the trust sponsors put together a largely fixed/unmanaged portfolio of securities and then sell ownership units in the portfolio to individual investors.

In the early 1990s, brokerage firms began aggressively marketing a new type of investment product—the *stock-oriented UIT.* These new equity trusts caught on quickly with investors seeking capital gains and attractive returns, and today account for over half the market. A popular theme among equity trusts is the "Dogs of the Dow" strategy of selecting (and holding) the five or ten companies in the DJIA paying the highest dividend yields—although growth stock, high yield, and market index trusts also do well. Stock trusts are normally offered with terms that range from 1 year (typical of the Dow Dogs products) to 5 years (found on many stock index trusts). Except for the shorter terms (1 to 5 years for equity trusts versus 15 to 30 years for fixed-income products), these trusts are really no different from the traditional bond-oriented UITs: Once the portfolios are put together, they usually remain untouched for the life of the trust.

Various sponsoring brokerage houses put together these diversified pools of securities and then sell units in the pool to investors (each *unit* being like a share in a mutual fund). For example, a brokerage house might put together a diversified pool of corporate bonds that amounts to, say, $100 million. The sponsoring firm would then sell units in this pool to the investing public at anywhere from $250 (for many equity trusts) to $1,000 per unit (common for fixed-income products). The sponsoring organization does little more than routine recordkeeping, and it services the investments by collecting coupons or dividends and distributing the income (often monthly) to the holders of the trust units. There is a dark side to UITs, however—*they tend to be very costly.* These products can have not only substantial up-front transaction costs, but hefty annual fees as well. For example, many equity UITs carry load charges of 1 to 3 percent and then another 1.5 to 2.5 percent in annual fees—both of which are well above what you'd pay for a typical equity mutual fund. Brokers argue that they earn those fat fees by removing fear and greed from the investment process, and by enabling investors to build a well-diversified portfolio at a reasonable cost.

smart.sites

If you want to invest in real estate without the hassle of buying property, consider a real estate investment trust (REIT), and learn more about these closed-end trusts at Invest in REITs, **http://www.investinreits.org**.

Real Estate Investment Trusts

real estate investment trust (REIT) A business that accumulates money for investment in real estate ventures by selling shares to investors; like a mutual fund, except that REITs confine their investments to real estate and/or mortgages.

A **real estate investment trust (REIT)** is a type of closed-end investment company that invests money in mortgages and various types of real estate investments. A REIT is like a mutual fund in that it sells shares of stock to the investing public and uses the proceeds, along with borrowed funds, to invest in a portfolio of real estate investments. The investor, therefore, owns a part of the real estate portfolio held by the real estate investment trust. The basic appeal of REITs is that they enable investors to receive both the capital appreciation and the current income from real estate ownership without all the headaches of property management. *REITs are also popular with income-oriented investors because of the very attractive dividend yields they provide.*

There are three basic types of REITs: those that invest in *properties*, such as shopping centers, hotels, apartments, and office buildings (the so-called *property*, or *equity*, REITs); mortgage REITs—those that invest in mortgages; and *hybrid* REITs, which invest in both properties and mortgages. Mortgage REITs tend to be more income-oriented—they emphasize their high current yields (which is to be expected from a security that basically invests in debt). In contrast, while equity REITs may promote their attractive current yields, most of them also offer the potential for earning varying amounts of capital gains (as their property holdings appreciate in value). In 2002, there were some 175 REITs, which together held over $160 billion in various real estate assets. Equity REITs dominate, accounting for about 85–90 percent of the market.

REITs must abide by the Real Estate Investment Trust Act of 1960, which established requirements for forming a REIT as well as rules and procedures for making investments and distributing income. Because they are required to pay out nearly all their earnings to the owners, they do quite a bit of borrowing to obtain funds for their investments (although, in today's market environment, they do try to keep the amount of leverage they employ to reasonable levels). A number of insurance companies, mortgage bankers, commercial banks, and real estate investment companies have formed REITs, many of which are traded on the major securities exchanges. The income earned by a REIT is not taxed, but *the income distributed to the owners is designated and taxed as ordinary income.* While dividends on common stocks normally are taxed at the new, low preferential rates (of 15 percent, or less), that's not the case with REITs, whose cash dividends are treated as ordinary income, and therefore subject to normal tax rates. REITs have become very popular as investment vehicles both for their portfolio diversification properties and for their very attractive dividend yields, which are well above the yields on common stocks (in fact, 65 percent of the total return from REITs comes from their dividends).

Some Important Cost Considerations

When you buy or sell shares in a *closed-end* investment company, or in *EFTs* for that matter, you pay a commission just as you would with any other listed or OTC common stock transaction. This is not so with *open-end* funds, however. In particular, the cost of investing in an open-end mutual fund depends on the types of fees and load charges that the fund levies on its investors.

Load Funds

Most open-end mutual funds are so-called **load funds**, because they charge a commission *when the shares are purchased* (such charges are often referred to as *front-end loads*). Front-end loads can be fairly substantial and amount to as much as 8½ percent of the *purchase price* of the shares. The fact is, however, very few funds today charge the maximum; instead, many funds charge commissions of only 2 or 3 percent—such funds are known as **low-load funds**. There is a commission to pay on low-load funds, but it's relatively small. The good news on front-end load funds is that there's normally no charge or commission to pay when you *sell* your shares! Occasionally, however, you will run into funds that charge a commission—or a so-called *redemption fee*—when you sell your shares. Known as **back-end load funds**, they may charge as much as 7¼ percent of the value of the shares sold, although back-end loads tend to decline over time and usually disappear altogether after 5 or 6 years. The purpose of such charges is to discourage investors from trading in and out of the funds over short periods of time.

load fund
A mutual fund on which a transaction cost (associated with the purchase of shares) is levied.

low-load fund
A mutual fund in which commissions charged on purchases of shares range between only 1 and 3 percent of the purchase price.

back-end load
A commission charged for redeeming mutual fund shares.

no-load fund
A mutual fund on which no transaction fees are charged.

12(b)-1 fee
A type of fee that's charged annually and which is supposed to be used to offset the promotion and selling expenses of a mutual fund; known as a hidden load because it's often used by funds as an indirect way of charging commissions.

No-Load Funds

Some open-end investment companies charge you nothing at all to buy their funds; these are known as **no-load funds**. Actually, relatively few pure no-loads are left today, charging nothing to buy, sell, or hold their funds. Less than 30 percent of the funds sold today are true no-loads; all the rest charge some type of load or fee. Indeed, even funds that don't have front-end loads (and, thus, may appear as no-loads) can have back-end load charges that you have to pay when you sell your fund shares, or something called a 12(b)-1 fee, which you would pay for as long as you hold your shares.

12(b)-1 Fees

Also known as *hidden loads*, **12(b)-1 fees** have been allowed by the SEC since 1980, and were originally designed to help no-load funds cover their distribution and marketing expenses. Not surprisingly, their popularity spread rapidly among fund distributors, so that they are now used by many open-end mutual funds. The fees are assessed annually and can amount to as much as 1 percent of assets under management. In good markets and bad, they're paid right off the top. And that can take its toll. Consider, for instance, $10,000 in a fund that charges a 1 percent 12(b)-1 fee. That translates into an annual charge of *$100 a year*, certainly not an insignificant amount of money.

The latest trend in mutual fund fees is the so-called *multiple class sales charge*. You'll find such arrangements at firms like American Express, Dreyfus, Merrill Lynch, MFS, Scudder, Putnam, and others. The way it works is that the mutual fund will issue different classes of stocks on the same fund or portfolio of securities. Thus, rather than having just one class of stock outstanding, there might be three of them: Class A shares might have normal (modest) front-end loads; Class B stock might have no front-end loads, but substantial back-end loads along with maximum annual 12(b)-1 fees; and finally, Class C shares might carry a small back-end load and modest 12(b)-1 fees. In other words, you choose your own poison.

To try and bring some semblance of order to fund charges and fees, in 1992 the SEC instituted a series of caps on mutual fund fees. Under the 1992 regulations, a mutual fund cannot charge more than 8.5 percent in *total sales charges and fees*, and that includes front- and back-end loads as well as 12(b)-1 fees. Thus, if a fund charges a 5 percent front-end load and a 1 percent 12(b)-1 fee, it can charge a maximum of only 2.5 percent in back-end load charges—otherwise, it will violate the 8.5 percent cap. In addition, the

SEC set a 1 percent cap on annual 12(b)-1 fees and, perhaps more significantly, stated that true "no-load" funds cannot charge more than 0.25 percent in annual 12(b)-1 fees (if they do, they have to drop the no-load label in their sales and promotional material).

Management Fees

management fee A fee paid to the professional money managers who administer a mutual fund's portfolio.

The **management fee** is the cost you incur to hire the professional money managers to run the fund's portfolio of investments. These fees are also assessed annually and usually range from less than .5 percent to as much as 3 or 4 percent of assets under management. All funds—whether they are load or no-load, open- or closed-end—have these fees; and, like 12(b)-1 fees, they bear watching, because high management fees will take their toll on performance. As a rule, the size of the management fee is totally unrelated to the fund's performance—you'll pay the same amount whether it's been a winning year or a real loser. In addition to these management fees, some funds may charge an *exchange fee*, whenever an investor transfers money from one fund to another within the same fund family, and/or an *annual maintenance fee*, to help defer the costs of providing service to low-balance accounts.

Keeping Track Of Fund Fees And Loads

Critics of the mutual fund industry have come down hard on the proliferation of fund fees and charges. Indeed, some would argue that all the different kinds of charges and fees are really meant to do one thing: confuse the investor. The fact is that a lot of funds were going to great lengths—lower a cost here, tack on a fee there, hide a charge somewhere else—to make themselves look like something they weren't. The funds were following the letter of the law, and, indeed, were fully disclosing all their expenses and fees. The trouble was that the funds were able to neatly hide all but the most conspicuous charges in a bunch of legalese. Fortunately, steps have been taken to bring fund fees and loads out into the open.

For one thing, fund charges are more widely reported now than they were in the past. Most notably, today you can find detailed information about the types and amounts of fees and charges on just about any mutual fund by accessing a variety of Web sites, such as **http://www.quicken.com/investments/mutualfunds/**, **http://www.kiplinger.com/investing/funds/**, or **http://www.morningstar.com/Funds/**. Alternatively, you can use the mutual fund quotes that appear daily in (most) major newspapers and in *The Wall Street Journal*. For example, take a look at *The Wall Street Journal* quotations in Exhibit 13.4; note the use of the letters "r," "p," and "t." If you see an "r" behind a fund's name, it means that the fund charges some type of *redemption fee*, or back-end load, when you sell your shares; this is the case, for example, with the Dreyfus MidCap Value Fund. The use of a "p," in contrast, means the fund levies a *12(b)-1 fee*, which you'll have to pay, for example, if you invest in the Domini Social Equity Fund. Finally, a "t" indicates funds that charge *both* redemption fees and 12(b)-1 fees. The point is, don't be surprised to find load funds that also charge redemption and/or 12(b)-1 fees; and the same goes for no-load funds, because they're allowed to charge annual 12(b)-1 fees of 0.25 percent

Financial Road Sign

The ABC's of Fund Fees

A shares, B shares, C shares—what's an investor to do? Here's a guide to use in deciding which type of mutual fund share is best for you.

1. ***A shares***: Usually involve modest front-end load charges and perhaps a small 12(b)-1 fee (typically 0.25%); *these shares usually make the most sense for long-term investors.*
2. ***B shares***: Normally have substantial back-end loads for a period of up to 6 years, plus maximum 12(b)-1 fees of 1 percent per year; the lack of a front-end load make them look attractive to investors, but the fact is *most investors should steer clear of them—they are a bad deal!!*
3. ***C shares***: Usually a small back-end load if you sell within a year, plus a 12(b)-1 fee of up to 1 percent; *these shares are normally a better deal than B shares.*

Bottom line: If you're a long-term investor, go for the A shares, if not, go for the C shares.

and still call themselves "no-load" funds. The quotations, of course, tell you only the *kinds* of fees charged by the funds; they don't tell you how much is charged. To get the specifics on the amount charged, you'll have to turn to other sources. Furthermore, these quotes (which are fairly representative of what you'd find in other major newspapers) *tell you nothing about the front-end loads*, if any, charged by the funds. Refer once again to the quotes in Exhibit 13.4 and compare the Dodge & Cox Balanced and FPA Capital funds. They look alike, don't they? But they're not. For even though neither of them charges redemption or 12(b)-1 fees, one of them is a no-load fund, the other is not: Dodge & Cox does not charge a front-end load, whereas the FPA fund comes with a hefty 5¼ percent front-end load. As a point of interest, the three other funds highlighted in Exhibit 13.4 don't charge front-end loads either, but you'd never know that from the quotes. (It should be noted that *The Wall Street Journal* also publishes a *Monthly Mutual Fund Review* [on the first or second Monday of each month] which, among other things, does provide some specifics on front-end loads and annual expense charges, including 12(b)-1 fees.)

In addition to the public sources noted above, the mutual funds themselves are required by the SEC to *fully disclose* all of their fees and expenses in a standardized, easy-to-understand format. Every fund prospectus must contain, right up front, a fairly detailed *fee table*, much like the one illustrated in Exhibit 13.5. Notice that this table has three parts. The first specifies all *shareholder transaction costs.* In effect, this tells you what it's going to cost to buy and sell shares in the mutual fund. The next section lists all the *annual operating expenses* of the fund. Showing these expenses as a percentage of average net assets, the fund must break out management fees, those elusive 12(b)-1 fees, and any other expenses. The third section provides a rundown of the *total cost over time* of buying, selling, and owning the fund. This part of the table contains both transaction and operating expenses and shows what the total costs would be over hypothetical 1-, 3-, 5-, and 10-year holding periods. To ensure consistency and comparability, the funds must follow a rigid set of guidelines when constructing the illustrative costs.

Buying And Selling Funds

Buying and selling shares of *closed-end investment companies*, or *ETFs*, is no different from buying shares of common stock. The transactions are executed on listed exchanges or in the OTC market through brokers or dealers who handle the orders in the usual way. They are subject to the normal transaction costs; and because they are treated like any other listed or OTC stock, their shares can even be margined or sold short.

The situation is considerably different, however, with *open-end funds.* There are several ways of acquiring such shares, depending on whether the fund is load or no-load. Regardless of type, however, the fund is required to provide you with basic information about its operations. According to rules recently adopted by the SEC, investors now have the choice of buying into a mutual fund on the basis of a brief (two- to six-page), concise, readable document called a *fund profile*, or requesting a more detailed *prospectus* from the fund company. The fund profile is designed to tell you (in plain English and a standardized format) the most important things you need to know about a fund (e.g., its investment objectives, principle risks, fees and expenses, etc.) without overwhelming you with a bunch of unnecessary legalese. Likewise, the fund prospectuses are now far more user-friendly, as they, too, must be simplified and downsized (by removing all the irrelevant "boiler-plates"); they must be written in plain English, as well.

Should you want more information than provided in either the profile or prospectus, you can always request a copy of the fund's *Statement of Additional Information*, which provides detailed information on the fund's investment objectives, portfolio

EXHIBIT 13.4

Mutual Fund Quotes

Open-end mutual funds are listed separately from other securities, and have their own quotation system, an example of which is shown here in quotes from *The Wall Street Journal*. Note that these securities are also quoted in dollars and cents and that the quotes include not only the fund's NAV, but year-to-date (YTD) and 3-year returns as well. Also included as part of the quotes is an indication of whether the fund charges redemption and/or 12(b)-1 fees.

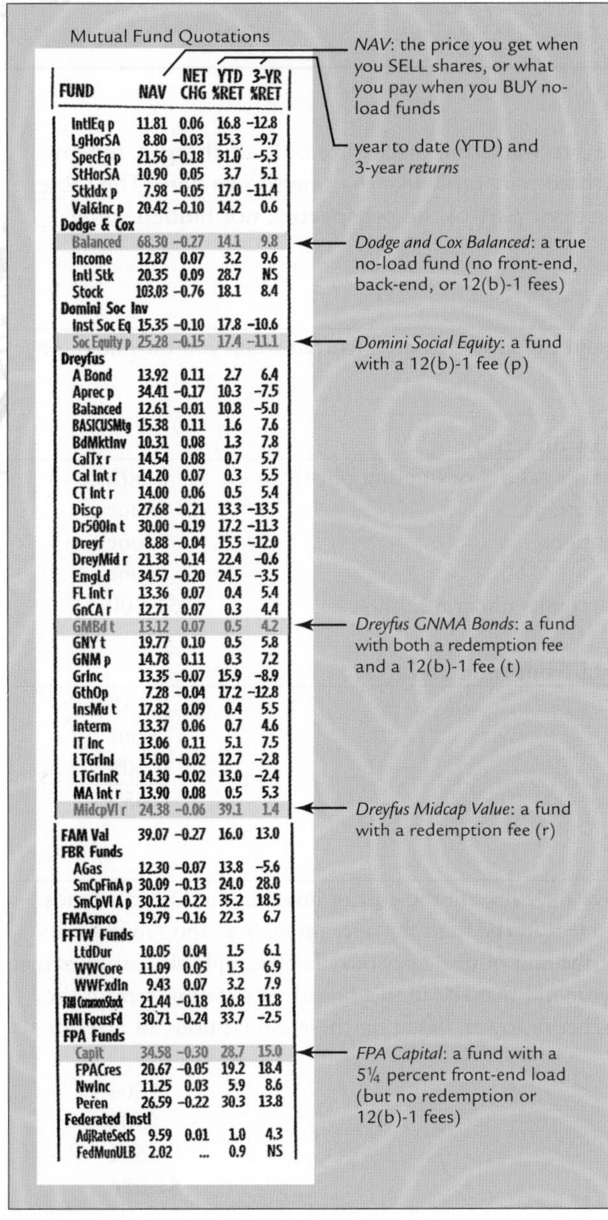

Mutual Fund Quotations

FUND	NAV	NET CHG	YTD %RET	3-YR %RET
IntlEq p	11.81	0.06	16.8	-12.8
LgHorSA	8.80	-0.03	15.3	-9.7
SpecEq p	21.56	-0.18	31.0	-5.3
StHorSA	10.90	0.05	3.7	5.1
StkIdx p	7.98	-0.05	17.0	-11.4
Val&Inc p	20.42	-0.10	14.2	0.6
Dodge & Cox				
Balanced	68.30	-0.27	14.1	9.8
Income	12.87	0.07	3.2	9.6
Intl Stk	20.35	0.09	28.7	NS
Stock	103.03	-0.76	18.1	8.4
Domini Soc Inv				
Inst Soc Eq	15.35	-0.10	17.8	-10.6
Soc Equity p	25.28	-0.15	17.4	-11.1
Dreyfus				
A Bond	13.92	0.11	2.7	6.4
Aprec p	34.41	-0.17	10.3	-7.5
Balanced	12.61	-0.01	10.8	-5.0
BASICUSMtg	15.38	0.11	1.6	7.6
BdMktInv	10.31	0.08	1.3	7.8
CalTx r	14.54	0.08	0.7	5.7
Cal Int r	14.20	0.07	0.3	5.5
CT Int r	14.00	0.06	0.5	5.4
Discp	27.68	-0.21	13.3	-13.5
Dr500In t	30.00	-0.19	17.2	-11.3
Dreyf	8.88	-0.04	15.5	-12.0
DreyMid r	21.38	-0.14	22.4	-0.6
EmgLd	34.57	-0.20	24.5	-3.5
FL Int r	13.36	0.07	0.4	5.4
GnCA r	12.71	0.07	0.3	4.4
GMBd t	13.12	0.07	0.5	4.2
GNY t	19.77	0.10	0.5	5.8
GNM p	14.78	0.11	0.3	7.2
GrInc	13.35	-0.07	15.9	-8.9
GthOp	7.28	-0.04	17.2	-12.8
InsMu t	17.82	0.09	0.4	5.5
Interm	13.37	0.06	0.7	4.6
IT Inc	13.06	0.11	5.1	7.5
LTGrInI	15.00	-0.02	12.7	-2.8
LTGrInR	14.30	-0.02	13.0	-2.4
MA Int r	13.90	0.08	0.5	5.3
MidcpVl r	24.38	-0.06	39.1	1.4
FAM Val	39.07	-0.27	16.0	13.0
FBR Funds				
AGas	12.30	-0.07	13.8	-5.6
SmCpFinA p	30.09	-0.13	24.0	28.0
SmCpVl A p	30.12	-0.22	35.2	18.5
FMAsmco	19.79	-0.16	22.3	6.7
FFTW Funds				
LtdDur	10.05	0.04	1.5	6.1
WWCore	11.09	0.05	1.3	6.9
WWFxdIn	9.43	0.07	3.2	7.9
FMI CommonStock	21.44	-0.18	16.8	11.8
FMI FocusFd	30.71	-0.24	33.7	-2.5
FPA Funds				
Capit	34.58	-0.30	28.7	15.0
FPACres	20.67	-0.05	19.2	18.4
NwInc	11.25	0.03	5.9	8.6
Peren	26.59	-0.22	30.3	13.8
Federated Instl				
AdjRateSecIS	9.59	0.01	1.0	4.3
FedMunULB	2.02	...	0.9	NS

Source: *The Wall Street Journal*, Sept. 8, 2003.

composition, management, and past performance. Whether it's the fund profile (which should be good enough for most investors), the fund's prospectus, or its Statement of Additional Information, the bottom line is these publications should be required reading for anybody who's thinking about investing in a mutual fund.

In the case of load funds, investors buy the stocks from a broker or through salespeople employed by the funds—not surprisingly, many of these funds carry substantial load charges. Most brokerage firms are authorized to sell shares in a variety of load funds, and this is the easiest and most convenient way of buying funds for investors who have established brokerage accounts. Sometimes, however, the fund may not be sold through brokerage houses, in which case the investor would deal directly with the fund's commissioned salespeople—individuals who are employed by the mutual fund for the sole purpose of selling its shares.

EXHIBIT 13.5

A Mutual Fund Fee Table

Mutual funds are required by the SEC to make full disclosure of load charges, redemption fees, and annual expenses in a three-part table like the one shown here. The table must be conspicuously placed in the front part of the prospectus, not hidden somewhere in the back.

Fee Table

The following table describes the fees and expenses that are incurred when you buy, hold, or sell shares of the fund.

Shareholder Fees (paid by the investor directly)	
Maximum sales charge (load) on purchases (as a % of offering price)	3.00%
Sales charge (load) on reinvested distributions	None
Deferred sales charge (load) on redemptions	None
Exchange Fees	None
Annual account maintenance fee (for accounts under $2,500)	$12.00

Annual fund operating expenses (paid from fund assets)	
Management fee	0.45%
Distribution and Service (12b-1) fee	None
Other expenses	0.20%
Total annual fund operating expenses	0.65%

Example:

This example is intended to help an investor compare the cost of investing in different funds. The example assumes a $10,000 investment in the fund for one, three, five, and ten years and then a redemption of all fund shares at the end of those periods. The example also assumes that an investment returns 5 percent each year and that the fund's operating expenses remain the same. Although actual costs may be higher or lower, based on these assumptions an investor's costs would be:

1 year	$364
3 years	$502
5 years	$651
10 years	$1,086

Financial Road Sign

Critical Rules for Mutual Fund Investors

1. *Do your homework.* Research the best investments to meet your goals.
2. *Don't buy the first mutual fund that looks good.* First identify your investment goals, return requirements, and risk tolerance.
3. *Don't look for quick profits.* Invest for the long term (5 to 10 years).
4. *Diversify.* This reduces your chances of losing money; but don't overdo it: That just means more costs and management problems.
5. *Invest regularly* with each paycheck. Use mutual funds' automatic investment programs.
6. *Avoid paying high commissions and fees* for mutual funds.
7. *Size counts.* A fund's size should be compatible with its investment objectives; some fund categories need to be big to operate efficiently.
8. *Wait for a new manager or fund to prove itself.* Choose a fund with at least a 3-year track record.
9. *Know when to sell* your mutual funds.
10. *Invest to beat the tax man.* Take advantage of an Individual Retirement Account (IRA) and other tax shelters.

Source: Adapted from Alan Lavine and Gail Liberman, *The Complete Idiot's Guide to Making Money with Mutual Funds*, excerpted at Brill's Mutual Fund Interactive, **http://www.brill.com/newbie2.html**.

If you happen to be interested in a no-load, or perhaps even a low-load fund, you may be pretty much on your own. You'll have to write or call the mutual fund directly (most have toll-free numbers) to obtain information. You will then receive an order form and instructions on how to buy shares; no salesperson will ever call on you. To complete the transaction, you simply mail your check, along with the completed order form, to the mutual fund or its designated agent. Before you go through all that, however, check with your bank; if it's a major (good-sized) commercial bank, it may be authorized to sell a wide variety of mutual funds. Indeed, during the past 5 to 10 years, a lot of big mutual funds have made arrangements to sell their products through major banking and other financial institutions around the country—and at no added cost to you. Thus, you may be able to find just the fund you're looking for right in your local bank.

smart.sites

Unlike many mutual fund Web sites, Fund Alarm (**http://www.fundalarm.com**) focuses not on what funds to buy but when to sell the funds you own. Its "3-Alarm Fund" lists highlight funds that have underperformed based on 3- or 5-year returns within each benchmark.

Selling shares in a fund is also a do-it-yourself affair, whether the fund is load or no-load. Because brokers and salespeople usually don't make anything on fund *sales*, they have little motivation to execute sell orders. As a result, you may find you'll have to redeem your fund shares by directly notifying the mutual fund of your intention to sell. The fund then buys the shares back and mails you a check. But before selling your fund shares this way, check to see if the fund offers *phone switching*. This service is available from a number of investment companies, and it enables you to simply pick up the phone to move money from one fund to another—the only constraint is that the funds must be managed by the same family of funds. Most companies charge little or nothing for these shifts, although funds that offer free exchange privileges often place a limit on the number of times you can switch each year. (We'll discuss this service in more detail later in the chapter when we cover *conversion privileges.*)

Concept ✓

13-1. What is a mutual fund? Discuss the mutual fund concept; why are diversification and professional management so important?

13-2. Briefly describe how a mutual fund is organized. Who are the key players in a typical mutual fund organization?

13-3. Briefly define each of the following:
  a. *Closed-end investment company*
  b. *Open-end investment company*
  c. *Exchange-traded funds*
  d. *Unit investment trust*
  e. *Real estate investment trust*

13-4. What is the difference between a load fund and a no-load fund? Are there some advantages to either type? What is a *12(b)-1* fund? Can such a fund operate as a no-load fund?

13-5. Briefly describe a *back-end load,* a *low load,* a *hidden load.* How can you tell what kind of fees and charges a fund has?

Stable-Value Funds: A Safe Harbor for Retirement Investors

How does an investment that returns close to 5 percent annually with virtually no risk sound? Although it might not sound like a big deal, for the past several years (including the 2002–'02 bear market) stable value funds have been offering just such a safe harbor to investors seeking to protect their profits from the roller-coaster ride of many stock and bond investments.

Stable-value funds are offered mainly through employer-sponsored retirement plans. In fact, about two-thirds of all 401(k) plans include stable value funds in their investment mix. Some of the larger stable-value fund providers include Fidelity Managed Income Portfolio, Vanguard Retirement Savings Trust, and the Wells Fargo Stable Return Fund. According to the Stable Value Investment Association, the pool of stable value funds held by investors currently tops $321 billion.

Stable-value funds differ from more traditional investment funds like money market and bond funds in several key ways. First, a typical stable-value fund holds a blend of high-quality, intermediate-term investments. These can include mortgage bonds, credit card receivables, and guaranteed-interest contracts (GICs) from insurance companies. However, the key difference between stable-value funds and other type of fund investments is a "wrapper," an insurance policy designed to allow the fund to redeem shares at a stable price even if the overall value of its investment drops.

For investors, this translates into the assurance that they will be able to maintain the net value of their initial principal—no matter how the fund performs overall. Another benefit for investors: low costs. Stable-value fund expenses usually average about 53 cents a year per $100 invested.

Before you rush to add stable-value funds to your investment portfolio, however, there are a few things to consider. Because stable-value funds tend to put money in longer-term fixed-income investments, earnings can easily be outpaced by inflation and overall yields often lag behind the overall equity market. Finally, some stable-value funds put

...continued on next page

TYPES OF FUNDS AND FUND SERVICES

LG3, LG4

Some mutual funds specialize in stocks and others in bonds; some funds have maximum capital gains as their investment objective, and some seek high current income. Some funds will appeal to speculators, and others primarily to income-oriented investors. Every fund has a particular investment objective, some of the more common ones being capital appreciation, income, tax-exempt income, preservation of investment capital, or some combination thereof. Disclosure of a fund's investment objective is required by the SEC, and each fund is expected to do its best to conform to its stated investment policy and objective.

Categorizing funds according to their investment policies and objectives is widely practiced in the mutual fund industry, as it tends to reflect similarities not only in how the funds manage their money, but also in their risk and return characteristics. Some of the more popular types of mutual funds include growth, aggressive growth, value, equity-income, balanced, growth-and-income, bond, money market, index, sector, socially responsible, international, and asset allocation funds. Still another type of mutual fund is the so-called stable-value fund. As explained in the nearby *Money in Action* box, these once obscure funds became the talk of Wall Street during the bear market of 2000–02; however, given the way these funds are structured, and what their investment portfolios are designed to do, it remains to be seen how long that popularity will last once we have another full-fledged bull market. So, let's now take a look at these and all the other types of mutual funds to see what they are and what they have to offer investors. After we do that, we'll look at the kinds of investor services these funds offer.

TYPES OF FUNDS

Growth Funds

The objective of a *growth fund* is simple—capital appreciation. Long-term growth and capital gains are the primary goals of such funds, and as a result they invest principally in common stocks that have above-average growth potential. Because of the uncertain nature of their investment income, growth funds involve a fair amount of risk exposure. They are usually viewed as long-term investment vehicles that are most suitable for the more aggressive investor who wants to build capital and has little interest in current income.

Aggressive Growth Funds

These are the so-called performance funds that tend to increase in popularity when the markets heat up. *Aggressive growth funds* are highly speculative investment vehicles that seek large profits from capital gains; in many respects, they are really an extension of the growth fund concept. Many are fairly small, with portfolios consisting mainly of high-flying common stocks. Also known as "capital appreciation" funds, they often buy stocks of small, unseasoned companies, stocks with relatively high price/earnings multiples, and stocks whose prices are highly volatile. Some of these funds even go so far as to use leverage in their portfolios (that is, they buy stocks on margin by borrowing part of the purchase price). All this is designed, of course, to yield big returns. However, aggressive growth funds are also highly speculative and are perhaps the most volatile of all the fund types. When the markets are good, these funds do well; when the markets are bad, they typically experience substantial losses.

restrictions on when and how investors can withdraw cash out of the fund, which could cause problems if those rules conflict with your plans.

In general, stable-value funds are best for retirees with conservative investment needs who are seeking maximum safety. However, they can also be useful for younger investors who are looking to build a safety net within a larger retirement portfolio. Most financial advisors suggest that you should limit the amount you have in stable-value funds to about 8% of the fixed-income portion of your investment portfolio. Finally, if you do decide that the safety of stable-value funds makes sense for you, it's wise to boost your savings in other areas to compensate for potentially lower returns over the long haul.

Critical Thinking Questions:

1. How do stable-value funds differ from more traditional investment funds?
2. What are the risks and benefits associated with stable-value funds?
3. Would you choose stable-value funds for your own investment portfolio? Why or why not?

Sources: James M. Clash, "Guaranteed!" *Forbes*, June 9, 2003, p. 118; Amy Feldman, "The Selling of Safety," *Money*, May 2003, p. 95; Jeffrey R. Kosnett, "Simple and Safe," *Kiplinger's Personal Finance Magazine*, July 2003, pp. 35–37; Briget O'Brian, "Stable-Value Funds See Big Inflows," *The Wall Street Journal*, July 25, 2002, p. D-13; "Questions about Stable Value Investments," Stable Value Investment Association web site, **http://www.stablevalue.org/help/faq_main.asp**, downloaded December 6, 2003.

Value Funds

Value funds confine their investing to stocks considered to be ***undervalued*** by the market; that is, the funds look for stocks that are fundamentally sound but have yet to be discovered, and as such, remain undervalued by the market. These funds, in effect, hold stocks as much for their underlying intrinsic values as their *growth potential.* In stark contrast to growth funds, value funds look for stocks with relatively low P/Es, high dividend yields, and moderate amounts of financial leverage. They prefer undiscovered companies that offer the potential for growth, rather than those that are already experiencing rapid growth. Value investing is not easy! It involves extensive evaluation of corporate financial statements and any other documents that will help fund managers *uncover value (i.e., investment opportunities) before the rest of the market does* (that's the key to getting the low P/Es). And the approach seems to work. For even though value investing is generally regarded as being *less risky* than growth investing (lower P/Es, higher dividend yields, fundamentally stronger companies all translate into reduced risk exposure), the long-term returns to investors in value funds is quite competitive with that earned from growth or even aggressive growth funds. Thus, value funds are often viewed as a viable investment alternative for relatively conservative investors who are looking for the attractive returns that common stocks have to offer, yet want to keep share price volatility and investment risk in check.

Equity-Income Funds

Equity-income funds emphasize current income, which they provide by investing primarily in high-yielding common stocks. Capital preservation is also a goal of these funds, and so is capital gains, although capital appreciation is not their primary objective. They invest heavily in high-grade common stocks, some convertible securities and preferred stocks, and occasionally even junk bonds or certain types of high-grade foreign bonds. They like securities that generate hefty dividend yields, but also consider potential price appreciation over the longer haul. In general, because of their emphasis on dividends and current income, these funds tend to hold higher-quality securities that are subject to less price volatility than the market as a whole. They're generally viewed as a fairly low-risk way of investing in stocks.

Balanced Funds

Balanced funds are so named because they tend to hold a balanced portfolio of both stocks and bonds, and they do so for the purpose of generating a well-balanced return of current income and long-term capital gains. In many respects, they're a lot like equity-income funds, except that balanced funds usually put much more into fixed-income securities; generally they keep at least 25 to 50 percent of their portfolios in bonds, and sometimes more. The bonds are used principally to provide current income, and stocks are selected mainly for their long-term growth potential. The funds can, of course, tilt the emphasis in their security holdings one way or the other. Clearly, the more the fund leans toward fixed-income securities, the more income oriented it will be. For the most part, balanced funds tend to confine their investing to high-grade securities, and are therefore usually considered a relatively safe form of investing, one where you can earn a competitive rate of return without having to endure a lot of price volatility.

Growth-And-Income Funds

Like balanced funds, *growth-and-income funds* also seek a balanced return made up of current income and long-term capital gains, but they place a greater emphasis on growth of capital. Moreover, unlike balanced funds, growth-and-income funds put most of their money into equities—indeed, it's not unusual for these funds to have 80 to 90 percent of their capital in common stocks. They tend to confine most of their investing to high-quality issues, so you can expect to find a lot of growth-oriented blue-chip stocks in their portfolios, along with a fair amount of high-quality income stocks. One big appeal of these funds is the fairly substantial returns many of them have been able to generate over the long haul. But then, these funds do involve a fair amount of risk, if for no other reason than the emphasis they place on stocks and capital gains. Consequently, growth-and-income funds are most suitable for those investors who can tolerate their risk and price volatility.

Bond Funds

As their name implies, *bond funds* invest in various kinds of fixed-income securities. Income is their primary investment objective, although they do not ignore capital gains. There are three important advantages to buying shares in bond funds rather than investing directly in bonds. First, bond funds generally are more liquid; second, they offer a cost-effective way of achieving a high degree of diversification in an otherwise expensive investment vehicle (most bonds carry minimum denominations of $1,000 to $5,000, or more); and third, bond funds will automatically reinvest interest and other income, thereby allowing the investor to earn fully compounded rates of return. There are more than 4,000 publicly traded bond funds which, together, have over $1.1 *trillion* worth of bonds under management.

Although bond funds are usually considered a fairly conservative form of investment, they are not totally without risk, because the prices of the bonds held in the funds' portfolios will fluctuate with changing interest rates. Although many of the funds are basically conservative, a growing number are becoming increasingly aggressive—in fact, much of the growth that bond funds have experienced in the recent past can be attributed to this new investment attitude. No matter what your tastes, you'll find a full menu of bond funds available, including:

- *Government bond funds*, which invest in U.S. Treasury and agency securities.
- *Mortgage-backed bond funds*, which put their money into various types of mortgage-backed securities issued by agencies of the U.S. government (such as GNMA issues). These funds appeal to investors not only because they provide diversification and a more affordable way to get into these securities, but also because they have a provision that allows investors (if they so choose) to reinvest the *principal* portion of the monthly cash flow, thereby enabling them to preserve, rather than consume, their capital.
- *High-grade corporate bond funds*, which invest chiefly in investment-grade securities rated triple-B or better.
- *High-yield corporate bond funds*, which are risky investments that buy *junk bonds* for the yields they offer.
- *Convertible bond funds*, which invest primarily in (domestic and possibly foreign) securities that can be converted or exchanged into common stocks; by investing in convertible bonds and preferreds, the funds offer investors some of the price stability of bonds, along with the capital appreciation potential of stocks.
- *Municipal bond funds*, which invest in tax-exempt securities and are suitable for investors looking for tax-free income. Like their corporate counterparts, municipals can also come out as either high-grade or high-yield funds. A special type of municipal bond fund is the so-called *single-state* fund, which invests in the municipal issues of only one state, thus producing (for residents of that state) interest income that is *fully* exempt from not only federal taxes, but state (and possibly even local/city) taxes as well.
- *Intermediate-term bond funds*, which invest in bonds with maturities of 7 to 10 years, or less, and offer not only attractive yields but relatively low price volatility as well; shorter (2- to 5-year) funds are also available and can be used as substitutes for money market investments by investors looking for higher returns on their money, especially when short-term rates are way down.

general-purpose money fund
A money market mutual fund that invests in virtually any type of short-term investment vehicle, so long as it offers an attractive rate of return.

tax-exempt money fund
A money market mutual fund that limits its investments to tax-exempt municipal securities with short maturities.

government securities money fund
A money market mutual fund that limits its investments to short-term securities of the U.S. government and its agencies, thus eliminating any default risk.

Money Market Mutual Funds

With the introduction of the very first *money fund* in 1972, the concept of investing in a portfolio of short-term money market instruments caught on like wildfire. The reason for their popularity is really quite simple: Money funds gave investors with modest amounts of capital access to the higher-yielding end of the money market, where many instruments require minimum investments of $100,000 or more. Today, there are over 1,000 publicly-traded money funds that, together, hold about $2.25 *trillion* in assets.

Actually, there are several different kinds of money market mutual funds. **General-purpose money funds** essentially invest in any and all types of money market investment vehicles, from Treasury bills to corporate commercial paper and bank certificates of deposit. They invest their money wherever they can find attractive short-term returns. The vast majority of money funds are of this type. The **tax-exempt money fund** limits its investments to tax-exempt municipal securities with very short (30- to 90-day) maturities. Because their income is free from federal income tax, they appeal predominantly to investors in high tax brackets. **Government securities money funds** were established as a way of meeting investors' concern for safety. In essence, these funds eliminate any risk of default by confining their investments to Treasury bills and other short-term securities of the U.S. government or its agencies (such as the Federal National Mortgage Association).

Money funds are highly liquid investment vehicles, and are very low in risk because they are virtually immune to capital loss. However, the interest income they produce tends to follow interest rate conditions, and as such, the returns to shareholders are subject to the ups and downs of market interest rates. (Money funds were discussed more fully in Chapter 4, along with other short-term investment vehicles.)

Index Funds

"If you can't beat 'em, join 'em." That saying pretty much describes the idea behind *index funds.* Essentially, an index fund is a type of mutual fund that buys and holds a portfolio of stocks (or bonds) equivalent to those in a market index like the S&P 500. An index fund that's trying to match the S&P 500, for example, would hold the same 500 stocks that are held in that index, in exactly (or very nearly) the same proportion. Rather than trying to beat the market, as most actively managed funds do, *index funds simply try to match the market*—that is, to match the performance of the index on which the fund is based. They do this through low-cost investment management; in fact, in most cases, the whole portfolio is run almost entirely by a computer that matches the fund's holdings with those of the targeted index. Besides the S&P 500, a number of other market indexes are used, including the S&P Midcap 400, Russell 2000, and Wilshire 5000, as well as value stock indexes, growth stock indexes, international stock indexes, and even bond indexes.

The approach of index funds is strictly buy-and-hold. Indeed, about the only time there's a change to the portfolio of an index fund is when the targeted market index alters its "market basket" of securities. (Occasionally an index will drop a few securities and replace them with new ones.) A pleasant by-product of this buy-and-hold approach is that the funds have extremely low portfolio turnover rates and, therefore, very little in *realized* capital gains. As a result, aside from a modest amount of dividend income, these funds produce very little taxable income from year to year, which leads many high-income investors to view them as a type of tax-sheltered investment.

In addition to their tax shelter, however, these funds provide something else. That is, as boring as the whole idea may sound, by simply trying to match the market, index funds actually produce *highly competitive returns* for investors! The fact is that it's very tough to outperform the market, whether you are a professional money manager or a seasoned individual investor. Index funds readily acknowledge this fact and, as such, don't even try to outperform the market; instead, all they try to do is match the returns. Surprisingly, the net result of this strategy, along with a *very low cost structure*, is that most index funds readily outperform the vast majority of all other types of stock funds. Indeed, historical data show that only abut 20 to 25 percent of stock funds outperform the market. Because a (true) index fund will pretty much match the market, these funds tend to produce better returns than 75 to 80 percent of competing stock funds. Granted, every now and then the fully managed stock funds will have a year (or two) when they outperform index funds, but those are the exception rather than the rule! Especially when you look at multi-year returns (covering periods of 3 to 5 years, or more), where you'll find that most fully managed stock funds just can't keep up with index funds.

smart.sites

At IndexFunds.com, **http://www.indexfunds.com**, you'll find a wealth of resources, articles, and a Fund Screener to search based on expense ratio, returns, net assets, or other criteria.

Sector Funds

As the name implies, a *sector fund* restricts its investments to a particular sector of the market. In effect, these funds concentrate their investment holdings in the one or more industries that make up the targeted sector. For example, a *healthcare* sector fund would confine its investments to those industries that make up this segment of the market: drug companies, hospital management firms, medical suppliers, and biotech concerns. Its portfolio would then consist of promising growth stocks from those industries. The underlying investment objective of sector funds is *capital gains.* In many respects, they are similar to growth funds and thus should be considered speculative in nature.

The idea behind the sector fund concept is that the really attractive returns come from small segments of the market. Thus, rather than diversifying the portfolio across wide segments of the market, you should put your money where the action is. This notion may warrant consideration by the more aggressive investor who is willing to take on the added risks that often accompany these funds. Among the more popular sector funds are those that concentrate their investments in real estate (REITs), technology, energy, financial services, leisure and entertainment, natural resources, electronics, chemicals, computers, telecommunications, utilities, and, of course, healthcare.

Socially Responsible Funds

For some, investing is far more than just cranking out some financial ratios. To these investors, the security selection process doesn't end with bottom lines, P/E ratios, growth rates, and betas; rather, it also includes the *active, explicit consideration of moral, ethical, and environmental issues.* The idea is that social concerns should play just as big a role in the investment decision as profits and other financial matters. Not surprisingly, there are a number of funds today that cater to such investors; known as **socially responsible funds**, they actively and directly incorporate morality and ethics into the investment decision.

socially responsible fund
A type of mutual fund that puts social concerns on the same level of importance as financial returns, investing only in companies that meet certain moral, ethical, and/or environmental tests.

These funds will consider only what they view as socially responsible companies for inclusion in their portfolios—if a company doesn't meet certain moral, ethical, or environmental tests, they simply won't consider buying the stock, no matter how good the bottom line looks. Generally speaking, these funds abstain from investing in companies that derive revenues from tobacco, alcohol, or gambling; are weapons contractors; or operate nuclear power plants. In addition, the funds tend to favor firms that produce "responsible" products and services, have strong employee relations, have positive environmental records, and are socially responsive to the communities in which they operate. Although these screens may seem to eliminate a lot of stocks from consideration, these funds (most of which are fairly small) still have plenty of securities to choose from, so it's not all that difficult for them to keep their portfolios fully invested.

As far as performance is concerned, the general perception is that there's a price to pay for socially responsible investing in the form of lower average returns. For example, in late 2003, year-to-date returns on 149 socially responsible funds averaged just under 14.0 percent, whereas domestic stock funds in general turned in year-to-date returns of 20.6 percent. Such comparative performance should come as no surprise, however, for as you add more investment hurdles or screens, you're likely to reduce return potential. But for those who truly believe in socially responsible investing, perhaps they really are willing to put their money where their mouths are!

smart.sites

If socially responsible funds appeal to you, the Social Investment Forum (**http://www.socialinvest.org**) is a good first stop. You'll find information, contacts, resources, and performance records on funds with a conscience.

International Funds

In their search for higher yields and better returns, American investors have shown a growing interest in foreign securities. Sensing an opportunity, the mutual fund industry was quick to respond with a proliferation of so-called **international funds**—a type of mutual fund that does all or most of its investing in foreign securities. Just look at the number of international funds around today versus a few years ago. In 1985, there were only about 40 of these funds; by 2003, that number had grown to nearly 1,900. The fact is, a lot of people would like to invest in foreign securities but simply don't have the experience or know-how to do so. International funds may be just the ticket for such investors, *provided they have at least a basic appreciation of international economics.* Because these funds deal with the international economy, balance of trade positions, and currency valuations, investors should have at least a fundamental understanding of what these issues are and how they can affect fund returns.

international fund
A mutual fund that does all or most of its investing in foreign securities; also includes global funds, a special type of international fund that invests in both international and domestic securities.

Technically, the term *international fund* is used to describe a type of fund that *invests exclusively in foreign securities*, often confining the fund's activities to specific geographical regions (such as Mexico, Australia, Europe, or the Pacific Rim). In contrast, there is also another class of international funds, known as *global funds*, which invest not only in foreign securities, *but also in U.S. companies*—usually multinational firms. As a rule, global funds provide more diversity and, with access to both foreign and domestic markets, can go wherever the action is.

Regardless of whether they're global or international (from here on, we'll use the term "international" to apply to both), you'll find just about any type of fund you could possibly want in the international sector. There are international *stock* funds, international *bond* funds, even international *money market* funds; in addition, there are aggressive growth funds, balanced funds, long-term growth funds, high-grade bond funds, and so forth. Thus, no matter what your investment philosophy or objective, you're likely to find what you're looking for in the international area.

Basically, these funds attempt to take advantage of international economic developments in two ways: (1) by capitalizing on changing foreign market conditions, and (2) by positioning themselves to benefit from devaluation of the dollar. They do so because they can make money not only from rising share prices in a foreign market, but, perhaps just as important, from a falling dollar (which, in itself, produces capital gains to American investors in foreign securities and international funds). Many of these funds, however, will attempt to protect their investors from currency exchange risks by using various types of *hedging strategies.* That is, by using foreign currency options and futures (or some other type of derivative product), the fund will try to eliminate (or reduce) the effects of currency exchange rates. Some funds, in fact, do this on a permanent basis—in essence, these funds hedge away exchange risk so they can concentrate on the higher returns that foreign securities offer. Most others are only occasional users of currency hedges and will employ them only if they feel there's a real chance of a substantial swing in currency values. But even with currency hedging, international funds are still considered fairly high-risk investments and should be used only by investors who understand and are able to tolerate such risks.

Asset Allocation Funds

Studies have shown that the most important decision an investor can make is to decide where to allocate his or her investment assets. This is known as *asset allocation*, and, as we saw in Chapter 11, basically involves deciding how you're going to divide your investments among different types of securities. For example, what portion of your money is going to be devoted to money market securities, what portion to stocks, what portion to bonds? Asset allocation deals in broad terms and does not address individual security selection. Even so, as strange as it may sound, asset allocation has been found to be a far more important determinant of total returns on a well-diversified portfolio than individual security selection.

Because a lot of individual investors have a tough time making asset allocation decisions, the mutual fund industry has, not surprisingly, created a product to do the job for them. Known as *asset allocation funds*, these funds spread investors' money across all different types of markets. That is, while most mutual funds concentrate on one type of investment—whether stocks, bonds, or money market securities—asset allocation funds put money into all these markets. Many of them also include foreign securities in their asset allocation scheme, and some may even include inflation-resistant investments such as gold or real estate.

These funds are designed for people who want to hire fund managers not only to select individual securities for them, but also to make the strategic decision of how to allocate money among the various markets. Here's how many asset allocation funds work. The money manager will establish a desired allocation mix—it might look something like this: 50 percent of the portfolio goes to U.S. stocks, 10 percent to foreign securities, 30 percent to bonds, and 10 percent to money market securities. Securities are then purchased for the fund in this proportion, and the overall portfolio maintains the desired mix. Actually, each segment of the fund is managed almost as a separate portfolio, so securities within, say, the stock portion are bought, sold, and held as the market dictates. Now, here's what really separates asset allocation funds from the rest of the pack: *As market conditions change over time, the asset allocation mix will change as well.* Thus, if the U.S. stock market starts to soften, funds will be moved out of stocks to some other area; as a result, the stock portion of the portfolio may drop to, say, 35 percent and the foreign securities portion may increase to 25 percent. Of course, there's no assurance that the money manager will make the right moves at the right time, but that's the idea behind these funds.

Asset allocation funds are supposed to provide investors with one-stop shopping; that is, just find an asset allocation fund or two that fits your needs and invest in it (or them), rather than going out and buying a couple stock funds, a couple bond funds, and so on. The success of these funds rests not only on how good a security picker the money manager is, but also on how good a job he or she does in timing the market and moving funds among different segments of the market.

Financial Road Sign

Test Drive a Life-Cycle Fund

If the idea of investing once and forgetting about it appeals to you, consider life cycle mutual funds that do most of the work for you. You choose a fund according to your target retirement date and it shifts assets from stocks into more conservative securities as you approach retirement age. Also called target date, target maturity, or morphing funds, most invest in other mutual funds to create a very widely diversified fund. The following pointers will help you decide if they belong in your portfolio and how to use them properly:

- Look at the asset mix carefully. Some funds use equities more aggressively than others.
- As with all funds, choose those with low expense ratios.
- Past performance won't predict future returns, because the fund assets will change over time to include more conservative–and hence, lower-yielding–securities.
- Life-cycle funds are designed as long-term investments, so don't trade them looking for better performance in the short term.
- Use life-cycle funds appropriately in your portfolio. They are widely diversified to stand on their own and serve as the major investment in your portfolio, rather than be part of an overall asset allocation strategy.

Sources: Harriet Johnson Brackey, "One-Stop Investing," *San Diego Union-Tribune*, November 9, 2003, p. H-3; and Rachel Emma Silverman, "Lifecycle Funds Lure Jittery Buyers," *The Wall Street Journal*, August 28, 2003, pp. D1, D2.

SERVICES OFFERED BY MUTUAL FUNDS

Ask most investors why they buy a particular mutual fund and they'll probably tell you that the fund provides the kind of income and return they're looking for. Now, no one would question the importance of return in the investment decision, but there are other reasons for investing in mutual funds, not the least of which are the valuable services they provide. Some of the most sought-after *mutual fund services* are automatic investment and reinvestment plans, regular income programs, conversion and phone-switching privileges, and retirement programs.

Automatic Investment Plans

It takes money to make money, and for an investor that means being able to accumulate the capital to put into the market. Unfortunately, that's not always the easiest thing in the world to do. Enter mutual funds, which have come up with a program that makes savings and capital accumulation as painless as possible. The program is the **automatic investment plan** and it allows fund shareholders to automatically funnel fixed amounts of money *from their paychecks or bank accounts* into a mutual fund. It's very much like a payroll deduction plan that treats savings a lot like insurance coverage—that is, just as insurance premiums are automatically deducted from your paycheck (or bank account), so too are investments to your mutual fund.

automatic investment plan
A type of automatic savings program that enables an investor to systematically channel a set amount of money into a given mutual fund; it provides investors with a convenient way to accumulate capital.

This fund service has become very popular, as it allows shareholders to invest without having to think about it. Just about every major fund group offers some kind of automatic investment plan. To enroll, a shareholder simply fills out a form authorizing the fund to siphon a set amount (usually it has to be a minimum of $25 to $100 per period) from your bank account or paycheck at regular intervals—typically monthly or quarterly. Once enrolled, you'll be buying shares in the funds of your choice every month or quarter (most funds deal in fractional shares); of course, if it's a load fund, you'll still have to pay normal sales charges on your periodic investments.

To remain diversified, you can divide your money among as many funds (within a given fund family) as you like; and you can get out of the program anytime you like, without penalty, by simply contacting the fund. Although convenience is perhaps the plans' chief advantage, they also make solid investment sense, because one of the best ways of building up a sizable amount of capital is to systematically add *funds to your investment program over time.* The importance of making regular contributions to your investment program cannot be overstated—it ranks right up there with compound interest!

Automatic Reinvestment Plans

This is one of the real draws of mutual funds, and it's a service that's offered by just about every open-ended mutual fund. Whereas automatic investment plans deal with money shareholders put into a fund, automatic *re*investment plans deal with the disposition of dividends and other distributions the funds pay to their shareholders. Much like the dividend reinvestment plans we looked at with stocks, the **automatic reinvestment plans** of mutual funds enable you to keep all your capital fully employed. Through this service, dividend and capital gains income is *automatically used to buy additional shares in the fund.* Keep in mind, however, that even though you reinvest your dividends and capital gains, the IRS still treats them as cash receipts and taxes them in the year in which they are paid.

automatic reinvestment plan
A plan offered by most mutual funds that allows share owners to elect to have dividends and capital gains distributions reinvested in additional fund shares.

The important point is that by plowing back profits (reinvested dividends and capital gains distributions), the investor can essentially put his or her profits to work in generating even more earnings. Indeed, the effects of these plans on total accumulated capital over the long haul can be substantial. Exhibit 13.6 shows the long-term impact of one such plan. (These are the actual performance numbers for a *real* mutual fund—Vanguard Health Care.) In the illustration, we assume that the investor starts with $10,000 and, except for the reinvestment of dividends and capital gains, *adds no new capital over time.* Even so, note that the initial investment of $10,000 grew to nearly $160,000 over a 15-year period (which, by the way, amounts to a compound rate of return of 20.26 percent). Clearly, so long as care is taken in selecting an appropriate fund, *attractive benefits can be derived from the systematic accumulation of capital offered by automatic reinvestment plans.*

Regular Income

Although automatic reinvestment plans are great for the long-term investor, how about the investor who's looking for a steady stream of income? Once again, mutual funds

EXHIBIT 13.6

The Effects of Reinvesting Income

Reinvesting dividends and/or capital gains can have tremendous effects on one's investment position. This graph shows the results of a hypothetical investor who initially invested $10,000 and, for a period of 15 years, reinvested all dividends and capital gains distributions in additional fund shares. (No adjustment has been made for any income taxes payable by the shareholder—which would be appropriate so long as the fund was held in, say, an IRA or Keogh account.)

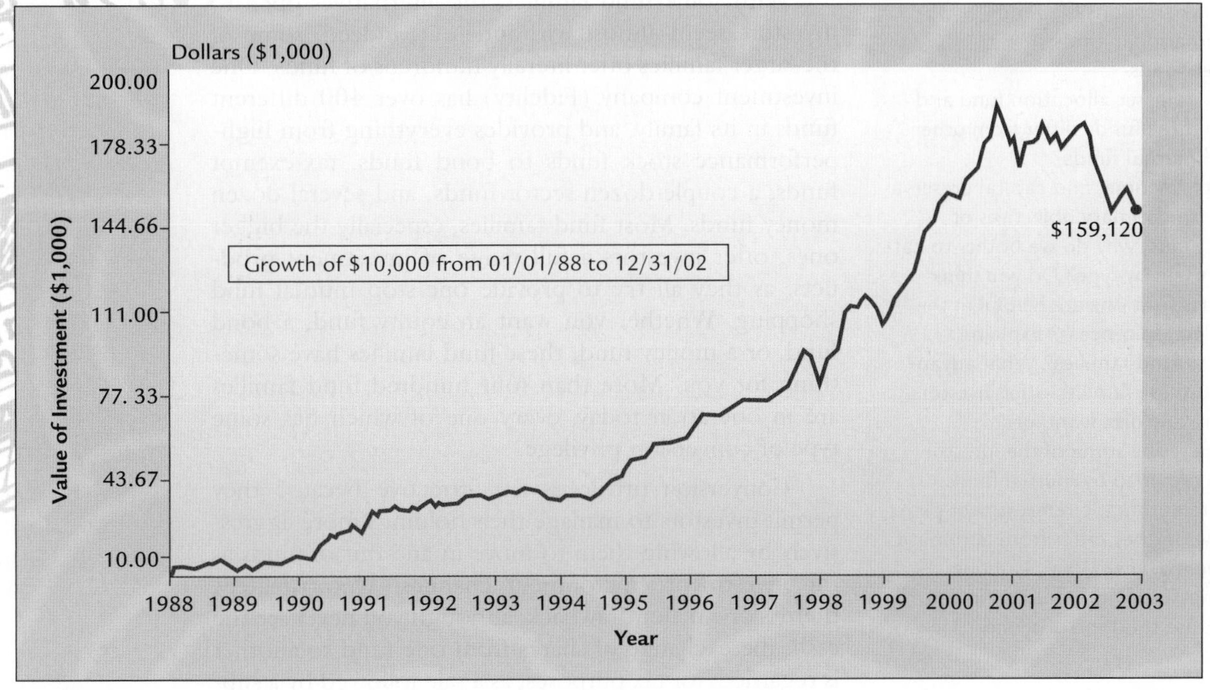

Source: *Morningstar Principia for Mutual Funds,* June 30, 2003.

systematic withdrawal plan A plan offered by mutual funds that allows shareholders to be paid specified amounts of money each period.

have a service to meet this kind of need. It's called a **systematic withdrawal plan**, and it's offered by most open-ended funds. Once enrolled in one of these plans, you will automatically receive a predetermined amount of money every month or quarter.

To participate, shareholders are usually required to have a minimum investment of $5,000 to $10,000, and the size of the withdrawal must usually be $50 or more per month. Depending on how well the fund is doing, the income derived from the fund may actually be greater than the withdrawals, thus allowing the investor not only to receive regular income but also enjoy an automatic accumulation of *additional* shares in the plan. On the other hand, if the fund is not performing well, the withdrawals could eventually deplete the original investment.

Conversion Privileges

Sometimes investors find it necessary to switch out of one fund and into another; for example, their investment objectives may change, or the investment environment itself may have

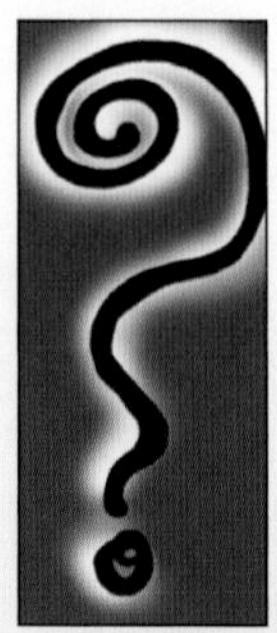

Concept ✓

13-6. Briefly describe each of the following types of mutual funds:
  a. Aggressive growth funds
  b. Equity-income funds
  c. Growth-and-income funds
  d. Bond funds
  e. Sector funds
  f. Socially responsible funds
  g. International funds
  h. Index funds

13-7. What is an asset allocation fund and how do these funds differ from other types of mutual funds?

13-8. If growth, income, and capital preservation are the primary objectives of mutual funds, why do we bother to categorize them by type? Do you think such classifications are helpful in the fund selection process? Explain.

13-9. What are fund families? What advantages do these families offer investors? Are there any disadvantages?

13-10. Briefly describe some of the investor services provided by mutual funds. What are automatic reinvestment plans and how do they differ from automatic investment plans? What is phone switching, and why would an investor want to use this type of service?

changed. **Conversion** (or **exchange**) **privileges** meet the needs of these investors in a convenient and economical manner. Investment companies that offer a number of different funds to the investing public—known as *fund families*—usually provide conversion privileges that enable shareholders to move easily from one fund to another; and, as we saw earlier, this is usually done by phone (as in *phone switching*). The only limitation is that the investor must confine the switches within the same *family* of funds. For example, an investor can switch from a Dreyfus growth fund to a Dreyfus money fund, or to its income fund, or to any other fund managed by Dreyfus.

conversion (exchange) privileges A feature offered by many investment companies that allows investors to switch from one mutual fund to another within a family of funds.

With some fund families, the alternatives open to investors seem almost without limit; indeed, some of the larger families offer literally hundreds of funds. One investment company (Fidelity) has over 400 different funds in its family, and provides everything from high-performance stock funds to bond funds, tax-exempt funds, a couple dozen sector funds, and several dozen money funds. Most fund families, especially the bigger ones, offer investors a full range of investment products, as they all try to provide one-stop mutual fund shopping. Whether you want an equity fund, a bond fund, or a money fund, these fund families have something for you. More than four hundred fund families are in operation today, every one of which has some type of conversion privilege.

Conversion privileges are attractive because they permit investors to manage their holdings more aggressively by allowing them to move in and out of funds as the investment environment changes. Unfortunately, there is one major drawback; although you never see the cash, the exchange of shares from one fund to another is regarded, for tax purposes, as a sale followed by a subsequent purchase of a new security. As a result, if any capital gains exist at the time of the exchange, the investor is liable for the taxes on that profit.

Retirement Plans

As a result of government legislation, self-employed individuals are permitted to divert a portion of their pretax income into self-directed *retirement plans.* And all working Americans, whether they are self-employed or not, are allowed to establish individual retirement accounts—either in the form of a standard tax-deductible IRA, or the newest type of retirement account, the Roth IRA (all of which we'll look at in the next chapter). Today all mutual funds provide a special service that allows individuals to quickly and easily set up tax-deferred retirement programs as either IRA or Keogh accounts—or, through their place of employment, to participate in a qualified tax-sheltered retirement plan, such as a 401(k), for example. The funds set up the plans and handle all the administrative details in such a way that the shareholders can take full advantage of available tax savings.

MAKING MUTUAL FUND INVESTMENTS

LG5, LG6

Suppose you are confronted with the following situation. You have money to invest and are trying to select the right place to put it. You obviously want to pick a security that meets your idea of acceptable risk, but also one that will generate an attractive rate of return. The problem is that you have to make the selection from a list of nearly 8,300 securities. Sound like a "mission impossible"? Well, that's basically what a typical investor is up against when trying to select a suitable mutual fund. But perhaps if the problem is approached systematically, it may not be so formidable a task after all. For as we will see, it is possible to whittle down the list of alternatives by matching one's investment needs with the investment objectives of the funds.

The Selection Process

When it comes to mutual funds, one question that every investor has to answer is: Why invest in a mutual fund to begin with; why not just go it alone (that is, buy individual stocks and bonds directly)? For beginning investors, or investors with little capital, the answer is pretty simple—mutual funds provide far more diversification than they could ever get on their own, plus they get the help of professional money managers, and at a very reasonable cost to boot.

For more seasoned, better-heeled investors, the answers are probably a bit more involved. Certainly, the diversification and professional money management come into play, but there are other reasons as well. The competitive returns that mutual funds offer have to be a factor with many investors, and so do the services they provide. A lot of well-to-do investors have simply decided that they can get better returns over the long haul by carefully selecting mutual funds than by trying to invest on their own. As a result, they put all, or a big chunk, of their money into funds. Many of these investors will use part of their capital to buy and sell individual securities on their own, and the rest will be used *to buy mutual funds that invest in areas they don't fully understand or don't feel well-informed about*—for example, they will use mutual funds to get into foreign markets or as the way to buy mortgage-backed securities. For more on the question of which way to go—mutual funds or individual securities—see the *Money in Action* box on pages 580–581.

Once a decision to use mutual funds has been made, the investor will then have to decide which funds to buy. The selection process itself (especially with regard to the *types* of funds to purchase) obviously plays an important role in defining the amount of success you will have with mutual funds. It means putting into action all you know about investing to gain as much return as possible from an acceptable level of risk. Given that you have an asset allocation strategy in place and you are trying to select funds compatible to your targeted mix, the selection process begins with an assessment of your own investment needs; this sets the tone for your investment program. Obviously, what you want to do is select from those 8,000 or so funds the one or two (or three or four) that will best meet your investment needs.

Objectives And Motives For Using Funds

Selecting the right investment means finding those funds that are most suitable to your investment needs. *The place to start is with your own investment objectives.* In other words, why do you want to invest in a mutual fund, and what are you looking for in a fund? Obviously, an attractive rate of return would be desirable, but there is also the matter of ensuring a tolerable amount of risk exposure. Face it, some investors are more willing to take risks than others, and this is certainly an important ingredient in the selection process. More than likely, when you look at your own risk temperament in relation to the various types of mutual funds available, you will discover that certain types of funds are more appealing to you than others. For instance, aggressive growth or sector funds will probably *not* be attractive to individuals who wish to avoid high exposure to risk.

Another important factor in the selection process is the intended use of the mutual fund. That is, do you want to invest in mutual funds as a way of *accumulating capital* over an extended period of time, to *speculate* with your money in the hopes of generating high rates of return, or to *conserve your capital* by investing in low-risk securities where preservation of capital is as important, or more so, than return on capital. This is helpful information, because it puts into clearer focus the question of exactly what you are trying to do with your investment dollars. Finally, there is the matter of the types of services provided by the fund. If there are services you are particularly interested in, you should be sure to look for them in the funds you select. Having assessed what you are looking for in a fund, you now want to look at what the funds have to offer.

What Funds Have To Offer

The ideal mutual fund would achieve maximum capital growth when security prices rise, provide complete protection against capital loss when prices decline, and achieve high levels of current income at all times. Unfortunately, such funds do not exist. Instead, just as each individual has a set of investment needs, each fund has its own *investment objective*, its own *manner of operation*, and its own *range of services*. These three parameters are useful in helping you assess investment alternatives. But where does the investor look for such information? One obvious place is the fund's *profile* (or its prospectus), where information on investment objectives, portfolio composition, management, and past performance can be obtained. In addition, publications such as *The Wall Street Journal*, *Barron's*, *Money*, *Fortune*, and *Forbes* provide all sorts of useful data and information about mutual funds. These sources publish a wealth of operating and performance statistics in a convenient and easy-to-read format. What's more, services are available that provide background information and assessments on a wide variety of different kinds of funds. Among the best in this category are *Morningstar's Mutual Funds* (an excerpt of which is shown in Exhibit 13.7), Wiesenberger's *Investment Companies* (an annual publication with quarterly updates), and *Value Line Mutual Fund Survey* (which produces reports similar to their stock reports, except they apply to mutual funds). In addition, all sorts of performance statistics are available on disks or on the Internet for easy use on home computers—for example, quarterly or annually updated software is available, at very low cost, from *Morningstar* or the American Association of Individual Investors (AAII). Using sources like these, investors can obtain information on such things as investment objectives, load charges and annual expense rates, summary portfolio analyses, services offered, historical statistics, and reviews of past performance.

Financial Road Sign

Profiles and Prospectuses Have the Answers

If mutual fund prospectuses seemed daunting in the past, you might want to give them another try. The fund industry, in response to new SEC rules, now prepares more readable, streamlined prospectuses and also offers fund profiles, briefer documents that provide key information in 2 to 6 pages. Whether you read the profile or opt for the longer prospectus, here are some guidelines to help sort through the material:

- **Expenses:** This critical section lists all the fees and their amounts, such as sales load (if any), and management and marketing fees.
- **Investment Objectives:** Here you find the fund's investment style—for example, growth, value, or income—and perhaps some information on the types of investments it will buy.
- **Risk:** The prospectus should also give you some idea of this fund's risk profile.
- **Long-term total returns:** Are they consistent or volatile? If they are missing from the prospectus, be wary; they might be low.
- **Management:** Look at the fund manager's biography. How long has he or she managed the fund? Past returns are meaningless if a new manager has just taken over.

Want to know even more? Request the *Statement of Additional Information*, which goes into much greater detail on these topics. The fund's annual or semiannual report is another good resource.

Whittling Down The Alternatives

At this point, fund selection becomes a process of elimination as investor needs are weighed against the types of funds available. A large number of funds can be eliminated

EXHIBIT 13.7

Mutual Fund Information

Investors who want in-depth information about the operating characteristics, investment holdings, and market performance of mutual funds can usually find what they're looking for in publications like *Morningstar Mutual Funds*, or, as shown here, from computer-based information sources like *Morningstar's Principia*.

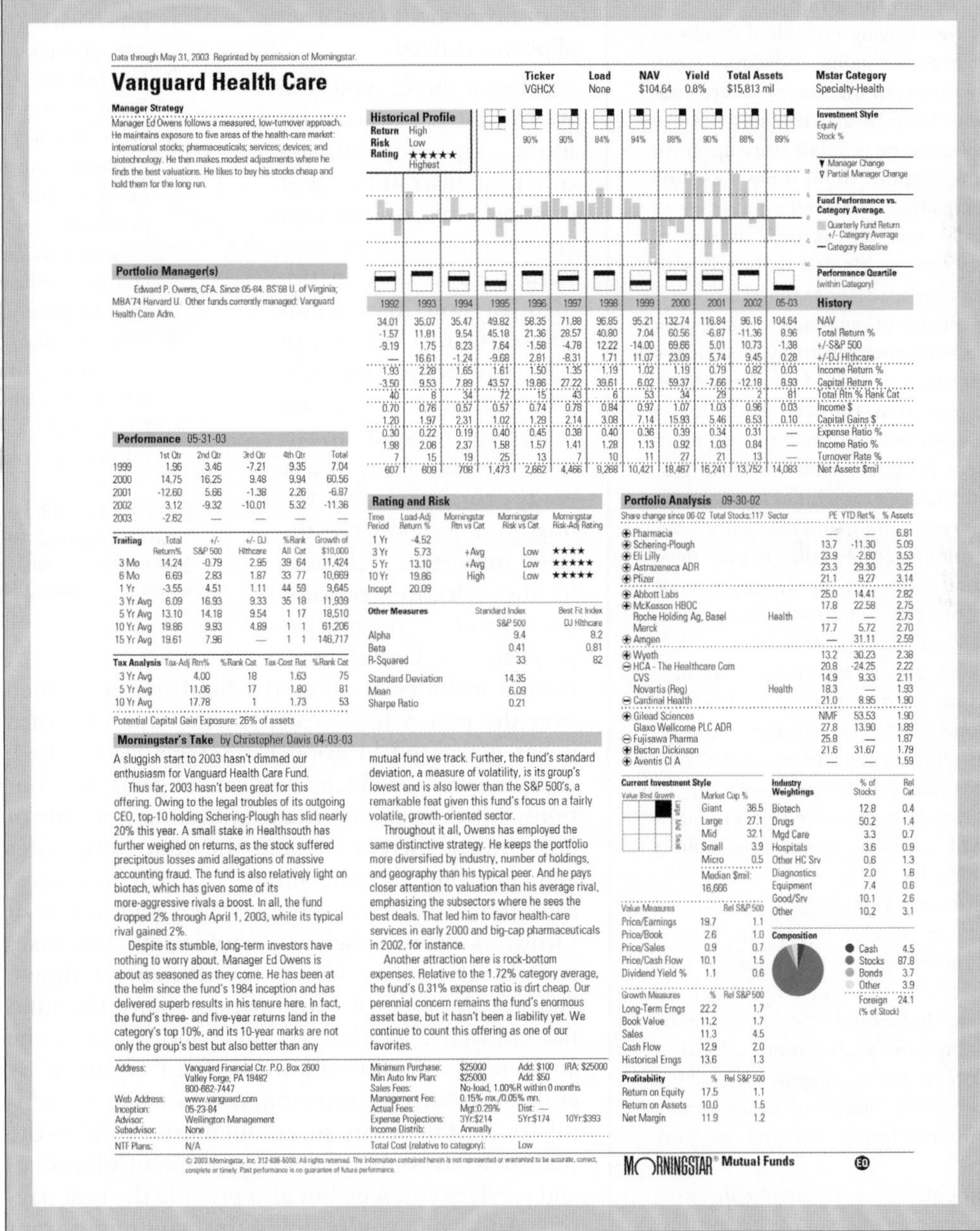

Data through May 31, 2003 Reprinted by permission of Morningstar.

Vanguard Health Care

Ticker	Load	NAV	Yield	Total Assets	Mstar Category
VGHCX	None	$104.64	0.8%	$15,813 mil	Specialty-Health

Manager Strategy

Manager Ed Owens follows a measured, low-turnover approach. He maintains exposure to five areas of the health-care market: international stocks; pharmaceuticals; services; devices; and biotechnology. He then makes modest adjustments where he finds the best valuations. He likes to buy his stocks cheap and hold them for the long run.

Historical Profile
Return High
Risk Low
Rating ★★★★★ Highest

Investment Style
Equity
Stock %: 90% 90% 84% 94% 88% 90% 88% 89%

▼ Manager Change
▽ Partial Manager Change

Fund Performance vs. Category Average.
Quarterly Fund Return +/- Category Average
— Category Baseline

Performance Quartile (within Category)

Portfolio Manager(s)

Edward P. Owens, CFA. Since 05-84. BS'68 U. of Virginia; MBA'74 Harvard U. Other funds currently managed: Vanguard Health Care Adm.

1992	1993	1994	1995	1996	1997	1998	1999	2000	2001	2002	05-03	History
34.01	35.07	35.47	49.82	58.35	71.88	96.85	95.21	132.74	116.84	96.16	104.64	NAV
-1.57	11.81	9.54	45.18	21.36	28.57	40.80	7.04	60.56	-6.87	-11.36	8.96	Total Return %
-9.19	1.75	8.23	7.64	-1.58	-4.78	12.22	-14.00	69.66	5.01	10.73	-1.38	+/-S&P 500
—	16.61	-1.24	-9.68	2.81	-8.31	1.71	11.07	23.09	5.74	9.45	0.28	+/-DJ Hlthcare
1.93	2.28	1.65	1.61	1.50	1.35	1.19	1.02	1.19	0.79	0.82	0.03	Income Return %
-3.50	9.53	7.89	43.57	19.86	27.22	39.61	6.02	59.37	-7.66	-12.18	8.93	Capital Return %
40	8	34	72	15	43	6	53	34	29	2	81	Total Rtn % Rank Cat
0.70	0.76	0.57	0.57	0.74	0.78	0.84	0.97	1.07	1.03	0.96	0.03	Income $
1.20	1.97	2.31	1.02	1.29	2.14	3.08	7.14	15.93	5.46	6.53	0.10	Capital Gains $
0.30	0.22	0.19	0.40	0.45	0.38	0.40	0.36	0.39	0.34	0.31	—	Expense Ratio %
1.98	2.06	2.37	1.58	1.57	1.41	1.28	1.13	0.92	1.03	0.84	—	Income Ratio %
7	15	19	25	13	7	10	11	27	21	13	—	Turnover Rate %
607	609	708	1,473	2,662	4,466	9,268	10,421	18,467	16,241	13,752	14,083	Net Assets $mil

Performance 05-31-03

	1st Qtr	2nd Qtr	3rd Qtr	4th Qtr	Total
1999	1.96	3.46	-7.21	9.35	7.04
2000	14.75	16.25	9.48	9.94	60.56
2001	-12.60	5.66	-1.38	2.26	-6.87
2002	3.12	-9.32	-10.01	5.32	-11.36
2003	-2.62	—	—	—	—

Trailing	Total Return%	+/- S&P 500	+/- DJ Hlthcare	%Rank All	%Rank Cat	Growth of $10,000
3 Mo	14.24	-0.79	2.95	39	64	11,424
6 Mo	6.69	2.83	1.87	33	77	10,669
1 Yr	-3.55	4.51	1.11	44	59	9,645
3 Yr Avg	6.09	16.93	9.33	35	18	11,939
5 Yr Avg	13.10	14.18	9.54	1	17	18,510
10 Yr Avg	19.86	9.93	4.89	1	1	61,206
15 Yr Avg	19.61	7.96	—	1	1	146,717

Tax Analysis	Tax-Adj Rtn%	%Rank Cat	Tax-Cost Rat	%Rank Cat
3 Yr Avg	4.00	18	1.63	75
5 Yr Avg	11.06	17	1.80	81
10 Yr Avg	17.78	1	1.73	53

Potential Capital Gain Exposure: 26% of assets

Rating and Risk

Time Period	Load-Adj Return %	Morningstar Rtn vs Cat	Morningstar Risk vs Cat	Morningstar Risk-Adj Rating
1 Yr	-4.52			
3 Yr	5.73	+Avg	Low	★★★★
5 Yr	13.10	+Avg	Low	★★★★★
10 Yr	19.86	High	Low	★★★★★
Incept	20.09			

Other Measures	Standard Index S&P 500	Best Fit Index DJ Hlthcare
Alpha	9.4	8.2
Beta	0.41	0.81
R-Squared	33	82
Standard Deviation	14.35	
Mean	6.09	
Sharpe Ratio	0.21	

Portfolio Analysis 09-30-02

Share change since 06-02 Total Stocks:117	Sector	PE	YTD Ret%	% Assets
Pharmacia		—	—	6.81
Schering-Plough		13.7	-11.30	5.09
Eli Lilly		23.9	-2.60	3.53
Astrazeneca ADR		23.3	29.30	3.25
Pfizer		21.1	9.27	3.14
Abbott Labs		25.0	14.41	2.82
McKesson HBOC		17.8	22.58	2.75
Roche Holding Ag, Basel	Health	—	—	2.73
Merck		17.7	5.72	2.70
Amgen		—	31.11	2.59
Wyeth		13.2	30.23	2.38
HCA - The Healthcare Com		20.8	-24.25	2.22
CVS		14.9	9.33	2.11
Novartis (Reg)	Health	18.3	—	1.93
Cardinal Health		21.0	8.95	1.90
Gilead Sciences		NMF	53.53	1.90
Glaxo Wellcome PLC ADR		27.8	13.90	1.89
Fujisawa Pharma		25.8	—	1.87
Becton Dickinson		21.6	31.67	1.79
Aventis Cl A		—	—	1.59

Current Investment Style
Value Blnd Growth / Large Mid Small

Market Cap %	
Giant	36.5
Large	27.1
Mid	32.1
Small	3.9
Micro	0.5
Median $mil:	16,666

Value Measures		Rel S&P 500
Price/Earnings	19.7	1.1
Price/Book	2.6	1.0
Price/Sales	0.9	0.7
Price/Cash Flow	10.1	1.5
Dividend Yield %	1.1	0.6

Growth Measures	%	Rel S&P 500
Long-Term Erngs	22.2	1.7
Book Value	11.2	1.7
Sales	11.3	4.5
Cash Flow	12.9	2.0
Historical Erngs	13.6	1.3

Profitability	%	Rel S&P 500
Return on Equity	17.5	1.1
Return on Assets	10.0	1.5
Net Margin	11.9	1.2

Industry Weightings	% of Stocks	Rel Cat
Biotech	12.8	0.4
Drugs	50.2	1.4
Mgd Care	3.3	0.7
Hospitals	3.6	0.9
Other HC Srv	0.6	1.3
Diagnostics	2.0	1.6
Equipment	7.4	0.6
Good/Srv	10.1	2.6
Other	10.2	3.1

Composition

Cash	4.5
Stocks	87.8
Bonds	3.7
Other	3.9
Foreign (% of Stock)	24.1

Morningstar's Take by Christopher Davis 04-03-03

A sluggish start to 2003 hasn't dimmed our enthusiasm for Vanguard Health Care Fund.

Thus far, 2003 hasn't been great for this offering. Owing to the legal troubles of its outgoing CEO, top-10 holding Schering-Plough has slid nearly 20% this year. A small stake in Healthsouth has further weighed on returns, as the stock suffered precipitous losses amid allegations of massive accounting fraud. The fund is also relatively light on biotech, which has given some of its more-aggressive rivals a boost. In all, the fund dropped 2% through April 1, 2003, while its typical rival gained 2%.

Despite its stumble, long-term investors have nothing to worry about. Manager Ed Owens is about as seasoned as they come. He has been at the helm since the fund's 1984 inception and has delivered superb results in his tenure here. In fact, the fund's three- and five-year returns land in the category's top 10%, and its 10-year marks are not only the group's best but also better than any mutual fund we track. Further, the fund's standard deviation, a measure of volatility, is its group's lowest and is also lower than the S&P 500's, a remarkable feat given this fund's focus on a fairly volatile, growth-oriented sector.

Throughout it all, Owens has employed the same distinctive strategy. He keeps the portfolio more diversified by industry, number of holdings, and geography than his typical peer. And he pays closer attention to valuation than his average rival, emphasizing the subsectors where he sees the best deals. That led him to favor health-care services in early 2000 and big-cap pharmaceuticals in 2002, for instance.

Another attraction here is rock-bottom expenses. Relative to the 1.72% category average, the fund's 0.31% expense ratio is dirt cheap. Our perennial concern remains the fund's enormous asset base, but it hasn't been a liability yet. We continue to count this offering as one of our favorites.

Address:	Vanguard Financial Ctr. P.O. Box 2600, Valley Forge, PA 19482, 800-662-7447
Web Address:	www.vanguard.com
Inception:	05-23-84
Advisor:	Wellington Management
Subadvisor:	None
NTF Plans:	N/A

Minimum Purchase:	$25000	Add: $100	IRA: $25000
Min Auto Inv Plan:	$25000	Add: $50	
Sales Fees:	No-load, 1.00%R within 0 months		
Management Fee:	0.15% mx./0.05% mn.		
Actual Fees:	Mgt:0.29%	Dist: —	
Expense Projections:	3Yr:$214	5Yr:$174	10Yr:$393
Income Distrib:	Annually		
Total Cost (relative to category):	Low		

MORNINGSTAR® Mutual Funds

Source: *Morningstar Principia*, Release Date: June 30, 2003.

Money in Action

Go It Alone or Join the Group?

Ready to invest in the markets? Then you have a choice to make: Should you go it alone or join the group?

Many investors view buying individual stocks as their best shot at big-time gains. Individual stock purchases do let you determine exactly where your money is going, whether it be a blue chip stock like IBM or General Electric or a small start-up company that you think is about to hit it big. Over the past century, equities have returned an average of 10 percent annually—but, as the bear market of the past few years shows, it's just as possible to lose your shirt in a market downswing.

Mutual funds, on the other hand, reduce your risk and provide a smoother return by diversifying your investment across a variety of equities. When you purchase shares in a mutual fund, you're essentially hiring a professional manager to manage your investment for you. Instead of having to keep track of a portfolio of individual stocks, your responsibilities for researching and managing your investments are minimized. Finally, if you need cash quickly, mutual funds are highly liquid, while it can be much more difficult to sell your stocks, depending on the kind you've invested in.

If you're thinking about investing in bonds, however, individual bonds are probably less volatile than a bond fund. The net asset value of bond funds tends to fall when interest rates rise. Although an individual bond's price will dip as interest rates rise, you may not care if you're holding the bond until maturity, content to collect income every six months.

So, which investment is right for you - individual stocks and bonds or mutual funds? Be honest about your goals, abilities, and tolerance for risk. If you don't have the time or knowledge to research and manage individual stock investments, then you're probably safer with a mutual fund. A mutual fund's professional management is also a big selling point if you're interested in something exotic such as international investing or junk bond funds.

Mutual funds are also best for smaller investors who are looking for a systematic way of building their

...continued on next page

from consideration simply because they fail to meet these needs. Some may be too risky; others may be unsuitable as a storehouse of value. Thus, rather than trying to evaluate 8,300 different funds, you can use a process of elimination to narrow the list down to two or three *types* of funds that best match your investment (and asset allocation) needs.

From here, you can whittle the list down a bit more by introducing other constraints. For example, because of cost considerations, you may want to deal only in no-load or low-load funds (more on this below), or you may be seeking certain services that are important to your investment goals. Now we're ready to introduce the final (but certainly not the least important) element in the selection process: *the fund's investment performance.* Useful information includes (1) how the fund has performed over the past 5 to 7 years; (2) the type of return it has generated in good markets as well as bad; (3) the level of dividend and capital gains distributions, which is an important indication not only of how much current income the fund distributes annually, but also the fund's *tax-efficiency* (as a rule, funds that have low dividends and low asset turnovers expose their shareholders to less taxes and therefore have higher tax-efficiency ratings); and (4) the type of investment stability the fund has enjoyed over time (or, put another way, the amount of volatility/risk in the fund's return). By evaluating such information, it is possible to identify some of the more successful mutual funds—the ones that not only offer the investment objectives and services you seek but also provide the best payoffs. And while you're doing this, you might want to keep in mind some of the fund facts noted in Exhibit 13.8.

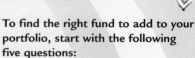

Financial Road Sign

Five Questions to Ask Before Buying a Mutual Fund

To find the right fund to add to your portfolio, start with the following five questions:

1. *How has the fund performed?* Compare fund returns with benchmarks (indexes, the fund's peer group).
2. *How risky has the fund been?* Some funds are more volatile than others.
3. *What does the fund own?* The fund's name may not tell you what it owns, so examine a fund's portfolio.
4. *Who runs the fund?* Who's in charge, for how long, and what's the investment strategy?
5. *What does the fund cost?* A fund may charge management fees, administrative fees, 12(b)-1 fees, front- and back-end loads, interest costs, brokerage fees, etc.

Source: Adapted from Susan Dziubinski, "Five Questions to Ask Before Buying a Fund" Morningstar University, June 8, 2000, downloaded from **http://news.morningstar.com**.

Stick With No-Loads Or Low-Loads

There's a longstanding "debate" in the mutual fund industry regarding load funds and no-load funds. The question is: do load funds add value? And if not, why pay the load charges? As it turns out, the results generally don't support load funds. Indeed, rather than producing superior returns, load fund returns, in general, don't seem to be any better than the returns from no-load funds and, in fact, in many cases, the funds with abnormally high loads and 12(b)-1 charges often produce returns that are far *less* than what you can get from no-loads! And, because of compounding, the differential returns tend to widen with longer holding periods.

That should come as no surprise, however, because big load charges and/or 12(b)-1 fees do nothing more than *reduce your investable capital* and, therefore, reduce the amount of money you have working for you. In fact, the only way a load fund can overcome this handicap is to *produce superior returns*—which is no easy thing to do, year in and year out. Granted there are a handful of load funds that have produced very attractive returns over extended periods of time, but they are the exception rather than the rule.

Obviously, it's in your best interest to pay close attention to load charges (and other fees) whenever you're considering an investment in a mutual fund. As a rule, to maximize returns, *you should seriously consider sticking to no-load funds, or low-loads* (funds that have total load charges, including 12(b)-1 fees, of 3 percent or less). Or at the very minimum, you should consider a more expensive load fund *only* if it has a much better performance record (and offers more return potential) than a less expensive fund. There may well be times when the higher costs are justified, but far more often than not, you're better off trying to minimize load charges. That shouldn't be all that hard to do, however, as there are literally thousands of no-load and low-load funds to choose from; and they come in all different types and sizes.

smart.sites

MAXfunds (**http://www.maxfunds.com**) offers investors an entertaining and educational site to help make better investing decisions. It also covers lesser-known and smaller funds. Much of its research is unique to the site, and the data is easy to understand.

assets. A mutual fund makes it easy to put 10 percent of your paycheck into the market every month simply by sending a check or arranging for a direct transfer from your checking account.

However, purchasing individual stocks can make sense for some investors. For example, if your goal is to buy and hold the ten largest stocks in the Fortune 500 or a handful of high-grade corporate-grade bonds, then you probably don't need a mutual fund. Investors with large amounts of money to invest may also prefer to buy individual stocks because they can afford to diversify their portfolio on their own. Large investors are also likely to receive more input and advise from stockbrokers to help them manage their portfolio.

It's also important to consider the cost differences between a mutual fund and an individual investment. If you buy and sell stocks in your portfolio frequently, you may find some of your profits eaten up by broker fees, although it is possible to reduce these costs by using a discount brokerage firm. Mutual funds, however, can be costly as well. Even if you stick with no-load mutual funds, you'll pay 1 to 2 percent of your fund's value to cover expenses each year. That particularly hurts in bond funds, because bond returns are typically in the single digits.

There are tax considerations as well. Individual stocks and bonds don't generate capital gains taxes until you actually sell them, but you'll pay taxes on the annual gains realized by a mutual fund whether or not you've actually redeemed shares. However, it is possible to delay mutual fund taxation by placing mutual funds into your tax-deferred retirement accounts.

Critical Thinking Questions

1. Why are individual stocks attractive to many investors? What are some of the drawbacks to buying them?
2. What are the main advantages and disadvantages of buying mutual funds?
3. Which investment do you think would fit best with your personal investment goals: mutual funds, individual stocks, or a combination of both? Explain your answer in light of your financial goals and investment experience.

Sources: "Funds: What Now?," *CNN/Money*, November 5, 2003, downloaded from **http://money.cnn.com**; Jeff D. Opdyke and Michelle Higgins, "Bond Bind: The 0% Rate You Really Don't Want," *The Wall Street Journal*, June 19, 2003, downloaded from **http://webreprints.djreprints.com**; Dustin Woodard, "The Mutual Fund Advantage," *About.com*, downloaded from **http://mutualfunds.about.com**; December 7, 2003; and Jason Zweig, "Funds You Can Trust," *Money*, November 2003, downloaded from **http://money.cnn.com**.

EXHIBIT 13.8

Some Mutual Fund Facts Every Investor Should Know

Mutual funds are meant to provide investors with a simple yet effective way of buying into the stock and bond markets. Unfortunately, fund investing isn't always as simple as it looks. So, here are a few fund facts every investor should keep in mind when making mutual fund investments.

- Stock funds that get hit hard in market crashes aren't necessarily bad investments.
- Even great funds have bad years now and then.
- Most stock (and bond) funds fail to beat the market.
- You don't need a broker to buy mutual funds.
- A fund that doesn't charge a sales commission isn't necessarily a no-load fund.
- If you own more than a dozen different funds, you probably own too many.
- Mutual fund names are often misleading.
- Bond funds with high yields don't necessarily produce high returns.
- Money market funds are not risk-free (you never know what kind of return you're going to earn with these things).
- If the market crashes, it will probably be too late to sell your fund shares (the damage will probably already have been done).
- Even bad funds sometimes rank as top performers.

GETTING A HANDLE ON MUTUAL FUND PERFORMANCE

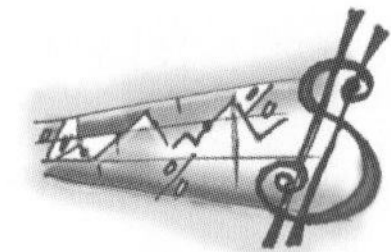

If you were to believe all the sales literature, you'd think there was no way you could go wrong by investing in mutual funds. Just put your money into one of these funds and let the good times roll! Unfortunately, the hard facts of life are that *when it comes to investing, performance is never guaranteed.* And that applies just as much to mutual funds as it does to any other form of investing. Perhaps even more so, because with mutual funds, the single variable that drives a fund's market price and return behavior is the performance of the fund's portfolio of securities.

Measuring Fund Performance

Basically, any (open- or closed-end) mutual fund has three potential sources of return: (1) dividend income, (2) capital gains distribution, and (3) change in the fund's share price. Depending on the type of fund, some will derive more income from one source than another; for example, we would normally expect income-oriented funds to have higher dividend income than capital gains distributions. Mutual funds regularly publish reports that recap investment performance. One such report is *The Summary of Income and Capital Changes*, an example of which is provided in Exhibit 13.9. This statement gives a brief overview of the fund's investment activities, including expense ratios and portfolio turnover rates. Of interest to us here is the top part of the report (which runs from "Net asset value, beginning of period" to "Net asset value, end of period"—lines 1 to 10). This is the part that reveals the amount of dividend income and capital gains distributed to the shareholders, along with any change in the fund's net asset value.

Dividend income (see line 7 of Exhibit 13.9) is the amount derived from the dividend and interest income earned on the security holdings of the mutual fund. When the fund receives dividends or interest payments, it passes these on to shareholders in the

EXHIBIT 13.9

A Summary of Income and Capital Changes

The return on a mutual fund is made up of (1) the (net) investment income the fund earns from dividends and interest and (2) the realized and unrealized capital gains the fund earns on its security transactions. Mutual funds provide such information to their shareholders in a standardized format (like the statement here), which highlights, among other things, key income, expense, and capital gains information.

	2004	2003	2002
1. **Net asset value, beginning of period:**	$24.47	$27.03	$24.26
2. **Income from investment operations:**			
3. Net investment income	$ .60	$ .66	$ .50
4. Net gains on securities (realized and unrealized)	6.37	(1.74)	3.79
5. Total from investment operations	6.97	(1.08)	4.29
6. **Less distributions:**			
7. Dividends from net investment income	($ .55)	($ .64)	($ .50)
8. Distributions from realized gains	(1.75)	(.84)	(1.02)
9. Total distributions	(2.30)	(1.48)	(1.52)
10. **Net asset value, end of period:**	$29.14	$24.47	$27.03
11. **Total return:**	28.48%	(4.00%)	17.68%
12. **Ratios/supplemental data:**			
13. Net assets, end of period ($000)	$307,951	$153,378	$108,904
14. Ratio of expenses to average net assets	1.04%	0.85%	0.94%
15. Ratio of net investment income to average net assets	1.47%	2.56%	2.39%
16. Portfolio turnover rate*	85%	144%	74%

**Portfolio turnover rate* measures the number of shares bought and sold by the fund against the total number of shares held in the fund's portfolio; a high turnover rate (for example, in excess of 100 percent) would mean the fund has been doing a lot of trading.

form of dividend payments. The fund accumulates all the current income it has received for the period and then pays it out an a prorated basis. Because the mutual fund itself is tax-exempt, any taxes due on dividend earnings are payable by the individual investor. For funds that are not held in tax-deferred accounts, like IRAs or 401(k)s, the amount of taxes due on dividends will depend on the source of such dividends. That is, *if these distributions are derived from dividends earned on the fund's common stock holdings, then they are subject to the preferential tax rate of 15 percent or less.* However, if these distributions are derived from interest earnings on bonds, dividends from REITs, or dividends from most types of preferred stocks, then such dividends do *not qualify for the preferential tax treatment*, but instead are taxed as ordinary income (see Chapter 4 for details).

Capital gains distributions (see line 8) work on the same principle as dividends, except that they are derived from the *capital gains actually earned* by the fund. (From a tax perspective, if the capital gains are long-term in nature, then they qualify for the preferential tax rate of 15 percent, or less; if not, then they're treated as ordinary income.) Note that these (capital gains) distributions apply only to *realized* capital gains—that is, where the securities holdings were actually sold and capital gains actually earned. *Unrealized* capital gains (or paper profits) are what make up the third and final element in a mutual fund's return, *for when the fund's securities holdings go up or down*

in price, its net asset value moves accordingly. This change (or movement) in the NAV is what makes up the unrealized capital gains of the fund. It represents the profit shareholders would receive (and are entitled to) if the fund were to sell its holdings.

A simple but effective way of measuring performance is to describe mutual fund returns in terms of the three major sources of return noted above—dividends earned, capital gains distributions received, and change in share price. These payoffs can be converted to a convenient return figure by using the standard ***approximate yield*** formula that was first introduced in Chapter 12. The calculations necessary for finding such a return measure can be shown by using the 2004 figures from Exhibit 13.9. Referring to the exhibit, we can see that this hypothetical no-load fund paid \$.55 per share in dividends and another \$1.75 in capital gains distributions; also, its price (NAV) at the beginning of the year (that is, at year-end 2003) of \$24.47 rose to \$29.14 by the end of the year (see lines 1 and 10, respectively). Putting this data into the familiar approximate yield formula, we see that the hypothetical mutual fund provided an annual rate of return of 26.0 percent.

$$\text{Approximate yield} = \frac{\text{Dividends and capital gains distributions} + \left[\dfrac{\text{Ending price} - \text{Beginning price}}{\text{1-year time period}}\right]}{\left[\dfrac{\text{Ending price} + \text{Beginning price}}{2}\right]}$$

$$= \frac{(\$.55 + \$1.75) + \left[\dfrac{\$29.14 - \$24.47}{1}\right]}{\left[\dfrac{\$29.14 + \$24.47}{2}\right]}$$

$$= \frac{\$2.30 + \$4.67}{\$26.80} = \frac{\$6.97}{\$26.80} = \underline{\underline{26.0\%}}$$

Calculator Keystrokes. You can just as easily find the ***exact return*** on this investment with a handheld financial calculator. Here's what you'd do: Using ***annual compounding***, to find the return on this mutual fund in 2004, we use the same input data as above; namely, we start with a price at the beginning of the year of \$24.47, add in total dividends and capital gains distributions of \$2.30 a share (i.e., \$.55 + \$1.75), and then using a year-end price of \$29.14, we punch the keystrokes shown in the margin, where:

N = number of *years* you hold the fund,

PV = the ***initial*** price of the fund (entered as a ***negative***),

PMT = ***total*** amount of dividends and capital gains distributions received,

FV = the ***ending*** price of the fund.

Note that our computed return (of 28.48 percent) is exactly the same as the "Total Return" shown on line 11 of Exhibit 13.9—that's because this is basically the same procedure that the mutual funds have to use to report their return performance. The approximate yield measure (26.0 percent) may be close to the actual return, but clearly it's not close enough for fund reporting purposes.

What About Future Performance?

There's no question that approximate yield or return on investment are simple, yet highly effective measures that capture all the important elements of mutual fund return. Unfortunately, looking at past performance is one thing, but how about the future? Ideally, we would want to evaluate the same three elements of return over the future much like we did for the past. The trouble is, when it comes to the future performance of a mutual fund, it's extremely difficult—if not impossible—to get a handle on what the future holds as far as dividends, capital gains, and NAV are concerned. The reason: a mutual fund's future investment performance is directly linked to the future makeup of its securities portfolio—which is impossible to predict. It's not like evaluating the expected performance of a share of stock, where you're keying in on one company. With mutual funds, investment performance depends on the behavior of many different stocks and bonds.

So, where do you look for insight into the future? Most market observers suggest you do two things. First, give careful consideration to the ***future direction of the market as a whole.*** This is important, because the behavior of a well-diversified mutual fund tends to reflect the general tone of the market. Thus, if the feeling is that the market is going to be generally drifting up, that should bode well for the investment performance of mutual funds.

Second, take a good hard look at the past performance of the mutual fund itself, as that's a good way to get an indication of how successful the fund's investment managers have been. In essence, the success of a mutual fund rests in large part ***on the investment skills of the fund managers.*** So, when investing in a mutual fund, look for consistently good performance, in up as well as down markets, over extended periods of time (5 to 7 years, or more). Most important, check to see if the same key people are still running the fund. Although past success is certainly no guarantee of future performance, a strong team of money managers can have a significant bearing on the level of fund returns. Put another way, when you buy a mutual fund, you're buying a formula (investment policy + money management team) that has worked in the past, in the expectation that it will work again in the future.

Concept ✓

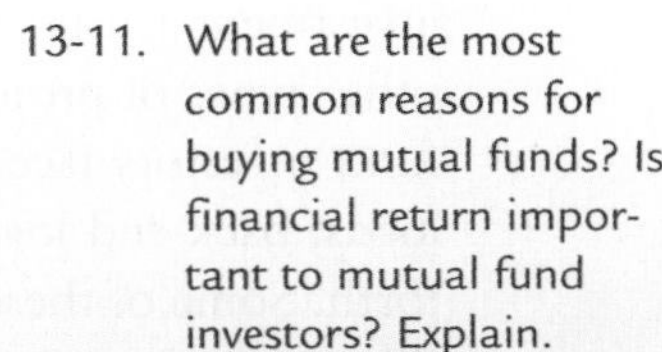

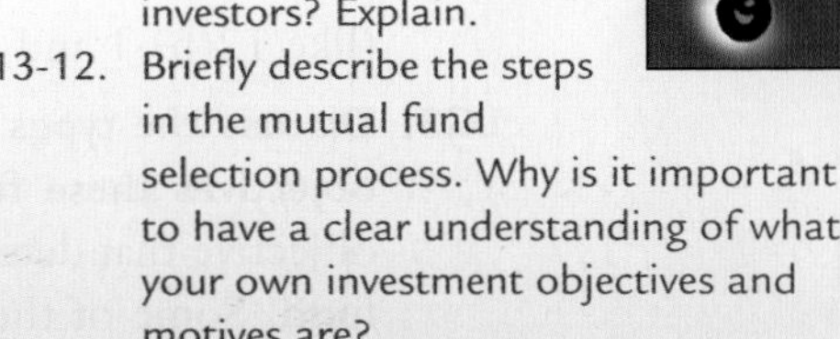

13-11. What are the most common reasons for buying mutual funds? Is financial return important to mutual fund investors? Explain.

13-12. Briefly describe the steps in the mutual fund selection process. Why is it important to have a clear understanding of what your own investment objectives and motives are?

13-13. Why does it pay to invest in no-load funds rather than load funds? Under what conditions might it make sense to invest in a load fund?

13-14. Identify three potential sources of return to mutual fund investors, and briefly discuss how each could affect total return to shareholders. Which would you rather have: $100 in dividend income or $100 in capital gains distribution? $100 in realized capital gains or $100 in unrealized capital gains? Explain.

13-15. How important is the general behavior of the market in affecting the price performance of mutual funds? Why is a fund's past performance so important to the mutual fund selection process? Does the future behavior of the market matter any in the selection process? Explain.

SUMMARY

LG1. Describe the basic features and operating characteristics of a mutual fund. Mutual fund shares represent ownership in a diversified, professionally managed portfolio of securities; many investors who lack the time, know-how, or commitment to manage their own money turn to mutual funds as an investment outlet. By investing in mutual funds, shareholders benefit from a level of diversification and investment performance they might otherwise find difficult to achieve.

LG2. Differentiate between open- and closed-end funds, as well as other types of professionally managed investment companies, and discuss the various types of fund loads and charges. Investors can buy either open-end funds, which have no limit on the number of shares they can issue, or closed-end funds, which have a fixed number of shares outstanding and which trade in the secondary markets like any other share of common stock. In addition, they can invest in exchange-traded funds, or ETFs, which possess characteristics of both open- and closed-end funds, REITs (which invest primarily in various types of real estate products), or unit investment trusts. There is a cost, however, to investing in mutual funds (and other types of professionally managed investment products). The fact is, mutual fund investors face a full array of loads, fees, and charges, including front-end loads, back-end loads, annual 12(b)-1 charges, annual management fees, and so forth. Some of these costs are one-time charges (like front-end loads), but others (like 12(b)-1 and management fees) are paid annually.

LG3. Discuss the types of funds available to investors, and the variety of investment objectives these funds seek to fulfill. Each fund has an established investment objective that determines its investment policy and identifies it as a certain type of fund. Some of the more popular types of funds are growth, aggressive growth, value, equity-income, balanced, growth-and-income, bond, money market, index, sector, socially responsible, asset allocation, and international funds. The different categories of funds have different risk-return characteristics and are important variables in the fund selection process.

LG4. Identify and discuss the different kinds of investor services offered by mutual funds. In addition to their investment returns, many investors buy mutual funds to take advantage of the various investor services they offer, such as automatic investment and reinvestment plans, systematic withdrawal programs, low-cost conversion and phone-switching privileges, and retirement programs.

LG5. Gain an understanding of the variables that should be considered when selecting funds for investment purposes. The fund selection process generally starts by assessing your own needs and wants; this sets the tone for your investment program and helps you decide on the types of funds to look at. Next, take a look at what the funds have to offer, particularly with regard to the fund's investment objectives and investor services—here, narrow down the alternatives by aligning your needs with the types of funds available. From this list of funds, introduce the final selection tests: fund performance and cost—other things being equal, look for high performance and low costs.

LG6. Identify the sources of return and calculate the rate of return earned on an investment in a mutual fund. The investment performance of mutual funds is largely a function of the returns the money managers are able to generate from their securities portfolios; generally speaking, strong markets translate into attractive returns for mutual fund investors. Mutual funds have three basic sources of return: (1) dividends, (2) capital gains distributions, and (3) changes in the fund's NAV (as accruing from unrealized capital gains). Both the approximate yield and total return measures recognize these three elements and provide a simple yet effective way of measuring the annual rate of return from a mutual fund.

Financial Planning Exercises

1. Contrast *mutual fund ownership* with the *direct investment in stocks and bonds.* Assume that your class is going to debate the merits of investing through mutual funds versus investing directly in stocks and bonds. Develop some pro and con arguments on each side of this debate and be prepared to discuss them in class. If you had to choose one side to be on, which would it be? Explain.

2. Using the mutual fund quotes in Exhibit 13.4, and assuming that you can buy these funds at their quoted net asset values, how much would you have to pay to buy each of the following funds?
   a. FBR Small Cap Value Fund-A (SmCpVlA)
   b. FMI Focus Fund (FMI FocusFd)
   c. Dodge & Cox International Stock Fund (IntlStk)
   d. Dreyfus S&P 500 Index Fund (Dr500In)
   e. Dreyfus MidCap Index Fund (DreyMid)

   According to the quotes, which of these five funds have 12(b)-1 fees? Which have redemption fees? Are any of them no-loads? Which fund has the highest year-to-date return? Which has the lowest? Which fund has the highest 3-year return? The lowest?
3. Let's imagine that you've just inherited $20,000 from a rich uncle. Now you're faced with the problem of trying to decide how to spend it. You could make a down payment on a condo, or, better yet, on that Corvette that you've always wanted. Or, you could spend your windfall more profitably by building a mutual fund portfolio. Let's say that after a lot of soul searching, you decide to do the latter: build a mutual fund portfolio. Your task at hand is to develop a $20,000 mutual fund portfolio—use actual funds and actual quoted prices, invest as much of the $20,000 as you possibly can, and be specific! Briefly describe the portfolio you end up with, including the investment objectives you are trying to achieve.
4. For *each pair* of funds listed below, select the fund that would be the *least* risky; briefly explain your answer:
   a. Growth versus growth-and-income
   b. Equity-income versus high-grade corporate bonds
   c. Intermediate-term bonds versus high-yield municipals
   d. International versus balanced
5. What investor service is most closely linked to the notion of a fund family? If a fund is not part of a family of mutual funds, can it still offer a full range of investor services? Explain. Using a source such as *The Wall Street Journal*, or perhaps your local newspaper, find two examples of fund families; list some of the mutual funds they offer.
6. Using a source like *Barron's*, *Forbes*, *Money*, or perhaps even *Morningstar* (if it's readily available to you), select five mutual funds—(a) a growth fund, (b) an index fund, (c) a sector fund, (d) an international fund, and (e) a high-yield corporate bond fund—that you feel would make good investments. Briefly explain why you selected each of the funds.

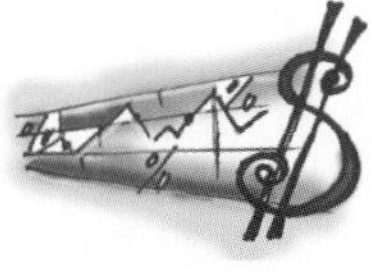

7. About a year ago, Dave Kidwell bought some shares in the Hi-Flyer Mutual Fund. He bought the stock at $24.50 a share, and it now trades at $26.00. Last year the fund paid dividends of 40 cents a share and had capital gains distributions of $1.83 a share. Using the approximate yield formula, what rate of return did Dave earn on his investment? Repeat the calculation using a hand-held financial calculator. Would he have made a 20 percent rate of return if the stock had risen to $30 a share?
8. Describe an ETF and explain how these funds combine the characteristics of open- and closed-end funds. Looking in the Vanguard family of funds, which one of their funds would most closely resemble a "Spider" (SPDR). In what respects are the Vanguard fund (that you selected) and Spiders the same; how are they different? If you could invest in only one of them, which would it be? Explain.

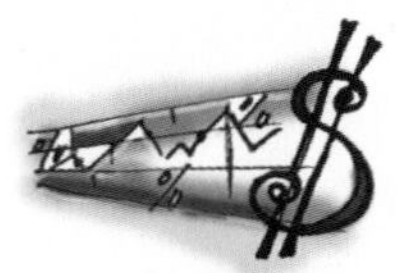

9. A year ago, the Full-Bore Growth Fund was being quoted at an NAV of $21.50 and an offer price of $23.35; today it's being quoted at $23.04 (NAV) and $25.04 (offer). Use the approximate yield formula, or a hand-held financial calculator, to find the rate of return on this load fund, given it was purchased a year ago and its dividends and capital gains distributions over the year totaled $1.05 a share. (*Hint:* You, as an investor, buy fund shares at the offer price and sell at the NAV.)

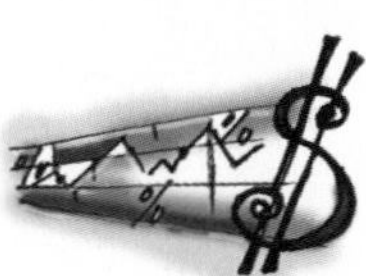

10. Listed below is the per-share performance record of the East Coast Growth-and-Income fund for 2004 and 2003:

	2004	2003
1. **Net asset value, beginning of period:**	$58.60	$52.92
2. **Income from investment operations:**		
3. Net investment income	$1.39	$1.35
4. Net gains on securities (realized and unrealized)	8.10	9.39
5. Total from investment operations	9.49	10.74
6. **Less distributions:**		
7. Dividends from net investment income	($ .83)	($1.24)
8. Distributions from realized gains	(2.42)	(3.82)
9. Total distributions	(3.25)	(5.06)
10. **Net asset value, end of period:**	$64.84	$58.60

Use this information to find the rate of return earned on the East Coast G-&-I fund in 2003 and in 2004. What is your assessment of the investment performance of this fund for the 2003–2004 period?

Applying Personal Finance

The Feeling's Mutual!

Mutual funds offer convenience, diversification, and the services of professional money managers and analysts. Mutual funds can be particularly appealing to small investors who don't have a lot of money and for those who are new to investing. The purpose of this project is to help you learn more about the various types of mutual funds and how to pick the funds that best suit your investment objectives.

Assume that you have just received a windfall of $25,000 and would like to invest it all in mutual funds. There are several ways to segment mutual funds, but for the purpose of this project, use the following eight categories:

1. Growth
2. Value
3. Equity-income
4. Bond
5. Balanced
6. Index
7. Socially responsible
8. International

Pick three or four categories that you believe best meet your financial needs and risk tolerance, and then select one fund from each category. You may use some of the reference sources mentioned in this chapter to help you make your selections. For each fund, find the following information:

a. Name of fund, its ticker symbol, the fund manager, and the tenure of the fund manager.

b. Category and size of the fund—try to find the *Morningstar* style box.
c. Loads, fees, and other charges; minimum investment required.
d. Performance of the fund over the past 1, 3, and 5 years. Compare the fund's performance to other funds in its category and to an appropriate index over these same time periods.
e. How much did the fund pay out last year in dividends and in short- and long-term capital gains distributions?
f. What was the approximate yield on the fund last year? (You may have to compute this yourself using the approximate yield formula or a handheld calculator, and by finding its price 1 year ago from a source such as **http://finance.yahoo.com**.)
g. What services does the fund offer, such as automatic reinvestment plans or phone switching?
h. Briefly explain why you selected this fund and how it meets your investment objectives.

Contemporary Case Applications

13.1 Dave's Dilemma: Common Stocks or Mutual Funds?

Dave Brubaker has worked in the management services division of Ace Consultants for the past 5 years. He currently earns an annual salary of about $65,000. At 33, he is still a bachelor and has accumulated about $60,000 in savings over the past few years. He keeps his savings in a money market account, where it earns about 3 percent interest. Dave wants to earn "a bigger bang for his buck" and thus is contemplating withdrawing $50,000 from his money market account and investing it in the stock market. He feels that such an investment can easily earn more than 3 percent. Marlene Bellamy, a close friend, suggests that he invest in mutual fund shares. Dave has approached you, his broker, for advice.

Questions

1. Explain to Dave the key reasons for purchasing mutual fund shares.
2. What special fund features might help Dave achieve his investment objectives?
3. What types of mutual funds would you recommend to Dave?
4. What recommendations would you make with respect to Dave's dilemma about whether to go into stocks or mutual funds? Explain.

13.2 Marge Ponders Mutual Funds

Marge Simmons is the director of a major charitable organization in Springfield, Ohio. A single mother of one young child, she earns what could best be described as a "modest income." Because charitable organizations are not notorious for their generous retirement programs, Marge has decided it would be best for her to do a little investing on her own. She would like to set up a program that enables her to supplement her employer's retirement program and, at the same time, provide some funds for her child's college education (which is still 12 years away). Although her income is modest, Marge feels that with careful planning, she could probably invest about $250 a quarter, and hopefully increase this amount over time. She presently has about $15,000 in a bank savings account, which she would be willing to use to kick off this program. In view of her investment objectives, she is not interested in taking a lot of risk. Because her knowledge of investments extends to savings accounts, series EE bonds, and a little bit about mutual funds, she approaches you for some investment advice.

Questions

1. In view of Marge's long-term investment goals, do you think mutual funds are an appropriate investment vehicle for her?
2. Do you think she should use her $15,000 savings to start off a mutual fund investment program?
3. What type of mutual fund investment program would you set up for Marge? Include in your answer some discussion of the types of funds you would consider, the investment objectives you would set, and any investment services (such as withdrawal plans) you would seek. Would taxes be an important consideration in your investment advice? Explain.

Money Online

Prosper with Mutuals!

Note: Web addresses change frequently, so you may need to determine the home page and do a site search to find the page or topic that's referenced.

1. **http://www.quicken.com/investments/mutualfunds/finder**

Find the mutual funds that best suit your needs! Work through Quicken's "Popular Searches," "EasyStep Search," or "Full Search" to find the mutual funds that match your investing goals. While you're there, click on "Top 25 Funds" to view the top 25 performing mutual finds in 50 different categories.

2. **http://www.morningstar.com**

How many stars does your fund rate? What do those stars mean, anyway? Find out from Morningstar how funds are analyzed and the stars assigned. Click on "Funds" to learn more about evaluating mutual funds and then on "Tools" to use their expertly prepared investing tools.

3. **http://www.thestreet.com**

What's happening on The Street—Wall Street, that is? How will happenings in the financial world affect your investments? Find the latest in financial news and analysis or pull up the "Economic Calendar" to learn of upcoming reports and events.

4. **http://www.brill.com**

Need to find a mutual fund's Web site? Brill's Mutual Funds Interactive provides "Fundlink" with links to thousands of mutual fund companies. Brill's also provides an "Experts" corner, "Profiles" of various fund managers, "Answers" under "Q&A," and "Funds 101" for beginning and experienced investors alike. Be sure to sign up for their free weekly Mutual Fund Alert newsletter to keep up with what's happening with mutual funds.

5. **http://www.etfconnect.com**

Like to know more about exchange traded funds? The ETF Connect Web site prepared by Nuveen Investments covers both closed-end and indexed ETFs in depth. First, click on the "Education Center" to explore the various characteristics, advantages, risks, and opportunities offered by these funds. Then, click on "Industry Links" to find even more sites dealing with ETFs.

6. **http://www.nareit.com/home.cfm**

Interested in real estate but don't want to own property directly? Consider real estate investment trusts for the improved liquidity and portfolio diversification that they provide. The Web site of the National Association of Real Estate Investment Trusts explains it all in "About REITs." If you feel REITs would make a good investment for you, then explore "Investing in REITs" to learn even more.

7. **http://www.sec.gov/info/advisers.shtml**

What are the laws in regard to mutual fund companies? Read through the various laws, rules, and regulations concerning both mutual funds and investment advisors at the

Web site of the Securities and Exchange Commission, the federal agency which regulates the securities markets.

8. **http://www.nasaa.org**
Need to make a complaint concerning an investment? You may do so electronically at the Web site of the North American Securities Administrators Association. Find the "Investment-Related Complaint Center" by clicking on "Enforcement" in the drop-down box at the top of the page. You may also find the name, address, phone number, and Web site of your state's securities regulator by scrolling down to "Find Regulator" at the home page.

9. **http://www.fabian.com**
Is your fund a lemon? Click on "Investing Tools" to find Fabian's "Lemon List." Whether it's an overcharger or an underachiever, find out if your fund is a loser! View the Lipper "Benchmark Chart," and then read the "Lemon Laws" to see how Fabian evaluates these funds.

Just for Fun!

10. **http://www.smartmoney.com/maps**
Color-code your investments! Scroll down to "Map Your Portfolio" to use SmartMoney's revolutionary color-coding tool to track your own portfolio and instantly see how your investments are performing in relation to one another! While you're there, click on "Mutual Fund Map" for a revealing view of the 1,000 most important funds. Track and compare performance, expenses, *Morningstar* rankings and more at this information-packed Web site. (Be patient while maps load!)

PART SIX

Retirement and Estate Planning

14
Planning for Retirement

15
Preserving Your Estate

CHAPTER 14

Planning for Retirement

Learning Goals

LG1. Recognize the importance of retirement planning and identify the three biggest pitfalls to good planning.

LG2. Establish your income needs in retirement, and estimate your retirement income.

LG3. Explain the eligibility requirements and benefits of the Social Security program.

LG4. Differentiate among the different types of basic and supplemental employer-sponsored pension plans.

LG5. Describe the various types of self-directed retirement plans.

LG6. Choose the right type of annuity for your retirement plan.

What a Difference a Decade Makes

When she was 35, Sandy Beach invested much of her portfolio in speculative stocks. Growing up in a family of active investors, some of whom retired in their 50s, Sandy knew she needed to redirect her investments if she had any hope of retiring in 2003 at age 55.

Sandy's retirement portfolio included two self-directed retirement accounts—a Keogh plan that she started in 1976 and funded from occasional freelance assignments, and an IRA to which she contributed $2,000 annually since 1982 and $3500 annually since 2001—and savings through her employer, the federal government. Sandy's only other savings were reinvested dividends from corporate stocks.

At 45, Sandy left her government job and began working solely as a consultant, increasing the need to become a disciplined saver to achieve her retirement goals. Every month she saved 25 percent of her gross earnings, investing 20 percent of net earnings, the maximum allowed by law, into her Keogh. She was very pleased with the annual returns of more than 20 percent during the late 1990s, when she aggressively invested 70 percent of her portfolio in high tech companies so that she could indeed retire at 55.

With only three years remaining until her planned retirement, Sandy watched with dismay as the value of her portfolio dropped 75 percent in 2000. She realized that she needed to reallocate her portfolio across different asset types so that she had a balance of mutual funds, stocks, and bonds. Sandy prepared a new income plan to figure out how to reallocate her portfolio and monitored her retirement holdings carefully. She diversified into more fixed income securities, cash equivalents, annuities, and international mutual funds to ride out any future market volatility and to help rebuild her nest egg.

Although unable to retire at 55 as originally planned, Sandy is more confident with the balance of assets in her retirement account. As she learned, today it is more important than ever to take control of your retirement funds and choose investments wisely. This chapter explains how to assess your own needs and develop your own plan, so that you, too, will be ready for retirement.

CRITICAL THINKING QUESTIONS

As you review the chapter, consider these questions in relation to Sandy Beach's financial planning:

- Why is it important to do long-range planning for retirement?
- Explain the difference in employer-sponsored and self-directed retirement plans.
- Discuss reasons for investing aggressively for retirement as Sandy did.

AN OVERVIEW OF RETIREMENT PLANNING

LG1, LG2

Do you know your life expectancy? Well, if you're in your late teens or early twenties, you'll probably live another 60 or 70 years. While this prospect may sound delightful, it also brings into focus the need for careful retirement planning. After all, you may only work for about 40 of those years—perhaps less—and spend 20 or more years in retirement. The challenge, of course, is to do it in style—and that is where retirement planning comes into play! But to enjoy a comfortable retirement, you must start *now*—for one of the biggest mistakes people make in retirement planning is waiting too long to begin. Yet the longer you wait, the harder it will be to reach the kind of retirement income you would like.

Make no mistake about it, accumulating adequate retirement funds is a daunting task that takes careful planning. Like budgets, taxes, and investments, retirement planning is vital to your financial well-being and is a critical link in your personal financial plans. Even so, it's difficult for most people under the age of 30 to develop a well-defined set of retirement plans. There are just too many years to go until retirement and too many uncertainties to deal with: inflation, Social Security, family size, the type of pension you'll receive—if any—and how much money you will have when you're ready to retire. However, it's just this kind of uncertainty that makes retirement planning so important. To cope with uncertainty, you must plan for a variety of outcomes, and monitor and modify your plans as your hopes, abilities, and personal finances change.

Role of Retirement Planning in Personal Financial Planning

The financial planning process would be incomplete without *retirement planning*. Certainly there is no financial goal more important than achieving a comfortable standard of living in retirement. In many respects, retirement planning captures the very essence of financial planning. It is forward looking (perhaps more so than any other aspect of financial planning), has an impact on both your current and future standard of living, and, if successful, can be highly rewarding and make a significant contribution to your net worth.

Okay, it's important; so where do you start? Well, like most aspects of financial planning, you need a goal or an objective—that is, the first step in retirement planning is to set *retirement goals* for yourself. Take some time to define the things you want to do in retirement, the standard of living you hope to maintain, the level of income you would like to receive, and any special retirement goals you may have (like buying a retirement home in Arizona, or taking an around-the-world cruise). Such goals are important because *they give direction to your retirement planning*. Of course, like all goals, they are subject to change over time as the situations and conditions in your life change.

Once you know what you want out of retirement, the next step is to establish the *size of the nest egg* you're going to have to build to achieve your retirement goals. In essence, how much money will you need to retire the way you would like?

The final step is to formulate an *investment program* that will enable you to build up your required nest egg. This usually involves creating some type of systematic savings plan (putting away a certain amount of money each year) and identifying the types of investment vehicles that will best meet your retirement needs. This phase of your retirement program is closely related to two other aspects of financial planning—investment and tax planning.

Investments and investment planning (see Chapters 11 through 13) are the vehicles through which you build up your retirement funds. They constitute the active, ongoing part of retirement planning in which you manage and invest the funds you have set aside for retirement. It is no coincidence that a major portion of most individual investor portfolios is devoted to building up a pool of funds for retirement. Taxes and tax planning (see Chapter 3) are also important, because one of the major objectives of sound retirement planning is to legitimately shield as much income as possible from taxes and, in so doing, maximize the accumulation of retirement funds.

The Three Biggest Pitfalls to Sound Retirement Planning

Human nature being what it is, people often get a little carried away with the amount of money they want to build up for retirement. Face it, having a nest egg of $3 million or $4 million would be great, but it's beyond the reach of all but a tiny fraction of the population. Besides, you don't need that much to live comfortably in retirement. So set a more realistic goal. But when you set that goal, remember: It's not going to happen by itself; you have to do something to bring it about. And this is precisely where things start to fall apart. Why? Because when it comes to retirement planning, people tend to make three big mistakes:

- They start too late.
- They put away too little.
- They invest too conservatively.

Many people in their twenties, or even thirties, find it hard to put money away for retirement. More often than not, that's because they have other, more pressing financial concerns to worry about—such as buying a house, retiring a student loan, or paying for child care. The net result is that they *put off retirement planning until later in life*—in many cases, until they're in their late thirties or forties. Unfortunately, the longer people put it off, the less they're going to have in retirement. Or, it means that they're not going to be able to retire as early as they'd hoped. Even worse, once people start a retirement program, *they tend to be too skimpy and put away too little.* Although this, too, may be due to pressing family needs, all too often it boils down to lifestyle choices. They'd rather spend for today than save for tomorrow. As a result, they end up putting maybe $1,000 a year into a retirement plan when, with a little more effective financial planning and family budgeting, they could easily afford to save two or three times that amount.

On top of all this, many *people tend to be far too conservative* in the way they invest their retirement money. Too often, people fail to achieve the full potential of their retirement programs because they treat them more like savings accounts than investment vehicles! The fact is, they place way too much of their retirement money into *low-yielding*, fixed-income securities such as CDs and treasury notes. While you should *never speculate* with something as important as your retirement plan, you do not have to totally avoid risk. There's nothing wrong with following an investment program that involves a reasonable amount of risk, so long as it results in a correspondingly higher level of return. Caution is fine, but being overly cautious can be very costly in the long run. Indeed, a low rate of return can have an enormous effect on the long-term accumulation of capital and, in many cases, may mean the difference between just getting by or enjoying a comfortable retirement.

Compounding the Errors

All three of these pitfalls become even more important when we introduce *compound interest.* Why is that so? Because *compounding essentially magnifies the impact of these mistakes.* To illustrate, consider the first variable—starting too late. If you were to start a retirement program at age 35 by putting away $2,000 a year, it would grow to more than $150,000 by the time you're 65 when invested at an average rate of return of 6 percent.

Not a bad deal, considering your total out-of-pocket investment over this 30-year period is only $60,000. But look at what you end up with if you start this investment program 10 years earlier, at age 25: That same $2,000 a year will grow to over $300,000 by the time you're 65. Think of it—for another $20,000 ($2,000 a year for an extra 10 years), you can double the terminal value of your investment! Of course, it's not the extra $20,000 that's doubling your money; rather, it's *compound interest* that's doing most of the work.

And the same holds true for the rate of return you earn on the investments in your retirement account. Take the second situation above—starting a retirement program at 25. Earning 6 percent means a retirement nest egg of over $300,000; increase that rate of return to 10 percent (a reasonable investment objective), and your retirement nest egg will be worth nearly $900,000! *You're still putting in the same amount of money,* but because your money is working harder, you end up with a much bigger nest egg. Of course, when you seek higher returns (as you would when go from 6 percent to 10 percent), that generally means you also have to take on more risks. But that may not be as much of a problem as it appears, because in retirement planning, *the one thing you have on your side is time* (unless you start your plan very late in life). And the more time you have, the less of a burden risk becomes. That is, the more time you have, the easier it is to recover from those temporary market setbacks.

On the other hand, if you simply cannot tolerate the higher risks that accompany higher returns (and, certainly, some people cannot), then stay away from the higher-risk investments. Rather, stick to safer, lower-yielding securities and find some other ways to build up your nest egg. For instance, contribute more each year to your plan or extend the length of your investment period. The only other option—and not a particularly appealing one—is to accept the fact that you will not be able to build up as big a nest egg as you had thought and, therefore, will have to accept a lower standard of living in retirement. All else being the same, it should be clear that the more you sock away each year, the more you're going to have at retirement. That is, put away $4,000 a year, rather than $2,000, and you are going to end up with twice as much money at retirement.

The combined impact of these three variables is seen in Exhibit 14.1. Note that it's really the combination of these three factors that determines the amount you will have at retirement. Thus, you can offset the effects of earning a lower rate of return on your money by increasing the amount you put in each year or by lengthening the period over which you build up your retirement account—meaning that you start your program earlier in life (or work longer and retire later in life). The table shows that *there are several different ways of getting to roughly the same result;* that is, knowing the kind of nest egg you'd like to end up with, you can pick the combination of variables (period of accumulation, annual contribution, and rate of return) that you're most comfortable with.

ESTIMATING INCOME NEEDS

Retirement planning would be much simpler if we lived in a static economy. Unfortunately (or perhaps fortunately), we don't, and as a result, both your personal budget and the general economy are subject to considerable change over time. All of which make accurate forecasting of retirement needs difficult at best. Even so, it is a necessary task, and one you can handle in one of two ways. One strategy is to plan for retirement over *a series of short-run time frames.* A good way to do this is to state your retirement income objectives as a percentage of your present earnings. For example, if you desire a retirement income equal to 80 percent of your final take-home pay, you can determine the amount necessary to fund this need. Then, every 3 to 5 years, you can revise and update your plan.

EXHIBIT 14.1

Building Up Your Retirement Nest Egg

The size of your retirement nest egg will depend on when you start your program (period of accumulation), how much you contribute each year, and the rate of return you earn on your investments. As seen in this table, you can combine these variables in a number of different ways to end up with a given amount at retirement.

	Amount of Accumulated Capital from							
	Contribution of $2,000/yr. at These Average Rates of Return				Contribution of $5,000/yr. at These Average Rates of Return			
Accumulation Period*	4%	6%	8%	10%	4%	6%	8%	10%
10 yrs. (55 yrs. old)	$ 24,010	$ 26,360	$ 28,970	$ 31,870	$ 60,030	$ 65,900	$ 72,440	$ 79,690
20 yrs. (45 yrs. old)	59,560	73,570	91,520	114,550	148,890	183,930	228,810	286,370
25 yrs. (40 yrs. old)	83,290	109,720	146,210	196,690	208,230	274,300	365,530	491,730
30 yrs. (35 yrs. old)	112,170	158,110	226,560	328,980	280,420	395,290	566,410	822,460
35 yrs. (30 yrs. old)	147,300	222,860	344,630	542,040	368,260	557,160	861,570	1,355,090
40 yrs. (25 yrs. old)	190,050	309,520	518,100	885,160	475,120	773,790	1,295,260	2,212,900

*Assumes retirement at age 65; parenthetical figure, therefore, is the age at which the person would start his or her retirement program.

Alternately, you can follow *a long-term approach* in which you actually formulate the level of income you would like to receive in retirement, along with the amount of funds you must amass to achieve that desired standard of living. Rather than addressing the problem in a series of short-run plans, this approach goes 20 or 30 years into the future—to the time when you will retire—to determine how much saving and investing you must do today to achieve your long-run retirement goals. Of course, if conditions or expectations should happen to change dramatically in the future (as they very well could), it may be necessary to make corresponding alterations to your long-run retirement goals and strategies.

smart.sites

CNNMoney's comprehensive retirement planning site, **http://www.moneycentral.msn.com/retire/home.asp**, includes educational articles on key topics as well as the latest news affecting retirement plans.

Determining Future Retirement Needs

To illustrate how future retirement needs and income requirements can be formulated, let's consider the case of Jack and Lois Spellman. In their mid-thirties, they have two children and an annual income of about $60,000 before taxes. Up to now, Jack and Lois have given only passing thought to their retirement. But even though it's still some 30 years away, they recognize it's now time to give some serious consideration to their situation to see if they will be able to pursue a retirement lifestyle that appeals to them. Worksheet 14.1 provides the basic steps to follow in determining retirement needs. This

worksheet 14.1

Estimating Future Retirement Needs

This worksheet will help you define your income requirements in retirement, the size of your retirement nest egg, and the amount you must save annually to achieve your given retirement goals.

PROJECTING RETIREMENT INCOME AND INVESTMENT NEEDS

Name(s) Jack & Lois Spellman Date June 2004

I. Estimated Household Expenditures in Retirement:	
A. Approximate number of years to retirement	30
B. Current level of annual household expenditures, excluding savings	$ 42,000
C. Estimated household expenses in retirement as a *percent* of current *expenses*	70%
D. Estimated annual household expenditures in retirement (B × C)	$ 29,400
II. Estimated Income in Retirement:	
E. Social security, annual income	$ 13,000
F. Company/employer pension plans, annual amounts	$ 9,000
G. Other sources, annual amounts	$ 0
H. Total annual income (E + F + G)	$ 22,000
I. Additional required income, or annual shortfall (D − H)	$ 7,400
III. Inflation Factor:	
J. Expected average annual rate of inflation over the period to retirement	5%
K. Inflation factor (in Appendix A): Based on 30 years to retirement (A) and an expected average annual rate of inflation (J) of 5%	4.32
L. Size of inflation-adjusted annual shortfall (I × K)	$ 32,000
IV. Funding the Shortfall:	
M. Anticipated return on assets held *after* retirement	10%
N. Amount of retirement funds required—size of nest egg (L ÷ M)	$ 320,000
O. Expected rate of return on investments *prior* to retirement	8%
P. Compound interest factor (in Appendix B): Based on 30 years to retirement (A) and an expected rate of return on investments of 8%	113.3
Q. Annual savings required to fund retirement nest egg (N ÷ P)	$ 2,824

Note: Parts I and II are prepared in terms of current (today's) dollars.

worksheet shows how the Spellmans have estimated their retirement income and determined the amount of investment assets they must accumulate to meet their retirement objectives.

Jack and Lois began their calculation by determining what their *household expenditures* will likely be in retirement. Their estimate is based on maintaining a "comfortable" standard of living—one that will not be extravagant yet will allow them to do the things they would like in retirement. A simple yet highly effective way to derive an estimate of expected household expenditures is to base it on the current level of such expenses. Assume that the Spellmans' annual household expenditures (excluding savings) currently run about $42,000 a year—this information can be readily obtained by referring to their most recent income and expenditures statement. Making some obvious adjustments for the different lifestyle they will have in retirement—their children will no longer be living at home, their home will be paid for, and so on—the Spellmans estimate that they will be able to achieve the standard of living they'd like in retirement at an annual level of household expenses equal to about 70 percent of the current amount. Thus, *in terms of today's dollars,* their estimated household expenditures in retirement will be $42,000 × .70 = $29,400. (This process is summarized in steps A through D in Worksheet 14.1.)

Estimating Retirement Income

The next question is: Where will they get the money to meet their projected household expenses of $29,400 a year? They have addressed this problem by estimating what their *income* will be in retirement—again *in terms of today's dollars.* Their two basic sources of retirement income are Social Security and employer-sponsored pension plans. Based on today's retirement tables they estimate that they will receive about $13,000 a year from Social Security (as we'll see later in this chapter, you can receive an estimate directly from the Social Security Administration of what your future Social Security benefits are likely to be when you retire) and another $9,000 from their employer pension plans, for a total projected annual income of $22,000. When this is compared to their projected household expenditures, it is clear the Spellmans will be facing an annual shortfall of $7,400 (see steps E through I in Worksheet 14.1). This is the amount of retirement income they must come up with; otherwise, they will have to reduce the standard of living they hope to enjoy in retirement.

At this point, we need to introduce the *inflation factor* to our projections in order to put the annual shortfall of $7,400 in terms of retirement dollars. Here we make the assumption that both income and expenditures will undergo approximately the same average rate of inflation, causing the shortfall to grow by that rate over time. In essence, 30 years from now, the annual shortfall is going to amount to a lot more than $7,400. How large it will grow to will, of course, be a function of what happens to inflation. Assume that the Spellmans think inflation, on average, over the next 30 years will amount to 5 percent—while that's a bit on the high side by today's standards, the Spellmans decide to use it anyway as they would rather overestimate the effects of inflation than underestimate them. Using the compound value table from Appendix A, we find that the *inflation factor* for 5 percent and 30 years is 4.32; multiplying this inflation factor by the annual shortfall of $7,400 gives the Spellmans an idea of what that figure will be by the time they retire: $7,400 × 4.32 = $31,970, or nearly $32,000 a year (see steps J to L in Worksheet 14.1). Thus, based on their projections, the shortfall will amount to $32,000

Financial Road Sign

Beat the Retirement Clock

These tips will help you take a hard look at your lifestyle, your resources, and many other things you may take for granted while you are still employed.

1. Know how much you will need to retire in comfort.
2. Think about where you want to live and the cost of living in those locations.
3. Find out about your Social Security benefits.
4. Learn about your employer's pension or profit sharing plan.
5. Contribute to a tax-sheltered savings plan.
6. Put money into an IRA.
7. Don't cash out your retirement plan every time you change jobs—instead roll it over to an IRA or some other tax-sheltered program.
8. Start now, set goals, and stick to them.
9. Understand basic investment principles.
10. Don't neglect insurance planning.

a year when they retire 30 years from now. *This is the amount they will have to come up with through their own supplemental retirement program.*

Funding the Shortfall

The final two steps in this estimation process are to determine (1) *how big the retirement nest egg must be* to cover the projected annual income shortfall, and (2) *how much to save each year* to accumulate the required amount by the time the Spellmans retire. To find out how much money they need to accumulate by retirement, they must estimate the rate of return they think they will be able to earn on their investments *after* they retire. This will tell them how big their nest egg will have to be by retirement in order to eliminate the expected annual shortfall of $32,000. Let's assume that this rate of return is estimated at 10 percent, in which case the Spellmans must accumulate $320,000 by retirement. This figure is found by *capitalizing* the estimated shortfall of $32,000 at a 10 percent rate of return: $32,000 ÷ .10 = $320,000 (see steps M and N). Given a 10 percent rate of return, such a nest egg will yield $32,000 a year: $320,000 × .10 = $32,000. And so long as the capital ($320,000) remains untouched, it will generate the same amount of annual income for as long as the Spellmans live and can eventually become a part of their estate.

smart.sites

Want an online approach to determine how much you'll need to retire? Use the T. Rowe Price Retirement Income Calculator, **http://www3.troweprice.com/ric/RIC/** to help you figure it out.

Now that the Spellmans know how big their nest egg has to be, the final question is: How are they going to accumulate such an amount by the time they retire? For most people, that means setting up a *systematic savings plan* and putting away a certain amount *each* year. To find out how much must be saved each year to achieve a targeted sum in the future, we can use the table of annuity factors in Appendix B. The appropriate interest factor is a function of the rate of return one can (or expects to) generate and the length of the investment period. In the Spellmans' case, there are 30 years to go until retirement, meaning that the length of their investment period is 30 years. If they feel they will be able to earn an average rate of return of 8 percent on their investments over this 30-year period, they will want to use an 8-percent, 30-year interest factor; from Appendix B, we see that this equals 113.3. Because the Spellmans must accumulate $320,000 by the time they retire, *the amount they will have to save each year* (over the next 30 years) can be found by *dividing* the amount they need to accumulate by the appropriate interest factor; that is, $320,000 ÷ 113.3 = $2,824 (see steps O to Q in Worksheet 14.1).

Calculator Keystrokes. As you might have suspected, the last few steps in the worksheet can just as easily be done on a good hand-held financial calculator. That is, with the calculator in the *annual mode*, to find the amount that must be put away annually to fund a $320,000 retirement nest egg in 30 years, given an expected return of 8 percent, use the keystrokes shown here, where:

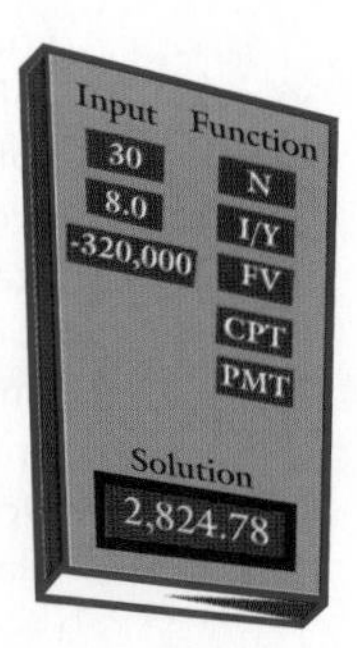

N = number of *years* over which the retirement nest egg is to be accumulated,

I/Y = *expected* annual return on invested capital,

FV = the size of the targeted nest egg, entered as a *negative*.

A value of 2,824.78 should appear in the calculator display, indicating the amount that must be put away annually to reach a target of $320,000 in 30 years. (*Note:* The size of the

Financial Road Sign

Time for a Plan Check Up!
Even the best retirement plan needs a review every few years to make sure it is performing to meet your retirement objectives. As you approach retirement age, you'll want to reevaluate your plan more frequently. Here are some questions to guide you.

- Do your original goals still apply, or do you need to revise them? The age at which you plan to retire or your health may have changed.
- Are the income projections and spending patterns you used to develop your plan still valid?
- Will you have to use retirement funds to finance your children's college education?
- Has your marital status changed?
- Have your investments performed in line with your expectations?
- Do you need to change your asset allocation to better reflect your current life stage?
- Have you reviewed your Social Security earnings statement for accuracy?
- Will you need different life and/or health insurance after you retire?
- Can you increase your retirement fund contributions if you are falling short of your goals?
- Should you convert your regular IRA to a Roth IRA?

inflation-adjusted annual shortfall [step L in Worksheet 14.1] can also be computed using a hand held financial calculator by letting **PV** = 7,400; **I/Y** = 5.0; **N** = 30; and then solve for/compute (**CPT**)**FV**. Try it. You should end up with an answer (**FV**) equal (or close) to $31,982.37.)

The Spellmans now know what they must do to achieve the kind of retirement they want: Put away $2,824 a year and invest it at an average annual rate of 8 percent over the next 30 years. If they can do that, they will have their $320,000 retirement nest egg in 30 years. Of course, they could have been more aggressive in their investing and assumed an average annual rate of 10 percent, in which case, either they'd end up with a bigger nest egg at retirement, or they could get away with saving less than $2,824 a year. Now, how they actually invest their money so as to achieve the desired 8 (or 10) percent rate of return will, of course, be a function of the investment vehicles and strategies they use. All the worksheet tells them is how much money they will need, not how they will get there; it is at this point that investment management enters the picture.

The procedure outlined here admittedly is a bit simplified and does take a few shortcuts, but considering the amount of uncertainty imbedded in the long-range projections being made, it does provide a viable estimate of retirement income and investment needs. The procedure certainly is far superior to the alternative of doing nothing! One important simplifying assumption in the procedure, though, is that it ignores the income that can be derived from the *sale of a house*. The sale of a house not only offers some special tax features (see Chapter 3) but can generate a substantial amount of cash flow as well. Certainly, if inflation does occur in the future (and it will!), it will very likely drive up home prices right along with the cost of everything else. A lot of people sell their homes around the time they retire and either move into smaller houses (often in Sun Belt retirement communities) or decide to rent in order to avoid all the problems of homeownership. Of course, the cash flow from the sale of a house can have a substantial effect on the size of the retirement nest egg. However, rather than trying to factor it into the forecast of retirement income and needs, we suggest that you *recognize* the existence of this cash flow source in your retirement planning, and consider it as a cushion against all the uncertainty inherent in retirement planning projections.

Computer-based Retirement Planning

Like many other aspects of our life, retirement planning has become a lot easier as a result of the computer. Most fully integrated financial planning software—such as *Quicken,* for example—contain retirement planning programs that perform many of the same forecasting functions found in Worksheet 14.1. In addition, there are so-called "dedicated" software packages that focus almost entirely on retirement planning. But it's the *Internet* that really brings retirement planning right to our doorsteps, because there are literally hundreds of Web sites that offer online retirement planning. For example, *Smartmoney.com* has its "Retirement Worksheets," *Quicken.com* offers a "Retirement Planner," and *Bloomberg.com* has its "Retirement Calculator." In essence, with most of these programs and Web sites, all you do is answer a few key questions about expected inflation, desired rate of return on investments, and current levels of income and expenditures, and the computer determines the size of any income shortfall, the amount of retirement funds that must be accumulated over time, and different ways to achieve the desired retirement nest egg.

As with any Web site or software, you should consider the features of each to find the one that works best for you. *An attractive feature of most of these programs is the ability to easily run through a series of "what-if" exercises.* By just punching a few buttons, you can change one or more key variables to see the impact they have on the size of your retirement nest egg and the amount of money you must put away annually. For example, you can find out what would happen if you failed to achieve the desired rate of return on your investments. In addition to this important retirement planning function, such software often allows you to track various retirement accounts to readily see how your performance is stacking up to your retirement goals—whether you are ahead of schedule, and, if not, what you can do to get back on track. Thus, modern, computer-based retirement planning assists you not only in establishing retirement goals and plans, but also in keeping track of your progress toward those objectives. Of course, as with other areas of financial planning, you should reevaluate your retirement needs whenever the underlying assumptions change—for example, if your personal circumstances change (job loss, divorce, and so on) or inflation rises.

Concept ✓

14-1. Discuss the relationship of retirement planning to financial planning; do investment and tax planning have a role in retirement planning? Identify and briefly discuss each of the steps in the retirement planning process.

14-2. Identify and briefly discuss the three biggest mistakes people tend to make when setting up retirement programs. Which of these three do you think is most important? Explain. What role does compound interest play in all this?

14-3. How do income needs fit in the retirement planning process? Discuss briefly the advantages of using PC programs or the Internet for retirement planning.

14-4. What are the most important sources of retirement income for most people?

Sources of Retirement Income

As Exhibit 14.2 reveals, the three principal sources of income for retired people are Social Security, assets (income-producing types, such as savings, stocks, and bonds), and pension plans. For the average retiree, these categories will account for about 90 percent of total retirement income. Just about every retired worker receives Social Security income, about 65 to 85 percent obtain at least some of their income from savings or investment assets, and, surprisingly, only about half (40 to 55 percent) receive benefits from some type of employer-provided pension plan. However, keep in mind these are *sources* of retirement income and not dollar amounts. The *amount* of income retired individuals will receive will, of course, vary from amounts that are barely above the poverty line to six-figure incomes. The amount received in retirement depends on a number of variables, the most important of which is the level of preretirement earnings. Obviously, the more individuals make before they retire, the more they will receive in Social Security benefits and from company-sponsored pension plans—and, very likely, the greater the amount of income-producing assets they will hold. In this chapter, we will examine Social Security and various types of pension plans and retirement programs. In addition, we will look briefly at an investment vehicle designed especially for retirement income: the *annuity.*

EXHIBIT 14.2

Sources of Income for the Average Retiree

Note that *government assistance* (which is made up mostly of Social Security benefits) is the single largest source of income for the average U.S. retiree. This source alone is almost as much as the average retiree receives from company pension plans *and* personal wealth/investment assets *combined.*

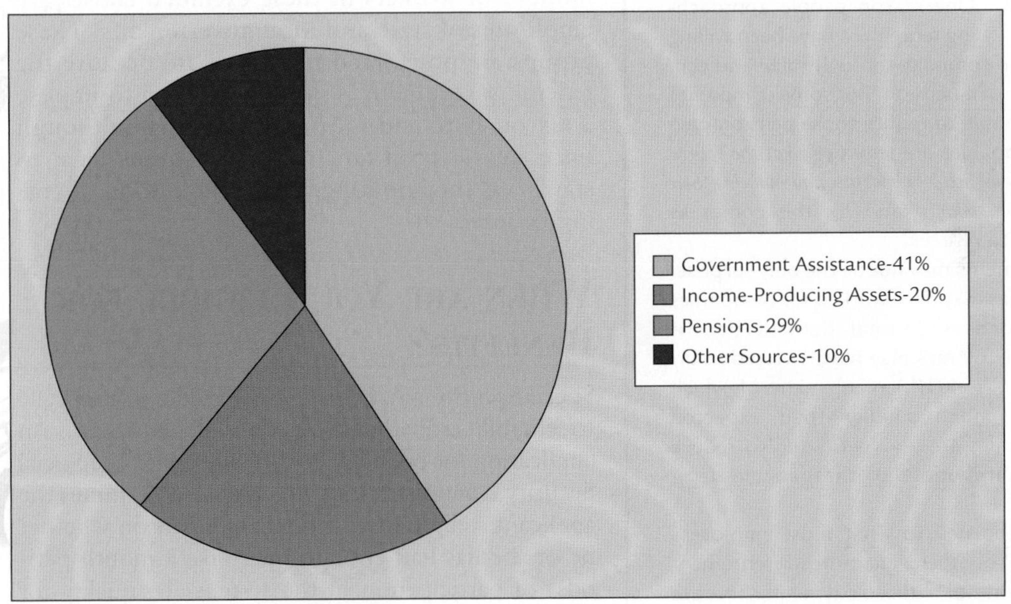

Source: *The Tenth Annual Retirement Confidence Survey*, cosponsored by the Employee Benefit Research Institute and the American Savings Education Council. Percentages reflect actual sources of income for current retirees.

LG3 SOCIAL SECURITY

The Social Security Act of 1935 was landmark legislation. Not only did it create a basic retirement program for working Americans at all income levels, it also established a number of other social programs, all of which are administered under the auspices of the *Old Age, Survivor's, Disability, and Health Insurance (OASDHI) program.* Some of the other services include supplementary security income (SSI), Medicare, unemployment insurance, public assistance, welfare services, and provision for black lung benefits. This chapter gives primary attention to the old age and survivor's portion of the act, because it has a direct bearing on retirement planning. The disability and health/Medicare benefits of Social Security are discussed in Chapter 9.

Who is Covered?

As mandated by Congress, Social Security coverage today extends to just about all gainfully employed workers. There are currently only two major classes of employees exempt from *mandatory* participation in the Social Security system: (1) federal

Money in Action

Social Security and Pension Benefits: There Are No Guarantees

One reason people approaching retirement have been willing to stick with one company through thick and thin was the promise of a pension. But some companies are using a loophole to reduce those pension payments. The companies are *projecting what the retiree would collect in Social Security benefits, and reducing their pensions dollar for dollar*. Naturally, this comes as quite a surprise to retirees.

Reduced payments may not be the only surprise. Some new retirees may have worked for companies that underfunded traditional defined benefit plans. Other new retirees may have invested solely in their company's 401(k) plan, many of which have provided much smaller than expected returns. Companies are now permitted to reduce their annual contributions to the possible detriment of retirees.

What has happened to what most employees believed would be their guaranteed retirement income? In the case of reduced payments, because employers contribute 7.65 percent of workers' pay, up to a maximum of $87,000 (in 2003) to fund Social Security benefits, many companies try to recover the costs of those benefits by reducing benefits paid. Such "integration" formulas affect more than half of the 44 million or so Americans covered by pensions in the private sector. Employees also contribute 7.65 percent of their wages toward Social Security benefits.

The Tax Reform Act of 1986 made it legal for employers to subtract Social Security from a pension plan, although they cannot reduce a benefit by more than half. Employees don't have a right to prohibit a company from using Social Security integration, although trade groups have tried to stop the practice.

The problem is most widespread for companies that offer defined benefit plans, which promise a fixed payment for life. It doesn't directly affect people with defined contribution plans, such as 401(k)s, in which the employee is primarily responsible for building his or her nest-egg. However, for companies with both defined

...continued on next page

civilian employees who were hired before 1984 and are covered under the Civil Service Retirement System and (2) employees of state and local governments who have chosen not to be covered (although the vast majority of these employees are covered through *voluntary participation* in Social Security). In addition, certain marginal employment positions, such as newspaper carriers under age 18 and full-time college students working in fraternity and sorority houses, are also exempt. But by far, the largest number of workers in these excluded classes are employees of state and local governments. These groups are not forced to participate because the federal government is not empowered to impose a tax on state and local governments—although once in the program, these employees have to stay in, as they no longer have the option of voting to leave.

When are You Eligible for Benefits?

Social Security payments are not paid automatically to eligible individuals (or their dependents). An application for benefits must be filed with the Social Security Administration, which then determines the applicant's eligibility for benefits based on whether he or she has had enough quarters (3-month periods) of participation in the system. To qualify for full retirement benefits, nearly all workers today must be employed in a job covered by Social Security for at least 40 quarters, or 10 years. These quarters need not be consecutive. Once this 40-quarter requirement is met, the worker becomes fully insured and remains eligible for retirement payments even if he or she never works again in covered employment. Note, however, that when yearly covered wages are computed, zeros are inserted for years in which no Social Security taxes were paid—which substantially reduces the size of future monthly benefit payments.

The surviving spouse and dependent children of a *deceased worker* are also eligible for monthly benefits if the worker was fully insured at the time of death or, in some special cases, if certain other requirements are met. Workers may be considered fully insured if they had six quarters of coverage during the 3-year period preceding the time of death.

Social Security Payroll Taxes

The cash benefits provided by Social Security are derived from the payroll (FICA) taxes paid by covered employees and their employers. The tax rate in 2003 was 7.65 percent—this is the amount paid by employees, and an equal amount was paid by employers. Self-employed people are also covered by Social Security and in 2003, they had to pay the total rate of 15.3 percent (that is, 7.65 percent × 2); because there are no employers to share the burden, self-employed people have to pay the full amount themselves.

Regardless of whether the individual is an employee or self-employed, the indicated tax rate stays in effect only until the employee reaches a maximum *wage base*, which increases each year. For 2003, basic Social Security taxes were paid on the first $87,000 of wages earned or self-employed income. Thus, the maximum Social Security tax paid by an employee in 2003 was $6,656 ($87,000 × .0765), and by the *self-employed* was $13,311 ($87,000 × .153). Note that starting in 1991, a second tax was added to cover the rising costs of Medicare. Now, once the Social Security wage base is passed, the new, higher Medicare wage base kicks in and employees are subject to a tax rate of 1.45 percent *on all earnings* over $87,000, whereas the added earnings of the self-employed are taxed at the rate of 2.9 percent.

Social Security Retirement Benefits

Basic Social Security benefits that are important to retired people and their dependents include (1) old-age benefits and (2) survivor's benefits. Both programs provide extended benefits to covered workers and their spouses; the major provisions of each program are briefly described in the material that follows.

benefit and defined contribution plans, the 401(k) balance is often used by employers to reduce the combined Social Security and defined benefit target they think a person should receive in retirement.

Since 2000, many defined benefit plans have been forced to go under. Starting in 1974, the federal Pension Benefit Guaranty Corporation (PBGC) has insured pension plans. But one danger is that retirees who turn to PBGC may get less than they would have if their own plans had remained solvent. Another is that PBGC could collapse because so many pension funds have either defaulted or are now gravely underfunded or without adequate assets to cover payouts (estimates range in the hundreds of billions of dollars).

In the case of smaller than expected returns from 401(k) plans, workers haven't been benefiting in proportion to market gains. Even during the 1980s and 1990s when the stock market rose astronomically, 401(k)s provided much lower returns. In fact, pension wealth in 1998 was either the same or less than it was 15 years earlier.

Critical Thinking Questions

1. What factors would you consider when evaluating a prospective employer's pension plan?
2. How could you guard against integrating Social Security benefits with other company benefits?
3. If you were a financial planner specializing in retirement, how would you advise people nearing retirement who have worked for the same company for most of their working years?

Sources: M.J. Andersen, "Pension Woes Are a Rising Flood," *Providence Journal*, August 22, 2003, p. B5; Melanie D. Goldman, "Integration: When the Check Isn't in the Mail," *Atlanta Business Chronicle*, June 30, 1997; "PBGC Announces Maximum Guarantee for the Year 2004," November 13, 2003, downloaded from **http://www.pbgc.gov**; Ellen E. Schultz, "The Pension Eraser: Integrating Social Security Can Cut Benefits," *The Wall Street Journal*, March 12, 1997, p. C1; and William Wolman, "The Great 401(k) Hoax, Continued," *Business Week Online*, October 15, 2003, downloaded from **http://www.businessweek.com**.

Old Age Benefits

Workers who are fully covered (that is, who have worked the required 40 quarters under Social Security) may receive old-age benefits for life once they reach full retirement age. For anyone born in 1960 or later, the Social Security Administration defines "full retirement age" as age 67. (If you were born before 1960, your full retirement age is between 65 and 67, and can be calculated at **http://www.ssa.gov**. For our discussion purposes here, we'll use 67 as the full retirement age.) In addition, workers who elect to retire early—at age 62—will receive reduced benefits, currently 70 to

80 percent of the full amount (again, depending on when they were born). If the retiree has a spouse 67 or older, the spouse may be entitled to benefits equal to one-half of the amount received by the retired worker. The spouse may also elect early receipt of reduced benefits at age 62.

In the case of two-income families, both the husband and wife may be eligible for full Social Security benefits. When they retire, they can choose to receive their benefits in one of two ways: each can (1) take the full benefits to which each is entitled from his or her account, or (2) take the husband and wife benefits of the higher-paid spouse. If each takes his or her own full share, there are no spousal benefits; if they take the husband and wife benefits of the higher-paid spouse, they effectively receive 1.5 shares. Obviously, two-income couples should select the option that provides the greatest amount of benefits (the amount of Social Security benefits will be described later).

Survivor's Benefits

If a covered worker dies, the spouse can receive survivor's benefits from Social Security. These benefits include a small lump-sum payment of several hundred dollars, followed by monthly benefit checks. The lump-sum amount is paid automatically upon application. To be eligible for monthly payments, the surviving spouse generally must be at least 60 years of age, or have a dependent and unmarried child of the deceased worker in his or her care. (To qualify for *full* benefits, the surviving spouse must be at least 67 years of age; reduced benefits are payable between ages 60 and 67.) If the children of a deceased worker reach age 16 before the spouse reaches age 60, the monthly benefits cease and do not resume until the spouse turns 60. This period during which survivor's benefits are not paid is sometimes called the *widow's gap*. (As we saw in Chapter 8, Social Security survivor's benefits play a key role in life insurance planning.)

How Much are Monthly Social Security Benefits?

The amount of Social Security benefits to which an eligible person is entitled is set by law and defined according to a fairly complex formula. But you don't need to worry about doing the math yourself, as the Social Security Administration has a computerized service that does the benefits estimating for you. Social Security Administration is required by law to provide all covered workers with a *Social Security Statement* containing information similar to that shown in Exhibit 14.3. This statement is sent out annually and is supposed to arrive about three months before the covered worker's birthday. (You can also request a statement by going to the Social Security Administration Web site: **http://www.ssa.gov**.) "Your Social Security Statement" lists the year-by-year Social Security earnings you've been credited with, and shows (in today's dollars) what benefits you can expect under three scenarios: (1) if you retire at age 62 and receive 80 percent of the full benefit (or less, depending on your age), (2) the full benefit at age 65 to 67 (depending on your year of birth), and (3) the increased benefit (of up to 8 percent per year) that's available if you delay retirement until age 70. The statement also estimates what your children and surviving spouse would get if you die, and how much you'd receive monthly if you became disabled.

EXHIBIT 14.3

Your Social Security Statement

The Social Security Administration keeps a lifetime record of your earnings; thus, when you apply for benefits, it checks your earnings record to see if you've worked long enough to qualify, and then determines the amount of your monthly benefits. The statement shown on this and the next page, prepared by the Social Security Administration, is intended to provide an estimate of what one's future benefits are likely to be (*Note:* Statement *excludes* record of Medicare credit.)

Facts About Your Social Security

We based your benefit estimates on these facts:

Your name	I.M. Somebody
Your date of birth	February 31, 1943
Your estimated taxable earnings per year after 2003	Over $87,000
Your Social Security number	000-00-0000

Your Earnings Record at a Glance

Years You Worked	Maximum Yearly Earnings Subject to Social Security Tax*	Your Taxed Social Security Earnings
1960	$ 4,800	$ 889
1961	4,800	259
1962	4,800	566
1963	4,800	1,840
1964	4,800	4,800
1965	4,800	4,800
1966	6,600	6,600
1967	6,600	6,600
1968	7,800	0
1969	7,800	0
1970	7,800	7,053
1971	7,800	7,800
1972	9,000	9,000
1973	10,800	10,800
1974	13,200	13,200
1975	14,100	14,100
1976	15,300	15,300
1977	16,500	16,500
1978	17,700	17,700
1979	22,900	22,900
1980	25,900	25,900
1981	29,700	29,700
1982	32,400	32,400
1983	35,700	35,700
1984	37,800	37,800
1985	39,600	39,600
1986	42,000	42,000
1987	43,800	43,800
1988	45,000	45,000

...continued on next page

EXHIBIT 14.3 (continued)

1989	48,000	48,000
1990	51,300	51,300
1991	53,400	53,400
1992	55,500	55,500
1993	57,600	57,600
1994	60,600	60,600
1995	61,200	61,200
1996	62,700	62,700
1997	65,400	65,400
1998	68,400	68,400
1999	72,600	72,600
2000	76,200	76,200
2001	80,400	80,400
2002	84,900	84,900
2003	87,000	87,000

Totals over your working career:

Estimated taxes for Social Security:

You Paid: $86,204 Your Employers Paid: $82,254

Retirement You have earned enough credits to qualify for benefits. At your current earnings rate, if you stop working . . .

At age 62, your payment would be about . . . . $1,367 a month

If you continue working until . . .

your full retirement age (65 and 4 months), your payment would be about . . . . $1,785 a month

age 70, your payment would be about . . . . $2,034 a month

Note: When you continue working beyond your full retirement age, your benefit amount increases because of your additional earnings and the special credits you will receive for delaying your retirement. This increased benefit can be important to you later in your life. It also can increase the future benefit amounts your family and survivors could receive.

Disability You have earned enough credits to qualify for benefits. If you become severely disabled right now . . .

Your payment would be about . . . . $1,765 a month

Family If you get retirement or disability benefits, your spouse and children may also qualify for benefits.

Survivors You have earned enough credits for your family to receive the following benefits if you die this year.

Total family benefits cannot be more than . . . . $3,122 a month
Your child . . . . $1,338 a month
Your spouse who is caring for your child . . . . $1,338 a month
Your spouse who reaches full retirement age . . . . $1,785 a month

Your spouse or minor child may be eligible for a special one-time death benefit of $255.

Medicare You have earned enough credits to qualify for Medicare at age 65. Even if you do not retire at age 65, be sure to contact Social Security three months before your 65th birthday to enroll in Medicare.

*Information added for this exhibit only; it is **NOT** part of the Social Security statement.

A Range of Benefits

Using information provided by the Social Security Administration, we can describe the *current level of benefits* (for someone who retired in 2003); this is done in Exhibit 14.4. The benefits, *as of 2003*, are for a retired worker, a retired worker and nonworking spouse, and a two-income couple for low, medium (average), and high career income levels (a *high* income worker is one whose annual earnings equaled or exceeded the maximum Social Security tax base). Bear in mind that the figures listed in the exhibit represent amounts that the beneficiaries will receive in the *first year* of their retirement. Those amounts will, of course, be adjusted upward each year with subsequent increases in the cost of living. But be careful! Don't just automatically assume that Social Security will provide you with an additional source of income during retirement. For as the *Money in Action* box on pages 618–619 reveals, with some pension plans your Social Security benefits may actually lead to *lower* pension benefits.

smart.sites

Do you qualify for Social Security benefits, and if so, how much will you get? The Social Security Administration's Web site, **http://www.ssa.gov/** has the answers.

EXHIBIT 14.4

Selected Monthly Social Security Retirement Benefits

The Social Security benefits listed here are initial, *first-year benefits*. As time passes, the beneficiary will receive correspondingly higher benefits as the cost of living goes up. For example, the maximum benefit payable to someone who retired in 1980 was $572 a month; by 2003 those benefits had grown to $1,721 a month.

	Career Earnings Level		
Latest Benefits (2003)	**Low**	**Average**	**Maximum**
Retired worker, age 65	$ 701	$1,158	$1,721
Retired worker, age 62	572	943	1,404
Family benefits:			
Retired worker and spouse, both 65	$1,051	$1,737	$2,581
Retired worker and spouse, both 62	858	1,414	2,106
Two-income couple[a]			
Both retire at 65	$1,402	$2,316	$3,442
Both retire at 62	1,144	1,886	2,808

[a] *Both* in the same career income category and *both* eligible for normal benefits at their career income levels.

Source: Based on data from *Understanding Social Security Benefits*, Social Security Administration, **http://www.ssa.gov**, 2003.

Note also that the benefits shown in Exhibit 14.4 *may be reduced* if the Social Security recipient is *under age 67 and still gainfully employed*—perhaps in a part-time job. In particular, retirees aged 62 through 66 are subject to a so-called "earnings test," which effectively limits the amount of income they can earn before they start losing some (or all) of their Social Security benefits. In 2003, that limit was $11,520 per year (this earnings limit rises annually with wage inflation). The rule states that if you're a

Social Security recipient aged 62 through 66, you'll lose $1 in benefits for every $2 you earn above the earnings test amount. Thus if you earned, say, $15,000 a year at a part-time job, you'd lose $1,740 in annual Social Security benefits—that is, $15,000 – $11,520 = $3,480 ÷ 2 = $1,740. That's $145 a month you'd lose simply because you hold a job that pays you more than the stipulated maximum. Not a very fair deal! But at least it applies only to early retirees. Once you reach "full retirement age", the earnings test no longer applies. (Now keep in mind the age 67 cut-off applies only to those recipients born *after 1960*; if you were born prior to that year, your cut-off will fall somewhere between ages 65 and 67, depending on your year of birth. For example, if you were born in 1940, your cut-off is 65½ years of age—if you defer retirement to that age, the earnings test doesn't apply, because you can earn any amount without penalty.)

The Senior Citizens' Freedom to Work Act of 2000 removed all earnings restrictions for anyone aged 65 to 67 (depending on date of birth) or older. Thus, effective January 2000, anyone aged 65 (to 67) or older can earn any amount they want, and not lose one penny in Social Security benefits. In contrast to earned income, there never have been any limits on so-called "unearned income" derived from such sources as interest, dividends, rents, or profits on securities transactions—a retiree can receive an unlimited amount of such income without any benefits reduction.

Taxes on Benefits

In 1984, Congress passed legislation to tax the benefits paid to "upper-income beneficiaries." Specifically, as the law presently stands, *Social Security retirement benefits are subject to federal income taxes if the beneficiary's annual income exceeds one of the following base amounts:* $25,000 for a single taxpayer, $32,000 for married taxpayers filing jointly, and zero for married taxpayers filing separately. In determining the amount of income that must be counted, the taxpayer starts with his or her *adjusted gross income* as defined by the present tax law (see Chapter 3) and then adds all nontaxable interest income (such as income from municipal bonds) plus a stipulated portion of the Social Security benefits received. Thus, if for single taxpayers the resulting amount is between $25,000 and $34,000, 50 percent of Social Security benefits are taxable. If income exceeds $34,000, 85 percent of Social Security benefits is subject to income tax. If the combined income of married taxpayers filing joint returns is between $32,000 and $44,000, 50 percent of the Social Security benefits is taxable. The percentage of benefits taxed increases to 85 percent when their combined income exceeds $44,000.

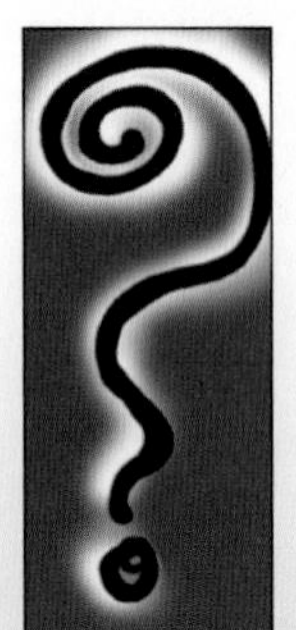

Concept ✓

14-5. What benefits are provided under the Social Security Act, and who is covered? Describe the basic operations of the Social Security system.

14-6. Discuss the old-age and survivor's benefits provided to retirees and their dependents under the Social Security program.

14-7. Does Social Security coverage relieve you of the need to do some retirement planning on your own? Explain. What is a *Social Security Statement*, and how would such a statement help you in your retirement planning?

Social Security and Retirement Planning

No one can accurately predict the amount of Social Security benefits that will be paid 30 or 40 years from now. For retirement planning purposes, however, it seems reasonable to expect Social Security to provide the average retired wage earner (who is married) with perhaps 40 to 60 percent of the wages that he or she was earning in the year before retirement—assuming, of course, that the retiree has had a full career working in covered employment. Social Security therefore should be viewed as *a foundation for your retirement income.* By itself, *it is insufficient to allow a worker and spouse to maintain their preretirement standard of living.* For people who earn in excess of the wage base, a lower percentage of total preretirement wages will be replaced by Social Security. Consequently, it's essential that average and upper-middle-income families plan to supplement their Social Security retirement benefits with income from other sources. Two popular sources are pensions (and retirement programs) and annuities. These topics are discussed in the next two sections.

LG4, LG5

PENSION PLANS AND RETIREMENT PROGRAMS

Accompanying the expansion of the Social Security system has been a corresponding growth in employer-sponsored pension and retirement plans. In 1940, when the Social Security program was in its infancy, fewer than 25 percent of the workforce had the benefit of an employer-sponsored plan. Today, better than 50 percent of all wage earners and salaried workers (in both the private and public sectors) are covered by some type of employer-sponsored retirement or profit-sharing plan.

In 1948, the National Labor Relations Board (NLRB) ruled that pensions and other types of insurance programs are legitimate subjects for collective bargaining. In response, many employers established new pension plans or liberalized the provisions of existing ones to meet or anticipate union demands. Qualified pension plans (discussed later) allow firms to deduct for tax purposes their contributions to employee retirement programs. Even better, the employees can also deduct these contributions from their taxable income; as a result, the participants are able to build up their own retirement funds on a tax-deferred basis. Eventually, of course, when the funds are paid out as benefits, the employees will have to pay taxes on this income.

Government red tape, however, has taken a toll on pension plans. In particular, the **Employee Retirement Income Security Act of 1974** (sometimes referred to as **ERISA** or the *Pension Reform Act*), established to protect employees participating in private employer retirement plans, has actually led to a reduction in the number of new retirement plans started among firms, especially the smaller ones. Indeed, the percentage of workers covered by company-sponsored plans has fallen dramatically since the late 1970s. It's estimated that today, *in the private sector*, only about 40 percent of all full-time workers are covered by company-financed plans—even worse, only about one-third (or less) of the part-time labor force is covered. In contrast, there has been a significant increase in salary-reduction forms of retirement plans (discussed later). In addition to ERISA, the widespread availability of Keogh plans, individual retirement arrangements (IRAs), and other programs has lessened the urgency of small firms (and bigger ones as well) to offer their own company-financed pension plans.

Employee Retirement Income Security Act (ERISA)
A law passed in 1974 to ensure that workers eligible for pensions actually receive such benefits; also permits uncovered workers to establish individual tax-sheltered retirement plans.

EMPLOYER-SPONSORED PROGRAMS: BASIC PLANS

Employers can sponsor two types of retirement programs—*basic plans*, in which employees automatically participate after a certain period of employment, and *supplemental plans*, which are mostly voluntary programs and which enable employees to increase the amount of funds being set aside for retirement. We will look first at some of the key characteristics of basic plans. Apart from financing, there are certain features of employer-sponsored pension plans that you should become familiar with, including participation requirements, contributory obligations, benefit rights, retirement age, and methods of computing benefits.

Participation Requirements

In most pension plans, employees must meet certain criteria before they become eligible for participation. Most common are requirements relating to years of service, minimum age, level of earnings, and employment classification. Years of service and minimum-age requirements are often incorporated into retirement plans in the belief that a much higher labor turnover rate applies to both newly hired and younger employees. Therefore, to reduce the administrative costs of the plans, employees in these categories are often excluded—at least, initially—from participation. Once these (or any other) participation requirements are met, the employee automatically becomes eligible to participate in the program.

What's Your Contribution?

Whether you, as an employee, must make payments toward your own pension depends on the type of plan you're in. If you belong to a **noncontributory pension plan**, the employer pays the total cost of the benefits—you don't have to pay a thing. Under a **contributory pension plan**, the cost is shared by both the employer and the employee. Today the trend is toward contributory plans. In addition, nearly all plans for employees of federal, state, and local governments require a contribution from the employee. In contributory plans, the employee's share of the costs is often between 3 and 10 percent of annual wages and is typically paid through a payroll deduction. Probably the most common arrangement is for the employer to match the employee's contribution such that the employee puts up half the annual contribution and the employer puts up the other half. When employees who have participated in a contributory retirement plan terminate employment prior to retirement, they are legally entitled to some benefit, based on the amount of their own contributions. Usually this benefit is a cash lump sum, but in some cases it can be taken as a monthly payment at retirement. Whether departing employees receive any benefit from the *employer's* contributions depends on the plan's benefit rights.

noncontributory pension plan
A pension plan in which the employer pays the total cost of the benefits.

contributory pension plan
A pension plan in which the employee bears a portion of the cost of the benefits.

Vested Interest: A Right to the Benefits

Not everyone who participates in a pension plan will earn the right to receive retirement benefits. Pension plans impose certain criteria that must be met before the employee can obtain a nonforfeitable right to a pension, known as **vested rights**. Prior to 1974, employers often required workers to be employed for 25 years or more before vesting would occur. An employee who left before completing this period of employment (and plenty did) would lose all the previously earned pension benefits. Because of the high mobility of labor and capital, many workers at retirement faced the prospect of having no pension. One of the principal purposes of ERISA was to eliminate this unfair practice (which indirectly contributed to the social problem of low incomes among the aged). ERISA required covered employers to grant employees vested rights after no more than 10 years of employment (when there was no partial vesting prior to 10 years of service), or alternately, 15 years, where partial vesting began after 5 years.

vested rights
Employees' nonforfeitable rights to receive benefits in a pension plan based on their own and their employer's contributions.

Although ERISA was certainly a step in the right direction, legislation passed in 2002 resulted in even better vesting requirements. As the law now stands, *full vesting* rights are required after only 3 to 6 years of employment. More specifically, companies must now choose between two vesting schedules. One, the so-called *cliff vesting*, requires full vesting after no more than 3 years of service—but you obtain no vesting privileges until then. It's sort of a "zero-one" proposition; there are no vesting privileges at all for the first 3 years, and then all of a sudden you're fully vested. Once vested, you're entitled to everything that's been paid in so far (your contributions *plus* your employer's) and everything that will be contributed in the future. Under the alternate procedure, the so-called *graded schedule*, vesting takes place gradually over the first 6 years of employment. At the minimum, after 2 years you would have a nonforfeiture right to at least 20 percent of the benefits, with an additional 20 percent each year thereafter until you're 100 percent vested after 6 years. Note, however, that these are minimum standards, and employers can grant more favorable vesting terms.

To illustrate the vesting process, assume that a medium-sized firm offers a plan in which full vesting of benefits occurs after 3 years. The plan is contributory, with employees paying 3 percent of their salaries and the employer paying an amount equal to 6 percent of the salaries. Under this plan, employees cannot withdraw the contributions made by the employer until they reach retirement. The plan provides annual benefits in the amount of $11 per year of service for each $100 of an employee's final monthly earnings—the amount earned during the final month in the employ of the firm. Therefore, an employee who worked a minimum of 3 years for the firm would be eligible for a retirement benefit from that company even if he or she left the company at, say, age 30.

However, because of inflation, the value of the benefit for a worker who left the firm long before retirement age would be very small. Consequently, the employee might be better off simply withdrawing his or her own contributions (which always vest immediately) and terminating participation in the plan at the same time he or she leaves the employer. Of course, any worker who leaves the firm prior to accumulating the required number of years of service would be entitled only to a return of his or her own contributions to the plan (plus nominal investment earnings). *And whenever you terminate employment, resist the urge to spend the money you have built up in your retirement account! Over time, that can have a devastating effect on your ability to accumulate retirement capital. Instead, when you take money out of one retirement account, roll it over into another one.*

Retirement Age

Nearly all retirement plans specify when an eligible employee is entitled to benefits—in most cases, at age 65. Often pension plans also provide an early retirement age. In these cases, employees may begin receiving reduced benefits prior to the normal retirement age. Many retirement plans for public employees give workers the option of retiring after a stated number of years of service (say, 30 or 35) at full benefits, regardless of their age at the time. In the past, the trend in pension plans was toward earlier permissible retirement ages. However, now that many have begun to argue in favor of increasing the age for mandatory retirement (that is, letting people work longer), it is expected that there will be little motivation to further reduce the normal retirement age.

Defined Contributions or Defined Benefits

The method used to compute benefits at retirement is spelled out in detail in every retirement plan. The two most commonly used methods are the defined contribution plan and the defined benefits plan. A **defined contribution plan** specifies the amount of contribution that the employer and employee must make. At retirement, the worker is awarded whatever level of monthly benefits those contributions will purchase. Although such factors as age, income level, and the amount of contributions made to the plan have a great deal to do with the amount of monthly benefits received at retirement, probably no variable is more important than the level of *investment performance* generated on the contributed funds.

defined contribution plan
A pension plan that specifies the amount of the contributions that both employer and employee must make; it makes no promises concerning the size of the benefits at retirement.

A defined contribution plan promises nothing at retirement except the returns the fund managers have been able to obtain. The only thing that's defined is the amount of contribution that the employee and/or employer have to make (generally stated as a percent of the employee's income). The benefits at retirement depend totally on investment results. Of course, there's a certain standard of care that's followed by the investment managers, so there is some protection provided to the plan participants (indeed, most of the investing is confined to high-quality investment vehicles). But even so, that still leaves a lot of room for variability in returns. There'll be a big difference in retirement benefits for someone who's in a fund that's earned 6 percent versus someone who's in a fund that's earned 12 percent.

Under a **defined benefits plan**, the formula for computing benefits, not contributions, is stipulated in the plan provisions. These benefits are paid out regardless of how well (or poorly) the retirement funds are invested. If investment performance falls short, the employer has to make up the difference to come up with the benefits agreed to in the plan. This type of plan allows employees to determine before retirement how much their monthly retirement income will be. Often the number of years of service and amount of earnings are prime factors in the formula. For example, a worker might be paid 2.5 percent of his or her final 3-year average annual salary for each year of service. Thus, the *annual* benefit to an employee whose final 3-year average annual salary was $65,000 and who was with the company for 20 years would be $32,500 (2.5 percent × $65,000 × 20 years).

defined benefits plan
A pension plan in which the formula for computing benefits is stipulated in its provisions.

Other types of defined benefits plans may simply pay benefits based on (1) a consideration of earnings excluding years of service, (2) a consideration of years of service excluding earnings, or (3) a flat amount with no consideration given to either earnings or years of service. Many defined benefits plans also increase retirement benefits periodically to help retirees keep up with the cost of living. In periods of high inflation, these increases are essential to maintain retirees' standards of living. Today, there are more than 44 million people (workers and retirees) covered by defined benefits plans. However, while the number of *people covered* by such plans continues to rise, the number of (private sector) defined benefit *plans in existence* has steadily declined, from about 115,000 plans in 1985 to less than 35,000 today. Not surprisingly, most of that decline has been among the smaller plans with 100 or fewer participants.

Regardless of the method used to calculate benefit amounts, the employee's basic concern should be with the percent of final take-home pay the plan is likely to produce at retirement. A pension is usually thought to be good if, when combined with Social Security, it will result in a monthly income equal to about 70 to 80 percent of preretirement net earnings. To reach this goal, however, today's employees must take some responsibility, because there's a growing trend for *companies to switch from defined benefits plans to defined contribution programs.* Whereas in 1975, about 85 percent of all plans were defined benefits plans, today fewer than half are. Companies don't like the idea of being faced with undefined future pension liabilities—after all, the pension/retirement payments that don't come from investment earnings have to be made up from company earnings, and that means lower profits. So more and more companies are avoiding these problems by changing over to defined contribution plans—indeed, there are far more defined contribution plans today than there are defined benefits plans. And in cases where the firms are sticking with their defined benefits plans, the benefits are often so meager that they don't come close to the desired 70 to 80 percent income target. (Some of the defined contribution plans don't either.)

In either case, *the employee is being forced to assume more responsibility for ensuring the desired level of postretirement income.* The logic from the company's perspective is that if obtaining a comfortable standard of living in retirement is a worthwhile objective, the employee should be willing to help achieve it. That might mean participating in a company-sponsored supplemental retirement plan or possibly even setting up your own self-directed program (we'll look at both supplemental and self-directed plans later). All this means that where you end up in retirement will depend, more than ever, on what *you've* done, rather than on what your employers have done. *Very likely, you're the one who is going to control not only how much goes into the company's retirement programs, but where it goes as well.*

Cash Balance Plans

One of the newest types of employer-sponsored retirement programs is the **cash-balance plan**. *These plans combine some of the features of defined contribution plans with those of defined benefit plans.* As is the case in a defined contribution plan, you as an employee

cash-balance plan
A type of employer-sponsored retirement program that combines features of defined contribution and defined benefit plans, and is well suited for a mobile work force.

have your own "account" in the cash balance plan. Your employer credits the account with an annual contribution usually set to a fixed percentage (for example, 5 percent) of your pay. The fixed contribution percentage allows employees to earn benefits evenly over their career.

Over time, these contributions are guaranteed to earn a minimum return, which might be a fixed percentage, or a variable return linked to inflation or interest rates. This guarantee means that the *employer* bears the downside risk of poor investment performance in these plans, which makes them similar to defined benefit plans. Another big advantage of these plans is that *when employees leave a firm, they can roll their account into their new employer's cash balance plans*, or into an IRA.

The portability of cash balance plans makes them better suited than traditional defined benefit plans to meet the needs of an increasingly mobile work force. Firms that currently offer traditional defined benefit plans are able to convert to cash balance plans, provided that the conversion does not reduce the value of pension benefits already earned by current employees. The conversions must also be "age-natural," meaning that they cannot provide more benefits for younger employees than for older ones. In any event, *cash balance plans have become quite popular, and experts expect them to replace the majority of defined benefit plans in the near future.*

Qualified Pension Plans

qualified pension plan A pension plan that meets specified criteria established by the Internal Revenue Code.

The Internal Revenue Code permits a corporate employer making contributions to a **qualified pension plan** to deduct from taxable income its contributions to the plan. As a result, the employees on whose behalf the contributions are made do not have to include these payments as part of their taxable income until the benefits are actually received. Further, in contributory plans, *the employee can also shelter his or her contributions from taxes.* In other words, such contributions are not counted as part of taxable income in the year in which they are made, but instead act to reduce the amount of taxable income reported to the IRS, and therefore lead to lower taxes for the employee.

Still another tax advantage of these plans is that any and all investment income is allowed to accumulate tax free; as a result, investment capital can build up quicker. Yet, in spite of all these tax benefits, a lot of firms still believe that the costs of regulation exceed any benefits that might result and therefore choose to forgo the procedures required for having a plan qualified. Probably the biggest disadvantage of nonqualified pension plans from the employee's perspective is that any contributions made to *contributory* plans are fully taxable and, as such, are treated just like any other type of income—in other words, the contributions are made on an after-tax basis and are therefore *not* sheltered from taxes.

Employer-Sponsored Programs: Supplemental Plans

In addition to basic retirement programs, many employers offer supplemental plans. These plans are often *voluntary* and enable employees to not only increase the amount of funds being held for retirement but also enjoy attractive tax benefits. Essentially, there are three types of supplemental plans: profit-sharing, thrift and savings, and salary reduction plans.

profit-sharing plan An arrangement in which the employees of a firm participate in the company's earnings.

Profit-Sharing Plans

Profit-sharing plans permit employees to participate in the earnings of their employer. A **profit-sharing plan** may be qualified under the IRS and become eligible for essentially the same tax treatment as other types of pension plans. An argument in support of the use of profit-sharing plans is that they encourage employees to work harder because the employees benefit when the firm prospers. Whether these types of plans

Money in Action

Are There Cracks in Your Nest Eggs?

Some people rely solely on the pension funds of their employers (401(k)s) to support them during retirement. Many of these people have worked for the same company for most of their working lives and know that the 401(k) is invested solely in that company's stock. For example, Paul and Mary Petersen, both 62, each worked for one company. Paul, in product distribution for Proctor & Gamble (P&G) for 30 years; Mary in sales for WorldCom. She started working for MCI in the early 1970s, shortly after the company first offered their stock to the public. Neither Paul nor Mary had an individual retirement account (IRA). Thus, their entire nest egg was invested in only two stocks, and they assumed the stocks would hold their value.

Although the Petersons are a hypothetical couple, they are representative of many company employees who took it for granted that their pensions would support their retirement. Their story has been repeated countless times and reflects what happens when people rely too heavily on company stock—or any one investment—to provide for retirement.

Most investors know that it's important to diversify. Yet, millions of workers overload their 401(k) or other employer-sponsored retirement plan with company stock. Employees commonly hold almost all of their plan assets in company stock, and some compound the problem by holding additional stock options.

Let's continue to follow the Petersons' investment progress. In only a few years, the price of P&G stock dropped approximately 50 percent. The company requires employees over age 50 to hold at least 40 percent of the assets in the profit sharing plan as company stock. The picture for WorldCom, which was hit by a major corporate scandal, was much worse: Mary's retirement plan was wiped out. It was then that the Petersens sought help from a financial planner.

The planner explained that overloading a retirement plan with employer stock puts workers in double jeopardy because it links both their job security and retirement security to the fortunes of

...continued on next page

accomplish this goal is debatable. One advantage of profit-sharing plans from the firm's viewpoint, however, is that they do not impose any specific levels of contribution or benefits on the part of the employer. When profits are low, the employer makes smaller contributions to the plan, and when profits are high, the firm pays more.

To provide reasonable returns, many employers establish minimum and maximum amounts to be paid as contributions to profit-sharing plans, regardless of how low or high corporate earnings are. Contributions to profit-sharing plans can be invested in certain types of fixed-interest products, stocks and bonds, or, in many cases, securities issued by the employing firm itself. Employees who receive the firm's securities may actually benefit twice. When profits are good, larger contributions are made to the profit-sharing plan *plus* the price of the shares already owned is likely to increase.

A number of big-time, major firms offer *voluntary profit-sharing plans* that invest heavily in their own stock. It's not unusual in many of these cases for long-term career employees to accumulate several hundred thousand dollars worth of the company's stock. And we're not talking about highly paid corporate executives here; rather, these are just average employees who had the discipline to consistently divert a portion of their salary to the company's profit-sharing plan. *There is a very real and important downside to this practice, however*—that is, as more fully explained in the nearby *Money in Action* box, if the company should hit hard times, not only could you face salary cuts (or even worse, the loss of a job), but the value of your profit-sharing account very likely will take a big tumble as well. Just look what happened to employees in the tech sector during the 2000–02 bear market!

Thrift And Savings Plan

thrift and savings plan A plan established by an employer to supplement pension and other fringe benefits, in which the firm makes contributions in an amount equal to a set proportion of the employee's contribution.

Thrift and savings plans were established to supplement pension and other fringe benefits. Most plans require the employer to make contributions to the savings plan in an amount equal to a set proportion of the amount contributed by the employee. For example, an employer might match an employee's contributions at the rate of 50 cents on the dollar up to, say, 6 percent of salary. Thus, an employee making $40,000 a year could pay $2,400 into the plan annually, and the employer would kick in another $1,200. These contributions are then deposited with a trustee, who invests the money in various types of securities, including stocks and bonds of the employing firm. With IRS-qualified thrift and savings plans, the *employer's* contributions and earnings on the savings are not included in the *employee's* taxable income until he or she withdraws these sums. Unfortunately, this attractive tax feature does not extend to the employee's contributions, and, as a result, any money put into one of these savings plans is still considered part of the employee's taxable income—subject to regular income taxes.

Thrift and savings plans usually have more-liberal vesting and withdrawal privileges than pension and retirement programs. Often the employee's right to the contributions of the employer becomes nonforfeitable immediately upon payment, and the total savings in the plan can be withdrawn by giving proper notice. Employees who terminate participation in such a plan, however, are frequently prohibited from rejoining it for a specified period, such as 1 year. An employee who has the option should seriously consider participation in a thrift plan, because the returns are usually pretty favorable—especially when you factor in the added kicker provided by the *employer's* contributions.

smart.sites

You'll find several useful retirement calculators, tools, and an asset-allocation worksheet at Fidelity Investments' 401(k) site, **http://www.401k.com/401k/tools/tools.htm**.

one company. With WorldCom's collapse, Mary lost both her job and her retirement. P&G, however, had regained almost its full value by year end 2003. Holding too much in a single stock—employer stock or otherwise—is risky.

The Petersens' nest egg cracked from the risk. Others, however, who have IRAs in addition to company-funded pensions have the opportunity to mitigate some of that risk. They need to look at the company stock in relationship to their entire nest egg. The company stock in their employer's 401(k) may, in fact, represent a reasonably small portion of investment vehicles such as mutual funds, fixed income securities, and stocks from other companies. If the Petersens had known about and followed the general rule of holding no more than 20-30 percent in a single stock in an entire portfolio, they could have avoided cracking their nest egg.

Critical Thinking Questions

1. Discuss pitfalls from investing half or even an entire nest egg in a single stock.
2. Discuss differences in retirement planning strategies for people in their early 20s and early 40s.
3. What steps can Mary Petersen take for the years she continues to work to rebuild a retirement portfolio?

Sources: "Investing for Retirement in Volatile Markets," *TIAA-CREF Participant*, May 2001, pp. 12–13; Christine Dugas, "Company Stock Fills 401(k)s," *USA Today*, January 2, 2003, downloaded from **http://www.usatoday.com**; Paul J. Lim, "Losing Altitude," *U.S. News & World Report*, April 21, 2003, pp. 58–60.

Salary Reduction Plans

salary reduction, or 401(k), plan An agreement under which a portion of a covered employee's pay is withheld and invested in some qualified form of investment; the taxes on both the contributions and the account earnings are deferred until the funds are withdrawn.

Another type of supplemental retirement program—and certainly the most popular judging by employee response—is the **salary reduction plan**, or the so-called **401(k) plan** as it's more popularly known. Although our discussion here will center on 401(k) plans, similar programs are available for employees of public, nonprofit organizations. Known as *403(b) plans* or *457 plans*, they offer many of the same features and tax shelter provisions as 401(k) plans. (Workers at public schools, colleges, universities, nonprofit hospitals, and similar organizations have 403(b) plans, whereas those who work for a state or local government probably have a 457 plan, as do employees at some tax-exempt organizations.)

Today, more and more companies are cutting back on their contributions to traditional (defined benefits) retirement plans and are turning, instead, to 401(k) plans, a type of defined contribution plan. More than 80 percent of all companies with more than 200 employees now offer 401(k) plans. In 2002, the amount of assets held in 401(k) plans exceeded \$1.5 trillion, up from just \$300 billion in 1990 (in addition, another \$700 billion or so was held in 403(b) and 457 plans).

A 401(k) plan basically gives the employee the option to divert a portion of his or her salary to a company-sponsored, tax-sheltered savings account. In this way, the earnings diverted to the savings plan accumulate tax free. Taxes must be paid eventually, but not until the employee starts drawing down the account at retirement, presumably when he or she is in a lower tax bracket. In 2003, an individual employee could put as much as $12,000 (up to 25 percent of salary, to this maximum) into a tax-deferred 401(k) plan—this annual dollar cap will increase $1,000 per year before topping out at $15,000 in 2006. (The contribution limits for 403(b) and 457 plans will be the same as those for 401(k) plans.)

To see how such tax-deferred plans work, consider an individual who earned, say, $75,000 in 2003, and would like to contribute the maximum allowable—$12,000—to the 401(k) plan where she works. Doing so reduces her taxable income to $63,000 and, assuming she's in the 28 percent tax bracket, lowers her federal tax bill by some $3,360 (i.e., $12,000 × .28). Such tax savings will offset a good portion—28 percent—of her contribution to the 401(k) savings plan. In effect, she will add $12,000 to her retirement program with only $8,640 of her own money; the rest will come from the IRS via a reduced tax bill! Further, all the *earnings* on her savings account will accumulate tax free as well.

These plans are generally viewed as highly attractive *tax shelters* that offer not only substantial tax savings but also a way to save for retirement. As a rule, as long as you can afford to put the money aside, *you should seriously consider joining a 401(k)/403(b)/457 plan if offered at your place of employment.* This is especially true considering the matching features that many of these plans offer. That is, a special attraction of 401(k) plans is that the firms offering them can sweeten the pot by matching all or a part of the employee's contributions. The vast majority of companies that offer 401(k) plans have some type of matching contributions program, often putting up 50 cents (or more) for every dollar contributed by the employee. Such matching plans provide both tax and savings incentives to individuals and clearly enhance the appeal of 401(k) plans. (Matching contributions by employers are far less common with 403(b) plans and virtually nonexistent with 457 plans.)

smart.sites

mPower Cafe, (**http://www.mpower.com**) is dedicated to helping investors manage their retirement investments—401(k), 403(b), and 457 plans and individual retirement arrangements.

401(k) plans offer participants several investment options, such as equity and fixed-income mutual funds, company stock, and other interest-bearing vehicles, such as bank CDs or similar insurance company products. The typical 401(k) has about 10 choices, and some plans have as many as 20 or more. Today the trend is toward giving plan participants more options and providing seminars and other educational tools to help employees make informed retirement plan decisions.

Financial Road Sign

Steps to a Healthy 401(k)

Many employers now let you design your retirement fund portfolio to meet your particular needs and investment style. The number of investment options available in 401(k) plans has increased, too. If all those options feel overwhelming, use the following steps to help narrow your investment choices to a manageable number.

1. **Max out:** Contribute as much as your plan allows and invest enough to receive the full employer match.
2. **Know your investment options:** Most plans offer choices such as different types of mutual funds; some also include individual stocks—most often, your employer's.
3. **Allocate your assets:** Before selecting funds, know what asset categories you need. Many sites offer asset allocation worksheets to help you with this task.
4. **Cut, cut, cut:** Review your plan's offerings and delete funds that don't match your asset allocation.
5. **Hunt for bargains:** Funds with low expense ratios are likely to outperform their peers.
6. **Use index funds:** Index funds, with their low fees, generally do better than actively managed funds in the long run.
7. **Trust the old standbys:** Funds from well-regarded families like Fidelity, Vanguard, and American are usually good bets.
8. **Checks and balances:** You should have about 10 or so funds on your list. Investigate these more carefully to be sure the fund is in the right style category; don't rely on fund names.

Evaluating Employer-Sponsored Pension Plans

When you participate in a company-sponsored pension plan, you're entitled to certain benefits in return for meeting certain conditions of membership—which may or may not include making contributions to the plan. Whether your participation is limited to the firm's basic plan or includes one or more of the supplemental programs, *it's vital that you take the time to acquaint yourself with the various benefits and provisions* of these retirement plans. And be sure to familiarize yourself not only with the basic plans (even though participation is mandatory, you ought to know what you're getting for your money), but also with any (voluntary) supplemental plans you may be eligible to join.

So, how should you evaluate these plans? Most experts agree that although there are many aspects that go into a typical company-sponsored pension plan (some of which are a bit complex and difficult to evaluate), you can get a pretty good handle on essential plan provisions and retirement benefits by taking a close look at these features:

- **Eligibility requirements:** Precisely what are they, and if you're not already in the plan, when will you be able to participate?
- **Defined benefits or contributions:** Which one is defined? If it's the benefits, exactly what formula is used to define them? Pay particular attention to how Social Security benefits are treated in the formula. If it's a defined contribution program, do you have any control over how the money is invested? If so, what are your options? *What you would like to have*: a lot of attractive stock/equity mutual funds to choose from; *what you don't need:* a bunch of low-yielding investment options, such as bank CDs, money market mutual funds, or fixed annuities.
- **Vesting procedures:** Does the company use a cliff or graded procedure, and precisely when do you become fully vested?
- **Contributory or noncontributory:** If the plan is contributory, how much comes from you and how much from the company; and what is the total of this contribution, as a percentage of your salary? If it is noncontributory, what is the company's contribution, as a percentage of your salary?
- **Retirement age:** What is the normal retirement age, and what provisions are there for *early retirement*? What happens if you leave the company before retirement? Are the pension benefits *portable*—that is, can you take them with you if you change jobs?
- **Voluntary supplemental programs:** How much of your salary can you put into one or more of these plans, and what, if anything, is *matched* by the company? Remember, these are like defined contribution plans, so there's nothing guaranteed as far as benefits are concerned.

Getting answers to these questions will help you determine where you stand and what, if any, improvements need to be made in your retirement plans. As part of this evaluation process, you should try to work up, as best as you can, *a rough estimation of what your benefits are likely to be at retirement*—you'll need to make some projections about future income levels, investment returns, and so on, but it's an exercise well worth taking (before you start cranking out the numbers, however, check with the people who handle employee benefits at your place of work; they'll often give you the help you need). Then, using a procedure similar to what we did with Worksheet 14.1, you can estimate what portion of your retirement needs will be met from your company's basic pension plan. If there's a shortfall—*and there likely will be*—it will indicate the extent to which you need to participate in some type of company-sponsored supplemental program, such as a 401(k) plan, or (alternatively) how much you're going to have to rely on your own savings and investments to come up with the kind of standard of living you're looking for in retirement. *Such insights will enable you to more effectively dovetail the investment characteristics and retirement benefits of any company-sponsored retirement plans you're entitled to with the savings and investing that you do on your own.*

smart.sites

Paying too much in 401(k) fees? Head over to the Motley Fool's 401(k) section (**http://www.fool.com/money/401k/401k.htm?source=LN**) which helps plan participants evaluate their retirement plans.

SELF-DIRECTED RETIREMENT PROGRAMS

In addition to participating in company-sponsored retirement programs, individuals can also set up their own tax-sheltered retirement plans. There are two basic types of self-directed retirement programs: *Keogh* and *SEP plans*, which are for self-employed individuals, and *individual retirement arrangements (IRAs)*, which can be set up by just about anybody.

Keogh And Sep Plans

Keogh plan
An account to which self-employed persons may make payments, up to the lesser of $40,000 or 25 percent of earned income per year, that may be taken as deductions from taxable income; the earnings on such accounts also accrue on a tax-deferred basis.

Keogh plans were introduced in 1962 as part of the Self-Employed Individuals Retirement Act, or simply the Keogh Act. Keogh plans allow self-employed individuals to set up tax-deferred retirement plans for themselves and their employees. Like contributions to 401(k) plans, payments to Keogh accounts may be taken as deductions from taxable income. As a result, they reduce the tax bills of self-employed individuals. The maximum contribution to this tax-deferred retirement plan in 2003 was $40,000 per year, or 25 percent of earned income, whichever is less.

Any individual who is self-employed, either full- or part-time, is eligible to set up a Keogh account. They can also be used by individuals who hold full-time jobs and "moonlight" on a part-time basis—for instance, the engineer who has a small consulting business on the side or the accountant who does tax returns in the evenings and on weekends. If the engineer, for example, earns $10,000 a year from his part-time consulting business, he can contribute 25 percent of that income ($2,500) to his Keogh account and, in so doing, reduce both his taxable income and the amount he pays in taxes. Further, he is still eligible to receive full retirement benefits from his full-time job, and to have his own IRA (though, as we'll see below, contributions to his IRA may not qualify for tax shelter).

Keogh accounts can be opened at banks, insurance companies, brokerage houses, mutual funds, and other financial institutions. Annual contributions must be made at the time the respective tax return is filed or by April 15 of the following calendar year (for example, you have until April 15, 2004, to make the contribution to your Keogh for 2003). Although a designated financial institution acts as custodian of all the funds held in a Keogh account, *the actual investments held in the account are under the complete direction of the individual contributor.* These are self-directed retirement programs where the *individual* decides which investments to buy and sell (subject to a few basic restrictions).

The income earned from the investments must be reinvested in the account and it, too, accrues tax free. All Keogh contributions and investment earnings must remain in the account until the individual turns 59½, unless he or she becomes seriously ill or disabled—early withdrawals for any other reason are subject to 10 percent tax penalties. However, the individual is *not required* to start withdrawing the funds at age 59½; the funds can stay in the account (and continue to earn tax-free income) until the individual is 70½ at which time the individual *must* begin withdrawing funds from the account—unless he or she continues to be gainfully employed past the age of 70½ (technically, a participant in a Keogh plan must begin to receive distributions from the plan by April 1 of the year that follows the *latter of:* (1) the year in which the participant turns 70½ or (2) the year in which the participant retires). Of course, once an individual starts withdrawing funds (upon or after turning 59½), all such withdrawals are treated as ordinary income and subject to normal income taxes. Thus, the taxes on all contributions to and earnings from a Keogh account will eventually have to be paid, a characteristic of any tax-*deferred* (as opposed to tax-*free*) program.

A program that's similar in many respects to the Keogh account is something called a *Simplified Employee Pension Plan*—or SEP-IRA for short. It's aimed at small-business owners, particularly those with *no employees*, who want a plan that is simple to set up and administer. SEP-IRAs *can be used in place of Keoghs*, and although they are simpler to administer, they have the same annual contribution caps as a Keogh account—that is, $40,000 per year, or 25 percent of earned income, whichever is less.

Individual Retirement Arrangements (IRAs)

individual retirement arrangement (IRA) A retirement plan, open to any working American, to which a person may contribute a specified amount each year; also known, more popularly, as an *individual retirement account*.

Some people mistakenly believe that an IRA is a specialized type of investment. It is not. Actually, an **individual retirement arrangement (IRA)**, or individual retirement *account*, as it's more commonly known, is virtually the same as any other investment account you open with a bank, credit union, stockbroker, mutual fund, or insurance company, except that it's clearly designated as an IRA. That is, the form you complete designates the account as an IRA and makes the institution its trustee. That is all there is to it. Basically, any gainfully-employed person (and his/her spouse) can have an IRA account, though the type of accounts that a person can have and the tax status of those accounts depend on a number of variables. All IRAs, however, have one thing in common: They're designed to encourage retirement savings on the part of individuals, which they do by sheltering the investment income earned in these accounts from income taxes.

Actually, the whole IRA landscape was altered dramatically in 1997–98, with the introduction of *Roth IRAs*. As it now stands, the individual has a full menu of different types of IRAs to choose from, including the following:

- **Traditional (Deductible) IRA**, which can be opened by anyone without a retirement plan at his or her place of employment, regardless of income level, or by couples filing jointly who, even if they are covered by retirement plans at their places of employment, have adjusted gross incomes of less than $54,000 (or single tax payers with AGIs of less than $34,000). Those individuals who qualify may make tax deductible contributions of up to $3,000 a year to their accounts (an equal tax deductible amount can be contributed by a nonworking spouse). This maximum annual contribution increases to $4,000 in 2005, and $5,000 in 2008 and beyond (and there's a catch-up contribution of an additional $500 to $1,000 per year that can be made by individuals age 50 or older). All earnings in the accounts grow tax free until withdrawn, when ordinary tax rates apply (though a 10 percent penalty normally applies to withdrawals made before age 59½).
- **Nondeductible (After-Tax) IRA**, which is open to anyone, regardless of their income level or whether they are covered by a retirement plan at their place of employment; contributions of up to $3,000 a year in 2003, rising (as with the traditional IRA) to $5,000 in 2008, can be made to this account, but they are made with after-tax dollars (that is, the contributions are not tax deductible). However, the earnings do accrue tax free and are not subject to tax until they are withdrawn, after the individual reaches age 59½ (funds withdrawn before age 59½ may be subject to the 10 percent penalty).

- **Roth IRA**, the newest kid on the block (available only since 1998), can be opened by couples filing jointly with adjusted gross incomes of up to $150,000 (singles up to $95,000), regardless of whether they have other retirement or pension plans. But the neatest part of the Roth account is its tax features—although the annual contributions of up to $3,000 a person in 2003, rising (as with the traditional IRA) to $5,000 in 2008, are made with nondeductible/after-tax dollars, all earnings in the account grow tax free and *all withdrawals from the account are also tax free, as long as the account has been open for at least 5 years and the individual is past the age of 59½*. In other words, as long as these conditions are met, you won't have to pay taxes on any withdrawals you make from your Roth IRA!

The key features and provisions of all three of these IRAs are outlined in Exhibit 14.5.

EXHIBIT 14.5

Qualifying for an IRA

In 1998, the ground rules for opening an IRA changed dramatically with the introduction of the new Roth IRAs. Individuals can now select from three different types of individual retirement accounts.

- **Deductible IRA**
  - For 2003, annual contributions of up to $3,000 by a working taxpayer and $3,000 by a nonworking spouse are fully deductible if the taxpayer is not covered by an employer's pension plan or has adjusted gross income of less than $34,000 a year on a single taxpayer return or $54,000 on a joint return. The maximum annual contribution will increase to $4,000 in 2005, and $5,000 in 2008, and there is an additional $500 to $1,000 per year catch-up contribution that can be made by those age 50 or older.
  - Partial tax deductible contributions are available to joint filers with AGIs (in 2003) of $54,000 to $64,000, and to single filers with AGIs (in 2003) of $34,000 to $44,000—essentially, the deductible contribution is reduced at higher levels of AGI and phases out completely at AGI of $44,000 for single taxpayers and $64,000 for joint returns.
  - The AGI ranges noted above are scheduled to rise annually through 2005/2007 so that the phase out range will rise to $50,000–$60,000 for single filers by 2005, and $80,000–$100,000 for joint filers by 2007.
  - The nonworking spouse of a taxpayer covered by a deductible IRA can also contribute from $3,000 (in 2003) to $5,000 (in 2008) per year to a fully deductible IRA, provided the couple's AGI is $150,000 or less.
- **After-Tax IRA**
  - Working taxpayers who fail to qualify for deductible IRAs, and their nonworking spouses, can make annual nondeductible IRA contributions of up to $3,000 each in 2003, rising (as outlined previously) to $5,000 in 2008.
- **Roth IRA**
  - A working taxpayer with AGI of up to $95,000 on a single return or $150,000 on a joint return can make nondeductible contributions of up to $3,000 (in 2003) to $5,000 (in 2008).
  - The contribution phases out at $110,000 single and $160,000 joint; partial contributions are available to single filers with AGIs of $95,000–$110,000, and joint filers with AGIs of $150,000–$160,000.
  - A nonworking spouse can make after-tax contributions of up to $3,000 per year (in 2003) to $5,000 per year (in 2008) to a Roth IRA with AGI of less than $150,000 on a joint return.

Regardless of the type, and notwithstanding the conditions set out above, penalty-free withdrawals (of up to $10,000) are generally allowed from an IRA as long as the funds are being used for first-time home purchases, qualifying educational costs, certain major medical expenses, or other qualified emergencies. Also, with both the traditional/deductible and nondeductible IRAs, you must start making withdrawals from your account once you reach age 70½—though this requirement does not apply to Roth IRAs. Finally, in addition to the three retirement-based IRAs, 1998 also brought us the so-called *Education IRA*, which can be set up and used to meet the future education (college) cost of a child or grandchild. Specifically, these accounts, which more formally are known as *Coverdell Education Savings Accounts* (or ESAs), can be opened by couples with AGIs of up to $190,000 (or singles with AGIs up to $95,000) for the benefit of a child under the age of 18. Nondeductible annual contributions of up to $2,000 per child are allowed in 2003. As with Roth IRAs, the earnings grow tax free as long as they remain in the account, and all withdrawals (which must be made by the time the beneficiary reaches age 30) are also made tax free and penalty free, as long as the funds are used for qualifying education expenses.

Self-Directed Accounts

IRAs are like Keogh and SEP plans in that they are *self-directed accounts*—meaning you are free to make just about whatever investment decisions you want. Actually, as with any investment, an individual can be conservative or aggressive in choosing securities for an IRA (or Keogh), though the nature of these retirement programs generally favors a more conservative approach. In fact, conventional wisdom favors funding your IRA (and Keogh) with *income-producing assets*; this would also suggest that if you are looking for capital gains, it is best to do so *outside* your retirement account. The reasons are twofold: (1) Growth-oriented securities are by nature *more risky*, and (2) you *cannot write off losses* from the sale of securities held in an IRA (or Keogh) account. This does not mean, however, that it would be altogether inappropriate to place a good-quality growth stock or mutual fund in a Keogh or IRA—in fact, many advisors contend that growth investments should always have a place in your retirement account due to their often impressive performance and ability to counteract inflation. Such investments may pay off handsomely, because they can appreciate totally free of taxes.

In the end, of course, *it is how much you have in your retirement account that matters rather than how your earnings were made along the way*. Also, regardless of what type of investment vehicle you use, keep in mind that once you place money in an IRA, it's meant to stay there for the long haul. For like most tax-sheltered retirement programs, there are restrictions on when you can withdraw the funds from an IRA. Specifically, as noted earlier, any funds withdrawn from an IRA prior to age 59½ are subject to a

Concept ✓

14-8. Which basic features of employer-sponsored pension plans should you be familiar with? Explain.

14-9. Discuss the distinguishing features of (a) *basic*, (b) *qualified*, (c) *defined benefit*, and (d) *contributory pension plans*. Under which procedure will you become fully vested most quickly—cliff or graded vesting? Explain.

14-10. What is the difference between a *profit-sharing plan* and a *salary reduction*, or *401(k), plan?* Are these basic or supplemental plans?

14-11. Why is it important to evaluate and become familiar with the pension plans and retirement benefits offered by your employer? Identify and briefly discuss at least six different plan provisions that you feel would be important in such an evaluation.

14-12. Briefly describe the tax provisions of *401(k) plans* and *Keogh plans*. Would you describe these plans as tax-deferred or tax-free programs? Explain. Describe and differentiate between Keogh plans and *individual retirement arrangements*; what's the difference between a *nondeductible IRA* and an *education IRA?*

10 percent tax penalty, on top of the regular tax paid on the withdrawal. (Note, however, that you can avoid the 10 percent tax penalty and still start withdrawals before age 59½ by setting up a systematic withdrawal program that essentially pays you equal amounts over the rest of your life expectancy; obviously, unless you have a substantial amount of money in your IRA, the annual payments under this program are likely to be pretty small.) In addition, when you move your IRA account to a new firm (this is known as a "roll-over"), the transfer is subject to a *20 percent withholding tax* if the proceeds from the transfer are paid to you directly—the rule is very clear on this: If you take possession of the funds (even for just a few days), you will be hit with the withholding tax. Thus, the best way to handle IRA roll-overs is to *arrange for the transfer of funds from one firm to another.*

So, should you contribute to an IRA or not? Obviously, so long as you qualify for either a traditional/tax-deductible IRA or a Roth IRA (as per the provisions spelled out above), you should seriously consider making the maximum payments allowable. There are no special recordkeeping requirements or forms to file, and the IRA continues to be an excellent vehicle for sheltering income from taxes. Indeed, probably the biggest decision you're going to have to make is which IRA is right for you—the traditional or the Roth? *Hint*: the Roth is probably most appropriate for people in their thirties or forties.

ANNUITIES

LG6

An annuity is just the opposite of life insurance. As we pointed out in Chapter 8, life insurance is the systematic accumulation of an estate that is used for protection against financial loss resulting from premature death. In contrast, an **annuity** is the systematic *liquidation* of an estate in such a way that it provides protection against the economic difficulties that could result from outliving personal financial resources. The period during which premiums are paid toward the purchase of an annuity is called the **accumulation period**; correspondingly, the period during which annuity payments are made is called the **distribution period**.

annuity
An investment product, created by life insurance companies, that provides a series of payments over time.

accumulation period
The period during which premiums are paid for the purchase of an annuity.

distribution period
The period during which annuity payments are made to an annuitant.

survivorship benefit
On an annuity, the portion of premiums and interest that has not been returned to the annuitant prior to his or her death.

Under a pure life annuity contract, a life insurance company will guarantee regular monthly payments to an individual for as long as he or she lives. These benefits are composed of three parts: principal, interest, and survivorship benefits. The *principal* consists of the premium amounts paid in by the *annuitant* (person buying the annuity) during the accumulation period. *Interest* is the amount earned on these funds between the time they are paid and distributed. The interest earnings on an annuity accrue (that is, accumulate) tax free—note, however, while the earnings in an annuity accumulate on a tax-sheltered basis, the amounts paid into an annuity are all made with *after-tax dollars* (that is, there is no special tax treatment given to the capital contributions). The portion of the principal and interest that has not been returned to the annuitant prior to death is the **survivorship benefit**. These funds are available to those members of the annuity group who survive in each subsequent period. By using mortality tables and estimated investment returns, life insurance companies can calculate for a group of annuitants of a given age the amount of monthly payment they can guarantee to each individual without prematurely depleting the total amount accumulated. Consequently, the risk of outliving one's income is eliminated.

CLASSIFICATION OF ANNUITIES

Annuities may be classified according to several key characteristics, including the way the premiums are paid, the disposition of proceeds, inception date of benefits, and the method used in calculating benefits. Exhibit 14.6 presents a chart of this classification system.

EXHIBIT 14.6

Different Types of Annuity Contracts

The different types of annuity contracts vary according to how you pay for the annuity, how the proceeds will be disbursed, how earnings accrue, and when you will receive the benefits.

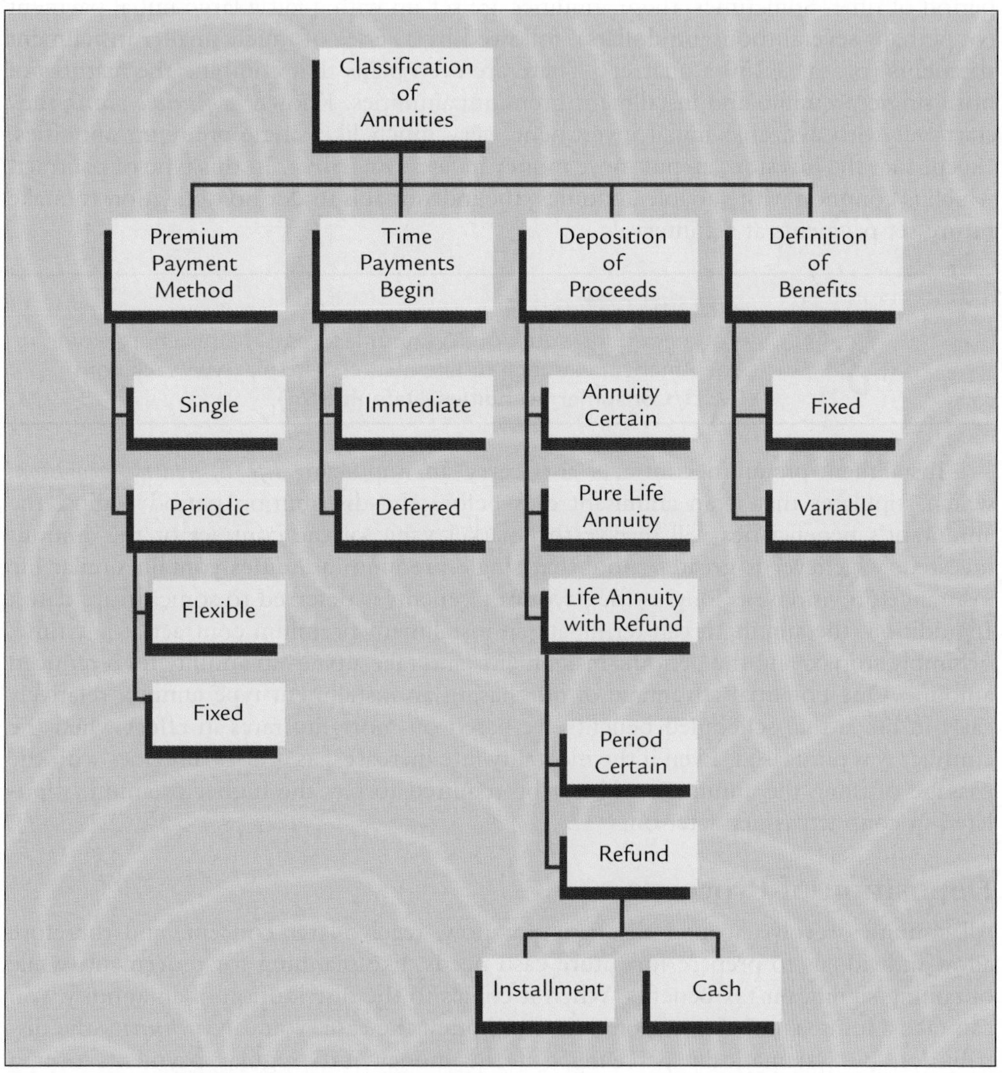

Source: Adapted from Black & Skipper, *Life & Health Insurance*, Thirteenth Edition (Prentice Hall, 2000), p. 163.

single-premium annuity contract An annuity contract purchased with a lump-sum payment.

Single Premium or Installments

There are two ways to pay the premiums when you purchase an annuity contract: you can make a large single (lump-sum) payment right up front, or pay the premium in installments. The **single-premium annuity contract** usually requires a ***minimum investment*** of anywhere from $2,500 to $10,000, with $5,000 the most common figure. These annuities have become very popular, primarily because of the attractive tax features they offer. They are often purchased just before retirement as a way of creating a future stream of income. Sometimes the cash value of a life insurance policy will be used at retirement to acquire a single-premium annuity. This is a highly effective use of a life insurance policy: you get the insurance coverage when you *need* it the most (while you're raising and educating your family) and then a regular stream of income when you can probably *use* it the most (after you've retired).

Although the majority of *group* annuity policies are funded with single premiums, many *individuals* still buy annuities by paying for them in installments. With these so-called **installment-premium annuity contracts**, set payments, starting as low as $100, are made at regular intervals (monthly, quarterly, or annually) over an extended period of time. Sometimes, these annuities are set up with a fairly large initial payment (of perhaps several thousand dollars), followed by a series of much smaller installment payments (of, say, $250 a quarter). There are even plans that combine the features of both single-premium and installment-premium annuities. Known as *flexible plans*, they start out with a sizable initial investment, very much like single-premium annuities, except that the investor can put more money in later, *as desired*. In this type of contract, which is common with variable annuities, the individual is under no obligation to make future set payments at set intervals.

installment-premium annuity contract An annuity contract purchased through periodic payments made over a given period of time.

life annuity with no refund (pure life) An option under which an annuitant receives a specified amount of income for life, regardless of the length of the distribution period; in turn, no payments or refunds are made to the person's family or estate upon his or her death.

guaranteed-minimum annuity An annuity that provides a guaranteed minimum distribution of benefits.

life annuity, period certain A type of guaranteed-minimum annuity in which the annuitant is guaranteed a stated amount of monthly income for life and the insurer agrees to pay that amount for a minimum number of years, regardless of whether the annuitant survives.

smart.sites

For a good introduction to annuities, read the brochure from the American Council of Life Insurers (**http://www.acli.com/ACLI/Consumer/Annuities/Default.htm**).

Installment-premium contracts also carry an important *life insurance provision*, which stipulates that if an annuitant dies before the distribution period begins, the annuitant's beneficiaries will receive the market value of the contract or the amount invested, whichever is greater (note that single-premium annuities contain similar life insurance provisions, as long as the payout of benefits is deferred to some future date). In addition, the annuitant can terminate an installment-premium contract at any time, or simply stop paying the periodic installments and take a paid-up annuity for a reduced amount. One potential advantage of purchasing an installment-type annuity relatively early in life is that scheduled benefits are based on mortality rates in effect when the contract was purchased. Even if the mortality rate increases, as it normally does with the passage of time, the annuitant will not be required to pay the higher premium stipulated in contracts issued later on.

Deposition of Proceeds

All annuities revolve around the basic pay-now, receive-later concept, and therefore allow individuals to prepare for future cash needs, like planning for retirement, while obtaining significant tax benefits. When it comes to the distribution of an annuity, you can take a lump-sum payment, or, as is more often the case, you can *annuitize* the distribution by systematically parceling out the money into regular payments over a defined or open-ended period. Because most people choose to annuitize their proceeds (which is conceptually the way an annuity should be used), let's look at the most common annuity disbursement options:

- **Life annuity with no refund (pure life):** The annuitant receives a specified amount of income for life, whether the disbursement period turns out to be 1 year or 50 years. The estate or family receives no refunds when the annuitant dies. This results in the largest monthly payments of any of the distribution methods, because the issuer (a life insurance company) does not have to distribute the principal, if any, to the annuitant's heirs.

- **Guaranteed minimum annuity (life annuity with refund):** In this type of contract, the benefits (future cash flows) are not limited to the annuitant only, but may also extend to named beneficiaries. There are two forms of this annuity. With a **life annuity, period certain**, the annuitant gets a guaranteed monthly income for life, with the added provision that the insurance company will pay the monthly benefits for at least a minimum number of years (five or ten, for example). If the annuitant dies soon after the distribution begins, his or her beneficiaries receive the monthly benefits for the balance of the "period certain." With a **refund annuity**, if the annuitant dies, the designated beneficiary receives monthly payments (or in some cases, a lump-sum cash refund) until the total purchase price of the annuity has been refunded.
- **Annuity certain:** This type of annuity pays a set amount of monthly income for a specified number of years, thereby filling a need for monthly income that will expire after a certain length of time. An annuitant selecting a 10-year annuity certain receives payments for 10 years after retirement, regardless of whether he or she lives for 2 or 20 more years. For example, a widow, age 52, could use a 10-year annuity certain contract to provide income until she reaches age 62 and can apply for Social Security benefits.

refund annuity A type of guaranteed-minimum annuity that, upon the annuitant's death, makes monthly payments to the designated beneficiary until the total purchase price of the annuity has been refunded.

annuity certain An annuity that provides a specified monthly income for a stated number of years, without consideration of any life contingency.

Immediate Versus Deferred Annuity

An annuitant usually has the choice of receiving monthly benefits immediately upon buying an annuity or of deferring receipt for a number of years. Logically, the first type is called an immediate annuity and the latter a deferred annuity. An **immediate annuity**, purchased with a single premium, is most often used in conjunction with the cash value or death proceeds of a life insurance policy to create a stream of cash receipts needed for retirement or to support a survivor or dependent children.

A **deferred annuity**, in contrast, can be bought with either a single payment or through an installment plan. This contract is quite flexible and can be issued with numerous options for paying the premiums and receiving the proceeds. The big advantage of a deferred annuity is that your savings can build up over time, free of taxes. With no taxes to pay, you have more money working for you and, thus, can build up a bigger retirement nest egg (of course, you'll have to pay taxes on your earnings eventually, but not until you start receiving payments from your annuity). Most annuities purchased under group contracts are immediate annuities, whereas those purchased by individuals are usually of the *deferred* type. In fact, because of their attractive tax features, a lot of people buy deferred annuities—and especially single-premium deferred annuities—more as a tax-sheltered *investment vehicle* than anything else.

immediate annuity An annuity in which the annuitant begins receiving monthly benefits immediately.

deferred annuity An annuity in which benefit payments are deferred for a certain number of years.

Fixed Versus Variable Annuity

When you put your money into an annuity, the premium is invested on your behalf by the insurance company, much as a mutual fund invests the money you put into it. From the time you pay the annuity premium until it is paid back to you as a lump sum or as an annuitized monthly benefit, you'll earn a rate of return on your investment. How that rate of return is figured determines whether you own a fixed or variable annuity. In a **fixed rate annuity** the insurance company safeguards your principal and agrees to pay a guaranteed minimum rate of interest over the life of the contract—which often amounts to little more than prevailing money market rates that existed at the time you bought the contract. These are conservative, very low risk annuity products that essentially promise to return *the original investment plus interest* when the money is paid out to the annuitant (or any designated beneficiaries). Unlike bond mutual funds, fixed annuities do not fluctuate in value when interest rates rise or fall; your principal is therefore secure at all times. These *interest-earning annuities*, as

fixed rate annuity An annuity in which the insurance company safeguards your principal and agrees to pay a guaranteed rate of interest on your money.

they're also called, are ideally suited for the cautious investor who likes the secure feeling of knowing what his or her monthly cash flow will be.

Imagine an investment vehicle that lets you move between stocks, bonds, and money funds and, at the same time, accumulate profits tax free. That, in a nutshell, is a variable annuity. With a **variable annuity** contract, the amount that's ultimately paid out to the annuitant varies with the investment results obtained by the insurance company—*nothing* is guaranteed, not even the principal! When you buy a variable annuity, *you decide* where your money will be invested, based on your investment objectives and tolerance for risk; you can usually choose from stocks, bonds, money market securities, or some combination thereof. Insurance companies typically offer five or six stock and bond funds, as well as money market investments for short-term safety; some companies even offer a relatively exotic fleet of alternatives, ranging from zero coupon bonds to real estate and foreign securities. As an annuity holder, you can stay put with a single investment for the long haul, or, as with most variable annuities, you can aggressively play the market by switching from one fund to another. Obviously, when the market goes up, investors in variable annuities do well; but, when the market falters, the returns on these policies can go down as well.

variable annuity An annuity in which the monthly income provided by the policy varies according to the actual investment experience of the insurer.

Because the payoff from a variable annuity depends to such an extent on the fate of the markets, ***the annuitants take a chance that their monthly income will be less than anticipated.*** Of course, most people who participate in variable annuity plans fully expect to be able to outperform fixed annuities. But that doesn't always happen, as we saw in the nasty 2000–02 bear market, which had a devastating effect on variable annuities and caused variable annuity returns to fall well below the returns on corresponding fixed-rate plans. Annuitants, however, do have some control over this type of risk exposure, because they can choose to go with high- or low-risk investment vehicles and, in so doing, influence the certainty of return. In effect, if you go with an account that stresses high-risk securities, you should expect a good deal of uncertainty in return—the potential for high return might be there, but so is the chance for loss. If you're uncomfortable with that, stick to annuities that offer safer investment choices (such as zero coupon bonds or Treasury securities).

Also, although there's nothing to prohibit you from staying with market-sensitive variable annuities during both the accumulation and distribution periods, in most cases you can convert to a fixed annuity at distribution. What you do, in effect, is use the cash value in your variable annuity to buy a paid-up fixed annuity. In this way, you use a ***variable annuity during the accumulation period*** to build up your capital as much as possible, and then switch to a ***fixed annuity for the distribution period*** to obtain a certain, well-defined stream of future income.

smart.sites

How large an annuity do you need to buy to get a $1,300 monthly payment? The annuities calculator at ImmediateAnnuities.com, **http://www.immediateannuities.com**, provides a quick answer as well as companies offering the product in your state.

Financial Road Sign

Are Annuities Right for You?

You may want to consider annuities if you:

1. Have contributed the maximum to your 401(k) plans and IRAs, but want more tax-deferred investment gains
2. Prefer investing in mutual funds over individual securities
3. Will keep the annuity for at least 15 to 20 years
4. Are in a 28 percent or higher income tax bracket today, but expect to be in a lower tax bracket in retirement
5. Don't need the annuity proceeds prior to age 59½
6. Are unconcerned that your heirs must pay ordinary income taxes on any appreciation
7. Desire a "guaranteed" income for life in retirement

Source: Adapted from "Annuities: What's to Like?" *The Motley Fool*, **http://www.fool.com/retirement/annuities/annuities.htm**.

Sources and Costs of Annuities

Annuities are administered by life insurance companies, and, for that reason, it should come as no surprise that they're also the leading sellers of these financial products. Annuities can also be purchased from stock brokers, mutual fund organizations, banks, and financial planners. When you buy an annuity, the cost will vary with the age of the annuitant at issue, the age of the annuitant when payments begin, the method used to distribute benefits, the number of lives covered, and the sex of the annuitant. Exhibit 14.7 provides some real-life examples of the lump-sum costs of two types of immediate annuities. Note the substantial differences that exist among the companies' premiums. These differences confirm the need to shop around before making an annuity purchase. Note, too, that in every category the cost to females is higher than the cost to males, because of the lower mortality rates among women.

In addition, as with mutual funds, there are some annual fees you should be aware of. In particular, be prepared to pay insurance fees of 1 percent or more—and that's on top of annual management fees of perhaps 1 to 2 percent paid on variable annuities. That's a total of 2 to 3 percent—or more—taken right off the top, year after year. And then there's also a *contract charge* (or maintenance fee) that's deducted annually to cover various contract-related expenses; these fees usually run from about $30 to $60 per year. Obviously, these fees can drag down returns and reduce the advantage of tax-deferred income. Finally, as we'll see later, most annuities charge hefty *penalties for early withdrawal*; meaning that in order to get out of a poorly performing annuity, you'll have to forfeit a chunk of your money.

EXHIBIT 14.7

Lump-Sum Costs Necessary for Funding Payments of $100 a Month

Annuity costs vary not only by the type of annuity and the sex and age of the beneficiary, but also by the company selling the contract. Clearly, it pays to shop around. Here are some costs quoted by four life insurance companies; note that it would cost a 55-year-old male about 22 percent less to buy a life annuity contract from Company 2 than from Company 3.

	Life Annuity with No Refund					
	Male			Female		
Company	55	65	75	55	65	75
1	$13,110	$11,170	$8,510	$13,930	$12,280	$9,700
2	11,820	10,250	8,010	12,450	11,140	8,980
3	15,020	11,970	8,420	16,510	13,440	9,580
4	12,900	10,960	8,480	13,660	11,860	9,270
	Life Annuity—10 Years Certain					
	Male			Female		
Company	55	65	75	55	65	75
1	$13,400	$11,840	$10,170	$14,070	$12,660	$10,770
2	12,050	10,800	9,390	12,560	11,440	9,870
3	N/A	N/A	N/A	N/A	N/A	N/A
4	13,190	11,570	9,940	13,790	12,200	10,300

The Investment and Income Properties of Annuities

A major attribute of most types of annuities is that they provide a source of income that cannot be outlived. Although individuals might be able to create a similar arrangement by simply living off the interest or dividends from their investments, they would find it difficult to engage in the systematic liquidation of their principal in a manner that would be timed to coincide closely (or exactly) with their death. Also viewed very positively is the fact that the income earned in an annuity is allowed to accumulate tax free; thus, it provides a form of *tax-sheltered investment.* Actually, the income from an annuity is *tax deferred*, meaning that taxes on the earnings will have to be paid when the annuity is liquidated.

Although shelter from taxes is an attractive investment attribute, there is a hitch. You may be faced with a big tax penalty if you close out or withdraw money from an annuity before it's time. Specifically, the IRS treats annuity withdrawals like withdrawals from an individual retirement arrangement, meaning that except in cases of serious illness, *anybody who takes money out before reaching age 59½ will incur a 10 percent tax penalty.* Thus, if you're under age 59½ and in the 28 percent tax bracket, you'll end up paying a 38 percent tax rate on any funds withdrawn from an annuity. (The IRS views withdrawals *as taxable income* until the account balance falls to the amount of original paid-in principal—after which any further withdrawals are tax free.) Short of some type of serious illness, about the only way to tap your account penalty-free before you're 59½ is to *annuitize.* Unfortunately, the annuity payments must be spread out over your estimated remaining life span, which means the size of each monthly payment could end up being pretty small. All of which only reinforces the notion that *an annuity should always be considered a long-term investment.* Assume that it's a part of your retirement program (that's the way the IRS looks at it) and that you're getting in for the long haul, because it's not that easy to get out before you turn 59½.

From an investment perspective, the returns generated from an annuity can, in some cases, prove to be a bit disappointing. For instance, as we discussed earlier, the returns on *variable annuities* are tied to returns in the money and capital markets; even so, they are still no better than what you can get from other investment vehicles—and, as you can see in Exhibit 14.8, they are often lower, due in part to higher annuity fees. And keep in mind, these differential returns aren't due to tax features, because in both cases returns were measured on a before-tax basis. But *returns from annuities are tax-sheltered*, so that makes those lower returns look a lot more attractive. If you're considering a variable annuity, go over it much the same way you would a traditional mutual fund: Look for superior past performance, proven management talents, and the availability of attractive investment alternatives that you can switch in and out of. And *pay particular attention to an annuity's total expense rate.* For although these products have a (bad) reputation for being heavily loaded with fees and

Concept ✓

14-13. What is an annuity? Briefly explain how an *annuity* works, and also how it differs from a life insurance policy. Differentiate between a *single-premium annuity* and an *installment-premium annuity*.

14-14. Briefly explain the three procedures that are most widely used in the distribution of annuity proceeds. Which one results in the highest monthly payment?

14-15. Describe and differentiate among (a) an *immediate annuity*, (b) a *deferred annuity*, (c) a *straight life annuity*, and (d) a *refund annuity*.

14-16. What is a *fixed-rate annuity*, and how does it differ from a *variable annuity*? Does the type of contract (whether it's fixed or variable) have any bearing on the amount of money you'll receive at the time of distribution? Explain. Which type of contract would probably be most suitable for someone who wants a minimum amount of risk exposure? What's the purpose of a bailout provision in a fixed-rate annuity?

14-17. How do variable annuity returns compare to mutual fund returns? Can you offer any logical reasons as to why there would be any difference in comparable returns? Explain.

charges, it is possible to find annuities with above-average performance and relatively low fee structures! That's the combination you're looking for.

EXHIBIT 14.8

The Comparative Returns of Variable Annuities Versus Mutual Funds

Variable annuities are structured and operate very much like mutual funds, so you'd expect their performance to be comparable. But as we see here, that's not always the case.

	Average Annual Return (Over 5-Year Period Ending 6/30/03)	
Variable Annuity or Mutual Fund Category	**Variable Annuities**	**Mutual Funds**
Aggressive Growth	–3.10%	0.61%
Growth	–2.05	0.47
Growth and Income	–1.98	–0.71
International Stocks	–3.52	–2.85
Balanced	0.63	1.42
Corporate Bonds	4.96	7.56
Government Bonds	5.47	7.05
High-Yield Bonds	–0.73	7.34
International Bonds	5.01	8.70

Source: *Morningstar.*

As far as *fixed-rate annuities* are concerned, although many of them advertise high rates of return, a close look at the fine print reveals that such rates are guaranteed only for the first 1 to 5 years, after which time they drop to something closer to money market yields—or less. True, there are minimum guaranteed rates that the annuities have to stand behind, but these are usually so low that they're really not much help. Investors generally have little choice but to accept the going rate or surrender the policy. Surrendering can be painful, however, not only because of IRS penalties, but also because of the hefty *surrender fees* that are found on many of these contracts (these fees often amount to 5 to 10 percent of the account balance in the first year and then gradually decline to zero, normally over a period of 5 to 7 years).

It's possible to get around a surrender fee if the annuity has a *bailout* clause. Such a provision allows you to withdraw your money, free of any surrender fees, if the rate of return on the annuity falls below a certain level (say, a point or so below the initial rate). But you have to act fairly quickly, because the bailout provision may exist for only a limited period. Of course, even if you exercise a bailout provision, you may still have to face a tax penalty for early withdrawal—unless you transfer the funds to another annuity through what is known as a *1035 exchange.*

How Good is the Insurance Company?

One final point: If you're seriously considering buying an annuity, make sure you carefully read the contract and see what the guaranteed rates are, how long the initial rate applies, and if a bailout provision exists. Just as important, because *the annuity is only as good as the insurance company that stands behind it,* check to see how the company is rated by Best's, Standard & Poor's, or Moody's. It's important to make sure that the insurance company itself is financially sound before buying one of its annuity products. After all, there is no FDIC or other federal agency to step in and pick up the pieces.

In Chapter 8 we provided a list of some of the stronger life insurance companies; *that same list can be used to check out the issuer of a fixed or variable annuity.* You can also do the checking yourself by referring to Best's, Standard & Poor's, or Moody's. These independent rating agencies provide quality ratings (on hundreds of insurance companies) that are much like those found in the bond market and are meant to reflect the financial strength of the firm. Letter grades are assigned on the principle that the stronger the company, the lower the risk of loss—accordingly, if security is important to you, stick with insurers that carry one of the top ratings (A++ or A+ for Best's; AAA or AA for S&P; and Aaa or Aa for Moody's); see Chapter 8 for more discussion on these insurance ratings and how they work.

SUMMARY

LG1. Recognize the importance of retirement planning and identify the three biggest pitfalls to good planning. Retirement planning plays a vital role in the personal financial planning process. It employs many of the same basic principles and concepts of effective financial planning, including the establishment of financial goals and strategies, the use of savings and investment plans, and the use of certain insurance products, such as annuities. The three biggest pitfalls to sound retirement planning are starting too late, not saving enough, and investing too conservatively.

LG2. Establish your income needs in retirement, and estimate your retirement income. Rather than address retirement planning in a series of short-run (3- to 5-year) plans, it's best to take a long-term approach and look 20 to 30 years into the future to determine how much saving and investing you must do today to achieve the retirement goals you've set for tomorrow. Implementing a long-term retirement plan involves determining future retirement needs, estimating retirement income from known sources (such as Social Security and company pension plans), and deciding how much to save and invest each year to build up a desired nest egg.

LG3. Explain the eligibility requirements and benefits of the Social Security program. Social Security forms the basic foundation for the retirement programs of most families; except for a few exempt classes (mostly government employees), almost all gainfully employed workers are covered by Social Security. Upon retirement, covered workers are entitled to certain monthly benefits, as determined mainly by the employee's earning history and age at retirement.

LG4. Differentiate among the different types of basic and supplemental employer-sponsored pension plans. Employer-sponsored pension and retirement plans provide a vital source of retirement income to many individuals. Such plans can often spell the difference between enjoying a comfortable standard of living in retirement or a bare subsistence. In *basic* retirement programs, all employees participate after a certain period of employment. These plans can be defined contribution or defined benefits plans. There are also several forms of *supplemental* employer-sponsored programs, including profit-sharing plans, thrift and savings plans, and, perhaps the most popular of all, salary reduction plans such as the so-called 401(k) plans.

LG5. Describe the various types of self-directed retirement plans. In addition to company-sponsored retirement programs, individuals can set up their own self-directed tax-sheltered retirement plans; it is through such plans that most individuals can build up the nest eggs they will need to meet the retirement objectives they have set for themselves. The basic types of self-directed retirement programs are Keogh and SEP plans for self-employed individuals, and various forms of IRAs, which can be set up by any salary or wage earner.

LG6. Choose the right type of annuity for your retirement plan. Annuities are also an important source of income for retired people. Basically, an annuity is an investment vehicle that allows investment income to accumulate on a tax-deferred basis, and provides for the systematic liquidation (payout) of all invested capital and earnings over an extended period of time. A wide variety of annuities exists, including single payment and installment-premium, fixed and variable, and immediate and deferred; different payout options also exist.

FINANCIAL PLANNING EXERCISES

1. DeShawn Thomas, a 25-year-old personal loan officer at First State Bank, understands the importance of starting early when it comes to saving for retirement. She has designated $3,000 per year for her retirement fund and assumes she will retire at age 65.
   a. How much will she have if she invests in CDs and similar money market instruments that earn 4 percent on average?
   b. How much will she have if she invests in equities instead and earns 10 percent on average?
   c. DeShawn is urging her friend, Mark Randolph, to start his plan right away, too, because he is 35. What would his nest egg amount to if he invested in the same manner as DeShawn and he, too, retires at age 65? Comment on your findings.

2. *Use Worksheet 14.1* to help Al and Linda Gonzales, who would like to retire while they are still relatively young—in about 20 years. Both have promising careers, and both make good money. As a result, they are willing to put aside whatever is necessary to achieve a comfortable lifestyle in retirement. Their current level of household expenditures (excluding savings) is around $75,000 a year, and they expect to spend *even more* in retirement; they think they'll need about 125 percent of that amount (*note*: 125 percent equals a multiplier factor of 1.25). They estimate that their Social Security benefits will amount to $20,000 a year in today's dollars and they will receive another $35,000 annually from their company pension plans. They feel that future inflation will amount to about 3 percent a year; in addition, they think they will be able to earn about 12 percent on their investments prior to retirement and about 8 percent afterward. Use Worksheet 14.1 to find out how big their investment nest egg will have to be and how much they will have to save annually in order to accumulate the needed amount within the next 20 years.
3. Many critics of the Social Security program feel that participants are getting a substandard investment return on their money. Discuss why you agree or disagree with this point of view.
4. Use Exhibit 14.4 to determine the amount of Social Security retirement benefits that Elwood Cheeseater would receive annually if he had a high (that is, "maximum") level of career earnings, is age 62, has a dependent wife (also age 62), and a part-time job that pays him $24,000 a year. If Elwood also receives another

$47,500 a year from a company pension and some tax-exempt bonds that he holds, will he be liable for any tax on his Social Security income? Explain.

5. Diane Fein has just graduated from college and is considering job offers from two companies. Although the salary and insurance benefits are similar, the retirement programs are not. One firm offers a 401(k) plan that matches employee contributions with $.25 for every $1 contributed by the employee, up to a $10,000 limit. The other has a contributory plan that allows employees to contribute up to 10 percent of their annual salary through payroll deduction and matches it dollar for dollar. The plan vests fully after 5 years. Because Diane is unfamiliar with these plans, explain the features of each to her so she can make an informed decision.
6. John Yee is an operations manager for a large manufacturer. He earned $68,500 in 2003 and plans to contribute the maximum allowed to the firm's 401(k) plan. Assuming that John is in the 28 percent tax bracket, calculate his taxable income and the amount of his tax savings. How much did it actually cost John on an after-tax basis to make this retirement plan contribution?
7. At what age would you like to retire? What type of lifestyle do you envision (for example, where do you want to live, do you want to work part-time, and so on)? Discuss the steps you think you should take to realize this goal.
8. Describe the three basic types of IRA (traditional, Roth, and nondeductible), including their respective tax features and what it takes to qualify for each. Which is most appealing to you personally? Explain.
9. Dave Jones is in his early thirties and is thinking about opening an IRA; however, he can't decide whether to open a traditional/deductible IRA or a Roth IRA, so he turns to you for help.
   a. To help you in your explanation, you decide to *run some comparative numbers on the two types of accounts*; for starters, use a 25-year period to show Dave what contributions of $3,000 per year will amount to (after 25 years), given he can earn, say, 10 percent on his money. Will the type of account he opens have any impact on this amount? Explain.
   b. Given Dave is in the 30 percent tax bracket (and will remain there for the next 25 years), determine the annual and total (over 25 years) tax savings he will enjoy from the $3,000-a-year contributions to his IRA; contrast the (annual and total) tax savings he would generate from a traditional IRA with that from a Roth IRA.
   c. Now, fast-forward 25 years. Given the size of Dave's account in 25 years (as computed in part **a**), assume he takes it all out in one lump sum. If he's still in the 30 percent tax bracket, how much will he have, *after taxes*, with a traditional IRA compared with a Roth IRA? How do the taxes computed here compare with those computed in part **b**? Comment on your findings.
   d. Based on the numbers you computed above, as well as any other factors, what kind of IRA would you recommend Dave set up? Explain. Would the fact that maximum contributions are scheduled to increase to $5,000 per year make any difference in your analysis? Explain.
10. Explain how the purchase of a variable annuity is much like an investment in a mutual fund. Do you, as a buyer, have any control over the amount of investment risk to which you're exposed in a variable annuity contract? Explain.
11. Briefly explain why annuities are a type of tax-sheltered investment. Is there anything you have to give up to obtain this tax-favored treatment? (*Hint:* age 59½)

12. Why is it important to check the financial ratings of an insurance company when buying an annuity? Why should you look at past performance when considering the purchase of a variable annuity?
13. Briefly describe the main characteristics of defined contribution and defined benefit pension plans, and discuss how they differ from cash balance plans. In each of these plans, does the employee or employer bear the risk of poor investment performance?
14. Use Exhibit 14.4 to determine the annual Social Security benefit for Chester Atherton, assuming that he had an "average" career earnings level. Chester is 65 years old and earns $18,000 a year at a part-time job. (Note that Chester is already at "full retirement age," since he was born well before 1960.) What would Chester's annual benefit be if he were only 62 years old?

15. ***Use Worksheet 14.1*** to assist Linda Bailey with her retirement planning needs. She plans to retire in 15 years, and her current household expenditures run about $50,000 per year. Linda estimates that she will spend 80 percent of that amount in retirement. Her Social Security benefit is estimated at $15,000 per year, and she will receive $12,000 per year from her employer's pension plan (both in today's dollars). Additional assumptions include an inflation rate of 4 percent, and a rate of return on retirement assets of 9 percent a year prior to retirement and 6 percent afterward. Use Worksheet 14.1 to calculate the required size of Linda's retirement nest egg, and the amount that she must save annually over the next 15 years in order to reach that goal.
16. What are the main differences between fixed-rate and variable annuities? Which type is more appropriate for someone who is 60 years old and close to retirement?

APPLYING PERSONAL FINANCE

Your Ideal Retirement Plan!

Many people have little or no money set aside for their retirement needs. Those who do may find their retirement funds insufficient for them to maintain their desired standard of living during retirement. The purpose of this project is for you to contemplate the type and features of a retirement program that would best meet your needs.

Looking back over this chapter, review the features of both employer-sponsored and self-directed retirement programs. Depending on your career, you may actually have both kinds. Develop an outline of your ideal retirement plan or plans, being sure to give due consideration to the following issues:

1. Would the plan be contributory or noncontributory?
2. Stated as a *percent* of your base salary, how much would be put into your retirement plan each year? Remember that there are certain allowable limits.
3. What would be the eligibility and vesting provisions? Would your plan be portable? Under what conditions?
4. What would be the earliest retirement age? Would there be provisions for early retirement?
5. Would your plan be a defined contribution or a defined benefit plan? You could also have a combination of the two types.
6. Would the plan be qualified?
7. Would you want a voluntary supplemental plan as part of your program? If you could have only one supplemental plan, what would it be?

What would be the advantages and disadvantages of your ideal plan? This research will help you understand the retirement benefits that you may have with your current job or of job offers you may receive in the future.

Contemporary Case Applications

14.1 Comparing Pension Plan Features: Which Plan Is Best?

Mary Maloney and Ellen Saperstein are neighbors in Kansas City. Mary works as a systems engineer for United Foods Corporation, while Ellen works as an executive assistant for U.S. Steel and Castings. Both are married, have two children, and are well paid. Before Mary and Ellen joined their respective companies, there had been some employee unrest and strikes. To counteract these problems, their firms had developed job enrichment and employee motivation programs. Of particular interest are the portions of these programs that deal with pensions and retirement.

United Foods Corp., Mary's company, has a contributory plan under which 5 percent of the employees' annual wages is deducted to meet the cost of the benefits. An amount equal to the employee contribution is also contributed by the company. The plan uses a 5-year graded vesting procedure; it has a normal retirement age of 60 for all employees, and the benefits at retirement are paid according to a defined contribution plan.

Although U.S. Steel and Castings, Ellen's company, has a minimum retirement age of 60, it provides an extension period of 5 to 6 years before compulsory retirement. Employees (full-time, hourly, or salaried) must meet participation requirements. Further, in contrast to the United Foods plan, the U.S. Steel and Castings program has a noncontributory feature. Annual retirement benefits are computed according to the following formula: 2 percent of the employee's final annual salary for each year of service with the company is paid upon retirement. The plan vests immediately.

Questions

1. Discuss the basic features of the retirement plans offered by United Foods Corp. and U.S. Steel and Castings.
2. Which plan do you think is more desirable? Consider the basic features, retirement age, and benefit computations as explained above.
3. Explain how you would use each of these plans in developing your own retirement program.
4. What role, if any, could the purchase of annuities play in these retirement programs? Discuss the pros and cons of using annuities as a part of retirement planning.

14.2 Evaluating Lydia Sanchez's Retirement Prospects

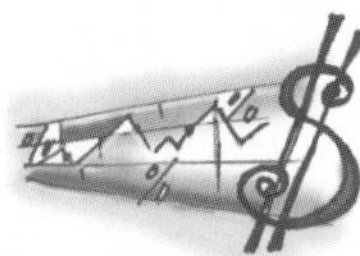

Lydia Sanchez is 57 years old and has been widowed for 13 years. Never remarried, she has worked full-time since her husband died—in addition to raising her two children, the youngest of whom is now finishing college. Forced back to work in her forties, her first job was in a fast-food restaurant. Eventually, she upgraded her skills sufficiently to obtain a supervisory position in the personnel department of a major corporation, where she is now earning $58,000 a year.

Although her financial focus for the past 13 years has, by necessity, been on meeting living expenses and getting her kids through college, she feels she can now turn her attention to her retirement needs. Actually, Lydia hasn't done too badly in that area either. Due to some shrewd investing of the proceeds from her husband's life insurance policy, Lydia has accumulated the following investment assets:

Money market securities, stocks, and bonds	$72,600
IRA and 401(k) plans	$47,400

Other than the mortgage on her condo, the only other debt she has is $7,000 in college loans.

Lydia would like to retire in 8 years and recently hired a financial planner to help her come up with an effective retirement program. He has estimated that for her to live comfortably in retirement, she'll need about $37,500 a year (in today's dollars) in retirement income.

Questions

1. Use Exhibit 14.5 to estimate the amount of annual income Lydia can expect from Social Security.
2. After taking into account the income she'll receive from Social Security and her company-sponsored pension plan, the financial planner has estimated that Lydia's investment assets will need to provide her with about $15,000 a year to meet the balance of her retirement income needs. Assuming a 6 percent after-tax return on her investments, how big of a nest egg will she need to earn that kind of income?
3. Given she can invest the money market securities, stocks, and bonds (the $72,600) at 5 percent after taxes, and the amount she's presently accumulated in her tax-sheltered IRA and 401(k)—the $47,400—at 9 percent, how much will her investment assets be worth in 8 years, when she retires?
4. Lydia's employer matches her 401(k) contributions dollar for dollar, up to a maximum of $3,000 a year. If she continues to put $3,000 a year into that program, how much more will she have in 8 years, given a 9 percent rate of return?
5. What would you advise Lydia about her ability to retire in eight years, as she hopes to?

MONEY ONLINE

Retire in Style!

Note: Web addresses change frequently, so you may need to determine the home page and do a site search to find the page or topic that's referenced.

1. **http://www.quicken.com/retirement/planner**

How much do you need to save for retirement? Find out by using Quicken's "Retirement Planner" to determine how much you will need in order to meet your retirement goals. While you're there, look under "Investing Education" to learn more about 401(k)s, IRAs, and retirement in general.

2. **http://www.financenter.com/consumertools**

How much of an effect can inflation have on retirement plans? What happens if tax laws change? Which savings should be used first in retirement? The FinanCenter provides calculators to help you with these and many other retirement planning issues. Under "Calculators," click on "Retirement," and start planning for your retirement today!

3. **http://www.ssa.gov**

What are the latest issues concerning Social Security? Find out at the Web site of the Social Security Administration. While you're there, learn about the services they provide for businesses, read up on Social Security laws and regulations, or report Social Security fraud.

4. **http://www.smartmoney.com/retirement**

Should you borrow from your 401(k)? How should you handle a lump-sum distribution? What are five things you should know about your 401(k)? Scroll down to the "Index" at the bottom of SmartMoney's "Retirement" page to find numerous articles concerning every aspect of retirement and retirement plans.

5. **http://www.pbgc.gov**
What happens when a pension plan runs out of money or is terminated? What type of plan does the PBGC insure? What guarantees are provided? Click on "Publications" and then on "Fact Sheets" to learn the role of the Pension Benefit Guaranty Corporation in protecting defined benefit plans. Click on "Pension Search" to find names of people owed unclaimed benefits from pension plans that were closed.

6. **http://quicken.com/retirement/RIRA/planner**
Do you qualify for a Roth IRA? Which IRA option is best for you? What income should you expect from an IRA during retirement? Let Quicken's "IRA Analyzer" help you with these and other IRA questions.

7. **http://www.sec.gov/investor/pubs/varannty.htm**
Are variable annuities right for you? Understand the features and complexities of these confusing investments *before* you buy one! The Securities and Exchange Commission offers a general description of variable annuities, how they work, the fees and charges involved, and questions you should ask before purchasing one.

8. **http://www.fidelity.com**
Set up a retirement plan of your own if you're self-employed or own a small business. Under "Planning & Retirement," click on "Retirement Resource Center" to learn more about "Fidelity's Retirement Plans for Small Business." Find an overview of the types of plans available to business owners and the advantages, features, and responsibilities of each.

9. **http://personal.vanguard.com**
Tap into Vanguard's wealth of investor educational material! Click on "Planning & Advice" and find investment basics, investment guides, investor resources, and answers to top financial questions. Read their "Plain Talk" brochures online or order them by mail. Find a list of books for recommended reading or find links to many other investor Web sites.

Just for Fun!

10. **http://www.lib.lsu.edu/gov/fedgov.html**
Ever wonder how to find or contact a federal agency? Consult the U.S. Federal Government Agencies Directory compiled by the Louisiana State University Libraries and find links to federal agencies on the Internet. Pull up sites belonging to the White House, the U.S. Supreme Court, or the U.S. Senate or House of Representatives. Search by Keyword to find the agency of your choice. Another great resource for finding information is **http://www.firstgov.gov**, the U.S. government's official Web portal.

CHAPTER 15 Preserving Your Estate

Learning Goals

LG1. Describe the role of estate planning in personal financial planning and identify the seven steps involved in the process.
LG2. Recognize the importance of preparing a will and other documents to protect you and your estate.
LG3. Explain how trusts are used in estate planning.
LG4. Determine whether a gift will be taxable and use planned gifts to reduce estate taxes.
LG5. Calculate federal and state taxes due on an estate.
LG6. Use effective estate-planning techniques to minimize estate taxes.

The Dreaded Phone Call

When the phone rang at 4 a.m. on March 31, 2004, Carolyn Robbins knew immediately that it was bad news. Her 60-year-old father, Frederick, had suffered massive injuries in a traffic accident and was in a coma. The doctors did not know if he would recover. Her stepmother was devastated, because she and Carolyn's dad had been married only 1 year. Carolyn flew from Los Angeles to Chicago to be with her brother at her father's bedside and to see what steps they needed to take next.

Like so many families, Carolyn's found it very hard to discuss money matters, and talking about wills and dying was even worse. Her stepmother said that the newlyweds had been meaning to revise their wills and prepare living wills and durable powers of attorney for healthcare but hadn't yet gotten around to them. Now they did not know what, if any, life-sustaining measures he would want taken. Fortunately—or unfortunately as the case may be—they did not have to make educated guesses as to his wishes because he died 2 days later without regaining consciousness.

Until they contacted his lawyer and found out where Frederick kept all his important papers, they were unsure how to proceed with funeral arrangements. He had left no letter of last instructions, so the family was unsure of the type of funeral he would have liked. His will named Carolyn as his executor, but he had never discussed this with his children, and her older brother was upset that he had not been chosen. When they found his life insurance policy, they got another surprise. He had never changed the beneficiary of his life insurance policy when he remarried, so his ex-wife was still named and would receive the proceeds. In addition, Frederick had not kept up with changing estate-planning laws or the latest estate-planning techniques, nor had he taken any steps to minimize the costs of estate administration or estate taxes. As currently structured, his estate totaled $1.65 million—above the allowable exclusion amount and therefore subject to estate taxes—and would have to go through the probate process, which could cost more and certainly would take longer than if he had established a living trust.

Her dad's poor planning made Carolyn realize that no matter what your age, you need an estate plan that includes an up-to-date will. In this chapter, you will learn how to protect your assets through estate planning.

CRITICAL THINKING QUESTIONS

- What preparation in terms of estate planning should Frederick and his family have made to make sure that his estate was handled according to his wishes?
- How could Frederick have benefited from keeping up with estate planning laws?
- What documents should have been included as part of his estate plan, and why?

PRINCIPLES OF ESTATE PLANNING

LG1

Like it or not, no one lives forever. Although this thought may depress you, safeguarding the future of the people you care about is one of the most important aspects of financial planning. Unless you develop plans and take steps during your lifetime to accumulate, preserve, and distribute your wealth on your death, chances are that your heirs and beneficiaries will receive only part of your estate. The rest will go (often unnecessarily) to taxes and various administrative costs. This process, called *estate planning*, requires knowledge of wills, trusts, and taxes.

Understanding these components and their interrelationships will help you minimize estate shrinkage after your death, while still achieving your lifetime personal financial goals. Also, keep in mind that not only wealthy people but also individuals of modest or moderate means need to plan their estates. Those who start saving for retirement early are likely to have sizable retirement accounts. Without proper planning, taxes could consume much of what is left in those accounts after your death.

Estate planning is the process of developing a plan to administer and distribute your assets on death in a manner consistent with your wishes and the needs of your survivors, while minimizing taxes. This process helps people accumulate enough capital to meet college education costs and other special needs, provide financial security for family members in the event of the death of the head of household, take care of themselves and their family during a long-term disability, and provide for a comfortable retirement. However, estate planning goes beyond financial issues. It also includes plans to manage your affairs if you become disabled and a statement of your personal wishes for medical care should you become unable to make them clear yourself.

estate planning The process of developing a plan to administer and distribute your assets on death in a manner consistent with your wishes and the needs of your survivors, while minimizing taxes.

As with other financial planning activities, one of the major objectives of estate planning is to eliminate or minimize tax exposure. Doing so, of course, will increase the amount of your estate that ultimately will be passed on to your heirs and beneficiaries. Estate planning is closely related to insurance and retirement planning. Certainly the most important reason for buying life insurance is to provide for your family in the event of your premature death. Likewise, one of the principal challenges of effective retirement planning is to achieve a comfortable standard of living in retirement, while preserving as much of your accumulated wealth as possible. This not only reduces the chances of you (or your spouse) outliving your financial resources, but also leaves an estate that can be passed on to your heirs and designated beneficiaries in accordance with your wishes.

Planning occurs in every estate. The estate owner and his or her professional counselors control some parts of the plan, and federal and state governments may control other parts of the plan. If one fails to plan, state and federal laws will control the disposition of assets, and determine who bears the burden of expenses and taxes. Indeed, the taxes may be higher because of the lack of planning. Individuals who wish to plan their estates must systematically uncover problems in a number of important areas and provide solutions for them. Exhibit 15.1 lists the major types of problems and their associated causes or indicators. Techniques to avoid or minimize these problems are discussed in later sections.

WHO NEEDS ESTATE PLANNING?

Estate planning should be part of everyone's financial plan, whether they are married or single, have five children or none. For example, married couples who own many assets jointly and have designated beneficiaries for assets such as retirement funds and life insurance policies may think that they don't need wills. However, a will covers many other important details, such as naming an executor to administer the estate and a

EXHIBIT 15.1

Potential Estate-Planning Problems and Major Causes or Indicators

Careful estate planning can prevent many problems that arise during the settlement of an estate. The first step toward preventing problems is an awareness and understanding of their major causes or indicators.

Problem	Major Cause or Indicator
• Excessive transfer costs	Taxes and estate administrative expenses higher than necessary.
• Lack of liquidity	Insufficient cash. Not enough assets that are quickly and inexpensively convertible to cash within a short period of time to meet tax demands and other costs.
• Improper disposition of assets	Beneficiaries receive the wrong asset or the proper asset in the wrong manner or at the wrong time.
• Inadequate income at retirement	Capital insufficient or not readily convertible to income-producing status.
• Inadequate income, if disabled	High medical costs, capital insufficient or not readily convertible to income-producing status, difficulty in reducing living standards.
• Inadequate income for family at estate owner's death	Any of the above causes.
• Insufficient capital	Excessive taxes, inflation, improper investment planning.
• Special problems	A family member with a serious illness or physical or emotional problem, children of a prior marriage, beneficiaries who have extraordinary medical or financial needs, beneficiaries who can't agree on how to handle various estate matters, business problems or opportunities.

guardian for children, clarifying how estate taxes will be paid, and distributing property that doesn't go directly to a joint owner.

Partners who are not married and single persons will discover that estate planning is especially important, particularly if they own a home or other assets that they want to leave to specific individuals or to charity. Unmarried couples need to put extra effort into their estate plans. They may need to make special arrangements to be sure they can indeed leave assets to a partner.

The two main areas of estate planning are *people planning* and *asset planning*.

People Planning

People planning means anticipating the psychological and financial needs of those people you love and providing enough income or capital or both to ensure a continuation of their way of life. People planning also means keeping Mother's cameo brooch in the family and out of the pawnshop, or preserving the business that Granddad started in the early 1900s. People planning is especially important to those individuals with children who are minors; children who are exceptionally artistic or intellectually gifted; children or other dependents who are emotionally, mentally, or physically handicapped; and

Money in Action

Having "The Talk"—the Adult Version

Remember when your parents sat you down to have "The Talk?" Now it's your turn, but this time about money, their wills, and other estate-planning matters–topics that are just as hard to discuss as sex. Even though most parents plan to leave assets to their heirs, the American Association of Retired Persons (AARP) reports that almost two-thirds have not discussed end-of-life issues with family members. "When you put money, love, and death together, it's like a triple whammy," says Olivia Mellan, a Washington psychotherapist.

The recent stock market slide has made it doubly important to talk with your parents about family finances and estate planning. If their investment and retirement accounts took a big hit, they may be worried about having enough to continue their current lifestyle after they retire. As uncomfortable as it is to bring up financial and end-of-life issues, you and your parents need to keep the lines of communication open with regard to these matters. When children have no idea of their parents' wishes, helping the parents make different living arrangements when their health fails or handling an estate becomes a tremendous emotional and financial burden. In addition to coping with parents who can no longer function physically or mentally or losing a parent, the children must try to guess what the parent wanted and also take on additional tasks such as paying immediate expenses.

Your parents may be uncomfortable when you bring up money, illness, and death. You can use an article, book, news story, or an event in your own or their life to start a discussion. A news event, such as the September 11, 2001 terrorist attacks or a personal event such as the death of neighbor can give you the opportunity to chat about being prepared for the unexpected. That provides the opening to say, "I don't want to be like that family." You can also tell them about your own estate plans: "We're thinking of rewriting our wills and would like your advice." Parents love to be consulted, and they may then share their own plans. Otherwise, you will have to take a direct approach,

...continued on next page

spouses who cannot or do not want to handle money, securities, or a business.

Minor children cannot legally handle large sums of money or deal directly with real estate or securities. Custodial accounts, guardianships, or trusts will provide administration, security, financial advice, and the legal capacity to act on behalf of minors. Few children are exceptionally artistic or intellectually gifted, but those who are often need—or should have—special (and often expensive) schooling, travel opportunities, or equipment. Emotionally, mentally, or physically handicapped children (and other relatives) may need nursing, medical, or psychiatric care. Clearly, outright gifts of money or property to those who cannot care for themselves are foolishly inappropriate. These individuals may need more (or less) than other children. An individual who gives all of his or her children equal shares may not be giving them equitable shares.

How many of us have handled hundreds of thousands of dollars? Think of the burden we place on others when we expect a spouse who cannot—or does not want to—handle such large sums of money or securities to do so. This is particularly burdensome when the assets being handled are his or her only assets. Engaging in people planning demonstrates a high degree of caring. People planning also involves talking about estate planning with your loved ones, as the *Money in Action* box at the left explains.

Asset Planning

From the standpoint of wealth alone, estate planning is essential for anyone—single, widowed, married, or divorced—with an estate exceeding the "applicable exclusion amount," which is $1,500,000 in 2004 and increases in steps until it reaches $3,500,000 in 2009. (Note that the 2001 Tax Act provides for the complete repeal of the estate tax in 2010; of course, this is subject to change by the legislature at any time.) When an estate involves a closely held business, estate planning is essential to stabilize and maximize its asset and income-producing values, both during the owner's lifetime and at the owner's death or disability. Likewise, estate planning is essential to avoid the special problems that occur when an estate owner holds title to property in more than one state; these problems include incurring attorneys' fees in each state and being taxed on the same assets by more than one state.

The estate-planning process gets more complicated if you are part of a blended family or have special requests. With careful planning, you can be sure that your assets will go to the desired beneficiaries.

smart.sites

What should you do first when someone close to you dies? Download the University of Pittsburgh Medical Center's comprehensive guide, "When a Loved One Dies," to help you through these difficult times: **http://patienteducation.upmc.com/Pdf/LovedOneDies.pdf**.

Financial Road Sign

Excuses, Excuses, Excuses!

It's easy to put off estate planning. After all, who wants to think about dying? Don't let any of the following excuses keep you from moving forward.

- I don't have time.
- Thinking about death is morbid.
- I don't have enough assets to need estate planning.
- I'm too young to need a will.
- I have no kids/I'm not married.
- My spouse and I can't agree on a guardian for our children.
- My life insurance policy takes care of my estate planning.
- It costs too much.

Without an estate plan, your relatives will be left with a messy situation, will have no guidance as to your wishes, and could owe more taxes than necessary. The state will appoint a guardian for your children and decide who gets which assets. Accidents and disease can strike at any age. And life insurance is just one component of an estate plan; you need to look at the other areas, such as tax planning, and end-of-life planning.

Why Does an Estate Break Up?

Quite often, when people die, their estates die with them—not because they have done anything wrong but because they have not done anything. There are numerous forces that, if unchecked, tend to shrink an estate, reduce the usefulness of its assets, and frustrate the objectives of the person who built it. These include death-related costs, inflation, lack of liquidity, improper use of vehicles of transfer, and disabilities.

1. **Death-Related Costs.** When someone dies, the estate incurs certain types of death-related costs. For example, medical bills relating to a final illness and funeral expenses are good examples of *first-level death-related costs. Second-level death-related costs* consist of fees for attorneys, appraisers, and accountants along with

as Jim Towey, president of Aging with Dignity in Tallahassee, Florida, suggests: "Mom, Dad, I love you, and I want to be there when you need me, and I'd like to know what you want. I don't want to have to guess."

If your parents still won't share this information with you, they may feel more comfortable talking instead to an objective nonfamily person such as a professional financial planner. "A professional can hold their hand, give them confidence, and help them make decisions to ensure their money lasts," says Lynn O'Shaughnessy, author of the *Retirement Bible*.

Your discussions should cover the following areas:

1. *Where do they keep their important documents?* You need to locate birth and marriage certificates, the names of financial and legal advisers, insurance policies, lists of bank accounts and investments, and a letter of last instructions.
2. *Will they have enough money to live on?* This is very important now that people are living longer. Do they want to move to a particular retirement or assisted care facility, or have they set aside funds for in-home care. Do they have long-term care insurance to cover nursing home or in-home care?
3. *Do they have a durable power of attorney?* This gives someone appointed by the parents access to their bank accounts to pay bills in case they become incapacitated. Keep the originals at home and put copies of these documents in the safe-deposit box.
4. *Have they each prepared a healthcare proxy or living will?* This sets forth decisions on the kind of care and life-prolonging procedures the parent prefers in the event of hospitalization.
5. *Have they written wills or established any trusts?* Where can you find these documents?
6. *What are their wishes with regard to funeral and burial arrangements?*

Encourage your parents to share their intentions and the facts. What may be clear to them while they are writing their wills may not be so apparent to the heirs. For example, leaving different amounts to children without explaining why often leads to anger and can destroy relationships between siblings. Help your parents realize that by discussing how they want to live, they are giving a precious gift to the family, advises Deborah E. Banda, AARP's Massachusetts state director. "It lets the adult children know what to do and it also tells them exactly how they can help. And it reduces stress on everyone."

...continued on next page

Critical Thinking Questions

1. Why is it important to discuss end-of-life issues with family members?
2. When discussing retirement and estate plans with your parents, what specific information should you obtain?
3. Why should you learn your parents' intentions as well as facts?

Sources: Kathleen Adams, "Balancing Tact and Tactics," *Time,* May 15, 2000, p. F2; Shannon Buggs, "Your Money Column," *Houston Chronicle*, March 3, 2003, downloaded from ProQuest, **http://www.proquest.com**; "Don't Keep Your Estate Plans a Secret," *Kiplinger's Retirement Report,* January 2000, downloaded from **http://www.kiplinger.com/retreport**; Robert Frick, "Talking to Your Parents About Money," *Kiplinger's Personal Finance,* August 1999, downloaded from **http://www.kiplinger.com**; Eileen Alt Powell, "Checking Parents' Financial Health," *AP Online*, October 10, 2002, downloaded from BigChalk Library, **http://library.bigchalk.com;** Art Simas, "Can We Talk about What Might Happen in Five or 10 Years?" *Telegram & Gazette* (Worcester, Mass.), August 17, 2001, p. 6.

probate expenses—so-called administrative costs, federal estate taxes, and state death taxes. Most people also die with some current bills unpaid, outstanding long-term obligations (such as mortgages, business loans, and installment contracts), and unpaid income taxes and property taxes.

2. **Inflation.** Death-related costs are only the tip of the estate-impairment iceberg. Failure to continuously reappraise and rearrange an estate plan to counter the effects of inflation can impair the ability of assets—liquid, real, and personal property and investments—to provide steady and adequate levels of financial security.
3. **Lack of Liquidity.** Insufficient cash to cover death costs and other estate obligations has always been a major factor in estate impairment. Sale of the choicest parcel of farmland or a business that has been in the family for generations, for instance, often has undesirable psychological effects on the heirs. The outcome can be a devastating financial and emotional blow.
4. **Improper Use of Vehicles of Transfer.** Assets are often put into the hands of beneficiaries who are unwilling or unable to handle them. Improper use of vehicles of transfer may pass property to unintended beneficiaries or to the proper beneficiaries in an improper manner or at an incorrect time. For example, spendthrift spouses or minors may be left large sums of money outright in the form of life insurance, through joint ownership of a savings account, or as the beneficiaries of an employee fringe benefit plan.
5. **Disabilities.** A prolonged and expensive disability of a family wage earner is often called a *living death.* Loss of income due to disability is often coupled with a massive financial drain caused by the illness itself. The financial situation is further complicated by inadequate management of currently owned assets. This not only threatens the family's financial security but also diminishes the value of the estate at an incredible speed.

What Is Your Estate?

Your estate is your property—whatever you own. Your **probate estate** consists of the real and personal property you own in your own name that can be transferred at death according to the terms of a will, or under intestate laws if you have no valid will. The probate estate is distinct from the gross estate (a tax law term that may encompass a considerably larger amount of property). Your **gross estate** includes all the property—both probate and nonprobate—that might be subject to federal estate taxes at your death. Life insurance, jointly held property with rights of survivorship, and property passing under certain employee benefit plans are common examples of nonprobate assets that might be subject to federal (and state) estate taxes.

probate estate The real and personal property owned by a person that can be transferred at death according to the terms of a will, or under intestate laws in the absence of a valid will.

gross estate All property—both probate and nonprobate—that might be subject to federal estate taxes at a person's death.

In addition, you may provide for property that is not probate property and will not be part of your estate for federal estate tax purposes yet will pass to your family and form part of their financial security program. There are two types of such assets. One is *properly arranged* life insurance. For instance, you could give assets to your daughter to allow her to purchase, pay the premiums for, and be the beneficiary of a policy on your life. At your death, the proceeds would not be included as part of your estate. The other type of financial asset that falls into this category is *Social Security*. Social Security payments to a surviving spouse and minor children generally are neither probate assets nor subject to any federal (or state) estate taxes. Because of the freedom from administrative costs and taxes, this category of assets provides unique and substantial estate-planning opportunities.

smart.sites

The sample estate plan outlined at Castleman Law Firm's site, **http://www.castlelaw.com/samplan.htm**, provides a good overview of what an estate plan should contain.

THE ESTATE-PLANNING PROCESS

The estate-planning process consists of seven important steps, as summarized in Exhibit 15.2. First, you must assess your family situation, evaluating its strengths and weaknesses, and set estate-planning goals. Next, gather comprehensive and accurate data on all aspects of the family. Exhibit 15.3 on page 651 summarizes the data that professionals require to prepare detailed estate plans. Most professional estate planners provide forms to help their clients compile this information. Then, you should take inventory and determine the value of your estate. Next, you must designate beneficiaries of your estate's assets, estimate estate transfer costs, and formulate and implement your plan. The final step is ongoing: Review your estate plan periodically—at minimum every 3 to 5 years, and revise it as circumstances dictate. Key events that should also trigger a review include the death or disability of a spouse or family member, moving to another state, changing jobs, getting married or divorced, having children, or acquiring new assets.

EXHIBIT 15.2

Steps in the Estate-Planning Process

The estate-planning process consists of seven important steps listed below in the sequence they would be performed.

1. Assess your family situation and set estate-planning goals.
2. Gather comprehensive and accurate data.
3. List all assets and determine the value of your estate.
4. Designate beneficiaries of your estate's assets.
5. Estimate estate transfer costs.
6. Formulate and implement your plan.
7. Review the plan periodically and revise it as necessary.

Concept ✓

15-1. Discuss the importance and goals of estate planning. Explain why estates often break up. Distinguish between the *probate estate* and the *gross estate.*

15-2. Briefly describe the steps involved in the estate-planning process.

The objective of estate plans, of course, is to maximize the usefulness of people's assets during their lives and to achieve their personal objectives after their deaths. Once the plan has been implemented, however, you must reevaluate it on a regular basis. An estate plan is good only as long as it fits the needs, desires, and circumstances of the parties involved. As these elements change, you must modify your estate plan. Marriage or remarriage, divorce, the birth of a child, a change of job or location, and substantial changes in income, health, or living standards are the types of events that indicate a need for a review. Even if none of these occur, you should automatically review life insurance needs at least once every 2 years and perform a full estate audit at least once every 3 to 5 years (or whenever there has been a major change in the federal or state death-tax laws). Because of the general complexity of the laws relating to estate transfer, the assistance of estate planners, life insurance professionals, certified financial planners (CFP®s), chartered financial consultants (ChFCs), accountants, and attorneys is often necessary in the planning and evaluation process. Due to the individual nature of estate planning, we cannot include more-specific guidelines in this chapter.

THY WILL BE DONE...

LG2

As the Robbins family learned, having an up-to-date will is an important aspect of personal financial planning and estate planning. Without it, you have no assurance that your assets will be divided according to your desires. A **will** is a written, legally enforceable expression or declaration of a person's wishes concerning the disposition of his or her property on death. Unfortunately, about 70 percent all Americans do not have valid wills. The importance of a valid will becomes very apparent when we examine what happens when someone dies without one.

will
A written and legally enforceable document that expresses how a person's property should be distributed on his or her death. It is also used to name a personal representative to guide the disposition of the estate, to name a guardian for persons and property, and to specify the distribution of tax burdens to beneficiaries.

ABSENCE OF A VALID WILL: INTESTACY

Suppose that Frederick Robbins had died without a valid will, a situation called **intestacy.** State intestacy laws "draw the will the decedent failed to make" to determine the disposition of the probate property of persons who have died intestate. These statutes set forth certain preferred classes of survivors. Generally, the decedent's spouse is favored, followed by the children and then other offspring. If the spouse and children or other offspring, such as grandchildren or great-grandchildren, survive, they will divide the estate, and other relatives will receive nothing. If no spouse, children, or other offspring survive, the deceased's parents, brothers, and sisters will receive a share of the estate.

Exhibit 15.4 on page 652 provides an example of the disposition of a typical intestate estate. After paying debts and taxes and deducting state-defined family exemptions, that individual's separately owned property would be distributed in the order and percentages shown. Where property goes to the state due to the absence of a will, the property is said to *escheat to the state.* If a person without relatives dies with a valid will, his or her property will probably go to friends or to charity, rather than to the state.

intestacy
The situation that exists when a person dies without a valid will.

Aside from having lost control of the disposition of the property, the person who dies intestate also forfeits the privileges of naming a personal representative to guide the disposition of the estate, naming a guardian for persons and property, and specifying which beneficiaries would bear certain tax burdens. In addition, estate planning and a valid will may minimize the amount of estate shrinkage through transfer taxes. Having a valid will—regardless of the size of an estate—is a critical element in the personal financial planning process.

EXHIBIT 15.3

Factual Data Required for Estate Planning

The second step in developing an effective estate plan involves gathering comprehensive and accurate data on all aspects of the family. The types of factual data required by professionals are listed below.

Personal data:	Names, addresses, phone numbers, family consultants, family birth dates, occupations, health problems, support needs, citizenship, marital status, marital agreements, wills, trusts, custodianships, trust beneficiary, gifts or inheritances, Social Security numbers, education, and military service
Property (except life insurance or business):	Classification, title, indebtedness, basis, date and or manner of acquisition, value of marketable securities, and location
Life insurance:	Name of the insured, kind of policies, amounts, insurance company, agents' names and addresses
Health insurance:	Medical expense insurance: insurance company, policy benefits; disability income insurance
Business interest:	Name, address, ownership, valuation factors, desired survivorship control; name, address, and phone number of business attorney and accountant
Employee benefits:	Group insurance plans, pension benefits
Family income:	Income of client, spouse, dependent children, income tax information
Family finances:	Budget information, investment preferences, ranking of economic objectives, capital needs, other objectives
Income and capital needs:	Retirement: planned retirement age, required amount, potential sources; disability: required amount, sources; death: expected sources of income
Liabilities:	Classification of liabilities, creditors, amounts, whether insured or secured
Factors affecting plan:	Gift propensity, charitable inclinations, emotional maturity of children, basic desires for estate distribution
Authorization for information:	Life insurance
Receipt for documents:	Personal and business

Source: Copyright © 1995 by The American College, Bryn Mawr, PA. Adapted from Confidential Personal and Financial Data form, Advanced Estate Planning Course. All rights reserved.

smart.sites

TD Waterhouse's estate-planning section (**http://www.tdwaterhouse.com**) explains the differences among various types of wills. It also has a calculator to help you estimate estate size, taxes, and probate costs.

PREPARING THE WILL

testator
A person whose will directs the disposition of property at his or her death.

A will allows a person, called a **testator**, to direct the disposition of property at his or her death. The testator can change or revoke a will at any time prior to his or her death. On the death of the testator, the will becomes operative.

Will preparation, or drafting, varies with respect to difficulty and cost, depending on individual circumstances. In some cases, a two-page will costing $150 may be adequate although in others, a complex document costing $1,500 or more may be necessary. A

EXHIBIT 15.4

Distribution of a Typical Intestate Estate

If a person dies intestate (without a valid will), the estate will be distributed according to established state laws of intestate succession. The summary that follows is based on Utah's probate code.

Survivors	Distribution*
Spouse and offspring—children, grandchildren, etc.—not of the surviving spouse	The first $50,000 plus 50% of the balance to the surviving spouse and the other 50% of the balance to the decedent spouse's offspring by right of representation (the spouse's share is reduced by any nonprobate transfers to him or her)
Spouse and no offspring or decedent's offspring all by the surviving spouse	100% to surviving spouse
No spouse but offspring	To decedent's descendants per capita at each generation.
No spouse and no offspring, but parent(s)	To parent or parents equally
No spouse, no offspring, no parents, but offspring of parents	To parents' descendants per capita at each generation
No spouse, no offspring, no parents, and no offspring of parents, but grandparents or offspring of grandparents	Divided half to maternal grandparents (or their offspring, if neither survives) and half to the paternal grandparents (or their offspring, if neither survives). If one side predeceased and there are no offspring, the other side takes all.
None of the above	The intestate estate passes to the state for the benefit of the state school fund.

* Because intestate laws vary from state to state, the actual distribution of assets may differ from what is shown here; however, the Utah Probate Code is based upon the Uniform Probate Code that has been adopted by at least 18 states.

will must not only effectively accomplish the objectives specified for distributing assets, but it must also take into consideration income, gift, and estate tax laws. Will preparation also requires a knowledge of corporate, trust, real estate, and securities laws. Note that a will, important as it is, may be ineffective or misstate the testator's estate plan if it does not consider and coordinate assets passing outside its limits.

A properly prepared will should meet three important requirements. It should:

- Provide a plan for distributing the testator's assets in accordance with his or her wishes, the beneficiaries' needs, and federal and state dispositive and tax laws
- Consider the changes in family circumstances that might occur after its execution
- Be unambiguous and complete in describing the testator's desires

By following these general guidelines, the testator generally can develop a satisfactory will.

Will drafting, no matter how modest the size of the estate, should not be attempted by a layperson. The complexity and interrelationships of tax, property, domestic relations, and other laws make the homemade will a potentially dangerous document. Nowhere is the old adage, "He who serves as his own attorney has a fool for a client," more true, and few things may turn out more disastrous in the long run than the do-it-yourself will.

smart.sites

For a "Crash Course in Wills and Trusts" and general estate-planning advice, visit the award-winning site of Michael T. Palermo, an attorney and CFP®, at **http://www.mtpalermo.com**.

Common Features of the Will

Although there is no absolute format that must be followed when preparing a will, most wills contain similar distinct sections. Exhibit 15.5, which presents the will of John Steven Fabian, includes generalized examples of each of these clauses. Refer to the exhibit as you read the following descriptions of the clauses. *These clauses must be tailored to individual needs and circumstances by an attorney familiar with the testator's situation.*

- **Introductory Clause.** An introductory clause, or preamble, normally states the testator's name and residence; this determines the county that will have legal jurisdiction and be considered the testator's domicile for tax purposes. The revocation statement nullifies old and forgotten wills and *codicils*—legally binding modifications of an existing will.
- **Direction of Payments.** This clause directs the estate to make certain payments of expenses. As a general rule, however, the rights of creditors are protected by law, and such a clause is largely useless.
- **Disposition of Property.** Fabian's will has three examples of clauses dealing with disposition of property:

  1. *Disposition of personal effects:* A testator may also make a separate detailed and specific list of personal property and carefully identify each item, and to whom it is given, as an informal guide to help the executor divide the property. (This list generally should not appear in the will itself because it is likely to change frequently.)
  2. *Giving money to a specifically named party:* Be sure to use the correct legal title of a charity.
  3. *Distribution of residual assets after specific gifts have been made:* Bequests to close relatives (as defined in the statute) who die before the testator will go to the relative's heirs unless the will includes other directions. Bequests to nonrelatives who predecease the testator will go to the other residual beneficiaries.

- **Appointment Clause.** Appointment clauses name the *executors* (the decedent's personal representatives who administer the estate), guardians for minor children, and trustees and their successors:
- **Tax Clause.** In the absence of a specified provision in the will, so-called *apportionment statutes* of the testator's state will allocate the burden of taxes among the beneficiaries. The result may be an inappropriate and unintended reduction of certain beneficiaries' shares or adverse estate tax effects. Earlier statutes tended to charge death taxes on the residual of the estate, but today the trend is toward statutes that charge each beneficiary based on his or her share of the taxable estate. Because the spouse's share and the portion going to a charity are deducted from the gross estate before arriving at the taxable estate, neither is charged with taxes.
- **Simultaneous Death Clause.** This clause describes what happens in the event of simultaneous death. The assumption that the spouse survives is used mainly to permit the

EXHIBIT 15.5

A Representative Will for John Steven Fabian

John Steven Fabian's will illustrates the eight distinct sections of most wills.

The Last Will and Testament of John Steven Fabian

Section 1 — Introductory Clause

I, John Steven Fabian, of the city of Chicago, state of Illinois, do, hereby make my last will and revoke all wills and codicils made prior to this will.

Section 2 — Direction of Payments

Article 1: Payment of Debts and Expenses

I direct payment out of my estate of all just debts and the expenses of my last illness and funeral.

Section 3 — Disposition of Property

Article 2: Disposition of Property

I give and bequeath to my wife, Sally Warren Fabian, all my jewelry, automobiles, books, and photography equipment, as well as all other articles of personal and household use.

I give to the Chicago Historical Society the sum of $100,000.

All the rest, residue, and remainder of my estate, real and personal, wherever located, I give in equal one-half shares to my children, Charles Elliot and Lara Sue, their heirs and assigns forever.

Section 4 — Appointment Clause

Article 3: Nomination of Executor and Guardian

I hereby nominate as the Executor of this Will my beloved wife, Sally Warren Fabian, but if she is unable or unwilling to serve then I nominate my brother, Winston James Fabian. In the event both persons named predecease me, or shall cease or fail to act, then I nominate as Executor in the place of said persons, the Northern Trust Bank of Chicago, Illinois.

If my wife does not survive me, I appoint my brother, Eugene Lawrence Fabian, Guardian of the person and property of my son, Charles Elliot, during his minority.

Section 5 — Tax Clause

Article 4: Payment of Taxes

I direct that there shall be paid out of my residuary estate (from that portion which does not qualify for the marital deduction) all estate, inheritance, and similar taxes imposed by a government in respect to property includable in my estate for tax purposes, whether the property passes under this will or otherwise.

Section 6 — Simultaneous Death Clause

Article 5: Simultaneous Death

If my wife and I shall die under such circumstances that there is not sufficient evidence to determine the order of our deaths, then it shall be presumed that she survived me. My estate shall be administered and distributed in all respects in accordance with such assumption.

Section 7 — Execution and Attestation Clause

In witness thereof, I have affixed my signature to this, my last will and testament, which consists of five (5) pages, each of which I have initialed, this 15th day of September, 2005.

John Steven Fabian

Section 8 — Witness Clause

Signed, sealed, and published by John Steven Fabian, the testator, as his last will, in the presence of us, who, at his request, and in the presence of each other, all being present at the same time, have written our names as witnesses.

(*Note:* Normally the witness signatures and addresses would follow this clause.)

marital deduction, which offers a tax advantage. Other types of clauses are similarly designed to avoid double probate of the same assets—duplication of administrative and probate costs. Such clauses require that the survivor live for a certain period, such as 30 or 60 days, to be a beneficiary under the will.

- **Execution and Attestation Clause.** Every will should be in writing and signed by the testator at its end as a precaution against fraud. Many attorneys suggest that the testator also initial each page after the last line or sign in a corner of each page.
- **Witness Clause.** The final clause helps to affirm that the will in question is really that of the deceased. All states require two witnesses to the testator's signing of the will, with the exception of Vermont, which requires three. Most states require witnesses to sign in the presence of one another, after they witness the signing by the testator. Their addresses should be noted on the will. If the testator is unable to sign his or her name for any reason, most states allow the testator to make a mark and to have another person (properly witnessed) sign for him or her.

smart.sites

AIM Trimark Investor's estate planning section has several good articles and checklists to help you get started, including a checklist to help select your children's guardian and provide guidance to him or her as to your wishes: **http://www.aimtrimark.com/AIM/Retail/InvestorEd/intergeneral_planning.cfm**.

REQUIREMENTS OF A VALID WILL

To be valid, a will must be the product of a person with a sound mind, there must have been no *undue influence* (influence that would remove the testator's freedom of choice), the will itself must have been properly executed, and its execution must be free from fraud.

1. **Mental Capacity.** You must be of "sound mind" to make a valid will. This means that you:
   (1) know what a will is and are aware that you are making and signing one
   (2) understand your relationship with persons for whom you would normally provide, such as a spouse or children
   (3) understand what you own
   (4) are able to decide how to distribute your property and have knowledge of the persons who would generally be expected to receive the estate (even though the testator is not required to leave anything to them); generally, such capacity is presumed

   Setting aside a will requires clear and convincing proof of mental incapacity, and the burden of proof is on the person contesting the will.
2. **Freedom of Choice.** When you prepare and execute your will, you must not be under the undue influence of another person. Threats, misrepresentations, inordinate flattery, or some physical or mental coercion employed to destroy the testator's freedom of choice are all types of undue influence.
3. **Proper Execution.** To be considered properly executed, a will must meet the requirements of the state's wills act or its equivalent. It must also be demonstrable that it is in fact the will of the testator. Most states have statutes that spell out who may make a will (generally any person of sound mind, age 18 or older but 14 in Georgia and 16 in Louisiana), the form and execution the will must have (most states require a will to be in writing and signed by the testator at the logical end), and requirements for witnesses. Generally, a beneficiary should not serve as a witness. Although the will is otherwise valid, about 60 percent of the states penalize

the beneficiary-witness in some way, such as limiting the beneficiary-witness' bequest to the intestate share that he or she would receive.

Most states now provide for a *self-proving will* that states in the attestation clause that the correct formalities for will execution were observed. A self-proving will eliminates the need to have the witnesses sign, after the testator's death, a declaration verifying their signatures and that of the testator. This saves time, money, and often a great deal of inconvenience to the executor.

Financial Road Sign

Choosing Your Children's Guardian

The personal guardian you choose for your children should:

1. Be old enough (18 years old in most states)
2. Have the confidence of you and your children
3. Have similar family values and style of child rearing
4. Have a genuine concern for your children's welfare
5. Have the emotional and physical capability, as well as the time, to handle the job
6. Have kids close in age to your children if possible
7. Share your moral beliefs and religion
8. Be willing to accept the responsibility of guardianship

Also consider:

9. Can you provide enough assets to raise the children? If not, can your prospective guardian afford to bring them up?
10. Would your kids have to move? Can siblings stay together?

Sources: Adapted from "Choosing a Guardian for Your Children," *Nolo's Legal Encyclopedia*, **http://www.nolo.com/lawcenter/ency/index.cfm**; and Andrew E. Tanenbaum "Choosing a Guardian," She Knows.com, downloaded December 16, 2003, from **http://sheknows.com.**

Changing or Revoking the Will: Codicils

As life circumstances change, so should your will. Because a will is inoperative until the testator's death, the testator can change it at any time, as long as he or she has the mental capacity. In fact, periodic revisions should occur at certain times, including the following:

- His or her (or the beneficiaries') health or financial circumstances change significantly
- Births, deaths, marriages, or divorces alter the operative circumstances
- The testator moves to a state other than where the will was executed
- An executor, trustee, or guardian can no longer serve
- Substantial changes occur in the tax law

Only the testator can change a will. By reviewing your will regularly, you can be sure that it accurately reflects your current wishes.

Changing the Will

To make minor changes to an existing will, the testator draws up a **codicil.** This simple and convenient legal means of modifying a will is often a single-page document that reaffirms all the existing provisions in the will except the one to be changed. The codicil should be executed and witnessed in the same formal manner as a will.

codicil
A document that legally modifies a will without revoking it.

When a will requires substantial changes, a new will is usually preferable to a codicil. In addition, if a gift in the original will is removed, it may be best to draw a new will and destroy the old, even if substantial changes are not required. This avoids offending the omitted beneficiary. Sometimes, however, the prior will should not be destroyed even after the new will has been made and signed. If the new will fails for some reason (because of the testator's mental incapacity, for example), the prior will may qualify. Also, a prior will could help to prove a "continuity of testamentary purpose"—in other words, that the latest will (which may have provided a substantial gift to charity) continued an earlier intent and was not an afterthought or the result of an unduly influenced mind.

Revoking the Will

When he remarried, Frederick Robbins might have wanted to make significant changes to his will. In that case, he would have been better off revoking his will and writing a new one, rather than doing a series of codicils. A will may be revoked either by the testator or automatically by the law. A testator can revoke a will in one of four ways:

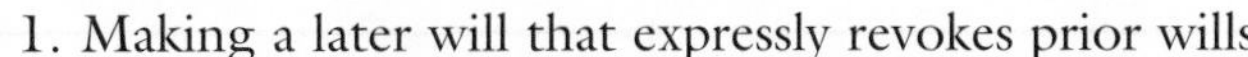

1. Making a later will that expressly revokes prior wills
2. Making a codicil that expressly revokes all wills earlier than the one being modified
3. Making a later will that is inconsistent with a former will
4. Physically mutilating, burning, tearing, or defacing the will with the intention of revoking it

The law automatically modifies a will under certain circumstances, which vary from state to state but generally revolve around divorce, marriage, birth or adoption, and murder. In many states, if a testator becomes divorced after making a will, all provisions in the will relating to the spouse become ineffective. If a testator marries after making a will, the spouse receives that portion of the estate that would have been received had the testator died without a valid will—unless the will gives the spouse a larger share. If a testator did not provide for a child born or adopted after the will was made (unless it appears that such lack of provision was intentional), the child receives that share of the estate not passing to the testator's spouse that would have been given to him or her had the deceased not had a will. Finally, almost all states have some type of slayer's statute forbidding a person who commits murder from acquiring property as the result of the deed.

Financial Road Sign

Will-Writing Pointers

Here are some tips to help you write your will in a way that will prevent problems later:

Take stock: Compile lists of your assets, outstanding debts, and family members and other beneficiaries.

Evaluate your findings: Take your time considering how to distribute your assets in an equitable manner.

Consider taxes: A carefully designed will and estate plan can reduce the taxes your heirs will owe.

Talk about your will and your intentions: Letting family members know what you're leaving them and why could avoid hard feelings afterward.

Create a trust: Evaluate whether trusts make sense for estate administration and to reduce estate taxes.

Be reasonable: You don't have to divide everything equally among your children, but strive for fairness in asset distribution. Again, explain the rationale behind your decisions.

Spread the wealth: Try to bequeath something to all those with a valid interest in your estate. Otherwise they might try to contest the will.

Review and update regularly: Life circumstances change and your will may no longer be appropriate.

Leave more than money: An ethical will that discusses the values you hope to have left your survivors can be a wonderful gift to will in addition to one that deals with possessions.

Safeguarding the Will

In most cases, you should keep your original will in a safe-deposit box, with copies in a safe and accessible place at home and with the attorney who drafted it. Although some authorities and many attorneys recommend leaving the original will with the attorney who drafted it, this may make it awkward for the executor to exercise the right to choose his or her own attorney. Further, it may discourage the estate owner from changing the will or engaging a new attorney even if he or she moves out of the state in which the will is drawn.

Worksheet 15.1 contains an executor's checklist of documents and information that should be kept in a safe-deposit box. If each spouse has a separate safe-deposit box, the couple may want to keep their wills in each other's boxes. Some states provide for *lodging* of the will, a mechanism for filing and safekeeping it in the office of the probate court (also called *orphan's* or *surrogate's court*). In those states, this procedure satisfies the need to safeguard the will.

Letter of Last Instructions

People often have thoughts they want to convey and instructions they wish others to carry out that are not appropriate to include in their wills. For example, Frederick Robbins might have explained why he chose Carolyn to be his executor rather

worksheet 15.1

A Checklist of Items to Keep in a Safe-Deposit Box

This checklist itemizes the various documents and information that the executor may need to effectively carry out the terms of the will. These items should be kept in a safe-deposit box.

EXECUTOR'S CHECKLIST

Name (Testator)____________________ Date__________

______ 1. Birth certificates
______ 2. Marriage certificates (including any prior marriages)
______ 3. Your will (and spouse's will) and trust agreements
______ 4. Listing of life insurance policies or certificates
______ 5. Your Social Security numbers
______ 6. Military discharge papers
______ 7. Bonds, stocks, and securities
______ 8. Real estate deeds
______ 9. Business (buy-sell) agreements
______ 10. Automobile titles and insurance policies
______ 11. Property insurance policies
______ 12. Letter of last instructions
______ 13. Additional documents

List all checking and savings account numbers, including bank addresses and location of safe-deposit boxes:

List name, address, and phone number of property and life insurance agents:

List name, address, and phone number of attorney and accountant:

List name, address, and phone number of (current or past) employer. State date when you retired if applicable. Include employee benefits booklets:

List all debts owed to *and* owed by you:

List the names, addresses, telephone numbers, and birth dates of your children and other beneficiaries (including charitable beneficiaries):

Source: Stephan R. Leimberg, Jerry A. Kasner, Stephen N. Kandell, Morey S. Rosenbloom, and Herbert L. Levy, *The Tools & Techniques of Estate Planning*, 12th ed. (Upper Saddle River, NJ: Prentice Hall, 2002). Reprinted with permission of the publisher.

letter of last instructions An informal memorandum separate from the will and containing suggestions or recommendations for carrying out the decedent's wishes.

probate process The court-supervised process of liquidation that occurs when a person dies; it consists of collecting money owed the decedent, paying his or her debts, and distributing the remaining assets to the appropriate individuals and organizations.

executor The personal representative of an estate designated in the decedent's will.

administrator The personal representative of the estate appointed by the court if the decedent died intestate (without a valid will).

than her brother. A **letter of last instructions** is the best way to communicate these suggestions or recommendations. It typically takes the form of an informal memorandum separate from the will. (This letter of last instructions should not contain any bequests, because it has no legal standing.) Usually it is best to make several copies of the letter, keeping one at home and the others with the estate's executor or attorney, who can deliver it to beneficiaries at the appropriate time.

A letter of last instructions might provide directions with respect to such items as:

1. Location of the will and other documents
2. Funeral and burial instructions (often a will is not opened until after the funeral)
3. Suggestions or recommendations as to the continuation, sale, or liquidation of a business (it is easier to freely suggest a course of action in such a letter than in a will)
4. Personal matters that the testator might prefer not to be made public in the will, such as statements that might sound unkind or inconsiderate but would prove of great value to the executor (for example, comments about a spendthrift spouse or a reckless son)
5. Legal and accounting services (executors are free, however, to choose their own counsel—not even testators can bind them in that selection)
6. An explanation of the actions taken in the will, which may help avoid litigation (for instance, "I left only $1,000 to my son, Ramon, because . . ." or "I made no provisions for my oldest daughter, Melissa, because . . .")
7. Suggestions on how to divide the personal property

Administration of an Estate

When people die, they usually own property and owe debts. Often, they will have claims (accounts receivable) against other persons. A process of liquidation, called the **probate process,** similar to that which occurs when a corporation is dissolved, might be required. In this process, money owed the decedent is collected, creditors (including the tax authorities) are satisfied, and what remains is distributed to the appropriate individuals and organizations. A local court generally supervises the probate process through a person designated as an **executor** in the decedent's will, or, if the decedent died intestate (without a valid will), through a court-appointed **administrator.**

An executor or administrator, who is sometimes also referred to as the *decedent's personal representative,* must collect the assets of the decedent, pay debts or provide for the payment of debts that are not currently due, and distribute any remaining assets to the persons entitled to them by will or by the intestate law of the appropriate state. Estate administration is important for many reasons. The executor or administrator becomes the decedent's legal representative, taking care of such matters as collecting bank accounts and other contracts, releasing liability, and creating clear title to make real estate marketable. Due to the importance of the estate administration process, you should select executors who are not only familiar with the testator's affairs but also can effectively handle the responsibilities of being an executor.

Other Important Estate-Planning Documents

power of attorney Legal document that authorizes another person to take over one's financial affairs and act on his or her behalf.

In addition to your will and the letter of last instructions, you should have several other documents to protect yourself and your family: a power of attorney, a living will, a durable power of attorney for healthcare, and an ethical will.

Power of Attorney

If you are incapacitated by a serious illness, a **power of attorney** allows you to name as your agent the person you consider best suited to take over your financial affairs—perhaps a spouse or other relative. Although this is a simple document, it transfers enormous power to your designated appointee, so be sure you can rely on the person you choose to manage your finances responsibly. If you have investments, your power of attorney should include language that covers powers of investment on your behalf. You may want to clear your power of attorney with the brokerage firms and mutual funds where you have accounts.

living will
A document that states, in very precise terms, the treatments that a person wants and to what degree he or she wishes them continued if he or she becomes terminally ill.

durable power of attorney for healthcare
A written power of attorney authorizing an individual (an *agent*) to make healthcare decisions on behalf of the principal during such times, either temporarily or permanently, when the principal is unable to make such decisions.

Living Will and Durable Power of Attorney for Healthcare

Had Frederick Robbins lingered in a coma with little or no hope of recovery, his family could have faced very difficult decisions regarding his medical care. He had not prepared a *living will* or *durable power of attorney for healthcare* to give them guidance as to his preferences. These documents address another important aspect of estate planning: determining the medical care you wish to receive, or *not* receive, if you become seriously ill and are unable to give informed consent. The **living will** states, in very precise terms, the treatments that you want and to what degree you wish them continued. You must be as specific as possible so that your wishes are clear; otherwise, a living will might be put aside because it is too vague. For example, you should define what you mean by "terminal illness." Each state has its own form for a living will, and you can usually complete it yourself.

Many experts prefer the **durable power of attorney for healthcare** instead of the living will; some advise having both to reinforce each other. Through the durable power of attorney for healthcare, you authorize an individual (your *agent*) to make healthcare decisions for you if you are unable to do so, either temporarily or permanently. Unlike the living will, it applies in any case where you cannot communicate your wishes, not just when you are terminally ill. You can limit the scope of the durable power of attorney and include specific instructions as to the desired level of medical treatment. You should spend some time making these decisions and then review your ideas and philosophy concerning these matters with your family and the person you designate as your agent. These documents, copies of which should be held by your designated agent and your doctor, can make it easier for your family to deal with these difficult issues.

smart.sites
Partnership for Caring offers advice to express how you want to be treated if you are seriously ill and unable to speak for yourself. Find out more at: **http://www.partnershipforcaring.com**.

Ethical Wills

ethical will
An informal personal statement left for family, friends, and community that shares your values, blessings, life's lessons and hopes and dreams for the future.

In addition to a traditional will that covers the distribution of tangible assets, today many people also prepare **ethical wills** to leave family, friends, and community a personal statement of values, blessings, life's lessons, and hopes and dreams for the future. Sometimes called *legacy statements*, ethical wills are informal documents, usually added to formal wills and read at the same time. They offer a way to share your morals, business ethics, life experiences, family stories and history, and more with future generations. They can take various forms, such as handwritten letters or journals, personal essays written on a computer, or even videotaped or audiotaped conversations.

Writing an ethical will can be a daunting project and may perhaps be even more difficult than writing a regular will. Experts suggest dividing it into smaller steps. You might prepare a list of questions about the impact of certain experiences on shaping your life and values, how you want to be remembered, the lessons you wish to pass on to your family and friends, and any other important messages.

It's a good idea to review your ethical will with the lawyer who handles your estate planning. An ethical will that can be interpreted in a way that seems to contradict the intentions of the formal will may lead to a challenge of the formal will.

smart.sites

If the idea of writing an ethical will appeals to you but you don't know where to start, the resources at EthicalWill.com, **http://www.ethicalwill.com**, will help.

right of survivorship The right of surviving joint owners of property to receive title to the deceased joint owner's interest in the property.

joint tenancy A type of ownership by two or more parties, with the survivor(s) continuing to hold all such property on the death of one or more of the tenants. Each joint tenant can unilaterally sever the tenancy.

tenancy by the entirety A form of ownership by husband and wife, recognized in certain states, in which the property automatically passes to the surviving spouse. Tenancy can be severed only by mutual agreement, divorce, or conveyance by both spouses to a third party.

tenancy in common A form of joint ownership under which there is *no right of survivorship,* and each co-owner can leave his or her share to whomever he or she desires.

What about Joint Ownership?

Many people take title to property jointly either through a *joint tenancy* or as *tenants by the entirety.* These two forms of joint ownership have the following characteristics:

1. The interest of a decedent passes directly to the surviving joint tenant(s) [that is, to the other joint owner(s)] by operation of the law and is free from the claims of the decedent's creditors, heirs, or personal representatives. This is called the **right of survivorship.**
2. A **joint tenancy** may consist of any number of persons. The joint owners do not have to be related. A **tenancy by the entirety,** on the other hand, can exist only between husband and wife.
3. In the case of joint tenancy, each joint tenant can unilaterally sever the tenancy. This is not the case with a tenancy by the entirety, which can be severed only by mutual agreement, divorce, or conveyance by both spouses to a third party. In some states a tenancy by the entirety can exist only with respect to real property, whereas others do not recognize such tenancies at all.
4. The co-owners have equal interests.

Joint tenancy, the more common form of joint ownership, offers a sense of family security, quick and easy transfer to the spouse at death, exemption of jointly owned property from the claims of the deceased's creditors, and avoidance of delays and publicity in the estate-settlement process. The key disadvantage of joint tenancy is the inability to control jointly owned property by a will so that the first joint owner to die cannot control the property's disposition and management on his or her death. Another disadvantage is the potential for higher tax costs often incurred in creating and severing a joint tenancy.

For example, a father who purchases and pays for property and places it in his own and his daughter's name is making a gift to her of one half of the value. On the termination of the tenancy, if the daughter receives the entire proceeds (for example, on the sale of a jointly owned home), the father is making a *second* gift to her—of *his* half interest in the property. In both situations, he will have gratuitously transferred an interest to her that she did not have before. Fortunately, because federal gift tax law does not tax most interspousal transfers, the problem will not arise on a federal level between a married couple (although some states may tax such gifts). Although the property passes to the surviving spouse tax free, larger estate taxes could be due when the second spouse dies—if the estate is worth more than $1,500,000 (in 2005). Because most people believe the advantages of joint ownership of major assets, such as a home or automobile, far outweigh the potential disadvantages, it is commonly used by married couples.

You should also be familiar with two other forms of ownership: *tenancy in common* and *community property.*

Tenancy in Common

A third common form of co-ownership is called **tenancy in common.** There is *no right of survivorship,* and each co-owner can leave his or her share to whomever he or she desires. Thus the decedent owner's will controls the disposition of the decedent's partial interest in the asset. If the decedent dies without a will, the intestate succession laws

Concept ✓

15-3. What is a *will*? Why is it important? Describe the consequences of dying *intestate*.

15-4. Describe the basic clauses that are normally included as part of a will and the requirements with respect to who may make a valid will.

15-5. How can changes in the provisions of a will be made legally? In what four ways can a will be revoked?

15-6. Indicate what is meant by each of the following: (a) *intestacy*, (b) *testator*, (c) *codicil*, (d) *letter of last instructions*.

15-7. What is meant by the *probate process*? Who is an *executor*, and what role does the executor play in estate settlement?

15-8. Describe briefly the importance of the following documents for estate planning: (a) *power of attorney*, (b) *living will*, (c) *durable power of attorney for healthcare*, and (d) *ethical will*.

15-9. Define and differentiate between *joint tenancy* and *tenancy by the entirety*. Discuss the advantages and disadvantages of joint ownership. How does *tenancy in common* differ from joint tenancy?

15-10. What is the *right of survivorship*? What is *community property* and how does it differ from joint tenancy with regard to this right?

of the state where the property is located will determine who inherits the decedent's interest. Tenancy in common interests can be unequal; a property owned by three co-owners could be apportioned such that their respective shares are 50 percent, 30 percent, and 20 percent of the property.

Community Property

Just as tenancy by the entirety is a special form of marital property co-ownership found only in common law states (that is, states that trace their property law to England), community property is a form of marital property co-ownership based on Roman law and found primarily in the southwestern states, which had a Spanish or French influence.

Community property is all property acquired by the effort of either or both spouses during marriage while they are domiciled in a community property state. For example, wages and commissions earned and property acquired by either spouse while living in a community property state are automatically owned equally by both spouses, even if only one was directly involved in acquiring the additional wealth. Property acquired before marriage or by gift or inheritance can be maintained as the acquiring spouse's separate property.

By agreement, which typically must be in writing to be enforceable, the couple can change community property into separate property, and vice versa. Each spouse can leave his or her half of the community property to whomever he or she chooses, thus there is *no right of survivorship* inherent in this form of ownership.

community property
A form of marital property co-ownership wherein all wages and commissions earned and property acquired by either spouse while living in a community property state are automatically owned equally by both spouses.

trust
A legal relationship created when one party, the *grantor*, transfers property to a second party, the *trustee*, for the benefit of third parties, the *beneficiaries*, who may or may not include the grantor.

TRUSTS

LG3

Trusts, another important tool for estate planning, facilitate the transfer of property and the income from that property to another party. Although trusts were once considered estate-planning techniques only for the wealthy, today even those of more modest means use trusts to their advantage in estate planning. This change is attributed to rising real estate values, the bull markets of the 1980s and 1990s, and marketing by estate-planning attorneys. Also, as people live longer and are more likely to marry more than once, they need ways to protect and manage assets.

A **trust** is a legal relationship created when one party, the **grantor** (also called the *settlor, trustor,* or *creator*), transfers property to a second party, the **trustee** (an organization or individual), for the benefit of third parties, the **beneficiaries,** who may or may not include the grantor. The property placed in the trust is called *trust principal* or *res* (pronounced "race"). The trustee holds the legal title to the property in the trust and must use the property and any income it produces solely for the benefit of trust beneficiaries. The trust generally is created by a written document.

The grantor spells out the substantive provisions (such as how to allocate the property in the trust and how to distribute income) and certain administrative provisions. A trust may be *living* (funded during the grantor's life) or *testamentary* (created in a will

grantor
A person who creates a trust and whose property is transferred into it. Also called *settlor, trustor,* or *creator.*

trustee
An organization or individual selected by the *grantor* to manage and conserve property placed in trust for the benefit of the *beneficiaries.*

beneficiaries Those who receive benefits—property or income—from a trust or from the estate of a decedent; may or may not include the *grantor*.

and funded by the probate process). It may be *revocable* or *irrevocable*. The grantor can regain property placed into a revocable trust and alter or amend the terms of the trust. The grantor cannot recover property placed into an irrevocable trust during its term.

Let's now look at how trusts solve various estate-planning problems.

Why Use a Trust?

Trusts are designed for a variety of purposes. The most common motives are to attain income and estate tax savings and manage and conserve property over a long period.

Income and Estate Tax Savings

Under certain circumstances, a grantor who is a high-bracket taxpayer can shift the burden of paying taxes on the income produced by securities, real estate, and other investments to a trust itself or to its beneficiary, both of whom are typically subject to lower income tax rates than the grantor. However, the *Tax Reform Act of 1986* severely limited the ability of a person to shift income in this manner. Specifically, with certain types of trusts, the beneficiary must be more than 14 years of age; otherwise, the income from the trust will be taxed at the same rate as the beneficiary's parents. In addition to possible income tax benefits, impressive *estate tax* savings are also possible because the appreciation in the value of property placed into such a trust can be entirely removed from the grantor's estate and possibly benefit several generations of family members without incurring adverse federal estate tax consequences.

Financial Road Sign

Trust-worthy Tips

These tips will help you use trusts to protect assets and save taxes:

1. Avoid unneeded trusts: If none of your heirs is a minor you may not need a trust.
2. Make sure to name the trust correctly.
3. Verify that title to the assets has been transferred properly to the trust.
3. Be sure that the trustee of an insurance trust purchases the policy and transfers the asset to the trust.
4. If you name the trust's beneficiary as trustee, you can avoid having the trust's assets become part of the beneficiary's estate by limiting the use of proceeds to education, support, health, and maintenance.
5. Be aware that retaining control of spending decisions for a minor's trust may result in a tax liability for parents.
6. Include a spendthrift clause to protect the trust against a beneficiary's creditors.
7. Consider co-trustees and also create a way for beneficiaries to replace poorly performing trustees.

Management and Conservation of Property

Minors, spendthrifts, and those who are mentally incompetent need asset management for obvious reasons. However, busy executives and others who cannot or do not want to spend the countless hours necessary to handle large sums of money and other property often use trusts to relieve themselves of those burdens. The trustee assumes the responsibility for managing and conserving the property on behalf of the beneficiaries. In some cases, management by the trustee is held in reserve in case a healthy and vigorous individual is unexpectedly incapacitated and becomes unable or unwilling to manage his or her assets.

Selecting a Trustee

Five qualities are essential in a trustee. He or she must:

1. Possess sound business knowledge and judgment
2. Have an intimate knowledge of the beneficiary's needs and financial situation
3. Be skilled in investment and trust management
4. Be available to beneficiaries (specifically, this means that the trustee should be young enough to survive the trust term)
5. Be able to make decisions impartially

A corporate trustee, such as a trust company or bank that has been authorized to perform trust duties, may be best able to meet these requirements. A corporate trustee is likely to have investment experience and will not impose the problems created by death, disability, or absence. Unlike a family member, a corporate trustee is impartial and obedient to the directions of the trust instrument. Such objectivity adds value if there are several beneficiaries. On the other hand, a corporate trustee may charge high fees or be overly conservative in investments, be impersonal, or lack familiarity with and understanding of family problems and needs. Often a compromise involves the appointment of one or more individuals and a corporate trustee as co-trustees.

Common Types and Characteristics of Trusts

Although there are various types of trusts, the most common are the *living trust,* the *testamentary trust,* and the *irrevocable life insurance trust,* each of which is described in the following sections. Exhibit 15.6 describes seven other popular trusts.

EXHIBIT 15.6

Seven Popular Trusts

Trusts shift assets (and thus appreciation) out of one's estate while retaining some say in the future use of the assets. The drawback is that trusts can be cumbersome and expensive to arrange and administer. Here are brief descriptions of seven popular trusts:

- **Credit Shelter Trust.** Most common trust for estate planning; couples with combined assets worth more than the "applicable exclusion amount" can gain full use of each partner's exclusion by having that amount placed in a bypass trust, that is, one that bypasses the surviving spouse's taxable estate. It is called a *credit shelter trust* because of the way the taxes are calculated using a method called the *unified credit.* The surviving spouse is usually given the right to all the trust income and, in an emergency, even has access to the principal. Thus, if the first death occurred in the year 2005, the trust would be funded with assets worth $1,500,000.
- **Qualified Terminable Interest Property (QTIP) Trust.** Usually set up in addition to a *credit shelter trust* to ensure that money stays in the family; it receives some or all of the assets in the estate over the applicable exclusion amount ($1,500,000 in 2005). Assets left outright to a spouse who remarries could be claimed by the new spouse. The survivor receives all income from the property until death, at which point the assets go to the persons chosen by the first spouse to die. Estate taxes on QTIP trust assets can be delayed until the second spouse dies. Also useful for couples with children from prior marriages.
- **Special Needs Trust.** An irrevocable trust established for the benefit of a person with disabilities. It is designed to provide extra help and life enrichment without reducing state and federal government help to the beneficiary.
- **Minor's Section 2503(c) Trust.** Set up for a minor, often to receive tax-free gifts. However, assets must be distributed to the minor by the time he or she turns 21.
- **Crummey Trust.** Used to make tax-free gifts up to the annual exclusion amounts to children; unlike a *minor's section 2503(c) trust,* these funds do not have to be distributed at age 21. However, the beneficiary can withdraw the funds placed into the trust for a limited time (for example, for up to 30 days), after which the right to make a withdrawal ceases. (The annual exclusion amount is the annual amount that can be given each year without being subject to gift tax—for example, $11,000 in 2005.)
- **Charitable Lead (or Income) Trust.** Pays some or all of its income to a charity for a period of time. Then, the property is distributed to noncharitable beneficiaries. Grantor gets immediate income tax deduction based on expected future pay-out to charity.
- **Charitable Remainder Trust.** Similar to a *charitable lead trust,* except that income goes to taxable beneficiaries (for example, the grantor or the grantor's children) and principal to a charity when the trust ends.

Living Trusts

A **living (inter vivos) trust** is one created and funded during the grantor's lifetime. It can be either revocable or irrevocable and can last for a limited period or continue long after the grantor's death. These come in two forms, revocable and irrevocable.

living (inter vivos) trust
A trust created and funded during the grantor's lifetime.

Revocable Living Trust

revocable living trust
A trust in which the grantor reserves the right to revoke the trust and regain trust property.

The grantor reserves the right to revoke the trust and regain trust property in a **revocable living trust.** For federal income tax purposes, grantors of these trusts are treated as owners of the property in the trust—in other words, just as if they held the property in their own names—and are therefore taxed on any income produced by the trust.
Revocable living trusts have three basic advantages:

1. Management continuity and income flow are ensured even after the death of the grantor. No probate is necessary because the trust continues to operate after the death of the grantor just as it did while he or she was alive.
2. The trustee assumes burdens of investment decisions and management responsibility. For example, an individual may want to control investment decisions and management policy as long as he or she is alive and healthy but sets up a trust to provide backup help in case he or she becomes unable or unwilling to continue managing the assets.
3. The terms and the amount of assets placed into the trust do not become public knowledge, as they would during the probate process.

The principal disadvantages of these trusts include the fees charged by the trustee for managing the property placed into the trust and the legal fees charged for drafting the trust instruments.

Irrevocable Living Trust

irrevocable living trust
A trust in which the grantor relinquishes the title to the property placed in it and gives up the right to revoke or terminate the trust.

Grantors who establish an **irrevocable living trust** relinquish title to the property they place in it and give up the right to revoke or terminate the trust. (The grantor may retain the income from certain types of irrevocable trusts.) Such trusts have all the advantages of revocable trusts plus the potential for reducing taxes. Disadvantages of such a trust relate to the fees charged by trustees for managing assets placed in it, possible gift taxes on assets placed into it, in some cases the grantor's complete loss of the trust property and any income it may produce, and the grantor's forfeiture of the right to alter the terms of the trust as circumstances change.

Living Trusts and Pour-Over Wills

pour-over will
A provision in a will that provides for the passing of the estate—after debts, expenses, taxes, and specific bequests—to an existing living trust.

A will can be written so that it "pours over" designated assets into a previously established revocable or irrevocable living trust. The trust may also be named beneficiary of the grantor's insurance policies. The **pour-over will** generally contains a provision passing the estate—after debts, expenses, taxes, and specific bequests—to an existing living trust. The pour-over will ensures that the property left out of the living trust, either inadvertently or deliberately, will make its way into the trust (that is, "pour over" into it). The trust contains provisions as to how those assets (together with insurance proceeds payable to it) will be administered and distributed. Such an arrangement provides for easily coordinated and well-administered management of estate assets.

Concept ✓

15-11. Describe the basic trust arrangement, and discuss purposes for which trusts are typically established. What essential qualities should a trustee possess?
15-12. What is a *living (inter vivos) trust?* Distinguish between a *revocable living trust* and an *irrevocable living trust.*
15-13. Explain what is meant by each of the following: (a) *grantor,* (b) *trustee,* (c) *beneficiary,* (d) *pour-over will,* (e) *testamentary trust,* and (f) *irrevocable life insurance trust.*

Testamentary Trust

testamentary trust
A trust created by a decedent's will and funded through the probate process.

A trust created by a decedent's will is called a **testamentary trust**. Such a trust comes into existence only after the will is probated. A court order directs the executor to transfer the property to the trustee to fund the trust. This type of trust does not provide any tax savings for the grantor because he or she continues to own the property until his or her death.

Irrevocable Life Insurance Trust

A wealthy individual can establish an **irrevocable life insurance trust** where the major asset of the trust is life insurance on the grantor's life. To avoid having the proceeds of the policy included in the grantor's estate, the independent trustee usually acquires the policy. The terms of the trust make it possible for the trustee to use the proceeds to pay the grantor's estate taxes and to take care of the grantor's spouse and children.

FEDERAL UNIFIED TRANSFER TAXES

LG4

Federal tax law establishes a **gift tax** on the value of certain gifts made during one's lifetime and an **estate tax** on "deathtime" gifts. For decades, the gift tax and estate tax gave very similar treatment to wealth transfers, regardless of whether the transfer was during life (a gift) or at death (part of an estate). Indeed, these taxes are still officially part of what is called the Uniform Transfer Tax within the Internal Revenue Code. While the tax rate is the same for gifts and estates and is known as the **unified rate schedule** (see the graduated table of rates in Exhibit 15.7), the difference in the applicable exclusion amount will make large gifts more expensive than estate transfers for the period between 2004 and 2010.

The *Economic Growth and Tax Relief Reconciliation Act of 2001 (EGTRRA)* has greatly complicated estate planning for wealthy families because it initially increases the amount that can pass free of estate taxes, temporarily eliminates the estate tax altogether for the year 2010, and then, in 2011, returns the tax to what it would have been had the Act never been passed. In addition, EGTRRA makes gift taxes more costly than estate taxes as the amount that can pass tax free, called the applicable exclusion amount, is frozen at $1 million for gifts, while it increases in increments from $1 million in 2002 to $3.5 million for estates in 2009.

Consider these two examples:

1. Fred gives his daughter a $4,000,000 taxable gift in 2005. Gift taxes equal $1,395,000.
2. Mary dies in 2005 and leaves her son a $4,000,000 estate. The estate tax equals $1,185,000.

Due to the difference in the respective applicable exclusion amounts (see Exhibit 15.8 on page 670); in the previous examples the gift tax is $210,000 higher than the estate tax—even though the transferred amount is the same.

Therefore, as a result of the 2001 Tax Act, many estate planners recommend against giving sizable lifetime gifts. Many planners expect Congress to revisit this area of the law to "fix" the estate tax so that it does not disappear for the year 2010 only to have it reappear the following year for estates over $1 million. The fix is likely to include having the estate applicable exclusion amount set permanently (well, as permanent as things get in tax law) at $4 million, perhaps with that amount being indexed for inflation.

irrevocable life insurance trust
An irrevocable trust, typically established by a wealthy individual, where the major asset of the trust is life insurance on the grantor's life.

gift tax
A tax levied on the value of certain types of gifts made during the giver's lifetime.

estate tax
A tax levied on the value of property transferred at the owner's death.

unified rate schedule
A graduated table of rates applied to all taxable transfers after a number of adjustments and computations; used for *both* federal gift and estate tax purposes.

GIFTS AND TAXES

Gifting can be a good way to transfer property to a beneficiary before you die. However, most transfers will be subject to gift taxes. There is no gift tax on services that one person performs for another, nor is the rent-free use of property a taxable transfer. A tax may be payable on cash gifts, gifts of personal or real property, and both direct and indirect gifts. For example, if a father makes the mortgage payments on his adult son's home, the payment is an indirect gift from father to son. In fact, almost any shifting of financial advantage in which the recipient does not provide full consideration in money or money's worth may be considered a gift. For example, suppose that your

EXHIBIT 15.7

Federal Unified Transfer Tax Rates

The *unified rate schedule* below defines the amount of federal gift and estate taxes that estates of various sizes would have to pay; it incorporates the rates passed in the *Economic Growth and Tax Relief Reconciliation Act of 2001*. The rates and amounts remain the same through 2009 for estates worth up to $2,000,000. Estates under the exclusion amount pay no federal tax; anything over that amount is currently taxed at 45 to 50 percent. The exclusion amount increases annually from $1,000,000 in 2002 to $3,500,000 in 2009 (see Exhibit 15.8 on page 670). From 2002 to 2009, the top tax rates for estates worth more than $2,000,000 decrease as shown below.

Taxable Estate Value		Tentative Tax		
More Than	But Not More Than	Base Amount	+Percent	On Excess Over
$ 0	$ 10,000	$ 0		
10,000	20,000	1,800	20%	$ 10,000
20,000	40,000	3,800	22	20,000
40,000	60,000	8,200	24	40,000
60,000	80,000	13,000	26	60,000
80,000	100,000	18,200	28	80,000
100,000	150,000	23,800	30	100,000
150,000	250,000	38,800	32	150,000
250,000	500,000	70,800	34	250,000
500,000	750,000	155,800	37	500,000
750,000	1,000,000	248,300	39	750,000
1,000,000	1,250,000	345,800	41	1,000,000
1,250,000	1,500,000	448,300	43	1,250,000
1,500,000	2,000,000	555,800	45	1,500,000
Top Rates, 2002				
2,000,000	2,500,000	780,800	49	2,000,000
2,500,000		1,025,800	50	2,500,000
Top rate, 2003				
2,000,000		780,800	49	2,000,000
Top rate, 2004				
2,000,000		780,800	48	2,000,000
Top rate, 2005				
2,000,000		780,800	47	2,000,000
Top rate, 2006				
2,000,000		780,800	46	2,000,000
Top rate, 2007–2009				
2,000,000		780,800	45	2,000,000
2010	Repealed for Estates. The maximum rate for gifts is 35% starting at $500,000.			
2011 and beyond	Returns to pre-2001 tax law levels unless otherwise modified by Congress.			

Source: Adapted from material in John C. Bost, *Estate Planning and Taxation, 2003–2004 Edition* (Dubuque, Iowa: Kendall Hunt, 2003).

father gave you a summer home valued at $175,000 in exchange for $125,000. This type of transaction is called a *bargain sale*. The $50,000 excess value received over the consideration paid is treated as a gift. Of course, if you didn't pay your dad anything for the house, the gift would be equal to its market value ($175,000).

Usually a gift is considered to be made *when the donor relinquishes dominion and control over the property or property interest transferred.* For example, if a mother places cash in a bank account held jointly with her son, no gift is made until the son makes a withdrawal. Until that time, the mother can completely recover the entire amount placed in the account. Therefore, when parents place property into a revocable trust for their children, no gift occurs because they have not relinquished control over the assets placed in it. However, if they later make the trust irrevocable and thereby relinquish their right to control the gift, the transfer will be considered a completed gift.

Is It Taxable?

All that is transferred by an individual is not necessarily subject to a gift tax. Annual exclusions, gift splitting, charitable deductions, and marital deductions are all means of reducing the total amount for tax purposes.

- **Annual exclusions.** The gift tax law allows a person to give gifts up to a specified annual amount—currently $11,000 per calendar year (increased from $10,000 in 2002 and indexed for inflation)—to any number of donees. For example, a person could give gifts of $11,000 each to 30 recipients, for a total of $330,000, without using up any of the donee's applicable exclusion amount (and of course not paying any gift tax). Further, the ability to give tax-free gifts of $11,000 per donee renews annually. This annual exclusion applies only for gifts given with "no strings attached."
- **Gift splitting.** This is a method of reducing gift taxes whereby a gift given by one spouse, with the consent of his or her spouse, can be treated as if each had given one-half of it.
- **Charitable deductions.** There is no limit on the amount that can be given gift-tax free to a qualified charity (one to which deductible gifts can be made for income tax purposes). Therefore, people could give their entire estates to charity and receive gift tax deductions for the total amount. There would be no federal gift taxes regardless of the type or amount of assets transferred.
- **Marital deductions.** Federal law permits an unlimited deduction for gift tax and estate tax purposes on property given or left to a spouse who is a U.S. citizen. Special rules apply in the case of transfers to a spouse who is not a U.S. citizen. These prevent tax-avoidance if the noncitizen spouse returns to his or her native country, where the bequest would then escape taxation in the United States.

annual exclusion
Under the federal gift tax law, a deduction of up to $11,000 (indexed for inflation since 1998) per donee from gross gifts for gifts by any donor to any number of donees in a given calendar year.

gift splitting
A method of reducing gift taxes whereby a gift given by one spouse, with the consent of his or her spouse, can be treated as if each had given one-half of it.

Reasons for Making Lifetime Gifts

There are several tax-oriented reasons why estate planners recommend gift giving:

- **Gift exclusion.** As noted above, a single individual can give any number of donees up to $11,000 (2005 amount) each year with no tax costs to either the recipient or the donor.
- **Gift tax exclusion escapes estate tax.** Fortunately, property that qualifies for the annual exclusion is not taxable and is therefore free from gift and estate taxes. Estate tax savings from this exclusion can be significant. Regardless of a gift's size—and even if it is made within 3 years of the donor's death—it typically will not be treated as part of the donor's gross estate. However, the taxable portion of lifetime gifts (technically called *adjusted taxable gifts*) pushes up the rate at which the donor's estate will be taxed.
- **Appreciation in value.** Generally, the appreciation on a gift, from the time it is made, is excluded from the donor's estate. Suppose that Larry gives his son Steve a gift of stock worth $25,000 in 2003. At the time of Larry's death 2 years later, the stock is worth $60,000. The amount subject to transfer taxes will be $14,000, the amount of

the gift that exceeded the $11,000 annual exclusion at the time the gift was made. None of the appreciation would be subject to gift or estate taxes.

- **Credit limit.** Because of the credit that is used to offset otherwise taxable gifts, gift taxes do not have to be paid on cumulative lifetime gifts up to the applicable exclusion amount (for example, up to $1,500,000 in 2005 and increasing through 2009, per Exhibit 15.8 on page 670). To the extent that the credit is used against lifetime gift taxes, it is not available to offset estate taxes.
- **Impact of marital deduction.** The transfer tax marital deduction allows one spouse to give the other spouse an unlimited amount of money or other property entirely tax free without reducing the applicable exclusion amount that can be transferred to others tax free.

Concept ✓

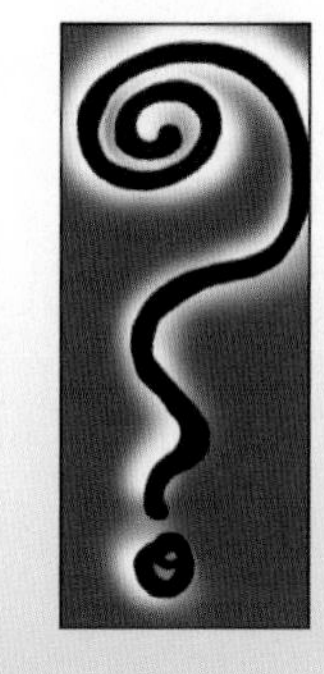

15-14. What is a gift, and when is a gift made? Describe the following terms as they relate to federal gift taxes: (a) *annual exclusion*, (b) *gift splitting*, (c) *charitable deduction*, and (d) *marital deduction*.

15-15. Discuss the reasons estate planners cite for making lifetime gifts. How and in what ways might gift giving help reduce estate shrinkage?

LG5 CALCULATING ESTATE TAXES

Estate taxes may be generated when property is transferred at the time of death, so one of the goals of effective estate planning is to minimize the amount of estate taxes paid. The federal estate tax is levied on the transfer of property at death. The tax is measured by the value of the property that the deceased transfers (or is deemed to transfer) to others. The parenthetical phrase "deemed to transfer" is important because the estate tax applies not only to transfers that a deceased actually makes at death but also to certain transfers made during the person's lifetime. In other words, to thwart tax-avoidance schemes, the estate tax is imposed on certain lifetime gifts that in essence are the same as dispositions of property made at death.

Although most gifts made during one's life are not part of the decedent's gross estate, there are some exceptions. A major exception pertains to life insurance if the owner is also the insured. If the owner-insured gives away the policy within 3 years of his or her death, the proceeds will be included in the insured's gross estate.

For example, 2 years before his death, Max gives his son Eric a $1 million term insurance policy on Max's life. At the time of the gift, Max was in good health, and the value of the term insurance policy for gift tax purposes was clearly less than the annual exclusion amount. Therefore, Max did not have to file a gift tax return. Because Max died within 3 years of gifting the life insurance policy, the $1 million proceeds amount is included in his gross estate for estate tax purposes. Had Max outlived the transfer by more than 3 years, the proceeds would not have been included in his gross estate.

COMPUTATION OF THE FEDERAL ESTATE TAX

The computation of federal estate taxes involves six steps:

1. Determine the *gross estate*, the total of all property in which the decedent had an interest and that is required to be included in the estate.
2. Find the *adjusted gross estate* by subtracting from the gross estate any allowable funeral and administrative expenses, debts, and other expenses incurred during administration.
3. Calculate the *taxable estate* by subtracting any allowable marital deduction or charitable deduction from the adjusted gross estate.

4. Compute the *estate tax base*. After determining the value of the taxable estate, any "adjusted taxable gifts"—which are the taxable gifts (gifts above the annual exclusion) made after 1976—are added to the taxable estate. The unified rate schedule—the one applicable to gift taxes shown in Exhibit 15.7—is then applied to determine a *tentative tax on estate tax base*.
5. After the tentative tax is found, subtract any gift taxes the decedent paid on certain gifts and the **unified tax credit** (described below). The result is the *total death taxes*.
6. Determine the *federal estate tax due*. Certain credits are allowed against the total death taxes, which result in a dollar-for-dollar reduction of the tax. The dominant credit is the state death-tax credit. After reducing the total death taxes by any eligible credits, the federal estate tax due is payable by the decedent's executor, generally within 9 months of the decedent's death.

unified tax credit
The credit that can be applied against the *tentative tax-on-estate tax base*; the unified credit amount for any year absorbs all of the tentative tax on taxable transfers up to the exclusion amount.

You can use Worksheet 15.2 to estimate federal estate taxes. The worksheet shown here depicts the computations for a hypothetical situation involving a death in 2004, when the applicable exclusion of $1.5 million applies. Note that the applicable exclusion amount is not subtracted from the gross estate. The worksheet is useful in following the flow of dollars from the gross estate to the federal estate tax due.

Over the period from 1997 to 2009, the *Taxpayer Relief Act of 1997* and *Economic Growth and Tax Relief Reconciliation Act of 2001* increased the amount that can pass free of transfer taxes. Exhibit 15.8 shows the increasing applicable exclusion amount for estates and the unified credit—the credit that is applied against the tentative tax. The tentative tax is calculated on the estate tax base. Using the rates shown in Exhibit 15.7, you can determine the tentative tax on an estate. For a taxable estate of $1,500,000 in the year 2004, no tax is owed because the unified tax credit for that year is $555,800, which exactly matches the tentative tax on $1,500,000 (calculated using Exhibit 15.7). If the taxable estate in 2004 is $1,700,000, the tentative tax is $645,800, and the estate tax is $90,000 ($645,800 tentative tax − $555,800 unified credit). Notice that a taxable estate of $1,700,000 is $200,000 above the applicable exclusion amount, so the excess is taxed at the marginal rate of 45 percent. Hence the tax owed is $90,000 (.45 × $200,000).

EXHIBIT 15.8

Unified Credits and Applicable Exclusion Amounts for Estates and Gifts

The *Economic Growth and Tax Relief Reconciliation Act of 2001* increased the applicable exclusion amount on a scheduled basis over the period from 2002 to 2009, with a complete repeal of the estate tax in 2010. This table shows the step-ups in the exclusion amount from 2002 through repeal in 2010. Also shown are the unified tax credit amounts over the 2002 to 2011 period.

Year	Unified Tax Credit—Estates	Applicable Exclusion Amount—Estates	Unified Tax Credit—Gifts	Applicable Exclusion Amount—Gifts
2002	$345,800	$1,000,000	$345,800	$1,000,000
2003	$345,800	$1,000,000	$345,800	$1,000,000
2004	$555,800	$1,500,000	$345,800	$1,000,000
2005	$555,800	$1,500,000	$345,800	$1,000,000
2006	$780,800	$2,000,000	$345,800	$1,000,000
2007	$780,800	$2,000,000	$345,800	$1,000,000
2008	$780,800	$2,000,000	$345,800	$1,000,000
2009	$1,455,800	$3,500,000	$345,800	$1,000,000
2010	Estate tax repealed for 2010		$330,800	$1,000,000
2011	$345,800	$1,000,000	$345,800	$1,000,000

Worksheet 15.2 factors the unified credit for the year 2004 into the calculation at line 9b. The $555,800 shown on that line is equal to the tentative tax on an estate tax base of $1,500,000. If the tentative tax shown on line 8 is less than the unified credit available for the decedent's year of death, there will be no federal estate tax due.

worksheet 15.2

Computing Federal Estate Tax Due

This worksheet is useful in determining federal estate tax due. Note that taxes are payable at the marginal tax rate applicable to the estate tax base (line 7), which is the amount that exists before the tax-free exclusion is factored in.

COMPUTING FEDERAL ESTATE TAX DUE

Name Mary Widow Date June 10, 2004

Line	Computation	Item	Amount	Total Amount
1		*Gross estate*		$3,500,000
2	Substract sum of:	(a) Funeral expenses	$ 6,000	
		(b) Administrative expenses	25,000	
		(c) Debts	130,000	
		(d) Other expenses	0	
		Total		(161,000)
3	Result:	*Adjusted gross estate*		$ 3,339,000
4	Subtract sum of:	(a) Marital deduction	—	
		(b) Charitable deduction	—	
		Total		(0)
5	Result:	*Taxable estate*		$ 3,339,000
6	Add:	*Adjusted taxable gifts (post-1976)*		$ 0
7	Result:	*Estate tax base*		$ 3,339,000
8	Compute:	*Tentative tax on estate tax base*[a]		$ 1,423,520
9	Subtract sum of:	(a) Gift tax payable on post-1976 gifts	$ —	
		(b) Unified tax credit[b]	555,800	
		Total		($ 555,800)
10	Result:	*Total death taxes*[c]		$ 867,720
11	Subtract:	State death-tax credit[d]		($ 53,436)
12	Result:	*Federal estate tax due*		$ 814,284

[a]Use Exhibit 15.7 to calculate the tentative tax: $780,800 + [48% × ($3,339,000 − $2,000,000)] = $780,800 + (48% × $339,000) = $1,423,520.

[b]Use Exhibit 15.8 to determine the appropriate unified credit.

[c]Note that the tax amount shown on line 10 is the significant number, because most states are "pickup tax" states, meaning that the state simply collects the state death tax credit, a dollar-for-dollar credit.

[d]Use Exhibit 15.9 to calculate the state death tax credit: $47,700 + [2.4% × ($3,339,000 − $3,100,000)] = $47,700 + (2.4% × $239,000) = $53,436.

STATE DEATH TAXES

Some individual's estates are also subject to state death taxes. About one-third of the states have an inheritance tax that is separate from the federal estate tax. Most states have switched to the pickup estate tax, which allows them to collect the amount of the federal credit for state death taxes, which is shown in Exhibit 15.9. Taxable estates just above the applicable exemption amount may pay more to the state than to the federal government. When the federal credit for state death taxes is phased out in 2005, only those states with separate inheritance taxes will collect any taxes.

For example, in the year 2004, a state that has a pickup tax rather than an inheritance tax (a tax calculated on the value of the property the beneficiary receives) would collect $97,900 on a taxable estate of $5,000,000. But if the death occurred in 2005, the state would collect no death taxes since the state death tax credit expires that year.

Concept ✓

15-16. Explain the general nature of the federal estate tax. How does the *unified tax credit* affect the amount of estate tax owed?

15-17. What is the difference, in terms of calculation, between the state pickup tax and the state inheritance tax? Does your home state impose either of these taxes?

ESTATE-PLANNING TECHNIQUES

LG6

As with income taxes, you can minimize the estate taxes owed by applying appropriate tax avoidance strategies. The federal and state tax laws described in the preceding paragraphs provide both problems and opportunities for you and your estate planner. Judicious use of certain tax-oriented strategies will minimize estate shrinkage and maximize financial security. Two basic techniques of estate planning are dividing your estate and deferring income to minimize income taxes and leave a larger amount to accumulate for the estate. Life insurance is another estate-planning tool.

DIVIDING

Each time you create a new tax-paying entity, you will save income taxes and stimulate estate accumulation. Some of the more popular techniques are:

1. **Giving income-producing property to children, either outright or in trust.** Because each child can receive a specified amount of unearned income each year, some income tax savings may be realized each year even by persons who are not in high tax brackets.
2. **Establishing a corporation.** Incorporation may permit individuals in high tax brackets, such as doctors or other professionals, to save taxes by accumulating income in a manner subject to relatively lower income tax rates.
3. **Properly qualifying for the federal estate tax marital deduction.** This marital deduction allows an individual to pass—estate tax free—unlimited amounts to a spouse, taking full advantage of both spouses' unified credits. Properly qualifying in some estates may mean something less than fully qualifying. In other words, there are circumstances in which an advisor will properly recommend passing less than an individual's entire estate to the surviving spouse.

DEFERRING

Progressive tax rates (rates that increase as the amount of income or size of the estate increases) penalize taxpayers whose maximum earnings (or estates) reach high peaks. This makes it more difficult to gain and maintain financial security. Techniques to minimize the total tax burden by spreading income over more than 1 tax year or deferring

EXHIBIT 15.9

Federal Estate Tax Credit for State Death Taxes, 2003–2004

Credit is given on federal estate tax returns for state death taxes paid up to certain maximum amounts, as specified in the table below. *The Economic Growth and Tax Relief Reconciliation Act of 2001* reduced the state death-tax credit from pre-2002 levels in three annual steps (25% in 2002, 50% in 2003, and 75% in 2004), as shown for 2003 and 2004 in the following table. After 2005, the state death-tax credit is repealed and replaced by a deduction for death taxes actually paid to any state or the District of Columbia.

Taxable Estate		Tax Year 2003		Tax Year 2004	
At Least	But Not More Than	Base Amount	Rate on Excess Over Base	Base Amount	Rate on Excess Over Base
$100,000	$150,000	$0	0.4%	$0	0.2%
$150,000	$200,000	$200	0.8%	$100	0.4%
$200,000	$300,000	$600	1.2%	$300	0.6%
$300,000	$500,000	$1,800	1.6%	$900	0.8%
$500,000	$700,000	$5,000	2.0%	$2,500	1.0%
$700,000	$900,000	$9,000	2.4%	$4,500	1.2%
$900,000	$1,100,000	$13,800	2.8%	$6,900	1.4%
$1,100,000	$1,600,000	$19,400	3.2%	$9,700	1.6%
$1,600,000	$2,100,000	$35,400	3.6%	$17,700	1.8%
$2,100,000	$2,600,000	$53,400	4.0%	$26,700	2.0%
$2,600,000	$3,100,000	$73,400	4.4%	$36,700	2.2%
$3,100,000	$3,600,000	$95,400	4.8%	$47,700	2.4%
$3,600,000	$4,100,000	$119,400	5.2%	$59,700	2.6%
$4,100,000	$5,100,000	$145,400	5.6%	$72,700	2.8%
$5,100,000	$6,100,000	$201,400	6.0%	$100,700	3.0%
$6,100,000	$7,100,000	$261,400	6.4%	$130,700	3.2%
$7,100,000	$8,100,000	$325,400	6.8%	$162,700	3.4%
$8,100,000	$9,100,000	$393,400	7.2%	$196,700	3.6%
$9,100,000	$10,100,000	$465,400	7.6%	$232,700	3.8%
$10,100,000		$541,400	8.0%	$270,700	4.0%

Source: Adapted from material in John C. Bost, *Estate Planning and Taxation, 2003–2004 Edition* (Dubuque, Iowa: Kendall-Hunt, 2003).

the tax to a later period—so the taxpayer can invest the tax money for a longer period of time—apply to estate planning as well as to income tax planning. Examples include:

1. *Nonqualified deferred-compensation plans* for selected individuals in corporate businesses and private contractors.
2. *Making installment sales* instead of cash sales to spread the taxable gain over several years.
3. *Private annuities*, which are arrangements whereby one person transfers property to another, usually a younger family member. This recipient promises in return to pay an annuity to the original owner for as long as he or she lives. The income tax attributable to such an annuity can thereby be spread over a number of years.

Money in Action

Making Your IRA a Survivor

For many people, their IRA will account for most of their estates—in some cases, as much as 80 percent of total assets. If you start your retirement savings early and maximize your contributions to employer-sponsored 401(k) plans or other tax-deferred programs such as Keogh and 403(b) plans, your savings will compound over your career to reach a sizable sum. Each time you change jobs and also when you retire, you must roll the proceeds from your plans into an IRA.

However, retirement accounts often get short shrift in the estate-planning process. The same people who agonize over who will get Mom's jewelry typically neglect this important area of estate planning. They mistakenly assume that their wills also cover their retirement accounts. In fact, the disposition of these funds is governed by the beneficiary designation on each account.

Unlike assets governed by a will, the IRA does not go through the probate process. Any IRA assets that remain after you die go to the beneficiary or beneficiaries you name, as specified by the IRA contract and the custodial agreement with the bank or mutual fund company.

"The key is to pass IRA savings on to heirs intact so that the money keeps growing long after you are gone," says Ed Slott, editor of *Ed Slott's IRA Advisor.* Good IRA estate planning avoids paying taxes from the IRA itself and allows an heir to stretch mandatory distributions over his or her remaining lifetime, so the savings continue to grow tax free.

Some financial planners recommend drafting a separate document called a *retirement asset will (RAW)* with details of beneficiaries and distribution arrangements. The RAW is especially useful when it comes to control of retirement assets. Without instructions from you to the contrary, the custodial agreement might allow a beneficiary to change heirs or prevent the beneficiary from changing to another money manager.

To make sure that your IRA is handled according to your wishes, follow these guidelines:

- **Designate a beneficiary and contingent beneficiary on every IRA account and keep copies of the beneficiary forms with your will.** Without proof that you named a beneficiary, your IRA could be

...continued on next page

Furthermore, when the original owner dies, the property transferred is not part of the transferrer's estate, and the annuity's value drops to zero.

4. *Qualified pension and profit-sharing plans* that allow tax deferral on the income and gains from investments.
5. *Government Series EE bonds* because their earnings can be treated as taxable income at maturity rather than yearly as earned.
6. *Stocks that pay no or low dividends* but provide high price appreciation because they invest retained earnings in profitable projects.
7. *Life insurance policies* in which lifetime growth is not taxed and death values are income tax free. If the insured survives, earnings inherent in policy values become taxable only as received, thus the tax on any gain can be deferred over a lifetime.
8. *Depreciable real estate* that yields high write-offs in years when the estate owner is earning high levels of taxable passive income.
9. *Installment payment of federal estate taxes* applicable to a business interest that equals or exceeds 35 percent of the adjusted gross estate. Payments can be spread over as many as 14 years with only the interest being paid on the unpaid tax during the first 4 years.
10. *Possible elimination of the estate tax* in the near future, or at least additional significant increases in the applicable exclusion amount. (This is discussed in greater detail in a later section.)

Because of the popularity of tax-deferred retirement programs, these assets may compose the bulk of a person's estate. The *Money in Action* box at the left discusses how to protect those accounts and make sure that your heirs get the maximum benefit.

Life Insurance as an Estate-Planning Tool

Life insurance can be a valuable component of your estate plan. A policy can be purchased for an annual premium of from 3 to 6 percent of the face (death) value of the policy. If someone other than the insured owns the policy, the proceeds of such insurance can pass to the decedent's beneficiaries free of income tax, estate tax, inheritance tax, and probate costs. For example, the trustee of an irrevocable life insurance trust might be selected to apply for and own the policy. After the insured's death, the trustee uses the insurance proceeds for the benefit of the surviving family members, who in turn might use them to pay death taxes, debts, administrative expenses, or other family expenses such as college costs, mortgage balances, and other major expenditures. What's more, whole life and universal life insurance policies are an attractive form of loan collateral. As pointed out in Chapters 7 and 8, some lending institutions and other creditors require borrowers to obtain life insurance in an amount sufficient to repay them in the event that borrowers die before fully repaying their loans.

Future of the Estate Tax

The estate tax law passed in 2001 raised the applicable exclusion amounts and decreased the transfer tax rates, with a complete repeal of the estate tax taking place in 2010 but lasting for just one year. The estate tax springs back to life for decedents dying in 2011 or later with a taxable estate that is in excess of $1 million. While it is likely that Congress will revisit the estate tax issue before then, it is too early to predict what the future holds.

As we've learned in this chapter, estate planning goes beyond minimizing taxes. It is the best way to take care of the people you love, help charitable organizations, transfer property, and spell out your wishes if you die or become disabled. Regardless of what happens to the estate tax in the future, estate planning will continue to be a key component of personal financial planning.

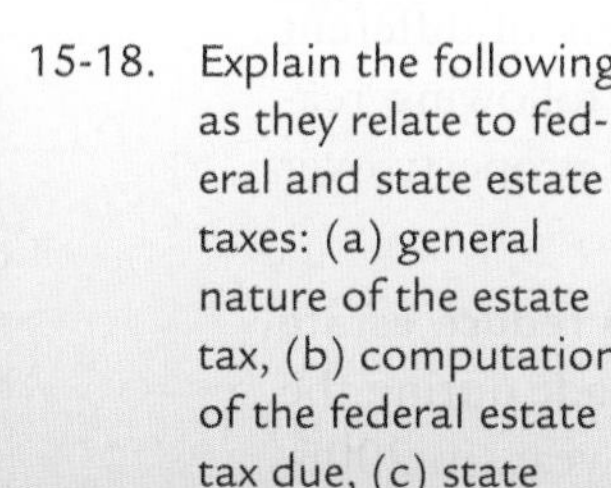

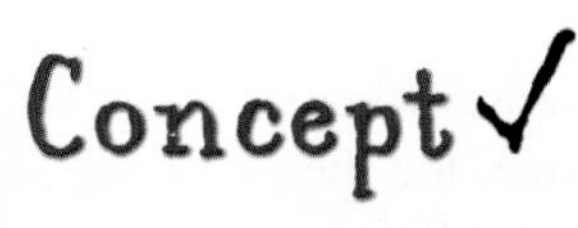

15-18. Explain the following as they relate to federal and state estate taxes: (a) general nature of the estate tax, (b) computation of the federal estate tax due, (c) state inheritance tax, (d) state estate tax, (e) sponge tax, (f) pickup estate tax, (g) amount of exemptions and deductions, (h) multiple taxation, and (i) state death-tax rates.

15-19. The techniques of estate planning can be summarized by the three Ds: divide, defer, and discount. Describe and discuss each of the three Ds and their associated strategies.

liquidated, taxed, rolled into your estate, and taxed again.

- **Update beneficiary forms if you move your IRA to another custodian or have a change in your marital status.**
- **Provide assets to pay estate taxes without taking an IRA distribution that generates hefty taxes.** A life insurance policy that pays when the second spouse dies is one option. The policy should be put in the heir's name and funded through annual tax-free gifts.
- **Make sure that beneficiaries can move the account to another bank or fund custodian.** Some custodians may balk at this; be sure before you open an account that the custodian will honor your detailed instructions.
- **Do not name your estate as beneficiary of your IRA.** The estate must liquidate the account within a specified time and pay taxes on it.
- **Leave an IRA to younger beneficiaries to take advantage of the new stretch IRAs.** *Stretch IRAs* allow you to pass on your wealth for two more generations and reduce the amount you must withdraw during your lifetime. For example, if a mother names her son as beneficiary, at age 70½ she can choose to stretch benefits out over her life and her son's life. On her death, her son gets the IRA, can spread withdrawals over his remaining life expectancy, and pays only income taxes on the amount he withdraws every year. If the son names his own beneficiary, the proceeds can be spread to a third generation (but no further). Most custodians now allow stretch IRAs, but a company 401(k) plan might not.

Critical Thinking Questions

1. Why is it important to clearly specify beneficiary designations in your IRA?
2. Why do some financial planners recommend drafting a *retirement asset will (RAW)*? How is the RAW useful?
3. What is a *stretch IRA*? How can you take advantage of it?

Sources: Neil Downing, "With an IRA, You Can Name Your Beneficiary," *Providence Journal*, August 12, 2002, p. E-01; Ashlea Ebeling, "The Stretch IRA," *Forbes Magazine*, October 13, 2003, p. 138; "IRAs Sometimes Complicate Estate Planning," *The Record* (Bergen County, NJ) February 3, 2002, p. B6; Mike McNamee, "Passing on Your IRA," *Business Week*, April 9, 2001, p. 104; Ronaleen R. Roha, "Your Will Be Done," *Kiplinger's Personal Finance Magazine*, January 1, 2003, p. 82.

SUMMARY

LG1. Describe the role of estate planning in personal financial planning and identify the seven steps involved in the process. Estate planning involves the accumulation, preservation, and distribution of an estate in a manner that will most effectively achieve an estate owner's personal goals. The seven major steps to estate planning are: (1) assess the family situation and set estate-planning goals, (2) gather comprehensive and accurate data, (3) list all assets and determine estate value, (4) designate beneficiaries of estate's assets, (5) estimate estate transfer costs, (6) formulate and implement a plan, and (7) review the plan periodically and revise it as necessary.

LG2. Recognize the importance of preparing a will and other documents to protect you and your estate. A person who dies without a valid will forfeits important privileges, including the right to decide how property will be distributed at death and the opportunity to select who will administer the estate and bear the burden of estate taxes and administrative expenses. The will should provide a clear and unambiguous expression of the testator's wishes, be flexible enough to encompass possible changes in family circumstances, and give proper regard to minimizing income, gift, and estate taxes. A will is valid only if properly executed by a person of sound mind. Once drawn up, wills can be changed by codicil or be fully revoked. The executor, named in the will, is responsible for collecting the decedent's assets, paying his or her debts and taxes, and distributing any remaining assets to the beneficiaries in the prescribed fashion. In addition to the will, other important estate-planning documents include the letter of last instructions, power of attorney, living will, durable power of attorney for healthcare, and an ethical will.

LG3. Explain how trusts are used in estate planning. The trust relationship arises when one party, the grantor, transfers property to a second party, the trustee, for the benefit of a third party, the beneficiary. Although there are a variety of different types of trusts, each is designed primarily for one or both of the following reasons: to save income and estate taxes and to manage and conserve property over a long period.

LG4. Determine whether a gift will be taxable and use planned gifts to reduce estate taxes. Gifts of cash, financial assets, and personal or real property made during the donor's lifetime are subject to federal taxes. A gift of $11,000 per year (in 2005, and indexed for inflation) to each recipient is excluded from the donor's gift tax calculation. Generally, donations to qualified charities and gifts between spouses are also excluded from the gift tax.

LG5. Calculate federal and state taxes due on an estate. Federal estate taxes are essentially a levy on the transfer of assets at death. They are unified (coordinated) with the gift tax—which imposes a graduated tax on the transfer of property during one's lifetime—so that the rates and credits are the same for both. Today, as a result of the 2001 Tax Act, the gift tax exclusion amount stays at $1,000,000, and the estate tax exclusion amount is rising from $1,000,000 in 2002 to $3,500,000 in 2009, will be eliminated in 2010, and drops back to $1,000,000 in 2011. (Congress is likely to reconsider estate taxes before that date.) Once federal estate taxes are computed, certain credits are allowed, and the resulting amount is payable in full generally within 9 months of the decedent's death. States also impose taxes on estates.

LG6. Use effective estate-planning techniques to minimize estate taxes. Most well-defined estate plans use three basic estate-planning techniques. Dividing involves the creation of new tax entities. Deferring gives an individual the use of money that would otherwise have been paid in taxes. Life insurance proceeds can be used to pay estate taxes or to provide heirs with funds for specific purposes.

Financial Planning Exercises

1. Generate a list of estate-planning objectives that apply to your personal family situation. Be sure to consider the size of your potential estate and both people planning and asset planning.
2. Renée and Steve Burrows are in their mid-thirties and have two children, ages 8 and 5. They have combined annual income of $95,000 and own a house in joint tenancy with a market value of $310,000, on which they have a mortgage of $250,000. Steve has $100,000 in group term life insurance and an individual universal life policy for $150,000. However, the Burrowses have not yet prepared their wills. Steve plans to do one soon, but they think that Renée doesn't need one because the house is jointly owned. As their financial planner, explain why it is important for both Steve and Renée to draft wills as soon as possible.
3. Prepare a basic will for yourself, using the guidelines presented in the text; also prepare your brief letter of last instructions.
4. Your best friend has asked you to be executor of his estate. What qualifications do you need, and would you accept the responsibility?
5. Joe Phillips, 48 and a widower, and Amy Parsons, 44 and divorced, were married 5 years ago. Joe has two children and Amy has one from their prior marriages. Their estate totals $1.4 million, including a house valued at $475,000, a vacation home in the mountains, investments, antique furniture that has been in Amy's family for many years, and jewelry belonging to Joe's first wife. Discuss how they could use trusts as part of their estate planning, and suggest some other ideas for them to consider when preparing their wills and related documents.

6. ***Use Worksheet 15.2.*** When Jim Levitt died in 2004, he left an estate valued at $3,650,000, as follows: $10,000 to the local hospital, $60,000 to his alma mater, and the remainder to his three adult children. Death-related costs and expenses were: $6,800 for funeral expenses, $40,000 paid to attorneys, $5,000 paid to accountants, and $30,000 paid to the trustee of his living trust. In addition, there were debts of $115,000. Use Worksheet 15.2 and Exhibits 15.7, 15.8, and 15.9 to calculate the state death-tax credit and the federal estate tax due on his estate.
7. Summarize any recent legislation affecting estate taxes and briefly describe its impact on estate planning. Explain why getting rid of the estate tax does not eliminate the need for estate planning.

Applying Personal Finance

Prepare Your Will!

If you die without a valid will, the laws of the state in which you live will determine what happens to your property. That may be fine with people who have few assets, but it's not fine for people who care what happens to their property, and it's certainly not fine for people with dependents. The purpose of this project is for you to consider what your current will should contain and what changes you should make to your will in accordance with your future circumstances.

Look back through this chapter and review the common features of a will, then write your own will based on the sample clauses and examples of a representative will given in the text. List the property that you currently have or expect to have in the future, and name a beneficiary for each. Be sure to name your personal representative, and charge him or her with disposing of your estate in accordance with your wishes. If you have children or expect to have children, or if you have other dependents such as an elderly parent or disabled sibling, be sure to name a guardian and a back-up guardian for them. Also prepare a letter of last instruction to convey any personal thoughts or instructions that you feel cannot be properly included in your will. Remember, this exercise should help you think about the orderly disposition of your estate, which is the final act in the implementation of your personal financial plans.

CONTEMPORARY CASE APPLICATIONS

15.1 A Long Overdue Will for Theo

During the early 1970s, Theo Pappadopolus, originally from Greece, migrated to the United States where he is now a citizen. A man of many talents and deep foresight, he has built a large fleet of ocean-going oil tankers during his stay in the United States. Now a wealthy man in his sixties, he resides in Palm Springs, Florida, with his second wife, Veronica, age 35. He has two sons, who are both high-school seniors. For quite a while, Theo has considered preparing a will to ensure that his estate will be properly distributed if some unforeseen tragedy or natural cause takes his life. A survey of his estate—all legally owned by him—reveals the following:

Ranch in Amarillo, Texas	$ 800,000
Condominium in San Francisco	400,000
House in Palm Springs	600,000
Franchise in ice cream stores	2,000,000
Stock in Seven Seas International	5,000,000
Shares in Fourth National Bank	1,000,000
Corporate bonds	3,000,000
Other assets	200,000
Total assets	$13,000,000

In addition to $1 million for their education and welfare, he would like to leave each of his sons 20 percent of his estate. He wishes to leave 40 percent of the estate to his wife. The rest of the estate is to be divided among relatives, friends, and charitable institutions. He has scheduled an appointment for drafting his will with his attorney and close friend, Leonard Wiseman. Theo would like to appoint Leonard and his cousin, Plato Jones, as coexecutors of his estate. If one of them predeceases Theo, he would like his bank, Fourth National Bank, to act as coexecutor.

Questions

1. Does Theo really need a will? Explain why or why not? What would happen to his estate if he were to die without a will?
2. Explain to Theo the common features that need to be incorporated into a will.
3. Is a living trust an appropriate part of his estate plan? How would a living trust change the nature of Theo's will?
4. What are the options available to Theo if he decides to change or revoke the will at a later date? Is it more difficult to change a living trust?
5. What duties will Leonard Wiseman and Plato Jones have to perform as coexecutors of Theo's estate?

15.2 Estate Taxes on Philip Colburn's Estate

Philip Colburn of Arlington Heights, Delaware, was 65 when he retired in 1998. His wife of 35 years passed away shortly thereafter. Her will left everything to Philip. Although her estate was valued at $1,750,000, there was no estate tax due because of the 100 percent marital deduction. Their only child, Mark Colburn, is married to Alice, and they have four children, two in college and two in high school. When Philip died in 2004, his home was valued at $650,000, his vacation cabin on the lake was valued at $85,000, his investments in stocks and bonds at $890,000, and his pension funds at $345,000 (Mark was named beneficiary). Philip also owned a life insurance policy that paid proceeds of $250,000 to Mark. He left $60,000 to his church and $25,000 to his high school to start a scholarship fund in his wife's name. The rest of the estate was left to Mark. Funeral costs were $5,000. Debts and expenses totaled $90,000. Four years prior to his death, Philip made a gift of XYZ stock worth $170,000 jointly to Mark and Alice. Because of the annual exclusions and the unified credit, no gift taxes were due. Use Worksheet 15.2 to guide your calculations as you answer the following questions.

Questions

1. Compute the value of Philip's *probate estate.*
2. Compute the value of Philip's *gross estate* at the time of his death.
3. Determine the total allowable deductions.
4. Calculate the *estate tax base*, taking into account the gifts given to Mark and Alice (remember the annual exclusions).
5. Use Exhibit 15.7 to determine the *tentative tax on estate tax base.*
6. Subtract the appropriate *unified tax credit* (Exhibit 15.8) for 2004 from the tentative tax on estate tax base to arrive at the total death taxes. Note that there is no credit for gift tax payable on post-1976 gifts because no gift taxes had to be paid.
7. Determine the *state death-tax credit.*
8. Subtract the state death-tax credit from the total death taxes to arrive at the *federal estate tax due.*
9. Comment on the estate shrinkage experienced on Philip's estate. What might have been done to reduce this shrinkage? Explain.

Money Online

My Will Be Done!

1. **http://www.northwesternmutual.com**

Maximize the wealth you pass on to your loved ones. Click on "Network Services" and then on "Estate Planning" at Northwestern Mutual's Web site for information on the entire estate planning process. Learn the basic concepts involved in estate planning and the various techniques which can be utilized.

2. **http://www.usaaedfoundation.org**

What documents are essential in a comprehensive estate plan? Click on "Financial" and then on "Estate Planning" to find an explanation of these necessary legal documents. Read on through the article to learn how trusts and life insurance are used as estate planning tools, how to plan for probate, and how to use property ownership laws in estate planning.

3. **http://www.findlaw.com**

Need legal information? The Find Law Web site provides resources for professionals, students, businesses, or the public. Topics of interest include Elder Law and Aging, Estate Planning, Wills, and Probate and Estates.

4. **http://www.nolo.com**

What can you NOT do in your will? Click on "Wills & Estate Planning" and look under "Wills" for the answer to this and other estate planning questions. Access Nolo's extensive and comprehensive encyclopedia to find topics such as "Special Property Rules for Married People," "Using Roth IRAs to Avoid Probate," and "You May Not Need a Living Trust."

5. **http://www.mtpalermo.com**
Take a crash course in wills and trusts! This legal Web site presents a practical guide not only to wills and trusts, but also to the entire estate planning process. Written in easy-to-understand language, this course discusses living trusts, tax issues, specialized trusts and estate planning tools, and preserving the estate with long-term care insurance.

6. **http://www.seniorlaw.com/resource.htm**
What legal resources are available on the Internet for the elderly? The Senior Law site provides an unbelievable amount of links to all types of resources. Find general legal resources, federal agencies, and estate planning sites, to name only a few.

7. **http://www.bradynordgren.com**
Are you fiscally fit? Click on "Articles—Estate Planning" to find the "Estate Planning Checklist" at this legal Web site. Be sure to examine "Estate Planning Concepts" for a thorough discussion of estate and gift tax provisions. Then read through "Talking with Adult Children" for a discussion on the importance of involving one's children in the estate planning process.

8. **http://www.nafep.com**
What are the estate planning considerations for business owners? How can you protect your estate's assets from lawsuits and judgments? What about establishing a charitable family foundation? These estate planning concerns and others are addressed at the Web site of the National Association of Financial and Estate Planning.

9. **http://www.prudential.com**
What are the various types of trusts and how can they be used in estate planning? Read through the "Estate Planning Tutorial" presented by Prudential Securities. Click on "Financial Planning" and then on "Your Estate" to learn more about protecting the transfer of your assets to your loved ones or to charity.

10. **http://www.estateplanninglinks.com**
Links and more links! The Estate Planning Links Web site has links for virtually every estate planning need. Find links to legal resources, definitions, calculators, tax information, and much more.

Just for Fun!

11. **http://www.courttv.com/people/wills**
Read the wills of famous people. Court TV gives you a glimpse. Find out what a chief justice forgot to put in his own will or which baseball player established a foundation for destitute children. Above all, be sure to find out who got Jerry Garcia's guitars!

APPENDICES

Appendix A

Table of Future Value Factors

Instructions: To use this table, find the future value factor that corresponds to both a given time period (year) and an interest rate. To illustrate, if you want the future value factor for 6 years and 10 percent, move across from year 6 and down from 10 percent to the point at which the row and column intersect: 1.772. Other illustrations: For 3 years and 15 percent, the proper future value factor is 1.521; for 30 years and 8 percent, it is 10.062.

	Interest Rate											
Year	2%	3%	5%	6%	8%	9%	10%	12%	15%	20%	25%	30%
1	1.020	1.030	1.050	1.060	1.080	1.090	1.100	1.120	1.150	1.120	1.250	1.300
2	1.040	1.060	1.102	1.120	1.166	1.190	1.210	1.254	1.322	1.440	1.562	1.690
3	1.061	1.090	1.158	1.190	1.260	1.290	1.331	1.405	1.521	1.728	1.953	2.197
4	1.082	1.130	1.216	1.260	1.360	1.410	1.464	1.574	1.749	2.074	2.441	2.856
5	1.104	1.160	1.276	1.340	1.469	1.540	1.611	1.762	2.011	2.488	3.052	3.713
6	1.126	1.190	1.340	1.420	1.587	1.670	1.772	1.974	2.313	2.986	3.815	4.827
8	1.172	1.260	1.477	1.590	1.851	1.990	2.144	2.476	3.059	4.300	5.960	8.157
10	1.219	1.340	1.629	1.790	2.159	2.360	2.594	3.106	4.046	6.192	9.313	13.786
12	1.268	1.420	1.796	2.010	2.518	2.810	3.138	3.896	5.350	8.916	14.552	23.298
15	1.346	1.560	2.079	2.390	3.172	3.640	4.177	5.474	8.137	15.407	28.422	51.185
20	1.486	1.810	2.653	3.210	4.661	5.600	6.727	9.646	16.366	38.337	86.736	190.047
25	1.641	2.090	3.386	4.290	6.848	8.620	10.834	17.000	32.918	95.395	264.698	705.627
30	1.811	2.420	4.322	5.740	10.062	13.260	17.449	29.960	66.210	237.373	807.793	2619.936
35	2.000	2.810	5.516	7.690	14.785	20.410	28.102	52.799	133.172	590.657	2465.189	9727.598
40	2.208	3.260	7.040	10.280	21.724	31.410	45.258	93.049	267.856	1469.740	7523.156	36117.754

Note: All factors are rounded to the nearest 1/1000 as shown to agree with values used in the text.

Appendix B

Table of Future Value of Annuity Factors

Instructions: To use this table, find the future value of annuity factor that corresponds to both a given time period (year) and an interest rate. To illustrate, if you want the future value of annuity factor for 6 years and 10 percent, move across from year 6 and down from 10 percent to the point at which the row and column intersect: 7.716. Other illustrations: For 3 years and 15 percent, the proper future value of annuity factor is 3.472; for 30 years and 8 percent, it is 113.282.

	Interest Rate											
Year	2%	3%	5%	6%	8%	9%	10%	12%	15%	20%	25%	30%
1	1.000	1.000	1.000	1.000	1.000	1.000	1.000	1.000	1.000	1.000	1.000	1.000
2	2.020	2.030	2.050	2.060	2.080	2.090	2.100	2.120	2.150	2.200	2.250	2.300
3	3.060	3.090	3.152	3.180	3.246	3.270	3.310	3.374	3.472	3.640	3.813	3.990
4	4.122	4.180	4.310	4.380	4.506	4.570	4.641	4.779	7.993	5.368	5.766	6.187
5	5.204	5.310	5.526	5.630	5.867	5.980	6.105	6.353	6.742	7.442	8.207	9.043
6	6.308	6.460	6.802	6.970	7.336	7.520	7.716	8.115	8.754	9.930	11.259	12.756
8	8.583	8.890	9.549	9.890	10.637	11.030	11.436	12.300	13.727	16.499	19.842	23.858
10	10.950	11.460	12.578	13.180	14.487	15.190	15.937	17.549	20.304	25.959	33.253	42.619
12	13.412	14.190	15.917	16.870	18.977	20.140	21.384	24.133	29.001	39.580	54.208	74.326
15	17.293	18.600	21.578	23.270	27.152	29.360	31.772	37.280	47.580	72.035	109.687	167.285
20	24.297	26.870	33.066	36.780	45.762	51.160	57.274	72.052	102.443	186.687	342.945	630.157
25	32.030	36.460	47.726	54.860	73.105	84.700	98.346	133.333	212.790	471.976	1054.791	2348.765
30	40.567	47.570	66.438	79.060	113.282	136.300	164.491	241.330	434.738	1181.865	3227.172	8729.805
35	49.994	60.460	90.318	111.430	172.314	215.700	271.018	431.658	881.152	2948.294	9856.746	32422.090
40	60.401	75.400	120.797	154.760	259.052	337.870	442.580	767.080	1779.048	7343.715	30088.621	120389.375

Note: All factors are rounded to the nearest 1/1000 as shown to agree with values used in the text.

Appendix C

Table of Present Value Factors

Instructions: To use this table, find the present value factor that corresponds to both a given time period (year) and an interest rate. To illustrate, if you want the present value factor for 25 years and 7 percent, move across from year 25 and down from 7 percent to the point at which the row and column intersect: .184. Other illustrations: For 3 years and 15 percent, the proper present value factor is .658; for 30 years and 8 percent, it is .099.

	Interest Rate											
Year	2%	3%	5%	7%	8%	9%	10%	12%	15%	20%	25%	30%
1	.980	.971	.952	.935	.926	.917	.909	.833	.870	.893	.800	.769
2	.961	.943	.907	.873	.857	.842	.826	.797	.756	.694	.640	.592
3	.942	.915	.864	.816	.794	.772	.751	.712	.658	.579	.512	.455
4	.924	.888	.823	.763	.735	.708	.683	.636	.572	.482	.410	.350
5	.906	.863	.784	.713	.681	.650	.621	.567	.497	.402	.328	.269
6	.888	.837	.746	.666	.630	.596	.564	.507	.432	.335	.262	.207
8	.853	.789	.677	.582	.540	.502	.467	.404	.327	.233	.168	.123
10	.820	.744	.614	.508	.463	.422	.386	.322	.247	.162	.107	.073
12	.789	.701	.557	.444	.397	.356	.319	.257	.187	.112	.069	.043
15	.743	.642	.481	.362	.315	.275	.239	.183	.123	.065	.035	.020
20	.673	.554	.377	.258	.215	.178	.149	.104	.061	.026	.012	.005
25	.610	.478	.295	.184	.146	.116	.092	.059	.030	.010	.004	.001
30	.552	.412	.231	.131	.099	.075	.057	.033	.015	.004	.001	*
35	.500	.355	.181	.094	.068	.049	.036	.019	.008	.002	*	*
40	.453	.307	.142	.067	.046	.032	.022	.011	.004	.001	*	*

*Present value factor is zero to three decimal places.

Note: All factors are rounded to the nearest 1/1000 as shown to agree with values used in the text.

Appendix D

Table of Present Value of Annuity Factors

Instructions: To use this table, find the present value of annuity factor that corresponds to both a given time period (year) and an interest rate. To illustrate, if you want the present value of annuity factor for 30 years and 7 percent, move across from year 30 and down from 7 percent to the point at which the row and column intersect: 12.409. Other illustrations: For 3 years and 15 percent, the proper present value of annuity factor is 2.283; for 5 years and 8 percent, it is 3.993; for 30 years and 8 percent, it is 11.258.

	Interest Rate											
Year	2%	3%	5%	7%	8%	9%	10%	12%	15%	20%	25%	30%
1	.980	.971	.952	.935	.926	.917	.909	.893	.870	.833	.800	.769
2	1.942	1.913	1.859	1.808	1.783	1.759	1.736	1.690	1.626	1.528	1.440	1.361
3	2.884	2.829	2.723	2.624	2.577	2.531	2.487	2.402	2.283	2.106	1.952	1.816
4	3.808	3.717	3.546	3.387	3.312	3.240	3.170	3.037	2.855	2.589	2.362	2.166
5	4.713	4.580	4.329	4.100	3.993	3.890	3.791	3.605	3.352	2.991	2.689	2.436
6	5.601	5.417	5.076	4.767	4.623	4.486	4.355	4.111	3.784	3.326	2.951	2.643
8	7.326	7.020	6.463	5.971	5.747	5.535	5.335	4.968	4.487	3.837	3.329	2.925
10	8.983	8.530	7.722	7.024	6.710	6.418	6.145	5.650	5.019	4.192	3.570	3.092
12	10.575	9.954	8.863	7.943	7.536	7.161	6.814	6.194	5.421	4.439	3.725	3.190
15	12.849	11.938	10.380	9.108	8.560	8.061	7.606	6.811	5.847	4.675	3.859	3.268
20	16.352	14.878	12.462	10.594	9.818	9.129	8.514	7.469	6.259	4.870	3.954	3.316
25	19.524	17.413	14.094	11.654	10.675	9.823	9.077	7.843	6.464	4.948	3.985	3.329
30	22.396	19.601	15.373	12.409	11.258	10.274	9.427	8.055	6.566	4.979	3.995	3.332
35	24.999	21.487	16.378	12.948	11.655	10.567	9.844	8.176	6.617	4.992	3.998	3.333
40	27.356	23.115	17.159	13.332	11.925	10.757	9.779	8.244	6.642	4.997	3.999	3.333

Note: All factors are rounded to the nearest 1/1000 as shown to agree with values used in the text.

Appendix E

Using a Financial Calculator

Important Financial Keys on the Typical Financial Calculator

The important financial keys on a typical financial calculator are depicted and defined below. On some calculators the keys may be labeled using lowercase characters for "N" and "I". Also, "I/Y" may be used in the place of the "I" key.

CPT — Compute Key; Used to initiate financial calculation once all values are input
N — Number of Periods
I — Interest Rate per Period
PV — Present Value
PMT — Amount of Payment; Used only for annuities
FV — Future Value

The handheld financial calculator makes it easy to calculate time value. Once you have mastered the time value of money concepts using tables, we suggest you use such a calculator. For one thing, it becomes very cumbersome to use tables when calculating anything other than annual compounding. For another, calculators rather than tables are used almost exclusively in the business of personal financial planning.

You don't want to become overly dependent on calculators, however, because you may not be able to recognize a nonsensical answer in the event that you accidentally push the wrong button. The important calculator keys are shown and labeled in the above exhibit. Before using your calculator to make the financial computations described in this text, be aware of the following points.

1. The keystrokes on some of the more sophisticated and expensive calculators are menu-driven: after you select the appropriate routine, the calculator prompts you to input each value; a compute key (CPT) is not needed to obtain a solution.
2. Many calculators allow the user to set the number of payments per year. Most of these calculators are preset for monthly payments—12 payments per year. Because we work primarily with annual payments—one payment per year—it is important to *make sure that your calculator is set for one payment per year.* Although most calculators are preset to recognize that all payments occur at the end of the period, it is important to *make sure your calculator is in the END mode.* Consult the reference guide that accompanies your calculator for instructions for setting these values.
3. To avoid including previous data in current calculations, *always clear all registers of your calculator before inputting values and making each computation.*
4. The known values *can be punched into the calculator in any order*; the order specified in this and other calculator use demonstrations included in this text results merely from convenience and personal preference.

Calculator Keystrokes Let's go back to the future value calculation on page 53, in which we're trying to calculate the future value of $5,000 at the end of 6 years invested at 10 percent. Here are the steps to solve the problem with a calculator:

1. Punch in 5000 and press **PV**.
2. Punch in 6 and press **N**.
3. Punch in 10 and press **I**.
4. To calculate the future value, press **CPT** and then **FV**. The future value of 8,857.81 should appear on the calculator display.

On many calculators, this value will be preceded by a minus sign, which is a way of differentiating cash inflows from outflows. For our purposes, this sign can be ignored.

To calculate the yearly savings (the amount of an annuity), let's continue with the example on pages 53 and 54. This time, you're given the interest rate of 10 percent, the number of periods is 6, and the future value is $26,140. Your job is to solve the equation for the annuity. The steps using the calculator are:

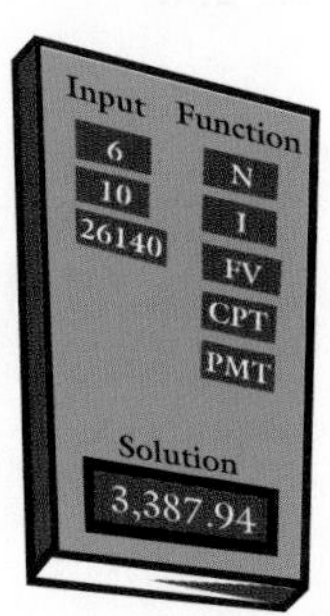

1. Punch in 6 and press **N**.
2. Punch in 10 and press **I**.
3. Punch in 26140 and press **FV**.
4. To calculate the yearly payment or annuity, press **CPT** and then **PMT**.

The annuity of 3,387.94 should appear on the calculator display. Again, *a negative sign can be ignored.*

A similar procedure is used to find present value of a future sum or an annuity, except you would input the **FV** or **PMT** and press **CPT** and then **PV** to calculate the desired result. To find the equal annual future withdrawals from an initial deposit, the **PV** would be input and you would solve for the **PMT** by pressing **CPT** and then **PMT**.

Index

C

E

G

H

I

J

K

L

Q

R

S